ENCYCLOPEDIA OF
THE UNITED NATIONS

ENCYCLOPEDIA OF THE UNITED NATIONS

JOHN ALLPHIN MOORE, JR.
California State Polytechnic University

JERRY PUBANTZ
Salem College

☑® Facts On File, Inc.

Encyclopedia of the United Nations

Facts On File, Inc.
132 West 31st Street
New York NY 10001

Library of Congress Cataloging-in-Publication Data

Moore, John Allphin, 1940–
Encyclopedia of the United Nations / John Allphin Moore, Jr., Jerry Pubantz.
p. cm.
Includes bibliographical references and index.
ISBN 0-8160-4417-1
1. United Nations—Encyclopedias. 2. International relations—Encyclopedias.
I. Pubantz, Jerry, 1947– II. Title.

KZ4968.M66 2002
341.23′03—dc21   2002072222

Facts On File books are available at special discounts when purchased in bulk quantities for businesses, associations, institutions, or sales promotions. Please call our Special Sales Department in New York at (212) 967-8800 or (800) 322-8755.

You can find Facts On File on the World Wide Web at http://www.factsonfile.com

Text and cover design by Cathy Rincon

Printed in the United States of America

VB Hermitage 10 9 8 7 6 5 4 3 2 1

This book is printed on acid-free paper.

Dedicated
to
Our National Model United Nations Teams over the last 25 years
in Pomona and Winston-Salem
We have surely learned more from them about
the possibilities for international cooperation than
they from us

And to
Linda Christ Moore and Gloria Pubantz
for their loving patience
with our preoccupation on this special project

CONTENTS

PREFACE

On September 11, 2001, the United Nations was due to convene the 56th session of the General Assembly in New York City. That meeting would have opened, as it had every September since 1981, with a moment of silence in recognition of the Assembly's self-proclaimed International Day of Peace. That act of reverence for 20 years had commemorated "the ideals of peace both within and among all nations and peoples." At the appointed moment of 3 P.M., however, the Assembly Hall stood silent and empty, its expected occupants tragically focused on the gruesome events unfolding just 50 blocks south, where the smoking rubble of the World Trade Center towers lay as reminder that peace was hardly secure at the beginning of the new millennium.

The terrorism from the air that wreaked that terrible calamity was a very different insult to the world's peace than the ashes of war out of which the United Nations had been born. Yet, in those harrowing hours, if anyone thought to ask whether the 56-year-old institution would likely address this new global challenge as it had so many other threats to international peace and security since 1945, that person would have predicted "of course." It is an extraordinary thing that, while other international organizations, alliances, and even states of the cold war era have vanished or have had to remake themselves wholly, the United Nations shows the durability that makes it as potentially relevant today as when Franklin Roosevelt, Joseph Stalin, and Winston Churchill first agreed to replace the far more mortal League of Nations. With all of its warts and weaknesses, the United Nations simply is part of our expected reality and an expression of our hoped-for future. It is, as well, a universal focus of what is called "globalization." So, if terrorism has been globalized, then whatever global antidotes are available must of necessity absorb the attention of the wider world. In fact, at the millennium, this suggestion obtains for any number of issues, including rescuing disintegrating states, addressing economic dislocations, extending human rights, avoiding environmental degradation, containing arms races, resolving border disputes, calming ethnic and religious hatreds, and

more. These are not issues isolated in parochial locales. They belong to the entire globe.

Thus, in a new era of international politics, the United Nations has taken on new visibility. Its expansion of peacekeeping operations, the reinvigoration of great power cooperation in the Security Council, and the organization's central role in contemporary international diplomacy have revived interest in UN affairs unparalleled since its founding in 1945. The transformation in world politics brought on by the breakup of the Soviet Union raised the promise and expectations of the United Nations that now require a careful understanding by policy makers and the general public of the world body. The United Nations, unlike any comparable multistate organization in history, has remained with us for an unprecedented half century, expanding its membership to virtual universality. For many it has sustained the hope of a future democratic and peaceful world, for others it has served as the arena or agent for the pursuit of national interests. It is in the firm belief that the United Nations has been, and will continue to be, central to world politics that we have crafted this encyclopedia in order to provide an authoritative source on the UN's structure, functions, and history.

An encyclopedia differs from a dictionary in that the latter is primarily devoted to words; an encyclopedia is, of course, dependent on words, but it is necessarily committed to the use of words for the transmission of comprehensive information. This encyclopedia, in the tradition of those of the past, aspires to a particular kind of breadth, that is, to the compilation of extensive and useful knowledge about the United Nations. We hasten to add that while encyclopedias must be complete, they must also be selective. Everything cannot be described, because then nothing can be highlighted. This reference volume provides a comprehensive guide to the UN's institutions, procedures, policies, specialized agencies, historic personalities, initiatives, and involvement in world affairs. We intend that it set into context the past six decades of major world happenings and the role the United Nations has played in them. We also intend to demonstrate to the careful reader that there is a "new" United Nations. Secretary-General Kofi Annan best captured its transformation when he talked about it as part of an emerging international civil society. In this volume we present the new UN through thematic essays on topics that would not have been part of an encyclopedia on the institution during its first few decades. Women, environment, human rights, globalization, sustainable development, indigenous peoples, and terrorism, among other topics, have joined traditional UN concerns such as disarmament and the development of international law.

Laid out in alphabetical order for easy access, entries include brief references, longer explanatory essays, and detailed data on the United Nations. For many of the entries we have provided references to some of the most current scholarship and also seminal works on the topic. This is enhanced by a lengthy bibliography divided by subject fields. And in this Internet age, many entries provide websites to which students of the institution may turn for even more current information.

The truly lasting encyclopedic works since the time of the Enlightenment have been collections of scholarship by a community of scholars. We have attempted to follow in that tradition. The strength of this work arises from the genius and expertise of its 25 contributors. Their thoughtful essays on critical topics, agencies, people, and themes are each noted by their names at the end of the entry. Their affiliations can be found in the list of Contributors. Three shared qualities bind our contributors: their scholarship, their willingness to let us liberally edit their work to give the volume a consistent style and tone, and their empathy for the institution. This last attribute has been shown in many ways, not the least of which is that several of the contributors are Model United Nations advisers. They have worked together as colleagues, most particularly in the setting of the National Model United Nations in New York, the oldest simulation of its kind in the world. More important, they have taught generations of students the merits, demerits, and broad possibilities for the United Nations in a diverse but globalized world. Those who have not served as Model UN advisers have written extensively in their fields, have been advocates for international cooperation, or have tended to the vineyards of international life in UN agencies, related bodies, or non-governmental organizations. We are deeply in their debt for their contribution to this project. Entries not attributed to a specific author were written by the editors.

As in any effort to put together a meaningful encyclopedia, we found one of our most daunting tasks to be deciding what to put in and what to leave aside. We trust that we have compensated for missed opportunities by providing a useful set of appendices, including important UN documents such as the Charter of the United Nations, the Universal Declaration of Human Rights, and the Statute of the International Court of Justice. Also in the appendices readers will find (1) a list of the member states and their years of accession, (2) a list of the UN's Secretaries-General, their terms, and their biographical dates, and (3) an index of resolutions that either changed the ways in which the United Nations works (e.g., Uniting for Peace Resolution) or were overwhelmingly critical to world affairs (e.g., Security Council Resolutions 242 and 678). A chronology of important UN dates and the events associated with them is also provided, with capitalization of items that have their own entries in the volume. This should assist the student who wishes to construct a history on a specific UN topic.

Of all the websites available on the "net," none is more comprehensive than that offered by the United Nations. "www.un.org" opens an unending cornucopia of information, topics, and links to all the nooks and crannies of the world. But like most things on the Internet, "more" is often confusing and beguilingly misdirecting. To help guide the interested student, we have provided an extensive table of the most useful websites. Of course, we know that some will disappear, and some will change their URLs, but at least the serious searcher now can know where to start.

Because the entries are organized alphabetically, a user of the encyclopedia should have little trouble making contact with a specific topic. For further guidance, we have included within entries a wealth of cross-references indicated by capitalization, and at the conclusion of most entries a specific bibliography and directions for the reader to "see also" related entries. In most cases the cross-reference directs the student to a full entry, in others to yet more entries that further describe the topic. The cross-referenced entry will appear in exactly the same form in the alphabetical listing, with only two exceptions to this rule. When the cross-referenced item appears in an entry in the plural form, we have placed that item in small capitals (e.g., TREATIES), however, the reader should turn to the entry in its singular form (e.g., Treaty). Second, sometimes a cross-referenced entry will be preceded by "UN" (e.g., UN ENVIRONMENT PROGRAMME) for the purposes of making the entry more readable. Unless the cross-reference is to a resolution (e.g., UN SECURITY COUNCIL RESOLUTION 242) readers should assume that "UN" abbreviates "United Nations" and should turn to the entry with that in mind (e.g., United Nations Environment Programme).

As the previous sentence demonstrates, from time to time the reader will discover a word spelled differently from that normally found in American English. This occurs because the United Nations by tradition and formal agreement employs certain words such as "programme" and "labour" in all of its English-language texts. While the encyclopedia generally employs American usage and spelling, we have conformed to the UN practice of British or French spelling when referring to official UN bodies with these words in their names or when quoting from UN documents. This may appear strange to the American reader, or even inconsistent, since two different forms of the same word (*program* or *programme*, for instance) will be used at different points in this volume. Nonetheless, it is important to record accurately UN practice in this regard.

This large project owes much to many. Along with our contributors we owe primary thanks to the efforts of the editorial staff at Facts On File, most particularly to our gifted editor Owen Lancer. We have worked with Owen on other projects in the past and, frankly, we have been spoiled by the alertness, direction, and subtle if humane pressure only the best of editors can bring to bear on their authors. We have savored our meetings in New York with Owen. And we owe a debt of gratitude to the copy editor, marketing people, and diligent staff at Facts On File. Colleagues at California State Polytechnic University who offered dependable insight, help, and encouragement include Mahmood Ibrahim, Steve Englehart, Griet Vankeerberghen, Zuoyue Wang, John Lloyd, Amanda Podany, and Gayle Savarese. The dean's office at the College of Letters, Arts, and Social Sciences graciously provided partial release time in the fall term of 2000 to allow concentrated work on the project, and the library staff at the university, as always, provided steady support to the enterprise. Wide-ranging, accessible research material was at our fingertips because of librarian Kate Seifert's unfailing and good-natured tutoring on uses of the library's unsurpassed website. Once again, John Stephen Moore proved indispensable as an expert computer escort. The researcher at Salem College is always assured success if he or she has the talented assistance of Susan Taylor, Salem's reference librarian. Her devoted help on this project has given it a richness and an accuracy that every author and editor hopes for. Also at Salem the Faculty Affairs Committee generously provided research funds that made possible many happy and useful hours of study at UN headquarters. While he is duly listed among the expert contributors for his superb historical entries in the encyclopedia, Errol Clauss, professor of history at Salem, provided invaluable counsel throughout the project.

And finally, the unerring hand of Fran Swajkoski, Salem faculty secretary, assured that all drafts and final documents arrived where they needed to be, and when they needed to be there.

The manuscript simply could not have appeared in its final form without the substantial contribution of the Dag Hammarskjöld Library at the UN Headquarters in New York. We spent several hours on separate occasions in the alluring setting of the library, making full use of the photographic library with its unprecedented collection of pictures. Several reproductions from this historic collection grace the pages of this encyclopedia. We extend our appreciation to Mr. Pernacca Sudhakaran, head of the Photography Unit. A very special "thank you" must go to Ms. Anne Cunningham in the UN Department of Public Information. Her graciousness, her intercessions on our behalf, her advice, and her support all made working with the UN Secretariat a professional and delightful experience.

Finally, in a shared spirit that we think will not fade from the present moment, we acknowledge the city of New York. As faculty advisers to the National Model UN conference, we first met in New York some quarter of a century ago. We have visited regularly since then, attending to the UN Headquarters at least once a year for that quarter of a century. We do research and turn in manuscripts in New York. We met most of our contributors there. There we have celebrated successes and commemorated tragedy. In New York the United Nations endures and from New York this encyclopedia issues forth. If it carries omissions, oversights, or errors, those belong alone to the editors.

— John Allphin Moore, Jr.
Pomona, CA
— Jerry Pubantz
Winston-Salem, NC

INTRODUCTION
The United Nations and World History

Perhaps the most famous encyclopedia, the French rendition of the late 18th century, edited by Denis Diderot, surfaced during a period later generations called "enlightened." If the Enlightenment brought modern rationality to learning, it also imposed upon international affairs fresh notions that eventually would sway world leaders and lead to the United Nations. Eighteenth-century developments in politics, economics, international law, science, and conceptions of individual rights led to what some have called modern liberal democratic nationalism.[1] In turn, influenced by liberals in the American and French revolutionary traditions, and by German philosopher Immanuel Kant, thinkers envisioned a peaceful world that would be characterized by democracy, economic interdependence, and international law and institutions.[2] Such notions may strike the 21st century reader as commonplace examples of what the current age calls "globalization." But it would take some two centuries, sanguinary conflict, and agonizing efforts to effect a world organization that conformed to the prescriptions of enlightened notions of diplomacy. And still the world would not be perfect.

However, with the subtle deception nonaligned history can on occasion tease, world affairs by the early 1990s conspired to suggest the triumph of Kant's vision. The year 1989 brought the end of the Berlin Wall, the Warsaw Pact, and the cold war. A united Security Council authorized military action against Iraq, pushing the aggressor out of tiny Kuwait. U.S. president George Bush proclaimed a "New World Order," by which he and his listeners meant a world more nearly conforming to the political and economic norms we associate with enlightened Western society: the rule of law, democratic elections, market economics, rising standards of living, and the advancement of human rights, all within the context of a world of interdependent, cooperating sovereign nations. The United Nations was seen as the energizing institution of that new world, just as its founders had intended, and just as it had only recently, against the aggressor Saddam Hussein, proved it could be. By 2002 the United Nations could count 190 member states and numerous international organizations and non-governmental organizations that considered themselves part of the UN family. Composed of and dependent on individual nation-states, it nonetheless seemed poised to transcend distinct state desires for more wide-ranging global purposes.

Crisis at the Millennium

Yet, at the turn into the new millennium such a heady assessment seemed premature. Early unpleasantness in Somalia, Bosnia, Chechnya, and Cambodia was followed by the specter of other states around the globe disintegrating—in Indonesia, the former Yugoslavia, and elsewhere in Africa. The Arab-Israeli dispute, calmed by the Oslo Agreement of 1993 and mutual Palestinian-Israeli recognition and the onset of negotiations, degenerated by the end of the decade into a mutual bloodbath. World economic and financial crises emerged in Asia and Latin America, AIDS became an epidemic in much of sub-Saharan Africa, and angry protesters showed up in larger and larger numbers at meetings of international financial and economic organizations to voice strong opposition to globalization. Violence accelerated at these international meetings and then, on September 11, 2001, the unimaginable happened as terrorists commandeered four American airplanes on the east coast and slammed two of them into New York's World Trade Center and one into the Pentagon in Washington, D.C., causing unspeakable death and destruction. Within the month U.S. and British aircraft were bombing Afghanistan, protests against the bombings were spreading throughout the Islamic world, and anthrax, a deadly bio-

---

[1] Jack C. Plano and Robert E. Riggs, *Forging World Order* (New York: Macmillan, 1967), 7.

[2] Bruce Russett and John R. Oneal, *Triangulating Peace; Democracy, Interdependence, and International Organizations* (New York: Norton, 2001), 10, 29, 35.

logical agent, was showing up in a number of mailboxes in the United States.

The United Nations remained as an institution accepting of appeal to still the noise and to medicate the victims. But the euphoric moment of the early 1990s seemed long ago, and much more pessimistic appraisals of international possibility entered the public discourse. Some, such as former U.S. secretary of state Henry Kissinger, simply dismissed the United Nations as an insignificant factor for addressing the world's pains.[3] Professor Samuel P. Huntington provided an even darker assessment, beginning with his stunning essay "The Clash of Civilizations?" Huntington challenged the notion of a universal liberalism ever organizing the world. Instead he offered a more disquieting suggestion, namely, that the future world would be plagued by serious clashes between and among deeply different "civilizations" and cultures. Western civilization was but one of some seven or eight distinct civilizations, each with its own unique cluster of political and social ideas, standards of behavior, and, above all, religion. He predicted the certain and perilous collision of incompatible and suspicious civilizations and urged an end to soft optimism, including any expectation that a flawed United Nations could somehow gloss over such differences.[4] Huntington experienced something of a revival in 2001, as, despite vigorous efforts of the Americans and others to maintain wide cooperation—including within the United Nations—tension between Islamic and Western nations seemed to materialize following the terrorist actions in the United States and the U.S. military response, the Arab-Israeli situation deteriorated, religious and ethnic violence erupted in Southeast Asia, and the Balkans split along religious lines.

Other critics were equally depressing. Princeton professor Paul Kennedy, in his widely read book *Preparing for the Twenty-first Century*,[5] offered up a dreary recital of unmanageable worldwide demographic explosion, rampant environmental despoliation, risky biotechnological advances, malnutrition, uncured diseases, ethnic strife, and more. Journalist Robert Kaplan's *The Ends of the Earth* added more misery to the picture. Traveling in remote areas in Africa, the Middle East, and South and Southeast Asia, Kaplan found a nether world in perilous disintegration, plagued by overpopulation, lack of education, disease, environmental disasters, rampant crime and corruption, anarchy, and civic collapse. "The idea," he insisted, "that a global elite like the UN can engineer reality from above is … absurd."[6]

Toward Internationalism

Undoubtedly, as we proceed to face the new century more crises will occur and more voices will be raised to find wanting any claim that human society collectively and through international organizations can reasonably address world problems and make life for the world's inhabitants a bit better. We must concede that conflict in the formal relations between and among nations, empires, and peoples has characterized human activity since the millennia before the common era.[7] The diffusion and ultimate availability of texts and treaties dealing with such relations suggests a pattern in world history, however, of cross-cultural intercourse among political elites the world over that led in time to what might be called international relations. Basic principles and precedents emerged as different communities sought to impose order on their mutual relations and to resolve disagreements without the resort to force, unless those principles or their interests might allow or require it.

Empire

Still, for most of history public order was maintained by hierarchical imperial administrations whose dominance was punctuated by sporadic uprisings and dissolution, too often resulting in violence.[8] As a rule the great periods of Chinese history are considered to be those times when powerful consolidating empires brought pervasive peace, some prosperity, Confucianist (or later, Maoist) standards of conduct, artistic grandeur, and systematic rule to a society that nonetheless intermittently plunged into chaotic and disruptive civil strife. The Roman Empire is the prototypical administrative unit of the Western legacy. Rome brought stability, peace (the Pax Romana), law, infrastructure, a common language, and eventually Christianity to the known Western world. Byzantium was the imperial reflection of Rome in much of Eastern Europe, and it lasted longer and left an impressive legacy of Slavic orthodox culture neither nationalist nor liberal in configuration. The Ottoman Empire imposed a flexible bureaucracy on a wide swath of land with an extremely diverse population. And great Russian empires, whether Romanov or Bolshevik, brought to heel the squabbling medley of ethnic groups covering its large landmass. As a rule, when the imperial power was challenged the consequence was unwel-

[3] Henry Kissinger, *Diplomacy* (New York: Simon and Schuster, 1994), 249–50.

[4] Samuel P. Huntington, *The Clash of Civilizations and the Remaking of World Order* (New York: Simon and Schuster, 1996).

[5] Paul Kennedy, *Preparing for the Twenty-first Century* (New York: Random House, 1993).

[6] Robert Kaplan, *The Ends of the Earth* (New York: Random House, 1996), 436.

[7] See Raymond Cohen and Raymond Westbrook, eds., *Amarna Diplomacy: The Beginnings of International Relations* (Baltimore: Johns Hopkins 2000); and James B. Pritchard, ed., *Ancient Near Eastern Texts Relating to the Old Testament* (Princeton, N.J.: Princeton University Press, 1969), 199–206, 529–41.

[8] Here and elsewhere in this Introduction liberal use has been made of chapter 1 of John Allphin Moore, Jr., and Jerry Pubantz, *To Create a New World? American Presidents and the United Nations* (New York: Peter Lang Publishers, 1999).

come disruption (the 19th-century Taiping rebellion in China provides an example). Empire, whether imposed willingly and brutally or reluctantly and benignly, seemed the common solution to international disorder. In fact, as late as the turn of the last century, international diplomacy was something characteristically conducted among empires (Romanovs in Eurasia, Manchus in China, Ottomans in the Middle East, Hapsburgs in south-central Europe, Hohenzollerns in Germany and east-central Europe, and the British and French worldwide).

Nation-States

What might be termed the "post-empire" era of political organization is more familiar to the modern world. The idea of "national sovereignty" provided nation-states the ultimate authority over populations within discernible boundaries. The nation-state, considered to have originated in Europe in the 15th and 16th centuries, heralded what some scholars have called "international anarchy." Since no commanding sovereign authority rested above the nations, international order depended on the good faith of its individual sovereign members. In the West this phenomenon led to the development of modern international relations and international law. Scholars and practitioners such as Hugo Grotius (1583–1645) and Emmerich de Vattel (1714–67) sought to codify rules of international behavior, on the understanding that each sovereign state would determine whether to abide by them. This "state of nature" in international matters posited an underlying possibility of conflict. An initial response to this problem was the theory of "balance of power." This meant that if any one nation were to gain overwhelming power so as to represent a danger to others, they would join together to restrain—that is balance—the powerful entity. In addition to balance of power, early European theorists proffered notions of what we might call international human rights law. The earliest approaches to this issue came from alarm about the treatment of civilians during the brutal religious wars, particularly the Thirty Years' War (1618–48). Grotius and Vattel, and their readers in Europe and America, sought to codify into an embryonic international law accepted practices against what we have come to call "war crimes." Moreover, by way of the Peace of Westphalia that ended the Thirty Years' War, sovereignty became the criterion for authority in any political entity. Thus, sovereign rulers were authorized to determine the religion of any state, in order to avoid internal wars between competing religions, which too often had drawn in outside forces. As a consequence, by the "Westphalian" settlement, Europe came to be characterized by sovereign nation-states theoretically abiding by an international law regarding the rules of war.

Following World War I, new nation-states surfaced in central Europe. In 1947 India and Pakistan became independent of Great Britain, while various states emerged out of the former Ottoman Empire and the mandates administered there by Britain and France. By the 1960s many new states in the "developing world" gained independence. The nation-state had become the accepted mode of political organization.

The Concert of Europe

The American and French Revolutions brought to world politics the idea of universal principles applicable at all times and to all peoples. The idea that all human beings were, by nature, equal inspired but also disturbed existing politics. The French Revolution culminated in a long world war and the age of Napoleon. The victorious allies who finally defeated the French general met at Vienna during 1814–15 and restructured Europe and its diplomatic practices in an attempt to bring order to the continent and avoid another descent into violence. The Congress of Vienna crafted a complex plan to build a peaceful Europe. Diplomats agreed on a new and transformed balance of power, complemented by territorial compromise among all the former belligerents, monarchical legitimacy and restoration, and an agreement to meet in the future to consult on actions to take to meet disruptive crises (signaling the so-called congress system of European affairs).[9] Often considered a conservative settlement, the Vienna program was followed by a reasonably tranquil 19th century, which experienced a creative expansion of international organizations. Early river commissions, such as the Central Rhine Commission (1815) and the European Danube Commission (1856) were examples. The International Red Cross was in place by the middle of the century, and the International Telegraphic Union (1865) and the Universal Postal Union (1874) paved the way for numerous future international agencies in fields as diverse as narcotic drugs, agriculture, health, weights and measures, railroads, time zones, and tariffs. The 1883 Paris Convention for the Protection of Industrial Property and the Berne Convention for the Protection of Literary and Artistic Works (1886) brought issues of protecting patents and copyrights into the larger realm of international law. In 1899 and 1907, the Hague conferences marked a culminating phase in the arbitration movement, establishing the Permanent Court of Arbitration and expanding rules governing arbitral procedures.

Twentieth-Century Crisis

But crises challenged the arrangements of the Concert of Europe and the progress in international cooperation right up to the plunge into the Great War of 1914–18. When that disastrous war ended, a new participant encroached into the

---

[9] Paul W. Schroeder, *The Transformation of European Politics, 1763–1848* (Oxford: Clarendon, 1994).

club of the more traditional great powers to attempt a solution to the disorder that had caused the war. American president Woodrow Wilson joined others at the Paris Peace Conference in 1918–19. He brought with him positions he had earlier articulated in his Fourteen Points, including an outline for a new worldwide organization—a League of Nations—committed to collective security and to the elimination of war. When the peacemakers arrived in the Paris suburb of Versailles to sign the completed agreement, there were several compromises that troubled Wilson's most resolute supporters. Wilson, who had been welcomed to Europe as a savior, became by the end of the negotiations the target of nationalist frustrations abroad and partisan bickering at home. Almost no one was happy with the final national boundaries, and opponents in the United States complained that the president had made too many compromises in Paris and feared that he had overcommitted the country to international collective security. In September 1919, campaigning for Senate approval of the League, the president collapsed following a stroke in Colorado. His resulting illness and the growing opposition to his plans resulted in the Senate's refusal to ratify the peace agreement and thus deny U.S. entrance into the new League of Nations. Still, without doubt the Wilsonian principles of "self-determination" and "internationalism," though from a certain perspective ominously antipodal, had been clearly presented to the world's peoples.

The Versailles settlement may have been doomed to failure irrespective of the American snub. Statesmen at Paris had before them a dangerously disintegrating world. Most of the major organizing empires of the previous century were gone. The Manchu dynasty in China had collapsed in 1911, replaced by a weak republican government, and a disruptive civil war followed. In Russia, a Bolshevik revolution ended the rule of the Romanovs but found itself in control of a truncated state, the former empire having lost considerable territory to the Germans months before the war ended. By war's end, the Hohenzollerns in Germany and the Hapsburg rulers of the Austro-Hungarian Empire were likewise gone, as was the Ottoman Empire, now completely dissolved. Within the resulting vacuums in the center of Europe, in the Middle East, and elsewhere left by these disappearances were a variety of religions and a myriad of ethnic entities that now demanded sovereign national independence along religious and ethnic lines. From a certain perspective, world leaders have since 1918 been trying to restore order out of the chaos left by World War I.

Despite the American rebuff, the League, guided by its Covenant (its founding document), came into being and functioned until the world descended into the next round of world discord in the late 1930s. Three permanent organs marked the originality of the new experiment—an Assembly with equal representation from all member states, a Council of four permanent members (Britain, France, Italy, and Japan) comprising at first four and then six nonpermanent seats, and a Secretariat. Each of these signified advances in the development of international institutions. Although earlier international conferences had made some use of secretariats, the League Secretariat, providing centralized administration, expert advice, and day-to-day coordination, embodied a novel concept of a permanent international civil service. Outside the Covenant framework, but related to the League, were a Permanent Court of International Justice (the so-called World Court) and the International Labour Organization. Despite its ultimate failure, the League's organizational structure and its various activities provided a basis for its UN progeny.

By the end of the 1930s the League became effectively inoperative and World War II erupted. Seeds for a new organization were planted in the Atlantic Charter of August 14, 1941, issued by U.S. president Franklin Roosevelt and British prime minister Winston Churchill. The document obliquely referred to the future "establishment of a wider and permanent system of general security." On January 1, 1942, with the United States now in the war, 26 nations joined in signing a Declaration by United Nations (a term coined by Roosevelt), reaffirming the principles of the Atlantic Charter and committing themselves to defeat of the Axis powers. At a meeting in Moscow in October 1943, the foreign ministers of the United States, the Soviet Union, Great Britain, and China signed the Moscow Declaration on General Security, explicitly recognizing "the necessity of establishing at the earliest practicable date a general international organization." Planning for the new body had been centered in the U.S. State Department, where Secretary of State Cordell Hull organized a special committee of advisers to draft a proposal as the new organization's governing document. The committee's draft charter became the outline that subsequently was crafted into the final UN Charter. Talks in August and September 1944, at Dumbarton Oaks, an estate in Washington, D.C., furthered planning. At the crucial Yalta Conference, held in the Russian Crimea in February 1945, Roosevelt, Churchill, and Stalin hammered out the final compromises that became the basis for the San Francisco Conference on International Organization, which, in June 1945, witnessed the signing of the completed charter. With sufficient ratifications, the United Nations came into being at 4:50 P.M. on October 24, 1945.

The challenges confronting the UN's founders were not the same as those facing the world community at the start of the 21st century, but they were no less momentous: Western leaders needed to assuage Russian suspicions of any Western-bred organization to which Moscow would be asked to commit; the United States was obliged to convince its own people and the rest of the world that it would not again retreat from leadership in this postwar period; Britain required encouragement to complete the Wilsonian dream of the dismantling of worldwide empires, the largest of which was administered from London; the defeated nations needed to be reconstructed and fused into the new global framework; urgent rebuilding and rehabilitation of a war-devastated world required action; displaced persons and roaming refugees had want of immediate attention; the world's economy demanded restitution and rational orderliness; and the globe awaited a general, broad, and forceful commitment to those fundamental human rights so long promised by enlightened liberals and so clearly desecrated in recent times. Whatever criticisms can be mounted against the early United Nations, we must remark that it—and its associated organs—met and resolved every one of those challenges within a few short years following the most destructive war in history.

To the Millennium

Although the League of Nations was a model for the United Nations, in important respects the new organization was different from its predecessor. The League had been ensconced in the full Treaty of Versailles; thus to reject the League a nation had to reject the entire peace agreement, as was the case in 1919 with the United States. The United Nations, conversely, was purposely separated from the peace treaties that ended World War II; President Roosevelt, informed by Wilson's lack of success, determined on a separate process of ratification to assure U.S. participation in the new world organization. The League Covenant had been a traditional agreement among governments, called in the Covenant "The High Contracting Parties." The Preamble of the later Charter begins, "We the *peoples* of the United Nations."[10] The League required unanimous votes in both the Assembly and the Council, but decision making in the United Nations is more flexible.[11] Parties to a dispute before the League were prohibited from voting because of the obvious conflict of interest. In the United Nations, in a concession to the realities of power politics, member states had no such limitations. When coupled with the veto, this meant that a permanent member of the Security Council could block UN action.

The organization of the United Nations, which was initially something of a mystery to Soviet leader Stalin, rings familiar to citizens of the Western world or those conversant with presidential or Westminster-style parliamentary systems of government. For example there are legislative (the General Assembly), executive (the Secretariat combined with the Security Council), and judicial (the International Court of Justice) branches, and the Charter emphasizes equal trade and the "territorial and administrative integrity" of sovereign states (Article 2) and, supplemented by the Universal Declaration of Human Rights, individual freedoms.

All this notwithstanding, the United Nations too often is marginalized in discussions of world affairs. Part of this disregard undoubtedly is due to certain misconceptions about the organization. It is useful to remember that the United Nations is a "confederation," not a unitary or federally organized government. That is, it is made up of sovereign members; it has no overarching authority apart from those states, and it is then only what its members make of it. Thus it acts effectively only by way of consensus, not majoritarianism. Moreover, it cannot fulfill "utopian notions" of world peace and order because, as former Israeli representative Abba Eban has reminded, it is an "international organization ... a *mechanism,* not a policy or principle."[12] Or, as Secretary-General Dag Hammarskjöld once explained: "The United Nations is not ... a superstate, able to act outside the framework of decisions by its member governments. It is an instrument for negotiation ... [it] can serve, but not substitute itself for the efforts of its member governments."[13]

Also, it may be instructive to note that in the aftermath of the cold war, the United Nations is not alone at a pinnacle above all other institutions that connect the world; rather, it serves as a consolidating axis for all those organizations. The intricate international order purposely crafted following World War II has proved durable and mature. By 2002, the General Agreement on Tariffs and Trade (GATT) had become the World Trade Organization (WTO); the World Bank and the International Monetary Fund (IMF) had extended their activities; at Vienna in 1993 human rights were proclaimed and accepted by most nations as "universal"; the North Atlantic Treaty Organization (NATO) was expanding its membership far to the east; other regional groupings from the North American Free Trade Association (NAFTA) to the Association of Southeast Asian Nations (ASEAN) to the Asian Pacific Economic Cooperation Organization (APEC) to the European Union (EU) linked sovereign states into ever-widening and more closely knit international units. And the United Nations, unlike any comparable multistate organization in history, remained operative for an unprecedented half century, expanding its membership to virtual universality. As this expansion continued to the turn of the millennium, the organization found itself at the forefront in some of the most significant international developments. Apart from the oft-remarked activities of UN agencies in bringing about social and health reforms, consider, just for example, the following: (1) Israel came into being by the Jewish Agency's unilateral implementation of a UN resolution, initiating the modern Middle East quandary; the UN has been the central institution in defining, in international legal

---

[10] See the entries for "Charter" and "Covenant."

[11] See the entry for "Voting."

[12] "The U.N. Idea Revisited," *Foreign Affairs* (September–October 1995), 40.

[13] *New York Times Magazine* (September 15, 1957), 21. Quoted in Plano, *Forging World Order,* 8.

terms, the nature of the Middle East problem. From the establishment of Israel to the crisis of 1956, UN Resolutions 242 and 338, the Camp David Accords, the handshake at the White House in 1993, and the impasse of 2001, the internationally recognized legal basis of any possible resolution of this seemingly intractable dilemma rests in a long-term connection with the United Nations. (2) The remarkable developments in South Africa and Namibia over the last decade of the 20th century, resulting in the purging of apartheid and the introduction of democratic government in South Africa and full independence of Namibia, were conditional upon UN resolutions. (3) The 1993 elections in troubled Cambodia took place under the legal rubric of UN resolutions and with UN administration, and again in 1998 international monitors returned to watch over another election and the United Nations remained involved as part of the international effort to establish a war crimes tribunal to address the forced deaths of some 1.5 million Cambodians during the 1970s. (4) The ongoing negotiations to settle the Cyprus problem are based in UN resolutions. (5) By the mid-1990s the United Nations, by passing resolutions and establishing observer groups to provide supervision, guided the end of civil wars and the ultimate general elections in three beleaguered Central American countries: Nicaragua, El Salvador, and Guatemala. (6) The Gulf War in 1991, which removed Iraqi forces from Kuwait, was based on UN Security Council resolutions (particularly 678); thus, the war was a genuine "collective security" operation designed to uphold the sovereignty of a UN member. (7) The Dayton Accords of 1995 were U.S.-led impositions to implement the UN's insistence on ending the brutal fighting in the former Yugoslavia; as of the turn of the century, the UN Mission in Bosnia and Herzegovina was still in place, coordinating a wide range of responsibilities, including provision of humanitarian and relief supplies, human rights enforcement, removal of land mines, monitoring of elections, and rebuilding infrastructure. (8) In Kosovo, the UN Kosovo Force (KFOR), starting in spring 1999, supervised the final peace settlement following the NATO war against Serbian domination of the province, and the UN Interim Administration for Kosovo, which monitored the relatively peaceful municipal elections in the province in October 2000, was considered an example of successful nation-building by the United Nations. (9) In 1999 the United Nations took over administration in the embattled territory of East Timor, setting up a transitional authority in the area as it proceeded to separate from Indonesia; in late August, 2001, UN monitors administered a trouble-free election for East Timor, providing self-rule for its inhabitants for the first time since the Portuguese arrived 400 years earlier. (10) UN war crimes tribunals were, as of 2001, active in The Hague and in Arusha, Tanzania, prosecuting and trying alleged war criminals from the Balkan and Rwandan civil wars.

It is almost trite to say that something called "globalization," which began long ago, has accelerated in our own time, conforming to a conscious policy initiated in the bleak year of 1945 to attract the world into a cooperative international diplomacy. Today the world and individual nations are characterized by both integrating and fragmenting pressures, occasionally at the same time. Along with alarming evidence of ethnic tension, national rivalries, religious fanaticism, ancient prejudices, and powerful grievances, we also have centripetal forces such as the World Wide Web, extensive travel, CNN International and Al-Jazeera television networks, unprecedented mixing of peoples and cultures, and a substantive, developing, credible set of international norms, agreed to at least rhetorically by most nations. The United Nations finds itself at the pivot of this maelstrom.

Of course the human experiment is problematic. Whether we are on the verge of unmitigated disaster or not remains questionable. Whether we are capable of grasping with sharp discernment the challenges to our existence, and dealing with them sensibly, while providing a life just a little bit better for just a few more of our fellow human beings, remains open to debate. Cassandras always have the advantage, since misery and disappointment are constants. Idealists, or even realists who seek orderliness and progress in human affairs, can never be satisfied. And, of course, in the end, as J. M. Keynes so famously reminded us, we are all dead.

But we must insist on applauding united efforts to relieve the downtrodden, expand opportunity to ever more of our earth's citizens, promote self-government, assure human rights everywhere, and provide peace, so that all of us, individually if we wish, and collectively if we will, can savor our moment on Earth. The dense web of international connection represented by the United Nations and its affiliated institutions is, in our time, perhaps the principal mechanism for performing these commendable labors.

CONTRIBUTORS

Douglas J. Becker
Colgate University

Marjorie W. Bray
California State University, Los Angeles

Marie I. Chevrier
University of Texas, Dallas

Errol MacGregor Clauss
Salem College

Cynthia C. Combs
University of North Carolina, Charlotte

Patrick M. Grady
Global Economics Ltd.

Kenneth J. Grieb
University of Wisconsin, Oshkosh

Annette Skovsted Hansen
Columbia University

Irina Kebreau
Pace University

Daniel K. Lewis
California State Polytechnic University, Pomona

Michael S. Lindberg
Elmhurst College

Andrei I. Maximenko
Benedict College

Sean F. McMahon
University of Alberta

Robert E. McNamara
Sonoma State University

Amy S. Patterson
Calvin College

Megan E. Reif
University of Michigan

Sandra C. Rein
University of Alberta

Donna M. Schlagheck
Wright State University

G. Sidney Silliman
California State Polytechnic University, Pomona

Malinda S. Smith
Athabasca University

Karen J. Vogel
Hamline University

Thomas J. Weiler
University of Bonn

Shelton L. Williams
Austin College

ACRONYMS

A21	Agenda 21
ACABQ	Advisory Committee on Administrative and Budgetary Questions
ACC	Administrative Committee on Coordination
ADF	African Development Fund
AfDB	African Development Bank
ALD	Assignment of Limited Duration (short-term UN contract)
AOSIS	Alliance of Small Island States
AsDB	Asian Development Bank
BC	Basel Convention on the Control of Transboundary Movements of Hazardous Wastes and Their Disposal
BDPA	Beijing Declaration and Platform for Action
BOAD	West African Development Bank
BONUCA	United Nations Office in the Central African Republic
BWC	Convention on the Prohibition of the Development, Production and Stockpiling of Bacteriological (Biological) and Toxin Weapons and on Their Destruction
BWIs	Bretton Woods Institutions
C24	Committee of Twenty-Four
CAB	Conventional Arms Branch, DDA
CABEI	Central American Bank for Economic Integration
CAT	Committee on Torture
CBD	Convention on Biological Diversity
CCAQ	Consultative Committee on Administrative Questions, ACC
CCD	Conference of the Committee on Disarmament
CCD	Convention to Combat Desertification
CCPCJ	Commission on Crime Prevention and Criminal Justice
CCPOQ	Consultative Committee on Programme and Operational Questions, ACC
CCW	Convention on Certain Conventional Weapons

CD	Conference on Disarmament
CDB	Caribbean Development Bank
CDF	Comprehensive Development Framework, World Bank
CDP	Committee on Development Planning, ECOSOC
CEB	UN System Chief Executives Board for Coordination
CEDAW	Committee on the Elimination of Discrimination Against Women, also Convention on the Elimination of All Forms of Discrimination Against Women
CERD	Committee on the Elimination of Racial Discrimination
CESCR	Committee on Economic, Social and Cultural Rights
CFA	Committee on Freedom of Association, ILO
CHR	Commission on Human Rights
CICP	Centre for International Crime Prevention
CIDIE	Committee of International Development Institutions on the Environment
CITES	Convention on International Trade in Endangered Species of Wild Fauna and Flora
CLCS	Commission on the Limits of the Continental Shelf
CMS	Convention on the Conservation of Migratory Species of Wild Animals
CND	Commission on Narcotic Drugs
CO	Country Office
CONGO	Conference of Non-governmental Organizations
COP	Conference of the Parties to a UN Convention
COPUOS	Committee on the Peaceful Uses of Outer Space
CPC	Committee for Programme and Co-ordination

CPR	Committee of Permanent Representatives, UNEP	ECOSOC	Economic and Social Council
CRC	Convention on the Rights of the Child	ECOWAS	Economic Community of West African States
CROC	Committee on the Rights of the Child	ECWA	Economic Commission for Western Asia
CSD	Commission on Sustainable Development	EIB	European Investment Bank
CSocD	Commission for Social Development	EIT	Economies in Transition
CSTD	Commission on Science and Technology for Development	ENDC	Eighteen Nation Disarmament Committee
		ENRIN	Environment and Natural Resources Information Networking, UNEP
CSW	Commission on the Status of Women	EPTA	Expanded Program of Technical Assistance
CTBT	Comprehensive Test Ban Treaty	ESAF	Enhanced Structural Adjustment Facility, IMF
CTBTO	Comprehensive Test Ban Treaty Organization		
CWC	Convention on the Prohibition of the Development, Production, Stockpiling and Use of Chemical Weapons	ESCAP	Economic Commission for Asia and the Pacific
		ESCWA	Economic and Social Commission for Western Asia
DAC	Development Assistance Committee	ESP	Committee on Employment and Social Policy, ILO
DAM	Department of Administration and Management		
		EU	European Union
DAW	Division for the Advancement of Women, DESA	FAO	Food and Agriculture Organization
		FYROM	Former Yugoslav Republic of Macedonia
DDA	Department for Disarmament Affairs	G-21	Group of Twenty-one in the Conference on Disarmament
DDSMS	Department for Development Support and Management Services		
		G-77	Group of Developing States in the United Nations Conference on Trade and Development
DESA	Department of Economic and Social Affairs		
DESD	Department of Economic and Social Development		
		GA	General Assembly
DGAACS	Department of General Assembly Affairs and Conference Services	GAINS	Gender Awareness Information and Networking System, INSTRAW
DHA	Department of Humanitarian Affairs	GATT	General Agreement on Tariffs and Trade
DOALOS	Division for Ocean Affairs and the Law of the Sea	GCD	General and Complete Disarmament
		GDP	Gross Domestic Product
DOMREP	Mission of the Special Representative of the Secretary-General in the Dominican Republic	GEF	Global Environment Facility
		GEMS	Global Environment Monitoring System, UNEP
DPA	Department of Political Affairs	GNP	Gross National Product
DPCSD	Department for Policy Coordination and Sustainable Development	GPA	Global Programme on AIDS
		GRIPP	*Global Review and Inventory of Population Policies*, DESA
DPI	Department of Public Information		
DPKO	Department of Peacekeeping Operations	GSDF	Global Sustainable Development Facility
DSB	Dispute Settlement Board/WTO	HABITAT	United Nations Centre for Human Settlements
DSG	Deputy Secretary-General		
EADB	East African Development Bank	HIPC	Heavily Indebted Poor Country
EBRD	European Bank for Reconstruction and Development	HLCM	High-Level Committee on Management, ACC
ECA	Economic Commission for Africa	HLCOMO	High-Level Committee of Ministers and Officials, UNEP
ECE	Economic Commission for Europe		
EC-ESA	Executive Committee on Economic and Social Affairs	HLCP	High-Level Committee on Programmes, ACC
ECLAC	Economic Commission for Latin America and the Caribbean	HONLEA	Subcommission on Illicit Drug Traffic Enforcement Agencies
ECOFIN	Second Committee: Economic and Financial	IACSD	Inter-Agency Committee on Sustainable Development
ECOMOG	Economic Community of West African States Monitoring Group	IACWGE	Inter-Agency Committee on Women and Gender Equality

IADB	Inter-American Development Bank	INCB	International Narcotics Control Board
IAEA	International Atomic Energy Agency	INCD	Intergovernmental Negotiating Committee on Desertification
IASC	Inter-Agency Standing Committee		
IATF	Inter-Agency Task Force	INSTRAW	International Research and Training Institute for the Advancement of Women
IBE	International Bureau of Education		
IBRD	International Bank of Reconstruction and Development (World Bank)	IOC	Intergovernmental Oceanographic Commission, UNESCO
ICAO	International Civil Aviation Organization	IPCC	Intergovernmental Panel on Climate Change
ICBL	International Campaign to Ban Landmines		
ICC	International Computing Centre	IPF	Intergovernmental Panel on Forests
ICC	International Criminal Court	IPTF	United Nations International Police Task Force, UNMIBH
ICCPR	International Covenant on Civil and Political Rights		
		IRPTC	International Register for Potentially Toxic Chemicals
ICESCR	International Covenant on Economic, Social, and Cultural Rights	ISAF	International Security Assistance Force
ICGFI	International Consultative Group on Food Irridation	ISBA	International Seabed Authority
		ISCC	Information Systems Coordination Committee, ACC
ICJ	International Court of Justice		
ICPD	International Conference on Population and Development	ITC	International Trade Centre UNCTAD/WTO
		ITLOS	International Tribunal for the Law of the Sea
ICRC	International Committee of the Red Cross		
ICS	International Centre for Science and High Technology	ITTA	International Tropical Timber Agreement
		ITTO	International Tropical Timber Organization
ICSC	International Civil Service Commission	ITU	International Telecommunications Union
ICSID	International Centre for Settlement of Investment Disputes	JAG	Joint Advisory Group, International Trade Centre UNCTAD/WTO
ICTR	International Criminal Tribunal for Rwanda	JIAS	Joint Interim Administrative Structure, UNMIK
ICTY	International Criminal Tribunal for the Former Yugoslavia		
		JIU	Joint Inspections Unit
IDA	International Development Association	JSAP	Judicial System Assessment Program, UNMIBH
IDB	Inter-American Development Bank, or Islamic Development Bank		
		JUNIC	Joint United Nations Information Committee, ACC
IDNDR	International Decade for Natural Disaster Reduction		
		JUSSCANNZ	Non-EU industrialized states
IDP	Internally Displaced Person	KFOR	Kosovo Force
IEFR	International Emergency Food Reserve	LDC	Less Developed Country, and Least Developed Country
IFAD	International Fund for Agricultural Development		
		LDCR	Least Developed Country Report
IFC	International Finance Corporation	LILS	Committee on Legal Issues and International Labour Standards, ILO
IFOR	Implementation Force: Yugoslavia		
IGO	Inter-Governmental Organization	LLDC	Land-locked Least Developed Country
ILC	International Law Commission	MDI	Monitoring, Database and Information Branch, DDA
ILO	International Labour Organization		
ILOAT	International Labour Organization Administrative Tribunal	MICAH	United Nations Civilian Support Mission in Haiti
IMCO	Inter-Governmental Maritime Consultative Organization	MICIVIH	International Civilian Mission in Haiti
		MIGA	Multilateral Investment Guarantee Agency
IMF	International Monetary Fund	MINUGUA	United Nations Verification Mission in Guatemala
IMG	International Management Group		
IMIS	Integrated Management Information System	MINURCA	United Nations Mission in the Central African Republic
IMO	International Maritime Organization		
INC	Intergovernmental Negotiating Committee for the UNFCCC	MINURSO	United Nations Mission for the Referendum in Western Sahara
		MINUSAL	United Nations Mission in EI Salvador

MIPONUH	United Nations Civilian Police Mission in Haiti
MONUA	United Nations Observer Mission in Angola
MONUC	United Nations Organization Mission in the Democratic Republic of the Congo
MOP	Meeting of the Parties of a UN Convention
MOU	Memorandum of Understanding
NAM	Non-Aligned Movement
NATO	North Atlantic Treaty Organization
NBC	Nuclear, Biological, and Chemical (Weapons)
NDF	Nordic Development Fund
NGO	Non-governmental Organization
NIB	Nordic Investment Bank
NIDS	New International Development Strategy
NIEO	New International Economic Order
NIIO	New International Information Order
NIICO	New International Information and Communication Order
NNWS	Non-Nuclear Weapons State
NPT	Non-Proliferation of Nuclear Weapons Treaty
NWS	Nuclear Weapons State
OAS	Organization of American States
OAU	Organization of African Unity
OC	Organizational Committee, ACC
OCHA	Office for the Coordination of Humanitarian Affairs
ODA	Official Development Assistance
ODCCP	Office for Drug Control and Crime Prevention
OECS	Organization of Eastern Caribbean States
OEOA	Office of Emergency Operations in Africa
OHCHR	Office of the United Nations High Commissioner for Human Rights
OIOS	Office of Internal Oversight Services
OLA	Office of Legal Affairs
ONUC	United Nations Operation in the Congo
ONUCA	United Nations Observer Group in Central America
ONUMOZ	United Nations Operation in Mozambique
ONUSAL	United Nations Observer Mission in EI Salvador
ONUVEH	United Nations Observer Mission to Verify the Electoral Process in Haiti
ONUVEN	United Nations Observer Mission to Verify the Electoral Process in Nicaragua
OOSA	Office for Outer Space Affairs
OPANAL	Organization for the Prohibition of Nuclear Weapons in Latin America and the Caribbean
OPCW	Organization for the Prohibition of Chemical Weapons
OPE	Office for Projects Execution, UNDP
OSCAL	Office of the Special Coordinator for Africa and the Least Developed Countries, DESA
OSCE	Organization for Security and Cooperation in Europe
PACD	Plan of Action to Combat Desertification
PAERD	Programme of Action for African Economic Recovery and Development
PAROS	Preventing an Arms Race in Outer Space
PAS	Performance Appraisal System
PCA	Permanent Court of International Arbitration
PFA	Programme, Financial and Administrative Committee, ILO
PKO	Peacekeeping Operation
POPIN	*Population Information Network,* DESA
PrepCom	Preparatory Committee
PRGF	Poverty Reduction and Growth Facility, IMF
PUNE	Peaceful Uses of Nuclear Energy
RAMSAR	Convention on Wetlands
RDB	Regional Disarmament Branch, DDA
RDMHQ	Rapid Deployable Mission Headquarters
SADC	Southern African Development Community
SAF	Structural Adjustment Facility, IMF
SC	Security Council
SCITECH	Commission on Science and Technology
SDR	Special Drawing Right
SEATO	Southeast Asia Treaty Organization
SFOR	Stabilization Force: Yugoslavia
SG	Secretary-General
SHIRBRIG	Multinational Standby Forces High Readiness Brigade
SIA	Special Initiative in Africa
SIDS	Small Island Developing States
SMG	Senior Management Group, SG
SNPA	Substantial New Programme of Action
SOCHUM	Third Committee: Social, Cultural, and Humanitarian
SPECPOL	Fourth Committee: Special Political
SPLOS	States Parties to the Law of the Sea Convention
SRSG	Special Representative of the Secretary-General
SSOD	Special Session on Disarmament
SUNFED	Special United Nations Fund for Economic Development
SU/TCDC	Special Unit/Technical Cooperation Among Developing Countries
SWAPO	South-West Africa People's Organization
TC	Trusteeship Council
TFAP	Tropical Forestry Action Plan
UDHR	Universal Declaration of Human Rights
UN/NGLS	United Nations Non-Governmental Liaison Service
UNA	United Nations Association

UNAIDS	Joint United Nations Programme on HIV/AIDS	UNESCO	United Nations Educational, Scientific and Cultural Organization
UNAMET	United Nations Mission in East Timor	UNFCCC	United Nations Framework Convention on Climate Change
UNAMIC	United Nations Advance Mission in Cambodia	UNFICYP	United Nations Force in Cyprus
UNAMIR	United Nations Assistance Mission for Rwanda	UNFIP	United Nations Fund for International Partnerships
UNAMSIL	United Nations Mission in Sierra Leone	UNFPA	United Nations Population Fund
UNASOG	United Nations Aouzou Strip Observer Group	UNFSDT	United Nations Fund for Science and Technology for Development
UNAT	United Nations Administrative Tribunal	UNGOMAP	United Nations Good Offices Mission in Afghanistan and Pakistan
UNAVEM	United Nations Angola Verification Mission	UNHCHR	United Nations High Commissioner for Human Rights
UNCAST	United Nations Conference on Applications of Science and Technology for the Benefit of Less Developed Areas	UNHCR	United Nations High Commissioner for Refugees
UNCC	United Nations Compensation Commission	UNICEF	United Nations Children's Fund
UNCCD	United Nations Convention to Combat Desertification	UNICPO	United Nations Open-ended, Informal, Consultative Process on Ocean Affairs
UNCDF	United Nations Capital Development Fund	UNICRI	United Nations Interregional Crime and Justice Research Institute
UNCED	United Nations Conference on Environment and Development (Earth Summit)	UNIDIR	United Nations Institute for Disarmament Research
UNCF	United Nations Command in Korea	UNIDO	United Nations Industrial Development Board
UNCG	Convention on the Prevention and Punishment of the Crime of Genocide	UNIFEM	United Nations Development Fund for Women
UNCHS	United Nations Centre for Human Settlements	UNIFIL	United Nations Interim Force in Lebanon
UNCI	United Nations Commission for Indonesia	UNIIMOG	United Nations Iran-Iraq Military Observer Group
UNCIO	United Nations Conference on International Organization (San Francisco Conference)	UNIKOM	United Nations Iraq-Kuwait Observation Mission
UNCIP	United Nations Commission for India and Pakistan	UNIPOM	United Nations India-Pakistan Observation Mission
UNCITRAL	United Nations Commission on International Trade Law	UNISPACE	United Nations Conference on the Exploration and the Peaceful Uses of Outer Space
UNCLOS	United Nations Convention on the Law of the Sea	UNITAF	Unified Task Force
UNCOD	United Nations Committee on Desertification	UNITAR	United Nations Institute for Training and Research
UNCRO	United Nations Confidence Restoration Operation	UNITeS	United Nations Information Technology Service
UNCTAD	United Nations Conference on Trade and Development	UNKRA	United Nations Korean Reconstruction Agency
UNDAFs	United Nations Development Assistance Frameworks	UNLDC	United Nations Conference on Least Developed Countries
UNDC	United Nations Disarmament Commission	UNMEE	United Nations Mission in Ethiopia and Eritrea
UNDCP	United Nations International Drug Control Programme	UNMIBH	United Nations Mission in Bosnia and Herzegovina
UNDG	United Nations Development Group	UNMIH	United Nations Mission in Haiti
UNDOF	United Nations Disengagement Observer Force	UNMIK	United Nations Interim Administration Mission to Kosovo
UNDP	United Nations Development Programme	UNMOGIP	United Nations Military Observer Group in India and Pakistan
UNDRO	United Nations Disaster Relief Coordinator		
UNEF	United Nations Emergency Force		
UNEP	United Nations Environment Programme		

UNMOP	United Nations Mission of Observers in Prevlaka		UNSCO	Office of the United Nations Special Coordinator for the Middle East
UNMOT	United Nations Mission of Observers in Tajikistan		UNSCOB	United Nations Special Committee on the Balkans
UNMOVIC	United Nations Monitoring, Verification and Inspection Commission		UNSCOM	United Nations Special Commission on Iraq
UN-NADAF	United Nations New Agenda for the Development of Africa in the 1990s		UNSCOP	United Nations Special Commission on Palestine
UNOA	United Nations Office in Angola		UNSD	United Nations Statistical Division, DESA
UNOB	United Nations Office in Burundi		UNSDRI	United Nations Social Defence Research Institute
UNOCHA	United Nations Office for the Coordination of Humanitarian Assistance to Afghanistan		UNSECOORD	Office of the United Nations Security Coordinator
UNOG	United Nations Office at Geneva		UNSF	United Nations Security Force
UNOGBIS	United Nations Peace-building Support Office in Guinea-Bissau		UNSMA	United Nations Special Mission to Afghanistan
UNOGIL	United Nations Observer Group in Lebanon		UNSMIH	United Nations Support Mission in Haiti
UNOIP	United Nations Office of the Iraq Programme		UNSO	United Nations Office to Combat Desertification/United Nations Sudano-Sahalian Office
UNOL	United Nations Peace-building Support Office in Liberia		UNTAC	United Nations Transitional Authority in Cambodia
UNOMIG	United Nations Observer Mission in Georgia		UNTAES	United Nations Transitional Authority in Eastern Slavonia, Baranja and Western Sirmium
UNOMIL	United Nations Observer Mission in Liberia			
UNOMSIL	United Nations Observer Mission in Sierra Leone		UNTAET	United Nations Transition Administration in East Timor
UNOMUR	United Nations Observer Mission for Uganda-Rwanda		UNTAG	United Nations Transition Assistance Group
UNON	United Nations Office at Nairobi		UNTCOK	United Nations Temporary Commission on Korea
UNOPS	United Nations Office for Project Services		UNTEA	United Nations Temporary Executive Authority
UNOSOM	United Nations Operations in Somalia			
UNOV	United Nations at Vienna		UNTMIH	United Nations Transition Mission in Haiti
UNPAN	United Nations Public Administration Network		UNTOP	United Nations Tajikistan Office of Peace-Building
UNPKO	United Nations Peacekeeping Operations		UNTSO	United Nations Truce Supervision Organization
UNPOB	United Nations Political Office in Bougainville			
UNPOS	United Nations Political Office for Somalia		UNU	United Nations University
UNPREDEP	United Nations Preventive Deployment Force in the former Yugoslav Republic of Macedonia		UNV	United Nations Volunteers
			UNWCHR	United Nations World Conference on Human Rights
UNPROFOR	United Nations Protection Force		UNYOM	United Nations Yemen Observation Mission
UNPSG	United Nations Civilian Police Support Group		UPOV	International Union for the Protection of New Varieties of Plants
UNRFNRE	United Nations Revolving Fund for Natural Resources		UPU	Universal Postal Union
			USG	Under Secretary-General
UNRISD	United Nations Research Institute for Social Development		WAEC	West African Economic Community
			WB	World Bank
UNRRA	United Nations Relief and Rehabilitation Administration		WCED	World Commission on Environment and Development
UNRWA	United Nations Relief and Works Agency		WEOG	Western European and Other States Group
UNSAS	United Nations Standby Arrangements System		WFC	United Nations World Food Council
			WFP	World Food Programme
UNSCEAR	United Nations Scientific Committee on the Effects of Atomic Radiation		WFUNA	World Federation of United Nations Associations

WHO	World Health Organization	WSC	World Summit for Children
WIPO	World Intellectual Property Organization	WSSD	World Summit for Social Development
WMD	Weapons of Mass Destruction	WTO	World Trade Organization
WMO	World Meteorological Organization	WTO/OMT	World Tourism Organization
WP/SDG	Working Party on the Social Dimension of Globalization, ILO	WWW	World Weather Watch
		ZC	Zangger Committee

A

abstention from voting   *See* VOTING.

accession

The term *accession,* in international parlance, refers to adherence to or formal acceptance of a TREATY, CONVENTION, international organization, or other form of international agreement. Thus new members may "accede" to an intergovernmental organization—such as the United Nations—or to an international statute. For example, the six original members of the European Economic Community signed a Treaty of Accession to the European Communities in 1972, and in September 2000 the UN MILLENNIUM SUMMIT in New York witnessed several accessions to major international treaties.

See also CONVENTION ON THE PROHIBITION OF THE USE, STOCKPILING, PRODUCTION AND TRANSFER OF ANTI-PERSONNEL MINES AND THEIR DESTRUCTION.

Acheson, Dean (1893–1971)

An imposing figure in American foreign policy comparable to John Quincy Adams and Woodrow Wilson, Dean Acheson was the quintessential American realist. The most important of President Harry S. Truman's "Wise Men" who shaped postwar U.S. foreign policy, he served as undersecretary of state under James Byrnes and George Marshall from 1945 to 1947 and as secretary of state from 1949 to 1953. Acheson was indeed "present at the creation" of the post–World War II Pax Americana.

An unlikely intimate of President Truman, the aristocratic Acheson was instrumental in creating the postwar international financial institutions at BRETTON WOODS, in organizing the Marshall Plan to restore the economic viability of Western Europe, and in drafting the Truman Doctrine to contain any Soviet advance into the Middle East and Mediterranean. He provided the intellectual basis for the North Atlantic Treaty Organization (NATO) as well as Truman's decision to confront North Korean AGGRESSION in 1950.

Although perceived as a rigid cold warrior by many, Acheson also endured the wrath of the McCarthyites for his initial pragmatic attitudes toward Moscow, Beijing, and the need to avoid a nuclear arms race. Secretary of State Byrnes put Acheson in charge of a committee to draft a proposal for the international control of atomic energy, to be submitted to the United Nations Atomic Energy Commission (UNAEC). The undersecretary convened a working group of experts and politically savvy individuals who drafted what became known as the ACHESON-LILIENTHAL REPORT. The plan envisaged an Atomic Development Authority (ADA), which would own and control all uranium mines, fissionable materials, and processing facilities around the world. Acheson proposed phasing the plan in. The United States would not turn over its weapons until all states had submitted their facilities and resources to the authority. The proposal became the basis for the BARUCH PLAN, which was submitted to the UN and quickly rejected by the Soviet Union.

Acheson eventually adopted a rhetoric of anticommunism designed to make his proposals "clearer than truth" to a reluctant Congress. As a realist, he frowned on a "crusade against any ideology." He declined to attend the San Francisco Conference where the CHARTER of the United Nations was created in the spring of 1945. Despite his deep skepticism over the UN's ability to resolve great international conflicts, and his stern opposition to a cabinet seat for the UN ambassador, Acheson dutifully lobbied for congressional approval of the Charter. He regarded the creation of the United Nations as the most recent example of "the nineteenth-century faith in the perfectibility of man and the advent of universal peace and law." Acheson blamed Woodrow Wilson for the "grand fallacy" that democratic procedures and institutions could be applied effectively to international relations. For Dean Acheson, the United Nations was at best "an aid to diplomacy."

Further Reading: Acheson, Dean. *Present at the Creation: My Years in the State Department.* New York: W.W. Norton, 1969. Chace, James. *Acheson: The Secretary of State Who Created the American World.* New York: Simon and Schuster, 1998. McGlothlen, Ronald. *Controlling the Waves: Dean Acheson and U.S. Foreign Policy in Asia.* New York: W.W. Norton, 1993.

— *E. M. Clauss*

Acheson-Lilienthal Report

Submitted by the UNITED STATES to the inaugural meeting of the United Nations Atomic Energy Commission (UNAEC) in June 1946, the report served as the basis for early UN deliberations on the control of nuclear weapons. Written by a committee headed by U.S. undersecretary of state Dean ACHESON and David Lilienthal, the former head of the Tennessee Valley Authority, the American proposal called for the creation of a new United Nations body, the Atomic Development Authority (ADA). The authority would own and control all uranium mines, processing facilities, and fissionable materials worldwide. The ADA would then distribute "denatured" nuclear materials to national governments for peaceful uses. Acheson and Lilienthal envisioned the transfer of American, Soviet, and all other national nuclear assets to the United Nations in a phased process.

The U.S. representative to the UNAEC, Bernard Baruch, incorporated the elements of the Acheson-Lilienthal Report into his own BARUCH PLAN, calling for penalties against states that violated ADA authority. The Soviet Union rejected the American initiative as an effort to maintain the U.S. monopoly on nuclear capability. While the UNAEC

approved the U.S. plan by a vote of 10 to 0 in December 1946, the Soviet Union abstained, making any further progress impossible.

In December 1953 President Eisenhower revised the American position, calling on nuclear powers to transfer a small percentage of their nuclear materials to a new INTERNATIONAL ATOMIC ENERGY AGENCY (IAEA) under the ultimate authority of the United Nations but largely independent of its control. He suggested that as trust among the nuclear powers and in the agency increased more and more plutonium could be transferred to the United Nations, ultimately meeting the goals of the Acheson-Lilienthal Report. He offered to transfer U.S. stockpiles at a rate of 5 to 1 of that turned over by the USSR. While the Soviet Union rejected the proposal, Eisenhower's initiative led to the establishment of an IAEA Preparatory Committee and the creation of the UN agency in 1957.

See also DISARMAMENT.

Further Reading: Acheson, Dean. *Present at the Creation: My Years at the State Department.* New York: W.W. Norton, 1969. Clarfield, Gerard H., and William M. Wiecek. *Nuclear America.* New York: Harper and Row, 1984.

Administrative Committee on Coordination (ACC)

The UN ECONOMIC AND SOCIAL COUNCIL (ECOSOC) created the Administrative Committee on Coordination in 1946 to supervise implementation of recently signed agreements with SPECIALIZED AGENCIES being brought into the UNITED NATIONS SYSTEM under the CHARTER's Articles 57 and 63. Over the next 50 years the ACC was greatly expanded in MEMBERSHIP and purpose, becoming the primary organ for cooperation at the policy level among all UN bodies. By the end of the 20th century the committee included representation from 25 UN system organizations, PROGRAMMES AND FUNDS, as well as members from the BRETTON WOODS institutions, and all specialized agencies. Its metamorphosis led SECRETARY-GENERAL Kofi ANNAN to propose as part of his REFORM effort a review of the committee's structure, subordinate bodies, and even its name. The ACC, in 2002, was renamed the UN System Chief Executives Board for Coordination (CEB).

Not part of the UN's SECRETARIAT, the committee brings together leaders of all UN system secretariats under the chairmanship of the Secretary-General semiannually for a two-day meeting. At its sessions it discusses coordinated efforts that can be taken to implement UN initiatives, WORLD CONFERENCE recommendations, and needed responses to new international challenges. In the spring the CEB meets at the headquarters of one of its member agencies, and in the fall at UN HEADQUARTERS in New York City. Biennially it holds a "retreat" for its membership. It issues the *Annual*

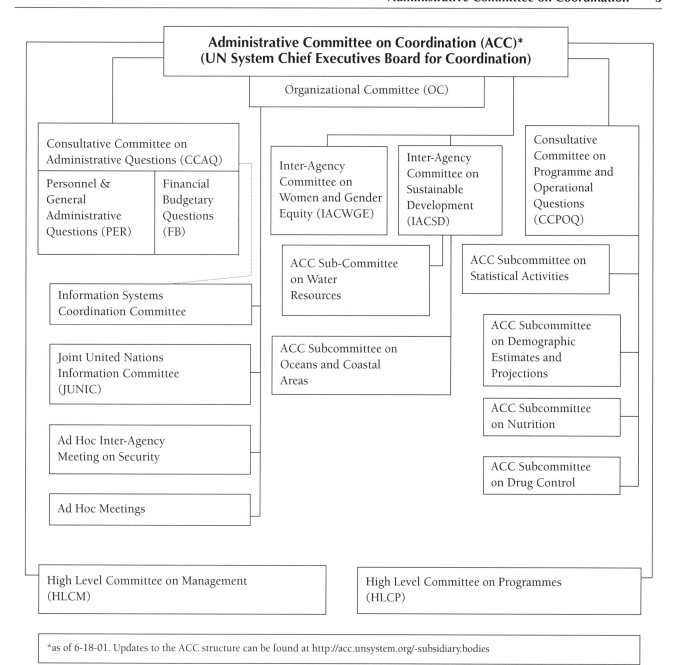

Administrative Committee on Coordination (ACC)*
(UN System Chief Executives Board for Coordination)

Organizational Committee (OC)

Consultative Committee on Administrative Questions (CCAQ)

| Personnel & General Administrative Questions (PER) | Financial Budgetary Questions (FB) |

Inter-Agency Committee on Women and Gender Equity (IACWGE)

Inter-Agency Committee on Sustainable Development (IACSD)

Consultative Committee on Programme and Operational Questions (CCPOQ)

Information Systems Coordination Committee

Joint United Nations Information Committee (JUNIC)

Ad Hoc Inter-Agency Meeting on Security

Ad Hoc Meetings

ACC Sub-Committee on Water Resources

ACC Subcommittee on Oceans and Coastal Areas

ACC Subcommittee on Statistical Activities

ACC Subcommittee on Demographic Estimates and Projections

ACC Subcommittee on Nutrition

ACC Subcommittee on Drug Control

High Level Committee on Management (HLCM)

High Level Committee on Programmes (HLCP)

*as of 6-18-01. Updates to the ACC structure can be found at http://acc.unsystem.org/-subsidiary.bodies

Overview Report, in which it highlights the critical issues on which it believes the UN system should focus in the near term. In May 2000, the ACC's report identified the following issues that should be central to UN decision making: (1) the implications of globalization for development, (2) the economic and social causes of conflict in the world, (3) peace and SUSTAINABLE DEVELOPMENT in Africa, (4) poverty eradication, (5) HIV/AIDS, (6) UN staff security, and (7) the negative impact on third countries of UN-imposed SANCTIONS under CHAPTER VII.

The CEB's identification of the critical issues to be addressed by the UN system has great weight because it reflects the consensus of the heads of all important UN agencies. In 2001, in addition to Mr. Annan, the committee included the executive leaders of the following organizations: INTERNATIONAL LABOUR ORGANIZATION, FOOD AND AGRICULTURE ORGANIZATION, UNITED NATIONS EDUCATIONAL, SCIENTIFIC AND CULTURAL ORGANIZATION, INTERNATIONAL CIVIL AVIATION ORGANIZATION, WORLD HEALTH ORGANIZATION, WORLD BANK, INTERNATIONAL MONETARY FUND, UNIVERSAL POSTAL UNION, INTERNATIONAL TELECOMMUNICATION UNION, WORLD METEOROLOGICAL ORGANIZATION, INTERNATIONAL MARITIME ORGANIZATION, WORLD INTELLECTUAL PROPERTY ORGANIZATION, INTERNATIONAL

FUND FOR AGRICULTURAL DEVELOPMENT, UNITED NATIONS INDUSTRIAL DEVELOPMENT ORGANIZATION, INTERNATIONAL ATOMIC ENERGY AGENCY, WORLD TRADE ORGANIZATION, UNITED NATIONS CONFERENCE ON TRADE AND DEVELOPMENT, UNITED NATIONS ENVIRONMENT PROGRAMME, UNITED NATIONS DEVELOPMENT PROGRAMME, UNITED NATIONS POPULATION FUND, UNITED NATIONS CHILDREN'S FUND, WORLD FOOD PROGRAMME, UNITED NATIONS INTERNATIONAL DRUG CONTROL PROGRAMME, Office of the UNITED NATIONS HIGH COMMISSIONER FOR REFUGEES, and UNITED NATIONS RELIEF AND WORKS AGENCY for Palestine refugees in the Near East.

The size of the membership and broad scope of its mandate have led the CEB to develop a complex administrative structure of its own. It has five major subsidiary committees: The Organizational Committee (OC) proposes the agenda and organizes the meetings of the CEB. Each agency on the CEB has a representative on the OC, which meets just prior to and following regular meetings of the full committee. The Consultative Committee on Administrative Questions (CCAQ) advises the CEB on management and administrative policy questions, and works to create system-wide policies on personnel, budgetary, and financial matters. The Inter-Agency Committee on Women and Gender Equity (IACWGE) is a response to the 1995 FOURTH WORLD CONFERENCE ON WOMEN, held in Beijing, CHINA. Replacing an earlier Ad Hoc Inter-Agency Meeting on WOMEN, the IACWGE is meant to implement the Beijing Platform for Action and to bring about a gender perspective throughout the UN System. In this regard, at the end of the century it formulated a medium-term plan for the advancement of women in all UN agencies. The INTER-AGENCY COMMITTEE ON SUSTAINABLE DEVELOPMENT (IACSD) advises the CEB on ways that the UN system might coordinate efforts to carry out the decisions of the UNITED NATIONS CONFERENCE ON ENVIRONMENT AND DEVELOPMENT (UNCED), including AGENDA 21 and the Plan of Action for the SUSTAINABLE DEVELOPMENT of small island developing states (SIDS). The Consultative Committee on Programme and Operational Questions (CCPOQ) was created in 1993, merging two earlier committees. It is an "inter-secretariat coordinating body" that seeks to mobilize the complementary capabilities of the different UN agencies in order to accomplish the goals of all UN initiatives, particularly at the field level. In addition to all CEB members being represented on CCPOQ, so too are the UNITED NATIONS UNIVERSITY, the WORLD TOURISM ORGANIZATION, and the United Nations Staff College.

In the 1990s each subsidiary committee of the CEB developed its own set of subcommittees and ad hoc meetings. This trend made the Administrative Committee on Coordination an example of the redundancy and bureaucratization in the United Nations that critics decried. At the CEB's October 2000 meeting the committee accepted Secretary-General Annan's recommendation and created two high-level committees—one to oversee management functions

(HLCM), and one to supervise programmatic work (HLCP). Their creation was part of a general review of the committee's structure in an effort to streamline the CEB's operation by December 2001. The change in name in 2002 also reflected an effort to reform the committee.

Further Reading: New Zealand Ministry of Foreign Affairs. *United Nations Handbook.* Wellington, N.Z.: Ministry of Foreign Affairs and Trade, published annually. ACC website: <acc.unsystem.org>.

administrative tribunals

Employees who work for the United Nations and its associated bodies are international civil servants. As such, they are not regulated or protected by the labor laws of their own countries. In order to protect their rights and to impose common personnel policy, the UNITED NATIONS SYSTEM has several administrative tribunals to which employees, who believe the terms of their contract or appointment have been violated, may appeal.

There are three significant administrative tribunals in the United Nations System. The UN Administrative Tribunal (UNAT), created by the GENERAL ASSEMBLY in 1949, has seven members appointed for three-year terms by the Assembly on the recommendation of the FIFTH COMMITTEE. The tribunal of the INTERNATIONAL LABOUR ORGANIZATION (ILOAT) is the oldest of the three, founded by the ILO in 1946 as the successor to the High Administrative Tribunal of the LEAGUE OF NATIONS. The WORLD BANK and INTERNATIONAL MONETARY FUND maintain an administrative tribunal that hears appeals not only from their employees but also appointees at the INTERNATIONAL FINANCE CORPORATION and the INTERNATIONAL DEVELOPMENT ASSOCIATION. UNAT and ILOAT serve both the employees within their organizations and the workforce of several other SPECIALIZED AGENCIES. UNAT is available to the employees of the INTERNATIONAL CIVIL AVIATION ORGANIZATION and the INTERNATIONAL MARITIME ORGANIZATION in addition to UN SECRETARIAT staff. The ILO has similar agreements with the following agencies: FOOD AND AGRICULTURE ORGANIZATION, UNITED NATIONS EDUCATIONAL, SCIENTIFIC, AND CULTURAL ORGANIZATION, WORLD HEALTH ORGANIZATION, INTERNATIONAL TELECOMMUNICATIONS UNION, WORLD METEOROLOGICAL ORGANIZATION, WORLD INTELLECTUAL PROPERTY ORGANIZATION, INTERNATIONAL ATOMIC ENERGY AGENCY, and UNIVERSAL POSTAL UNION. These tribunals, although established by major bodies of the UN system, are not considered "subsidiary" bodies, but rather "judicial" organs. They are, therefore, independent of their parent organizations, and their decisions may not be reversed by those organizations. The INTERNATIONAL COURT OF JUSTICE (ICJ) decided this question in 1954, when it issued an advisory opinion in the case of 11 employees who had been awarded

$180,000 in compensation by UNAT for illegal dismissal. The Court held that the General Assembly could not reverse the tribunal's award and had to authorize payment. On the other hand, employees have an appeal process from the tribunal that allows their cases to be taken to the ICJ.

In the 1954 ICJ case UNAT found itself caught up in the politics of McCarthyism in the UNITED STATES. SECRETARY-GENERAL Trygve LIE had fired 18 American nationals in 1952 for exercising their Fifth Amendment right against self-incrimination by refusing to testify before the U.S. Senate's Internal Security Subcommittee. They had been accused of being members of the American Communist Party. Lie argued that their behavior violated the requirement that they act in a manner "befitting their status as international civil servants." On appeal to UNAT the fired employees were exonerated and compensated. The United States led the fight in the General Assembly to bar the compensation, but the Court eventually upheld the UNAT decision. That judgment gave the administrative tribunals an independence not enjoyed by other UN-created bodies.

Further Reading: Simma, Bruno, ed. *The Charter of the United Nations. A Commentary.* New York: Oxford University Press, 1994. Stoessinger, John G. *The United Nations and the Superpowers: China, Russia, and America.* 4th ed. New York: Random House, 1977. United Nations Department of Public Information. *Everyone's United Nations; A Handbook on the Work of the United Nations.* New York: United Nations Department of Public Information, 1986.

admission of members

In addition to the founding members of the United Nations, as defined in Article 3 of the CHARTER, the UN, in keeping with the idea of universality, is open to new members, provided the applicant is a peace-loving state, accepts the obligations of the Charter, is able to carry out these obligations, and is willing to do so. In an opinion on May 28, 1948, the INTERNATIONAL COURT OF JUSTICE (ICJ) ruled that "All these conditions [of Art. 4 para 1] are subject to the judgment of the Organization, i.e., of the SECURITY COUNCIL (SC) and of the GENERAL ASSEMBLY (GA) and, in the last resort, of the members of the organization." In this context, the ICJ also declared that an application request cannot be denied for any reason other than those stated in Article 4. The ICJ further held in an advisory opinion on March 3, 1950, that the GA could not admit a member without a recommendation given by the Security Council. With the admission of Tuvalu at the MILLENNIUM SESSION in September 2000, the number of member states rose to 189. In March 2002, Switzerland's citizens, in a referendum, voted to enter the United Nations. By September 2002, East Timor was also poised to join the world body. The addition of these two states would produce near universality, with 191 UN members.

Applicants for MEMBERSHIP are evaluated by the Committee on Admission of New Members, a standing committee of the Security Council. Based on its findings, new members may be recommended by the Security Council to the General Assembly, which then votes on their admission. A two-thirds majority in the GA is required to admit new members.

Especially during the first decade of the UN, permanent members' VETOs blocked admission of new members in the Security Council. Given the parliamentary nature of GA procedures, it was important for both the UNITED STATES and the Soviet Union to secure working majorities in the body. For this reason the USSR sought an expansion of UN membership to overcome the initial advantage the United States had among the founding members. The PERMANENT FIVE were also under pressure from the UN's first SECRETARY-GENERAL Trygve LIE and his successor Dag HAMMARSKJÖLD to make the world body truly universal by adding new members. Finally, the newly liberated states themselves conducted public diplomacy toward that end.

In December 1955 the logjam was broken by both sides agreeing to admit 16 nations, 4 from the Soviet bloc and the rest from the ranks of Africa, Asia, and the Arab world. For the first time since INDONESIA's admission in 1950, the General Assembly had enlarged its membership. The first wave of new members was quickly followed by other successful applicants, such that African and Asian nations achieved a majority of seats in the General Assembly in 1963. The enlargement meant new voices, points of view, and policy emphases would now be advanced in the United Nations. The problems of the LESS DEVELOPED COUNTRIES—poverty, political instability, NORTH-SOUTH trade, and multilateral aid—all moved to the forefront.

A particularly heated controversy was the admission of the People's Republic of CHINA. It was critical to the Soviet Union to seat the representatives of the People's Republic in place of the delegation from the Republic of China (Taiwan). The USSR had boycotted the Security Council for a good part of 1950 over this issue, with the consequence of letting the United States achieve Council support for intervention in Korea. The admission of "Red China" was an emotional issue in American politics. Mao's introduction of troops in the KOREAN WAR, coupled with the anticommunist mood of the country, produced overwhelming opposition to the seating of a Beijing delegation in New York. If the Mainland Chinese took China's seat in the Security Council it would also mean another certain veto of Western proposals in that body. The American administration sought to maintain a GA majority in opposition to seating the Beijing government. When that no longer seemed achievable, Washington was willing to use all parliamentary procedures available toward this end. This American tactic continued until the presidency of Richard Nixon. Faced with an overwhelming majority in favor of China's admission, and seeking accommodation with the Chinese government itself, the United States sought to accede to the admission of the PRC while maintaining membership of the Republic of China in the General Assembly. In October 1971 the GA majority rejected that approach and gave Taiwan's seat in the UN, and particularly on the Security Council, to the government in Beijing.

Rights and privileges of membership may be suspended and a state can be excluded from the United Nations if the member state either is subject to ENFORCEMENT MEASURES imposed by the Security Council or has "persistently" violated the principles of the Charter (Articles 5 and 6). In the case of EXCLUSION, readmission is possible under the provisions of Article 4. A suspension of UN rights and privileges was imposed on Yugoslavia during the 1990s for the violation of UN RESOLUTIONS pertaining to the Balkans. The Socialist Federal Republic of Yugoslavia was an original member of the United Nations until its dissolution during the crisis in that region. Following the overthrow of President Milosevic, the Republic of Yugoslavia was readmitted on November 1, 2000.

See also COLD WAR.

Further Reading: Simma, Bruno, ed., *The Charter of the United Nations: A Commentary.* New York: Oxford University Press, 1994.

— *T. J. Weiler*

Advisory Committee on Administrative and Budgetary Questions (ACABQ)

At its first session in 1946 the UN GENERAL ASSEMBLY created two standing committees to assist with its work during and between regular Assembly meetings. They were the Advisory Committee on Administrative and Budgetary Questions and the COMMITTEE ON CONTRIBUTIONS. The first of these advises the Assembly, by way of its FIFTH COMMITTEE, on financial and budgetary matters related to the administration of the United Nations and its programs. ACABQ has 16 members, who are nominated by their governments but serve as private individuals. They are elected by the Assembly to three-year renewable terms based on their expertise, with due regard for geographical representation. Their terms expire on a rotating basis in order to assure continuity. In 2000, ACABQ was chaired by C. S. M. Mselle from Tanzania. He was joined on the committee by members from Romania, Jordan, Mali, Barbados, Costa Rica, Pakistan, India, the United Kingdom, Japan, Italy, France, CUBA, the RUSSIAN FEDERATION, the UNITED STATES, and Cameroon. The committee meets several times a year and in different places around the world. In June 2000 alone, it met in Geneva, Switzerland; Turin, Rome, and Brindisi, Italy; Pristina, Yugoslavia; and Vienna, Austria.

Given its expertise and longevity, the committee has achieved increased authority and prestige within the UN

STRUCTURE. It can call upon the Secretary-General's office and the heads of UN PROGRAMMES AND FUNDS to meet with it and provide needed information. With regard to those programmes financed with voluntary funds, ACABQ reports to their governing bodies on the programmes' administrative budgets, personnel, and procedures. Its functions also include the examination of the regular UN BUDGET, and of extra-budgetary expenditures. It evaluates and reports on the financing of PEACEKEEPING operations and international tribunals and carries out any other assignments given to it by the SECRETARY-GENERAL. It has the decision-making authority to authorize start-up expenditures by the Secretary-General on peacekeeping operations that need rapid implementation even though related budgetary matters have not yet been resolved. As an example, in July 2000, the SECURITY COUNCIL established the United Nations Mission in Ethiopia and Eritrea (UNMEE), calling for the deployment of 4,200 troops. While it would take some months for the General Assembly process to approve the estimated $199 million budget through June 2001, ACABQ released an immediate $50 million for the dispatch of reconnaissance and liaison teams to the region, and for the creation of an initial UN presence. It also made recommendations to the Fifth Committee on permanent personnel and spending allocations for the mission.

The Advisory Committee played a key role in the implementation of Secretary-General Kofi ANNAN's REFORM program. It promoted "results-based budgeting" throughout the UNITED NATIONS SYSTEM. Particularly in the SPECIALIZED AGENCIES ACABQ urged new cost-accounting procedures, the use of cost-saving technologies, and the sharing of administrative experiences to enhance efficiency. It even recommended that the various UN bodies develop common terminology for practices and phenomena so that communication and documentation could be standardized. It also became a major advocate of enhanced support services within the United Nations, including improvement in physical facilities. It argued that continued reductions in spending on UN buildings, including HEADQUARTERS in New York, were shortsighted savings that would reduce UN effectiveness in the long term. The reputation of the committee for professional expertise generally produces endorsement of its recommendations by the Fifth Committee, the Assembly as a whole, the Secretary-General, and the rest of the UN system.

Further Reading: See the reports of ACABQ and the remarks of its members to the GA Fifth Committee at the Fifth Committee website:<www.un.org/ga/56/fifth/>. For preceding and succeeding years, substitute the GA session number in the website URL.

advisory opinion   *See* INTERNATIONAL COURT OF JUSTICE.

Afghanistan

Afghanistan became a member of the United Nations on November 19, 1946. Active UN involvement in Afghanistan began on January 5, 1980, when the SECURITY COUNCIL met to consider the Soviet Union's December 27, 1979, invasion of the country. Claiming that the Afghan government requested Soviet assistance under terms of their 1978 friendship TREATY, the USSR vetoed a RESOLUTION condemning the intervention. Invoking the General Assembly's 1950 UNITING FOR PEACE RESOLUTION, the Council moved the question to the GENERAL ASSEMBLY, which voted on January 14, 1980, for withdrawal of foreign troops and soon thereafter authorized the SECRETARY-GENERAL to seek a solution to the conflict.

In February 1981, Secretary-General Kurt WALDHEIM named a personal representative on Afghanistan, Javier PÉREZ DE CUÉLLAR, who—after becoming Secretary-General himself in 1982—appointed Diego Cordovez to succeed him as personal representative. In April 1988, after 12 rounds of negotiations, the governments of Pakistan and Afghanistan signed the Geneva Accords, with the UNITED STATES and USSR as guarantors. The accords provided for Soviet troop withdrawal, noninterference in Afghanistan's internal affairs, and the voluntary return of refugees. On February 15, 1989, the UN Good Offices Mission in Afghanistan and Pakistan (UNGOMAP) verified the Soviet withdrawal, but civil conflict continued with Soviet assistance to the communist regime and U.S. aid to resistance groups.

In November 1989, the General Assembly encouraged the Secretary-General to facilitate internal settlement, resulting in the 1991 appointment of Benon Sevan, head of the Office of the Secretary-General in Afghanistan and Pakistan (OSGAP), as personal representative. The superpowers agreed in 1991 to end aid to all parties by January 1, 1992, and supported a transition plan in accordance with the Secretary-General's May 1991 statement calling for an "intra-Afghan dialogue" ultimately leading to "free and fair elections." For the first time, some Afghan resistance groups were involved in and supported the UN negotiations, but the Soviet Union collapsed and resistance forces captured Kabul in April 1992 before the communist regime's planned abdication to a transitional council. Soviet-sponsored president Najibullah obtained sanctuary at the UN's Kabul office and, on May 6, 1992, resistance groups established the Afghan Interim Government, headed for two months by Sebghatullah Mujadeddi before he transferred power to Burhanuddin Rabbani, whose government continued to hold Afghanistan's UN seat through the 1990s with annual approval by the CREDENTIALS COMMITTEE.

Factional fighting intensified and UN efforts lapsed until December 1993, when a General Assembly resolution established the UNITED NATIONS SPECIAL MISSION TO AFGHANISTAN (UNSMA). UNSMA was headed by Mahmoud Mestiri (February 1994–May 1996) and later by Norbert Holl (May 1996–October 1997). Secretary-General Kofi ANNAN elevated UN involvement with the appointment of a special envoy, a position held first by Lakhdar Brahimi (July 1997–October 1999), and assumed in February 2000 by Francesc Vendrell. In 1997, with Brahimi's support, Annan convened the "Six-Plus-Two" group, comprised of Afghanistan's six neighbors—CHINA, Iran, Pakistan, Tajikistan, Turkmenistan, and Uzbekistan, as well as Russia and the United States. From 1984, the UN COMMISSION ON HUMAN RIGHTS regularly renewed the mandate of the SPECIAL RAPPORTEUR for Afghanistan and became increasingly involved in direct investigation of specific rights violations. Yet these UN efforts brought limited achievements and a civil war continued through the 1990s. The Taliban Islamic movement originated in 1994 and gained military ascendance over competing Afghan parties in 1996.

Sometimes lauded as a UN success, the Geneva Accords, accompanied by the Secretary-General's GOOD OFFICES, have been credited with maintaining a critical CONFLICT RESOLUTION mechanism during a period when a PERMANENT MEMBER's VETO (the Soviet Union's) paralyzed the Security Council. However, the troop withdrawal was the only fully implemented element of the accords and, some argue, an inevitable result of a changed international system—that is, a thaw in the COLD WAR—and internal Soviet politics. The accords' exclusion of Afghan resistance parties—either as direct participants or signatories—the absence of mechanisms for enforcement and intra-Afghan settlement, and the guarantors' immediate violation of the agreement through continued aid to their clients contributed to the failure of the UN missions that followed.

The UN missions—some more than others—also were criticized for misapprehending Afghanistan's complexities, for reluctance to address misbehavior of UN member states, and for inconsistent coordination with the UN's humanitarian operations. The UNITED NATIONS HIGH COMMISSIONER FOR REFUGEES, which began assisting refugees in 1978, appeared to reinforce U.S.-supported elements of the Afghan resistance to Soviet occupation and may have undermined the neutrality of UN MEDIATION. During the 1990s, a group of UN committees adopted Afghanistan as a test case for strengthened coordination of UN crisis operations, including the application of a unitary funding mechanism and "principled common programming" on gender, minorities, and other issues. Yet the effort to unify UN humanitarian and political efforts met with limited success.

Afghanistan continued to present obstacles to UN humanitarian operations, including limited UN access to WOMEN imposed by the Taliban's gender restrictions, looting of UN offices, and violent reaction for the August 1998 U.S. missile attacks on the suspected residence of Osama bin Laden. The attacks were carried out in retaliation for bin Laden's alleged complicity in the terrorist bombing of two U.S. embassies in Africa. In 1999 the Security Council placed SANCTIONS on Afghanistan. Over the years meantime, frequent evacuations and suspensions of operations, although usually justified, compromised the UN's image when agencies such as the International Red Cross remained in Kabul. Nevertheless, UNOCHA, the United Nations Office for the Coordination of Humanitarian Assistance to Afghanistan, as the longest standing UN special body charged with promoting and coordinating assistance in a complex emergency, came to serve as a model for other global humanitarian efforts.

Successive UN missions argued with increasing vigor that their ultimate ineffectiveness was a result of the absence of international political and financial support and a lack of interest in ending the fighting on the part of some Afghans and influential regional powers. In November 1997, Kofi Annan said "it could be argued that . . . the role of the United Nations in Afghanistan is little more than that of an alibi to provide cover for the inaction—or worse—of the international community at large." He later questioned the usefulness of the Six-Plus-Two process when a major Taliban offensive followed the July 1999 Tashkent Declaration on Fundamental Principles for a Peaceful Settlement of the Conflict in Afghanistan, in which Afghanistan's neighbors for the first time pledged publicly to cease military interference in Afghanistan.

With the post–cold war convergence of member interests in the region, the Security Council, in an unprecedented direct action, passed a resolution on October 15, 1999, banning nonhumanitarian flights and freezing Taliban assets to persuade the regime to extradite U.S.-indicted terrorist Osama bin Laden. As it gained increasing control of much of Afghanistan's territory by September 2000, the Taliban renewed efforts to obtain Afghanistan's UN seat and proposed alternatives to the extradition of bin Laden, while the Security Council contemplated further sanctions.

On September 11, 2001, hijackers, reputedly part of bin Laden's al-Qaeda terrorist network, seized control of four U.S. civilian airliners. They crashed two of them into the World Trade Center towers in New York City, bringing both towers to the ground and killing approximately 3,000 people. The third plane crashed into the U.S. Pentagon in Arlington, Virginia, after circling major government sites in Washington, D.C. The fourth airliner crashed in western Pennsylvania with the loss of all on board. President George W. Bush declared the events "acts of war" and made harsh demands on the Taliban government in Afghanistan, believing that the regime was harboring bin Laden.

The United States sought UN support for any actions it might take in reprisal. On September 12 the Security Council unanimously adopted Resolution 1368, condemning the assault and finding it a threat to international peace and security. Council members invoked CHAPTER VII, making the resolution's provisions mandatory on all member states. The General Assembly, once it convened on September 13,

followed with a condemnation of the attack. The Council also passed Resolution 1373 on September 28, calling on all states to "prevent and suppress the financing of terrorist acts."

The United States issued an ultimatum to the Taliban demanding the extradition of bin Laden and his senior associates, the closing of his training bases in Afghanistan, and the stationing of U.S. personnel on Afghan territory to investigate and destroy terrorist camps. The regime in Kabul rejected these demands, closed all international aid programs in the country, requested proof of bin Laden's complicity, and seized UN facilities. The Bush administration organized a large coalition in support of its demands, including Afghanistan's neighboring states of Pakistan and Uzbekistan. The North Atlantic Treaty Organization declared the attack on the United States an act requiring COLLECTIVE SELF-DEFENSE. On October 7, 2001, the United States and Great Britain launched intensive air attacks on major cities, military targets, and training areas inside Afghanistan.

Under pressure from the attacks, the Taliban leaders called on all Muslim nations to defend Afghanistan from American "AGGRESSION." At the same time they offered to negotiate turning over Osama bin Laden to a third country in return for a cessation of the bombing. The offer was rejected by Washington. Faced with a growing refugee and humanitarian crisis, and with calls from UN officials among others to assist innocent Afghan victims of the attack, the U.S. administration made airdrops of food rations and offered to assist with humanitarian relief. Also recognizing the need to assure stability in Afghanistan if the Taliban was driven from power, President Bush lent support to future UN efforts at NATION-BUILDING in Afghanistan, reversing the position of the administration on this aspect of contemporary UN PEACEKEEPING activities.

Known as Operation Enduring Freedom, the American military attack in cooperation with the Afghan Northern Alliance drove Taliban forces from power during November and December. Meeting under UN auspices in Bonn, Germany, Afghan factions agreed on December 5, 2001, to create an Interim Authority for the purposes of governing the country during a six-month transition period. The agreement appointed Hamid Karzai as the interim head of government and called for international forces to provide security for the Karzai administration. The Security Council responded on December 20 by approving Resolution 1386 establishing the International Security Assistance Force (ISAF). Karzai's government took power on December 22. The Bonn agreement committed the parties to the convocation of a Loya Jirga—a national assembly of representatives—to craft a new permanent government. As a product of the Bonn meeting, Chairman Karzai inaugurated a special commission on January 29 to organize the gathering. Local and regional elections of representatives were conducted under UN auspices in the spring, and the Loya Jirga met in June 2002.

While humanitarian, political, economic, and social challenges confronted the new government at the beginning of 2002, the restoration of peace and security remained the highest priority for Afghan and international leaders. The United Kingdom offered to serve as the lead nation in the ISAF for the purposes of protecting "Kabul and its surrounding areas," and to do so through April 30, 2002. The London government urged Secretary-General Annan to identify another member state willing to take over leadership responsibilities at that time. Turkey agreed to succeed Great Britain in the leadership of the security force. The ISAF, while authorized by the UN Security Council, functioned under the operational military authority of the U.S. Central Command, which continued attacks on suspected al-Qaeda and Taliban enclaves. Following an outbreak of factional violence in the northern and eastern parts of the country, Annan and his re-appointed special representative Lakhdar Brahimi urged a deployment of the ISAF throughout Afghanistan. On February 1 the United Nations brokered a demilitarization agreement between groups in Mazar-i-Sharif, avoiding conflict over control of the city. A similar effort in Gardez, however, failed. In Kabul itself the government was shaken in mid-February by the brazen assassination of the minister of aviation at the capital's airport. Although the victim was ostensibly murdered at the hands of Muslim pilgrims angered by delays in their departure for Mecca, Hamid Karzai later accused senior members of his government of being responsible for the crime. A day after the assassination violence broke out in Kabul among Afghans during a soccer game meant to demonstrate the return of peace and normalcy.

Secretary-General Annan reported to the Security Council on February 6 that the ability of the interim government to restore order depended heavily on the willingness of the international community to increase funding for Afghan government operations. The Karzai administration was without resources even for the purpose of filling short-term needs, such as salary payments to government employees. Annan's appeal came in the wake of the Tokyo Conference on Afghanistan Reconstruction in January 2002, at which several states pledged more than $4.5 billion combined. Believing the Tokyo commitments were insufficient, and fearing the new regime would lose credibility unless it could address pressing economic problems quickly, the Secretary-General followed up the conference with a trip to Afghanistan, Japan, Pakistan, and Iran seeking more international aid. With renewed factional violence and limited progress in finding and capturing leaders of the previous regime, American and UN officials warned in mid-February that restoring stability in Afghanistan would be a long, difficult, and expensive process.

Further Reading: Khan, Riaz M. *Untying the Afghan Knot: Negotiating Soviet Withdrawal.* Durham, N.C.: Duke University Press, 1991. Maley, William. "The UN and Afghanistan: 'Doing Its Best' or Failure of a Mission?" In *Fundamentalism Reborn: Afghanistan and the Taliban,* 182–98. Edited by William Maley. New York: New York University Press, 1998. Rubin, Barnett R. *The Search for Peace in Afghanistan: From Buffer State to Failed State.* New Haven, Conn.: Yale University Press, 1995. ———. "Afghanistan under the Taliban," *Current History* 98, no. 625 (February 1999): 79–91.

— M. E. Reif

Africa *See* ANGOLA, APARTHEID, DEPARTMENT OF PEACEKEEPING OPERATIONS, DESERTIFICATION, ECONOMIC COMMUNITY OF WEST AFRICAN STATES, GROUP OF 77, HIV/AIDS, LEAST DEVELOPED COUNTRIES, NAMIBIA, NATIONAL LIBERATION, ORGANIZATION OF AFRICAN UNITY, PEACEKEEPING, RWANDA CRISIS, SIERRA LEONE, SOMALIA.

Africa Industrialization Day
Celebrated annually on November 20, the day is meant to generate support in the international community for the industrialization of Africa.

African Development Bank (ADB) *See*
REGIONAL DEVELOPMENT BANKS.

Agenda for Development
The Agenda for Development, adopted by a special meeting of the GENERAL ASSEMBLY on June 20, 1997, was the result of more than four years of extensive deliberations by member states and the SECRETARIATs of the UNITED NATIONS SYSTEM. The final document represented the product of a special working group of the General Assembly established in December 1994 to provide a forum among UN members for the exchange of views on development.

The idea for an agenda for development emerged in 1992, in the wake of SECRETARY-GENERAL Boutros BOUTROS-GHALI's elaboration of *AN AGENDA FOR PEACE.* At that time, there had been a strong feeling by many in the global south that development was being marginalized in favor of peace and security. These developing nations felt that there was a continued need to assert the United Nation's primacy in the area of development. The South had demanded an agenda for development and Boutros-Ghali made an attempt to produce one. The Secretary-General's own vision of development was set out in May 1994 in a report to the General Assembly entitled *An Agenda for Development.* The report addressed peace, the economy, the ENVIRONMENT, society, and democracy as the five foundations of development. The Secretary-General also examined the multiplicity of actors engaged in development work and outlined his vision of the role of the United Nations in development in an increasingly complex world. His report declared that universal respect for and protection of HUMAN RIGHTS was an integral part of development, and that particular human rights, including group rights such as those of INDIGENOUS PEOPLES, WOMEN, children, and the disabled, should be emphasized. In November 1994, in response to the request of the General Assembly, the Secretary-General issued his recommendations for the implementation of *An Agenda for Development*. However, some nations considered the recommendations incomplete. As a result, member states chose to negotiate key parameters of the agenda. To facilitate this effort, a working group on an agenda for development was established on December 19, 1994, by UN resolution GA 49/126.

Given the background of concern about the development partnership between the North and South, reaching agreement on broad desirable outcomes was a significant achievement. The working group saw its main task as forging a framework for a partnership that would hold together, rather than trying to articulate plans with great detail. The working group hoped that under such a partnership specifics could be sorted out as it developed agreed-upon goals. One of the key stumbling blocks was the fear among Southern states that the emphasis on protecting the environment might stifle their economic growth. As a result of compromise, the document attempted to balance the need for SUSTAINABLE DEVELOPMENT with the need for sustained economic growth.

In UN Secretary-General Kofi ANNAN's words, the Agenda for Development, adopted after intense and extended consultations, "represent[ed] one of the most far-reaching agreements on the central issue of development ever attained by the international community." Developing countries, fearing that the United Nations had become marginalized by the BRETTON WOODS institutions, saw the core thrust of the agenda as reaffirming the importance of development for the United Nations, and they sought to resituate the organization's central role toward the encouragement of development. The agenda not only addressed the familiar components of development, such as economic growth, trade, finance, science and technology, poverty eradication, employment and human resources development, but also placed new emphasis on the role of democracy, human rights, popular participation, good governance, and the empowerment of women. As such, it provided, according to Annan, "an all-encompassing framework for international cooperation on development—a central and evolving concern of the United Nations since its inception."

Further Reading: Bergesen, Helge Ole, Goerg Parmann, and Oystein B. Thommessen. *Yearbook of International Cooperation on Environment and Development, 1999/2000.* London:

Earthscan Publications, 1999. Weiss, Thomas G., David P. Forsyth, and Roger A. Coate. *The United Nations and Changing World Politics.* Boulder, Colo.: Westview Press, 2000.
— *A. I. Maximenko*

Agenda for Peace

In January 1992 a unanimous SECURITY COUNCIL requested that the SECRETARY-GENERAL prepare a report that included "analysis and recommendations on ways of strengthening and making more efficient within the framework and provisions of the CHARTER the capacity of the UN for preventive diplomacy, for peacemaking and for peacekeeping." The result of the request was *An Agenda for Peace*. Secretary-General Boutros BOUTROS-GHALI authored and released the report in June 1992.

An Agenda for Peace detailed a REFORM agenda. It sought to reinvigorate the United Nations in the post–COLD WAR era. Boutros-Ghali recommended that the United Nations identify "at-risk" states and act early to avoid the collapse of state SOVEREIGNTY and internal order. He proposed that military forces be placed at the disposal of the United Nations for rapid action in times of crisis. The report outlined problems in the LESS DEVELOPED COUNTRIES and the need for a humanitarian, political, economic, and military response by the United Nations. As a result of the report, new terms such as "preventive diplomacy," "state-building," and "peace making" entered the lexicon of potential UN activities.

The report highlighted four concepts: preventive diplomacy, peace making, PEACEKEEPING, and post-conflict peace-building. Preventive diplomacy attempted to resolve intra- and interstate conflicts before violence erupted, or to limit the spread of violence; it was intended to be proactive peacekeeping. Peace making sought to bring hostile parties to agreement through negotiation and MEDIATION. Peacekeeping was defined as UN deployment into potential or actual zones of conflict. Post-conflict peace-building was popularized by this report. Peace-building aimed to construct an environment that sustained durable peace. This was done through developments that addressed the economic, social, cultural, and humanitarian problems that underpinned violent conflict. Preventive diplomacy tried to avoid crisis; peace-building strove to prevent a recurrence.

A supplement to *An Agenda for Peace* was presented in 1995. It reviewed UN experience with peace operations over a two-and-one-half-year period following the original report.

See also AGENDA FOR DEVELOPMENT.

Further Reading: Boutros-Ghali, Boutros. *An Agenda for Peace.* 2d ed. New York: United Nations Department of Public Information, 1995. Kars, D. "The [UN] Agenda for Peace: A 1995 Evaluation." *European Security* 5, no. 1 (Spring 1996): 98–112. Weiss, Thomas. "New Challenges for UN

Military Operations: Implementing an Agenda for Peace."
Washington Quarterly 16, no. 1 (Winter 1993): 51–66.

— *S. F. McMahon*

Agenda 21

Agenda 21 was the Plan of Action approved by the 1992 UNITED NATIONS CONFERENCE ON ENVIRONMENT AND DEVELOPMENT (UNCED) that provided a set of objectives and strategies for attaining SUSTAINABLE DEVELOPMENT in the 21st century. Filling more than 800 pages, Agenda 21 was the most comprehensive statement of international consensus as of 1992 on the intersections between environmental protection and DEVELOPMENT in the LESS DEVELOPED COUNTRIES (LDCs) of the world. It struck a pragmatic balance between the needs of states in early stages of development and the developed states of the North that sought to avoid environmental damage from unwise development practices.

Agenda 21 was divided into four substantive sections comprising 40 chapters on a myriad of environmental and development topics. Each chapter outlined the environmental/developmental challenge, set international and national objectives, and provided a number of programmatic activities meant to achieve the objectives. Section I (Chapters 1–8: preamble; international cooperation to accelerate sustainable development; combating poverty; changing consumption patterns; demographic dynamics and sustainability; promoting and protecting human health; promoting sustainable human settlement; integrating ENVIRONMENT and development in decision making) presented the "Social and Economic Dimensions of Sustainable Development." Section II on "Conservation and Management of Resources for Development" included Chapters 9–22 (protection of the atmosphere; planning and management of land resources; combating deforestation; combating DESERTIFICATION and drought; sustainable mountain development; promoting sustainable agriculture and rural development; conservation of biological diversity; environmentally sound management of biotechnology; protection of the oceans and the protection and rational development of their living resources; protection of freshwater resources; environmentally sound management of toxic chemicals; environmentally sound management of hazardous wastes; environmentally sound management of solid wastes; sound management of radioactive wastes). Section III (Chapters 23–32) on "Strengthening the Role of Major Groups" included among those groups WOMEN (24), children and youth (25), INDIGENOUS PEOPLES (26), NON-GOVERNMENTAL ORGANIZATIONS (27), local authorities (28), workers and trade unions (29), business and industry (30), the scientific and technological community (31), and farmers (32). Section IV (Chapters 33–40) identified the means of implementation for the whole agenda. Most important, chapter 33 established the financial

mechanisms to be encouraged and chapter 38 called for the creation of the COMMISSION ON SUSTAINABLE DEVELOPMENT (CSD). Other chapters encouraged education (36), the transfer of environmentally friendly technology (34), and the creation of science for sustainable development. They also promoted national capacity building (37) and the development of international environmental law (39).

In Agenda 21, Earth Summit participants committed UN bodies to incorporating sustainable development into their areas of responsibility. In particular, Agenda 21 assigned strategic planning, the development of international environmental law, and the provision of scientific/technical/legal advisory services to the UNITED NATIONS ENVIRONMENT PROGRAMME (UNEP). The UNITED NATIONS DEVELOPMENT PROGRAMME (UNDP) was given the lead role in obtaining donor assistance, accumulating expertise in sustainable development, working on desertification and drought, and developing new capacities in poor countries for sustainable development. Agenda 21 called for a network of cooperation among UNEP, UNDP, the WORLD BANK, the UNITED NATIONS CONFERENCE ON TRADE AND DEVELOPMENT (UNCTAD), the GLOBAL ENVIRONMENTAL FACILITY (GEF), the INTERNATIONAL DEVELOPMENT ASSOCIATION (IDA), and REGIONAL DEVELOPMENT BANKS in the effort to carry out more than 1,000 specific recommendations. Most importantly, UNCED's Plan of Action urged the GENERAL ASSEMBLY to create a new functional Commission on Sustainable Development (CSD) under the auspices of the ECONOMIC AND SOCIAL COUNCIL (ECOSOC) that would give continuing international attention to the problems associated with the environment and development. The Assembly fulfilled its charge in this regard the following year.

The negotiations on Agenda 21 were long and difficult. Three sets of issues limited a stronger and more specific list of recommendations. First, the growing conflict between developed states with an interest in global environmental protection and less developed states that did not want any environmental limitations on their development programs meant that consensus on recommendations was only possible if they were vague, or if contradictory recommendations were included in the document. Second, the effort to protect the global environment naturally impinged on the sovereign rights of states to pursue their own internal policies. Agenda 21 generally protected the latter at the expense of the former. Third, the estimated costs of the recommendations to make sustainable development a reality went far beyond the will of the donor states to give. LDCs had hoped for the creation of a "Green Fund" at UNCED with the major industrialized powers making substantial contributions. The conference SECRETARIAT estimated the cost of Agenda 21's proposals at $600 billion annually, well beyond the then current combination of domestic spending and assistance to the developing world. While Europe and Japan announced at the conference they would increase funding by $5 billion per year, there was no major contribution from the UNITED STATES. Of the total amount estimated by the secretariat, $125 billion was foreign assistance 10 times the 1992 levels of global concessional aid. That figure, however, was close to the official UN target for Official Development Assistance (ODA) of 0.7 percent of rich countries' GNP. This being so, chapter 33 called on states to achieve the 0.7 percent figure "as soon as possible," and made the GEF the interim mechanism for Agenda 21 funding.

See also RIO DECLARATION.

Further Reading: Brenton, Tony. *The Greening of Machiavelli: The Evolution of International Environmental Politics.* London: Earthscan Publications, 1994. Campiglio, Luigi, Laura Pineschi, Domenico Siniscalco, and Tullio Treves. *The Environment After Rio.* London: Graham and Trotman, 1994. Grubb, Michael, Matthias Koch, Koy Thomson, Abby Manson, and Francis Sullivan. *The 'Earth Summit' Agreements: A Guide and Assessment.* London: Earthscan Publications, 1993.

aggression

Since one of the principal purposes of the United Nations is to maintain international peace and security, identifying nations that commit aggression constitutes a basis for SECURITY COUNCIL action. CHAPTER VII, Article 39, of the CHARTER states that "The Security Council shall determine the existence of any threat to the peace, breach of the peace, or act of aggression, and shall make recommendations or decide what measures shall be taken." Unfortunately, the Charter contains no definition of aggression, and reaching agreement on a meaningful definition has proven difficult. Various actions can be construed as aggression. While all agree that the unjustified or improper use of force against another nation constitutes aggression, there is always room for debate about whether the use of force was provoked by actions of the other party. While there is widespread agreement that aggression is wrong, nations engaged in armed conflict consistently contend that they act in self-defense. Even Adolf Hitler claimed that Poland attacked Germany at the start of World War II in 1939. Only twice has the Security Council, under the provisions of Article 39, identified an aggressor and then used force to halt the aggression. The first was North Korea in 1950. The second was Iraq in 1990, when it invaded Kuwait.

Since Security Council decisions often entail determining which of the parties to a conflict is the aggressor, it is scarcely surprising that the GENERAL ASSEMBLY established a commission to write a definition shortly after it began functioning. Reaching agreement among all member states on exactly what constituted aggression proved so difficult that the commission negotiated for almost 30 years before arriving at a consensus in 1974. It required almost 500 words to define aggression, and achieving accord required language of such ambiguity and extensiveness that the commission produced an umbrella definition subsuming almost all possible acts as well as exceptions, providing the Security Council with little guidance. The definition stated that "the use of force against the SOVEREIGNTY, territorial integrity or political independence of another state, or in any other manner inconsistent with the Charter of the United Nations" constituted aggression. The definition applied particularly to the state first resorting to force. However, it also described several uses of force that did not constitute aggression, such as "acts by and in support of peoples struggling to achieve self-determination, freedom, and independence" from "colonial and racist regimes or other forms of alien domination."

The broad 1974 definition left each member state to reach its own conclusions about what constituted aggression and effectively left the Security Council to reach a determination on a case-by-case basis. It proved impossible to define the term more effectively, and no new commissions have attempted to grapple with the issue since. The United Nations, and for that matter the world, has no working definition of aggression that is binding under INTERNATIONAL LAW, or is accepted by more than a few nations.

See also APPEALS TO THE SECURITY COUNCIL, COLLECTIVE SECURITY, COLLECTIVE SELF-DEFENSE, FOURTEEN POINTS, GULF WAR, IRAN-IRAQ WAR, *JUS COGENS,* KOREAN WAR, SOUTHEAST ASIA TREATY ORGANIZATION, TEHERAN CONFERENCE, UNITING FOR PEACE RESOLUTION.

Further Reading: Nyiri, Nicolas. *The United Nations' Search for a Definition of Aggression.* New York: Peter Lang, 1989. Simma, Bruno, ed. *The Charter of the United Nations: A Commentary.* New York: Oxford University Press, 1994.

— *K. J. Grieb*

AIDS   *See* HIV/AIDS, JOINT UNITED NATIONS PROGRAMME ON AIDS.

Amendments to the Charter of the United Nations   *See* CHARTER OF THE UNITED NATIONS.

An Agenda for Development   *See* AGENDA FOR DEVELOPMENT.

Angola

Located on the southwest coast of Africa, Angola was colonized by the Portuguese in 1583. Portugal began settling the colony in earnest in the early 20th century and relied heavily on the wealth, particularly the oil and diamonds, found within the colony. Beginning in the 1960s, insurgent groups demanded Angola's independence. After 15 years of guerrilla warfare, Portugal left Angola in January 1975. However, a brutal civil war, complicated by differences among several ethnic groups (Ovimbundi, at about 35 percent, represented the largest single group), ensued between the guerrilla groups, further fueled by support from external sources, namely, the UNITED STATES, the Soviet Union, South Africa, and CUBA. The Movimento Popular de Libertação de Angola (MPLA), a Marxist-oriented party, successfully achieved power over the Frente Nacional de Libertação de Angola (FNLA) and the Uniâo Nacional para a Independência Total de Angola (UNITA) in November 1975 and established the first independent government in Angola.

The MPLA's dominance, however, did not end the civil war within Angola's borders, nor did it successfully terminate the external COLD WAR interests that continued to support insurgency movements within Angola. UNITA, under the leadership of Jonas Savimbi, an Ovimbundi, and supported by South Africa and the United States, became the foremost threat to the MPLA's hold on power (the MPLA enjoyed the support of Cuba and the Soviet Union). As the United States and the Soviet Union played out their rivalry by proxy, Angola became one of the most heavily land-mined regions in the world. By the close of the 1980s, cold war tensions had diminished significantly and the United Nations was invited to verify the withdrawal of Cuban troops in 1988.

Although the Cuban withdrawal signaled an important opportunity to realize peace in Angola, progress was slow. In 1991, the MPLA and UNITA negotiated a set of peace accords, which were intended to lead to national reconciliation and democratic elections. Elections were subsequently held in 1992, under UN observation; however, Savimbi alleged widespread electoral fraud and refused to accept the results—which clearly favored the MPLA over UNITA. In an attempt to salvage the peace process, a series of negotiations were held between UNITA and the government of Angola (under the leadership of President Jose Eduardo dos Santos) that resulted in the Lusaka PROTOCOL (May 1994, effective November 1994).

Between 1988 and 1999, the United Nations initiated three verification missions to the country (UNAVEM I, II, III) and one observer mission, UN OBSERVER MISSION IN ANGOLA (MONUA). At best, these operations provided short buffer periods between intensified conflict. One of these respites came to an end with particularly tragic consequences for the United Nations. During the last week of 1998 rebel forces shot down two UN cargo airplanes, killing more than 20 passengers and crew. In 1999, the government of Angola indicated that it no longer believed such UN Missions were productive. On February 26, the SECURITY COUNCIL ended MONUA's presence in Angola, after a total

expenditure of $1.5 billion and the loss of 60 staff members trying to bring peace to the country.

Under pressure from the NON-GOVERNMENTAL ORGANIZATION Human Rights Watch, the Council agreed to open a small UN Office in Angola (UNOA) in October 1999. UNOA's purpose was to liaise with military, police, political, and civilian authorities. UNITA, however, continued to control significant territory and showed no real commitment to peace. General elections were scheduled for 2002, but without a significant improvement in domestic security, the possibility for free and fair elections was severely compromised.

If there was some small cause for hope, it arose from the Security Council's commitment to enforcing SANCTIONS against UNITA and from the growing international condemnation of the purchasing of diamonds from groups such as UNITA. Sponsored by the Canadian representative on the Security Council, the Council unanimously approved in April 2000 a CHAPTER VII monitoring mechanism to investigate violations of the diamond ban and to penalize countries that circumvented the sanctions. Constraining UNITA's ability to profit from illegal diamond and resource exchange held the potential of eventually forcing Savimbi to surrender. Also, by the turn of the century the Angolan government indicated that it was willing to consider amnesty for former UNITA activists—a move that could help the cause of national reconciliation. In February 2002, Savimbi was killed in a fire fight with government troops, raising hopes of an end to the fighting. However, the twists and turns of Angola's civil war over the previous 26 years defied prediction. As a result, Angola's conflict earned the dubious distinction of being Africa's longest running civil war.

See also CONGO, NAMIBIA, PÉREZ DE CUÉLLAR, UNITED NATIONS ANGOLA VERIFICATION MISSION.

Further Reading: Ciment, James. *Angola and Mozambique: Postcolonial Wars in Southern Africa.* New York: Facts On File, 1997. Hodges, Tony. *African Issues: Angola from Afro-Stalinism to Petro-Diamond Capitalism.* Bloomington: Indiana University Press, 2001.

— S. C. Rein

Annan, Kofi Atta (1938–)

The seventh SECRETARY-GENERAL, Annan was the first person to be elected to the office from the ranks of the United Nations staff, the first black, and the first from sub-Saharan Africa. *Time* magazine called Annan "a miracle of our internationalized world." Born in Ghana, educated in the UNITED STATES and Europe, Annan became a career diplomat with the United Nations, spent much of his career in Europe, Africa, and New York, and ascended to the position of Secretary-General in 1997. This well-traveled international civil servant was born in 1938 in Kumasi, Ghana—at the time a British colony called the Gold Coast. His father, Henry

Secretary-General Kofi Annan (UN/DPI Photo by Milton Grant)

Reginald Annan—whose first and second names were a legacy of British colonialism—was a highly respected noble of the Fante tribe. The son studied at the University of Science and Technology at Kumasi and then, in 1961, completed a bachelor's degree in economics at Macalester College in St. Paul, Minnesota. He pursued graduate studies at the Institut Universitaire des Hautes Études Internationales in Geneva, and in 1971–72 was a Sloan Fellow at the Massachusetts Institute of Technology where he earned a Master of Science degree in management. Fluent in English, French, and several African languages, Annan in 1984 married his second wife, the Swedish artist and lawyer, Nane Lagergren, whose uncle, Swedish diplomat Raoul Wallenberg, helped thousands of Hungarian Jews escape from the Nazis during World War II.

Annan began his career with the United Nations in 1962 as an administrative and budget officer with the GENERAL AGREEMENT ON TARIFFS AND TRADE (GATT)—now the WORLD TRADE ORGANIZATION (WTO)—in Geneva. He went on to serve in a number of posts around the world. For a brief time in the mid-1970s he directed the Ghana Tourist Development Company, but then returned to UN service, rising to assistant secretary-general for human resources man-

agement and security coordinator for the UNITED NATIONS SYSTEM from 1987 to 1990 and assistant secretary-general for programme planning, BUDGET and finance, and controller from 1990 to 1992. Secretary-General Boutros BOUTROS-GHALI appointed him to a special assignment to negotiate safe passage for some half-million stranded Asian workers and release of hostages during the GULF WAR of 1990–91. In 1993 he became assistant secretary-general for peacekeeping operations and then, in early 1994, UNDER SECRETARY-GENERAL. As under secretary he witnessed the considerable growth in size and scope of UN PEACEKEEPING operations and oversaw 17 military operations and a $3.5 billion budget, 15 times larger than the budget of 1988. He also supervised the removal of UN forces from SOMALIA in 1995 and served as Boutros-Ghali's SPECIAL REPRESENTATIVE to the FORMER YUGOSLAVIA, in which capacity he worked to organize peacekeeping efforts with the UN ambassadors from the United States, Britain, France, and Russia and, thus, he oversaw the transition in BOSNIA and Herzegovina from the United Nations Protection Force (UNPROFOR) to the multinational Implementation Force (IFOR), led by NATO (North Atlantic Treaty Organization).

By late 1996 it was clear that the United States, alone among the PERMANENT MEMBERS of the SECURITY COUNCIL, unalterably opposed reappointment of Boutros-Ghali, forcing the Council to consider other candidates. There was high interest in considering sub-Saharan African diplomats, since no Secretary-General had ever come from the region. Annan's reputation, his long residence in New York, and perhaps as important, his acceptability to conservative forces in the United States (led by North Carolina senator Jesse Helms, chair of the Senate Foreign Relations Committee) gained him the firm support of the Clinton administration and made him the consensus favorite, although the French would have preferred a leader from a francophone country. By late December, France withdrew its reticence when all three African nations on the Security Council indicated their support of Annan, who was chosen by the Council on December 17, 1996. After election by the GENERAL ASSEMBLY, Annan assumed the post on January 1, 1997.

The Secretary-General's first major initiative was his REFORM plan, *RENEWING THE UNITED NATIONS*. Unveiled in July 1997, the plan called for restructuring and pruning the UN's bureaucracy. He recommended consolidating and reorganizing 24 agencies into five divisions, to report to the Secretary-General but also to a new position called DEPUTY SECRETARY-GENERAL. (In January 1998, Louise FRÉCHETTE, Canada's deputy minister of national defense, became the first deputy secretary-general.) In November 1997 the General Assembly approved the first package of reforms, designed to save the United Nations some $123 million. Although there continued to be critics in American political circles, the U.S. Congress, in response, passed budget legislation in November 1999 appropriating $819 million for partial repayment of the $1 billion back dues owed by Washington.

By early 1998 the issue of WEAPONS inspections in Iraq brought the threat of confrontation between Baghdad and the United States. Saddam HUSSEIN insisted that he would deny access to weapons inspectors unless the UN-imposed economic SANCTIONS on his country were lifted. The United States threatened air strikes on Iraq unless the country cooperated with the inspectors. Annan, in an attempt to resolve the standoff diplomatically, met with Hussein. Although criticized in the West, Annan was able to gain from the Iraqi leader the so-called Memo of Understanding of February 22, 1998, whereby Iraq accepted all previous Security Council RESOLUTIONS pertaining to the issue and agreed to "unconditional and unrestricted" inspections. As a consequence the Security Council lifted the annual limit on Iraqi oil sales, on condition that the extra income be used to buy food and medicine and pay for repairs to the country's infrastructure. But in August 1998, Hussein again halted inspections and the unresolved standoff persisted.

The new Secretary-General tirelessly set out to address other stubborn problems facing the United Nations. In March 1998 he visited the Middle East. Speaking to the Palestinian Legislative Council in Gaza City, he urged nonviolence and patience regarding peace talks with Israel; then he spoke to the Israeli Foreign Relations Council in Jerusalem, where he apologized for past unfair UN actions toward Israel but criticized settlements in Palestinian areas and undue hardships imposed on Palestinians. In April of the same year he presented a detailed report to the Security Council entitled "The Causes of Conflict and the Promotion of Durable Peace and SUSTAINABLE DEVELOPMENT in Africa." When the peace process collapsed in the Middle East in October 2000, Annan led a feverish diplomatic shuttle among the parties and brokered an emergency summit at Sharm El-Sheik, Egypt, where he brought together Israeli prime minister Ehud Barak, Palestinian Authority chairman Yasser Arafat, U.S. president Bill Clinton, and Egyptian president Hosni Mubarak.

In April 1998 the Secretary-General traveled to his native Africa, visiting eight countries. In Rwanda, before that country's parliament, he sought to repair an abiding ill-will by acknowledging the delinquency of the United Nations in responding to the horrific massacre of Tutsis during disturbances in 1994, a time when he was Under Secretary-General. And, in September 1998, at the opening of the General Assembly, he recommended intervention in the escalating conflict between Serbs and Albanians in Kosovo. By June 1999 the Security Council approved the NATO-led peacekeeping force in Kosovo, and the UN INTERIM ADMINISTRATION MISSION TO KOSOVO (UNMIK) acquired the difficult responsibility of forming a multinational police force, setting up a justice system, and restoring order in that unhappy province. The Secretary-General also welcomed the establishment of the INTERNATIONAL CRIMINAL COURT (ICC) in Rome to bring justice to those committing "crimes against humanity." When, in the fall of 1999, EAST TIMOR voted to secede from INDONESIA, violence erupted as pro-Jakarta militias fought against independence, and a fearful chaos descended over multiethnic and religiously diverse Indonesia. Annan negotiated with the government of President Habibie, who had recently replaced long-ruling General Suharto, to allow UN forces to enter the province. Eventually a UN-sanctioned force, led by Australians, did begin to restore order. But as the century ended, and the United Nations found itself once again in the difficult position of trying to sustain civil order in a dangerous place, the island of Timor remained devastated, and an ominous, seemingly uncontrolled Indonesian militia continued to threaten Timorese. The discredited government of Abdurraham Wahid in Jakarta collapsed in the summer of 2001.

These and other problems related to the challenge of disintegrating states led the Secretary-General to support and build upon certain ideas regarding peacekeeping that were associated with his predecessor, Boutros Boutros-Ghali. In the fall of 2000 the United Nations issued a report, drawn from an international panel of experts, headed by Lakhdar Brahimi, that had been appointed by the Secretary-General, reflecting Annan's vision for peacekeeping. The BRAHIMI REPORT recommended formalizing the UN's peacekeeping activities and ending ad hoc deployments. One of the central recommendations was to create a new information-gathering and analysis office within the United Nations to assemble databases and act as a professional policy planning staff. The panel further recommended the establishment of an integrated task force for each mission, combining analysis, military operations, civilian police, aid programs, finance, electoral assistance, and more. The panel also urged that definitions of self-defense be stretched to allow UN peacekeeping missions to take a more offensive posture in dangerous situations. The expert group that drew up these proposals was made up of members from 10 nations, including the United States and Russia, and its recommendations were praised by, among others, Richard C. Holbrooke, U.S. ambassador to the United Nations.

The forward recommendations for improved UN peacekeeping were ready for timely presentation at the moment of the historic meeting of the MILLENNIUM SUMMIT. This largest gathering of world leaders in history was the brainchild of Secretary-General Annan. Meeting at the UN's New York HEADQUARTERS in September 2000, the meeting entertained some 200 speeches from about 150 prime ministers, presidents, and potentates from most of the world's countries, plus other diplomats. Delegates, in both formal sessions and informal meetings, discussed, and occasionally attempted to resolve, many of the greatest challenges to the world, including reforming peacekeeping, eliminating poverty, reversing the spread of AIDS, promoting DISARMAMENT, advancing the Middle East peace process, making certain that economic globalization left no one behind, and more. When the summit ended on September 8, delegates from countries of often divergent views adopted a wide-ranging DECLARATION containing six "fundamental values" deemed essential to international relations: freedom, equality, solidarity, tolerance, respect for nature, and a sense of shared responsibility. Although some critics scoffed at the apparent ambiguity of the document, the very fact that the United Nations had been able to command the attendance of such a large number of world leaders and keep the summit on the front pages of most major newspapers and on the screens of television and Internet news outlets must have pleased the conference's initiator, Kofi Annan.

And his pleasure must have been enhanced many fold on the following June 27, six months before his first term was to conclude, when the Security Council unanimously renominated Annan and forwarded his name to the General Assembly, where, on June 29, 2001, he was reelected to his post by enthusiastic acclamation. Annan's reelection broke UN tradition. The vote for a Secretary-General normally occurs at the very end of the year, and according to an implicit rotation schedule, Asia could have expected a nominee from its region that December. But Bangladeshi ambassador Anwarul Chowdhury, SECURITY COUNCIL PRESIDENT for June, with the full concurrence of his colleagues, proposed moving the nomination process forward one-half year. This move signaled the growing regard that had been reaped by the Secretary-General and also, of symbolic significance, allowed a developing country to preside over the selection. He had succeeded in meeting the expectations of member states, rich and poor, North and South. Richard Holbrooke captured the attitude of many people around the world, when he referred to Annan as "the international rock star of diplomacy." That stardom received further credence when the Secretary-General and the United Nations garnered the Nobel Peace Prize in 2001, the 100th anniversary of the award. The prize committee praised Annan for "bringing new life to the organization."

See also ADVISORY COMMITTEE ON ADMINISTRATIVE AND BUDGETARY QUESTIONS, AFGHANISTAN, GLOBAL COMPACT, SENIOR MANAGEMENT GROUP, SOVEREIGNTY, SUBSIDIARITY.

Further Reading: Annan, Kofi. *Renewing the United Nations: A Programme for Reform.* UN Document A/51/950, July 16, 1997. ———. *We the Peoples: The Role of the United Nations in the 21st Century.* New York: United Nations Department of Public Information, 2000. Farley, Maggie. "Annan Nominated for 2nd Term as Secretary-General." *Los Angeles Times,* June 28, 2001. Moore, John Allphin, Jr., and Jerry Pubantz. *To Create a New World? American Presidents and the United Nations.* New York: Peter Lang Publishers, 1999. *New York Times Magazine,* March 29, 1998. Tessitore, John. *Kofi Annan: The Peacekeeper.* New York: Franklin Watts, 2000. *Time.* September 4, 2000.

Antarctic Treaty

The Antarctic Treaty was signed in Washington, D.C., on December 1, 1959. Its 14 articles came into force on June 23, 1961, upon ratification by all signatory states—Argentina, Australia, Belgium, Chile, France, Japan, New Zealand, Norway, South Africa, the USSR, the United Kingdom, and the UNITED STATES. Under this legal framework, Antarctica, which was defined in the TREATY as the area "south of 60 degrees South Latitude" (Article 6), could only be used for peaceful purposes (Article 1). WEAPONS testing was forbidden, and military personnel and equipment could be used only for scientific research or other peaceful purposes. Article 5 prohibited nuclear tests and explosions and the disposal of nuclear waste, making Antarctica the first NUCLEAR-WEAPONS-FREE ZONE Articles 2 and 3 guaranteed scientific freedom and encouraged scientific cooperation and exchange. Under Article 7, treaty-state observers were given free access to all stations and installations and could conduct inspections of any facility. Contracting parties agreed to undertake efforts consistent with the UN CHARTER to ensure that no one engaged in activities contrary to the principles or purposes of the treaty (Article 10). Should a dispute arise it was to be settled peacefully by the parties concerned. If necessary, it could be submitted to the INTERNATIONAL COURT OF JUSTICE (ICJ).

As of August 2001, there were 44 treaty members: 27 consultative and 17 acceding. The consultative (that is, VOTING) members included those seven nations (Argentina, Australia, Chile, France, New Zealand, Norway, and Great Britain) that claimed portions of Antarctica as their national territory and 20 nonclaimant nations (Belgium, Brazil, Bulgaria, People's Republic of CHINA, Ecuador, Finland, Germany, India, Italy, Japan, South Korea, the Netherlands, Peru, Poland, Russia, South Africa, Spain, Sweden, Uruguay, and the United States). Parties to the treaty have held regular consultative meetings at which new PROTOCOLS have been considered, with more than 200 adopted. In 1999 treaty members met in Peru, and in July 2001 in St. Petersburg, Russia.

Among the additions to the treaty, the parties approved the following accords: Agreed Measures for the Conservation of the Antarctic Flora and Fauna (1964), the CONVENTION for the Conservation of Antarctic Seals (1972), the Convention on the Conservation of Antarctic Marine and Living Resources (1980), and a Protocol on Environmental Protection (1991). This last agreement was also known as the Madrid Protocol, entering into force on January 14, 1998. Its aim is to preserve the status of Antarctica as a "natural reserve devoted to peace and science." The protocol prohibited all activities relating to mineral resources unless they were of a scientific research nature. The Antarctic ENVIRON-MENT was to be protected further through specific annexes on marine pollution, fauna, flora, waste management, protected areas, and environmental impact assessments. These measures were taken in part because of scientific warnings that tourism—despite heavy penalties assessed for damaging the ecosystem—increasingly threatened the continent.

See also DISARMAMENT, TREATY OF TLATLELOCO.

Further Reading: Joyner, Christopher C. "Recommended Measures under the Antarctic Treaty: Hardening Compliance with Soft International Law." *Michigan Journal of International Law* 19 (Winter 1998): 401–28. Simma, Bruno. "The Antarctic Treaty as a Treaty Creating an 'Objective Regime.'" *Cornell International Law Journal* 19, no. 2 (1986): 189–209. Stokke, Olav Schram, and Davor Vidas, eds. *Governing the Antarctic: The Effectiveness and Legitimacy of the Antarctic Treaty System.* New York: Cambridge University Press, 1996.

apartheid

From 1946 to 1994, the United Nations addressed the issue of apartheid in more than 220 General Assembly Resolutions and with a mandatory arms embargo. During this period, UN bodies such as the ECONOMIC AND SOCIAL COUNCIL and the ECONOMIC COMMISSION ON AFRICA, and SPECIALIZED AGENCIES like the WORLD HEALTH ORGANIZATION, the INTERNATIONAL LABOUR ORGANIZATION, and the INTERNATIONAL ATOMIC ENERGY AGENCY voted to restrict South Africa's MEMBERSHIP. The GENERAL ASSEMBLY also recognized diplomats from the African National Congress and Pan African Congress liberation movements, granting them legitimacy and providing them with needed financial assistance. Over time, South Africa became increasingly ostracized in the United Nations.

South Africa's racial policies were first debated in the United Nations in 1946, when India raised the issue of the treatment of Indian nationals in the Union of South Africa. In response, South Africa invoked the UN CHARTER's principle of noninterference in matters of "domestic JURISDICTION" (Article 2, paragraph 7), and was supported by the UNITED STATES, several European countries, and six Latin American countries. Even though South Africa requested that the INTERNATIONAL COURT OF JUSTICE issue an advisory opinion on the UN's competency, the Indian-sponsored resolution passed the General Assembly. In 1952, India introduced another resolution specifically concerning the practice of apartheid. By 1960, after the Sharpeville massacre, in which 69 people were killed, the General Assembly passed Resolution 1598, almost unanimously, which rejected apartheid as "reprehensible and repugnant to human dignity." Because of increasing global acceptance of racial equality, and the growing number of African states in the UN, support for South Africa's call for

noninterference in the face of UN action declined. In 1962, the General Assembly set up the Special Committee on the Policies of Apartheid of the Government of South Africa, which played a crucial role in keeping the apartheid issue before both the General Assembly and the SECURITY COUNCIL. In Resolution 1761 (1962), the General Assembly placed voluntary SANCTIONS on South Africa, including breaking diplomatic relations, boycotting South African goods, and refusing landing rights to South African aircraft. General Assembly Resolution 2398 (1968) discouraged immigration into South Africa and advocated the end of economic linkages with the country. Though voluntary, these sanctions served to heighten South Africa's ostracism by the global community. By 1983, the General Assembly stridently condemned the "illegitimate racist minority regime" of South Africa and termed apartheid a "crime against humanity."

The Security Council also addressed the issue of apartheid. In 1961, the Council considered a resolution to expel South Africa from the United Nations, but it was

Segregated sports arena in South Africa, 1969 (UN PHOTO 177913/H. VASSAL)

defeated by several PERMANENT MEMBERS. In 1963, with abstentions by France and the United Kingdom, the Council called on South Africa to abandon apartheid, claimed these policies seriously disturbed international peace and security, and set a voluntary arms embargo on the country (Res. 181). With no abstentions, the Council passed Resolution 418 in 1977 to make the arms embargo mandatory. Though the Council condemned apartheid and domestic violence in the wake of the 1976 Soweto riots (Res. 417), the permanent members justified the arms embargo by citing South Africa's confrontational foreign policy toward its neighbors. Yet, the Security Council continued to reject mandatory economic sanctions, even when the 1985 South African state of emergency received international condemnation. Several Security Council draft resolutions on sanctions reached the VOTING stage, but they were always rejected by the United States, United Kingdom, and France. In addition to their concerns about COLD WAR confrontations in southern Africa if South Africa was economically weakened, these permanent members expressed a belief that economic sanctions violated the norm of non-interference and would be ineffective.

In February 1990, the new prime minister of South Africa, Frederik W. de Klerk, ordered the release of the black nationalist leader Nelson Mandela, who had been incarcerated for almost three decades. A year later, de Klerk, in compliance with UN resolutions, announced the end of all apartheid laws. Mandela went on to be elected the first black president of South Africa on May 10, 1994. On May 24, the Security Council terminated the arms embargo against South Africa. In June 1994, the General Assembly approved the credentials of the South African delegation, terminated the mandate of the Special Committee Against Apartheid, and removed from its agenda the item on the "elimination of apartheid and the establishment of a united, democratic and non-racial South Africa." Within days, the Security Council removed the item on "the question of South Africa" from its agenda.

Despite the unwillingness of the Security Council to act more forcefully against the South African apartheid regime, the UN did much to shape international opinion about South Africa and the larger norms of racial equality. Between 1946 and 1990, no issue was more enduring, more debated, or more time consuming within the UN than apartheid.

See also NAMIBIA.

Further Reading: Bissell, Richard. *Apartheid and International Organizations.* Boulder, Colo.: Westview Press, 1977. Boutros-Ghali, Boutros, and Nelson Mandela. *The United Nations and Apartheid.* New York: United Nations Department of Public Information, 1996. Stultz, Newell. "Evolution of the United Nations Anti-Apartheid Regime." *Human Rights Quarterly,* no. 13 (1991): 1–23.

— A. S. Patterson

Appeal to the Security Council

Article 35 of the UN CHARTER allows any member state of the United Nations to bring "any dispute or any situation" that is likely to endanger the maintenance of international peace and security to the attention of the SECURITY COUNCIL. Non–member states may also bring disputes as long as they accept in advance the obligations of pacific settlement laid out in CHAPTER VI. While the Council is not obligated to discuss or act on every complaint brought to it, the use of Article 35 has been one of the usual means by which international conflicts have been placed on its agenda.

Iran's complaint in 1946 that, in the aftermath of World War II, Soviet troops still occupied its northernmost province, was the first appeal to the Council under Article 35. In Africa, states often appealed to the Council to end colonialism or to resolve conflicts between neighboring states. Great powers have also used the procedure to obtain UN endorsement for collective or unilateral action against another state. Conversely, small states have appealed to the Security Council to condemn the actions of major powers. GUATEMALA in 1954 and CUBA in 1960 used this procedure against the UNITED STATES, alleging AGGRESSION in each case.

The question of whether to include an item on the Council's agenda is a procedural matter. It may not be vetoed by one of the PERMANENT MEMBERS. While most appeals are accepted for Council discussion, some have not been. Often prolonged debate occurs over the wisdom of Council action or its JURISDICTION under the Charter. If the Council accepts the appeal, it may invite non-Council members to participate in the debate. It must allow parties to the dispute to address the Council. Once the item is on the Council agenda, the GENERAL ASSEMBLY may make no recommendations concerning it (Article XII), unless the UNITING FOR PEACE RESOLUTION is successfully invoked. In several cases the dispute has remained on the Council's agenda for more than five years.

The Security Council may suggest a traditional means of settling the dispute, including negotiation, INQUIRY, MEDIATION, CONCILIATION, or ARBITRATION. It may also refer the parties to the other bodies of the United Nations, including sending legal disputes to the INTERNATIONAL COURT OF JUSTICE, or to REGIONAL ORGANIZATIONS. In the most serious cases, when it appears that pacific methods are insufficient, it may invoke CHAPTER VII ENFORCEMENT MEASURES and use force to settle the dispute. One strategy, not mentioned in the Charter, but used regularly by the Council when the parties are already locked in battle, has been to call upon the combatants to honor a cease-fire. In a number of Middle East crises this was the approach adopted by the Council, halting the fighting in order to allow for behind-the-scenes diplomacy to find at least a temporary resolution of the conflict.

See also KOREAN WAR.

Further Reading: Bennett, A. LeRoy. *International Organizations: Principles and Issues.* 4th ed. Englewood Cliffs, N.J.: Prentice Hall, 1988. Riggs, Robert E., and Jack C. Plano. *The United Nations: International Organization and World Politics.* Pacific Grove, Calif.: Brooks/Cole Publishing Co., 1988. Simma, Bruno, ed. *The Charter of the United Nations: A Commentary.* New York: Oxford University Press, 1994.

Arab-Israeli dispute

The struggle between the state of Israel and the Palestinian community, the latter supported by surrounding Arab states in the Middle East, has been the longest running conflict facing the United Nations. The British government first handed the problems of the area over to the fledgling UN when it announced in 1947 its intention to withdraw from its LEAGUE OF NATIONS mandate in Palestine. The central problem then, and over the following 60 years, was the conflict between two peoples who claimed one land—the struggle between the indigenous Palestinian Arabs and the Zionist Jews who had been settling in the region since the late 19th century. Between 1948 and 2002 the United Nations found itself embroiled in five international wars, several local uprisings and civil conflicts, terrorist acts, refugee flows, and superpower politics because of the dispute.

Waves of Jewish immigrants poured into Palestine in the first decades of the 20th century and were further encouraged by a British policy statement in 1917 (the Balfour DECLARATION) committing the United Kingdom to the eventual creation of a Zionist state in the mandate. Faced with British departure the following year, the United Nations established the Special Commission on Palestine (UNSCOP) in 1947 to find a solution to the growing conflict between the two peoples. The commission recommended the partition of Palestine into Jewish and Arab states with Jerusalem under international administration. The GENERAL ASSEMBLY approved Resolution 181 on November 29, 1947, endorsing UNSCOP's proposals. In order to give each side approximately the same amount of land while not requiring the massive movement of local populations, the proposed states were carved out of the territory with irregular borders and separated regions. Zionist leaders of the Jewish Agency quickly accepted the plan, but Palestinians and regional Arab leaders rejected it as the "theft" of Palestinian land. Despite the strategic difficulties of the borders proposed by the partition plan, and the lack of Arab support, both the UNITED STATES and the Soviet Union voted for the RESOLUTION.

Violence escalated dramatically in Palestine following passage of Resolution 181. As tensions led to open warfare in the spring of 1948, both sides frantically prepared for the imminent end of British control. On May 14, Zionist leaders declared the independence of the new Israeli state within its assigned borders of the UN partition plan. The United States and the USSR granted diplomatic recognition within hours.

Arab states responded with military intervention. Armies from Egypt, Transjordan, Iraq, and Syria joined Palestinian fighters in an effort to reclaim the land for the Arab community. Despite their overwhelming advantage in numbers, the Arab militaries proved no match for the determined Israelis. During the summer the United Nations attempted to establish a cease-fire through the diplomacy of its mediator, Swedish count Folke Bernadotte. His efforts met with only temporary success. In June the SECURITY COUNCIL created the UNITED NATIONS TRUCE SUPERVISION ORGANIZATION (UNTSO), the UN's first observer mission. UNTSO was directed to assist the UN mediator in his efforts to strengthen the cease-fire. Tragically, Bernadotte was assassinated in Jerusalem on September 17 by Israeli ultranationalists. His successor, Ralph BUNCHE, finally achieved an armistice in spring 1949. By the time the fighting ended, Israel's forces were in control of nearly all of Palestine, with the exceptions of East Jerusalem, the West Bank of the Jordan River, parts of the Golan Heights, and the Gaza Strip.

Equally as important, huge flows of Palestinian refugees, numbering nearly 700,000 individuals, were created by the war, leading to the establishment of refugee camps in surrounding Arab states. On November 19, 1948, the General Assembly created UN Relief for Palestine Refugees (UNRPR), sought $25 million in voluntary contributions for it, and gave the effort nine months to assist the refugees. When it became obvious that refugee assistance would have to extend well into the future, UNRPR was replaced by the UNITED NATIONS RELIEF AND WORKS AGENCY FOR PALESTINE REFUGEES IN THE NEAR EAST (UNRWA). It began operation on May 1, 1950, and its mandate, which included the provision of education and work projects in addition to humanitarian assistance, was regularly renewed through 2002.

The uneasy peace following the 1948 war lasted until 1956. Anti-Israeli policies became a staple of Arab foreign policy. The regional opposition to Israel was spearheaded by Egypt and its nationalist leader, Gamal Abdel NASSER. He had come to power in 1952 with a group of army officers who had staged a coup in the name of national independence and Egyptian modernization. Much of Nasser's domestic support came from his antagonistic stand against the powers that had controlled Egypt for more than 100 years. The most egregious symbol of European imperialism in Egypt was the Suez Canal, built by Napoleon III and controlled later by the British. Unable to obtain American assistance for significant development projects, Nasser first threatened, then nationalized the Suez Canal (July 26, 1956) in order to secure the income from operating the waterway. Both Britain and France saw the seizure of the canal as a mortal threat to their presence not only in the Middle East but also in Asia. Egyptian control of the canal was also perceived as constituting a death grip on the Israeli economy, given the amount of shipping that passed through it on its way to the port of Eilat on the Gulf of Aqaba.

Collusion among Britain, France, and Israel produced a secret arrangement that called for an invasion of Egypt by the latter and a reaction from the European powers that would involve the stationing of an Anglo-French contingent of troops in the canal zone. Israel invaded Egypt on October 29, 1956, and the European forces landed at Port Said and Port Faud on November 5 and 6. Egypt made an APPEAL TO THE SECURITY COUNCIL that led to a resolution vetoed by Britain and France. In response, the Soviet Union invoked the UNITING FOR PEACE RESOLUTION, calling for an emergency session of the General Assembly.

The EMERGENCY SPECIAL SESSION urged a cease-fire, the withdrawal of invading forces, and the reopening of the canal. Canada proposed to the Assembly that it replace foreign forces along the canal with a UN force. On November 4, the Assembly approved Resolution 998 (ES-1) directing SEC-RETARY-GENERAL HAMMARSKJÖLD to submit within 48 hours a plan "for the setting up, with the consent of the nations concerned, of an emergency international United Nations force (later known as UNEF) to secure and supervise the cessation of hostilities." The intent of the operation was to place a neutral force between the combatants and to monitor the cease-fire. Thus was born on November 5, 1956, the United Nations's first PEACEKEEPING operation. The UN effort, combined with pressure from the United States, led to a British and French announcement on December 3 that they would withdraw, and a similar Israeli announcement on March 1, 1957.

UNEF's presence on Egyptian soil (Israel would not allow the peacekeeping force on its territory) ended direct conflict between Israel and its most important Arab neighbor. The next decade witnessed an evolution in the violence to terrorist attacks, bombings, and brief border skirmishes. The Arab states sponsored new Palestinian organizations. Nasser, in particular, made the Palestinian cause a central tenet of his efforts to mobilize a pan-Arab movement in the Middle East. He took the lead in the creation of the Palestine Liberation Organization (PLO) in 1964. With Arab support, Palestinian groups such as al-Fatah launched increasingly severe attacks on Israeli domestic sites.

Hostilities reached a critical point between Israel and two of its foes, Egypt and Syria, in the spring of 1967. There were armed Israeli-Syrian clashes in April. On May 16 Nasser asked UN Secretary-General U THANT to remove from the Sinai the peacekeepers who had been there since the armistice of 1956. Thant acceded, much to the consternation of many world leaders. On May 22 Egypt closed the Strait of Tiran and the Gulf of Aqaba, putting a death grip on Israel's economy. Although U Thant had been warning for several months about the rising threat of violence in the Middle East, the PERMANENT MEMBERS of the Security Council did little prior to the outbreak of war in June.

The MIDDLE EAST WAR OF 1967 began June 5 and ended June 10. It was initiated by Israel's preemptive attack on Egypt, Iraq, Jordan, and Syria in which Israeli forces seized the Sinai Peninsula, Syrian territory in the Golan Heights, and the land designated by the 1947 UN partition plan as the territory for the Arab state in Palestine. Israel's air force simultaneously attacked 17 major Egyptian air bases, destroying the bulk of Egypt's airpower within hours of the initiation of hostilities. Similar success against its other Arab enemies led to Israeli occupation of East Jerusalem and the West Bank, producing new waves of Palestinian refugee emigration and adding the issues of Jerusalem's future and that of the occupied territories to the general dispute between Israel and the Arabs.

Israel accepted a UN cease-fire on June 10. It was not until November that the Security Council was able to arrive at a resolution acceptable to all of the parties. RESOLUTION 242, adopted unanimously on November 22, called for a withdrawal of Israel's forces from occupied territories to safe and secure borders, a termination of the state of belligerency and mutual recognition, freedom of navigation, and a settlement of the refugee problem. The recalcitrance of both the Israelis and the Arabs required strong pressure from both the United States and the Soviet Union on their respective allies to get this agreement. Later, there would be acrimony among the parties over the meaning of Resolution 242, specifically concerning whether it required the Israelis to withdraw from *ALL* occupied territories or only from those that would not jeopardize Israel's security. The resolution was premised on the idea of "land for peace," which became one of the cornerstones for all subsequent regional peace negotiations.

The 1967 war marked the emergence of the Arab-Israeli dispute as a central issue in COLD WAR politics between the two superpowers. Lyndon Johnson would be the last U.S. president of the 20th century to believe that this region, as it had been in 1948, was essentially a responsibility of the world's representatives in New York. The "War of Attrition," as it was called, which followed the 1967 conflict, witnessed the division of the region into ideological camps with the Arabs largely dependent on the USSR. In the Soviet-American confrontation each side attempted to manipulate the dispute to its own advantage.

In 1970 Egyptian president Nasser died and was succeeded by Anwar Sadat. In the wake of a confrontation with Egypt's patron, the Soviet Union, Sadat decided that the return of the Sinai depended on a successful demonstration of his country's military strength against Israel and a shift in diplomatic alliances, which would lead to a new and positive relationship with the United States. In Washington the new Nixon administration was pleased that Sadat had removed more than 10,000 Soviet advisers, and it hoped to supplant both Soviet and UN influence over the Arab-Israeli dispute.

At the United Nations, support for Israel, which was increasingly seen as the aggressor and illegal occupier of Arab lands by the growing Third World majority in UN MEMBERSHIP, declined precipitously after 1967. The world body steadily shifted toward support for the Palestinian cause, culminating in the recognition of the Palestine Liberation Organization as the "legitimate representative of the Palestinian people" in 1974, and its achievement of "OBSERVER STATUS" at the UN. Anti-Israeli sentiment peaked with the passage of the ZIONISM IS RACISM RESOLUTION in November 1975. The General Assembly resolution passed by a large majority and equated Israel with the racist regimes then in power in Zimbabwe and South Africa.

The hesitant peace after the 1967 war lasted only until October 6, 1973. On Yom Kippur, the Day of Atonement in the Jewish calendar, Syria and Egypt opened two fronts against Israel seeking to liberate lands captured in the previous conflict. Egypt established a line across the Suez Canal, allowing President Sadat to claim a rare Arab victory against Israeli forces. Within 10 days, however, the balance of forces had shifted and both Syria and Egypt were in retreat. In a daring move Israeli forces crossed the canal, surrounded Suez City, and threatened to march north toward Cairo. The change in military fortune gave incentive to both sides to seek a cease-fire. At the United Nations the USSR offered a draft Security Council resolution calling for (1) a cease-fire in place, (2) withdrawal of Israeli forces to borders implied in Resolution 242, and (3) the commencement of consultations on a peace agreement. After lengthy negotiations between the Soviets and the Nixon administration the Security Council passed Resolution 340, calling for a "return" to the original cease-fire lines as provided in Resolution 338. Following a meeting in the Sinai between Israeli and Egyptian negotiators under UN auspices, a cease-fire was restored.

President Nixon and Secretary of State Kissinger wanted the United States to play the dominant role in bringing a settlement to the troubled area. Despite American sponsorship of Resolution 338, and the Sinai talks under UN auspices, the administration largely ignored the UN machinery in succeeding years as Kissinger launched "Shuttle Diplomacy," hurrying among Middle East capitals, offering American GOOD OFFICES, and brokering several interim peace arrangements. By the time Kissinger left office in 1977, he had engineered a military disengagement between the Egyptians and the Israelis on the Sinai Peninsula (January 1974) and a similar agreement between the Israelis and the Syrians on the Golan Heights (May 1974). In the Golan Heights the United Nations Disengagement Observer Force (UNDOF) monitored the agreement. On September 4, 1975, Kissinger successfully cobbled together an acceptable buffer zone in the Sinai, originally to be maintained by U.S. civilian technicians stationed between the antagonists. U.S. domination of international efforts to resolve the Arab-Israeli dispute continued into the presidency of Jimmy Carter. While a strong advocate of the United Nations, Carter played the central role in the negotiation of the Camp David Accords, which included a "Framework for Peace" between Israelis and Palestinians and a draft peace TREATY between Israel and Egypt.

Anwar Sadat surprised the world in November 1977 when he became the first Arab leader to make a visit to Israel. In an effort to advance the American-shepherded peace process, in which he had invested much political capital, Sadat addressed the Israeli Knesset and declared his desire for peace. Determined not to let the momentum provided by Sadat's visit slip, Carter invited Sadat and Israeli prime minister Menachem Begin to convene at Camp David, the presidential retreat in rural Maryland. Meetings commenced on September 5, 1978, and lasted 13 days. In the end, the two antagonists agreed to two documents: first, a historic peace agreement between Israel and Egypt, by which the two nations would exchange ambassadors and the Israelis would return occupied portions of the Sinai Peninsula to Egypt; and second, a "Framework for Peace," based on UN Resolutions 242 and 338, detailing procedures to complete a comprehensive peace for the region. The framework called for negotiations involving the United States, Egypt, Israel, and Jordan for the purposes of granting a "homeland" to the Palestinians and securing the border of Israel. In the framework agreement the parties recognized the right of Palestinian representatives to participate in negotiations aimed at establishing an "elected self-governing authority in the West Bank and Gaza." The framework called on the UN Security Council to ensure that its provisions were carried out. The framework laid the basis for a political settlement of the land dispute between Israelis and Palestinians, but it left the question of Jerusalem to future negotiations.

Final approved treaties were scheduled to be completed within three months. But they were not. In the ensuing months, the parties quibbled, and Begin backpedaled on crucial details of the accords. His government also pursued a controversial policy of creating Jewish settlements on the West Bank, drastically changing the demographic and political character of the territory. Rejectionists among Palestinians and the Arab states condemned the framework. Matters were not made easier in March 1978 when Begin ordered an invasion of Lebanon in retaliation for attacks on Israel from guerrilla bases in the southern regions of that tormented country. In the attack, Israel had used American-supplied cluster bombs. Carter was irate, and the United States took the lead in proposing Security Council Resolution 425, which condemned the invasion.

In March 1979, Carter traveled to Cairo and Jerusalem. Once again he used considerable personal pressure to force the parties to an agreement. On March 26, 1979, at the White House, with Carter between them, Sadat and Begin signed the two documents, the first such PACT between an Arab country and Israel since the latter's founding more than 30 years earlier.

In an effort to disrupt the Camp David Accords, the PLO stepped up guerrilla attacks on Israel from southern Lebanon and Syrian territory. In response the Israeli government annexed the Golan Heights in December 1981. Then, on June 6, 1982, it launched a full-scale invasion of Lebanon and headed to Beirut to rout the Palestinians. That same day, the UN Security Council passed Resolution 509, demanding that "Israel withdraw all its military forces forthwith and unconditionally to the internationally recognized boundaries of Lebanon." Ignoring the UN action, Israeli forces within a few days had advanced to the outskirts of Beirut and occupied most of the southern half of the country.

The United States, which had brokered the peace process since the 1973 war, found itself pressured by moderate Arab states to save the Palestine Liberation Organization from complete defeat. The new U.S. secretary of state, George Shultz, and his special envoy in Lebanon, Philip Habib, worked out a plan for the PLO to evacuate the capital city under the protection of a multinational force made up of French, Italian, and American marines. On September 1, President Reagan articulated a new American Middle East policy. He proposed a formula of "peace in exchange for territory," with Israel giving up the West Bank, which would become a Palestinian "homeland" to be confederated with Jordan. The Arab states endorsed the Reagan autonomy plan as a good first step. The Israeli government, however, rejected it outright. With no agreement on the Palestinian issue, Israel was bogged down in Lebanon with no obvious way to declare victory and leave.

The frustrations of continued iron-fisted Israeli occupation on the West Bank and Gaza, coupled with new Jewish settlements in the territories and no signs of progress in the peace process, produced the 1987 intifada, a persistent, spontaneous, and widely supported uprising by Palestinians under occupation. Fearing the loss of allegiance from Palestinians in the territories, the PLO indicated its readiness to accept the legitimacy of, and negotiate directly with, Israel. At the end of July 1988, King Hussein announced that Jordan would cut all legal and administrative ties to the West Bank. There was, then, by late summer, considerable activity around the Israeli-Palestinian issue, much of which seemed to suggest the possibility of positive movement. Added to this was the new friendliness between the Soviet Union and the United States, which made senseless any continuing interpretation of the Middle East problem as part of the cold war.

In the fall of 1988, the PLO representative at the United Nations, Zehdi Terzi, informed the Security Council that he would request a visa for Yasser Arafat to come to the regular session of the General Assembly. By treaty with the United Nations, the United States had agreed not to block such visas unless a security risk was involved. At the same time, U.S. law forbade representatives of the PLO from visiting unless the secretary of state recommended an exception. This Shultz was unwilling to do, unless the PLO renounced TERRORISM and accepted the provisions of Resolution 242. While Arafat did not attend the General Assembly meeting,

in December he met American conditions that Shultz indicated could result in negotiations with the United States. The new administration of George Bush, thus, opened direct talks with the PLO the following year.

The American-orchestrated peace process was put on hold by Saddam Hussein's invasion of Kuwait in August 1990. The allied victory in the ensuing GULF WAR, however, gave the United States new persuasive power in both Israel and the Arab states, as well as with the PLO. Secretary of State James Baker shuttled between capitals in hope of a breakthrough, an effort culminating in the Madrid Conference in 1991. PLO representatives from the occupied territories joined Israeli government officials and representatives of the Arab states at the negotiating table with President Bush and Soviet president Mikhail Gorbachev. Bush also urged the full participation of the United Nations in the conference, a position adamantly opposed by the Israeli government. In the end the UN was granted a meager "observer" status. The conference operated on two tracks: direct negotiations between Israel and its individual Arab adversaries, and multilateral talks on broader regional issues. Importantly, the Madrid Conference provided the umbrella structure for secret talks between the PLO and the Israeli government, largely conducted away from the Madrid venue. These talks culminated in the Oslo Accords of 1993, which formally accepted the long-endorsed UN principle of partition in Palestine.

As part of the accords, formally signed in Washington on September 13, the PLO conceded Israel's right to exist, and Israel recognized the Palestine Liberation Organization as the representative of the Palestinian people. The Declaration of Principles established a Palestinian Authority in the Gaza Strip and in the West Bank city of Jericho, where Arafat then established his new government. The accords contemplated the eventual transfer of most of the occupied territories to Palestinian control, the negotiation of a final status agreement on Jerusalem, and the refugees' right of return. The momentum of the agreement led to a peace treaty between Israel and Jordan in 1994. A second Oslo Agreement, encouraged by the United States, was negotiated in September 1995.

The peace process suffered a severe blow when Yigal Amir shot Israeli prime minister Yitzhak Rabin to death on November 4, 1995. A fanatical religious nationalist, Amir admitted at his trial that he assassinated the prime minister in an effort to halt the movement toward peace. He reflected the deep animosity in segments of both the Israeli and the Palestinian communities against the terms established in the Oslo Accords. Most of the opposition in Palestinian society came from Hamas and other Islamic fundamentalist groups. While the interim government of Shimon Peres attempted to move ahead on the peace process, Israeli elections brought to power Benjamin Netanyahu, who opposed any additional concessions to the Palestinian Authority. The new Likud government emphasized security and settlements in the territories. In the spring of 1997 the United States found it necessary to VETO a Security Council resolution condemning the construction of an Israeli settlement at Har Homa. President Clinton, however, went to great lengths to explain this veto, arguing that the insertion of the United Nations into the issue could jeopardize the ongoing peace negotiations between the Israelis and the Palestinians.

Clinton convened a second Camp David Summit in the summer of 2000, bringing together Arafat and Ehud Barak, Netanyahu's successor. All three leaders had conveyed optimism that a final agreement resolving all of the remaining issues of the Arab-Israeli dispute could be reached. Unfortunately, the meeting ended in failure. While Barak made major concessions on land and Palestinian control over the Holy Sites, Arafat refused to accept an agreement that did not recognize the refugees' right of return and did not grant full SOVEREIGNTY in Jerusalem. The collapse of the summit contributed to the disenchantment in the territories, which in turn produced a second intifada in the fall. Sparked by Israeli politician Ariel Sharon's untimely appearance in September atop the holiest (and most contentious) site in Jerusalem—the Temple Mount, or Haram al-Sharif—Palestinians took to the streets and attacked Israeli security forces and settlers. Israel responded with heavy military force.

As hostilities grew in the streets of the West Bank, U.S. secretary of state Madeleine Albright hurried to Paris and tried to convince assembled Middle East leaders to do something to salvage the faltering peace process. She had no success. On another front, for the first time since 1973 an American administration sought the active leadership of the UN Secretary-General. Kofi ANNAN, who had been shuttling between Jerusalem, Tel Aviv, and Gaza City, and traveling elsewhere in the Middle East, in a quest to ease tensions, stepped into the US/Israeli/Palestinian standoff. With a calm persistence that had become his trademark, Annan persuaded Barak, Arafat, and Egyptian president Hosni Mubarak to convene a summit at Sharm al-Sheik on October 14, 2000. The Israeli government and the Palestinian Authority had come to trust Annan. According to Israel's ambassador to the United Nations, Yehuda Lanery, Annan had "opened the door to Israel. He [was] perceived by Israel as a man of reason, displaying the greatest moral authority possible." The Israeli confidence in Annan was based in part on his expression of regret for the tone of past UN resolutions toward Israel, which he had made during a visit to Jerusalem early in his term. Annan particularly had expressed pleasure at the repeal of the 1975 "Zionism is Racism" resolution in 1991.

At Sharm al-Sheik the United States and the United Nations worked in tandem. President Clinton served as chairman of the summit and Secretary-General Annan provided the quiet diplomacy that led to a tenuous agreement. Arafat and Barak agreed, orally—not in signed form—to call for a halt to the violence; Barak agreed to withdraw Israeli military forces to positions held before the beginning of the unrest, to lift the closure of the West Bank and Gaza, and to reopen the Gaza airport. Security forces from both sides agreed to resume a dialogue that had been interrupted by the crisis. Clinton also announced the creation of a U.S.–controlled fact-finding committee to investigate the causes of the crisis. Clinton appointed the members of the commission after consulting with the parties and Annan. The president designated George Mitchell, former U.S. senator and negotiator of the "Good Friday" agreement in Northern Ireland, as the chairman of the commission. The text of the commission's report, then, was to be shown to Annan and UN officials before being published, and the final decision on the wording of the report was to be made by the United States. A new triangulation had emerged among the White House, UN headquarters, and Middle East leaders.

Unfortunately, the Sharm al-Sheik accord only produced a brief pause in the violence, which soon took the form of Palestinian attacks on settlers and retaliatory Israeli security measures. Faced with opposition from within Palestinian ranks, and with no evidence his commitments at Sharm al-Sheik on their own could halt protests in the streets, Arafat proposed a UN peacekeeping presence in the territories. He sought 2,000 UN peacekeepers to separate the parties on the West Bank and particularly in Gaza, and to limit police actions by the Israeli occupation forces. Tel Aviv immediately rejected the idea. Arafat, however, found support for the proposal not only in Arab capitals but also in Paris, London, and Moscow. Only the threat of a U.S. veto in the Security Council held Britain, France, and Russia to a mere abstention on the final resolution. The resolution failed by only one vote on December 18.

The Israeli electorate chose Ariel Sharon as its new prime minister in the spring of 2001, largely on his promise to end the intifada. Sharon refused to negotiate further with Arafat until the Palestinian Authority controlled the violence. Arafat was hesitant to do so until there was an Israeli promise to withdraw its security forces as agreed at the summit. When the Mitchell Commission issued its report, it called for an end to the violence and a halt to the Israeli construction of settlements in the territories. Both UN and U.S. officials endorsed the commission's recommendations. The new Bush administration sent Secretary of State Colin Powell to the region. On June 28, he announced a change in American policy, endorsing the placement of an observer mission to monitor a cooling-off period until peace negotiations could resume. The creation of such a monitoring force would likely mean a new level of UN involvement in the Middle East crisis. Powell's announcement seemed to foretell a new model of cooperation between New York and Washington in trying to end the Arab-Israeli dispute, which the United Nations first addressed more than 50 years earlier.

Despite concerted UN and U.S. efforts, violence escalated during summer 2001. A series of deadly suicide bombings orchestrated by Palestinian groups and reprisal military assassinations by the Sharon government of Palestinian leaders on the West Bank and the Gaza Strip ended the possibility of an early resumption of peace talks. The terrorist attack on the World Trade Center in New York City on September 11, and the strong American response against terrorist organizations in AFGHANISTAN, encouraged the Israeli government to move military forces into territories controlled by Yasser Arafat's Palestine Authority. Prime Minister Sharon claimed that Arafat was responsible for terrorism against Israeli civilians and could no longer be a partner in the peace process. His contention was reinforced in January 2002 by the interception of a large arms shipment to the Palestinians ostensibly from Iran. Israeli forces surrounded Arafat's headquarters on the West Bank, barring his free movement in the territories and abroad. Israeli policies, however, did not stem the violence. In late February, Sharon announced that the government would attempt to create "buffer zones" between Palestinian and Israeli communities, effectively segregating the warring sides. Arab nations, in support of the Palestinian cause, introduced in the UN Security Council a resolution condemning Israeli actions, but the council instead passed Resolution 1397 on March 12, calling for an end to the violence and the creation of two states side by side. Palestinian claims of genocide by Israeli forces in Jenin led to efforts by Secretary-General Annan to dispatch a fact-finding mission, but Israel's opposition made that impossible.

See also MIDDLE EAST WAR OF 1973, SUEZ CRISIS, ZIONISM.

Further Reading: Bailey, Sydney D. *Four Arab-Israeli Wars and the Peace Process.* London: Macmillan, 1990. Bickerton, Ian, and Carla Klausner. *A Concise History of the Arab-Israeli Conflict.* 2d edition. Englewood Cliffs, N.J.: Prentice Hall, 1995. Laqueur, Walter, and Barry Rubin. *The Israel-Arab Reader: A Documentary History of the Middle East Conflict.* New York: Penguin Books, 2000. Moore, John Allphin, Jr., and Jerry Pubantz. *To Create a New World? American Presidents and the United Nations.* New York: Peter Lang Publishers, 1999. Shlaim, Avi. *The Iron Wall. Israel and the Arab World.* New York: W.W. Norton, 2001.

arbitration

Arbitration is the process of settling a dispute by using an impartial party or tribunal chosen by the opposing sides that decides the differences between them and adjudicates a solution. Adversaries usually agree in advance to accept the arbitrator's judgment (so-called compulsory arbitration). In international disagreements, arbitrators may be selected from the PERMANENT COURT OF INTERNATIONAL ARBITRATION (PCA), created by the Hague Peace Conferences of 1899 and 1907, or may be selected ad hoc by the disputants. Arbitration is typically conducted on the basis of the rules, practices, and precedents of INTERNATIONAL LAW.

Arbitration is an antique arrangement, used most notably from the late 18th century into the interwar period of the 20th century. The Jay TREATY of 1794, negotiated by Great Britain and the UNITED STATES, introduced the modern practice of arbitration as a means of peaceful dispute resolution between two states, and the procedure was used on a few occasions, most notably in the settlement of an American claim from the Civil War period, resulting in the so-called Alabama Arbitration of 1872. Between 1900 and 1932, 20 international disputes utilized the PCA procedures. Since then, only three cases have been resolved in this manner. The proliferation of established arrangements for international judicial settlement, such as the INTERNATIONAL COURT OF JUSTICE, a range of international tribunals, the European Court of Justice, the INTERNATIONAL CRIMINAL COURT, and various MEDIATION procedures in regional and trade organizations, rendered arbitration less practical by the late 20th century.

In 1958 the United Nations GENERAL ASSEMBLY adopted the Model Rules on Arbitral Procedure, formulated by the INTERNATIONAL LAW COMMISSION. The most serious use of arbitration in the contemporary period was the establishment of the Iran–United States Claims Tribunal in 1981 to adjudicate property claims by nationals in each country against the other government. The tribunal was a component in the resolution of the IRAN HOSTAGE CRISIS.

See also CHAPTER VI, CONCILIATION, CONFLICT RESOLUTION, GOOD OFFICES, INDONESIA, ORGANIZATION OF AFRICAN UNITY, UNITED NATIONS CONFERENCE ON THE LAW OF THE SEA.

arms control   *See* DISARMAMENT.

arms race   *See* DISARMAMENT.

Asian Development Bank (ADB)   *See* REGIONAL DEVELOPMENT BANKS.

assessments   *See* SCALE OF ASSESSMENTS.

Atlantic Charter

The Atlantic Charter was the joint DECLARATION of purpose issued by Franklin Delano ROOSEVELT and Winston CHURCHILL at the Atlantic Conference held at Placentia Bay, Newfoundland, on August 9–12, 1941. FDR desired a public statement of fundamental American political convictions regarding a just and peaceful international order that would rally public support for an increasingly dangerous foreign policy in both the Atlantic and the Pacific regions. He also sought a joint statement with Britain (unlike Woodrow

Winston Churchill and Franklin Roosevelt at Atlantic Conference (UN/DPI Photo)

Wilson's unilateral FOURTEEN POINTS) that could serve as a rallying point for an anti-Axis coalition.

The United States and Britain pledged territorial nonaggrandizement, self-determination, freedom of trade, freedom of the seas, the abandonment of the use of force, DISARMAMENT, and ultimately, in some form, a world security organization. The joint declaration was not a state paper in the usual sense of the term. Technically, it was nothing more than a press release, of which there was no official copy.

Nevertheless, the Charter was cabled to Joseph STALIN for his endorsement and on January 1, 1942, at U.S. secretary of state Cordell HULL's suggestion, 26 nations pledged their support for the principles of the Charter in the "DECLARATION BY UNITED NATIONS." This document not only avoided the troubling domestic issue of a formal alliance with Great Britain but also it served as the foundation stone for the later United Nations Organization. The first four signatures on the declaration were those of the representatives of the UNITED STATES, the United Kingdom, the Soviet Union, and CHINA, privately referred to by FDR as "THE FOUR POLICEMEN."

Further Reading: Dallek, Robert. *Franklin D. Roosevelt and American Foreign Policy* 1932–1945. New York: Oxford University Press, 1979. Hoopes, Townsend, and Douglas Brink-ley. *FDR and the Creation of the U.N.* New Haven, Conn.: Yale University Press, 1997. Kimball, Warren. *The Juggler.* Princeton, N.J.: Princeton University Press, 1991. Langer, William, and S. Everett Gleason. *The Undeclared War. 1940–1941.* New York: Harper and Brothers, 1953.

— E. M.Clauss

Atomic Energy Commission (United Nations Atomic Energy Commission)   *See* DISARMAMENT.

Atoms for Peace proposal

U.S. president Dwight D. Eisenhower addressed the UN GENERAL ASSEMBLY on December 8, 1953, and proposed that the nuclear powers gradually transfer a percentage of their fissionable materials to a new INTERNATIONAL ATOMIC ENERGY AGENCY (IAEA), which would be under the ultimate authority of the United Nations. The proposed agency, according to Eisenhower, would safeguard the plutonium deposits and look for ways to use them for the "peaceful pursuits of mankind," such as the generation of electricity "in the power-starved areas of the world." He envisioned scientists and experts mobilized to transform the materials of nuclear destruction into the assets of peaceful world construction. He offered to put U.S. stockpiles under IAEA control at a ratio of 5 to 1 of that turned over by the Soviet Union. Eisenhower's speech provided impetus to UN DISARMAMENT negotiations that led to the 1957 creation of the IAEA and its "safeguards" system for monitoring nuclear material used for peaceful purposes.

During the previous April, the president had directed his advisers to draft a major speech for him on the destructive potential of atomic and hydrogen bombs. In an address that same month to the American Society of Newspaper Editors, he argued that there was a "chance for peace" in the COLD WAR if the USSR was willing to follow a policy of "goodwill." In that case, the two sides could pursue nuclear disarmament, and the savings from that cooperative course of action could be used by the United Nations for a "total war . . . on the brute forces of poverty and need." He laid out the prospect that the end of the arms race could produce the resources for "roads and schools, hospitals and homes, food and health" and could "make the United Nations an institution that can effectively guard the peace and security of all peoples."

It was this formula of responsible Soviet behavior, superpower disarmament, and UN use of armaments savings for humanitarian and development assistance in the Third World that underlay Eisenhower's proposal to the General Assembly in December of his first year in office. Moscow's immediate reaction to the "Atoms for Peace" proposal was negative, as it had been to the Truman administration's BARUCH PLAN. That proposal had also contemplated the transfer of national nuclear assets to UN supervision. Any reduction, however, in nuclear stockpiles by the two sides, even if it drew more heavily from the American arsenal, would still have left the UNITED STATES with an advantage, and consequently the Soviet government was opposed to it. Nonetheless, the United Nations established an IAEA Preparatory Commission in 1954, and the Soviet Union agreed to serve on it, along with the United States, Czechoslovakia, the Vatican, India, and Australia. Eisenhower's speech also created sufficient momentum for the convocation of the first UN Conference on the "Peaceful Uses of Nuclear Energy" (PUNE) in the summer of 1955. After lengthy negotiations the Statute of the IAEA was approved on October 23, 1956, and the agency began operations in 1957. It had no authority to take possession of fissionable materials, but it was authorized to develop nuclear safety standards, and, based on those standards, to assist its member states in the use of nuclear science and technology for peaceful purposes. The agency, which was an outgrowth of Eisenhower's proposal, encompassed 132 member states as of June 2001.

See also ACHESON-LILIENTHAL REPORT.

Further Reading: Ambrose, Stephen E. *Eisenhower: The President.* Vol. 2. New York: Simon and Schuster, 1984. Pruden, Caroline. *Conditional Partners: Eisenhower, the United Nations, and the Search for a Permanent Peace.* Baton Rouge: Louisiana State University Press, 1998. Atoms for Peace Speech website:<www.iaea.org/worldatom/About/atoms.html>.

B

bacteriological weapons   *See* DISARMAMENT, WEAPONS OF MASS DESTRUCTION.

Baruch Plan

This proposal, presented to the United Nations ATOMIC ENERGY COMMISSION (UNAEC) on June 14, 1946, by American industrialist Bernard Baruch, the U.S. representative to the commission, was the first plan ever proposed for the control of nuclear weapons. The commission itself had been created by the UN's first RESOLUTION as an effort to rid "national armaments of atomic WEAPONS and all major weapons adaptable to mass destruction."

The Baruch proposal derived from a committee appointed by President Harry S. Truman, and headed by Dean ACHESON and David Lilienthal (the administrator of the Tennessee Valley Authority). The ACHESON-LILIENTHAL REPORT provided for an international body to control the raw materials and the production facilities used for atomic energy. Truman then appointed Baruch to present the plan to the UN Atomic Energy Commission. The industrialist altered the original proposal by inserting a VOTING procedure that in effect would have given the UNITED STATES considerable influence over every step in the plan—including the peaceful use of atomic energy in countries like the Soviet Union. On December 30, 1946, the commission approved the Baruch Plan, thereby rejecting an alternative proposal,

the so-called Gromyko Plan (named for Soviet ambassador to Washington Andrei Gromyko) that the USSR had offered. The two sides' objections to the other's plan hardened into a pattern that permeated arms control and DISARMAMENT negotiations between the two superpowers throughout almost the entirety of the COLD WAR.

Specifically, the Baruch Plan called for the creation of an International Atomic Development Authority (IADA) that would own and manage all aspects of atomic energy "potentially dangerous to world security." According to the plan no nation would be allowed nuclear weapons and the SECURITY COUNCIL VETO would not extend to the IADA's decisions. The IADA would verify compliance of the peaceful uses of nuclear materials by on-site inspection and any state refusing inspections would suffer economic SANCTIONS. Once the IADA was operating and the inspections regime was in place, the United States would destroy its own atomic stockpile. The Soviets resisted allowing the United States even momentary exclusive control over atomic weaponry and found distasteful the inspections regime. The Gromyko Plan, conversely, called for a speedy abolition of the U.S. nuclear arsenal, rejected the inspection provisions, and demanded the extension of the veto power to the new authority. The United Nations Atomic Energy Commission suspended its meetings on July 29, 1947, due to the deadlock between the United States and the Soviet Union, and the Baruch Plan was never implemented.

Further Reading: Baruch, Bernard M. *Baruch.* Vol. 2. *The Public Years.* New York: Holt, Rinehart and Winston, 1960. Bechhoefer, Bernard. *Postwar Negotiations for Arms Control.* Washington, D.C.: Brookings Institution, 1961. Herken, Gregg. *The Winning Weapon: The Atomic Bomb in the Cold War, 1945–1950.* New York: Vintage Books, 1980. Holloway, David. *The Soviet Union and the Arms Race.* New Haven, Conn.: Yale University Press, 1984.

— S. L. Williams

Basel Convention on the Control of Transboundary Movements of Hazardous Wastes and Their Disposal (BC)

Public disclosure in the 1980s that Western industrialists had been dumping toxic wastes in the developing world, mostly in African countries, led to an international effort to ban or regulate the practice. Sponsored by the UNITED NATIONS ENVIRONMENT PROGRAMME (UNEP), the 1987 Cairo Guidelines on Waste Management were drafted to assist states in their own development of waste policies. Two years later a UNEP conference in Basel, Switzerland, adopted the Basel Convention, which did not ban transboundary movement of hazardous waste, but did place stiff regulations on the practice and created a SECRETARIAT to implement its provisions. UNEP provided financing and staffing for the CONVENTION, with the Secretariat's HEADQUARTERS in Geneva. On January 28, 2001, Dr. Sachiko Kuwabara-Yamamoto of Japan became the new BC executive secretary.

The objectives of the convention were to reduce the production, transboundary movement, and distant disposal of hazardous waste, including materials containing arsenic, lead, mercury, asbestos, and other dangerous chemicals. BC also prohibited shipment of this type of waste to countries without the legal, administrative, and technical capability to handle it safely. In addition, the secretariat assisted states with the development of environmentally sound management practices.

By August 2001, 148 nations had joined the convention. Signatories were obligated to put in place national enforcement measures to fulfill the aims of the PACT. Each transboundary shipment of hazardous waste had to be accompanied by a movement document from the exporting state to the national authorities of the importing nation. Moreover, states were required to identify appropriate disposal and storage sites with sufficient environmental safeguards and to provide enforcement personnel trained in the identification of hazardous waste, with a knowledge of normal companies' operations and a familiarity with international documentation requirements. The Basel Convention established regional centers in Argentina, CHINA, Egypt, EL SALVADOR, India, INDONESIA, Nigeria, Senegal, Slovak Republic, South Africa, RUSSIAN FEDERATION, Trinidad and Tobago, and Uruguay in order to assist governments in these tasks.

The convention created a Conference of the Parties (COP) to meet biennially as the governing body. COP-6 was scheduled for 2002. In previous sessions the COP had added new PROTOCOLS to the convention, strengthening its regulatory functions. The most important of these was the 1995 Ban Amendment, which prohibited export of hazardous waste for any purpose from EU and OECD countries and from Liechtenstein to any other signatory states. In order to enter into force, the ban needed ratification from 62 of the parties present at the time of adoption. As of August 9, 2001, this goal had not been achieved. On that date the U.S. government announced it would seek Senate consent for ratification of the 1989 convention but not of the 1995 amendment. Without American support the prospects for the ban were seriously diminished.

See also AGENDA 21, COMMISSION ON SUSTAINABLE DEVELOPMENT, ENVIRONMENT.

Further Reading: Eco'Diagnostic, Geneva. *International Geneva Yearbook, 2000–2001.* Geneva: United Nations, 2000. BC website: <www.basel.int>.

Beijing Conference   *See* WORLD CONFERENCES ON WOMEN.

Beijing Declaration   *See* WORLD CONFERENCES ON WOMEN.

Beijing +5

In June of 2000, a SPECIAL SESSION of the UN GENERAL ASSEMBLY convened in New York to appraise and assess the progress achieved in the implementation of the Nairobi Forward-looking Strategies for the Advancement of WOMEN and the Beijing Declaration and Platform for Action. The Special Session became known as "Beijing +5" since it was intended to consider what had been accomplished and what was still needed following the Beijing Global Conference on Women, which had been held in 1995. Participants in the Special Session included UN member states, associate members of regional economic commissions, UN SPECIALIZED AGENCIES, NON-GOVERNMENTAL ORGANIZATIONS (NGOs), and intergovernmental organizations (IGOs) in CONSULTATIVE STATUS with the ECONOMIC AND SOCIAL COUNCIL (ECOSOC), including NGOs that were accredited to the FOURTH WORLD CONFERENCE ON WOMEN in Beijing, and new NGOs that had achieved accreditation since 1995.

Delegates to Beijing +5 considered 12 areas of concern cited in the Beijing Platform for Action. The topics were poverty, education and training, health, violence, armed conflict, economy, decision making, institutional mechanisms, HUMAN RIGHTS, media, ENVIRONMENT, and the plight of the girl-child. The Platform for Action had spelled out strategic objectives and actions to be taken by governments, non-governmental organizations, the private sector, and the international community. Beijing +5 provided the opportunity to reflect, compare experiences, review commitments, and examine problems and obstacles faced as well as useful practices achieved in putting the Platform of Action into effect. The report of the Special Session recognized the accelerated progress made in some areas of the platform and the problems of discrimination and human rights yet to be addressed.

See also WORLD CONFERENCES ON WOMEN.

Further Reading: Beijing +5 website:<www.un.org/womenwatch/followup/beijing5/about.htm>.

— *K. J. Vogel*

Bernadotte, Folke   *See* ARAB-ISRAELI DISPUTE.

biological weapons (BW)

Biological WEAPONS are living organisms, most commonly bacteria and viruses, deliberately disseminated to cause death or disease in humans, animals, or plants. Biological weapons are considered WEAPONS OF MASS DESTRUCTION because they have the potential to destroy life equaled only by nuclear weapons. They could also be used for much smaller scale effect and in clandestine operations. An important distinction between biological weapons and nuclear weapons is that the former do not have the ability to destroy a country's infrastructure or industrial capacity. Despite the concern about BW TERRORISM in recent years, the power of governments to build, maintain, and hide offensive BW programs still constitutes the most serious biological weapons' threat to international peace and security. Advances in the biological sciences in the last quarter century have added to the risk that such expertise could be misused.

The 1925 Geneva PROTOCOL prohibited the use of biological weapons in warfare. The 1972 Convention on the Prohibition of the Development, Production, and Stockpiling of Bacteriological (Biological) and Toxin Weapons and on Their Destruction (BWC) went further by prohibiting their development and possession. The United Nations provides conference services for the BWC and has strongly encouraged its members to strengthen the TREATY's effectiveness through a legally binding protocol. The UN SECRETARY-GENERAL has the authority to investigate the alleged use of biological weapons, ascertain facts regarding such alleged use, and report his findings to the member states.

Prior to the 20th century and the widespread understanding of the role of germs in causing disease, the use of biological weapons was extremely rare. In certain instances, however, their use was well documented, most notably in the deliberate spread of disease among the INDIGENOUS PEOPLE in North America. The 20th century was characterized by state efforts to develop, produce, and, to a lesser extent, use biological weapons. Germany used veterinary biological weapons for sabotage purposes in World War I. Japan had a sophisticated BW program directed against humans with large-scale experimentation and use in CHINA in the 1940s. The UNITED STATES, United Kingdom, Canada, and France all had BW research, development, and production programs in the years preceding and/or during World War II, but none of these countries used the weapons they developed.

A number of countries violated their obligations under the BWC by initiating or continuing to develop and produce biological weapons following the treaty's entry into force. The Soviet Union maintained a massive secret BW program, South Africa produced biological weapons in the 1980s and 1990s, and Iraq, while a signatory of the BWC, developed an offensive biological program in the 1980s. In 1991 the UN SECURITY COUNCIL required Iraq to accept the unconditional destruction of its biological weapons and all components of its BW program. Despite years of inspections and extensive evidence and documentation of Iraq's BW program, its complete destruction could not be confirmed. Following complaints from CUBA to the Secretary-General that the United States had used these types of weapons against it, a formal consultative meeting took place in 1997. The meeting was officially inconclusive; however, substantial credible evidence contradicted Cuba's claim.

See also DISARMAMENT.

Further Reading: "Biological Weapons: From the BWC to Biotech." *Disarmament Forum* no. 4 (2000): 7–50. Geissler, Erhard, and John Ellis van Courtland Moon, eds. *Biological and Toxin Weapons: Research, Development and Use from the Middle Ages to 194,* Stockholm Peace Research Institute (SIPRI) Chemical & Biological Warfare Studies, no. 18. Oxford, U.K.: Oxford University Press, 1999. Lederberg, Joshua, ed. *Biological Weapons: Limiting the Threat.* Cambridge, Mass.: MIT Press, 1999. Zilinskas, Raymond A., ed. *Biological Warfare: Modern Offense and Defense.* Boulder, Colo.: Lynne Rienner, 2000.

— *M. I. Chevrier*

Biological Weapons Ban   *See* BIOLOGICAL WEAPONS (BW), DISARMAMENT.

Blue Helmets

Military personnel serving as UN peacekeepers wear a familiar blue helmet to distinguish themselves from all other military or PEACEKEEPING operations. Increasingly joined by civilian colleagues, the mandates of these so-called Blue Helmets became more challenging as the world moved into the 21st century. Blue-helmeted UN peacekeeping forces administered cease-fires, managed the separation of hostile forces, aided in encouraging national and ethnic reconciliation, promoted HUMAN RIGHTS, monitored elections, and became involved in "nation-building," as in AFGHANISTAN, East Timor, the FORMER YUGOSLAVIA, the Middle East, and many other locales. Blue Helmets have been active since 1948, when they were dispatched to Palestine. In 1988, the UN's Blue Helmets—that is its peacekeeping forces—won the Nobel Peace Prize.

See also CHAPTER VI ½ PROVISIONS, SUEZ CRISIS, UNITED NATIONS EMERGENCY FORCE.

Further Reading: *The Blue Helmets.* 3rd ed. New York: United Nations Department of Public Information, 1996. Hillen, John, *Blue Helmets: The Strategy of UN Military Operations.* 2nd ed. Washington, D.C.: Brassey's, 2000.

Board of Chief Executives of the United Nations System *See* ADMINISTRATIVE COMMITTEE ON COORDINATION.

Bonn Convention *See* CONVENTION ON THE CONSERVATION OF MIGRATORY SPECIES OF WILD ANIMALS (CMS).

Bosnia

Bosnia is one of the former Yugoslav republics born out of the Yugoslav civil war of the 1990s. It declared its secession following a plebiscite in February 1992. On May 22, 1992, Bosnia and Herzegovina was officially recognized as a member state of the United Nations. But its three largest communities—Muslims (44 percent of the population), Croats (17 percent), and Serbs (31 percent)—disagreed about the future of an independent Bosnia, resulting in a bloody civil war.

In the early days of Yugoslavia's breakup, the Yugoslav National Army (JNA), comprised mostly of Serbs, sought to maintain the territorial integrity of the nation. But with the successes of Slovenia and Croatia in establishing their independence, the JNA shifted its emphasis to aiding Serb irredentist sentiment (that is, the JNA insisted that all Serbs should be united under the same government—the postwar "rump" Yugoslavia). When Bosnia attempted to establish an independent government headed by President Alija Izetbe-

govic, the Serbs within Bosnia revolted and sought to establish their own state or to join their territories with the rest of Yugoslavia. The difficulty of this task, and the ensuing ethnic violence, arose from the interconnectedness of the two communities within Bosnia. In an effort to assure Serb majorities in the parts of Bosnia they controlled, Serbs engaged in ethnic cleansing. They imprisoned many Bosnian Muslims, killed others, and terrorized the rest, forcing them to leave their homes for predominately Muslim areas.

In response to the violence and to Serb policies, the United Nations deployed the UN Protection Force (UNPRO-FOR) and sought to create "safe havens" in which Muslims would be protected from Serb assaults. The United Nations was unsuccessful at protecting the enclaves. Perhaps the greatest atrocity of the war occurred at the "safe haven" of Srebrenica. During July 1995, Serb forces entered the town, took UN peacekeepers hostage, and systematically murdered hundreds of Muslim men and boys. Out of concern for the remaining foreign peacekeepers' safety, neither European governments nor UN officials would accept American proposals for military retaliation.

In the midst of the fighting, the United Nations and the European Union collaborated on a peace proposal, authorizing former U.S. secretary of state Cyrus Vance to negotiate for the United Nations, and former British foreign minister Lord David Owen to negotiate for the EU. The Vance-Owen peace plan, however, proved ineffective, due in part to its territorial complexity as well as to the Serb determination to continue fighting the war. In August 1995 Bosnian Serb forces carried out a particularly heinous attack on Sarajevo, shelling the marketplace and killing 35 people. To protect Bosnian Muslims, the North Atlantic Treaty Organization (NATO) began bombing Serb positions within Bosnia. In the wake of the NATO bombing the Croats attacked the Serbs in Croatia along the Krajina strip and retook much of the land the Serbs had won in battle in 1992. The West did little to oppose this Croatian attack, revealing how isolated the Serbs were. Additionally, Bosnian Muslims and Croats agreed to a federated Bosnia, meaning each ethnic group would have autonomous powers within its region should they agree to the territorial integrity of Bosnia. Under intense international pressure, including economic SANCTIONS that created record inflation in Yugoslavia, the Serbian leader, Slobodan Milosevic, agreed to accept an American invitation to meet in Dayton, Ohio, with Izetbegovic and Croatian president Franjo Tudjman. In November 1995 the DAYTON PEACE ACCORDS ended the civil war in Bosnia.

The Dayton Accords had a number of important provisions: (1) that all nationals be repatriated to their original homes, so that ethnic cleansing would not be rewarded, (2) that the Serbs recognize the SOVEREIGNTY of the Muslim-led government of President Izetbegovic, (3) that the United Nations send a PEACEKEEPING force (first called IFOR, for Implementation Force, later SFOR, for Stabilization Force) to monitor the peace, and (4) that all war criminals indicted by the INTERNATIONAL CRIMINAL TRIBUNAL FOR YUGOSLAVIA be extradited to The Hague for trial. NATO troops totaling 60,000 were to supervise the implementation of the agreement. The long process of building the Bosnian nation had begun.

That same year, the SECURITY COUNCIL established the UN International Police Task Force as part of a larger UNITED NATIONS MISSION IN BOSNIA AND HERZEGOVINA (UNMIBH), which supervised the demilitarization of the region and organized elections. Serious problems, however, continued to confront Bosnia and Herzegovina at the turn of the century, including resettling refugees, rebuilding the economy, establishing a working government, locating indicted war criminals who were still at large, and dealing with the fact of a rump Serbian entity within the country (the Srpska Republic). In a positive move, however, in October 2001 the parliament of the Bosnian Serb enclave approved the arrest of individuals under indictment by the international tribunal in The Hague. And there continued to be a steady return of refugees to their homes.

See also FORMER YUGOSLAVIA, LAND MINES, RUSSIAN FEDERATION, WAR CRIMES TRIBUNALS

Further Reading: Daalder, Ivo H. *Getting to Dayton: The Making of America's Bosnia Policy.* Washington: Brookings Institution, 1999. Holbrooke, Richard. *To End a War.* New York: Random House, 1999. Rieff, David. *Slaughterhouse: Bosnia and the Failure of the West.* New York: Simon and Schuster, 1996. Rohde, David. *Endgame: The Betrayal and Fall of Srebenica, Europe's Worst Massacre since World War II.* Boulder, Colo.: Westview Press, 2000. Woodward, Susan L. *Balkan Tragedy: Chaos and Dissolution After the Cold War.* Washington, D.C.: Brookings Institution, 1993. Dayton Peace Accords websites: <www1.umn.edu/humanrts/icty/Dayton/daytoncompl.html>,<www.state.gov/www/regions/eur/bosnia/bosagree.html>. UNMIBH website:<www.un.org/Depts/DPKO/Missions/unmibh/>.

— *D. J. Becker*

Boutros-Ghali, Boutros (1922–)

The sixth SECRETARY-GENERAL, Boutros Boutros-Ghali was the first Arab and first African to hold the post. He was born in Cairo, Egypt, in 1922 into a distinguished Coptic Christian family. His grandfather had been prime minister of Egypt and his father finance minister. Boutros-Ghali studied political science, economics, and law at Cairo University, where he received a Bachelor of Law degree in 1946. In 1949 he earned a Ph.D in INTERNATIONAL LAW from the University of Paris (Sorbonne). He then held professorships at Cairo University and lectured on international law and international affairs at several universities in Europe, the UNITED STATES, India, the Middle East, and Africa. He also authored numer-

ous scholarly books and articles on international affairs—most written in French—was a Fulbright scholar at Columbia University in New York for the 1954–55 academic year, and was a director of the HAGUE ACADEMY OF INTERNATIONAL LAW in the Netherlands, 1963–64.

Boutros-Ghali, appointed as minister of state for foreign affairs in 1977, accompanied Egyptian president Anwar Sadat that year on the historic trip to Jerusalem, and he is considered one of the main architects of the Camp David Accords of 1978, which led to the Egyptian-Israeli peace TREATY of the following year. By 1991, he had been elevated to deputy prime minister of Egypt.

When Javier PÉREZ DE CUÉLLAR's retirement neared in late 1991, Boutros-Ghali emerged as one of several possible successors. The ORGANIZATION OF AFRICAN UNITY (OAU) pressed for appointment of an African to the position of Secretary-General. Breaking with tradition, Boutros-Ghali openly campaigned for nomination. Although he was an Arab, he was acceptable to Israel (and the United States) because of his work on the Egyptian-Israeli peace negotiations and because he had married into a prominent Egyptian-Jewish family. The OAU, preferring a sub-Saharan choice, nonetheless accepted Boutros-Ghali as an adequate alternative. Egyptian president Hosni Mubarak lobbied heavily with U.S. president George Bush on behalf of his countryman, who at the same time was enthusiastically supported by France. Meantime, most of the Third World found little to protest, and CHINA and the Soviet Union decided to go along with the nomination. Thus, although 14 sound candidates were presented to the SECURITY COUNCIL at a closed-door session on November 21, 1991, Boutros-Ghali won nomination on the first ballot.

Within a few months of his assuming office in January 1992, Boutros-Ghali forwarded the concepts of "peace enforcement" and "peace-building" as distinct from "PEACE-KEEPING." This shift in UN policy, interpreted as not requiring the consent of all parties to a conflict, even if the conflict was internal to a sovereign state, resulted in an expansion of UN peacekeeping operations, with the most notable, and difficult, taking place in SOMALIA and the FORMER YUGOSLAVIA. Indeed, in 1988, there were fewer than 10,000 UN peacekeepers on duty in world hot spots, costing the organization $364 million annually. By early 1992 the number had barely nudged up to 11,500. But by the summer of that year, UN troops around the world had risen to 44,000, and by early 1993 approached 80,000, with a total cost of $4 billion.

With the conclusion of the GULF WAR in mind, world leaders met in January 1992 in the first Heads of Government Council meeting to consider the future role of the United Nations in the post–COLD WAR environment. The leaders directed the new Secretary-General to prepare recommendations on ways of strengthening the United Nations and making it more efficient in "PREVENTIVE DIPLOMACY" and peacekeeping. The Council requested that the report be submitted in six months. In June, Boutros-Ghali published his recommendations. Entitled *AGENDA FOR PEACE*, the report outlined the most ambitious UN program of peacekeeping in the organization's history. According to the report, the United Nations needed to identify "at risk" states and act early to avoid the collapse of state SOVEREIGNTY and internal order. The Secretary-General proposed that military forces be placed at the disposal of the United Nations for rapid action in times of crisis.

Boutros-Ghali then became the prime mover in mobilizing the world community to deal with the collapse of order in the east African nation of Somalia. At his initiative, Security Council RESOLUTION 751 (April 1992) created UNOSOM I, a small, unarmed, peacekeeping force for Somalia. But the situation continued to deteriorate. In late November the Secretary-General wrote to President Bush seeking immediate American action to secure food supplies in Somalia and to restore order. On December 3 the Security Council—at U.S. urging—approved Resolution 794 invoking CHAPTER VII. Under its authorization, and at the conclusion

of the president's term in December 1992, he inserted U.S. forces, allegedly to lead the UN contingent for a limited time. The Americans soon became enmeshed in a nasty civil conflict between rival warlords. On October 3, 1993, the new Clinton administration was confronted with tragic front-page news stories of 18 U.S. soldiers being trapped in a firefight and killed, and a lurid photograph of one of them being dragged through the streets of Mogadishu. American support for more vigorous UN peacekeeping efforts now waned, troops were home within the year, and criticism mounted that the United Nations was incapable of ordering the internal affairs of any country.

For Rwandans the shifting mood was particularly perilous, since a brutal, genocidal civil conflict had broken out between the rival Tutsi and Hutu tribes. Although the Clinton administration had originally supported the UNITED NATIONS ASSISTANCE MISSION FOR RWANDA (UNAMIR), the outbreak of massacres in April 1994 caused it to propose the cutting back of the number of peacekeepers in the region out of fear for their safety. Meantime, the degenerating situation

Secretary-General Boutros Boutros-Ghali (UN PHOTO 186266/FABRIC RIBERE)

in the FORMER YUGOSLAVIA increasingly appeared to be beyond UN remedy. The 1994 off-year congressional elections in the United States, bringing Republicans into a majority in both houses for the first time in almost half a century, now brought the Secretary-General, and his ideas about an invigorated United Nations, into direct conflict with the world's most powerful nation.

In response to growing criticism about UN bureaucratic wastefulness, Boutros-Ghali froze the UN BUDGET and took a number of other steps to allay concerns, particularly those being expressed in Washington. By 1993 U.S. arrears to the organization reached $1 billion. In hopes of ending the freeze on American contributions to the UN, Boutros-Ghali appointed Richard Thornburgh, a former U.S. attorney-general, UNDER SECRETARY-GENERAL for administration and management. He gave Thornburgh carte blanche to review all operations in the world body. The new appointee, in turn, asked the Ford Foundation to conduct an external review of the United Nations. It set up a commission headed by Paul Volcker, a former chairman of the U.S. Federal Reserve, and Shiguro Ogata, the former deputy governor of the Japan Development Bank. Within a year both Thornburgh and the Volcker-Ogata Commission issued reports highlighting many of the same weaknesses in the United Nations. Both called for tighter quality control of the UN staff, and budgetary reforms. The Thornburgh Report also suggested the appointment of an inspector-general to root out fraud, waste, and abuse. Seeking greater efficiency, the Ford Foundation group called for a unified peacekeeping budget. When the Clinton administration signaled its support of both reports, Boutros-Ghali indicated he would take steps to implement many of the recommendations. In 1994, Boutros-Ghali supported the creation of the OFFICE OF INTERNAL OVERSIGHT SERVICES (OIOS), headed by an under secretary-general. The new director of OIOS was given a five-year term and virtual independence from the Secretary-General with a mandate to conduct broad investigations and evaluations throughout the UNITED NATIONS SYSTEM. None of these moves, however, stopped the growing criticism from conservative U.S. senators, who saw the United Nations as inefficient, inept, yet bent on gaining too much power at the expense of U.S. SOVEREIGNTY. The Secretary-General and Senator Jesse Helms of North Carolina—new chair of the powerful Senate Foreign Relations Committee—now engaged in a public argument in the pages of the respected journal *Foreign Affairs*. In the spring of 1996 Boutros-Ghali penned a defense of his ideas regarding an active Secretary-General at the head of a more vigorous United Nations. Five months later, in the same journal, Helms used highly blunt language to lambaste the United Nations and excoriate its executive leader.

Although Boutros-Ghali had disavowed a second term when he entered office in 1992, a number of nations, including some of America's closest allies, strongly supported his continuing in 1997. But the political climate in Washington clearly made such continuance impossible. The Secretary-General, the object of unkind remarks during the American presidential campaign of 1996, had become the lightning rod in the United States for displeasure at all that seemed wrong with the United Nations. There was no way his nomination could avoid a U.S. VETO in the Security Council. Having entered office at a high point of optimism regarding the possibilities of the international organization, Boutros Boutros-Ghali, the victim of a spate of uncontrollable in-state collapses and the decline of UN financing, left office after one tumultuous term.

See also AGENDA FOR DEVELOPMENT, ANNAN, REFORM OF THE UNITED NATIONS, SECRETARIAT.

Further Reading: Boutros-Ghali, Boutros. *Unvanquished: A U.S.–U.N. Saga.* New York: Random House, 1999. Moore, John Allphin, Jr., and Jerry Pubantz. *To Create a New World? American Presidents and the United Nations.* New York: Peter Lang Publishing, 1999.

Brahimi Report

On August 23, 2000, the Panel on United Nations Peace Operations published a 70-page report calling for dramatic REFORM of the UN's PEACEKEEPING missions, its DEPARTMENT OF PEACEKEEPING OPERATIONS (DPKO), the process by which the SECURITY COUNCIL and the SECRETARY-GENERAL implemented decisions to intervene in conflicts, and the funding mechanisms for peacekeeping efforts. The panel was chaired by Algerian ambassador and former foreign minister Lakhdar Brahimi, who had also served as UN SPECIAL REPRESENTATIVE to AFGHANISTAN. Secretary-General Kofi ANNAN appointed the panel on March 7, 2000. Made up of 10 experts on peace operations, including representatives from the UNITED STATES and Russia, Brahimi's panel issued its report on the eve of the MILLENNIUM SUMMIT. The report's recommendations elicited the most earnest and sustained discussion among the attending heads of government.

Consisting of nearly 60 proposals, the report reflected Secretary-General Annan's desire to strengthen and make more effective UN peacekeeping. Pressured particularly by the United States, the Secretary-General asked Brahimi to prepare frank and specific recommendations that would narrow the gap between the UN's burgeoning peacekeeping responsibilities and its limited financial and organizational resources.

The Brahimi Report recommended formalizing the UN's peacekeeping activities and ending ad hoc deployments. One of the central recommendations was to create a new information-gathering and analysis office within the United Nations to assemble databases and act as a professional policy planning staff. The panel further recommended the establishment of an integrated task force for each mission, combining political analysis, military operations, civilian police, electoral assistance, aid to refugees, finance, logistics, public information, and streamlined procurement procedures. The panel also urged that definitions of self-defense be stretched to allow UN peacekeeping missions to take a more offensive posture in dangerous situations. It recommended that traditional UN "impartiality" between combatants in a conflict not be allowed to "amount to complicity with evil." According to the panel, the credibility of UN peacekeeping depended on being able "to distinguish victim from aggressor."

While it did not call for a standing UN army, the Brahimi Report advocated reform of the United Nations Standby Arrangements System (UNSAS) in order to ensure that the UN could fully deploy a peacekeeping force within 30 days of a Security Council decision to do so. In order to fund rapid deployment, the panel recommended that the Secretary-General be authorized to commit up to $50 million in advance of a contemplated Security Council decision to undertake a new operation.

The report encouraged "a substantial increase in resources for HEADQUARTERS support of peacekeeping operations," and called upon Annan to submit a financing proposal to the GENERAL ASSEMBLY, as well as a plan for implementation of the report's other recommendations. Annan welcomed the report's findings and directed DEPUTY SECRETARY-GENERAL Louise FRÉCHETTE to proceed with implementation. He requested that the General Assembly authorize expenditure of $22 million to carry out all of the recommendations. In January 2001 it granted a first installment of $9.5 million for this purpose. The General Assembly's willingness to fund the reforms was due in part to a fall review by the Security Council's Special Committee on Peacekeeping Operations that had endorsed them, a Security Council resolution on November 13 approving them, and Annan's subsequent steps toward implementation.

The General Assembly's action marked a victory for Annan and for the United States, which had sought significant reform before it would support any new operations or pay its assessments arrears. Initial reaction to the report among developing states had been cool, fearing the new rules for peacekeeping might amount to a form of UN "colonialism" at the behest of U.S. foreign policy and might take funds away from development. Among the PERMANENT MEMBERS of the Security Council, concern was initially reflected in the demur from Chinese president Jiang Zemin and Russian president Vladimir Putin. But a vigorous public relations effort by Annan and Brahimi, combined with the promise of U.S. funding if the recommendations were accepted, dispelled the opposition. By the spring of 2001, most national leaders supported the activist peacekeeping vision of Secretary-General Annan and Ambassador Brahimi.

Further Reading: Report of the Panel on United Nations Peace Operations website: <www.un.org/peace/reports/peace_operations/>. Millennium Report of the Secretary-General website: <www.un.org/millennium/sg/report/index.html>.

Bretton Woods

The United Nations Monetary and Financial Conference convened in Bretton Woods, New Hampshire, from July 1 to 22, 1944. The conference drafted agreements establishing three institutions meant to create a postwar global free trade system: the INTERNATIONAL MONETARY FUND (IMF), the International Bank of Reconstruction and Development (IBRD)—better known as the WORLD BANK—and the GENERAL AGREEMENT ON TARIFFS AND TRADE (GATT). The last of these was supposed to be an "interim" agreement until an International Trade Organization (ITO)—which would provide a more ambitious regulatory framework for world trade—could be established. GATT, however, remained in place until January 1, 1995, when it was superseded by the WORLD TRADE ORGANIZATION (WTO).

Sponsored by the UNITED STATES, the Bretton Woods Conference and its ensuing agreements attempted to create a new international monetary and trade regime that was stable and predictable. Negotiators structured the IMF to limit the fluctuation of foreign currency exchange rates while using the World Bank to pump needed capital investment into nations devastated by the war. American planners hoped to avoid the economic nationalism of the interwar years by gradually removing protectionist barriers to free trade. Through "rounds" of negotiation members of GATT eliminated tariffs, quotas, and other impediments to international commerce. The success of the measures initiated at Bretton Woods depended, however, on the willingness of the United States, whose economy accounted in 1944 for more than half of world domestic product, to fund these institutions and to maintain monetary policies conducive to world economic growth.

The Bretton Woods meeting was held nearly in tandem with the DUMBARTON OAKS CONFERENCE, which prepared the draft CHARTER OF THE UNITED NATIONS. Each was undertaken by the United States to create a postwar international framework that would avoid the instability that followed World War I. Soon after the Bretton Woods institutions came into being, Washington pegged the dollar to gold at $35 an ounce, enacted large foreign aid programs in order to pump liquidity into the international economic system, and made the largest subscription of funds of any IBRD member to the assets of the World Bank. IMF, GATT, and the World Bank, while independent institutions, were considered part of the UNITED NATIONS SYSTEM.

See also ACHESON, ADMINISTRATIVE COMMITTEE ON COORDINATION, INTERNATIONAL LAW, NEW INTERNATIONAL ECONOMIC ORDER, PASVOLSKY.

Further Reading: Schild, Georg. *Bretton Woods and Dumbarton Oaks: American Economic and Political Postwar Planning in the Summer of 1944.* New York: St. Martin's, 1995. Schwartz, Herman M. *States versus Markets. History, Geography, and the Development of the International Political Economy.* New York: St. Martin's, 1994.

Bricker Amendment

During the post–World War II era a major American constitutional issue arose out of the potential impact of the United Nations CHARTER and the UN COVENANT on Human Rights upon U.S. federal-state relations. The problem first attracted notice in the Supreme Court case *Oyama v. California* (1948), which argued that a California law denying aliens ineligible to become citizens the right to own land was void because it conflicted with Article 55 of the UN Charter. Under Article 55 the United States pledged itself to "promote . . . universal respect for, and observance of, HUMAN RIGHTS and fundamental freedoms for all without distinction as to race, sex, LANGUAGE, or religion." A California court subsequently ruled the state law invalid on this ground.

The decision initiated a widespread legal discussion over whether the UN Charter was a self-executing TREATY and capable, as the supreme law of the land, of setting aside state and federal statutes in areas of civil rights and property rights. One view held that the Charter was merely a vague DECLARATION of national intent, to be effective only when implemented by congressional statute. Others insisted that it was indeed a self-executing treaty and thus supreme law. The pending International Covenant on Human Rights would have gone further, essentially binding signatory states to an elaborate series of guarantees, in the form of an international bill of rights.

In response to widespread public agitation over the issue, Senator John Bricker (R-Ohio) in 1952 introduced a constitutional amendment to limit the scope of the federal treaty power. The Bricker Amendment sought to negate any treaty that conflicted with the U.S. Constitution, to demand appropriate enabling legislation to make a treaty valid as internal law, and to regulate all executive and other agreements with any foreign power or international organization.

Critics of the amendment insisted that it would interfere with the president's conduct of foreign affairs so decisively as to make an effective foreign policy impossible. Despite growing popularity, Bricker's initiative was confounded when President Eisenhower and Secretary of State John Foster Dulles announced their opposition to the proposal. Nevertheless, in February 1954 the Senate voted 60 to 31, one vote short of the required two-thirds constitutional majority, for a modified and weakened version of the Bricker Amendment. Subsequently, the issue rapidly lost its political appeal and became a dead issue.

Further Reading: Eisenhower, Dwight D. *The White House Years.* Vol. 1. *Mandate for Change, 1953–1956.* Garden City, N.Y.: Doubleday, 1963. Tannenbaum, Duane A. "The Bricker Amendment Controversy: Its Origins and Eisenhower's Role." *Diplomatic History* 9 (Winter 1985): 73–93.
— *E. M. Clauss*

Brundtland Commission   *See* WORLD COMMISSION ON ENVIRONMENT AND DEVELOPMENT.

Brundtland, Gro Harlem (1939–   )

The chairperson of the WORLD COMMISSION ON ENVIRONMENT AND DEVELOPMENT (WCED) in the 1980s, Dr. Gro Harlem Brundtland gave birth to one of the United Nations's most enduring programmatic ideas, that of "SUSTAINABLE DEVELOPMENT." Brundtland, a medical doctor and former prime minister of Norway, led the effort to link development and environmental protection on a global scale, and in compatible ways that would preserve the earth and the economic prospects of future generations. As a result of her efforts, she became one of the most visible WOMEN working within the UNITED NATIONS SYSTEM, becoming DIRECTOR-GENERAL of the WORLD HEALTH ORGANIZATION (WHO) in 1998.

Gro Harlem Brundtland was born in Oslo, Norway, in April 1939. After becoming a doctor and a Master of Public Health (MPH) she pursued advanced studies at Harvard University. When she returned to Norway she held a succession of public health positions. In 1974 she was appointed Norway's minister of the ENVIRONMENT. In 1981 she became the country's youngest and first female prime minister. She served in that post at different times for more than 10 years between 1981 and 1996.

Dr. Brundtland's public expressions of concern about global issues related to the environment led UN SECRETARY-GENERAL Javier PÉREZ DE CUÉLLAR to appoint her the chair of the WCED in 1983. In an effort to revitalize the program of action proposed by the 1972 UNITED NATIONS CONFERENCE ON THE HUMAN ENVIRONMENT (UNCHE), he urged Brundtland's commission to establish "a global agenda for change." The commission held nearly two years of public hearings and interviewed thousands of individuals and organizations on the problems of environment and development. In 1987 it issued its final report, *Our Common Future*, which became the bedrock statement for sustainable development, the central doctrine around which all future UN efforts in the two fields would be built. The "Brundtland Commission," as it became known, defined sustainable development as "development that meets the needs of the present without compromising the ability of future generations to meet their own needs." *Our Common Future* called upon governments to include environmental concerns in the process of development, and the document noted the intrinsic link between economic growth, and socioenvironmental factors such as health, population growth water and air purity, and natural beauty. The WCED recommended that the United Nations convene a global conference on sustainable development, which it did in Rio in 1992. Known as the Earth Summit, the meeting enshrined Brundtland's concept as the centerpiece for future UN development efforts.

After she stepped down as Norwegian prime minister in 1996 Brundtland sought, and achieved, appointment as director-general of WHO in May 1998. In so doing, she returned to her professional roots in public health. She restructured the organization to include "Sustainable Development and Healthy Environment" as one of WHO's primary "clusters" of activity, demonstrating the breadth to which the concept could be applied. She told the World Health Assembly in her 1998 acceptance speech that the organization needed "to unleash development and alleviate suffering." It should do this by "promoting sustainable and equitable health systems in all countries." Her leadership of WHO along these lines had the effect of expanding sustainable development from a concept focused solely on development and environment to one that included Sustainable Human Development in all of its dimensions.

See also COMMISSION ON SUSTAINABLE DEVELOPMENT, UNITED NATIONS CONFERENCE ON ENVIRONMENT AND DEVELOPMENT, UNITED NATIONS ENVIRONMENT PROGRAMME.

Further Reading: Elliott, Lorraine. *The Global Politics of the Environment.* New York: New York University Press, 1998. World Commission on Environment and Development. *Our Common Future.* New York: Oxford University Press, 1987.

budget of the United Nations

There are three major budgets for UN operations: the regular budget funded by assessment of contributions from member states, a budget for international tribunals, and a PEACEKEEPING budget. For the biennium of 2000–01 the regular budget of the United Nations was slightly more than $2.5 billion, the eighth "no growth" budget in a row. On December 24, 2001, the GENERAL ASSEMBLY, using a new "results-based format" that focused on expected accomplishments by UN bodies over the next two years, approved an increase in the budget for 2002–03 to $2.63 billion. The Assembly added $1.58 million to peacekeeping operations and set aside $16.1 million for 121 new peacekeeping positions; $242.79 million was allocated for the INTERNATIONAL CRIMINAL TRIBUNAL FOR YUGOSLAVIA and $192.31 million was budgeted for the Rwandan WAR CRIMES TRIBUNAL.

Each of these budgets is approved by the General Assembly upon the recommendation of panels of experts that have reviewed proposals from the SECRETARY-GENERAL. In addition there are many voluntary program FUNDS to which

states may make contributions. These funds provide resources for UN PROGRAMMES and special initiatives. Often "pledging conferences" and other solicitation techniques will be used to raise sufficient voluntary contributions. In the wider UNITED NATIONS SYSTEM, SPECIALIZED AGENCIES maintain separate budgets with some effort at system-wide coordination of budgetary and administrative policies.

Since its founding, the United Nations has employed "the capacity to pay" as its primary budgetary principle, with the consequence that rich industrialized states are charged significant percentages of UN expenses while new developing states are responsible for an insignificant proportion of the budget. Beyond a state's gross domestic product, its per capita income and level of debt are also factored into determining its assessment. The unwillingness of states large and small to pay their assessments, however, has left the world body regularly on the brink of financial collapse. At the time of the MILLENNIUM SUMMIT in 2000, unpaid assessments to the regular budget totaled in excess of $244 million, to tribunals $31 million, and to peacekeeping more than $1.3 billion. Within a year the deficit in the regular budget rose to $723 million with 103 members delinquent in their payments. A significant part of Secretary-General Kofi ANNAN's REFORM program after 1997 was directed at restoring confidence by nonpaying states in the effectiveness of the United Nations in order to importune payment of arrearages, and to find cost savings through the results-based budgeting technique.

It is the FIFTH COMMITTEE of the General Assembly that recommends the regular two-year budget to the plenary body. In its deliberations, the committee depends heavily on the oral and written reports of the ADVISORY COMMITTEE ON ADMINISTRATIVE AND BUDGETARY QUESTIONS (ACABQ), which is made up of 16 financial experts, and those of the 34-member Committee for Programme and Coordination. The Fifth Committee has the responsibility of recommending the SCALE OF ASSESSMENTS every three years, which establishes how much each state must pay to the organization. This is done on the recommendation of the COMMITTEE ON CONTRIBUTIONS, one of the two standing committees of the General Assembly. The "ceiling" that any member was required to pay, as of June 2001, was 22 percent of the regular budget and 27 percent of the peacekeeping budget. As the largest contributor, only the UNITED STATES was affected by these ceilings. The "floor," or lowest assessment assigned, was .001 percent and was applied to the poorest states in the United Nations.

The most problematic of the three UN budgets has been peacekeeping. With no direct authorization in the CHARTER for this activity, some states have refused to accept responsibility for such costs. Beginning with the creation of the UNITED NATIONS EMERGENCY FORCE (UNEF) during the 1956 SUEZ CRISIS, the world body has had difficulty obtaining the needed funds to carry out its assigned duties. During

Outstanding Debts to the UN Regular Budget, 1971–2000

Source: Global Policy Forum, February 2001

the 1960 Congolese civil war, the Soviet Union ceased making payments, generating the institution's first financial crisis, and requiring other states through voluntary contributions to make up the difference.

The United States contributed more than 30 percent of the total budget at its peak. The huge expansion of peacekeeping operations in the wake of the COLD WAR imposed costs far exceeding anticipated contributions, placing increased budgetary strains on the organization. At the end of August 2001 the United Nations had a cash deficit of $75 million, forcing it to move funds from one account to another in order to pay salaries, and requiring states that contributed peacekeeping troops to cover their own costs.

Growing dissatisfaction with UN activities and with the proportion of the budget paid by the United States led in the 1980s to American refusal to pay as much as UN officials argued it owed. By 1993 the United States had become the UN's largest debtor and Washington demanded institutional reform before it would pay arrearages. The U.S. debt to the United Nations reached more than $1.1 billion before a package of reforms and repayments was negotiated between Washington and UN HEADQUARTERS. The final payment fulfilling past commitments was made in October 2001.

See also BOUTROS-GHALI, BOUTROS; GOLDBERG RESERVATION; IMPORTANT QUESTION; PÉREZ DE CUÉLLAR, JAVIER; SECRETARIAT, SUSPENSION AND EXPULSION OF MEMBERS.

Further Reading: McDermott, Anthony. *The New Politics of Financing the UN.* Basingstoke, U.K.: Macmillan, 2000. Tessitore, John, and Susan Woolfson. *A Global Agenda: Issues before the 55th General Assembly of the United Nations.* 2000–01 edition. New York: Rowman and Littlefield, 2001. Fifth Committee website: <www.un.org/ga/fifth/>.

budget process   *See* BUDGET OF THE UNITED NATIONS.

Bunche, Ralph (1903–1971)

Ralph Johnson Bunche was born on August 7, 1903 (some records list 1904), in Detroit, Michigan. In the 1930s he organized the first department of political science at any historically black university, at Howard University. In 1945 he became the first African American to head a division in the UNITED STATES Department of State. His work with the United Nations began that same year during the UN conference in San Francisco, where he drafted the sections of the CHARTER on decolonization and trusteeship issues. The next year, despite offers of a high position at the State Department, Bunche joined the permanent SECRETARIAT in New York when he accepted the call to direct the Trusteeship Division. In 1947 he became the principal secretary for the Commission for Palestine. After the assassination of Count Folke BERNADOTTE in Jerusalem in 1948, Bunche was

Ralph Bunche in Palestine (OFFICIAL UN PHOTO DEPARTMENT OF PUBLIC INFORMATION)

RETARY-GENERAL (USG) for Special Political Affairs. During the early years of his service, besides working with the UN program for the peaceful use of atomic energy, he was mainly occupied with bringing stability to war-ridden regions. Bunche established the guiding principles for PEACEKEEPING missions. He served as supervisor for the deployment of the UNITED NATIONS EMERGENCY FORCE (UNEF) to the Suez Canal zone in December 1956. In 1960, he tried to negotiate a peaceful settlement in the CONGO and was responsible for the ill-fated UN peacekeeping effort ONUC (UNITED NATIONS OPERATION IN THE CONGO) as SPECIAL REPRESENTATIVE for the Secretary-General, overseeing both the military and the civilian aspects of the undertaking. In 1964, Bunche directed the UN mission to intervene between hostile Greek and Turkish Cypriots and their respective countries (UNITED NATIONS FORCE IN CYPRUS [UNFICYP]).

Despite growing health problems Bunche participated in the Civil Rights movement in the United States, serving as a board member of the National Association for the Advancement of Colored People (NAACP) for many years. Notes that he kept during his career have been published, and they are available to scholars and students. Ralph Bunche died on December 9, 1971, in New York City. To honor his countless achievements, a small park across from the UN HEADQUARTERS has been dedicated to him.

See also ARAB-ISRAELI CONFLICT, CYPRUS DISPUTE, SUEZ CRISIS.

entrusted by SECRETARY-GENERAL Trygve LIE with the position of chief mediator to negotiate a truce between Israel and its Arab adversaries (Egypt, Jordan, Lebanon, and Syria). For his diligent diplomacy between February and May 1949 (on Rhodes) in bringing stability to Palestine he was awarded the Nobel Prize for Peace in December 1950.

Bunche worked under Secretaries-General Dag HAMMARSKJÖLD and U THANT, serving after 1958 as UNDER SEC-

Further Reading: Rivlin, Benjamin, ed. *Ralph Bunche: The Man and His Times.* New York: Holmes and Meier, 1990. Urquhart, Brian. *Ralph Bunche: An American Odyssey.* New York: W.W. Norton, 1998.

— *T. J. Weiler*

Cairo Declaration

Franklin Delano ROOSEVELT, Winston CHURCHILL, and Chiang Kai-shek issued the Cairo Declaration at the Cairo Conference held from November 23 to 26 and December 3 to 7, 1943 (before and after the TEHERAN CONFERENCE). The Soviet Union, although not represented at Cairo, had been consulted before it was issued.

The "Three Great Allies" in the Asian war announced their intent to strip Japan of all islands taken in World War I, of all territories "stolen" from CHINA, such as Manchuria, Formosa, and the Pescadores, and all other lands "taken by violence and greed." In addition, Korea was to be liberated and "in due course" become free and independent. The purpose of this sweeping statement was to boost the morale of the faltering Chiang government and forestall any efforts at a separate peace with Japan. In addition, this was part of a larger strategy by Roosevelt to elevate China to a great power in the postwar world in order to play her assigned role as one of the FOUR POLICEMEN in the international security organization-to-be.

In order to head off an effort by the Republican Party to formulate a postwar foreign policy statement for the 1944 election, FDR used the MOSCOW FOREIGN MINISTERS CONFERENCE (October 1943) to introduce Cordell HULL's Four-Power DECLARATION on a postwar world organization. China comprised a crucial component, not only to serve as the Asian "policeman" but also as an ally of the UNITED STATES in its efforts to establish a security system of international trusteeships for colonies and mandates in the region. The Cairo Declaration was central to this vision.

Further Reading: Dallek, Robert. *Franklin D. Roosevelt and American Foreign Policy, 1932–1945.* New York: Oxford University Press, 1979. Feis, Herbert. *Churchill. Roosevelt. Stalin; The War They Waged and the Peace They Sought.* Princeton, N.J.: Princeton University Press, 1957. Kimball, Warren F. *Forged in War: Roosevelt, Churchill, and the Second World War.* New York: William Morrow, 1997.

— *E. M. Clauss*

Cambodia

Present-day Cambodia came under Khmer rule in the early seventh century, following which it became the center of a vast empire stretching over much of Southeast Asia. In the 12th century Buddhism was introduced into the region. In 1863 France colonized the area, joining Cambodia, Laos, and Vietnam into a protectorate called French Indochina. After World War II, Cambodia, along with other countries of Indochina recently freed from Japanese influence, sought independence, which was granted by France in 1953. Cambodia became a member of the United Nations in 1955. During the French Indochina War, which persisted until the Geneva Accords of 1954, Prince Norodom Sihanouk ascended to power, and he did his utmost first to achieve independence and then to secure Cambodian neutrality from all parties to the ongoing conflict in Vietnam. In 1970, General Lon Nol, with the concurrence of the UNITED STATES, overthrew Prince Sihanouk in a coup. Five years later, as the United States retreated from Southeast Asia, the Khmer Rouge, a Communist guerrilla movement led by Pol Pot, ousted Lon Nol.

Regional alignments shaped the UN's relationship with Cambodia in the 1980s, while the end of the COLD WAR and increased international cooperation facilitated UN action in the early 1990s to resolve Cambodia's internal conflict. After signing a mutual assistance TREATY with the Soviet Union in November 1978, Vietnam invaded Cambodia in December and replaced the Beijing-backed Pol Pot government with the Heng Samrin–Hun Sen regime. The USSR subsequently protected its ally by vetoing UN SECURITY COUNCIL condemnation of the Vietnamese occupation of a sovereign country. UN recognition of Vietnam's client government in Cambodia was blocked, however, through lobbying by the Association of Southeast Asian Nations (ASEAN) even though this appeared to legitimize the autogenocide inflicted on the Cambodian people by the Pol Pot group after it came to power in 1975. ASEAN also guided RESOLUTIONS through the UN GENERAL ASSEMBLY that called on Vietnam to withdraw its troops and to permit the Cambodians to select their own government. After the three Cambodian factions opposing the Hun Sen regime formed the Coalition Government of Democratic Kampuchea (CGDK) in 1982 at the urging of ASEAN, the United States, and CHINA, the United Nations seated the delegation from this government-in-exile as the legal representative of Cambodia.

The United Nations was involved early in seeking a political settlement of the conflict that followed the installation of the Hun Sen government. An international conference on Kampuchea was convened in 1981 at the urging of the General Assembly but failed to achieve concrete results. SECRETARY-GENERAL Javier PÉREZ DE CUÉLLAR instructed Rafeeuddin Ahmed, his SPECIAL REPRESENTATIVE for humanitarian affairs in Southeast Asia, to offer the UN's GOOD OFFICES. By 1985, Ahmed's consultations produced the outline of a solution to the conflict. Yet a significant UN role only became possible in the late 1980s with the end of the cold war and increased cooperation among the PERMANENT MEMBERS OF THE SECURITY COUNCIL. By August 1990, the permanent members reached agreement on a framework for a political settlement, and by September, the Cambodian parties, which had met informally as early as 1988 at talks hosted by INDONESIA, accepted the framework. After a series of meetings to negotiate the details, the Agreement on a Comprehensive Political Settlement of the Cambodian Conflict was approved on October 23, 1991, at the reconvened Paris International Conference on Cambodia. The Security Council approved the documents of the Paris conference

within days and in February 1992 authorized the UNITED NATIONS TRANSITIONAL AUTHORITY IN CAMBODIA (UNTAC) to ensure implementation of the Paris agreements. As the transitional authority over Cambodia for 15 months, UNTAC took on an unprecedented set of responsibilities to institutionalize the reconciliation of the parties to the Cambodian conflict. It managed daily administration of Cambodian foreign and defense policy, provided domestic government services, and stationed more than 20,000 UN personnel in the country.

Prince Sihanouk was appointed leader of an interim council to run the country pending elections, which, under the tutelage of UNTAC, took place in May 1993. Although Hun Sen lost the election, he insisted on, and achieved, a power-sharing arrangement with his co-prime minister, Prince Norodom Ranariddh, Sihanouk's son. Differences among the various factions of Cambodia continued. In 1997, Hun Sen executed a coup, removing his opponents from the power-sharing arrangement. The United Nations then refused to seat Cambodia's delegation to the General Assembly. Intricate internal negotiations ensued and in July 1998, again with international monitors present, another, controversial, election was held, won by Hun Sen. Following this election Cambodia regained its seat in the United Nations and in 1999 was accepted as a member of the Association of Southeast Asian Nations. As of the turn of the century, the United Nations remained engaged with Cambodia as part of the international effort to establish a WAR CRIMES TRIBUNAL to hold the Pol Pot group accountable for the 1.5 million Cambodians who were executed or who died from starvation and disease during the rule of the Khmer Rouge.

See also LAND MINES, LEAST DEVELOPED COUNTRIES, SOUTHEAST ASIA TREATY ORGANIZATION, UNITED NATIONS ADVANCE MISSION IN CAMBODIA, UNITED NATIONS OFFICE FOR PROJECT SERVICES, WALDHEIM.

Further Reading: *Agreements on a Comprehensive Political Settlement of the Cambodia Conflict, Paris, 23 October 1991.* New York: United Nations Department of Public Information, 1992. Kiernan, Ben. *The Pol Pot Regime: Race, Power, Genocide in Cambodia under the Khmer Rouge, 1975–1979.* New Haven, Conn.: Yale University Press, 1996. Permanent Mission of the Kingdom of Cambodia website: <www.un.int/cambodia>.

— G. S. Silliman

Caribbean Development Bank (CDB)   See
REGIONAL DEVELOPMENT BANKS.

caucus groups
Since the United Nations is the meeting site of sovereign nations, it is a place where the majority of business is con-

ducted through informal negotiations in halls, lounges, and meeting rooms. National representatives informally discuss their concerns and work out the precise wording of resolutions and reports to be adopted by the bodies in the United Nations. Most of the preparatory negotiations occur in caucus groups organized by geographical proximity, national identification with internationally recognized political or economic issues, or shared interests. The intense talks outside of the formal sessions continue until agreement is reached on a single RESOLUTION on each topic, whose wording and actions are, if not acceptable to all, at least not so offensive or objectionable to any single nation that it is compelled to vote no. Because the United Nations is a universal organization in which virtually every nation of the world is represented, a wide range of viewpoints must be reconciled and included during negotiation regarding any issue. Typically such reconciliation must be accomplished informally, as it would be too cumbersome to attempt to reach agreement and hear all nations in formal session.

In any negotiation in a large body the delegates separate into smaller groups of representatives who share similar concerns and viewpoints, and caucusing groups are simply these smaller groups. They perform in the United Nations the function provided by political parties in a legislative body. Such groups are formed, both formally and informally, on a number of commonalities, which vary with any particular issue. The most influential caucusing groups are the NON-ALIGNED MOVEMENT and the GROUP OF 77, which represent the developing nations and exert considerable influence because of the large number of such nations.

Additionally the United Nations recognizes several geographical area groups for purposes of organization of, and election to, various UN positions. Election to posts such as the SECURITY COUNCIL, the ECONOMIC AND SOCIAL COUNCIL (ECOSOC), the GENERAL ASSEMBLY vice presidents, the chairs of the various committees, and even the SECRETARY-GENERAL and the SECRETARIAT's senior staff positions are apportioned according to geographical blocs. In practice this means that regional groups select the candidates for the various positions prior to election by the General Assembly or by particular committees. The recognized geographical blocs, assuring "equitable geographical representation" in the world body, are the African, Asian, Latin American and Caribbean, East European, and the West European and Other groups. The latter is so named to allow it to represent nations that share Western culture and levels of development despite being located in other parts of the world, such as Australia and New Zealand. In 2000, Israel was added to this group. It should be noted that these are geographical, not regional groups, since the Middle East is divided between Africa and Asia. In practice these groups are also the points at which diplomatic negotiations begin on any given issue. Each group agreeing on a common position presents it to the body at large. The organization of these groups varies, with

some meeting frequently during sessions of the various UN bodies. Such groups are particularly important to small and mid-sized nations that find it difficult to exert influence individually and hence are more likely to agree on a common position representing the entire group.

There are also subgroups within geographical groups (such as the Nordic Group), and other caucusing groups that span the geographical regions, such as the Middle Eastern Group. In addition, a number of other less formally organized groups exist, such as the Islamic Group. Specific groupings often may emerge on any given issue, and several have assumed considerable importance on individual issues. These include the Group of Seven (G-7)—now the Group of Eight (G-8)—on economic matters, the Nuclear Powers Group in DISARMAMENT matters, the so-called Contact Group on issues involving the FORMER YUGOSLAVIA, the Organization of Petroleum Exporting Countries (OPEC), the least developed countries, the Small Island Developing States, and many other special issue groups formed by nations that share a particular concern with and usually a similar viewpoint on any given issue. On one topic, there was even a bloc named "the Group of Like Minded States." While all nations are members of an officially recognized geographical group, most nations are also members of several different blocs, which at times overlap and vary with each issue under consideration.

See also NORTH-SOUTH RELATIONS.

Further Reading: Flores, Fernando A. *A Guide to Delegate Preparation. 1998–99.* New York: United Nations Association of the USA, 1998.

— *K. J. Grieb*

Centre for Human Rights   *See* HUMAN RIGHTS.

***Chance for Peace* Speech**   *See* ATOMS FOR PEACE PROPOSAL.

Chapter VI

Chapter VI, comprising Articles 33 through 38 of the United Nations CHARTER, describes mechanisms for noncoercive measures to settle disputes peacefully between nations. It provides rules for the implementation of one of the overriding aims of the United Nations as described in Article 1 (1): eliminating threats to global peace and ensuring the settlement or adjustment of potential conflicts that could develop into a threat to international peace and security. In this context, the United Nations acts as a facilitator to help states solve their disputes through the nonuse of force.

Acting under Chapter VI, the SECURITY COUNCIL can decide to investigate a dispute or situation that could lead to a dispute to ascertain if it is likely to develop into a threat to international peace and security (Article 34), or a member state may bring a case to the attention of the Council under Article 35 (1). According to Article 35 (2), a non-member—since it has not ratified the UN CHARTER—must subject itself first to the principles of a peaceful solution in order to bring a dispute before the world organization. Also, the SECRETARY-GENERAL can alert the Security Council to such a case under Article 99. The SECRETARIAT, although not mentioned in Chapter VI, implements Chapter VI decisions, usually with a mandate but no clear plan from the Security Council.

All measures under Chapter VI described below are not legally binding for the parties involved and can be discussed by both the Security Council and the GENERAL ASSEMBLY. Once the Council takes up the matter, however, Article 12 (1) decrees that the General Assembly shall not pass any recommendations regarding it. The term "peace" used throughout this chapter, unlike in Article 1 (2) of the Charter, is to be understood in the negative sense, that is, it describes the state of an absence of war or other use of military force between two nations or parties to a dispute. Chapters VI and VII do not address the goal of establishing good and amicable relations between nations, only the aim of preventing war. Also, although the friction normally has been of an international nature, in some instances—such as the situation in Rhodesia after 1966—the Security Council has dealt with problems that did not directly threaten international peace and security but in fact were internal to a state. In some cases, the threat was not even clearly defined or established, but recommendations regarding it were passed nonetheless.

Once the Council has established that a threat exists, the following options present themselves for action. First are the measures mentioned in Article 33 (1): negotiation, MEDIATION, CONCILIATION, ARBITRATION, and judicial decisions, as well as using regional institutions and other peaceful means for resolving the threat. The United Nations urges the parties to avail themselves of these options (Article 33 [2]), and encourages the parties to settle peacefully the dispute themselves by direct bilateral negotiations. Mediation would include a third party, such as the United Nations, to serve as a facilitator. A judicial resolution would require the parties to take the dispute to the INTERNATIONAL COURT OF JUSTICE. Second, according to Articles 36 (1) and 37 (2), respectively, the Council can make recommendations regarding the procedure or method of adjustments and terms of settlement for disputes. It can also, finally, make recommendations of a more general nature if the parties request it (Article 38).

During the COLD WAR, with the Security Council often locked in a superpower stalemate, Chapter VI provisions became the only measures that could be agreed upon. In most of these cases the Security Council or the General Assembly passed RESOLUTIONS providing compromises or principles for resolving a certain dispute. The parties, under the obligations of Article 33, were urged to come to a peaceful settlement. Chapter VI also became the authorization for UN PEACEKEEPING operations, thus creating what became known as CHAPTER VI $^1/_2$ PROVISIONS. The end of the cold war did not lessen the Security Council's desire to use Chapter VI when dealing with matters of peace and security. Given the failure of CHAPTER VII ENFORCEMENT MEASURES mandated in recent years by the UN, such as in Kosovo and SOMALIA, this trend is likely to continue.

Chapter VI decisions, unlike those taken under Chapter VII, do not become part of INTERNATIONAL LAW but are recommendations. In this respect, this part of the UN Charter provides much less power to UN organs than Chapter VII gives to the Security Council. The persuasive role of Chapter VI, therefore, is to be seen against the background of more forceful action pending if UN actions within this context are ineffective. Both parts of the Charter were drafted at the DUMBARTON OAKS negotiations in 1944 and show a compromise between granting more power to the United Nations than the world community had given to the LEAGUE OF NATIONS on the one hand and assuring a state's right to maintain its sovereign authority over its actions and territory on the other hand. Most of the resolutions passed under Chapter VI have had limited impact, unless enforced by other means, such as meaningful peacekeeping operations, or the threat of SANCTIONS. Thus, Chapter VI efforts have led to "gray areas" of UN action, somewhere between Chapter VI and VII and not clearly mandated.

See also APPEALS TO THE SECURITY COUNCIL.

Further Reading: Lepgold, Joseph, and Thomas G. Weiss, eds., *Collective Conflict Management and Changing World Politics.* Albany, N.Y.: State University of New York Press, 1998. Ratner, Steven R. "Image and Reality in the UN's Peaceful Settlement of Disputes." *European Journal of International Law* 6, no. 3 (1995): 426. Roberts, A., and B. Kingsbury, eds. *United Nations, Divided World: The UN's Roles in International Relations.* 2d ed. New York: Oxford University Press, 1994. Simma, Bruno, ed. *The Charter of the United Nations. A Commentary.* New York: Oxford University Press, 1994.

— *T. J. Weiler*

Chapter VI $^1/_2$ provisions

Peacekeeping operations (PKOs) are not explicitly mentioned in the United Nations CHARTER. However, provisions regarding the SECURITY COUNCIL, the GENERAL ASSEMBLY, and the SECRETARY-GENERAL (SG) may be interpreted as a legal basis for the institution of PEACEKEEPING. It is widely believed that peacekeeping is in line with the spirit of CHAPTER VI, but also close to CHAPTER VII. The term "Chapter VI $^1/_2$" has, therefore, been used to describe the guiding principles for PKOs.

The evolution of peacekeeping missions and their rules can be classified in four stages: The first missions (so-called First-Generation PKOs) were conducted according to guiding principles that had been codified in the latter half of the 1950s by Ralph BUNCHE, who at that time served as UNDER SECRETARY-GENERAL (USG) for Special Political Affairs. Until 1986, the person holding this position was also responsible for the general supervision of all such missions. Bunche first developed these principles in crafting a response to the SUEZ CRISIS in 1956. Then in the CONGO (1960) and in CYPRUS (1964) he refined the UN model for all future COLD WAR peacekeeping operations. PKOs were to be conducted along conflict lines between states to disengage the warring parties and prevent a renewed outbreak of hostilities. Three principles had to be adhered to: (1) The parties involved had to agree to the stationing of UN peacekeeping and to a cease-fire or truce between them. (2) The troops deployed had to be only lightly armed, if at all, and were only authorized to use their WEAPONS in self-defense. (3) The UN had to be strictly impartial.

Because of these restrictions, advanced military capabilities were deemed unnecessary. Unarmed observers were sent to oversee agreements and report on the situation, or a peacekeeping force, lightly armed for purposes of self-defense, was established to act as a buffer between front lines of an international dispute. Theirs was a moral rather than military authority. These rules, although they were not always observed strictly, guided PKOs until the end of the cold war.

With the change of the global situation after the collapse of the Soviet bloc, "Second Generation" PKOs came into being. Although based on the same principles, PKOs now included the help of the UN in the transition period toward the establishment of a lasting peace. The tasks and responsibilities were diversified and included, inter alia, the supervision of elections and the rebuilding of countries. The missions also included civilian personnel to provide the capabilities necessary for these "peace-building" efforts. As had been the case with the UNITED NATIONS OPERATIONS IN THE CONGO (ONUC), a SPECIAL REPRESENTATIVE of the SG was appointed to oversee both parts of the operation. The control over the missions was shifted from the USG for Special Political Affairs to the executive office of the SG in 1986; in 1992, a separate DEPARTMENT OF PEACEKEEPING OPERATIONS (DPKO), headed by an Under Secretary-General for Peacekeeping, was created.

Shortly thereafter, the nature of some missions changed toward peace enforcement, "Third Generation" PKOs, in which the UN coerced the parties to come to a peaceful settlement. These were ordered by the Security Council under Chapter VII of the Charter, which gives the Council authority to use force even when the parties oppose UN intervention. The mission in SOMALIA (UNOSOM) was the first to be conducted under the new guidelines, which allowed for the disarming of warring factions and so-called mission-defense. That is, peacekeepers were authorized to use force in order to reach the established goal of the operation. The failure of the UN in Somalia discredited Third-Generation PKOs and induced greater caution in subsequent missions.

Nonetheless, current peacekeeping operations can be classified as a Fourth Generation in the sense that better trained and equipped troops are called upon to conduct "robust" missions, thus combining aspects of Chapter VI and Chapter VII PKOs. Troops have to be well trained and equipped to be able to defend not only themselves but also serve as a shield for refugees or uphold HUMAN RIGHTS with force, should the necessity arise. Operations at the turn of the century in BOSNIA, Kosovo, and East Timor reflected this new strategy. Specifically, the BRAHIMI REPORT was established to guide new missions. At the direction of Secretary-General Kofi ANNAN, Lakhdar Brahimi, the SG's Special Representative to AFGHANISTAN, prepared and submitted in 2000 a set of recommendations for future operations. The report established three rules: (1) The "BLUE HELMETS" should not cede the initiative to an attacker, (2) the UN's impartiality should have its limits, and (3) the PKO should only be authorized after the necessary resources are available.

Further Reading: Benton, Barbara, ed. *Soldiers for Peace: Fifty Years of United Nations Peacekeeping.* New York: Facts On File, 1996. Durch, William J., ed. *The Evolution of UN Peacekeeping: Case Studies and Comparative Analysis.* New York: St. Martin's, 1993. United Nations. *The Blue Helmets: A Review of United Nations Peace-Keeping.* 3d ed. New York: United Nations Publications, 1996. ————. *UN Peacekeeping: 50 Years, 1948–1998.* New York: United Nations Publications, 1998.

— *T. J. Weiler*

Chapter VII

Chapter VII of the United Nations CHARTER is essential to the UN's functioning as an effective system of global COLLECTIVE SECURITY. Providing further reaching powers than those in the ill-fated COVENANT of the LEAGUE OF NATIONS, it establishes the UN's ability to take collective measures in order to uphold or restore international peace and security. Article 39 gives the SECURITY COUNCIL the authority under INTERNATIONAL LAW to "determine the existence of any threat to the peace, breach of the peace, or act of AGGRESSION," and to "decide what measures shall be taken" to halt the threat or punish the aggressor. In enabling the Security Council to take coercive measures to achieve these tasks, Chapter VII installs the United Nations as the international guarantor of peace and security.

A number of conditions have to be satisfied before the Security Council can act under the provisions of Chapter

VII: First, it must be established that either an act of aggression or a threat to or breach of the peace has occurred (Article 39). The Charter does not contain definitions of these terms, thus the Council itself is the sole defining power. Consequently, the classification of a certain case as a threat to international peace has been among the most complicated matters throughout UN history. The fact that decisions of the Security Council are subject only to very limited judicial review by the INTERNATIONAL COURT OF JUSTICE (ICJ) is evidence for the broad margin of power Chapter VII grants to the Security Council.

The Security Council also has considered the following factors in its deliberations on whether to invoke Chapter VII ENFORCEMENT MEASURES: the international value or right endangered in the particular case, the extent and immediacy to which this right or value is being threatened or violated, and the international, transboundary character of the threat. Due to Article 2 (7), which prohibits UN intervention in the internal affairs of states, "peace" in Chapter VII is understood as "international peace." For this reason, actions being contemplated by the Security Council must be weighed against the right of SOVEREIGNTY of those states such actions would affect.

While in theory a differentiation among the three violations of international order mentioned in Article 39 is required, by definition, the term "act of aggression" demands that one of the parties to a conflict be classified as an aggressor. Thus the Security Council has been hesitant to be precise in its statements about transgressions of the article. So far, only North Korea in 1950, Argentina in 1982, and Iraq in 1990 have been identified as "aggressors," or rather invaders/attackers; in 1960, while an aggression was identified, Belgium was not mentioned as the perpetrator. As in CHAPTER VI, "peace" is understood to mean the absence of war, rather than harmonious relations between nations.

Chapter VII gives the Security Council four possible actions if it determines that a threat to international peace exists: Article 40 empowers it to take provisional measures to prevent an escalation or aggravation of the situation. Such actions may include calls for a cease-fire or armistice, withdrawal of troops, or similar actions. These recommendations are not binding, but if they are ignored, coercive nonmilitary or military actions may be taken. Article 41 (actions not involving military force) and Article 42 (military actions) describe a gradual increase in coerciveness. Article 41 enumerates, in a nonexclusive way, steps that do not involve the use of WEAPONS, such as the cessation of diplomatic relations and economic SANCTIONS up to a blockade. The latter has been instituted only in a few cases, as in the post–GULF WAR sanctions against Iraq. The effectiveness of sanctions in general remains in dispute, the case of South Africa often cited as perhaps the only successful operation of this kind. Should sanctions not be adequate, Article 42 provides for even harsher measures as it authorizes the United Nations to take military action. It is common practice to empower individual states or other organizations/regional groups to take such action, usually in the form of an ad hoc "coalition of the willing" (Art. 48; cf. also Chapter VIII) in order to carry out the mandate issued by the Security Council.

All member states are asked and, at least according to the letter of Articles 43 and 44, are obliged to contribute troops and equipment to UN-led operations. In practice, however, setting up the forces necessary to conduct such operations as authorized by the Council is problematic, as numerous problems with PEACEKEEPING operations have shown. Finally, intending to ensure the UN's ability for swift action, Articles 45–47 call for the establishment of a UN military force. The PERMANENT MEMBERS discussed in vain this possibility during the founding period of the United Nations. Due to member states' unwillingness to confer command authority and independent forces to the United Nations, and because of the emergence of COLD WAR politics in the world body, troops being sent to war by the United Nations remained at the end of the century but a theoretical possibility. While the Charter mandated a MILITARY STAFF COMMITTEE (Art. 47), the only military action ever undertaken under the UN FLAG (although under U.S. command) occurred in the KOREAN WAR. In contrast, the 1991 Gulf War against Iraq was not, strictly speaking, a UN operation. It was conducted by a U.S.-led coalition of member states on the basis of Article 42, sentence 2, and Article 48.

All of the enforcement measures described above can be instituted only if none of the five permanent members use their VETO power, as all decisions under Chapter VII are substantive (Article 27). The veto power vitiated any Security Council response to international crises during the cold war, as the superpowers often were unable to come to an agreement. Even in the "new world order," the Security Council would be unable to offer protection against aggression or threats committed by any of the permanent members. Article 51, finally, clarifies that the right to individual or COLLECTIVE SELF-DEFENSE even outside of the UNITED NATIONS SYSTEM is left untouched by the provisions of Chapter VII. For example, Article 5 of the North Atlantic Treaty Organization (NATO) explicitly refers to this provision.

See also CHAPTER VI, CHAPTER VI ½ PROVISIONS, SOMALIA.

Further Reading: Freudenschuss, Helmut. "Article 39 of the UN Charter Revisited." *Austrian Journal of Public and International Law,* no. 46 (1993). Lepgold, Joseph, and Thomas G. Weiss, eds. *Collective Conflict Management and Changing World Politics.* Albany, N.Y.: State University of New York Press, 1998. Simma, Bruno, ed. *The Charter of the United Nations—A Commentary.* New York: Oxford University Press, 1994. Weiss, Thomas G., et al. *The United Nations and Changing World Politics; Part One: International Peace and Security.* Boulder, Colo.: Westview Press, 1997.

— *T. J. Weiler*

Charter of the United Nations

The UN Charter is the "constitution" of the United Nations. Member states agree to abide by its principles and its procedures, laid out in a preamble and 19 chapters containing 111 articles. The Charter was signed on June 26, 1945, in San Francisco, at the conclusion of the UN CONFERENCE ON INTERNATIONAL ORGANIZATION. It came into force on October 24, 1945.

Article 108, in Chapter XVIII, provides the method for amending the Charter, which has been employed on only a few occasions. For an AMENDMENT to be added, it must be adopted by a vote of two-thirds of the members of the GENERAL ASSEMBLY (GA) and then ratified according to the respective constitutional processes of two-thirds of the member states, including all of the PERMANENT MEMBERS OF THE SECURITY COUNCIL (P5). Amendments to the Charter as of 2001 included alterations to Articles 23, 27, and 61, adopted by the General Assembly on December 17, 1963, and coming into force on August 31, 1965. An additional change in Article 61 was adopted on December 20, 1971, and entered into force on September 24, 1973. Article 109 was amended by the General Assembly on December 20, 1965, and the amendment came into force June 12, 1968. The amendment to Article 23 enlarged the MEMBERSHIP of the SECURITY COUNCIL (SC) from 11 to 15, and changes in Article 27 altered VOTING requirements in the Security Council—from seven to nine votes to pass procedural and all other matters. The VETO for the five permanent members remained. The two revisions of Article 61 enlarged the membership of the ECONOMIC AND SOCIAL COUNCIL (ECOSOC) from 18 to 27, and then to 54. The change in Article 109 increased the number from seven to nine of Security Council votes necessary to call a General Conference for the purpose of reviewing the Charter. The two-thirds vote required of the General Assembly remained.

It is useful in analyzing the Charter to distinguish the word *charter* from COVENANT. The latter term, used for the foundation document of the LEAGUE OF NATIONS, carries a more metaphysical and spiritual meaning than does charter. A covenant is a voluntary agreement entered into by two or more parties to do or refrain from some action or actions. In law, a covenant is a promise or contract of legal validity. In theology, a covenant is a contract or commitment between God and human beings, such as the biblical covenant between God and Israel, or the covenant entered into between the 17th-century American Puritans and their God. The League Covenant was a traditional agreement among governments, called in the Covenant "The High Contracting Parties," whereas the Preamble of the UN Charter begins "We the peoples of the United Nations."

The word *charter* customarily denotes the granting or gaining of rights, powers, or functions. A charter may be bestowed by the sovereign body of a state to a lower political level, to a corporation, to a university, or so on. One of the most legendary of all charters was the Magna Carta, famous in British constitutional history, which, in 1215, provided protection of certain rights for landed Englishmen against monarchal interference. This example gives evidence of the Latin origin of the word. One approximate—and telling—synonym, according to the *Oxford English Dictionary,* is "written constitution." In the UN's case, in the Preamble and thus in essence—if not with juridical precision—the world's peoples granted themselves the rights, powers, and responsibilities contained in the Charter.

Comparing the League's Covenant and the UN's Charter draws attention to certain new, or elaborated, principles of INTERNATIONAL LAW introduced by the latter. For example, the Covenant essentially suggested a voluntary commitment not to resort to force, while the Charter, in Article 2, paragraph 4, confirms the nonresort to war as an established principle: "All members shall refrain in their international relations from the threat or use of force against the territorial integrity or political independence of any state, or any other manner inconsistent with the purposes of the United Nations." The Covenant's Preamble speaks of the dealings of "organized peoples with one another," as though there were "disorganized," or perhaps, "less civilized" peoples in the world. As Nagendra Singh, former president of the INTERNATIONAL COURT OF JUSTICE, has pointed out, the Charter disavows an international "class" system by provisions devoted to decolonization (especially Chapters XI, XII, and XIII), to the equal SOVEREIGNTY of states (Article 2), and by its encouragement of universal membership (Chapter II). Of equal significance is the principle of obligatory registration of treaties at a single, universally visible place and with a single institution—the United Nations—as provided in Article 102. This article additionally directs the SECRETARIAT to accumulate and publicize all registered treaties.

However, two of the Charter's accentuated themes sometimes have seemed to operate at cross-purposes. First is the principle of the independence and sovereignty of equal member states (Article 2) and the concomitant principle of noninterference in the domestic or internal affairs of states, as explicated in Article 2, paragraph 7: "Nothing contained in the present Charter shall authorize the United Nations to intervene in matters which are essentially within the domestic JURISDICTION of any state or shall require the Members to submit such matters to settlement under the present Charter." But second is the promotion of universal respect for HUMAN RIGHTS and fundamental freedoms, as found in Article 1, paragraph 3, in Article 13, paragraph 1, and in Article 55, section C, which, in succession, promotes and encourages "respect for human rights," advocates "assisting in the realization of human rights," and calls on the United Nations to promote "universal respect for, and observance of, human rights." Of course, sovereignty and noninterference appear to denote the right of a NATION-STATE to enforce its own version of human rights.

Yet the UNIVERSAL DECLARATION OF HUMAN RIGHTS and several provisions of the Charter seem to proclaim rights as universal rather than culturally or nationally determined. In 1999 SECRETARY-GENERAL Kofi ANNAN maintained that such human rights could not be abridged in the name of state sovereignty. By the conclusion of the 20th century the proposition that sovereignty and the principle of non-interference deny any other nation, group of nations, or the United Nations, the right—even duty—to interfere in a state's domestic affairs came under increased challenge as the world community found itself dealing with human tragedies in collapsing and dysfunctional states in the FORMER YUGOSLAVIA, INDONESIA, and areas of Africa. The Security Council, for example, authorized direct humanitarian intervention in SOMALIA, Rwanda, and East Timor, not always at the clear invitation of any central government. Moreover, the BRAHIMI REPORT, prepared by a special committee on PEACEKEEPING operations and available for international consideration at the MILLENNIUM SUMMIT of 2000, underscored Annan's view and recommended strengthening UN peacekeeping and a more robust and offensive posture in dangerous and out-of-control situations in disintegrating states.

The Charter's original authors may well not have foreseen these recent developments. The basic framework for the Charter derived from discussions among the main Allies during World War II. The idea for a new world organization began to take form once it was clear that the League of Nations had collapsed. U.S. president Franklin ROOSEVELT used the words "United Nations" in early 1942 to refer to those countries aligned against the Axis powers. During the war U.S. secretary of state Cordell HULL convened an Advisory Committee to deal with issues of a new international organization. Hull presented a completed working paper—called "Charter of the UN"—in August 1943. This was the first time the word "Charter" had been used in reference to the proposed new organization, and the document became the focus of negotiations and discussions from that time forward. The Moscow DECLARATION of October 30, 1943, issued by CHINA, the United Kingdom, the UNITED STATES, and the Soviet Union represented the first official statement from the Allies on the need for a new international organization. On November 5, 1943, the U.S. Senate adopted the Connally Resolution, 85 to 5, calling for establishment of an international authority after the war. During the summer of 1944, the same four countries that had issued the Moscow Declaration sent representatives to the six and a half week conference held at DUMBARTON OAKS in Washington, D.C., where preliminary proposals for a Charter were drafted. At the YALTA CONFERENCE in February 1945, Roosevelt, Winston CHURCHILL, and Joseph STALIN reached further agreement on Charter provisions. At the founding conference in San Francisco in June 1945, all nations that had adhered to the original January 1, 1942,

DECLARATION BY UNITED NATIONS, or who had declared war on Germany and Japan by March 1, 1945—totaling 50 nations—were invited to help draft the finished Charter. According to Article 110, paragraph 3, the Charter was to enter into force once it had received ratification by the five permanent Security Council members (United States, United Kingdom, China, USSR, and France) and a majority of all other signatories. The United States was the first to deposit its instrument of ratification (August 8) and the Soviet Union, Ukraine, Byelorussia, and Poland the last, on October 24, 1945, making the latter date the official "UNITED NATIONS DAY."

The Preamble indicates that the Charter is an agreement not among "governments" or "states," but among the "peoples" of the world, a notion that caused considerable debate in San Francisco. Less deliberation was directed to the remaining paragraphs of the Preamble, dealing with saving the future world from the "scourge of war," emphasizing human rights and the legitimacy of treaties and international law, and promoting social progress and better standards of living.

Chapter I outlines the UN's "Purposes and Principles," including the maintenance of international peace and security, respect for equal rights and self-determination, the encouragement of rights and freedoms, and the principle of sovereign equality of all member states. It establishes a COLLECTIVE SECURITY system among its members, requiring them to "settle their international disputes by peaceful means."

Chapter II deals with membership, the qualification for which is to be a "peace-loving" state. ADMISSION requires Security Council recommendation followed by General Assembly approval. It also allows for the SUSPENSION of the membership of a state against which the UN has taken some ENFORCEMENT MEASURES. Under the most dire circumstances, a state may be expelled by the General Assembly upon recommendation of the Security Council.

Chapter III lists the PRINCIPAL ORGANS and explicitly commands that there be no restriction on "the eligibility of men and women to participate" in any principal or subsidiary organ. The Charter creates five principal organs: the General Assembly, the Security Council, the Economic and Social Council, the TRUSTEESHIP COUNCIL, and the Secretariat.

Chapters IV and V detail provisions for the General Assembly and the Security Council, including voting procedures for both bodies and the jurisdiction of actions each can take. Membership in the General Assembly is completely equal, since each country, whatever its size, has one vote. While a majority vote effects most actions, the more important decisions made by the GA are made on "IMPORTANT QUESTIONS," which require a two-thirds vote of those members present and voting (Article 18). In the 15-member Security Council, nine votes are required to pass a procedural matter, while "all other matters" require that the five permanent members concur (the veto provision in Article 27).

Chapters VI and VII constitute the core precepts for the historic development of UN peacekeeping policies and outline the collective security measures that the United Nations may employ to restore peace. CHAPTER VI describes the procedures for dealing with the "Pacific Settlement of Disputes" and threats to the peace. It lists the traditional methods in international diplomacy that the parties should use to resolve their differences. They are negotiation, MEDIATION, CONCILIATION, ARBITRATION, and judicial decisions. CHAPTER VII emphasizes the role of the Security Council under international law to "determine the existence of any threat to the peace, breach of the peace, or act of AGGRESSION," and to "decide what measures shall be taken" to halt the threat or punish the aggressor. In enabling the Security Council to take coercive measures to achieve these tasks, Chapter VII installs the United Nations as the international guarantor of peace and security.

Chapters VIII and IX define and sanction REGIONAL ORGANIZATIONS to keep the peace and encourage economic and social cooperation. Article 57 encourages SPECIALIZED AGENCIES to develop a relationship with the United Nations and to expedite raising living standards, resolving economic and social problems, and enhancing human rights. These chapters are followed by the related Chapter X, which defines and sets the parameters for action of the Economic and Social Council.

Chapters XI and XII deal with NON-SELF-GOVERNING TERRITORIES (typically colonies). The first of these two chapters is a declaration of UN intent to promote decolonization and the progressive development of "free political institutions." Chapter XIII establishes the Trusteeship Council and defines its membership (those states administering trust territories, the remaining permanent members of the Security Council that do not administer any territories in the system, and sufficient member states elected by the General Assembly to assure an equal number of administering and non-administering governments on the Council).

Chapter XIV provides for the International Court of Justice, the judicial arm of the United Nations. By Article 92, the ICJ replaced the PERMANENT COURT OF INTERNATIONAL JUSTICE (PCIJ), became an integral part of the United Nations, and gained its own statute, annexed to the UN Charter and based on the statute of the PCIJ.

Chapter XV creates the Secretariat, to be headed by a SECRETARY-GENERAL appointed by the General Assembly upon the recommendation of the Security Council. In addition to being the chief administrative officer of the United Nations, the Secretary-General plays an important political role. Article 99 allows him to bring to the Security Council's attention any matter that he believes threatens peace and security. The Secretariat is designed to be the administrative

arm of the United Nations. Its members are "international officers responsible only to the Organization" (Article 100).

Chapter XVI outlines miscellaneous provisions for UN members. Chapter XVII, with the title "Transitional Security Arrangements," sorted out specific matters that concluded World War II, and Chapter XVIII explicates the method of amending the Charter (see above) while the Charter concludes with Chapter XIX, which describes the time line and process of ratification (see above).

See also CHAPTER VI $^1/_2$, REFORM OF THE UNITED NATIONS, STRUCTURE OF THE UNITED NATIONS, UNITED NATIONS SYSTEM, UNITING FOR PEACE RESOLUTION.

Further Reading: Gross, Leo. "The Development of International Law through the United Nations." *The United Nations; Past, Present, and Future.* Edited by James Barros. New York: The Free Press, 1972. Nicholas, H. G. *The United Nations as a Political Institution.* 5th ed. Oxford: Oxford University Press, 1975. Russell, Ruth B. *A History of the United Nations Charter: The Role of the United States, 1940–1945.* Washington, D.C.: Brookings Institution, 1958. Simma, Bruno. *The Charter of the United Nations: A Commentary.* Oxford: Oxford University Press, 1994. Singh, Nagendra. "The UN and the Development of International Law." *United Nations, Divided World; The UN's Roles in International Relations.* 2d ed. Edited by Adam Roberts and Benedict Kingsbury. Oxford: Clarendon Press, 1993.

Chechnya   *See* RUSSIAN FEDERATION.

chemical weapons (CW)

In April 1915, the German army first used chemical WEAPONS, in the form of chlorine gas. From then until the end of World War I, these WEAPONS OF MASS DESTRUCTION (WMD) killed or maimed tens of thousands of people. In what constituted the first arms race, each side developed methods of deployment and agents that even rendered gas masks worn by the enemy useless. At that time mostly chlorine and phosgene were used, both usually in gaseous form. Accordingly, chemical warfare was often called "Gas War." Most CW agents, however, were liquids or solids, like the so-called mustard gas, which was used later in World War I. Often, chemical weapons were used in their atomized form as aerosols, entering the body via the respiratory organs or penetrating the skin. Chemical weapons were not used during World War II, even though all sides possessed huge quantities of them.

With the onset of the COLD WAR, even more deadly agents were developed, mainly in the Warsaw PACT states. In 1969, the United Nations defined chemical warfare agents as "chemical substances, whether gaseous, liquid or solid, which might be employed because of their direct toxic effects on man, animals and plants." Not only the toxic chemicals but also the equipment for their dispersal was classified as a chemical weapon. In recent years, the Iraqi government used CW agents against the Iraqi Kurds (in Halabja in 1988) and during the IRAN-IRAQ WAR. Also, the chemical Sarin was used in a terrorist attack on the Tokyo subway in 1995.

On November 30, 1992, the GENERAL ASSEMBLY adopted the "Convention on the Prohibition of the Development, Production, Stockpiling and Use of Chemical Weapons and on their Destruction" (Res. 39), an accord submitted and recommended by the CONFERENCE ON DISARMAMENT. The Chemical Weapons Convention (CWC) was opened for signature in Paris on January 13, 1993. It entered into force on April 29, 1997, six months after Hungary became the 65th state to sign it. As of July 2001, the CWC counted 143 states that had become or were in the process of becoming parties to the agreement.

The CWC regulates assistance to states that might be attacked with chemical agents and also regulates trade relationships among the parties in the field of chemicals and related equipment. The obligations imposed on signatory states are unprecedented in their scope. The CWC prohibits the development, acquisition, production, stockpiling, and use of chemical weapons. States are required to destroy all chemical weapons (including those left within the territory of another state) and production facilities that they may possess. The CONVENTION is the first international DISARMAMENT agreement with the purpose of eliminating an entire category of WMDs.

The ORGANIZATION FOR THE PROHIBITION OF CHEMICAL WEAPONS (OPCW), headquartered in The Hague, was created to implement the CWC, including providing international verification and a forum for international cooperation in this field. The organization trains inspectors and promotes universal ACCESSION to the convention. The verification provisions of the CWC are far-reaching. They affect the military sector as well as the civilian chemical industry by imposing obligations and restrictions on the production, processing, and consumption of all chemicals that potentially could be used in weapons production.

Further Reading: *Chemical Disarmament: Basic Facts.* 1999 edition. The Hague: Organization for the Prohibition of Chemical Weapons, 2000. Moodie, Michael, and Javed Ali, eds. *Synthesis 2000: A Year in Review.* The Hague: Organization for the Prohibition of Chemical Weapons, 2001. Tucker, Jonathan B., ed. *Toxic Terror: Assessing Terrorist Use of Chemical and Biological Weapons.* Cambridge: MIT Press, 2000. ———. *The Chemical Weapons Convention: Implementation Challenges and Solutions.* Monterey, Calif.: Monterey Institute of International Studies Center for Nonproliferation Studies, 2001. OPCW website:<www.opcw.org>.

— *T. J. Weiler*

China

China was one of the 26 countries that joined in the January 1, 1942, DECLARATION BY UNITED NATIONS to overcome the Axis powers. The country then joined with the UNITED STATES, the United Kingdom, and the Soviet Union in the MOSCOW DECLARATION of October 30, 1943—the first official statement on the necessity of creating a new international organization to replace the LEAGUE OF NATIONS. Subsequently, China participated with the same three countries in drafting specific proposals for the UN CHARTER at the DUMBARTON OAKS CONFERENCE of 1944, and, although not in attendance at the YALTA CONFERENCE of February 1945, achieved at that meeting the status of PERMANENT MEMBER OF THE SECURITY COUNCIL. For a nation that had suffered Japanese occupation of much of its territory from 1931 to the end of World War II, and repeated humiliations at the hands of other nations since the early 19th century, this surfacing international respectability appeared extraordinary. Yet this high point was followed immediately by a brutal internal civil war, ending in 1949 with Mao Zedong's Chinese Communist Party victorious and the rival Republic of China's leader Jiang Jieshi (Chiang Kai-shek)—who had participated in all the wartime negotiations—removed to the island of Taiwan (Formosa). From 1949 to 1971, Jiang's republic officially represented China at the United Nations and as a permanent member in the SECURITY COUNCIL. But a dramatic GENERAL ASSEMBLY vote in 1971 removed the republic and elevated Mao's People's Republic of China (PRC) to fill China's seat. For the remainder of the 20th century, the PRC conducted China's business in the United Nations and in the myriad global organizations it joined.

Active diplomacy and collaboration across international boundaries were recent modi operandi for a country that for centuries had seen itself as the "Middle Kingdom" and superior to all others. Ethnocentrism, certainly not unique to the Chinese, rested in the Celestial Empire's expansiveness and centrality, as well as in its unusually long and continuous history, unmatched by most other civilizations. By the end of the 18th century, Manchu China extended to Tibet, beyond Xinjiang to Turkestan, and included Mongolia, Taiwan, a vassal state in Korea, and tributary control over northern Vietnam and Burma. China was at its greatest territorial extent. Between 1700 and 1800 the population doubled to about 300 million, making China from then until the opening of the 21st century the most populous country on earth.

But by the end of the 19th century China had suffered three humiliating losses in wars and a subsequent loss of sovereign control over "spheres of influence," territories within the country administered by outside nations. Western-educated Sun Zhongshan (Sun Yat-sen) instigated a nationwide revolution against the weakened Manchus, who were overthrown in 1911. Sun became the first president of the new Provisional Chinese Republic. But soon he resigned in favor of strongman Yuan Shikai, whose death in 1916 was followed by years of factional civil war among aspiring warlords. Sun's hopes to forge a republican solution to China's problems seemed stillborn. Moreover, during World War I, Japan had successfully extracted further concessions, and in 1919 anger mounted when Chinese learned that the Treaty of Versailles ending World War I had granted former German concessions in China to the Japanese. Generalissimo Jiang Jieshi, who guided Sun's Guomindang (Nationalist) Party following the latter's death in 1925, defeated remaining warlords. He then turned on his erstwhile allies in the Chinese Communist Party (founded by Mao Zedong in 1921) and brought some unity to the country. But it was short-lived. In 1931 Japan invaded Manchuria and turned it into the puppet state of Manzhouguo (Manchukuo). (After the invasion Mao voiced his disdain for international organizations by referring to the League of Nations as "a League of Robbers by which the various imperialisms are dismembering China.") In a reborn but fragile united front with the Communists, Jiang tried to resist Japanese incursion. Then, in 1937, Tokyo began its full-scale AGGRESSION on the Chinese mainland. Japan occupied Manchuria and much of the coastal region of China for the duration of World War II.

The Communist-Guomindang front began to crumple during the war and the disintegration simply merged into a civil conflict that continued after World War II had ended. On October 1, 1949, in Beijing, victorious Mao Zedong, announcing that at last China had "stood up," proclaimed the People's Republic of China. Meantime, Jiang crossed to the island of Taiwan, where in his capital of Taipei, he headed what he and the United States—and the United Nations—were to consider, for the next two decades, the legitimate government of China.

Taipei joined with the United States and the West in the rivalry now called the COLD WAR, while the Soviet Union and its allies recognized the new government in Beijing and urged its seating in the United Nations. The outbreak of the KOREAN WAR solidified cold war divisions. Documents released in 2000 from Soviet archives show that Soviet leader Joseph STALIN approved North Korea's June 25, 1950, invasion of the South, emphasizing to North Korean leader KIM II SUNG that the victory of the Chinese Communists the previous year demonstrated that Americans were weak and would not respond to such an invasion, and that Chinese troops would be made available to fight with the North. In October 1950, following General Douglas MacArthur's landing at Inchon, Mao enthusiastically agreed to intervene (but wanted prior Soviet assurance of air cover, which never came, and marked an initial strain in the Sino-Soviet alliance signed in February of that year). The upshot was that the PRC found itself technically at war with the United Nations, whose U.S.-dominated forces were the main defenders of the South. Sino-American hostility deepened, and Washington used all its political muscle to assure exclusion of Beijing from the United Nations.

Seating of PRC delegation, November 15, 1971 (UNITED NATIONS)

Meantime China reabsorbed Tibet (1951), tried and sentenced "class enemies," and confiscated land from landowners to give to peasants. Cut off from the new international financial and trade regimes, China in the late 1950s experienced Mao's "Great Leap Forward," a self-generated economic growth plan that established rural communes in place of peasant ownership and called for a crash program for village industrialization, all directed from the central government. Consequences were disastrous. The country suffered from widespread famine and economic downturn. When INDONESIA's leader Sukarno removed that country from the United Nations in 1965, Mao called for an alternate "revolutionary United Nations" made up only of leftist countries. A border dispute with India, Russia's friend, further isolated the regime. Mao attempted to reenergize revolutionary fervor by activating the Great Proletarian Cultural Revolution in 1966. Schools were closed down. Officially sanctioned and ideologically pure Red Guard units, made up of rowdy, faithful youth, roamed the country engaging in nasty purges of wrong ideas and impure customs, and challenged any remnant signs of bourgeois capitalism, including those allegedly within the entrenched party bureaucracy. Formerly powerful leaders were placed under house arrest. Others, like future leader Deng Xiaoping, were exiled to distant rural areas.

China seemed to turn completely within itself, and to be highly combustible.

Then three important developments began to alter China's position with the wider world and hint at a long-term effect on the nation's internal life as well as on its external diplomacy. One was the growing estrangement with the Soviet Union, whose invasion of Czechoslovakia in 1968 finally convinced the Chinese that Moscow was more dangerous than the United States. The second was the changing nature of UN MEMBERSHIP; as many former colonial nations entered the organization, support for Taiwan became more tenuous, and support for seating Beijing grew. The third important development was the departure of the revolutionary generation leadership, and particularly that of Mao, who died in 1976, just short of the age of 83.

U.S. president Richard Nixon sensed an opportunity to exploit the Sino-Soviet unfriendliness and draw China closer to the United States. By early 1971 the two countries were engaged in secret talks. In July 1971 Nixon sent Henry Kissinger, his national security adviser, on a trip to China. In February 1972, the president himself was in the country, where he met with Mao and signed the historic Shanghai Communiqué, recognizing Beijing's SOVEREIGNTY in China and disavowing a "two-China" policy. These events enveloped one of the more interesting moments in UN history, as the annual GENERAL ASSEMBLY vote on China's representation came up in October 1971. The U.S. Department of State, long publicly committed to Taiwan, was prepared to pursue its regular procedural tactic of making the issue of seating Beijing an IMPORTANT QUESTION, thus requiring a two-thirds vote. This strategy had until then restrained a United Nations increasingly sympathetic to the PRC. Now, however, with the highest U.S. officials unexpectedly linked with the mainland, the U.S. position seemed at least confused, and the Third World pro-PRC coalition of representatives was able to surmount the two-thirds barrier. On October 25 the General Assembly, in a dramatic late night ballot, removed Taiwan and seated Beijing as China's UN representative.

For the most part, the PRC's behavior as a new member of the United Nations revealed a traditional, pragmatic posture of attention first to national interests and then, usually fairly quietly, endorsement of nonthreatening consensus actions. The first VETO exercised by Beijing in the Security Council was against the admission of Bangladesh, formed out of East Pakistan after the India-Pakistan War of 1971. The veto underscored the Pakistan-China friendship and the recurrent Sino-Indian hostility. Also early, Beijing positioned itself to take a leadership role among the smaller Third World nations by supporting RESOLUTIONS and initiatives against the white minority governments in South Africa and Rhodesia (now Zimbabwe). Of the 21 vetoes China cast from 1971 to 1996, 19 had to do with nominations for SECRETARY-GENERAL. Beijing consistently supported Third World candidates. At the 1972 Stockholm conference that established the UNITED NATIONS ENVIRONMENT PROGRAMME (UNEP), China played a surprisingly active role, and, consistent with its courting of the developing world, was a crucial influence on having UNEP's headquarters placed in Nairobi, Kenya.

Following Mao's death in 1976, the once dishonored Deng Xiaoping emerged from intraparty rivalry to the top leadership position in the country (as deputy premier, chief of staff of the army, and member of the central committee of the party). He achieved full diplomatic relations with the United States in 1979 and engineered a remarkable reinterpretation of communist ideology, leading to sweeping economic changes. In 1978 the government announced the policy of the "Four Modernizations" (agriculture, industry, science and technology, and defense). The new policy encouraged foreign investment and technology transfer. In a drive to modernize, Western management and market practices replaced Maoist tenets. By breaking up rural communes and returning land to individuals under long leases, China realized extraordinary progress in agricultural production during the 1980s. In 1993, the party's central committee called for the conversion of state-owned enterprises into joint-stock companies and the eventual creation of a central bank and modern tax system. Official Chinese estimates showed by 1994 an economic growth rate of 12 percent (retreating to an estimated 7.9 percent by 2001). From 1978 to 1998, economic output quadrupled, and by then China had the world's second largest gross domestic product (an estimated $4.8 trillion in 1999).

But internal problems remained. With decreasing public-sector support, large groups of Chinese, particularly in rural areas, found themselves unemployed. Economic REFORMS were not followed by loosening political control from the central party. In the spring of 1989 student demonstrations took place in Beijing to mourn the death of disgraced former reformist party secretary Hu Yaobang. The demonstrations quickly took on a life of their own and student leaders and others convened in Tiananmen Square to demand wide-ranging democratic reforms. Protests spread to other parts of the country. Deng and a handful of powerful leaders replaced wavering party secretary Zhao Ziyang with Jiang Zemin and ordered military repression of the demonstrations. Beginning with the crackdown on June 3–4, thousands of protesters and dissidents were arrested and an unknown number killed.

For the next decade, China tried to put the Tiananmen unpleasantness behind it. After an initial explosion of outrage around the world, followed by some SANCTIONS, China's international economic and political relations resumed unhampered. They were guided by Jiang Zemin, who became president in 1993 and dominant party leader upon the death of Deng in February 1997. On July 1, 1997, the United Kingdom returned Hong Kong to Chinese sovereignty, and on December 20, 1999, China regained administrative control of Macao, the oldest permanent European enclave in Asia. Responding to President Bill Clinton's urgings, the U.S. Congress in 2000 granted China permanent most-favored-nation trading status, opening the way for Beijing's entry into the WORLD TRADE ORGANIZATION, scheduled for early 2002. In 2001 China was chosen to host the 2008 Olympic Games.

From within the UNITED NATIONS SYSTEM came further evidence of the nation's full integration into world affairs. In the 1980s Beijing joined almost all important international governmental organizations, including the WORLD BANK and the INTERNATIONAL MONETARY FUND. China began participating in the CONFERENCE ON DISARMAMENT in 1980, the COMMISSION ON HUMAN RIGHTS in 1982, and in late 1984 a Chinese national—jurist Ni Zhengyu—became a judge on the INTERNATIONAL COURT OF JUSTICE. China acceded to several human rights CONVENTIONS, including those on racial discrimination, APARTHEID, WOMEN, GENOCIDE, torture, refugees, and the child (but not the INTERNATIONAL COVENANT ON ECONOMIC, SOCIAL AND CULTURAL RIGHTS or the INTERNATIONAL COVENANT ON CIVIL AND POLITICAL RIGHTS). By the turn of the century, China was a signatory to several international environmental agreements, including the Antarctic Environmental PROTOCOL, the ANTARCTIC TREATY, the UN CONVENTION ON THE LAW OF THE SEA, and UN Conventions on Biological Diversity, climate change, DESERTIFICATION, Hazardous Wastes, the Ozone Layer, and more. By 2001 China had signed, but not yet ratified the KYOTO PROTOCOL. On the occasion of the 40th anniversary of the United Nations, in 1985, Zhao Ziyang became the first PRC prime minister to address the General Assembly. Prime Minister Li Peng participated in the first-ever Security Council summit in January 1992, the first Earth Summit at Rio in 1992, and the first WORLD SUMMIT ON SOCIAL DEVELOPMENT at Copenhagen in 1995. President Jiang Zemin attended the 50th anniversary meeting in 1995 and addressed the UN's MILLENNIUM SUMMIT in New York in September 2000.

Scholars noted a subtle shift in China's UN policy from a highly visible attempt to assume a leadership role among Third World nations to a concentration on Chinese national interests. Core issues for China appeared to include (1) an emphasis on state sovereignty and noninterference from outside powers in the internal affairs of member states, (2) a determination to maintain, solidify, and/or realize Chinese control over Tibet, Hong Kong, and Taiwan, (3) national security, (4) participation in global economic growth, and (5) maintenance of great power status.

These core interests mixed subtly when China considered specific issues. Typically, Beijing argued that all UN activities, including PEACEKEEPING and HUMAN RIGHTS formulations, should strictly observe the principles of state sovereignty and noninterference. For China these principles were crucial in order to assure no interference in China's

policies toward its own people or its control over Tibet and other regions. Thus, China was not sympathetic to notions of extending INTERNATIONAL LAW in ways that would result in outside intrusion into the internal affairs of states. Yet, within the Security Council, China demonstrated a cooperative stance in VOTING for the extension of the UN peacekeeping force in Cyprus (UNFICYP) in 1981, in agreeing in 1989 to dispatch Chinese military observers to serve in the UN TRUCE SUPERVISION ORGANIZATION (UNTSO) in the Middle East, in participating in the UN TRANSITIONAL GROUP (UNTAG) to help monitor the independence process in NAMIBIA, and in supporting the establishment of the UN TRANSITIONAL AUTHORITY IN CAMBODIA (UNTAC). And, by abstaining on Security Council RESOLUTION 827, it allowed the creation of the INTERNATIONAL TRIBUNAL FOR THE FORMER YUGOSLAVIA. China to all intents and purposes abandoned its treasured policy of the inviolability of state sovereignty. Also, China—as seen in its acceptance of various DECLARATIONS, such as that negotiated at the WORLD CONFERENCE ON HUMAN RIGHTS in Vienna (1993)—gradually accepted the principles of JUS COGENS and agreed that there is a common heritage of the world's peoples that can be conceptualized in an expanding international law.

The Gulf Crisis of 1990–91 was the most serious test for China's position on noninterference. Its solution was to abstain on UN SECURITY COUNCIL RESOLUTION 678, which authorized punitive action against Iraq. In effect this meant an approval of Security Council action. Subsequently, China found useful the tool of abstention, which students of the Security Council have come to see as a practiced and positive behavior in diplomacy among the great powers. The United States lifted its post-Tiananmen economic sanctions on China in gratitude for Beijing's abstention/cooperation on Security Council resolutions dealing with Iraq in the early 1990s. Both nations achieved important national priorities diplomatically.

The PRC's original support of Third World issues became more rhetorical than substantive as the century moved on. Accordingly, while offering moral support for greater Third World representation on the Security Council, China became clearly comfortable with not diluting its veto power by expanding the number of permanent seats on the Council. In fact, China seemed to relish its status as the only non-Western country in the center of UN great power politics. That status, with the veto, proved useful in affording considerable leverage that could be used in China's interest.

China's shift in UN policy to a more concentrated concern with national interest could be seen as well in budgetary politics. In 1973, but two years a UN member, China thrilled the world (and embarrassed the United States) by requesting to have its assessment rate raised from 4 percent to 5.5 percent. Then, in 1978, two years after Mao's death, China abandoned its economic policy of self-reliance and requested aid from the UN DEVELOPMENT PROGRAMME

(UNDP) and then asked that its SCALE OF ASSESSMENT be revised downward. Following its entry into the World Bank and the International Monetary Fund in 1980, China proceeded to obtain the largest number of multilateral aid projects, becoming the world's leading recipient of multilateral aid and largest borrower from the World Bank.

Resolution of two crisis events at the turn of the century suggested the long way Chinese relations with the outer world had progressed from the early 1970s. On May 7, 1999, U.S. aircraft mistakenly bombed the Chinese embassy in Belgrade while on a raid during the NATO war to rescue Kosovo. And on March 31, 2001, PRC fighter planes intercepted a U.S. Navy E-P 3 surveillance aircraft in the South China Sea, forcing a landing on Hainan island. In each instance emotions on either side ran high. But quick and adroit diplomacy relieved tensions and the crises both waned. China's march to the WTO remained on track. During the summer of 2001, in a speech commemorating the 80th anniversary of the founding of the Chinese Communist Party, President Jiang Zemin made a proposal that capitalists be encouraged to join the party. In mid August, Jiang, anticipating the invitation to host the 2008 Olympics, gave an extraordinarily expansive interview to the *New York Times*, accompanied by a cover story entitled "Chinese President Expresses Optimism on Relations with U.S." Less than a month later, Jiang flew to North Korea, Beijing's communist ally in its war with UN forces in the early 1950s, and encouraged that secluded country to seek closer ties with South Korea and join in the Asia Pacific Economic Cooperation forum (APEC), which, coincidentally, included a number of nations, like the United States, considered in days past dangerous enemies of the Chinese.

There remained at the turn of the 21st century distinguished scholars and public officials who saw China as a future danger to international order. Others insisted that the current regime would collapse within a very short time. What seemed clear was that China, impacted by its UN experiences, had moved far beyond the isolation so embedded in its history.

See also ADMISSION OF MEMBERS; AFGHANISTAN; FOUR POLICEMEN PROPOSAL; FOURTH WORLD CONFERENCE ON WOMEN; NATIONAL LIBERATION; NON-ALIGNED MOVEMENT; PÉREZ DE CUÉLLAR, JAVIER; STIMSON DOCTRINE; UNITED NATIONS CONFERENCE ON INTERNATIONAL ORGANIZATION; WALDHEIM, KURT; WORLD HEALTH ORGANIZATION.

Further Reading: Cohen, Warren I. *America's Response to China.* New York: Columbia University Press, 2000. Economy, Elizabeth, and Michel Oksenberg, eds. *China Joins the World: Progress and Prospects.* New York: Council on Foreign Relations Press, 1999. Fairbank, John King, and Merle Goldman. *China: A New History.* Cambridge: Belknap Press, 1998. "In Jiang's Words: 'I Hope the Western World Can Understand China Better.'" *New York Times*, August 10, 2001. Stoessinger, John G. *The United Nations and the Superpowers: China, Russia, and America.* 4th ed. New York: Random House, 1977. CIA World Factbook on China website: <www.cia.gov/cia/publications/factbook/geos/ch.html>. Permanent Mission of PRC to UN website: <un.fmprc.gov.cn/eng/index.html>.

China Representation   *See* CHINA.

Churchill, Winston (1874–1965)

Winston Churchill served as British prime minister from 1940 to 1945 and again from 1951 to 1955. He had first gained the attention of the British public as a reporter covering foreign events. His capture and imprisonment by the Boers of South Africa, while he was reporting the British-Boer conflict, raised his visibility sufficiently to win election to Parliament in 1900 as a Conservative. He switched to the Liberal Party during World War I, and he served in several capacities in the government. For much of the interwar period he was out of politics, but earlier than others he began to warn of the dangers of Adolf Hitler. He returned to Parliament (again as a Conservative) as war broke out and replaced Neville Chamberlain as prime minister.

As the leader of one of the "Big Three" wartime allies—the UNITED STATES, the United Kingdom, and the Soviet Union—he played a central role in crafting the United Nations. Churchill developed what he perceived to be a "special relationship" with President Franklin D. ROOSEVELT both before and during U.S. involvement in World War II. America's "nonbelligerent" relationship with war-beleaguered Britain reached a peak with the Atlantic Conference, when the two men met in August 1941 aboard the naval vessel *Prince of Wales* in Placentia Bay near the harbor of Argentia, Newfoundland. There, Churchill and Roosevelt discussed strategic issues and announced war aims and a joint vision of the postwar world. The most famous product of the meeting was the eight-point concluding statement called the ATLANTIC CHARTER. Churchill had brought to the meeting hopes for a closer U.S. alignment with the British war effort. In a noteworthy statement in the Atlantic Charter Roosevelt accepted Churchill's proposal of an "effective international organization" after the war.

When the United States entered the war in December 1941, Churchill journeyed to Washington to coordinate Anglo-American strategy in a more formal manner. At the suggestion of U.S. secretary of state Cordell HULL, the two leaders signed a DECLARATION BY UNITED NATIONS and invited, first CHINA and the Soviet Union, and then 22 smaller nations to join them in this initiative. The DECLARATION created a wartime alliance against the Axis powers but failed to announce a postwar international organization as many had hoped. Neither Churchill nor Roosevelt were as yet committed to such a proposition, although key figures in both the British Foreign Office and the U.S. State Department were keen enthusiasts. The two leaders concentrated on winning the war in the desperate year of reverses, 1942.

When the tide of war turned more in favor of the Allies in late 1942 and early 1943, Churchill began to think of regional councils to stabilize the postwar world (and to protect the British Empire). Roosevelt, on the other hand, began to develop his concept of the "FOUR POLICEMEN"—the United States, the United Kingdom, the Soviet Union, and China—to win the war and ensure the peace by way of a great power-dominated association of nations. Neither vision reflected the idealism of Woodrow Wilson's LEAGUE OF NATIONS.

The year 1943 was not only the turning point of Allied fortunes of war but also the embryonic phase of the United Nations. In March, Churchill delivered an important radio address and at the same time sent an aide-memoire to Washington, each outlining his vision of the postwar world. Dismissive of China and suspicious of the Soviet Union, the prime minister expressed the hope that the three major powers (that is, minus China) would create some sort of vague umbrella organization after victory, with the focus on a Council of Europe and a Council of Asia to ensure regional stability. Churchill's initiative compelled Roosevelt to begin focusing his attention on postwar issues, and by the time of the QUADRANT CONFERENCE in Quebec in August, his advisers had devised a counterproposal to present to the British that combined elements of FDR's Four Policemen with Churchill's regional approach. Foreign Minister Anthony EDEN was especially receptive to the American proposal.

Joseph STALIN, however, was uninterested in any schemes that went beyond the wartime coalition against Germany. It was Churchill who suggested that the best approach to the Soviet leader was to present postwar plans as merely a continuation of wartime collaboration and to do so while the war was still going on. Attracted first by Churchill's regional approach and then Roosevelt's Four Policemen proposal, Stalin came to accept the concept of the United Nations at both the October 1943 MOSCOW CONFERENCE OF FOREIGN MINISTERS and the TEHERAN CONFERENCE in December.

During the course of 1944 it became apparent to Churchill, to Stalin (both realists), and, importantly, to the American people that Franklin Roosevelt's United Nations, dominated by the Four Policemen, reflected the realism of Theodore Roosevelt rather than the idealism of Woodrow Wilson. Nevertheless, the YALTA CONFERENCE in January 1945 revealed a surprising divergence of opinion between the Anglo-American powers. Churchill agreed with Stalin that the Big Four should be granted an absolute VETO power over the discussion of disputes presented to the SECURITY COUNCIL. U.S. secretary of state Edward STETTINIUS and British foreign secretary Anthony Eden spent the first evening of the conference attempting to change Churchill's mind. The prime minister finally accepted Eden's view that

the small nations would refuse to participate in such an arrangement of raw power.

On the third day of the Yalta Conference, Churchill backed the American proposal that the Security Council must accept the principle of free discussion in order to affirm great power confidence in each other as well as in the sentiments of lesser nations. On February 12, 1945, Churchill, Roosevelt, and Stalin met for the last time and announced that all nations that had signed the United Nations Declaration would be invited to a conference at San Francisco on April 12, 1945, to create a new world organization.

But troubling Churchill was American insistence on a role for the United Nations in the self-determination of colonial peoples. Ever an advocate of the civilizing role that Britain had played in the reaches of its empire, Churchill was concerned about the threat to British national interest if the United Nations promoted decolonization. As early as 1943, Roosevelt approved a State Department draft adding an "agency for trusteeship responsibilities" to the contemplated UN CHARTER. British objections, however, postponed final acceptance of the UN's TRUSTEESHIP COUNCIL until the UNITED NATIONS CONFERENCE ON INTERNATIONAL ORGANIZATION in 1945. In the final negotiations Churchill's government accepted a UN commitment to "self-government," but not "independence" of colonial peoples. During the remainder of his time in office he rebuffed efforts by U.S. presidents Truman and Eisenhower to soften his position on this issue.

Churchill was one of the finest orators of the 20th century. Among his most legendary speeches was his "Iron Curtain" address, delivered at Fulton, Missouri, on March 5, 1946, which heralded the onset of the COLD WAR. He was also an accomplished writer, whose publications, including multivolume historical works on World Wars I and II and on the history of English-speaking peoples won him wide commendation and, in 1953, the Nobel Prize for Literature.

See also CAIRO CONFERENCE, TRUSTEESHIP SYSTEM.

Further Reading: Divine, Robert. *Second Chance: The Triumph of Internationalism in America during World War II.* New York: Atheneum, 1967. Eubank, Keith. *Summit at Teheran.* New York: Morrow, 1985. Gilbert, Martin. *Churchill: A Life.* New York: Holt, 1991. Gilbert, Martin, and Winston S. Churchill. *Road to Victory. 1944–1945.* Vol. 7. New York: Houghton Mifflin, 1986.

— E. M. Clauss

climate change   *See* UNITED NATIONS FRAMEWORK CONVENTION ON CLIMATE CHANGE, ENVIRONMENT.

cold war

The "cold war" refers to the U.S.–USSR rivalry following World War II (1939–45) to about 1991. The two superpowers, as they became known, engaged in a global competition with political, military, economic, ideological, and diplomatic dimensions that was called a cold war rather than a "hot" or shooting war. Each side attracted allies, and the contest came to be seen as a struggle between the "West" (the UNITED STATES and its allies) and the East (the Soviet Union and its allies). Other nations, declining to join either side, began calling themselves "non-aligned" in the cold war. As it shaped the global environment into a sharply divided "bipolar" arrangement, the cold war greatly influenced the work and development of the United Nations. It differed sharply from earlier great power conflicts in its intense ideological struggle between communism on the one side and democracy and capitalism on the other, and further manifested itself in a conventional arms race as well as massive stockpiling of WEAPONS OF MASS DESTRUCTION (nuclear, biological, and CHEMICAL WEAPONS) by both sides; rivalry also was waged in the United Nations.

The United States declared its plan to "contain" communism until it would be forced to collapse or change, a policy recommended by diplomat George Kennan and first launched by President Harry S. Truman. Containment became the main aim of both the Truman Doctrine (1947) and the rebuilding of former World War II foes by way of the Marshall Plan (1947), and it found expression in military alliances, such as the North Atlantic Treaty Organization (NATO) initiated in 1949. The United States blocked the ADMISSION of pro-Soviet applicants to the United Nations, such as Albania, Bulgaria, Hungary, and Romania, and

Nikita Khrushchev addresses the United Nations, 1959 (UNITED NATIONS)

insisted that the Republic of CHINA, seated in Taiwan—not the communist regime in Beijing—was the "legitimate" representative of the Chinese people at the UN. Meantime, the USSR objected to the admission of pro-Western countries such as Austria, Italy, Ireland, and Japan. This deadlock was broken in 1955, when several NATION-STATES from each rival bloc were admitted to the organization. However, mainland China did not achieve admittance until 16 years later.

The cold war rivalry dominated the functioning of the SECURITY COUNCIL most intensely, beginning with its first session in 1946, which was called to address the failure of the USSR to remove its troops from northern Iran. During World War II both Britain and the Soviet Union had stationed troops in Iran to guard against a Nazi seizure of oil resources located there; British troops had withdrawn from the country, complying with an agreement with Soviet leader Joseph STALIN, who, nonetheless, subsequently refused to pull out Red Army forces occupying northern Iran. The Security Council struggled to find a viable role in mediating the conflict consistent with its charge in the CHARTER to "maintain international peace and security, and to that end, to take effective collective measures for the prevention and removal of threats to the peace" (Article 1). But since the cold war had "divided" the UN members into competitive "East" and "West" camps, authentic collective action became difficult, if not impossible. Because of the ideological divide and the superpower VETO, the Security Council did not take up matters such as the French or American conflict in Vietnam, or the Soviet dispatch of troops and tanks to Hungary (1956) and Czechoslovakia (1968) to suppress anticommunist movements. Nor did the Soviets or Americans participate with significant troop deployments to UN PEACEKEEPING operations (PKO).

An early indication of the cold war's impact on the United Nations occurred with reference to Korea. The GENERAL ASSEMBLY first considered the question of Korea at its session in 1947, with unsuccessful efforts to reestablish a unified country via elections. By 1948 two separate countries came into being, divided at the 38th parallel. The General Assembly called for the withdrawal of all foreign troops and established the UNITED NATIONS TEMPORARY COMMISSION ON KOREA (UNTCOK). When, in June 1950, North Korean troops invaded the South, the Security Council, with staunch U.S. encouragement, recommended that member states furnish assistance to repel the attack. The UNITED NATIONS COMMAND IN KOREA (UNC) carried the UN FLAG although it was not a UN peacekeeping operation under the SECRETARY-GENERAL, but, in fact, a unified force under American command. The Soviet Union, which had been absent from Security Council meetings in protest of the seating of the Republic of China in the United Nations instead of the government in Beijing, declared the Council's action illegal because adopted without the presence of two PERMANENT MEMBERS (the USSR and China). Moscow refused to provide any assessed funding for the operation, and, by all accounts, supported the North Koreans during the conflict. UN peace-keeping became, in the eyes of the Russians at least, U.S. warfare against an ally, and a demonstration of the unwelcome control of the organization by a cold war enemy. Troops from the People's Republic of China also entered the war as allies of the North Koreans, and Americans (under a UN flag) found themselves in direct combat with these Chinese forces. Thus the KOREAN WAR has come to be seen as a "hot" war within the larger context of the global cold war. Fighting ended with an armistice in 1953, but the country remained—into the twenty-first century, long after the end of the cold war—the last divided country dating from the end of World War II.

In 1960 U.S. spy planes (a U-2 surveillance craft piloted by Francis Gary Powers and an RB-47 lost over the Arctic) were shot down over Soviet territory, sending the cold war into a deep freeze. Each side proceeded to use the United Nations for bombastic speeches about the perfidy of its opponent. Soviet leader Nikita Khrushchev showed up at the General Assembly annual meeting in 1960 where he banged his shoe on a desk to protest Western treachery, while in the Security Council U.S. ambassador Henry Cabot Lodge accused the Russians of planting secret microphones in the U.S. embassy in Moscow. Television viewers were entranced. Nonaligned nations decried the inability of the United Nations to meet their needs or temper the contest between Moscow and Washington.

The CONGO crisis of the early 1960s further underscored the challenge of the cold war to the United Nations. When the Congo in 1960 became independent from Belgium, a complicated civil war broke out, with one side being supported by the Soviet Union, one side by Washington, and a third side trying to secede. In the confusion Secretary-General Dag HAMMARSKJÖLD tried to insert a UN presence to bring the disorder to an end. Believing the Secretary-General to be carrying out the wishes of the United States and its cold war partners in the West, the Soviet Union demanded a reorganization of the office of Secretary-General, replacing the single secretary with a troika, whereby there would be a three-person executive with equal representation from the Western bloc, the Eastern bloc, and the neutral countries in the United Nations. Deflecting the Soviet challenge, Hammarskjöld persisted in his efforts, in the event dying in a plane crash in a remote part of Northern Rhodesia (now Zambia). The Congo dissolution persisted into the middle of the decade, after which the country was kept together, but was left under the rule of a dictatorship. The center of Africa continued to be a place where cold war differences disrupted any UN attempts at resolution. UN efforts in the Congo and elsewhere raised serious questions about the efficacy of UN peacekeeping, particularly in the era of cold war tension.

Perhaps the most dangerous encounter between the superpower rivals occurred during the CUBAN MISSILE CRISIS

in 1962. In October of that year, U.S. intelligence discovered that the Soviet Union was placing intermediate range nuclear weapons in CUBA. The Kennedy administration challenged the Soviets to remove the WEAPONS under clear threat of military action against Cuba, and of necessity, against the Soviet Union. Adlai Stevenson, the U.S. ambassador to the United Nations, argued with vigor the American position in the Security Council and worked in private with Secretary-General U THANT, in an effort to craft a liaison role for the Secretary-General in ending the crisis. Soviet leader Nikita Khrushchev also suggested using the Secretary-General as intermediary. The American administration, imposing a naval quarantine on Cuba, hoped to incorporate the United Nations into its efforts to avoid war while assuring the removal of the missiles. Meanwhile urgent secret negotiations transpired in New York and Washington to defuse this most serious challenge of a possible nuclear exchange in the cold war's history. By the end of October, the Russians agreed to remove the weapons, and the United States, in response, was poised to dismantle its own nuclear weapons in Turkey. The incident seemed to have a deep impact on the rival leaders in the cold war—President John Kennedy and Soviet leader Khrushchev—who, in mid-1963, agreed to sign a nuclear test ban TREATY.

Following the Cuban Missile Crisis, relations between the cold war adversaries never reached such dire peril again, but within the United Nations the competition continued to have an effect. Each side was interested in using the United Nations to criticize the other in its foreign adventures—the United States in Vietnam, the Soviets in AFGHANISTAN. The United Nations had virtually no impact on the American involvement in Southeast Asia, but the United States and its allies were able to gain RESOLUTIONS in the General Assembly criticizing the Russian involvement in Afghanistan. Earlier, in 1971, the United States witnessed an embarrassing reversal of its cold war China policy when, by an overwhelming vote in the General Assembly, the government of Beijing replaced the Republic of China in the organization, becoming an official permanent member of the Security Council.

It was at the United Nations, in December 1988, that Soviet leader Mikhail Gorbachev made an important gesture toward bringing the cold war to an end. After a genial meeting on Governor's Island in New York with outgoing President Ronald Reagan, the Soviet president addressed the full General Assembly, insisting that it was now "high time to make use of the opportunities provided by this universal organization." By the time of the crisis engendered by the Iraqi invasion of Kuwait in 1990 and the GULF WAR in 1991, Gorbachev's anticipation of an effective United Nations seemed prescient as Moscow and Washington cooperated within the Security Council in ways that would have astonished earlier diplomats in both countries. Evidence of the end of the cold war was visible early in 1991, before the

Soviet Union's demise that year, when the Russian delegation did not veto a British and American resolution before the Security Council authorizing the use of "any means necessary" (Res. 678) against Iraq to restore the SOVEREIGNTY of Kuwait. Iraq had been a Soviet ally. The Russians also joined a UN-sponsored multilateral peacekeeping operation in BOSNIA in 1995, and helped end the NATO bombing of Yugoslavia in 1999 by convincing the government led by Slobodan Milosevic to withdraw his forces from Kosovo.

Upon the collapse of the Berlin Wall (1989) and the dissolution of the Soviet Union (1991), the cold war was declared over, and shock waves rippled through the international system and within the United Nations. The disintegration of two communist states, the USSR and Yugoslavia, in 1991, contributed to the swelling MEMBERSHIP of the United Nations. With the end of the cold war, peacekeeping and peace-making became central concerns of the United Nations, as demand for UN intervention in conflicts continued to rise. The September 2000 summit of 150 heads of state at UN HEADQUARTERS in New York (the MILLENNIUM SUMMIT) affirmed the importance of peacekeeping operations, now no longer blocked by issues of superpower proxies and rivalry. The importance of arms control and weapons proliferation also moved to the forefront of the United Nations' agenda with the COMPREHENSIVE TEST BAN TREATY (CTBT) signed by the American and Russian governments in 1996, and the NON-PROLIFERATION TREATY's (NPT) extension in 1995.

See also DISARMAMENT, KOREAN WAR, RUSSIAN FEDERATION, UNITING FOR PEACE RESOLUTION.

Further Reading: Gaddis, John Lewis. *We Now Know, Rethinking Cold War History.* Oxford: Clarendon Press, 1998. Mingst, Karen, and Margaret Karns. *The United Nations in the Post–Cold War Era, Dilemmas in World Politics.* Boulder, Colo.: Westview Press, 2000. Moore, John Allphin, Jr., and Jerry Pubantz. *To Create a New World? American Presidents and the United Nations.* New York: Peter Lang Publishers, 1999. Muldoon, James P., JoAnn Fagot Aviel, Richard Reitano, and Earl Sullivan. *Multilateral Diplomacy and the United Nations Today.* Boulder, Colo.: Westview Press, 1999.

— *D. M. Schlagheck*

collective security

Collective security refers to agreements and actions among several states uniting them against an aggressor. Collective security guarantees each state's security; an attack on one means an attack on all; and all nations party to the agreement agree to resist any AGGRESSION. It works on the assumption that no state would use force against any member of the collective security system, as any aggression would be met by overwhelming international force and therefore would be fruitless.

The United Nations is a "universal" collective security system, having nearly all of the world's NATION-STATES as its members. However, throughout its history the UN has found it difficult to fulfill its collective security obligations. There are several reasons. First, member states have never met their obligations under Article 43 of the CHARTER "to make available to the SECURITY COUNCIL . . . in accordance with a special agreement or agreements, armed forces . . . for the purpose of maintaining international peace and security." Thus, the Security Council has had to depend on voluntary contributions of personnel, supplies, and funds in order to undertake COLLECTIVE SELF-DEFENSE efforts. Furthermore, all actions authorized by the United Nations in this respect are subject to the VETO power created in Article 27. The practical consequence of the veto is that no action can be taken against any of the permanent five members of the Security Council. During the COLD WAR this limitation meant that the concept of collective security had to be exercised through PREVENTIVE DIPLOMACY, PEACEKEEPING, pacific settlement methods authorized by CHAPTER VI, and CHAPTER VI ½ PROVISIONS.

With the end of the cold war during the last decade of the 20th century, the United Nations faced both the opportunity and the challenge of meeting threats to collective security through the original provisions laid down in the Charter for this purpose. The collective action taken against Iraq in 1991 marked the first use of CHAPTER VII's ENFORCEMENT MEASURES since the "police action" in the KOREAN WAR (1950–53) and went much further than any previous peacekeeping effort.

See also GULF WAR, LEAGUE OF NATIONS.

Further Reading: Freudenschuss, Helmut. "Between Unilateralism and Collective Security: Authorizations of the Use of Force by the UN Security Council," *European Journal of International Law* 5, no. 4 (1994): 492–531. Lepgold, Joseph, and Thomas G. Weiss, eds, *Collective Conflict Management and Changing World Politics.* Albany: State University of New York Press, 1998. Weiss, Thomas G., ed. *Collective Security in a Changing World.* Lynne Rienner, 1994.

— *T. J. Weiler*

collective self-defense

Article 51 of the UN CHARTER grants member states "the inherent right of individual or collective self-defense" against an armed attack until the SECURITY COUNCIL can undertake ENFORCEMENT MEASURES against the aggressor. Given that the maintenance of peace and security is one of the main functions of the United Nations, it may also exercise collective self-defense by acting militarily under CHAPTER VII. Additionally, a group of countries acting together in an alliance or through a REGIONAL ORGANIZATION may also undertake collective self-defense activities. However, they must report their action immediately to the Security Council.

The ability to act on a regional basis to deter AGGRESSION was important to the UNITED STATES and to other members of the ORGANIZATION OF AMERICAN STATES at the time of the 1945 San Francisco Conference. Many of the founding member states worried that the delegation of enforcement powers to the Security Council would limit the formation of regional alliances. Article 51's recognition of the right to collective self-defense and the Charter's Chapter VIII provisions on regional organizations provided a compromise on the issue.

The United Nations lacks a standing military force, and therefore in order to act decisively against aggression it must rely on coalitions of member states to carry out collective enforcement. This was the case in both the KOREAN WAR and the GULF WAR against Iraq. Military operations in these cases were authorized by Security Council RESOLUTIONS that called upon member states to defend the international community by any necessary means against an identified aggressor. States, according to the Charter, are obliged to place forces at the disposal of the United Nations for the purposes of collective self-defense. However, none have done so on a standing basis, forcing the UN to seek voluntary troop commitments on an ad hoc basis in order to carry out its mandates.

See also COLLECTIVE SECURITY, MILITARY STAFF COMMITTEE, SOUTHEAST ASIA TREATY ORGANIZATION.

Further Reading: Gottlieb, Gidon. *Nation against State*. New York: Council on Foreign Relations, 1994. Lepgold, Joseph, and Thomas G. Weiss, eds. *Collective Management and Changing World Politics*. Albany: State University of New York Press, 1988.

— *T. J. Weiler*

Commission for Social Development (CSocD)

The Commission for Social Development is one of nine functional commissions of the ECONOMIC AND SOCIAL COUNCIL (ECOSOC). As the new millennium began, the commission was the main intergovernmental body of the United Nations focused on social concerns and their relationship to development. Its duties include advising governments and ECOSOC on the enhancement of national social policies, with a special emphasis on dependent groups such as the elderly, youth, the disabled, minorities, and INDIGENOUS PEOPLES.

Created in 1946 as the Social Commission, it received its current name in 1966. During its lengthy history its mandate and MEMBERSHIP have expanded. Originally consisting of 18 members, the commission grew to 21 in 1961, 32 in 1966, and 46 in 1996 with each member state elected to a four-year term. In order to assure appropriate geographical representation 12 Commission seats are allocated to Africa, 10 to Asia,

five to Eastern European nations, nine to LATIN AMERICA and the Caribbean, and 10 to Western European and Other states. The commission meets annually in New York City, where since 1996 it has had responsibility for reviewing progress on the implementation of the 1995 Copenhagen DECLARATION on Social Development and the agreements made at the follow-up Copenhagen +5 Social Summit held in Geneva in 2000. The Commission also reviews the work of the UNITED NATIONS RESEARCH INSTITUTE FOR SOCIAL DEVELOPMENT (UNRISD) and nominates new members to UNRISD for election by ECOSOC.

Each year following the 1995 WORLD SUMMIT FOR SOCIAL DEVELOPMENT in Copenhagen, CSocD established a thematic agenda for its work based on the Copenhagen Programme for Action—the eradication of poverty (1996), productive employment (1997), promotion of social integration (1998), social services (1999), contributions made by the commission (2000), social protection and vulnerability during globalization, the role of volunteerism (2001), and the integration of social and economic policy (2002). At its 39th session in February 2001, the commission agreed on a multiyear program of work through 2006, continuing its thematic approach.

During its 54th session the UN GENERAL ASSEMBLY decided that the commission would serve as the preparatory committee for the Second World Conference on Ageing, held in Madrid, April 8–12, 2002. The meeting was scheduled to correspond with the 20th anniversary of the first WORLD CONFERENCE on the topic that convened in Vienna. CSocD worked closely with the UN SECRETARY-GENERAL's Technical Committee of Experts in preparation for the conference. It set as its goal for the conference a revision of the 1982 International Plan of Action on Ageing; a revision that would take into account the growing number of ageing people in the developing countries and the incapacity of governments in these countries both to sustain national development and to provide for the well-being of this sector of the population.

See also DEPARTMENT OF ECONOMIC AND SOCIAL AFFAIRS.

Further Reading: New Zealand Ministry of Foreign Affairs. *United Nations Handbook*. Wellington, N.Z.: Ministry of Foreign Affairs, published annually. CSocD website: <www.un.org/esa/socdev/csd/index.html>.

Commission on Human Rights (CHR)

In 1946 the ECONOMIC AND SOCIAL COUNCIL (ECOSOC) created the UN Commission on Human Rights as one of its functional commissions. Chaired by Eleanor ROOSEVELT, the commission realized its first major achievement with its composition of, and its subsequent securing of, international acceptance for the UNIVERSAL DECLARATION OF HUMAN

RIGHTS, approved by the GENERAL ASSEMBLY on December 10, 1948.

The commission, made up of 53 members elected by ECOSOC for three-year terms on the basis of equitable geographical representation, meets for about six weeks every March and April in Geneva. Some 3,000 delegates from member and observer delegations attend the commission's meetings. The commission has the authority to meet between regular sessions in exceptional SPECIAL SESSIONS to deal with urgent matters if a majority of the 53 members of the CHR agree. During regular annual sessions the commission adopts about 100 or so RESOLUTIONS, decisions, and statements on issues related to HUMAN RIGHTS. A subcommission on the promotion and protection of human rights and a number of working groups support the work of the commission.

With the Universal Declaration and other international instruments as guidelines, the commission reviews observance of human rights around the world, receives reports of violations of rights, and discusses ways to assure and protect them. In 1967 ECOSOC authorized CHR to investigate complaints from individuals about violations of rights in particular countries. The commission's mandate allows it to appoint SPECIAL RAPPORTEURS to investigate and report back to the commission on specific human rights problems in identifiable countries as well as on "thematic" questions, such as slavery, torture, religious intolerance, arbitrary detention and executions, state-sponsored "disappearances," violence against WOMEN, and more. Working groups from the CHR have drafted COVENANTS, CONVENTIONS, and DECLARATIONS for General Assembly approval and for ratification by UN member states. Among the most important of these are the INTERNATIONAL COVENANT ON CIVIL AND POLITICAL RIGHTS (and its first and second Optional PROTOCOLS) and the INTERNATIONAL COVENANT ON ECONOMIC, SOCIAL, AND CULTURAL RIGHTS (both entering into force in 1976), which together with the Universal Declaration make up the International Bill of Human Rights. Other international instruments initiated by the commission include the CONVENTION AGAINST TORTURE AND OTHER CRUEL, INHUMAN OR DEGRADING TREATMENT OR PUNISHMENT (1984), and the Convention on the Rights of the Child (1989). The commission remains cognizant and supportive of a number of other conventions, including the CONVENTION ON THE PREVENTION AND PUNISHMENT OF THE CRIME OF GENOCIDE (1948), the CONVENTION RELATING TO THE STATUS OF REFUGEES (1951), the International Convention on the Elimination of All Forms of Racial Discrimination (1966), and the CONVENTION ON THE ELIMINATION OF ALL FORMS OF DISCRIMINATION AGAINST WOMEN (1979). As of 2001, a working group of the commission was deliberating on a draft declaration regarding the rights of INDIGENOUS PEOPLES.

In a surprising development in 2001, the UNITED STATES, for the first time in the history of the CHR, was not elected to MEMBERSHIP on the commission. This seemed a setback for Washington, which found itself suffering international criticism for lack of attention to the commission's work. After a one-year hiatus the United States was reelected to the commission on April 29, 2002.

See also AFGHANISTAN, COMMITTEE OF 24, INQUIRY, INTERNATIONAL LAW, UNITED NATIONS CONFERENCE ON INTERNATIONAL ORGANIZATION.

Further Reading: United Nations. *The United Nations and Human Rights: 1945–1995.* New York: United Nations, 1995. CHR website: <www.unhchr.ch/html/menu2/2/chr.htm>.

Commission on Human Settlements (HABITAT)

The Commission on Human Settlements replaced the Committee on Housing, Building and Planning in 1977. It was created by the UN GENERAL ASSEMBLY. Its membership is representative of equitable geographical distribution, with its 58 members elected from Africa (16 members), Asia (13), Eastern Europe (six), LATIN AMERICA and the Caribbean (10), and Western European and Other States (13). Members serve four-year terms and have primary responsibility for policy guidance of the UNITED NATIONS CENTRE FOR HUMAN SETTLEMENTS (UNCHS). The commission meets every two years.

Commission on Narcotic Drugs (CND)

The ECONOMIC AND SOCIAL COUNCIL (ECOSOC) created the Commission on Narcotic Drugs in 1946 by way of RESOLUTION 9 (I). One of ECOSOC's first functional commissions, CND was authorized to advise the Council on issues of narcotic drugs and to prepare and draft agreements relating to the topic. CND is the main UN policy-making body for all drug-related matters, including analyses of drug abuse globally and efforts to enhance international drug control. The commission supervises application of international treaties and CONVENTIONS related to narcotic drugs and works to effect cooperation in drug-related law enforcement efforts at regional levels. Pursuing the latter goal, the CND has created subsidiary bodies, including the Subcommission on Illicit Drug Traffic Enforcement Agencies (HONLEA). It also directs the activities of the UN INTERNATIONAL DRUG CONTROL PROGRAMME (UNDCP), founded in 1991.

Membership of CND initially was 15 but, by 2001, had expanded to 53 by ECOSOC resolution. Members are elected every two years by ECOSOC for staggered four-year terms from among UN member states, members of SPECIALIZED AGENCIES, and parties to the Single Convention on Narcotic Drugs (1961). In electing the members, ECOSOC takes into account a concern for adequate representation from countries directly affected by illicit drug production, trafficking, and addiction. CND's headquarters is in Vienna. It meets annually.

See also OFFICE FOR DRUG CONTROL AND CRIME PREVENTION.

Further Reading: UNDCP website: <www.undcp.org>.

Commission on Population and Development

See INTERNATIONAL CONFERENCE ON POPULATION AND DEVELOPMENT.

Commission on Sustainable Development (CSD)

The United Nations GENERAL ASSEMBLY (GA) authorized the creation of the commission in 1992 (Res. 191). The Assembly made the commission one of the nine permanent commissions reporting to the ECONOMIC AND SOCIAL COUNCIL (ECOSOC), and by way of ECOSOC to the GA SECOND COMMITTEE. In so doing, the Assembly fulfilled the most important structural recommendation to come out of the UNITED NATIONS CONFERENCE ON ENVIRONMENT AND DEVELOPMENT (UNCED) that convened in Rio de Janeiro in 1992. The conference, also known as the Earth Summit, recommended the creation of the commission to monitor global progress on one of the summit's approved programs, AGENDA 21. The purpose of the agenda was to promote development in the less developed countries (LDCs) in ways that sustained environmental resources for their needed use by future generations. The UNCED sought ways to harmonize economic development with global environmental concerns. The commission was also directed to encourage NON-GOVERNMENTAL ORGANIZATIONS (NGOs), business, industry, and governments to implement Agenda 21. Given the nature of its work, the commission collaborates with the UNITED NATIONS CONFERENCE ON TRADE AND DEVELOPMENT (UNCTAD), the WORLD TRADE ORGANIZATION (WTO), the UNITED NATIONS ENVIRONMENT PROGRAMME (UNEP), and other UN bodies involved with environmental or development issues.

The Commission on Sustainable Development comprises 53 member governments elected to three-year terms by ECOSOC. One-third of the body is elected annually, and members may be reelected. The size of the commission constituted a matter of debate between the developed states of the North and the developing countries of the south. The former pushed for a small efficient commission in which the developed states would not be outvoted, while the LDCs wanted a large body with geographical representation. With a membership of 53 the CSD has one fewer participant than ECOSOC and allows for extensive participation from the South. Membership is regionally allocated with 13 seats assigned to elected African states, 11 seats for Asian governments, 6 to Eastern Europe, 10 to

LATIN AMERICA and the Caribbean, and 13 for the Western European and Others caucus. The 47th session of the General Assembly also directed that non-governmental organizations, other UN bodies, and intergovernmental economic organizations, both on global and regional levels, participate in the work of the commission. NGOs are authorized to submit written reports, address the commission with the permission of the chairman, and conduct "consultations" with members at the invitation of the chair or the United Nations SECRETARY-GENERAL. More than 1,000 NGOs are accredited to CSD.

The commission meets each year to review national reports from member states on meeting the targets of Agenda 21. These reports are submitted voluntarily and sporadically. Some participants at the Earth Summit had hoped to make such reporting mandatory, but opposition from developing states, worried about possible international pressure to alter their development programs, vetoed the requirement.

In all of its work, CSD has faced two overriding dilemmas: the apparent conflict between environmental protection and economic development, and the intrusiveness of international efforts to preserve the ENVIRONMENT on the one hand and the inviolability of SOVEREIGNTY on the other. Environmental issues are inherently global concerns. National borders do not restrict the deleterious effects of bad environmental practices from migrating. Furthermore, any efforts to limit these effects require the international community to focus on internal practices of NATION-STATES. Consequently, sovereignty, the bedrock principle of the international system, must give way to some extent if the environment is to be protected. Environmental protection can also run contrary to development strategies put in place by developing states. These strategies may cause environmental problems, or the effort to accommodate them to environmentally friendly techniques may be too costly. Thus, developing nations often see the demand that states alter their development programs to meet international environmental standards as unwarranted and counterproductive intrusion in their internal affairs.

Faced with these countervailing pressures, the Commission on Sustainable Development has had limited success in implementing Agenda 21 objectives. It has established two working groups that meet frequently to review each of the areas given priority by that document, however. In addition, there have been intersessional meetings sponsored by member states on a variety of topics before the commission. These meetings, held around the world, have considered issues related to health, the transfer of technology, water and environmental sanitation, chemical safety, finance, and sustainable consumption, among other items suggested by Agenda 21.

Between 1994 and 1996 the CSD reviewed each area identified by Agenda 21, including DESERTIFICATION, health, toxic chemicals and hazardous waste, biodiversity, human settlements, the atmosphere, and oceans and seas. It also held sessions on the overlapping issues of trade and the environment, poverty, demographic pressures on the environment, financial resources and mechanisms, and the transfer of environmentally sound technology to the underdeveloped world. In 1997 the Earth+5 SPECIAL SESSION OF THE GENERAL ASSEMBLY directed CSD to monitor carefully a few major identified provisions of Agenda 21. At its eighth session in April 2000 the commission reviewed agriculture, finance, land management, and trade. The 2001 meeting focused on the atmosphere, energy, transport, and information for decision making and participation. The commission also prepared reports and agenda for other UN activities in environment and development. In 1999 it prepared the plan for the General Assembly's review of SUSTAINABLE DEVELOPMENT of small island developing countries.

Earth+5 directed the commission to begin work on the identification of "Indicators of Sustainable Development" that could be used to measure progress toward the goals of the RIO DECLARATION. Three types of indicators were agreed to. The commission identified "Driving Force" indicators that it defined as "human activities, processes and patterns that impact on sustainable development." They included unemployment rates, adult literacy rates, population growth rates, annual energy consumption, per capita gross domestic product (GDP), emission of greenhouse gases, and the generation rate of hazardous wastes. The commission also identified "State" indicators as measures of the status of sustainable development within individual nations. They included population density, poverty indices, life expectancy, average rainfall, changes in land conditions, energy reserves, debt as a ratio of gross national product, the nutritional status of children, arable land per capita, and the percentage of the population in urban areas. Finally, CSD established "Response" indicators that measured the range of policy options a state had to use in meeting its current sustainable development challenges. Among them were GDP spent on education, immunization against childhood diseases, national health care expenditures as a ratio of GDP, infrastructure expenditures per capita, waste water treatment coverage, and environmental protection expenditures as a percent of GDP. The effort to develop these indicators, as well as to review progress on Agenda 21 topics, was scheduled to continue through 2002.

Further Reading: Elliott, Lorraine. *The Global Politics of the Environment.* New York: New York University Press, 1998. Mensah, Chris. "The United Nations Commission on Sustainable Development." In *Greening International Institutions.* Edited by Jacob Werkman. London: Earthscan Publications, 1996. Sands, Philippe, ed. *Greening International Law.* New York: The New Press, 1994. Commission on Sustainable Development website: <http://www.un.org/esa/sustdev/index.html>.

Commission on the Status of Women (CSW)

By RESOLUTION 11 (II) of June 21, 1946, the ECONOMIC AND SOCIAL COUNCIL created the Commission on the Status of Women, making it one of the first functional commissions of ECOSOC. Committed to the principle that WOMEN and men should have equal rights, CSW forwards recommendations and reports to the Council promoting women's civil and social rights, emphasizing gender equity in politics, education, and economics. Additionally, the commission alerts ECOSOC to pressing challenges for women that may require prompt attention, and drafts treaties, CONVENTIONS, and other instruments designed to elevate the status of women.

ECOSOC has periodically expanded CSW's mandate. Beyond defining women's rights, the commission also studies the underlying causes of gender discrimination and makes recommendations for remedying them. In 1993 the GENERAL ASSEMBLY adopted a DECLARATION ON THE ELIMINATION OF VIOLENCE AGAINST WOMEN that had been recommended by the commission.

The CSW has prepared several WORLD CONFERENCES ON WOMEN. After the fourth of these, the 1995 WORLD CONFERENCE on Women in Beijing, the General Assembly authorized the commission to review progress in the areas of concern articulated in the Beijing Platform for Action. The commission has worked to eliminate gender discrimination and violence against women, to advance the status of women, including the achievement of a 50 percent gender balance at the highest professional levels in the UN SECRETARIAT, as well as to continue the promotion of political, social, and economic rights for women.

Beginning with 15 members, the commission expanded its MEMBERSHIP to 45 by 2001. As of 2001, membership was accorded on a geographic basis: 13 from Africa, 11 from Asia, 4 from Eastern Europe, 9 from LATIN AMERICA and the Caribbean, and 8 from Western Europe and Other States. ECOSOC elects CSW's members for four-year terms from a pool appointed by UN member governments. The commission usually meets once a year for about eight days. Its officers—a chairperson and four vice chairs—are chosen by its members, and its headquarters is in Vienna.

See also BEIJING +5, CONVENTION ON THE ELIMINATION OF DISCRIMINATION AGAINST WOMEN.

Further Reading: CSW website: <www.un.org/women-watch/daw/csw>.

Committee of International Development Institutions on the Environment (CIDIE)

The Committee coordinated the work of international organizations involved in environmental affairs with the activities of the WORLD BANK and other development agencies. The United Nations does not have direct control over the affiliated bodies of the World Bank Group, and, therefore, must negotiate cooperative policies with those entities. On February 1, 1980, the Bank and several UN bodies signed the "Declaration of Environment Policies and Procedures Relating to Economic Development" in recognition of the critical impact that development projects have on the ENVIRONMENT. The signatories established CIDIE at that time to carry out the objectives of the DECLARATION.

In particular, the committee sought to resolve the competing interests between development in LESS DEVELOPED COUNTRIES and the global environmental initiatives launched at the 1972 UNITED NATIONS CONFERENCE ON THE HUMAN ENVIRONMENT in Stockholm. It also attempted to improve the work of the different intergovernmental organizations focused on environmental matters. Despite its purposes, the committee had only limited success because economic incentives in development programs generally override environmental concerns. The membership of the committee included the UNITED NATIONS ENVIRONMENT PROGRAMME (UNEP), the World Bank, the African Development Bank, the Arab Bank for Economic Development in Africa, the Asian Development Bank, the Caribbean Development Bank, the Inter-American Development Bank, the Commission of the European Community, the ORGANIZATION OF AMERICAN STATES, the European Investment Bank, and the UNITED NATIONS DEVELOPMENT PROGRAMME (UNDP).

See also REGIONAL DEVELOPMENT BANKS.

Further Reading: Caldwell, Lynton Keith. *International Environmental Policy, Emergence and Dimensions.* Durham, N.C.: Duke University Policy Studies, 1984. Elliott, Lorraine. *The Global Politics of the Environment.* New York: New York University Press, 1998. Sands, Philippe, ed. *Greening International Law.* New York: The New Press, 1994.

Committee of 24

The UN GENERAL ASSEMBLY in 1960 adopted the DECLARATION ON THE GRANTING OF INDEPENDENCE TO COLONIAL COUNTRIES AND PEOPLES, urging a faster pace in the process of decolonization. While one of the PRINCIPAL ORGANS OF THE UNITED NATIONS—the TRUSTEESHIP COUNCIL—was created to preside over the self-determination of NON-SELF-GOVERNING TERRITORIES, relatively few territories were under the Council's JURISDICTION, and half of the Council's members were administering powers. The Asian and African states that had only recently become members of the United Nations believed that neither the Council nor the United Nations as a whole was doing enough to encourage independence. In the effort to realize the goals of the DECLARATION, the General Assembly established the Special Committee on the Implementation of the Declaration on Decolonization. The original MEMBERSHIP in 1961 included 17 members, largely from the developing world. The committee was

enlarged to 24 in 1962 (Res. 1810), and thus became known as the Committee of 24. The total membership has varied from 23 to 25 during the committee's life, but it has retained the same name.

The committee became the primary voice in the UN STRUCTURE for the end to colonialism. The stridency of its debates, public pronouncements, and agenda drove all colonial and administering powers from its membership by 1971. The committee established two subcommittees to focus attention on particular colonial holdings and to receive petitions from inhabitants in non-self-governing territories. Those petitions were used to shed light on what the committee saw as violations of indigenous populations' rights. It was particularly harsh in its criticism of Portuguese colonial policy in Africa, and South African control of NAMIBIA. In the latter case the committee regularly called for economic SANCTIONS against South Africa. It was also at the forefront of UN efforts to sanction the breakaway state of Rhodesia under Ian Smith's APARTHEID regime. In addition to receiving and debating petitions, the committee created visiting missions to colonial territories and held local forums for the inhabitants to express their sentiments. On a very constructive note, the Committee of 24 sponsored talks between the United Kingdom and Argentina over the Falkland (Malvinas) Islands from 1965 to 1982.

As the number of colonial possessions declined, the impact on UN policies by the Committee of 24 shifted from mobilizing decolonization efforts to spurring HUMAN RIGHTS protections both in the remaining non-self-governing territories and in the developing world. In 1947 the UN COMMISSION ON HUMAN RIGHTS (CHR) concluded that "it had no power to take any action in regard to any complaints concerning human rights" by individuals against their own governments. This was known as the doctrine of impotency and was quickly endorsed by the ECONOMIC AND SOCIAL COUNCIL (ECOSOC). In 1965 the Committee of 24 urged ECOSOC to look at the violations of human rights in southern Africa that had been submitted to the committee by petitioners. ECOSOC, influenced by the new African and Asian voices in the United Nations, directed the Human Rights Commission, as a matter of importance and urgency, to take up these allegations, which it did. Since then, both ECOSOC and CHR have asserted the authority of UN bodies to protect individual rights. The Committee of 24 was also instrumental in the 1970s in getting the Human Rights Commission to take special notice of conditions in Western Sahara. In that case, the committee, the CHR, and the INTERNATIONAL COURT OF JUSTICE all concluded that people had an inherent human right to self-determination. The human rights focus of the committee continued in 2000 under the leadership of its chairman, Peter D. Donigi from Papua New Guinea.

Further Reading: Baehr, Peter R., and Leon Gordenker. *The United Nations in the 1990s.* 2d ed. New York: St. Martin's,

1994. United Nations Department of Public Information. *Everyone's United Nations*. New York: United Nations Department of Public Information, 1986. *United Nations Handbook*. Wellington, N.Z.: Ministry of External Affairs, published annually.

Committee of 24 at the World Bank and International Monetary Fund   *See* GROUP OF 77.

Committee on Contributions

One of two STANDING COMMITTEES OF THE GENERAL ASSEMBLY (GA), the Committee on Contributions recommends to the Assembly the SCALE OF ASSESSMENTS that determines the amount each member state must contribute to the regular BUDGET of the United Nations. The 18-member committee is made up of financial experts who work closely with the GA's FIFTH COMMITTEE and the ADVISORY COMMITTEE ON ADMINISTRATIVE AND BUDGETARY QUESTIONS to determine the budgetary needs of the organization. It determines each country's contribution on the "capacity to pay" principle—as determined by measuring a state's total national income in comparison to other states. The Committee on Contributions also takes into consideration low per capita income, giving affected states relief up to 85 percent of their assessment. A state's level of debt is factored into the determination. The committee also makes recommendations on the application of Article 19 of the CHARTER, which allows for the removal of a state's right to vote in the GENERAL ASSEMBLY if it is in arrears equaling a full two years of assessed contributions.

See also COMMITTEE SYSTEM OF THE GENERAL ASSEMBLY.

Committee on Non-Governmental Organizations

According to Article 71 of the UN CHARTER, the ECONOMIC AND SOCIAL COUNCIL (ECOSOC) may grant CONSULTATIVE STATUS to NON-GOVERNMENTAL ORGANIZATIONS (NGOs) whose concerns fall within the COMPETENCE of ECOSOC and its subsidiary bodies. Although the DEPARTMENT OF ECONOMIC AND SOCIAL AFFAIRS (DESA) at UN HEADQUARTERS processes requests for consultative status, applicant organizations must complete a questionnaire that is then presented to the Committee on Non-governmental Organizations. ECOSOC RESOLUTION 1996/31 established the principles required for gaining consultative status and provides guidance for the Committee on NGOs.

The members of the committee are elected by ECOSOC on the basis of equitable geographic representation. In 2001 it had 19 members. The committee selects its own officers. It carries a mandate to monitor the growing relationship between NGOs and the United Nations. It consults with NGOs and issues reports to ECOSOC regarding those consultations. The committee is also expected to confer with the SECRETARY-GENERAL on matters arising under Article 71 of the Charter, and it may receive referrals from ECOSOC for consideration and recommendations on matters regarding NGOs. The committee considers applications for consultative status at its annual meeting before the substantive sessions of ECOSOC. Every fourth year organizations with consultative status must submit to the committee a report on their activities with specific explanation of their support of UN activities. On the basis of these reports, the committee may recommend reclassification in the status of an NGO.

See also CONFERENCE OF NON-GOVERNMENTAL ORGANIZATIONS IN CONSULTATIVE RELATIONSHIP WITH THE UNITED NATIONS.

Further Reading: Willetts, Peter, ed. *The Conscience of the World: The Influence of Non-governmental Organizations in the UN System*. Washington, D.C.: Brookings Institution, 1996.

Committee on the Elimination of Racial Discrimination (CERD)

The 1965 International Convention on the Elimination of all Forms of Racial Discrimination created the Committee on the Elimination of Racial Discrimination (Articles 8 and 9). Made up of 18 experts "of high moral standing and acknowledged impartiality," CERD receives reports from its member states on the status of racial discrimination and efforts to abolish it within their countries. The committee meets twice a year, usually in Geneva. Under the convention's OPTIONAL CLAUSE (Article 14), private citizens of CONVENTION signatories may submit complaints about government policies and incidents of racial discrimination. States may also submit complaints about other convention members. The committee then may conduct investigations and discuss the complaints, bringing pressure on states to correct any violations of the TREATY. The Optional Clause entered into effect in 1982. CERD reports on its work to the UN GENERAL ASSEMBLY annually.

Committee on the Elimination of Discrimination Against Women (CEDAW)

See CONVENTION ON THE ELIMINATION OF DISCRIMINATION AGAINST WOMEN.

Committee on the Peaceful Uses of Outer Space (COPUOS)

In 1958, following the Soviet Union's successful launching of *Sputnik*, the first artificial space satellite, the GENERAL ASSEMBLY established an ad hoc Committee on the Peaceful

Uses of Outer Space. The 18-member committee was charged with considering how the United Nations and its SPECIALIZED AGENCIES, plus other international bodies, might provide help and guidance in promoting international cooperation, legal advice, and organizational arrangements to assure the peaceful uses of outer space in what was seen to be a future of space exploration. In Resolution 1472 (XIV) of 1959, the General Assembly made the committee a permanent body, with headquarters in Vienna and a membership of 24.

By instruction from the General Assembly (Res. 1721 of 1961), COPUOS was expected to maintain close contact with governments and NON-GOVERNMENTAL ORGANIZATIONS active in outer space, encourage full exchange of information and research about outer space activities, support the study of methods to assure cooperation in outer space, and play a role in the development of international space law. By the same RESOLUTION, the SECRETARY-GENERAL was authorized to maintain a public registry of space launchings.

Membership in COPUOS grew to 61 by 2001. Also, several international organizations and non-governmental organizations gained OBSERVER STATUS. The committee has two standing subcommittees of the whole—the Scientific and Technical Subcommittee and the Legal Subcommittee. The former of these subcommittees discusses topics such as remote sensing by satellite, nuclear power in outer space, the challenge of space debris, environmental concerns relating to space exploration, and space and planetary exploration. The Legal Subcommittee is interested in the legal definition of space and its boundaries, and reviews the status and effectiveness of international agreements, treaties, and CONVENTIONS governing outer space. As of 2001, due to the work of the committee and its Legal Subcommittee, there were in force five international instruments that were part of INTERNATIONAL LAW: the Treaty on Principles Governing the Activities of States in the Exploration and Use of Outer Space, including the Moon and Other Celestial Bodies (the "Outer Space Treaty" of 1966), the Agreement on the Rescue of Astronauts, the Return of Astronauts and the Return of Objects Launched into Outer Space (the "Rescue Agreement" of 1967), the Convention on International Liability for Damage Caused by Space Objects (the "Liability Convention" of 1971), the Convention on Registration of Objects Launched into Outer Space (the "Registration Convention" of 1974), and the Agreement Governing Activities of States on the Moon and Other Celestial Bodies (the "MOON AGREEMENT" of 1979).

Also, over the years COPUOS has embraced an array of principles to guide the international community in its conduct toward outer space. These principles complement the international agreements listed above. They address such matters as respect for state SOVEREIGNTY and equitable dissemination of information during direct television broadcasting and remote sensing activities from outer space,

guidelines for the safe use of nuclear power in space and for notification of malfunctions during reentry of radioactive material, and cooperation in space exploration.

COPUOS and its subcommittees meet annually, often in the late spring. Both work on the basis of consensus, both receive reports from member states and queries from the General Assembly, and the full body makes recommendations to the General Assembly. Annual reports from the committee and its subcommittees detail their work. In Vienna, the UN Office for Outer Space Affairs serves as the SECRETARIAT for the committee.

Further Reading: COPUOS website: <www.oosa.unvienna. org/COPUOS>.

Committee on Torture (CAT)   *See* CONVENTION AGAINST TORTURE AND OTHER CRUEL, INHUMAN OR DEGRADING TREATMENT OR PUNISHMENT.

Committee System of the General Assembly

The GENERAL ASSEMBLY (GA), one of the PRINCIPAL ORGANS OF THE UNITED NATIONS, has a committee system that allows most agenda items to be considered initially by one of its six main committees. All UN members are represented on each of the committees, and all member states have an equal vote on each committee. Committee decisions are made by a majority of those present and VOTING. At the beginning of the annual session, the GA president, with the formal approval of the Assembly, assigns agenda items to the committees. Normally, the General Assembly considers only RESOLUTIONS passed by its committees, although a few items are placed directly on its agenda without committee referral.

In the committees diplomats negotiate intensely to arrive at a consensus on agenda items, usually recommending one resolution on each topic. Members of each delegation consult each other regularly in order to assure that the content of each committee resolution is acceptable to their government. The primary GA debate on international issues occurs in committee. Since all states participate in committee work, consensus resolutions from committees tend to pass with ease through the full General Assembly.

The main committees of the General Assembly, each with its own topical specialization, are: FIRST COMMITTEE (DISARMAMENT and International Security), SECOND COMMITTEE (Economic and Financial), THIRD COMMITTEE (Social, Humanitarian, and Cultural), FOURTH COMMITTEE (Special Political and decolonization), FIFTH COMMITTEE (Administrative and Budgetary), and SIXTH COMMITTEE (Legal). Designated the Political and Security Committee under its original mandate, the First Committee deals almost exclusively with disarmament affairs. GA member states decided that this topic was so central to the international system that it required its own committee. A separate Special Political Committee formerly considered all other political questions, but it was merged in the 1990s with the TRUSTEESHIP committee, creating a new mandate for the Fourth Committee. Developing countries consider the Second Committee one of the most pivotal bodies in the United Nations, since it addresses questions of DEVELOPMENT and international trade and finance. Topics before the Third Committee each year include, among other issues, HUMAN RIGHTS, the impediments to WOMEN, INDIGENOUS PEOPLES, children, and minorities, drug trafficking and other social problems, and refugees and trans-boundary migration. The Fifth Committee reviews the proposed UN BUDGETs and SCALE OF ASSESSMENTS sent to it by the ADVISORY COMMITTEE ON ADMINISTRATIVE AND BUDGETARY QUESTIONS (ACABQ), and forwards its recommendations to the General Assembly. The Sixth Committee deals with the intricacies of INTERNATIONAL LAW, negotiating the texts of treaties and the meaning of legal concepts, as well as reviewing the work of UN judicial and legal bodies.

The General Assembly is empowered to establish other committees and working groups to deal with specific issues or to handle procedural matters. Each session, the GA creates several ad hoc and subsidiary committees in order to assure that important and controversial questions are negotiated before being brought to the full Assembly for a final vote. In 2000, there were 36 such bodies. The Assembly has two permanent PROCEDURAL COMMITTEES: the GENERAL COMMITTEE, made up of the president of the General Assembly and its 21 vice presidents, and the CREDENTIALS COMMITTEE, which is responsible for accrediting delegations to the UN.

See also IMPORTANT QUESTION, STRUCTURE OF THE UNITED NATIONS.

Further Reading: Mingst, Karen A., and Margaret P. Karns. *The United Nations in the Post–Cold War Era.* Boulder, Colo.: Westview, 1995. Muldoon, James P. Jr., JoAnn Fagot Aviel, Richard Reitano, and Earl Sullivan, eds. *Multilateral Diplomacy and the United Nations Today.* Boulder, Colo.: Westview, 1999. Peterson, M. J. *The General Assembly in World Politics.* Boston: Allen and Unwin, 1986. GA website: <www.un.org/ga/>.

— *K. J. Grieb*

competence of United Nations organs

Lawful competence of a political organization is the grant of responsibility for designated functions, usually by some authoritative source such as a constitution or decree. The organization itself must be seen as "legitimate" by those persons and entities subject to its decisions. In the case of an international organization, competence arises from the organization having an "international legal personality" and being authorized by its founding document to do certain

things, such as make treaties, adjudicate disputes, and allocate funds for approved activities. Closely intertwined with the concept of JURISDICTION, competence is not synonymous with it. The latter describes the legal authority upon which the organization, or a component of it, asserts a legitimate right to consider and act within a particular area of the organization's mission. It is a state of being, while jurisdiction describes a range of meaningful control, which may be large or small, over people, territory, and human behavior as the body exercises its competence.

In the 1949 *Reparations for Injuries Suffered in the Service of the United Nations* case, the INTERNATIONAL COURT OF JUSTICE (ICJ) decided that the states that created the United Nations, "by entrusting certain functions to it, with the attendant duties and responsibilities, . . . clothed it with the competence required to enable those functions to be effectively discharged." The Court concluded that the United Nations had an "objective international personality" that gave it a competence in international affairs going beyond a legitimacy solely among the states that founded it. In other words, the ICJ held that the United Nations was an independent actor in international relations with expressed and implied powers.

Within the United Nations different organs are competent to undertake certain specified actions. The CHARTER grants the broadest competence to the GENERAL ASSEMBLY. It may "discuss any questions or any matters within the scope of the . . . Charter or relating to the powers and functions of any organs" of the United Nations. All other bodies report to it. It may also pass RESOLUTIONS and convene international meetings. The SECURITY COUNCIL is competent under the Charter to deal with all threats to international peace, even to the exclusion of all other UN organs. Administrative competence is lodged in the SECRETARIAT. The International Court of Justice is the "judicial" organ of the United Nations, and draws its competence to define INTERNATIONAL LAW through rulings on cases brought before it, not only from the Charter but also from a separate statute to which all UN members are parties.

Comprehensive Nuclear Test Ban Treaty (CTBT)

The Comprehensive Nuclear Test Ban Treaty was negotiated in Geneva at the CONFERENCE ON DISARMAMENT (CD) and adopted by the UN GENERAL ASSEMBLY on September 10, 1996. The idea for a comprehensive nuclear test ban was first suggested by Prime Minister Jahwaharlal Nehru to the Indian parliament as a "standstill agreement" on nuclear explosions. The CTBT's ultimate journey to the General Assembly resulted because India, along with Iran, blocked a consensus regarding test bans in the Conference on Disarmament. The purpose of the TREATY was to stop nuclear testing in all environments and, as such, represented the definitive treaty in a series of accords dating back to the Partial Test Ban Treaty of 1963, and including the Threshold Test Ban Treaty concluded bilaterally between the UNITED STATES and the Soviet Union in 1974. At the 1995 NUCLEAR NON-PROLIFERATION TREATY Review and Extension Conference, the five Nuclear Weapons States—CHINA, France, Russia, the United Kingdom, and the United States (NWS)—agreed to conclude a CTBT by 1996. This decision both facilitated the indefinite extension of the Non-Proliferation Treaty (NPT) and coordinated the Nuclear Weapons States' stances on a test ban treaty.

The CTBT provided for a comprehensive verification system. It included as well a network of both land- and sea-based sensor stations, using four different technologies, called the International Monitoring System (IMS). The purpose of the IMS was to detect "anomalous events" worldwide. The treaty established a Comprehensive Test Ban Treaty Organization (CTBTO) with 51 seats on an executive council, apportioned geographically, whose functions included considering data from the IMS and implementing the treaty's provisions in conjunction with national authorities and a technical staff. The detection of any anomalous event within the territory of a state party to the treaty would require an effort to determine the exact nature of the occurrence, perhaps to distinguish it from a mine explosion, earthquake, or other natural or man-made event. An unexplained incident could trigger a request for an on-site inspection, which could be initiated within 72 hours with an affirmative vote of at least 30 of the executive council members. Other provisions of the treaty included standard administrative and withdrawal procedures. But the topic of greatest concern and controversy was the entry-into-force provision. According to Article XIV of the CTBT, all of the 44 states that participated in the work of the 1996 session of the Conference on Disarmament and that appeared in the 1996 INTERNATIONAL ATOMIC ENERGY AGENCY's April 1996 edition of *Nuclear Powers of the World* were required to sign and ratify the treaty before it could enter into force. India and Pakistan were among that group and, as of the turn of the century, remained vocal critics of the treaty. Moreover, the U.S. Senate rejected the treaty for consent to ratification on October 13, 1999. As of mid 2001, only 31 of the 44 necessary states had ratified the CTBT, so that its actual entry into force was subject to an uncertain future. Although work to establish the IMS stations and the CTBTO continued to take place, no inspections were supposed to occur until the treaty entered into force. Nonetheless, as of 2001, all nuclear weapons states were following a voluntary moratorium on the testing of nuclear weapons.

See also DISARMAMENT.

Further Reading: Ghose, Arundhati. "Negotiating the CTBT: India's Security Concerns and Nuclear Disarmament." *Journal of International Affairs* (Summer 1997). Hawkins, Wohlety K. "Visual Inspection for CTBT Verification." *Los Alamos Lab* Report 15244-MS, Spring 1997. York, Herbert F. *The CTBT and Beyond.* New York: United Nations Department of Public Information, 1994.

— *S. L. Williams*

Comprehensive Test Ban Treaty Organization (CTBTO)   *See* COMPREHENSIVE NUCLEAR TEST BAN TREATY.

compulsory jurisdiction

Because NATION-STATES are sovereign, they are not required to submit legal disputes with other states to any court, panel, or tribunal. However, they may agree to do so as part of a TREATY or the PROTOCOL to a multilateral CONVENTION. Even in these circumstances, a state may decline to be sued or to accept the judgment made by the judicial body that heard the case. Despite these limitations on judicial resolution of international disputes, since the founding of the United Nations many agreements have included compulsory jurisdiction provisions. The most famous is OPTIONAL CLAUSE 36 (paragraphs 2 and 3) in the STATUTE OF THE INTERNATIONAL COURT OF JUSTICE. Countries that have signed the Optional Clause agree to adjudicate before the INTERNATIONAL COURT OF JUSTICE (ICJ) legal disputes concerning: (1) the interpretation of a treaty, (2) any question of INTERNATIONAL LAW, (3) the existence of any fact which may constitute a breach of an international obligation, or (4) the nature and extent of a reparation for such a breach. However, states may withdraw their consent to the Optional Clause, as the United States did in the 1984 case of *Nicaragua v. U.S.A.*, refusing for two years to accept prior compulsory jurisdiction of the International Court in matters relating to Central America.

Some tribunals created by international conventions have grappled with the question of when a state may withdraw its consent to the agreement's compulsory jurisdiction requirements. In 1999 the Inter-American Court of HUMAN RIGHTS held that if a signatory of the 1969 American Convention on Human Rights had agreed to compulsory jurisdiction, its only option for withdrawing its consent was through the process of denouncing the convention itself. If this principle were to apply universally, it would undermine the principle of SOVEREIGNTY central to the "Westphalian" system of independent states. This problem was addressed in another 1999 case involving the LAW OF THE SEA Convention (LOS). Under its terms, states agree to the compulsory jurisdiction of LOS ARBITRATION procedures. But the convention's provisions overlap with many other international agreements and regional treaties. When a case was brought before the LOS Arbitral Tribunal on a matter also covered by a regional agreement that did not have a compulsory jurisdiction provision, the tribunal held that it did not have JURISDICTION, severely limiting the enforcement mechanisms of the Law of the Sea regime. As these cases demonstrated, the evolution of the compulsory jurisdiction principle at the turn of the century was closely intertwined with broader conceptions of the international system as either a collection of independent nation-states or an emerging international civil society in which sovereignty could be limited by international agreement.

Further Reading: Oxman, Bernard H. "Complementary Agreements and Compulsory Jurisdiction." *American Journal of International Law* 95, no. 2 (April 2001): 277–312.

conciliation

In international affairs conciliation refers to the process of seeking agreement between or among parties without recourse to ARBITRATION. Conciliation may be accomplished by having a dispute examined in depth by an impartial INQUIRY or "conciliation commission," leading to a nonbinding resolution. The General Act on the pacific settlement of International Disputes in 1928 provided elaborate measures for international conciliation efforts, but these techniques enjoyed a short period of notoriety during the interwar years. Nonetheless, some treaties still provide for well-defined conciliation practices, as does the LAW OF THE SEA (1982). Also, since 1975, the European Union has used a joint "conciliation committee" to resolve disagreements between the EU's Council of Ministers and the European Parliament.

See also CHAPTER VI, CONFLICT RESOLUTION, GOOD OFFICES, MEDIATION, ORGANIZATION OF AFRICAN UNITY.

Conference of Non-Governmental Organizations in Consultative Relationship with the United Nations (CONGO)

The Conference of Non-Governmental Organizations is an independent, not-for-profit association of non-governmental organizations (NGOs) dedicated to facilitating the participation of NGOs in UN activities. CONGO is active at UN HEADQUARTERS in New York and Geneva as well as elsewhere around the world. Founded in 1948, CONGO has mobilized NGOs in a number of efforts, including worldwide forums on HUMAN RIGHTS. Although not taking positions on substantive matters, it does represent the interests of its member NGOs in seeking influence on UN debates and decisions. Its membership comprises national, regional, and international non-governmental organizations who are in CONSULTATIVE STATUS with the UN ECONOMIC AND SOCIAL COUNCIL (ECOSOC). CONGO associate membership is open to NGOs not holding consultative status.

See also COMMITTEE ON NON-GOVERNMENTAL ORGANIZATIONS.

Conference of the Committee on Disarmament (CCD)   *See* CONFERENCE ON DISARMAMENT.

Conference on Disarmament (CD)

Located in Geneva, Switzerland, the Conference on Disarmament is the world's principal multilateral DISARMAMENT negotiating forum. While the United Nations provides conference services for the CD and the GENERAL ASSEMBLY makes recommendations that may become part of the CD's focus, the CD has its own rules, procedures, work program, and dynamics. Principal among its negotiating rules is a policy of consensus. Established in 1978 by consultations among members of its predecessor body, the CONFERENCE OF THE COMMITTEE ON DISARMAMENT (CCD, 1969), at the first UN SPECIAL SESSION ON DISARMAMENT, the CD was called the Committee on Disarmament until 1983. The EIGHTEEN NATION DISARMAMENT COMMITTEE (ENDC, 1962) and the Ten Nations Disarmament Committee (1960) were also predecessor bodies. By 1996, the CD had expanded from its original 38 member states to 61. Its set agenda, known as "the Decalogue," establishes 10 broad areas of disarmament for annual review. When the CD wishes to negotiate a specific topic, as it did successfully with the CHEMICAL WEAPONS CONVENTION (CWC, 1992) and the COMPREHENSIVE NUCLEAR TEST BAN TREATY (CTBT, 1996), it creates an ad hoc committee with a negotiating mandate to establish the TREATY's exact provisions. Reflecting a COLD WAR legacy, three groups act as informal negotiating parties within the CD. They are the East, West, and the non-aligned blocs. CHINA serves as a "group of one."

Several events in the mid-1990s affected the status and effectiveness of the CD. Perhaps most importantly, the CONVENTION ON THE PROHIBITION OF THE USE STOCKPILING, PRODUCTION, AND TRANSFER OF ANTI-PERSONNEL MINES AND THEIR DESTRUCTION (1997) was debated, negotiated, and adopted for ratification outside the CD in a "fast track" set of negotiations known as "The Ottawa Process." Moreover, in 1996 the UN General Assembly gave final approval to the Comprehensive Nuclear Test Ban Treaty when India refused to join the consensus for the treaty at the CD. Finally, in the years following the decision of the 1995 Review and Extension Conference of the NUCLEAR NON-PROLIFERATION TREATY (NPT) to extend the treaty's terms indefinitely, the CD was unable to achieve a consensus on a treaty banning the production of fissile materials; the Western Group refused a demand from the non-aligned Group of 21 within the CD to establish an ad hoc committee to discuss the abolition of nuclear weapons; and the UNITED STATES, Britain, and France resisted one on the prevention of an arms race in outer space. The stalemate inside the CD and events outside the CD, including India's and Pakistan's testing of nuclear weapons and the success of the Ottawa Process, led to widespread speculation among experts about the need either to maintain the status quo at the CD, to change the CD's rules and procedures, or to endorse the establishment of alternative negotiating fora to address a range of disarmament questions. The 1999 and 2000 sessions of the CD ended without consensus on a new negotiating mandate or an agreement to expand the conference's MEMBERSHIP.

See also UNITED NATIONS INSTITUTE FOR DISARMAMENT RESEARCH, WEAPONS OF MASS DESTRUCTION.

Further Reading: Carle, Christophe, and Patricia Lewis. "Arms Control and Disarmament Mechanisms." *First Conference of the PfP Consortium of Defence Academies and Security Study Institutes,* Kongresshaus Zurich, Switzerland, October 18–21, 1998. Cordon, Pierce. "The Future of the Conference on Disarmament and Multilateral Arms Control." *Center for Nonproliferation Studies; China–US Conference on Arms Control, Disarmament, and Nonproliferation,* September 24–25, 1998. Conference on Disarmament, CD/8/Rev.8, August 17, 1999. Johnson, Rebecca. "CD Writes Off 1999 with Hopes for 2000." *Disarmament Diplomacy,* Issue no. 39. Sethi, Manpreet. "Conference on Disarmament: Groping Its Way Around." *Strategic Analysis 23,* no. 8 (November 1999). United Nations Institute for Disarmament Research. "Electronic Conference on the Future of the Conference on Disarmament and Its Agenda," January 13–27, 1998.

— *S. L. Williams*

conflict resolution

Unlike MEDIATION and CONCILIATION, with which it is sometimes compared, conflict resolution relies more on "academic" or even "social psychology" techniques. It depends less on an outside agent and suggests an approach and analysis of the causes and possible solutions to conflict as much as the final resolution itself. Implied in conflict resolution is that for a settlement of a conflict to be successful, the parties to the disagreement must redefine their relationship so as to perceive a way they can avoid conflict and deal reasonably with one another. Thus, conflict resolution requires that adversaries maintain contact, ongoing discussion, and even joint activities to resolve their differences. As an example, some Palestinian and Israeli groups in the Middle East have attempted to initiate formal associations to practice conflict resolution.

The United Nations has promoted conflict resolution as a necessary ingredient in trying to mitigate intrastate violence in unstable nations (such as in the FORMER YUGOSLAVIA, AFGHANISTAN, INDONESIA, and elsewhere) where ethnic, religious, and national rivalries have brought novel challenges to the maintenance of civil societies. In his *AGENDA FOR PEACE,* SECRETARY-GENERAL Boutros BOUTROS-GHALI called

for "peace-building" in which the United Nations would play a critical role in the establishment of "social peace" among warring groups. The key problem seems to be that for conflict resolution to work, the parties to a dispute must demonstrate a committed resourcefulness and agree to enter into the process. Most critics see this as unlikely and thus deem conflict resolution as more an ideal to be sought after than a practical modus operandi.

See also ECONOMIC COMMUNITY OF WEST AFRICAN STATES.

Congo

There have been two periods of United Nations involvement in the Congo. The first period (1960–64) followed Congo's independence from Belgium on June 30, 1960. On July 4, the Armée Nationale Congolaise (ANC) mutinied against its Belgian officers and began attacking European civilians. Against the wishes of the Congo government, Belgium sent 10,000 paratroopers to restore order. On July 10, Congolese prime minister Patrice Lumumba asked UN Secretary-General Dag HAMMARSKJÖLD for technical assistance to help restore order. On July 11, President Moise Tshombe of the mineral-rich Katanga province declared independence. With heavy fighting between Belgian and Congolese troops, both Lumumba and the Belgians requested the dispatch of UN troops to restore order on July 12. For the first time, the SECRETARY-GENERAL invoked Article 99 of the CHARTER to bring to the SECURITY COUNCIL's (SC) attention the Congo situation. Security Council RESOLUTIONS 4387 and 4405 urged the withdrawal of Belgian troops and established the UNITED NATIONS OPERATION IN THE CONGO (ONUC) to promote order. The SC passed Resolution 4426 in August in response to Katanga's refusal to allow ONUC troops to enter the province.

The UN became more involved in the civil war after a constitutional crisis emerged in late 1960 and Lumumba was murdered. On February 15, 1961, Hammarskjöld declared that ONUC could act to investigate the assassination, protect civilians, prevent clashes between armed units, reorganize the ANC, and remove Belgians from Katanga. On February 21, the SC authorized the use of force, if necessary, to prevent civil war in the Congo (Res. 4741). After abortive UN attempts to expel Belgian political and military advisers and mercenaries from Katanga in August–September 1961, most Belgian troops left the Congo. In response to an increasingly radical and violent secessionist movement, the SC extended ONUC's authorization to use force to detain and apprehend mercenaries and confiscate their arms (Res. 5002). In December 1961, the Katangans attacked the Elisabethville airport and ONUC retaliated, killing 50 civilians. Some member states criticized ONUC's use of force as beyond its mandate. After Hammarskjöld's death in a plane crash near Ndola, Rhodesia, Acting Secretary-General U THANT continued to mediate peace talks between the Congolese government and Katanga throughout 1962. In response to a UN budgetary crisis in 1963, the Congo government sought bilateral military aid from Belgium, Israel, Italy, and the UNITED STATES to counter the rebellion. On June 30, 1964, ONUC forces left Congo.

From 1960 to 1964, more than 93,000 troops served in ONUC, with 20,000 present at any one time; the total cost of military operations was $402 million. The Congo mission raised constitutional questions about PEACEKEEPING and military enforcement under CHAPTERS VI and VII of the UN Charter and helped to define the role of the Secretary-General regarding peace and security issues.

The second period of UN involvement in the Congo was precipitated by the 1994 Rwandan GENOCIDE and the consequent exodus of one million primarily Hutu ethnic refugees into eastern Congo (then called Zaire). By 1997, the refugee camps had become a staging ground for Hutu extremists who had committed the genocide to attack Rwanda and Uganda. Zaire's long-time dictator Mobutu Sese Seko was unable to control the camps and faced rebel movements in eastern Zaire. In a move orchestrated by Rwandan president Paul Kagame and supported by Angolan and Ugandan troops, Laurent Kabila's Alliance of Democratic Forces for the Liberation of Congo (ADFL) overthrew President Mobutu in May 1997. In the process, ADFL forces attacked the refugee camps and killed more than 200,000 people. In April 1997, the UN COMMISSION ON HUMAN RIGHTS (CHR), with the support of the SC, established a mission headed by Roberto Garreton (Chile) to investigate alleged HUMAN RIGHTS abuses in the Democratic Republic of Congo (DRC; formerly Zaire). For almost a year, UN officials were detained, threatened, and denied access to the sites where refugees were massacred. On April 17, 1998, Secretary-General Kofi ANNAN announced the permanent withdrawal of the UN investigators because of the lack of cooperation from the Kabila government.

In August 1998, fighting broke out between the Kabila government and the insurgent Congolese Rally for Democracy (RCD), which was supported by Uganda and Rwanda. Past allies of Kabila, Rwanda and Uganda were disappointed that the new president had not secured the borders of eastern Congo. ANGOLA, Zimbabwe, and NAMIBIA sent troops to aid Kabila, and Chad and Sudan sent military advisers. In May 1999, the RCD broke into two factions, one backed by Rwanda (RCD-Goma) and the other supported by Uganda (RCD-Kisangani). The Movement for the Liberation of the Congo (MLC), a rebel movement backed by Uganda, also became involved in the conflict.

In April 1999, the Secretary-General appointed Moustapha Niasse of Senegal as UN special envoy to assist in peace negotiations. In Resolution 1234 (1999), the SC supported the appointment of the special envoy, called for an immediate cease-fire, and condemned the presence of foreign state intervention in the DRC. On July 10, 1999, in Lusaka, Zambia, the DRC, Angola, Namibia, Rwanda, Uganda, and Zimbabwe signed a cease-fire agreement; the MLC and both RCD factions signed the agreement in early August. The Lusaka Agreement called for an inter-Congolese dialogue on the country's future, normalization of the DRC border, militia DISARMAMENT, and the establishment of a Joint Military Commission (JMC) of two representatives from each party under a neutral chairman. In Resolution 1258 (1999), the SC welcomed the Lusaka Agreement and authorized the deployment of 90 UN liaison personnel to the capitals of signatory states and the JMC provisional headquarters. After a recommendation by the Secretary-General, the SC extended the mandate of the UN liaison personnel until January 15, 2000 (Res. 1973) and then in Resolution 1979 decided that these personnel would constitute the UNITED NATIONS ORGANIZATION MISSION IN THE DRC (MONUC). In February 2000, the SC extended the mandate of MONUC until August 31, 2000, and authorized the expansion of the mission to 5,537 military personnel. When deployed, the mission would work with the JMC to monitor the cease-fire, facilitate humanitarian assistance, verify the disengagement of the contending parties' forces, and protect civilians (Security Council Res. 1291).

Despite the Lusaka Agreement, fighting continued between the parties. After another cease-fire was signed on April 8, 2000, JMC officials and the leaders of the signatory states urged the SC to deploy the MONUC peacekeepers. In an April 18 report, the Secretary-General expressed his concerns for human rights violations, the limited progress on the inter-Congolese dialogue, and the uncertain environment in which to deploy UN troops. On May 4–8, 2000, seven SC members visited the region and met with the leaders of the involved parties to discuss the peace process. In spring 2000, fighting also erupted between Ugandan and Rwandan forces near Kisangani, killing more than 200 Congolese and injuring 1,000. In response, the SC called for the immediate withdrawal of Rwandan and Ugandan forces from Congo (Res. 1304).

On June 12, 2000, the Secretary-General reported that only 200 MONUC observers had been sent to the DRC. Plans to deploy additional troops were postponed indefinitely in July after Kabila refused to allow MONUC into some parts of the country. In response to Kabila's lack of cooperation with the UN and the JMC, the South African Development Community threatened SANCTIONS against the DRC on August 15, 2000. Kabila continued to insist that peacekeepers could not be deployed until Rwanda and Uganda withdrew from the DRC. On August 18, Secretary-General Annan sent former Nigerian ruler Abdulsalami Abubakar to the DRC to discuss Kabila's failure to provide for MONUC's security and his continued propaganda campaign against MONUC. Though he initially signaled his willingness to allow peacekeepers in all areas of the DRC, Kabila appeared to change his mind on August 25.

Member states have been leery of committing troops to MONUC, especially in light of Kabila's animosity toward the UN and his refusal to participate in the inter-Congolese dialogue. In order to give the SC and the Secretary-General time to reconsider the mission, the Security Council passed Resolution 1316 (2000), which extended the mandate of MONUC until October 15, 2000. In January 2001, a presidential bodyguard assassinated Kabila. Parliament immediately chose his son, Joseph, as his successor, and hopes rose that a UN-brokered cease-fire and withdrawal of forces accord could be achieved. But tensions continued. As the new century began, more than 1.7 million Congolese had died of disease, malnutrition, and violence in the civil war. Africa's first war, as the conflict has been termed, challenged the UN's ability to promote peace, defend state SOVEREIGNTY, and protect human rights. As of March 31, 2002, the UN had deployed more than 3,600 military personnel as part of MONUC, and had budgeted in excess of $462 annually for the operation.

Further Reading: Boulden, Jane. *The United Nations Experience in Congo, Somalia, and Bosnia.* Westport, Conn.: Praeger, 2001. Dayal, R. *Mission for Hammarskjöld: The Congo Crisis.* London: Oxford University Press, 1976. Lefever, Ernest. *Crisis in the Congo.* Washington, D.C.: Brookings Institution, 1965. Shearer, David. "Africa's Great War." *Survival 41, no. 2* (1999): 89–106.

— A. S. Patterson

Congolese Civil War   *See* CONGO.

consultative status

Article 71 of the UN CHARTER allows the ECONOMIC AND SOCIAL COUNCIL (ECOSOC) to "make suitable arrangements for consultation with NON-GOVERNMENTAL ORGANIZATIONS (NGOs) which are concerned with matters within its COMPETENCE." Under this authority, as of October 2001, nearly 2,100 NGOs had been admitted to consultative status with ECOSOC and an additional 400 to the same status with ECOSOC's COMMISSION ON SUSTAINABLE DEVELOPMENT. The growth in the number and diversity of non-governmental organizations formally affiliated with the United Nations reflected the growth in international civil society and the UN's effort to develop ties with additional entities beyond the NATION-STATES that make up its membership.

Three categories of consultative status exist: General, Special, and Roster. These classifications were established in 1996 by the adoption of ECOSOC Resolution 31. The RESOLUTION considerably expanded the privileges that NGOs traditionally had maintained under the original system created shortly after the United Nations was founded. According to the resolution, organizations in the General Category must "be concerned with most of the activities of the ECOSOC and

its subsidiary bodies." They receive the provisional agenda of the council and of its commissions and may propose items to be added. They may designate representatives who sit as observers at council meetings and may submit written statements to both the council and subsidiary bodies. Reflecting a democratization of UN procedures, non-governmental organizations accredited in the General Category may address the Council on subjects of interest. "Special" NGOs, while unable to address ECOSOC, may speak at commission meetings and may circulate written materials. NGOs may be placed in this category if they have a competence or are concerned with "only a few of the fields of activity covered by the ECOSOC." NGOs with a very narrow or technical focus are placed on the "Roster," and have limited rights. But they are invited, along with General and Special NGOs, to send delegates to UN conferences and to appoint representatives to UN bodies.

While Article 71 links non-governmental organizations only to the Economic and Social Council, the United Nations has encouraged an expansion in NGO participation with all UN agencies. At WORLD CONFERENCES, they are urged to hold companion forums. They are also included in the implementation work of program agencies, such as the JOINT UNITED NATIONS PROGRAMME ON HIV/AIDS (UNAIDS). Those NGOs with an information distribution capability are also associated with the UN DEPARTMENT OF PUBLIC INFORMATION. Most SPECIALIZED AGENCIES have followed the pattern established by ECOSOC and have created consultative status for relevant private groups. Among the agencies to have done so are the INTERNATIONAL LABOUR ORGANIZATION, the UNITED NATIONS CONFERENCE ON TRADE AND DEVELOPMENT, the WORLD INTELLECTUAL PROPERTY ORGANIZATION, the INTERNATIONAL TELECOMMUNICATION UNION, the WORLD HEALTH ORGANIZATION, the FOOD AND AGRICULTURE ORGANIZATION, and the INTERNATIONAL MARITIME ORGANIZATION. In 1999 UN SECRETARY-GENERAL Kofi ANNAN launched an initiative to bring private enterprises into a special relationship with the United Nations through the GLOBAL COMPACT. Corporations could commit to nine principles established in important UN CONVENTIONS, and in so doing be given recognition and involvement in the work of the world body. Annan established a special bureau in his office for this liaison relationship.

See also BEIJING +5, COMMITTEE ON NON-GOVERNMENTAL ORGANIZATIONS, DEPARTMENT OF ECONOMIC AND SOCIAL AFFAIRS, INDIGENOUS PEOPLES, UNITED NATIONS ASSOCIATION.

Further Reading: Weiss, Thomas, and Leon Gordenker, eds. *NGOs, the UN, and Global Governance.* Boulder, Colo.: Lynne Rienner, 1996. Willetts, Peter, ed. *The Conscience of the World: The Influence of Non-governmental Organizations in the UN System.* Washington, D.C.: Brookings Institution, 1996. NGOs and ECOSOC website: <www.un.org/partners/civil_society/ngo/n-ecosoc.htm#top>.

Contact Group for Namibia   *See* NAMIBIA.

convention

In the language of international affairs, *convention* is a term for an international agreement, bilateral or multilateral. Conventions may be open or closed for other states that have not participated in their preparation. There are several examples in the UNITED NATIONS SYSTEM, such as the CONVENTION ON THE ELIMINATION OF ALL FORMS OF DISCRIMINATION AGAINST WOMEN.

Convention Against Torture and Other Cruel, Inhuman or Degrading Treatment or Punishment

The UN Convention against Torture, which was adopted and opened for signature, ratification, or ACCESSION by the GENERAL ASSEMBLY on December 10, 1984, codified the process of combating the practice of torture. The CONVENTION entered into force on June 26, 1987, after the 20th instrument of ratification was deposited with the SECRETARIAT in accordance with Article 27(1) of the convention. As of November 2001, 65 states had ratified the convention. Fifteen additional states and nine non-state parties had signed, but not yet ratified it. The convention defined torture as "the deliberate infliction of severe physical or mental pain or suffering by public officials in order to intimidate, punish or obtain a confession or information from the victim." It required member states to take effective legal and other measures to prevent the practice.

To monitor compliance and implementation of the convention, the Committee on Torture was established. The committee met for the first time in April 1988 in Geneva and subsequently carried out intensive activities. The committee consists of 10 experts of high moral standing and recognized COMPETENCE in the field of HUMAN RIGHTS, who are elected by secret ballot by the state parties. The convention sets out a number of obligations designed to strengthen the sphere of protection of human rights and fundamental freedoms, while conferring upon the Committee on Torture broad powers of examination and investigation. The committee may invite SPECIALIZED AGENCIES, United Nations bodies concerned, REGIONAL ORGANIZATIONS, and NON-GOVERNMENTAL ORGANIZATIONS in CONSULTATIVE STATUS with the ECONOMIC AND SOCIAL COUNCIL to submit information, documentation, and written statements, as appropriate, relevant to the committee's activities. It submits an annual report on its activities to the state parties and to the UN General Assembly.

The work of the committee has been debilitated by the refusal of many parties to ratify the convention in full. Only 29 states had ratified the convention by autumn 2001 without declarations under Articles 22 or 28. A DECLARATION under Article 22 allows private individuals to submit complaints to the committee, whereas a declaration under Article 28 indicates that the state does not recognize the competence of the committee to investigate allegations of widespread torture within its borders. By late 2001, 28 states had ratified the convention and made declarations under Article 22, and eight states had ratified with declarations under Article 28. Fifteen states, including the UNITED STATES, signed but did not ratify the convention.

See also INTERNATIONAL DAY IN SUPPORT OF VICTIMS OF TORTURE, WAR CRIMES TRIBUNALS.

Further Reading: Burgers, Herman, and Hans Danelius. *United Nations Convention against Torture: A Handbook on the Convention against Torture and Other Cruel, Inhuman, or Degrading Treatment or Punishment.* The Hague: Kluwer Academic Publishers, 1988.

Convention on Biological Diversity (CBD)

See UNITED NATIONS CONFERENCE ON ENVIRONMENT AND DEVELOPMENT (UNCED).

Convention on International Trade in Endangered Species of Wild Fauna and Flora (CITES)

On March 3, 1973, 80 nations meeting in Washington, D.C., agreed on the text of the Convention on International Trade in Endangered Species of Wild Fauna and Flora. The CONVENTION, drafted 10 years earlier at a meeting of the World Conservation Union, entered into force on July 1, 1975. As of 2001 CITES counted more than 150 parties and accorded protection to more than 30,000 species. The convention is an international agreement intended to assure the survival of specimens of wild animals and plants that constitute a growing part of international trade. That trade, estimated to be in the billions of dollars annually, ranges widely from live plants and animals to a variety of wildlife by-products such as food, leather goods, musical instruments, curios, medicine, and more. CITES underscores a concern with resisting habitat loss and protecting species from extinction. Since it came into force in 1975 no species listed under its provisions has become extinct as the result of trade practices.

CITES is administered by its own SECRETARIAT, which acts in an advisory role, is the repository for reports dealing with issues covered by the convention, distributes information relevant to the parties to the convention, and arranges meetings of the Conference of the Parties and the permanent committees of the conference. The Conference of the Parties, made up of all member states to the convention, meets every two or three years for about two weeks to review the implementation of the convention. These meetings are also attended by observers and by representatives of relevant UN agencies, who can participate in the meetings at the discretion of the member parties. The conference has established four permanent committees: a Standing Committee, an Animals Committee, a Plant Committee, and a Nomenclature Committee. The Standing Committee comprises VOTING representatives from member countries apportioned according to geographic region (Africa, Asia, Europe, North America, Central and South America and the Caribbean, and Oceania), with the number of committee members determined according to the number of participating parties in each region. The Standing Committee elects its chairperson and vice chair, meets once a year, provides policy guidance to the secretariat, oversees the secretariat's BUDGET, drafts RESOLUTIONS, and coordinates the efforts of the other committees and working groups. The Animals and Plants committees, composed of experts from the six geographic regions who are elected at meetings of the conference, provide knowledge and technical assistance regarding species. The Nomenclature Committee, made up of volunteers appointed by the conference, works to standardize the classification and standard naming of species and regularly reviews the convention's appendices to maintain correct use of zoological and botanical designations.

See also UNITED NATIONS ENVIRONMENT PROGRAMME.

Further Reading: CITES website: <www.cites.org>.

Convention on the Conservation of Migratory Species of Wild Animals (CMS)

Known as the Bonn Convention, or by its shortened title of Convention on Migratory Species, the Convention on the Conservation of Migratory Species of Wild Animals entered into force on November 1, 1983. As of 2001 membership was 76 NATION-STATES from Africa, Central and South America, Asia, Europe, and Oceania. Three of the largest nations in the world—the RUSSIAN FEDERATION, CHINA, and the UNITED STATES—were, as of 2001, "non-parties in participation." That is, they had not ratified the CONVENTION but were abiding by its provisions. Members of CMS aspire to conserve migratory species and their sensitive habitats. CMS is guided by a list of endangered migratory species listed in the convention's Appendix I (85 species as of 2001). It seeks to achieve international agreements to promote conservation and reasonable management practices for the protection of migratory species listed in Appendix II and it encourages cooperation in research and dissemination of information on endangered species and protections for migratory wildlife.

A number of agreements have been composed under the auspices of CMS. They intend to conserve specific species, including bats in Europe, cetaceans in the Mediterranean and Black Seas, small cetaceans in the Baltic and North Seas, seals in the Wadden Sea, migratory waterbirds in Africa and

Eurasia, the Siberian crane, the slender-billed curlew, and marine turtles.

Administrative support for the convention comes from a SECRETARIAT authorized by the UNITED NATIONS ENVIRONMENT PROGRAMME (UNEP). The Conference of the Parties, which holds periodic meetings, is the decision-making body for CMS. Between regular meetings of the conference a Standing Committee administers CMS's affairs. Member states appoint experts to a Scientific Council that provides technical and scientific advice to CMS bodies.

Further Reading: CMS website: <www.wcmc.org.uk/cms>.

Convention on the Elimination of All Forms of Discrimination Against Women (CEDAW)

During the UNITED NATIONS DECADE FOR WOMEN (1976 to 1985), the United Nations recognized WOMEN as important players in society. To endorse that view, the members of the HUMAN RIGHTS COMMISSION promoted a broad CONVENTION on the rights of women. In 1979 the GENERAL ASSEMBLY passed the United Nations Convention on the Elimination of All Forms of Discrimination Against Women. The convention extended the earlier 1952 CONVENTION ON THE POLITICAL RIGHTS OF WOMEN by prohibiting any distinction, exclusion, or restriction made or the basis of sex that impeded HUMAN RIGHTS and fundamental freedoms for women.

The process of ratification and implementation is monitored by the Committee on the Elimination of Discrimination Against Women (also known as CEDAW), which holds regular meetings to review reports from member states. U.S. president Bill Clinton's administration supported CEDAW, but the U.S. Senate failed to ratify the convention. Supporters claimed that the convention would help protect women from many abuses, such as domestic violence, political oppression, and being sold into sexual slavery. Critics of the convention argued that it forced societies to adapt to UN notions of gender roles. Women's groups in the UNITED STATES such as NOW (National Organization of Women) favored the convention and pressed Congress to ratify it, but by the time Clinton left office, no action had been taken. Meantime, as of May 2001, 168 countries had ratified or acceded to the convention.

In the fall of 1999, an additional Optional PROTOCOL was added to the convention. The Optional Protocol acknowledged the right to submit petitions to the United Nations and provided for individual complaint procedures. States that recognized the Optional Protocol accepted the COMPETENCE of the CEDAW Committee to consider petitions from individual women or groups of women who had exhausted all other national channels. The committee could conduct inquiries into grave or systematic violations of the convention. The Protocol, which was opened for signature and ratification, had an "opt-out clause," allowing states upon ratification or ACCESSION to declare that they did not accept the INQUIRY procedure. As of fall 2000, the Optional Protocol had been signed by 62 states. The Optional Protocol officially entered into force on December 22, 2000.

See also COMMISSION ON THE STATUS OF WOMEN, MILLENNIUM SUMMIT.

Further Reading: Cooper, Mary H. "Women and Human Rights." *Congressional Quarterly* 9, no. 16 (April 30, 1999): 353. UN WomenWatch website: <www.un.org/womenwatch/daw/cedaw/op2609.html>.

— *K. J. Vogel*

Convention on the Elimination of All Forms of Racial Discrimination   *See* HUMAN RIGHTS, WORLD CONFERENCES TO COMBAT RACISM AND RACIAL DISCRIMINATION.

Convention on the Political Rights of Women

In July of 1954, the Convention on the Political Rights of Women entered into force. Considered at the time as a landmark effort in the push for political equality, the CONVENTION called for member states to allow WOMEN to vote and to hold public office on equal terms with men and without any discrimination. The convention, however, did not deal with broader concerns of discrimination, such as denial of equal pay for equal work or issues of violence against women. Negotiated in 1952, the convention did not provide any guidelines for enforcement and did not recognize the role of women in DEVELOPMENT, population policy, or food issues.

During the UNITED NATIONS DECADE FOR WOMEN (1976 to 1985), awareness of the key role of women in society grew, and UN participants, particularly those serving on the HUMAN RIGHTS COMMISSION, urged establishing a broader convention to deal with gender discrimination. In 1979, the GENERAL ASSEMBLY passed the UN CONVENTION ON THE ELIMINATION OF ALL FORMS OF DISCRIMINATION AGAINST WOMEN (CEDAW). This convention, generally characterized as an international bill of rights for women, prohibited any distinction, exclusion, or restriction made on the basis of sex that impeded HUMAN RIGHTS and fundamental freedoms for women.

See also COMMISSION ON THE STATUS OF WOMEN.

Further Reading: Cooper, Mary H. "Women and Human Rights." *Congressional Quarterly* 9, no. 16 (April 30, 1999): 353. UN Women/Watch website: <www.un.org/womenwatch>. UN High Commissioner for Human Rights website: <www.unhchr.ch/html/menu3/b/22.htm>.

— *K. J. Vogel*

Convention on the Prevention and Punishment of the Crime of Genocide (UNCG)

The UN GENERAL ASSEMBLY unanimously adopted the Convention on the Prevention and Punishment of the Crime of Genocide on December 9, 1948, opening it for signature, ratification, or ACCESSION. The CONVENTION entered into force on January 12, 1951, in accordance with Article 13. As of November 2001, there were 41 signatories and 132 parties to the convention.

The term "genocide" derives from the combination of the Greek word for group or tribe—"genos"—and the Latin for killing—"cide." It was first used in 1944, when the jurist Raphael Lemkin published *Axis Rule in Occupied Europe,* in which he detailed the extermination policies pursued by the Third Reich and its allies. He called for the international prohibition of the "practice of extermination of nations and ethnic groups." Lemkin was instrumental in lobbying UN officials and representatives to secure the passage of a RESOLUTION by the General Assembly affirming that "genocide is a crime under INTERNATIONAL LAW which the civilized world condemns, and for the commission of which principals and accomplices are punishable." The matter was referred for consideration to the ECONOMIC AND SOCIAL COUNCIL, its deliberations culminating with the signing of the 1948 United Nations Convention on Genocide.

The convention's definition of genocide as acts committed with intent to destroy—in whole or in part—a national, ethnic, racial, or religious group was intended in large part to prevent the systematic destruction of specific peoples, particularly as was the case with Jews and other groups in the Holocaust. As such, many experts, legal and academic, considered the criteria for genocide deficient in that the criteria were too narrow. For instance, it excluded the physical destruction of certain subgroups that regularly have been the victims of extensive killing programs. But vagueness of definition was to be expected in any legal instrument that was the outcome of negotiations among parties holding conflicting views as to the proper scope of the definition.

Because the Holocaust was so central to the conception of the UNCG, its application to other situations after 1948 was problematic. Situations such as the massacre of Armenians by the Turks during World War I, the destruction of the intelligentsia and others by the Khmer Rouge in CAMBODIA from 1975 to 1978, and the Ukrainian famine of the 1930s share some elements with the Nazi genocidal program. However, there were also important differences that raised questions about the applicability of the criteria specified by Article II of the UNCG. The slaughter of 800,000 Tutsis during the 1994 RWANDA CRISIS renewed interest in a broad definition of genocide. In the FORMER YUGOSLAVIA, as well, the international community sought the arrest and punishment of Serbian, Croatian, and Bosnian leaders for genocidal crimes. Most important among those detained was Slobodan Milosevic, former president of Yugoslavia, who was arrested and turned over to the INTERNATIONAL CRIMINAL TRIBUNAL FOR YUGOSLAVIA in the summer of 2001.

See also HUMAN RIGHTS, INTERNATIONAL COVENANT ON CIVIL AND POLITICAL RIGHTS, INTERNATIONAL CRIMINAL COURT.

Further Reading: Kuper, Leo. *Genocide: Its Political Use in the Twentieth Century*. Harmondsworth: Penguin Books, 1981. Minow, Martha. *Between Vengeance and Forgiveness: Facing History after Genocide and Mass Violence*. Boston: Beacon Press, 1998. Office of the High Commissioner for Human Rights. *Basic Human Rights Instruments*. Geneva: United Nations, 1998. United Nations *Manual on Human Rights Reporting under Six Major International Human Rights Instruments*. Geneva: United Nations, 1997. United Nations Department of Public Information. *Report of the Independent Inquiry into the Actions of the United Nations during the 1994 Genocide in Rwanda*. New York: United Nations Department of Public Information, 1999.

— *I. Kebreau*

Convention on the Prohibition of the Development, Production, and Stockpiling of Bacteriological (Biological) Weapons *See* BIOLOGICAL WEAPONS.

Convention on the Prohibition of the Development, Production, Stockpiling and Use of Chemical Weapons (CWC) *See* CHEMICAL WEAPONS.

Convention on the Prohibition of the Use, Stockpiling, Production and Transfer of Anti-Personnel Mines and Their Destruction

The Convention on the Prohibition of the Use, Stockpiling, Production and Transfer of Anti-Personnel Mines and Their Destruction is also known as the Ottawa Convention. The CONVENTION was opened for signature in Ottawa, Canada, on December 3, 1997. Under Article 15, the TREATY remained open for signature until its entry into force, which was March 1, 1999. After that date states could no longer sign it; rather, they could join the convention without signature through a one-step procedure known as ACCESSION. As of March 1, 2001, 139 states had signed or acceded to the convention, and 111 of those had ratified the agreement. Among the states notably absent

from the list of signatories were the UNITED STATES, Israel, and Russia.

The 1997 convention prohibited in all circumstances any use of anti-personnel LAND MINES. It also required the destruction of stockpiles within four years of the treaty's entry into force, and that mines already in the ground be destroyed within 10 years.

In October 1996, Canada's foreign minister Lloyd Axworthy initiated the Ottawa Process. This process consisted of conferences in Vienna, Brussels, and Oslo involving like-minded international actors determined to ban land mines. The Ottawa Treaty was drafted in Oslo and the process returned to Canada in December 1997 for the signing ceremony.

A coalition of state and non-state actors championed the Ottawa Process/Treaty, with Canada and Belgium leading the effort to establish a land mine ban. NON-GOVERNMENTAL ORGANIZATIONS (NGOs) such as the International Committee of the Red Cross (ICRC), Medecins sans Frontières (MSF), and the International Campaign to Ban Landmines (ICBL) also advocated on behalf of the process/treaty. This last group was awarded the Nobel Peace Prize for its work.

The UN's role in the Ottawa Treaty was contradictory, yet notable. The UN had been involved in the movement to ban land mines since the 1970s. In 1980, it negotiated the Convention on Certain Conventional Weapons (CCW). The General Assembly, however, had established the UN's CONFERENCE ON DISARMAMENT (CD) in 1978 as the only global arms control negotiating forum. Frustration with the slow peace of the CD led several states to pursue negotiations on the Ottawa Treaty outside of the UN STRUCTURE. Paradoxically, the United Nations then circumvented its own negotiating forum by joining the Ottawa Treaty process. The UN acted as a policy partner with the NGOs. One example of such cooperation was the Survey Action Center. This represented the combined efforts of the UN Mine Action Service and NGOs such as Landmine Survivors Network and Norwegian Peoples' Aid. The Survey Action Center monitored standards and facilitated the international coordination of resources and expert personnel for the completion of the Global Landmine Survey in the most mine-affected countries.

See also UNITED NATIONS OFFICE OF PROJECT SERVICES.

Further Reading: Short, N. "The Role of NGOs in the Ottawa Process to Ban Landmines." *International Negotiation* 4, no. 3 (1999): 481–500. Sundararaman, S. "The Landmines Question: An Overview of the Ottawa Process." *Strategic Analysis* 22, no. 1 (April 1998): 17–33. Thakur, R, and W. Maley. "The Ottawa Convention on Landmines: A Landmark Humanitarian Treaty in Arms Control?" *Global Governance: A Review of Multilateralism and International*

Organizations. 5, no. 3 (July–September 1999): 273–302. International Campaign to Ban Landmines website: <www.icbl.org>.

— *S. F. McMahon*

Convention Relating to the Status of Refugees (Refugee Convention)

The basis for the right of return for refugees under INTERNATIONAL LAW is found in the Convention Relating to the Status of Refugees (1951) and its PROTOCOL of 1967. The CONVENTION, adopted by the GENERAL ASSEMBLY on December 14, 1950, was subsequently adopted by the UN Conference of Plenipotentiaries on the Status of Refugees and Stateless Persons at a meeting in Geneva in July 1951. The convention entered into force on April 22, 1954, and by 2001 it had 137 parties.

According to international refugee law and international HUMAN RIGHTS law, the right of return is fundamental, although instruments of law usually emphasize voluntary repatriation. The issue of refugee repatriation grew out of the large displacement of persons during World War II. The concern continued to face the international community as the 20th century proceeded. The Refugee convention uses the concept of "country" rather than "nation" or "state" as the locale for return, since the former is more inclusive and considers ties and associations that an individual may have with a territory. Thus the convention recognizes the right of a stateless person to return to a country of "former habitual residence," suggesting that nationality is not necessarily an unquestionable standard to verify the right of repatriation. Refugee law, according to the convention as well as other international instruments, does not clearly obligate a state to bestow nationality, so, a returnee could be considered a resident and not a citizen. International protection ceases once a refugee has "reavailed himself of the protection of the country of his nationality," has "voluntarily re-acquired it," or when the circumstances that caused the refugee status in the first place no longer exist. Also a key provision of refugee law is the principle of "non-refoulment," which prohibits the forceful expulsion or forceful return of persons to a country where they would have reason to fear persecution.

See also UN HIGH COMMISSIONER FOR REFUGEES, UN RELIEF AND WORKS AGENCY FOR PALESTINE REFUGEES IN THE NEAR EAST, WORLD REFUGEE DAY.

Further Reading: Nicholson, Frances, and Patrick Twomey, eds. *Refugee Rights and Realities: Evolving International Concepts and Regimes.* Cambridge: Cambridge University Press, 1999. United Nations High Commissioner for Refugees. *Collection of International Instruments and Other Legal Texts Concerning Refugees and Displaced Persons.* Geneva: United Nations High Commissioner for Refugees, 1995. ———.

State of the World's Refugees. New York: United Nations, issued every two years.

Convention to Combat Desertification (CCD and UNCCD)

In June 1992, the UNITED NATIONS CONFERENCE ON ENVIRONMENT AND DEVELOPMENT (UNCED or the Earth Summit) recommended the establishment of an Intergovernmental Negotiating Committee on Desertification (INCD), which drafted the Convention to Combat Desertification in Those Countries Experiencing Serious Drought and/or Desertification, Particularly in Africa. The committee approved the CONVENTION on June 17, 1994. It was opened for signature in Paris on October 14–15, 1994, and entered into force on December 26, 1996, 90 days after the 50th country had ratified it. In the meantime, many of the convention's provisions were carried out voluntarily on the basis of a Committee RESOLUTION calling for urgent action in Africa.

The convention offered new hope in the struggle against DESERTIFICATION. It was to be implemented through action programs addressing the underlying causes of desertification and drought and identifying measures to prevent and reverse these causes on the national level. Regional and subregional programs were also supposed to complement national programs, particularly where transboundary resources such as lakes and rivers were involved. Action programs were detailed in the four regional implementation annexes to the convention: Africa, Asia, LATIN AMERICA and the Caribbean, and the Northern Mediterranean.

The convention established a number of institutions and procedures for guiding international action. The Conference of the Parties (COP) oversees the implementation of the convention. The COP held its first session in October 1997 in Rome and meets once a year. While only national governments that ratify the convention are members of the COP, other bodies and organizations also participate. The convention made special provision for national and international agencies and qualified NGOs (NON-GOVERNMENTAL ORGANIZATIONS) to attend the COP's meetings and to contribute to its work. One of the COP's main functions is to review reports submitted by the member states detailing how they are carrying out their commitments. The COP makes recommendations on the basis of these reports. It also has the power to make AMENDMENTS to the convention or to launch negotiations for new annexes, such as additional regional implementation annexes. In this way, the COP guides the convention as global circumstances and national needs change. To assist the COP, the convention provided for several other supporting bodies and allowed the COP to establish additional ones if necessary.

The COP is supported by a SECRETARIAT. Like other convention secretariats, the CCD secretariat arranges COP meetings, prepares documents, provides coordination with other relevant bodies, compiles and transmits information, and facilitates consultations. Affected developing countries are also able to rely on the secretariat for information or advice on, for example, organizing their national consultation process.

The Committee on Science and Technology advises the COP on scientific and technological matters. It identifies priorities for research and recommends ways of strengthening cooperation among researchers. It also advises on such issues as joint research programs for new technologies. The COP may set up ad hoc panels to assist with specialized issues. The panels draw their members from a roster of government-nominated experts.

A Global Mechanism helps the COP promote funding for convention-related activities and programs. This mechanism does not raise or administer funds. Instead, it encourages and assists donors, recipients, development banks, non-governmental organizations, and others to mobilize funds and to channel them to where they are most needed. It seeks to promote greater coordination among existing sources of funding and greater efficiency and effectiveness in the use of funds.

The convention radically departed from the traditional approaches to desertification in its strong emphasis on a "bottom-up" approach with strong local participation in decision making. Traditionally, local communities have been relatively passive participants in development projects. The convention put them on an equal footing with other actors in the development process. Communities and their leaders, as well as non-governmental organizations, experts, and government officials, work closely together to formulate action programs.

NGOs have not only played a prominent role in the convention process, but they continue to raise public awareness of the convention and to lobby parliamentarians for its speedy ratification. For their part, international and REGIONAL ORGANIZATIONS provide crucial information, expertise, contacts, and research and managerial capabilities in the fight against desertification.

See also ENVIRONMENT, WORLD METEOROLOGICAL ORGANIZATION.

Further Reading: Scherl, Lea M. *Relationships and Partnerships among Governments, NGOs, CBOs and Indigenous Groups in the Context of the Convention to Combat Desertification and Drought.* Nairobi, Kenya: Environment Liaison Centre International, 1996. Convention to Combat Desertification website: <www.unccd.int/convention/menu.php>.

— I. Kebreau

covenant

A covenant is a voluntary agreement entered into by two or more parties to do or refrain from some action or actions. In law, a covenant is a contract or a promise—rather like a sacred promise—of legal weight. In the Bible, and in theology more generally, a covenant is a contract or engagement between God and human beings. For example, the "covenant" between God and Israel is fundamental to Jewish religious tradition, and the original 17th-century Puritan settlers in America "covenanted" together to create their civil and religious societies. Thus covenant takes on a more metaphysical and spiritual meaning than CHARTER or TREATY, which are more clearly secular documents. The LEAGUE OF NATIONS originated in a covenant, the United Nations in a charter. The League Covenant was a traditional agreement among governments, called in the Covenant "The High Contracting Parties." The preamble of the UN Charter begins, "We the peoples of the United Nations."

See also PACT, *and for examples of covenants* BRICKER AMENDMENT, INTERNATIONAL COVENANT ON CIVIL AND POLITICAL RIGHTS, INTERNATIONAL COVENANT ON ECONOMIC, SOCIAL, AND CULTURAL RIGHTS.

Credentials Committee of the General Assembly

The Credentials Committee is one of two PROCEDURAL COMMITTEES of the UN GENERAL ASSEMBLY (GA). Its nine members are appointed at the beginning of the Assembly's annual session on the recommendation of the GA president. The committee has the responsibility of recommending to the Assembly the seating of delegations and representatives. A routine task normally, the acceptance or rejection of a national delegation's credentials has been used to exclude or seat a controversial government. While the UN CHARTER allows for the SUSPENSION OR EXPULSION of a member, the UN MEMBERSHIP has been unwilling to take either drastic action. Instead, on occasion it has informally "suspended" the participation of states that it believes have violated UN principles by challenging the credentials of the representatives sent to New York. This was done to the South African delegation in 1974 and the Israeli delegation in 1982, effectively excluding them from participation in GA debate and VOTING. At the close of the century, the Credentials Committee also effectively had denied recognition to the Taliban government of AFGHANISTAN by continuing to seat the previous interim Afghan government's representatives.

See also COMMITTEE SYSTEM OF THE GENERAL ASSEMBLY.

Cuba

Cuba joined the United Nations as one of the body's original members on October 24, 1945. Its representatives were active in the first decade of the UN's development and operations. It supported failed efforts to limit the authority of the PERMANENT MEMBERS OF THE SECURITY COUNCIL and supported attempts to gain guaranteed regional representation within the SECURITY COUNCIL for the Latin American states.

Cuba gained notoriety for the loyalty that it offered to the UNITED STATES during the early COLD WAR. Its positions were especially anticommunist. For example, during cease-fire negotiations at the end of the KOREAN WAR, Cuba was one of only two delegations to vote against the participation of Mao Zedong's People's Republic of CHINA. Its cold war allegiance to the United States within the United Nations was an extension of the Batista dictatorship's foreign policy. When the Cuban Revolution forced Fulgencio Batista from power in 1959, Cuba transformed itself into an antagonist of the United States.

The transformation began with Fidel Castro's speech before a SPECIAL SESSION OF THE GENERAL ASSEMBLY in September 1960. Attacking American imperialism and asserting Cuban independence, the leader's speech accelerated the deterioration of Cuban-American relations. As the years passed, the United Nations became a forum for the new rivalry.

The abortive April 1961 Bay of Pigs invasion of the island became the first serious crisis between the American government and Cuba after its revolutionary shift. The United States, having sponsored the invasion, faced condemnation within the GENERAL ASSEMBLY. Washington's representatives, who argued that the ORGANIZATION OF AMERICAN STATES (OAS), as a recognized regional authority, held JURISDICTION over the matter, headed off all challenges with the threat of a VETO in the Security Council. A RESOLUTION did pass the Assembly, but its language merely urged all states to seek peaceful settlement of their differences.

In 1962, the United States imposed an economic embargo that blocked all U.S. trade with Cuba, and pressured its allies in LATIN AMERICA and Europe to follow suit. The Cuban government initially sought UN condemnation of the American action, but was unsuccessful. Thirty years later, the General Assembly did approve a resolution that called for the end of the embargo that, nonetheless, still remained in force at the turn of the century.

Cuban-American relations at the United Nations worsened again during the missile crisis in October 1962. The crisis arose when U.S. intelligence discovered Soviet missile sites on the island. Cuba first inserted itself into the center of this superpower confrontation when Fidel Castro wrote to SECRETARY-GENERAL U THANT asserting Cuba's ability, willingness, and right to defend its territory from American AGGRESSION, referencing the downing of a U-2 spy plane over the island on October 27th. As tension mounted, however, Soviet and American representatives worked directly to defuse the crisis without any Cuban involvement.

In the years that followed, Cuba used the United Nations as a venue for two projects. First, through its representatives' votes, it demonstrated its support for the Soviet Union, which became the revolutionary regime's financial and mili-

tary prop for two decades. Second, upon gaining membership in the GROUP OF 77 in 1971, it worked to forge alliances with its members, and more generally with the nations of the NON-ALIGNED MOVEMENT, particularly in the UN CONFERENCE ON TRADE AND DEVELOPMENT (UNCTAD).

Pursuing these two strands in its UN policy often proved counterproductive. Cuban support within the United Nations for the Soviet Union's invasions of Czechoslovakia in 1968 and of AFGHANISTAN in 1979 went against the sentiments of the majority of nonaligned states and reinforced efforts made by the United States and its allies to depict Cuba as a mere Soviet satellite. Also within the United Nations the Cuban delegation offered support for most NATIONAL LIBERATION movements, including those involving Vietnam, the African National Congress in South Africa, and the independence movement in Puerto Rico. Cuba's military assistance for resistance and liberation movements in Africa and the Americas strained its relations with other nations within the United Nations.

During the last two decades of the 20th century Cuba found its policies challenged in the United Nations by significant numbers of former supporters. In 1980, facing threats from the Bahamas and other English-speaking Caribbean nations, it apologized for its sinking of a Bahamian coast guard vessel in order to head off a Security Council resolution that would have sanctioned its actions. The UN COMMISSION ON HUMAN RIGHTS (CHR), under pressure from the United States, annually challenged Cuba for its treatment of political dissidents. In 1988, the CHR accepted an invitation from the Cuban government to investigate HUMAN RIGHTS conditions there. Cuban military involvement in ANGOLA complicated UN efforts to end that country's civil war. Security Council resolutions had sanctioned South Africa for its intervention in Angola. In 1984, the Cuban government agreed to withdraw its troops and civilian advisers once South Africa accepted the UN mandate. A UN settlement moved Angola toward peace after 1988. UN monitors reported the final withdrawal of all Cuban forces in 1991.

The collapse of the Soviet Union and the curtailment of its economic and military assistance led Cuba to adopt a more pragmatic approach within the United Nations. It obtained, despite U.S. opposition, financial and programmatic support from the UN DEVELOPMENT PROGRAMME (UNDP), the UN EDUCATIONAL, SCIENTIFIC AND CULTURAL ORGANIZATION (UNESCO), and the UN CHILDREN'S FUND (UNICEF). It also scaled back its public and private support for radical and revolutionary groups in the Americas and in Africa. However, the United Nations remained a forum for the continuing conflict between the United States and Cuba. The General Assembly endorsed the Cuban position in 1992 and again in 1997 with resolutions that condemned the U.S. trade embargo. In reaction, Washington continued to bring pressure against the Castro regime in the world body. Castro returned to the United Nations in 1995 to offer an address during the body's 50th anniversary. In 1996, U.S. efforts led to a UN investigation of the downing of a civilian aircraft flown from Miami over international waters.

See also APPEAL TO THE SECURITY COUNCIL, CUBAN MISSILE CRISIS, MILLENNIUM SUMMIT, NAMIBIA, NUCLEAR NONPROLIFERATION TREATY, NUCLEAR-WEAPONS-FREE ZONES, ORGANIZATION OF AMERICAN STATES, TREATY OF TLATLELOCO, UNITED NATIONS ANGOLA VERIFICATION MISSION, UN SECURITY COUNCIL RESOLUTION 678.

Further Reading: Dominguez, Jorge I. *To Make a World Safe for Revolution: Cuba's Foreign Policy.* Cambridge, Mass.: Harvard University Press, 1989. Erisman, H. Michael. *Cuba's Foreign Relations in a Post-Soviet World.* Gainesville: University of Florida Press, 2000. Sadri, Houman A. *Revolutionary States, Leaders, and Foreign Relations: A Comparative Study of China, Cuba, and Iran.* Westport, Conn.: Praeger Publishers, 1977.

— *D. K. Lewis*

Cuban missile crisis

On October 15, 1962, American reconnaissance planes flying over CUBA discovered Soviet missile sites under construction. Immediately the U.S. administration of President John F. Kennedy decided to force the removal of these sites. What ensued were 13 days in which the world stood on the brink of nuclear war. President Kennedy estimated that the chances for war were "somewhere between one in three and fifty-fifty." During the crisis neither side made much use of the United Nations, except to utilize the SECURITY COUNCIL for propaganda statements meant to sway world public opinion. Only U.S. PERMANENT REPRESENTATIVE to the UN Adlai E. Stevenson made the case that diplomacy through the world body should be employed before resorting to the threat of force.

Soviet premier Nikita Khrushchev had decided to place nuclear missiles in Cuba for strategic reasons. The Soviet Union lagged behind the UNITED STATES in nuclear weapons warheads and sought to minimize this disparity. It sought to do so by placing missiles in Cuba with the range to hit almost anywhere in the United States. Prior to October 1962 its missiles had limited range and much of the United States was beyond their reach. Khrushchev also was annoyed that the United States had placed Jupiter missiles on the soil of geographically close Soviet rival Turkey. The Soviet leader reportedly considered deployment of Soviet missiles in Cuba to be, for Americans, a "taste of their own medicine." The Cubans, led by Fidel Castro, sought to use the missiles as a way to defend against another American invasion. In 1961 the United States had armed anti-Castro Cubans in an abortive effort to overthrow the regime. An American-sponsored invasion in April at the Bay of Pigs had been repelled by Cuban forces. By fall 1962, Castro, certain that the United

States was planning another incursion, wanted to avoid a repetition of 1961 and considered the missiles to be the ultimate defense for his country.

Following the discovery of the missiles, Kennedy convened his National Security Council's Executive Committee (EXCOMM) to consider responses. EXCOMM debated the merits of an air strike as well as a blockade around the island. While most members of EXCOMM initially favored an air strike, the president's brother (and U.S. attorney-general) Robert Kennedy, declaring that "I will not have my brother be another Tojo," advocated instead a naval blockade of the island. Concerned that a blockade was an act of war, President Kennedy chose to call the action a "quarantine" and announced that Soviet ships headed to Cuba would be subject to American inspection. In the end, Khrushchev ordered Soviet ships not to run the blockade, occasioning U.S. secretary of state Dean Rusk to declare that "we stood eyeball to eyeball and the other guy blinked."

During the crisis Khrushchev floated the idea of using UN SECRETARY-GENERAL U THANT as an intermediary, but the Kennedy administration demurred. The most important diplomatic exchanges were kept directly between Moscow and Washington. At UN HEADQUARTERS the United States requested a session of the Security Council. During that televised meeting, Stevenson used surveillance photographs to make the U.S. case. In the most dramatic moment of the debate Stevenson asked Soviet ambassador Valery Zorin repeatedly whether there were offensive missiles in Cuba. Zorin gave no reply. At one point in a tense confrontation, Stevenson turned to Zorin and said that he "was prepared to wait until hell freezes over for your reply." Beyond the drama, negotiations in New York were limited to out-of-view discussions.

As the crisis unfolded, Khrushchev offered two different proposals. On October 25 he offered to remove the missiles if Kennedy would make a "no-invasion" pledge regarding Cuba. The next day Khrushchev added a second demand— the removal of American missiles in Turkey. According to popular history, Robert Kennedy suggested accepting the first proposal while ignoring the second. The president directed Stevenson to explore with Secretary-General Thant the possibility of the United Nations providing observation teams to oversee any missile withdrawal. He also let his UN ambassador suggest that if an exchange of missile sites in Turkey for those in Cuba became necessary, then the proposal to do so would best come from Thant. As it happened, Robert Kennedy met on October 27 with Soviet ambassador to the United States Anatoly Dobrynin and agreed to both conditions, but insisted that the Soviets keep the second condition confidential. Kennedy dropped the idea of UN observation teams as well, depending on Central Intelligence Agency overflights to verify the dismantling of the missiles. On October 28 both sides announced that the crisis had been defused; the missiles

Meeting of the Security Council during the Cuban Missile Crisis, 1962 (UNITED NATIONS)

would be withdrawn and the United States would make clear it had no intention of invading Cuba in the future. As a result of the crisis, the two countries agreed to the installation of a "hot line" telephone connection so that in the future negotiations could be initiated instantly, before an awkward situation became a crisis.

See also COLD WAR, LATIN AMERICA.

Further Reading: Allison, Graham T. *The Essence of Decision: Explaining the Cuban Missile Crisis.* New York: Addison, Wesley, Longman, 1999. Allyn, Bruce J., Georgy Shakhnazarov, David A. Welch, and James G. Blight, eds. *Back to the Brink: Proceedings of the Moscow Conference on the Cuban Missile Crisis, January 27–28, 1989.* Lanham, Md.: University Press of America, 1992. Garthoff, Raymond L. *Reflections on the Cuban Missile Crisis.* Washington, D.C.: Brookings Institution, 1990. Kennedy, Robert. F. *Thirteen Days: A Memoir of the Cuban Missile Crisis.* New York: W.W. Norton and Company, 1999. May, Ernest R., and Philip D. Zelikow, eds. *The Kennedy Tapes: Inside the White House during the Cuban Missile Crisis.* Cambridge, Mass.: Harvard Uni-

versity Press, 1998. Nathan, James A., ed. *The Cuban Missile Crisis Revisited.* New York: St. Martin's, 1993.

— *D. J. Becker*

Cyprus dispute

Controlled by the Turkish Ottoman Empire from the 16th century, Cyprus, the third largest island of the Mediterranean Sea, was annexed by Great Britain during World War I. For centuries, the majority ethnic Greek population considered Greece the mother country of Cyprus. The country became independent in 1960, and full rights were promised to its minority Turkish population. In 1964 communal clashes occurred between Greek and Turkish Cypriots, and a temporary UN PEACEKEEPING force was sent to the island to help end the dispute. From 1964 to 1974 the United Nations pursued a single-state solution based on the agreements among the United Kingdom, Greece, and Turkey that granted independence to the island.

In 1974 Archbishop Makarios, the Cypriot president, was overthrown by a military coup apparently seeking merger with Greece. Turkey responded with an invasion to protect the Turkish minority. From 1974 until the turn of the century, the UNITED NATIONS FORCE IN CYPRUS (UNFICYP) sought a bi-zonal solution, supervising and maintaining a buffer zone between the Greek Cypriot National Guard and Turkish forces. Makarios eventually returned to power in late 1974, but Turkish troops remained in the north, controlling about 40 percent of the country, and in 1983 proclaimed a separate "Turkish" Republic. The UN SECURITY COUNCIL declared this action invalid, and the SECRETARY-GENERAL and his special adviser on the island continued to try to draw the opposing forces into direct discussions to end the long stalemate and initiate meaningful negotiations leading to a comprehensive settlement. The lengthy presence of UNFICYP, separating the two communities, had the ironic consequence of lessening incentives for reunification. Talks resumed in 1999, but the de facto division of the island continued into the next century.

See also BUNCHE, RALPH, DEPARTMENT OF PEACEKEEPING OPERATIONS.

Further Reading: Richmond, Oliver P. *Mediating in Cyprus. The Cypriot Communities and the United Nations.* London: Frank Cass, 1998. UNFICYP website: <www.un.org/Depts/DPKO/Missions/unficyp/body_unficyp.htm>.

Dag Hammarskjöld Library

Located on the southwest corner of UN HEADQUARTERS in New York City, the UN's main library, a gift of the Ford Foundation, is dedicated to the memory of the second SECRETARY-GENERAL, Dag HAMMARSKJÖLD, who died in Africa in 1961 while on a PEACEKEEPING mission to the CONGO.

The library was an addition to the larger project for the headquarters that included the GENERAL ASSEMBLY building, the conference building, and the 39-story SECRETARIAT building. The lead architect for the entire enterprise, Wallace K. Harrison, of New York, was the chief designer of the library, which opened officially in 1962, one year after the death of Hammarskjöld. Built of marble, the library has an expansive view north of UN headquarters and adjacent buildings and open spaces. It is not open to the public but is mandated to serve the information needs of UN permanent mission staffs and the Secretariat. It is also accessible to scholars to provide materials not available at other depository libraries.

The library contains about 380,000 volumes, as well as a newspaper collection, a microfilm laboratory, tape recording services, an extensive photography library, reading rooms, and an auditorium. The library is open Monday through Friday, 9 A.M. to 5:30 P.M. except when the General Assembly is in session, when the hours of operation are extended to 6 P.M. during the workweek. By its mandate, the library maintains bibliographic control over the documentation of the United Nations. It provides, through the United Nations Bib-liographic Information System (UNBIS), indexing for UN documents and publications issued in New York, Geneva, and Vienna, as well as documents released by regional commissions and other UN bodies.

See also DEPARTMENT OF PUBLIC INFORMATION.

Further Reading: Hammarskjöld Library website: <www.un.org/Depts/dhl/services.htm>.

Dayton Peace Accords

The death in 1980 of Marshall Josip Broz Tito, the post–World War II leader of the FORMER YUGOSLAVIA, foreshadowed a fractured future for the Balkan country, one in which BOSNIA and Herzegovina—one of the six original republics of the Socialist Federal Republic of Yugoslavia—would suffer miserably until the Dayton accords of 1995 formally ended a three-pronged civil war.

A disappointing economy and the end of the COLD WAR brought a splintering of Yugoslavia. DECLARATIONS of independence by Slovenia and Croatia in 1991 and Bosnia and Herzegovina in 1992 initiated a civil war, when the dominant Yugoslav republic Serbia attempted to thwart the secessions. As early as 1991 the UN SECURITY COUNCIL imposed an arms embargo on Yugoslavia and in early 1992 established the UNITED NATIONS PROTECTION FORCE (UNPROFOR), authorized by mid-year to protect the delivery of humanitarian aid in Bosnia. All three of the newly declared NATION-STATES were admitted to the United Nations in 1992. But, unlike the other seceding states, Bosnia and Herzegovina was not composed of a homogenous ethnic population. A plurality (44 percent) were Muslims, 31 percent Serbs, and 17 percent Croats. Croatian president Franjo Tudjman and Serbian strongman Slobodan Milosevic set out to partition the area between themselves, all to the disadvantage of the Muslim population, led by Bosnian president Alija Izetbegovic.

The siege of Sarajevo, Bosnia's capital, and the practice of "ethnic cleansing," carried out by Bosnian Serbs, shocked the world. By the middle of 1992, Serbs controlled more than 60 percent of the country, and the number of refugees and displaced persons mounted to more than 2 million, the largest refugee crisis in Europe since World War II. In May 1993, the Security Council declared Sarajevo and other Bosnian towns as "safe areas," but the devastating war continued. In August 1995 the North Atlantic Treaty Organization (NATO) intervened militarily following Bosnian Serb attacks on civilians in the UN enclaves at Srebrenica and Goradze—where they took UN peacekeepers hostage and systematically murdered civilian men and boys—after a brutal mortar attack on the marketplace in Sarajevo. NATO bombed Serb positions around the capital. A joint Bosnian Muslim and Croat military offensive followed NATO action and diminished Serbian areas of control.

In October, faced with military defeat, the government in Belgrade agreed to a U.S.–initiated peace conference in Dayton, Ohio, at Wright-Patterson Air Force Base. The following month, the three presidents—Izetbegovic, Tudjman, and Milosevic—agreed to end the fighting, to respect each other's SOVEREIGNTY and independence, and to accept a Muslim-Croat federation and a separate Serb entity (Republika Srpska) within the larger federation of Bosnia. Additional provisions of the accord, officially signed in Paris on December 14, 1995, included promises by all sides to allow displaced persons to return to their homes, release all persons still detained, cooperate with the work of the INTERNATIONAL CRIMINAL TRIBUNAL FOR THE FORMER YUGOSLAVIA, allow working journalists to perform their professional functions, resume commercial air travel between Bosnia and Herzegovina and the Federal Republic of Yugoslavia, and continue discussions toward the establishment of full diplomatic relations between Sarajevo and Belgrade at meetings of the Ministerial Contact Group (formed in 1994 by France, Germany, the RUSSIAN FEDERATION, the United Kingdom, and the UNITED STATES). NATO troops numbering 60,000 were to supervise the implementation of the agreement. Fighting abated, and in elections in September 1996, Izetbegovic was chosen president of the new country. The same year, by act of the Security Council, the United Nations International Police Task Force became part of a larger UNITED NATIONS MISSION IN BOSNIA AND HERZEGOVINA (UNMIBH), which attempted to implement the Dayton accords, supervising the demilitarization of the region and organizing and administering elections.

Serious problems continued to confront Bosnia and Herzegovina at the turn of the century, including resettling refugees, rebuilding the economy, establishing a working government, locating indicted war criminals who were still at large, and dealing with the fact of a rump Serbian entity within the country. Still, after Dayton there was, as of spring 2002, no further outbreak of ruinous civil war in the country, and by late summer 2000, UN officials could report that a record 25,000 refugees had returned to their homes since the start of that year.

See also INTERNATIONAL CRIMINAL COURT.

Further Reading: Holbrooke, Richard. *To End a War.* New York: Random House, 1998. Dayton peace accords websites: <www1.umn.edu/humanrts/icty/Dayton/daytoncompl.html>, <www.state.gov/www/regions/eur/bosnia/bosagree.html>.

Decade for Women   *See* UNITED NATIONS DECADE FOR WOMEN.

declaration
In the UNITED NATIONS SYSTEM, *declaration* is a term applied to legal statements made by governments or groups of governments. In the United Nations it typically refers to unanimously agreed upon statements, in contrast to RESOLUTIONS, which are adopted usually by a majority of votes. That is, a declaration is rather like a public proclamation, much in the manner of the U.S. Declaration of Independence (1776), or France's Declaration of the Rights of Man and the Citizen (1789). Nearly all UN-sponsored world conferences conclude with the publication of a declaration of agreed principles, such as the RIO DECLARATION issued at the conclusion of the Earth Summit in 1992.

Declaration by United Nations
The UNITED STATES, the United Kingdom, CHINA, and the Soviet Union signed the DECLARATION by United Nations in Washington on January 1, 1942. The next day 22 other nations at war with the Axis powers signed the declaration. The decision to put the "Big Four" ahead of the lesser states in the signatory process reflected President ROOSEVELT's belief that the great powers would have a unique responsibility for the war effort and the postwar peace. This principle guided future U.S. planning for the United Nations organization. Secretary of state Cordell HULL and his aides in the U.S. State Department initially had suggested this statement, and when British prime minister Winston CHURCHILL arrived in Washington in late December, he and Roosevelt immediately agreed, making numerous changes in the draft. Hull insisted that Russia and China be invited to serve as joint sponsors with the United States and Great

Britain. Roosevelt himself thought of the name "United Nations."

The declaration created a wartime alliance of "United Nations," each promising to wage war against the Axis powers with all of its resources and not to sign a separate peace. The signatories accepted the principles of the ATLANTIC CHARTER as a "common program of purposes," and promised "to defend life, liberty, independence and religious freedom, and to preserve HUMAN RIGHTS and justice in their own lands as well as in other lands." Many supporters of the subsequent 1945 United Nations CHARTER were later disappointed when this language was left out of the founding document. The formal expression of the world community's commitment to these values would be left to the promulgation of the UNIVERSAL DECLARATION OF HUMAN RIGHTS. A final clause in the declaration permitted other countries that entered the war in the future to join the United Nations. Eventually eight other nations signed the document.

Despite the jubilation of internationalists over the declaration by United Nations, there was also disappointment at the neglect to mention a postwar international organization. Roosevelt remained cool to the idea of such an organization. He made reference only to his hopes for a just postwar peace based on the Four Freedoms and the Atlantic Charter. Nevertheless, the declaration introduced the term "United Nations" to the American public and it slowly came to represent a conception of world organization.

See also ARTICLE 3 OF THE UNITED NATIONS CHARTER (Appendix A).

Further Reading: Divine, Robert A. *Second Chance: The Triumph of Internationalism in America during World War II.* New York: Atheneum, 1967. Kimball, Warren F. *The Juggler: Franklin Roosevelt as Wartime Statesman.* Princeton, N.J.: Princeton University Press, 1991. Sherwood, Robert. *Roosevelt and Hopkins: An Intimate Portrait.* New York: Harper, 1948.
— E. M. Clauss

Declaration on the Elimination of Violence against Women

On December 20, 1993, the GENERAL ASSEMBLY adopted the Declaration on the Elimination of Violence against Women. The DECLARATION defined "violence against women" as any act of gender-specific brutality that causes, or is likely to result in, physical, sexual, or psychological injury or torment. Threats, coercion, or arbitrary denial of freedom in private or public qualified as a violation of the declaration. Particular, but not exclusive, areas denoting violence included: physical, sexual, or psychological violence within the family, the general community, or that carried out by a state.

The declaration also provided a mandate for a SPECIAL RAPPORTEUR on violence against WOMEN. In 1994, the Office

of the UN HIGH COMMISSIONER FOR HUMAN RIGHTS appointed Ms. Radhika Coomaraswamy of Sri Lanka to the post and authorized her to collect and analyze data and make recommendations regarding the causes for and the elimination of violence against women. At the 57th session of the COMMISSION ON HUMAN RIGHTS in April 2001, the Special Rapporteur submitted her annual report, focusing on violence against women perpetrated and/or condoned by the state during times of armed conflict. She also presented a report of her fall 2000 mission to Bangladesh, Nepal, and India to investigate the issue of trafficking of women and girls, and a further report detailing country-by-country reviews of allegations and appeals that had been forwarded to specific governments, and the replies of those governments.

See also COMMISSION ON THE STATUS OF WOMEN, CONVENTION ON THE ELIMINATION OF ALL FORMS OF DISCRIMINATION AGAINST WOMEN, INTERNATIONAL DAY FOR THE ELIMINATION OF VIOLENCE AGAINST WOMEN, WORLD CONFERENCES ON WOMEN.

Further Reading: Bunch, Charlotte, and Niamh Reilly. *Demanding Accountability: The Global Campaign and Vienna Tribunal for Women's Human Rights.* New Brunswick, N.J.: Center for Women's Global Leadership, 1994. Reilly, Niamh, ed. *Testimonies of the Global Tribunal on Violations of Women's Human Rights at the United Nations World Conference on Human Rights, Vienna, June 1993.* New Brunswick, N.J.: Center for Women's Global Leadership, 1994. Declaration website: <www.unhchr.ch/women/focus-violence.html>.

Declaration on the Granting of Independence to Colonial Countries and Peoples

On December 14, 1960, the UN GENERAL ASSEMBLY adopted the Declaration on the Granting of Independence to Colonial Countries and Peoples, urging a faster pace in the process of decolonization. The Asian and African states that had only recently become members of the United Nations believed that neither the TRUSTEESHIP COUNCIL nor the United Nations as a whole was doing enough to encourage independence. Their impatience with the colonial powers was reflected in the declaration's demand that independence be granted even where there was an "inadequacy of political, economic, social or educational preparedness." The emerging majority in the General Assembly from the newly independent states of the developing world used the DECLARATION to reenforce the principle of self-determination as a central tenet of the UN CHARTER. The text of the declaration follows.

The General Assembly,

Mindful of the determination proclaimed by the peoples of the world in the Charter of the United Nations to reaffirm faith in fundamental HUMAN RIGHTS, in the dignity and worth of the human person, in the equal rights of men and WOMEN and of nations large and small and to promote social progress and better standards of life in larger freedom,

Conscious of the need for the creation of conditions of stability and well-being and peaceful and friendly relations based on respect for the principles of equal rights and self-determination of all peoples, and of universal respect for, and observance of, human rights and fundamental freedoms for all without distinction as to race, sex, language or religion,

Recognizing the passionate yearning for freedom in all dependent peoples and the decisive role of such peoples in the attainment of their independence,

Aware of the increasing conflicts resulting from the denial of or impediments in the way of the freedom of such peoples, which constitute a serious threat to world peace,

Considering the important role of the United Nations in assisting the movement for independence in Trust and NON-SELF-GOVERNING TERRITORIES,

Recognizing that the peoples of the world ardently desire the end of colonialism in all its manifestations,

Convinced that the continued existence of colonialism prevents the development of international economic cooperation, impedes the social, cultural and economic development of dependent peoples and militates against the United Nations ideal of universal peace,

Affirming that peoples may, for their own ends, freely dispose of their natural wealth and resources without prejudice to any obligations arising out of international economic cooperation, based upon the principle of mutual benefit, and INTERNATIONAL LAW,

Believing that the process of liberation is irresistible and irreversible and that, in order to avoid serious crises, an end must be put to colonialism and all practices of segregation and discrimination associated therewith,

Welcoming the emergence in recent years of a large number of dependent territories into freedom and independence, and recognizing the increasingly powerful trends towards freedom in such territories which have not yet attained independence,

Convinced that all peoples have an inalienable right to complete freedom, the exercise of their SOVEREIGNTY and the integrity of their national territory,

Solemnly proclaims the necessity of bringing to a speedy and unconditional end colonialism in all its forms and manifestations;

And to this end

Declares that:

1. The subjection of peoples to alien subjugation, domination and exploitation constitutes a denial of fundamental human rights, is contrary to the Charter of the United Nations and is an impediment to the promotion of world peace and cooperation.

2. All peoples have the right to self-determination; by virtue of that right they freely determine their political status and freely pursue their economic, social and cultural development.

3. Inadequacy of political, economic, social or educational preparedness should never serve as a pretext for delaying independence.

4. All armed action or repressive measures of all kinds directed against dependent peoples shall cease in order to enable them to exercise peacefully and freely their right to complete independence, and the integrity of their national territory shall be respected.

5. Immediate steps shall be taken, in Trust and Non-Self-Governing Territories or all other territories which have not yet attained independence, to transfer all powers to the peoples of those territories, without any conditions or reservations, in accordance with their freely expressed will and desire, without any distinction as to race, creed or colour, in order to enable them to enjoy complete independence and freedom.

6. Any attempt aimed at the partial or total disruption of the national unity and the territorial integrity of a country is incompatible with the purposes and principles of the Charter of the United Nations.

7. All States shall observe faithfully and strictly the provisions of the Charter of the United Nations, the UNIVERSAL DECLARATION OF HUMAN RIGHTS and the present Declaration on the basis of equality, non-interference in the internal affairs of all States, and respect for the sovereign rights of all peoples and their territorial integrity.

Declaration on the Right to Development

Adopted by the GENERAL ASSEMBLY in RESOLUTiON 128 of December 4, 1986, the Declaration on the Right to Development proclaimed development "an inalienable HUMAN RIGHT by virtue of which each person and all peoples are entitled to participate in, contribute to and enjoy economic, social, cultural and political development in which all human rights and fundamental freedoms can be fully realized." The Assembly's action came five years after the adoption of the African Charter of Human and Peoples' Rights, also known as the Banjul Charter, which was the first international document to assert the right. Several WORLD CONFERENCES subsequently reaffirmed the principle in their final documents. Among them the RIO DECLARATION (Principle 3) of the 1992 Earth Summit, the 1993 Vienna DECLARATION and Programme of Action at the WORLD CONFERENCE ON HUMAN RIGHTS, and the Declaration of the Third UN CONFERENCE ON THE LEAST DEVELOPED COUNTRIES in 2001 were the most important.

See also SECOND COMMITTEE OF THE GENERAL ASSEMBLY.

Declaration on the Rights of the Child

On November 20, 1959, the UN GENERAL ASSEMBLY adopted 10 principles, dedicated to the well-being of every child "without distinction or discrimination." The Assembly's

DECLARATION was unusually specific concerning the policies NATION-STATES should implement on behalf of their young people. In subsequent years the United Nations regularly focused world attention on the plight of children in many parts of the world. It declared 1979 the International Year of the Child, directed the UNITED NATIONS CHILDREN'S FUND (UNICEF), the institution's lead agency on children's issues, to prepare a CONVENTION on the Rights of the Child, and urged relevant SPECIALIZED AGENCIES to develop assistance programs for children. The text of the declaration follows.

Principle 1
The child shall enjoy all the rights set forth in this Declaration. Every child, without any exception whatsoever, shall be entitled to these rights, without distinction or discrimination on account of race, colour, sex, LANGUAGE, religion, political or other opinion, national or social origin, property, birth or other status, whether of himself or of his family.

Principle 2
The child shall enjoy special protection, and shall be given opportunities and facilities, by law and by other means, to enable him to develop physically, mentally, morally, spiritually and socially in a healthy and normal manner and in conditions of freedom and dignity. In the enactment of laws for this purpose, the best interests of the child shall be the paramount considerations.

Principle 3
The child shall be entitled from his birth to a name and a nationality.

Principle 4
The child shall enjoy the benefits of social security. He shall be entitled to grow and develop in health; to this end, special care and protection shall be provided both to him and to his mother, including adequate pre-natal and post-natal care. The child shall have the right to adequate nutrition, housing, recreation and medical services.

Principle 5
The child who is physically, mentally or socially handicapped shall be given the special treatment, education and care required by his particular condition.

Principle 6
The child, for the full and harmonious development of his personality, needs love and understanding. He shall, wherever possible, grow up in the care and under the responsibility of his parents, and, in any case, in an atmosphere of affection and of moral and material security; a child of tender years shall not, save in exceptional circumstances, be separated from his mother. Society and the public authorities shall have the duty to extend particular care to children without a family and to those without adequate means of support. Payment of State and other assistance towards the maintenance of children of large families is desirable.

Principle 7
The child is entitled to receive education, which shall be free and compulsory, at least in the elementary stages. He shall be given an education which will promote his general culture, and enable him, on a basis of equal opportunity, to develop his abilities, his individual judgement, and his sense of moral and social responsibility, and to become a useful member of society.
The best interests of the child shall be the guiding principle of those responsible for his education and guidance; that responsibility lies in the first place with his parents.
The child shall have full opportunity for play and recreation, which should be directed to the same purposes as education; society and the public authorities shall endeavour to promote the enjoyment of this right.

Principle 8
The child shall in all circumstances be among the first to receive protection and relief.

Principle 9
The child shall be protected against all forms of neglect, cruelty and exploitation. He shall not be the subject of traffic, in any form.
The child shall not be admitted to employment before an appropriate minimum age; he shall in no case be caused or permitted to engage in any occupation or employment which would prejudice his health or education, or interfere with his physical, mental or moral development.

Principle 10
The child shall be protected from practices which may foster racial, religious and any other form of discrimination. He shall be brought up in a spirit of understanding, tolerance, friendship among peoples, peace and universal brotherhood, and in full consciousness that his energy and talents should be devoted to the service of his fellow men.

decolonization   *See* NATIONAL LIBERATION.

Department for Disarmament Affairs (DDA)
After a hiatus of six years the Department for Disarmament Affairs was reestablished in 1998 on the recommendation of the GENERAL ASSEMBLY (GA) as one of the UN SECRETARIAT's major departments. It had earlier existed (1982–92) as a product of the Assembly's Second SPECIAL SESSION ON DISARMAMENT. Headed by UNDER SECRETARY-GENERAL Jayantha Dhanapala from Sri Lanka, in 2001 DDA had five branches: WEAPONS OF MASS DESTRUCTION (WMD), Conventional Arms including Practical DISARMAMENT Measures (CAB), Regional Disarmament (RDB),

Monitoring, Database and Information (MDI), and CON-FERENCE ON DISARMAMENT (CD). Secretariat and Conference Support are located in Geneva. With the overall goal of promoting global norms of disarmament, DDA branches provide informational and administrative assistance to the GA's FIRST COMMITTEE, the Conference on Disarmament, the DISARMAMENT COMMISSION, and other UN disarmament bodies and conferences. The department also promotes public education on disarmament issues by publishing the *Disarmament Yearbook, Disarmament Notes,* and a quarterly *DDA Update.*

Following its reestablishment, the Department for Disarmament Affairs emphasized certain issues for international negotiation and public debate. Among them were transparency and openness in military affairs, confidence-building measures, disarmament verification, regional disarmament, curbs on the flow of small arms and arms trafficking, and containing the proliferation of WEAPONS OF MASS DESTRUCTION. This last topic led DDA to work closely with the ORGANIZATION FOR THE PROHIBITION OF CHEMICAL WEAPONS, the INTERNATIONAL ATOMIC ENERGY AGENCY, and the Preparatory Committee of the COMPREHENSIVE TEST BAN TREATY Organization. Its efforts to slow regional arms buildups were bolstered by the creation of UN Regional Centres for Peace and Disarmament in Africa, Asia and the Pacific, and LATIN AMERICA, which DDA oversaw and coordinated.

At the turn of the century DDA had identified three "emerging" issues it intended to address in its work: Disarmament and development, Gender Perspectives on Disarmament, and Disarmament Education. As part of SECRETARY-GENERAL Kofi ANNAN's Steering Group on Disarmament and Development, DDA assisted in the preparation of the Secretary-General's report on the subject and coordinated its activities with other agencies involved in aspects of the issue. Given that gender and disarmament linkages were not readily apparent, DDA launched a series of research projects including "Gender Perspectives on Weapons of Mass Destruction," "Gender Perspectives on Small Arms," and "Gender Perspectives on LAND MINES." Finally, it provided administrative support for a GA-authorized "United Nations Study on Disarmament and Non-Proliferation Education." To be carried out by a panel of 10 governmental experts from Egypt, Hungary, India, Japan, Mexico, New Zealand, Peru, Poland, Senegal, and Sweden, the study was scheduled to be the basis of a report by Secretary-General Annan to the General Assembly in 2002. The first two working sessions of the 10-member group were organized by DDA in August 2001.

Further Reading: DDA website: <www.un.org/Depts/dda/dda.htm>. *Disarmament Notes* website: <www.un.org/Depts/dda/DDAHome.htm>.

Department of Economic and Social Affairs (DESA)

One of the departments of the UN SECRETARIAT, DESA provides administrative services for the many commissions and committees of the ECONOMIC AND SOCIAL COUNCIL (ECOSOC). Created as a consolidation of three former departments, DESA is directed by an UNDER SECRETARY-GENERAL—in 2001, Mr. Nitin Desai of India—who also chairs the Secretariat's Executive Committee on Economic and Social Affairs, which brings together 18 UN agencies working in the field. In addition to its administrative services the department has a number of normative, policy analysis, and advisory duties that its carries out in its nine divisions.

Entering the new millennium, the Department of Economic and Social Affairs sought to promote SUSTAINABLE DEVELOPMENT, with a particular emphasis on Africa, small island developing states, and North-South cooperation. As the focal point for UN SECRETARY-GENERAL Kofi ANNAN's promotion of development in Africa, DESA houses the Office of the Special Coordinator for Africa and the LEAST DEVELOPED COUNTRIES (OSCAL). DESA emphasizes gender-related issues, ENVIRONMENT, population effects, and social dimensions of development. In all of these areas the department works to translate the Plans of Action and Final DECLARATIONS of recent WORLD CONFERENCES into practical steps that governments could take to meet conference goals. This requires working closely with SPECIALIZED AGENCIES and bodies created by UN conferences, as well as with the Second and THIRD COMMITTEES OF THE GENERAL ASSEMBLY, and ECOSOC and its commissions.

Particularly under Annan's REFORM program, DESA has developed extensive coordination and support functions. As the lead agency of one of Annan's four newly created thematic executive committees, the Executive Committee on Economic and Social Affairs, DESA promotes coherence and efficiency in the work of the committee's members. The Executive Committee membership includes the United Nations OFFICE FOR DRUG CONTROL AND CRIME PREVENTION (ODCCP), the UNITED NATIONS DEVELOPMENT PROGRAMME (UNDP), the UN regional economic commissions, HABITAT, the UNITED NATIONS CONFERENCE ON TRADE AND DEVELOPMENT (UNCTAD), UNITED NATIONS UNIVERSITY (UNU), the UNITED NATIONS RESEARCH INSTITUTE FOR SOCIAL DEVELOPMENT (UNRISD), the United Nations INTERNATIONAL RESEARCH AND TRAINING INSTITUTE FOR THE ADVANCEMENT OF WOMEN (INSTRAW), the UNITED NATIONS ENVIRONMENT PROGRAMME (UNEP), and the Office of the UN HIGH COMMISSIONER FOR HUMAN RIGHTS (UNHCHR). Additionally, DESA's Division for Public Economics and Public Administration manages the UN's Programme in Public Administration and Finance. Its Division for Social Policy and Development provides guidance to ECOSOC's COMMIS-

SION FOR SOCIAL DEVELOPMENT (CSocD). As of 2001, the division had also convened four sessions of the World Youth Forum to enhance ties between youth NON-GOVERNMENTAL ORGANIZATIONS (NGOs) and youth-related UN bodies. Its Population Division provides the secretariat for the COMMISSION ON POPULATION AND DEVELOPMENT, undertaking research studies and preparing public reports on the topic. Its Division for the Advancement of WOMEN (DAW) provides administrative support for the COMMITTEE ON THE ELIMINATION OF DISCRIMINATION AGAINST WOMEN (CEDAW); its Division for Sustainable Development provides the secretariat for the COMMISSION ON SUSTAINABLE DEVELOPMENT (CSD), and supplies data and policy recommendations to CSD; and its Division for ECOSOC Support and Coordination provides system-wide guidance on ECOSOC activities, oversight and coordination of subsidiary bodies, and support for the NGOs that have CONSULTATIVE STATUS with the Council.

DESA has an independent research and policy analysis function that provides extensive data and reports to the world community, assisting governments and NGOs engaged in the development process. Among its more important publications is the United Nations *WORLD ECONOMIC AND SOCIAL SURVEY*, published annually by its Division for Development Policy Analysis. The *Survey* analyzes topical global economic issues and provides UN forecasts on the world economy and world trade. DESA's Statistical Division publishes the *Statistical Yearbook,* the *World Statistics Pocketbook,* and statistical publications on international merchandise trade, national accounts, demography, gender, population, energy, environment, human settlements, disability, social indicators, and industry. Additionally, DESA maintains major databases, such as its Population Division's *World Population Projections to 2150,* the *Global Review and Inventory of Population Policies* (GRIPP), and the *Population Information Network* (POPIN).

See also INTER-AGENCY COMMITTEE ON SUSTAINABLE DEVELOPMENT.

Further Reading: United Nations Department of Public Information. *Basic Facts about the United Nations.* New York: United Nations Department of Public Information, 2000. DESA website: <www.un.org/esa>.

Department of General Assembly Affairs and Conference Services (DGAACS)   *See* SECRETARIAT.

Department of Management (DM)   *See* SECRETARIAT.

Department of Peacekeeping Operations (DPKO)

The Department of Peacekeeping Operations was created in 1992 as an integral part of the Executive Office of the UN SECRETARY-GENERAL. Prior to 1992 the UNDER SECRETARY-GENERAL (USG) for Special Political Affairs controlled missions authorized by the SECURITY COUNCIL or GENERAL ASSEMBLY. The department has administrative, managerial, planning, and preparation responsibilities for PEACEKEEPING missions. It is headed by the Under Secretary-General for Peacekeeping—in 2001, USG Jean-Marie Guéhenno of France—and has divisions for operations, planning and support, training and evaluation, and assessment of past operations. This last division is officially known as the Lessons Learned Unit, established in April 1995 by UN Secretary-General Kofi ANNAN, himself a former USG for Peacekeeping. The Training and Evaluation Office was established by the General Assembly to coordinate and standardize training for national peacekeeping units. It provides courses, publications, and training exercises for those member states that contribute forces to peacekeeping operations.

The end of the COLD WAR occasioned a significant increase in peacekeeping operations. Following apparent peacekeeping successes in ANGOLA and NAMIBIA, there was confidence that the United Nations could intervene effectively in disintegrating states, not only to restore peace but to undertake state-building. Failures, however, in SOMALIA and Rwanda, induced strong pressures for an evaluation of DPKO operations and the UN peacekeeping function in general. The department struggled with inadequate resources trying to meet new mandates that went far beyond the original idea of peacekeeping. The UNITED STATES, in particular, urged an overhaul of DPKO, including the creation of a rapidly deployable headquarters team, the maintenance of a database of available forces, and a modest airlift capability. An initial response to these recommendations was the creation of the Lessons Learned Unit, with the mandate to study past peacekeeping operations, discover the strengths and weaknesses of those efforts, and make recommendations for administrative improvement.

In March 2000, Secretary Annan appointed a panel of experts to study the new challenges facing UN peacekeeping. He hoped the experts would complement the work of the Lessons Learned Unit. The panel's report, issued just before the September 2000 meeting of the MILLENNIUM SUMMIT, recommended formalizing the UN's peacekeeping activities, ending ad hoc deployments, and creating a new information-gathering and analysis office within the United Nations to act as a professional policy planning staff for DPKO.

Past and present peacekeeping and peace-building operations include:

Africa

Angola	UN ANGOLA VERIFICATION MISSION (UNAVEM I)	December 1988–May 1991
	UN Angola Verification Mission (UNAVEM II)	May 1991–February 1995
	UN Angola Verification Mission (UNAVEM III)	February 1995–June 1997
	UN Observer Mission in Angola (MONUA)	June 1997–February 1999
	UN Office in Angola (UNOA)	October 1999–
Central African Republic	UN Mission in the Central African Republic (MINURCA)	April 1998–February 2000
	UN Office in the Central African Republic (BONUCA)	February 2000–
Chad/Libya	UN Aouzou Strip Observer Group (UNASOG)	May 1994–June 1994
CONGO	UN Operation in the Congo (ONUC)	July 1960–June 1964
Democratic Republic of the Congo	UN ORGANIZATION MISSION IN THE DEMOCRATIC REPUBLIC OF THE CONGO (MONUC)	December 1999–
Ethiopia/Eritrea	UN Mission in Ethiopia and Eritrea (UNMEE)	July 2000–
Guinea-Bissau	UN Peace-building Support Office in Guinea-Bissau (UNOGBIS)	March 1999–
Liberia	Observer Mission in Liberia (UNOMIL)	September 1993–
	UN Peace-building Support Office in Liberia (UNOL)	September 1997 November 1997–
MOZAMBIQUE	UN Operation in Mozambique (ONUMOZ)	December 1992–December 1994
Namibia	UN TRANSITION ASSISTANCE GROUP (UNTAG)	April 1989–March 1990
Rwanda	UN ASSISTANCE MISSION FOR RWANDA (UNAMIR)	October 1993–March 1996
Rwanda/Uganda	UN Observer Mission for Uganda-Rwanda (UNOMUR)	June 1993–September 1994
SIERRA LEONE	UN Observer Mission in Sierra Leone (UNOMSIL)	July 1998–October 1999
	UN Mission in Sierra Leone (UNAMSIL)	October 1999–
SOMALIA	UN OPERATIONS IN SOMALIA (UNOSOM I)	April 1992–March 1993
	UN Operations in Somalia (UNOSOM II)	March 1993–March 1995
	UN Political Office for Somalia (UNPOS)	April 1995–
Western Sahara	UN Mission for the Referendum in Western Sahara (MINURSO)	April 1991–

LATIN AMERICA and the Caribbean

Central America	UN OBSERVER GROUP IN CENTRAL AMERICA (ONUCA)	November 1989–January 1992
Dominican Republic	Mission of the SPECIAL REPRESENTATIVE of the SECRETARY-GENERAL in the Dominican Republic (DOMREP)	May 1965–October 1966
EL SALVADOR	UN OBSERVER MISSION IN EL SALVADOR (ONUSAL)	July 1991–April 1995
GUATEMALA	UN VERIFICATION MISSION IN GUATEMALA (MINUGUA)	January 1997–May 1997
HAITI	UN Mission in Haiti (UNMIH)	September 1993–June 1996
	UN Support Mission in Haiti (UNSMIH)	July 1996–July 1997
	UN Transition Mission in Haiti (UNTMIH)	August 1997–November 1997
	UN CIVILIAN POLICE MISSION IN HAITI (MIPONUH)	December 1997–March 2000
	UN Civilian Support Mission in Haiti (MICAH)	December 1999–

Asia

AFGHANISTAN	International Security Assistance Force (ISAF)	December 2001–
Afghanistan/Pakistan	UN GOOD OFFICES Mission in Afghanistan and Pakistan (UNGOMAP)	March 1988–March 1990
	UN SPECIAL MISSION TO AFGHANISTAN (UNSMA)	December 1993–
CAMBODIA	UN Advance Mission in Cambodia (UNAMIC)	October 1991–March 1992
	UN TRANSITION AUTHORITY IN CAMBODIA (UNTAC)	March 1992–September 1993
EAST TIMOR	UN TRANSITIONAL ADMINISTRATION IN EAST TIMOR (UNTAET)	October 1999–
Georgia	UN Observer Mission in Georgia (UNOMIG)	August 1993–
India/Pakistan	UN INDIA-PAKISTAN OBSERVATION MISSION (UNIPOM)	September 1965–March 1996
	UN MILITARY OBSERVER GROUP IN INDIA AND PAKISTAN (UNMOGIP)	January 1949–
Tajikistan	UN Mission of Observers in Tajikistan (UNMOT)	December 1994–May 2000
	UN Tajikistan Office of Peace-building (UNTOP)	June 2000–
West New Guinea	UN SECURITY FORCE (UNSF)	October 1962–April 1963

Europe

BOSNIA and Herzegovina	UN MISSION IN BOSNIA AND HERZEGOVINA (UNMIBH)	December 1995–
	UN Mission of Observers in Prevlaka (UNMOP)	January 1996–

(continues)

Croatia	UN Confidence Restoration Operation (UNCRO)	March 1995–January 1996
	UN Transitional Authority in Eastern Slavonia, Baranja, and Western Sirmium (UNTAES)	January 1996–January 1998
	UN Civilian Police Support Group (UNPSG)	January 1998–October 1998
Cyprus	UN PEACEKEEPING FORCE IN CYPRUS (UNFICYP)	March 1964–
Former Yugoslav Republic of Macedonia	UN PREVENTIVE DEPLOYMENT FORCE IN THE FORMER YUGOSLAV REPUBLIC OF MACEDONIA (UNPREDEP)	March 1995–February 1999
FORMER YUGOSLAVIA	UN PROTECTION FORCE (UNPROFOR)	February 1992–March 1995
	UN INTERIM ADMINISTRATION MISSION IN KOSOVO (UNMIK)	June 1999–
Georgia	UN Observer Mission in Georgia (UNOMIG)	August 1993–

Middle East

Golan Heights	UN Disengagement Observer Force (UNDOF)	June 1974–
Iran/Iraq	UN Iran-Iraq Military Observer Group (UNIIMOG)	August 1988–February 1991
Iraq/Kuwait	UN IRAQ-KUWAIT OBSERVATION MISSION (UNIKOM)	April 1991–
Lebanon	UN Observer Group in Lebanon (UNOGIL)	June 1958–December 1958
	UN INTERIM FORCE IN LEBANON (UNIFIL)	March 1978–
Middle East	UN EMERGENCY FORCE (UNEF I)	November 1956–June 1967
	UN Emergency Force (UNEF II)	October 1973–July 1979
Yemen	UN YEMEN OBSERVATION MISSION (UNYOM)	July 1963–September 1964

See also BRAHIMI REPORT, SECRETARIAT.

Further Reading: Report of the Panel on United Nations Peace Operations website: <www.un.org/peace/reports/peace_operations/>. DPKO website: <www.un.org/Depts/dpko/>.

Department of Political Affairs   *See* SECRETARIAT.

Department of Public Information (DPI)

The GENERAL ASSEMBLY created the Department of Public Information in 1946. It is a department within the United Nations's administrative organ, the SECRETARIAT. The mandate of DPI is to enlist public support for the United Nations by building awareness and understanding of the purpose and activities of the organization among the peoples of the world. The department functions as the catalyst for information related to the United Nations and its system. It assists all the other UN departments, commissions, committees, programs, and SPECIALIZED AGENCIES in gathering, coordinating, preparing, and disseminating information in the form of teaching guides, exhibits, documentary films, reports, press releases, topical promotional campaigns, and newsletters, such as *African Recovery.* The information includes photographs, maps, and regional statistics collected by the economic and social commissions of the United Nations.

The Department of Public Information disseminates information through its Media Division, which uses a wide variety of channels, such as online, print, television, and radio. DPI has information centers in more than 130 countries, including 50 in Africa, 35 in Asia and Oceania, and 15 in Europe. The UN-guided tours began with the opening of UN HEADQUARTERS in 1952 and are now also conducted at the UN offices in Geneva and Vienna. Some 300 depository libraries throughout the world make UN documents accessible locally to researchers, students, and parliamentarians. Furthermore, since the launching of the UN website in 1997, an increasing number of documents have been made available directly on the Internet. The Public Inquiries Unit provides information over the phone or by e-mail free of charge. Media accreditation and press kits ensure that the world press has the opportunity to cover UN events. The Office of the Spokesman of the SECRETARY-GENERAL briefs international journalists and press officers of the member states on a daily basis and coordinates the media-related activities of the Secretary-General, such as press conferences and interviews. Besides enlisting the press to help disseminate UN information, DPI coordinates the relationship of NON-GOVERNMENTAL ORGANIZATIONS (NGOs) with the United Nations. The NGOs, in exchange for varying degrees of CONSULTATIVE STATUS with the ECONOMIC AND SOCIAL COUNCIL, disseminate UN-related information to their members.

In addition to its Media Division, DPI has a Division of Promotion and Public Services, and a Division for Library and Publications. The latter is responsible for the Dag HAMMARSKJÖLD RESEARCH LIBRARY, which is the documentation, research, and reference facility of the UN. The Promotion and Public Services Division conducts public awareness campaigns and conferences.

The UNDER SECRETARY-GENERAL (USG) for Communication and Public Information coordinates the work of DPI with other UN bodies and programs.

On May 31, 2002, Secretary-General Kofi ANNAN elevated the interim department head, Shashi Tharoor of India, to the USG position. The department translates its message into a variety of languages. All UN documents are written in the two working languages of the United Nations—French and English—and many documents are translated into the other four official languages: Arabic, Chinese, Russian, and Spanish. UN radio broadcasts are prepared in 18 languages, public tours are conducted in approximately 30 languages, and the information centers provide the translation of UN documents into local languages.

See also STRUCTURE OF THE UNITED NATIONS.

Further Reading: United Nations Department of Public Information. *Basic Facts about the United Nations.* New York: United Nations Department of Public Information, published periodically. Department of Public Information websites: <www.un.org/Depts/>; <www.un.org/MoreInfo/>.

— *A. S. Hansen*

Deputy Secretary-General (DSG)

On March 2, 1998, Louise FRÉCHETTE became the United Nations's first Deputy Secretary-General (DSG). The GENERAL ASSEMBLY had authorized SECRETARY-GENERAL Kofi ANNAN's creation of the post under Article 101 of the CHARTER the previous December (Res. 12). The Assembly's action was part of the general REFORM OF THE UNITED NATIONS first proposed by Annan in September 1997.

The duties of the Deputy Secretary-General are to assist the Secretary-General (SG) in managing the SECRETARIAT, act for the SG at United Nations HEADQUARTERS when he or she is not there, enhance coherence and cooperation among UN bodies, provide leadership in economic and social activities of the UN, represent the Secretary-General at conferences and official functions, and "undertake such assignments as may be determined by the Secretary-General." The Deputy Secretary-General serves only during the term of the Secretary-General who appointed him or her.

As the first occupant of the office, Fréchette defined by her actions and assigned duties the initial parameters of the position. Annan's reform proposal, *RENEWING THE UNITED NATIONS,* called for the Deputy Secretary-General to be his senior adviser who would oversee day-to-day operations at UN headquarters. Responding largely to demands from the UNITED STATES for greater efficiency and accountability, the Secretary-General established a cabinet of his most senior staff. Fréchette served on this SENIOR MANAGEMENT GROUP and other secretariat committees. She was given responsibility for implementing the rest of the UN reforms approved by the General Assembly, including chairing the Steering Committee on Reform and Management Policy. In addition to her responsibilities for reform, she focused attention on UN social, economic, and development activities. She was also given a major role in Annan's efforts to develop cooperation between the United Nations and "civil society," including partnerships with NON-GOVERNMENTAL ORGANIZATIONS and private businesses. She was appointed chair of the Advisory Board of the United Nations Fund for International Partnerships (UNFIP). Among the special assignments given to Fréchette was implementation of the BRAHIMI REPORT. Named for the chairman of the Panel on United Nations Peace Operations, the report recommended structural reforms of UN PEACEKEEPING, requiring the acquisition and expenditure of $22 million over several years.

Fréchette, much experienced in UN affairs after lengthy service in the Canadian External Affairs Department and as Canada's PERMANENT REPRESENTATIVE to the United Nations, quickly acquired a public presence that was not required by the position. She regularly spoke in favor of creating a "new" United Nations, that is, an institution increasingly focused on "human beings, respect for their rights, and the satisfaction of their basic needs." As the first Deputy Secretary-General, she gave the post a public legitimacy that made the DSG more than just another senior member of the UN Secretariat. In the budding view of UN members the Deputy Secretary-General and the Secretary-General were seen as a team giving direction to the institution as a whole.

See also PRINCIPAL ORGANS OF THE UNITED NATIONS, STRUCTURE OF THE UNITED NATIONS.

Desert Shield *See* GULF WAR.

Desert Storm *See* GULF WAR.

desertification

As defined in chapter 12 of the 1992 Earth Summit's AGENDA 21, "desertification is land degradation in arid, semi-arid and dry sub-humid areas resulting from various factors, including climatic variations and human activities." By the close of the 1990s, Asia possessed the largest land area affected by desertification. In the areas of Asia suffering from desertification 71 percent was moderately to severely degraded. For LATIN AMERICA, this proportion was 75 percent. In Africa, two-thirds of which was desert or drylands, 73 percent of the agricultural drylands were moderately to severely degraded. Africa was under the greatest desertification threat, with a rate of disappearance of forest cover of 1.4 to 1.9 million square miles per year depleting both surface and groundwater resources, and with half the continent's farmland suffering from soil degradation and erosion.

Desertification presented a credible threat to the sustainability of human development. In 2002, desertification and drought seriously threatened the livelihood of 1.2 billion people who depended on land for most of their needs. More than 23 million people were at risk of famine as a consequence of the continuing drought in the Horn of Africa, Kenya, Tanzania, and ANGOLA. Half of the population of Tajikistan faced severe food access problems due to severe drought and inadequate irrigation systems. CHINA was losing 984 square miles of land every year to desertification and 2 percent of its territory was already desert. Dust from desertification-affected areas of India and Pakistan covered much of East Asia, reaching as far as Japan. Water scarcity and land degradation increased in southern European countries.

The attention of the international community shifted at the millennium from the climatic factors of desertification to its human causes. Desertification was also linked to the security concerns of many developing countries. Soil erosion and water scarcity clearly led to urban migration, overpopulation, poverty, and instability. It also produced famine, leading to the displacement of civilians, which, in turn, threatened the stability of entire regions. As neighboring countries not experiencing desertification become hosts to migrating refugees, the difficulty of feeding several million more people each year put food security ahead of military security as the principal preoccupation of many governments. Thus, the issue of combating desertification was at the forefront among the agendas of many nations and international organizations, including the United Nations.

The United Nations Committee on Desertification (UNCOD) took the first major step on the international level in 1977, by approving a Plan of Action to Combat Desertification (PACD). The plan was modified and expanded at the 1992 UNITED NATIONS CONFERENCE ON ENVIRONMENT AND DEVELOPMENT (UNCED) in Rio de Janeiro, Brazil (the Earth Summit). One hundred heads of state met in Rio de Janeiro, endorsed the RIO DECLARATION and the STATEMENT OF FOREST PRINCIPLES, and adopted AGENDA 21, a 300-page plan for achieving SUSTAINABLE DEVELOPMENT in the 21st century. The conference gave the UNITED NATIONS DEVELOPMENT PROGRAMME (UNDP) the lead role in working on desertification and drought. An Intergovernmental Negotiating Committee on Desertification (INCD), initiated by UNCED, created the CONVENTION TO COMBAT DESERTIFICATION in those countries experiencing serious drought and/or desertification, particularly in Africa (UNCCD or CCD), which entered into force on December 26, 1996. Its CHARTER created four regional annexes in Africa, Asia, LATIN AMERICA and the Caribbean, and the Northern Mediterranean, and the document provided for the implementation of action programs on national, regional, and subregional levels.

The Committee on Desertification identified four different levels of drought: meteorological (or climatological), agricultural, hydrological, and socioeconomic. The work of UNCCD concentrated predominantly on socioeconomic aspects of desertification because this final category of drought encompassed all other categories. This approach emphasized that the most constructive action to combat desertification needed to be done on a local level. The CONVENTION provided for research and education efforts on both global and regional levels. The 2000 meeting of the convention's conference of parties (COP) in Bonn, Germany, emphasized full involvement of civil society and science as essential for success in combating desertification worldwide.

At the turn of the century the problem of desertification was so overwhelming that other UN bodies and agencies joined the UNITED NATIONS ENVIRONMENT PROGRAMME (UNEP) and the CCD organization in their efforts to combat the growing crisis. The FOOD AND AGRICULTURE ORGANIZATION (FAO) created and enabled databases containing information about desertification and related subjects. Organizations involved in combating the effects of desertification included the UNITED NATIONS CHILDREN'S FUND (UNICEF), the WORLD FOOD PROGRAMME (WFP), and the UNITED NATIONS HIGH COMMISSIONER FOR REFUGEES (UNHCR). The WORLD HEALTH ORGANIZATION (WHO) focused on the impact of desertification and droughts on human health and devised health policies that would minimize their devastating effects. As part of its campaign to arrest global environmental deterioration, particularly by combating the degradation of drylands, the UN General Assembly designated June 17th as "WORLD DAY TO COMBAT DESERTIFICATION AND DROUGHT."

See also ENVIRONMENT, REGIONAL DEVELOPMENT BANKS, SECOND COMMITTEE OF THE GENERAL ASSEMBLY, WORLD METEOROLOGICAL ORGANIZATION.

Further Reading: Biswas, Margaret R., and Asit K. Biswas. *Desertification: Associated Case Studies Prepared for the United Nations Conference on Desertification.* New York: Pergammon Press, 1980. Minguet, Monique. *Desertification: Natural Background and Human Mismanagement.* Spring Study Edition. New York: Springer-Verlag, 1994. Mouat, David A., and Charles F. Hutchinson, eds. *Desertification in Developing Counties: International Symposium and Workshop on Desertification in Developing Countries.* The Hague: Kluwer Academic Publishers, 1996.

— *I. Kebreau*

development   *See* COMMITTEE OF INTERNATIONAL DEVELOPMENT INSTITUTIONS ON THE ENVIRONMENT, ECONOMIC AND SOCIAL COUNCIL, SUSTAINABLE DEVELOPMENT, UNITED NATIONS CONFERENCE ON ENVIRONMENT AND DEVELOPMENT, UNITED NATIONS CONFERENCE ON LEAST DEVELOPED COUNTRIES, UNITED NATIONS CONFERENCE ON TRADE AND DEVELOPMENT, UNITED NATIONS DEVELOPMENT PROGRAMME.

development account

UN SECRETARY-GENERAL Kofi ANNAN proposed the creation of a Development Account as part of his 1997 REFORM proposals for the world organization. In RENEWING THE UNITED NATIONS, Annan suggested that the account should be funded with savings from the implementation of contemplated cost-cutting measures in the administration of the United Nations. The GENERAL ASSEMBLY created the Development Account in October 1999 and directed that its resources be used for "supplementary development activities." By 2001 more than $30 million had been generated by streamlining the SECRETARIAT and its activities, better coordination of entities in the UNITED NATIONS SYSTEM, and the expanded use of electronic information technologies. The UNDER SECRETARY-GENERAL for Economic and Social Affairs serves as the program manager for the account.

Projects funded by the account are approved by the General Assembly. During its first two years of operation the account supported more than 20 projects focused on capacity-building through regional cooperation of developing states. They included the promotion of electronic commerce, the creation of the United Nations Public Administration Network (UNPAN), and the convocation of several international workshops on aspects of capacity-building. In 2001 the UN DEPARTMENT OF ECONOMIC AND SOCIAL AFFAIRS announced that the next set of projects would focus on "capacity-building for managing globalization."

Development Decades

Beginning in 1961 the UN GENERAL ASSEMBLY established four consecutive Development Decades in order to bring attention to the plight of developing countries. Originally conceptualized as an economic planning rubric, the Development Decades' greatest service was to give visibility to UN efforts to assist the LEAST DEVELOPED COUNTRIES and to inspire international campaigns meant to pressure rich nations into increasing foreign assistance. Particularly during the Second and Third Decades (1971–90) there was a concerted effort by the General Assembly majority to promote the agenda of the NEW INTERNATIONAL ECONOMIC ORDER (NIEO). Central to the urgings of the developing SOUTH was an annual transfer of 1 percent of GDP from the developed world to the Third World. At first they sought that aid in the form of multilateral grants, but by the 1980s they stressed debt relief.

The NIEO described the principal problems facing the LESS DEVELOPED COUNTRIES (LDC) and concluded that only a drastic revision of global trading rules and processes could improve their lot. Beginning with the premise that the existing system had been developed by the major industrialized states before most of the developing nations achieved their independence, and, therefore, unfairly discriminated against LDC, the NIEO called for the replacement of the BRETTON WOODS system with a new set of rules to assure that the voices of developing nations were heard. Much of the developing states' efforts to replace the international trade system came in the UNITED NATIONS CONFERENCE ON TRADE AND DEVELOPMENT (UNCTAD), which convened for its first session in 1964 during the First Development Decade, and then met every four years through the end of the century.

The momentum created by the Development Decades contributed to the creation or adoption of several UN bodies and programs. During the First Decade two pivotal organizations were established: the UNITED NATIONS DEVELOPMENT PROGRAMME (UNDP) in 1965 and the UNITED NATIONS INDUSTRIAL DEVELOPMENT ORGANIZATION in 1967. In the early years of these organizations both emphasized industrialization. This gave way in the wake of the 1992 UNITED NATIONS CONFERENCE ON ENVIRONMENT AND DEVELOPMENT to the pursuit of SUSTAINABLE DEVELOPMENT. In the Third Development Decade, the United Nations adopted the SUBSTANTIAL NEW PROGRAMME OF ACTION for least developed countries and the New Industrial Development Strategy. As part of the effort to keep the Development Decades at the forefront of world attention the United Nations also launched a number of new publications through the DEPARTMENT OF PUBLIC INFORMATION and UNDP. Of particular note were *Development Forum* and *Development Update*.

Further Reading: United Nations Department of Public Information. *Everyone's United Nations; A Handbook on the Work of the United Nations.* New York: United Nations Department of Public Information, 1986. Riggs, Robert E., and Jack C. Plano. *The United Nations: International Organization and World Politics.* Pacific Grove, Calif.: Brooks/Cole Publishing Co., 1988.

director-general

A necessary concomitant of emerging intergovernmental organizations (IGOs) in the 19th and early 20th centuries was the development of permanent SECRETARIATs to implement the policies of these organizations, to maintain their international headquarters, and to prepare meetings, budgets, and agenda. The chief administrator was known by different titles, including executive secretary or executive director. The most common appellation, however, was director-general. This administrator was considered to be the servant of the organization and not of his or her national state, was paid out of the agency's regular budget, and was expected to maintain impartiality in the administration of the organization. During early planning for the United Nations, many draft CHARTER proposals included the post of director-general as head of the organization, in part to dissociate the new body from the out-of-favor LEAGUE OF NATIONS that was administered by a SECRETARY-GENERAL.

Those who argued for the title suggested that "Director-General" conveyed a dynamic political leadership role not evident in "Secretary-General," such as that played by the director-general of the International Labour Office after World War I.

The appointment of a director-general to head an IGO continues to be a normal practice in the SPECIALIZED AGENCIES of the United Nations. Since specialized agencies are autonomous organs of the world body, directors-general are not accountable to the UN Secretariat, but to their individual agency organs as defined in the organizations' constitutional documents. Usually elected by the agency's plenary body, the director-general has extensive latitude in the appointment, supervision, and activities of the body's bureaucracy. The director-general also maintains the diplomatic immunities and benefits that are accorded to international civil servants under INTERNATIONAL LAW. Some of the most important of the UN specialized agencies are headed by directors-general, including the WORLD TRADE ORGANIZATION (WTO), the WORLD HEALTH ORGANIZATION (WHO), the INTERNATIONAL ATOMIC ENERGY AGENCY (IAEA), the FOOD AND AGRICULTURE ORGANIZATION (FAO), the ORGANIZATION FOR THE PROHIBITION OF CHEMICAL WEAPONS (OPCW), and the UNITED NATIONS EDUCATIONAL, SCIENTIFIC AND CULTURAL ORGANIZATION (UNESCO).

While an agency's director-general is independent of UN Secretariat control, in 1946 the United Nations established the ADMINISTRATIVE COMMITTEE ON COORDINATION (ACC). Renamed the UN System Chief Executives Board for Coordination (CEB) in 2002, it is chaired by the UN Secretary-General and made up of executive leaders from the specialized agencies. The CEB has a complex structure of subsidiary committees on which many of the directors-general or their representatives serve. Through this body, which meets semi-annually, the UN Secretariat tries to bring about a coordinated effort to implement UN initiatives, WORLD CONFERENCE recommendations, and agency responses to new international challenges. Directors-general's discretion is also limited by the relationship agreements between their agencies and the United Nations, which contain specific provisions on terms of employment and service, headquarters agreements, and stipulations on the privileges and immunities of the agencies' civil servants. A "Common System" for budget, staffing, and personnel policy has emerged that restricts the discretion of a director-general when hiring, removing, promoting, and disciplining agency personnel. Employees are also protected through a system of ADMINISTRATIVE TRIBUNALS.

disarmament

Disarmament, a major focus of the United Nations from the beginning, by definition refers to the actual destruction, removal, or deactivation of existing WEAPONS. Agreements achieving this ultimate end were very difficult and very few until the end of the COLD WAR allowed the two former antagonists—the UNITED STATES and the Soviet Union—seriously to engage in deep and mutual disarmament, starting with the Intermediate Nuclear Forces Agreement of 1987. Negotiations, however, within and without the UNITED NATIONS SYSTEM, have also taken place to effect arms *control* regimes, arms *limitation* agreements (which sometimes simply limited the *growth* in armaments), non-proliferation of existing weapons and weapons technologies, and weapons-free areas. Often these efforts have been subsumed under the general category of "disarmament."

The UN effort has been a continuation of pre–World War II diplomacy that sought to reduce the threat of war by reducing the modern weapons possessed by states. The COVENANT of the LEAGUE OF NATIONS had committed the organization to the pursuit of world disarmament. In the 1920s efforts were also made by the United States and other major powers to negotiate limits on armed forces, most notably to seek naval disarmament. The rise of military dictatorships in Europe and Asia only reenforced the belief that the reduction of armaments was crucial to the maintenance of peace and to the replacement of the use of force with the rule of law.

In 1945 the new UN CHARTER committed the United Nations to global efforts to achieve disarmament. Article 11 authorized the GENERAL ASSEMBLY (GA) to "consider the general principles . . . governing disarmament." Article 26 charged the SECURITY COUNCIL (SC) with the responsibility for "formulating . . . a system for the regulation of armaments." The American use of nuclear weapons against Japan in August 1945, only four months after the Charter signing in San Francisco, generated strong interest in a UN initiative to pursue nuclear disarmament and to promote nuclear energy for peaceful purposes. As the wartime amity between the United States and the Soviet Union faded, and the prospects of a superpower nuclear arms race emerged, the United Nations seemed the suitable venue for working out what U.S. president Harry S. Truman called "a satisfactory arrangement for the control of this discovery."

The establishment in 1946 of the ATOMIC ENERGY COMMISSION (UNAEC) initiated a permanent UN effort to limit the growth of nuclear arsenals. At its inaugural meeting in June the United States proposed the international control of all nuclear materials, uranium mines, and processing facilities. Known as the BARUCH PLAN—it was named for Bernard Baruch, the U.S. representative to the UNAEC who presented the U.S. proposal—the contemplated UN authority would have the power to impose SANCTIONS and fines on offending states, and would operate independent of the VETO power in the Security Council. The USSR immediately rejected the proposal as an effort by the United States to maintain its monopoly on nuclear weapons. Soviet delegate Andrei Gromyko proposed the alternative of a moratorium on atomic development prior to any plan for nuclear internationalization. Americans saw this as a ploy by the Soviets to limit U.S. defense efforts while pursuing a nuclear buildup undetected by international inspections.

Negotiations in the Atomic Energy Commission in the summer of 1946 foreshadowed the general pattern of UN nuclear disarmament efforts during the cold war. The deadlock produced by the competing interests of the United States and the Soviet Union undermined the possibility of fruitful negotiations. It also demonstrated the central role of the superpowers to any disarmament arrangement, and therefore the limited peripheral roles non-nuclear member states could play in promoting disarmament and arms control. In 1952 the Atomic Energy Commission and the UN's Commission on Conventional Armaments were merged into the UN DISARMAMENT COMMISSION, but this forum served as little more than a setting for Soviet and American propaganda bombasts, the former power calling for "general and complete disarmament," the latter insisting on verifiable and intrusive inspection under any disarmament plan—with neither state expecting its proposals to be accepted by the other side.

The UN's impact on disarmament in the 1950s was negligible. Serious discussions within the Disarmament Commission occurred only in the Subcommittee on Disarmament, created in 1954 and made up of the United States, the Soviet Union, the United Kingdom, France, and Canada. These states conducted their talks in secret. Otherwise, the commission was reduced to debating proposals by non-nuclear and non-aligned states. To be sure, the growing number of new UN members from the Third World and the desire to maintain influence in these countries led the superpowers to make organizational concessions to the UN MEMBERSHIP, but substantive issues were monopolized by the nuclear powers. In August 1959 the subcommittee was enlarged, becoming the Ten Nation Disarmament Committee with the addition of Bulgaria, Czechoslovakia, Poland, and Romania from the Warsaw PACT, and Italy from the North Atlantic Treaty Organization. Eight non-aligned nations were added in 1961, creating the EIGHTEEN NATION DISARMAMENT COMMITTEE (ENDC). The only serious negotiations, however, were conducted in bilateral contacts between Washington and Moscow.

As a product of U.S.–USSR talks a number of agreements were reached in the 1960s and early 1970s. Following the dangerous confrontation in the CUBAN MISSILE CRISIS, the two sides agreed to the 1963 Partial Test Ban TREATY and a communications hotline between the two capitals to assure no misunderstandings on the deployment or use of weapons and personnel. In 1972 they reached agreement on the Anti-Ballistic Missile Treaty.

In the nuclear field UN negotiations were relegated to what were then seen as peripheral matters. Two topics

Poster for Second Special Session on Disarmament, 1982 (UN PHOTO)

dominated UN diplomacy: NUCLEAR-WEAPONS-FREE ZONES (NFZ) and nuclear non-proliferation. The ANTARCTIC TREATY of 1959 was the first agreement to ban nuclear weapons on a regional basis. Sponsored by the nuclear weapons states, the treaty prohibited weapons or weapons testing on the Antarctic continent. Signatories pledged to demilitarize Antarctica. Recognizing the fragile ENVIRONMENT of the region, the treaty also banned the dumping of radioactive wastes. Verification provisions included required inspections. This was followed in 1976 by the TREATY OF TLATLELOCO, negotiated among Latin American nations, prohibiting nuclear weapons in Central and South America and the Caribbean. In later decades NFZ accords were reached in Africa (Treaty of Pelindaba, 1996), Southeast Asia (Treaty of Bangkok, 1995), and the South Pacific (Treaty of Rarotonga, 1985). Obstacles to equivalent agreements in the Middle East and on the broader Asian continent, however, proved more intractable. Conflicts between Israel and Arab states made a Middle East Nuclear-

Weapons-Free Zone unattainable. In Asia, due to the presence of India and Pakistan—two states with a history of deep mutual hostility and divided by ongoing tension in the disputed Kashmir province, and each possessing a nuclear arsenal—an NFZ treaty was not a possibility.

The UN's single greatest achievement in restraining the nuclear arms race was the NUCLEAR NON-PROLIFERATION TREATY (NPT, opened for signature on July 1, 1968) that entered into force in 1970. The PACT was the direct result of multilateral negotiations on a joint draft submitted by the United States and the Soviet Union to the ENDC on August 24, 1967. The NPT's intention was to halt and then reverse the spread of independent control over nuclear weapons. It established in Article IX that only states that had acquired nuclear weapons by January 1, 1967, qualified as Nuclear Weapons States (NWS). All others were considered Non-Nuclear Weapons States (NNWS) and any such state adhering to the NPT was obligated to subject its entire peaceful nuclear program to the INTERNATIONAL ATOMIC ENERGY AGENCY (IAEA) material accountancy safeguards, and to pledge only to acquire nuclear materials and equipment for peaceful purposes. Conversely the NWS, which happened to be the five PERMANENT MEMBERS OF THE SECURITY COUNCIL, pledged not to transfer nuclear weapons to any NNWS or to assist it in manufacturing or acquiring nuclear weapons (Article I); to share the benefits of the "Peaceful Atom" with any NNWS party to the treaty (Articles IV and V); and to pledge to make a "good faith" effort to end the arms race at an "early date" (Article VI).

The treaty called for five-year review conferences (Article VIII) and for a conference 25 years from entry into force for the parties to the treaty to determine whether it should be extended indefinitely or for a defined period (Article X). That conference, held at the UN HEADQUARTERS in 1995, reached a consensus that a majority of the parties wished to extend the NPT indefinitely. The parties also agreed to an "enhanced" review process to hold all parties "accountable" for their NPT obligations, and the NWS further committed to achieve a COMPREHENSIVE NUCLEAR TEST BAN TREATY (CTBT). The CTBT was opened for signature on September 24, 1996. During the 1990s adherence to the NPT accelerated as long-time holdouts like France (1992), CHINA (1992), and South Africa (1991) signed and ratified the treaty. By 2000, only four states stood outside the treaty's framework: CUBA, India, Pakistan, and Israel.

Following the adoption of the Nuclear Non-Proliferation Treaty, the General Assembly expanded the ENDC to include all UN members, changing the name to the Conference of the Committee on Disarmament (CCD). The CCD, in turn, was replaced by the CONFERENCE ON DISARMAMENT (CD) in 1978. Located in Geneva, the Conference on Disarmament became the world's principal multilateral disarmament negotiating forum. While the General Assembly, as of 2001, had convened three SPECIAL SESSIONS ON DISARMAMENT since 1978, and had maintained its FIRST COMMITTEE as a forum for disarmament issues, it was the Conference on Disarmament that served as the UN's initiating body for disarmament agreements. The UN SECRETARIAT's DEPARTMENT FOR DISARMAMENT AFFAIRS (DDA) provided administrative services for the CD, and the General Assembly made recommendations that became part of the CD's agenda.

Several events in the mid-1990s, however, affected the status and effectiveness of the CD. Perhaps most importantly, the CONVENTION ON THE PROHIBITION OF THE USE, STOCKPILING, PRODUCTION AND TRANSFER OF ANTI-PERSONNEL MINES AND THEIR DESTRUCTION (1997) was debated, negotiated, and adopted for ratification outside the conference in a "fast track" set of negotiations known as "The Ottawa Process." Moreover, in 1996 the General Assembly gave final approval to the Comprehensive Nuclear Test Ban Treaty when India refused to join the consensus for the Treaty at the CD. The stalemate inside the CD led to widespread speculation among experts about the need to change the CD's rules and procedures or to endorse the establishment of alternative negotiating forums to address the range of disarmament questions.

The Conference on Disarmament categorizes the critical weapons systems as nuclear weapons, other WEAPONS OF MASS DESTRUCTION (WMD) such as chemical and biological agents, and conventional weapons. While nuclear disarmament efforts have overshadowed UN attempts to limit other arsenals, the United Nations has pursued arms reductions in each of these areas. In 1969, the United Nations defined CHEMICAL WEAPONS as "chemical substances, whether gaseous, liquid or solid, which might be employed because of their direct toxic effects on man, animals and plants." Not only the toxic chemicals but also the equipment for their dispersal was classified as a chemical weapon. On November 30, 1992, the General Assembly adopted the Convention on the Prohibition of the Development, Production, Stockpiling and Use of Chemical Weapons and on Their Destruction (CWC). As of July 2001, 143 states had become or were in the process of becoming parties to the CONVENTION. It was the first international disarmament agreement with the goal of eliminating an entire category of WMDs. To enforce its provisions the convention established the ORGANIZATION FOR THE PROHIBITION OF CHEMICAL WEAPONS (OPCW) with the authority to conduct surprise inspections. The dual use nature of chemicals and the ease of their production, however, made the exclusion of chemical weapons from the world's arsenals nearly impossible.

BIOLOGICAL WEAPONS (BW) are living organisms, most commonly bacteria and viruses, deliberately disseminated to cause death or disease in humans, animals, or plants. Biological weapons are considered weapons of mass destruction because they have the potential to destroy life equaled only by nuclear weapons. The 1925 Geneva PROTOCOL prohibited the use of biological weapons in warfare. The 1972 CONVEN-

TION ON THE PROHIBITION OF THE DEVELOPMENT, PRODUC-
TION AND STOCKPILING OF BACTERIOLOGICAL (BIOLOGICAL)
AND TOXIN WEAPONS AND ON THEIR DESTRUCTION (BWC)
went further by prohibiting their development and possession. The UN SECRETARY-GENERAL has the authority under
the treaty to investigate the alleged use of biological weapons,
ascertain facts regarding such alleged use, and report the findings to member states. A number of countries violated their
obligations under the BWC by initiating or continuing to
develop and produce biological weapons following its entry
into force. The Soviet Union maintained a secret BW program; South Africa produced biological weapons in the 1980s
and 1990s; and Iraq, while a signatory of the BWC, developed
an offensive biological program in the 1980s.

The expanded use of conventional weapons such as
LAND MINES and small arms in the post–cold war context of
sectarian violence caused heightened concern among UN
member states in the 1990s. In 1997 the United Nations
opened for signature the Landmines Convention. It prohibited in all circumstances any use of antipersonnel land
mines. It also required the destruction of stockpiles within
four years of the treaty's entry into force and mandated that
mines already in the ground be destroyed within 10 years. As
of March 1, 2001, 139 states had signed or acceded to the
convention, and 111 of those had ratified the agreement.
Among the states notably absent from the list of signatories
were the United States, Israel, and the RUSSIAN FEDERATION.

The United Nations had been involved in the movement
to ban land mines since the 1970s. In 1980, it negotiated the
Convention on Certain Conventional Weapons (CCW).
Frustration, however, with the slow pace of developing a specific land mine agreement in the Conference on Disarma-
ment led several states to pursue negotiations outside the UN
STRUCTURE. Beginning in October 1996, a coalition of states
and non-state actors championed the Ottawa Process, with
Canada and Belgium leading the effort to establish a land
mine ban. NON-GOVERNMENTAL ORGANIZATIONS (NGOs)
such as the International Committee of the Red Cross
(ICRC), Medecins sans Frontières (MSF—"Doctors without
Borders"), and the International Campaign to Ban Landmines
(ICBL) also advocated on behalf of a treaty. Following conferences in Vienna, Brussels, and Oslo, the process returned to
Canada in December 1997 for the signing ceremony. In the
negotiations the United Nations acted as a policy partner
with the NGOs. One example of such cooperation was the
work of the Survey Action Center. It monitored standards
and facilitated the international coordination of resources
and expert personnel for the completion of the Global Landmine Survey in the most mine-affected countries. That data
was then used to urge completion of the treaty.

Conflicts in the post–cold war era have been fought
almost exclusively with light or small arms. Clandestine
arms brokers found these types of weapons the easiest to sell
and deploy, exacerbating international efforts to limit their

numbers. The disintegration of states and the weakening of
central control over national arsenals also produced a huge
dispersion of these armaments. In 2001 the United Nations
convened a WORLD CONFERENCE to address this type of
weapon, but participating states could not arrive at a consensus on how to cut small arms quantities or how to regulate
their movement.

See also ACHESON-LILIENTHAL REPORT, ATOMS FOR PEACE
PROPOSAL, COMMITTEE ON THE PEACEFUL USES OF OUTER
SPACE, HAMMARSKJÖLD, JUS COGENS, MOON AGREEMENT,
UNITED NATIONS INSTITUTE FOR DISARMAMENT RESEARCH.

Further Reading: *Chemical Disarmament: Basic Facts.* 1999
edition. The Hague: Organization for the Prohibition of
Chemical Weapons, 2000. Cirincione, Joseph, ed. *Repairing
the Regime: Preventing the Spread of Weapons of Mass Destruction.* New York: Routledge, 2000. Lederberg, Joshua, ed. *Biological Weapons: Limiting the Threat.* Cambridge, Mass.: MIT
Press, 1999. United Nations Department of Public Information. *The United Nations and Nuclear Non-Proliferation.* Volume 3 of the United Nations Bluebook Series. New York:
United Nations Department of Public Information, 1995.
United Nations Treaty Series. New York: United Nations,
updated regularly. United Nations. *Verification and the United
Nations: The Role of the Organization in Multilateral Arms
Limitation and Disarmament Agreements.* New York: United
Nations, 1991. United Nations Disarmament Treaty website:
<domino.un.org/TreatyStatus.nsf>. UNIDIR website: <www.
unog.ch/unidir>. DDA website: <www.un.org/Depts/dda/dda.
htm>. *Disarmament Notes* website: <www.un.org/Depts/dda/
DDAHome.htm>.

Disarmament and International Security Committee   *See* FIRST COMMITTEE.

Disarmament Commission (UNDC)

In 1952 the ATOMIC ENERGY COMMISSION and the Commission on Conventional Armaments were merged into the UN
Disarmament Commission. But this forum served as little
more than a setting for Soviet and American propaganda, the
former power calling for "general and complete DISARMA-
MENT," the latter insisting on verifiable and intrusive inspection under any disarmament plan. Serious discussions
within the Disarmament Commission occurred only in the
Subcommittee on Disarmament, created in 1954 and made
up of the UNITED STATES, the Soviet Union, the United Kingdom, France, and Canada. These states conducted their talks
in secret. Otherwise, the commission was reduced to debating proposals by non-nuclear and non-aligned states.

In August 1959 the commission's subcommittee was
enlarged, becoming the Ten Nation Disarmament Commit-

tee, and then in 1961 the EIGHTEEN NATION DISARMAMENT COMMITTEE (ENDC). The ENDC was largely an independent venue for negotiations on a number of disarmament and arms control issues. Most important, it served as the institutional setting for the negotiation of the 1968 NUCLEAR NON-PROLIFERATION TREATY.

The SPECIAL SESSION OF THE GENERAL ASSEMBLY on Disarmament (SSOD-I) in 1978 attempted to revive the Disarmament Commission as "a deliberative body, a subsidiary body of the GENERAL ASSEMBLY, the function of which [is] to consider and make recommendations in the field of disarmament." All UN member states are represented on the commission. Without a clear focus to its agenda, however, the commission has been eclipsed both by the FIRST COMMITTEE OF THE GENERAL ASSEMBLY and the CONFERENCE ON DISARMAMENT in Geneva. The commission normally meets for three weeks annually in May and June, and is provided SECRETARIAT services by the DEPARTMENT FOR DISARMAMENT AFFAIRS. At the close of the 1990s the commission had on its agenda not only nuclear weapons but also conventional small arms.

Further Reading: United Nations. *Compilation of All Texts of Principles, Guidelines or Recommendations on Subject Items Adopted Unanimously by the Disarmament Commission.* New York: United Nations, 1999. UNDC website: <www.un.org/Depts/dda/UNDC/UNDC.htm>.

dispute settlement   *See* CHAPTER VI.

domestic jurisdiction clause

Article 2, Paragraph 7 of the UN CHARTER reads in part: "Nothing contained in the present Charter shall authorize the United Nations to intervene in matters which are essentially within the domestic jurisdiction of any state." This so-called Domestic JURISDICTION of states provision was first introduced in 1919 in the COVENANT of the LEAGUE OF NATIONS in Article 15, Paragraph 8. By the same UN Charter clause, the only exception to the principle occurs when there are breaches of peace and acts of AGGRESSION. At that point, CHAPTER VII of the charter becomes operative, and the SECURITY COUNCIL may apply mandatory ENFORCEMENT MEASURES, including intervention with military force. An assertion of the principle of state SOVEREIGNTY, the domestic jurisdiction clause came under challenge at the close of the century as the United Nations increasingly defended the HUMAN RIGHTS of men and WOMEN against violations by their own governments, pursued NATION-BUILDING in disintegrating states, and established WAR CRIMES TRIBUNALS to try NATION-STATE leaders charged with crimes against humanity and GENOCIDE inside their countries' borders.

See also CHAPTER VI $^1/_2$, INTERNATIONAL LAW, PEACEKEEPING.

Further Reading: Simma, Bruno, ed. *The Charter of the United Nations; A Commentary.* New York: Oxford University Press, 1995.

double veto

Matters considered by the SECURITY COUNCIL are defined in the UN CHARTER as "procedural" or "non-procedural." The latter, often referred to as "SUBSTANTIVE QUESTIONS," are subject to the VETO by any of the Council's PERMANENT MEMBERS. Procedural matters are not, and are decided by a simple majority vote of the Council MEMBERSHIP. According to the Statement of the Sponsoring Powers at the 1945 San Francisco Conference, certain items are clearly procedural in nature. However, when a dispute arises about the procedural or substantive character of a particular question before the Security Council, that matter itself is considered a substantive question, and, therefore, subject to the veto. This creates the possibility of a "double veto" by the UNITED STATES, CHINA, the United Kingdom, France, or the RUSSIAN FEDERATION. Theoretically, each can keep the council from even taking up a matter that it finds objectionable.

The Soviet Union used the double veto successfully three times in the late 1940s. However, in 1950 when the Republic of China attempted the stratagem to keep supporters of the People's Republic of China from addressing the Security Council, the council president summarily ruled that the matter was a procedural question. The Chinese representative was unable to muster the necessary seven votes to overrule the chair, and the decision stood. The device of a ruling from the chair was used several times after the 1950 experience, greatly limiting the use of the double veto to thwart council action.

drug control   *See* COMMISSION ON NARCOTIC DRUGS,
OFFICE FOR DRUG CONTROL AND CRIME PREVENTION.

Dumbarton Oaks Conference

The Dumbarton Oaks Conference convened in Washington, D.C., from August 21 to October 7, 1944. Representatives from CHINA, the Soviet Union, the United Kingdom, and the UNITED STATES participated in the conference. The aim of the negotiations was to establish a postwar international institution. The conference gave rise to the Dumbarton Oaks Proposals for the Establishment of a General International Organization.

The Dumbarton Oaks Proposals are important for three reasons. First, the proposals outlined the STRUCTURE of the evolving international organization. Chapter IV of the proposals established the GENERAL ASSEMBLY, SECURITY COUNCIL, INTERNATIONAL COURT OF JUSTICE, and SECRETARIAT as the PRINCIPAL ORGANS OF THE UNITED NATIONS. Second, the proposals assigned different responsibilities to each of these organs. Most important, Chapter VI conferred responsibility for international peace and security on the proposed Security Council, while Chapter V indicated that the General Assembly should be more involved in the economic and social spheres and supervise the operations of the organization. This division of labor is reflected in CHAPTER V, Article 24 of the UN CHARTER, where "primary responsibility for the maintenance of international peace and security" is conferred on the Security Council. Third, the proposals articulated the idea that the PERMANENT MEMBERS OF THE SECURITY COUNCIL—China, France, the United Kingdom, the United States, and the USSR—should be able to VETO any substantive (nonprocedural) matters before the body. The Dumbarton Oaks Proposals, like the UN Charter, did not use the term "veto." Rather, Chapter VI, Section C3 stated that an affirmative vote of the Council required the "concurring votes of the permanent members." A negative vote by any of the permanent members meant the failure of the proposed RESOLUTION. It is arguable whether the Dumbarton Oaks Conference settled the issue of the veto, since the subsequent YALTA CONFERENCE in February 1945 took up the matter again among the three wartime allied leaders: Franklin Delano ROOSEVELT, Winston CHURCHILL, and Joseph STALIN. Ultimately, however, the permanent members did receive their vetoes in the adopted UN Charter.

The Yalta Conference resolved issues left outstanding from the Dumbarton Oaks Conference. Specifically, Soviet insistence that each of its 16 constituent republics be given VOTING rights was addressed. An arrangement that gave the Ukraine and Byelorussia special voting status was agreed to by the United States, the United Kingdom, and the Soviet Union.

At the UN founding conference in San Francisco in 1945 some changes were made to the Dumbarton Oaks Proposals. This was done to make the proposed international organization more acceptable to the wider range of participants. Arguably the most significant modification involved the establishment of the TRUSTEESHIP COUNCIL. Despite such changes, the proposals that originated at the Dumbarton Oaks Conference constituted the basis of the UN Charter.

See also CHAPTER VI; MOSCOW CONFERENCE OF FOREIGN MINISTERS; PEARSON, LESTER.

Further Reading: For the text of the Dumbarton Oaks Proposals, see *Postwar Foreign Policy Preparation, 1939–1945,* Department of State Publication 3580 (Washington, D.C.: U.S. Government Printing Office, 1949). Claude, Inis. *Swords into Plowshares: The Problems and Progress of International Organization.* 4th ed. New York: Random House, 1971. Krasno, J. "A Step Along an Evolutionary Path: The Founding of the United Nations." *Global Dialogue* 12, no. 2 (Spring 2000): 9–18.

— *S. F. McMahon*

E

Earth Summit   *See* UNITED NATIONS CONFERENCE ON ENVIRONMENT AND DEVELOPMENT (UNCED).

East Timor dispute

The United Nations, beginning in 1976, annually adopted RESOLUTIONS demanding that Indonesian troops withdraw from East Timor and that the right to self-determination be given to the East Timorese. Beginning in the early 1980s, the UN SECRETARY-GENERAL's office arranged a series of negotiations in an attempt to find an acceptable solution to the dispute over the status of this former Portuguese colony. Through Resolution 1246, adopted on June 11, 1999, the SECURITY COUNCIL established the UNITED NATIONS MISSION IN EAST TIMOR (UNAMET) to ensure that the people of East Timor could choose their future through a secret ballot. When violence increased in the territory after 78.5 percent of East Timorese voters opted to reject the "special autonomy" proposal offered by INDONESIA, the Security Council, in September 1999, authorized a multinational force (INTERFET) to restore peace and security. The Security Council, through Resolution 1272 of October 1999, then established the UNITED NATIONS TRANSITIONAL ADMINISTRATION IN EAST TIMOR (UNTAET) to administer the territory during the transition to independence.

The United Nations's interest in East Timor stems from Indonesia's invasion of the eastern half of the island of Timor in 1975, Indonesia's 1976 annexation of the territory, and the heavy human costs inflicted on the East Timorese people during the reign of President Suharto. Nationalists and military hard-liners in Indonesia viewed the April 1974 overthrow of the Caetano dictatorship in Portugal as an opportunity to bring East Timor into the Indonesian fold. The East Timorese, however, viewed the Lisbon coup as an opportunity to end Portuguese rule. Nationalists in East Timor differed in their approach to autonomy, yet independence was the common goal of the two most popular parties, the Timorese Democratic Union (UDT) and the Revolutionary Front for an Independent East Timor (FRETILIN). When civil war broke out between UDT and FRETILIN in August 1975, Indonesia gave support to the Association for the Integration of Timor into Indonesia (Apodeti) and, on December 7, 1975, invaded East Timor. Although Indonesia formed a provisional government headed by an Apodeti official and hand-picked delegates to a people's assembly voted for integration with Indonesia, FRETILIN, with the support of much of the Timorese population, resisted the imposition of Indonesian rule through a guerrilla campaign. It is estimated that more than 100,000 Timorese died between 1976 and 1980 as a result of Indonesia's military actions and its resettlement of nearly 300,000 Timorese.

While the United Nations considered Portugal to be the administrating power in East Timor and repeatedly called for Indonesia to withdraw its forces, Jakarta refused to relax its control over the island. In 1983, the Secretary-General initiated a series of tripartite talks involving Indonesia and Portugal to improve the humanitarian situation in the territory and to achieve a resolution of the dispute. In 1995, the Secretary-General promoted the formation of the All-Inclusive Intra-East-Timorese Dialogue as a forum for East Timorese consultations. But success for the United Nations came only after President Suharto's forced resignation in 1998 and the formation of a successor government under President Habibie. On May 5, 1999, as a result of ministerial-level talks led by the personal representative of the Secretary-General (Jamsheed Marke), representatives of the Indonesian and Portuguese foreign ministries signed an agreement specifying that the East Timor question would be resolved through a popular consultation on Timorese acceptance or rejection of autonomy within Indonesia. On August 30, 1999, 344,580 Timorese cast their ballot for independence; only 94,388 (21.5 percent) voted in favor of the "special autonomy" proposal. The last Indonesian Army troops left East Timor on November 1, 1999. In September 2001, the United Nations administered the first parliamentary elections in East Timor's history. UN administration ended on May 20, 2002, as the new state of East Timor was proclaimed. The Timorese parliament immediately submitted a request for MEMBERSHIP in the United Nations.

See also ANNAN, KOFI; CHAPTER VI ¹/₂ PROVISIONS; PEACE-KEEPING.

Further Reading: Hainsworth, Paul, and Stephen McCloske. *The East Timor Question: The Struggle for Independence from Indonesia.* London: I.B. Tauris, 2000. Krieger, Heike. *East Timor and the International Community: Basic Documents.* Cambridge: Research Centre for International Law, Cambridge University Press, 1997.

— *G. S. Silliman*

Economic and Financial Committee *See* SECOND COMMITTEE OF THE GENERAL ASSEMBLY.

Economic and Social Affairs Executive Committee *See* DEPARTMENT OF ECONOMIC AND SOCIAL AFFAIRS.

Economic and Social Commission for Asia and the Pacific (ESCAP) *See* REGIONAL COMMISSIONS OF THE ECONOMIC AND SOCIAL COUNCIL.

Economic and Social Council (ECOSOC)

The Economic and Social Council is one of the six PRINCIPAL ORGANS OF THE UNITED NATIONS. It is charged with overseeing the considerable UN activities in the economic and social fields. Perhaps because of the breadth of its functions and

the fact that the GENERAL ASSEMBLY can take up any issue, the functions and role of ECOSOC are less clear than the other main organs, and member states have very different views about its role.

In essence, ECOSOC is the UN body most concerned with economic and social development. While industrialized nations regard development as secondary to the maintenance of international peace and security, developing nations regard it as the central purpose of the United Nations, believing that it constitutes a necessary precondition to the maintenance of international peace and security. Hence discussions of strengthening or reforming the United Nations often focus on the role and powers of ECOSOC. The importance of the Economic and Social Council is indicated by the fact that two of the only five AMENDMENTS to the UN CHARTER have dealt with the size of ECOSOC. In reaction to the expansion in UN MEMBERSHIP following decolonization, and to meet the desires of newly independent nations to be represented within the United Nations in proportion to their numbers, the Charter was amended twice to expand membership in ECOSOC. In 1965 membership rose from 18 to 27, and in 1971 to 54. This membership growth clearly reflected the priority developing nations placed on ECOSOC. Currently there are 54 nations represented on ECOSOC serving three-year terms, with one-third elected annually by the General Assembly, in accordance with a formula guaranteeing regional representation.

The opening paragraph of the Charter, following the phrase "We the peoples of the United Nations," lists the UN's purposes: to preserve international peace and security, to reaffirm HUMAN RIGHTS, to preserve INTERNATIONAL LAW as the basis for international relations, and "to promote social progress and better standards of life." Industrialized nations have focused on the initial three purposes, regarding development as secondary. But developing nations have regarded the promotion of development as equal in priority to preserving international peace and security, contending that these are the two preeminent purposes of the United Nations. In fact, developing nations have always preferred that the United Nations concentrate on development. In their view, strengthening ECOSOC is one of the most effective ways to do this.

Despite ECOSOC's broad responsibilities, its powers are quite limited, and its decisions are considered recommendations to the General Assembly. The functions of ECOSOC are primarily designed to focus discussion on issues and thereby to direct attention to economic and social problems. Specifically, ECOSOC conducts studies, drafts treaties, calls conferences dealing with economic and social issues, and makes recommendations to the General Assembly. It is up to the individual member states to decide how best to address these issues, in the General Assembly, at a summit conference, or by signing and ratifying a TREATY. Yet the function of ECOSOC is highly important, since its studies and reports set the agenda, guide prepara-

ECOSOC Chamber (UN/DPI by Ron Da Silva)

tions, and identify the terms of discussion at conferences, in other bodies, and in international documents. Article 62 of the Charter states that ECOSOC is to deal with "international economic, social, cultural, educational, health, and related matters," defining a very comprehensive mandate. ECOSOC also coordinates the activities of the independent SPECIALIZED AGENCIES, and accredits the NON-GOVERNMENTAL ORGANIZATIONS that play an important role in ECOSOC and the specialized agencies.

In addition to recommending and initiating actions, ECOSOC monitors the actions of member states in implementing decisions by its commissions and in meeting commitments made through treaties. It assists nations in drafting the necessary legislation to implement internationally agreed upon standards required by these decisions and treaties. This role is viewed as part of the UN's mission of "harmonizing the actions of nations" (Article 1 [4] of the Charter). ECOSOC's primary means of exerting influence is through requiring and reviewing reports from member states, providing the governments of those nations with advice, and assessing their progress on the implementation of international agreements. The Economic and Social Council publicizes the progress or lack thereof of member states in living up to their commitments to the international community, thus relying on the moral force of disclosure to achieve its aims.

ECOSOC has created a broad range of both regional and functional commissions to address specific challenges in the economic and social realms. Regional commissions are designed to promote cooperation and coordination among geographically proximate governments regarding economic and social matters. There are also functional commissions dealing globally with specific topics, such as the COMMISSION ON HUMAN RIGHTS, the COMMISSION ON THE STATUS OF WOMEN, and the COMMISSION ON SOCIAL DEVELOPMENT, each the primary UN agency in its field. ECOSOC's commissions include among their functions making international rules, drafting treaties, and monitoring the measures to carry out agreements. ECOSOC and its commissions serve to promote agreements setting voluntary norms and minimum standards that become standards of behavior by which the efforts of each government are assessed. ECOSOC and its commissions also publish informational material and model legislation in various fields.

FUNCTIONAL COMMISSIONS OF THE ECONOMIC AND SOCIAL COUNCIL

Statistical Commission
Commission on Population and Development
Commission for Social Development
Commission on Human Rights
Commission on the Status of Women

Commission on Narcotic Drugs
Commission on Crime Prevention and Criminal Justice
Commission on Science and Technology for Development
Commission on Sustainable Development

REGIONAL COMMISSIONS OF THE ECONOMIC AND SOCIAL COUNCIL

Economic Commission for Africa (Addis Ababa, Ethiopia)
Economic and Social Commission for Asia and the Pacific (Bangkok, Thailand)
Economic Commission for Europe (Geneva, Switzerland)
Economic Commission for Latin America and the Caribbean (Santiago, Chile)
Economic and Social Commission for Western Asia (Beirut, Lebanon)

STANDING COMMITTEES OF THE ECONOMIC AND SOCIAL COUNCIL

Committee for Programme and Coordination
Commission on Human Settlements
Committee on Non-governmental Organizations
Committee on Negotiations with Inter-governmental Agencies
Committee for Development Planning

See also STRUCTURE OF THE UNITED NATIONS.

Further Reading: South Centre. *Enhancing the Role of the United Nations.* Geneva: South Centre, 1992. ———. *For a Strong and Democratic United Nations: A South Perspective on UN Reform.* London: Zed Books, 1995. ———. *The United Nations at a Critical Crossroads: Time for the South to Act.* Geneva: South Centre, 1993.

— *K. J. Grieb*

Economic Commission for Africa (ECA) *See* REGIONAL COMMISSIONS OF THE ECONOMIC AND SOCIAL COUNCIL.

Economic Commission for Europe (ECE) *See* REGIONAL COMMISSIONS OF THE ECONOMIC AND SOCIAL COUNCIL.

Economic Commission for Latin America and the Caribbean (ECLAC)

Originally named the Economic Commission for Latin America (ECLA, CEPAL in Spanish), the organization was created by the UN ECONOMIC AND SOCIAL COUNCIL (ECOSOC) in 1948 to promote regional economic development. In order to gain approval for its establishment, the proposers of ECLA

included in its initial membership nations with colonial territories in the region (France, Great Britain, the Netherlands, and the UNITED STATES) as well as regional nations. In 1984, recognizing the inclusion of independent former colonies of Great Britain and the Netherlands, ECOSOC redesignated the organization as the Economic Commission for Latin America and the Caribbean. It became a leader in theory building, policy promotion, and gathering economic data for nations largely lacking the resources to engage in such activities themselves. Its economists came to occupy policy-making positions in most countries of the region.

The organization was profoundly influenced by the thought of its initial SECRETARY-GENERAL, Raúl PREBISCH, and the dominant thrust of its initial work involved promoting cooperation among the region's nations and encouraging the adoption of policies designed to modernize national economies through the policy of import substitution. It was anticipated that discouraging imports of manufactured goods through tariffs and targeted exchange rates would make the preexisting market for exports available for domestically produced consumer items and that the market would expand as workers in the new industries also became consumers. Successive ripple effects would render the process self-sustaining. The Latin American Free Trade Area (LAFTA) and the Central American Common Market were to implement the program regionally. The scenario did not materialize, although the level of industrialization did increase substantially. By the end of the 20th century, ECLAC had shifted its position away from protectionism and accepted the prevailing neoliberal doctrine of open markets.

ECLAC's headquarters is in Santiago, Chile. The membership in 2000 included 41 nations, also including Italy, Spain, and Portugal, and seven non-independent associate members from the Caribbean. The organization's secretary-general is appointed by the UN Secretary-General. In 1998 Secretary-General ANNAN appointed José Antonio Ocampo from Colombia to the post. Meetings of ECLAC occur every two years with a Committee of the Whole meeting between sessions. The 28th session was held in Mexico City in April 2000; the next meeting was scheduled for Brazil in 2002.

In 1995 ECLAC's executive secretary noted that the organization's work "had become part of the intellectual heritage of LATIN AMERICA;" that it had changed "the economic theories in vogue in the world . . . adapting them to the actual conditions of Latin America." The following year its member countries expanded ECLAC's mission to include provision of expert analysis of the development process. In addition to the full commission sessions, ECLAC does much of this work through the Latin American and Caribbean Institute for Economic and Social Planning, and the Latin American Demographic Centre. These organs provide research, training, and policy advice to member states. The organization has also established the following subsidiary bodies: the Central American Economic Co-operation Committee, the Committee of High-Level Government Experts from developing member countries for analysis of the achievement of the International Development Strategy in the Latin American region, the Caribbean Development and Co-operation Committee, the Conference on the Integration of WOMEN into the Economic and Social Development of Latin America and the Caribbean, and the Regional Council for Planning.

See also REGIONAL DEVELOPMENT BANKS, REGIONAL COMMISSIONS OF THE ECONOMIC AND SOCIAL COUNCIL.

Further Reading: Cayuela, Jose. *ECLAC 40 Years (1948–1988)*. Santiago, Chile: Economic Commission for Latin America and the Caribbean, 1988. Rosenthal, Gert. "The United Nations and ECLAC at the Half-Century Mark." *CEPAL Review*, no. 57 (December 1995): 7–15. Santa Cruz, Hernan. "The Creation of the United Nations and ECLAC." *CEPAL Review*, no. 57 (December 1995): 17–33. ECLAC website: <*www.eclac.cl/index1.html*>.

— *M. W. Bray*

Economic Commission for Western Asia

(ECWA)   *See* REGIONAL COMMISSIONS OF THE ECONOMIC AND SOCIAL COUNCIL.

Economic Community of West African States (ECOWAS)

The Treaty of Lagos established the Economic Community of West African States in May 1975. The 15 original signatories included Benin, Côte d'Ivoire, Gambia, Ghana, Guinea, Guinea-Bissau, Liberia, Mali, Mauritania, Niger, Nigeria, Senegal, SIERRA LEONE, Togo, and Upper Volta (Burkina Faso). Cape Verde joined in 1977; Mauritania withdrew its membership in 2001.

The main aim of ECOWAS is to promote regional cooperation "in all fields of economic activity, particularly industry, transport, telecommunications, energy, agriculture, natural resources, commerce, monetary and financial questions, social and cultural matters." During 1991 and 1992, member states revised the original TREATY to strengthen regional integration, in both the political and economic spheres. The revised treaty was signed in July 1993. Its main political goal has been the creation of a West African parliament to enhance regional governance, identity, and citizenship. Its main economic goal has been to create a common market and a single currency.

Institutions in ECOWAS include the Authority of Heads of States and Government that meets once a year; the Fund for Cooperation, Compensation and Development (Fund); the Executive Secretariat with representatives elected for four-year terms; the Council of Ministers with two representatives from each country; the Community Parliament; the Economic and Social Council; and the Community Court of Justice. The SECRETARIAT, located in Abuja, Nigeria, and the fund located in Lomé, Togo, are two of ECOWAS's most important governance and policy-making bodies.

There are five specialized commissions of the secretariat responsible for various sectoral activities in the region: (1) trade, customs, immigration, and monetary payments; (2) transportation, telecommunications, and energy; (3) industry, agriculture, and natural resources; (4) social and cultural affairs; and (5) administration and finance. In the area of energy, ECOWAS has planned to establish regional centers to disseminate information on alternative and renewal energy resources. In agriculture, its goal of self-sufficiency by 2000 was not realized. However, regional centers were established to provide information on seed selection and livestock, and to increase overall agricultural productivity. In the social and cultural areas, there are organizations for health, trade unions, youth, universities, WOMEN, and annual sports events.

The fund has entered into a number of agreements to promote regional economic development, integration, and external investments to the region. In 1988, the fund signed an agreement with the African Development Bank and the Islamic Development Bank to cofinance projects both for regional and nonregional entrepreneurs and microenterprises. Private investment to the region is promoted through the private regional investment bank, Ecobank Transnational Inc., located in Lomé, Togo.

The Economic Community of West African States has tried to enhance both intraregional and international cooperation. In the 1990s ECOWAS and the United Nations cooperated on CONFLICT RESOLUTION and management in Liberia, Guinea-Bissau, and Sierra Leone. In August 1990, ECOWAS's Standing MEDIATION Committee established ECOMOG, a cease-fire monitoring group to oversee the implementation of the Abuja Agreement for Liberia. Subsequently, a joint UN-ECOWAS-Sierra Leone government coordination mechanism was established for conflict management in Sierra Leone.

ECOWAS member states agreed to two measures: a Moratorium on the Importation, Exportation, and Manufacture of Light WEAPONS in West Africa, which became effective in November 1998, and the Mechanism for Conflict Prevention, Management, Resolution, PEACEKEEPING and Security in December 1999. In March 2001, ECOWAS met with a 17-member UN Inter-Agency Mission to West Africa to explore continued cooperation in the areas of good governance, national reconciliation, arms reduction, and human security, including HIV/AIDS, malaria, refugees, displaced persons, and war-affected children.

See also ORGANIZATION OF AFRICAN UNITY.

Further Reading: Dutt, Sagarika. *Africa at the Millennium: An Agenda for Mature Development.* New York: Palgrave, 2000. Ezenwe, Uka. *ECOWAS and the Economic Integration of West Africa.* New York: St. Martin's, 1983. Senghor, Jeggan Colley. *ECOWAS: Perspectives on Treaty Revision and Reform.* Dakar: United Nations African Institute for Economic Development and Planning, 1999. Shaw, Timothy M., and Julius Emeka Okolo. *The Political Economy of Foreign Policy in ECOWAS.* New York: St. Martin's, 1994.

— *M. S. Smith*

Eden, Anthony (1897–1977)

As British foreign secretary from 1941 to 1945, Eden was a supporter of a new postwar international organization and worked with U.S. secretary of state Cordell HULL at the MOSCOW CONFERENCE OF FOREIGN MINISTERS in 1943 to persuade the Soviets to accept the general terms of the Four Power DECLARATION that had been drafted earlier at the Quebec Conference. It recognized the "necessity" of a postwar "international organization" to keep the peace. In Moscow, representatives of the great powers, including CHINA, committed themselves to forming a general international organization composed of "all peace-loving states . . . for the maintenance of international peace and security." Eden attended the founding San Francisco conference, expressing a strong desire to serve as the SECRETARY-GENERAL of the new United Nations.

In later years, however, Eden expressed skepticism about the efficacy of international organizations in thwarting AGGRESSION. As British prime minister (1955–57) he played a central role in attempting to bypass the United Nations in the ill-considered international crisis prompted by Egypt's Gamal Abdul NASSER's nationalization of the Suez Canal in 1956. Despite efforts to halt UN action against British, French, and Israeli military initiatives by the first Western use of the VETO power, pressure from the United Nations and the UNITED STATES forced the Western allies to yield their positions on the Suez Canal to the first United Nations PEACEKEEPING force in November 1956. Despite Eden's proposal that British and French troops make up the force, the UNITED NATIONS EMERGENCY FORCE (UNEF) consisted of troops from small neutral states, establishing the model for all future UN peacekeeping units during the COLD WAR.

See also SUEZ CRISIS.

Further Reading: Dutton, David. *Anthony Eden: A Life and Reputation.* New York: St. Martin's, 1997. Ostrower, Gary. *The United Nations and the United States.* New York: Twayne, 1998. Thomas, Hugh. *Suez.* New York: Harper, 1967.

— *E. M. Clauss*

Egypt   *See* ARAB-ISRAELI DISPUTE, SUEZ CRISIS.

Eighteen Nation Disarmament Committee (ENDC)

Created in 1961 as a replacement for the Ten Nation Disarmament Committee, the ENDC for the first time brought the voice of the non-aligned states into the UN DISARMAMENT debate, which to that point had been the sole preserve of the two superpowers and their closest allies. Ostensibly a subordinate committee to the United Nations DISARMAMENT COMMISSION, the ENDC was largely an independent venue for negotiations on a number of disarmament and arms control issues. Most important, it served as the institutional setting for the negotiation of the 1968 NUCLEAR NON-PROLIFERATION TREATY.

The UNITED STATES and the USSR had monopolized nuclear disarmament negotiations within the Disarmament Commission by relegating those talks to a subcommittee consisting of the two states and the United Kingdom. The subcommittee was expanded in 1959 with the addition of seven new members, but little changed, because care was taken to assure that each side could count on five votes on the committee. The additional members were Bulgaria, Czechoslovakia, Italy, Canada, Poland, Romania, and France. SECRETARY-GENERAL Dag HAMMARSKJÖLD, among others, complained on several occasions that the UN's responsibilities were being undermined by the East-West domination of arms control.

By 1961, however, the United States was interested in developing good relations with the newly independent states of the Third World. So too, Nikita Khrushchev's government in Moscow sought to appeal to the nonaligned nations. Under pressure from those states and from the GENERAL ASSEMBLY, the U.S. and USSR agreed to expand the committee to 18 nations with the superpowers as the co-chairs. The new members were Brazil, Burma, Ethiopia, India, Mexico, Nigeria, Sweden, and the United Arab Republic.

The lesser powers were concerned particularly with the problem of "horizontal" proliferation, the spread of nuclear WEAPONS to non-nuclear states. In 1959 the General Assembly passed RESOLUTION 1380, proposed by Ireland, calling upon the Ten Nation Disarmament Committee to consider "the feasibility of an international agreement . . . whereby the Powers producing nuclear weapons would refrain from handing over control of such weapons to any nation not possessing them, and whereby the Powers not possessing such weapons would refrain from manufacturing them." The ENDC became the new STRUCTURE through which the non-nuclear states initiated non-proliferation proposals. The idea of a "non-atomic club" gained credence, and that group helped clarify the necessary aspects of any successful non-proliferation treaty.

On May 25, 1962, the ENDC co-chairs placed "Measures to Prevent Further Dissemination of Nuclear Weapons" on the committee's agenda. The eight nonaligned members outlined the main principles a non-proliferation TREATY should have, among them an agreement that it should embody an acceptable balance of mutual responsibilities and obligations for nuclear and non-nuclear states. The ENDC negotiations reached a critical point in August 1967 when the Soviet Union and the United States tendered a joint draft treaty on non-proliferation. It prohibited the transfer of nuclear weapons to non-nuclear states and barred non-nuclear signatories from obtaining them by any means. Nonaligned states on the committee, however, balked at the one-sided nature of the proposal. It created, in their view, a world of nuclear "haves" and "have nots," without placing any restrictions on the arsenals of the nuclear powers. The nonaligned committee members, led by Brazil, emerged as representatives for the prevalent views of the General Assembly majority.

Brazil and other states argued that there was no "acceptable balance of responsibilities" in the draft between nuclear and non-nuclear states. Nothing in the draft committed the United States and the Soviet Union to decreasing "vertical" proliferation, that is, the size of their already existing stockpiles. Without revision, the smaller states made clear they would not accept the treaty. The superpowers had hoped to ignore the question of vertical proliferation, since this would call for extensive deprivation of their own freedom of action in the nuclear sphere. But the need for acceptance by the non-nuclear states of the draft in order to give it any value led to a major concession. Article Six of a revised treaty was added. It required the nuclear powers "to pursue negotiations in good faith on effective measures relating to cessation of the nuclear arms race at an early date and to nuclear disarmament." Article Six, imposed by the will of the ENDC's nonaligned states, laid the basis for the next stage in arms control negotiations, the Strategic Arms Limitation Talks between Washington and Moscow.

Further Reading: Bader, William. *The United States and the Spread of Nuclear Weapons.* New York: Pegasus, 1968. Beker, Avi. *Disarmament without Order.* Westport, Conn.: Greenwood, 1985. Larson, Thomas B. *Disarmament and Soviet Policy, 1964–1968.* Englewood Cliffs, N.J.: Prentice Hall, 1969. United Nations Department of Public Information. *The United Nations and Disarmament, 1945–1965.* New York: United Nations Department of Public Information, 1967.

El Salvador

El Salvador entered the United Nations as an original member on October 24, 1945. Its participation within the organization during the UN's first decades of operations showed it to be a close ally of the UNITED STATES in the developing COLD WAR confrontations with the Soviet Union and its allies.

A brutal civil war in El Salvador escalated after 1981. The country's military, backed by the United States, worked to block an increasingly effective guerrilla movement. A military stalemate and the success of UN-brokered agreements elsewhere in Central America led to deeper UN involvement in the country. Working in concert with the Contadora Peace initiative launched in 1985, SECRETARY-GENERAL Boutros BOUTROS-GHALI backed the efforts of the "Friends of the Secretary General" to reach a negotiated settlement to the conflict. In 1989, Secretary-General Javier PÉREZ DE CUÉLLAR urged the presidents of the Central American countries to focus their efforts toward achieving a settlement. Working both directly and through representatives, the Secretary-General helped craft the San José HUMAN RIGHTS Accord in 1990 and gained acceptance from the Salvadoran government for UN observers in the country's transition from civil war to democratic elections.

Successful negotiations that ended the civil war then led to more direct UN involvement. In May 1991, a SECURITY COUNCIL RESOLUTION authorized the creation of the UN OBSERVER MISSION IN EL SALVADOR (ONUSAL). ONUSAL helped ensure the successful application of a peace agreement between the Salvadoran government and the Frente Faribundo Martí para la Liberación Nacional (FMLN). It then stationed observers throughout the country to help certify a national election. Representatives signed a final version of the peace TREATY in 1992. This treaty granted a "Peace Commission" (the National Commission for Consolidation of Peace, or COPAZ) authority over the demilitarization of the guerrilla forces and their integration into Salvadoran society and political affairs. It also established a "Truth Commission" to investigate human rights violations connected with the civil war. The treaty gave ONUSAL a cooperative role in this process. The observer mission remained in place to monitor the 1994 elections and to facilitate continuing negotiations between the two sides in the conflict. It was replaced in April 1995 with the United Nations Mission in El Salvador (MINUSAL), a small civilian contingent to provide UN GOOD OFFICES to the parties.

See also BASEL CONVENTION ON THE CONTROL OF TRANS-BOUNDARY MOVEMENTS OF HAZARDOUS WASTES AND THEIR DISPOSAL, LATIN AMERICA.

Further Reading: Johnston, Ian. *Rights and Reconciliation: UN Strategies in El Salvador.* Boulder, Colo.: Lynn Rienner, 1995. Roberts, Adam, and Benedict Kingsbury, eds. *United Nations, Divided World: The UN's Roles in International Relations.* Oxford: Clarendon Press, 1993. Tulchin, Joseph, ed. *Is There a Transition to Democracy in El Salvador?* Boulder, Colo.: Lynn Rienner, 1992.

— *D. K. Lewis*

emergency special sessions of the General Assembly

Under the terms of the 1950 UNITING FOR PEACE RESOLUTION, when the UN SECURITY COUNCIL is unable to act on a threat to peace and security because of a lack of unanimity among the PERMANENT MEMBERS, nine members of the Council may request the convocation of an emergency SPE-

CIAL SESSION of the GENERAL ASSEMBLY. The RESOLUTION urged states to keep representatives in New York City so that the session could be convened within 24 hours. The Assembly could then discuss the issue and make recommendations for restoring peace, including a recommendation that armed force be used. The UNITED STATES proposed the procedure during the KOREAN WAR when it appeared that vetoes by the Soviet Union would block effective action on the Korean peninsula and in subsequent COLD WAR conflicts. While the Soviet Union protested the constitutionality of the procedure—because the CHARTER prohibits Assembly consideration of any issue involving the maintenance of peace and security while the Security Council has it on its agenda—the USSR subsequently employed the Uniting for Peace Resolution to convene emergency special sessions in 1956 and 1967, respectively. France also objected to any ENFORCEMENT MEASURES or expenses associated with them undertaken by the United Nations as a product of General Assembly action. Paris argued that only the Security Council could authorize CHAPTER VII measures and require member states to honor or pay for them. Following the 1960 emergency session on the Congolese civil war, France and the Soviet Union, using these arguments, refused to pay their assessments for the Congolese PEACEKEEPING operation, precipitating a financial crisis for the United Nations. The provision for emergency special sessions of the General Assembly amounted to an informal AMENDMENT of the Charter, reflecting a need to make the United Nations a viable guarantor of peace in the midst of cold war hostility between the USSR and the United States. Between 1956 and 2000, 10 emergency special sessions convened on the following topics.

Emergency Special Session	Topic	Date of the Session
First	SUEZ CRISIS	November 1–10, 1956
Second	Hungarian Crisis	November 4–10, 1956
Third	Lebanon and Jordan	August 8–21, 1958
Fourth	CONGO Question	September 17–19, 1960
Fifth	MIDDLE EAST WAR OF 1967	June 17–September 18, 1967
Sixth	AFGHANISTAN	January 10–14, 1980
Seventh	Palestine	July 22–29, 1980; April 20–28, June 25–26, August 16–19, September 24, 1982
Eighth	NAMIBIA	September 3–14, 1981
Ninth	Occupied Arab Territories	January 29–February 5, 1982
Tenth	Occupied East Jerusalem and the Rest of the Occupied Palestinian Territories	April 24–25, July 15, November 13, 1997; March 17, 1998; February 5, 8 and 9, 1999; October 18–20, 2000

enforcement measures

The United Nations CHARTER establishes a COLLECTIVE SECURITY system, and lodges in the SECURITY COUNCIL the authority to take any action that might be necessary to maintain international peace and security. All members are obligated to carry out the Council's decisions when it imposes military or nonmilitary measures to halt an aggressor or to restore international peace. This authority is granted under CHAPTER VII of the Charter (Articles 41 and 42). Among the nonmilitary measures the Council may take are economic SANCTIONS, the severance of diplomatic relations, and the full or partial disruption of communications between the states responsible for the breach of the peace and the outside world. If the Security Council believes these measures would be inadequate, it may enforce its decisions with military "air, land, and sea forces" of UN member states, and may also impose embargoes, blockades, or any other measures deemed necessary.

Generally the Security Council has sought to resolve international disputes by employing the more traditional diplomatic means of pacific settlement outlined in CHAPTER VI. During the COLD WAR, when a breach of the peace called for the use of Chapter VII, the Council's PERMANENT MEMBERS often deadlocked, sometimes leading to no action being taken, the use of the UNITING FOR PEACE RESOLUTION to allow the GENERAL ASSEMBLY to make a recommendation for action, or the ad hoc creation of PEACEKEEPING efforts—referred to as CHAPTER VI $^1/_2$ PROVISIONS. When enforcement measures were used, they were applied in a graduated manner, beginning with less threatening sanctions. Economic and military sanctions were imposed against the APARTHEID regime in South Africa during the 1970s. They remained in place until the presidential election of Nelson Mandela in 1994. At later times, and for a variety of reasons, the Council imposed economic sanctions on SIERRA LEONE, Iraq, FORMER YUGOSLAVIA, Libya, HAITI, Liberia, AFGHANISTAN, Ethiopia, Sudan, and Rwanda. The effectiveness of economic sanctions, however, was often hard to measure, and usually slow to materialize. Quite often they were insufficient to force compliance with Council mandates.

Only four times between 1945 and 2001 did the Council invoke Chapter VII to declare a threat to international peace and security, or to identify an act of AGGRESSION requiring UN members to act "by any means necessary" to restore the peace. In 1950, the Council called for the world community to repel North Korean aggression against South Korea. In 1991, the Security Council declared Iraq the aggressor and urged the liberation of Kuwait. In 1992, Council members found the instability in SOMALIA to be a threat to international peace and authorized intervention under U.S. leadership. Finally, following the September 11, 2001, terrorist attack on the World Trade Center in New York City, the UNITED STATES shepherded through the Council Resolution 1368, which declared the attacks a threat to international peace and expressed the Council's "readiness to take all necessary steps to respond to the terrorist attacks . . . and to combat all forms of TERRORISM." Based on this RESOLUTION and its inherent right to self-defense the United States mobilized a large coalition of states and launched military attacks on the suspected perpetrator, Osama bin Laden, his international network of operatives, and the Taliban government in Afghanistan that was accused of harboring him. The Resolution also required all member states to confiscate the assets of terrorist organizations, and to cooperate with the international community in the effort to end terrorism.

The end of the cold war occasioned a new interest among the permanent members of the Security Council in employing Chapter VII enforcement measures. They encouraged SECRETARY-GENERAL Boutros BOUTROS-GHALI to draft proposals on ways the Council, and the United Nations in general, might act more forcefully to maintain peace. In 1992 Boutros-Ghali submitted his report, An AGENDA FOR PEACE, in which he promoted "preventive diplomacy." He encouraged the Council to act early in order to assist "states at risk." He also urged member states to earmark military contingents for quick UN activation. While many of the Secretary-General's proposals were neglected, Council members did show an interest in authorizing particular states—such as the United States in the GULF WAR, and Australia in the EAST TIMOR secession crisis—or other organizations, for example, the North Atlantic Treaty Organization in BOSNIA, to take the lead in UN-sanctioned military endeavors.

See also APPEALS TO THE SECURITY COUNCIL, COLLECTIVE SELF-DEFENSE, EMERGENCY SPECIAL SESSIONS OF THE GENERAL ASSEMBLY, KOREAN WAR, SUSPENSION AND EXPULSION OF MEMBERS.

Further Reading: Conlon, Paul. *United Nations Sanction Management: A Case Study of the Iraq Sanctions Committee, 1990–1994.* Ardsley, N.Y.: Transnational Publishers, 2000. Freudenschuss, Helmut. "Between Unilateralism and Collective Security: Authorizations of the Use of Force by the UN Security Council." *European Journal of International Law* 5, no. 4 (1994): 492–531. Maley, William. "The UN and Afghanistan: 'Doing Its Best' or Failure of a Mission?." *Fundamentalism Reborn: Afghanistan and the Taliban.* Edited by William Maley. New York: New York University Press, 1998. Roberts, Adam, and Benedict Kingsbury, eds. *United Nations, Divided World: The UN's Roles in International Relations.* 2nd ed. New York: Oxford University Press, 2000.

environment

Nothing in the United Nations CHARTER specifically authorizes the organization to deal with global environmental issues. In 1945 the founders of the United Nations were primarily concerned with creating an institution that could maintain international peace and security. While the Char-

ter's Preamble committed UN members "to promote social progress, and better standards of life in larger freedom," and "to employ international machinery for the promotion of the economic and social advancement of all peoples," environmental issues were perceived to be matters for national governments and organizations outside the UN STRUCTURE. Yet, beginning in the 1970s the United Nations became the initiator and primary sponsor of global efforts to protect the environment from detrimental human activities, and to assure that its protection was compatible with social and economic development. Pressured by NON-GOVERNMENTAL ORGANIZATIONS (NGOs), SPECIALIZED AGENCIES, developed states, and growing scientific evidence of environmental damage, the United Nations sponsored WORLD CONFERENCES, panels of experts, the initiation of environmental CONVENTIONS, and the creation of new environmental law and concepts that came to define the international regime of environmental politics by the end of the century.

Interest by the United Nations in environmental affairs was part of the emerging "Other UN," as contrasted with the primary institutional focus on questions of war and peace. In the context of a COLD WAR that limited UN success in political and military areas, environmental policy became part of the United Nations's growing "THEMATIC DIPLOMACY," which emphasized areas of functional human activity and included, in addition to the environment, HUMAN RIGHTS, economic development, health, humanitarian assistance, the transfer of technology, and issues involving WOMEN and dependent populations.

The United Nations's active and direct participation in environmental politics began with the 1972 UNITED NATIONS CONFERENCE ON THE HUMAN ENVIRONMENT (UNCHE), held in Stockholm. Earlier meetings, sponsored by private groups and by some of the UN's specialized agencies—particularly the 1968 Biosphere Conference convened by the UNITED NATIONS EDUCATIONAL SCIENTIFIC AND CULTURAL ORGANIZATION (UNESCO)—had put pressure on the GENERAL ASSEMBLY to convene a world conference focused on natural resource conservation. Also, at the 1968 U.S.–Soviet Summit meeting in Glassboro, New Jersey, the two superpowers called for international cooperation on environmental matters as a way to promote cooperation in East-West diplomacy. Finally, growing European concerns that unrestricted development in the Third World would damage the global commons and, consequently, the quality of life in the developed world led the United Nations to accept a Swedish invitation to host the Stockholm Conference.

UNCHE focused on conservation and pollution issues, viewing the natural environment as fundamentally under threat from economic development. The conference issued the "Stockholm Declaration," outlining the environmental obligations and duties of states, and a Plan of Action with 109 recommendations. The conference documents suggested that development and environmental protection were laudable movements that unfortunately required trade-offs between the two. Furthermore, because economic development was essentially within the domestic JURISDICTION of states, protecting the environment on a global scale constituted an assault on the principle of state SOVEREIGNTY. The Stockholm meeting attempted to balance the conflicting interests in the final DECLARATION. Principle 21 asserted that "States have . . . a sovereign right to exploit their own resources pursuant to their own environmental policies . . . [States have] the responsibility to ensure that activities within their jurisdiction or control do not cause damage to the environment of other States, or of areas beyond the limits of national jurisdiction."

The most important institutional outcome of the meeting was the establishment of a new environmental agency. In December 1972 the General Assembly created the UNITED NATIONS ENVIRONMENT PROGRAMME (UNEP). Its expenses were to be paid through a voluntary fund, and its headquarters was located in Nairobi, Kenya, to ease concerns in the developing world that the UN body might represent developed states' desires to limit development policies. During its first decade of activity UNEP became an effective and visible actor in promoting environmental awareness and in attracting major contributions from the industrialized states to international environmental projects. It formed partnerships with the WORLD BANK and the UNITED NATIONS DEVELOPMENT PROGRAMME (UNDP).

On the 10th anniversary of the Stockholm Conference, 70 government representatives met in Nairobi to assess the amount of progress that had been made on environmental matters. They concluded that a reinvigorated international effort was needed, and they called on the General Assembly to initiate a new study of the relationship between the environment and development. In 1983 the Assembly established the WORLD COMMISSION ON ENVIRONMENT AND DEVELOPMENT (WCED). SECRETARY-GENERAL Javier PÉREZ DE CUÉLLAR appointed Norwegian prime minister Gro Harlem BRUNDTLAND as the commission's chairperson. The Secretary-General charged the commission with establishing "a global agenda for change."

The 21-member commission, and its panel of experts, held open hearings and interviewed thousands of individuals and groups over a two-year period. The commission's final report (1987), entitled OUR COMMON FUTURE, proved to be one of the most widely read and influential UN publications. The report recognized the direct links between development and the environment. It called for SUSTAINABLE DEVELOPMENT, defined as "development that meets the needs of the present without compromising the ability of future generations to meet their own needs." Sustainable development became the bedrock objective for all future UN efforts to address global environmental challenges. While imprecisely defined, "sustainable development" appealed to political leaders in states with environmental concerns because it

seemed to put a natural limit on economic development strategies. For developing countries it officially recognized for the first time the legitimate competing claims of environmental preservation and development.

Dr. Brundtland's commission called upon the United Nations to convene another world conference, this one with the expressed purpose of drafting an international convention on the rights and duties of states in terms of sustainable development. The General Assembly, in its 44th session (1989), authorized the calling of the UNITED NATIONS CONFERENCE ON ENVIRONMENT AND DEVELOPMENT (UNCED), later known as the Earth Summit. When it convened in Rio de Janeiro in 1992, it proved to be the largest, most expensive, and most widely covered UN meeting in history. National delegations from 178 countries and two-thirds of the world's heads of state attended. More than 1,400 NONGOVERNMENTAL ORGANIZATIONS (NGOs) were accredited to UNCED. The NGOs, with UN blessing, also staged a Global Forum in tandem with the conference that attracted 30,000 participants.

The field of environmental politics has provided an expanding opportunity for non-governmental organizations to be involved in UN affairs. At the Stockholm Conference more than 400 NGOs participated. Stockholm's secretary-general, Maurice Strong, also appointed to chair the subsequent Earth Summit in Rio, made sure that NGOs would have an even greater presence at the 1992 meeting. Strong believed that NGOs were critical to the formation of international public opinion and to effective implementation on the subnational level of international environmental programs.

UNCED produced three important international agreements—the RIO DECLARATION, AGENDA 21, and the STATEMENT OF FOREST PRINCIPLES—and served as the venue for the signing of the FRAMEWORK CONVENTION ON CLIMATE CHANGE (UNFCCC) and the CONVENTION ON BIOLOGICAL DIVERSITY (CBD). It also called upon the United Nations to create a new institutional body to oversee the successful implementation of sustainable development in all of its dimensions. This led to the General Assembly's establishment of the COMMISSION ON SUSTAINABLE DEVELOPMENT (CSD) in 1993. UNCED directed key UN bodies to make sustainable development a central part of their responsibilities (Chapter 38). In particular, it identified the United Nations Environment Programme, the United Nations Development Programme, the World Bank, the UNITED NATIONS CONFERENCE ON TRADE AND DEVELOPMENT (UNCTAD), the GLOBAL ENVIRONMENT FACILITY (GEF), the INTERNATIONAL DEVELOPMENT ASSOCIATION (IDA), and the REGIONAL DEVELOPMENT BANKS as the central agencies for future UN activity.

The primary documents produced by the Earth Summit attempted to balance the concerns of developed states for greater environmental protection—and their desire to avoid huge new financial responsibilities associated with the global effort—with the LESS DEVELOPED COUNTRIES' (LDCs) efforts to protect their sovereignty and pursue unrestrained national economic policies. LDCs also demanded increased international aid to cover additional costs imposed by sustainable development requirements. However, led by the UNITED STATES, which remained largely hostile to the UNCED negotiations, major powers refused to include increased environmental aid in the final conference report.

The Rio Declaration proclaimed that "human beings are at the centre of concerns for sustainable development." It recognized the right to development. The declaration gave support to the creation of international environmental law and standards. It recognized the "Polluter Pays Principle" (PPP), which required states to pay not only for pollution prevention on their territory but also for damage costs from pollution. It reaffirmed the idea, first asserted in principle 21 of the 1972 Stockholm Declaration, that states were accountable for practices that injured the environment beyond their borders. Agenda 21, an 800-page document filled with more than 1,000 specific recommendations to achieve a "comprehensive plan for global action in all areas of sustainable development," set international and national objectives, and provided programmatic suggestions on how to fulfill the objectives. The areas for action included world trade, poverty eradication, population, cities, atmospheric pollution, deforestation, drought, DESERTIFICATION, marine resource management, waste management, agriculture, biodiversity, and the transfer of technology. UNCED also issued the "Non-legally binding authoritative statement of principles for a global consensus on the management, conservation and sustainable development of all types of forests." The document fell far short of the World Convention on Forests that developed states and NGOs sought. Developing states resisted international restrictions on the use of forests. With no possibility of an agreement between developing and developed states, the Statement of Forest Principles simply called for the protection of forests, but recognized the right of states to use their forests as they wished.

The signing by 153 nations and the European Union (EU) of the United Nations Framework Convention on Climate Change, and by the EU and 155 countries of the Convention on Biological Diversity provided much of the perceived "success" of the Rio conference. Global media coverage, particularly of the climate change agreement, provided impetus for many national governments to establish domestic environmental programs and agencies. It also encouraged the General Assembly to endorse the negotiation of additional environmental conventions. The United Nations Conference on Environment and Development laid the foundation for UN activity in many fields of environmental policy. Over the succeeding decade the United Nations and its affiliated bodies sponsored environmental meetings, conventions, and implementation programs in each of the following areas:

SUSTAINABLE DEVELOPMENT

Between 1994 and 1996 the Commission on Sustainable Development reviewed each area identified by Agenda 21, including desertification, health, toxic chemicals and hazardous waste, biodiversity, human settlements, the atmosphere, and oceans and seas. It also held sessions on the overlapping issues of trade and the environment, poverty, demographic pressures on the environment, financial resources and mechanisms, and the transfer of environmentally sound technology to the underdeveloped world. In 1997 the Earth+5 SPECIAL SESSION OF THE GENERAL ASSEMBLY directed CSD to monitor carefully a few major identified provisions of Agenda 21. Earth+5 also directed the commission to begin work on the identification of "Indicators of Sustainable Development" that could be used to measure progress toward the goals of the Rio Declaration.

While the UN created the commission specifically to oversee sustainable development goals laid out at the Earth Summit, it proved to be UNEP that took the lead in promoting sustainable development projects. In 1997 UNEP approved the Nairobi Declaration, which declared it the "principal United Nations body in the field of environment." In the 1990s UNEP was assigned responsibility for providing SECRETARIAT, scientific, and technical assistance for several environmental agreements and mechanisms. The success of UNEP could be credited in significant part to its development of scientific and technical expertise, which it employed in a number of successful monitoring and information-sharing programs. For example, through its *Infoterra* network it provided a national environmental information service to more than 170 states.

In January 1999 Secretary-General Kofi ANNAN proposed a GLOBAL COMPACT between the United Nations and multinational corporations to fulfill the environmental principles established in the Rio Declaration. In particular, he called upon those companies joining the compact to support sustainable development's precautionary approach to environmental challenges, and to undertake greater diffusion of environmentally friendly technologies to the developing world. Within a year more than 50 transnational corporations had signed the compact. Secretary-General Annan wrote in 1998 that the United Nations was "focusing on the importance of sustainability—on sustainable development—in all aspects of [its] work, [even] including peace and security."

ATMOSPHERE AND CLIMATE CHANGE

The WORLD METEOROLOGICAL ORGANIZATION (WMO) and the United Nations Environment Programme played the central roles in the 1980s and 1990s in the world's efforts to halt the interrelated problems of ozone layer depletion and global warming. Under their sponsorship the VIENNA CONVENTION FOR THE PROTECTION OF THE OZONE LAYER was adopted in 1985. The convention, ratified by 173 states as of May 2000, made a general commitment to protect the ozone layer by reducing ozone-depleting chemical compounds from the atmosphere. It was amended several times at subsequent Meetings of the Parties (MOPs). The most important was the MONTREAL PROTOCOL in 1987, which set specific production and consumption limits on refrigerant and industrial substances known as CFCs.

Ozone depletion and its recovery are closely associated with climate change. In the late 1980s UNEP and WMO launched two important initiatives to deal with the deleterious aspects of the latter. The first was the creation of the INTERGOVERNMENTAL PANEL ON CLIMATE CHANGE (IPCC) in 1988, made up of more than 1,000 scientists, policy makers, legal experts, and climate specialists from more than 60 nations. The two organizations hoped the IPCC would bring new attention to the growing phenomenon and would produce momentum toward a new international convention. The work of the panel led to the United Nations Framework Convention on Climate Change. The second was the promotion of a World Climate Conference that convened in November 1990, setting the stage for several climate agreements during the decade. The most important was the KYOTO PROTOCOL to the UNFCCC. Adopted in 1997 the PROTOCOL set specific greenhouse gas (GHG) emission targets for industrialized states to be achieved by 2012. The goal was to lower overall emissions of carbon dioxide, nitrous oxide, methane, hydrofluorocarbons, perfluorocarbons, and sulphur hexafluoride to at least 5 percent below 1990 levels. Kyoto's provisions were specifically directed at the industrialized states, which produced the overwhelming bulk of effluents responsible both for global warming and ozone depletion. Post-Kyoto meetings were aimed at developing operational plans for implementing the Protocol, but the unwillingness of the United States and several other major states to ratify the agreement kept the Protocol from entering into force.

MARINE RESOURCES AND WATER POLLUTION

The Stockholm Declaration gave special emphasis to protecting the marine environment. Consequently, its successor organization, the United Nations Environment Programme, developed a number of programs to improve marine fish stocks, ocean and freshwater bodies, and transboundary waterways. Under UNEP auspices, efforts to protect the world's oceans resulted in a number of regional seas agreements. Nine were signed in the 1970s, beginning with an agreement among countries bordering the Mediterranean. Six more agreements were signed in the 1980s covering many of the regional seas of the world. In addition to UNEP, the ECONOMIC COMMISSION FOR EUROPE (ECE) played a critical role in developing the 1992 Convention on the Protection and Use of Transboundary Watercourses and International Lakes.

Central to the UN's activity to protect the ocean environment was the LAW OF THE SEA Convention, adopted in 1982. By the mid-20th century, various pressures on the oceans brought about several challenges to the long-standing custom of "freedom of the seas." Specifically, concerns over exploitation of global fish stocks by expanded distant fishing fleets, the realization that offshore areas contained significant supplies of natural resources (especially oil and natural gas), and increased potential for damage to the marine environment from various sources (especially increased oil tanker traffic) contributed to the realization that there was a need for modification of the existing law of the sea. Part XII of the convention dealt specifically with the protection of the marine environment. It was augmented in 1995 with an Agreement for the Implementation of the Provisions of the UNCLOS (UNITED NATIONS CONFERENCE ON THE LAW OF THE SEA) of December 10, 1982, Relating to the Conservation and Management of Straddling Fish Stocks and Highly Migratory Fish Stocks. The effort to build on the Law of the Sea Convention in order to enhance marine protection was largely driven by the MEMBERSHIP of the Commission on Sustainable Development.

BIODIVERSITY AND NATURAL RESOURCES

Pressed to do so by many environmental NGOs, UNEP sponsored negotiations beginning in 1987 on a convention to protect biological diversity. Those negotiations resulted in the Convention on Biological Diversity being opened for signature at the 1992 Earth Summit. The convention, while couched in general terms, sought to conserve biodiversity and to provide for the fair and equitable sharing of genetic resources and technology. Under the terms of the convention nations were required to make national inventories of biodiversity, develop national plans for the sustainable use of biodiversity, restore degraded ecosystems, and regulate the release of genetically modified organisms. The convention established a Conference of the Parties (COP) to implement and enhance the PACT through subsequent negotiations. By 2000, 176 nations had ratified the agreement and joined the COP.

In addition to UNEP, the United Nations Conference on Trade and Development (UNCTAD) played an important role in promoting the CBD. At the 1996 conference of the CBD signatories, UNCTAD launched its "Biotrade Initiative," meant to stimulate trade and investment in biological resources in the developing world. UNCTAD established Biotrade country programs to help governments identify opportunities for sustainable resource development. Based on a 1997 Memorandum of Understanding between the Convention on Biological Diversity Secretariat and UNCTAD, the two organs identified partnerships that could be developed among governments, NGOs, and international agencies that had the potential to turn the protection of biodiversity into a development asset for LDCs.

DEFORESTATION AND DESERTIFICATION

While there often has been a conflict between economic development and environmental protection, one area where the two reenforced each other was the slowing of land degradation. In Africa the steady growth of the Sahara Desert has diminished arable land and, thus, undercut agricultural production and lowered the standard of living. According to a 2000 FOOD AND AGRICULTURE ORGANIZATION (FAO) report, 44 percent of sub-Saharan Africa was at high risk of devastating drought. Led by states in the Sahel region during the 1980s, African nations pressed for international action. The 1992 Earth Summit recommended that the United Nations create a negotiating committee to draft a convention on the problem of desertification. The product of the committee's work was the CONVENTION TO COMBAT DESERTIFICATION (CCD), which was opened for signature in Paris in October 1994. The TREATY entered into force in December 1996 following ratification by 50 states. The CCD established its secretariat headquarters in Bonn, Germany, in 1999. Activities recommended by the convention required extensive new funding, which proved difficult to raise. The Conference of Parties, which directed the work of the convention, set up a "Global Mechanism" in conjunction with the INTERNATIONAL FUND FOR AGRICULTURAL DEVELOPMENT (IFAD) in Rome to seek funds and channel them into desertification projects. Major goals of these projects included efforts to reduce poverty in arid and semi-arid areas in the belief that poverty led to agricultural practices that exacerbated desertification.

At the time of the Rio meeting, the positive connections between environmentally sound policies concerning forests and economic development in the underdeveloped world were not as clear. Industrialized states had become concerned by reports of significant damage to the rain forests and to tropical stands of timber as the result of land clearing, the sale of mahogany and other precious lumber, and development practices that threatened this part of the global commons. While deforestation produced land degradation, often in the form of erosion, LDCs argued that this was a necessary practice if, first, land were going to be made available for agricultural and industrial development, and, second, if forest products were going to comprise a part of the nation's export production. Led by Brazil and INDONESIA, developing states not only blocked a convention on forests in 1992 but subsequently kept any consensus from emerging on how to meet Agenda 21's call for the protection of forested terrain. In May 1999 the International Forum on Forests met in Geneva and discussed the incentives created by the Kyoto Protocol's "sinks" provisions, which would reward states for planting and restoring forests. The forum hoped to establish a funding mechanism to emulate Kyoto's incentives, but no agreement was reached.

FINANCING

At the conclusion of UNCED the conference secretariat estimated that $125 billion in foreign assistance to developing countries would be needed to implement all of the recommendations in Agenda 21. This was nearly 10 times the 1992 level of global aid. Yet no large contributions to a "Green Fund" were made at the conference by the major industrialized states. One of the reasons that LDCs urged the creation of the Commission on Sustainable Development was their hope that the new UN body could be used to encourage greater financial aid from the donor states. When it became clear that the rich nations were not going to give any significant new funds to implement Agenda 21, and that the CSD could not raise the sums needed, the world community fell back on using the World Bank's GLOBAL ENVIRONMENT FACILITY (GEF) as an interim mechanism.

In 1990 the World Bank set up the Global Environment Facility to meet the Brundtland Commission's concerns about insufficient international financing of environmentally friendly development projects. The bank provided $1.4 billion in initial funding for projects focused on biodiversity, global warming, ocean pollution, and ozone depletion. Following the Earth Summit the agency was designated as the financial mechanism for the implementation of both the Convention on Biological Diversity and the United Nations Framework Convention on Climate Change.

As of December 2000, the facility included 167 member states and was based in Washington, D.C. GEF established 12 operational programs, ranging from plans to protect biodiversity to efforts to lower long-term costs associated with low greenhouse gas emitting energy technologies. Between 1991 and 1999 GEF provided more than $2 billion in grants, as well as $7 billion in co-financing. In developing funding projects, GEF worked closely with the United Nations Environment Programme, the United Nations Development Programme, the WORLD TRADE ORGANIZATION, and UNCTAD.

See also COMMITTEE OF INTERNATIONAL DEVELOPMENT INSTITUTIONS ON THE ENVIRONMENT, REGIONAL DEVELOPMENT BANKS.

Further Reading: Chasek, Pamela S. *The Global Environment in the Twenty-first Century: Prospects for International Cooperation.* New York: United Nations University Press, 2000. Elliott, Lorraine. *The Global Politics of the Environment.* New York: New York University Press, 1998. Victor, David G., Kal Raustiala, and Eugene B. Skolnikoff. *The Implementation and Effectiveness of International Environmental Commitments: Theory and Practice.* Cambridge, Mass.: MIT Press, 1998. Werksman, Jacob. *Greening International Institutions.* London: Earthscan Publications, 1996. World Commission on Environment and Development. *Our Common Future.* New York: Oxford University Press, 1987. United Nations Environment Programme website: <www.unep.org>. UNFCCC and Kyoto Protocol website: <www.unfccc.de/>. Commission on Sustainable Development website: <www.un.org/esa/sustdev/index.html>.

Executive Committee on Economic and Social Affairs   *See* DEPARTMENT OF ECONOMIC AND SOCIAL AFFAIRS.

Expanded Program of Technical Assistance (EPTA)

U.S. president Harry S. Truman proposed in his 1949 inaugural address a new American program of economic assistance under the aegis of Article 56 of the UN CHARTER. Responding to this initiative, the GENERAL ASSEMBLY created the Expanded Program of Technical Assistance in November of that year. Based on a U.S. proposal, EPTA was placed under the JURISDICTION of the UN's ECONOMIC AND SOCIAL COUNCIL (ECOSOC). It commenced operations in 1950 as the UN's single largest program, with $20 million contributed by 54 nations. The UNITED STATES initially provided 60 percent of the agency's budget. By 1964, the last year of EPTA's existence, pledges from 108 NATION-STATES brought its budget to $50 million.

EPTA was made up of "participating organizations," which included the United Nations itself, the FOOD AND AGRICULTURE ORGANIZATION (FAO), the INTERNATIONAL LABOUR ORGANIZATION (ILO), the WORLD HEALTH ORGANIZATION (WHO), the INTERNATIONAL CIVIL AVIATION ORGANIZATION (ICAO), the UNIVERSAL POSTAL UNION (UPU), the INTERNATIONAL ATOMIC ENERGY AGENCY (IAEA), the UNITED NATIONS EDUCATIONAL, SCIENTIFIC AND CULTURAL ORGANIZATION (UNESCO), the WORLD METEOROLOGICAL ORGANIZATION (WMO), the INTERNATIONAL TELECOMMUNICATION UNION (ITU), and the INTERNATIONAL MARITIME ORGANIZATION (IMO). These SPECIALIZED AGENCIES were represented on EPTA's Technical Assistance Board. In an effort to limit ideological controversy over its work, the board met in private, debated possible funding projects, and then submitted the list as a package for an up or down vote. The Expanded Program provided technical training for people in the Third World. It also sponsored experts who could contribute development advice in LESS DEVELOPED COUNTRIES. Since it did not make capital grants or loans, developing countries often criticized EPTA for constituting a limited effort by the developed world. It was merged with the SPECIAL UNITED NATIONS FUND FOR ECONOMIC DEVELOPMENT (SUNFED) in 1965 to form the UNITED NATIONS DEVELOPMENT PROGRAMME (UNDP).

See also POINT FOUR PROGRAM.

Further Reading: Riggs, Robert E., and Jack C. Plano. *The United Nations. International Organization and World Politics.* Pacific Grove, Calif.: Brooks/Cole Publishing Company, 1988. Stoessinger, John G. *The United Nations and the Superpowers: China, Russia, and America.* 4th ed. New York: Random House, 1977.

expulsion from the United Nations   *See* SUSPENSION AND EXPULSION OF MEMBERS.

F

Fifth Committee of the General Assembly

The Fifth Committee of the GENERAL ASSEMBLY, one of its six main committees, considers an agenda relating to the budgetary and administrative matters of the United Nations. Like all General Assembly main committees, it consists of representatives of every member state, each with an equal vote. Its function is to consider and negotiate draft RESOLUTIONS before they are placed before the full General Assembly.

Budgetary matters are highly specialized and detailed, requiring expert representatives. The Fifth Committee functions by consensus, adopting all measures in this manner. It addresses the financing of the various UN bodies, and each year spends extensive time dealing with lengthy reports on the Regular, PEACEKEEPING, and PROGRAMME BUDGETS of the United Nations. It examines and approves the institution's financial audits, prepared by the UN Board of Auditors, and its procurement procedures. It also considers resolutions concerning the financing of all peacekeeping missions, programme planning, and international WAR CRIMES TRIBUNALS. In its deliberations, the committee depends heavily on the oral and written reports of the ADVISORY COMMITTEE ON ADMINISTRATIVE AND BUDGETARY QUESTIONS (ACABQ), which is one of the two standing committees of the General Assembly.

Since the United Nations and its bodies are dependent on contributions from member states, the Fifth Committee has the responsibility of recommending to the General Assembly the SCALE OF ASSESSMENTS every three years, which establishes how much each state must pay to the organization. Many states have failed to pay their assessed contributions, or have been slow in doing so. Thus the committee has focused on methods to cover the continuing expenses of the United Nations, while reforming the assessment procedure. The committee also makes recommendations to the General Assembly on the appointment of individuals to fill vacancies on the COMMITTEE ON CONTRIBUTIONS, the ACABQ, the Board of Auditors, the United Nations ADMINISTRATIVE TRIBUNAL, the International Civil Service Commission, and the Staff Pension Committee.

See also COMMITTEE SYSTEM OF THE GENERAL ASSEMBLY, STRUCTURE OF THE UNITED NATIONS.

Further Reading: Fifth Committee website: <www.un.org/ga/fifth/>.

— *K. J. Grieb*

financing the United Nations   *See* BUDGET, SCALE OF ASSESSMENTS.

First Committee of the General Assembly

The First Committee is one of the six main committees that present RESOLUTIONS to the GENERAL ASSEMBLY (GA) for final approval or rejection. Each of these committees consists of equal representation from all member states of the United Nations. The First Committee was known originally as the Political and Security Committee. However, the committee, quickly overwhelmed by the range of issues assigned to it, came to focus its work on the field of DISARMAMENT. Given the importance of disarmament and, in particular, issues of nuclear arms reduction, the General Assembly decided in the wake of the 1978 SPECIAL SESSION on Disarmament that the First Committee should concentrate on this topic. Political issues were shunted to the SPECIAL POLITICAL COMMITTEE, and subsequently the title of the First Committee was changed to "Disarmament and International Security."

Debates about disarmament were highly contentious during the COLD WAR and particularly in the early years of nuclear weapons development, when international diplomats were trying to work out a set of rules and agreements to deal with a new and frightening topic that threatened global survival. Key negotiations occurred among the two superpowers and the five nuclear powers (UNITED STATES, United Kingdom, Union of Soviet Socialist Republics, France, and the People's Republic of CHINA). The First Committee and the CONFERENCE OF THE COMMITTEE ON DISARMAMENT offered the only forums where the non-nuclear states could express their views and be heard by the larger world community.

The First Committee considers all disarmament related topics on the agenda of the General Assembly's regular session. Annually it adopts more than 40 resolutions dealing with the NUCLEAR NON-PROLIFERATION regime, the various proposals for regional NUCLEAR-WEAPONS-FREE ZONES, nuclear test bans, all aspects of the arms trade, chemical and BIOLOGICAL WEAPONS, and all types of WEAPONS OF MASS DESTRUCTION and conventional arms. It also considers the implementation of existing disarmament agreements and General and Complete Disarmament. At the turn of the century the committee emphasized the need for full ratification of the Comprehensive Test Ban TREATY. Beyond disarmament, the 55th session of the General Assembly (2000–01) asked the First Committee to consider the following security agenda items: development of good neighborly relations among the Balkan states, the violent disintegration of NATION-STATES, developments in telecommunications in the context of international security, confidence-building measures in central Africa, and strengthening security and cooperation in the Mediterranean region.

See also COMMITTEE SYSTEM OF THE GENERAL ASSEMBLY, STRUCTURE OF THE UNITED NATIONS.

Further Reading: First Committee website: <www.un.org/ga/55/first/>. For preceding and succeeding years, substitute the GA session number in the website URL.

— *K. J. Grieb*

First Development Decade   *See* DEVELOPMENT DECADES.

First and Third Worlds

In 1952 the French demographer Alfred Sauvy coined the expression "Third World" *(tiers monde)* to distinguish the world's poorer countries from its richer and more dominant ones. Sauvy saw the term as analogous to the "third estate," or the class of commoners in France before and during the French Revolution. In that historical case, the First Estate and the Second Estate (equivalent to the First World and SECOND WORLD of the late 20th century) consisted of the most dominant classes, such as priests and nobles.

While Third World came to refer to the economically underdeveloped countries of Asia, Africa, Oceania, and LATIN AMERICA, the "First World" signified the richer developed capitalist world, including countries such as the UNITED STATES, Canada, Western European nations, Japan, Australia, and New Zealand. Unlike the last two, most First World nations reside in the northern hemisphere, while the bulk of Third World countries are in the south. The "Second World" comprised the communist bloc, led by the Soviet Union; with the collapse of the USSR in the early 1990s, the Second World ceased to exist.

The First World typically refers to those NATION-STATES that historically were in the forefront of economic and political modernization, that is, those who benefited most from the industrial revolution. Several First World nations were also colonial powers. And, many Third World nations were those that had been colonized. While some observers prefer the terms "developed" and "developing" to denote differences, the terms First and Third World were widely used as the 20th century ended.

Within the United Nations, particularly in the GENERAL ASSEMBLY and the ECONOMIC AND SOCIAL COUNCIL, these classifications have had some procedural meaning. For example, the GROUP OF 77 was originally organized by Third World nations as a CAUCUS GROUP to promote common interests and highlight common concerns. During the COLD WAR, these nations tended to be non-aligned, refusing to join either Western alliances of the First World, such as NATO, or Soviet-inspired alliances, such as the Warsaw PACT. Within the UNITED NATIONS SYSTEM, these Third World countries often acted together as the largest bloc, frequently frustrating more powerful First World nations, who, interestingly, had been most active in initiating the United Nations in the mid-1940s. To promote their interests within UN bodies, most of the First World states joined the West European and Other States caucus group.

See also LEAST DEVELOPED COUNTRIES, LESS DEVELOPED COUNTRIES, NEW INTERNATIONAL ECONOMIC ORDER, NORTH-SOUTH RELATIONS.

Five Power Disarmament Committee   *See* DISARMAMENT.

Food and Agriculture Organization (FAO)

One of the largest SPECIALIZED AGENCIES in the UNITED NATIONS SYSTEM, the Food and Agriculture Organization is an intergovernmental organization that, as of 2001, comprised 180 member countries plus one member organization, the European Union. The FAO is located in Rome and carries a mandate to raise levels of nutrition and standards of living, aid productivity in agriculture, and enhance living conditions in rural areas of the world.

In 1943, 44 governments met in Hot Springs, Virginia, and committed themselves to setting up a permanent organization for the support of food and agricultural improvements worldwide. The first session of the FAO Conference, attended by the original 44 nations, convened in Quebec City, Canada, in 1945 to create the Food and Agriculture Organization as a UN Specialized Agency. The founding date of October 16, 1945, was observed after 1981 as WORLD FOOD DAY. In 1951, FAO headquarters moved from Washington, D.C., to Rome.

A conference of member nations governs the Food and Agriculture Organization and meets every two years to review the organization's work, approve a program of work, and determine a budget for the next two years. The conference elects a DIRECTOR-GENERAL for a six-year term, and a council, made up of 49 member nations, that acts as an interim body to direct the FAO's operations between conference meetings. Elected members of the council serve three-year terms. In 2000 Dr. Jacques Diouf of Senegal was reelected director-general for a second six-year term.

More than 3,700 staff personnel worked for the FAO by the turn of the century. The organization had five regional offices, five subregional ones, five liaison offices, and almost 80 country offices in addition to its Rome headquarters. At any given time it had about 1,800 field operations in place. Its budget was divided into a "Regular Programme" budget, which was $650 million in 2001, and a "Field Programme" budget, amounting to just under $300 million in 1999.

The FAO is active in promoting SUSTAINABLE DEVELOPMENT. It provides help to developing nations by way of a range of assistance programs; it collects, analyzes, and disseminates information about nutrition, food production, agricultural issues, and forestry and fisheries matters; and it acts as a clearinghouse for farmers, scientists, and governments in food and agriculture developments. It encourages nations to seek its advice on strategies for rural development, food security, and reducing poverty, particularly in rural areas. In 1996 the FAO hosted the WORLD FOOD SUMMIT in Rome, where 186 nations approved a DECLARATION and Plan of Action on World Food Security, outlining a set of commitments intended to achieve universal food security

and halve hunger by 2015. However, in June 2002 the FAO announced that without the commitment of an additional $24 billion annually by the world community, this goal could not be met. Nearly 600 million hungry people would remain without additional contributions.

In 1962 the organization joined with the WORLD HEALTH ORGANIZATION (WHO) to establish the FAO/WHO Codex Alimentarius (Food Code) Commission, to set international food standards. The commission seeks to protect the health of consumers and promote fair practices in the food trade by way of a set of international standards of behavior and by coordinating world food standards.

See also ADMINISTRATIVE COMMITTEE ON COORDINATION, ADMINISTRATIVE TRIBUNALS, DESERTIFICATION, EXPANDED PROGRAM OF TECHNICAL ASSISTANCE, INTER-AGENCY COMMITTEE ON SUSTAINABLE DEVELOPMENT, STATEMENT OF FOREST PRINCIPLES, WORLD FOOD PROGRAMME.

Further Reading: New Zealand Ministry of Foreign Affairs *United Nations Handbook.* Wellington, N.Z.: Ministry of Foreign Affairs and Trade, published annually. FAO website: <www.fao.org>.

former Yugoslavia

Yugoslavia emerged as a nation through the Paris Peace Conference ending World War I, realizing a long dream of Serbs to create a country for South Slav peoples. It united a mix of ethnic groups in the Balkan regions under a Serb monarch, and the country remained a monarchy until World War II. The ultimate breakup of Yugoslavia may well have been destined in 1919, and clearly the balancing act required to hold the nation together was at best difficult, at worst, monumental. During World War II, the Axis powers conquered Yugoslavia and pitted nationality against nationality. Italy occupied Kosovo and Macedonia and gave the areas to Albania, and encouraged the Albanians to display their national icons. Croat Ustache collaborated with the Nazis and waged a bitter war against both Serbs and Muslims. The largely Serb, pro-royalist Chetnik resistance waged war with both the Nazis and communist partisans, led by Marshall Josip Broz Tito and drawing from all nationalities as a class-based movement.

The success of the communists by the end of the war, and the subsequent trial and execution of Chetnik militia leader Dragoljub (Draza) Mihailovic, signaled the end of nationalist politics. Mihailovic had promised a Yugoslav kingdom led by the Serb royal family. Tito countered with the need for a federalist state under communist rule. Tito won the day politically, but the contradictions of his politics could not outlast his rule. On one hand, he called for a strong central state, consistent with the communist program. Also consistent with communism was his call for a new Yugoslav identity, and his assertion that nationalism was an ideology of capitalism. The six republics—BOSNIA and

Herzegovina, Croatia, Macedonia, Montenegro, Serbia, and Slovenia—each contained different ethnic and different religious populations, including Roman Catholics in Slovenia and Croatia, Orthodox Christians in Serbia, a plurality of Muslims in Bosnia (and a large majority of Muslim Albanians in Kosovo province). Tito insisted that workers of all nations shared a common bond, and therefore brotherhood and unity were the keys to the state. But he also provided for governments at the republic level, and he rotated key positions within the state to placate the different nationalities. The Tito-led Yugoslav postwar government entered the United Nations as an original member on October 24, 1945. Tito's personality was strong enough to hold this contradiction together for many years, but upon his death, the foundation was shaken considerably. After his death in 1980, the call was "After Tito, Tito," but the stage was set for the breakup of the country.

The course of the breakup was set as the COLD WAR was ending, at the height of Mikhail Gorbachev's perestroika and glasnost in 1987. The rise of Slobodan Milosevic within the Serb Republic in Yugoslavia signaled an end of Tito's dream of a multiethnic socialist state. Milosevic's speech to a group of Serbs in Kosovo on April 24, 1987, in which he declared to the Serbian minority of the province that "no one should dare beat you," vaulted the nationalist to the forefront of Yugoslav politics, marshaled the ouster of then-president Ivan Stambolic, and sparked the violence that finally tore the country apart.

By the time that Milosevic made his famous speech in Kosovo, tensions in every republic had risen. The federal government seized on Milosevic's stirring of Serb emotions to remove Kosovo's autonomy. Kosovo occupied a unique place in Yugoslavia because historically it was a part of Serbia. The battle of Kosovo in 1389 marked the foremost political date on the Serb calendar. But Kosovo was predominantly Albanian. The abolition of Kosovar autonomy signaled the other republics that Serbia intended to use the federal government as a means to dominate Yugoslavia.

Following Tito's death in 1980 the Yugoslav federal presidency became a collective of the heads of the different republics, each taking a turn in the presidential chair. In spring 1991 the Serb president, Borisav Jovic, refused to step down in order to allow the Croat Stipe Mesic to hold the presidency as scheduled. Because Serbia controlled four of the eight votes in the collective presidency (Kosovo, Montenegro, and Vojvodina were controlled by Milosevic allies),

UNPROFOR ambulances in Croatia, 1992 (UN PHOTO 159206/S. WHITEHOUSE)

the vote to seat Mesic was deadlocked and Jovic was granted an additional term. This was, in essence, a Serb coup d'état, and on May 19, 1991, Croatia first voted for independence from Yugoslavia. Despite intense lobbying from both the European Union and the UNITED STATES, Croatia and Slovenia carried through with their DECLARATIONS of independence. Milosevic responded with force and "ethnic cleansing" in Serb-dominated parts of Croatia.

The first fighting took place in Slovenia, which had a very small percentage of Serbs. To placate Yugoslavia's largest ethnic group, Tito had allowed Serbs to dominate the officer corps of the Yugoslav National Army (JNA), and by 1991 Serbs represented the dominant group in the army. As the country verged on collapse, the strongest pro-unity sentiment was in the army. Milosevic used this to his advantage as he shifted from a policy of Serb-dominated unity of Yugoslavia to one of disintegration but with the largest "rump" state remaining. At first, the JNA attacked Slovenia to maintain the state's unity, but as the war progressed badly for the JNA, Milosevic quickly withdrew the army and prepared to unite all Serbs in the rump state. Slovenia gained its independence by the time the JNA withdrew on July 18, 1991.

Croats and Serbs had been bitter enemies in World War II. Croat Ustache militia had, with the help of the German army, rounded up Serbs and placed them in the Jasenovac concentration camp. This history served as the backdrop for the violence of the war, in which the JNA forcibly resettled (ethnically cleansed) Croats out of the Krajina region of Croatia and united that area with the rump state. Croatian militia responded by driving Serb farmers off their land. By December 1991, Croatia gained international recognition but lost about one-third of its prewar territory. On May 22, 1992, both Slovenia and Croatia became members of the United Nations. The low-level guerrilla war that ensued claimed countless lives, and, by May 1995, most of the Krajina territory was under Croatian control.

The hope for Western unity on policy toward Yugoslavia disintegrated in 1991. The United States and most of its European allies worked to hold Yugoslavia together as a loosely bound democracy. Involved in the war with Iraq, the United States left the matter to European resolution, and the European Union sought United Nations action, largely of a humanitarian character. It was Germany, however, that first broke ranks with the Western effort to maintain the federal Yugoslav state. Faced with massive Serbian HUMAN RIGHTS violations in Slovenia and Croatia, and little evidence that international efforts were succeeding, the government of Chancellor Helmut Kohl announced that it would support independence for the two republics. That Germany was leading the recognition charge only further fueled Serb suspicions about the European Union's intentions. In December, German foreign minister Hans Dietrich Genscher announced to the European Union that, if there was no unified policy about how and when to recognize the new states, Germany would

act unilaterally. On December 17, the European Union rushed into place a policy of recognition, and the key component was that any republic wishing independence had to state that intention by December 24, 1991. With a timetable set by the European Union, Croatia and Slovenia immediately confirmed their intention to become independent, and Bosnia, under the leadership of Alija Izetbegovic, made clear its intention to hold a referendum on independence in the spring. The European Union recognized Slovenia and Croatia, while the United States withheld recognition.

The UN's initial involvement came in September 1991, as the SECURITY COUNCIL imposed an arms embargo on Yugoslavia. The SECRETARY-GENERAL then appointed a personal envoy, former U.S. secretary of state Cyrus Vance (replaced later by Thorvald Stoltenberg) to coordinate UN cooperation with European Union peace efforts, led by veteran British diplomat and politician Lord Owen. The Vance-Owen Plan concentrated on finding a solution to the brewing Bosnian crisis. In the end they recommended the cantonization of Bosnia, dividing the republic among Bosnian Muslim, Bosnian Serb, and Bosnian Croatian communities. None of the parties was willing to accept the proposed subdivisions, and the mission failed. In 1993 the Security Council created the INTERNATIONAL CRIMINAL TRIBUNAL FOR THE FORMER YUGOSLAVIA (ICTY) as the first institution of international criminal prosecution since the end of World War II. The ICTY issued its first indictment on November 11, 1994. It cited Dragan Nikolic, a Bosnian Serb who was alleged to have been the commander of a small prison camp in eastern Bosnia.

Bosnia proved to be the battleground for the most brutal fighting and the most violent war crimes. Bosnia and Herzegovina declared independence in March 1992 and also became a member of the United Nations on May 22, 1992. Because Bosnia was an ethnically mixed republic, the principle that all Serbs should live in a rump Yugoslavia was considerably more difficult to achieve than in Krajina. Muslim populations were removed and driven to the smaller center of the Republic as the Serb militias moved to ethnically cleanse areas and make them majority Serb. The Serb militias, led by General Ratko Mladic, killed Muslim men, WOMEN, and children, carried out a systematic campaign of rape and terror, and created death and detention centers at Omarska, Trnopolje, and Manjaca. When images of these camps were displayed in Western media centers, it reminded the international community of Nazi concentration camps. Western governments were aware of the camps in April 1992, and the press publicized them in July, raising the demand for justice to a fever pitch.

UN efforts proved unsuccessful in attempting to end the violence. The North Atlantic Treaty Organization (NATO) also proved incapable of a consensus on military measures that would halt the Serbian attacks. Throughout 1992 and 1993, Bosnian calls for stronger action were met with international indifference, and the Serb violence continued. Bosnian Croats joined their Pale counterparts in declaring an independent state in southwestern Bosnia, and the nation threatened to break up along ethnic and religious lines. A PEACEKEEPING force, the United Nations Protection Force (UNPROFOR), established by the Security Council in early 1992, was sent to Yugoslavia, but proved ineffective. The Muslim populations moved from the countryside to UNPROFOR "protected areas" or safe havens in Mostar, Gorazde, Srebrenica, and elsewhere, believing in the UN promise of protection, only to find the peacekeepers unable to fight off the Serb militias. At Srebrenica, Mladic's forces rounded up men and boys, marched them out of the town as UN peacekeepers were held hostage, and summarily executed the civilians in the surrounding fields.

After a brutal mortar attack on the marketplace in Sarajevo, NATO bombed Serb positions around the capital in August 1995. Coupled with a successful Croatian offensive that reclaimed large territories held by the Serbs, the NATO action forced Milosevic to the bargaining table. Invited by U.S. president Bill Clinton to Dayton, Ohio, the leaders of Serbia, Croatia, and Bosnia hammered out an agreement. The Bosnian war ended with negotiation of the DAYTON PEACE ACCORDS, which provided that the United Nations monitor the agreement through the Implementation Force (IFOR) made up of NATO troops, to be replaced by the Stabilization Force (SFOR). In October 2001 the parliament of the Bosnian Serb enclave approved the arrest of individuals under indictment by the international tribunal in The Hague.

Milosevic, constitutionally banned from an additional term as president of Serbia, manipulated an election in July 1997 to have himself elected president of Yugoslavia, by then made up only of the former republics of Serbia and Montenegro, as well as, presumably, Kosovo. He then moved to crush the ethnic Albanian drive for independence in Kosovo. Fighting between Serbia's JNA and the Kosovo Liberation Army (KLA) reached fever pitch in 1999 with thousands of Kosovar refugees forced to flee to the Albanian mountains and to Macedonia. When a peace proposal (arranged by Richard Holbrooke, U.S. PERMANENT REPRESENTATIVE to the United Nations) could not be negotiated between the two sides, NATO, citing UN RESOLUTIONS empowering it to promote peace in the region and protect civilian victims from ethnic cleansing, bombed Yugoslav targets in both Kosovo and Serbia, beginning on March 25, 1999. Milosevic accepted a UN-approved peace agreement on June 3. By then, according to the UN HIGH COMMISSIONER FOR REFUGEES, at least 850,000 people had been displaced from their homes in Kosovo. The final settlement called for a UN force—called the Kosovo Force (KFOR)—to monitor that peace.

Tensions ran high in Macedonia as well, a former Yugoslav republic that had declared its independence and become a UN member in 1992. By summer 2001, Macedonia faced a potential civil war between its majority of Macedonians and minority Muslim Albanians. A NATO/European Union negotiated settlement concluded in the late summer called for an end to conflict and internal reforms to allow more equitable representation in government for Albanian Macedonians. By the agreement, the United Nations was to join with troops from NATO, largely veterans of KFOR, to monitor the DISARMAMENT of all sides.

Earlier, in September 2000, Vojislav Kostunica, a Serb reformer, was elected president of Yugoslavia, finally ending the reign of Milosevic, who in 2001 was arrested and handed over to the UN's International Criminal Tribunal for the Former Yugoslavia, in The Hague, to be tried for war crimes. Kostunica committed his government to internal democracy and to resolving tensions in Kosovo peacefully. Yugoslavia, which had not been allowed automatically to accede to the UN MEMBERSHIP of the defunct Yugoslav Socialist Republic, was admitted to membership on November 1, 2000. The arms embargo imposed in March 1998 was lifted by the Security Council on September 10, 2001, ending all international SANCTIONS on the regime. In March 2002, leaders from the two remaining republics of the former Yugoslavia signed a PACT creating a weak confederation to be called Serbia and Montenegro. By thus abandoning the name Yugoslavia, the rump confederation, if approved by parliaments of both republics, would officially end the eight decade long attempt to create a unification of south Slavs.

See also SUSPENSION AND EXPULSION OF MEMBERS, UNITED NATIONS INTERIM ADMINISTRATION MISSION TO KOSOVO, UNITED NATIONS MISSION IN BOSNIA AND HERZEGOVINA, UNITED NATIONS PREVENTIVE DEPLOYMENT FORCE IN THE FORMER YUGOSLAV REPUBLIC OF MACEDONIA, UNITED NATIONS SPECIAL COMMITTEE ON THE BALKANS, WAR CRIMES TRIBUNALS.

Further Reading: Holbrooke, Richard. *To End a War.* New York: Random House, 1998. Meier, Viktor. *Yugoslavia: A History of Its Demise.* London: Routledge Books, 1999. Rogel, Carole. *The Breakup of Yugoslavia and the War in Bosnia.* Westport, Conn.: Greenwood Press, 1998. Silber, Laura, and Allan Little. *Yugoslavia: Death of a Nation.* New York: Penguin Books, 1995. Udovicki, Jasminka, and James Ridgeway; eds. *Burn This House: The Making and Unmaking of Yugoslavia.* Revised and expanded. Durham, N.C.: Duke University Press, 2000.

— *D. J. Becker*

"Four Policemen" proposal

U.S. president Franklin ROOSEVELT first used this term in reference to the four major powers that initially had signed the DECLARATION BY UNITED NATIONS on January 1, 1942. Following the UNITED STATES, the United Kingdom, CHINA, and the Soviet Union, representatives of 22 other nations at war with the Axis powers signed the document the next day in Washington, D.C. This distinction between great and small nations soon became a fundamental axiom in Roosevelt's thinking about postwar planning for peace.

Determined to avoid the excessive idealism of Woodrow Wilson's plan for a universal family of nations, the president emphasized the need for the use of military power by the Big Four of the wartime Grand Alliance in order to insure postwar peace. With a growing indication of public approval for some sort of organization of nations after the war, Roosevelt, in November 1942, revealed his plan for the Four Policemen to disarm and patrol the postwar world to Clark Eichelberger, one of the leading internationalist leaders in the nation.

During the course of 1943, Roosevelt shared his views of a great power–dominated association of nations with Winston CHURCHILL (a supporter of regional security arrangements), Joseph STALIN (soon a convert) at the TEHERAN CONFERENCE, and, in veiled terms, with the American people in a series of public speeches from January to December 1943. That year marked the turning point of the world conflict and, thus, 1944 and 1945 were the critical years of postwar planning for peace. At the State Department a planning group proposed a "United Nations Authority" with a security commission consisting of the four great powers, thus incorporating Roosevelt's idea into a more general universal organization.

During 1944, policy makers in Washington carefully monitored American public opinion regarding international organization. The Hollywood feature film *Wilson* sparked a popular internationalist revival, while best-selling books and articles by Wendell Willkie, Sumner Welles, Walter Lippmann, and Nicholas Spykman prompted a lively debate about the nature and goals of U.S. foreign policy. By mid-1944 American public opinion had moved quite far from the idealism of Wendell Willkie's *One World* and other internationalists' proposals. Although accepting the need for a universal world organization, Americans seemed to reject the ideal of the full equality of all nations and embraced instead Roosevelt's realpolitik of Big Four hegemony. The president finally revealed publicly his concept of the "Four Policemen" in a two-part interview in *The Saturday Evening Post* in May 1944. The author, Forrest Davis, concluded that the new United Nations "presupposes that the powers able to make war are convinced their self-interest demands peace."

Roosevelt thus enjoyed overwhelming public support in his struggles against both liberal internationalists and conservative opponents of postwar cooperation with the Soviet Union. As the century turned, the STRUCTURE of the UN SECURITY COUNCIL remained a testament to the durability of the concept of the "Four Policemen."

See also CAIRO DECLARATION.

Further Reading: Divine, Robert A. *Second Chance: The Triumph of Internationalism in America during World War II.* New York: Atheneum, 1967. Hoopes, Townsend, and Douglas Brinkley. *FDR and the Creation of the U.N.* New Haven, Conn.: Yale University Press, 1997. Kimball, Warren F. *Forged in War: Roosevelt, Churchill, and the Second World War.* New York: William Morrow, 1997. Ostrower, Gary. *The United Nations and the United States.* New York: Twayne, 1998.

— E. M. Clauss

Four Power Declaration   *See* RUSSIAN FEDERATION.

Fourteen Points

In a speech to both houses of the U.S. Congress on January 8, 1918, President Woodrow Wilson introduced the Fourteen Points by which he sought to build a peace at the conclusion of the "war to end all war." His statement of "what we demand in this war" declared that the Allies sought to make the world safe for democracy, one that was "safe for every peace-loving nation." Wilson's Fourteen Points unveiled the idea of an international organization through which the nations of the world would preserve peace, thereby leading directly to the LEAGUE OF NATIONS, the predecessor of the United Nations.

Wilson was president of the UNITED STATES from 1913 to 1921. In the early 20th century, Americans viewed Europe with suspicion and initially sought to stay out of World War I, but the effort proved hopeless. In early 1917, while the United States was still officially neutral, Wilson called for a "peace without victory" and enunciated what he considered the kind of peace the American people would support.

Once the United States was in the war, the Fourteen Points appeared to express distinctive American views about war and international relations and changed public opinion about the nature of diplomacy. Wilson listed objectives that became the basis of U.S. foreign policy in the American public mind and influenced the role of the United States in the world well beyond World War I. Although the president presented the Fourteen Points as Allied objectives, he did not consult any of the Allied governments prior to his speech to Congress.

The first five points reflected Wilson's desire for the rule of law in international politics. He called for (1) open COVENANTS of peace, openly arrived at, and an end to all secret diplomacy and secret treaties, (2) freedom of the seas, meaning the right of the ships of all nations to sail on any international waters, (3) removal of economic barriers and the establishment of equal trading rights for all nations, constituting one of the initial statements of the most-favored-nation trading principle that became the basis of international trade rules after World War II, (4) reduction of armaments "to the lowest point consistent with domestic safety," thus stating the American objective of DISARMAMENT, and (5) adjustment of all colonial claims based on the interests of the colonial peoples, which were to be considered equally with the claims of the colonial powers.

Points 6 through 13 dealt with European territorial settlements among the combatants, based on the principles of nationality and self-determination. Boundaries should now be established in order to unite peoples of a given nationality (or ethnicity) within a single state where they would constitute the majority of the population and hence be guaranteed the right to govern themselves. Such "self-determined" nations would replace political entities based on natural features, conquest, and dynasties, and be an important step toward worldwide decolonization. Achieving this would entail the breakup of Germany, Austria-Hungary, and the Ottoman Empire. The latter two multinational states would be carved up into several new states whose frontiers would be based on nationality. When implemented after the conclusion of the war, this restructuring required the forced relocation of large populations. Nations based on ethnically kindred populations would replace the empires of central Europe that had ignored nationalities in order to unite within a single state all the resources needed to achieve economic security and power.

Most significant, the 14th point called for the establishment of "A general association of nations . . . for the purpose of affording guarantees of political independence and territorial integrity" to all countries. This point became the basis of the League of Nations, embodying the principle of COLLECTIVE SECURITY through universal action against AGGRESSION, whereby all members would agree to protect the boundaries of all other members.

The League of Nations, established by the Allies at the 1919 Versailles Peace Conference, launched a new era in international organization. Ironically, after President Wilson forced inclusion of the League in the peace settlement over the objections of the reluctant Europeans, the U.S. Senate rejected the treaty. Thus the United States did not join the entity it had helped create. World War II exposed the weaknesses of the League, but, for many Americans, the collapse of international order leading to the war likewise revealed the need for their country to enter forcefully into international affairs in a leadership role as anticipated by Wilson in his Fourteen Points. A major result was the establishment of the United Nations.

See also ATLANTIC CHARTER, NATION-STATE.

Further Reading: Bailey, Thomas A. *Wilson and the Peacemakers.* New York: Macmillan, 1947. Cooper, John Milton, Jr. *Breaking the Heart of the World: Woodrow Wilson and the Fight for the League of Nations.* New York: Cambridge University Press, 2001. Hoover, Herbert. *The Ordeal of Woodrow Wilson.* New York: McGraw Hill, 1958. Knock, Thomas J. *To End All War: Woodrow Wilson and the Quest for a New World Order.* Princeton, N.J.: Princeton University Press, 1995. Link, Arthur S. *Wilson the Diplomatist.* Baltimore: Johns Hopkins University Press, 1957.

— *K. J. Grieb*

Fourth Committee of the General Assembly

The Fourth Committee of the GENERAL ASSEMBLY (GA) is one of the GA's six main committees, and is also known as the Special Political and Decolonization Committee. Like all General Assembly main committees, it has representatives from every member state, each with an equal vote. Its function is to consider and negotiate draft RESOLUTIONS before they are placed before the full General Assembly. By GA Resolution 233 in 1993 the General Assembly merged the Special Political Committee (formerly the Seventh Committee) with that of the Fourth Committee, adding the work of the former to the latter's existing agenda on trusteeship issues. This was done because, with the independence of most colonial, and all trust territories, there was little business left for the Fourth Committee. The Special Committee itself had been created in the early years of the United Nations, when the FIRST COMMITTEE found that it needed to devote its attention to DISARMAMENT.

Since the end of the COLD WAR, despite the existence of an expanding number of ethnic conflicts and the increasing involvement of the United Nations in internal civil wars, the newly merged Fourth Committee has developed a high level of cooperation and consensus on its agenda topics. The committee addresses all conflict situations appearing before the General Assembly, invariably passing resolutions on each one. It also deals with all aspects of PEACEKEEPING, and the issues of NON-SELF-GOVERNING TERRITORIES. Each year it invariably passes several resolutions relating to various aspects of the situation in the Middle East. It also considers matters relating to the Geneva CONVENTIONS regarding the laws of war, and issues concerning cooperation in outer space.

See also COMMITTEE SYSTEM OF THE GENERAL ASSEMBLY, STRUCTURE OF THE UNITED NATIONS, TRUSTEESHIP COUNCIL.

Further Reading: Fourth Committee website: <www.un.org/ga/fourth/>.

— *K. J. Grieb*

Fourth Development Decade   *See* DEVELOPMENT DECADES.

Fourth World Conference on Women   *See* WORLD CONFERENCES ON WOMEN.

Framework Convention on Climate Change (UNFCCC)   *See* UNITED NATIONS FRAMEWORK CONVENTION ON CLIMATE CHANGE.

Fréchette, Louise (1946–)

On March 2, 1998, Louise Fréchette became the first DEPUTY SECRETARY-GENERAL of the United Nations. The post had been created in December 1997 by the GENERAL ASSEMBLY as part of the REFORM package put forward by SECRETARY-GENERAL Kofi ANNAN. According to the plan set forth in *RENEWING THE UNITED NATIONS*, the Deputy Secretary-General would serve as the Secretary-General's primary adviser, have assigned responsibilities for daily administration of the SECRETARIAT—particularly of the reform process—coordinate coherence and cooperation among UN bodies, represent the Secretary-General at conferences and official functions, and take on special assignments. With her appointment,

Deputy Secretary-General Louise Fréchette (UN/DPI PHOTO BY ESKINDER DEBEBE)

Fréchette became the highest-ranking woman within the institution in UN history.

Louise Fréchette was born in Montreal, Canada, on July 16, 1946. She earned a bachelor of arts degree from College Basile Moreau and a history degree from the University of Montreal (1970). She also earned a diploma in economic studies from the College of Europe in Bruges, Belgium. Following her graduation from the University of Montreal, Fréchette commenced a long career in the Canadian government, rising to the position of deputy minister of national defense immediately prior to her appointment as Deputy Secretary-General. As a member of Canada's Department of External Affairs in 1972 she served on the delegation to the UN General Assembly. She then served as second secretary in the Canadian embassy in Athens. Following a tour of service in the External Affairs Department's European Division (1975–77), Fréchette became Canadian first secretary at its UN mission in Geneva until 1982. In 1985 she was appointed ambassador simultaneously to Argentina, Uruguay, and Paraguay. Her work in South America led to an appointment as assistant deputy minister for Latin American and Caribbean affairs. From 1992 to 1995 Fréchette served as Canada's PERMANENT REPRESENTATIVE to the United Nations in New York.

In addition to overseeing the UN reform process, Fréchette served on Annan's SENIOR MANAGEMENT GROUP and other secretariat leadership committees. Her primary responsibilities centered on social, economic, and development activities. She supervised the Office for Development Financing in the effort to find additional financial support for UN projects. She was also given a major role in Annan's efforts to develop cooperation between the United Nations and "civil society," including partnerships with NON-GOVERNMENTAL ORGANIZATIONS and private businesses. She was a major advocate of the UN's GLOBAL COMPACT, an initiative by Annan to obtain the formal commitment by world business leaders to respect UN-established HUMAN RIGHTS, labor, and environmental norms. The most important of these liaison relationships for which Fréchette had special responsibility was with American broadcast entrepreneur Ted Turner's United Nations Foundation, which bestowed a gift of $1 billion to the UN in 1999. In the area of peace and security, the Secretary-General put his deputy in charge of implementing the recommendations of the BRAHIMI REPORT, a sweeping set of reforms in the area of UN PEACEKEEPING.

Fréchette became an ardent spokesperson for what she called the emerging "New" United Nations, an institution increasingly focused on "human beings, respect for their rights, and the satisfaction of their basic needs," and for gender equality in all societies. Speaking in April 2001, she argued for the THEMATIC DIPLOMACY of the UN that went "beyond the CHARTER," and was enshrined in the DECLARATION of the MILLENNIUM SUMMIT, convened in September 2000. Beyond the traditional concerns of NATION-STATE diplomacy the United Nations in her view was now rightly focused on human problems associated with peace missions, globalization, poverty, democratization, environmental activities, human settlements, population growth, drug trafficking, disease, migration, climate change, and the information revolution. Noting the critical importance of the United Nations to a topic "that is dear to me," namely, women's rights, Fréchette suggested that the UN's engagement with global civil society had "created for the WOMEN of world a set of standards against which to measure performance in their own countries."

Further Reading: Hampson, Fen Osler, and Maureen Appel Molot, eds. *Big Enough to Be Heard: Canada among Nations.* Ottawa: Carleton University Press, 1996.

funds   *See* PROGRAMMES AND FUNDS.

G

General Agreement on Tariffs and Trade (GATT)

The General Agreement on Tariffs and Trade was a PACT originally adopted at Geneva on October 30, 1947. It governed tariff concessions on industrial products as agreed to among its 23 original signatories. These initial GATT partners included the most important countries allied in World War II against the Axis powers. The negotiations were driven by the postwar agenda of the main Allied powers, the UNITED STATES, the United Kingdom, and Canada, to create postwar institutions to prevent a reemergence of war and depression. This aim could be accomplished, in their view, only by ending economic nationalism and the extensive protectionist policies that had characterized the interwar period.

The GATT was supposed to be an "interim" agreement until an International Trade Organization (ITO), which would provide a more ambitious regulatory framework for world trade, was established to join the INTERNATIONAL MONETARY FUND (IMF) and the INTERNATIONAL BANK FOR RECONSTRUCTION AND DEVELOPMENT (World Bank) in overseeing the international economy. While the Final Act of the United Nations Conference on Trade and Employment at Havana, CUBA, establishing an ITO, was signed on March 24, 1948, this so-called Havana Charter was withdrawn from consideration by the Truman administration in 1950 because of the almost certain defeat it faced in the U.S. Senate. This left the GATT by default as the mainstay of the international

trading system. It, along with the IMF and the WORLD BANK, was intended to promote a global free trade system.

To underline its "interim" status, secretarial support for the GATT was provided by the UN's Interim Committee for International Trade Organization. Over its almost 50-year lifetime, the GATT SECRETARIAT, which remained very small by UN standards, had four executive secretaries (subsequently upgraded to the more prestigious title of DIRECTOR-GENERAL): Eric Wyndham White, Olivier Long, Arthur Dunkel, and Peter Sutherland. Another sign of the provisional nature of GATT was that its secretariat did not actually have a permanent home until 1977 when it moved into the Centre William Rappard on the shores of Lake Geneva in Switzerland.

There were several key principles embodied in the various articles of GATT. It established the principle of nondiscrimination in international trade as expressed in most-favored-nation (MFN) treatment (Article I) and national treatment (Article III). Under "MFN treatment," signatories to GATT agreed to extend the lowest tariff rate that was generally applicable to the imports from all other GATT countries. Under "national treatment," member countries agreed that tax and regulatory policies should not be applied to imported or domestic products so as to afford protection to domestic production. Additionally, the agreement required the publication and transparency of trade regulations (Article X); the use of tariffs—not nontariff barriers— to regulate trade (Articles III through XXIII); the objective of a progressive reduction of tariffs (Article XXVIII); the private, and not governmental, nature of trade; the acceptance of barriers against dumped or subsidized imports (Article VI); the settlement of disputes through consultation and negotiation (Articles XXII and XXIII); and the avoidance of retaliation.

Over eight rounds of negotiations, culminating in the 1986–94 Uruguay Round, progress was made in lowering average tariff rates on manufactured goods levied by industrialized countries from 40 percent before GATT to around 4 percent. Progress was also made in eliminating barriers to trade such as exchange controls, import licensing, quotas, and other quantitative restrictions that were even more damaging than tariffs. But it was not until the Uruguay Round that significant separate agreements were reached covering the two key excluded areas of agriculture and services.

In its negotiations, the GATT employed an easy three-step recipe to reduce the overall level of protectionism in the world economy. First, less visible nontariff trade barriers were, wherever possible, replaced with tariffs or, better still, eliminated. Second, maximum (or "bound") tariff rates were negotiated. The "binding of tariffs" results in countries agreeing not to increase a tariff after it has been lowered. Third, the bound rates continued to be lowered over time in subsequent rounds of negotiations.

For most industrialized countries, under GATT rules, bound tariff rates were the same as MFN tariff rates. But for developing countries, bound tariff rates were often much higher than the actual "applied" rates, that is, the existing rates then in place, and consequently the bound rates served as a ceiling. This gave these poorer countries the flexibility to raise tariffs arbitrarily and unexpectedly if they so chose. In contrast, countries that bound their tariffs at applied levels were required to compensate their trading partners if for any reason they raised their tariffs. During the Uruguay Round, there were detailed schedules of bound tariffs by Harmonized System classification for each individual country participating in the negotiations.

The Uruguay Round tariff cuts, which were fully phased in by the year 2000, averaged almost 40 percent and lowered the average tariff on industrial products levied by developed countries from 6.3 percent to 3.8 percent. The proportion of the value of these products that were duty free rose from 20 percent to 44 percent. The proportion facing high tariffs—above 15 percent—fell from 7 percent to 5 percent. The proportion of these tariff lines that were bound increased from 78 percent to 99 percent.

According to a 1997 Organization for Economic Cooperation and Development (OECD) study, average tariffs would be reduced substantially when the Uruguay Round cuts were fully in place. For the four largest economies (the United States, the European Union, Japan, and Canada), tariffs would average in the 4 to 7 percent range and be higher in the European Union and Canada than in Japan and the United States. Excepting Switzerland and Sweden, bound tariff rates would be significantly higher in other advanced OECD countries, averaging from 9 to 25 percent. And bound tariffs would be even higher in the developing countries of Mexico and Turkey, averaging 35 to 45 percent, which would be representative of bound tariff rates in the developing world. Applied tariff rates only averaged 14 percent in Mexico and 10 percent in Turkey.

While much progress had been made in eliminating or lowering nontariff barriers (NTBs), at the turn of the century they still existed and were important. The OECD examined the prevalence of NTBs among OECD countries. The NTBs considered fell under two rubrics: price controls and quantitative restrictions (QRs). Price controls covered Voluntary Export Restrictions (VERs) like those used for automobiles and textiles, variable charges, and antidumping and countervailing duties. QRs included nonautomatic licensing, export restraints, and other quotas and import prohibitions. The OECD study showed that QRs were still very prevalent.

The GATT and its secretariat were subsumed into the WORLD TRADE ORGANIZATION (WTO) on January 1, 1995. The GATT and its related understandings and agreements became parts of Annex 1A to the "Marrakesh Agreement Establishing the World Trade Organization." Consequently, future GATT negotiations will take place under the auspices of the WTO, the GATT will be administered by the WTO, and disputes will be resolved under the new rules of the WTO's dispute settlement understanding.

See also ANNAN, KOFI, BRETTON WOODS.

Further Reading: Hart, Michael. *Fifty Years of Canadian Statecraft: Canada at the GATT 1947–1997.* Ottawa: Centre for Trade Policy and Law, 1998. Organization for Economic Cooperation and Development. *Indicators of Tariff and Nontariff Trade Barriers: Update 1997.* Paris: Organization for Economic Cooperation and Development, 1997.

— P. M. Grady

General and Complete Disarmament (GCD)

See DISARMAMENT.

General Assembly (GA)

CHAPTER IV, Articles 9 through 22 of the UN CHARTER, provides for the composition, functions, powers, and procedures of the General Assembly. The GA, meeting in formal session every fall at UN HEADQUARTERS in New York, is the single most important of the six PRINCIPAL ORGANS OF THE UNITED NATIONS. It is the sole forum in which all member states are represented and in which each member state, regardless of its physical size or population, has an equal vote. For this reason most nations consider the Assembly the focal point of the United Nations. Its importance has grown

General Assembly Hall, New York City (UN/DPI Photo by Eskinder Debebe)

with the expansion of United Nations MEMBERSHIP, which has ensued following the end of Western colonialism, particularly during the 1960s. The consequence has been a dramatic increase in the number of independent nations in the world, and hence in the UN membership, which reached 189 in the year 2000. The General Assembly prepared to act in 2002 on yet two more membership applications—from Switzerland and East Timor.

The General Assembly is often referred to as the "Town Meeting of the World," where all residents of the planet theoretically are represented by their governments. Small and middle-sized nations place a great value on the equality of VOTING, reflecting the principle of the sovereign equality of states, which constitutes the basis of INTERNATIONAL LAW and, hence, of the UNITED NATIONS SYSTEM. Each member state is allowed five representatives and five alternate representatives to the General Assembly, with these individuals serving on the various committees as well as meeting in the full Assembly.

Since four of the remaining principal organs report to the General Assembly, it plays a role in all the main functions of the United Nations. Only the SECURITY COUNCIL (SC) and the INTERNATIONAL COURT OF JUSTICE (ICJ) do not submit their decisions for review. The General Assembly deals with a wide range of topics spanning all fields of international affairs. It employs a system of plenary committees, with all topics originally debated, reviewed, and voted upon by these committees. Committee RESOLUTIONS are then presented to the Assembly for plenary consideration.

There are six main committees. The FIRST COMMITTEE, designated the Political and Security Committee under its original mandate, in fact deals almost exclusively with DISARMAMENT affairs. The member states found that this topic was so central to the international system that it required its own committee. The First Committee is now charged with addressing "disarmament and international security." A separate Special Political Committee was established early in the history of the United Nations to consider all other political questions. The other main committees are the SECOND COMMITTEE: Economic and Financial (ECOFIN); THIRD COMMITTEE: Social, Humanitarian, and Cultural (SOCHUM); FOURTH COMMITTEE: Trusteeship, which in the late 1990s was merged with the Special Political Committee to become the Special Political and Decolonization Committee; FIFTH COMMITTEE: Administrative and Budgetary; and SIXTH COMMITTEE: Legal. The General Assembly also has established special committees and working groups to deal with specific issues, or to carry out procedural and administrative duties. The most important are the GENERAL COMMITTEE, the CREDENTIALS COMMITTEE, the ADVISORY COMMITTEE ON ADMINISTRATIVE AND BUDGETARY QUESTIONS (ACABQ), and the COMMITTEE ON CONTRIBUTIONS. The General Assembly may also call SPECIAL SESSIONS to deal with specific issues.

The annual meeting usually convenes on the first or second Tuesday after the first Monday of September each year, and usually concludes in mid-December. This three and a half month period includes the most intense portion of the session when the majority of the agenda items are considered. It is not unusual for less frequent meetings to resume in January and continue through April to deal with additional items. The September session begins with each nation making an opening statement in what is called a period of GENERAL DEBATE. These statements constitute formal policy DECLARATIONS regarding the items that nations consider the most important issues before the United Nations and in the international arena. Opening statements are of such importance that most nations send their president, prime minister, or minister of foreign affairs to deliver the address.

The agenda of the General Assembly consists of matters proposed by any member state, as well as continuing items resulting from previously adopted General Assembly resolutions. Hence, the member states determine the agenda, although the SECRETARY-GENERAL can also suggest additional items for consideration. Some continuing items are brought directly to the General Assembly without reference to a committee. The overwhelming majority of the resolutions considered by the full Assembly have been previously discussed in detail and passed by the various committees. The Assembly elects its own president annually, along with 17 vice presidents. The latter are chosen on a proportional basis according to geographical regions, to assure representation of all areas of the world. Collectively they, along with the president and the elected chairmen of each of the six main committees, constitute the General Committee, which functions as a steering committee of the session and sets the agenda order.

The General Assembly functions by consensus rather than by majority vote. While a majority vote can assure passage, the United Nations is not a sovereign body, meaning that General Assembly resolutions are not binding but are dependent on the will of the participating governments to carry them out. Whereas in a government of a sovereign state the majority may have the right to impose its will on the minority through binding laws, in the greater global community, as represented in the United Nations, only those nations agreeing to be bound by a resolution are committed to carrying out its provisions. A majority vote can therefore be meaningless unless all member states are willing to abide by the terms of the approved resolution. As a result, the General Assembly functions as a negotiating body rather than a parliamentary body; the objective is to seek the agreement of all participating nations to the resolution, which is the only way to ensure that all sovereign nations agree to carry it out. This necessity often requires lengthy negotiations among representatives of all member states in order to establish language that is acceptable—or at least tolerable—to all, and to reach agreement on declarations that all member states are willing and likely to fulfill. Usually, the General Assembly negotiations continue until the initial proposals by the various nations are combined to reach agreed compromise on a single resolution on each agenda topic. As a result, negotiations regarding the wording continue until unanimous agreement is achieved, or until it is evident that unanimous consent is impossible and that the number of nations dissenting is reduced to a handful. Only after negotiations reach these stages is an item brought to a vote. Generally, a resolution that lacks the support of an overwhelming majority of the body will be withdrawn rather than being brought to a vote, and votes take place only when there are only a small number of holdouts that cannot accept the language of the resolution.

Consensus agreement is frequently reached on global issues, and since the end of the COLD WAR more than 70 percent of the resolutions adopted by the General Assembly each year have been adopted by unanimous consent, without a formal recorded vote. In about half the cases where votes are necessary, only a handful of negative votes (fewer than 10) are recorded, along with a larger group of abstentions, as nations vote negatively only in cases where their national interests or perceived national security is endangered. Abstentions are far more common than are negative votes. Thus, while the Charter provides that the Assembly functions by majority rule, it in fact functions by unanimous consent, and therefore does indeed serve as a town meeting of the world. The Charter further stipulates that "IMPORTANT QUESTIONS" must pass in the GA by a two-thirds majority. Yet, this requirement has little impact, since resolutions are rarely adopted with less than a two-thirds majority, especially in the years since the end of the cold war. Important questions are those involving international peace and security, trusteeship questions, questions involving membership and the SUSPENSION of the rights and privileges of membership, budgetary questions, and various electoral functions for the other principal organs of the United Nations.

The General Assembly elects the NON-PERMANENT MEMBERS OF THE SECURITY COUNCIL, the members of the ECONOMIC AND SOCIAL COUNCIL, and the TRUSTEESHIP COUNCIL, and, acting upon the recommendation of the SECURITY COUNCIL, elects the Secretary-General, as well as the judges of the International Court of Justice in concurrence with the Council. A two-thirds vote of the General Assembly is also required to propose AMENDMENTS to the Charter, which then must be ratified by the governments of the member states, or to set the place and time of a General Conference to be held for the purpose of proposing Charter amendments. While the Security Council normally deals with questions affecting international peace and security, the General Assembly may consider such questions and make recommendations to the Security Council, and under the 1950 UNITING FOR PEACE RESOLUTION may make recommendations in cases when a VETO prevents the Security Council from taking action, although this latter measure is rarely invoked.

In addition to its official functions, the General Assembly offers a meeting place for the governments of the world to share ideas on global concerns. It also can be the vital setting for informal, behind-the-scenes diplomacy, even between nations that have technically broken relations or may be at war. The resulting opportunities for confidential exchanges can play, and have played, a central role in enabling nations to cooperate in addressing a wide range of global, multilateral, and bilateral issues.

See also PROCEDURAL COMMITTEES.

Further Reading: Bailey, Sydney D. *The United Nations: A Concise Political Guide.* 3d ed. Lanham, Md.: Barnes and Noble, 1995. Mingst, Karen A., and Margaret P. Karns. *The United Nations in the Post–Cold War Era.* Boulder, Colo.: Westview, 1995. Muldoon, James P. Jr., et al., eds. *Multilateral Diplomacy and the United Nations Today.* Boulder, Colo.: Westview, 1999. Peterson, M. J. *The General Assembly in World Politics.* Boston: Allen and Unwin, 1986.

— *K. J. Grieb*

General Committee

The General Committee is one of the PROCEDURAL COMMITTEES of the GENERAL ASSEMBLY (GA), and consists of the Assembly's president, 21 vice presidents, and the elected chairmen of the six main committees of the General Assembly. Members are elected at the beginning of the GA session in September. The president serves for one annual session, and is usually a leading statesman from a middle power or small state, with the position rotating by region. No representative of the PERMANENT MEMBERS OF THE SECURITY COUNCIL has ever been elected to the presidency.

Following selection of the president, the General Assembly elects 17 vice presidents for one-year terms. They are allocated by geographical region, according to a formula that assures equitable representation reflecting the VOTING strength of each region in the MEMBERSHIP of the United Nations. Specifically, there are seven vice presidents from Africa and Asia, three from LATIN AMERICA, two from the Western Europe and Other States CAUCUS GROUP, and one from Eastern Europe (reflecting the fact that the distribution was agreed upon during the COLD WAR). Since the Middle East is not considered a "geographical area" in UN parlance, one of the seven seats assigned to Asia and Africa is by agreement held by a Middle Eastern country, thereby allowing accommodation to a significant political bloc within a formula based exclusively on geographical representation. Thus, the seat allocated to the Middle East rotates between Africa and Asia. The "Other" category is used to add the Western democracies located outside Western Europe and includes Canada, Australia, and New Zealand. In 2000 Israel was added to the Other group, becoming eligible for election as a vice president for the first time since the United Nations was formed. The region from which the president of the General Assembly is drawn receives one less vice president. The five remaining vice presidencies are allotted to the permanent members of the SECURITY COUNCIL.

The General Committee functions as the steering committee for the annual session of the General Assembly, making decisions regarding the agenda and the order in which items will be considered. Items are placed on the agenda at the request of member states, or by previous decisions and continuing actions of the General Assembly.

Further Reading: United Nations Department of Public Information. *Basic Facts about the United Nations.* New York: United Nations Department of Public Information, periodically.

— *K. J. Grieb*

General Debate

Each session of the GENERAL ASSEMBLY (GA) opens in September with what is called General Debate. During this two- or three-week period, each member state makes an opening address before the full General Assembly in the GA Hall at UN HEADQUARTERS. These statements are formal policy DECLARATIONS regarding the items that each government considers the most important issues before the United Nations and in the international arena. The speeches are not confined to items on the agenda, nor do they attempt to address all agenda topics. Rather each nation has the option to focus on a single item, or on several issues that it regards as of particular consequence.

Opening statements are of such importance that most nations send their president, prime minister, or minister of foreign affairs to deliver the address. The length of general debate speeches has varied over the years. While diplomatic courtesy requires limiting the length of statements, it is difficult to silence a head of state once at the podium. However, as the number of member states has expanded over the years, limits have been agreed upon and are generally respected.

— *K. J. Grieb*

Geneva Headquarters of the United Nations

Considered the second UN center in the world after the UN HEADQUARTERS in New York, the Palais des Nations in Geneva, Switzerland, became the headquarters of the LEAGUE OF NATIONS in 1936. At its initiation in 1919 the League chose Geneva as its central location. Designed by a team of architects from four European countries, the Palais was built between 1929 and 1936. When, after World War II the United Nations assumed the place of the League as the universal COLLECTIVE SECURITY organization of the world's nations, it took possession of the Palais des Nations as its European seat. Officially called the UN Office at Geneva (UNOG), the Palais is situated in Ariana Park overlooking Lake Geneva. Since 1936 it has remained a major center of international activity, and surrounding it in the city of Geneva are several international organizations, almost all of which are affiliated with the United Nations. More than 300 conferences convene annually at the Palais, and, as of 2001, national representatives from more than 140 nations were accredited to the Geneva Office. Here as well are found several OBSERVER missions, intergovernmental organizations such as the European Union, the ORGANIZATION OF AFRICAN UNITY, and the Arab League. There is a library at the headquarters, established by a donation from American entrepreneur John D. Rockefeller Jr., containing more than one million volumes and, since 1997, state-of-the-art connections with the World Wide Web. The Palais also serves as Geneva's international press center and contains a post office, bank, restaurants, media services, and a UN philatelic museum.

In the Palais's most spacious room—the Assembly Hall, accommodating more than 2,000 delegates—SPECIAL SESSIONS of the United Nations, such as the WORLD SOCIAL SUMMIT of 2000, as well as annual plenary gatherings of several UN SPECIALIZED AGENCIES have been held over the

Palais des Nations (UN/DPI PHOTO BY P. KLEE)

years. The CONFERENCE ON DISARMAMENT usually holds its annual sessions in the smaller Council Chamber, where other historic conferences have occurred, including the conference on Indochina in 1954, the conference on Korea in 1954, and the AFGHANISTAN peace conference of 1988.

Like the New York Headquarters the Palais is open to the public and provides guided tours and information programs. SECRETARY-GENERAL Kofi ANNAN appointed Sergei Ordzhonikidze as the new UNOG DIRECTOR-GENERAL beginning March 1, 2002, succeeding Vladimir Petrovsky, who had held the post for the previous nine years.

See also INTERNATIONAL LAW COMMISSION, INTERNATIONAL TRADE CENTRE UNCTAD/WTO, UNITED NATIONS ASSOCIATION, UNITED NATIONS RESEARCH INSTITUTE FOR SOCIAL DEVELOPMENT.

Further Reading: Eco'Diagnostic, Geneva. *International Geneva Yearbook.* Geneva: United Nations, published annually. UNOG website: <www.unog.ch>. Geneva Headquarters Guide website: <www.genevabriefingbook.com/chapters/palais>.

genocide   *See* CONVENTION ON THE PREVENTION AND PUNISHMENT OF THE CRIME OF GENOCIDE.

Global Compact

The United Nations is an international organization of sovereign NATION-STATES that serves as a forum for interstate diplomacy and collective action. However, as the new millennium approached, the organization expanded its involvement with the private sector and NON-GOVERNMENTAL ORGANIZATIONS (NGOs). Particularly in the area of development, there was a new UN effort to engage private corporations and NGOs in the work of the United Nations. Decreases in donor state funding made this a necessity. The focus on private actors in the international arena was also a recognition by the UN leadership that an emerging international civil society would have a significant impact on the success or failure of UN initiatives. It was within this context that SECRETARY-GENERAL Kofi ANNAN proposed a Global Compact between the United Nations and multinational corporations to protect HUMAN RIGHTS, international labor standards, and the global ENVIRONMENT. Speaking on January 31, 1999, to the World Economic Forum in Davos, Switzerland, Annan urged corporations to work directly with the world body, bypassing national governments, to fulfill nine principles established in the RIO DECLARATION of the Earth Summit, the INTERNATIONAL LABOUR ORGANIZATION's Fundamental Principles on Rights of Work, and the UNIVERSAL DECLARATION OF HUMAN RIGHTS.

Corporations joining the Global Compact commit themselves to: (1) support and respect the protection of international human rights within their sphere of influence, (2) make sure their own corporations are not complicit in human rights abuses, (3) uphold freedom of association and the right to collective bargaining, (4) promote the elimination of all forms of forced and compulsory labor, (5) work for the effective abolition of child labor, (6) support the elimination of discrimination in respect to employment and occupation, (7) support a precautionary approach to environmental challenges, (8) undertake initiatives to promote greater environmental responsibility, and (9) encourage the development and diffusion of environmentally friendly technologies. The program requires the chief executive officer to submit a letter to the executive office of the Secretary-General committing the corporation to these nine principles and agreeing to post them on the premises of the enterprise. Other private organizations, ranging from chambers of commerce and labor organizations to activist environmental and human rights NGOs are allowed to join as well.

Within a year of Annan's speech more than 50 transnational corporations had signed the compact, and by fall 2001 MEMBERSHIP approached 1,000. Annan established a Global Compact office within his executive office, which began operations on July 26, 2000. Supporting the work of the new bureau—headed until March 2002 by a special adviser to the Secretary-General on the Global Compact, Gören Lindhal—were its sponsoring organizations: UNITED NATIONS ENVIRONMENT PROGRAMME (UNEP), UNITED NATIONS DEVELOPMENT PROGRAMME (UNDP), UN FUND for International Partnership, International Labour Organization (ILO), and the Office of the UN HIGH COMMISSIONER FOR HUMAN RIGHTS (UNHCHR).

The Global Compact set as its overall goals the promotion of international corporate citizenship and social responsibility, the establishment of corporate "good practices," and the development of the United Nations, the "world's only truly global political forum, as authoritative convener and facilitator" of international civil societal organizations. To these ends the Global Compact office staged policy dialogues during its first operating years—in 2000 on the role of the private sector in zones of conflict (with business leaders in 30 countries participating), and in 2001 on transparency, voluntary initiatives, and revenue sharing agreements. In October 2001, the Global Compact also launched the Global Compact Learning Forum, an on-line service for sharing experiences and discussing lessons learned in private corporate efforts.

See also FRÉCHETTE, SUSTAINABLE DEVELOPMENT.

Further Reading: Tessitore, John, and Susan Woolfson, eds. *A Global Agenda. Issues before the 55th General Assembly of the United Nations.* New York: Rowman and Littlefield, 2000. Global Compact website: <www.unglobalcompact.org>.

Global Environment Facility (GEF)

The GEF is one of the leading international agencies for the global ENVIRONMENT. It was established in November 1990 by the WORLD BANK, with participation by the UNITED NATIONS DEVELOPMENT PROGRAMME (UNDP) and the UNITED NATIONS ENVIRONMENT PROGRAMME (UNEP). The Global Environment Facility's primary purpose is to provide grants to developing countries for environment-related projects and to facilitate networking and cooperation among donors. Also, the agency serves as the financial mechanism for the implementation of two international conventions adopted at the 1992 UNITED NATIONS CONFERENCE ON ENVIRONMENT AND DEVELOPMENT (UNCED) in Rio: the Convention on Biological Diversity and the UNITED NATIONS FRAMEWORK CONVENTION ON CLIMATE CHANGE.

As of December 2000, the facility had 167 member states. GEF's operations are directed by an assembly, composed of all member states, which meets every three years, and a council, functioning as a board of directors and representing 32 constituencies (16 from developing countries, 14 from developed countries, and 2 from transitional economies), that meets twice a year and also conducts business by mail. Daily activities are managed by a permanent SECRETARIAT consisting of a staff of 40, headed by a chief executive officer, and based in Washington, D.C. The World Bank is the trustee of the GEF trust fund. It acts as one of the facility's three implementing agencies, and it provides administrative support for the secretariat. The other two GEF implementing agencies are UNDP and UNEP.

Restructured in 1994, GEF implements 12 operational programs (OPs) through which it provides grants. Eleven of these reflect the facility's primary focal areas: four on biodiversity, four on climate change, and three on international waters. OP 12—integrated ecosystem management—encompasses cross-sectoral projects. In addition, GEF funds projects to combat ozone depletion that are not grouped among the OPs. Biodiversity OPs include: arid and semi-arid zone ecosystems; coastal, marine, and freshwater ecosystems; forest ecosystems; and mountain ecosystems. Climate change OPs include: removal of barriers to energy efficiency and energy conservation; promoting the adoption of renewable energy by removing barriers and reducing implementation costs; reducing the long-term costs of low greenhouse gas emitting energy technologies; and promoting environmentally sustainable transport. International waters OPs include: waterbody-based, integrated land and water multiple focal area and contaminant-based operational programs. Between 1991 and 1999 GEF provided $991 million in grants for biological diversity projects, and $884 million for climate change projects, as well as $1.5 billion and $4.7 billion in co-financing in these same areas, respectively. It also allocated $360 million to international water initiatives. In addition, it provided $155 million to projects to phase out ozone depleting substances.

In accordance with the Global Environment Facility's policy, any individual or group may propose a project, which must meet two key criteria: it must improve the global environment or advance the prospect of reducing risks to it and it must reflect national or regional priorities and have support of the country or countries involved. GEF project ideas may be proposed directly to any of its implementing agencies. Country eligibility to receive funding is determined in two ways. Developing countries that have ratified the relevant CONVENTION are eligible to propose biodiversity and climate change projects. Other countries, primarily those with economies in transition, are eligible if the country is a party to the appropriate TREATY and is eligible to borrow from the World Bank or receives technical assistance grants from UNDP.

See also AGENDA 21, SUSTAINABLE DEVELOPMENT, WORLD COMMISSION ON ENVIRONMENT AND DEVELOPMENT.

Further Reading: Aggarwal-Khan, Sheila. *Promoting Coherence: Towards an Effective Global Environment Facility.* Amsterdam: Netherlands Committee for IUCN, 1997. Chasek, Pamela S. *The Global Environment in the Twenty-first Century: Prospects for International Cooperation.* New York: United Nations University Press, 2000. *Introduction to the GEF.* Washington, D.C.: The Global Environment Facility, 2000. Sjeoberg, Helen. *From Idea to Reality: The Creation of the Global Environment Facility.* Washington, D.C.: The Global Environment Facility, 1994.

— A. I. Maximenko

globalization   *See* BRETTON WOODS, GLOBAL COMPACT, INTERNATIONAL MONETARY FUND, MILLENNIUM SUMMIT, WORLD TRADE ORGANIZATION.

Goldberg Reservation

In 1960 the United Nations intervened with PEACEKEEPING forces in the Congolese civil war. Meant to restore order, the UN operation was seen by the Soviet Union as an effort on the part of UN SECRETARY-GENERAL Dag HAMMARSKJÖLD to support Western forces in the CONGO. In protest, and despite a ruling by the INTERNATIONAL COURT OF JUSTICE that peacekeeping expenses could be drawn from the regular BUDGET OF THE UNITED NATIONS, the USSR refused to pay its associated UN assessment. According to Article 19 of the UN CHARTER, "A Member of the United Nations which is in arrears to the payment of its financial contributions to the Organization shall have no vote in the GENERAL ASSEMBLY if the amount of its arrears equals or exceeds the amount of the contributions due from it for the preceding two full years." Once the Soviet Union fell far enough behind in payments to trigger the implementation of Article 19 the UNITED STATES pressed for the denial of Soviet VOTING privileges.

Led first by Adlai Stevenson, and then by Arthur J. Goldberg, U.S. PERMANENT REPRESENTATIVES to the United Nations during the Johnson administration, the American effort made little progress since the growing pro-Soviet majority in the United Nations, largely from the developing world, saw no value in excluding the Soviet Union from the General Assembly. The United States gave up its effort in 1965, but Ambassador Goldberg took the occasion to assert a new American policy toward the world body. He told the SECURITY COUNCIL, "If any member can insist on making an exception to the principle of collective financial responsibility with respect to certain activities of the United Nations, . . . the United States reserves the same option to make exceptions if, in our view, strong and compelling reasons exist to do so."

This threat, known as the Goldberg Reservation, simply appeared to be an expression of disgust and an admission of defeat. By the end of Lyndon Johnson's term as president of the United States, the U.S. government was paying nearly one-third of all UN bills. However, following the 1980 election of President Ronald Reagan, the Goldberg Reservation was exercised. Disillusionment with the United Nations led the administration to withdraw U.S. MEMBERSHIP from some UN agencies, charging that they had been "politicized," and to limit payment of its assessment, particularly for peacekeeping, until institutional REFORMS were made. The Goldberg Reservation was reenforced with the Kassebaum Amendment, which cut U.S. payments to UN organs until their staffs were reduced significantly, and until they made revisions to their charters in order to allow weighted representation based on the size of the financial contributions of the members. In 1985, 20 years after Goldberg enunciated U.S. policy, President Reagan signed congressional legislation unilaterally reducing the U.S. contribution to the UN budget from 25 percent to 20 percent. This action led to a growing U.S. debt owed to the United Nations that by 2000 left the United States on the verge of losing its vote in the General Assembly. Only a final compromise between Washington and the United Nations led to a payment of U.S. arrearages in 2001.

See also SCALE OF ASSESSMENTS.

good offices

In international affairs when a party independent of a disagreement intervenes to help bring about negotiation and eventual resolution of the disagreement, the third party is expected to act with "good offices." That is, the outsider's "good offices" suggest impartiality, a desire to avoid conflict and initiate discussions, and a genuine commitment to an eventual resolution of the dispute. Good offices should be distinguished from MEDIATION and ARBITRATION, both of which imply active participation by the third party in reaching settlement. Good offices is less participatory and is usually limited to offering channels of communication between those in disagreement. Thus it seeks to create diplomatic conversation preliminary to any possible settlement.

While the "good offices" function of the SECRETARY-GENERAL is not mentioned in the UN CHARTER, each Secretary-General has exercised this function, authorized to do so by the SECURITY COUNCIL or the GENERAL ASSEMBLY, by agreement of the parties to a dispute, or on his own initiative. Secretaries-General have exercised "good offices" in disputes involving Cyprus, Libya, CAMBODIA, EAST TIMOR, NAMIBIA, YUGOSLAVIA, the Falkland Islands, SOMALIA, Iran, Lebanon, and Iraq. The first-ever summit meeting of the Security Council in 1992 recommended that the Secretary-General "make greater use . . . of his good offices in settling post–COLD WAR disputes."

See also AFGHANISTAN, CONCILIATION, CONFLICT RESOLUTION, INDONESIA, IRAN-IRAQ WAR, IRAN HOSTAGE CRISIS, ORGANIZATION OF AFRICAN UNITY, UNITED NATIONS COMMISSION FOR INDONESIA, WALDHEIM.

Group of 77

The Group of 77 is a CAUCUS of the nations of the Third World or the global south within the United Nations that came into being in 1964 during the first meeting of the UNITED NATIONS CONFERENCE ON TRADE AND DEVELOPMENT (UNCTAD). The group, which originally consisted of 75 Third World nations, became officially the Group of 77 at its first ministerial meeting in 1977 that issued the Charter of Algiers. Although the membership grew to 133 by the end of the century, the name was retained for its historic significance. The organizational STRUCTURE of the Group has gradually expanded and chapters have been established in several locations in association with United Nations agencies most significant to the concerns of developing nations, including New York (at UN HEADQUARTERS), Rome (at the FOOD AND AGRICULTURAL ORGANIZATION [FAO]), Vienna (at the UN INDUSTRIAL DEVELOPMENT ORGANIZATION [UNIDO]), and Paris (at the UN EDUCATIONAL, SCIENTIFIC AND CULTURAL ORGANIZATION [UNESCO]). There is also a Committee of 24 located in Washington, D.C., to represent the group's interests at the INTERNATIONAL MONETARY FUND and WORLD BANK. Its objectives are to articulate and promote the collective interests of the nations of the Third World and to enhance their joint negotiating capacity on economic issues in the UNITED NATIONS SYSTEM. This committee, however, should not be confused with the Special Committee on the Implementation of the Declaration on Decolonization, also known as the COMMITTEE OF 24. The latter is also made up of many members from the Group of 77, but it is an official committee of the GENERAL ASSEMBLY, with responsibilities for implementing the 1960 DECLARATION on decolonization. In addition to their presence in these UN bodies, Group of 77 nations seek to expand economic and technical cooperation among themselves.

Important to the effectiveness of the ministerial meetings of the Group of 77 have been preliminary meetings on a regional basis in LATIN AMERICA, Africa, and Asia. At first the activities of the group related primarily to negotiations with industrialized nations; the importance of South to South cooperation was recognized in 1976 when a Conference on Economic Co-operation among Developing Countries was held in Mexico City. Despite the many forces that have existed to undermine the group's cohesiveness—regional differences, differences in size and wealth that confer advantages on larger nations, privileged economic relationships of former colonies with their one-time colonizers, and ideological disagreements—the value of the group to its members has been demonstrated by its continued existence.

In April 2000 the first meeting of the heads of state of the Group of 77 was held in Havana. The issues highlighted at this South Summit were the need for renewed North-South dialogue, the North's domination of the BRETTON WOODS organizations (the IMF and the World Bank), the nontransparency of the WORLD TRADE ORGANIZATION (WTO), the need for food security and rural employment, and the problem of AIDS. It was resolved to strengthen the Group of 77 and to hold a second South Summit in 2005.

See also NON-ALIGNED MOVEMENT, NORTH-SOUTH RELATIONS.

Further Reading: Sauvant, Karl P. *The Group of 77: Evolution, Structure, Organization.* New York: Oceana, 1981. ———. *Chronology, Bibliography and Index for the Group of 77 and the Non-Aligned Movement.* New York: Oceana, 1993. Sauvant, Karl P., and Joachim Miller, eds. *The Third World without Superpowers: The Collected Documents of the Group of 77, 2nd Series.* New York: Oceana, 1891–1995. Williams, Marc. *Third World Cooperation: The Group of 77 in UNCTAD.* New York: St. Martin's, 1991. Group of 77 website: <www.g77.org>.

— M. W. Bray

Guatemala

Guatemala joined the United Nations as one of the body's original members on October 24, 1945. It became a concern of the SECURITY COUNCIL in 1954 as a result of a military coup mounted against the democratically elected president, Jacobo Arbenz Guzmán. The UNITED STATES provided military, financial, and diplomatic support for the coup. Protest over U.S. involvement and support led Guatemala to request the intervention of the Security Council. Honduras, Nicaragua, Colombia, and Brazil challenged the request. Citing Article 33 of CHAPTER VI and Article 52 (2) of Chapter VIII of the UN CHARTER, Guatemala's opponents argued that as a regional dispute the matter fell under the JURISDICTION of the ORGANIZATION OF AMERICAN STATES (OAS). A VETO by the USSR blocked a RESOLUTION offered by Brazil and

Colombia that would have officially called on the OAS to open discussion concerning the situation in Guatemala. In its place, France authored a resolution that called for an end to military action and a commitment from all parties to block any and all assistance to the disputing parties. This resolution passed unanimously.

The Soviet Union and Guatemala continued to call for UN action, but a U.S. veto stalled Security Council deliberations. The fall of the Arbenz government led to an end of UN discussion of the crisis.

Conflict between the Guatemalan government and indigenous communities residing in the country generated extended concern within the United Nations after 1980. Systematic HUMAN RIGHTS violations and political corruption led first to GENERAL ASSEMBLY Resolution 184 on December 17, 1982, that expressed the body's concern over the human rights situation in the country. With the formation of the Rio Group in 1986, which involved representatives from the Contadora Group, the Contadora Support Group, the secretary-general of the OAS, and the SECRETARY-GENERAL of the United Nations, the latter organization became directly involved in the push to bring peace to Guatemala. In 1994 the General Assembly established the United Nations Verification Mission in Guatemala (MINUGUA) to monitor the human rights treatment of INDIGENOUS PEOPLES.

Both the Guatemalan government and its civilian opposition preferred UN involvement in the peace process over that of the OAS. Following the successfully negotiated settlements in Nicaragua and EL SALVADOR, the United Nations Observer Group in Central America helped coordinate talks involving the Guatemalan government and the guerrilla movement. These efforts culminated with the signing of a peace accord in 1996. MINUGUA then took responsibility for verifying that the agreement was being fulfilled.

Further Reading: McCoubrey, Hilaire, and Justin Morris. *Regional Peacekeeping in the Post–Cold War Era.* Boston: Kluwer Law International, 2000. Permanent Mission of Guatemala to the United Nations website: <www.un.int/guatemala>. MINUGUA website: <www.minugua.guate.net>.

— D. K. Lewis

Gulf War

On August 2, 1990, 150,000 Iraqi armed forces invaded the neighboring country of Kuwait, claiming its territory as an integral part of Iraq, driving the ruling al-Sabah family into exile, occupying all of Kuwait within less than two days, and marshaling a huge military force on the Kuwait–Saudi Arabia border. The invasion culminated several months of growing tension between the Iraqi government, headed by Saddam HUSSEIN, and the Kuwaiti regime. The invasion was met with

Burning oil well and destroyed Iraqi tank (UN/DPI PHOTO 158181/J. ISAAC)

an unprecedented coalition of Western and Arab nations, led by the UNITED STATES, that first defended Saudi Arabia and then liberated Kuwait in the spring of 1991. Iraq was branded the "aggressor" in the war by the UN SECURITY COUNCIL and subjected to a series of Council RESOLUTIONS mandating CHAPTER VII ENFORCEMENT MEASURES—the most dramatic exercise of UN authority and power since the KOREAN WAR.

Despite an historical objection by Iraq to the legitimacy of Kuwait's independence and SOVEREIGNTY, the two countries had maintained good relations during the IRAN-IRAQ WAR (1980–87). Kuwait lent several billion dollars to Iraq in an effort keep Iranian Shi'ite influence in the Gulf region confined. When the war was over, however, old tensions reemerged. War-torn Iraq balked at requested repayment of Kuwaiti loans. Instead, it accused Kuwait of keeping international oil prices low (to the detriment of Iraqi postwar reconstruction) by selling oil in excess of Kuwait's OPEC–approved quotas, by opposing higher cartel prices on the world market, and by using slant drilling techniques to "steal" Iraqi oil from the transboundary Rumeilah fields. Arguing that it had defended the Gulf Arab states from Iranian domination, Baghdad sought concessions from Kuwait, including control of two strategic Kuwaiti islands at the northern end of the Persian Gulf. The al-Sabah rulers declined to lease the islands or to make any concessions on oil policy. As the confrontation escalated in the summer of 1990, Hussein held a fateful meeting with the U.S. ambas-

sador to Iraq, April Glaspie. Based on that discussion, including her reference to the nonexistence of a mutual defense PACT between the United States and Kuwait, Hussein and his advisers miscalculated that the international reaction to an Iraqi invasion would be muted.

On August 2 U.S. president George Bush directed the U.S. PERMANENT REPRESENTATIVE to the United Nations, Thomas Pickering, to request an emergency meeting of the Security Council. The occupation of Kuwait directly threatened American interests, it endangered a significant proportion of the world's oil supply, and it jeopardized the security of several American allies in the region. The American initiative found near unanimity of support among UN members and a consensus for action among the Council's five PERMANENT MEMBERS. Over the next three months the Security Council passed 10 RESOLUTIONS meant to isolate Iraq, and to prepare the legal groundwork for collective military action. Among the most important were Resolutions 660 (a condemnation of the invasion), 661 (the imposition of mandatory economic SANCTIONS), 662 (a DECLARATION that the annexation of Kuwait was null and void), 665 (the establishment of a naval blockade and the invitation to member states to make use of the UN MILITARY STAFF COMMITTEE for military preparations), and 678. This last resolution was passed on November 29 and gave Iraq 48 days to withdraw from Kuwait or face military retaliation. For only the second time in its history the United Nations authorized member states to use "all necessary means . . . to restore peace and security in the area." Resolution 678 legitimized the American sponsored military coalition then massing in the Saudi desert. The UN action was reinforced by equivalent condemnations from other international organizations: the ORGANIZATION OF AFRICAN UNITY (August 3), the Gulf Cooperation Council (August 3), the Organization of the Islamic Conference (August 5), and the League of Arab States (August 10).

By August 9 the U.S. military had accepted an invitation from the Saudi government and took up defensive positions along the Saudi-Kuwaiti border. Dubbed "Desert Shield," the first phase of preparations included the dispatch of more than 200,000 U.S. troops to Saudi Arabia. President Bush adroitly worked to put together a coalition of states, unusual in its combination. By January 1991 troop levels had grown to 715,000, with personnel from the United States, the United Kingdom, France, Egypt, Syria, Italy, Morocco, Bangladesh, Bahrain, Qatar, Algeria, Kuwait, Turkey, Senegal, the United Arab Emirates, Saudi Arabia, Oman, Niger, and Pakistan. During the buildup U.S. secretary of state James Baker secured the nonmilitary support of the Soviet Union and Israel. At Bush's direction, he also met with Iraq's foreign minister Tariq Aziz to warn of the consequences of noncompliance with UN resolutions. UN SECRETARY-GENERAL PÉREZ DE CUÉLLAR also traveled to Baghdad to urge compliance. Iraq could count on support only from Libya and the Palestine Liberation Organization, with neutral positions taken by Jordan and Yemen.

The deadline established in Resolution 678 having passed, the coalition commenced Desert Storm on January 16, 1991, a military effort that drove Iraq from Kuwait, beginning with a powerful five and a half week air campaign. Using the most technologically advanced WEAPONS, the UN coalition carried out more than 10,000 sorties in the first week, dropping more than 800,000 tons of munitions. Targets in all parts of Iraq were hit, including civilian sites in Baghdad. Two days into the fighting Iraq launched SCUD missiles against sites in Israel, hoping to draw the Israelis into the war, and to transform the conflict into an Arab struggle against Israel and the United States. Promising to address the ARAB-ISRAELI DISPUTE when the war was over, and dissuading the Israelis from retaliation, President Bush maintained the coalition's resolve to liberate Kuwait. On February 24 the land phase of military operations began. With unexpected ease the coalition forces liberated Kuwait in four days and moved into the southern quarter of Iraq.

Offensive operations ended on February 28 following Iraq's announcement that it would accept all UN resolutions passed since August 2. There was some criticism, especially in the United States, that the allied forces had not marched all the way to Baghdad to force the removal of Saddam Hussein. However, nothing in the UN resolutions that held the multilateral coalition together authorized such action. Arab states in particular would not support efforts beyond the liberation of Kuwait and the implementation of penalties contained in the relevant Security Council resolutions.

In the spring of 1991 the Security Council adopted Resolution 687 establishing the conditions and modalities of a cease-fire. It affirmed Iraq's liability under INTERNATIONAL LAW "for any direct loss, damage, . . . or injury to foreign governments, nationals and corporations, as a result of Iraq's unlawful invasion and occupation of Kuwait." The resolution created a number of bodies to implement its directives. Pursuant to Resolution 687, the Security Council created a Compensation fund to pay claims, its assets coming from 30 percent of Iraqi oil export revenues. As of 2001 the fund had paid more than $300 billion to satisfy 2.6 million claims. The resolution also authorized the Council's Sanctions Committee, created in August 1990 to enforce the mandated embargo, to supply humanitarian materials for civilian use. Also created was the UN Iraq-Kuwait Observation Mission (UNIKOM) to monitor the demilitarized border between the two countries. In addition the Council created the UN SPECIAL COMMISSION ON IRAQ (UNSCOM) to verify Iraqi compliance with all UN resolutions and to carry out no-notice inspections inside of Iraq for the purpose of finding and destroying all WEAPONS OF MASS DESTRUCTION. Finally,

UNSCOM was charged with establishing a permanent system of monitoring and verification to assure that Iraq could not rebuild nuclear, biological, or CHEMICAL WEAPON capabilities. UNSCOM conducted its work under continuing challenge and obstruction from the Baghdad government until Iraq ended all cooperation with the UN agency in 1998. During its seven years of operation UNSCOM's demands on the regime often were buttressed with air reprisals, largely carried out by U.S. and British warplanes, before Hussein would allow the commission's inspections.

The collapse of Iraqi resistance to the coalition assault sparked secessionist efforts in both southern and northern Iraq. The Shia community in the Basra area seized the opportunity to break with Baghdad. In the north Kurds sought to fulfill their long sought goal of an independent Kurdish state. Hussein responded with air attacks against both groups. At the end of March 1991 the Iraqi army launched a massive attack against rebels in the northern part of the country. The attack produced more than 200,000 Kurdish REFUGEES fleeing to the region along Iraq's border with Turkey and 500,000 crossing into Iran. On April 5 the Security Council condemned the attacks and called upon "the Secretary-General to use all the resources at his disposal . . . to address urgently the critical needs of the refugees." The United States, with the assistance of Turkey, Great Britain, and France, established "no-fly" zones in both the north and the south. The four powers launched Operation Provide Comfort, creating a massive humanitarian air-drop operation and protective "enclaves" for Kurds inside Iraq. Almost immediately thereafter the allies urged the United Nations to take over administration of the enclaves. Pérez de Cuéllar was hesitant to do so without the consent of the Iraqi government. To this end he negotiated an agreement with Baghdad on April 18, 1991. With the agreement in place the allied states ceded control of the camps. Unwilling to allow the destabilization of the region that a breakup of Iraq would produce, the United Nations imposed a near protectorate over large parts of the country.

See also COLD WAR, COLLECTIVE SELF-DEFENSE, INTERNATIONAL ATOMIC ENERGY AGENCY, UN SECURITY COUNCIL RESOLUTION 678.

Further Reading: Andersen, Roy R., Robert F. Seibert, and Jon G. Wagner. *Politics and Change in the Middle East: Sources of Conflict and Accommodation.* 6th ed. Upper Saddle River, N.J.: Prentice Hall, 2001. Hiro, Dilip. *Desert Shield to Desert Storm: The Second Gulf War.* London: Paladin, 1992. Moore, John Allphin Jr., and Jerry Pubantz. *To Create a New World? American Presidents and the United Nations.* New York: Peter Lang Publishing, 1999. Sifry, Micah L., and Christopher Cerf. *The Gulf War Reader: History, Documents, Opinions.* New York: Times Books, 1991.

H

habitat   See UNITED NATIONS CENTRE FOR HUMAN SETTLEMENTS.

Hague Academy of International Law

Housed in the Peace Palace at The Hague, Netherlands, with its neighbors the INTERNATIONAL COURT OF JUSTICE (ICJ) and the PERMANENT COURT OF ARBITRATION (PCA), the Hague Academy of International Law provides training for advanced students of INTERNATIONAL LAW. Admission to the academy's programs is granted only to those who have studied law for at least four years or have an equivalent qualification acceptable to the curatorium of the academy, and who are fluent in one of the two working languages of the academy—English or French, the same languages used by the ICJ. The academy's highly regarded summer course program in public international law is open to a selective number of scholars, who are usually supported in their applications by references made to the academy's SECRETARIAT. Participants in the summer program, numbering about 300, come from a wide range of countries and backgrounds, including law professors, diplomats, judges, and practicing lawyers. Lecturers in the program are among the most well known and eminent of international lawyers, including judges from the International Court of Justice. Additionally, the academy has established a respected diploma for those candidates who possess advanced knowledge of international law and pass a rigorous qualifying examination. Since 1950 the academy has awarded the diploma to a limited number of applicants from 54 countries.

Further Reading: The Hague Academy of International Law website: <www.hagueacademy.nl/Eng>.

Haiti

Haiti joined the United Nations as an original member on October 24, 1945. Regarded as the least developed country in the Western Hemisphere, its government first requested assistance from the UN ECONOMIC AND SOCIAL COUNCIL (ECOSOC) in 1948 in an effort to identify and recommend solutions that would assist in the improvement of Haitian economic conditions.

In the 1990s, a political and military crisis in Haiti led to the intervention of UN PEACEKEEPING forces. In the wake of a military coup against the democratically elected government of Father Jean-Bertrand Aristide in September 1991, the United Nations acted in concert with the ORGANIZATION OF AMERICAN STATES (OAS) to defend the right of self-determination and preserve democracy. The GENERAL ASSEMBLY approved economic and trade SANCTIONS and established an embargo against oil and fuel shipments in June 1993. The sanctions led to the Governors Island Accord in July that committed the Haitian military to a gradual relinquishing of power and to Aristide's eventual return to office. As part of the agreement the United Nations established the UN Mission in Haiti (UNMIH) for the purpose of assisting the returned democratic government. However, the continued resistance of the Haitian military and police forces to any return to civilian rule led first to an extension of economic and military sanctions and then to a postponement of UNMIH's deployment. In July 1994, the SECURITY COUNCIL approved the use of military force against the Haitian dictatorship. Before an invasion of U.S. armed forces took place, Haitian officers agreed to a peace settlement on September 17, 1995.

The UN peacekeeping force, comprised of troops from the UNITED STATES, Bangladesh, and India, supervised the transition to civilian rule, which resulted in the election of René Préval as the new president on December 17, 1995. UNMIH was replaced in July 1996 by the United Nations Support Mission in Haiti (UNSMIH) with the mandate of assisting in the professionalization of the Haitian National Police. Under UNSMIH's command, foreign soldiers remained on duty in Haiti until July 1997, and police from Canada and other nations recruited and trained police and security forces within Haiti that would reinforce the authority of the new government. UNSMIH was succeeded by yet four more UN peacekeeping operations to assure Haitian domestic stability to the end of the century: United Nations Transition Mission in Haiti—UNTMIH (August to November, 1997), UNITED NATIONS CIVILIAN POLICE MISSION IN HAITI—MIPONUH (December 1997 to March 2000), International Civilian Support Mission in Haiti—MICAH (succeeded MIPONUH in March 2000), and INTERNATIONAL CIVILIAN MISSION IN HAITI—MICIVIH (a joint UN/OAS operation).

See also LATIN AMERICA.

Further Reading: Perusse, Roland I. *Haitian Democracy Restored, 1991–1995.* Lanham, Md.: University Press of America, 1995. United Nations. *Mission to Haiti: Report of the United Nations Mission of Technical Assistance to the Republic of Haiti.* United Nations Publication 1949, IIB, 2. Lake Success, N.Y.: United Nations Publications, 1949. MICIVIH website: <www.un.org/rights/micivih/first.htm>. MIPONUH website: <www.un.org/Depts/dpko/dpko/co_mission/miponuh.htm>.

— D. K. Lewis

Hammarskjöld, Dag Hjalmar Agne Carl (1905–1961)

The second SECRETARY-GENERAL of the United Nations served from April 10, 1953, until his untimely death on September 18, 1961, while on a peace mission to the recently independent Congo. Hammarskjöld was born in 1905 in Jönköping, Sweden. The son of the Swedish prime minister during World War I—Hjalmar Hammarskjöld—he was brought up in the university town of Uppsala, near Stock-

Secretary-General Dag Hammarskjöld in the Congo (UNITED NATIONS)

holm. At the university in Uppsala he studied French literature, political economy, and law, and in 1934 he completed a doctor's degree in economics at the university in Stockholm. He then joined the Swedish civil service, served in the Ministry of Finance, and eventually became chairman of the board of the bank of Sweden. As World War II ended, he was appointed adviser to the cabinet on financial and economic matters. In 1947 he entered the Foreign Office with the rank of under-secretary, that year participating as a delegate to the Paris Conference that organized the Marshall Plan program for Europe. The following year he was Sweden's head delegate to the Paris Conference that initiated the Organization for European Economic Cooperation. By 1951 he had ascended to the post of deputy foreign minister, and from 1951 to 1953 he represented Sweden at the Sixth and Seventh GENERAL ASSEMBLY sessions held, consecutively, in Paris and New York. In early April 1953, five months after the resignation of Trygve LIE of Norway as Secretary-General, the General Assembly, on the recommendation of the SECURITY COUNCIL, unanimously appointed Hammarskjöld to the post Lie had vacated. In September 1957, the General Assembly, again unanimously, reelected him to a five-year term.

Hammarskjöld's term as Secretary-General was marked by considerable activity, and he approached the job with vigor and dedication. Although tactful and quiet, Hammarskjöld demonstrated an energetic commitment to international diplomacy, and, in the event, extended the influence of the United Nations and enhanced the reputation and visibility of the institution's Secretary-General. On several occasions he criticized the superpowers for ignoring the UN's role in the maintenance of COLLECTIVE SECURITY. In 1954, for example, he urged the UNITED STATES, to no avail, to bring its dispute with the Arbenz government in GUATEMALA to the Security Council. The Eisenhower administration, however, kept the matter out of the Council, preferring the friendlier setting of the ORGANIZATION OF AMERICAN STATES (OAS). Hammarskjöld also complained on several occasions that the UN's responsibility for DISARMAMENT and arms control was being undermined by the American and Soviet monopolization of negotiations.

The Secretary-General traveled extensively in his efforts to lessen tensions in the world. In 1955 he visited Beijing, after which CHINA released 15 detained U.S. flyers who had served with the United Nations forces in Korea. Twice he visited the Middle East in ongoing efforts to stabilize armistice agreements between Israel and the Arab states and to promote peace in the region. Following his efforts (with cooperation from Canadian prime minister Lester PEARSON) to resolve the SUEZ CRISIS of 1956, he guided the launching of the UNITED NATIONS EMERGENCY FORCE (UNEF), sent to the Middle East to help maintain peace and order after the crisis; he led in the creation of the UNITED NATIONS OBSERVATION GROUP IN LEBANON (UNOGIL), dispatched to Lebanon in 1957, and he appointed a SPECIAL REPRESENTATIVE to Jordan in 1958.

His continuing travels took him to numerous countries throughout the world. On one trip, from mid-December 1959 to the end of January 1960, he visited 21 countries and territories in Africa, a "study" trip, he called it, to obtain a "cross-section of every sort of politically responsible opinion in the Africa of today." In fact, Hammarskjöld was committed to making the United Nations a truly universal organization. When, in April 1955, 25 African and Asian countries initiated the "NON-ALIGNED MOVEMENT," pressure for expanding UN MEMBERSHIP grew. In December 1955 Hammarskjöld presided over an agreement between the opposing sides in the COLD WAR—each fearing that the other would profit by membership growth—and realized a dramatic increase in membership, as 16 new nations were admitted, four from the Soviet bloc and the rest from Africa, Asia, and the Arab world. But the biggest challenge confronting the Secretary-General, the one that would result in his death, emerged from the center of Africa.

The Belgian Congo became the independent country of the CONGO on June 30, 1960, and almost immediately civil strife broke out between various factions, some eventually associated with the major cold war competitors. Hopes for stability were particularly endangered when soldiers in the national army revolted against remaining Belgian soldiers, and the southern province of Katanga, led by Moise Tshombe, seceded. The Secretary-General, fearful that Washington and Moscow might once again circumvent the UN, quickly assumed an active role in the crisis. The Congo's new president, Joseph Kasavubu, and his prime minister, Patrice Lumumba, both issued a cable to New York on July 12 urging immediate UN military assistance. In a novel but dramatic moment, Hammarskjöld, exercising Article 99 of the UN CHARTER, convened a night meeting of the Security Council on July 13, urging "utmost speed" in meeting the request. The Security Council called on Belgian forces to withdraw and opposed the secession of Katanga province. Hammarskjöld then helped craft the UN force in the Congo, and personally made four trips to the area in connection with UN operations there. In the meantime, the Secretary-General obtained authority to replace Belgian troops and, going beyond a neutral PEACEKEEPING role, moved to support the central government. But Belgian forces delayed leaving, and Prime Minister Lumumba sent an appeal to Soviet leader Nikita Khrushchev for help. Khrushchev began airlifting WEAPONS and technical advisers to the Congo and called for the United Nations to leave the country. The United States saw Lumumba as a tool of the Soviet Union and persuaded President Kasavubu to dismiss him. Lumumba refused to go and, in the midst of the chaos, Congolese general Joseph Mobutu seized power. The United States now gave its full support to Hammarskjöld's efforts to shore up the central government. At one point, UN forces arrested Lumumba and turned him over to the Kasavubu government, now backed by Mobutu. Kasavubu then callously turned the former prime minister over to Katangan rebels, who promptly executed him. By September 1960, the Soviet Union had determined that the Secretary-General was a tool of U.S. foreign policy, pursuing policies in the Congo that were unneutral and antithetical to its interests. Moscow denounced Hammarskjöld and demanded that he be replaced by a three-person board (the TROIKA PROPOSAL), equally representing the West, Soviet bloc nations, and neutral countries. But Hammarskjöld, with Western support, persisted in his efforts to bring peace and stability to central Africa.

On September 12, 1961, he began what would be the last trip of his unusually vigorous diplomatic career. He was on his way to urge Moise Tshombe, leader of the breakaway province of Katanga, to pursue peace and to drop his plans to secede. He died on September 18, when his plane crashed in a remote area of Northern Rhodesia (now Zambia). Almost immediately, Hammarskjöld became a martyred symbol of the noblest, yet most frustrating, possibilities of international cooperation. His writings, including his popular *Markings*, published in English in 1964, enhanced his fame and further elevated his reputation. Initially, some Third World countries, aggravated by the murder of Patrice Lumumba, and angry Soviet leaders, would not join in the praise. Meantime, a widely performed play by the Irish writer Conor Cruise O'Brien (who had been the Secretary-General's representative in Katanga in 1961) entitled *Murderous Angles; A Political Tragedy and Comedy in Black and White* (1968) raised doubts about the late Secretary-General's character and his Congo policy. Nonetheless, Hammarskjöld's reputation survived. Posthumously he was awarded the 1961

Nobel Peace Prize, and today the DAG HAMMARSKJÖLD MEMORIAL LIBRARY at UN HEADQUARTERS in New York and the nearby Dag Hammarskjöld Plaza reflect the legacy of the second Secretary-General.

Further Reading: Cordier, Andrew W., and Wilder Foote. *Public Papers of the Secretaries-General of the United Nations.* New York: Columbia University Press, 1969–1977. Foote, Wilder, ed. *Servant of Peace; A Selection of the Speeches and Statements of Dag Hammarskjöld, Secretary-General of the United Nations, 1953–1961.* New York: Harper and Row, 1962. Hammarskjöld, Dag. *Markings.* New York: Knopf, 1964. Urquhart, Brian. *Hammarskjöld.* New York: Knopf, 1972. Zacher, Mark W. *Dag Hammarskjöld's United Nations.* New York: Columbia University Press, 1970.

Hammarskjöld Library *See* DAG HAMMARSKJÖLD LIBRARY.

Headquarters of the United Nations

Although the United Nations maintains operations in various parts of the world and several of its PROGRAMMES, SPECIALIZED AGENCIES, and other organizations have headquarters in major international cities—for example, in Paris, The Hague, Rome, Vienna, Nairobi, Washington, D.C., and, most significantly, in Geneva—the official headquarters is in New York City, on First Avenue, between 42nd and 48th Streets. This scenic location adjacent to the East River is the permanent nerve center of the organization, and includes the GENERAL ASSEMBLY building—featuring the GA's magnificent Assembly Hall—the Conference building, with the SECURITY COUNCIL, TRUSTEESHIP COUNCIL, and ECONOMIC AND SOCIAL COUNCIL chambers, the DAG HAMMARSKJÖLD MEMORIAL LIBRARY, and the 39-story SECRETARIAT building.

The inaugural UN General Assembly met in Central Hall, Westminster, London, on January 10, 1946; the Security Council met for the first time in London exactly one week later. There was at that time no permanent location for the new organization. In December 1946, John D. Rockefeller, Jr., offered a gift of $8.5 million to the United Nations to purchase the present site, an 18-acre area known as Turtle Bay. Construction costs, provided in most part by an interest-free loan from the UNITED STATES, came close to $70 million. The complex was designed by a group of international architects led by Wallace K. Harrison of New York, and included Le Corbusier of France, Oscar Niemeyer of Brazil, and Sven Markelius of Sweden. Under the direction of city planner Robert Moses, New York made way for the buildings by diverting First Avenue's through traffic into a tunnel under United Nations Plaza on the west side of the avenue. SECRETARY-GENERAL Trygve LIE and chief architect Harrison laid the cornerstone on October 24, 1949 (the second anniversary of official "United Nations Day"). The Secretariat building opened in 1950 and the General Assembly and Security Council were able to begin meeting there two years later. By 1953 the headquarters was declared finished and ready for full occupancy, but the library was not completed until 1962.

The final product became a major feature of the New York skyline, and an early example of the so-called "international style" of architecture, represented by tall, unadorned rectangular structures typically sheathed in glass. The Secretariat building gave evidence of the new style. A 544-foot-high slab only 72 feet thick, it dominates the group of buildings, with the library to the south and the General Assembly building to the north. Constructed of white Vermont marble and glass and aluminum panels, the Secretariat building, by the turn of the century, accommodated an extensive operation, including the office of the Secretary-General and more than 7,000 international civil servants from many countries, counting among its employees interpreters and translators, experts in INTERNATIONAL LAW and economics, press officers, security officers, tour guides, and more.

Visitors enter the headquarters via one of seven doors at the northern side of the low-lying General Assembly building. Here one finds the great Assembly Hall, the setting for

UN Headquarters, New York City (UN PHOTO/Y. NAGATA/ARA)

annual fall meetings of the largest organ of the United Nations. From its speaker's podium, the world has heard from the most powerful, most famous, and most infamous of national and international leaders, watched over by representatives from some 200 countries, observer groups, and NON-GOVERNMENTAL ORGANIZATIONS (NGOs) who fill the hall, as well as by the president of the General Assembly, an UNDER SECRETARY-GENERAL for political affairs, and the Secretary-General, who are perched above the speakers on a high dais surmounting the rostrum. Behind them is a large emblem of the United Nations, placed between two illuminated boards that indicate the electronic VOTING of members. To either side, in an upper floor behind glassed panels, reside simultaneous translators and representatives of the media. No matter where one is in the great hall, one has a panoramic view of the 75-foot high, 165 feet by 115 feet oval interior.

To enter the United Nations complex is to enter international territory. The land belongs not to just one country, but to all member countries. It has its own security and fire forces, issues its own postage stamps, and conducts business in the six official LANGUAGES of the United Nations. The site is one of the most visited tourist destinations in the world. By 2001, almost 40 million people had taken the tour of the headquarters. Tour guides from some 30 countries conduct tours in more than 20 different languages. Visitors see the Assembly Hall, conference rooms, including the Security Council meeting chamber, and the many exhibits of art, sculpture, and photographs bequeathed to the United Nations by several countries.

Further Reading: Churchill, Henry Stern. "United Nations Headquarters." *Architectural Record* 112 (July 1952). Dudley, George A. *A Workshop for Peace: Designing the United Nations Headquarters.* Cambridge, Mass.: MIT Press, 1994. United Nations Headquarters website: <www.greatbuildings.com/buildings/United_Nations_Headquarter.html>.

Hiss, Alger (1904–1996)

Alger Hiss was an active participant in the U.S. State Department's efforts to create the United Nations, and the central figure in one of the most celebrated espionage cases in early COLD WAR America. A Harvard Law School graduate and protégé of Felix Frankfurter, Oliver Wendell Holmes, and Dean ACHESON, he rose rapidly through the ranks of Franklin ROOSEVELT's New Deal agencies, entering the State Department in 1936.

With the outbreak of World War II in 1939, the State Department began an effort at postwar planning, which intensified when Cordell HULL appointed Leo PASVOLSKY, a special assistant to the secretary, to head a new Division of Special Research. Assisted by Sumner Welles, Pasvolsky became the major architect of what came to be the UN CHAR-

TER. Alger Hiss served as the deputy director of the division and in that role was one of Roosevelt's advisers at the YALTA CONFERENCE. In 1945 he was appointed the secretary-general of the UN's founding San Francisco Conference. Indeed, the Soviet Union proposed that he be elected the first SECRETARY-GENERAL of the United Nations. Leaving the State Department, he went on to serve as president of the Carnegie Endowment of International Peace until 1949.

In 1948 the liberal establishment in America was stunned when Hiss was accused of being a Communist Party member as well as a Soviet spy by *Time* magazine editor Whittaker Chambers, a former party member. Although denying the charge until his death, Hiss was convicted of perjury and jailed for several years. The case became an important icon in the rise of McCarthyism in postwar America, pitting liberals against conservatives for decades to come.

Evidence gleaned from Soviet archives after the end of the cold war convinced most historians that Hiss, indeed, had been an agent of Soviet military intelligence (GRU) since the mid-1930s. With access to the records of the State, War, and Navy Departments, he was a major source for Soviet intelligence operations in the UNITED STATES. During the course of 1945 and 1946 Hiss made extraordinary efforts to acquire top secret reports on atomic energy that were clearly outside of his duties as a specialist on United Nations diplomacy. Occasional suspicions of Alger Hiss were always allayed by his impeccable credentials and ties to the New Deal–Fair Deal elite.

Further Reading: Haynes, John, and Harvey Klehr. *Venona: Decoding Soviet Espionage in America.* New Haven, Conn.: Yale University Press, 1999. Weinstein, Allen, and Alexander Vassiliev. *The Haunted Wood: Soviet Espionage in America—The Stalin Years.* New York: Random House, 1999.

— E. M. Clauss

HIV/AIDS (Human Immunodeficiency Virus/Acquired Immune Deficiency Syndrome)

AIDS was first identified in 1981 among homosexual men in the UNITED STATES. After 20 years, AIDS had become a pandemic disease with cases diagnosed in most regions of the world and primarily among heterosexuals through either sexual intercourse or intravenous drug use. By the year 2001 the disease would infect 58 million people, killing 22 million of them.

There have been distinctive phases in the spread of HIV/AIDS and the subsequent global response. In the first phase, from the mid-1970s until 1981, the epidemic spread silently since its presence was unknown. When AIDS was authoritatively defined in 1981, cases began appearing in various parts of the world—Africa, the Caribbean, Europe,

LATIN AMERICA, and the United States. The scientific community embarked upon a sustained effort to identify the cause of this mysterious illness. The period of discovery of HIV lasted from 1981 to 1984 during which time the medical community was able to identify modes of transmission and those behaviors associated with increased risk of HIV infection. The next phase of global mobilization started in 1985 when the WORLD HEALTH ORGANIZATION (WHO) drafted the global strategy for the prevention and control of HIV/AIDS. Many countries also created national AIDS programs. On a local level, community-based organizations sprang up with programs to deal with HIV prevention and to administer to the needs of those suffering and dying from AIDS.

A gradual realization that HIV/AIDS was rapidly affecting every corner of the world provoked calls for a more concerted international response. The UNITED NATIONS SYSTEM, with its experience in health as well as social and economic DEVELOPMENT issues, was soon compelled to mount an international plan of action. Many believed that the United Nations was best equipped to help mobilize national governments and international organizations, including NON-GOVERNMENTAL ORGANIZATIONS (NGOs), to develop policies both for prevention of HIV transmission and for the mitigation of social and economic consequences of the growing pandemic. The UN response to HIV/AIDS began in the mid-1980s with a coordinated effort between the UNITED NATIONS DEVELOPMENT PROGRAMME (UNDP) and WHO. In February 1987, WHO set up its Special Programme on AIDS, which later received the more permanent title of the Global Programme on AIDS (GPA). In October 1987, the UN GENERAL ASSEMBLY held an extraordinary session on AIDS calling for all parts of the UN system to become engaged in a coordinated effort to address global HIV/AIDS problems.

Despite inter-agency agreements under the leadership of the World Health Organization, coordinating policies, strategies, and support activities became increasingly difficult. In response to these difficulties and to the growing awareness that HIV/AIDS was not only a medical problem but also an epidemic with social, economic, and political complexities, a new UN program, the JOINT UNITED NATIONS PROGRAMME ON HIV/AIDS (UNAIDS), was created in 1996. With seven agencies operating under the leadership of a program SECRETARIAT, UNAIDS recognized the need for greater program coordination to combat the increasingly complex nature of this global pandemic. Important features of the UNAIDS program design included cooperation with the numerous NGOs active in HIV prevention worldwide as well as the active participation of national HIV/AIDS programs.

The UN SECURITY COUNCIL also recognized the potentially destabilizing force of HIV/AIDS, particularly among those communities ravaged by conflicts and warfare. Through a number of RESOLUTIONS, AIDS was identified by the Security Council as the first health and development issue to be considered a threat to global peace and security. Particular attention was focused on the links between regional conflicts in sub-Saharan Africa and the incidence of HIV/AIDS.

The United Nations continued to evolve in its response to the HIV/AIDS pandemic. A "Country Response Monitoring Project" launched in 2000 was just one of the UN's efforts, in collaboration with national governments and NGOs, to provide the latest information on the epidemic in specific countries. In June 2001, the United Nations General Assembly held its first SPECIAL SESSION on HIV/AIDS. The Final Document, known as the Declaration of Commitment, recognized the HIV/AIDS pandemic as much more than a medical problem. With references to political challenges, HUMAN RIGHTS, and economic threats posed by the pandemic, the DECLARATION called for an increased emphasis on prevention efforts bearing in mind the particular vulnerability of WOMEN to HIV disease. In addition, the Special Session called for the immediate implementation of the Heavily Indebted Poor Country Initiative (HIPC) and cancellation of all bilateral debts of HIPC countries, especially those heavily impacted by HIV/AIDS.

Despite these efforts, as of 2001 the AIDS pandemic continued unabated in regions hardest hit. The developing world bore the brunt of this pandemic with 95 percent of those living with HIV/AIDS residing in the Third World. Africa alone accounted for nearly 75 percent of the 36 million people living with HIV/AIDS; another 18 percent lived in South and Southeast Asia. Developing countries lacked the resources to overcome the HIV/AIDS challenges and, less able to take advantage of medical and scientific developments, experienced reverses in many of the economic and social gains achieved through decades of efforts. According to the WORLD BANK, widespread international support was required to help these countries establish viable national HIV/AIDS programs that included basic prevention, treatment, and care. And while promising antiviral drugs had extended the lives of some infected with the HIV virus, the overwhelming majority in the developing world were too poor ever to expect this type of treatment. Of the estimated 36 million HIV-infected people living in 2001, at least 30 million of them were classified as poor (living on less than $2 a day). Most government health programs were incapable of providing the necessary drugs and infrastructure to deal with AIDS in the developing world. Recognizing the urgency of the poorer countries facing the devastation of AIDS, the United Nations called for a Global AIDS and Health Fund to generate between $8 billion and $10 billion annually to respond to the AIDS pandemic. In addition, AIDS activists put political pressure on international pharmaceutical companies to lower the price on HIV/AIDS drug therapies for the developing world. Still, prevention efforts constituted the mainstay in the fight against AIDS. Yet these too were hampered, primarily by poverty but also by cultural norms in some instances and by political considerations in others. The UN General Assembly's Declaration of Commitment in 2001 reflected the controversies surrounding prevention efforts with its notable omission of language on certain "high risk" groups such as homosexuals and sex workers. UNAIDS/WHO reported that at the new millennium 16,000 people—almost half of whom were between the ages of 15 and 24 years old—became newly infected everyday with HIV.

See also ADMINISTRATIVE COMMITTEE ON COORDINATION.

Further Reading: Bastos, Cristiana. *Global Responses to AIDS: Science in Emergency.* Bloomington: Indiana University Press, 1999. Mann, Jonathan, and Daniel Tarantola, eds. *AIDS in the World II.* New York: Oxford University Press, 1996. Smith, Raymond. *Encyclopedia of AIDS: A Social, Political, Cultural, and Scientific Record of the HIV Epidemic.* Chicago: Fitzroy Dearborn Publishers, 2000.

— *R. E. McNamara*

Hull, Cordell (1871–1955)

In 1945 Cordell Hull was awarded the Nobel Peace Prize for his role in establishing the United Nations. Appointed secretary of state by President Franklin ROOSEVELT in 1933, Hull served until 1944, longer than any other secretary in U.S. history. Roosevelt, joining in wide recognition, called him the "Father of the United Nations."

Hull was born in a log cabin in Pickett County, Tennessee. He was educated at the Montvale Academy at Celina, Tennessee, the Normal School at Bowling Green, Kentucky, and the National Normal University at Lebanon, Ohio. He obtained a law degree in 1891 upon completing a one-year course at Cumberland University at Lebanon, Tennessee. Elected to the Tennessee House of Representatives in 1893, he later fought in the Spanish-American War, served in the U.S. Congress from 1907 to 1931, and was elected to the U.S. Senate in 1930, but he resigned upon his appointment as secretary of state in 1933. He actively pursued the Roosevelt administration's "Good Neighbor" policy with LATIN AMERICA, attending several hemispheric meetings during the 1930s. A proponent of liberalized international trade, Hull urged the Reciprocal Trade Agreements Act of 1934, which reversed the high tariff policies of the 1920s. He negotiated numerous treaties under authority of the act that lowered tariff barriers and stimulated international commerce.

Shortly after the outbreak of World War II, Hull proposed that a new international organization be created to replace the failed LEAGUE OF NATIONS. A supporter and admirer of President Woodrow Wilson's moralistic and legalistic visions of world affairs, Hull was also keenly mindful of that president's failure with the League. Determined to have the UNITED STATES participate in the new postwar organization, Hull in 1941 formed a bipartisan Advisory Committee on Postwar Foreign Policy to assure that a wide spectrum of the country's political views were represented in discussions. The committee included members of Congress, senators, experts from the private sphere, and State Department officials. Hull, chairman of the group, pressed for public discussions of the plans being considered, and oversaw the formulation of detailed proposals.

Hull's efforts within the State Department began as early as 1939. He was approached by the Council on Foreign Relations (CFR) with a proposal that the CFR form a group of experts to research postwar issues under the "general guidance" of the department. Hull accepted the idea, and the Council established the War and Peace Studies Project. Hull set up a department committee for postwar planning in December 1939, and he appointed Under Secretary of State Sumner Welles to chair it. In early 1943 he appointed a close confidant—Leo PASVOLSKY—as his "special adviser" in charge of preparatory work for the proposed international organization. His efforts resulted in composition of a State Department draft document in August 1943, entitled "CHARTER of the United Nations." This document became the basis for discussions at the DUMBARTON OAKS CONFERENCE in 1944.

At the MOSCOW CONFERENCE OF FOREIGN MINISTERS in October 1943, Hull successfully brought the issue forward, and for the remainder of his service in the department he was chiefly occupied with forwarding plans for a United Nations. Following the conference, the Secretary of State established an "Informal Political Agenda Group," which crafted the outlines of the world body. President Roosevelt approved the group's recommendations early in 1944.

Although President Roosevelt and Prime Minister Winston CHURCHILL early indicated a penchant for a postwar world of more or less independent regional councils and SPECIALIZED AGENCIES, with all but four nations—the United States, the United Kingdom, the Soviet Union, and CHINA—disarmed, Hull insisted that the new peace organization be universal in character, and that no parts be greater than the whole. With the Four-Power Declaration of the Dumbarton Oaks Conference, Hull's views triumphed in language that called for "a general international organization, based on the . . . sovereign equality of all peace-loving states, and open to MEMBERSHIP by all such states, large and small."

On November 27, 1944, Hull, citing ill health, resigned, and he was replaced by Edward STETTINIUS, who faithfully carried on his predecessor's work. Hull, who had seemed to lose influence with the president as the war proceeded, nonetheless received from Roosevelt praise as "the one person in all the world who has done the most to make this great plan for peace an effective fact."

See also DECLARATION BY UNITED NATIONS, INTERNATIONAL COURT OF JUSTICE, MOSCOW DECLARATION, TRUSTEESHIP SYSTEM.

Further Reading: Drummond, Donald F. "Cordell Hull." In *An Uncertain Tradition: American Secretaries of State in the Twentieth Century.* Edited by Norman A. Graebner. New York: McGraw Hill, 1961. Gellman, Irwin F. *Secret Affairs: Franklin Roosevelt, Cordell Hull, and Sumner Welles.* Baltimore: Johns Hopkins University Press, 1995. Hull, Cordell. *The Memoirs of Cordell Hull.* Two vols. New York: Macmillan, 1948. Pratt, Julius W. *Cordell Hull, 1933–1944.* New York: Cooper Square Publishers, 1964.

human rights

The United Nations was the first international organization to address the issue of human rights, and it has remained a central concern of the institution since its founding. Before World War II, human rights were rarely addressed in international relations. For example, the COVENANT of the LEAGUE OF NATIONS did not use the term "human rights." International diplomats previously had addressed only narrow questions of what might be called "worst practices," such as when banning the slave trade in 1815, which led much later to the Slavery Convention of 1926. The Hague Convention of 1907 dealt with a government's treatment of foreign nationals, but the document said nothing about treatment of its own citizens. Under the principle of SOVEREIGNTY, the relations between a government and its people were considered an internal matter, and, even in the view of a number of nations at the turn of the 21st century, outside intrusion on that relationship continued to be regarded as a violation of INTERNATIONAL LAW.

Addressing human rights on an international level involved two problematic challenges. The first was that NATION-STATES held different views regarding the role of the international community in the area of rights. Second, while many people agreed that there was a set of basic human rights, not all agreed on what was included under the term "rights." Dissimilar cultures placed different definitions and different priorities on the claim of rights, and indeed even on the basis from which such rights derived. Initially, the impetus for the idea of human rights was Western-based, and since the CHARTER was drawn up by a small group of wartime allies, it reflected Western views of this concept.

Although the UN Charter did not contain specific definitions and procedures regarding this issue, it was the first international agreement in which the signatory nations made a commitment to promote human rights at the international level. The fundamental nature of this issue was indicated in the Preamble. It declared that one of the UN's purposes was "to reaffirm faith in the fundamental human rights, in the dignity and worth of the human person, in equal rights of men and WOMEN and of nations large and small."

The Charter contains several references to human rights. The term is used in Articles 13, 55, 56, 62, 68, and 76. The Charter authorizes the United Nations to make recommendations to member states regarding human rights policies, and it declares that the states have an obligation to consider its proposals carefully. The Charter limits the organization to making recommendations, since only treaties can create legally binding obligations. Under the Charter all the PRINCIPAL ORGANS of the United Nations can deal with human rights, and each of them has addressed this topic at one time or another.

Yet while Article 68 of the Charter empowers the ECONOMIC AND SOCIAL COUNCIL (ECOSOC) to set up commissions to promote human rights it made no effort to define the term "Human Rights," and reaching agreement on what constituted such rights required a prolonged effort that gradually expanded the meaning of the term. The deliberations reflected the sensitivity of the issue and the new departure represented by the Charter. The founding San Francisco Conference shunned proposals to define the term, reflecting the challenge posed by the concept of national sovereignty. At its initial session in 1946, the COMMISSION ON HUMAN RIGHTS, created that year by ECOSOC, established a small drafting group to prepare the UNIVERSAL DECLARATION OF HUMAN RIGHTS (UDHR). Eleanor ROOSEVELT, wife of U.S. president Franklin D. Roosevelt, chaired the drafting committee. Mrs. Roosevelt played a central role in the evolution of the document, along with John Humphrey of Canada, the first director of the SECRETARIAT's Division of Human Rights, Charles Malik, rapporteur of the commission, Dr. Peng-chun Chang, who represented an Asian perspective on rights, and Frenchman René Cassin, who in 1968 won the Nobel Peace Prize for his involvement in the drafting of the DECLARATION. Throughout the drafting, the Soviet Union and its Eastern European allies resisted the idea of defining human rights.

Western nations and their citizens, drawing on a tradition of democratic politics that accentuates the primacy of the individual, place strong emphasis on civil and political rights. That is, they stress the rights of the person, and tend to view human rights as protecting the individual from actions by the state. They emphasize protection of minority groups against overweening majority power. This viewpoint advocates that human rights be articulated and proclaimed in print, and, furthermore, ascertained and protected by judicial process. Such an outlook emphasizes rights such as free speech, freedom of religion, freedom of assembly, specific rights of the accused, and the right to organize.

Developing nations, on the other hand, emphasize economic, social, and cultural rights. In part, this viewpoint is based on their living conditions. Theirs is a collective outlook that holds that societies, as groups, have rights, and that the rights of the group as a whole supercede the rights of the individual. In this view, the good of the majority transcends the protection of the minority. Developing nations and their citizens also believe that the state offers the only prospect for development of the society, and hence view human rights as the basis for state action, rather than as designed to protect the individual from the state. This approach to human rights speaks to the goals and responsibilities of the state, requiring government action to provide citizens with the conditions and facilities essential for the full realization of rights. Developing nations view economic rights, particularly the right to development, as the most basic rights, and therefore essential to the exercise of all other rights. Developing nations also view these rights as creating obligations for the international system as a whole, including the provision of needed resources for development. Developing nations have emphasized the primacy of rights such as adequate food, tolerable living standards, and requisite shelter, which they regard as essential to human dignity. Western nations tend to reject development as a right equivalent to individual freedoms. The Western nations have resisted elevating economic rights to a position of primacy, since they view this as an effort to redistribute wealth to their disadvantage.

On December 10, 1948, the GENERAL ASSEMBLY adopted the Universal Declaration of Human Rights as "a common standard of achievement for all peoples and all nations, to the end that every individual and every organ of society, keeping this Declaration constantly in mind, shall strive by teaching and education to promote respect for these rights and freedoms and by progressive measures, national and international, to secure their universal and effective recognition and observance, both among the peoples of Member States themselves and among the peoples of territories under their JURISDICTION." Reflecting the predominantly Western MEMBERSHIP of the United Nations in 1948, prior to decolonization, 22 of the Declaration's 30 articles deal with individual, civil, and political rights, and only six articles deal with economic, social, and cultural rights. The declaration stresses the "inherent dignity" of the individual, the principle of equality, and the three interrelated fundamental rights of life, liberty, and the security of the person. It also recognizes the need for social order, and therefore that individuals also have duties, which impose certain limitations on the exercise of their rights. Since those limitations are determined by national law, the declaration accepts the principle that states can limit human rights, providing that such laws are "solely for the purpose of securing due recognition and respect for the rights" of others, and establishing "the just requirements of morality, public order and the general welfare in a democratic society." The Universal Declaration set the direction for all subsequent agreements in the field of human rights.

It required elaborate negotiations spanning another 18 years to produce the other documents that comprise the composite "International Bill of Human Rights." In 1948, the CONVENTION ON THE PREVENTION AND PUNISHMENT OF THE CRIME OF GENOCIDE was opened for signature. The much more specific INTERNATIONAL COVENANT ON CIVIL AND POLITICAL RIGHTS (ICCPR) and the INTERNATIONAL COVENANT ON ECONOMIC, SOCIAL, AND CULTURAL RIGHTS (ICESCR), which, with the Universal Declaration, collectively comprise the International Bill of Human Rights, were only adopted by the General Assembly in 1966. Another 10 years elapsed before the covenants were ratified by the requisite 35 nations to come into force, and then they were binding only on those nations that had ratified them. The International Covenants were adopted as two separate documents rather than as a single CONVENTION because Western nations objected to the inclusion of economic, social, and cultural rights, which they contended were goals that were not enforceable. Developing nations insisted on including economic and social rights, since they considered these to be the most fundamental. As a compromise, two separate documents were composed and introduced simultaneously. Reflecting the NORTH-SOUTH controversy, there were a few "no" votes to each.

The two covenants spelled out in more detail the rights involved in each category. Unlike the Universal Declaration, they were written in the form of treaties, requiring ratification by the member states, and consequently creating legally binding obligations. The ICCPR detailed the freedoms of speech, press, worship, assembly, security of person and property, political participation, and procedural due process, protecting the individual against arbitrary and unreasonable government action. Each state assumed the obligation to submit regular reports to the HUMAN RIGHTS COMMITTEE, which reviewed them in detail and made recommendations to governments for improvement and additional legislation. The ICESCR provided guarantees of "the right of everyone to the enjoyment of an adequate standard of living for himself and his family, including adequate food, clothing, and housing, and to the continuous improvement of living conditions." It also guaranteed access by all to adequate education, social security, medical care, employment, shelter, mental health, and leisure, requiring an expansion of governmental functions. At the insistence of the developing nations, which by 1966 made up a majority of UN membership, both documents recognized the right of self-determination. By December 31, 1995, ratifications of the two covenants had reached 132, or about two-thirds of the member states of the United Nations.

Regional efforts revealed the differing viewpoints regarding human rights. The Western Hemisphere acted first, when the ORGANIZATION OF AMERICAN STATES unanimously approved the American Declaration on the Rights and Duties of Man on May 2, 1948. It was the first international human rights document to include a detailed enumeration of those rights. The document reflected the region's Western heritage, and consequently emphasized civil and political rights. But it insisted on an individual's duties as well. Reflecting Western traditions, it included the right to life and to asylum. However, it also stressed the protection of the family, its mothers and children, and the inviolability of the home. In 1948 the Western Hemisphere nations also adopted the Inter-American Charter of Social Guarantees, protecting workers' rights and stressing the goal of raising the standard of living. The American Convention on Human Rights of 1969, also known as the PACT of San José, entered into force in 1976. It established the Inter-American Court of Human Rights and the Inter-American Commission of Human Rights. The commission investigates complaints and makes recommendations to signatory governments. The court can adjudicate complaints brought by other states. Individual complaints can be made to the commission, which has the power to place cases before the Inter-American Court.

The European Convention for the Protection of Human Rights and Fundamental Freedoms was drafted by the Council of Europe and entered into force in 1953. At the time, its application was confined to Western Europe, since it was written when the COLD WAR divided the continent. It established the European Commission of Human Rights, which reviewed complaints by individuals as well as NON-GOVERN-MENTAL ORGANIZATIONS (NGOs), and the European Court of Human Rights, whose decisions were binding among signatories. Individuals could bring complaints before the court.

In many respects the most significant regional agreement was the African Charter of Human and Peoples' Rights, also known as the Banjul Charter, signed in 1981, which came into force in 1986. The African Charter was a major document reflecting the views of the developing nations and former colonies. It was notable for its statement of the collective rights of peoples, as revealed in its title, pointing out that the rights of the nation as a collective take primacy over the rights of individuals. It stressed that individuals have duties to their families and the society as a whole, and consequently that the "rights and freedoms of each individual, shall be exercised with due regard to the rights of others, COLLECTIVE SECURITY, morality, and common interest." The charter placed considerable emphasis on economic, social, and cultural rights. The African Charter was the first international agreement to include both classes of rights, civil and political, as well as economic, social, and cultural, within a single document. It was also the first international document to identify the right to development as the most fundamental right of all. It included the right of peoples to peace and security, and the right to an ENVIRONMENT supportive of the health of its citizens. In 1988 the ORGANIZATION OF AFRICAN UNITY established the African Commission on Human and Peoples' Rights, which was primarily a body to study and collect information on "African problems in human and peoples' rights."

Other regions acted in a more limited manner. In the Middle East, the issue of human rights has been more contentious than in other regions, echoing the conflict that has polarized the region since the end of World War II. Middle Eastern countries were divided in their attitudes toward the adoption of the Universal Declaration. Initial resistance came from fundamentalist Islamic states that objected to the right of religious conversion. However, the League of Arab States established the Arab Commission on Human Rights in 1968 that was empowered to draft regional agreements in this field. The Islamic Conference adopted the broader Cairo Declaration on Human Rights in Islam in 1990.

Countries in Asia have shown the strongest inclination to abstain from Western notions of the universality of human rights. Asian states' firmness on asserting the inviolability of national sovereignty has meant that no agreement on an Asian human rights instrument has ever been reached. At the turn of the century Asia remained the only continent without such a document.

The UN's role has been to formulate standard and voluntary norms through conferences and declarations, and then to encourage conformity, while having little enforcement power. It carries out its mission by promoting international agreements that set standards, and then urges member states to report on their progress. The United Nations supplies information and assists nations in meeting human rights standards through technical missions and by developing model codes and programs. These procedures depend on monitoring to encourage states to develop legislation to implement the rights involved. The Commission on Human Rights serves as the main monitoring body. Compliance with universal standards is voluntary, and implementation is up to individual governments.

In 1967, the Economic and Social Council authorized the Commission on Human Rights to move beyond general discussion, and to consider human rights violations in individual countries. While no enforcement was possible, both the commission and the General Assembly passed RESOLUTIONS condemning the worst abuses on a country-specific basis each year. In 1979–80 the commission expanded its efforts by establishing special procedures to enable investigations, which led to the appointment of SPECIAL RAPPORTEURS to investigate and compile reports for the commission. Rapporteurs were employed both to investigate thematic issues such as torture, summary executions, violence against women, racial discrimination, and religious discrimination, and to investigate the situation in particular countries. This procedure ensured discussion of the topic, and often led to resolutions on the subject. In 2000 there were 15 Special Rapporteurs covering a range of topical and country situations. A number of non-governmental organizations, which served as advocates for human rights, also monitored situations throughout the world and submitted their own reports to the various UN bodies.

Throughout its existence the United Nations has negotiated and adopted a long list of conventions and declarations regarding specific rights that have sought to extend and clarify the meaning of "human rights." Some were drafted by the commission, some by other bodies, and several resulted from UN conferences or came from SPECIALIZED AGENCIES. Among the principal documents on the long list are the conventions on the Elimination of All Forms of Racial Discrimination (1966), the Suppression and Punishment of the Crime of APARTHEID (1973), the Political Rights of Women (1953), the Elimination of All Forms of Discrimination Against Women (1979), the Suppression of the Traffic in Persons (1950), the Status of Refugees (1951), the Status of Stateless Persons (1954), against Torture and other Cruel and Inhuman or Degrading Treatment or Punishment (1984), the Rights of the Child (1989), and the Protection of the Rights of All Migrant Workers (1990). Declarations were issued dealing with the Eradication of Hunger and Malnutrition (1974), the Protection of Women and Children in Emergency and Armed Conflict (1974), the Rights of Disabled Persons (1975), the Right to Development (1986), and the Rights of Persons Belonging to National, Ethnic, Religious, and Linguistic Minorities (1992). These joined the initial Convention on Genocide to constitute a body of humanitarian law. Additional PROTOCOLs were added to several of the existing covenants. All set standards and required reporting by governments, although all nations had not ratified all agreements.

Other agencies and organizations within the UNITED NATIONS SYSTEM also have negotiated agreements relating to human rights. For example, several treaties regarding the rights of labor, including the right to organize, were formulated through the INTERNATIONAL LABOUR ORGANIZATION (ILO). Other agencies include the UNITED NATIONS CHILDREN'S FUND (UNICEF), the United Nations COMMISSION ON THE STATUS OF WOMEN, and the UNITED NATIONS HIGH COMMISSIONER FOR REFUGEES (UNHCR). In 1993 the WORLD CONFERENCE ON HUMAN RIGHTS, known as the Vienna Conference, conducted a global review of human rights and the UN work in this area. The Vienna Declaration and Program of Action, adopted by participants representing 171 nations, highlighted the links among development, democracy, and the promotion of human rights, bridging the differing interpretations of the West and the developing nations. It emphasized the universality, indivisibility, and interdependence of civil, cultural, economic, political, and social rights, declaring all to be the responsibility of governments and requiring governments to promote all human rights and fundamental freedoms. The declaration reaffirmed the right to development as a universal, inalienable, integral, and fundamental part of human rights. The signatories of the Vienna Declaration agreed that the development of the poorest nations was the collective responsibility of the international community. The Final Document asserted that extreme poverty and social exclusion constituted a "violation of human dignity." The declaration emphasized the rights of all vulnerable groups, especially women, and extended this protection to INDIGENOUS PEOPLES.

In one of its most controversial decisions, the Vienna Declaration recommended the creation of the position of UN HIGH COMMISSIONER FOR HUMAN RIGHTS, a new office to advocate human rights and to coordinate UN programs, agencies, and offices involved in this field. Established in 1993, the High Commissioner serves as the focal point for all United Nations human rights activities, and acts as the SECRETARIAT for all treaty bodies monitoring compliance with human rights covenants and agreements. The CENTRE FOR HUMAN RIGHTS became part of the Office of the High Commissioner. Located in Geneva, the centre conducts studies and provides recommendations, information, and analysis to all UN organs dealing with human rights issues.

The various UN and regional human rights bodies are assisted by a large number of non-governmental organizations that serve as advocates of human rights and work to protect them. At times the NGOs intervene to protect individuals who are denied their rights. These NGOs constantly monitor the situation in each of the world's nations, and they submit informative reports to the various monitoring bodies. While functioning separately, they therefore are indirectly a part of the global monitoring system for human rights. Human rights is an area of concern for one of the largest number of non-governmental organizations.

In the course of developing human rights treaties, the United Nations adopted the Nuremberg Tribunal Charter, under which World War II war criminals were tried for "crimes against humanity." These were defined as crimes of "murder, extermination, enslavement, deportation, and other inhumane acts committed against any civilian population, before or during a war . . . whether or not in violation of the domestic law of the country where perpetrated." Both the Convention on Genocide and the Convention on the Suppression and Punishment of the Crime of Apartheid (1973) defined these as crimes against humanity.

Following the conclusion of the cold war, the United Nations established judicial bodies to deal with this type of crime. The SECURITY COUNCIL established the INTERNATIONAL CRIMINAL TRIBUNAL FOR THE FORMER YUGOSLAVIA in 1993, with headquarters in The Hague. The INTERNATIONAL CRIMINAL TRIBUNAL FOR RWANDA, with headquarters in Arusha, Tanzania, was established in 1994. Each had jurisdiction involving only the specified countries, and in the Rwandan case for Rwandan citizens who may have committed war crimes in neighboring states. The creation of these tribunals embodies an expression of the worldwide horror at the GENOCIDE practiced in both crises, which differentiated them from other conflicts. In 1998, a conference of 100 countries approved the Rome Statute of the INTERNATIONAL CRIMINAL COURT (ICC) establishing a permanent court, independent of the United Nations, to investigate and decide cases involving individuals responsible for the most serious crimes of concern to the international community. Its statute extended the court's jurisdiction to genocide, war crimes, and crimes against humanity, and provided definitions for these crimes. On April 11, 2002, 10 nations deposited their ratifications of the statute, bringing the ICC into existence as of July 1. While there was considerable controversy about the jurisdiction and powers of the court, its creation constituted a significant new departure in the enforcement and definition of human rights.

The General Assembly declared 1995–2004 as the UN Decade for Human Rights Education. The decade sought to encourage the establishment of national committees composed of representatives from both public and private sectors in each country to promote education about and awareness of human rights.

See also AFGHANISTAN, AGENDA FOR DEVELOPMENT, BEIJING +5, BRICKER AMENDMENT, CHAPTER VI ¹/₂, COMMITTEE OF 24, CONGO, CONVENTION AGAINST TORTURE AND OTHER CRUEL, INHUMAN OR DEGRADING TREATMENT OR PUNISHMENT, CONVENTION ON THE ELIMINATION OF ALL FORMS OF DISCRIMINATION AGAINST WOMEN, CONVENTION ON THE ELIMINATION OF ALL FORMS OF RACIAL DISCRIMINATION, CONVENTION ON THE POLITICAL RIGHTS OF WOMEN, DECLARATION BY UNITED NATIONS, GLOBAL COMPACT, *JUS COGENS,* MILLENNIUM SUMMIT, OFFICE FOR THE COORDINATION OF HUMANITARIAN AFFAIRS, PEACEKEEPING, RWANDA CRISIS, SIERRA LEONE, UNITED NATIONS DEVELOPMENT FUND FOR WOMEN, UNITED NATIONS MISSION IN BOSNIA AND HERZEGOVINA, UNITED NATIONS TRANSITIONAL ADMINISTRATION IN EAST TIMOR.

Further Reading: Alston, Philip, ed. *The United Nations and Human Rights: A Critical Appraisal.* Oxford: Oxford University Press, 1992. Donnelly, Jack. *International Human Rights.* Boulder, Colo.: Westview Press, 1998. Langley, Winston E. *Encyclopedia of Human Rights Issues since 1945.* Westport, Conn.: Greenwood Press, 1999. United Nations. *The United Nations and Human Rights: 1945–1995.* New York: United Nations, 1995.

— *K. J. Grieb*

Human Rights Commission   *See* COMMISSION ON HUMAN RIGHTS.

Human Rights Committee (HRC)

Article 28 of the INTERNATIONAL COVENANT ON CIVIL AND POLITICAL RIGHTS established the Human Rights Committee to monitor the progress made by signatory states in ensuring "the equal rights of men and WOMEN to the enjoyment of all civil and political rights." The 18 committee members are elected by the states party to the COVENANT, but they do not represent their states. They serve in their personal capacity as individuals of high moral character and with expertise in the field of HUMAN RIGHTS. Sometimes confused with the

UN COMMISSION ON HUMAN RIGHTS, which was created in 1946 and drafted the UNIVERSAL DECLARATION OF HUMAN RIGHTS, the Human Rights Committee was established in 1976, meets three times yearly in New York or Geneva, and considers reports on human rights conditions in the specific nations that have signed the covenant.

The International Covenant detailed the freedoms of speech, press, worship, assembly, security of person and property, political participation, procedural due process, and individual protection against arbitrary and unreasonable government action. Each state assumed the obligation to submit regular reports to the Human Rights Committee, which reviews them in detail and makes recommendations to governments for improvement and additional legislation. In addition, as of 2001, 95 states had accepted the covenant's First Optional PROTOCOL that gave the committee the COMPETENCE to receive petitions from individuals alleging human rights abuses by their own governments. The committee also has oversight of the Second Optional Protocol, which entered into force in 1991, seeking to eliminate the use of the death penalty. Forty-three states had approved that protocol by 2001.

Under the committee's rules of procedure, the HRC provides guidelines to signatory states for the preparation of national reports. Those reports are then discussed by the committee with the state's representatives present. The committee publishes a summary of its findings in what are called "general comments." These commentaries are written in broad, vague terms. Specific criticisms and recommendations are conveyed under terms of confidentiality to the government concerned.

Further Reading: Langley, Winston E. *Encyclopedia of Human Rights Issues since 1945.* Westport, Conn.: Greenwood Press, 1999. United Nations Centre for Human Rights, and United Nations Institute for Training and Research. *Manual on Human Rights Reporting under Six Major International Human Rights Instruments.* New York: United Nations, 1991.

Human Rights Conventions   *See* HUMAN RIGHTS.

Human Rights Day

Celebrated on December 10 annually, HUMAN RIGHTS Day marks the anniversary of the GENERAL ASSEMBLY'S adoption of the UNIVERSAL DECLARATION OF HUMAN RIGHTS in 1948. It has been celebrated since 1950.

Hussein, Saddam (1937–)

Saddam Hussein was born in 1937 in Tikrit, Iraq. He was educated at the Universities of Cairo and Baghdad and became a member of Iraq's Ba'ath Socialist Party in 1957. Following imprisonment in 1964, Hussein participated in General Bakr's 1968 revolution. Hussein succeeded Bakr to become chairman of Iraq's Revolution Command Council and, in 1979, president of Iraq. He proceeded to establish a harsh system of one-man rule, making use of an extended family from Tikrit and favored military personnel to maintain tight control on the country.

In 1980 Hussein initiated the IRAN-IRAQ WAR (1980–88) by ordering Iraqi forces into Iran. It was during this conflict that Hussein used poison gas against Iranian troops as well as Kurds in northern Iraq. The muted UN response to this conflict stands in stark contrast to the international outcry that accompanied Hussein's 1990 invasion of Kuwait.

During the Iran-Iraq War, Saudi Arabia, Kuwait, and several Western states, desiring to preserve a balance of power in the Persian Gulf region between Iraq and the larger Islamic revolutionary government of Iran, provided financial and military assistance to Hussein's regime. One factor that prompted Hussein to invade Kuwait was a Kuwaiti refusal to forgive $14 billion in loans extended to Iraq to help fight Iran. Hussein's invasion of Kuwait was met with an avalanche of UN SECURITY COUNCIL resolutions. In accordance with these resolutions, a U.S.-led coalition forcibly removed Iraqi forces from Kuwait.

Following a March 1991 cease-fire, the United Nations imposed crippling SANCTIONS on Iraq. American administrations, and their allies in the Security Council, maintained that these sanctions were necessary to prevent Hussein from replenishing his arsenal of WEAPONS OF MASS DESTRUCTION. As such, the UNITED STATES refused to allow the Security Council to revisit the RESOLUTION that imposed the sanctions, despite the hardship they caused to ordinary Iraqi citizens. Hussein used the unpopularity of the sanctions to maintain his grip on power in Iraq. Repeatedly he challenged the inspections regime imposed by the United Nations, and the no-fly zones maintained by the coalition partners both in the northern and southern areas of Iraq. In 1998 he permanently expelled the UN WEAPONS inspectors. By 2001 Saddam Hussein had gained some support in the Arab world and among outside powers for a relaxation of the sanctions or, in some instances, a normalization of relations. U.S. secretary of state Colin Powell, who entered office in early 2001, began a diplomatic effort to refine the UN sanctions so as to meet growing criticisms. In the spring of 2002 Hussein's government began negotiations with UN officials about the possibility of readmitting weapons inspectors, ostensibly in return for an easing of the sanctions.

See also GULF WAR, UNITED NATIONS IRAQ-KUWAIT OBSERVER COMMISSION, UNITED NATIONS MONITORING, VERIFICATION, AND INSPECTION COMMISSION, UNITED NATIONS SPECIAL COMMISSION ON IRAQ, UN SECURITY COUNCIL RESOLUTION 598, UN SECURITY COUNCIL RESOLUTION 678.

Further Reading: Makiya, Kanan. *Republic of Fear: The Politics of Modern Iraq.* Berkeley: University of California Press, 1998. Moore, John Allphin Jr., and Jerry Pubantz. *To Create a New World? American Presidents and the United Nations.* New York: Peter Lang Publishers, 1999. Pérez de Cuéllar, Javier. *Pilgrimage for Peace: A Secretary General's Memoir.* New York: St. Martin's, 1997.

—*S. F. McMahon*

I

IAEA Safeguards *See* INTERNATIONAL ATOMIC ENERGY AGENCY.

Implementation Force (IFOR) *See* BOSNIA.

important question

Article 18 of the UN CHARTER has three paragraphs. The second of these refers to "important questions" which require a two-thirds vote of those "present and VOTING" in any session of the GENERAL ASSEMBLY (GA). The GA's Rules of Procedure define the words "members present and voting" as "members casting an affirmative or negative vote. Members which abstain from voting are considered as not voting." Thus, the two-thirds vote mandated for Important Questions could actually be less than a majority of all the members of the General Assembly.

The distinction in Article 18 between "important" and "other" questions is detailed in the second paragraph, where Important Questions are specified, and in the third paragraph, which allows the General Assembly, by majority vote, to determine what "other" questions must be decided by a two-thirds vote of those present and voting. According to the second paragraph, a two-thirds vote **must** be obtained on the following Important Questions: matters relating to international peace and security, electing NON-PERMANENT MEM-BERS to the SECURITY COUNCIL (SC) and all members of the ECONOMIC AND SOCIAL COUNCIL (ECOSOC) and the TRUSTEESHIP COUNCIL, the ADMISSION OF MEMBERS to the United Nations, the SUSPENSION AND EXPULSION OF MEMBERS, issues regarding the operation of the TRUSTEESHIP SYSTEM, and budgetary questions. Also, the General Assembly Rules of Procedure require a two-thirds vote in order to reconsider proposals that have been adopted or rejected, and in order to add items to the supplementary list or the agenda of an EMERGENCY SPECIAL SESSION. By Rule 84 of the Rules of Procedure, amendments to proposals relating to Important Questions must obtain a two-thirds vote of those present and voting.

Over the years the General Assembly, using the provisions of the third paragraph of Article 18, has, by a simple majority vote, determined that "other" questions are, in fact, "important" and require a two-thirds vote of those present and voting. (This is a practice only recognized in the General Assembly; none of the GA main committees has such a rule; their decisions are made by a simple majority.) Numerous examples include: consideration of new trusteeship agreements, questions relating to racial conflict in South Africa, questions relating to South-West Africa, and issues of decolonization. Perhaps the most legendary use of this procedure dealt with the representation of CHINA in the United Nations. From 1961 on the UNITED STATES used the third paragraph of Article 18 to make any consideration of changing Chinese representation an Important Question, requiring

147

a two-thirds vote. By assuring a simple majority vote to resolve that the issue of representation was an "important question," Washington was able to insist on an insurmountable two-thirds vote to seat the People's Republic of China and to remove the government of the Chinese Republic on Taiwan from the United Nations (and the Security Council). The procedure worked until 1971. On October 25 of that year the vote on the Important Question RESOLUTION regarding Chinese representation narrowly lost for the first time, 59 to 55, with 15 abstentions, and on the next vote, the General Assembly seated Beijing as the official Chinese representative and removed Taiwan.

Further Reading: Simma, Bruno, ed. *The Charter of the United Nations: A Commentary.* New York: Oxford University Press, 1994.

India

See DEPARTMENT OF PEACEKEEPING OPERATIONS, KASHMIR, UNITED NATIONS INDIA-PAKISTAN OBSERVATION MISSION, UNITED NATIONS MILITARY OBSERVER GROUP IN INDIA AND PAKISTAN.

indigenous peoples

The United Nations defines indigenous peoples as "those people having a historical continuity with pre-invasion and pre-colonial societies, [who] consider themselves distinct from other sectors of the societies now prevailing in those territories or parts of them." Indigenous peoples consider themselves "non-dominant sectors of society" and are usually determined "to preserve, develop and transmit to future generations, their ancestral territories, and their ethnic identity."

Indigenous peoples can be found in many areas of the world. As of 2001 they numbered about 300 million and lived in about 70 countries on five continents. Indigenous, or "aboriginal" peoples are considered descendants of those who lived in a region before new and different peoples arrived. The new arrivals typically became dominant by way of conquest or settlement. Indigenous peoples include the Indians of the Americas, the Inuit and Aleutians of the polar regions, the Saami in Scandinavia, the Aborigines and Torres Strait Islanders of Australia, and the Maori of New Zealand.

Between March 1997 and August 2001, 15 organizations of indigenous peoples gained CONSULTATIVE STATUS with the ECONOMIC AND SOCIAL COUNCIL (ECOSOC). Representatives of other indigenous peoples have come to participate in UN meetings, particularly in the UN Working Group on Indigenous populations, established in 1982, following the first international conferences of NON-GOVERNMENTAL ORGANIZATIONS on indigenous issues held in Geneva in 1977 and again in 1981. The Working Group meets for one

week each year before the annual session in Geneva of the UN Sub-commission on Prevention of Discrimination and Protection of Minorities. The Working Group has two formal tasks: first, to review national developments regarding protection of HUMAN RIGHTS for indigenous peoples, and second, to develop international standards concerning the rights of indigenous peoples.

In 1990 the GENERAL ASSEMBLY (GA) proclaimed 1993 to be the International Year of the World's Indigenous People. And in 1993 the GA proclaimed the International Decade of the World's Indigenous People to be 1995–2004. The goal of the decade was to strengthen international cooperation in seeking solutions to the problems confronting indigenous populations.

In 1995, the COMMISSION ON HUMAN RIGHTS and the Economic and Social Council established an open-ended inter-sessional Working Group to develop a draft DECLARATION on the rights of indigenous peoples. The group was composed of representatives of member states, and NGOs and indigenous organizations that had gained consultative status. Also in 1995 the General Assembly established the UN Voluntary fund for the International Decade of the World's Indigenous People, and directed it to administer voluntary contributions during the decade and to assist indigenous communities and organizations to participate in the activities of the Working Group on the draft declaration. Finally, by a 1994 RESOLUTION, the General Assembly designated August 9 of each year as International Day of the World's Indigenous People for the duration of the International Decade.

See also GUATEMALA, LATIN AMERICA.

Further Reading: New Zealand Ministry of Foreign Affairs. *United Nations Handbook.* Wellington, N.Z.: Ministry of Foreign Affairs and Trade, published annually. UNHCR Indigenous Peoples website: <www.unhchr.ch/indigenous/ind>.

Indonesia

The struggle between the Netherlands, which sought to reassert its control over the East Indies after Japan's defeat in World War II, and Indonesian nationalists, who had declared a republic in 1945, was one of the first colonial disputes to elicit extensive United Nations involvement. Security Council Resolution 27 of August 1, 1947, called for a cease-fire in the armed conflict and urged the parties "to settle their disputes by ARBITRATION or other peaceful means." By Resolution 31 (August 21, 1947), the SECURITY COUNCIL created the Committee of GOOD OFFICES (the Committee of Three, composed of the UNITED STATES, Belgium, and Australia) to facilitate an agreement. The continued use of force by the Dutch, however, negated the Renville Agreement of January 1948 and signified that the Security Council could no longer persevere with its good offices approach. Instead, through

Resolution 67 (January 28, 1949), the Security Council outlined a detailed recommendation for a settlement of the dispute and established the UNITED NATIONS COMMISSION FOR INDONESIA (UNCI). The Netherlands, under pressure from the United States, ultimately accepted the RESOLUTION and, on December 27, 1949, transferred SOVEREIGNTY to the Republic of Indonesia. Indonesia was admitted to the United Nations on September 29, 1950.

The subsequent conflict between the Netherlands and Indonesia over the status of West New Guinea (West Irian) was also resolved with UN assistance. Indonesia brought the issue to the United Nations in 1954, claiming that West New Guinea should have come under its JURISDICTION in 1950 as stipulated by the 1949 agreement that recognized Indonesian independence. The Netherlands contended that the Papuans of West New Guinea were not Indonesians and that they should be permitted to decide their own fate at some future date. After years of resistance to Indonesian claims that the territory should be freed from Dutch colonial rule, the Netherlands, under pressure from the United States, finally agreed to give up West New Guinea and to use the United Nations as a mechanism for the transfer. The August 1962 agreement—reached through the good offices of UN SECRETARY-GENERAL U THANT and the MEDIATION of Ellsworth Bunker—committed the Netherlands to transfer the administration of West New Guinea to a UNITED NATIONS TEMPORARY EXECUTIVE AUTHORITY (UNTEA) on October 1. In May of the following year, New Guinea was placed under Indonesian jurisdiction, subject to the right of the native Papuans to determine their own political fate by a plebiscite before the end of 1969. At the initiative of U Thant, but ultimately with the approval of the UN GENERAL ASSEMBLY, a UNITED NATIONS SECURITY FORCE (UNSF) was assembled to effect a cease-fire and to serve as the "police arm" of UNTEA in maintaining order during the transfer of authority. Comprised largely of 1,500 Pakistani troops, UNSF was a supplement to the Papuan police force in preserving law and order. UNTEA transferred full administrative control over West New Guinea (Irian Jaya) to Indonesia on May 1, 1963. In 1969, the government of Indonesia reported to the UN Secretary-General that consultative councils representative of the Papuan population had "expressed their wish to remain with Indonesia."

In January 1965, President Sukarno ordered Indonesia to leave the United Nations in protest against the election of Malaysia to a seat on the Security Council. Sukarno viewed Malaysia as a neocolonial creation of what he termed the "old established forces" of the West and, in 1963, he declared a policy of "confrontation" toward its Southeast Asian neighbor. While Indonesia is the only state to have announced its withdrawal from the United Nations, the Jakarta government reversed its position on September 19, 1966, and resumed full participation in UN activities.

In the 1990s, Indonesia served a term on the UN Security Council and joined the UN COMMISSION ON HUMAN RIGHTS. Indonesia was elected, as well, to chair the NON-ALIGNED MOVEMENT for a three-year term and, in September 1992, President Suharto addressed the UN General Assembly as a representative of the developing countries. Indonesia played a key role in getting the warring factions in CAMBODIA to agree to UN-sponsored elections in 1993 and contributed troops to UN PEACEKEEPING efforts in BOSNIA and Cambodia. President Suharto hosted the 1994 heads-of-state meeting of the Asia Pacific Economic Cooperation (APEC) forum and was instrumental in securing the agreement of APEC states (the Bogor Declaration) to create a tariff-free trading regime in the region by 2020 for developing countries and 2010 for developed countries.

Yet Indonesia's international reputation in the 1990s was marred by its continued and brutal occupation of East Timor. The United Nations repeatedly denounced Indonesia's 1975 invasion of East Timor and demanded that Indonesia withdraw its forces from the eastern portion of the island. In March 1993, a UN Human Rights Commission resolution censured Indonesia for its poor HUMAN RIGHTS record in the territory. With the fall of the Suharto government in 1998 and the new government's openness to possible independence for East Timor, the UN Security Council established the UNITED NATIONS MISSION IN EAST TIMOR (UNAMET) to oversee a popular consultation on the question of autonomy for the Timorese. The UNITED NATIONS TRANSITIONAL ADMINISTRATION IN EAST TIMOR (UNTAET) was formed to administer the territory during the transition to independence after the majority of East Timorese voters rejected autonomy within Indonesia. East Timor proclaimed its independence on May 31, 2002.

See also ANNAN, KOFI; EAST TIMOR DISPUTE; STATEMENT OF FOREST PRINCIPLES; UNITED NATIONS OPERATION IN SOMALIA.

Further Reading: McMullen, Christopher J. Mediation of the West New Guinea Dispute, 1962: A Case Study. Washington, D.C.: Institute for the Study of Diplomacy, Edmund A. Walsh School of Foreign Service, Georgetown University, 1981. Schwarz, Adam. A Nation in Waiting: Indonesia's Search for Security. 2d ed. Boulder, Colo.: Westview Press, 2000.

— G. S. Silliman

inquiry

One of the methods for the pacific settlement of disputes available to states under Article 33 of the UN CHARTER, inquiry is a fact-finding process conducted by reputable neutral observers meant to provide the basis for the resolution of a contentious issue between parties to a dispute. The Charter's reference to inquiry, along with negotiation, MEDIATION, and other traditional diplomatic means to resolve conflicts between states, was a continuation of 20th-century international practice beginning with the Hague CONVENTIONS of 1899 and 1907, and maintained by the LEAGUE OF NATIONS. The parties to a dispute might appoint or agree to a third-party appointment of a "commission of inquiry," which would investigate the factual matters underlying the beginnings of a conflict and then prepare a report for the disputants. The hope is that the elucidation of the objective circumstances will provide the basis for a negotiated settlement. In addition to the UN's authorization of this peaceful resolution method, the 1949 Geneva Conventions for the Protection of Victims of War, and their 1977 PROTOCOL endorsed the method, going further than the Charter by laying out specific procedures for its use.

While a century of diplomatic practice made inquiry an accepted principle of INTERNATIONAL LAW, the frequency of its use has been limited. By its nature it allows third-party involvement in a dispute with the likelihood that the neutral party will produce a report injurious to the interests of one of the disputants. It is also the case that most disputes arise not from a misunderstanding between states over factual matters but rather from a conflict of perceived national interests that inquiry cannot resolve. Most successfully used in 1904 to resolve a dispute between Russia and Great Britain over a mistaken Russian attack on British fishing ships, inquiry was used only twice between 1945 and 2000. The first time was in 1962 in the "*Red Crusader* Incident," when a panel of legal experts investigated an incident between British and Danish military ships. The second was part of the resolution of the IRAN-IRAQ WAR (1980–87). The two sides accepted a cease-fire demanded by the SECURITY COUNCIL in part on the condition that the United Nations establish a fact-finding commission to determine who started the hostilities. The commission reported in 1993 that Iraq was responsible for the commencement of the war.

Separate from its pacific settlement context, inquiry as a non-judicial process has found increased use in UN bodies as a means of bringing world public attention to HUMAN RIGHTS abuses, or to circumstances that could produce ethnic or religious conflict. Reversing a 1947 decision by the UN COMMISSION ON HUMAN RIGHTS (CHR) that "it had no power to take any action in regard to any complaints concerning human rights" by individuals against their own governments (Doctrine of Impotency), the ECONOMIC AND SOCIAL COUNCIL (ECOSOC) in 1967 directed the commission, as a matter of importance and urgency, to take up these allegations. Since then, both ECOSOC and CHR have asserted the authority of UN bodies to protect individual rights.

In its 1979–80 session, the commission established special procedures, known as "Mechanisms," to facilitate such investigations. These procedures led to the appointment of SPECIAL RAPPORTEURS to investigate and prepare reports for the commission. Through the appointment of special rapporteurs, an organ of the United Nations or a SPECIALIZED AGENCY seeks an inquiry into a specific global problem or area of concern. The rapporteur's report is normally extensive and consists of an explanation of the historical background, economic, social, political, and demographic information, assessment of the current situation, information received from relevant countries, reports of field or site visits, and, frequently, recommendations for UN action. The commission has appointed special rapporteurs to investigate thematic issues, such as torture, summary executions, violence against WOMEN, racial discrimination, and religious discrimination. In 2000 there were 15 special rapporteurs conducting inquiries into a broad range of topics and inspecting specific countries.

See also APPEAL TO THE SECURITY COUNCIL, CHAPTER VI, CONCILIATION, CONVENTION ON THE ELIMINATION OF ALL FORMS OF DISCRIMINATION AGAINST WOMEN, IRAN HOSTAGE CRISIS, RWANDA CRISIS, SECRETARY-GENERAL.

Further Reading: Shaw, Malcolm N. *International Law.* 3d ed. Cambridge: Cambridge University Press, 1994. Simma, Bruno, ed. *The Charter of the United Nations. A Commentary.* New York: Oxford University Press, 1994. United Nations. *Report of the Independent Inquiry into the Actions of the United Nations during the 1994 Genocide in Rwanda.* New York: United Nations, 1999.

Inter-Agency Committee on Sustainable Development (IACSD)

The United Nations ADMINISTRATIVE COMMITTEE ON COORDINATION (ACC), renamed the UN System Chief Executives Board for Coordination (CEB) in 2002, created the IACSD in October 1993 to advise it on ways that the UNITED NATIONS SYSTEM might coordinate efforts to carry out the decisions of the UNITED NATIONS CONFERENCE ON ENVIRONMENT AND DEVELOPMENT (UNCED), including AGENDA 21 and the Plan of Action for the SUSTAINABLE DEVELOPMENT of small island developing states (SIDS). The Inter-Agency Committee meets semi-annually and includes among its members most of the important UN funds, PROGRAMMES, and SPECIALIZED AGENCIES working in the fields of ENVIRONMENT and DEVELOPMENT. Sessions of the IACD are also open to all CEB members at the level of senior officials, and, as observers, to related organizations such as the GLOBAL ENVIRONMENT FACILITY (GEF). The CEB Subcommittees on Water Resources and on Oceans and Coastal Areas report to the IACSD.

The SECRETARIAT is located at UN HEADQUARTERS in New York. It prepares analytical studies and reports for the COMMISSION ON SUSTAINABLE DEVELOPMENT (CSD), promotes joint programming among UN agencies, and fulfills assessment and reporting functions for the Inter-Agency Committee. The IACSD monitors financing requirements associated with Agenda 21. It also issues directives to "task managers" from each of the represented organizations who then are expected to take responsibility for implementing specific aspects of the UNCED and CSD agendas. For example, the UNITED NATIONS EDUCATIONAL, SCIENTIFIC, AND CULTURAL ORGANIZATION (UNESCO) is responsible for trade and environment, the UNITED NATIONS DEVELOPMENT PROGRAMME (UNDP) for capacity building, and the FOOD AND AGRICULTURE ORGANIZATION (FAO) for land management, forestry, sustainable mountain development, and agriculture. The Inter-Agency Committee is chaired by an UNDER SECRETARY-GENERAL; in 2001 the chair was Nitin Desai from the UN Secretariat DEPARTMENT OF ECONOMIC AND SOCIAL AFFAIRS (DESA).

Inter-American Development Bank (IDB) *See* REGIONAL DEVELOPMENT BANKS.

Intergovernmental Maritime Consultative Organization (IMCO) *See* INTERNATIONAL MARITIME ORGANIZATION.

Intergovernmental Panel on Climate Change (IPCC)

In November 1988 the UNITED NATIONS ENVIRONMENT PROGRAMME (UNEP) and the WORLD METEOROLOGICAL ORGANIZATION (WMO) jointly sponsored the creation of the Intergovernmental Panel on Climate Change, made up of more than 1,000 scientists, policy makers, legal experts, and climate specialists from more than 60 nations. The two organizations hoped the IPCC would bring new attention to the growing phenomenon of climate change, and would produce momentum toward a new international CONVENTION in response to the problem. UNEP and WMO charged IPCC with assessing the scientific, technical, and socioeconomic information relevant to understanding the risks of human-induced climate change, its potential impact, and the options for adaptation and mitigation. Its reports were to be neutral with respect to policy, although objective in their analysis of the effects of policies currently employed.

The IPCC published its *First Assessment Report* in August 1990, noting the dangers implicit in climate change due to global warming. Its report provided the basis of discussion for the World Climate Conference convened by the WMO the following November. It also created the impetus for the establishment of the Intergovernmental Negotiating Committee (INC) that, in turn, made the commitment to the negotiation of a climate change TREATY by the time of the contemplated 1992 Earth Summit. Officially known as the UNITED NATIONS CONFERENCE ON ENVIRONMENT AND DEVELOPMENT (UNCED), the meeting in Rio provided the venue for signing the UNITED NATIONS FRAMEWORK CONVENTION ON CLIMATE CHANGE (UNFCCC).

Since 1992, the Intergovernmental Panel on Climate Change has continued its preparation of Assessment Reports—the second and third reports were released in 1995 and 2001—and special studies on aspects of climate change. Of special importance, the IPCC develops methods for calculating greenhouse gas emissions through its National Greenhouse Gas Inventories Programme, and its Task Force on Scenarios for Climate Impact Assessment (TGCIA) facilitates cooperation among experts on modeling future climate change. The panel meets yearly in plenary session to approve work done by the organization's working groups, of which there are three. Special attention is given to geographical representation on all of the units of the IPCC. The three working groups conduct no independent research or data collection. They review public scientific data and research results. Working Group I assesses the scientific aspects of climate change. Working Group II focuses on the impact of climate change on socioeconomic and natural systems, and the possibilities for adaptation to the changed conditions. Working Group III analyzes options for mitigating climate change and limiting greenhouse gases. The IPCC SECRETARIAT is hosted at WMO headquarters in Geneva, and the organization's work is directed by the IPCC secretary and bureau. The WMO and UNEP provide much of the funding for the IPCC, although member states of both organizations also make contributions to the IPCC Trust Fund based on their SCALE OF ASSESSMENT set by the UN GENERAL ASSEMBLY.

IPCC reports have had a significant impact on international policy-making concerning climate change. Its *Second Assessment Report* in 1995 led to the 1997 KYOTO PROTOCOL of the UNFCCC that set specific greenhouse gas emission limits on individual countries, which they agreed to meet by 2002. Its third report in 2001 found "there [was] stronger evidence [that greenhouse gases produced by human activity] have contributed substantially to the observed warming over the last 50 years." Preliminary word of the IPCC's warning in the report that if emissions were not lowered significantly temperatures could climb 50 percent higher than predicted in its 1995 report put intense pressure on the representatives of 180 countries meeting at the UN Climate Change Summit in The Hague during November 2000. The IPCC has also worked with specific sectors of the world economy to find mitigation strategies. Its 1999 report on the effects of aviation on climate change was the first to be undertaken in partnership with airlines, air industries, and air transportation engineers, with the consequence that its recommendations reflected an implicit commitment by those groups to implement the mitigation proposals. Furthermore, the report was forwarded to the parties of the UNFCCC and the INTERNATIONAL CIVIL AVIATION ORGANIZATION (ICAO) for additional action by those bodies.

See also ENVIRONMENT.

Further Reading: Elliott, Lorraine. *The Global Politics of the Environment.* New York: New York University Press, 1998. Grubbs, Michael, Matthias Koch, Koy Thomson, Abby Manson, and Francis Sullivan. *The 'Earth Summit' Agreements: A Guide and Assessment.* London: Earthscan Publications Ltd., 1993. Imber, Mark F. *Environment, Security and UN Reform.* New York: St. Martin's, 1994. Young, Oran B. *International Governance. Protecting the Environment in a Stateless Society.* Ithaca, N.Y.: Cornell University Press, 1994. IPCC website: <www.ipcc.ch/>.

International Atomic Energy Agency (IAEA)

U.S. president Dwight Eisenhower delivered his "ATOMS FOR PEACE" speech to the UN GENERAL ASSEMBLY in December 1953 and proposed that the nuclear powers gradually transfer a percentage of their fissionable materials to a new INTERNATIONAL ATOMIC ENERGY AGENCY, which would be under the authority of the United Nations. After nearly four years of diplomatic efforts, the required 18 nations had ratified the Statute of the IAEA, and it went into force on July 29, 1957. Because of the arms race at the time between the UNITED STATES and the Soviet Union, there was never a serious possibility that the superpowers would turn over part of their nuclear arsenals to the proposed agency. Instead, the only common ground that could be found was for a body committed to cooperation in the use of nuclear science and technology for peaceful development purposes. It was also not to be a subsidiary organ of the United Nations, but rather an independent inter-governmental organization under UN aegis. By 2001, 132 states had joined the International Atomic Energy Agency. Best known for its "Safeguards" system, the IAEA was increasingly used as a monitor in international agreements to guarantee that states were not diverting nuclear materials from peaceful purposes to military WEAPONS.

The IAEA's Statute commits the agency "to accelerate and enlarge the contribution of atomic energy to peace, health and prosperity throughout the world." To that end the agency maintains programs on verification, nuclear safety, the uses of nuclear energy, and technological exchange. Its Safeguards system was developed to implement the verification provisions of the 1968 NON-PROLIFERATION TREATY (NPT). Since then NATION-STATES have employed the system to enforce the compliance terms of international treaties, including NUCLEAR-WEAPONS-FREE ZONE agreements in Africa, LATIN AMERICA, and the South Pacific. Following the 1991 GULF WAR, IAEA safeguard inspectors enforced nuclear provisions of the armistice agreement imposed on Iraq. By 2001, more than 900 nuclear facilities were under IAEA Safeguards.

IAEA headquarters is in Vienna, Austria. It has additional offices in Toronto, New York, Trieste, Monaco, and Tokyo. The agency employs more than 2,000 people. Its General Conference and Board of Governors are the policy-making bodies of the IAEA. They approve the programs and budget, and appoint the DIRECTOR-GENERAL. The General Conference is the agency's plenary organ, consisting of all member states. It meets annually to debate the report of the Board of Governors and other agenda items presented by individual states. The board meets five times yearly, and its 35 members have reflected due regard for geographical representation. In 1999 the General Conference approved an expansion of the board to 43 members, which will occur when the approval process is completed. Among other duties, the board considers applications for MEMBERSHIP and nominates the director-general to the General Conference. The IAEA's regular budget reached $230 million in 2001, and it sought an additional $73 million in voluntary contributions during that same year.

See also ACHESON-LILIENTHAL REPORT, DISARMAMENT.

Further Reading: Imber, Mark. *The USA, ILO, UNESCO, and IAEA: Politicization and Withdrawal in the Specialized Agencies.* London: Macmillan, 1989. Pruden, Caroline. *Conditional Partners: Eisenhower, the United Nations, and the Search for a Permanent Peace.* Baton Rouge: Louisiana State University Press, 1998. *United Nations Handbook 2000.* Wellington, N.Z.: New Zealand Ministry of External Affairs and Trade, 2000. IAEA website: <www.iaea.org/worldatom>.

International Bank of Reconstruction and Development (IBRD) *See* WORLD BANK.

International Centre for Settlement of Investment Disputes *See* WORLD BANK.

International Civil Aviation Day

In 1996, the GENERAL ASSEMBLY proclaimed December 7 as International Civil Aviation Day. It marks the anniversary of the adoption of the Chicago CONVENTION in 1944, which brought into being the INTERNATIONAL CIVIL AVIATION ORGANIZATION (ICAO).

International Civil Aviation Organization (ICAO)

The International Civil Aviation Organization became a SPECIALIZED AGENCY of the United Nations in October 1947. It originated three years earlier at the International Civil Aviation Conference hosted by the UNITED STATES in Chicago. Fifty-two nations signed the Chicago Convention on December 7, 1944, which served as the constitution of the new organization. With the receipt of the required 26th ratification the ICAO came into being on April 4, 1947. The CON-VENTION dedicated the organization to providing safety in civilian air travel and cooperation among NATION-STATES to assure standard air transport principles and regulations. The ICAO headquarters was established in Montreal, Canada. As of August 2001, 185 nations belonged to the ICAO.

The organization is made up of an assembly, a council, and a SECRETARIAT. The assembly is the plenary body, made up of all members, which sets ICAO policies and approves the budget. It meets every three years, with its 34th session set for the fall of 2004. The council is the agency's executive body, has 33 members elected for three-year terms, and meets three times a year. Members are elected from three categories: states of chief importance in air transport, states that make the largest contribution to facilities for air travel, and states whose election will assure that all regions of the globe are represented. This last category is a reflection of an early decision to provide a universal organization dealing with air travel while also grouping states in regions where common air travel networks exist. The council has a number of committees that assist with policy making in areas of the organization's responsibilities. They are the Air Navigation Commission, the Air Transport Committee, the Legal Committee, the Committee on Unlawful Interference, and the Technical Cooperation Committee. The ICAO secretariat is headed by a SECRETARY-GENERAL. Renato Cláudio Costa Pereira was appointed to that post in 1997. Senior secretariat personnel are selected based on technical expertise and regard for geographical representation. The secretariat in Montreal works closely with regional offices around the world. It also works with specialized agencies and NON-GOV-ERNMENTAL ORGANIZATIONS that can contribute to air safety such as the WORLD METEOROLOGICAL ORGANIZATION, the INTERNATIONAL TELECOMMUNICATION UNION, the INTERNA-TIONAL MARITIME ORGANIZATION, the International Air Transport Association, and the International Federation of Air Line Pilots' Associations.

The primary work of the International Civil Aviation Organization is standardization of air rules and practices. Once the organization adopts a standard, it is then put into practice by all member states. Areas of standardization include operation of aircraft, personnel licensing, air traffic services, navigation rules, aeronautical communications, search and rescue, accident investigation, airworthiness, and regulating transport of dangerous goods. ICAO is also involved in the development of satellite-based navigation systems, regional planning, the facilitation of passenger movement through national terminals of entry and egress, and the development of international air law. Additionally, ICAO convenes diplomatic conferences for the purpose of developing consensus on important areas of civil aviation. In November 2001 it held a conference in Cape Town, South Africa, to adopt a Mobile Equipment Convention, and scheduled a conference for early 2003 to consider ways to liberalize air transport as part of the development of globalization.

The ICAO convened its first security conference in February 2002 with delegates from 144 countries and 22 international organizations attending the meeting in Montreal. Chaired by ICAO president Assad Kotaite, the conference urged a security audit for all member states in the wake of the September 11, 2001, terrorist attacks on New York City and Washington, D.C. The conference marked a shift in the organization's focus from safety issues to security both for airline passengers and people on the ground. ICAO estimated that the proposed audits would cost $17 million over three years. Initially the organization planned to seek voluntary donations to cover these costs but would include continuing audit expenses in its regular budget after the first three-year period.

Further Reading: *Yearbook of the United Nations. Special Edition, UN Fiftieth Anniversary, 1945–1995.* The Hague: Martinus Nijhoff Publishers, 1995. ICAO website: <www.icao.int>.

International Civilian Mission in Haiti (MICIVIH)

Initiated February 1993, the International Civilian Mission in Haiti was the first joint mission between the United Nations and a REGIONAL ORGANIZATION, the ORGANIZATION OF AMERICAN STATES (OAS). MICIVIH's director, an OAS representative, and its deputy director from the UN were jointly appointed by the two organizations, and an equal number of staff from each organization were assigned to its work. In the wake of the military seizure of power in September 1991, MICIVIH's mandate was to verify Haitian compliance with the human rights CONVENTIONs to which the country was a party. At its peak in 1995 the operation had more than 193 HUMAN RIGHTS monitors (89 OAS, 104 UN) in HAITI, including 26 UNITED NATIONS VOLUNTEERS, posted in 13 offices throughout the country.

The 1991 overthrow of Haiti's president, Jean-Bertrand Aristide, challenged the OAS commitment to the maintenance of democracy in the Western Hemisphere asserted just three months earlier in the Santiago Commitment to Democracy and the Renewal of the Inter-American System. The Santiago Commitment required the OAS Permanent Council to respond to "sudden or irregular interruptions of the democratic process." The organization already had been involved in assuring the fair election process that had brought Aristide to power in 1990. Following the coup, the Organization of American States sent several high-level delegations to Port-au-Prince to pressure the de facto leader of Haiti, Lieutenant-General Raoul Cédras, to accept an OAS presence on the island. In July 1992 OAS secretary-general Joán Baena Soares extended an invitation to UN SECRETARY-GENERAL Boutros BOUTROS-GHALI to send a representative as part of a joint delegation, an invitation Boutros-Ghali accepted. In January 1993 ousted president Aristide asked first the OAS and then the United Nations to expand the international presence in Haiti. The GENERAL ASSEMBLY responded with a RESOLUTION directing the UN Secretary-General to work out the modalities of a joint UN/OAS Mission.

MICIVIH's assignment was to verify that the regime was honoring Haiti's commitments under the INTERNATIONAL COVENANT ON CIVIL AND POLITICAL RIGHTS, and the American Convention on Human Rights. It worked in tandem with the separately deployed UNITED NATIONS CIVILIAN POLICE MISSION IN HAITI (MIPONUH), which sought to professionalize the Haitian National Police as a neutral security force in the country, and provided security for MICIVIH's personnel. MICIVIH's duties included assisting the judicial system in its administration of justice, receiving complaints from Haitian citizens and groups about violations of human rights, conducting unannounced inspections of any site in Haiti (mission observers regularly used this power to inspect Haitian prisons), and making recommendations to the Haitian government concerning ways to ameliorate human rights abuses.

Following the restoration of the Aristide government in October 1994, MICIVIH added to its responsibilities democratic institution-building and civic education. It held workshops and seminars for local residents in preparation for parliamentary and local elections. At the time of elections OAS representatives served as election monitors and UN personnel provided technical assistance in staging the elections. With the restoration of civilian domestic government MICIVIH presence was reduced and finally withdrawn in early 2000, when it and MIPONUH were both replaced with the International Civilian Support Mission in Haiti (MICAH). The latter was not a usual SECURITY COUNCIL mandated PEACEKEEPING operation, but a special mission, without any military or police component, created by consensus vote of the General Assembly to oversee upcoming parliamentary elections.

Further Reading: MICIVIH website: <www.un.org/rights/micivih/first.htm>.

International Commission of Inquiry   *See* RWANDA CRISIS.

International Conference on Population and Development (ICPD)

The International Conference on Population and Development convened in Cairo, September 5–13, 1994. Chaired by Dr. Safis Nadik, executive director of the UNITED NATIONS POPULATION FUND (UNFPA), the conference attracted 179 government participants, and 4,200 representatives of 1,500

NON-GOVERNMENTAL ORGANIZATIONS (NGOs). The WORLD CONFERENCE was the fifth global meeting on population, with the previous conferences having been held in Rome (1954), Belgrade (1965), Bucharest (1974), and Mexico City (1984). The conference sought to demonstrate the reenforcing links between population policies and development. It endorsed the rights of all people to reproductive freedom, and it encouraged policies that would slow population growth, including the empowerment of WOMEN, expanded educational opportunities, gender equality, and the reduction of poverty.

The conference adopted a program of action to guide international population efforts for the next 20 years. It called for universal availability of family planning by 2015—calling it a basic HUMAN RIGHT—and encouraged adolescent access to reproductive and family planning information. ICPD called upon individual countries and the international community to commit up to $21 billion by 2015 to population projects and services. UNFPA was decreed the lead agency for the implementation of the ICPD recommendations and an Inter-Agency Task Force was established to coordinate efforts throughout the UNITED NATIONS SYSTEM. The agency became part of the UN's ADMINISTRATIVE COMMITTEE ON COORDINATION in 1996.

The Cairo meeting, while reasserting many of the consensus recommendations of previous conferences, found itself embroiled in controversy over the issues of abortion and reproductive rights. Nations with sizable Roman Catholic populations, Right to Life NGOs, and the Vatican opposed any language in the final conference statement that might imply endorsement of abortion. Compromise language was achieved that urged governments "to deal with the health impact of unsafe abortion as a major public health concern and to reduce the recourse to abortion through expanded and improved family planning services." It also declared that "in no case should abortion be promoted as a method of family planning." Islamic nations sought to limit conference recommendations that might interfere with gender relationships and laws distinctive to certain cultures and nations. The Programme of Action sought a middle ground by affirming "the right of men and women to be informed and to have access to safe, effective, affordable and acceptable methods of family planning of their choice, as well as other methods of their choice for the regulation of fertility *which are not against the law.*" [Italics added.]

As follow-up to the Cairo Conference, the Intergovernmental Commission on Population was renamed in 1995 the UN Commission on Population and Development, and given responsibility for monitoring progress on different aspects of the Programme of Action. It approached its work in much the same way that its parallel body, the ECONOMIC AND SOCIAL COUNCIL's COMMISSION FOR SOCIAL DEVELOPMENT (CSocD) approached review of the outcomes from the WORLD SUMMIT FOR SOCIAL DEVELOPMENT (WSSD). That is, it established a topical yearly agenda and focused its assessment on one set of

ICPD meets in Cairo, 1994 (UN/DPI PHOTO)

recommendations at a time. In 1999 a full review of progress was released as a report (ICPD+5). An international forum organized by UNFPA was held in The Hague the same year, leading to a SPECIAL SESSION OF THE UN GENERAL ASSEMBLY, June 30 to July 2, 1999, that considered ICPD+5 and made some specific recommendations for future action. The Assembly set benchmarks for measuring progress through 2015. The session adopted recommendations that the 1990 illiteracy rate for women and girls should be halved by 2005, the primary school enrollment ratio for all children should be 90 percent by 2010, 60 percent of all family planning facilities should offer comprehensive services by 2005 (80 percent by 2010, and 100 percent by 2015), and the gap between the proportion of individuals using contraceptives and the proportion expressing a desire to space or limit their families should be reduced gradually to zero percent by 2015. On the matter of HIV/AIDS the Special Session called for 90 percent of men and women between the ages of 15 and 24 to have access to preventive methods by 2005.

Further Reading: Johnson, Stanley. *The Politics of Population: The International Conference on Population and Development, Cairo 1994.* London: Earthscan Publications, 1995. Schechter, Michael G. *United Nations-Sponsored World Conferences. Focus on Impact and Follow-up.* Tokyo: United Nations University Press, 2001. Taub, Nadine. *International Conference on Population and Development.* Washington, D.C.: American Society of International Law, 1994. United Nations Department of Public Information. *UN Briefing Papers: The World Conferences, Developing Priorities for the 21st Century.* New York: United Nations Department of Public Information, 1997. ICPD website: <www.unfpa.org/icpd/index.htm>.

International Court of Justice (ICJ)

Established in 1945 in the CHARTER OF THE UNITED NATIONS (Chapter XIV) as the successor to the PERMANENT COURT OF INTERNATIONAL JUSTICE (PCIJ), the ICJ is the UN's principal judicial organ. While the Court functions as the UN's legal arm, it is an independent institution. Its governing document—the STATUTE OF THE INTERNATIONAL COURT OF JUSTICE—accentuates that independence. The Statute is an integral part of, and usually appended to, any published copy of the UN Charter and itself is based on the 1922 Statute of the Permanent Court of International Justice. The Statute details the organization, procedures, and JURISDIC- TION of the Court. The ICJ, like the PCIJ, is often called the "World Court," which draws attention to its ancestral con- nection to the earlier institution.

The outbreak of general European war in 1939 damaged the reputation not only of the LEAGUE OF NATIONS but also the Permanent Court of International Justice, which met for the last time on December 4, 1939. In 1942 U.S. secretary of state Cordell HULL and the foreign minister of the United Kingdom, Anthony EDEN, declared their support for a post- war reestablishment of an international court. In early 1943 the United Kingdom invited a number of experts to London to discuss the subject. Forming the so-called Inter-Allied Committee, under the chairmanship of Sir William Malkin, the group held 19 meetings and published a report on Febru- ary 10, 1944. Among other recommendations, the committee suggested that the statute of any new court be based on that of the PCIJ. Later that year, at the DUMBARTON OAKS CON- FERENCE in the U.S. capital, the four attending powers agreed on including an international court of justice into the emerging STRUCTURE OF THE UNITED NATIONS. In April 1945, a meeting of jurists from 44 nations convened in Washington, D.C. Chaired by G. H. Hackworth of the UNITED STATES, the committee composed a draft statute for the new court, which was then submitted to the UN's orga- nizing conference in San Francisco in the spring of 1945. At this meeting the delegates determined on creating a new court, with its own statute, to become the principal judicial organ of the United Nations. In order to retain a sensible continuity with evolving INTERNATIONAL LAW, the authors of the UN Charter made clear in Article 92 that the ICJ Statute was based on that of the PCIJ. The old Court convened in October 1945 in order to dissolve itself and transfer its archives to the new Court. The sixth and last president of the Permanent Court of International Justice, Judge J. Gustavo Guerrero, presided over this closing session and then became the first elected president of the new International Court of Justice.

The ICJ is the only PRINCIPAL ORGAN OF THE UNITED NATIONS not based in New York. The seat of the Court, like that of the PCIJ, is at the Peace Palace (a gift of American entrepreneur Andrew Carnegie) in The Hague, the Nether- lands. It may hold sessions elsewhere if it so determines, but as of 2002 it had not. Its first session took place on April 18, 1946. Since then the ICJ has been considered in continuous session. As an autonomous body it determines its own rules of procedure, elects its own president and vice president, and appoints a registrar (with the equivalent rank of an assistant secretary-general of the United Nations) and other registry staff and officers. The registry maintains all records of the Court, makes available its publications, communicates with outside organizations, acts as a press office, and keeps a web- site. Appointees to the registry must be proficient in both French and English, the official LANGUAGES of the Court.

All UN members are parties to the ICJ's Statute and some non-members are parties to the Statute as well. Additionally, a non-member may become a party to the Statute on condi- tions recommended by the SECURITY COUNCIL (SC) and approved by the GENERAL ASSEMBLY (GA). There are 15 judges on the Court, elected by the General Assembly and the Security Council for nine-year terms. The procedure of nominating and electing candidates for judgeships on the court is complex and is detailed in Article 4 of the Statute. All NATION-STATES party to the ICJ Statute are allowed to put forward candidates, although the nominations are made not by a government but by a group of four members from the PERMANENT COURT OF ARBITRATION who are from the nominating state. If a country is not represented on the Per- manent Court of Arbitration it may still make a nomination through a similar national group of legal experts that would clearly qualify to serve on the ARBITRATION tribunal. Each group can propose up to four candidates, not more than two of its own nationality. The names are then forwarded to the UN SECRETARY-GENERAL who submits the names to the General Assembly and the Security Council for vote. For this election the PERMANENT MEMBERS OF THE SECURITY COUNCIL retain no right of VETO; the required majority vote for a judge in that body is eight. Both the General Assembly and the Security Council vote simultaneously but separately. To be elected, a candidate must obtain an absolute majority in both chambers (in 2002 that amounted to 95 votes in the GA, eight in the SC). As a consequence, there often must be several votes before an election is decided. The elections are almost always held—in three-year cycles—at the HEAD- QUARTERS in New York during the annual fall session of the General Assembly. The term of office begins on February 6 of the next year. Judges may be reelected, but no two from the same country may serve simultaneously. (Should two candidates of the same nationality be elected at the same time, the elder of the two receives the appointment.) In accord with Article 13 of the Statute, elections for the first Court, meeting in 1946, resulted in three groups of five judges each being selected for first a three-year, then a six- year, and finally the normal nine-year term, initiating stag- gered terms to be filled every three years hence. Judges of the Court may not, according to Article 16 of the Statute, engage in any other administrative or political position nor in any other occupation of a professional nature. Members of the Court do not represent their governments; they are independent. Still, they should have qualifications for appointment to the highest judicial offices in their respec- tive countries or be recognized as experts in international law. No judge may be dismissed except by the unanimous decision of the other judges. The United Nations has persis- tently tried to apportion the judgeships on an equitable geo- graphical basis. In 2000 the allocation of seats on the Court was three Africans, two Latin Americans, three Asians, two east Europeans, and five from Western Europe and Other States, a distribution that exactly paralleled the Security Council membership. There is no entitlement to membership, but normally, with the exception of CHINA, the Court has always had judges from the permanent members of the Security Council.

The Court considers itself an organ of and contributor to international law. It decides disputes consistent with international law, the sources of which, according to Article 38 of the Statute, are international CONVENTIONS, international custom, general principles of law recognized by civilized nations, and judicial decisions and teachings of the most qualified publicists on the topic. All judgments of the Court are published in French and English. The Court's rules of procedure were updated on December 5, 2000.

The Court deals only with disputes between sovereign states; no private party may present a case. Moreover, the Court is not expected to resolve all international conflicts, but only specific legal disputes brought before it. It has COMPULSORY JURISDICTION in cases involving countries that have signed OPTIONAL CLAUSE 36 (paragraphs 2 and 3) of the

ICJ's Statute, allowing the Court to adjudicate legal disputes concerning (1) the interpretation of a TREATY, (2) any question of international law, (3) the existence of any fact which may constitute a breach of an international obligation, or (4) the nature and extent of a reparation for such a breach. This is the so-called optional clause, allowing "DECLARATIONS of acceptance of the compulsory jurisdiction of the Court." But the two affected states usually must agree to bring the case, and no state may be sued before the Court unless it consents to such an action. In fact, the jurisdiction and effectiveness of an international tribunal depend on the consent of the states concerned.

Most often cases are initiated either by the disputants, who notify the Court of a special agreement reached by each to seek Court action, or by the unilateral initiation of one party, acknowledging that the opposing party has not recognized the Court's jurisdiction, but asking it to do so. In the latter case, the lone litigant writes to the Court's registrar. Nation-states have no permanent official representatives at the ICJ. As a rule, a state's foreign minister, or ambassador to the Netherlands, communicates with the Court's registrar. Parties before the Court are not required to pay fees or

International Court of Justice (UNITED NATIONS PHOTO/170055)

administrative expenses; these costs fall to the United Nations.

In proceedings before the Court, there is both a written phase, when the parties file and exchange pleadings, and an oral stage, when there are public hearings and when counsel address the Court. The Court may hear witnesses and authorize investigations by commissions of experts. The Court deliberates in private, but all judgments—arrived at by majority vote—are made public in the Court's chambers. A judge in the minority may file a dissenting opinion, although majority judgments are final; there is no appeal. Yet the Court has no power of enforcement. Article 94 of the UN Charter provides recourse to the Security Council for a successful disputant unhappy at non-compliance with a decision. The Council then may forward recommendations or take measures to effect the judgment. But, in fact, given the reality of a world of sovereign nations, the Court's verdicts depend wholly on compliance by the litigants. Nonetheless, as of 2000 there had been only two recorded instances in which a disappointed party to a decision had failed to comply with the Court. The very first decision, in the *Corfu Channel* case of 1946, was rebuffed by Albania when it failed to pay the United Kingdom the £843,947 mandated by the Court as compensation for damages suffered. And the United States, reacting to the 1984 case of *Nicaragua v. U.S.A.*, refused for two years to accept prior compulsory jurisdiction of the Court in matters relating to Central America and, following the Court's insistence (by a 12–3 majority) that the United States had violated international law in its dealings with Nicaragua and should pay reparations to that country, blocked any APPEAL TO THE SECURITY COUNCIL. Yet one must bear in mind that on several occasions, by request of one of the litigants, cases have been removed from the Court's list before a judgment has been rendered.

Under provisions of Article 26 of the Statute, the Court may establish a special chamber composed of three or more judges. This might be done either at the request of the parties in an individual case, or in order to deal with particular categories of cases. Such a procedure was used for the first time in 1982 and has been used infrequently since. However, in July 1993 the Court set up a special seven-member chamber to deal with environmental cases falling within its jurisdiction.

Article 65 of the Statute also authorizes the Court to deliver "advisory opinions" if so requested by one of the five principal organs of the United Nations, or by a SPECIALIZED AGENCY. After receiving such a request, the Court seeks useful information from various organizations and requests written and oral statements on the issue. Otherwise, the procedures for dealing with advisory opinions and the legal sources employed are the same as for adversarial cases. Nonetheless, advisory opinions are consultative in nature and thus not binding. A nation may simply disregard an advisory opinion, as happened, for example, when in 1948 the Court advised the General Assembly that the Soviet Union could not use its veto to deny membership in the United Nations to the qualified states of Italy and Finland. Moscow ignored the decision and ultimately struck a compromise with Western nations that resulted in the two countries being admitted along with several other nations. As of 2001 the Court had rendered 24 advisory opinions concerning a variety of topics, including issues of UN membership, reparation for injuries in the service of the United Nations, the territorial status of NAMIBIA and Western Sahara, expenses of various UN operations, the status of human rights SPECIAL RAPPORTEURS, and the legality of the threat or use of nuclear weapons.

From 1946 to 2001, more than 95 contentious cases were referred to the Court, although several were subsequently removed from the Court's list or were still pending. Of the 75 countries that had been litigants in these cases, the United States was involved most often (about 20), with the United Kingdom and the FORMER YUGOSLAVIA ranking second and third.

Three specific cases give example to the Court's workings. In its first case, *Corfu Channel (United Kingdom v. Albania)*, the Court proffered three judgments. First, on March 25, 1948, it asserted its jurisdiction over the case—involving a British grievance against Albania for explosions in the Corfu Channel in 1946 that had damaged a British warship and killed members of the crew. Second, on April 9, 1949, it found Albania responsible under international law for the explosions. And third, on December 15, 1949, the Court assessed Albania a reparation payment to be paid to the United Kingdom. However, as noted above, Albania refused to observe the judgment.

In 1979 the United States requested that the Court take the case *U.S. Diplomatic and Consular Staff in Tehran (U.S.A. v. Iran)*. Washington brought the case following the occupation of its embassy by Iranian militants on November 4, 1979, and the capture and holding of hostages of its diplomatic and consular staff. The Court immediately held that there was no more fundamental requirement for international relations than the inviolability of diplomatic envoys and embassies. In a judgment of May 24, 1980, the Court found that Iran had violated obligations to the United States according to international law and under existing conventions. However, the Court was not called upon to deliver any further judgment on reparation, and, on May 12, 1981, the case was removed from the Court's list. Ultimately negotiations between Iran and the United States took place to resolve outstanding grievances on both sides. The result was the establishment of the Iran–U.S. Claims Tribunal to handle claims by nationals of either country. By the end of the century the tribunal had dealt with more than 3,900 cases.

A final example is the *LaGrand Case (Germany v. United States of America)*, decided on June 27, 2001. Citing Article

36 of the Statute (explained above) the Court determined that the United States had violated international law when it failed to grant consular services to two German brothers executed in Arizona in 1999. Also, the Court found that the United States had ignored an ICJ order to stay one of the executions. The two brothers were charged with murder in a 1982 holdup. Washington conceded during the proceedings that it had neglected the 1963 Vienna Convention on Consular Relations in prosecuting the LaGrand brothers without informing diplomats from their homeland, but insisted that the brothers had received a fair trial and that the verdicts would have been unaffected by consular intervention. But ICJ president Gilbert Guillaume, speaking for the Court's overwhelming majority, reprimanded the United States for denying defendants their international rights regardless of the likely outcome of a trial. The ruling was also noteworthy because it pronounced, for the first time in the Court's history, that provisional orders of the ICJ, such as the ignored injunction against Walter LaGrand's execution, were legally binding.

See also ADMINISTRATIVE TRIBUNALS, IRAN HOSTAGE CRISIS, JUS COGENS.

Further Reading: Bowett, D. W., et al. *The International Court of Justice: Process, Practice and Procedure.* London: British Institute of International and Comparative Law, 1997. International Court of Justice. *Yearbook.* The Hague, published annually. Rosenne, Shabtai. *The Law and Practice of the International Court, 1920–1996.* Boston: Martinus Nijhoff Publishers, 1997. ICJ website:<www.icj-cij.org/icj>.

International Covenant on Civil and Political Rights (ICCPR)

The International Covenant on Civil and Political Rights codified and expanded on rights listed in the UNIVERSAL DECLARATION OF HUMAN RIGHTS. As a formal TREATY, the COVENANT carried the force of INTERNATIONAL LAW, requiring signatories to live up to its terms. It was adopted by the GENERAL ASSEMBLY on December 16, 1966, and went into force in 1976. At the time of its adoption, the Assembly also opened for signature the INTERNATIONAL COVENANT ON ECONOMIC, SOCIAL AND CULTURAL RIGHTS (ICESCR), which together with the Universal Declaration and the ICCPR form what is often called the "International Bill of Human Rights." Excerpts from the covenant follow.

PREAMBLE
The States Parties to the present Covenant,
Considering that, in accordance with the principles proclaimed in the CHARTER OF THE UNITED NATIONS, recognition of the inherent dignity and of the equal and inalienable rights of all members of the human family is the foundation of freedom, justice and peace in the world,

Recognizing that these rights derive from the inherent dignity of the human person,

Recognizing that, in accordance with the Universal Declaration of Human Rights, the ideal of free human beings enjoying civil and political freedom and freedom from fear and want can only be achieved if conditions are created whereby everyone may enjoy his civil and political rights, as well as his economic, social and cultural rights,

Considering the obligation of States under the Charter of the United Nations to promote universal respect for, and observance of, HUMAN RIGHTS and freedoms,

Realizing that the individual, having duties to other individuals and to the community to which he belongs, is under a responsibility to strive for the promotion and observance of the rights recognized in the present Covenant,

Agree upon the following articles:

PART I

Article 1
1. All peoples have the right of self-determination. By virtue of that right they freely determine their political status and freely pursue their economic, social and cultural development.

2. All peoples may, for their own ends, freely dispose of their natural wealth and resources without prejudice to any obligations arising out of international economic cooperation, based upon the principle of mutual benefit, and international law. In no case may a people be deprived of its own means of subsistence.

3. The States Parties to the present Covenant, including those having responsibility for the administration of NON-SELF-GOVERNING and Trust Territories, shall promote the realization of the right of self-determination, and shall respect that right, in conformity with the provisions of the Charter of the United Nations.

PART II

Article 2
1. Each State Party to the present Covenant undertakes to respect and to ensure to all individuals within its territory and subject to its JURISDICTION the rights recognized in the present Covenant, without distinction of any kind, such as race, colour, sex, LANGUAGE, religion, political or other opinion, national or social origin, property, birth or other status.

2. Where not already provided for by existing legislative or other measures, each State Party to the present Covenant undertakes to take the necessary steps, in accordance with its constitutional processes and with the provisions of the present Covenant, to adopt such legislative or other measures as may be necessary to give effect to the rights recognized in the present Covenant.

3. Each State Party to the present Covenant undertakes:

(a) To ensure that any person whose rights or freedoms as herein recognized are violated shall have an effective remedy, notwithstanding that the violation has been committed by persons acting in an official capacity;

(b) To ensure that any person claiming such a remedy shall have his right thereto determined by competent judicial, administrative or legislative authorities, or by any other competent authority provided for by the legal system of the State, and to develop the possibilities of judicial remedy;

(c) To ensure that the competent authorities shall enforce such remedies when granted.

Article 3

The States Parties to the present Covenant undertake to ensure the equal right of men and WOMEN to the enjoyment of all civil and political rights set forth in the present Covenant.

Article 4

1. In time of public emergency which threatens the life of the nation and the existence of which is officially proclaimed, the States Parties to the present Covenant may take measures derogating from their obligations under the present Covenant to the extent strictly required by the exigencies of the situation, provided that such measures are not inconsistent with their other obligations under international law and do not involve discrimination solely on the ground of race, colour, sex, language, religion or social origin.

2. No derogation from articles 6, 7, 8 (paragraphs 1 and 2), 11, 15, 16 and 18 may be made under this provision.

3. Any State Party to the present Covenant availing itself of the right of derogation shall immediately inform the other States Parties to the present Covenant, through the intermediary of the SECRETARY-GENERAL of the United Nations, of the provisions from which it has derogated and of the reasons by which it was actuated. A further communication shall be made, through the same intermediary, on the date on which it terminates such derogation.

Article 5

1. Nothing in the present Covenant may be interpreted as implying for any State, group or person any right to engage in any activity or perform any act aimed at the destruction of any of the rights and freedoms recognized herein or at their limitation to a greater extent than is provided for in the present Covenant.

2. There shall be no restriction upon or derogation from any of the fundamental human rights recognized or existing in any State Party to the present Covenant pursuant to law, CONVENTIONS, regulations or custom on the pretext that the present Covenant does not recognize such rights or that it recognizes them to a lesser extent.

PART III

Article 6

1. Every human being has the inherent right to life. This right shall be protected by law. No one shall be arbitrarily deprived of his life.

2. In countries which have not abolished the death penalty, sentence of death may be imposed only for the most serious crimes in accordance with the law in force at time of the commission of the crime and not contrary to the provisions of the present Covenant and to the CONVENTION ON THE PREVENTION AND PUNISHMENT OF THE CRIME OF GENOCIDE. This penalty can only be carried out pursuant to a final judgement rendered by a competent court.

3. When deprivation of life constitutes the crime of genocide, it is understood that nothing in this article shall authorize any State Party to the present Covenant to derogate in any way from any obligation assumed under the provisions of the Convention on the Prevention and Punishment of the Crime of Genocide.

4. Anyone sentenced to death shall have the right to seek pardon or commutation of the sentence. Amnesty, pardon or commutation of the sentence of death may be granted in all cases.

5. Sentence of death shall not be imposed for crimes committed by persons below eighteen years of age and shall not be carried out on pregnant women.

6. Nothing in this article shall be invoked to delay or to prevent the abolition of capital punishment by any State Party to the present Covenant.

Article 7

No one shall be subjected to torture or to cruel, inhuman or degrading treatment or punishment. In particular, no one shall be subjected without his free consent to medical or scientific experimentation.

Article 8

1. No one shall be held in slavery; slavery and the slave-trade in all their forms shall be prohibited.

2. No one shall be held in servitude.

3. (a) No one shall be required to perform forced or compulsory labour;

(b) Paragraph 3 (a) shall not be held to preclude, in countries where imprisonment with hard labour may be imposed as a punishment for a crime, the performance of hard labour in pursuance of a sentence to such punishment by a competent court;

(c) For the purpose of this paragraph the term "forced or compulsory labour" shall not include:

(i) Any work or service, not referred to in subparagraph (b), normally required of a person who is under detention in consequence of a lawful order of a court, or of a person during conditional release from such detention;

(ii) Any service of a military character and, in countries where conscientious objection is recognized, any national service required by law of conscientious objectors;

(iii) Any service exacted in cases of emergency or calamity threatening the life or well-being of the community;

(iv) Any work or service which forms part of normal civil obligations.

Article 9

1. Everyone has the right to liberty and security of person. No one shall be subjected to arbitrary arrest or detention. No one shall be deprived of his liberty except on such grounds and in accordance with such procedure as are established by law.

2. Anyone who is arrested shall be informed, at the time of arrest, of the reasons for his arrest and shall be promptly informed of any charges against him.

3. Anyone arrested or detained on a criminal charge shall be brought promptly before a judge or other officer authorized by law to exercise judicial power and shall be entitled to trial within a reasonable time or to release. It shall not be the general rule that persons awaiting trial shall be detained in custody, but release may be subject to guarantees to appear for trial, at any other stage of the judicial proceedings, and, should occasion arise, for execution of the judgement.

4. Anyone who is deprived of his liberty by arrest or detention shall be entitled to take proceedings before a court, in order that that court may decide without delay on the lawfulness of his detention and order his release if the detention is not lawful.

5. Anyone who has been the victim of unlawful arrest or detention shall have an enforceable right to compensation.

Article 10

1. All persons deprived of their liberty shall be treated with humanity and with respect for the inherent dignity of the human person.

2. (a) Accused persons shall, save in exceptional circumstances, be segregated from convicted persons and shall be subject to separate treatment appropriate to their status as unconvicted persons;

(b) Accused juvenile persons shall be separated from adults and brought as speedily as possible for adjudication.

3. The penitentiary system shall comprise treatment of prisoners the essential aim of which shall be their reformation and social rehabilitation. Juvenile offenders shall be segregated from adults and be accorded treatment appropriate to their age and legal status.

Article 11

No one shall be imprisoned merely on the ground of inability to fulfill a contractual obligation.

Article 12

1. Everyone lawfully within the territory of a State shall, within that territory, have the right to liberty of movement and freedom to choose his residence.

2. Everyone shall be free to leave any country, including his own.

3. The above-mentioned rights shall not be subject to any restrictions except those which are provided by law, are necessary to protect national security, public order (*ordre public*), public health or morals or the rights and freedoms of others, and are consistent with the other rights recognized in the present Covenant.

4. No one shall be arbitrarily deprived of the right to enter his own country.

Article 13

An alien lawfully in the territory of a State Party to the present Covenant may be expelled therefrom only in pursuance of a decision reached in accordance with law and shall, except where compelling reasons of national security otherwise require, be allowed to submit the reasons against his expulsion and to have his case reviewed by, and be represented for the purpose before, the competent authority or a person or persons especially designated by the competent authority.

Article 14

1. All persons shall be equal before the courts and tribunals. In the determination of any criminal charge against him, or of his rights and obligations in a suit at law, everyone shall be entitled to a fair and public hearing by a competent, independent and impartial tribunal established by law. The press and the public may be excluded from all or part of a trial for reasons of morals, public order (*ordre public*) or national security in a democratic society, or when the interest of the private lives of the parties so requires, or to the extent strictly necessary in the opinion of the court in special circumstances where publicity would prejudice the interests of justice; but any judgement rendered in a criminal case or in a suit at law shall be made public except where the interest of juvenile persons otherwise requires or the proceedings concern matrimonial disputes or the guardianship of children.

2. Everyone charged with a criminal offence shall have the right to be presumed innocent until proved guilty according to law.

3. In the determination of any criminal charge against him, everyone shall be entitled to the following minimum guarantees, in full equality:

(a) To be informed promptly and in detail in a language which he understands of the nature and cause of the charge against him;

(b) To have adequate time and facilities for the preparation of his defence and to communicate with counsel of his own choosing;

(c) To be tried without undue delay;

(d) To be tried in his presence, and to defend himself in person or through legal assistance of his own choosing; to be informed, if he does not have legal assistance, of this right; and to have legal assistance assigned to him, in any case where the interests of justice so require, and without payment by him in any such case if he does not have sufficient means to pay for it;

(e) To examine, or have examined, the witnesses against him and to obtain the attendance and examination of witnesses on his behalf under the same conditions as witnesses against him;

(f) To have the free assistance of an interpreter if he cannot understand or speak the language used in court;

(g) Not to be compelled to testify against himself or to confess guilt.

4. In the case of juvenile persons, the procedure shall be such as will take account of their age and the desirability of promoting their rehabilitation.

5. Everyone convicted of a crime shall have the right to his conviction and sentence being reviewed by a higher tribunal according to law.

6. When a person has by a final decision been convicted of a criminal offence and when subsequently his conviction has been reversed or he has been pardoned on the ground that a new or newly discovered fact shows conclusively that there has been a miscarriage of justice, the person who has suffered punishment as a result of such conviction shall be compensated according to law, unless it is proved that the non-disclosure of the unknown fact in time is wholly or partly attributable to him.

7. No one shall be liable to be tried or punished again for an offence for which he has already been finally convicted or acquitted in accordance with the law and penal procedure of each country.

Article 15

1. No one shall be held guilty of any criminal offence on account of any act or omission which did not constitute a criminal offence, under national or international law, at the time when it was committed. Nor shall a heavier penalty be imposed than the one that was applicable at the time when the criminal offence was committed. If, subsequent to the commission of the offence, provision is made by law for the imposition of the lighter penalty, the offender shall benefit thereby.

2. Nothing in this article shall prejudice the trial and punishment of any person for any act or omission which, at the time when it was committed, was criminal according to the general principles of law recognized by the community of nations.

Article 16

Everyone shall have the right to recognition everywhere as a person before the law.

Article 17

1. No one shall be subjected to arbitrary or unlawful interference with his privacy, family, home or correspondence, nor to unlawful attacks on his honour and reputation.

2. Everyone has the right to the protection of the law against such interference or attacks.

Article 18

1. Everyone shall have the right to freedom of thought, conscience and religion. This right shall include freedom to have or to adopt a religion or belief of his choice, and freedom, either individually or in community with others and in public or private, to manifest his religion or belief in worship, observance, practice and teaching.

2. No one shall be subject to coercion which would impair his freedom to have or to adopt a religion or belief of his choice.

3. Freedom to manifest one's religion or beliefs may be subject only to such limitations as are prescribed by law and are necessary to protect public safety, order, health, or morals or the fundamental rights and freedoms of others.

4. The States Parties to the present Covenant undertake to have respect for the liberty of parents and, when applicable, legal guardians to ensure the religious and moral education of their children in conformity with their own convictions.

Article 19

1. Everyone shall have the right to hold opinions without interference.

2. Everyone shall have the right to freedom of expression; this right shall include freedom to seek, receive and impart information and ideas of all kinds, regardless of frontiers, either orally, in writing or in print, in the form of art, or through any other media of his choice.

3. The exercise of the rights provided for in paragraph 2 of this article carries with it special duties and responsibilities. It may therefore be subject to certain restrictions, but these shall only be such as are provided by law and are necessary:

(a) For respect of the rights or reputations of others;

(b) For the protection of national security or of public order (*ordre public*), or of public health or morals.

Article 20

1. Any propaganda for war shall be prohibited by law.

2. Any advocacy of national, racial or religious hatred that constitutes incitement to discrimination, hostility or violence shall be prohibited by law.

Article 21

The right of peaceful assembly shall be recognized. No restrictions may be placed on the exercise of this right other than those imposed in conformity with the law and which are necessary in a democratic society in the interests of national security or public safety, public order (*ordre public*), the protection of public health or morals or the protection of the rights and freedoms of others.

Article 22

1. Everyone shall have the right to freedom of association with others, including the right to form and join trade unions for the protection of his interests.

2. No restrictions may be placed on the exercise of this right other than those which are prescribed by law and which are necessary in a democratic society in the interests of national security or public safety, public order (*ordre public*), the protection of public health or morals or the protection of the rights and freedoms of others. This article shall not prevent the imposition of lawful restrictions on members of the armed forces and of the police in their exercise of this right.

3. Nothing in this article shall authorize States Parties to the INTERNATIONAL LABOUR ORGANIZATION Convention of 1948 concerning Freedom of Association and Protection of the Right to Organize to take legislative measures which would prejudice, or to apply the law in such a manner as to prejudice, the guarantees provided for in that Convention.

Article 23

1. The family is the natural and fundamental group unit of society and is entitled to protection by society and the State.

2. The right of men and women of marriageable age to marry and to found a family shall be recognized.

3. No marriage shall be entered into without the free and full consent of the intending spouses.

4. States Parties to the present Covenant shall take appropriate steps to ensure equality of rights and responsibilities of spouses as to marriage, during marriage and at its dissolution. In the case of dissolution, provision shall be made for the necessary protection of any children.

Article 24

1. Every child shall have, without any discrimination as to race, colour, sex, language, religion, national or social origin, property or birth, the right to such measures of protection as are required by his status as a minor, on the part of his family, society and the State.

2. Every child shall be registered immediately after birth and shall have a name.

3. Every child has the right to acquire a nationality.

Article 25

Every citizen shall have the right and the opportunity, without any of the distinctions mentioned in article 2 and without unreasonable restrictions:

(a) To take part in the conduct of public affairs, directly or through freely chosen representatives;

(b) To vote and to be elected at genuine periodic elections which shall be by universal and equal suffrage and shall be held by secret ballot, guaranteeing the free expression of the will of the electors;

(c) To have access, on general terms of equality, to public service in his country.

Article 26

All persons are equal before the law and are entitled without any discrimination to the equal protection of the law. In this respect, the law shall prohibit any discrimination and guarantee to all persons equal and effective protection against discrimination on any ground such as race, colour, sex, language, religion, political or other opinion, national or social origin, property, birth or other status.

Article 27

In those States in which ethnic, religious or linguistic minorities exist, persons belonging to such minorities shall not be denied the right, in community with the other members of their group, to enjoy their own culture, to profess and practice their own religion, or to use their own language.

PART IV

Article 28

1. There shall be established a HUMAN RIGHTS COMMITTEE (hereafter referred to in the present Covenant as the Committee). It shall consist of eighteen members and shall carry out the functions hereinafter provided.

2. The Committee shall be composed of nationals of the States Parties to the present Covenant who shall be persons of high moral character and recognized COMPETENCE in the field of human rights, consideration being given to the usefulness of the participation of some persons having legal experience.

3. The members of the Committee shall be elected and shall serve in their personal capacity...

Article 40

1. The States Parties to the present Covenant undertake to submit reports of the measures they have adopted which give effect to the rights recognized herein and on the progress made in the enjoyment of those rights:

(a) Within one year of the entry into force of the present Covenant for the States Parties concerned;

(b) Thereafter whenever the Committee so requests.

2. All reports shall be submitted to the Secretary-General of the United Nations, who shall transmit them to the Committee for consideration. Reports shall indicate the factors and difficulties, if any, affecting the implementation of the present Covenant.

3. The Secretary-General of the United Nations may, after consultation with the Committee, transmit to the SPECIALIZED AGENCIES concerned copies of such parts of the reports as may fall within their field of competence.

4. The Committee shall study the reports submitted by the States Parties to the present Covenant. It shall transmit its reports, and such general comments as it may consider appropriate, to the States Parties. The Committee may also transmit to the ECONOMIC AND SOCIAL COUNCIL these comments along with the copies

of the reports it has received from States Parties to the present Covenant.

5. The States Parties to the present Covenant may submit to the Committee observations on any comments that may be made in accordance with paragraph 4 of this article.

Article 41

1. A State Party to the present Covenant may at any time declare under this article that it recognizes the competence of the Committee to receive and consider communications to the effect that a State Party claims that another State Party is not fulfilling its obligations under the present Covenant. Communications under this article may be received and considered only if submitted by a State Party which has made a declaration recognizing in regard to itself the competence of the Committee. No communication shall be received by the Committee if it concerns a State Party which has not made such a DECLARATION. Communications received under this article shall be dealt with in accordance with the following procedure:

(a) If a State Party to the present Covenant considers that another State Party is not giving effect to the provisions of the present Covenant, it may, by written communication, bring the matter to the attention of that State Party. Within three months after the receipt of the communication the receiving State shall afford the State which sent the communication an explanation, or any other statement in writing clarifying the matter, which should include, to the extent possible and pertinent, reference to domestic procedures and remedies taken, pending, or available in the matter;

(b) If the matter is not adjusted to the satisfaction of both States Parties concerned within six months after the receipt by the receiving State of the initial communication, either State shall have the right to refer the matter to the Committee, by notice given to the Committee and to the other State;

(c) The Committee shall deal with a matter referred to it only after it has ascertained that all available domestic remedies have been invoked and exhausted in the matter, in conformity with the generally recognized principles of international law. This shall not be the rule where the application of the remedies is unreasonably prolonged;

(d) The Committee shall hold closed meetings when examining communications under this article;

(e) Subject to the provisions of subparagraph (c), the Committee shall make available its GOOD OFFICES to the States Parties concerned with a view to a friendly solution of the matter on the basis of respect for human rights and fundamental freedoms as recognized in the present Covenant...

Article 42

1. (a) If a matter referred to the Committee in accordance with article 41 is not resolved to the satisfaction of the States Parties concerned, the Committee may, with the prior consent of the States Parties concerned, appoint an *ad hoc* CONCILIATION Commission (hereinafter referred to as the Commission). The good offices of the Commission shall be made available to the States Parties concerned with a view to an amicable solution of the matter on the basis of respect for the present Covenant...

7. When the Commission has fully considered the matter, but in any event not later than twelve months after having been seized of the matter, it shall submit to the Chairman of the Committee a report for communication to the States Parties concerned...

Article 44

The provisions for the implementation of the present Covenant shall apply without prejudice to the procedures prescribed in the field of human rights by or under the constituent instruments and the conventions of the United Nations and of the specialized agencies and shall not prevent the States Parties to the present Covenant from having recourse to other procedures for settling a dispute in accordance with general or special international agreements in force between them.

Article 45

The Committee shall submit to the General Assembly of the United Nations, through the Economic and Social Council, an annual report on its activities.

PART V

Article 46

Nothing in the present Covenant shall be interpreted as impairing the provisions of the Charter of the United Nations and of the constitutions of the specialized agencies which define the respective responsibilities of the various organs of the United Nations and of the specialized agencies in regard to the matters dealt with in the present Covenant.

Article 47

Nothing in the present Covenant shall be interpreted as impairing the inherent right of all peoples to enjoy and utilize fully and freely their natural wealth and resources...

International Covenant on Economic, Social and Cultural Rights (ICESCR)

The International Covenant on Economic, Social and Cultural Rights codified and expanded on rights listed in the UNIVERSAL DECLARATION OF HUMAN RIGHTS. As a formal TREATY, the COVENANT carried the force of INTERNATIONAL LAW, requiring signatories to live up to its terms. It was adopted by the GENERAL ASSEMBLY on December 16, 1966, and went into force in 1976. At the time of its adoption, the Assembly also opened for signature the INTERNATIONAL COVENANT ON CIVIL AND POLITICAL RIGHTS (ICCPR), which together with the Universal Declaration and the ICESCR form what is often called the "International Bill of Human Rights." The text of the covenant follows.

PREAMBLE

The States Parties to the present Covenant,

Considering that, in accordance with the principles proclaimed in the CHARTER OF THE UNITED NATIONS, recognition of the inherent dignity and of the equal and inalienable rights of all members of the human family is the foundation of freedom, justice and peace in the world,

Recognizing that these rights derive from the inherent dignity of the human person,

Recognizing that, in accordance with the Universal Declaration of Human Rights, the ideal of free human beings enjoying freedom from fear and want can only be achieved if conditions are created whereby everyone may enjoy his economic, social and cultural rights, as well as his civil and political rights,

Considering the obligation of States under the Charter of the United Nations to promote universal respect for, and observance of, HUMAN RIGHTS and freedoms,

Realizing that the individual, having duties to other individuals and to the community to which he belongs, is under a responsibility to strive for the promotion and observance of the rights recognized in the present Covenant,

Agree upon the following articles:

PART I

Article 1

1. All peoples have the right of self-determination. By virtue of that right they freely determine their political status and freely pursue their economic, social and cultural development.

2. All peoples may, for their own ends, freely dispose of their natural wealth and resources without prejudice to any obligations arising out of international economic cooperation, based upon the principle of mutual benefit, and international law. In no case may a people be deprived of its own means of subsistence.

3. The States Parties to the present Covenant, including those having responsibility for the administration of NON-SELF-GOVERNING and Trust Territories, shall promote the realization of the right of self-determination, and shall respect that right, in conformity with the provisions of the Charter of the United Nations.

PART II

Article 2

1. Each State Party to the present Covenant undertakes to take steps, individually and through international assistance and cooperation, especially economic and technical, to the maximum of its available resources, with a view to achieving progressively the full realization of the rights recognized in the present Covenant by all appropriate means, including particularly the adoption of legislative measures.

2. The States Parties to the present Covenant undertake to guarantee that the rights enunciated in the present Covenant will be exercised without discrimination of any kind as to race, colour, sex, LANGUAGE, religion, political or other opinion, national or social origin, property, birth or other status.

3. Developing countries, with due regard to human rights and their national economy, may determine to what extent they would guarantee the economic rights recognized in the present Covenant to non-nationals.

Article 3

The States Parties to the present Covenant undertake to ensure the equal right of men and WOMEN to the enjoyment of all economic, social and cultural rights set forth in the present Covenant.

Article 4

The States Parties to the present Covenant recognize that, in the enjoyment of those rights provided by the State in conformity with the present Covenant, the State may subject such rights only to such limitations as are determined by law only in so far as this may be compatible with the nature of these rights and solely for the purpose of promoting the general welfare in a democratic society.

Article 5

1. Nothing in the present Covenant may be interpreted as implying for any State, group or person any right to engage in any activity or to perform any act aimed at the destruction of any of the rights or freedoms recognized herein, or at their limitation to a greater extent than is provided for in the present Covenant.

2. No restriction upon or derogation from any of the fundamental human rights recognized or existing in any country in virtue of law, CONVENTIONS, regulations or custom shalt be admitted on the pretext that the present Covenant does not recognize such rights or that it recognizes them to a lesser extent.

PART III

Article 6

1. The States Parties to the present Covenant recognize the right to work, which includes the right of everyone to the opportunity to gain his living by work which he freely chooses or accepts, and will take appropriate steps to safeguard this right.

2. The steps to be taken by a State Party to the present Covenant to achieve the full realization of this right shall include technical and vocational guidance and training programmes, policies and techniques to achieve steady economic, social and cultural development and full and productive employment under conditions safeguarding fundamental political and economic freedoms to the individual.

Article 7

The States Parties to the present Covenant recognize the right of everyone to the enjoyment of just and favourable conditions of work which ensure, in particular:

(a) Remuneration which provides all workers, as a minimum, with:

(i) Fair wages and equal remuneration for work of equal value without distinction of any kind, in particular women being guaranteed conditions of work not inferior to those enjoyed by men, with equal pay for equal work;

(ii) A decent living for themselves and their families in accordance with the provisions of the present Covenant;

(b) Safe and healthy working conditions;

(c) Equal opportunity for everyone to be promoted in his employment to an appropriate higher level, subject to no considerations other than those of seniority and competence;

(d) Rest, leisure and reasonable limitation of working hours and periodic holidays with pay, as well as remuneration for public holidays.

Article 8

1. The States Parties to the present Covenant undertake to ensure:

(a) The right of everyone to form trade unions and join the trade union of his choice, subject only to the rules of the organization concerned, for the promotion and protection of his economic and social interests. No restrictions may be placed on the exercise of this right other than those prescribed by law and which are necessary in a democratic society in the interests of national security or public order or for the protection of the rights and freedoms of others;

(b) The right of trade unions to establish national federations or confederations and the right of the latter to form or join international trade-union organizations;

(c) The right of trade unions to function freely subject to no limitations other than those prescribed by law and which are necessary in a democratic society in the interests of national security or public order or for the protection of the rights and freedoms of others;

(d) The right to strike, provided that it is exercised in conformity with the laws of the particular country.

2. This article shall not prevent the imposition of lawful restrictions on the exercise of these rights by members of the armed forces or of the police or of the administration of the State.

3. Nothing in this article shall authorize States Parties to the INTERNATIONAL LABOUR ORGANIZATION Convention of 1948 concerning Freedom of Association and Protection of the Right to Organize to take legislative measures which would prejudice, or apply the law in such a manner as would prejudice, the guarantees provided for in that Convention.

Article 9

The States Parties to the present Covenant recognize the right of everyone to social security, including social insurance.

Article 10

The States Parties to the present Covenant recognize that:

1. The widest possible protection and assistance should be accorded to the family, which is the natural and fundamental group unit of society, particularly for its establishment and while it is responsible for the care and education of dependent children. Marriage must be entered into with the free consent of the intending spouses.

2. Special protection should be accorded to mothers during a reasonable period before and after childbirth. During such period working mothers should be accorded paid leave or leave with adequate social security benefits.

3. Special measures of protection and assistance should be taken on behalf of all children and young persons without any discrimination for reasons of parentage or other conditions. Children and young persons should be protected from economic and social exploitation. Their employment in work harmful to their morals or health or dangerous to life or likely to hamper their normal development should be punishable by law. States should also set age limits below which the paid employment of child labour should be prohibited and punishable by law.

Article 11

1. The States Parties to the present Covenant recognize the right of everyone to an adequate standard of living for himself and his family, including adequate food, clothing and housing, and to the continuous improvement of living conditions. The States Parties will take appropriate steps to ensure the realization of this right, recognizing to this effect the essential importance of international cooperation based on free consent.

2. The States Parties to the present Covenant, recognizing the fundamental right of everyone to be free from hunger, shall take, individually and through international cooperation, the measures, including specific programmes, which are needed:

(a) To improve methods of production, conservation and distribution of food by making full use of technical and scientific knowledge, by disseminating knowledge of the principles of nutrition and by developing or reforming agrarian systems in such a way as to achieve the most efficient development and utilization of natural resources;

(b) Taking into account the problems of both food-importing and food-exporting countries, to ensure an equitable distribution of world food supplies in relation to need.

Article 12

1. The States Parties to the present Covenant recognize the right of everyone to the enjoyment of the highest attainable standard of physical and mental health.

2. The steps to be taken by the States Parties to the present Covenant to achieve the full realization of this right shall include those necessary for:

(a) The provision for the reduction of the stillbirthrate and of infant mortality and for the healthy development of the child;

(b) The improvement of all aspects of environmental and industrial hygiene;

(c) The prevention, treatment and control of epidemic, endemic, occupational and other diseases;

(d) The creation of conditions which would assure to all medical service and medical attention in the event of sickness.

Article 13

1. The States Parties to the present Covenant recognize the right of everyone to education. They agree that education shall be directed to the full development of the human personality and the sense of its dignity, and shall strengthen the respect for human rights and fundamental freedoms. They further agree that education shall enable all persons to participate effectively in a free society, promote understanding, tolerance and friendship among all nations and all racial, ethnic or religious groups, and further the activities of the United Nations for the maintenance of peace.

2. The States Parties to the present Covenant recognize that, with a view to achieving the full realization of this right:

(a) Primary education shall be compulsory and available free to all;

(b) Secondary education in its different forms, including technical and vocational secondary education, shall be made generally available and accessible to all by every appropriate means, and in particular by the progressive introduction of free education;

(c) Higher education shall be made equally accessible to all, on the basis of capacity, by every appropriate means, and in particular by the progressive introduction of free education;

(d) Fundamental education shall be encouraged or intensified as far as possible for those persons who have not received or completed the whole period of their primary education;

(e) The development of a system of schools at all levels shall be actively pursued, an adequate fellowship system shall be established, and the material conditions of teaching staff shall be continuously improved.

3. The States Parties to the present Covenant undertake to have respect for the liberty of parents and, when applicable, legal guardians to choose for their children schools, other than those established by the public authorities, which conform to such minimum educational standards as may be laid down or approved by the State and to ensure the religious and moral education of their children in conformity with their own convictions.

4. No part of this article shall be construed so as to interfere with the liberty of individuals and bodies to establish and direct educational institutions, subject always to the observance of the principles set forth in paragraph 1 of this article and to the requirement that the education given in such institutions shall conform to such minimum standards as may be laid down by the State.

Article 14

Each State Party to the present Covenant which, at the time of becoming a Party, has not been able to secure in its metropolitan territory or other territories under its JURISDICTION compulsory primary education, free of charge, undertakes, within two years, to work out and adopt a detailed plan of action for the progressive implementation, within a reasonable number of years, to be fixed in the plan, of the principle of compulsory education free of charge for all.

Article 15

1. The States Parties to the present Covenant recognize the right of everyone:

(a) To take part in cultural life;

(b) To enjoy the benefits of scientific progress and its applications;

(c) To benefit from the protection of the moral and material interests resulting from any scientific, literary or artistic production of which he is the author.

2. The steps to be taken by the States Parties to the present Covenant to achieve the full realization of this right shall include those necessary for the conservation, the development and the diffusion of science and culture.

3. The States Parties to the present Covenant undertake to respect the freedom indispensable for scientific research and creative activity.

4. The States Parties to the present Covenant recognize the benefits to be derived from the encouragement and development of international contacts and cooperation in the scientific and cultural fields.

PART IV

Article 16

1. The States Parties to the present Covenant undertake to submit in conformity with this part of the Covenant reports on the measures which they have adopted and the progress made in achieving the observance of the rights recognized herein.

2. (a) All reports shall be submitted to the SECRETARY-GENERAL of the United Nations, who shall transmit copies to the ECONOMIC AND SOCIAL COUNCIL for consideration in accordance with the provisions of the present Covenant;

(b) The Secretary-General of the United Nations shall also transmit to the SPECIALIZED AGENCIES copies of the reports, or any relevant parts therefrom, from States Parties to the present Covenant which are also members of these specialized agencies in so far as these reports, or parts therefrom, relate to any matters which fall within the responsibilities of the said agencies in accordance with their constitutional instruments.

Article 17

1. The States Parties to the present Covenant shall furnish their reports in stages, in accordance with a programme to be established by the Economic and Social Council within one year of the entry into force of the present Covenant after consultation with the States Parties and the specialized agencies concerned.

2. Reports may indicate factors and difficulties affecting the degree of fulfillment of obligations under the present Covenant.

3. Where relevant information has previously been furnished to the United Nations or to any specialized agency by any State Party to the present Covenant, it will not be necessary to reproduce that information, but a precise reference to the information so furnished will suffice.

Article 18

Pursuant to its responsibilities under the Charter of the United Nations in the field of human rights and fundamental freedoms, the Economic and Social Council may make arrangements with the specialized agencies in respect of their reporting to it on the progress made in achieving the observance of the provisions of the present Covenant falling within the scope of their activities. These reports may include particulars of decisions and recommendations on such implementation adopted by their competent organs.

Article 19

The Economic and Social Council may transmit to the COMMISSION ON HUMAN RIGHTS for study and general recommendation or, as appropriate, for information the reports concerning human rights submitted by States in accordance with articles 16 and 17, and those concerning human rights submitted by the specialized agencies in accordance with article 18.

Article 20

The States Parties to the present Covenant and the specialized agencies concerned may submit comments to the Economic and Social Council on any general recommendation under article 19 or reference to such general recommendation in any report of the Commission on Human Rights or any documentation referred to therein.

Article 21

The Economic and Social Council may submit from time to time to the General Assembly reports with recommendations of a general nature and a summary of the information received from the States Parties to the present Covenant and the specialized agencies on the measures taken and the progress made in achieving general observance of the rights recognized in the present Covenant.

Article 22

The Economic and Social Council may bring to the attention of other organs of the United Nations, their subsidiary organs and specialized agencies concerned with furnishing technical assistance any matters arising out of the reports referred to in this part of the present Covenant which may assist such bodies in deciding, each within its field of COMPETENCE, on the advisability of international measures likely to contribute to the effective progressive implementation of the present Covenant.

Article 23

The States Parties to the present Covenant agree that international action for the achievement of the rights recognized in the present Covenant includes such methods as the conclusion of conventions, the adoption of recommendations, the furnishing of technical assistance and the holding of regional meetings and technical meetings for the purpose of consultation and study organized in conjunction with the Governments concerned.

Article 24

Nothing in the present Covenant shall be interpreted as impairing the provisions of the Charter of the United Nations and of the constitutions of the specialized agencies which define the respective responsibilities of the various organs of the United Nations and of the specialized agencies in regard to the matters dealt with in the present Covenant.

Article 25

Nothing in the present Covenant shall be interpreted as impairing the inherent right of all peoples to enjoy and utilize fully and freely their natural wealth and resources.

PART V

Article 26

1. The present Covenant is open for signature by any State Member of the United Nations or member of any of its specialized agencies, by any State Party to the STATUTE OF THE INTERNATIONAL COURT OF JUSTICE, and by any other State which has been invited by the General Assembly of the United Nations to become a party to the present Covenant.

2. The present Covenant is subject to ratification. Instruments of ratification shall be deposited with the Secretary-General of the United Nations.

3. The present Covenant shall be open to ACCESSION by any State referred to in paragraph 1 of this article.

4. Accession shall be effected by the deposit of an instrument of accession with the Secretary-General of the United Nations.

5. The Secretary-General of the United Nations shall inform all States which have signed the present Covenant or acceded to it of the deposit of each instrument of ratification or accession.

Article 27

1. The present Covenant shall enter into force three months after the date of the deposit with the Secretary-General of the United Nations of the thirty-fifth instrument of ratification or instrument of accession.

2. For each State ratifying the present Covenant or acceding to it after the deposit of the thirty-fifth instrument of ratification or instrument of accession, the present Covenant shall enter into force three months after the date of the deposit of its own instrument of ratification or instrument of accession.

Article 28

The provisions of the present Covenant shall extend to all parts of federal States without any limitations or exceptions.

Article 29

1. Any State Party to the present Covenant may propose an amendment and file it with the Secretary-General of the United Nations. The Secretary-General shall thereupon communicate any proposed amendments to the States Parties to the present Covenant with a request that they notify him whether they favour a conference of States Parties for the purpose of considering and VOTING upon the proposals. In the event that at least one third of the States Parties favours such a conference, the Secretary-General shall convene the conference under the auspices of the United Nations. Any amendment adopted by a majority of the States Parties present and voting at the conference shall be submitted to the General Assembly of the United Nations for approval.

2. AMENDMENTS shall come into force when they have been approved by the General Assembly of the United Nations and accepted by a two-thirds majority of the States Parties to the present Covenant in accordance with their respective constitutional processes.

3. When amendments come into force they shall be binding on those States Parties which have accepted them, other States Parties still being bound by the provisions of the present Covenant and any earlier amendment which they have accepted.

Article 30

Irrespective of the notifications made under article 26, paragraph 5, the Secretary-General of the United Nations shall inform all States referred to in paragraph 1 of the same article of the following particulars:

(a) Signatures, ratifications and accessions under article 26;

(b) The date of the entry into force of the present Covenant under article 27 and the date of the entry into force of any amendments under article 29.

Article 31

1. The present Covenant, of which the Chinese, English, French, Russian and Spanish texts are equally authentic, shall be deposited in the archives of the United Nations.

2. The Secretary-General of the United Nations shall transmit certified copies of the present Covenant to all States referred to in article 26.

International Criminal Court (ICC)

The International Criminal Court is a permanent court that is intended to investigate and bring to justice individuals, not countries, who commit the most serious crimes of concern to the international community, such as GENOCIDE, war crimes, and crimes against humanity—including widespread murder of civilians, torture, and mass rape. The Rome Statute, negotiated by the world community over a two-year period and adopted on July 17, 1998, created the ICC as a global judicial institution with an international JURISDICTION complementing national legal systems. The key element of the ICC is that it is designed to be permanent, rather than an ad hoc body. The current tribunals for the FORMER YUGOSLAVIA and for Rwanda are ad hoc, created by the United Nations SECURITY COUNCIL, with defined historical periods and geographical areas as jurisdiction. The ICC would have no restrictions on time or geography.

The precedents for the International Criminal Court were the International Military Tribunal at Nuremberg and the Tokyo War Crimes Trial that concluded World War II. As early as October 1946, international legal meetings discussed the possibility of a permanent WAR CRIMES TRIBUNAL to sustain the momentum created at Nuremberg and Tokyo. By 1948, the INTERNATIONAL LAW COMMISSION (ILC) of the United Nations began discussions for the creation of a criminal court, and this sentiment was given greater momentum with the signing of the Geneva CONVENTIONs on December 9, 1948. The issue remained on the ILC agenda throughout the COLD WAR. In 1993, the ILC submitted a draft statute RESOLUTION to the GENERAL ASSEMBLY to create an international criminal court.

The General Assembly passed several resolutions that led to the Rome Conference. These included Resolution 73 on December 9, 1994, creating the initial ad hoc committee for the conference; Resolution 46 on December 11, 1995, making this committee permanent; and Resolution 160 on December 15, 1997, establishing the dates of the conference and selecting Rome as the host city. Between June 15 and July 17, 1998, 160 countries participated in the UN Diplomatic Conference of Plenipotentiaries on the Establishment of an International Criminal Court. On February 2, 1999,

Senegal became the first country to ratify the Rome Statute. By April 2001, 139 nations had signed the statute, and 29 had ratified it. It required 60 ratifications to take effect.

The most serious controversy to arise over the negotiation of the Rome Statute centered on U.S. objections to the jurisdiction of the court. The UNITED STATES declared that it would ratify the statute only if its jurisdiction were limited to cases referred to it by the UN Security Council. The statute, as opened for signature in 1998, had no such provisions and claimed universal jurisdiction on the basis of INTERNATIONAL LAW. In December 2000, President Bill Clinton signed the Rome Statute, but noted the need for amendments to it. Clinton's successor, President George W. Bush, was not expected to submit the Statute to the U.S. Congress for ratification until U.S. concerns were met.

The eighth Preparatory Commission of the ICC met in the aftermath of the September 11, 2001, terrorist attack on the United States of America. SECRETARY-GENERAL Kofi ANNAN addressed the commission, categorizing the assault as a crime against humanity, one of the crimes under the jurisdiction of the court.

Despite the intent of the commission to finalize the terms of the Rome Statute at the meeting, many issues were left open, including the definition of AGGRESSION, the issues of the Victims Trust fund and the first-year BUDGET of the court. Some of the difficulties resulted from the continuous references by the SECRETARIAT and the delegates to the work of the existing tribunals as a guide to the anticipated work of the court. However, the inadequacy of such analogies became evident from the presentations by the representatives of the tribunals as well as by the NON-GOVERNMENTAL ORGANIZATIONS participating in the meeting. The work of the commission was further handicapped by the decision of the American government to seek national legislation that effectively would prevent U.S. cooperation with the court and bar U.S. assistance to nations parties to the Rome Statute. The U.S. delegation participated in the work of two working groups, but its activities were severely limited by the U.S. policy position.

The meeting of the commission, however, ended on a positive note. The 42nd ratification instrument was deposited with the secretariat on the last day of the conference. On April 11, 2002, BOSNIA, Bulgaria, CAMBODIA, CONGO, Ireland, Jordan, Mongolia, Niger, Romania, and Slovakia deposited their ratifications in New York, making the court a reality. The ICC came into existence on July 1, 2002, in The Hague.

See also HUMAN RIGHTS, INTERNATIONAL CRIMINAL TRIBUNAL FOR RWANDA, INTERNATIONAL CRIMINAL TRIBUNAL FOR THE FORMER YUGOSLAVIA.

Further Reading: Beigbeder, Yves, and Theo Von Boven. *Judging War Criminals: The Politics of International Justice.* New York: St. Martin's, 1999. Frye, Alton. *Toward an International Criminal Court?: A Council Policy Initiative.* New York: Council on Foreign Relations, 2000. Lee, Roy S., ed. *The International Criminal Court: The Making of the Rome Statute Issues, Negotiations, Results.* The Hague: Kluwer Law International, 1999. Sewall, Sarah B., and Carl Kaysen, eds. *The United States and the International Criminal Court: National Security and International Law.* Lanham, Md.: Rowman and Littlefield Publishers, 2000. International Criminal Court website: <www.un.org/law/icc/>.

— *D. J. Becker*

International Criminal Tribunal for Rwanda (ICTR)

The UN SECURITY COUNCIL created the International Criminal Tribunal for Rwanda on November 8, 1994 (Res. 955), as the second institution of international criminal prosecution since the Nuremberg Tribunal at the end of World War II. It followed the establishment of the INTERNATIONAL CRIMINAL TRIBUNAL FOR THE FORMER YUGOSLAVIA (ICTY) and closely resembled it in STRUCTURE and procedures. Article 1 of its statute states that "The International Tribunal for Rwanda shall have the power to prosecute persons responsible for serious violations of international humanitarian law committed in the territory of Rwanda and Rwandan citizens responsible for such violations committed in the territory of neighbouring states between 1 January 1994 and 31 December 1994." As such, it had a limited time JURISDICTION, but its mandates extend beyond the borders of Rwanda to incorporate crimes against Rwandans in refugee camps in the Republic of CONGO and in Burundi. The crimes it specifically was empowered to prosecute included grave breaches of the 1949 Geneva Convention, war crimes, GENOCIDE, and crimes against humanity.

The ICTR operated with primary jurisdiction over national courts under the principle of *non-bis-in-idem*, which holds that one may not be tried twice for the same crime, and prohibits national courts from hearing the cases of those standing trial in the WAR CRIMES TRIBUNAL. At any time the ICTR formally could request that national courts surrender their jurisdiction over an individual to be tried at the tribunal. The ICTR was organized like the ICTY, with three offices: the chambers of judges (with both a trial chamber and an appeals chamber), the office of the prosecutor, and the registry. The two tribunals shared the judges of the appeals chamber as well as the lead prosecutor—in 2001, the Swiss jurist Carla Del Ponte. Also in 2001 the president of the tribunal was Judge Navanethem Pillay of South Africa and the vice-president was Judge Erik Møse of Norway.

The ICTR issued its first indictments, charging eight persons, on November 28, 1995. The tribunal also charged Jean-Paul Akayesu, a high government official, with inciting others to commit rape, recognizing the offense as a "war crime" for the first time in history. Former Rwandan prime minister Jean Kambanda was tried and convicted by the tribunal on September 4, 1998. The first head of government to be convicted for such crimes, Kambanda was sentenced to life imprisonment. The convictions of Akayesu and Kambanda were the first ever rendered by an international court for genocide. By 2001, the tribunal had secured the arrest of more than 40 individuals accused of involvement in the 1994 Rwandan massacre.

Mali was the first country to provide prison facilities for the enforcement of the tribunal's sentences. Benin, Swaziland, Belgium, Denmark, Norway, and some other African countries subsequently indicated their willingness to incarcerate persons convicted by the tribunal, under certain conditions. The ICTR was authorized to give a maximum punishment of life in prison, but no death penalty.

The budget for the ICTR in 2001 was just over $87 million for operations. The International Criminal Tribunal for Rwanda was housed at Arusha, Tanzania, and the Office of the Prosecutor was in Kigali, Rwanda.

See also HUMAN RIGHTS, INTERNATIONAL CRIMINAL COURT, RWANDA CRISIS.

Further Reading: Gourevitch, Philip. *We Wish to Inform You That Tomorrow We Will Be Killed with Our Families: Stories from Rwanda.* New York: St. Martin's, 1999. Morris, Virginia, and Michael P. Scharf. *International Criminal Tribunal for Rwanda.* Vols. 1 and 2. Irvington, N.Y.: Transnational Publishers, 1998. Jones, John R. W. D. *The Practice of the International Criminal Tribunals for the Former Yugoslavia and Rwanda.* Irvington, N.Y.: Transnational Publishers, 1999.

— *D. J. Becker*

International Criminal Tribunal for the Former Yugoslavia (ICTY)

The United Nations SECURITY COUNCIL created the International Criminal Tribunal for the Former Yugoslavia in 1993 (Res. 827) as the first institution of international criminal prosecution since the Nuremberg Tribunal at the end of World War II. An earlier decision by the council (Res. 780) had created the Kalshoven Commission of Experts to study and document crimes committed in the FORMER YUGOSLAVIA. The commission, headed by Mr. Cherif Bassiouni from Egypt, recommended that the Security Council establish an international tribunal to try those responsible for war crimes in the conflict. Both RESOLUTIONS passed unanimously. The tribunal was located in The Hague. The tribunals at Nuremberg and Tokyo were the precedents for this court. Article 1 of its statute stated that "The International Tribunal shall have the power to prosecute persons responsible for serious violations of international humanitarian law committed in the territory of the former Yugoslavia since 1991" until the UN Security Council decided to withdraw its mandate. The crimes it specifically was empowered

to prosecute included grave breaches of the 1949 Geneva Convention, violations of the laws and customs of war, GENOCIDE, and crimes against humanity.

The ICTY, operating under the principle of *non-bis-in-idem,* which holds that one may not be tried twice for the same crime, prohibits national courts from hearing the cases of those standing trial in the WAR CRIMES TRIBUNAL. The ICTY could also prosecute persons already under accusation in a national court if the accused was charged only with an "ordinary" offense (that is, not a war crime), or if the national trial had not been impartial.

The ICTY had three organs: the chambers of judges (with both a trial chamber and an appeals chamber), the office of the prosecutor, and the registry. Each of these bodies was established under the terms of the international agreement that created the tribunal. The trial chamber had five judges, and the appeals chamber had three judges. The Security Council, upon recommendation of the SECRETARY-GENERAL, selected the judges and the lead prosecutor. The prosecutor in 2001 was the Swiss jurist Carla Del Ponte, who followed South African Richard Goldstone and Canadian Louise Armour in this role. The president of the tribunal was Judge Claude Jorda of France, and the vice-president was Judge Florence Ndepele Mwachande Mumba of Zambia. The registry was the bookkeeping office of the tribunal, and served as the repository of all motions, arguments, judgments, and organizational records of the ICTY.

The International Criminal Tribunal for the Former Yugoslavia could not try defendants in absentia, but a Rule 61 proceeding allowed the prosecutor to present evidence publicly and to call witnesses. The stated purpose was to reconfirm the indictment against the defendant and to permit the judges to issue an international arrest warrant. Rule 61 served two functions. First, it provided a documentary account of alleged acts. Second, it increased pressure on alleged war criminals, who would not be able to travel out of the country without fear of detention by a UN member.

The ICTY issued its first indictment on November 11, 1994. It was for Dragan Nikolic, a Bosnian Serb who was alleged to have been the commander of a small prison camp in eastern BOSNIA. The first conviction was Dusko Tadic, who was convicted of every count established by the statute except genocide. Other notable indictments included former Yugoslav president Slobodan Milosevic, and Bosnian Serb leaders Radovan Karadzic and General Ratko Mladic, the latter two of whom remained at large by early 2002. The ICTY relied on other institutions, most notably the North Atlantic Treaty Organization (NATO), to apprehend and extradite indicted individuals. As of March 15, 2001, the tribunal had publicly indicted 98 individuals, detained 36, and conducted 14 trials. Of those found guilty, Tihomir Blaskic (a former general in the Croatian Defense Council) received the most severe sentence. The ICTY sentenced him to 45 years' imprisonment for three counts of crimes against humanity, six counts of grave breaches of the Geneva conventions, and ten counts of violations of the laws or customs of war.

Earlier, in September 2000, Vojislav Kostunica, a Serb reformer, was elected president of Yugoslavia, ending the reign of Slobodan Milosevic. The new government arrested and handed over the former president to the ICTY in 2001. Milosevic, charged with war crimes, crimes against humanity, and genocide, denied the legal authority of the tribunal and vigorously served as his own defense counsel during his trial in spring 2002.

The ICTY could pronounce a maximum punishment of life in prison. Once sentenced, defendants served their terms in nations that volunteered prison space and were approved by the tribunal. Once a criminal passed into the prison system of one of these countries, the ICTY relinquished JURISDICTION.

The BUDGET for the tribunal began very modestly, at only $276,000 in 1993, but it had escalated to $95 million by 2001.

See also INTERNATIONAL CRIMINAL COURT, INTERNATIONAL CRIMINAL TRIBUNAL FOR RWANDA, UNITED NATIONS MISSION IN BOSNIA AND HERZEGOVINA, UNITED NATIONS PROTECTION FORCE.

Further Reading: Ackerman, John E., and Eugene O'Sullivan. *Practice and Procedure of the International Criminal Tribunal for the Former Yugoslavia.* Boston: Kluwer Law International, 2000. Ball, Howard. *Prosecuting War Crimes and Genocide: The Twentieth Century Experience.* Lawrence: University of Kansas Press, 1999. Minow, Martha. *Between Vengeance and Forgiveness: Facing History after Genocide and Mass Violence.* Boston: Beacon Press, 1998. Neier, Aryeh. *War Crimes: Brutality, Genocide, Terror, and the Struggle for Justice.* New York: Times Books, 1998. Osiel, Mark. *Mass Atrocity, Collective Memory, and the Law.* New Brunswick, N.J.: Transaction Publishers, 1997. Paust, Jordan J., et al., eds. *International Criminal Law: Cases and Materials.* Durham, N.C.: Carolina Academic Press, 1996. ICTY website: <www.un.org/icty/>.

— *D. J. Becker*

International Day Against Drug Abuse

First observed in 1988, the International Day Against Drug Abuse is held annually on June 26.

International Day for Biological Diversity

The GENERAL ASSEMBLY has proclaimed May 22 of each year as the International Day for Biological Diversity. The date marks the anniversary of the adoption of the Convention on Biological Diversity in 1992.

International Day for the Elimination of Racial Discrimination

Observed annually on March 21, this International Day was proclaimed in 1966 in remembrance of the 69 people killed by police gunfire on March 21, 1960, in Sharpeville, South Africa. They were part of a peaceful demonstration against APARTHEID.

International Day for the Elimination of Violence against Women

The GENERAL ASSEMBLY has designated November 25 as International Day for the Elimination of Violence against WOMEN. That date was chosen to remember the 1961 assassination of three Mirabal sisters, political activists in the Dominican Republic, on orders of Dominican ruler Rafael Trujillo.

International Day for the Eradication of Poverty

Observed on October 17 annually, the day replaced the World Day for Overcoming Extreme Poverty, observed in many countries. The GENERAL ASSEMBLY created the day to promote awareness of the need to eradicate poverty and destitution in all nations, particularly in developing countries.

International Day for the Preservation of the Ozone Layer

Observed on September 16 annually, the day marks the anniversary of the signing of the MONTREAL PROTOCOL ON SUBSTANCES THAT DEPLETE THE OZONE LAYER in 1987.

International Day in Support of Victims of Torture

Observed on June 26, the date in 1987 when the CONVENTION AGAINST TORTURE AND OTHER CRUEL, INHUMAN OR DEGRADING TREATMENT OR PUNISHMENT entered into force, the day raises world public attention to the continuing problem of torture.

International Day of Cooperatives

In 1994, recognizing that cooperatives were becoming an indispensable factor in the economic and social development of the Third World, the GENERAL ASSEMBLY declared the first Saturday of July every year as the International Day of Cooperatives. The date marks the anniversary of the founding of the International Cooperative Alliance, an umbrella group of organizations comprising 760 million members of cooperatives in 100 countries in 1892.

International Day of Older Persons

First celebrated in 1991, the International Day of Older Persons is held annually on October 4.

International Day of Peace

In 1981, the UN GENERAL ASSEMBLY declared that the opening day of its regular session in September each year "shall be officially dedicated and observed as the International Day of Peace and shall be devoted to commemorating and strengthening the ideals of peace both within and among all nations and peoples." The General Assembly convenes each year, usually on the first Tuesday after September 1.

International Day of Solidarity with the Palestinian People

Celebrated annually on November 29, the day marks the anniversary of RESOLUTION 181, passed by the GENERAL ASSEMBLY in 1947 calling for the partition of Palestine.

International Day of the World's Indigenous People

In 1994 the GENERAL ASSEMBLY proclaimed August 9 for the duration of the International Decade of the World's Indigenous People (1995–2004) as the day in the UN calendar to recognize INDIGENOUS PEOPLES.

International Development Association (IDA)

See WORLD BANK

International Finance Corporation (IFC)   *See* WORLD BANK.

International Fund for Agricultural Development (IFAD)

The 1974 World Food Conference initiated the International Fund for Agricultural Development as a UN SPECIALIZED AGENCY. The conference sought to respond to the food crises of the early 1970s that especially affected the Sahelian area of Africa. Believing that economic structural problems and the concentration of poor populations in remote rural areas accounted for much food deficiency, insecurity, and famine, the conference advanced a RESOLUTION stating that "an International Fund for Agricultural Development should be established immediately to finance agricultural development projects primarily for food production in the developing countries." Thus, to ease scarcity in rural settings, improve nutrition, and deal with poverty and hunger, IFAD was to target the poorest people in the world. The FUND began operation as an international financial institution in 1977.

IFAD works with other institutions, including the WORLD BANK, REGIONAL DEVELOPMENT BANKS, and regional and UN agencies. Many of these bodies co-finance projects initiated by IFAD. Low-income countries obtain loans and grants from the fund on concessional terms, repaid usually over 40 years, with an initial grace period of 10 years and a very low annual service charge. From the time it began work in 1977 through 2001, IFAD financed more than 580 projects in some 115 countries and territories. The cost of these projects was about $7 billion in grants and loans. The fund's resources come, in roughly equal share, from three major sources: member contributions, loan repayments, and investment income.

MEMBERSHIP in IFAD is open to any member of the United Nations or one of its specialized agencies. A Governing Council—made up of all 162 members (as of 2001)—is the fund's highest authority. The council holds sessions annually and may call SPECIAL SESSIONS. A governor and alternate governor represent the council when it is not in session. An executive board of 18 members and 18 alternates oversees daily operations and approves loans and grants. The Governing Council elects a president for a four-year term, renewable for one further term. In February 2001, the council elected Mr. Lennart Båge its president. Its HEADQUARTERS is in Rome.

See also ADMINISTRATIVE COMMITTEE FOR COORDINATION, FOOD AND AGRICULTURE ORGANIZATION, WORLD FOOD PROGRAMME.

Further Reading: McGovern, George. *The Third Freedom, Ending Hunger in Our Time.* New York: Simon and Schuster, 2001. IFAD website: <www.ifad.org>.

International Labour Organization (ILO)

The constitution of the International Labour Organization was incorporated in Part XIII of the 1919 Versailles Peace Treaty ending World War I. International commitment to such an organization grew out of the strong labor and social movements of the late 19th century. The first meeting of the ILO was in Washington, D.C., on October 29, 1919. It subsequently opened its permanent HEADQUARTERS—operated by its SECRETARIAT, the International Labour Office—in Geneva. On December 14, 1946, the International Labour Organization became the first SPECIALIZED AGENCY of the newly created United Nations. With an original MEMBERSHIP of 45 countries, the ILO grew to near universal NATION-STATE participation by 2002. In 1969, during its 50th anniversary year, the agency was awarded the Nobel Peace Prize.

Not only governments are represented in the organization but also employer and worker delegates participate with equal VOTING rights. Each member state has four representatives to the ILO: two government delegates, one employer and one worker delegate. Members of the delegation are not required to speak or vote with one national voice, but may and do cast differing votes on issues brought before the organization. This arrangement is unique among UN specialized agencies. Delegates meet annually in the International Labour Conference, held each June in Geneva. Approximately 3,000 people participate. The conference is the chief legislative body. Each year the conference adopts several CONVENTIONS and RESOLUTIONS focused on international labor standards and working conditions.

Between sessions of the conference, the work of the ILO is directed by the Governing Body, a committee that meets three times a year (March, June, and November) and has 56 members (28 government, 14 employer, and 14 worker representatives). Ten of the government seats are held by "members of chief industrial importance": the UNITED STATES, the United Kingdom, France, CHINA, RUSSIAN FEDERATION, Brazil, Italy, Japan, India, and Germany. The remaining 18 seats are allocated on the basis of equitable geographic distribution: Africa (6), Americas (5), Asia (4), and Europe (3). Member countries are elected for three-year terms. The Governing Body prepares the agenda for the annual conference, drafts the budget, and undertakes ILO initiatives. It also elects the DIRECTOR-GENERAL.

The third important body in the ILO is the International Labour Office. As of 2002, it had been headed by nine directors-general since 1919: Albert Thomas (France, 1919–32), Harold Butler (Great Britain, 1932–38), John G. Winant (United States, 1939–41), Edward Phelan (Ireland, 1941–48), David Morse (United States, 1948–70), C. Wilfred Jenks (Great Britain, 1970–73), Francis Blanchard (France, 1974–89), Michel Hansenne (Belgium, 1989–99), and Juan Somavia (Chile, 1999–   ). The director-general oversees a staff of approximately 2,000, working both in Geneva and in 40 field offices around the world, and administers the organization's budget, which was $467 million in 2000–01. The office directs research and training programs, prepares reports, and provides secretariat services to the many committees of the organization. Among the most important of these subordinate bodies is the Committee on Freedom of Association (CFA). Created in 1951, the nine-member CFA meets three times a year to hear complaints (more than 2,000 since its founding) about violations of freedom of association. The secretariat carries out investigations and writes reports on these complaints, as well as preparing reports on individual countries' compliance with ILO standards and conventions.

The work of the ILO is guided by three of its most important documents: the constitution found in the Versailles Treaty, its 1944 "Philadelphia DECLARATION," and the 1998 "Declaration on Fundamental Principles and Rights at Work and its Follow-up." These statements of purpose give the

organization three broad duties. First, throughout its history the ILO has drafted and promoted conventions and treaties that establish international labor standards. By 2001 it had promulgated 183 conventions, and made 191 official "recommendations" to the international community. Once a member state ratified an ILO convention, it was obligated to implement its recommendations in domestic law. These conventions covered such topics as occupational safety and health, working conditions, industrial relations, minimum wage, social security, HUMAN RIGHTS, the employment of WOMEN, children, and the disabled, and collective bargaining. Second, the ILO provides technical assistance to national governments and the private sector, particularly in the developing world. To this end it works closely with the UNITED NATIONS DEVELOPMENT PROGRAMME. It also became one of the sponsoring organizations for UN SECRETARY-GENERAL Kofi ANNAN's "GLOBAL COMPACT" program, launched in 1999 and meant to bring private companies into a working relationship with the United Nations. Under the program, participating enterprises commit themselves to uphold nine principles, four of them (freedom of association and the right to collective bargaining, promotion of the elimination of all forms of forced and compulsory labor, effective abolition of child labor, and the elimination of discrimination in respect to employment and occupation) coming directly from the ILO's 1998 Declaration. Third, the ILO sponsors research, training, education, and publication of labor related materials. In 1960, the organization created the International Institute for Labour Studies in Geneva to conduct much of the research function. In 1965 it set up the International Training Centre in Turin, Italy, in order to train senior and mid-level managers in both private and public enterprises. During its first 35 years of operation, the Centre trained more than 70,000 individuals.

The work of the ILO has not been without controversy. Given the differences in labor laws and ideologies among nations, ILO standards have often offended particular member states. During the COLD WAR, when the world community had both capitalist and socialist systems vying for international dominance, the International Labour Organization was often accused of being "politicized." From 1977 to 1980 the United States refused to participate in the ILO for this reason and withdrew its funding, accounting for nearly one-fourth of the organization's budget. Successive American governments insisted on major reforms in the ILO, along with several other specialized agencies, before it would pay past and continuing assessments. Most of these had been met by the end of the century under Secretary-General Annan's REFORM program, and U.S. arrearages were scheduled to be paid in 2001.

See also ADMINISTRATIVE COMMITTEE ON COORDINATION, ADMINISTRATIVE TRIBUNALS, APARTHEID, EXPANDED PROGRAM OF TECHNICAL ASSISTANCE, INTERNATIONAL COVENANT ON CIVIL AND POLITICAL RIGHTS.

Further Reading: Imber, Mark. *The USA, ILO, UNESCO, and IAEA: Politicization and Withdrawal in the Specialized Agencies.* London: Macmillan, 1989. Lubin, Carol Riegelman, and Anne Winslow. *Social Justice for Women: The International Labor Organization and Women.* Durham, N.C.: Duke University Press, 1990. ILO website: <www.ilo.org>.

international law

The body of rules and norms regulating activities between and among NATION-STATES—often called "the law of nations"—was entitled "International Law" by the English philosopher Jeremy Bentham (1748–1832). Bentham's became the preferred term by the middle of the 20th century, although it was often expanded to "public international law" to contrast it with "private international law," or the "conflict of laws," regulating private matters affected by more than one legal JURISDICTION. By the beginning of the 21st century, due in part to quickening developments in the international community, and particularly due to activities within the UNITED NATIONS SYSTEM, international law's province experienced an expansion, in some instances including areas of jurisdiction once thought to be outside its realm. For example, recent years have witnessed a development in the field of international economic law that constitutes a mix of public and private international law. The expansion can be seen also in the establishment of WAR CRIMES TRIBUNALS to take to court individuals accused of violating HUMAN RIGHTS, even within their own country. Nonetheless, the apparent applicability of international law has not resulted in any comparable super-national means of enforcement. Whereas law within nations is enforced via the police function of the state, there is no such mechanism in an international community that continues to be composed of sovereign nations.

According to Article 38 of the STATUTE OF THE INTERNATIONAL COURT OF JUSTICE, the sources of international law are international CONVENTIONS, international custom, general principles of law recognized by civilized nations, judicial decisions, and teachings of the most qualified publicists on the topic. Of these, ratified international conventions and treaties tend to carry the most weight. Some legal experts also consider ARBITRATION awards and decisions by the ICJ as precedents for developing law in the international arena. International law is usually considered part of national or municipal law. (For example, Article 6, paragraph two of the U.S. Constitution declares "all treaties made, or which shall be made, under the authority of the UNITED STATES, shall be the supreme law of the land; and the Judges in every State shall be bound thereby, anything in the Constitution or laws of any State to the contrary notwithstanding.")

The development of formal relations between and among nations, empires, and peoples has characterized human activity since the millennia before the common era. The diffusion and ultimate availability of texts and treaties dealing with such relations suggests a pattern in world history of cross-cultural intercourse among political elites the world over that led to what might be called international affairs or even "international law." Basic principles and precedents emerged as different communities sought to impose order on their mutual relations, and to resolve disagreements without the resort to force, except as those principles might allow or require it.

Although law-like relations existed among political units in antiquity and throughout the world, the modern concept of international law emerged at the end of the Middle Ages in European history. It referred to a body of rules considered binding in relations among princely states. Typically, international law regulated diplomatic practices (that is, protection of diplomatic personnel, rules of seniority among ambassadors to a specific country, and related diplomatic matters), maritime intercourse, restrictions on WEAPONS, and the commencement and conduct of war. In 1625, the Dutch jurist Hugo Grotius (1583–1645) published his *De jure belli ac pacis* (Concerning the law of war and peace), the first comprehensive text of international rules. His views were frequently studied and on occasion applied in subsequent international interactions.

It is of note that Grotius, and many early publicists on international law who followed him—including Dutchman Cornelius van Bynkershoek (1673–1743), German philosopher Christian von Wolff (1679–1754), Swiss jurist Emerich de Vattel (1714–67), and German Georg Friedrich von Martens (1756–1821)—highlighted the SOVEREIGNTY and legal equality of states, principles later ensconced in the UN CHARTER (Article 2, paragraph 1). The concept of the sovereign state was enshrined in the 1648 Treaty of Westphalia, which prohibited interference by outside powers in a state's internal affairs. In the Westphalian system states took on obligations in the international community only by their voluntary commitments made largely through treaties. By the late 18th century, the mounting use of treaty agreements had furthered the course of international law considerably. Even the newly independent United States, emphasizing the value of treaty arrangements, contributed to its elaboration in the areas of international trade, freedom of the seas, and the meaning of neutrality.

Grotius developed many of his concepts of modern international law from an empirical study of what nations actually did in his time. For example, his rules on the LAW OF THE SEA were drawn from contemporaneous Dutch practice that emphasized oceanic free trade. But the Dutch scholar also premised his work on the assertion that international law was a reflection of the natural law, divorced from earlier theological conceptions of higher law, but nonetheless a reflection of the law of nature based on reason. Accordingly, Grotius's 1625 work invigorated an already existing "naturalist" school of international law. Found in the works of Francisco Vitoria (1480–1546), Father Suarez (1548–1617), and

Samuel Pufendorf (1632–94), naturalists argued that international law should codify not simply what states do, but rather what states *should* do to conform to the principles of justice. Pufendorf in particular denied the value of treaties and urged a conception of international law that recognized absolute values. The natural law tradition espoused by these scholars remained a secondary thread of Grotius's teachings until the 1940s, when the horror of the Nazi era produced a new interest in using international law to defend HUMAN RIGHTS, protect values even if states had not officially agreed to them in treaties, and punish states for "crimes against humanity." In this spirit, the Preamble of the UN Charter "reaffirm(ed) faith in fundamental human rights, in the dignity and worth of the human person, [and] in the equal rights of men and WOMEN."

The period of the Napoleonic Wars in the early 19th century witnessed a disregard for the law of nations, until the Congress of Vienna (1814–15), which concluded those wars, attempted a reassertion of European order through the restoration of older rules of diplomacy, and introduced newer and more standardized legal principles, such as respect for the freedom of navigation on international waterways and the more precise classification for and protection of diplomatic personnel. What had been "customary" international law—accepted practice—was clarified in legally binding international agreements. This marked the beginning of the long era of "legal positivism." The DECLARATION of Paris (1856) following the Crimean War represented the first major attempt to codify the rules of maritime warfare. It made privateering illegal, determined that a neutral flag protected all goods on board a ship—except contraband of a belligerent during times of war—and made neutral goods free from capture even when under an enemy's flag. A blockade was considered binding only if it was functional; that is, a belligerent could no longer appeal to a "paper" blockade. The Declaration of Paris was the accepted rule of law on the high seas until it became unfeasible with the introduction of submarines in World War I. As the century proceeded, multilateral agreements were negotiated establishing international rules for weights and measures, trademarks, copyrights, patents, and other matters for which legal uniformity was desirable. New technologies resulted in international conferences that established the International Telegraph Union (at Paris in 1865) and the Universal Postal Union (at Berne, Switzerland, in 1874). In the post–World War II period these became the UN SPECIALIZED AGENCIES of the INTERNATIONAL TELECOMMUNICATIONS UNION and the UNIVERSAL POSTAL UNION, respectively.

Meantime, arbitration as a means of settling disputes became fashionable. With the Jay Treaty of 1794, the United States and Great Britain initiated the practice of setting up mixed commissions to settle disagreements unyielding to normal diplomacy. The post–American Civil War *Alabama Claims* arbitration in 1872 between the United Kingdom and the United States marked a decisive phase in the arbitration movement that culminated with the establishment of the PERMANENT COURT OF ARBITRATION at the Hague Conference of 1899. A second Hague Conference in 1907 expanded rules governing arbitral procedures. The two Hague Conferences also issued a number of declarations and conventions dealing with the laws of war, including banning aerial bombardment, submarine mines, and poison gas. Meantime, Pan American Congresses in the Western Hemisphere established several continent-wide diplomatic practices.

But the onset of World War I brought this progress to a halt. Many provisions of international law were violated and new problems arose—for example, submarine warfare and the use of CHEMICAL WEAPONS—for which existing standards of international behavior were inadequate. The creation of the LEAGUE OF NATIONS and the PERMANENT COURT OF INTERNATIONAL JUSTICE following the war were attempts to create multinational institutions to deal with the extraordinary problems that had arisen during the conflict. The League represented the first attempt in history to maintain a permanent organization committed to a sustained effort to develop and codify international law. That is, unlike functional organizations of the 19th century dealing with a single purpose, and unlike time-bound congresses or conferences, the League was a multipurpose, permanent organization, with a SECRETARIAT, and a mandate to deal with all international law matters. League conferences brought forth more than 120 international understandings covering a range of subjects. Although many failed of full ratification, they became a model for the future United Nations, and some—such as those dealing with control of narcotics, traffic in persons, economic statistics, and slavery—remained in force with UN AMENDMENTS or further treaty action. Moreover, the UN SECRETARY-GENERAL's office became responsible for the depository of extant League documents.

Also in the interwar period other multilateral activities extended the reach of international law. The Washington Naval Conference of 1921–22 disarmed the world's most powerful navies (the last actual "DISARMAMENT" agreement until the 1987 Intermediate Nuclear Forces Agreement signed by the Soviet Union and the United States, although in the interim there were "arms limitations" and "arms control" initiatives), abolished the Anglo-Japanese alliance, provided for mutual respect for Pacific territories, and endorsed the Open Door Policy in CHINA to preserve China's territorial integrity and assure equal trade in the country. The Kellogg-Briand PACT (Paris Pact) of 1928, ultimately signed by 62 nations, outlawed war as national policy. These multilateral agreements had no enforcement mechanisms. They depended on compliance or moral suasion. The rise of fascism and nazism in Europe and of militarism in Japan and then the collapse of international order in the 1930s wrought discredit to the agreements of the 1920s and damaged the reputation of the League of Nations. The advent of World War II tainted international law with the darkest of hues.

Yet, phoenix-like, out of the war came the United Nations, the new INTERNATIONAL COURT OF JUSTICE (ICJ), a congeries of international economic institutions, and a renewed dedication to reclaim and build upon the efforts of former years. Indeed, during the post–World War II period, the concepts and procedures constituting international law were to undergo considerable maturation and affect the entire globe. From those early concerns with state practices during wartime through the development of a balance of power conception of international relations, international law was, by the 21st century, a remarkably transformed system, featuring a permanent multilateral framework for the resolution of disputes; preservation of the peace; the rules of war; the establishment of war crimes tribunals; financial, economic, environmental, and technological cooperation; and even the promulgation of individual and human rights. While this momentum clearly did not and could not promise a world utopia, the long-term crafting of such an international framework represented one of the extraordinary achievements of human endeavor. And, from 1945, the United Nations stood at the heart of these developments.

Since the end of World War II there have been differing opinions about exactly what international law is and how it is to be executed. One straightforward view is that all nations should obey international law, just as individuals should obey domestic (or "municipal") law. Yet some lofty thinkers—Samuel Pufendorf and Thomas Hobbes in the 17th century, John Austin in the 19th, and Henry Kissinger in the 20th—have challenged the very notion of an international "law," because there is no legitimate enforcer. Sociological responses have emphasized the behavior of states rather than overarching principle. Thus, since states seek first their own preservation, then their increased power, and only afterward world order, international law, according to some sociologists, cannot shape international politics but merely adjust to it. Marxists have regarded international law as but an instrument of class oppression; Chinese scholars, whether or not followers of Mao Zedong, have described international law as a set of platitudes that historically have been ruinous to non-Western cultures such as China's; many citizens of Third World nations have felt themselves victimized by Eurocentered notions of international law (as Saddam HUSSEIN said he was in 1990 while trying to correct a British-dictated boundary line between Iraq and Kuwait); feminists have argued that "the rules of international law privilege men," that women are "marginalized," and that international law is "a thoroughly gendered system"; and "post modernism," emphasizing relativism, difference, and the problematic nature of language itself, has questioned any "universalist" assumption of a fundamental international law deriving from a narrow, elitist political tradition in the Western First World. And, of course, a common commitment to a single conception of legal principles is less likely when one nation's core interests diverge from the interests of other nations.

Yet in practice international law is widely recognized and most nations have participated in its evolution. The penalties for failing to comply, although less severe than in national cases, and often unenforceable, are economic SANCTIONS, the constraint of public opinion, intervention by third states, international condemnation—as by way of UN RESOLUTIONS—and, as a last resort, war.

The wider reach of international law by the late 20th century was due in no small part to the activities of UN-related organizations. The International Court of Justice, which replaced the Permanent Court of International Justice after World War II and is popularly known as the World Court, has made modest but significant contributions to the development of international law, through countless judgments and advisory opinions that, although usually narrow, have affected maritime law, questions of diplomatic immunity, the legitimacy of mandates under the League of Nations, the COMPETENCE of the United Nations, the jurisdiction of its PRINCIPAL ORGANS, and other matters. Article 102 of the UN Charter requires member states to register all treaties with the Secretariat, which must then publish them. This represents a continuation of the practice of the League of Nations. It means that there is a central depository for all international agreements and that there should be no "secret" arrangements unobserved by the international community. By Article 13, paragraph 1 of the Charter, the GENERAL ASSEMBLY (GA) acquired the obligation to initiate studies and make recommendations for "encouraging the progressive development of international law and its codification." In 1947 the Assembly entrusted this Charter function to the INTERNATIONAL LAW COMMISSION, an auxiliary but autonomous organ of the Assembly, which began the slow but steady process of codification. The General Assembly SIXTH COMMITTEE works closely with the International Law Commission; it reviews the work of the UN COMMISSION ON INTERNATIONAL TRADE LAW (UNCITRAL), negotiates relevant treaties and agreements to submit to the General Assembly Plenary (the Sixth Committee spent 30 years in intricate negotiations to determine an internationally acceptable definition of AGGRESSION), and deals with reports from all UN bodies regarding legal matters. UNCITRAL, created by the General Assembly in 1966, develops conventions, rules, and legal guides to harmonize international trade law. The UN OFFICE OF LEGAL AFFAIRS (OLA), initiated in 1946, serves the Secretariat and provides legal advice to the Secretary-General. The WORLD INTELLECTUAL PROPERTY ORGANIZATION (WIPO), established in 1970, promotes the protection of intellectual property worldwide, and the INTERNATIONAL MARITIME ORGANIZATION (IMO), begun in 1959, is the only UN agency solely involved with issues of shipping safety and securing environmentally sound oceans.

The UN's efforts to internationalize outer space and bring it into the realm of recognized international law resulted in the 1966 Treaty on Principles Governing the Activities of States in the Exploration and Use of Outer Space, including the Moon and Other Celestial Bodies (Outer Space Treaty) and the 1979 Agreement Governing Activities of States on the Moon and Other Celestial Bodies (the MOON AGREEMENT). The COMMITTEE ON THE PEACEFUL USES OF OUTER SPACE, set up by the General Assembly in 1959 to review and encourage international cooperation, has adopted several additional treaties and conventions to regulate outer space, and in 1974 the committee set up the Office for Outer Space Affairs, which maintains a registry of space objects.

Other important areas of developing international law less directly connected with the United Nations derived from various arms agreements (beginning with the Limited Test Ban Treaty of 1963), from the internationalization of Antarctica (1959), and from a number of agreements regarding international economic and financial relations. The GENERAL AGREEMENT ON TARIFFS AND TRADE (GATT), a negotiating regime initiated in 1948 to encourage lowering trade barriers around the world, became the WORLD TRADE ORGANIZATION (WTO) in 1995. GATT/WTO, along with related organizations (the INTERNATIONAL MONETARY FUND and the WORLD BANK) founded at the BRETTON WOODS Conference (the UN Monetary and Financial Conference) in 1944, sought to bring harmonization and common rules to world trade and finance. The Bretton Woods institutions and the WTO became controversial in the late 1990s as some environmentalists, labor activists, and socialists came to view these institutions as promoting only the interests of wealthy capitalist nations to the disadvantage of developing countries, laboring people, and the ecosystem. Defenders insisted that these institutions, by bringing the rule of law to the world economy, providing banking resources for troubled economies, establishing transparent rules of trade among ever more nations, and lowering barriers to trade, travel, and investment, offered the best antidote to persistent poverty and the most sensible stimulus to economic growth worldwide.

One of the most comprehensive agreements affecting the development of international law was the UN CONVENTION ON THE LAW OF THE SEA. The convention, affording a uniform rule in the uses of the sea, established a framework to deal with questions of sovereignty, jurisdiction, use, and national rights and obligations in ocean areas. The convention was opened for signature in 1982 and entered into force in 1994. In like manner, the United Nations has been involved in the growth of international environmental law. Usually the UNITED NATIONS ENVIRONMENT PROGRAMME administers the many treaties brokered by the United Nations, including agreements on DESERTIFICATION, biological diversity, movement of hazardous wastes, protection of the ozone layer, and controlling acid rain. The KYOTO PROTOCOL, negotiated at a UN conference in 1997, would, if ratified by a sufficient number of states, set standards for states to curtail greenhouse emissions in order to combat global warming. In 2001 the PROTOCOL was renegotiated, but as of the end of that year it had not gone into force.

Undoubtedly, the most celebrated contribution by the United Nations to the creation of new international law is in the broad area of human rights. The contemporary effort to develop international law as an expression of a higher law that governs all human activity found its first modern expression in the international war crimes trials at Nuremberg and for Japanese enemies in Tokyo. Whereas a precedent of sorts had been established in the Versailles Treaty after World War I (providing for international tribunals for offending Germans, but left to German courts, where prosecution dissipated), nothing like them had happened before and nothing like them took place again until the late 20th century. Captured German and Japanese leaders were not charged with violating any particular treaty commitment, or even with violating their own domestic laws. They were tried, convicted, and punished for crimes against humanity. Following the trials, there developed over time an abundance of international agreements and rules that seemed to proscribe those atrocities classified as human rights violations.

In 1946 the General Assembly affirmed "the principles of international law recognized by the Charter of the Nuremberg Tribunal and the judgment of the Tribunal." At the same time the Assembly declared that "GENOCIDE is a crime under international law," and in 1948 the GA approved the Genocide Convention (CONVENTION ON THE PREVENTION AND PUNISHMENT OF THE CRIME OF GENOCIDE). In 1946 the ECONOMIC AND SOCIAL COUNCIL (ECOSOC) established the UN COMMISSION ON HUMAN RIGHTS, which was chaired by Eleanor ROOSEVELT and given a mandate to compose a UNIVERSAL DECLARATION OF HUMAN RIGHTS. Working with a group of celebrated international legal minds from a variety of cultures, Mrs. Roosevelt discovered that conceptualizing rights and fleshing out international law were multicultural, even multicivilizational endeavors. Peng-chung Chang, a Chinese philosopher, brought an Asian and Confucianist perspective to discussions; Charles Malik a view from the Arab Middle East; Hernán Santa Cruz was from Chile and from the Latin American political left; and Hansa Mehta brought an Indian outlook and an insistence that women's equality be clearly articulated. René Cassin, a French Jew, possessed a unique outlook, colored by the most recent, and appalling, example of human rights violations, When, in late 1948, the General Assembly passed the Universal Declaration without a dissenting vote, no longer could it be asserted without challenge that the notion of rights and the practice of international law were strictly Western conceits. René Cassin noted the most significant, if subtle, breakthrough in his 1968 acceptance speech upon receiving the Nobel Peace Prize: After the Universal Declaration, nations still retained jurisdiction over their citizens, he said, but it would "no longer be exclusive." From the 17th century to 1948, absolute state sovereignty had been the underpinning of international law. With the ascension of the primacy of rights, international law had entered a new, uncertain, phase. Combined with the declaration, the INTERNATIONAL COVENANT ON ECONOMIC, SOCIAL AND CULTURAL RIGHTS, and the INTERNATIONAL COVENANT ON CIVIL AND POLITICAL RIGHTS, both opened for signature in 1966 and both brought into force in 1976, made up the "International Bill of Human Rights." Other conventions and declarations announcing an assortment of human rights continued to pass in UN organs. By the summer of 1993, more than 170 nations, meeting in Vienna, adopted a sweeping declaration affirming the principle that "all human rights are universal," and that "it is the duty of states, regardless of their political, economic and cultural systems, to promote and protect all human rights and fundamental freedoms." Add to this the establishment of war crimes tribunals (The INTERNATIONAL TRIBUNAL FOR RWANDA and the INTERNATIONAL CRIMINAL TRIBUNAL FOR THE FORMER YUGOSLAVIA) that at the turn of the century were prosecuting individuals for crimes against humanity *in their own countries,* and the adoption in Rome in 1998 of a statute calling for an INTERNATIONAL CRIMINAL COURT to try individuals for genocide, crimes against humanity, war crimes, and aggression, and the implication Cassin discerned comes into fuller relief. As the third millennium began, international law was on a trajectory far beyond anything imaginable but a century earlier.

See also ACCESSION, CHAPTER VI, CHAPTER VII, HAGUE ACADEMY OF INTERNATIONAL LAW, INQUIRY, IRAN HOSTAGE CRISIS, *JUS COGENS,* MILLENNIUM SUMMIT, NATION-STATE, PEACEKEEPING, SECURITY COUNCIL, STIMSON DOCTRINE, STRUCTURE OF THE UNITED NATIONS, UNITED NATIONS CONFERENCE ON THE HUMAN ENVIRONMENT.

Further Reading: Beck, Robert J., et al., eds. *International Rules: Approaches from International Law and International Relations.* New York: Oxford University Press, 1996. Bentham, Jeremy, "Principles of International Law" (original, 1786–1789). In Bowring, John, ed. *The Works of Jeremy Bentham.* Vol. 2. New York: Russell and Russell, 1962. Glendon, Mary Ann. *A World Made New: Eleanor Roosevelt and the Universal Declaration of Human Rights.* New York: Random House, 2001. Gross, Leo. "The Development of International Law through the United Nations." In *The United Nations; Past, Present, and Future.* Ed. by John Barros. New York: Free Press, 1972. Hannikainen, Lauri. *Peremptory Norms (Jus Cogens) in International Law: Historical Development, Criteria, Present Status.* Helsinki: Finnish Lawyers' Publishing Company, 1988. Singh, Nagendra. "The UN and the Development of International Law." In Roberts, Adam, and Benedict Kingsbury, eds. *United Nations, Divided World.* New York: Oxford University Press, 1993. Research on international law website: <www.lib.uchicago.edu/~llou/forintlaw>. UN International Law website: <www.un.org/law>.

International Law Commission (ILC)

Article 13, paragraph 1 of the UN CHARTER directs the GENERAL ASSEMBLY (GA) to "initiate studies and make recommendations" to promote "the progressive development of INTERNATIONAL LAW and its codification." In response, GA RESOLUTION 174, in 1947, created an International Law Commission. The new permanent commission, charged with fulfilling the mandate of Article 13, began meeting on June 17, 1948. Since then, it has sought to make international law clear and acknowledged and to encourage its evolution. The commission's task is to forward the principles of the UN Charter. It engages chiefly in drafting articles on aspects of international law that may at some future point be acceptable in international CONVENTIONS or treaties.

The commission's membership, initially 15, was increased three times and as of 2001 consisted of 34 individuals of "recognized COMPETENCE" in international law, elected by the General Assembly to reflect "the principal forms of civilization and the principal legal systems of the world." Members serve for five-year terms (all of which terminated in 2001), no two of which may be nationals of the same NATION-STATE, and they may be reelected. The General Assembly receives nominees in the same manner as it does nominees to the INTERNATIONAL COURT OF JUSTICE, that is, from lists provided by UN member states. And as in the case of the ICJ, members of the commission serve as individuals, not as representatives of a specific government. Notwithstanding the requirement of impartiality, in 1981 the GA mandated the following geographical pattern of representation: nine members from African states, eight from Asia, three from Eastern Europe, six from LATIN AMERICA and the Caribbean, and eight from Western Europe and Other States. The commission is instructed by a statute that was drafted by the GA SIXTH COMMITTEE and adopted by the General Assembly on November 21, 1947. It usually meets in UN HEADQUARTERS in Geneva (Palais des Nations). The topics handled by the commission are often forwarded to it by the General Assembly or the Sixth Committee, or, on occasion, by other UN bodies. Since its founding, the commission has been one of the UN bodies to make use of SPECIAL RAPPORTEURS in aiding its research. When the commission completes draft articles on a particular topic, the General Assembly may convene an international conference of plenipotentiaries to consider incorporating the articles into a convention, and then open the convention to signature.

The idea of codifying and developing international law derives from long historic desires. For example, the British 18th-century philosopher Jeremy Bentham, who is credited with having coined the phrase "international law," proposed a full codification of all international laws. In 1924, the assembly of the LEAGUE OF NATIONS, with a view to fostering codification, created a committee of experts to compile a list of laws and obtain comments by various world governments on its work. In the spring of 1930, at The Hague, 47 governments participated in a "Codification Conference," which, however, ended with little in the way of accomplishment. Within a decade world war had broken out, and the labors of law codifiers seemed gravely weakened. But the UN's founders, with Article 13 of the Charter, determined to undertake another effort. The International Law Commission became a permanent manifestation of that endeavor.

By 2001 the commission had completed drafts on 19 topics and was considering five more. Its work was reflected in a number of agreements. For example, a UN conference in 1958 adopted the four conventions on the LAW OF THE SEA. In New York, the General Assembly adopted the Convention on the Prevention and Punishment of Crimes against Internationally Protected Persons, including Diplomatic Agents (1973) and the Convention on the Non-navigational Uses of International Watercourses (1997). Vienna has been the site of numerous meetings to consider and consolidate the commission's labors, including the Conventions on Diplomatic Relations (1961), on Consular Relations (1963), on the Law of Treaties (1969), on the Succession of States in Respect of State Property, Archives and Debts (1983), and on the Law of Treaties between States and International Organizations or between International Organizations (1986). In 1992 the General Assembly instructed the commission to provide a draft statute for an INTERNATIONAL CRIMINAL COURT (ICC), which led to the 1998 Rome conference that adopted the statute for the new court.

See also ARBITRATION, *JUS COGENS*, SIXTH COMMITTEE.

Further Reading: Morton, Jeffrey S. *The International Law Commission of the United Nations.* Columbia: University of South Carolina Press, 2000. *United Nations Handbook.* Wellington, N.Z.: Ministry of External Affairs, published annually. International Law Commission website: <www.un.org/law/ilc>.

International Maritime Organization (IMO)

The increase in international trade coupled with the growing number and size of the world's merchant fleets after World War II significantly heightened concerns about maritime safety. To address these concerns, a UN conference meeting in Geneva in 1948 established the Convention on the Inter-Governmental Maritime Consultative Organization (the name changed to International Maritime Organization in 1982). The CONVENTION entered into force in 1958 and the first meetings were held in 1959. Originally charged with updating existing maritime treaties and creating new ones to improve maritime safety and the efficiency of navigation, the IMO has since dealt with the prevention and control of marine pollution at sea, maritime traffic control, maritime education, technical issues, liability and compensation issues relating to marine pollution and accidents, and the prevention of crime on the high seas. The IMO is a SPECIALIZED AGENCY of the United Nations, and, as such, reports on its activities to the ECONOMIC AND SOCIAL COUNCIL.

The 158 member states constitute the Assembly, which meets every two years. The 32-member Council is the IMO's governing body and oversees the operations of the organization. There are five main committees (Maritime Safety, Environmental Protection, Legal, Technical Co-operation, and Facilitation) which deal with the organization's major areas of responsibility. Headquartered in London, the IMO has a permanent staff of 300. Since its inception, the IMO has produced 10 major conventions dealing with maritime safety, four with marine pollution, six with liability and compensation, two with maritime crime prevention, and three that address technical maritime issues. Many of these conventions have been ratified by more than 95 percent of the member states. Today most of the world's merchant vessels involved in international trade adhere to IMO building, maintenance, and operating regulations. As a result, the number and frequency of maritime accidents have been reduced considerably.

The IMO was the first UN agency to implement a Technical Co-operation Committee to assist member states in implementing the organization's conventions. This committee also has aided LESS DEVELOPED COUNTRIES with the development of their merchant fleets in accordance with IMO conventions. To facilitate further the implementation and maintenance of its regulatory and legislative work, the IMO has established the world's premier network of maritime educational institutions, including the International Maritime University in Malmö, Sweden, the International Maritime Academy in Trieste, Italy, and the International Maritime Law Institute in Valletta, Malta.

Further Reading: International Maritime Organization. *IMO: The First 50 Years.* London: International Maritime Organization, 1999. ———. *Convention on the IMO,* IMO 013E, London: International Maritime Organization Publishing Service, 1984. Simmonds, K. R. *The International Maritime Organization.* London: Simmonds and Hill Publishers, 1994.

— *M. S. Lindberg*

International Monetary Fund (IMF)

Created at the BRETTON WOODS Conference in New Hampshire in 1944, the International Monetary Fund is a UN SPECIALIZED AGENCY designed to promote international monetary cooperation; facilitate economic expansion, world trade, high employment, and income growth; promote stability and eliminate restrictions in international money exchange; and assist its members with temporary financial resources to solve balance of payments problems and other financial difficulties. It came into existence on December 27, 1945, when 29 nations signed the Articles of Agreement that had been proposed at Bretton Woods. The IMF often finds itself in close collaboration with the WORLD BANK, a group of four institutions made up of the International Bank for Reconstruction and Development (IBRD, initiated as well at the Bretton Woods Conference), the International Finance Corporation (IFC, founded in 1956), the International Development Association (IDA, founded in 1960), and the Multilateral Investment Guarantee Agency (MIGA, founded in 1988). These entities, all headquartered in Washington, D.C., along with the GENERAL AGREEMENT ON TARIFFS AND TRADE, which became the WORLD TRADE ORGANIZATION in 1995, serve as the primary international monetary and financial institutions in the global financial framework initiated after World War II.

At the conclusion of that war, economists, financiers, diplomats, and political leaders were determined to avoid the economic and financial pitfalls they believed had helped cause the collapse of international order leading to global conflict. They agreed to establish institutions to encourage freer trade in goods, money, and people, international rules to effect such liberalization, transparency in economic and financial arrangements, and the ability to locate and rectify sudden economic troubles in discrete areas of the world, so as to avoid their spreading infection. For the most part, these aims were astonishingly successful as the world economy grew substantially through the end of the 20th century. However, during the 1990s the work of the IMF, the World Bank, and the WTO became increasingly controversial because they were seen as promoters of a process called "GLOBALIZATION" that, critics believed, only benefited corporations in the wealthiest capitalist nations at the expense of Third World countries, laboring people, distinctive native cultures, and the ENVIRONMENT. Moreover, critics contended that IMF, World Bank, and WTO decisions were not those of democratically chosen governments, but rather of high-powered bankers and financiers, removed from the concerns and wishes of most people. The IMF was a particularly clear target because of its mode of operation and because of its role in setting financial terms for debt-ridden nations and imposing on them stringent conditions in order to receive help. Deep crises in Mexico (1995), throughout Asia (1997–98), and in Argentina (2001) led to IMF involvement, and to strong disagreement with its policies by national governments, NON-GOVERNMENTAL ORGANIZATIONS, other international institutions, and citizens' groups.

The IMF has tried to combine several roles that in their complexity, and possible incompatibility, make the institution controversial. It has taken on the role of an international bank, an insurance company, a regulator, and a charity. To begin, one may think of the IMF exactly as it is entitled: that is, it is a *fund*. The member countries of the IMF (183 as of 2001) grant an assessed quota to the IMF much as individu-

als deposit money into a bank or a credit union. The amount of the quota is based on each member's relative size in the world economy. The quotas so subscribed determine VOTING power in the IMF. So, richer nations wield more voting power when the IMF makes decisions. Members pay 25 percent of their quota subscription in acceptable international reserve assets (U.S. dollars, euros, Japanese yen, British pound sterling, or so-called Special Drawing Rights; see below for a definition). The remaining 75 percent is in the country's own currency. As with a bank or credit union, members may draw from the general resources of the fund derived from these quota subscriptions. Members with "structural maladjustments" (an inability to meet payments, an accelerating public debt, a dangerously fluctuating currency, a balance of trade problem, and so on) may enter into extended arrangements with the IMF for longer periods. The IMF can supplement its resources by borrowing from member countries that have strong economies. This may happen when the fund is in need of added capital to deal with an immediate and costly problem that endangers international financial stability. Finally, there is the "Structural Adjustment Facility" of the "Special Disbursement Account," under which funds may be made available on "concessional" terms to low-income, developing countries, at lower interest rates. Usually, these developing countries are engaged in fundamental structural REFORM of their economies. During the late 20th century, such structural readjustment normally meant moving from a more or less command style, socialist economy in which the government played the major role and outside trade was restricted by protectionist policies to a free market economy emphasizing private enterprise, freer trade, and an internationally convertible currency. Such "structural readjustments" typically were the conditions the IMF imposed on the borrowing countries, whose citizens, accustomed to government sustenance, sometimes suffered transitory discomfort or even prolonged hardship.

The IMF is governed by its member states. At the top is the Board of Governors, composed of one representative from each member, and an equal number of alternate governors. Governors are almost always the minister of finance or the head of the central bank of their country. Thus they represent their government. They gather only at annual meetings. Otherwise the governors stay in touch with the IMF executive board stationed at the headquarters in Washington. Twenty-four executive directors meet at least three times a week in formal session and carry out the policies of the Board of Governors. In 2001, eight executive directors represented individual countries: CHINA, France, Germany, Japan, Russia, Saudi Arabia, the United Kingdom, and the UNITED STATES. The 16 remaining directors represented groupings of the other member states. The executive board often makes decisions on the basis of consensus rather than majority vote. There is a staff of about 2,500 and a managing director (Horst Köhler, a German, in 2002), who is also chair of the executive board.

So-called Special Drawing Rights (SDR) are a novel creation of the IMF. The term implies that they can be "drawn" by a member state, much as one would "draw" a loan from a bank in which one had deposits. SDRs are a form of reserve asset invented by the IMF's Board of Directors in 1967. By 1969 enough members had ratified the new system to bring it into practice. SDRs are now the principal reserve of the IMF. In the practice of international finance, SDRs have replaced more traditional reserves such as gold. The value of the IMF's SDRs is measured against a "basket" of a few strong currencies (the dollar, yen, pound sterling, and euro), and it is based on current market exchange rates. Countries are accorded SDR allotments in the IMF, and consider them as assets within the fund. Although technically a paper reserve, SDRs have many of the characteristics of money. For example, SDRs are interest-bearing assets, and interest can be charged on IMF loans made in SDRs. In effect, SDRs represent a movement away from using the dollar as the world's reserve currency, implicit in the Bretton Woods system.

The IMF engages in several activities. It conducts "surveillance," which means that it constantly monitors, appraises, and reports its members' exchange rates to assure that they remain stable. It offers financial assistance, including credits and loans to members with financial needs. As of June 30, 2001, the fund had credit and loans outstanding to 90 countries for about $65 billion. (In August 2001, the IMF arranged a complex $8 billion loan to troubled Argentina.) And it provides technical assistance to its members to help with fiscal and monetary policy and structural reforms.

The IMF does not lend for specific purposes or projects as do REGIONAL DEVELOPMENT BANKS. Reserve assets that a member may borrow are normally deposited in the borrowing country's central bank and are available to the country as would be any other international reserves. When lending, the IMF provides reserve assets (in accepted foreign currencies and Special Drawing Rights) taken from other members of the fund. A borrower uses its own currency to "purchase" these assets from the fund that are obtained from quota subscriptions. To repay, the borrower "repurchases" its own currency with international reserve assets. So, from an accounting perspective, there is no variation in the fund's total resources. But financial aid is usually linked to specific, and sometimes onerous, conditions that the borrowing country must meet. This was the case with Mexico and afflicted Asian countries in the mid-1990s, and with Argentina in 2001. In each of these instances, because the richer nations of the world—most importantly the United States—held the controlling voting power in the IMF, and feared instability in world financial markets, the fund voted to provide "bailout" loans, determined to avert a serious world financial crisis.

See also DEVELOPMENT DECADES, MULTILATERALISM, SIERRA LEONE, UNITED NATIONS COMMISSION ON INTERNA-TIONAL TRADE LAW, UNITED NATIONS CONFERENCE ON TRADE AND DEVELOPMENT, UNITED NATIONS DEVELOPMENT PROGRAMME.

Further Reading: Matejka, Harriet, and Mihály Sima. *Aspects of Transition.* Helsinki: United Nations University, 1999. Micklethwait, John, and Adrian Wooldridge. *Future Perfect: The Challenge and Hidden Promise of Globalization.* New York: Crown Publishers, 2000. New Zealand Ministry of Foreign Affairs. *United Nations Handbook.* Wellington, N.Z.: Ministry of Foreign Affairs and Trade, published annually. O'Brien, Robert, et al. *Contesting Global Governance: Multilateral Institutions and Global Movements.* New York: Cambridge University Press, 2000. "Winners and Losers." *The Economist.* April 26, 2001. IMF website: <www.imf.org>.

International Research and Training Institute for the Advancement of Women (INSTRAW)

The UN ECONOMIC AND SOCIAL COUNCIL (ECOSOC) created the International Research and Training Institute for the Advancement of Women in 1976, fulfilling a recommendation made the previous year by the WORLD CONFERENCE of the International Women's Year, held in Mexico City. ECOSOC established INSTRAW as an autonomous institute within the framework of the UNITED NATIONS SYSTEM, joining by the end of the century the Division for the Advancement of Women (DAW), and the UNITED NATIONS DEVELOPMENT FUND FOR WOMEN (UNIFEM) as the three UN entities committed solely to promoting the advancement of WOMEN. In 1983 INSTRAW accepted the offer of facilities from the Dominican Republic for its permanent headquarters, situating it within the developing world, the focus of most of its efforts.

A board of 11 directors selected on the basis of equitable geographical distribution governs the Institute. Nominated by ECOSOC member states and appointed by the Council to three-year terms, they are individuals with international reputations and expertise in gender equity issues. The board meets annually to review the work of the staff, headed by a director appointed by the UN SECRETARY-GENERAL. It also approves the program, activities, and BUDGET (approximately $4 million in 1999) of the Institute. The Institute's training, research, and information dissemination programs are funded completely by voluntary contributions from governments, NONGOVERNMENTAL ORGANIZATIONS, and private contributors.

In 1999 the GENERAL ASSEMBLY approved a new working method for INSTRAW that allows it to make maximum use of information technology systems. Its Gender Awareness Information and Networking System (GAINS) serves as a "virtual workshop," producing and distributing information about women. GAINS also provides a mechanism for interactive research and training projects. With the new system INSTRAW set as one of its strategic work programs for 2001–02 "Closing the Digital Divide between Women and

Men." Close to its headquarters in the Dominican Republic, for example, it undertook in the Caribbean region two demonstration projects on developing women's skills in information and communications technologies. Other strategic topics established for the period were "Building Partnerships for Gender Equity," and "The Impact of Globalization." The latter of these was directed not only at the opportunities that globalization raises for women but also at the threats it can pose. Among other research agenda, INSTRAW undertook a study of the increasing role the Internet played in the migration of women as "e-mail order brides" worldwide, as well as research on the role of gender in the cycle of conflict in the FORMER YUGOSLAVIA.

INSTRAW also sponsors conferences on critical issues involving women and gender equity. In October 2001, it worked with the UNITED NATIONS CHILDREN'S FUND (UNICEF) and the UNITED NATIONS DEVELOPMENT PROGRAMME (UNDP) to organize a four-day conference on "Working with Men to End Gender-Based Violence." The meeting was held in Bellagio, Italy.

See also DEPARTMENT OF ECONOMIC AND SOCIAL AFFAIRS, PROGRAMMES AND FUNDS.

Further Reading: Anand, Anita, with Gouri Salvi. *Beijing! UN Fourth World Conference on Women.* New Delhi: Women's Feature Service, 1998. United Nations Department of Public Information. *The United Nations and the Advancement of Women, 1945–1996.* New York: United Nations Department of Public Information, 1996. ———. *Basic Facts about the United Nations.* New York: United Nations Department of Public Information, published periodically. INSTRAW website: <www.un-instraw.org>.

International Seabed Authority

On November 16, 1994, the United Nations CONVENTION on the Law of the Sea entered into force, some 12 years after it had been adopted following three rounds of meetings of the UN CONFERENCE ON THE LAW OF THE SEA. There were 135 states that were parties to the convention by 2001. An Implementing Agreement of July 28, 1994, on the application of provisions on seabed mining, supplemented the full convention. This latter agreement was meant to address requests for a more market-oriented approach to seabed issues, and refine decision-making procedures connected with the convention. The convention had established the International Seabed Authority, which, by virtue of the provisions of the convention, and the complementary Implementing Agreement, became responsible for organizing and controlling exploration for and exploitation of the mineral resources of the deep seabed.

Members of the International Seabed Authority are the parties to the convention on the Law of the Sea. They elect a Seabed Authority Council with representatives coming from geographical groupings identified in the UN Convention on the Law of the Sea. Council members serve for a term of four years. In 2001 the authority's SECRETARIAT had a staff of 19 professionals and 18 general service personnel. Its managing SECRETARY-GENERAL was Mr. Satya N. Nandan from Fiji, and its headquarters is in Kingston, Jamaica.

See also OBSERVER STATUS.

Further Reading: International Seabed Authority website: <www.isa.org.jm>.

International Telecommunication Union (ITU)

Founded in 1865 in Paris by 20 European nations as the International Telegraph Union, the ITU received its present name in 1934 and in 1947 became a SPECIALIZED AGENCY of the United Nations. It is the oldest intergovernmental organization in the world, with headquarters in Geneva. It encourages the development and efficient use of telecommunications and the seamless exchange of information around the world, promotes technical assistance in the field of telecommunications to developing countries, and endorses a broad approach to issues of telecommunications in the changing environment of the global information society. The ITU is particularly interested in assuring that progress in telecommunications advances the global movement and coordination of services, banking, tourism, transportation, and information.

As of 2002, in addition to its 189 member NATION-STATES, the ITU was also composed of more than 600 nongovernmental members (called "sector members") that included scientific and business groups, public and private operators, broadcasters, and regional and international organizations. It is governed by a plenipotentiary conference that convenes every four years, often amends its constitution, its CONVENTION, and its rules of procedure, establishes a budget, and elects a 46-member council that meets annually. The ITU is administered by a SECRETARY-GENERAL who in 2001 was Yoshio Utsumi of Japan, elected by the plenipotentiary conference of 1998.

The ITU seeks public-private cooperation in the development and use of telecommunications worldwide. The ITU has been involved in helping to develop a new system called "international freephone numbers" to help lower costs and make international communication more efficient. It has participated in the introduction of the third-generation mobile phone system (called MT-2000), developed global standards for connecting different telecommunications systems, and been active in the effort to restructure the domain-of-names system of the worldwide Internet. On January 9, 2002, the UN GENERAL ASSEMBLY designated the ITU as the lead agency in the convocation of a World Summit on the Information Society. The Summit was expected to promote global access to information technologies and was scheduled to hold its first session in Geneva in December 2003. A second session in Tunis in 2005 was planned in order to develop strategies for overcoming what Mr. Utsumi described as the "digital divide" both within and between nations.

See also ADMINISTRATIVE COMMITTEE ON COORDINATION, ADMINISTRATIVE TRIBUNALS, EXPANDED PROGRAM OF TECHNICAL ASSISTANCE.

Further Reading: United Nations Department of Public Information. *Basic Facts about the United Nations.* New York: United Nations Department of Public Information, 1998. ITU website: <www.itu.int>.

International Trade Centre UNCTAD/WTO (ITC)

The International Trade Centre is a "joint subsidiary organ" of the WORLD TRADE ORGANIZATION (WTO) and the United Nations, the latter acting through the UNITED NATIONS CONFERENCE ON TRADE AND DEVELOPMENT (UNCTAD). Created in 1964, the ITC provides technical assistance to enterprises in the field of trade promotion, being designated in 1973 by the UN GENERAL ASSEMBLY as the focal point in the UNITED NATIONS SYSTEM for this purpose. In particular, it implements trade promotion projects financed by the UNITED NATIONS DEVELOPMENT PROGRAMME (UNDP) in LEAST DEVELOPED COUNTRIES (LDC) and economies in transition (EITs). It also works closely with SPECIALIZED AGENCIES in the UN system, including the FOOD AND AGRICULTURE ORGANIZATION (FAO) and the UNITED NATIONS INDUSTRIAL DEVELOPMENT ORGANIZATION (UNIDO), and with REGIONAL DEVELOPMENT BANKS.

Among its other tasks, the International Trade Centre, headquartered at the Palais des Nations in Geneva, attempts to expand exports from developing countries. It also advises them on how to improve import operations. It provides trade information, needs assessment, and human resource development expertise. ITC specialists work with national and regional groups at the request of individual governments; projects last from several weeks to years.

ITC's executive director—in autumn 2001, J. Denis Bélisle—oversees a staff of more than 200, and several hundred consultants. The SECRETARIAT receives its funds in equal parts from the WTO and the United Nations. Project allocation of the funds are made on the recommendation of ITC's Joint Advisory Group (JAG), an inter-governmental board that meets annually. JAG also reviews the International Trade Centre's medium-term plan, which covers consecutive six-year periods.

Further Reading: New Zealand Ministry of Foreign Affairs. *United Nations Handbook.* Wellington, N.Z.: Ministry of Foreign Affairs and Trade, published annually. ITC website: <www.intracen.org/menus/mainhome.htm>.

International Tribunal for the Law of the Sea

See UNITED NATIONS CONFERENCE ON THE LAW OF THE SEA.

Iran hostage crisis

The Iran hostage crisis began on November 4, 1979, with the seizure of the American embassy in Tehran by followers of Ayatollah Khomeini. Students seized the embassy in response to an American decision to allow the deposed shah of Iran, Muhammad Reza Pahlavi, to receive medical treatment in the UNITED STATES. The embassy grounds were occupied and 66 American citizens taken hostage; 13 hostages were released shortly after the embassy was occupied while the remaining hostages were detained for a total of 444 days.

In 1979 there existed in the Iranian polity residual anger with U.S. involvement in the 1953 coup that reinstituted the shah, and as the crisis continued this discontent was exacerbated by Iranian fears that the United States would again intervene to reinstall the deposed shah. This anger was also compounded by American moves to freeze Iranian assets controlled by U.S. banks, the imposition of economic SANCTIONS on Iran, and an unwillingness on the part of the United States to return the shah to Iran to face prosecution.

The UN SECURITY COUNCIL was gravely concerned with the hostage crisis, seeing it as a serious threat to international peace. This sentiment is evident in Security Council Resolutions 457 and 461. Urgent calls for the release of the hostages appeared in both RESOLUTIONS as did demands that issues outstanding between the two states be resolved in accordance with the principles of the UN CHARTER. Resolution 457 in particular mentioned the Vienna CONVENTIONS of 1961 and 1963 on Diplomatic and Consular Relations as they pertain to the inviolability of diplomatic personnel.

The UN's SECRETARY-GENERAL, Kurt WALDHEIM, actively tried to resolve the Iran hostage crisis. Waldheim kept open channels of communication, met privately with U.S. secretary of state Cyrus Vance and with Iran's Revolutionary Council. He also traveled to Tehran to offer his GOOD OFFICES and to encourage compliance with Security Council Resolution 457 that demanded release of the hostages. Finally, he appointed a Commission of INQUIRY that visited Iran in early 1980 with no more success than he had achieved in his personal efforts. The INTERNATIONAL COURT OF JUSTICE (ICJ) was also involved in the crisis. On December 15, 1979, the Court ordered that the government of Iran should immediately release all American nationals held in Iran and that neither government should undertake any action that would aggravate extant tensions.

Following a failed rescue mission by the American government in April 1980, little progress toward a resolution occurred until Iran's prime minister, Muhammed Ali-Rajai, visited UN HEADQUARTERS in New York. He came seeking support for Iran in the war that had just broken out with Iraq.

Secretary-General Waldheim explained to him that as long as Tehran held the American hostages in violation of INTERNATIONAL LAW and UN resolutions, he could expect little support from member states. Within days of his return to Iran, Ali-Rajai designated Algeria as its official intermediary to negotiate a settlement with the United States. Waldheim wrote later that the prime minister's visit to the UN had been the turning point in the crisis. The highly negative attitude toward Iran presented by Third World countries in particular convinced Ali-Rajai of the need to settle the matter. After lengthy negotiations the hostages were released on January 20, 1981.

See also IRAN-IRAQ WAR.

Further Reading: Puchala, Donald, ed. *Issues Before the 35th General Assembly of the United Nations: 1980–1981.* New York: United Nations Association of the USA, 1980. Waldheim, Kurt. *In the Eye of the Storm: A Memoir.* Bethesda, Md.: Adler and Adler, 1986.

Iran-Iraq War

The Iran-Iraq war started in 1980 and raged until a UN-mediated cease-fire was agreed to by the combatants in July 1988. In accordance with UN SECURITY COUNCIL RESOLUTION 598, passed unanimously during that month, a peace settlement between Iran and Iraq, which tried to address issues such as an exchange of prisoners and the settlement of their shared international border, was agreed to in August 1990. The RESOLUTION also marked a high-water mark in American-Soviet cooperation on Middle East issues. The resolution imposed a threat of retaliation against either combatant who refused to comply.

Iraq initiated the Iran-Iraq war at the height of the IRAN HOSTAGE CRISIS but the conflict had its genesis in the imperial division of the Middle East earlier in the century. The border separating Iraq and Iran was a hotly contested issue in the region's immediate postcolonial period but was fixed after 1975 down the middle of the Shatt al Arab estuary. The repudiation of this agreement coupled with Iraq's invasion of Iran sparked the 1980 Iran-Iraq war.

Considering that the Iran-Iraq war was one of the longest and most costly conflicts of the 20th century, both in financial and human terms (estimates place total number of casualties as high as two million), the international community remained surprisingly silent on the conflagration. The UN SECURITY COUNCIL passed Resolution 479 a few weeks after hostilities were initiated and passed Resolutions 514, 522, 540, 582, 588, 598, 612, 616, 619, 620, 631, 642, 651, 671, 676, and 685 over the subsequent eight years; but while doing so (and calling on all states not to undertake actions that would contribute to the continuation and/or widening of the conflict) members of the Security Council were perpetuating, and profiting from, the conflict by rearming the combatants. American involvement in this enterprise was exposed as the Iran-contra affair.

UN silence and inaction resulted not because of apathy on the part of the SECRETARY-GENERAL but rather because of political calculations on the part of the permanent five (P5) in the Security Council. The Security Council did meet several days after the initial invasion but this was after Secretary-General Kurt WALDHEIM, under article 99 of the UN CHARTER, called the Security Council's attention to the conflict. Waldheim also immediately appealed to both sides to cease hostilities and offered the services of his GOOD OFFICES. As the conflict bogged down into a protracted stalemate the Secretary-General appointed as his SPECIAL REPRESENTATIVE—and sent to negotiate with both Iran and Iraq—the Swedish politician Olof Palme. Some of the political machinations that precluded Security Council action were American preoccupation with the hostages held in Iran; Soviet insistence that the Iraqi AGGRESSION had been launched at the behest of the West; and Chinese, Japanese, and West German concerns for their economic relations with the combatants.

Several of the Security Council's resolutions explicitly invoked the Geneva CONVENTIONS of 1949 as well as the 1925 Geneva PROTOCOL. The 1949 Geneva Convention prohibited attacks on civilian centers as well as the targeting of neutral shipping, both of which were occurring in the region. The council reaffirmed the Geneva Protocol of 1925 and its Protocol for the Prohibition of the Use in War of Asphyxiating, Poisonous or Other Gases, and of Bacteriological Methods of Warfare because of Iraq's repeated use of poison gas on Iranian troops, probably as early as 1983 and most certainly by 1986. It is in the context of this deployment of CHEMICAL WEAPONS that the UN CONFERENCE ON DISARMAMENT (CD) was cited in Resolution 620.

Also found in these documents—several of which merely extend the mandate of the UN Iran-Iraq Military Observer Group—is UN Security Council Resolution 616. This resolution, passed in July of 1988, expressed deep distress at the downing of Iran Air flight 655 over the Straits of Hormuz by a missile fired from the UNITED STATES warship USS *Vincennes* and welcomed an investigation by the INTERNATIONAL CIVIL AVIATION ORGANIZATION (ICAO) into the events that led to the destruction of the aircraft.

Further Reading: Pérez de Cuéllar, Javier. *Pilgrimage for Peace: A Secretary-General's Memoirs.* New York: St. Martin's, 1997. Simons, Geoff. *The United Nations: A Chronology of Conflict.* New York: St. Martin's, 1994. Urquhart, Brian. *Decolonization and World Peace.* Austin: University of Texas Press, 1989.

— *S. F. McMahon*

J

Joint Inspection Unit (JIU)

Located at the GENEVA HEADQUARTERS OF THE UNITED NATIONS, the Joint Inspection Unit is an external oversight body and subsidiary organ of the UN GENERAL ASSEMBLY (GA) that makes recommendations on improving management and coordination within the UNITED NATIONS SYSTEM. The General Assembly established JIU in 1968, giving it broad authority to investigate all SPECIALIZED AGENCIES and other bodies of the UN system, and to draft independent reports for consideration by the GA FIFTH COMMITTEE. By 2001, the Joint Inspection Unit had produced more than 300 reports on management issues, including personnel policy, planning, career development, budgeting, development cooperation, and performance assessment. Over three decades, JIU's guidelines and procedures became the standards used throughout the UN system.

The Joint Inspection Unit has 11 inspectors elected by the General Assembly to once-renewable five-year terms. In addition to assuring equitable geographical representation, the Assembly elects individuals with strong experience in administrative and financial matters. The inspectors have broad powers of investigation, using on-the-spot reviews of specialized agencies to assure that these organs are working efficiently and providing effective service. Among the UN bodies reviewed at the close of the 1990s were the INTERNATIONAL RESEARCH AND TRAINING INSTITUTE FOR THE ADVANCEMENT OF WOMEN (INSTRAW), the INTERNATIONAL CIVIL AVIATION ORGANIZATION (ICAO), and the INTERNATIONAL LABOUR ORGANIZATION (ILO). Its projected investigations for 2001 and beyond included the WORLD HEALTH ORGANIZATION (WHO), the UNITED NATIONS INDUSTRIAL DEVELOPMENT ORGANIZATION (UNIDO), and the UNITED NATIONS EDUCATIONAL, SCIENTIFIC AND CULTURAL ORGANIZATION (UNESCO). JIU also prepares reports on system-wide administrative and financial issues. It produced 27 such reports between 1994 and 1999. Its provisional work program at the beginning of the new century included studies on the administration of the UN OFFICE AT GENEVA (UNOG), the handling of oversight reports by legislative bodies in the UN system, the management of buildings, planning and budgeting in the UN system, a comparative analysis of the management of junior professionals in the system, and the administration of justice in UN ADMINISTRATIVE TRIBUNALS. The specialized agencies and the UN BUDGET cover the expenses of JIU, which generally range from $3 million to $9 million annually.

Further Reading: Eco'Diagnostic, Geneva. *International Geneva Yearbook, 2000–2001.* Geneva: United Nations, 2000. United Nations. *Reports of the Joint Inspection Unit: General Assembly Official Records,* Supplement No. 34 (each session). JIU website: <www.unsystem.org/jiu/>.

Joint United Nations Programme on HIV/AIDS (UNAIDS)

The Joint United Nations Programme on HIV/AIDS (UNAIDS) acts as the leading coordinating body for the United Nations's response to the worldwide AIDS epidemic. Prior to its creation in 1996, the WORLD HEALTH ORGANIZATION (WHO) was the primary agency responsible for addressing the epidemic. In 1987, the United Nations established a Special Programme on AIDS within WHO, later to be called the Global Programme on AIDS (GPA). Despite the leadership role of WHO and its coordinating efforts with the UNITED NATIONS DEVELOPMENT PROGRAMME (UNDP) and the WORLD BANK, it was decided within the United Nations that an expanded coordinating program was warranted to address the multifaceted nature of the AIDS epidemic. The consensus among the various UN organizations addressing the AIDS epidemic was that there needed to be one source of policy and technical guidance within the UN system that recognized the underlying causes and impact of AIDS, which go far beyond the health sector. The result was the creation of UNAIDS, which initially brought together six agencies belonging to or affiliated with the UN system—WHO, UNDP, UNICEF (UNITED NATIONS CHILDREN'S FUND), UNFPA (UNITED NATIONS POPULATION FUND), UNESCO (UNITED NATIONS EDUCATIONAL, SCIENTIFIC AND CULTURAL ORGANIZATION), and the World Bank—to coordinate their individual efforts in addressing the AIDS epidemic. In April 1999, recognizing the increasing impact of HIV transmission through needles shared by injecting drug users, the UN INTERNATIONAL DRUG CONTROL PROGRAMME (UNDCP) joined the Joint United Nations Programme on AIDS.

The goal of UNAIDS is to strengthen and orchestrate the expertise, resources, and influence that each of its constituent organizations offers. As the main advocate for global action on HIV/AIDS, the UNAIDS mission is to support a coordinated effort aimed at HIV prevention, provide care and support for people living with HIV/AIDS, and help alleviate the socioeconomic and human impact of AIDS. With this mission in mind, UNAIDS has identified four objectives: (1) To foster expanded national responses to HIV/AIDS, particularly in developing countries; (2) To promote strong commitment by governments to an expanded response to HIV/AIDS; (3) To strengthen and coordinate UN action on HIV/AIDS at the global and national levels; and (4) To identify, develop, and advocate international best practices for HIV prevention.

UNAIDS is governed by a Programme Coordinating Board with representatives of 22 governments from all regions of the world. In addition, the board includes representatives from the seven participating agencies and five representatives from NON-GOVERNMENTAL ORGANIZATIONS (NGOs), which include associations of people living with AIDS. As such, UNAIDS is the first United Nations program to include NGOs in its governing body.

With a relatively modest BUDGET of $60 million (for fiscal 2000), UNAIDS does not consider itself to be a direct funding or implementing agency. Rather, the UNAIDS SECRETARIAT, based in Geneva, operates on behalf of the participating agencies to provide the following services: (1) policy development and research; (2) technical support; (3) advocacy; and (4) coordination. Priority areas identified by the UNAIDS secretariat include: young people, high-risk populations, prevention of mother-to-child HIV transmission, development and implementation of community standards of AIDS care, vaccine development, and the creation of special initiatives for heavily impacted regions in the developing world where approximately 95 percent of HIV cases are found.

In the developing nations, UNAIDS operates through a United Nations Theme Group on AIDS, consisting of representatives of the participating UN agencies. The representatives work with national government agencies as well as NGOs to support the host governments' efforts to develop a comprehensive response to HIV/AIDS.

Further Reading: Bastos, Cristiana. *Global Responses to AIDS: Science in Emergency*. Bloomington: Indiana University Press, 1999. Feldman, Douglas, and Julia Wang Miller. *The AIDS Crisis: A Documentary History*. Westport, Conn.: Greenwood Press, 1998. Stine, Gerald. *AIDS Update 2000*. Upper Saddle River, N.J.: Prentice Hall, 1999.

— R. E. McNamara

judicial settlement   *See* CHAPTER VI OF THE UN CHARTER, INTERNATIONAL COURT OF JUSTICE.

jurisdiction of the United Nations

Jurisdiction is the exercise of legitimate "authority"—rather than "force" or "power"—over people, territory, or a particular human activity. In international affairs, jurisdiction is associated with the legal principle of state SOVEREIGNTY, which gives NATION-STATES unfettered control over domestic affairs, and requires of them non-interference in the affairs of other states. Within a political system itself, jurisdiction over aspects of political, social, and economic life may be assigned by constitutional arrangement to different government agencies, bodies, or individuals.

The jurisdiction of the United Nations arises from an agreement among independent states, enshrined in the UN CHARTER and approved at the 1945 San Francisco Conference. According to the Preamble of the Charter, the world's "people," represented by their governments, established the United Nations to maintain international peace and security, granting it broad jurisdiction in world affairs. Historically, the domestic jurisdiction of the nation-state shielded it from regulation by international organizations and INTERNATIONAL LAW. The Charter recognized this reality in Article 2, stating "nothing contained in the present Charter shall authorize the United Nations to intervene in matters which are essentially within the domestic jurisdiction of any state." The article made only one exception to this proviso, allowing for Security Council ENFORCEMENT MEASURES under CHAPTER VII. Nonetheless, from its founding to the turn of the millennium the United Nations promoted policies and took decisions that increasingly brought into question the dividing line between its jurisdiction and that of its member states.

In the 1903 *Nationality Decrees in Tunis and Morocco* case, the PERMANENT COURT OF INTERNATIONAL JUSTICE (PCIJ) ruled that "the question of whether a certain matter is or is not solely within the jurisdiction of a state is an essentially relative question, it depends on the development of international relations." State sovereignty became increasingly constrained in the latter half of the 20th century by many factors, not the least of which was the assertion by the United Nations of its authority in certain areas. The United Nations passed RESOLUTIONS condemning states' internal policies such as APARTHEID, colonial rule, HUMAN RIGHTS violations, environmental degradation, and the treatment of dependent populations. In the case of war crimes, crimes against humanity, and crimes against peace, the United Nations asserted the same "universal jurisdiction" that every state had under international law to bring perpetrators to account. Having officially accepted in 1946 the legal principles established in the Nuremberg Trials, the United Nations created its own tribunals in the 1990s (INTERNATIONAL CRIMINAL TRIBUNAL FOR THE FORMER YUGOSLAVIA, INTERNATIONAL CRIMINAL TRIBUNAL FOR RWANDA, INTERNATIONAL CRIMINAL COURT) to try suspected violators.

From the beginning, UN efforts to assert its jurisdiction engendered disputes. They took three forms: disputes about which organs of the United Nations were competent to exercise jurisdiction in a particular case, disagreements between the United Nations and other international organizations over which group's jurisdiction applied in a given area, and disputes between the United Nations and specific states concerning, from the state's point of view, an illegal intervention by the world body in the nation's domestic affairs.

An organization may have an overarching jurisdiction, but this quality is usually exercised in its parts by different organs within the larger entity. The Charter assigned jurisdiction for different activities to its six PRINCIPAL ORGANS: the GENERAL ASSEMBLY, the SECURITY COUNCIL, the SECRETARIAT, the TRUSTEESHIP COUNCIL, the INTERNATIONAL COURT OF JUSTICE, and the ECONOMIC AND SOCIAL COUNCIL. The Security Council was the only body given COMPULSORY JURISDICTION over threats to the peace, with the power to use force to restore peaceful conditions. In 1950, however, faced with a deadlock among the PERMANENT MEMBERS of the council, the

General Assembly passed the UNITING FOR PEACE RESOLUTION, giving the Assembly authority to recommend measures when the VETO blocked council action. The Resolution was rejected by the Soviet Union as a violation of the Charter. France later also rejected any responsibility for the costs of UN operations that came from an invocation of the resolution, causing a serious financial crisis for the organization.

The UN's most serious jurisdictional disputes with other international organizations have been with REGIONAL ORGANIZATIONS and alliances. Under the Rio PACT of 1947 and the Pact of Bogotá (1948), the ORGANIZATION OF AMERICAN STATES (OAS) claimed jurisdiction when disputes arose among its members. The OAS also pointed to Article 52 of the UN Charter, which approved the existence of regional organizations and encouraged "pacific settlement of local disputes through such regional arrangements." However, during crises in GUATEMALA (1954), CUBA (1960), and the Dominican Republic (1965), various UN members invoked Articles 34, 35, and 39, which appeared to give the Security Council immediate jurisdiction whenever it determined there was a threat to international peace and security. Jurisdictional disputes in these cases arose out of the COLD WAR politics of the time, and made UN action nearly impossible. Following the close of the cold war, however, jurisdictional questions arose over the role of the North Atlantic Treaty Organization (NATO) in Kosovo, as opposed to UN undertakings there. When NATO forces attacked Yugoslavian installations and occupied Kosovo, Russia and other states opposed to the operation asserted that NATO actions usurped UN jurisdiction and were, therefore, illegal.

The final form of jurisdictional dispute has been between individual states, or their leaders, and the United Nations as a whole. The UN's condemnation of apartheid and its call for SANCTIONS against South Africa in the 1960s and 1970s were labeled illegitimate by the South African government. Pretoria also rejected the jurisdiction of the United Nations, and particularly of the International Court of Justice, in the matter of South Africa's control of NAMIBIA. UN efforts to encourage decolonization led Portugal and other colonial powers to question UN jurisdiction under the Charter. More recently, the UN's pursuit of war criminals, and their forcible detention and trial before international tribunals, brought the defense by those charged that the United Nations had no jurisdiction in their cases. In July 2001, the former president of Yugoslavia, Slobodan Milosevic, made that argument after his transfer to The Hague for trial, claiming his actions were solely a matter of domestic jurisdiction, protected by the principle of state sovereignty.

jus cogens

Article 53 of the 1969 Vienna Convention on Treaties recognized the existence of *jus cogens,* defined as a "peremptory norm of INTERNATIONAL LAW." The CONVENTION voided all

TREATY provisions in violation of these universal principles "accepted and recognized by the international community of states as a whole as [norms] from which no derogation is permitted." The convention's Article 64 allowed the INTER-NATIONAL COURT OF JUSTICE (ICJ) to accept any dispute brought to it by a party to a treaty in which an issue of *jus cogens* arose, and for which the parties were unable to agree to ARBITRATION. The ICJ's JURISDICTION arose from the STATUTE OF THE INTERNATIONAL COURT OF JUSTICE's Article 38, which required it to apply "the general principles of law recognized by civilized nations" as a source of international law.

First suggested by Hugo Grotius in the 16th century, the revival of *jus cogens* by UN bodies and conferences represented a renewed interest in the natural law theory of international law. Instead of law solely arising from the consent of states, *jus cogens* asserted a set of fundamental principles that reflected higher law and were binding on all governments. The principle became closely associated with the efforts to develop HUMAN RIGHTS law that could limit state discretion against its own citizens or other peoples.

The development of *jus cogens* proved to be controversial as to both content and the method of creation. Since "univer-sal acceptance" was the bedrock for the assertion of these peremptory norms, the list of accepted general principles remained short. The INTERNATIONAL LAW COMMISSION (ILC) served as the forum of *jus cogens* debate within the UNITED NATIONS SYSTEM after 1969. Many examples of universal norms were cited and discussed, including prohibitions against GENOCIDE, AGGRESSION, slave-trading, piracy, and APARTHEID, as well as positive norms such as the sovereign equality of states, and self-determination. The Soviet Union often proposed DISARMAMENT and peaceful coexistence as *jus cogens*, but they never achieved the broad acceptance across ideological and regional blocs necessary to be so designated. By the time of the UN MILLENNIUM SUMMIT in 2000, the right of development was being promoted within the ILC, among developing states, and in many reports of UN bodies, including the SECRETARIAT, as an emerging general norm of international law, and therefore as part of *jus cogens*.

Further Reading: Hannikainen, Lauri. *Peremptory Norms (Jus Cogens) in International Law: Historical Development, Criteria, Present Status.* Helsinki: Finnish Lawyers' Publishing Company, 1988. Shaw, Malcolm N. *International Law.* 3d ed. Cambridge: Cambridge University Press, 1994.

K

Kampuchea   *See* CAMBODIA.

Kashmir

Controversy between Pakistan and India over the territory of Kashmir and Jammu has been a concern of the United Nations since the dispute surfaced in the 1940s. When the British *raj*—that is, colonial control over the subcontinent exercised from London—ended in 1947 with the grant of independence to the two separate nations of India and Pakistan, the partition resulted in the largest migration in human history. As many as 17 million people fled across the borders in both directions, Muslims to Pakistan, Hindus to India, all in a desperate effort to escape bloody riots among sectarian groups. Simultaneously, conflict broke out over competing claims to the princely states of Jammu and Kashmir, initiating the longest running dispute between the two nations. India gained sovereign control over most of the area, which had a majority Islamic population. For the United Nations this quarrel would become one of the oldest, comparable to the ARAB-ISRAELI DISPUTE. Both began in 1947 and both continued to plague the world into the new century.

The SECURITY COUNCIL first addressed the Kashmir issue in 1948, responding to an Indian complaint that forces had invaded the province. Pakistan denied the allegation and further declared the ACCESSION of Kashmir to India to be unlawful. The Security Council forwarded recommendations for ending the fighting. It established the United Nations Commission for India and Pakistan (UNCIP), which proposed a cease-fire, troop withdrawals, and a plebiscite to decide the controversy. Although both sides appeared to accept the proposal generally, they could not agree on details and modalities. However, the disputants did accept the deployment of the UNITED NATIONS MILITARY OBSERVER GROUP IN INDIA AND PAKISTAN (UNMOGIP), which remained in place for the next half century and at the turn of the century was still monitoring the original cease-fire. Thus UNMOGIP was one of the longest peace operations in UN history.

In 1962 India found itself at war with CHINA over a border dispute (still unresolved as of 2001) along the Kashmir and Assam frontiers. During the summer of 1965 hostilities between India and Pakistan occurred again over the issue of Kashmir. The skirmish led to Security Council RESOLUTION 211 calling for a cease-fire and a withdrawal of military forces to pre-conflict lines. Secretary-General U THANT then established an adjunct mission to UNMOGIP, the UNITED NATIONS INDIA-PAKISTAN OBSERVATION MISSION (UNIPOM). With the Tashkent Agreement of January 10, 1966, the parties agreed to withdraw their forces to lines recommended by the Security Council. UNIPOM provided GOOD OFFICES for the arranged withdrawal, and then the mission was terminated in March of that same year.

By 1971 Indian-Pakistani relations had degenerated further. A civil war that year in Pakistan, aggravated by Indian interference, resulted in the loss of East Pakistan, which became Bangladesh. When the war began, Pakistani president Yahya Khan requested that the United Nations send observers to the Pakistani side of the line and take over refugee facilities in East Pakistan. But the great powers resisted making use of the organization at the initiation of fighting. By December 4, 1971, when it was clear that India was on the march and that Pakistan was to be truncated, a Security Council resolution called for an immediate cease-fire. Because of a Soviet Union VETO, the proposal had to be carried to the GENERAL ASSEMBLY, where, under the UNITING FOR PEACE formula, it passed overwhelmingly. Pakistan would lose its eastern province once the UN-decreed cease-fire went into effect.

In 1972, following the war of the previous year, the two countries signed an agreement defining a line of control in Kashmir. India then took the position that the mandate of UNMOGIP had lapsed; Pakistan insisted that it had not. The SECRETARY-GENERAL insisted that only the Security Council could terminate the mandate, and consistently recommended that both sides seek UN MEDIATION to resolve the conflict.

In 1989, Muslim separatists in Kashmir called for an end to Indian rule and either independence or merger with Pakistan. India accused Islamabad of supporting the rebels and called their guerrilla activities "TERRORISM"; tension accelerated. A Hindu nationalist party in India, the Bharatiya Janata Party (BJP), became more potent during the 1990s by proposing a stronger assertion of Indian claims over Kashmir and it advocated a more hardened policy toward separatists there. In 1999 Muslim insurgents mounted attacks on Indian forces in Kashmir that were met with strong retaliation. That summer in Indian elections the BJP won control of the parliament and Atal Behari Vajpayee became prime minister. Meantime in Pakistan, the military took an equally inflexible position on Kashmir and, in October 1999, General Pervez Musharraf executed a coup, overthrowing the civilian government. Still more ominous, in the previous year both India and Pakistan, to the distaste of other major nations and the United Nations, each conducted successful nuclear weapons tests, clearly raising the stakes in the ongoing battle over Kashmir. With both rivals now governed by hard-liners, the situation seemed more unpromising than ever. In July 2001, Prime Minister Vajpayee and General Musharraf met for the first time, in Agra in Uttar Pradesh, India. For a moment there was some optimism, but the talks collapsed. Pakistan had always sought the independence of the province from India and from the beginning supported the notion of a plebiscite to determine Kashmir's future, but India considered the issue of Kashmir to be an internal issue and rejected a plebiscite, such as that recommended as early as 1948 by the United Nations.

The issue was complicated by the crisis brought on with the terrorist attacks on the UNITED STATES on September 11, 2001. Washington brought intense pressure on AFGHANISTAN to extradite alleged terrorist Osama bin Laden, and then, on October 7, the United States commenced an air attack on the ruling Taliban in the country. Even though Pakistan had been one of the few nations to recognize the Taliban, President Musharraf made the crucial decision to support the United States. On October 1, less than a week before the U.S. offensive, a Pakistan-based group was implicated in a terrorist attack on the state legislature in the Indian part of Kashmir. Harsh comments flowed from both New Delhi and Islamabad and violence mounted in Kashmir at the very time that U.S. strikes against the Taliban accelerated. U.S. secretary of state Colin Powell made a hurried visit to the area in mid October, hoping to defuse the tension so as to solidify support from both Pakistan and India for America's antiterrorist campaign. His efforts, however, were eclipsed by a dramatic escalation of the violence on December 13. Five gunmen entered the parliament building in New Delhi and killed seven people, injuring 18 others. Indian officials blamed Lashkar-e-Taiba, a radical Islamic group with headquarters in Pakistan, for the attack. New Delhi demanded that Pakistan close down the operation of the group and arrest militant terrorists in the Pakistani parts of Kashmir. President Musharraf was also under pressure from the United States to disband separatist and militant groups operating out of the country. By December 24, Pakistan and India had moved troops to the border and sporadic exchanges of gunfire were reported. Secretary-General Kofi ANNAN made a hurried trip to both capitals and achieved limited commitments from both governments not to resort to war. Nonetheless, tensions remained high well into spring 2002, exacerbated by the continuing military activity in bordering Afghan territories. Despite determined diplomatic efforts by Secretary of State Powell in May and June to defuse the situation, both sides redeployed military forces in large numbers along the Kashmir border.

Perhaps a dozen Islamic militant groups were fighting Indian security forces in Kashmir by 2002. India continued to charge that Pakistan was providing funding and training to the guerrilla groups, while Pakistan insisted that it provided only diplomatic and moral support to "freedom fighters." Official tallies estimate that 30,000 lives had been lost since the latest insurgency began in 1989. Some HUMAN RIGHTS groups insisted that the toll was double those numbers.

See also DEPARTMENT OF PEACEKEEPING OPERATIONS, NUCLEAR-WEAPONS-FREE ZONES, PEACEKEEPING.

Further Reading: United Nations. *The Blue Helmets: A Review of United Nations Peace-Keeping.* 3d ed. New York: United Nations Department of Public Information, 1996. UNMOGIP website: <www.un.org/Depts/DPKO/Missions/unmogip/body_unmogip.htm>.

Kassebaum Amendment *See* REFORM OF THE UNITED NATIONS.

Kim Il-Sung (1912–1994)

Known as the "Great Leader" and, since his death, "Eternal Leader" of the Democratic People's Republic of Korea (North Korea), Kim Il-Sung provoked the only military conflict that directly involved the United Nations by his attack on the Republic of Korea (South Korea) on June 25, 1950. The KOREAN WAR or "police action" lasted from 1950 to 1953 with 17 UN members contributing troops and supplies, while the People's Republic of CHINA (PRC) intervened on behalf of Kim and the Soviet Union provided surreptitious military assistance.

With the sudden collapse of Japan in mid-August 1945 in the wake of two nuclear attacks by the UNITED STATES and the long-promised Soviet declaration of war, Washington proposed that Japanese-dominated Korea be assigned a northern Soviet occupation zone and an American southern zone, divided at the 38th parallel. In the postwar climate of the COLD WAR, the Soviets supported a leftist North Korean regime headed by former anti-Japanese partisan Kim Il-sung, while the United States supported the rightist elder nationalist Syngman Rhee in the south. As the two superpowers prepared to leave the peninsula in 1948–49, the United States turned to the United Nations as an avenue of multilateral withdrawal, in hopes of avoiding chaos and civil war.

Despite Soviet opposition, the UN GENERAL ASSEMBLY approved a RESOLUTION calling for elections in the spring of 1948 throughout Korea to establish a national assembly. A UN Temporary Commission on Korea (UNTCOK) was created to oversee the process. When the Soviets carried out their threat to deny UNTCOK entry into the north, Washington secured UN sanction, through the Interim Committee of the General Assembly, for elections in the south alone to create a "National Government." Consequently, the Syngman Rhee regime in the south was confirmed as the legitimate government of all Korea while the Kim Il-Sung regime remained isolated and drew close to both the PRC and the USSR. It sought military assistance in order to carry out a forceful unification of the two Koreas.

After repeated political efforts to gain support for unification among southerners as well as efforts to foment rebellion, Kim Il-Sung, with the permission of Moscow and Beijing, launched a massive military assault on the Republic of Korea. Under U.S. pressure the United Nations quickly branded North Korea the aggressor and called upon all member states to render assistance to South Korea to repel armed attack and "to restore international peace and security in the area."

The Korean War soon stalemated and finally ended in an armistice in July 1953 between the Kim regime (and China) and the United Nations forces (most notably U.S. forces, who made up the preponderance of military personnel and who were led by U.S. commanders). A major international conference at Geneva in 1954 failed to bring a final resolution to the Korean imbroglio. For the next 20 years Kim Il-Sung routinely denounced the United Nations as a tool of American imperialism.

In 1972 Kim initiated a North-South Coordinating Committee to discuss the issue of reunification but it was soon apparent that he sought northern control of the south. Given this impasse, President Chung Hee Park, in June 1973, announced his willingness to have both Koreas admitted to the United Nations as separate entities. Kim condemned Park's proposal as a formula for permanent national division and urged a union of the two regimes under a Confederal Republic of Koryo that could join the United Nations as a single state. Seoul's rejection of the proposal led to an assassination attempt on President Park by Kim's government and to a relentless North Korean tunneling program under the demilitarized zone between north and south.

During the 1970s Kim Il-Sung sought to distance himself from his wartime allies (and superiors) by reaching out to the non-aligned nations for recognition and support in the United Nations. Slowly he gained acceptance as the legitimate ruler of an independent nation in the eyes of the world, especially following South Korea's proposed simultaneous and separate UN MEMBERSHIP. With the support of Algeria and other non-aligned nations and the replacement at the United Nations of the Republic of China (Taiwan) by PRC representatives in 1971, Kim Il-Sung managed to gain a foothold for North Korea to secure status as an official UN observer, and he succeeded in having his government admitted as a full member in a number of SPECIALIZED AGENCIES, beginning with membership in the WORLD HEALTH ORGANIZATION. In 1991 both Koreas became full members of the United Nations. Following Kim's death in 1994, his son, Kim Jong-Il, became the new leader of the North Korean regime and continued the policy of easing relations with the outside world.

Further Reading: Cumings, Bruce. *Korea's Place in the Sun: A Modern History*. New York: Norton, 1997. Stueck, William. *The Korean War: An International History*. Princeton, N.J.: Princeton University Press, 1995. Suh, Dae-Sook. *Kim Il-Sung: The North Korean Leader*. New York: Columbia University Press, 1988.

— *E. M. Clauss*

Korean War

The United Nations initially became involved in Korea in the autumn of 1947 when the American government presented a RESOLUTION to the GENERAL ASSEMBLY calling for the Soviet Union and the UNITED STATES to hold elections in their respective post–World War II occupation zones in order to select members of a national assembly and a Korean national government. In November the General Assembly approved the proposal and established a UNITED NATIONS TEMPORARY COMMISSION ON KOREA (UNTCOK) to supervise the elec-

U.S. Marines in Korea, 1951 (UNITED NATIONS)

tions and report to the Assembly. As the COLD WAR surfaced, the United States and its allies became convinced that the Soviet Union would never cooperate with an American-sponsored plan under the auspices of the United Nations. Thus Washington's policy was aimed at creating a separate South Korean government under conservative Syngman Rhee and shielded by United Nations legitimacy.

Other members of UNTCOK, including U.S. allies Australia and Canada, opposed the decision for elections until they could be administered throughout the peninsula. Under pressure from the American military government, the General Assembly in February 1948 approved an American-sponsored resolution giving UNTCOK authority to supervise elections "in such parts of Korea as might be accessible to the Commission."

Elections were held in May 1948 and Rhee won a significant victory despite mixed assessments of its fairness by the members of UNTCOK. In July, the newly created legislative assembly promptly elected Syngman Rhee as the first president of the Republic of Korea (ROK). Although a separate regime, the Democratic People's Republic (DPR), headed by KIM Il-sung, was established in North Korea, the General Assembly declared the South Korean government to be the only lawful government in that part of Korea where UNTCOK had observed elections and thus the only legitimate government in Korea. As both regimes claimed JURISDICTION over the entire peninsula, violence loomed as the only available path to national unification. International politics mirrored the stalemate in Korea as Soviet-U.S. relations deteriorated into a cold war characterized by an American foreign policy of containment. The fate of the troubled peninsula was to be left in the hands of the United Nations.

When North Korea, with the foreknowledge and approval of the Soviet Union and the People's Republic of

CHINA, invaded South Korea on June 25, 1950, the United States responded immediately, sending combat troops to defend Seoul and calling for an emergency meeting of the UN SECURITY COUNCIL. A UN resolution of June 27 provided for military SANCTIONS against North Korea and called for member states to assist the Republic of Korea. The Security Council was able to act decisively because the Soviet ambassador was boycotting council meetings at the time. Protesting the seating of the Nationalist Government as the representative of China, his absence meant the Soviet VETO was not an obstacle to action. Once the Soviets returned to the table, the American delegation had to appeal to the General Assembly to legitimize military actions in Korea. The Truman administration pushed through the Assembly the UNITING FOR PEACE RESOLUTION, which allowed the members to "discuss" threats to the peace and "recommend" UN action or a response from individual states when the Security Council was deadlocked over an issue. Eventually 16 nations, including the United States, provided armed forces. Another Security Council resolution of July 7 established a unified command under the UN FLAG and delegated the authority for the command to the United States. President Harry S. Truman appointed General Douglas MacArthur as the Supreme United Nations Commander, and the UNITED NATIONS COMMAND (UNC) became the official title of the force.

After enduring initial defeats that drove UN forces to the southern tip of Korea in the Pusan perimeter, MacArthur's forces mounted spectacular counterattacks at Inchon and Pusan, resulting in the recapture of Seoul on September 28 and the pursuit by UN armies of North Korean forces fleeing across the 38th parallel. The Truman administration decided that, absent evidence of a major Soviet or Chinese intervention in the war, UN forces would pursue the North Koreans beyond the 38th parallel and unite the peninsula by force. Thus began the period of the UN offensive, approved by the Security Council on October 7, 1950.

Despite repeated Chinese warnings that it would not tolerate an advance toward its borders, MacArthur's forces moved deeper into North Korea and made preparations to establish a government of national unification.

In early November, the Chinese acted, hurling hundreds of thousands of veteran troops across the Yalu River to confront U.S. and ROK forces approaching the border. As UN forces reeled in retreat, President Truman shocked the world by raising the possibility of using nuclear weapons to stem the tide. Britain's prime minister Clement Attlee flew to Washington to secure assurances from Truman that nuclear decisions would not be made unilaterally.

At the United Nations in New York, efforts were underway to seek a negotiated settlement of the conflict, including, for the first time, representatives of the People's Republic of China. The United States was adamant, however, that a cease-fire must not include discussions of such outstanding issues as diplomatic recognition, Formosa, or a seat at the United Nations. Consequently, the Chinese departed the talks and declared on December 21, 1950, that all actions taken by the United Nations without Chinese participation were illegal.

As UN forces retreated south toward the 38th parallel in the freezing winter of 1950–51, a major foreign policy debate erupted in the United States that made Europeans apprehensive that Washington would retreat from its postwar role of world leadership. While encouraging a dialogue between Washington and Moscow, Western European governments were appalled over an American resolution at the United Nations to brand China as an "aggressor nation" and to impose sanctions on Beijing. On February 1, 1951, the General Assembly approved the American resolution. It was seen as a call to Beijing to desist from offensive action, yet it was also perceived as an indication of a potential peaceful settlement of the issue. An early end to the conflict, however, was precluded by Washington's insistence that outstanding East Asian issues be deferred until after a cease-fire.

During the late winter and early spring of 1951, the pressing military crisis facing the UN Command (UNC) was contained when the Chinese offensive was halted south of Seoul and UN forces were able to launch a counteroffensive, led by General Matthew Ridgeway, which regained territory above the 38th parallel once more. Officially, UN forces still operated on the basis of the October 7, 1950, directive to establish "a unified, independent, and democratic Korea." In reality, however, the Chinese intervention caused both the U.S. State Department and Defense Department to reevaluate their objectives in Korea. The State Department made it clear that it now sought to use military pressure to achieve a cease-fire agreement followed by UN negotiations leading to reimposition of the status quo before June 25, 1950. Offensive operations north of the 38th parallel would only be initiated with the approval of coalition partners, an unlikely prospect.

As the tide of battle appeared to be turning, a mood of optimism pervaded American public opinion. In March 1951, the Western allies, SECRETARY-GENERAL Trygve LIE, and the State Department and Defense Department convinced Truman to undertake a major peace initiative toward North Korea and China through the United Nations Command. When informed of the initiative, the commander of UN forces, General Douglas MacArthur, was irate. He directly challenged U.S. policy and urged an expansion of the war to force a Chinese surrender, thus precipitating the Truman-MacArthur crisis, which ended with President Truman's dismissal of the celebrated general.

Hopes for a negotiated settlement were further delayed by the renewal of fierce Chinese offensives in April and May 1951. After UN forces repelled this drive and once again reentered North Korea, the Truman administration decided to halt the UN advance in order to probe the possibilities for a cease-fire.

Responding to the growing pressure of world opinion and confident that it could negotiate from a position of military strength, the Truman administration resumed the search for a diplomatic settlement. In May the State Department instructed diplomat George Kennan to meet with Jacob Malik, Soviet ambassador to the UN, and indicate that Washington was interested in seeking an armistice or cease-fire along the 38th parallel. On June 22, Moscow responded with a statement of interest. Despite determined resistance by South Korean president Syngman Rhee, negotiations between the United Nations and communist forces began on July 10, 1951, at Kaesong, the ancient capital of Korea.

A cease-fire, much less an armistice, was not close at hand. The military stalemate that had developed between the summer of 1951 and the winter of 1952 was reflected in the diplomatic impasse at the negotiation site in Panmunjom. In November, the U.S. National Security Council drafted a new policy statement on Korea (NSC-118/2), which concluded that the United States should continue its limited war in Korea while seeking an armistice. Flexibility in negotiations with the Chinese would be made possible by a "greater sanction" statement which threatened China with prompt retaliation in case of renewed AGGRESSION. The military stalemate was further complicated by heated controversies over the status of prisoners-of-war as well as charges of germ warfare lodged against the United States.

In November 1952, Republican Dwight Eisenhower won the U.S. presidential election in part because of a widespread belief that a new administration was necessary to bring a conclusion to the unpopular war in Korea. Keeping his campaign pledge, the president-elect flew to Korea in early December where he visited the troops and met with President Syngman Rhee and U.S. commander Mark Clark, making it clear that any escalation of the conflict would risk global war. Confident that the pivot of the cold war was Europe and not Asia, he was determined to take new initiatives to end the conflict in Korea.

Syngman Rhee's refusal to accept an armistice agreement and his threats to pursue a unilateral course forced the UN Command—and U.S. administration officials—to prepare plans for the possible withdrawal of ROK forces from the coalition. The U.S. 8th Army prepared plan EVERREADY that envisioned a military takeover if Rhee became openly hostile to UN forces. At the same time, the United States offered a mutual security PACT with South Korea if it would accept a UN proposed armistice and leave Korean forces under the control of the UN Command. In addition, Eisenhower subtly, but never directly, warned China of the possibility of nuclear retaliation.

The communists and the UN Command, but not Syngman Rhee, agreed to armistice terms in June 1953. Both President Eisenhower and his secretary of state, John Foster Dulles, sent notes to the South Korean leader indicating that the United States and the United Nations were prepared to conclude peace with or without the Seoul government. When armistice talks resumed on July 10, 1953, a leading issue involved the United States's ability to guarantee South Korea's conduct in the post-armistice period. The UN Command negotiators assured the Chinese and North Koreans that the UN Command would withdraw all military aid and support if ROK forces violated the armistice agreement. To insure good conduct, the Chinese launched a massive final assault against the ROK positions. Finally, the United States renewed its promise of a defense pact, a commitment from Eisenhower to South Korea to respond immediately to an unprovoked attack with a UN force and a pledge of major economic assistance.

The armistice ending the Korean War was signed in silence at Panmunjom on July 27, 1953. The next day, the 16 nations with armed forces in Korea signed the "greater sanction" statement reaffirming their intent to resist any attacks on South Korea from the north. In a report to the Security Council on August 7, 1953, General Mark Clark revealed that the allied nations had warned that a breach of the armistice would have consequences "so grave that in all probability, it would not be possible to confine hostilities within the frontiers of Korea."

A United Nations resolution of August 28, 1953, approving the armistice agreement, limited attendance to a postwar political conference to the former belligerents only, and the Soviet Union, which could participate "provided the other side desires it." Immediate postwar acrimony among China, North Korea, and South Korea prevented the realization of a postwar conference. Eventually, in 1954, agreement was reached to hold a conference of the Korean belligerents in Geneva in April of that year in order to discuss the final resolution of both the Korean and Indochina wars. The lack of a successful peace accord between the belligerent parties in Korea left the future unification of the nation in the hands of the United Nations, where it remains today.

See also CHAPTER VII OF THE UN CHARTER.

Further Reading: Foot, Rosemary. *The Wrong War: American Policy and the Dimensions of the Korean Conflict, 1950–1953.* Ithaca, N.Y.: Cornell University Press, 1985. Kaufman, Burton. *The Korean War: Challenges in Crisis, Credibility and Command.* New York: McGraw-Hill, 1997. Mazuzan, George. *Warren R. Austin at the UN, 1946–1953.* Kent, Ohio: Kent State University Press, 1977. Stueck, William. *The Korean War: An International History.* Princeton, N.J.: Princeton University Press, 1995.

— *E. M. Clauss*

Kosovo *See* FORMER YUGOSLAVIA, UNITED NATIONS INTERIM ADMINISTRATION MISSION FOR KOSOVO.

Kyoto Protocol

Adopted on December 11, 1997, by the Third Conference of the Parties (COP-3), the directing body of the UNITED NATIONS FRAMEWORK CONVENTION ON CLIMATE CHANGE (UNFCCC), the Kyoto Protocol set specific greenhouse gas (GHG) emission targets for industrialized states to achieve by 2012. Known as "Annex I Parties" to the UNFCCC, the developed states and states with economies in transition from socialist to capitalist systems agreed to lower overall emissions of six GHGs (carbon dioxide, nitrous oxide, methane, hydrofluorocarbons, perfluorocarbons, and sulphur hexafluoride) to at least 5 percent below 1990 levels between 2008 and 2012. Within this group individual states committed to realize differentiated emission reductions below the 1990 ceiling. Among them the UNITED STATES accepted a target of 7 percent reduction, Italy 6.5 percent, Germany 21 percent, Japan and Canada 6 percent each, and the United Kingdom 12.5 percent. Non-Annex I states were not required by the protocol to meet any specific targets.

Because of objections by industrialized states to the lack of mandated emission reductions by the LESS DEVELOPED COUNTRIES (LDCs), the PROTOCOL also established a number of innovative, flexible techniques for developed states to reach their targets. For example, it provided for "emissions trading," by which a country might transfer to another state emission reduction credits resulting from its own projects. Also, it had a "sinks" provision that provided credits to countries that planted forests or undertook other carbon dioxide absorbing activities. In addition, Kyoto allowed for "joint implementation" credits whereby an industrialized state could count emission reduction units achieved in another developed state if it helped finance the GHG-reducing project. Finally, at the urging of the United States and Brazil, negotiators created a "Clean Development Mechanism" that enabled a country to receive credit for emissions-avoiding projects that it undertook or that its private corporations undertook in other countries, presumably in the developing world.

The Kyoto Protocol was to enter into force after being ratified by a minimum of 55 states, among which were to be sufficient developed countries to account for at least 55 percent of global carbon dioxide (CO_2) emissions in 1990. Since the United States produced nearly 40 percent of the world's CO_2 emissions at the time of the Kyoto Protocol's signing, this provision gave Washington a near VETO over the measure. In July 1997 the U.S. Senate voted 95 to 0 to oppose ratification of any climate TREATY that did not include limitations on LDC emissions, effectively postponing early implementation of the agreement. While President Clinton later signed the protocol, chances for American ratification became more remote with the election of President George W. Bush, who announced, in early 2001, that he would not submit it to the Senate without significant changes.

Post-Kyoto annual meetings of the UNFCCC Conference of the Parties were aimed at developing operational plans for implementing the protocol and at generating public pressure on the United States and other developed countries to meet their Kyoto commitments. At COP-4 (1998) in Argentina, negotiators drew up the Buenos Aires Plan of Action, which established a calendar of negotiations on all outstanding issues. In November 2000, more than 7,000 participants gathered for the sixth COP meeting in The Hague, Netherlands. Despite two weeks of intense negotiations, however, the conference broke up without an agreement that would meet the needed requirements for the protocol to go into force. Delegates agreed to suspend the meeting until later in 2001, giving time for UN SECRETARY-GENERAL Kofi ANNAN and others to bring public pressure to bear on the United States and other states that had not ratified the Kyoto Protocol. On November 10, 2001, negotiators from 165 nations, meeting in Marrakech, Morocco, finally agreed on rules for implementing the protocol beginning in 2002. On June 4, 2002, Japan ratified the protocol, raising support for the agreement by countries responsible for 36 percent of 1990's global greenhouse gases. Japan's ratification raised hopes among supporters that sufficient country commitments could be reached to achieve the 55 percent goal, even without U.S. ratification, by the time of the World Summit on SUSTAINABLE DEVELOPMENT in August.

See also ENVIRONMENT, INTERGOVERNMENTAL PANEL ON CLIMATE CHANGE, MONTREAL PROTOCOL ON SUBSTANCES THAT DEPLETE THE OZONE LAYER.

Further Reading: Fletcher, Susan R. *Congressional Research Service Report for Congress. 98-2: Global Climate Change Treaty: The Kyoto Protocol.* Washington, D.C.: National Council for Science and the Environment, 2000. Kyoto Protocol website: <www.unfccc.de/resource/convkp.html>.

L

land mines

As of 2001, there were between 60 million and 110 million land mines deployed in more than 60 countries around the world. Some of the most heavily mine-affected states included AFGHANISTAN, BOSNIA, and CAMBODIA. By 2001, according to international experts, including those from the United Nations, land mines had caused 10,000 deaths and 15,000 injuries in those 60 states annually.

Land mines as a class of WEAPONS do not distinguish between combat forces and civilians. In fact, 80 to 90 percent of land mine victims have been civilians. Furthermore, land mines continue to kill and maim long after emplacement, well after hostilities have ended. In addition to their savage civilian toll, land mines hinder economic development and the repatriation of refugees and displaced persons. These devastating effects have prompted the United Nations to support numerous mine clearing projects. The UN Mine Action Service is a cooperative effort between the UN and NON-GOVERNMENTAL ORGANIZATIONS such as Handicap International and the Vietnam Veterans of America Foundation. The UN Mine Action Service has been involved in de-mining activities in states such as Azerbaijan, Cambodia, and Lebanon. The UNITED NATIONS OFFICE OF PROJECT SERVICES also provides extensive de-mining services in states where UN PEACEKEEPING operations are underway.

The SECRETARY-GENERAL and GENERAL ASSEMBLY have addressed the issue of land mines in reports and RESOLU-TIONS. In 1995, the Secretary-General issued a report entitled "Assistance in Mine Clearance." During the 1990s the General Assembly adopted resolutions 48/75K, 49/75D, 50/70O, 51/45S, 52/38A, 53/77N and 54/54B. Resolutions 49/75D and 50/70O made the elimination of anti-personnel land mines a goal of the international community. Together with resolution 48/75K, these resolutions urged a moratorium on a export of anti-personnel land mines. Resolution 51/45S urged states to pursue vigorously an effective, legally binding international agreement to ban the use, stockpiling, production, and transfer of anti-personnel land mines. This international agreement was realized in 1997 with the signing of the CONVENTION ON THE PROHIBITION OF THE USE, STOCKPILING, PRODUCTION AND TRANSFER OF ANTI-PERSONNEL MINES AND THEIR DESTRUCTION in Ottawa, Canada. Resolutions 52/38A, 53/77N, and 54/54B invited all states to sign the Ottawa Convention and urged signatories to ratify the CONVENTION without delay.

Further Reading: Cameron, M., R. Lawson, and B. Tomlin. *To Walk without Fear: The Global Movement to Ban Landmines.* Toronto: Oxford University Press, 1998. *Landmine Monitor Report 1999 or 2000: Toward A Mine-Free World.* Vines, A., and H. Thompson. "Beyond the Landmine Ban: Eradicating a Lethal Legacy." *Conflict Studies,* 316 (March 1999): 1–37. International Campaign to Ban Landmines website: <www.icbl.org>.

— S. F. McMahon

Deactivating mines in Cambodia (UN PHOTO 159491
J. BLEIBTREU)

languages, United Nations official and working

The official languages of the United Nations are Arabic, Chinese, English, French, Russian, and Spanish. Simultaneous translation into the official languages is provided in official meetings of UN organs and conferences. The UN website also is accessible in these languages. The working languages of the United Nations, however, are French and English. All UN documents are translated into these two languages. They, therefore, have more prominence in UN meetings, publications, and activities than the other four. There is even an intermixing of French and English in official titles and documents. For example, British English terms such as *centre* and *programme* are used universally in UN documents and publications.

Latin America

As a result of the region's participation in World War II as part of the Grand Alliance, 20 countries within the Western Hemisphere entered the United Nations as charter members on October 24, 1945: Argentina, Bolivia, Brazil, Chile, Colombia, Costa Rica, CUBA, the Dominican Republic, Ecuador, EL SALVADOR, GUATEMALA, HAITI, Honduras, Mexico, Nicaragua, Panama, Paraguay, Peru, Uruguay, and Venezuela.

Latin American leaders have been active in the leadership of the United Nations since its inception. Most notably, Javier PÉREZ DE CUÉLLAR served as SECRETARY-GENERAL between 1982 and 1992.

The region and its problems have been important concerns for a number of UN organizations. The Economic Commission for Latin America (ECLA), founded in 1948, helped promote policy shifts that aimed at the creation of sustained economic expansion and modernization within the region. In 1985, the body evolved into the ECONOMIC COMMISSION FOR LATIN AMERICA AND THE CARIBBEAN (ECLAC). Other UN bodies that have become involved in Latin American economic, social, and cultural issues include: UNESCO (UNITED NATIONS EDUCATIONAL AND CULTURAL ORGANIZATION, established in 1945), UNICEF (UNITED NATIONS CHILDREN'S FUND, 1946), UNIDO (UNITED NATIONS INDUSTRIAL DEVELOPMENT ORGANIZATION, 1966), and WHO (WORLD HEALTH ORGANIZATION, 1948).

Three controversies affecting the region marked the early history of the United Nations. The strained diplomatic relations between the UNITED STATES and Argentina as a result of the latter's neutrality in World War II led to a push to block Argentina from UN MEMBERSHIP. The Argentine government's decision on March 27, 1945, to declare war against the remaining Axis powers, and its subsequent ratification of the RESOLUTIONS issued at the Inter-American Conference on War and Peace Problems at Chapultepec Palace in Mexico City (February 11, 1945) settled existing differences and cleared the way for Argentina's membership.

The push for hemispheric solidarity involving the American states during the years preceding the UN's formation created a second and more serious problem. Latin American leaders sought special recognition from the body for their region's status, as well as guarantees that UN obstruction, resulting from the use of a VETO by a permanent member of the SECURITY COUNCIL or other means, would not interfere with inter-American issues and concerns. Facing an impasse, the United States orchestrated a compromise that recognized the authority of "regional arrangements" to manage local or regional affairs, provided that their activities were "consistent with the Purposes and Principles of the United Nations" (Chapter VIII, Article 52). Additionally, under Article 51 states were permitted to undertake "COLLECTIVE SELF-DEFENSE" until the Security Council had taken sufficient steps to restore peace. The new wording in the CHARTER, however, limited this grant of autonomy by asserting the right of the council to investigate and take action on any threat to the peace. It also allowed any state to bring any dispute directly to the council. Following its establishment in 1948, the ORGANIZATION OF AMERICAN STATES (OAS) took on primary responsibility for ensuring peace and security within Latin America in accordance with the Charter provisions.

Regional interests and concerns over the power of the PERMANENT MEMBERS OF THE SECURITY COUNCIL led to a third impasse. Latin American representatives sought a greater role within the Security Council from the outset. This push generated an effort, led by El Salvador and Brazil, to have Latin America guaranteed representation within the Security Council. El Salvador recommended the addition of more members to the council, which would have raised its original membership from 11 to 15. While the proposal gained support from small states in other regions, Brazil determined instead to seek a permanent seat on the Security Council for one Latin American country. The United States effectively blocked this proposed REFORM. Fearing that expansion would create concerns over a Western bloc within the council, Washington successfully argued that any attempt to alter the council's composition would upset existing settlements and delay the establishment of the United Nations. An informal compromise occurred. Latin American countries were in practice reserved two seats on the Security Council that the regional members shared through a regular rotation. Later, in 1965, the UN GENERAL ASSEMBLY adopted a resolution that increased the size of the Security Council to 15 and formally reserved two of the non-permanent seats for Latin American representatives.

While regional conflicts occasionally gained the attention of the United Nations, Latin America fell into a close partnership with the United States in almost all UN affairs. Rising COLD WAR tensions and the efforts of US policy makers to orchestrate Latin American support, produced a significant American VOTING bloc within the General Assembly that effectively countered challenges through the 1950s. In the first years of the body's operations, the Latin American bloc demonstrated its loyalty to Western interests through its votes on the ADMISSION of new members. Solidly supporting the candidates backed by the United States and its European allies, and voting with near unanimity against those put forward by the Soviet Union, the Latin American countries consistently demonstrated their allegiance to the anticommunist position. Latin American support for the series of resolutions that led to UN intervention in the KOREAN WAR in 1950 clearly demonstrated the success of American efforts to cultivate regional support.

The Guatemala crisis of 1954 strained the ties between the American members of the United Nations. Claiming that the Arbenz administration then ruling Guatemala was communist in its actions and character, the U.S. government helped foment a military coup. Guatemala sought the intervention of the United Nations. It claimed that the invasion of U.S.-backed mercenary groups from Nicaragua and Honduras was an act of AGGRESSION and it requested UN assistance. Honduras, Nicaragua, Colombia, and Brazil challenged the request. Citing Article 33 of CHAPTER VI and 52 (2) of Chapter VIII of the UN Charter, Guatemala's opponents argued that as a regional dispute the matter fell under the JURISDICTION of the Organization of American States. A veto by the USSR blocked a resolution offered by Brazil and Colombia that would have officially called on the OAS to open discussion concerning the situation in Guatemala. In its place, France authored a resolution that called for an end to military action and a commitment from all parties to block any and all assistance to the disputing parties. This resolution passed unanimously. The Soviet Union and Guatemala continued to call for UN action, but a U.S. veto stalled Security Council deliberations. The collapse of the Arbenz government led to an end of UN discussion of the crisis.

The fall of Fulgencio Batista in 1959 transformed Cuba into a catalyst of dramatic shifts in Latin America's role in the United Nations. The CUBAN MISSILE CRISIS of October 1962 brought about an emergency session of the UN Security Council. The United States used the session to justify its actions and establish a UN commission that was to supervise the removal of missiles and missile facilities from Cuba. The representatives of the Latin American delegations, with the exception of Cuba, supported the U.S. position. While a settlement negotiated by the United States and the USSR ended the crisis, the status of Cuba within Latin America and the United Nations generated challenges to the authority of the United States.

Rafael Trujillo's dictatorship in the Dominican Republic also created a crisis that altered inter-American relations. Declaring that civil war in the Dominican Republic threatened regional peace and its own national interests, the United States invaded the island in April 1965. In the wake of such a military intervention, the United Nations authorized its first observer mission. In May 1965 a resolution of the Security Council called for a cease-fire and for the UN Secretary-General to send a representative who would report on the situation. The Mission of the SPECIAL REPRESENTATIVE OF THE SECRETARY-GENERAL to the Dominican Republic remained in place until October 1966, after elections and the withdrawal of an inter-American PEACEKEEPING force had taken place.

Rising nationalist sentiment created a new source of tensions in Panama. Resentment over the continued control of the Canal Zone by the United States led to civil disturbances in the 1950s. Escalating riots in 1964 and the forceful response by U.S. military forces moved the Panamanian government to sever relations with the United States and appeal to the United Nations for redress. Stalled negotiations and intermittent violence led the UN Security Council to meet in Panama City in March 1973. The council aired a proposal to support Panamanian claims of SOVEREIGNTY over all its territories, but a threatened U.S. veto stalled any action. Bilateral negotiations eventually produced a TREATY that accelerated the transfer of authority over the Canal Zone in 1977.

Popular revolutions and fear of U.S. military interventions led Latin America to use the United Nations as a venue for negotiated settlements of recent and long-standing disagreements. The Nicaraguan revolution of 1979 toppled a regime closely allied with the United States. The U.S. government's concerns over the ideological orientation of the revolutionary government and its potential influence over politics in neighboring states led it to sponsor the Contra War. To bring peace and head off greater U.S. involvement in the military and political affairs of Central America, Latin American leaders launched the Contadora Peace Project. The UN issued resolutions first in 1983 supporting this effort. When the Contadora process stalled, Latin American leaders enlisted the involvement of the Secretary-General's office in an attempt to develop a regional settlement. The result was christened in 1986 the Rio Group, which launched negotiations and brokered settlements in Nicaragua, El Salvador, and Guatemala. The United Nations Observer Group in Central America, operating between 1989 and 1992, also established a system to demobilize and resettle combatants, verify elections, and reintegrate rebel groups into the political systems of the countries involved.

U.S. diplomatic and military actions weakened the allegiance of Latin America to the American position within the United Nations. The 1982 U.S. decision to aid Great Britain and to defend the British position in the United Nations in relation to the Malvinas (Falklands) Islands War angered many Latin American nations. The U.S. invasion of Grenada in 1983 led to a General Assembly resolution, supported by most Latin American nations, that condemned the intervention. A U.S. veto killed a similar proposal in the Security Council. The December 1989 invasion of Panama by the United States also generated broad criticism within Latin America. A Security Council resolution calling for the immediate withdrawal of U.S. forces failed to gain approval only as a result of vetoes from the United States, Great Britain, and France.

Latin American issues remained of primary importance within the United Nations as the new century began. The mounting debt of Latin American and other developing nations, which the interventions of the WORLD BANK and the INTERNATIONAL MONETARY FUND had not solved, became a growing concern of the United Nations beginning in the 1970s. In 1993, the General Assembly declared the "International Year of the World's INDIGENOUS PEOPLE," and in 1994 it inaugurated the "International Decade of the World's Indigenous People." Focusing UN attention on the rights and contributions of indigenous communities to world affairs, the General Assembly became increasingly active in Latin American conflicts. This attention was most pronounced concerning the central Andes, southern Mexico,

and Central America, as a result of discussions concerning government repression, the drug trade, and SUSTAINABLE DEVELOPMENT.

Within the United Nations, Latin America remained an important part of two recognized blocs. First, regional issues molded a Latin American and Caribbean group that often used the General Assembly as a venue for challenging the authority of the United States. Second, from the 1960s, Latin America increasingly joined in the NON-ALIGNED MOVEMENT when issues concerning economic development and the disparity between the Northern and Southern Hemispheres arose. These blocs were useful in the General Assembly for challenging U.S. policies. However, they have proven to be not particularly cohesive.

See also CAUCUS GROUPS, COMMISSION ON SUSTAINABLE DEVELOPMENT, DESERTIFICATION, DISARMAMENT, FIRST AND THIRD WORLDS, GENERAL COMMITTEE, GROUP OF 77, INTER-AMERICAN DEVELOPMENT BANK, INTERNATIONAL COURT OF JUSTICE, INTERNATIONAL LAW COMMISSION, NON-PERMANENT MEMBERS OF THE SECURITY COUNCIL, NUCLEAR-WEAPONS-FREE ZONES, ORGANIZATION FOR THE PROHIBITION OF CHEMICAL WEAPONS, PREBISCH, REGIONAL ORGANIZATIONS, TREATY OF TLATLELOCO, UNITED NATIONS CONFERENCE ON THE LAW OF THE SEA, UNITED NATIONS CONFERENCE ON TRADE AND DEVELOPMENT, UNITED NATIONS ENVIRONMENT PROGRAMME, YALTA CONFERENCE.

Further Reading: Houston, John A. *Latin America in the United Nations.* New York: Carnegie Endowment for International Peace, 1956. Mingst, Karen A., and Margaret P. Karns. *The United Nations in the Post–Cold War Era.* 2d ed. Boulder, Colo.: Westview Press, 2000. Roberts, Adam, and Benedict Kingsbury, eds. *United Nations, Divided World: The UN's Roles in International Relations.* 2d ed. Oxford: Clarendon Press, 1993.

— *D. K. Lewis*

Law of the Sea   *See* UNITED NATIONS CONFERENCE ON THE LAW OF THE SEA (UNCLOS).

League of Nations

Precursor to the United Nations, the League was founded at the end of World War I on the initiative of U.S. president Woodrow Wilson, who included in his FOURTEEN POINTS of 1918 (at number 14) a proposed league that would be the first world organization for maintaining peace and security, international cooperation, and the development of INTERNATIONAL LAW. The League virtually ceased to function with the outbreak of World War II and in 1946 it officially dissolved itself.

The unrivaled bloodshed and carnage of World War I convinced many leaders of the necessity of a world organization to avert another such conflict, but the intellectual and practical origins of the League preceded the eruption of war in 1914. Eighteenth-century German philosopher Immanuel Kant had envisioned a global organization, and the 19th century had witnessed the growth of numerous international cooperative ventures, including the International Telegraph Union, initiated in 1865, the UNIVERSAL POSTAL UNION, established in 1874, and the International Red Cross, urged by Swiss doctor Jean Henri Dunant after he witnessed the suffering of the wounded in the battle of Solferino in 1859. The Hague Peace Conferences at the beginning of the 20th century and the establishment of the PERMANENT COURT OF ARBITRATION gave further impetus to international cooperation. The war solidified opinion among an active group of diplomats, including South African Jan Smuts, Britain's Lord Robert Cecil, and Frenchman Léon Bourgeois, all advocating a society of nations. As early as 1914 Wilson had spoken with his closest adviser, Colonel Edward House, about the merits of a world association to avoid the kind of war just underway. The president may also have been influenced by the British writer Norman Angell with whom he spoke before publicly articulating his ideas on a league. In 1917, the American Institute of International Law issued a recommendation in Havana, CUBA, calling for a world organization that dovetailed agreeably with Wilson's proposal.

At the Paris Peace Conference in 1919, Wilson insisted on including the COVENANT of the new League in the text of the TREATY of Versailles, designed to end the war. The U.S. president headed a special committee at the conference that crafted the Covenant of the League and made it an "integral part of the General Peace Treaty." The Covenant, coming into force on January 10, 1920, included 26 articles, provided for an Assembly composed of all members, a Council to include PERMANENT MEMBERS from the great powers (at first the United Kingdom, France, Italy, and Japan, later joined by Germany and the Soviet Union), and a SECRETARIAT. Both the Assembly and the Council required unanimity on any decision. The Covenant called for DISARMAMENT, territorial integrity and political independence of NATION-STATES, the establishment of a PERMANENT COURT OF INTERNATIONAL JUSTICE, the end of colonialism by means of a mandate system (whereby existing colonial administrators would prepare colonial areas for independence), international cooperation in humanitarian affairs, and provisions for amending the Covenant. The most controversial provision of the Covenant, highlighted in Article 10, called for COLLECTIVE SECURITY to assure nations League protection against AGGRESSION.

The inaugural session of the League Council was held in Paris in January 1920, but Geneva became the permanent home of the new League, which met at first in the Hôtel National (before construction of the Palais des Nations, which opened in 1936). MEMBERSHIP could be extended to any state, dominion, or even self-governing colony by a two-thirds vote of the Assembly. The original members were the victorious nations from the war. There were 32 such countries, and 29 came into the League initially. The largest victor not to join was the UNITED STATES, which refused to ratify the Treaty of Versailles. In 1920 membership stood at 42 states. Several neutral nations, and the Soviet Union—isolated from world affairs following the Bolshevik Revolution—did not become members in 1920. Germany, unhappy with the peace treaty, did not enter the League until 1926. The Soviet Union joined in 1934, at the very time the strains on the organization were becoming unbearable. The greatest number of members, achieved in 1937, was 58; by 1943 there were only 10. The League's secretaries-general were Sir James Eric Drummond of Great Britain (1920–33), Joseph Avenol of France (1933–40), and Sean Lester of Ireland (1940–46).

The offices of the League Secretariat were in a building along Lake Geneva that in 1924 was renamed the Palais Wilson, following the death of the former president. Sir Drummond, the first, and longest serving, SECRETARY-GENERAL, assembled a genuinely international secretariat, and early on the League realized some successes. It settled a Finnish-Swedish dispute over the Aland Islands in the Gulf of Bothnia (1920–21), guaranteed the security of Albania (1921), aided Austria's economic reconstruction after the war, guided the peaceful division of Upper Silesia between Germany and Poland (1922), and helped prevent hostilities between Greece and Bulgaria in the Balkans (1925). It also extended help to refugees, worked to suppress the white slave trade and to restrain the traffic in opium, and published surveys and data on a number of pressing international issues such as world health, labor conditions, and economics. But intractable problems confronted the League. For one, without the United States as a member, the League lacked an influential player in world affairs. The problem of including the Soviet Union in international diplomacy was not resolved until quite late in the League's history. Moreover, the worldwide depression that engulfed most countries by the 1930s made it even more difficult to deal with nations seeking to look out for their own interests. Then, as the dismantling of world order ensued, the League seemed destined to sit aside as aggressions proceeded. The League could do nothing as the French and Belgians occupied the Ruhr in 1923, the Japanese invaded Manchuria in 1931 (when the League accepted the U.S. policy—called the STIMSON DOCTRINE—of simply not recognizing the occupation), the Japanese withdrew from League membership (1933), and Bolivia and Paraguay fought the Chaco War (1932–35). In 1935 the League completed a 15-year administration of the Saar territory with a plebiscite, but Germany had already left the League (1933), and in 1935 Italy invaded Ethiopia in defiance of League SANCTIONS. Adolf Hitler's remilitarization of the Rhineland and censure of the Treaty of Versailles foreshadowed an ominous future for the organization. The Spanish Civil War (1936–39), the Japanese invasion of mainland CHINA (1937), appeasement of Hitler at Munich concerning the dismemberment of Czechoslovakia (1938), and German demands on Danzig, Poland, which a League commissioner in the city could not resist, culminated in the outbreak of World War II and the end of the League experiment. The impotence of the League became obvious when in 1939 the Council—for the only time in the League's history—expelled a nation, the Soviet Union, for its attack on Finland, following the German-Soviet PACT of August 23, 1939, by which the two totalitarian regimes agreed to divide Eastern Europe. At the moment of the agreement, war became inevitable, as did the end of the League. Several affiliated organizations and powerful ideas of international cooperation did survive the crisis of World War II, and they merged with the new United Nations after that conflict.

Although the League served as a model for the later United Nations, in important respects the two organizations were different. The League had been ensconced in the full Treaty of Versailles; thus to reject the League the U.S. Senate of necessity had to reject the entire peace agreement. The United Nations, conversely, was purposely separated from the peace treaties that ended World War II; U.S. president Franklin ROOSEVELT, informed by Wilson's lack of success, determined on a separate process of ratification in the United States. The League Covenant had been a traditional agreement among governments, called in the Covenant "The High Contracting Parties." The Preamble of the UN CHARTER began, "We the *peoples* of the United Nations." The League required unanimous votes in both the League Assembly and the League Council, but decision making in the United Nations was deliberately made more flexible. Parties to a dispute before the League were prohibited from VOTING because of the obvious conflict of interest. In the United Nations, in a concession to the realities of power politics, member states have no such limitations. When coupled with the VETO, this means that a PERMANENT MEMBER OF THE SECURITY COUNCIL can block UN action. Finally, it is significant to note that in 1945 the United States, never a member of the League or the Permanent Court of International Justice, eagerly entered the United Nations and determined to play a major role in all the post–World War II international organizations.

See also ADMINISTRATIVE TRIBUNALS, CHAPTER VII, HUMAN RIGHTS, INTERNATIONAL LAW COMMISSION, MULTILATERALISM, NAMIBIA, TRUSTEESHIP SYSTEM, WORLD HEALTH ORGANIZATION.

Further Reading: Carr, E. H. *International Relations between the Two World Wars (1919–1939).* London: Macmillan, 1963. Moore, John Allphin, Jr., and Jerry Pubantz. *To Create a New World? American Presidents and the United Nations.* New York: Peter Lang, 1999. Northedge, F. S. *The League of Nations; Its Life and Times, 1920–1946.* New York: Holmes

and Meier, 1986. Rovine, Arthur W. *The First Fifty Years: The Secretary-General in World Politics, 1920–1970.* Leiden: A. W. Sijthoff, 1970.

least developed countries (LDC)

The term "Least Developed Country" is an official UN designation identifying the "poorest of the poor" countries with the greatest need of development assistance. The expression emerged in recognition of the inadequacy of the terms "Third World" and "developing nations," which served only to distinguish these nations from developed states, more correctly called industrialized countries. In recognition of the reality that the general category of "developing countries" included large numbers of nations with great differences among them, specialists regularly separated them into several subcategories. The United Nations Committee for Development Planning (CDP), a group of experts established by the ECONOMIC AND SOCIAL COUNCIL (ECOSOC), decided in 1971 that those nations ranking at the bottom of global living standards should be called "Least Developed." The governments of these countries are impoverished by a limited national economy and consequently have the fewest resources to assist their citizens.

The United Nations has developed a set of specific criteria for listing least developed countries. The first is extreme poverty, as demonstrated by a GDP (gross domestic product) per capita of $800 (U.S.) or less. Despite the official $800 ceiling, the vast majority of least developed countries had incomes under $400 in 2002. Indeed, the average per capita GDP of least developed countries is one-quarter of that of all developing countries, with 75 percent of the population in LDCs having an income of less than $2 per day. The second category is weak human resources and infrastructure, as measured by a composite Augmented Physical Quality of Life Index that combines life expectancy at birth, per capita calorie intake, combined primary and secondary school enrollment, and adult literacy. This category underscores the fact that such countries cannot afford to spend adequately on education or health care and usually are unable to produce enough food to feed their people. For example, primary school enrollment rates in least developed countries average 30 percentage points below the overall rate for all developing countries. Secondary school enrollments average 50 percentage points below, and adult literacy rates are less than two-thirds that of all developed countries. Least developed countries average four telephone lines per thousand people, which is one-fiftieth the average in all developing countries. The third criterion is a low level of economic diversification, as measured by a composite Economic Diversification Index, which combines the share of manufacturing in GDP, the share of the labor force employed in industry, annual per capita commercial energy consumption, and the UNCTAD (UNITED NATIONS CONFERENCE ON TRADE AND DEVELOPMENT) Merchandise Export

Concentration Index, measuring the degree of dependence on the export of single commodities and raw materials. Low performance relative to this standard indicates that such nations have very little industrialization and are dependent on the agricultural sector and the export of unprocessed or semi-processed primary commodities. Reflecting this single commodity dependence, the export instability price index of least developed countries is over 50 percent higher than that for all developing countries. LDCs derive the bulk of their energy from fuel-wood. Moreover, the per capita consumption of combined coal, natural gas, oil, and electricity in least developed countries averages one-tenth of the levels of developing countries as a whole.

At the turn of the century, small island developing states insisted that an additional criterion measuring LDCs' environmental vulnerability be added. Officially under consideration was a plan to replace the Economic Diversification Index with an Economic Vulnerability Index, which would reflect exposure to external shocks and highlight the difficulty of countries with very small and undiversified economies in responding to such shocks.

To be classified as "Least Developed," a nation must meet the inclusion thresholds for all three criteria. Countries qualify for "graduation" from the category when they surpass the thresholds for two of the three criteria. The number of least developed countries has remained surprisingly constant, with 49 countries so designated as of 2001. The majority of least developed countries are located in Africa, where more than 30 nations have been so classified, constituting more than half the nations on the continent. The 49 countries officially classified as least developed include: AFGHANISTAN, ANGOLA, Bangladesh, Benin, Bhutan, Burkina Faso, Burundi, CAMBODIA, Cape Verde, Central African Republic, Chad, Comoros, Democratic Republic of the CONGO, Djibouti, Equatorial Guinea, Eritrea, Ethiopia, The Gambia, Guinea, Guinea-Bissau, HAITI, Kiribati, Lao People's Democratic Republic, Lesotho, Liberia, Madagascar, Malawi, Maldives, Mali, Mauritania, Mozambique, Myanmar, Nepal, Niger, Rwanda, Samoa, Sao Tome and Principe, Senegal, SIERRA LEONE, Solomon Islands, SOMALIA, Sudan, Togo, Tuvalu, Uganda, United Republic of Tanzania, Vanuatu, Yemen, and Zambia.

Only Botswana has ever been declared to have "graduated" from the "Least Developed" to the "Middle Income" Category, although in 2001 Maldives was under consideration for the same change in designation. The Economic and Social Council upon recommendation by the CDP assigns countries to the LDC category, reviewing the list every three years. Eritrea was added to the list when it separated from Ethiopia in 1993. In 2000 ECOSOC declared Senegal eligible to be added to the list in 2001 with the requisite government approval.

Aid donors are expected to grant special consideration to least developed countries, providing them with more development assistance, and granting duty-free trade access to the home markets of industrialized donor states. LDCs also qualify for preferential debt relief terms. UN poverty eradication programs are especially targeted at least developed countries. In order to bring world attention and assistance to LDCs, the United Nations has sponsored three WORLD CONFERENCES on least developed countries—in Paris (1981 and 1990) and in Brussels (2001). These conferences have evaluated progress and developed programs and plans of action to address LDCs' problems.

See also CAUCUS GROUPS, SCALE OF ASSESSMENTS, SUSTAINABLE DEVELOPMENT, UNITED NATIONS DEVELOPMENT PROGRAMME.

Further Reading: United Nations Conference on Trade and Development. *The Least Developed Countries Report.* New York and Geneva: United Nations, issued annually. LDC website: <www.unctad.org/en/subsites/ldcs/ldc11.htm>.

— *K. J. Grieb*

Lebanon   *See* ARAB-ISRAELI DISPUTE, UNITED NATIONS INTERIM FORCE IN LEBANON.

Legal Committee   *See* SIXTH COMMITTEE OF THE GENERAL ASSEMBLY.

less developed countries (LDC)

"Less Developed Country" is a designation that applies to the middle segment of developing countries. The inclusive category of "developing countries" describes all states that are not classified as "industrialized countries," or "EITs" (Economies in Transition in the former socialist states of Eastern Europe). Developing countries, often referred to as the Third World, are in UN parlance divided into subcategories.

Congregated within the GROUP OF 77 (G 77) and the NON-ALIGNED MOVEMENT (NAM), developing countries nonetheless differ significantly in their economies and social infrastructure. The United Nations acknowledges these differences by enumerating several categories within the developing group. The official UN terms designate those with the most development as "Middle Income Countries," and the poorest as "LEAST DEVELOPED COUNTRIES." Nations that do not fall under either of these categories, but rather in between them, are the less developed countries. The WORLD BANK refers to them as "Lower-Middle Income Countries," defined as nations with a per capita annual gross domestic product (GDP) of between $750 and $2,995. The World Bank distinguishes this group from what it calls "Upper-Middle Income Countries." Less developed countries comprise about half of all developing countries.

Less developed countries are characterized by a lack of significant industrialization, the export of unprocessed or minimally processed primary commodities, single commodity dependence, a young population, widespread poverty, low government income, low spending in the education and health sectors, a lack of social services, a high degree of illiteracy, the absence of a social safety net for the populace, high debts, and a chronic negative balance of payments.

Less developed countries are not eligible for special aid programs targeted at least developed countries, but they are the recipients of extensive UN programmatic assistance. They are often exempt from international obligations, such as environmental rules, that are imposed on developed states.

See also ADMISSION OF MEMBERS, AGENDA FOR PEACE, AGENDA 21, ENVIRONMENT, EXPANDED PROGRAM OF TECHNICAL ASSISTANCE, FIRST AND THIRD WORLDS, KYOTO PROTOCOL, NEW INTERNATIONAL ECONOMIC ORDER, RIO DECLARATION, SPECIAL UNITED NATIONS FUND FOR ECONOMIC DEVELOPMENT, UNITED NATIONS CONFERENCE ON THE ENVIRONMENT AND DEVELOPMENT, UNITED NATIONS CONFERENCE ON THE HUMAN ENVIRONMENT, UNITED NATIONS DEVELOPMENT PROGRAMME, UNITED NATIONS FRAMEWORK CONVENTION ON CLIMATE CHANGE, UNITED NATIONS OFFICE FOR PROJECT SERVICES.

— K. J. Grieb

Lessons Learned Unit   *See* DEPARTMENT OF
PEACEKEEPING OPERATIONS.

Lie, Trygve Halvadan (1896–1968)

The first SECRETARY-GENERAL of the United Nations was born in Oslo, Norway, in 1896. He studied at Oslo University where he received a law degree in 1919. He became active in the Norwegian Labor Party as a youth, subsequently serving the party as legal adviser to the Norwegian Trade Union Federation and then as national executive secretary. During the 1930s, Lie won a seat in the Norwegian parliament and served as minister of justice in a labor government. When World War II broke out he became minister of supply and shipping, performing a crucial role in saving the Norwegian fleet for the Allies after the Germans had commenced their invasion in 1940. He then fled Norway and, during the war, acted as foreign minister for his homeland's exiled government in London. Lie was head of the Norwegian delegation to the San Francisco UN organizing conference in April 1945, where he played a prominent role in drafting the SECURITY COUNCIL provisions in the new CHARTER. Shortly after the San Francisco meeting, he was reelected to parliament and then chosen foreign minister in a new postwar Labor government, in which capacity he headed the Norwegian delegation to the UN GENERAL ASSEMBLY meeting in London in early 1946. Lie was elected the UN's first Secretary-General on February 1, 1946, being formally installed the next day by the General Assembly.

Lie considered the job of Secretary-General to be one of energetic leadership. During the crisis of the KOREAN WAR his active efforts in negotiations and his support of UN prosecution of the war annoyed the Soviet Union, which perceived him as a tool of American foreign policy. During the McCarthy era of the early 1950s Secretary-General Lie's willingness to fire American employees of the SECRETARIAT who came under suspicion as communist infiltrators reenforced the Soviet view. When 18 American employees asserted their fifth amendment rights against self-incrimination and refused to testify before the Senate Subcommittee on Internal Security in October 1952, Lie fired them on the grounds that they had violated Article 1.4 of the staff regulations, which required that they act in a manner befitting their status as international civil servants. Lie even allowed the U.S. Federal Bureau of Investigation to fingerprint and question all American UN officials at the HEADQUARTERS building in New York City.

At the close of his term in 1951 the USSR indicated it would VETO the reelection of Lie. The U.S. government responded that it would support no other candidate. The impasse was finessed by the General Assembly deciding by a vote of 46 in favor, 5 opposed, and 8 abstentions to "continue in office" the Secretary-General for another three years. The Soviet delegation considered the vote illegitimate and subsequently refused to work with Lie, hastening his early retirement. In 1953 he returned to Norway where, before his death in 1968, he continued an active political and diplomatic life, serving as governor of Oslo, minister of industries, and minister of commerce. In 1959 Norwegian king Olav V, asked by the General Assembly to expedite a settle-

Trygve Lie (UNITED NATIONS)

ment of a dispute between Italy and Ethiopia over the borders of SOMALIA, appointed Lie as mediator.

Further Reading: Barnes, James. *Trygve Lie and the Cold War: The UN Secretary-General Pursues Peace.* DeKalb: Northern Illinois University Press, 1989. Cordier, Andrew W., and Wilder Foote. *Public Papers of the Secretaries-General of the United Nations.* New York: Columbia University Press, 1969–1977. Lie, Trygve. *In the Cause of Peace.* New York: Macmillan, 1954.

MacArthur, Douglas   *See* KOREAN WAR.

Main Committees   *See* COMMITTEE SYSTEM OF THE GENERAL ASSEMBLY.

Mao Zedong   *See* CHINA, KOREAN WAR.

mediation
In international affairs mediation is a form of accommodation that involves an active search for a negotiated settlement to a conflict or disagreement between two or more states. Mediation specifically refers to having an agreed-upon impartial third party bring the rival disputants together and offer a settlement. The mediator may shuttle between the adversaries, call meetings, draw up an agenda, and propose solutions. In some instances the parties in disagreement may agree beforehand to accept the final solution of the mediator. The United Nations, particularly via the SECRETARY-GENERAL's office, has often been seen as a potential mediator, although usually with the full concurrence of the five PERMANENT MEMBERS OF THE SECURITY COUNCIL (P5). For example, the Secretary-General's office attempted to provide mediation in the SUEZ CRISIS of 1956, the IRAN HOSTAGE CRISIS (1979–1980), and AFGHANISTAN during the 1980s. U.S. president Jimmy Carter's activities

bringing the Egyptians and Israelis together in the Camp David agreement in the late 1970s was an example of energetic mediation.

See also ARBITRATION, CHAPTER VI, CONCILIATION, CONFLICT RESOLUTION, ECONOMIC COMMUNITY OF WEST AFRICAN STATES, GOOD OFFICES, INDONESIA, ORGANIZATION OF AFRICAN UNITY, PEACEKEEPING.

membership
The United Nations is a universal international organization that, under Article 4 of its CHARTER, is open to all peace-loving states willing and capable of fulfilling their charter obligations. Founded in 1945 with 51 original members, the United Nations included 189 members at the end of 2001. In March 2002, the electorate of Switzerland voted to seek membership. One day after achieving national independence, the East Timor parliament on June 1, 2002, submitted an application for ADMISSION to SECRETARY-GENERAL Kofi ANNAN. The growth in UN membership—the product of COLD WAR politics, decolonization, and the desire for universality—transformed the operations and relationship of the PRINCIPAL ORGANS of the institution from those contemplated by the founding states. It also affected significantly internal UN politics and the agenda of the world body.

CHINA, the UNITED STATES, the Soviet Union, and the United Kingdom committed themselves in the MOSCOW DECLARATION of October 30, 1943, to the creation of a uni-

206

versal organization of "peace-loving states," defined later as those states that had declared war on the Axis powers by March 1, 1945. However, the Charter approved at the San Francisco Conference applied stipulations for membership. According to Article 4, members "must accept the obligations contained in the present Charter and, in the judgment of the Organization, are able and willing to carry out those obligations." The judgment of the organization was to be exercised by a GENERAL ASSEMBLY vote to admit the member on the recommendation of the SECURITY COUNCIL. Following the San Francisco meeting, the allies at the Postdam Conference expanded the pool of potential members by including states that had been neutral during the war, and that had followed a general policy of neutrality, even though the Charter obligated members to support mandatory ENFORCEMENT MEASURES.

As the cold war deepened in the late 1940s, the USSR and the United States invoked these conditions to block the admission of members. Only nine states, out of 31 applicants, became members between 1946 and 1955. [A listing of UN members and the years in which they achieved membership can be found in Appendix C.] A large pro-American majority in the original UN membership allowed the United States to muster the needed votes in the Security Council to block East European candidates that Washington saw as satellite communist regimes, not free to participate in the United Nations independent of Soviet control. Moscow, in turn, used its VETO 47 times prior to 1955 to keep states friendly to the United States from being admitted. The deadlock was resolved in December 1955 with what was known as a "package deal," admitting 16 nations from both the Soviet and Western blocs and thus keeping the VOTING balance little changed.

Separate from cold war politics, rapid decolonization in the 1950s and 1960s placed pressure on the organization for enlargement. Membership grew from 76 at the end of 1955 to 110 in 1962. Almost all of the new members came from the developing world. With their admission, virtually all membership requirements, other than statehood, were set aside. Many of the new members were geographically small and poor, and each often represented only a minute portion of the world's population. By the turn of the century, more than 30 members had populations under one million people. Among the smallest, Tuvalu, admitted in 2000, had a population of 10,000, and Nauru, admitted in 1999, had 11,000.

These states' ability to fulfill Charter obligations was suspect. The General Assembly, however, was willing to accept their applications if they maintained friendly relations with other states, fulfilled other international obligations that they had made, and were committed to using pacific settlement methods to resolve disputes. Worried that it had lost its majority in the world body, the United States raised some precautionary concerns about admitting states that could offer little to preserving world peace and security. At its urging, the Security Council in 1969 established a committee to

consider the MINISTATE PROBLEM. The committee floated the idea of "associated" membership for some small states, but no change in membership requirements eventuated. After 1955 only a few "partitioned" states were initially barred from membership—East and West Germany, North and South Korea, and North and South Vietnam. The Germanies were admitted separately in 1973, and a unified Vietnam gained membership in 1977.

The growth in membership, coupled with the principle of sovereign equality that awarded an equal vote to each member, produced a new majority in the General Assembly, capable of passing sweeping RESOLUTIONS, but without the power or resources to fulfill new UN commitments. That majority also could, and did, shift the agenda of the world body from peace and security interests among the great powers to economic development concerns. The enlarged size of the world body also led to the formation of CAUCUS GROUPS, the expansion of membership on UN bodies like the ECONOMIC AND SOCIAL COUNCIL, and the proliferation of PROGRAMMES AND FUNDS for activities promoted by the new states.

The disintegration of communist regimes in Eastern Europe and of the Soviet Union itself occasioned a new surge in UN membership, raising interesting legal questions about successor states and continuing membership in the world body. When the Soviet Union dissolved in 1991, the Russian Federation notified the UN SECRETARY-GENERAL that it intended to take the Soviet Union's seat on the Security Council as a PERMANENT MEMBER with the veto power. This announcement was endorsed by the other former Soviet republics, and there was no objection from members of either the Security Council or the General Assembly. Ukraine and Belarus were original UN members and thus no action needed to be taken on their membership. All of the other republics were required to apply under Article 4 for membership, and were admitted (with the exception of Georgia) on March 2, 1992. Georgia, locked in a civil war, was finally admitted the following July. In the case of Czechoslovakia (an original member of the United Nations), which ceased to exist on December 31, 1992, two successor states were admitted, the Czech Republic and the Slovak Federal Republic.

Another original UN member, the Socialist Federal Republic of Yugoslavia, was suspended from exercising its rights and privileges in the General Assembly during the 1990s for the violation of UN resolutions pertaining to the Balkans. In 1992, when several of the seceding parts of Yugoslavia were immediately admitted as new members of the United Nations, the Security Council decided that the remaining "Yugoslavia" (Serbia and Montenegro) could not assume the FORMER YUGOSLAVIA's seat and would have to apply for new membership under Article 4. Following the overthrow of President Milosevic, the Republic of Yugoslavia was readmitted on November 1, 2000. In March 2002, leaders from the two remaining republics of the former

Yugoslavia signed a PACT creating a weak confederation to be called Serbia and Montenegro. By thus abandoning the name Yugoslavia, the rump confederation, if approved by parliaments of both republics, would officially end the eight decade long attempt to create a unification of south Slavs.

See also APARTHEID, ARAB-ISRAELI DISPUTE, DISARMAMENT, SUSPENSION AND EXPULSION OF MEMBERS, GROUP OF 77, HAMMARSKJÖLD, HULL, HUMAN RIGHTS, KIM IL-SUNG, LEAGUE OF NATIONS, NATIONAL LIBERATION, NATION-STATE, NEW INTERNATIONAL ECONOMIC ORDER, NON-PERMANENT MEMBERS OF THE SECURITY COUNCIL, PASVOLSKY, ROOSEVELT, SCALE OF ASSESSMENTS, SOVEREIGNTY, STRUCTURE OF THE UNITED NATIONS, UNIVERSAL DECLARATION OF HUMAN RIGHTS, YALTA CONFERENCE.

Further Reading: Riggs, Robert E., and Jack C. Plano. *The United Nations. International Organization and World Politics.* Pacific Grove, Calif.: Brooks/Cole Publishing Company, 1988. Simma, Bruno, ed. *The Charter of the United Nations; A Commentary.* New York: Oxford University Press, 1994. United Nations website: <www.un.org>.

Middle East

See AFGHANISTAN, ARAB-ISRAELI DISPUTE, GULF WAR, IRAN HOSTAGE CRISIS, IRAN-IRAQ WAR, MIDDLE EAST WAR OF 1967, MIDDLE EAST WAR OF 1973, SUEZ CRISIS, UNITED NATIONS INTERIM FORCE IN LEBANON, UN SECURITY COUNCIL RESOLUTION 242, UN SECURITY COUNCIL RESOLUTION 338.

Middle East War of 1967

The Middle East War of 1967 began June 5 and ended June 10. It was initiated by Israel's June 5, 1967, attack on Egypt, Iraq, Jordan, and Syria in which Israeli forces seized Egyptian territory in the Sinai Peninsula, Syrian territory in the Golan Heights, and the land designated by the 1947 UN partition plan for Palestine as the space for the Arab state in Palestine. There is contention as to whether Egyptian president Gamal Abdul NASSER's provocations (for example, his demand that the UN PEACEKEEPING force be removed from Egyptian territory) produced the regional environment for the war or whether Israel's "preemptive strikes" were a product of planned and intentioned belligerency; but what is not contested is that Israel's air force destroyed Egypt's surprised air force and through its territorial occupations tripled the size of 1949 Israel.

Two days after Israel initiated the conflict Jordan agreed to a UN SECURITY COUNCIL cease-fire RESOLUTION, as did Egypt on June 8 and Syria on June 9. Israel continued its attack and did not assent to the UN cease-fire until June 10. The cost to human life of this six-day engagement totaled 5,500 dead on the Israeli side, with Syria suffering 1,800

casualties, Jordan 3,100 casualties, and Egypt almost 18,000 casualties.

The short duration of the war precluded the Security Council from issuing any substantive resolutions. After Israel accepted the cease-fire, the Security Council became deadlocked; the Soviet Union condemned Israel's June 5th attacks on its neighbors and the UNITED STATES condemned subsequent breaches of the established cease-fire. The deadlock was tightened by American threats to VETO the proposals and resolutions emanating from non-permanent Security Council members.

This deadlock in the Security Council effectively handed the issue of the ARAB-ISRAELI CONFLICT over to the GENERAL ASSEMBLY. The futility of handling the conflict, however, spilled over into the larger UN organ and reduced its EMERGENCY SPECIAL SESSIONS into similarly ineffectual endeavors. A joint Soviet Union–Albania resolution was rejected as was an American resolution, a 17-member non-aligned resolution, and a 20-member Latin American resolution. Two resolutions, one a 26-member "humanitarian" resolution and the other a Pakistani resolution denouncing Israel's annexation of Jerusalem, were, however, passed overwhelmingly by the Assembly.

The most significant UN response to the war of 1967 was SECURITY COUNCIL RESOLUTION 242, which was adopted unanimously on November 22. This resolution was introduced by the United Kingdom and called for a withdrawal of Israel's forces from occupied territories, a termination of the states of belligerency, freedom of navigation and a settlement of the refugee problem. It also called on SECRETARY-GENERAL U THANT to designate a UN SPECIAL REPRESENTATIVE to the Middle East, later to be announced as Gunnar Jarring.

Resolution 242 was accepted by Israel, Egypt, and Jordan but rejected by Syria. Resolution 242 signaled Jordan's and Egypt's long withheld acknowledgment of Israel's existence and, because it was premised on the idea of "land for peace," it formed one of the cornerstones for the subsequent regional peace negotiations.

Further Reading: Bickerton, Ian, and Carla Klausner. *A Concise History of the Arab-Israeli Conflict,* 2d ed. Englewood Cliffs, N.J.: Prentice Hall, 1995. Meisler, Stanley. *United Nations: The First Fifty Years.* New York: Atlantic Monthly Press, 1995. Thant, U. *View from the UN.* Garden City, N.Y.: Doubleday, 1978.

— *S. F. McMahon*

Middle East War of 1973

October 6, 1973, was Yom Kippur, the Day of Atonement, the holiest day of the year for Jews. Syria and Egypt chose that date to attack Israel from two fronts. For three days the Arab coalition advanced; Egyptians crossed the Suez Canal,

UN Observer Force monitoring cease-fire in the Golan Heights (UNITED NATIONS/Y. NAGATA)

forced hundreds of Israeli troops to surrender, and recaptured land in the Sinai seized from them in the Israeli victory of 1967. Syria, in the north, nearly broke through Israeli defenses on the Golan Heights. During the first days of the war, neither the UNITED STATES nor the Soviet Union favored an immediate cease-fire RESOLUTION in the SECURITY COUNCIL. Egypt had established a line across the Suez Canal, and the Syrians were well into the Golan Heights, so neither was ready to halt its advance. Israel would not accept any cease-fire that left Arab enemies with gains on the ground. The tide of battle began to turn, however, as American assistance flowed to Tel Aviv. On October 16, Egypt, now under duress in the field, made contact through diplomatic channels with U.S. secretary of state Henry Kissinger, who recommended a cease-fire in place to be followed by "talks under the aegis of the SECRETARY-GENERAL with a view to achieving a settlement in accordance with SECURITY COUNCIL RESOLUTION 242 in all of its parts." Two days later, the Soviet Union offered a draft Security Council resolution calling for (1) a cease-fire in place, (2) withdrawal of Israeli forces to borders implied in Resolution 242, and (3) the commencement of consultations on a peace agreement. In a Moscow meeting

between Kissinger and Soviet leader Leonid Brezhnev a resolution was worked out, accepting the first and third of the Soviet proposals, but altering the second provision to a more equivocal call for the implementation of UN Resolution 242. The carefully calibrated compromise became SECURITY COUNCIL RESOLUTION 338 when it passed the Council at 12:50 A.M., October 22. But the attempted cease-fire did not hold, and on October 25 a message arrived from Egyptian president Anwar Sadat, who said that he would ask the United Nations, not the United States and the Soviet Union, to provide an international PEACEKEEPING force. The Security Council then passed Resolution 340, calling for a "return" to the original cease-fire lines as provided in Resolution 338, and for an augmentation of the international observers in the area to monitor compliance. Early Sunday morning, October 28, under the watchful eye of staff from the UNITED NATIONS TRUCE SUPERVISORY ORGANIZATION, Israeli and Egyptian military representatives faced one another in the Sinai. It was the first time in the 25 years of Israel's history that high-ranking officials from the two nations had met for direct talks.

See also ARAB-ISRAELI DISPUTE.

Further Reading: Bailey, Sydney D. *Four Arab-Israeli Wars and the Peace Process.* London: Macmillan, 1990. Laqueur, Walter, and Barry Rubin. *The Israel-Arab Reader: A Documentary History of the Middle East Conflict.* New York: Penguin Books, 2000.

Military Staff Committee

Article 47 of the UN CHARTER created the Military Staff Committee to "advise and assist" the SECURITY COUNCIL when it decided to use force under CHAPTER VII's provisions for the maintenance of peace and security. Clearly meant to provide the United Nations with its own military capability, Article 47 joined Articles 42, 43, 45, and 46 in producing an extraordinary innovation over previous international organizations such as the LEAGUE OF NATIONS. The Military Staff Committee provisions also were a realization of the wartime allies' expectation that the great powers would have the responsibility and authority to act militarily through UN machinery to preserve peace in the postwar period. The drafters of the Charter also contemplated in Article 26 the committee playing a role in the development of UN DISARMAMENT programs. Yet, despite the intentions of the founders in 1945, the Military Staff Committee quickly fell into disuse, largely ignored after 1946.

The membership of the committee consists of the military chiefs of staff of the Security Council's PERMANENT MEMBERS or their representatives. Charged with "the strategic direction of any armed forces placed at the disposal of the Security Council," the committee became an early victim of the COLD WAR. The permanent members were unable to agree on the kind of forces required or the size each should contribute to the committee's command. Article 43 calls upon member states to negotiate agreements with the United Nations on the provision of national forces and military facilities to the world organization, but no agreements were ever achieved, leaving the Military Staff Committee without troops to command.

During the cold war it was unimaginable that either the UNITED STATES or the Soviet Union, both essential to the effective application of Chapter VII's military articles, would relinquish national control over their armed forces. Only in 1950, while the USSR was boycotting the Security Council, did the committee meet briefly to discuss the response to North Korea's invasion of South Korea. Once the Soviet delegate returned, however, with the weapon of the VETO, military action in the KOREAN WAR had to be taken by individual member states, authorized by pertinent Security Council RESOLUTIONS and the recommendations of the GENERAL ASSEMBLY acting in accordance with the UNITING FOR PEACE RESOLUTION. Even at the close of the cold war, the Security Council preferred to authorize member states to "use all means necessary" to repel the 1990 Iraqi invasion of Kuwait. Some discussions occurred in the committee at the time, but

no effort then or in other operations during the 1990s was made to resuscitate the committee's role under the Charter.

In 1992 SECRETARY-GENERAL Boutros BOUTROS-GHALI alluded to the Military Staff Committee in his *AGENDA FOR PEACE,* a report to the UN membership on the new possibilities for the world body in the post–cold war era. He called upon the Security Council to negotiate agreements under Article 43 with NATION-STATES to place military forces at the disposal of the United Nations, and suggested a role in the use of those forces for the Committee—not in PEACEKEEPING operations, however, but in the application of ENFORCEMENT MEASURES against an aggressor. The Council members demonstrated no interest in Boutros-Ghali's recommendation, not even in giving the committee some capacity for contingency planning. And while Boutros-Ghali's successor, Kofi ANNAN—in his 1997 REFORM proposals—endorsed the previous Secretary-General's call for a UN rapid reaction force to meet immediate threats to the peace, he did not tie this recommendation to a revitalized Military Staff Committee. In stark contrast to expectations in 1945, Annan admitted to the gathering of world leaders at the 2000 MILLENNIUM SUMMIT that "We [the United Nations] are an organization without independent military capability," offering no recommendation to change that reality. The disregard with which the Military Staff Committee continued to be held was reflected in the summer of 2001 when its current members officially complained to the SECRETARIAT about a reallocation of its facilities. Its "changing room" at UN HEADQUARTERS, where its members changed from civilian clothes into their military uniforms prior to their regular meetings, had been converted into a "smoking lounge" for UN diplomats.

See also COLLECTIVE SECURITY, COLLECTIVE SELF-DEFENSE, GULF WAR.

Further Reading: New Zealand Ministry of Foreign Affairs. *United Nations Handbook.* Wellington, N.Z.: Ministry of Foreign Affairs and Trade, published annually. Roberts, Adam, and Benedict Kingsbury, eds. *United Nations, Divided World: The UN's Roles in International Relations.* Oxford: Clarendon Press, 1993.

Millennium Summit

From September 6 to 8, 2000, the Millennium Summit took place in a special room adjacent to the delegates' entrance to UN HEADQUARTERS in New York City. Although other international meetings had counted sizable numbers of delegates, the Millennium Summit reputedly attracted the largest number of heads of state—approximately 150—to a single gathering in the history of the world. They included some 100 presidents, including the president of Switzerland, whose electorate would vote in March 2002 to become a UN member, about 50 other government leaders, three crown princes, and a few vice presidents, deputy prime ministers, and "high ranking officials," a category that included Palestinian leader Yasser Arafat.

Following the urgings of SECRETARY-GENERAL Kofi ANNAN, General Assembly RESOLUTION 202 of December 17, 1998, called for convening the summit as an integral part of—and to initiate—the 2000 Millennium Assembly of the United Nations. By Resolution 254 (March 15, 2000) the GENERAL ASSEMBLY decided that the summit would be composed of plenary sessions and four interactive roundtable sessions, each held simultaneously with a plenary meeting. The UN SECRETARIAT also planned for every participating head of state to be provided time to make an address to the full summit.

Criticized by the conservative American newspaper the *Washington Times* as "a non-event … [and] amusingly reminiscent of an elementary class photo," the summit nonetheless witnessed a total of 273 TREATY actions by participants, resulting in 187 signatures and 86 ratifications or ACCESSIONS. Among those treaties that attracted the most media attention was the CONVENTION on the Rights of the Child, which obtained nearly 60 nations' signatures—and two instant ratifications—for two new optional PROTOCOLS seeking to prevent children under 18 from being recruited into armed conflict, and to bring to an end the sale of children, child prostitution, and child pornography. Also receiving support were the CONVENTION ON THE ELIMINATION OF ALL FORMS OF DISCRIMINATION AGAINST WOMEN (57 signatures and one ratification for an optional protocol), the Rome Statute of the INTERNATIONAL CRIMINAL COURT (12 signatures and four ratifications), the International Convention for the Suppression of the Financing of TERRORISM (10 signatures and two ratifications), and the Convention on the Safety of UN Personnel (seven ratifications and accessions). Observing this prodigious activity, Mary Robinson, the UN HIGH COMMISSIONER FOR HUMAN RIGHTS (UNHCHR) mused that "ratification of [these] treaties will be the first indicator of State willingness to embrace a rights-based order in the new millennium." In fact, at the summit world leaders, in major speeches and in informal comments, reaffirmed their determination to take responsibility for the fate of the United Nations and to try to imbue the world organization with a sense of hope and action for the new millennium.

Heads of Government Security Council Meeting (UN/DPI PHOTO BY MILTON GRANT)

By the conclusion of the summit, the assembled nations, often with very divergent views about issues like DEVELOPMENT and HUMAN RIGHTS, overwhelmingly approved a DECLARATION of the world's hopes for the 21st century. They agreed on six "fundamental values" essential to international relations: freedom, equality, solidarity, tolerance, respect for nature, and a sense of shared responsibility. The declaration also set specific goals, including to halve by 2015 the number of people living on less than $1 a day or living in hunger or having no access to clean water, to assure that by 2015 all children complete primary school and that there is no gender inequality in education, to reduce maternal mortality by three-fourths and the deaths of children under five by two-thirds, to stop the spread of HIV/AIDS, malaria, and other infectious diseases, to achieve significant improvement in the lives of at least 100 million slum dwellers, to promote gender equality and the empowerment of WOMEN, to encourage the pharmaceutical industry to make essential drugs more widely available, and to provide the benefits of new technologies to all the world's peoples.

Some 8,000 delegates and 4,500 Secretariat employees attended the summit, and 5,500 journalists covered the gathering. About 185 meetings between government leaders took place at UN headquarters. Dozens more were held at hotels and diplomatic MISSIONS around New York City.

Among the most prominently reported of these collateral meetings or encounters were a high profile handshake between U.S. president Bill Clinton and Cuban president Fidel Castro, and attendance by President Clinton and U.S. secretary of state Madeleine Albright at speeches delivered by Iranian president Mohammed Khatami. Secretary-General Kofi Annan, with the complicity of American and Iranian leaders, had worked with diligence to bring about the latter events. He worked up to the last minute to achieve contact between the two nations that had been locked in a pattern of distrust and diplomatic isolation since the Iranian Islamic Revolution began in 1979. The Secretary-General contacted Iranian and U.S. officials to urge the two presidents to sit through the other's major speech at the summit. President Clinton delayed talks with Vietnamese president Tran Duc Luong to remain for President Khatami's address, and Khatami arrived at the United Nations six hours earlier than scheduled to hear President Clinton. Annan also successfully encouraged Ms. Albright to attend President Khatami's address a day earlier at a UNESCO gathering.

Additionally, the various parties involved in the intractable Israeli-Palestinian negotiations, including President Clinton, Palestinian president Yasser Arafat, and Israeli prime minister Ehud Barak, met for extended discussions during the summit, and several leaders held side discussions and meetings over various other topics, including ballistic missile defense policies and all the challenges of globalization. Vladimir Putin's visit to the summit was his first trip to the UNITED STATES as Russian president, and he took the opportunity to call for a ban on militarization of space, offered to host international talks on halting an arms race in space, and engaged in one-on-one talks with a number of other world leaders.

Unfortunately, CONGO president Laurent Kabila was not in attendance, rendering any efforts at peace initiatives in war-plagued central Africa futile, and sad news met the opening of the summit, when an armed mob of 1,000 people stormed a UN refugee operation in West Timor, INDONESIA, demolishing the office and beating to death three unarmed UN workers. Embattled Indonesian president Abdurrahman Wahid, attending the summit, promised to reassert control in West Timor, but his words could hardly placate UN employees, who had seen 193 peacekeepers and civilian workers killed in the line of duty since 1992.

Given this grisly news, it seemed appropriate that, on the eve of the summit, the Secretary-General received a set of recommendations regarding UN PEACEKEEPING policy that he was able to place before the meeting for extended discussion. The international panel making the recommendations was drawn from 10 nations, including the United States and Russia. Named for its chairman, Lakhdar Brahimi, a former foreign minister of Algeria, the BRAHIMI REPORT reflected Secretary-General Annan's new vision for a more robust UN peacekeeping approach, including enhanced funding for such operations, a new information-gathering and analysis office within the United Nations, an integrated task force for each peacekeeping mission—combining political analysis, military operations, civilian police, electoral assistance, aid to refugees and displaced people, finance, logistics, and public information—and streamlined procurement procedures. When the SECURITY COUNCIL met during the summit, the member nations' government leaders occupied the seats normally filled by appointed envoys, and the discussion focused on broadening the role of the Security Council in peacekeeping. The Brahimi Report was central to the discussion and, while there was some demur from Chinese president Jiang Zemin and President Putin regarding more vigorous and intrusive peacekeeping by the UN, a significant number of national leaders echoed President Clinton's and British prime minister Tony Blair's support for the broader view of Secretary-General Annan.

When the summit ended, sober questions remained about the practical effectiveness of such a meeting to address seriously the major problems that afflict the world. As DEPUTY SECRETARY-GENERAL Louise FRÉCHETTE opined, "It is easy to be cynical about these meetings and say, 'Oh, they produce nothing.' But many such gatherings have made a real difference in focusing political energy and raising political will." The summit was certainly a media event, covered each day on television and in the major newspapers of the world. "This has been the mother of all summits," said Singapore's UN representative Kishore Mahbubani. "It also confirmed that the UN provides the only viable setting to develop a village council for a global village." Secretary-General Kofi Annan may have had reason to call the Millennium Summit a "Defining Moment" for the world.

Further Reading: Crossette, Barbara. "UN Meeting Ends with Declaration of Common Values." *New York Times*, September 9, 2000. Farley, Maggie. "Millennium Summit at UN to Draw 150 Leaders." *Los Angeles Times*, September 4, 2000. Schaefer, Bret. "United Nations Non-Event." *Washington Times*, September 23, 2000. The Millennium Summit website: <www.un.org/millennium/summit.htm>.

ministate problem

Beginning in 1955 the United Nations experienced an extraordinary growth in MEMBERSHIP that increased the size of the world body from 60 member states in that year to 189 by 2001. Several of the new members came from the Third World and had achieved their statehood through the process of decolonization. Many of them were poor, weak, and small—both in territory and population. Yet, because each state has an equal vote in the United Nations, by the mid-1960s the new members constituted a working UN majority. This was worrisome to several of the great powers who argued that small states, which could not carry the international responsibilities imposed by UN RESOLUTIONS, should not be able to establish by their votes policy, commitments, and agenda for the organization.

In 1969, at American urging, the SECURITY COUNCIL established a Committee of Experts to look at the ministate problem, and to consider suggested changes such as weighted VOTING. The committee held 11 meetings and recommended that a CHARTER revision be considered to allow for "Associated" membership. The matter was put on the Council agenda in 1970, but discussions among Council members resulted in no proposed AMENDMENTS, nor in an effort to tighten membership requirements. Amending the Charter would have required GENERAL ASSEMBLY agreement, which would not have been possible given the large number of small member states. Efforts by the UNITED STATES to impose greater scrutiny in the Security Council on candidates for membership in order to determine if they could meet Article 4's requirement that a member be "able" to carry out its Charter obligations were overwhelmed by the majority's wish to admit as many states as possible. As of December 2001, 41 of the UN's 189 members had populations under one million. When the 34 nations with one to four million people were added, these small states controlled 40 percent of the votes in the organization. The smallest of the ministate members were Tuvalu (10,000 people), Nauru (11,000), Palau (19,000), Liechtenstein (32,000), and Monaco (33,000).

Under the "parliamentary" procedures of UN bodies, ministates, in addition to their votes in the PRINCIPAL ORGANS, could influence policy dramatically through their membership in CAUCUS GROUPS. Small nations that found it difficult to exert influence individually were more likely to agree on a common position representing an entire group. The most influential caucusing groups at the turn of the century were the NON-ALIGNED MOVEMENT and the GROUP OF 77, which represented the developing nations and exerted considerable influence because of the large number of such nations.

missions to the United Nations

Each member state maintains a mission at UN HEADQUARTERS in New York City. Several states also have missions at the UNITED NATIONS OFFICE IN GENEVA (UNOG), where many SPECIALIZED AGENCIES and some UN bodies have their headquarters. Diplomats from the nation's foreign service staff the mission, and representatives from other governmental ministries, including the military, are often stationed there. Their duty is to represent the concerns of their government in all UN bodies.

Missions vary in size, according to the resources individual nations can budget to support them. Most missions include from 6 to 18 diplomats, plus support staff, although they can range from one or two individuals to several hundred. Generally speaking, major industrialized nations maintain the larger missions at the United Nations. Individual governments determine the precise numbers and the ranks of mission personnel. Nations that maintain smaller missions often bring in additional employees on temporary assignment during busy periods, such as when the GENERAL ASSEMBLY is in session.

The head of the mission is the PERMANENT REPRESENTATIVE to the United Nations and holds the rank of ambassador. The ambassador functions as the principal representative of the nation to all UN bodies. The second-ranking individual is the deputy permanent representative. In most missions this deputy will have the rank of minister. Larger missions may include several individuals with the rank of ambassador and have the option of choosing to appoint an individual with that rank as their deputy permanent representative. Major nations often assign an individual with the rank of ambassador to represent them in the ECONOMIC AND SOCIAL COUNCIL (ECOSOC). Most missions are organized into political, economic, and social sections, each headed by a counselor to coordinate diplomatic activity in these areas. Members of the mission serve on the main committees of the General Assembly, ECOSOC and its commissions, UN subcommittees, and other bodies located at UN headquarters.

A country's representatives have a broad range of responsibilities. They deliver speeches describing their nation's viewpoints on the various issues being debated at the United Nations, and they submit reports from their nation to the various UN organs. They also engage in constant negotiations with representatives of other nations in order to shape the RESOLUTIONS and actions of each body, and to reach the necessary consensus upon which all UN bodies function. This requires expertise on a broad range of subjects, since it involves detailed negotiations regarding the content and precise phraseology of each resolution or statement. The members of the mission are also collectively responsible for reporting to their home governments on all aspects of the issues under consideration, the views of their counterparts from other nations, and the status of all proposals and actions at the United Nations.

These diplomats serve not only as representatives to the United Nations but also as representatives interacting on a daily basis with their counterparts from other governments. This feature of the post contrasts to that of ambassadors in individual nations, who interact with only a single government. It is this larger task that endows missions to the United Nations with special status and importance. Smaller nations conduct a major part of their diplomacy at the United Nations, since they often cannot afford to maintain embassies in all nations. The country's UN mission becomes its principal point of contact with the other nations of the world. The permanent representative in this case functions as the member state's representative to the world, and can be called upon to conduct negotiations unrelated to the United Nations. It is for this reason that UN representatives are often seasoned diplomats, and that, for many countries, the UN permanent representative is the second most important member of the nation's foreign service, after the foreign minister. It is not unusual for permanent representatives to ascend to the position of their country's foreign minister, or become a senior member of the government. Even in major nations, the post of permanent representative to the United Nations is considered a senior post outranking ambassadorial appointments to individual countries. For example, in the UNITED STATES, it had become customary for the UN permanent representative to be accorded cabinet status, enabling that individual to participate in policy making at the highest level. President Bush, however, ended that practice in 2001.

Further Reading: UN member state website: <www.un.org/members/index.html>.

— *K. J. Grieb*

Montreal Protocol on Substances that Deplete the Ozone Layer

The Montreal Protocol on Substances that Deplete the Ozone Layer included 176 parties as of 2001. It supplemented the efforts of the VIENNA CONVENTION FOR THE PROTECTION OF THE OZONE LAYER by establishing the goal of using scientific knowledge and technical and economic tools to achieve total elimination of global emissions of ozone-depleting substances. The PROTOCOL was negotiated in 1987 and went into effect on January 1, 1989. For the first time, the international community set specific production and consumption limits on refrigerant and industrial substances known as chlorofluorocarbons (CFCs).

See also ENVIRONMENT, KYOTO PROTOCOL, UNITED NATIONS ENVIRONMENT PROGRAMME.

Moon agreement

The Agreement Governing Activities of States on the Moon and Other Celestial Bodies codified the principles relating to the moon laid out in the 1966 Treaty on the Exploration and Use of Outer Space. It was opened for signature on December 18, 1979, and went into force on July 11, 1984. The terms of the agreement were negotiated in the COMMITTEE ON THE PEACEFUL USES OF OUTER SPACE and its legal subcommittee. Excerpts from the agreement follow.

The States Parties to this Agreement,

Noting the achievements of States in the exploration and use of the moon and other celestial bodies,

Recognizing that the moon, as a natural satellite of the earth, has an important role to play in the exploration of outer space,

Determined to promote on the basis of equality the further development of co-operation among States in the exploration and use of the moon and other celestial bodies,

Desiring to prevent the moon from becoming an area of international conflict,

Bearing in mind the benefits which may be derived from the exploitation of the natural resources of the moon and other celestial bodies,

Recalling the TREATY on Principles Governing the Activities of States in the Exploration and Use of Outer Space, including the Moon and Other Celestial Bodies, the Agreement on the Rescue of Astronauts, the Return of Astronauts and the Return of Objects Launched into Outer Space, the CONVENTION on International Liability for Damage Caused by Space Objects, and the Convention on Registration of Objects Launched into Outer Space,

Taking into account the need to define and develop the provisions of these international instruments in relation to the moon and other celestial bodies, having regard to further progress in the exploration and use of outer space,

Have agreed on the following:

Article 1

1. The provisions of this Agreement relating to the moon shall also apply to other celestial bodies within the solar system, other than the earth, except in so far as specific legal norms enter into force with respect to any of these celestial bodies. . .

Article 2

All activities on the moon, including its exploration and use, shall be carried out in accordance with INTERNATIONAL LAW, in particular the CHARTER OF THE

UNITED NATIONS, and taking into account the DECLARATION on Principles of International Law concerning Friendly Relations and Co-operation Among States in accordance with the Charter of the United Nations, adopted by the GENERAL ASSEMBLY on 24 October 1970, in the interests of maintaining international peace and security and promoting international co-operation and mutual understanding, and with due regard to the corresponding interests of all other States Parties.

Article 3

1. The moon shall be used by all States Parties exclusively for peaceful purposes.

2. Any threat or use of force or any other hostile act or threat of hostile act on the moon is prohibited. It is likewise prohibited to use the moon in order to commit any such act or to engage in any such threat in relation to the earth, the moon spacecraft, the personnel of spacecraft or man-made space objects.

3. States Parties shall not place in orbit around or other trajectory to or around the moon objects carrying nuclear weapons or any other kinds of WEAPONS OF MASS DESTRUCTION or place or use such weapons on or in the moon.

4. The establishment of military bases, installations and fortifications, the testing of any type of weapons and the conduct of military manoeuvres on the moon shall be forbidden. The use of military personnel for scientific research or for any other peaceful purposes shall not be prohibited. The use of any equipment or facility necessary for peaceful exploration and use of the moon shall also not be prohibited.

Article 4

1. The exploration and use of the moon shall be the province of all mankind and shall be carried out for the benefit and in the interests of all countries, irrespective of their degree of economic or scientific DEVELOPMENT. Due regard shall be paid to the interests of present and future generations as well as to the need to promote higher standards of living and conditions of economic and social progress and development in accordance with the Charter of the United Nations.

2. States Parties shall be guided by the principle of co-operation and mutual assistance in all their activities concerning the exploration and use of the moon. International co-operation in pursuance of this Agreement should be as wide as possible and may take place on a multilateral basis, on a bilateral basis or through international intergovernmental organizations.

Article 5

1. States Parties shall inform the SECRETARY-GENERAL of the United Nations as well as the public and the international scientific community, to the greatest extent feasible and practicable, of their activities concerned with the exploration and use of the moon...

2. If a State Party becomes aware that another State Party plans to operate simultaneously in the same area of or in the same orbit around or trajectory to or around the moon, it shall promptly inform the other State of the timing of and plans for its own operations.

3. In carrying out activities under this Agreement, States Parties shall promptly inform the Secretary-General, as well as the public and the international scientific community, of any phenomena they discover in outer space, including the moon, which could endanger human life or health, as well as of any indication of organic life.

Article 6

1. There shall be freedom of scientific investigation on the moon by all States Parties without discrimination of any kind, on the basis of equality and in accordance with international law.

2. In carrying out scientific investigations and in furtherance of the provisions of this Agreement, the States Parties shall have the right to collect on and remove from the moon samples of its mineral and other substances. Such samples shall remain at the disposal of those States Parties which caused them to be collected and may be used by them for scientific purposes. States Parties shall have regard to the desirability of making a portion of such samples available to other interested States Parties and the international scientific community for scientific investigation. States Parties may in the course of scientific investigations also use mineral and other substances of the moon in quantities appropriate for the support of their missions...

Article 7

1. In exploring and using the moon, States Parties shall take measures to prevent the disruption of the existing balance of its ENVIRONMENT, whether by introducing adverse changes in that environment, by its harmful contamination through the introduction of extra-environmental matter or otherwise. States Parties shall also take measures to avoid harmfully affecting the environment of the earth through the introduction of extraterrestrial matter or otherwise...

Article 8

2 ...States Parties may, in particular:

(a) Land their space objects on the moon and launch them from the moon;

(b) Place their personnel, space vehicles, equipment, facilities, stations and installations anywhere on or below the surface of the moon.

Personnel, space vehicles, equipment, facilities, stations and installations may move or be moved freely over or below the surface of the moon...

Article 9

1. States Parties may establish manned and unmanned stations on the moon. A State Party establishing

a station shall use only that area which is required for the needs of the station and shall immediately inform the Secretary-General of the United Nations of the location and purposes of that station. Subsequently, at annual intervals that State shall likewise inform the Secretary-General whether the station continues in use and whether its purposes have changed…

Article 11

1. The moon and its natural resources are the common heritage of mankind, which finds its expression in the provisions of this Agreement and in particular in paragraph 5 of this article.

2. The moon is not subject to national appropriation by any claim of SOVEREIGNTY, by means of use or occupation, or by any other means.

3. Neither the surface nor the subsurface of the moon, nor any part thereof or natural resources in place, shall become property of any State, international intergovernmental or NON-GOVERNMENTAL ORGANIZATION, national organization or non-governmental entity or of any natural person. The placement of personnel, space vehicles, equipment, facilities, stations and installations on or below the surface of the moon, including structures connected with its surface or subsurface, shall not create a right of ownership over the surface or the subsurface of the moon or any areas thereof. The foregoing provisions are without prejudice to the international regime referred to in paragraph 5 of this article…

Article 18

Ten years after the entry into force of this Agreement, the question of the review of the Agreement shall be included in the provisional agenda of the General Assembly of the United Nations in order to consider, in the light of past application of the Agreement, whether it requires revision. However, at any time after the Agreement has been in force for five years, the Secretary-General of the United Nations, as depository, shall, at the request of one third of the States Parties to the Agreement and with the concurrence of the majority of the States Parties, convene a conference of the States Parties to review this Agreement. A review conference shall also consider the question of the implementation of the provisions of article 11, paragraph 5, on the basis of the principle referred to in paragraph 1 of that article and taking into account in particular any relevant technological developments…

See also DISARMAMENT.

Moscow Conference of Foreign Ministers

The first serious effort of the administration of U.S. president Franklin ROOSEVELT to convince America's major allies—the Soviet Union and the United Kingdom—of the merits of a postwar international organization was made in Moscow in October 1943. At the Moscow Conference of Foreign Ministers, Cordell HULL of the UNITED STATES, Anthony EDEN of Britain, V. I. Molotov of the USSR, and Foo Ping-sheung of CHINA signed the Moscow Declaration on General Security. The DECLARATION pledged continuing wartime cooperation "for the organization and maintenance of peace and security" and explicitly announced "the necessity of establishing at the earliest practicable date a general international organization."

U.S. secretary of state Hull had set up a special committee in the State Department to draw up a draft CHARTER for the new organization. By the fall of 1943 Roosevelt was prepared to have the secretary pursue the project with vigor. Hull traveled to Russia hoping to convince the Soviets that cooperation in a global organization would serve their interests. Up to that time Joseph STALIN's preference had been to ensure postwar military security by way of regional spheres of influence. Stalin's foreign minister, Vyacheslav Molotov, insisted on assurances from the American and British delegations that a western front in the war would be opened during 1944 and that the USSR would have freedom of action in Eastern Europe before the Soviets would consider the idea of a general international organization. Once agreement was reached on those matters, Stalin's government gave its support to the American proposal. Thus, of high significance at the Moscow conference was the commitment of the Soviet Union to the establishment of a world organization.

See also QUADRANT CONFERENCE, TEHERAN CONFERENCE.

Further Reading: Hoopes, Townsend, and Douglas Brinkley. *FDR and the Creation of the U.N.* New Haven, Conn.: Yale University Press, 1997. Moore, John Allphin, Jr., and Jerry Pubantz. *To Create a New World? American Presidents and the United Nations.* New York: Peter Lang Publishers, 1999.

Moscow Declaration   *See* MOSCOW CONFERENCE OF FOREIGN MINISTERS.

Mozambique   *See* UNITED NATIONS OPERATION IN MOZAMBIQUE.

Multilateral Development Bank (MDB)   *See* REGIONAL DEVELOPMENT BANKS.

Multilateral Financial Institution (MFI)   *See* REGIONAL DEVELOPMENT BANKS.

Multilateral Investment Guarantee Agency (MIGA)   *See* WORLD BANK.

multilateralism

Multilateralism is defined as the managing of relations among three or more states within the STRUCTURE of international institutions/organizations. Multilateralism is an organizing principle premised on the ideas of indivisibility (recognition that the effects of political and economic vicissitudes have the potential to spill over national boundaries), generalized principles of conduct (modifying behavior to conform to established norms), and diffuse reciprocity (more enduring expectation of benefits to be derived from coordination).

Multilateral activity has assumed the forms of congresses, conferences, and organizations and has addressed itself to myriad issues. Economic relations were and are the focus of such multilateral institutions as the BRETTON WOODS agreements (establishing the INTERNATIONAL MONETARY FUND [IMF] and WORLD BANK) and the WORLD TRADE ORGANIZATION (WTO). Matters of peace and security have been the concern of the Concert of Europe, the LEAGUE OF NATIONS, and the United Nations. Other examples of multilateralism in practice are the European Union (EU), the Association of Southeast Asian Nations (ASEAN), and the ORGANIZATION OF AFRICAN UNITY (OAU).

Conceptualizations and practices of multilateralism have changed and continue to change, and this morphing of multilateralism is often tied to REFORM OF THE UNITED NATIONS. Changing multilateralism and UN reform are connected because as the concept has proven malleable the practical deployment of the concept has increased. The conceptual definition has started to address demands for inclusion of non-state actors, particularly civil society organizations, and this is reflected practically in the UN's attempts to include NON-GOVERNMENTAL ORGANIZATIONS (NGOs) in its daily operations.

See also REGIONAL ORGANIZATIONS, UNITED NATIONS CONFERENCE ON INTERNATIONAL ORGANIZATION, WORLD CONFERENCES.

Further Reading: Cox, Robert. "Multilateralism and World Order." *Review of International Studies* 18, no. 2 (April 1992): 161–80. Knight, W. Andy. *Adapting the United Nations to a Post Modern Era: Lessons Learned.* London: Macmillan Press, 2000. Ruggie, John. *Multilateralism Matters: The Theory and Praxis of an Institutional Form.* New York: Columbia University Press, 1993.

— *S. F. McMahon*

Nairobi Conference   *See* WORLD CONFERENCES ON
WOMEN.

Namibia

Namibia, known until 1968 as South-West Africa, became a
colony of Germany in 1884. With Germany's defeat in World
War I, Namibia was classified under Article 22 of the LEAGUE
OF NATIONS Covenant as a class "C" mandate. This designation enabled South Africa to administer Namibia as a part of
its territory beginning in 1920. Directly contradicting the
League's ideas of self-determination, the white government
of South Africa required black Africans to carry passbooks
and live on segregated reserves, took traditional lands, and
appointed and dismissed black political leaders.

In 1946, the UN GENERAL ASSEMBLY (GA) passed Resolution 11(I) that encouraged all mandatory states to end their
trusteeship agreements. Instead of complying, South Africa
asked for UN consent to incorporate fully Namibia into its
territory on grounds that the region lacked the economic
and social development to achieve self-government. Refusing
to consent, the GA recommended that Namibia be placed
under the international TRUSTEESHIP SYSTEM (Res. 65[I]).
South Africa indicated that it would not incorporate Namibia
in 1947, though it would continue to apply the League of
Nations mandate to it. By 1949, the government in Pretoria
refused to submit reports on Namibia to the UN and formally imposed APARTHEID policies on the territory.

As a result, the GA requested that the INTERNATIONAL
COURT OF JUSTICE (ICJ) issue an advisory opinion regarding
the status of Namibia. In 1950, the ICJ ruled that Namibia
was still under the 1920 international mandate, but that the
UN could play a supervisory role over the territory. In 1956,
the ICJ decided that the GA had the right to adopt RESOLU-
TIONS and hear petitions concerning Namibia. Yet, in a disappointing 1966 decision, the ICJ ruled by one vote that
Ethiopia and Liberia (original League members) had no legal
right to charge South Africa with violating the spirit of the
League's mandate system through its indirect incorporation
of Namibia. By 1971, the composition of the ICJ had
changed, and the Court ruled that South Africa's occupation
of Namibia was illegal. In 1973, Pretoria devised its own
internal settlement, the Turnhalle system, which dispersed
the majority black population into distinct, separate ethnic
homelands. The UN rejected this proposal.

From the late 1960s until independence, the UN-recog-
nized South-West Africa People's Organization (SWAPO)
actively resisted South Africa's domination. The SWAPO
army—the People's Liberation Army of Namibia (PLAN)—
received arms from ANGOLA, Zambia, and the USSR. Reacting to PLAN, the South African Defense Force (SADF)
stepped up its repression in northern Namibia, deployed special forces, drafted blacks into the SADF, and invaded Angola
to destroy PLAN bases there. In response, Angola requested
military support from Cuban troops. As violence in the
region escalated in the late 1970s, the Western members on

Secretary-General Javier Pérez de Cuéllar in Namibia (UN PHOTO 156770 BY M. GRANT)

the SECURITY COUNCIL (the UNITED STATES, United Kingdom, France, West Germany, and Canada) tried to resolve the issue in order to avoid adopting SANCTIONS against South Africa. This Western Contact Group facilitated indirect talks between South Africa and SWAPO. The Security Council (SC) also passed two resolutions: Resolution 385 (1976), which called for a cease-fire and withdrawal of all forces to bases, and Resolution 435 (1978), which called for Namibia's independence and for free elections based on universal suffrage.

But COLD WAR politics enabled South Africa to stall Namibian independence for more than a decade. Fearing communism in Angola, the United States, during the 1980s, vetoed SC resolutions calling for mandatory sanctions on South Africa, refused to condemn SADF raids into neighboring states, and began to support militarily the UNITA (National Union for the Total Independence of Angola) rebels against the Angolan government (which was being aided by Cuban forces). Under U.S.-guided diplomatic efforts, South Africa's adherence to S/RES 385 and 435 was linked in negotiations to the removal of Cuban troops from Angola. By 1988, the high physical and monetary cost of war

and the changing relationship between the United States and the USSR led South Africa, Angola, and CUBA to sign the Geneva PROTOCOL and Tripartite Agreement. These set target dates for the implementation of S/RES 385 and 435, provided for a cease-fire, mandated South African and Cuban withdrawals from Namibia and Angola, and required free elections in Namibia.

The Security Council designed the UNITED NATIONS TRANSITIONAL ASSISTANCE GROUP (UNTAG) to assist with the independence process and to protect Namibians from South African biases during the transition. UNTAG educated and registered voters, oversaw the 1989 elections for a constituent assembly, assisted in Namibian refugee repatriation, and confirmed that troops were confined to bases. UNTAG contained 1,500 police monitors, 2,000 civilians, and 4,650 military personnel, though this last number was decreased from 7,500 at the final minute by the SC PERMANENT MEMBERS to save money. Delays prevented most UNTAG troops from being in Namibia on April 1, 1989, the official beginning date of the cease-fire. On that day, fighting broke out between SWAPO and SADF, almost derailing the peace settlement. Western pressure on South Africa and more rapid deployment of UNTAG forces helped the independence plan to continue. UNTAG declared the elections—in which 96 percent of eligible Namibians voted and SWAPO won a majority—to be free and fair. On March 21, 1990, Namibia achieved full independence and UNTAG left the country. Independent Namibia became a member of the UN in April 1990. With a total cost of $368 million, UNTAG was the first mission to go beyond traditional PEACEKEEPING by observing elections, educating voters, and assisting refugees; its success served as a model for UN missions in Central America and CAMBODIA.

See also CONGO; ORGANIZATION OF AFRICAN UNITY; PÉREZ DE CUÉLLAR, JAVIER.

Further Reading: Cliffe, Lionel. *The Transition to Independence in Namibia.* Boulder, Colo.: Lynne Rienner, 1994. Kaela, Laurent. *The Question of Namibia.* New York: St. Martin's, 1996.

— A. S. Patterson

narcotic drugs   *See* COMMISSION ON NARCOTIC DRUGS, OFFICE FOR DRUG CONTROL AND CRIME PREVENTION.

Nasser, Gamal Abdul   *See* ARAB-ISRAELI DISPUTE, SUEZ CRISIS.

nation-building   *See* AGENDA FOR PEACE.

nation-state

In the discourse of modern international affairs some countries or regions appear so dominant that the idea of co-equal nations often seems rather questionable, if not exceptional. Yet, according to Article 4 of the UN CHARTER, MEMBERSHIP in the United Nations is open to all "peace-loving" nation-states, and each is deemed equal with all other states in the world (Article 2).

A nation-state is an aggregation of citizens who share important phenomena in common—language, history, culture, a sense of destiny, sometimes a shared religion and ethnicity, and, most importantly, a definable geographic area. Such a nation-state is considered sovereign.

The nation-state is the prevailing political entity of modern history. Although it is a fairly recent historical occurrence, it remained, at the commencement of the third millennium, the principal unit of international relations. Before the 16th century most people were congregated into either large empires—the Roman Empire and the Ottoman Empire give example—large religious entities—Christendom, for example—smaller entities, such as city-states (ancient Athens, Venice in the early modern period, Singa-

pore in more recent times), or in ethnically based tribal entities (in the Americas, Africa, and in other localities). The nation-state developed in Europe from the 16th to the 19th centuries, first after the collapse of the Holy Roman Empire, and then, particularly with regard to Germany and Italy, in response to romantic notions of "national" solidarity in the face of other powerful nation-states, such as the United Kingdom and France, that had developed much earlier.

The nation-state early claimed exclusive and monopolistic authority, or SOVEREIGNTY, within a defined territorial area. Early nation-states were ruled by monarchs, usually "absolute" monarchs, such as Louis XIV in 17th-century France. With this development came the emergence of modern international relations, which featured the interaction of sovereign nation-states in all variety of political and economic matters. However, it was the 19th century that witnessed the fusion of "nation" with "state," dovetailing the idea of cultural homogeneity with supreme political organization and political grouping of a peculiar people, considered the "nation." In a world of colonial powers, the desire of subjugated peoples for their own independent states produced the phenomenon of self-determination movements. U.S. president Woodrow Wilson promoted self-determination as a legal principle among the FOURTEEN POINTS proclaimed in 1918. Article 1 of the UN Charter enshrined self-determination of the nation-state as a fundamental principle of INTERNATIONAL LAW. In the 20th century, this notion of a people and a geographic area merged, in various parts of the world, with a notion of a homogeneous or fused nationality, ominously in "Palestine," "Israel," and the fractured parts of the FORMER YUGOSLAVIA, as well as elsewhere, threatening the survival of multinational states.

The 20th century witnessed the trend toward cooperation among nation-states in the formation of increasingly formal international and supranational political organizations. Some of these were regional in nature, such as the European Union. The LEAGUE OF NATIONS, predecessor of the United Nations, was the first effort to create a "universal" international organization based on the rule of law and committed to limiting the anarchy of an international system made up of sovereign nation-states. Still, as the 21st century began, the nation-state was considered the most viable and vibrant force in international relations.

See also BOSNIA, COLLECTIVE SECURITY SYSTEM, EAST TIMOR DISPUTE, FORMER YUGOSLAVIA, NATIONAL LIBERATION.

national liberation

Emancipating a "nation" from outside or unwanted control is the aim of national liberation movements. Thus "national liberation" refers to the efforts of a people—sometimes an ethnic group, sometimes a political party, sometimes a self-defined "nation"—to free itself from colonial control or from any kind of oppressive rule. Wars of national liberation, then, seek to realize independence from outside or repressive regimes. The American and French Revolutions have often been considered the first successful "national liberation movements" of modern history in that the first event led to the liberation of 13 colonies from an external, imperial overlord and during the French upheaval a "people" freed themselves from an internal, authoritarian monarchy. In the post–World War II period, national liberation struggles became a common phenomenon in world politics and succeeded in establishing the independence of many former colonial possessions in Africa and Asia. Examples spanned the second half of the 20th century and included ancient civilizations such as India (gaining independence from the United Kingdom in 1947), former French colony Vietnam, where national liberation guerrillas fought first the French and then the Americans, and many other polities that became new states and usually were located in the geographic south.

In the 1950s and 1960s, newly liberated nations joined the United Nations, forming the majority of the UN's MEMBERSHIP. The UN CHARTER committed the world body to the principle of self-determination. At the San Francisco Conference in 1945 a DECLARATION on self-determination was included as Chapter V of the Charter. This reflected the Wilsonian principles embodied in the FOURTEEN POINTS. Typically the new states became members of the GROUP OF 77 (G-77) as well.

Other national liberation movements, usually of a leftist political persuasion, fought to overthrow their existing governments. For example, a Cuban rebellion, led by Fidel Castro, succeeded in ousting the existing, and pro-American, government in 1959 and assumed the Cuban membership in the United Nations. CUBA also became a supporter of other similarly motivated national liberation movements.

Some national liberation movements sought to resist and eliminate the "hegemonic" authority of international capitalism, fearing that external financial and commercial power eroded the national culture and subordinated the nation's peoples to the whim of distant financiers. CHINA, under the leadership of Mao Zedong, announced this intention at his Communist Party victory over the Chinese Republicans in 1949.

The Palestine Liberation Organization (PLO), founded in 1964, and led by Yasser Arafat from 1967 into the new century, represented several characteristics of national liberation movements. It sought to resist the intrusion of the State of Israel into territories it believed belonged to the Palestinian people. In effect the PLO defined an Arab population as "Palestinian" by virtue of its residence in the geographic area of Palestine. It organized a political infrastructure and a military arm for guerrilla resistance and it led a diplomatic effort to convince the world of the legitimate national aspirations of the Palestinians. It signed international agreements and succeeded in receiving considerable support in the United

Nations, particularly from nations recently successful in their own national liberation efforts, achieving OBSERVER STATUS in the GENERAL ASSEMBLY in 1974. As of 2001, however, the PLO had not achieved its final aim—a completely independent NATION-STATE.

See also ARAB-ISRAELI DISPUTE, FIRST AND THIRD WORLDS, SPECIAL SESSIONS OF THE GENERAL ASSEMBLY, TERRORISM, TRUSTEESHIP COUNCIL.

Further Reading: Singh, Lalita Prasad. *India and Afro-Asian Independence: Liberation Diplomacy in the United Nations.* New Delhi: National Book Organization, 1993.

NBC-weapons   *See* WEAPONS OF MASS DESTRUCTION.

New International Economic Order (NIEO)

The GROUP OF 77 developing nations (G-77) proposed the New International Economic Order in order to redress global trade imbalances and to REFORM the global trading system, which it perceived as unfair to the developing states. NIEO was proposed at the 1974 SPECIAL SESSION OF THE GENERAL ASSEMBLY on trade and development issues. The proposal described the principal problems facing the LESS DEVELOPED COUNTRIES (LDC) and concluded that only a drastic revision of global trading rules and processes would improve their lot. Beginning with the premise that the existing global trade rules had been developed by the major industrialized states before most of the developing nations received their independence, and, therefore, unfairly discriminated against LDC, the NIEO called for the replacement of the BRETTON WOODS system with a new set of rules to assure that the voices of developing nations were heard. G-77 nations sought more favorable terms of trade for primary commodities, which, they contended, were not priced fairly in the existing trading system. They anticipated that a revaluation of trade effectively would constitute a global redistribution of wealth, their only hope to escape poverty.

The NIEO was based on the theory of "dependency," which contended that the industrialized nations had manipulated the rules to keep the developing nations permanently impoverished and "dependent" on developed nations for goods and support. The existing system underpriced primary commodities, produced mainly in impoverished developing countries, relative to manufactured goods produced principally in wealthy industrialized states. On the basis of the dependency theory Third World countries also pressed for a code of conduct for transnational corporations, and for the CHARTER OF THE ECONOMIC RIGHTS AND DUTIES OF STATES.

The NIEO was proposed at the point when the decolonization process had transformed the MEMBERSHIP of the United Nations, resulting in developing nations becoming a majority in the GENERAL ASSEMBLY. Newly independent states sought to blame their domestic ills on their former colonizers, and to use the forum of the United Nations to criticize world trade policies that seemed to undermine their development policies. Both the G-77 and the NON-ALIGNED MOVEMENT (NAM) promoted the NIEO as the preferred international trade regime in their strident economic debates with the developed states of the FIRST WORLD. Among other changes in the free trade system, these groups, in cooperation with the UNITED NATIONS CONFERENCE ON TRADE AND DEVELOPMENT (UNCTAD), sought, as part of the NIEO, the establishment of commodity agreements, the transfer of technology to the developing world, a generalized system of preferences on tariffs for LDC, support for the creation of producer cartels to negotiate with importing countries, and increased financial aid from the developed North to the SOUTH.

By the mid-1980s, however, as it became apparent that withholding production had little effect on most commodity prices, and that the key to development was foreign direct investment, developing nations modified their objectives considerably and adopted more pragmatic goals. These goals were still based on the NIEO ideology. The most radical ideas—the development of an entire new trading system and a global redistribution of wealth—were abandoned and replaced with calls for debt reduction and debt forgiveness. LDC objectives continued to include special trade privileges, such as tariff exemptions, protection for infant industries in developing nations, commodity price supports, development assistance, export diversification, and guaranteed access to the markets of industrialized countries (especially for LEAST DEVELOPED COUNTRIES). The G-77 and NAM remained committed to its goals, but were more practical and pragmatic in their proposed solutions to the problems of development.

See also ORGANIZATION OF AFRICAN UNITY, RIO DECLARATION, WALDHEIM.

Further Reading: Murphy, Craig. *The Emergence of the NIEO Ideology.* Boulder, Colo.: Westview Press, 1984. Sauvant, Karl P., and Hajo Hasenpflug. *The New International Economic Order: Confrontation or Cooperation between North and South.* Boulder, Colo.: Westview Press, 1977.

— *K. J. Grieb*

Non-Aligned Movement (NAM)

The Non-Aligned Movement is the most significant CAUCUS GROUP in the UNITED NATIONS SYSTEM. Along with the GROUP OF 77, it represents the interests of the developing nations in global diplomacy and in all related meetings and conferences of the United Nations. Originally established to enable newly independent former colonies to resist COLD WAR pressures to affiliate with either of the two superpowers, the NAM is an informal organization without a regular SEC-RETARIAT. It was established at a summit conference in Belgrade, Yugoslavia, in 1961, after several preliminary meetings. The NAM, therefore, dates from the decade when the rapid end of colonialism brought independence to many African and Asian nations, most ruled by fragile governments in newly established nations. Though small when compared individually with the industrialized nations, these states collectively came to comprise the majority of the members of the United Nations. Since most could not afford diplomatic representation in all capitals, UN HEADQUARTERS became the focal point of their diplomacy and provided a means of contact with other nations and involvement in global affairs. In this situation, solidarity and joint action became essential to these nations.

The NAM was formed to coordinate cooperation in political affairs among developing nations. It sought to span the continental regional blocs. The number and diversity of its member nations in size, economies, characteristics, governments, and ideologies required it to adopt broad stances and focus on global issues. It led the movement against colonialism and APARTHEID, supported the Palestinian cause, and called for development assistance, while attempting to balance itself between the East and West blocs. While the later formation of the G-77 was intended to promote cooperation in economic matters, there was inevitably some overlap between the two groups; essentially they followed each other's lead and adopted identical stands, blurring the distinction between them. As of 2001 the NAM represented 105 member states and the Palestine Liberation Organization (a full member). The People's Republic of CHINA is not a member of the NAM, though it frequently associates itself with the group's positions.

NAM summits are held every three years, with foreign ministers' meetings in between (also held every three years so that the sessions fall midway between the summits). The summit host country becomes the leader and spokesman for the group and provides communications and coordination. The meetings (and hence the leadership) rotate among countries in Asia, Africa, and LATIN AMERICA, with negotiations determining the precise host.

With the end of the cold war, the NAM became the single most important political caucusing bloc at the United Nations, encompassing the largest grouping of member states. As the focus of global diplomacy shifted from the East-West cold war axis to the north-south axis based on economic well-being, the Non-Aligned Movement represented the developing and poor south in seeking concessions and assistance from the industrialized, developed North. Though critics often contended that there was no longer anyone to be non-aligned with, the NAM grew stronger and assumed a more pivotal role as the focus of global politics shifted to the North-South divide. The NAM deals with global issues, insisting that key questions be addressed in global rather than bilateral negotiations, and hence is particularly focused on and seeks prominence at the United Nations. Visitors to UN Headquarters frequently note posted schedules listing the NAM as one of the caucusing groups that meets most frequently.

The NAM stresses discussing all matters at the global level and making decisions at the United Nations by majority vote of all member states, where its members can effectively use their numbers to exert a greater influence. As a result it places particular priority on the GENERAL ASSEMBLY as a major decision-maker and regards the Assembly as the primary organ of the United Nations and the most representative body in the UN system. The NAM is the largest single VOTING bloc in the General Assembly, and its support, or at least forbearance, is required for any item to be adopted by that body, thereby guaranteeing the nations that collectively command less economic and military power but comprise the majority of the world's inhabitants an opportunity to influence the result and to prevent the imposition of the will of the larger economic and military powers. From the point of view of the developing nations, this means the application of the democratic process to decision making to assure that the views of all members, large and small, are able to influence the outcome. The NAM is also prominent in WORLD CONFERENCES and throughout all bodies of the UN system. It influences the selection of the SECRETARY-GENERAL and presses for equitable geographical representation in all UN committees, commissions, bodies, and working groups, and in the UN staff. The NAM is also highly important in the SECURITY COUNCIL, since all developing states that are members of the council regard themselves as representatives of the Non-Aligned Movement, even more so than of their respective regions.

Nations comprising the NAM are strong supporters of the United Nations. They place particular emphasis on the General Assembly, and on the economic and social portions of the UN CHARTER, seeing these issues as equal in importance to international peace and security. Consequently, the NAM seeks to give greater prominence to economic problems and assistance, and to promote greater representation of all nations and people in all UN bodies.

See also CONFERENCE ON DISARMAMENT, RWANDA CRISIS.

Further Reading: Jackson, Richard L. *The Non-aligned; The UN, and the Superpowers.* New York: Praeger, 1983. Kochler, Hans, ed. *The Principles of Non-Alignment.* London: Third World Center, 1982. Mortimore, Robert. *The Third World Coalition in International Politics.* Boulder, Colo.: Westview, 1984.

— *K. J. Grieb*

non-governmental organization (NGO)

A non-governmental organization is any nonprofit, voluntary citizens' group which is organized on a local, national, or international level. Task-oriented and driven by people with a common interest, NGOs perform a variety of services and humanitarian functions, bring citizens' concerns to governments, monitor policies, and encourage political participation at the community level. They provide analysis and expertise, serve as early warning mechanisms, and help monitor and implement international agreements. Some are organized around specific issues, such as HUMAN RIGHTS, the ENVIRONMENT, or health. Their relationship with offices and agencies of the UNITED NATIONS SYSTEM differs depending on their goals, their venue, and their mandate.

The importance of working with and through NGOs as an integral part of UN information activities was recognized when the DEPARTMENT OF PUBLIC INFORMATION (DPI) was first established in 1946. The GENERAL ASSEMBLY, in its Resolution 13 (I), instructed DPI and its branch offices to "actively assist and encourage national information services, educational institutions and other governmental and non-governmental organizations of all kinds interested in spreading information about the United Nations. For this and other purposes, it should operate a fully equipped reference service, brief or supply lecturers, and make available its publications, documentary films, film strips, posters and other exhibits for use by these agencies and organizations."

Non-governmental organizations may be admitted into a mutually beneficial working relationship with the United Nations by attaining CONSULTATIVE STATUS with the ECONOMIC AND SOCIAL COUNCIL (ECOSOC). This status is based on Article 71 of the CHARTER of the United Nations and on ECOSOC Resolution 31 adopted in 1996. The rights and privileges enumerated in detail in that RESOLUTION enable qualifying organizations to make a contribution to the work programs and goals of the United Nations by serving as technical experts, advisers, and consultants to governments and the SECRETARIAT. Sometimes, as advocacy groups, they espouse UN themes, implementing plans of action, programs, and DECLARATIONS adopted by the United Nations. In concrete terms this entails their participation in ECOSOC and its various subsidiary bodies through attendance at these meetings, and also through oral interventions and written statements on agenda items of those bodies. In addition, organizations qualifying for General Category consultative status may propose new items for consideration by ECOSOC. Organizations granted such status are also invited to attend international conferences called by the United Nations, General Assembly SPECIAL SESSIONS, and other inter-governmental bodies. The participation modalities for NGOs are governed by the rules of procedure of those bodies. By June 2002, there were 2,143 NGOs in consultative status with the Economic and Social Council (ECOSOC), and some 400 NGOs accredited to the COMMISSION ON SUSTAINABLE DEVELOPMENT, a subsidiary body of ECOSOC. Several UN agencies require NGO consultation in their deliberative processes. The JOINT UNITED NATIONS PROGRAMME ON HIV/AIDS (UNAIDS) was the first UN body to welcome NGO representatives to full MEMBERSHIP on its coordinating board.

NGOs that have an informational component in their programs can become associated with the UN Department of Public Information. NGOs associated with DPI disseminate information about the United Nations to their MEMBERSHIP, thereby building knowledge of and support for the organization at the grassroots level. This dissemination includes publicizing UN activities around the world on such issues as peace and security, economic and social development, human rights, humanitarian affairs, and INTERNATIONAL LAW; and promoting UN observances and international years established by the General Assembly to focus world attention on important issues facing humanity. More than 1,500 NGOs with strong information programs on issues of concern to the United Nations are associated with the Department of Public Information, giving the United Nations valuable links around the world.

NGOs at the United Nations have established several bodies to coordinate their activities, two of which deserve special mention. Congo, the Conference on Non-governmental Organizations in consultative status with the Economic and Social Council, serves as a representative voice of NGOs in consultative status before ECOSOC. Its aims are to ensure that they enjoy the fullest opportunities and appropriate facilities for performing their consultative functions, provide a forum on the consultative process, and convene meetings of member organizations to exchange views on matters of common interest. In addition, the DPI/NGO community elects an 18-member DPI/NGO Executive Committee to act in an advisory and liaison capacity to channel information and to represent the interests of NGOs associated with DPI. This committee is made up of NGOs from different parts of the world whose representatives in New York are elected for a period of two years. The Executive Committee collaborates with the DPI/NGO section on events, programs, and initiatives of mutual interest, including organization of the annual DPI/NGO conference.

See also COMMITTEE ON NON-GOVERNMENTAL ORGANIZATIONS, HIV/AIDS, UNITED NATIONS CONFERENCE ON ENVIRONMENT AND DEVELOPMENT, UNITED NATIONS CONFERENCE ON THE HUMAN ENVIRONMENT.

Further Reading: Korey, William. *NGOs and the Universal Declaration of Human Rights.* New York: St. Martin's, 1998. Weiss, Thomas, and Leon Gordenker, eds. *NGOs, the UN, and Global Governance.* Boulder, Colo.: Lynne Reinner, 1996. Willetts, Peter, eds. *The Conscience of the World: The Influence of Non-governmental Organizations in the UN System.* Washington, D.C.: Brookings Institution, 1996.

— *A. I. Maximenko*

non-permanent members of the Security Council

Article 23, Chapter V, of the UN CHARTER, which deals with the MEMBERSHIP of the SECURITY COUNCIL, established five PERMANENT MEMBERS, with the rest of the members of the Council elected by the GENERAL ASSEMBLY. The elected members are referred to as non-permanent members. Originally there were six such members, but the number of non-permanent members increased to 10 by Charter AMENDMENT in 1965 in order to reflect the expanding membership of the United Nations. The non-permanent members are elected for two-year terms and are not eligible for immediate reelection, so that the membership of the Council rotates. Five non-permanent members are elected each year in the fall, at the start of the General Assembly's regular session. Non-permanent members have full powers except for the VETO, which is held only by the five permanent members.

In practice, the member states of the United Nations have agreed on a formula, established by a General Assembly RESOLUTION, to assure that the Security Council is proportionately representative of the overall UN membership. Under this formula, five of the non-permanent seats are allocated to Asia and Africa, which are combined to assure representation of the Middle East, which is not a geographical bloc and spans two continents. This formula allows the single Middle Eastern seat to alternate between Africa and Asia. Two seats are allocated to LATIN AMERICA, two more to the Western Europe and Other group (the Other category is used to add the Western democracies located outside Western Europe, and includes Canada, Australia, and New Zealand), and one to Eastern Europe. Each geographical bloc rotates its allocated Security Council seats among its members.

— *K. J. Grieb*

Non-Self-Governing Territories   *See* TRUSTEESHIP COUNCIL.

North-South relations

The designations of *north* and *south* to indicate economic and political differences are roughly comparable to the terms *First World* and *Third World.* Typically, nations to the north of the equator are considered those that historically were in the forefront of economic and political modernization and benefited most by the industrial revolution. Also, colonial powers usually came from the Northern Hemisphere. Contrariwise, Third World nations and peoples are often located south of the equator, are economically underdeveloped, and often were those countries and areas colonized prior to the last half of the 20th century. Some observers employed the terms *developed* and *developing* to denote differences between nations of the North and nations of the South, although the labels First and Third World came to be more widely used as the 20th century ended. Of course the designations North and South have not always been of precise accuracy in describing the complete configuration of the world's countries. Some developing countries, for example, are found north of the equator, and some developed nations in the south—Australia and New Zealand for example. Also, during the COLD WAR, the Soviet Union and its allies in the Soviet bloc were sometimes placed in yet another category, then called the "Second World."

Still, within the United Nations the idea of different interests and aims between the North and the South have come to have some procedural meaning. Particularly in the GENERAL ASSEMBLY and in the ECONOMIC AND SOCIAL COUNCIL, CAUCUS GROUPS have formed to promote common interests and highlight common concerns for the so-called South. For instance, the GROUP OF 77 was originally organized by Third World nations of the south as a caucus bloc. As of the turn of the century, the group of 77 counted more than 100 countries and most of those were from the Southern Hemisphere. Several of the countries of the South also tended to be non-aligned during the cold war, neither joining Western alliances of northern states, nor Soviet-inspired alliances, such as the Warsaw PACT. These countries, becoming the majority from the 1960s on, often acted together as the largest bloc in UN organs, frequently frustrating the more powerful nations of the North who had instigated the United Nations in the 1940s, and who found it necessary to form their own caucus group, the West European and Other States bloc. During the 1970s, and with less vigor in later years, the countries of the South promoted in the United Nations the idea of a NEW INTERNATIONAL ECONOMIC ORDER in an attempt to create international measures to provide for a significant transfer of economic resources from the North to the South.

Nuclear Non-Proliferation Treaty (NPT)

The Nuclear Non-Proliferation Treaty (opened for signature on July 1, 1968) entered into force in 1970 after five years of negotiations at the EIGHTEEN NATION DISARMAMENT COMMITTEE (ENDC) in Geneva. The NPT, inspired by the "Irish Resolution" first introduced into the GENERAL ASSEMBLY in 1961, is often called the "cornerstone of the arms control nonproliferation regime." The PACT was the direct result of multilateral negotiations on a joint draft submitted by the UNITED STATES and the Soviet Union to the ENDC on August 24, 1967. The NPT's intention was to halt and then reverse the spread of independent control over nuclear weapons. It established in Article IX that only states that had acquired nuclear weapons by January 1, 1967, qualified as Nuclear Weapons States (NWS). All others were considered Non-Nuclear Weapons States (NNWS) and any such state adhering to the NPT was obligated to subject its entire peaceful

nuclear program to the INTERNATIONAL ATOMIC ENERGY AGENCY (IAEA) material accountancy safeguards, and to pledge only to acquire nuclear materials and equipment for peaceful purposes. Conversely the NWS, which happened to be the five PERMANENT MEMBERS of the SECURITY COUNCIL, pledged not to transfer nuclear weapons to any NNWS or to assist it in manufacturing or acquiring nuclear weapons (Article I); to share the benefits of the "Peaceful Atom" with any NNWS party to the TREATY (Articles IV and V); and to pledge to make a "good faith" effort to end the arms race at an "early date" (Article VI).

The treaty called for five-year review conferences (Article VIII) and for a conference 25 years from entry into force for the parties to the treaty to determine whether the treaty should be extended indefinitely or for a period or periods (Article X). That conference, held at the UN in 1995, reached a consensus that a majority of the parties wished to extend the NPT indefinitely. The parties also agreed to an "enhanced" review process to hold all parties "accountable" for their NPT obligations, and the NWS further committed to achieve a COMPREHENSIVE NUCLEAR TEST BAN TREATY (CTBT) by 1996. The CTBT was opened for signature on September 24, 1996. At the Sixth Review Conference in 2000, the NWS issued a statement that they were "unequivocally committed" to fulfilling "all" their obligations under the treaty. Most experts read this to be an affirmation of their agreement to reach a cessation of the nuclear arms race and universal DISARMAMENT, as called for in Article VI.

During the 1990s adherence to the NPT accelerated as long-time holdouts to the treaty like France (1992), CHINA (1992), and South Africa (1991) signed and ratified the treaty. By 2000, only four states stood outside the treaty's framework: CUBA, India, Pakistan, and Israel. Nevertheless, the treaty had vociferous critics. Indian leaders decried the NPT as an unequal treaty that created an unfair caste system of nuclear haves and have-nots. Others, especially in NON-GOVERNMENTAL ORGANIZATIONS (NGOs) and among certain NNWS, objected to the "pace" with which the NWS had moved to eliminate their own weapons and specifically demanded a "date certain" for the abolition of *all* nuclear weapons. On the other hand, some NNWS party to the treaty either violated the NPT (Iraq), attempted to withdraw from it (North Korea), or had their commitment to the treaty questioned by other parties (Iran). Continuing pressure from non-nuclear weapons states, proliferation challenges brought by India's and Pakistan's nuclear weapons tests in 1998, and events outside the treaty's parameters, such as U.S. efforts to alter or abrogate the 1972 Anti-Ballistic Missile Treaty and doubts about the future of the CTBT lowered expectations for success at the Seventh NPT Review Conference in 2005.

See also CONFERENCE ON DISARMAMENT.

Further Reading: Bader, William. *The United States and the Spread of Nuclear Weapons*. New York: Pegasus, 1968. Larson, Thomas. *Disarmament and Soviet Policy, 1964–1968.* Englewood Cliffs, N.J.: Prentice Hall, 1969. United Nations. *United Nations Treaty Series.* New York: United Nations. UN Disarmament Treaty website: <domino.un.org/TreatyStatus.nsf>.

— S. L. Williams

nuclear weapons   *See* DISARMAMENT, WEAPONS OF MASS DESTRUCTION.

nuclear-weapons-free zones

Eliminating, or at least limiting, the possession and use of nuclear WEAPONS has long been a focus of international diplomacy and a frequent subject of debate and negotiations at the United Nations. In view of the COLD WAR stalemate that slowed negotiation of a NUCLEAR NON-PROLIFERATION TREATY in the 1950s and 1960s, regional groupings of states established nuclear-weapons-free zones (NFZ) as a more rapid means of limiting the possession and spread of nuclear weapons. NFZ treaties enabled non-nuclear weapons states to take the initiative in nuclear DISARMAMENT. While limited to portions of the globe, these agreements were easier to reach because they were adopted in regions where none of the nuclear weapons states (that is, nations acknowledged to have nuclear weapons—the UNITED STATES, RUSSIAN FEDERATION, CHINA, the United Kingdom, and France—were located. Establishing such zones proved most difficult in regions that included states with the potential to develop their own nuclear weapons.

Nuclear-weapons-free zone treaties usually extend beyond pledges not to develop, manufacture, store, or station nuclear weapons on the territories of the signatory states. Some include test ban commitments, as well as PROTOCOLS requiring signatory nuclear weapons states to respect the provisions of the TREATY. Some of the accords contained provisions by which nuclear powers renounced the use of nuclear weapons or the threat to use them against nations in the zone.

The ANTARCTIC TREATY of 1959 was the first agreement to limit nuclear proliferation on a regional basis. Sponsored by the nuclear weapons states, the treaty banned the stationing or testing of nuclear weapons on the Antarctic continent. Signatories pledged to demilitarize Antarctica. Recognizing the fragile ENVIRONMENT of the region, the treaty also banned the dumping of radioactive wastes. Verification provisions included required inspections.

Latin American states negotiated the 1967 Treaty for the Prohibition of Nuclear Weapons in LATIN AMERICA and the Caribbean, more commonly referred to as the TREATY OF TLATLELOCO. All Latin American nations signed the treaty, but as of the turn of the century CUBA had not ratified it, the only signatory not to do so. Brazil and Argentina filed reservations, each fearing that the other would develop nuclear weapons, but they resolved their dispute in the 1990s. All five nuclear weapons states signed and ratified the appropriate protocols pledging to respect the zone.

Both Africa and the Middle East sought to develop similar agreements, but it proved far more difficult because of resistance from states in the region with the potential for nuclear weapons development. Although efforts to establish an NFZ in the Middle East continued, with annual RESOLUTIONS of the GENERAL ASSEMBLY calling for such action, the refusal of Israel to participate and its resistance to inspection prevented agreement. In response, several Arab nations declared that they could not sign a treaty regarding nuclear weapons until Israel did so. In the case of Africa, a similar problem existed with the APARTHEID regime in South Africa. The African Nuclear Weapons Free Zone Treaty, more commonly known as the Treaty of Pelindaba, was signed finally in 1996, after the new government of South Africa renounced its right to construct nuclear weapons and announced that it had destroyed all of its nuclear stockpile. When the treaty was first proposed there was another sensitive issue that blocked agreement, namely, French nuclear tests then being conducted in the Sahara Desert. But the progress of decolonization, removing France from its former colonial possessions in north Africa, and the construction of other facilities in the Pacific (for French use) removed this impediment by the time of the treaty signing in 1996, and all five nuclear weapons states agreed to the treaty. Although all African nations signed the accord, ratifications came slowly, and in 2001 the total was still far short of the number necessary to bring it into force.

Efforts to promote a nuclear-weapons-free zone in Asia also proved problematic, due to the presence of two states, India and Pakistan, that refused to renounce the possibility of developing nuclear weapons. The history of warfare between the two since gaining independence from Britain, and the ongoing tension in disputed KASHMIR province caused both to cite national security in preserving their options to develop such weapons. As a result, efforts in Asia moved from promoting a continent-wide NFZ to establishing smaller zones. The presence of the French nuclear-testing facilities in the South Pacific Islands raised particular problems but also strengthened regional resolve. The result was the South Pacific Nuclear Free Zone Treaty, more commonly known as the Treaty of Rarotonga, signed in 1985. This agreement encompassed the South Pacific islands states, Australia, and New Zealand. Four of the five nuclear weapons states signed the accord, with Russia not adhering. Although France signed the treaty, it later conducted a series of nuclear tests in the zone. Another Asian accord was added in 1995, with the signature of the Treaty of the Southeast Asia Nuclear Weapons Free Zone, more commonly known as the Treaty of Bangkok, which encompassed the members of the Association of South East Asian Nations (ASEAN). In the

1990s, after the collapse of the Soviet Union, the newly independent states of central Asia commenced negotiations on the establishment of a Central Asian nuclear free zone, although by July 2001 no treaty had resulted.

In addition to these agreements, related proposals included DECLARATIONS on the Indian Ocean as a zone of peace, and on the entire Southern Hemisphere as either a nuclear-weapons-free zone or a zone of peace. The General Assembly endorsed all such efforts and perennially included nuclear-weapons-free zones on its agenda.

See also FIRST COMMITTEE OF THE GENERAL ASSEMBLY, INTERNATIONAL ATOMIC ENERGY AGENCY.

Further Reading: Larsen, Jeffrey A., and Gregory J. Rattray, eds. *Arms Control: Toward the 21st Century.* Boulder, Colo.: Lynne Rienner, 1996. United Nations Department of Public Information. *The United Nations and Nuclear Non-Proliferation.* New York: United Nations Department of Public Information, 1995. ———. *The United Nations and Nuclear Non-Proliferation.* Volume III of the United Nations Bluebook Series. New York: United Nations Department of Public Information, 1995.

— *K. J. Grieb*

observer status

The United Nations is a universal international organization. As such, MEMBERSHIP is open only to NATION-STATES. However, in the search for universality, and in order to promote cooperation, the GENERAL ASSEMBLY (GA) and SECRETARY-GENERAL have created permanent "Observer Status" for various non-member states, regional groupings of states, and NATIONAL LIBERATION movements. Several SPECIALIZED AGENCIES have also been invited to participate in the Assembly's work, and each maintains a liaison office in New York City to facilitate that relationship. As of February 2002, there were 41 observers, 18 with MISSIONS at UN HEADQUARTERS, and 11 specialized agencies with liaison privileges. All had limited rights to participate in the work of the General Assembly and its subsidiary bodies. Without the privilege of VOTING, or submitting motions and RESOLUTIONS, observer groups could participate in debate and negotiation with member delegations, particularly when UN forums were discussing issues related to their interests and work.

The only reference in the UN CHARTER to non-members of the United Nations participating in UN activities is found in Article 35, which grants to non-member states the right to bring disputes to the attention of the General Assembly and the SECURITY COUNCIL. The creation of observer status, therefore, arose not from Charter provisions but from actions of the Assembly and the Secretary-General. States have achieved observer status by first sending a request to the Secretary-General, who in turn decided whether to grant the request. Using what came to be known as the "Vienna Formula," the Secretary-General granted observer status if the state had a high degree of diplomatic recognition and had a formal relationship with at least one specialized agency. In 2000, Switzerland and the Holy See maintained New York missions as non-member state observers. The former, however, decided in March 2002 to seek full membership in the United Nations.

Pursuant to Chapter VIII of the UN Charter, which recognizes the legitimacy of REGIONAL ORGANIZATIONS in the maintenance of peace and security and in cooperation with the United Nations, the General Assembly granted observer status to regional groupings of states at different points in its history. Observers include the ORGANIZATION OF AMERICAN STATES (Res. 253, October 16, 1948), the League of Arab States (Res., November 1, 1950), the ORGANIZATION OF AFRICAN UNITY (Res. 2011, November 11, 1965), the European Union (Res. 3208, November 11, 1974), the Organization of the Islamic Conference (Res. 3369, November 10, 1975), the Commonwealth Secretariat (Res. 3, October 18, 1976), and the Asian-African Legal Consultative Committee (Res. 2, October 10, 1980). Other inter-governmental organizations that have observer status include the INTERNATIONAL SEABED AUTHORITY, the International Tribunal for the LAW OF THE SEA, the International Union for the Conservation of Nature and Natural Resources, the Caribbean Community, the Commonwealth of Independent States, the Council of Europe, the Andean Community, the African

Development Bank, the PERMANENT COURT OF ARBITRATION, the Agency for the Prohibition of nuclear weapons in LATIN AMERICA and the Caribbean, the Customs Cooperation Council, the Economic Community of Central African States, the Central American Integration System, the Association of Caribbean States, the Latin American Parliament, the Community of Portuguese-Speaking Countries, the Latin American Economic System, the International Criminal Police Organization, the Black Sea Economic Cooperation Organization, the Inter-American Development Bank, the Organization for Economic Cooperation and Development, the Organization for Security and Cooperation in Europe, the Pacific Islands Forum, the Community of Sahelo-Saharan States, and the African, Caribbean and Pacific Group of States.

The General Assembly granted observer status to national liberation movements during the 1970s and 1980s in an effort to encourage decolonization, and to endorse self-determination and statehood. The Assembly "invited" participation by groups in Africa and the Middle East, giving those movements international visibility and legitimacy. In November 1974 the Assembly recognized the Palestine Liberation Organization (PLO) as the "sole legitimate representative of the Palestinian people," and granted it observer status. In December of that year GA Resolution 3280 granted observer status automatically to all national liberation movements recognized by the Organization of African Unity (OAU). That led to UN approval of the African National Congress and the Pan-Africanist Congress as observers. Two years later the SOUTH WEST AFRICAN PEOPLE'S ORGANIZATION was added to the list of observers from the African continent. As of 2001, the PLO—by now identifying its UN observer delegation as "Palestine"—was the only remaining movement with a mission in New York.

See also ARAB-ISRAELI DISPUTE.

Further Reading: Riggs, Robert E., and Jack C. Plano. *The United Nations: International Organization and World Politics.* Pacific Grove, Calif.: Brooks/Cole Publishing Co., 1988. Simma, Bruno, ed. *The Charter of the United Nations: A Commentary.* New York: Oxford University Press, 1994. United Nations Protocol and Liaison Service. *Permanent Missions to the United Nations.* New York: United Nations, 2000.

Office for Drug Control and Crime Prevention (ODCCP)

Founded in 1997 to provide coordination in UN efforts to combat illicit drug trafficking and related organized crime activities, ODCCP consists of the UN International Drug Control Programme (UNDCP) and the United Nations Centre for International Crime Prevention (CICP). ODCCP has a worldwide staff of about 350. Its HEADQUARTERS is in Vienna and it has 22 field offices worldwide. It depends on voluntary contributions for its BUDGET. Its executive director in 2001 was Pino Arlacchi.

The UN International Drug Control Programme, now part of the ODCCP, was founded in 1991. It provides educational materials about the dangers of drug abuse, works to strengthen international efforts against the production and trafficking of narcotic drugs, and encourages alternative DEVELOPMENT projects and crop monitoring programs. UNDCP works closely with more than 1,000 NON-GOVERNMENTAL ORGANIZATIONS to counter drug abuse around the world.

ODCCP's activities are complemented by several other UN bodies, including the COMMISSION ON NARCOTIC DRUGS (CND), established in 1946 by ECOSOC, and the International Narcotics Control Board (INCB), an independent, quasi-judicial body established by the Single Convention on Narcotic Drugs (1961). INCB implements UN drug CONVENTIONS.

Further Reading: United Nations Office for Drug Control and Crime Prevention. *Global Report on Crime and Justice.* New York: Oxford University Press, 1999. ———. *World Drug Report 2000.* New York: Oxford University Press, 2001. UNDCP website:<www.undcp.org>.

Office for the Coordination of Humanitarian Affairs (OCHA)

The United Nations has always been involved in assisting and protecting the civilian victims of conflicts and natural disasters, but such activity increased in volume and complexity in the years following the COLD WAR. With the expansion of PEACEKEEPING operations to include protecting civilians and providing security for humanitarian aid workers, the United Nations found it necessary to develop new, multidimensional institutional mechanisms. Establishing the Department of Humanitarian Affairs (DHA) in 1992 represented the initial effort to deal with these complex humanitarian emergencies.

In 1998 DHA was expanded and renamed the Office for the Coordination of Humanitarian Affairs. It is headed by the UNDER SECRETARY-GENERAL (USG) for humanitarian affairs, who also serves as the UN's emergency relief coordinator. In the latter capacity the USG chairs the Inter-Agency Standing Committee that includes representatives of all major UN offices, SPECIALIZED AGENCIES involved in humanitarian relief, and appropriate major NON-GOVERNMENTAL ORGANIZATIONS (NGOs).

The mandate of OCHA is to coordinate all international humanitarian assistance, contingency planning, and field responses to unexpected emergencies. It also seeks to protect the HUMAN RIGHTS of victims. OCHA designates a UN humanitarian coordinator to oversee efforts in countries where a UN resident coordinator is not already present. The coordinator conducts negotiations with the government of the affected nation in order to assure access to the needy population and security and facilities for relief workers.

OCHA monitors humanitarian developments throughout the world, particularly in vulnerable countries, in order to provide early warning of crises. It also undertakes inter-agency coordination to set priorities for relief efforts and assistance, and tries to assure that major humanitarian issues are addressed even if they fall between the existing mandates of humanitarian organizations. OCHA provides information to help raise global consciousness about humanitarian issues and crises, and works with other agencies to coordinate inter-agency appeals to fund relief efforts. It also serves as a policy advocate for the victims of humanitarian emergencies before all UN bodies and organs.

See also AFGHANISTAN, RWANDA CRISIS, SECRETARIAT, SOMALIA, UNIFIED TASK FORCE.

Further Reading: Inter-Agency Standing Committee. *Humanitarian Action in the 21st Century.* New York: United Nations, 2000. Weiss, Thomas G., and Cindy Collins. *Humanitarian Challenges and Intervention: World Politics and the Dilemmas of Help.* Boulder, Colo.: Westview Press, 1996. OCHA website: <www.reliefweb.int/ocha_ol/index.html>.

— *K. J. Grieb*

Office of Internal Oversight Services (OIOS)
See SECRETARIAT.

Office of Legal Affairs (OLA)   *See* SECRETARIAT.

Office of the United Nations Security Coordinator (UNSECOORD)   *See* SECRETARIAT.

Official Languages   *See* LANGUAGES, UNITED NATIONS OFFICIAL AND WORKING.

Open Skies Proposal   *See* QUANTICO MEETING.

optional clause
Often treaties, PROTOCOLS, and CONVENTIONS contain provisions that require specific assent by NATION-STATES before those states are subject to them, even if they are signatories to the agreement as a whole. This is often a useful device to attract support for the full agreement, while subjecting the state to a controversial provision in the convention only if it has specifically agreed to it. The most famous is Optional Clause 36 (paragraphs 2 and 3) in the STATUTE OF THE INTER-NATIONAL COURT OF JUSTICE. Countries that have accepted this provision allow the Court to adjudicate legal disputes concerning (1) the interpretation of a treaty, (2) any question of INTERNATIONAL LAW, (3) the existence of any fact that may constitute a breach of an international obligation, or (4) the nature and extent of a reparation for such a breach. In the case of the 1965 International Convention on the Elimination of all Forms of Racial Discrimination, Article 14 is an optional clause under which states agree to allow their citizens to submit complaints about domestic racial discrimination to the COMMITTEE ON THE ELIMINATION OF RACIAL DISCRIMINATION (CERD) for investigation and discussion.

See also COMPULSORY JURISDICTION.

Organization for the Prohibition of Chemical Weapons (OPCW)
The 1997 Chemical Weapons Convention (CWC) established the Organization for the Prohibition of Chemical Weapons in The Hague as its implementing institution. With more than 500 staff, including 200 inspectors, OPCW conducted 500 inspections at nearly 260 production and storage sites in 29 countries during its first two years of operation. Headed by José Bustani since its inception, OPCW's Conference of the State Parties (COP) gave him a new four-year term as DIRECTOR-GENERAL in May 2001. However, in April 2002 Bustani was removed from office under pressure from the UNITED STATES, which charged him with poor financial management of the organization. In addition to inspections, the OPCW promotes ACCESSION to the CONVENTION, which had 172 signatories as of the May 2001 COP meeting.

The Conference of the State Parties meets annually, and it is required to convene a review conference on the CWC in the sixth and 11th years after the agreement's entry into force—2003 and 2008, respectively. The COP elects the Executive Council, consisting of 41 states, each serving a two-year term. Seats are allocated on an equitable geographical basis, with Africa having nine seats, three of which must go to countries with the most significant chemical industry. Asia has nine seats with four assigned again to states with extensive chemical facilities. For Eastern Europe the equivalent seats are five and one, for LATIN AMERICA and the Caribbean, seven and three, for Western European and Other States, 10 and five, and an additional seat alternates between Asia and Latin America, including the Caribbean. The Council supervises the day-to-day activities of OPCW, and has policy responsibilities between meetings of the COP.

The director-general oversees the Technical SECRETARIAT and the Scientific Advisory Board. The first of these carries out the verification provisions of the Chemical Weapons Convention, and it is assigned responsibility for aiding any state that becomes a victim of chemical warfare. Given the dual-use character of chemical agents, the Technical Secretariat must be staffed with highly trained chemists, munitions experts, and industrial specialists. The OPCW puts together teams, averaging 14 members, of these experts to inspect military and civilian facilities in the member states. The places and materials to be inspected are selected based on the DECLARATION reports each signatory is required to submit regularly to OPCW. The convention not only prohibits the manufacture and possession of CHEMICAL WEAPONS but also requires the destruction of any existing stockpiles. The CWC provides a timetable spanning 10 years during which a country must eliminate these WEAPONS. The verification teams monitor this process, and they may carry out unscheduled "challenge" inspections when other members to the agreement believe a state is violating the convention. The Scientific Advisory Board consists of independent experts and provides specialized scientific and technological recommendations to the organization.

The OPCW has had difficulty convincing states to submit, in timely fashion, their reports on chemical agents in their possession and on plans for weapons destruction. In some cases, such as that of the RUSSIAN FEDERATION, states have declared a willingness to destroy their chemical weapons but have pleaded a lack of funds for the project. States also have been slow to establish a national authority, as required by the convention, to serve as the liaison with the organization in The Hague. It has also been difficult to obtain financial contributions from parties to the TREATY, as required by the CWC. With many states in arrears, OPCW has had a chronic budgetary shortfall, limiting its work. More ominously, several CWC member states have reinterpreted the treaty provisions in an effort to limit its impact on their military programs, and some suspected chemical weapons states have refused to join the treaty, including North Korea, Egypt, Iraq, Israel, Libya, and Syria.

See also DISARMAMENT.

Further Reading: Moodie, Michael, and Javed Ali, eds. *Synthesis 2000: A Year in Review.* The Hague: Organization for the Prohibition of Chemical Weapons, 2001. Organization for the Prohibition of Chemical Weapons. *Chemical Disarmament: Basic Facts.* 1999 Edition. The Hague: Organization for the Prohibition of Chemical Weapons, 2000. Tucker, Jonathan B., ed. *The Chemical Weapons Convention: Implementation Challenges and Solutions.* Monterey, Calif.: Monterey Institute Studies' Center for Nonproliferation Studies, 2001. OPCW website: <www.opcw.org>.

Organization of African Unity (OAU)

In 1963, the leaders of independent African states formed the Organization of African Unity (OAU). The OAU seeks to facilitate African solidarity and to encourage economic DEVELOPMENT and peace and security on the continent. The OAU secretary-general works closely with the UN SECRETARY-GENERAL on numerous issues, and OAU members play

an influential role in the United Nations. Closely linked to the UN CHARTER, OAU principles include promotion of sovereign equality, noninterference in the internal affairs of states, respect for SOVEREIGNTY and territorial integrity, peaceful settlement of disputes, and the end of colonialism in Africa. At its formation, the OAU agreed that the UN Charter takes precedence over any OAU policy document.

The 53 OAU members gain their strength in the UN from the fact that they comprise approximately one-third of the UN MEMBERSHIP. OAU members lobby the UN to pay attention to issues of African economic and social development and are particularly active in SPECIALIZED AGENCIES such as UNESCO (UNITED NATIONS EDUCATIONAL, SCIENTIFIC AND CULTURAL ORGANIZATION), WHO (WORLD HEALTH ORGANIZATION), UNEP (UNITED NATIONS ENVIRONMENT PROGRAMME), UNCTAD (UNITED NATIONS CONFERENCE ON TRADE AND DEVELOPMENT), UNHCR (UNITED NATIONS HIGH COMMISSIONER FOR REFUGEES), and UNDP (UNITED NATIONS DEVELOPMENT PROGRAMME). OAU members were instrumental in the 1974 GENERAL ASSEMBLY discussions of a NEW INTERNATIONAL ECONOMIC ORDER (NIEO), the development of UNCTAD, and the creation of the first DEVELOPMENT DECADE (A/16/1710; A/17/1785). In 1974, OAU members helped pass a RESOLUTION to prohibit South African participation in the General Assembly. More recently, the OAU created a common position on Africa's external debt and passed a DECLARATION on AIDS in Africa, both of which have informed UN debate on these issues.

The OAU has been closely involved with the UN in the arena of peace and security. The OAU founders established commissions for MEDIATION, CONCILIATION, and ARBITRATION, which have dealt with decolonization, border disputes, interstate conflicts, and internal conflicts. The OAU has also carried out two significant PEACEKEEPING missions: one in 1963 to observe the conflict between Algeria and Morocco, and one in 1981 during the Chad conflict. Since then, the OAU has worked with the United Nations and other subregional organizations such as the ECONOMIC COMMUNITY OF WEST AFRICAN STATES (ECOWAS) and the Southern African Development Community (SADC) to promote peace in Liberia, the Democratic Republic of CONGO, Rwanda, and NAMIBIA. Cooperation between the UN and the OAU has taken the form of consultation, diplomatic support, and technical support provided by the UN Secretary-General to the organization, and co-deployment of UN/OAU monitoring missions. The OAU has been closely involved with the United Nations in negotiation and mediation. In Western Sahara, the UN Secretary-General and the OAU used their GOOD OFFICES to facilitate a cease-fire and settlement agreement in 1988 and to set up a commission to determine eligible voters for a political referendum. In the SOMALIA conflict, OAU leaders met with factional leaders, as directed by SECURITY COUNCIL Resolution 733 of 1992; UNOSOM II also worked closely with the OAU to facilitate a political dialogue in the south.

The OAU provided 50 observers in Rwanda after the 1993 Arusha Accords, which the OAU and United Nations had helped to mediate. The Security Council consulted with OAU officials after the April 1994 GENOCIDE began in Rwanda, and the OAU unsuccessfully lobbied the Security Council in December 1995 to extend UNAMIR's (UNITED NATIONS ASSISTANCE MISSION FOR RWANDA) mandate to help repatriate refugees. The OAU also helped facilitate the peace process in Liberia in 1995, working with the UN Secretary-General's special envoy. As the United Nations seeks to REFORM peacekeeping missions, the OAU has agreed to the necessity of creating a multinational African Defense Force to respond militarily to African crises. Although questions about the force remain, OAU members and industrialized powers plan for Western aid to support the force, which will remain under the operational command of the OAU.

See also HUMAN RIGHTS, MULTILATERALISM, OBSERVER STATUS, REGIONAL ORGANIZATIONS, SIERRA LEONE.

Further Reading: El-Ayouty, Yassin, ed. *The Organization of African Unity after Thirty Years.* New York: Praeger, 1994. Nyangoni, Wellington. *Africa in the United Nations System.* London: Associated University Presses, 1975. United Nations. *Cooperation between the United Nations and the Organization of African Unity, Annual Report by the General Assembly.* New York: United Nations, 1998.

— A. S. Patterson

Organization of American States (OAS)

Created in the wake of World War II, the Organization of American States received special recognition as a regional representative body charged by the United Nations to handle disputes between nations in the Western Hemisphere. The special status of the OAS dates from the efforts by Latin American states to protect and preserve their regional authority within the international framework of interstate and interregional relations established under the auspices of the UN CHARTER. A definition of authority that established working boundaries between the United Nations and REGIONAL ORGANIZATIONS appears in Article 51, Chapter VIII of the Charter. This article approved the rights of individual and COLLECTIVE SELF-DEFENSE orchestrated through regional bodies, and also limited the intervention of the United Nations in regional conflicts only after the efforts of regional bodies had been exhausted.

The OAS was officially constituted at the Ninth International Conference of American States in Bogotá, Colombia, in 1948. Initially conceived as a body that would preserve local authority in the face of potential UN interest or intervention within the Americas, the OAS became increasingly tied to the interests and actions of the UNITED STATES during the COLD WAR. OAS RESOLUTIONS often provided the U.S. government with apparent support for unilateral actions within the Western Hemisphere that it then used to counter potential SANCTIONS from the United Nations. The case of GUATEMALA in 1954, and the series of actions against CUBA between 1959 and 1964 helped create the appearance of international support for the military, diplomatic, and economic actions of the United States through resolutions approved by the OAS.

The Cuban case created conflict between the OAS and the United Nations. As the revolutionary government moved openly toward the adoption of a communist model in the early 1960s, it was sanctioned by the OAS for parting from the group's commitment to anticommunism. The OAS attempt to isolate Cuba led its representatives to seek UN involvement in its escalating conflict with the United States. While the threat of a U.S. VETO effectively blocked SECURITY COUNCIL action, discussion and debate over the U.S.–Cuba conflict challenged the authority and called into question the actions of the OAS.

As cold war tensions eased after 1972, and as regional conflicts, such as those in Nicaragua (1979) and EL SALVADOR (1980) arose, the ability of the United States to command the unanimous approval of the OAS for its actions lessened. While the OAS continued to serve as a regional body recognized by the United Nations as holding authority over disputes within the Americas, its role since the end of the cold war was no longer clearly defined. Aggrieved parties within the hemisphere increasingly turned to the United Nations rather than to the OAS to seek redress.

The potential for contention between the United Nations and the OAS first arose in relation to the U.S. invasion of Grenada in October 1983. UN condemnation of U.S. sanctions against Nicaragua as well as for its continued support of the Contra rebels in the civil war during the mid-1980s again shattered OAS consensus and led Nicaragua to seek UN support for its case in 1984. The December 1989 invasion of Panama by the United States again paralyzed the OAS and led Latin American states to use the United Nations as a forum to criticize U.S. action.

Developed as a body that reserved the right of American states to defend peace and security of the hemisphere without intervention by the United Nations, the legacy, and ultimate end of the cold war left the OAS with an unclear mission. Efforts to defend the democratically elected government of HAITI between 1991 and 1996 once again brought into question the relationship between the United Nations and the OAS, and the responsibilities of each in regional disputes. Of the six PEACEKEEPING missions sent to Haiti, five were solely UN initiatives. Only the INTERNATIONAL CIVILIAN MISSION IN HAITI (MICIVIH) had active OAS participation. In a joint effort by the United Nations and the Organization of American States, MICIVIH sought to promote respect for HUMAN RIGHTS following the departure from office of the island's military leaders.

The OAS co-sponsorship of MICIVIH reflected a new emphasis on promoting democracy. Its 1991 GENERAL

ASSEMBLY meeting endorsed this trend by creating a mechanism, known as Resolution 1080, that required the OAS SECRETARY-GENERAL to convene the organization's Permanent Council and the members' foreign ministers within 10 days of a coup or interruption of a legitimate, elected government. Resolution 1080 was first used when the military seized power in Haiti, then in Peru in 1992, Guatemala in 1993, and Paraguay in 1996. Resolution 1080 provided a means for the OAS to take the initiative ahead of UN responses whenever a threat to democratic stability occurred in the Western Hemisphere. In September 2001 the OAS General Assembly went even further by endorsing a proposed Inter-American Democratic Charter that called for the SUSPENSION of a member nation if it altered its "constitutional regime," or interrupted the "democratic order." The measure was meant to forestall internal subversion of democratic systems by elected governments that were, in fact, "disguised dictatorships." OAS action came in the wake of President Fujimori's restrictions on the democratic process in Peru during the 1990s.

See also COMMITTEE OF INTERNATIONAL DEVELOPMENT INSTITUTIONS ON THE ENVIRONMENT, HAMMARSKJÖLD, JURISDICTION OF THE UNITED NATIONS, LATIN AMERICA, OBSERVER STATUS, REGIONAL ORGANIZATIONS.

Further Reading: Levin, Aida L. "The Organization of the American States and the United Nations." In *Regionalism and the United Nations.* Edited by Berhanykun Andemicael. Dobbs Ferry, N.Y.: Oceana Publications, 1979: 147–224. Wilson, Larman C., and David W. Dent. *Historical Dictionary of Inter-American Organizations.* Lanham, Md.: Scarecrow Press, 1998. OAS website: <www.oas.org>.

— *D. K. Lewis*

Ottawa Convention   *See* CONVENTION ON THE PROHIBITION OF THE USE, STOCKPILING, PRODUCTION AND TRANSFER OF ANTI-PERSONNEL MINES AND THEIR DESTRUCTION; *see also* LAND MINES.

Our Common Future   *See* WORLD COMMISSION ON ENVIRONMENT AND DEVELOPMENT (WCED).

P

P5 *See* PERMANENT MEMBERS OF THE SECURITY COUNCIL.

Pacific Settlement of Disputes *See* CHAPTER VI OF THE UN CHARTER.

pact

From Latin *pactum*, pact is very close in meaning to COVENANT and TREATY. It is an agreement between individuals or parties. As a particular type of treaty, a pact usually binds the parties to undertake some common activity or to pursue a generally positive relationship. The notorious Nazi-Soviet "pact" of August 1939 is an example. Unlike CONVENTIONS, pacts are not open for additional signature, but require further negotiation in order to include new partners. All pacts that are made by one or more members of the United Nations must be registered with the world body, and are published in the *UNITED NATIONS TREATY SERIES*.

Pakistan *See* AFGHANISTAN, DEPARTMENT OF PEACE-KEEPING OPERATIONS, KASHMIR, UNITED NATIONS INDIA-PAKISTAN OBSERVATION MISSION, UNITED NATIONS MILITARY OBSERVER GROUP IN INDIA AND PAKISTAN.

Palais des Nations *See* GENEVA HEADQUARTERS OF THE UNITED NATIONS.

Panel on United Nations Peace Operations
See BRAHIMI REPORT.

Pasvolsky, Leo (1893–1953)

Wartime planning for a postwar international body to keep the peace and the drafting of a charter for the proposed United Nations Organization were undertaken primarily by the UNITED STATES Department of State. Under the leadership of Secretary of State Cordell HULL, Leo Pasvolsky and other department officials crafted the proposals and shepherded the process that produced great power agreement at the DUMBARTON OAKS CONFERENCE (1944) on the STRUCTURE and purposes of the United Nations. Joining the State Department in 1938, Pasvolsky was one of the few senior officials to participate in every phase of the UN's development leading to the successful conclusion of the 1945 UNITED NATIONS CONFERENCE ON INTERNATIONAL ORGANIZATION at San Francisco.

Prior to his service at the U.S. State Department, Pasvolsky worked at the Brookings Institution in Washington, D.C., where he published many works on interwar economics and the effects of World War I on central Europe.

His writings included *The Economics of Communism with Special Reference to Russia's Experience* (1921), *Russian Debts and Russian Reconstruction* (1924), *World War Debt Settlements* (1926), *Economic Nationalism of the Danubian States* (1928), *War Debts and World Prosperity* (1932), and *Current Monetary Issues* (1933). In this period he was also a member of the Council on Foreign Relations (CFR), which, at the outbreak of World War II in Europe, launched a private effort to convince the American government to plan for a postwar successor to the ineffectual LEAGUE OF NATIONS. Pasvolsky drafted the council's proposal presented to the State Department on September 12, 1939, suggesting that the CFR form a group of experts to research postwar issues under the "general guidance" of the department. Hull accepted the idea, and the council established the War and Peace Studies Project with Pasvolsky as one of its research secretaries. A parallel structure was created within the State Department, and many CFR personnel were brought into the government. Pasvolsky was appointed director of the Special Research Division, and he became a confidant of Secretary Hull.

Hull set up a department committee for postwar planning in December 1939 with Pasvolsky as a member. The work of the committee soon came under the leadership of Under Secretary of State Sumner Welles, who joined Pasvolsky as the two strongest advocates for a new international organization. Pasvolsky was also involved in the State Department's discussions concerning an International Stabilization Fund to finance world commerce after the war. As part of the department's "Technical Committee," he helped draft the American proposals that later emerged as the BRETTON WOODS AGREEMENT, creating the major international postwar financial and monetary institutions.

In 1943 Leo Pasvolsky was given the title of "Special Adviser to the Secretary" in charge of preparatory work for the proposed international organization. Following the MOSCOW FOREIGN MINISTERS CONFERENCE in the fall, he was appointed to Hull's "Informal Political Agenda Group," which crafted the outlines of the world body based on the secretary's own draft of a "CHARTER OF THE UNITED NATIONS," written the previous August. President Franklin ROOSEVELT approved the plan in February 1944, and it served as the basis of the Dumbarton Oaks discussions in the fall of that year. Pasvolsky, Ralph BUNCHE, and Alger HISS served as the core of the U.S. preparation team for the conference. During the meeting Pasvolsky chaired the Joint Formulation Group, consisting of American, British, and Soviet officials charged with the technical drafting of the Charter. As the negotiations proceeded, it was within this group that most of the substantive discussions about the new organization occurred. Pasvolsky was particularly involved in discussions with Soviet ambassador Andrei Gromyko about the potential MEMBERSHIP of the 16 Soviet republics, and VOTING issues within the UN.

Pasvolsky accompanied Roosevelt to the YALTA CONFERENCE, and, immediately following that meeting, he went with Secretary of State STETTINIUS to the Mexico Conference, where the United States and its hemispheric neighbors drafted the Act of Chapultepec, dealing with the thorny problems of the relationship between the United Nations and a REGIONAL ORGANIZATION. He was appointed to the U.S. delegation to the San Francisco Conference in April 1945, where he chaired the critical Coordination Committee. Taking the recommendations from each of the conference commissions and committees, Pasvolsky's group decided on the structure of the Charter and drafted the final text. When the language of recommendations was unclear, the Coordination Committee recommended changes and standardized references in the Charter on social, economic, and HUMAN RIGHTS topics. Following the conference, Pasvolsky was one of the major advocates at the ratification hearings of the U.S. Senate Foreign Relations Committee.

Before leaving the State Department in 1946 to return to the Brookings Institution, Pasvolsky served on the key committee that prepared the recommendations for the creation of the Central Intelligence Agency. Back at Brookings, he headed up the International Studies Group that developed the draft outline for the Marshall Plan and its administration once Congress had approved the European recovery program. In 1951 he initiated a study program at Brookings on the United Nations that was projected to publish seven volumes on different aspects of the world body. He began work on the first volume, *The Charter of the United Nations,* but he died in 1953 before its completion. In all, five volumes were completed after his death, including his first volume, which was written by his associate, Ruth B. Russell, and dedicated to him. It became the seminal work on the drafting of the document.

Further Reading: Moore, John Allphin Jr., and Jerry Pubantz. *To Create a New World? American Presidents and the United Nations.* New York: Peter Lang Publishing, 1999. Russell, Ruth B. *A History of the United Nations Charter: The Role of the United States, 1940–1945.* Washington, D.C.: Brookings Institution, 1958. Simma, Bruno, ed. *The Charter of the United Nations. A Commentary.* New York: Oxford University Press, 1994. Brookings Institution archives website: <www.brookings.org/lib/archives.html>. National Archives and Administration search-page website: <search.nara.gov/>.

peacekeeping

Although peacekeeping is an endeavor often associated with the United Nations, it is an ad hoc undertaking that is not mentioned in the CHARTER. Peacekeeping is a concept that has evolved over the years, and the resulting changes in various peacekeeping missions account for many of the difficulties encountered by these efforts, for a great deal of misunderstanding of the United Nations, and for the rising criticism of the organization.

The founders of the United Nations did not envisage anything like peacekeeping. Consequently, while Chapter I, Article 1 of the Charter states that one of the purposes of the United Nations is "[T]o maintain international peace and security," the only methods elaborated in the Charter for achieving this objective are those of MEDIATION, investigation, and negotiation, as suggested in CHAPTER VI's provision for "pacific settlement of disputes," and the use of force by member states, as discussed in CHAPTER VII. Recognizing the need for forceful measures short of war, such as SANCTIONS, diplomats and UN staff members sought new methods to deal with the outbreak of international conflict. Peacekeeping was developed during the initial years of the UN as an action more intrusive than the peaceful settlement provisions of Chapter VI, yet short of Chapter VII's provisions authorizing member states to use force. Hence it is often referred to within the United Nations as coming under "CHAPTER VI ¹/₂."

Thus, international peacekeeping was a new concept developed by the United Nations. Since such measures had

not previously taken place in the history of the world, they required the development of a new method of operation, without the benefit of previous precedents that normally govern international activity. The idea of neutral international action to facilitate peace, rather than order being maintained by the extension of war based on national interests, was a new idea. During the latter half of the 20th century, distinctive "BLUE HELMETS" worn by UN peacekeepers became a vital symbol of the international security system, providing an important mechanism to preserve the global order, ensure the survival of small states, and protect HUMAN RIGHTS. In the year 2000 more than 30,000 peacekeepers were serving in multinational missions around the world. Of these, 22,000 were military troops, 5,700 were police, and 1,300 were observers. The nature of these missions included humanitarian assistance, civil administration, combatant separation, and truce observation.

As initially conceived in 1948 and 1949 and practiced for the first 40 years of the United Nations, peacekeeping was a narrowly focused process with limited and specific purposes. It normally involved an international action to assist in ending an international conflict (that is, a war between states) in

Peacekeeping in East Timor, 2000 (UN/DPI PHOTO BY ESKINDER DEBEBE)

an entirely voluntary action, carried out with the express permission of both sides to the conflict. Peacekeepers arrived after a cease-fire agreement or other settlement had been negotiated by both parties, positioning themselves between the combatants. The sole purpose of these early peacekeeping efforts was to supervise the implementation of truce agreements and specifically to verify that both sides took appropriate actions to carry out the agreements already reached. While military personnel were involved, only light arms were carried. Peacekeepers had no enforcement powers and were directed to use force only to defend themselves. The entire operation was based on voluntary consent and the cooperation of the parties to the conflict. Indeed, peacekeepers were sent only after the UN negotiated a "Status of Forces Agreement" by which the host state granted permission to use its territory, since it remained a sovereign nation. The agreement also defined the powers of the peacekeepers, their access to facilities, and the specific territory in which they would operate. Early peacekeeping operations were conducted by the United Nations in Egypt following the 1956 SUEZ CRISIS (UNITED NATIONS EMERGENCY FORCE, UNEF), during the 1960 Congolese civil war (UNITED NATIONS OPERATION IN THE CONGO, ONUC), and in the Cypriot crisis of 1964 (UNITED NATIONS FORCE IN CYPRUS, UNFICYP).

Troops involved in these operations were drawn from countries perceived as neutral in the conflict. Indeed, during the initial decades of peacekeeping, troops from the superpowers were never involved, with every effort made to draw troops from neutral nations. More than 110 nations have contributed troops to peacekeeping missions, and the increasing use of peacekeeping clearly demonstrates that it has filled a need in the international system.

As designed and practiced for the first 40 years of the UN, peacekeeping was a neutral operation to monitor or observe the combatants' steps to disengage and pull back after a cease-fire agreement had been reached, and to carry out agreements to end the conflict reached prior to the arrival of the peacekeeping mission. Initially peacekeeping was used sparingly, but over the years the number of missions proliferated as nations brought more and more disputes to the United Nations, and missions continued indefinitely because cease-fire agreements did not necessarily lead to negotiation of a final agreement. The costs of these peacekeeping operations were paid by all member states through a separate assessment, apart from the regular UN BUDGET, since the costs of such operations varied during any year depending on the number of crises the UN was asked to resolve. Objections to certain peacekeeping operations led to the withholding of assessment payments by many states, including major powers such as France and the Soviet Union.

The end of the COLD WAR brought an expansion of and notable changes in peacekeeping, as different types of disputes came before the United Nations. New challenges necessitated increasing the number of troops and raising the costs of financing the increased number of operations. The 1990s saw the launching of almost three times as many peacekeeping missions as were initiated during the previous 40 years, reflecting a period of increasing security crises and greater reliance on the United Nations by the nations of the world. Only 13 peacekeeping missions were authorized prior to 1988. From 1988 through 2000, more than 36 operations were undertaken. In this situation, merely raising the necessary troops and funding the costs of the operation became major concerns, in addition to conducting the missions. Other challenges included adequate training, equipping, and transporting of troops pledged by various nations. The increased number of missions also led to delays between authorization and deployment of forces, which caused further problems.

The nature of peacekeeping, the tasks involved, and the types of disputes that peacekeepers were asked to address also changed considerably during the period following 1988. The conflicts brought to the United Nations after 1988 mainly involved domestic, that is, internal civil wars, several disputing the legitimacy of an existing government or assaulting ethnic, religious, and minority groups, as in Rwanda, SOMALIA, BOSNIA, Kosovo, and East Timor. Although these conflicts often affected, or potentially affected, international peace and security, they fell outside the original scope of the United Nations, which dealt only with international disputes and interstate warfare. But this new form of peacekeeping, or "peacemaking," involved intervening in internal domestic disputes, and they thus challenged, if not violated, a nation's SOVEREIGNTY. More important, since at least one of the parties involved in the dispute was likely a rebel movement, and not a signatory of international agreements, it could consider itself outside the scope of INTERNATIONAL LAW. Hence, the United Nations was asked to get involved in disputes outside existing norms and with a party beyond the reach of normal international measures. Attempting to settle internal disputes also often meant that peacekeepers acted without the approval of all parties to the dispute, since the United Nations normally deals with the governments of its member states. The UN Charter does not provide explicit authority for the UN to act against the sovereignty of a member state without the permission of that government. Thus, interventions in disputes involving the potential emergence of new states meant entering entirely new legal ground. Inevitably difficulties ensued, due to the challenges of an entirely new type of peacekeeping.

Modern warfare also changed, with civilians increasingly the targets of efforts by rebels using unconventional methods of warfare, and this also brought new challenges. Peacekeepers were often asked to protect refugees and guard the delivery of humanitarian aid, as well as to investigate and seek to prevent violations of the human rights of the populace. While the United Nations did indeed seek to protect basic human rights and especially to prevent crimes against humanity, peacekeepers were not equipped and never intended to fight a conflict. Once peacekeepers attempted to protect victims or segments of the population, the neutrality on which their actions had previously been based was lost, and they were invariably perceived as parties to the conflict by at least one side. Efforts to protect civilians involved unprecedented cooperation of peacekeeping forces with SPE-CIALIZED AGENCIES and NON-GOVERNMENTAL ORGANIZA-TIONS, requiring complex coordination. In addition, the new mandates often involved lengthy deployments that included not merely troops but also police officers and legal officials.

Taking on vast new reponsibilities that were well beyond the original concept of peacekeeping, with little advance planning and few new resources, peacekeepers were now being asked to perform tasks that were at times contradictory. For example, protecting populations and delivering aid invariably caused a loss of the aura of neutrality. The relatively small DEPARTMENT OF PEACEKEEPING OPERATIONS (DPKO) struggled with inadequate resources trying to meet new mandates that went far beyond the original idea of peacekeeping. SECRETARY-GENERAL Kofi ANNAN appointed a panel of experts in March 2000 to study the new challenges facing UN peacekeeping operations. He hoped to avoid in future missions the errors, inefficiencies, and failures experienced in past UN efforts. Annan charged the panel with examining the ability of UN resources to meet the peacekeeping mandates given to the world body by the SECURITY COUNCIL in recent years. He hoped the experts would complement the work of the Lessons Learned Unit in DPKO. The panel's report, issued just before the September 2000 meeting of the MILLENNIUM SUMMIT, recommended formalizing the UN's peacekeeping activities, ending ad hoc deployments, creating a new information-gathering and analysis office within the United Nations to act as a professional policy planning staff, establishing an integrated task force for each new mission, and changing definitions of self-defense to allow missions to take a more offensive posture in dangerous situations. The panel drawing up these proposals included members from 10 nations, including the UNITED STATES and Russia. As a result of the UN's experiences and the SECRETARIAT's review of past missions, the relatively new phenomenon of peacekeeping, which dates from the mid-20th century, continued to evolve at the end of the century.

See also specific peacekeeping operations, listing of all peacekeeping operations in Department of Peacekeeping Operations entry; AGENDA FOR PEACE; BRAHIMI REPORT; BUNCHE, RALPH; PEARSON, LESTER.

Further Reading: Hill, Stephen M., and Shanin Malik. *Peacekeeping and the United Nations.* Aldershot, U.K.: Dartmouth, 1996. Ratner, Steven R. *The New UN Peacekeeping: Building Peace in Land of Conflict after the Cold War.* New York: St. Martin's, 1995. Ontunnu, Olara A., and Michael W. Doyle, eds. *Peacemaking and Peacekeeping for the New Century.* Lanham, Md.: Rowman and Littlefield, 1996. United Nations Depart-

ment of Public Information. *The Blue Helmets: A Review of United Nations Peace-Keeping.* 3d ed. New York: United Nations Department of Public Information, 1996.

— *K. J. Grieb*

Pearson, Lester (1897–1972)

Lester Bowles Pearson was born in Newton Brook, Ontario, Canada. Following university studies Pearson taught history at the University of Toronto from 1924 to 1928, after which he entered the Canadian foreign service. While employed by the foreign service during World War II, Pearson became involved with precursors to the United Nations. In 1943 he was a delegate to sessions of the UNITED NATIONS RELIEF AND REHABILITATION ADMINISTRATION (UNRRA) and chaired its supplies committee. He was also included in the planning sessions of the United Nations FOOD AND AGRICULTURE ORGANIZATION (FAO) and served in 1944 as Canada's senior adviser at the DUMBARTON OAKS CONFERENCE. In 1945 he was his nation's head delegate to the UN's founding conference in San Francisco.

In 1946 Pearson was appointed Canada's under-secretary of state for external affairs. Serving as chairman of the UN political and security committee in 1947, he played a decisive role in mediating the Palestinian crisis. From 1948 to 1956, Pearson served as head of the Canadian mission to the United Nations and was president of the seventh GENERAL ASSEMBLY during the 1952–53 session. Following Israel's attack on Egypt's Sinai Peninsula in 1956, Pearson proposed the deployment of a UN EMERGENCY FORCE (UNEF) to the Suez and volunteered a Canadian contingent of troops, thereby becoming the father of UN PEACEKEEPING. For his efforts Pearson was awarded the Nobel Peace Prize in 1957. The next year he became leader of the Liberal Party in Canada and, in 1963, prime minister, a position from which he retired in 1968.

Further Reading: English, John. *The Life of Lester Pearson: Shadow of Heaven (1897–1948) and Worldly Years (1949–1972).* Toronto: Lester and Orphen Dennys and A. A. Knopf, 1989–1992. Pearson, Lester B. *Mike: The Memoirs of the Right Honourable Lester B. Pearson.* 3 vols. Toronto: New American Library of Canada, 1972.

— *S. F. McMahon*

People's Republic of China   See CHINA.

Pérez de Cuéllar, Javier (1920–)

Pérez de Cuéllar, the fifth SECRETARY-GENERAL and first Latin American to hold that office, served two terms, from 1982 to 1991. He was born in Lima, Peru, in 1920 of a family descended from Spanish nobility. Educated early in life in

Roman Catholic schools, Pérez de Cuéllar developed a keen interest in Hispanic art, culture, and literature. While studying law at Catholic University in Lima, he took a position in the Peruvian Foreign Ministry as a clerk, commencing a long diplomatic career. From the mid-1940s he served successively in embassies in France, the United Kingdom, Bolivia, and Brazil, and in 1946 he was a member of Peru's delegation to the first United Nations GENERAL ASSEMBLY session. His career evinced a rapid rise within the foreign ministry. He was promoted to the rank of ambassador in 1962 and by the mid-1960s simultaneously held appointments as professor of diplomatic law at the Academia Diplomatica del Peru and professor of international relations at the Academia de Guerra Aerea del Peru, during which time he wrote *Manual de Derecho Diplomático* (Manual of international law). He served as ambassador to Switzerland from 1964 to 1966, and, following the establishment of full diplomatic relations with the Soviet Union in 1969, he became his nation's first ambassador to Moscow, serving concurrently as ambassador to Poland.

In 1971 he became Peru's PERMANENT REPRESENTATIVE to the United Nations, serving as president of the SECURITY COUNCIL during the CYPRUS DISPUTE of 1974. In the summer of that year, a military faction overthrew the government of Archbishop Makarios in an effort to bring about union of the island with Greece. Turkey immediately ordered an invasion to protect the Turkish minority. On September 18, 1975, Secretary-General Kurt WALDHEIM named Pérez de Cuéllar as his SPECIAL REPRESENTATIVE to Cyprus. Although the Cyprus dispute would persist as one of the most long-lasting concerns of the United Nations, Pérez de Cuéllar eventually convinced the leaders of the Greek and Turkish communities to initiate talks about their differences. In late 1977 he left the United Nations in order to assume the position of Peruvian ambassador to Venezuela, but in early 1979 returned to New York as UNDER SECRETARY-GENERAL for Special Political Affairs. In April 1981, Waldheim appointed him his personal representative to AFGHANISTAN and Pakistan, in an effort to defuse the tense relations between the two countries resulting from the Soviet invasion of Afghanistan in December 1979.

In 1981, at the age of 61, Pérez de Cuéllar intended to retire from his long and active diplomatic career, but events would conspire to delay his leaving the world stage. Kurt Waldheim's second term was coming to a close, and the United Nations now began the knotty process of designating a new Secretary-General. The selection was complicated by several factors. Waldheim wanted a third term, but he was vigorously opposed by several Third World countries, led by CHINA in the Security Council. The procedure provided in the CHARTER OF THE UNITED NATIONS (see Article 97) authorized the General Assembly to appoint the Secretary-General upon the recommendation of the Security Council. Since the five PERMANENT MEMBERS OF THE SECURITY COUNCIL retain

Secretary-General Javier Pérez de Cuéllar (UN PHOTO 169681/ J. ISAAC)

a VETO, it is conceivable that a nominee could receive 14 votes yet be an unsuccessful nominee. That is, all five permanent members must accede to any nomination. Tanzania's foreign minister, Salim Ahmed Salim, was a challenging candidate to Waldheim, and he would have become the first sub-Saharan African to serve in the post. The new, conservative, Reagan administration in Washington, resistant to the recent tilt in the United Nations toward what it perceived as Third-World radicalism, supported Waldheim, as did, interestingly, the Soviet Union. For six weeks the Security Council deadlocked on a nomination as either the UNITED STATES or China vetoed opposing candidates. Finally, upon the urging of Ugandan ambassador Olara Otunnu, president of the Security Council, both Salim and Waldheim withdrew from consideration. On December 11, 1981, the Council went into closed session for an arduous half day to consider nine candidates. By the end of the session, only one of those candidates proved acceptable to all of the permanent members—Javier Pérez de Cuéllar, who was quickly, and by acclamation, approved by the General Assembly. Here appeared a diplomat from a Latin American "Third World" country, yet of a "Western" cultural tradition, who had gained the confidence of the Soviet Union while serving as ambassador in Moscow. It is likely as well that, since he was

61, no one thought he would serve more than one term. Yet he would be reelected and would serve a full 10 years.

His first major challenge involved a military confrontation between Great Britain and Argentina over the Falkland Islands, called the Malvinas by the Argentineans, who invaded and claimed the islands in April 1982. Although his efforts at MEDIATION came to naught—by June 1982 Britain had defeated the Argentine army and reestablished control over the islands—he was widely praised in the international community for his labors. He continued with other personal initiatives, in Russian-occupied Afghanistan, in South African-occupied NAMIBIA, in Lebanon (plagued by Israeli invasion and internal civil strife), and in the Guyana-Venezuela border dispute, in the event continuing to win praise for his mediation efforts and enhancing his growing reputation as an impartial negotiator. He consistently advocated the use of the Security Council as a forum for negotiations and as the appropriate international tool to pursue PEACEKEEPING efforts, despite the persistent lack of funding for such efforts. During his tenure as well, the United Nations continued to emphasize refugee resettlement and HUMAN RIGHTS, and the Secretary-General initiated a program to bring relief to Ethiopia during a devastating famine in the late 1980s.

Most important, it was on his watch that the COLD WAR ended, providing the United Nations with the opportunity to be transformed from an international organization paralyzed by bipolarity into an institution that could more directly affect world affairs. Suddenly, at least for the moment, an environment more reflective of great power cooperation than the world had seen in some years seemed to provide the context for successful diplomacy orchestrated by an active and principled Secretary-General. The new opportunities for the organization over which Pérez de Cuéllar presided, however, brought with them the need for additional financial resources and more personnel. The Secretary-General expanded the UN bureaucracy and lobbied for increased funding.

Unfortunately, his efforts encountered growing hostility from the U.S. government, historically the United Nations's most important supporter. The Reagan administration, having come to office the same year as Pérez de Cuéllar's first appointment as Secretary-General, reversed decades of American financial support. Demanding reforms at the UN, President Reagan limited annual assessment payments, endorsed the KASSEBAUM AMENDMENT cutting contributions to UN SPECIALIZED AGENCIES, and demanded a 15 percent reduction in the UN staff. When the United States went so far as to withdraw from UNESCO (UNITED NATIONS EDUCATIONAL, SCIENTIFIC AND CULTURAL ORGANIZATION), arguing its mission had become too highly politicized and its staff and BUDGET bloated, the confrontation reached a crisis point. UNESCO appointed a new DIRECTOR-GENERAL and cut its activities by one-third. The Secretary-General agreed

REFORM and streamlining at the UN were needed. To accommodate American pressure, Pérez de Cuéllar even allowed the U.S. government's General Accounting Office (GAO) to review the work of the UN's auditing and evaluation unit. This was an unprecedented step, since nothing in the Charter allows national governments to review the management of the organization's agencies. In the end, however, none of Pérez de Cuéllar's efforts were sufficient to assuage the conservative Republican leadership in Washington.

On a brighter note for U.S.–UN relations, and with warmer relations developing between the United States and the USSR after the ascendancy of President Mikhail Gorbachev, several apparently intractable international problems were resolved through initiatives by the United Nations. In southern Africa, by the summer of 1988, all parties agreed to simultaneous withdrawals of forces by CUBA and South Africa from, respectively, ANGOLA and Namibia. This opened the way for full implementation of Security Council Resolution 435, providing for a UNITED NATIONS ANGOLA VERIFICATION MISSION (UNAVEM) and the placement of the UNITED NATIONS TRANSITION ASSISTANCE GROUP (UNTAG) in Namibia to help with the conversion to independence, achieved at the UN HEADQUARTERS in Geneva (the Palais des Nations) in December 1988. Meantime, Diego Cordovez, an assistant to the Secretary-General, worked quietly but effectively to mediate the conflict in Afghanistan and to help expedite the removal of Soviet forces from that country. At the Palais des Nations, a four-part agreement (Afghanistan, Pakistan, the United States, and the Soviet Union) was reached on April 14, 1988, providing for peace talks among the warring parties and removal of Soviet troops, which was completed by the following February.

Pérez de Cuéllar also oversaw the conclusion of the most devastating war in the post–World War II period. The IRAN-IRAQ WAR had begun in 1980 and had been characterized by extreme ferocity and brutality on both sides, resulting in hundreds of thousands of casualties. The war entered its final stages in early 1988 during the so-called war of the cities. In February, Iraqi leader Saddam HUSSEIN ordered the bombing of an oil refinery near Tehran, and Iran launched missiles into Baghdad in retaliation. Kurds in Iraq demanded autonomy and Hussein bombed their villages with poison gas. The war had completely degenerated into an unacceptable barbarity, and yet it was, by all accounts, a stalemate. Reluctantly, Ayatollah Khomeini, the Iranian religious leader, allowed his government to accept UN RESOLUTION 598, calling for a cease-fire and withdrawal of forces to pre-war boundaries. The RESOLUTION had been hammered out in an all-day session of the Security Council (July 20, 1987) that included the active participation of Pérez de Cuéllar. The action was historic; the United States and the Soviet Union for the first time jointly sponsored a Security Council resolution on the Middle East. The resolution even threatened retaliation against either of the combatants if they failed to accept its terms. Pérez de Cuéllar was entrusted with the diplomatic task of obtaining compliance. Iraq at first rejected the resolution and attempted yet another offensive, but the Secretary-General persisted in talks with the foreign ministers of each side and was finally able to announce agreement on August 20, 1988. The UN Security Council was now poised to act, cooperatively, to address the international crisis created when, in August 1990, Saddam Hussein directed an Iraqi invasion of neighboring Kuwait. UN SECURITY COUNCIL RESOLUTION 678 became the juridical basis of the U.S.-led coalition that drove Iraq out of Kuwait during the GULF WAR.

Once the war was concluded in the spring of 1991, a new humanitarian challenge presented itself. At the end of March the Iraqi army launched a massive attack against rebels in the northern part of the country. The attack produced more than 200,000 Kurdish refugees fleeing to the region along Iraq's border with Turkey and 500,000 crossing into Iran. On April 5 the Security Council condemned the attacks and called upon "the Secretary-General to use all the resources at his disposal . . . to address urgently the critical needs of the refugees." The United States, with the assistance of Turkey, Great Britain, and France, established a "no-fly" zone over the area, launched a massive humanitarian airdrop, and created protective "enclaves" inside Iraq for the Kurds. Almost immediately thereafter these powers urged the United Nations to take over administration of the enclaves. Pérez de Cuéllar was hesitant to do so without the consent of the Iraqi government. To this end he negotiated an agreement with Baghdad on April 18, 1991. With this in place the allied states ceded control of the camps to the UN. The episode proved to be another example of deft diplomacy by Pérez de Cuéllar, reminiscent of the successful approach he had used in international crises throughout his tenure as Secretary-General.

Further Reading: Pérez de Cuéllar, Javier. *Pilgrimage for Peace: A Secretary-General's Memoir.* New York: St. Martin's, 1997.

Permanent Court of Arbitration (PCA)

Often referred to as the "Hague Tribunal," the Permanent Court of Arbitration was initiated in 1899 by a CONVENTION of the First Hague Conference. The PCA arose from a developing interest in MEDIATION and ARBITRATION as methods of resolving international disputes. The 19th century witnessed a growth in the practice of inserting clauses in treaties calling for arbitration, and legal and political leaders considered proposals to create a permanent court to handle such cases. The Hague Peace Conference of 1899, convened to discuss peace and DISARMAMENT, adopted a Convention on the pacific settlement of International Disputes and called for a

permanent organization to enable the creation of arbitral tribunals. The resulting Permanent Court of Arbitration was established in 1900 and began operating in 1902 in The Hague, Netherlands. In 1913 it moved to the Peace Palace in that city, where it continues to function alongside its neighbors, the INTERNATIONAL COURT OF JUSTICE, the Carnegie Foundation (which originally provided the building), and the HAGUE ACADEMY OF INTERNATIONAL LAW. In 2000 there were 92 countries adhering to the convention. At the turn of the century, the PCA's services were available to resolve disputes between states, between states and private parties, and disputes in which inter-governmental organizations were involved.

The court consists of a panel of jurists designated by member countries. Each country is allotted up to four appointees, all of whom are expected to be experts in INTERNATIONAL LAW; they constitute what is called that country's PCA "National Group." From the full panel of all national groups, members of each arbitration tribunal may be chosen in a particular case. A case is initiated when two or more disputants sign an agreement to submit a disagreement to binding arbitration. They may then select arbiters from the PCA's panel to hear the case, or they may ask two panelists to pick an umpire before whom a hearing will take place.

On request, the PCA offers possibilities of arbitration (its original function), CONCILIATION, fact-finding commissions, GOOD OFFICES, and mediation. It also can provide administrative support to litigants, a private courtroom and hearing facilities at the Peace Palace, and access to the Peace Palace library.

The tribunal lost much of its original importance to the PERMANENT COURT OF INTERNATIONAL JUSTICE, established by the LEAGUE OF NATIONS after World War I, which was then superseded by the International Court of Justice after World War II. However, the Permanent Court of Arbitration regularly performs a role in nominating candidates for the ICJ. At the request of the UN SECRETARY-GENERAL, the "National Groups" can propose candidates for vacant positions on the Court. From these nominations the GENERAL ASSEMBLY and the SECURITY COUNCIL elect the ICJ's judges.

See also OBSERVER STATUS.

Further Reading: PCA website: <pca-cpa.org>.

Permanent Court of International Justice (PCIJ)

Often called the "World Court," the Permanent Court of International Justice was established by the LEAGUE OF NATIONS, pursuant to Article 14 of the League's COVENANT. In 1920 the League Assembly unanimously approved a statute for the new court and later that year called upon the League Council to submit a PROTOCOL to League members to adopt the statute. The required number of NATION-STATES (a majority of League members) ratified it by the next year. The Permanent Court began meeting at The Hague in February 1922, but it dissolved after World War II, when its functions, JURISDICTION, and, for the most part, its statute were transferred to the new INTERNATIONAL COURT OF JUSTICE (ICJ).

Like its progeny, the PCIJ received authorization from its statute to make judgments in cases submitted to it by states in disagreement over an issue of an international character and to give ADVISORY OPINIONS in any matter that the League's Council or Assembly referred to it. Thus its areas of activity were more extensive than that of the older PERMANENT COURT OF ARBITRATION (PCA)—often called the "Hague Tribunal." The latter, created by the Hague Peace Conference of 1899, dealt with ARBITRATION issues solely. Also unlike the Hague Tribunal, the PCIJ was a permanently constituted body, had its own statute and rules of procedure, and had a group of permanent judges rather than a large panel of jurists from which nations might select arbiters to hear a specific case. The PCIJ began with 11 regular judges and four deputies, but in 1931 the number increased to 15. The League Council and Assembly concurrently elected judges for nine-year terms. Nominees came from lists supplied by the Permanent Court of Arbitration, and no more than one citizen of a nation could serve at the same time. Judges were paid a salary and were barred from any occupation, government service, or legal activity other than their work on the World Court. The PCIJ had a permanent registry that served to keep records and make public all activities of the Court. The PCIJ was accessible to all states for judicial judgments in international disputes, and its statute specifically listed the sources of INTERNATIONAL LAW that were to apply to contentious cases and advisory opinions. All of these features of the PCIJ were transferred to the ICJ in 1946.

The UNITED STATES never joined the PCIJ because the U.S. Senate never ratified the original protocol. Yet an American always served on the Court's bench. By 1945, its last year, the statute of the PCIJ had an official adherence from 59 states. From 1922 until 1939, when the Court discontinued sitting, it received 66 cases, some of which were settled out of court and some left pending. Of the remaining, the Court handed down 32 judgments in contentious cases and 27 advisory opinions. Most of these, and particularly the advisory opinions, retained the sanctity of international law after the Permanent Court's demise, and were catalogued with the decisions subsequently made by the International Court of Justice. With the outbreak of World War II, the Permanent Court ceased to function, and its reputation, along with that of the League of Nations, suffered with the collapse of international order. It held its last meeting in October 1945, in order to transfer its archives and functions to the new International Court of Justice. The PCIJ's judges resigned on January 31, 1946, and election of the ICJ judges occurred the next week at the UN GENERAL ASSEMBLY's first session. April 1946 witnessed the formal dissolution of the PCIJ. Simultaneously, the ICJ, meeting at The Hague for the first time, chose as its inaugural president Judge J. Gustavo Guerrero, the last president of the PCIJ.

Further Reading: Hudson, Manley O. *The Permanent Court of International Justice, 1920–1942; A Treatise.* New York: Garland Publishers, 1972. Rosenne, Shabtai. *The World Court: What It Is and How It Works.* 5th rev. ed. Boston: Martinus Nijhoff Publishers, 1995.

Permanent Members of the Security Council (P5)

Article 23, CHAPTER V of the United Nations CHARTER specifies that five major powers shall be permanent members of the SECURITY COUNCIL. The five are the UNITED STATES, United Kingdom, France, Russia, and CHINA. Article 27 of the Charter endows the five permanent members with special powers on the Council by requiring a majority of nine votes and "the concurring votes of the permanent members" for the passage of all RESOLUTIONS on SUBSTANTIVE QUESTIONS. This provision effectively gave each of the five permanent members a VETO over Security Council action. While other nations often object to the veto, it was essential in order to win the approval of the U.S. Senate to ratification of the Charter, and to convince Marshal Joseph STALIN of the Soviet Union—wary of the U.S. idea of a United Nations—to pledge that the USSR would join the world body.

The veto has proven controversial, but has always remained intact, since Article 108 requires that AMENDMENTS TO THE CHARTER must obtain the ratification of the five permanent members. Also, in practice the decision to consider a topic or complaint has been considered procedural, and hence not subject to veto. However, whether an issue is a procedural or substantive matter is itself a substantive question, thus giving the permanent members a "DOUBLE VETO" on items before the Council. Over time, the Council adopted the interpretation that the words "concurring vote" in Article 27 meant that there had been no negative vote by any permanent member. That is, an abstention, not being a negative, indicated concurrence, and thus does not constitute a veto.

The veto was particularly important during the early years of the United Nations, when the COLD WAR protagonists used it to prevent condemnation of their actions and prevent action against their allies. It was used not only to block resolutions but also to thwart nominations for SECRETARY-GENERAL (43 cases) and to impede the ADMISSION of new members (59 vetoes). Only by the absence of a permanent member from a Council session or the exercise of the UNITING FOR PEACE RESOLUTION could the veto be circumvented. A total of 243 vetoes were cast prior to 1995. Of these, 82 occurred before 1955. Russia (the Soviet Union) cast the largest number of vetoes, with the United States casting the second largest. The use of the veto reflected the

MEMBERSHIP of the United Nations, since the overwhelming majority of the Russian vetoes were cast prior to 1965, when UN membership was pro-Western. By contrast, the United States did not cast a single veto prior to 1966, and found it necessary to do so only after the waning of colonialism resulted in increased UN membership of an anti-Western majority of newly independent former colonies during the mid-1960s. Vetoes have been rare since 1990. The end of the cold war led to negotiation and consensus among the P5 on most Security Council issues. Beginning with the GULF WAR, the five powers sought to reach a common position through informal consultations on matters of international peace and security, or at least a position that would garner nothing more than an abstention by a permanent member.

See also APARTHEID, APPEALS TO THE SECURITY COUNCIL, BOUTROS-GHALI, CHAPTER VII, DUMBARTON OAKS CONFERENCE, EMERGENCY SPECIAL SESSION OF THE GENERAL ASSEMBLY, GENERAL COMMITTEE, KOREAN WAR, LIE, SCALE OF ASSESSMENTS, TRUSTEESHIP COUNCIL, VOTING, YALTA CONFERENCE.

Further Reading: Jensen, Erik, and Thomas Fisher, eds. *The United Kingdom, The United Nations.* London: Macmillan, 1990. Karns, Margaret P., and Karen A. Mingst, eds. *The United States and Multilateral Institutions: Patterns of Changing Instrumentality and Influence.* Boston: Unwin Hyman, 1990. Moore, John Allphin Jr., and Jerry Pubantz. *To Create a New World? American Presidents and the United Nations.* New York: Peter Lang Publishing, 1999. Ostrower, Gary B. *The United Nations and the United States.* New York: Twayne, 1998. Stoessinger, John G. *The United Nations and the Superpowers: China, Russia, and America.* 4th ed. New York: Random House, 1977.

— *K. J. Grieb*

permanent observer   *See* OBSERVER STATUS.

permanent representative   *See* MISSIONS TO THE UNITED NATIONS.

Persian Gulf War   *See* GULF WAR.

personal representative   *See* SPECIAL REPRESENTATIVE OF THE SECRETARY-GENERAL.

Point Four program

Point Four of President Harry S. Truman's 1949 inaugural address urged international cooperation to teach self-help to poverty-stricken people in the underdeveloped world by pro-

viding technological knowledge and skills through private capital investment. The president argued that financial assistance was an American responsibility under Article 56 of the United Nations CHARTER, which pledged every member state to the promotion of higher standards of living and to the solution of economic and social problems. Although conceived as a weapon in the COLD WAR, the idea of economic aid to politically vulnerable areas of the world was still a novel idea confined to the Marshall Plan nations. By late 1948, the UNITED STATES offered no extensive aid to LATIN AMERICA, Asia, and Africa.

President Truman, however, felt that the absence of an aid program to the non-European world weakened American global policy. Its absence should be rectified, as he noted in his inaugural address. The brainchild of Benjamin Hardy, a State Department official, the idea of raising living standards for those peoples who would otherwise be "ripe for revolution" was brought to Truman's attention by advisers Clark Clifford and George Elsey.

An enthusiastic Truman embraced the concept for several reasons, both humanitarian and political. Point Four would encourage the extraction of critical raw materials in the noncommunist world—particularly oil, rubber, and metal ores—as well as stimulate more U.S. exports to these nations, paid for by dollars generated by investments from abroad. Finally, Point Four would contribute to the expansion and specialization of world trade; in a phrase, liberal internationalism.

Despite the president's enthusiasm for "a bold new program," the Point Four program was not easily implemented because of underfunding and a reliance on reluctant private investment. Secretary of State Dean ACHESON recalled that the "hyperbole of the inaugural outran the provisions of the budget." Congress shared the tepid interest of the business and banking communities in the program.

Senior staffer Walter S. Salant of the Council of Economic Advisers was responsible for recognizing the inadequacies of cautious private initiatives and urged instead the principle that extensive aid from the U.S. government was necessary to strengthen the economies of the underdeveloped nations. During the course of 1949, a series of crises forced a change in the orthodox international economic thinking of the Truman administration. Although ignoring calls by public figures for an Asian Marshall Plan, policy makers began to move away from the initially cautious Point Four legislation and toward Salant's advice for exports of government capital. The administration proposed an EXPANDED PROGRAM OF TECHNICAL ASSISTANCE (EPTA) under the JURISDICTION of the UN's ECONOMIC AND SOCIAL COUNCIL (ECOSOC).

By late 1949, the administration no longer regarded the difficulties of some underdeveloped nations as peripheral concerns. Truman's state of the union address of January 4, 1950, urged forceful government financial aid, the importance of such programs for Japanese and European economic recovery (the Marshall Plan was to end in 1952), and the critical importance of Southeast Asia as an object of economic stimulation. The Chinese revolution of October 1949 made all of these arguments compelling. The new demands placed on American foreign policy during 1949 required a more ambitious response, including capital assistance for the underdeveloped world and revitalization of commerce between the developed and underdeveloped nations. Financed by voluntary contributions, EPTA commenced operations in 1950 as the UN's single largest program. The United States initially provided 60 percent of the agency's $20 million BUDGET.

See also SPECIAL UNITED NATIONS FUND FOR ECONOMIC DEVELOPMENT, UNITED NATIONS DEVELOPMENT PROGRAMME.

Further Reading: Acheson, Dean. *Present at the Creation.* New York: Norton, 1969. Clifford, Clark. *Counsel to the President: A Memoir.* New York: Random House, 1991. Rotter, Andrew. *The Path to Vietnam: Origins of the American Commitment to Southeast Asia.* Ithaca, N.Y.: Cornell University Press, 1987.

— *E. M. Clauss*

population   *See* INTERNATIONAL CONFERENCE ON POPULATION AND DEVELOPMENT, UNITED NATIONS POPULATION FUND.

Prebisch, Raúl (1901–1986)

Prebisch, preeminent Third World economist of the post–World War II era, was an Argentine who helped manage his nation's economy during the Great Depression of the 1930s and World War II. His approach to economic issues was essentially Keynesian; that is, he advocated government economic intervention to break the bottlenecks of capitalist development. In 1948, as a consultant, he wrote for ECLA (ECONOMIC COMMISSION FOR LATIN AMERICA, now ECLAC) the groundbreaking *The Economic Development of Latin America and Its Principal Problems* and in 1949 the first part of the annual *Survey* of the region. In these works he amassed data to demonstrate the decline of trade between LATIN AMERICA—the "periphery"—and Europe and the UNITED STATES—the "center"—by aggregating the historical trade figures of Latin America with the two other regions and analyzing the trends. He proposed implementa-

UNCTAD Secretary-General Raúl Prebisch (third from left) (UNITED NATIONS/T. CHEN)

tion of import substitution measures to enable commodity producing nations to achieve more balanced economies by becoming industrialized. In 1950 he was appointed executive secretary of ECLA. His analysis and recommendations were to influence the economic policies of most of the nations of the region for several decades. Although ECLA participated in creating the failed Latin American Free Trade Area (LAFTA), he expressed grave doubts about the rigid nature of the organization, believing that the range of difference among the levels of development of the nations of the region made that arrangement one that would have great difficulty in succeeding. The theoretical approach of ECLA under his leadership became a dominant paradigm for the Third World in general.

His own role assumed world proportions when he became the first secretary-general of the UNITED NATIONS CONFERENCE ON TRADE AND DEVELOPMENT (UNCTAD) in 1963. There he played a more activist role than did the heads of most other UN organizations, promoting the interests of Third World countries according to his views. One of his major goals was to promote an integrated program for the support of an expanded number of commodity agreements that would regulate the production and sale of the principal products of developing nations. After retirement from UNCTAD in 1969 he remained active in various capacities with ECLAC and advised the government of Argentina until his death. To the end of his life his ideas continued to evolve in response to new circumstances and his own changing understanding of the problems of underdeveloped nations.

Further Reading: Meier, Gerald M., and Dudley Seers, eds. *Pioneers in Development.* New York: Oxford University Press, 1984: 175–91. Pinto, Anibal. "Raúl Prebisch 1901–1986." *CEPAL Review,* no. 29 (August 1986): 9–11. Prebisch, Raúl. "A Critique of Peripheral Capitalism." *CEPAL Review,* no. 1 (1976): 9–76. ——— "Notes on Trade from the Standpoint of the Periphery." *CEPAL Review,* no. 28 (April 1985): 203–14. Solis, Leopoldo. *Raúl Prebisch at ECLA: Years of Creative Intellectual Effort.* San Francisco: International Center for Economic Growth, 1988.

— M. W. Bray

president of the General Assembly   *See*
GENERAL COMMITTEE.

preventive diplomacy   *See AGENDA FOR PEACE.*

principal organs of the United Nations   *See*
ECONOMIC AND SOCIAL COUNCIL, GENERAL ASSEMBLY, INTERNATIONAL COURT OF JUSTICE, SECRETARIAT, SECURITY COUNCIL, STRUCTURE OF THE UNITED NATIONS, TRUSTEESHIP COUNCIL.

procedural committees of the General Assembly
The UN GENERAL ASSEMBLY has two permanent procedural committees: the GENERAL COMMITTEE and the CREDENTIALS COMMITTEE. The General Committee functions as the steering committee for the annual session of the General Assembly, making decisions regarding the agenda and the order in which items will be considered. It consists of the Assembly's president, 21 vice presidents, and the elected chairmen of the six main committees of the General Assembly. The Credentials Committee consists of nine members appointed at the beginning of the yearly session to consider and approve the credentials of representatives and delegations to the United Nations.

See also COMMITTEE SYSTEM OF THE GENERAL ASSEMBLY.

programmes and funds
The United Nations STRUCTURE includes a number of programmes and funds, created by the GENERAL ASSEMBLY to oversee and operate specific activities that are central to the organization's operations and purposes. Programmes and funds are differentiated from the SPECIALIZED AGENCIES in that they were created by and are part of the United Nations, whereas specialized agencies were established by separate treaties and have their own CHARTERS and executive boards. Both specialized agencies and UN programmes and funds rely on voluntary contributions from member states, and in some cases on private organizations and corporations. In addition to being formal parts of the United Nations rather than associated agencies, programmes and funds all report to both the GENERAL ASSEMBLY and the ECONOMIC AND SOCIAL COUNCIL (ECOSOC), while specialized agencies report only to ECOSOC and then exclusively for purposes of coordination with UN offices, activities, and organs.

United Nations programmes and funds include large operations that are among the principal dispensers of aid and assistance to developing countries, such as the UNITED NATIONS DEVELOPMENT PROGRAMME (UNDP). Smaller offices focus on problems of particular concern to the nations of the world. This latter group includes specialized research institutes extending knowledge regarding particular issues and assuring that the results are available to all nations. The broadest is the UNITED NATIONS INSTITUTE FOR TRAINING AND RESEARCH (UNITAR), which runs a large number of training seminars primarily for individuals from developing countries and new UN staff members. Others are more narrowly focused on particular specialties. They include the INTERNATIONAL RESEARCH AND TRAINING INSTITUTE FOR THE ADVANCEMENT OF WOMEN (INSTRAW), the UNITED NATIONS INSTITUTE FOR

DISARMAMENT RESEARCH (UNIDIR), the UNITED NATIONS INTERREGIONAL CRIME AND JUSTICE RESEARCH INSTITUTE (UNICRI), and the UNITED NATIONS RESEARCH INSTITUTE FOR SOCIAL DEVELOPMENT (UNRISD). All conduct extensive research programs in their areas of specialty, publishing reports that are made available to the governments of member states and conducting training seminars at various locations around the world.

The United Nations has also created offices that serve particular conferences and commissions, providing the specialized information and support necessary to the implementation of their missions. They supply the policy studies needed by governments to implement the programs of action adopted by the various WORLD CONFERENCES. The INTERNATIONAL TRADE CENTRE and the Centre for Transnational Corporations offer this type of service for the UNITED NATIONS CONFERENCE ON TRADE AND DEVELOPMENT (UNCTAD). Several also have their own governing boards or regular conferences, and hence constitute separate decision-making bodies within the United Nations, but all were established by the United Nations and are considered part of it.

The programmes include several large and pivotal agencies. The Office of the UNITED NATIONS HIGH COMMISSIONER FOR REFUGEES (UNHCR), established in 1993, is the primary body that provides assistance to refugees throughout the world and protects their rights. It has more than 5,000 personnel scattered throughout the world, wherever there is a refugee crisis. The UNHCR also seeks to coordinate the work of more than 450 independent NON-GOVERNMENTAL ORGANIZATIONS (NGOs) involved in refugee aid. The NGOs are designated officially as "partners" of the UNHCR. The United Nations Conference on Trade and Development promotes and represents the interests of developing nations in international trade negotiations. The UNITED NATIONS ENVIRONMENT PROGRAMME (UNEP) is the principal UN body in protecting the ENVIRONMENT. The UNITED NATIONS CHILDREN'S FUND (UNICEF) is the only UN body dedicated exclusively to the protection of children. It supports and conducts programs aimed at improving the rights of children everywhere, particularly in developing countries. It relies, like nearly all UN programmes, on voluntary contributions.

The UNITED NATIONS RELIEF AND WORKS AGENCY FOR PALESTINE REFUGEES IN THE NEAR EAST (UNRWA), one of the earliest UN offices, was established in 1949. It provides assistance to Palestinians who lost their homes and livelihood as a result of the 1948 ARAB-ISRAELI conflict, which led to the establishment of Israel and the dispersal of Palestinian refugees to the neighboring countries and throughout the Middle East, where many still remain. The UNITED NATIONS POPULATION FUND (UNFPA) is the largest multilateral source of population assistance for developing countries. It promotes efforts to improve reproductive health for WOMEN and

to encourage family planning. This work reflects its commitment to women's equality, as a critical factor in slowing global birth rates. The WORLD FOOD PROGRAMME (WFP) extends food assistance to people living in poverty and emergency relief to countries and areas affected by natural and man-made disasters.

The United Nations Development Programme (UNDP), established in 1965, is one of the UN's largest and most important offices. UNDP is the world's leading source of aid to governments to assist economic and social DEVELOPMENT, drawing on voluntary contributions. Developing countries generally prefer multilateral aid, such as that made available by the UNDP, because aid from specific countries often comes with conditions that restrict the recipient's freedom of action. The UNDP operates more than 100 country offices in developing nations, which constitute the heart of UN activities in support of development. The UNDP also manages several associated funds and programmes, including the UNITED NATIONS DEVELOPMENT FUND FOR WOMEN (UNIFEM), the UNITED NATIONS VOLUNTEERS (UNV), the Office to Combat DESERTIFICATION and Drought (UNSO), the United Nations Capital Development Fund (UNCDF), the United Nations Fund for Science and Technology for Development (UNFSDT), and the United Nations Revolving Fund for Natural Resources (UNRFNRE).

The Office of the High Commissioner for Human Rights, established in 1993, is officially designated as the focal point of all HUMAN RIGHTS activities in the United Nations. It is charged with coordinating UN efforts for the promotion of civil, cultural, political, economic, and social rights. The UNITED NATIONS CENTRE FOR HUMAN SETTLEMENTS (Habitat), originally created in 1978, was designated in 1996 as the focal point for the implementation of the Habitat Agenda adopted by the Second UN Conference on Human Settlements. It works in partnership with governments and local authorities. The UNITED NATIONS UNIVERSITY engages in research and postgraduate education, and it operates a publications program for the dissemination of knowledge. It includes several institutes and specialized programs disbursed throughout the world dealing with development, the environment, and technology.

See also ADMINISTRATIVE COMMITTEE ON COORDINATION, ADVISORY COMMITTEE ON ADMINISTRATIVE AND BUDGETARY QUESTIONS, EXPANDED PROGRAM IN TECHNICAL ASSISTANCE, GLOBAL ENVIRONMENT FACILITY, HIV/AIDS, INTER-AGENCY COMMITTEE ON SUSTAINABLE DEVELOPMENT, INTERGOVERNMENTAL PANEL ON CLIMATE CHANGE, JOINT UNITED NATIONS PROGRAMME ON AIDS, LANGUAGES, SOMALIA, SPECIAL SESSIONS OF THE GENERAL ASSEMBLY, SPECIAL UNITED NATIONS FUND FOR ECONOMIC DEVELOPMENT, SUSTAINABLE DEVELOPMENT, UNITED NATIONS CONFERENCE ON ENVIRONMENT AND DEVELOPMENT, UNITED NATIONS CONFERENCE ON THE HUMAN ENVIRONMENT, UNITED NATIONS OFFICE FOR PROJECT SERVICES.

Further Reading: United Nations Department of Public Information. *Basic Facts about the United Nations.* New York: United Nations Department of Public Information, published periodically. ———. *Everyone's United Nations.* New York: United Nations Department of Public Information, published periodically.

—*K. J. Grieb*

protocol

Protocol is a more ambiguous international term than TREATY and CONVENTION. It refers to agreed-upon rules governing diplomatic conduct or written international instruments, such as statements of principle, preliminary agreements, or authenticated minutes of an international conference, all of which might become part of a formal treaty in the future, provided the parties ratify the protocol. The KYOTO PROTOCOL of 1997 called for international agreement to cut energy emissions in the future in order to abate global warming. The protocol required formal ratification by the participating nations. As of 2001, the UNITED STATES—responsible for 40 percent of such emissions—had declined to ratify.

See also examples of protocols in BIOLOGICAL WEAPONS, IRAN-IRAQ WAR, MONTREAL PROTOCOL ON SUBSTANCES THAT DEPLETE THE OZONE LAYER, NAMIBIA, SOUTHEAST ASIA TREATY ORGANIZATION.

Quadrant Conference (Quebec Conference)

U.S. president Franklin D. ROOSEVELT (FDR) and British prime minister Winston CHURCHILL met in a wartime summit in Quebec, Canada, on August 17–24, 1943. The primary purpose of the conference was to review war plans, with particular attention to the coming invasion of Normandy in France (June 1944). However, the Quadrant Conference also proved to be an important occasion in the creation of the United Nations. Two critical matters were resolved: the British and the Americans arrived at a common conception of the general nature and outline of the organization, and the two leaders decided upon a strategy to convince Soviet Marshal Joseph STALIN that the USSR should join the new organization.

To this point, 1943 had been a year of planning for a postwar international organization in both Washington and London. In March, Churchill delivered an important radio address and at the same time sent an aide-memoire to Washington, each outlining his vision of the postwar world. Dismissive of CHINA and suspicious of the Soviet Union, the prime minister expressed the hope that the three major powers (that is, minus China) would create some sort of vague umbrella organization after victory, with the focus on a Council of Europe and a Council of Asia to ensure regional stability. The prime minister sought maximum regional autonomy, in part to assure London's independent control of the British Empire. Churchill was a geopolitician who placed his faith in great power dominance, rather than in a univer-

salist organization. Churchill's initiative compelled Roosevelt's advisers to devise a counterproposal that combined elements of FDR's "FOUR POLICEMEN" with Churchill's regional approach. It also had to reflect the general approach that Roosevelt had approved in January 1943 in meetings with Sumner Welles, his primary State Department architect for postwar organization. Welles had garnered FDR's agreement for an institution constructed in the mode of Woodrow Wilson's LEAGUE OF NATIONS, a universal COLLECTIVE SECURITY SYSTEM.

At Quebec, Roosevelt and Churchill approved the draft of a four-power DECLARATION (UNITED STATES, United Kingdom, China, and the Soviet Union), to be forwarded to Stalin, that called for a permanent global organization with an executive council heavily representing great power influence in the body. They also decided it was critical to achieve the Soviet leader's assent for the new organization before the war was won. Churchill, knowing Stalin would want to be unfettered after the war, thought the incentive of continuing Western war assistance would be essential to winning Soviet participation. Attracted first by Churchill's regional approach and then by Roosevelt's Four Policemen proposal, Stalin came to accept the concept of the United Nations at both the October 1943 MOSCOW CONFERENCE OF FOREIGN MINISTERS and the TEHERAN CONFERENCE in December. At the latter, Roosevelt outlined to Stalin what had been decided in Quebec about the STRUCTURE of the organization—it would have an assembly of all the United Nations that would discuss major world problems, but lack the authority to act, an executive committee composed of the Big Four, and six regional representatives to deal with social and economic issues. Finally, the four great powers would have sole authority to enforce the peace and prevent AGGRESSION.

Further Reading: Hoopes, Townsend, and Douglas Brinkley. *FDR and the Creation of the U.N.* New Haven, Conn.: Yale University Press, 1997. Moore, John Allphin, Jr., and Jerry Pubantz. *To Create a New World? American Presidents and the United Nations.* New York: Peter Lang Publishing, 1999.

Quantico meeting

To the extent that there was a serious discussion between the UNITED STATES and the Soviet Union during the first two decades of the COLD WAR, it occurred in the context of UN DISARMAMENT negotiations. U.S. president Dwight Eisenhower undertook his first initiative in this area with his "ATOMS FOR PEACE" SPEECH to the UN GENERAL ASSEMBLY in December 1953. At the heart of the American disarmament position was a requirement that any arms control agreement with the USSR include a verifiable inspection regime. On May 10, 1955, the Soviet delegate to the United Nations DISARMAMENT COMMISSION announced that the Soviet Union would accept many of the U.S. proposals for ground inspections. Eisenhower directed a group of advisers, headed by Nelson Rockefeller, to draft a response to be delivered at the scheduled July Geneva Summit of France, Great Britain, the United States, and the USSR, the first four-power meeting since the Potsdam Conference in 1945.

Rockefeller's group met in Quantico, Virginia, and crafted a counterproposal meant to test Soviet intentions. The included items were intended to be so tough that only if the Soviet Union were committed to ending the cold war would they be acceptable. At the center of the Quantico recommendations was a proposal to have both sides allow unfettered surveillance of their national territories. President Eisenhower, without prior U.S.–Soviet negotiation, presented the Quantico formulation to the summit in what became known as his "Open Skies" proposal. He called upon the Soviet Union to join the United States in providing to each other the complete blueprints of their military installations, and to allow each side to conduct aerial photography of the other country. He proposed complete transparency to avoid surprise attack or a breakout by one side or the other to nuclear superiority. Two weeks after the summit the president's special assistant for disarmament, Harold Stassen, introduced the Open Skies proposal to the UN Disarmament Commission. On August 18, however, the Soviet delegation rejected the Quantico recommendations as nothing but a ruse for American spying. It returned to the persistent Soviet position that only "general and complete disarmament" under UN auspices could end the nuclear threat.

Further Reading: Rostow, Walt W. *Open Skies.* Austin: University of Texas Press, 1982. Statement on Disarmament Presented at the Geneva Conference, July 21, 1955. *Public Papers of the Presidents of the United States.* Washington, D.C.: U.S. Government Printing Office, published annually.

Quebec Conference   *See* QUADRANT CONFERENCE.

R

Ramadan War   *See* ARAB-ISRAELI DISPUTE, MIDDLE EAST WAR OF 1973.

reform of the United Nations

When the world community convened for the MILLENNIUM SUMMIT and assembly at UN HEADQUARTERS in September 2000, it found the United Nations in the midst of the most far-reaching reform process in its history. The September gathering itself was an endorsement of the changes that had occurred over the previous two and a half years and of the reforms' architect, UN SECRETARY-GENERAL Kofi ANNAN. Elected Secretary-General in 1996, in part because of his commitment to undertake long-proposed revisions in the operation, staffing, and financing of the United Nations, Annan launched the latest era in UN evolution on July 16, 1997, with the publication of *Renewing the United Nations*, a compendium of reform proposals.

Throughout its history the United Nations has been subject to criticism by member states and elements of world public opinion who believe that the organization has served other interests than their own, or that revision of its purposes and STRUCTURE would make the United Nations more effective. Five times in the 20th century the UN CHARTER was formally amended. Informal "AMENDMENT" also occurred in 1950 with the adoption of the UNITING FOR PEACE RESOLUTION that allowed the GENERAL ASSEMBLY to convene EMERGENCY SPECIAL SESSIONS when the SECURITY COUNCIL was deadlocked over how to respond to a threat to international peace. Dag HAMMARSKJÖLD's tenure as Secretary-General (1953–61) enlarged the political role of that post beyond the expectations of the founding states. In the 1960s and 1970s there occurred an invigoration of the General Assembly's role in UN affairs, largely sponsored by the growing non-aligned bloc, the GROUP OF 77, and other developing country CAUCUS GROUPS. The new members of the world body hoped to limit the dominance of the great powers in the organization. Out of that same era came the development of PEACEKEEPING, an activity unmentioned in the Charter. By cobbling together aspects of the Charter's CHAPTERs VI and VII, the institution, in effect, created a "CHAPTER VI $^1/_2$" in order to authorize peacekeeping missions.

The reform movement at the close of the century was driven by four forces: demands from the U.S. government, the UN's largest contributor, for substantial institutional changes, a long-term financial crisis aggravated by the decision of the UNITED STATES to limit payments to the world body, the expansion of the number and nature of UN peacekeeping operations in the post–COLD WAR era to include nation-building, peace-making, and war-fighting, and the emergence of an activist Secretary-General who made reform the hallmark of his first term in office. The first of these—U.S. demands for change—served as the trigger not only for reform proposals, first by Secretary-General Boutros BOUTROS-GHALI in 1992, but also by Boutros-

Ghali's replacement, Kofi Annan. The United States, believing Boutros-Ghali too reluctant to carry out fundamental changes, engineered the election of Annan, thus imposing on the latter an inescapable expectation that he would lead a reform movement.

Driving the American interest in UN reform was the link between money and responsibility. With the inauguration of Ronald Reagan as president of the United States in 1981, the American public sentiment, persistent since the 1960s, that the United Nations wasted excessive U.S. contributions to the world body on policies and programs inimical to U.S. national interests became administration policy. The conservative wing of the Republican Party accused the UN majority of anti-American bias, and the institution as a whole of being ineffective. In 1985 Reagan halted expected U.S. payments—without UN consent lowering the American contribution from 25 percent of the BUDGET to 20 percent—and withdrew U.S. participation from the UNITED NATIONS EDUCATIONAL, SCIENTIFIC AND CULTURAL ORGANIZATION (UNESCO), which it accused of being too politicized. Reagan's actions were reenforced with the passage on Capitol Hill of the Kassebaum Amendment, which cut U.S. payments to UN organs until their staffs were reduced significantly, and until they made revisions to their charters in order to allow weighted VOTING based on the size of the financial contributions of the members. The State Department suggested that the United States would return to UNESCO and pay its assessments when both the SPECIALIZED AGENCY and the UN reformed themselves.

U.S. arrears neared $1 billion by 1993. Faced with potential bankruptcy without U.S. contributions, UN Secretary-General Boutros-Ghali attempted to meet U.S. demands, and opened UN internal operations to unprecedented scrutiny by a member state. In 1992 he appointed a former U.S. attorney-general, Richard Thornburgh, UNDER SECRETARY-GENERAL for administration and management. Thornburgh was allowed to review the entire organization with a view to proposing changes in operation. He, in turn, asked the Ford Foundation to study the United Nations and make recommendations for administrative change. Paul Volcker, former chairman of the U.S. Federal Reserve, and Shiguro Ogata, former deputy governor of the Japan Development Bank, headed the study, which focused on financial operations at the United Nations.

Thornburgh recommended the elimination of "dead-wood" in the UN staff, a streamlining of the personnel system, and the creation of an inspector-general's office, which would be autonomous from the Secretary-General and would root out fraud and waste. The Volcker-Ogata Report additionally recommended a unified peacekeeping budget. Separately the U.S. government sought "zero real growth" in the budgets of all UN bodies and agencies. Boutros-Ghali responded by freezing the UN budget in 1994 and supporting the creation of the OFFICE OF INTERNAL OVERSIGHT SERVICES, headed by an under secretary-general largely independent of Boutros-Ghali's control. These actions were not sufficient, however, to restore American confidence in his commitment to reform. U.S. opposition to his continued leadership of the UN was solidified further when Boutros-Ghali's proposals in 1992's AGENDA FOR PEACE, outlining a reinvigorated United Nations in preventing the outbreak of conflict along the lines contemplated by the PERMANENT MEMBERS OF THE SECURITY COUNCIL, met strong resistance in American public opinion.

Kofi Annan's Renewing the United Nations program went further than any previous attempt to remake the institution, proposing reform in four broad areas: the SECRETARIAT, the UN structure, finances, and COLLECTIVE SECURITY capabilities. His 1997 proposals included the appointment of a DEPUTY SECRETARY-GENERAL who would manage the Secretariat when the Secretary-General was away from headquarters, spearhead the reform movement inside the organization, and promote coherence among the disparate components of the UNITED NATIONS SYSTEM. In 1998 Annan appointed Louise FRÉCHETTE from Canada to the post. He also recommended the creation of a SENIOR MANAGEMENT GROUP to serve as the Secretary-General's cabinet and of a Strategic Planning Unit in his office to identify emerging global issues. He urged the strengthening of four thematic executive committees he had created in January 1997 to bring together key agencies in the different sectors of UN work. His other recommendations called for the establishment of a revolving credit fund of $1 billion to assure financial solvency, the integration of 12 Secretariat entities into five, the elimination of 1,000 staff positions (a 25 percent cut in personnel from a decade earlier), a reduction in administrative costs by 33 percent, with a share of savings going into a new DEVELOPMENT ACCOUNT for projects in the developing world, the "decentralization of decision-making at the country level while consolidating the UN presence under 'one flag,'" the adoption of "results-based budgeting" in order to assure accountability, the imposition of "sunset" provisions on new UN programs, and the reform of the DEPARTMENT OF PEACEKEEPING OPERATIONS (DPKO), including the provision for rapid deployment forces and centralization of control over the increasing number of peacekeeping efforts.

The new collective security function played by the United Nations in peacekeeping garnered special attention from Secretary-General Annan. As assistant secretary, and then under secretary-general for peacekeeping operations from 1993 to 1995, he witnessed the considerable growth in size and scope of those missions and oversaw 17 military operations with a $3.5 billion budget, 15 times larger than the budget of 1988. In his 1997 report he called for significant changes in how DPKO managed operations. He also suggested that the UN strengthen its capacity for nation-building. Echoing Boutros-Ghali's ill-fated Agenda for Peace, Annan called for a UN High Readiness Brigade in order to establish a credible UN presence at an early stage of a conflict. He recommended that the Security Council draft a model Status of Forces Agreement (SOFA) to be used when peacekeeping operations were contemplated.

The General Assembly substantially approved the Secretary-General's proposals in December 1997. Its RESOLUTION also recognized "that reform of the United Nations will be an ongoing process and that there is a need for the United Nations to consider changes of a more fundamental nature and other broader issues." The Assembly invited the Secretary-General to recommend changes in the TRUSTEESHIP COUNCIL and the United Nations system, and even to submit needed amendments to the Charter. Demonstrating extraordinary bureaucratic and public relations skills, Annan managed to put most of his reforms in place in time for the Millennium Summit, and to accomplish them with little in the way of criticism. Annan's continuing efforts at reform included the appointment in April 2002 of Patricia Durrant from Jamaica as the UN's first ombudsman. The endorsement of his reforms was best reflected in the Security Council's and General Assembly's decisions, well before his term expired, to reelect him as Secretary-General for another five-year period. The United States, believing the reforms to be permanent and real, reached agreement with the United Nations on a repayment package of its arrears. There was a difference in opinion between Washington and New York over exactly how much the United States owed, but the account was settled with a final payment by the United States in October 2001.

See also ADMINISTRATIVE COMMITTEE ON COORDINATION; BRAHIMI REPORT; ECONOMIC AND SOCIAL COUNCIL; GOLDBERG RESERVATION; MULTILATERALISM; PÉREZ DE CUÉLLAR, JAVIER; SCALE OF ASSESSMENTS; SUBSIDIARITY; TROIKA PROPOSAL; VETO.

Further Reading: Annan, Kofi. *Renewing the United Nations: A Programme for Reform.* UN Document A/51/950, July 16, 1997. ———. *We the Peoples: The Role of the United Nations in the 21st Century.* New York: United Nations Department of Public Information, 2000. Fassbender, Bodo. *UN Security Council Reform and the Right of Veto.* The Hague: Kluwer Law International, 1998. Gordon, Wendell. *The United Nations at the Crossroads of Reform.* Armonk, N.Y.: M. E. Sharpe, 1994. Hoffmann, Walter. *United Nations Security Council Reform and Restructuring.* Livingston, N.J.: Center for U. N. Reform Education, 1994. Moore, John Allphin, Jr., and Jerry Pubantz. *To Create a New World? American Presidents and the United Nations.* New York: Peter Lang, 1999. Taylor, Paul, Sam Daws, and Ute Adamczick-Gerteis, eds. *Documents on Reform of the United Nations.* Brookfield, Vt.: Dartmouth, 1997. Volker, Paul, and Shituro Ogata, et al. *Financing an Effective United Nations.* New York: Ford Foundation, 1993.

Refugee Convention   *See* CONVENTION RELATING TO THE STATUS OF REFUGEES.

refugees   *See* CONVENTION RELATING TO THE STATUS OF REFUGEES, UNITED NATIONS HIGH COMMISSIONER FOR REFUGEES, UNITED NATIONS RELIEF AND WORKS AGENCY FOR PALESTINE REFUGEES IN THE NEAR EAST.

regional development banks

In addition to the WORLD BANK Group, there are four major regional development banks that provide financial support and expertise for economic development activities in the Third World. Along with the World Bank, subregional banks, and multilateral financial institutions (MFIs), these banks make up a complex lending STRUCTURE for UN development activities. They are the African Development Bank, created in 1964 with its headquarters in Abidjan, Côte d'Ivoire, the Asian Development Bank, founded in 1966, the Inter-American Development Bank, created in 1959, and the newest of the four, the European Bank for Reconstruction and Development, established in 1991. Each bank has its own mandate, board of directors, and independent status. However, the banks have overlapping members, including both borrowing developing countries and developed states that invest in the institutions.

Also known as multilateral development banks (MDBs), these banks have large memberships, ranging in 2001 from 57 shareholders in the Asian Development Bank to 86 in the European Bank. Each institution makes several different types of loans: long term loans to developing countries in their region at market rates, very long term loans—referred to as "credits"—at interest rates well below the international market, and grant financing, which pays for ancillary expenses associated with development projects. The MDBs borrow in the world capital markets and then re-lend these funds. They also use donor contributions to make loans that are not financially viable in the market. Loans and credits made in the late 1990s totaled from $1 billion to $5 billion annually for each bank.

Within the UNITED NATIONS SYSTEM the banks have been integrated into a coordinated framework to assure the greatest cooperation and efficient use of financial resources. They work closely with the multilateral financial institutions, the most important of which are the European Investment Bank, the INTERNATIONAL FUND FOR AGRICULTURAL DEVELOPMENT, the Islamic Bank, the Nordic Development Fund, the Nordic Investment Bank, and the OPEC Fund for International Development. These bodies have narrower memberships than the regional development banks and focus on specialized activities. The banks are also closely associated with REGIONAL ORGANIZATIONS in their area. For example, the African Development Bank and the Islamic Development Bank entered into an agreement with the ECONOMIC COMMUNITY OF WEST AFRICAN STATES (ECOWAS) to finance projects both for regional and non-regional entrepreneurs and microenterprises. The regional banks also worked with the World Bank on the COMMITTEE OF INTERNATIONAL DEVELOPMENT INSTITUTIONS ON THE ENVIRONMENT (CIDIE), created in the 1980s, to resolve the competing interests between development in LESS DEVELOPED COUNTRIES and the global environmental initiatives launched at the 1972 UNITED NATIONS CONFERENCE ON THE HUMAN ENVIRONMENT in Stockholm.

The ENVIRONMENT has become a special concern to the MDBs. AGENDA 21, promulgated by the 1992 Earth Summit, called for cooperation among the UNITED NATIONS ENVIRONMENT PROGRAMME (UNEP), the UNITED NATIONS DEVELOPMENT PROGRAMME (UNDP), the UNITED NATIONS CONFERENCE ON TRADE AND DEVELOPMENT (UNCTAD), the GLOBAL ENVIRONMENT FACILITY (GEF), the INTERNATIONAL DEVELOPMENT ASSOCIATION (IDA), and the regional development banks in the effort to carry out more than 1,000 specific recommendations. Each bank has set up an environmental department to focus attention on methods of financing that contribute to SUSTAINABLE DEVELOPMENT. The banks have also been important actors in the global mechanism set up to finance the battle against DESERTIFICATION.

Further Reading: Culpepper, Roy. *Titans or Behemoths? The Multilateral Development Banks.* Ottawa: North South Institute, 1997. Upton, Barbara. *The Multilateral Development Banks. Improving U.S. Leadership.* Washington, D.C.: Center for Strategic and International Studies, 2000.

regional economic commissions of the economic and Social Council

In 1947, faced with the devastation of World War II, the UN ECONOMIC AND SOCIAL COUNCIL (ECOSOC) at the urging of the GENERAL ASSEMBLY created the Economic Commission for Europe (ECE) and the Economic Commission for Asia and the Far East—renamed in 1974 the Economic and Social Commission for Asia and the Pacific (ESCAP). These institutions served as mechanisms to encourage regional cooperation in postwar reconstruction. Pressed by Latin American states to acknowledge as equally important economic DEVELOPMENT in other parts of the world, the United Nations created the Economic Commission for LATIN AMERICA in 1948, redesignating it in 1984 as the ECONOMIC COMMISSION FOR LATIN AMERICA AND THE CARIBBEAN (ECLAC). ECOSOC created the Economic Commission for AFRICA (ECA) in 1958 and the Economic Commission for Western Asia (ECWA) in 1974, renamed the Economic and Social Commission for Western Asia (ESCWA) in 1985. The five regional commissions include countries within their respective regions and work with REGIONAL MULTILATERAL BANKS, other REGIONAL ORGANIZATIONS, the WORLD BANK Group, and NON-GOVERNMENTAL ORGANIZATIONS in an effort to develop regional responses to economic and social challenges.

All of the regional commissions are funded by the regular UN BUDGET. They provide technical expertise, planning services, and sponsorship of regional agencies. The 53-member Economic Commission for Africa has been particularly active in promoting new economic initiatives. It was instrumental in the establishment of the African Development Bank, the ECONOMIC COMMUNITY OF WEST AFRICAN STATES (ECOWAS), the African Institute for Economic Development and Planning, and the Community of Eastern and Southern Africa (COMESA). By the turn of the century the Economic Commission for Europe had sponsored more than 30 CONVENTIONS and PROTOCOLS, and more than 250 regional regulations on matters ranging from consumer welfare to environmental protection.

Each of the commissions has a self-designed organizational STRUCTURE, usually including a ministerial-level governing board that reports to ECOSOC, a SECRETARIAT, and specialized committees to carry out commission projects. ESCAP, the largest of the commissions, has thematic committees on regional economic cooperation, environmental concerns, and socioeconomic measures to alleviate poverty. It also has committees on tourism, communications, transport, and infrastructure development. The Economic Commission for Europe, which includes in its MEMBERSHIP the UNITED STATES, Israel, and Canada, has committees on sustainable energy, human settlements, inland transport, and trade. The executive director of each commission is appointed by the SECRETARY-GENERAL of the United Nations.

See also APARTHEID, DEPARTMENT OF ECONOMIC AND SOCIAL AFFAIRS, ENVIRONMENT, PREBISCH, SENIOR MANAGEMENT GROUP.

Further Reading: ECE website: <www.unece.org>. ESCAP website: <www.unescap.org>. ECLAC website: <www.eclac.org>. ECA website: <www.uneca.org>. ESCWA website: <www.escwa.org.lb>.

regional organizations

Regional organizations, a form of intergovernmental organization, have played varying roles in international politics. There are several different types of regional organizations, reflecting the primary goals of states in the geographical areas they represent. Some trace their origins to political issues, whereas others began as regional trading blocs. They have evolved differently. Some are continental in scope while others deal with cultural regions or small areas. At times a debate over the value and role of regionalism as opposed to globalism has caused tension between regional groups and global institutions like the United Nations. The purposes of both types of organization often overlap. Proponents of regional organizations draw attention to the benefits of allowing common issues to be addressed by neighboring states who share similar cultures and values, facilitating consensus. They believe that regional MULTILATERALISM is a necessary precursor to universalism. Supporters of universal international organizations, on the other hand, argue that peace is indivisible, that it must be preserved on a worldwide level, and that a global approach enables a more advantageous pooling of resources. They also point out that disputes are more likely to occur with one's neighbors, and that it may prove difficult for regional groupings to address issues as effectively and impartially as can more comprehensive organizations.

This tension was present at the very founding of the United Nations. The United Nations was originally proposed, and its basic STRUCTURE designed, in negotiations among the major powers of World War II, primarily by the UNITED STATES, Great Britain, and the Soviet Union, with some participation by CHINA. The mid-sized powers and smaller states were not involved in the conference at DUMBARTON OAKS or the YALTA CONFERENCE when the big powers worked out the details of the new global organization. Latin American nations objected that the proposed CHARTER contained no reference to regional organizations. The nations of the Western Hemisphere were proud of having formed the earliest regional organization in 1889: the Pan American Union, which had functioned with success during the recent war. Latin Americans wished to preserve the role of the Pan American Union, and initially stated their intentions in the Act of Chapultepec, drafted at the Inter-American Conference on Peace and Security held in Mexico in 1945.

Latin American insistence on provisions allowing regional organizations and dispute settlement became a major issue at the San Francisco Conference, and led directly to Chapter VIII of the UN Charter dealing with "Regional Arrangements." Article 52 stated "Nothing in the present Charter precludes the existence of regional arrangements or agencies for dealing with such matters relating to the maintenance of international peace and security as are appropriate for regional action." Correspondingly, Article 51 acknowledged the right of COLLECTIVE SELF-DEFENSE and allowed regional arrangements such as the Rio PACT for defense of the Americas against external attack, and served expressly to prevent a Security Council VETO from interfering with regional action under such treaties. Several delegations, however, objected to the Latin American proposals, fearful that regional organizations would undercut the authority of the United Nations to intervene when there was a threat to international peace and security. As a compromise, provisions of the Charter allowed a nation to take a dispute either to the appropriate regional organization or to the UN SECURITY COUNCIL. While this bargain did not allay some initial tensions, the issue cooled with time as both the United Nations and the regional organizations gained experience.

Regional organizations of diverse types were formed as colonialism ended and more nations gained independence.

The Pan American Union evolved in 1948 into the ORGANIZATION OF AMERICAN STATES (OAS), which emphasized political stability, and progressively added other issues of concern to its agenda. The ORGANIZATION OF AFRICAN UNITY (OAU) was formed in 1963, focusing initially on continental cooperation to end colonialism and resistance to extra-continental interference. Both the OAS and OAU adopted provisions preserving the existing NATION-STATE borders, since all nations recognized that any attempt to change colonial boundaries would lead to continental warfare and chaos. Both Africa and LATIN AMERICA later developed a series of subregional organizations that began as free trade groups, since continent-wide economic cooperation proved difficult. Some of these groups, such as the ECONOMIC COMMUNITY OF WEST AFRICAN STATES (ECOWAS) later added security matters to their agendas.

The pattern differed on other continents. The European Union was originally founded on the basis of economic cooperation and free trade. At its formation, it consisted only of a small number of West European nations with democratic governments, reflecting the division of Europe during the COLD WAR. The Organization for Security and Cooperation in Europe (OSCE), a continent-wide group, played a limited role until the end of the cold war. The North Atlantic Treaty Organization, founded in 1949, was also regarded as a regional organization, although it was based on a military alliance, differentiating it from other regional groupings. The Arab League and the Organization of the Islamic Conference (OIC) were both based on cultural and religious affinity spanning more than a single continent. In Asia, intense nationalism, the sensitivities resulting from World War II, and differences between large and small nations in power and development prevented the emergence of a single continent-wide organization. However, in 1967 Indonesia, Malaysia, the Philippines, Singapore, and Thailand formed a loose, consultative inter-governmental organization, the Association of South East Asian Nations (ASEAN), which by 2001 had expanded to include a total of 10 members in that subregion.

During the 1990s, cooperation between the United Nations and regional organizations increased. The Organization of African Unity established the OAU Mechanism on Conflict Prevention, Management, and Resolution in 1993, in an effort to deal with the many conflicts on the continent. It represented an important step in implementing the founding concept of the OAU, which was to find "African solutions to African problems." It also provided an alternative to direct UN involvement. Africans considered its establishment part of an effort to prevent external intervention on the continent. The mechanism also constituted a significant step in the evolution of regional organizations. It meant that African states had agreed to OAU intervention in internal conflicts in order to preserve continental peace and stability. Since its creation, the mechanism has been involved in efforts to settle all African conflicts, with varying degrees of success. These efforts have led to close cooperation with the United Nations. ECOWAS developed in a similar manner, and became active in conducting its own PEACEKEEPING operations in the region. During the 1990s the United Nations engaged in co-deployments and joint peacekeeping operations with the OAU and ECOWAS in SIERRA LEONE and Liberia, and in joint election monitoring with the OAS in HAITI and EL SALVADOR. Cooperative and joint actions typified the leadership of UN SECRETARY-GENERAL Kofi ANNAN. By the turn of the century, it was not uncommon to find cooperation between the United Nations and regional organizations in a wide range of projects and actions. This represented a significant development and reflected the growing importance of regional organizations in the post–cold war world and in the UNITED NATIONS SYSTEM.

In addition to joint action, regional organizations have also served as the focal points for regional caucuses to promote cooperation on global and regional issues before the United Nations. The OAU, OIC, and Arab League maintain their own MISSIONS at UN HEADQUARTERS. Other regional organizations rely on the nation serving as chairman of the group to represent the organization's interest in the world body.

See also APPEAL TO THE SECURITY COUNCIL, JURISDICTION OF THE UNITED NATIONS, SOUTHEAST ASIA TREATY ORGANIZATION, TERRORISM.

Further Reading: El-Ayouty, Yassin, ed. *The Organization of African Unity after Thirty Years.* New York: Praeger, 1994. Falk, Richard K., and Saul H. Mendlovitz, eds. *Regional Politics and World Order.* San Francisco: Freeman, 1973. United Nations. *Cooperation between the United Nations and the Organization of African Unity, Annual Report by the General Assembly.* New York: United Nations, 1998. See annual reports of the UN Secretary-General on the work of the organization, for information on joint activities with regional organizations.

— *K. J. Grieb*

Regular Budget   *See* BUDGET OF THE UNITED NATIONS.

Renewing the United Nations   *See* ANNAN, KOFI; REFORM OF THE UNITED NATIONS.

Republic of China   *See* CHINA.

resolution

An international term for a formal decision or expression of opinion by a legislative assembly, committee, or public meeting of some kind, passed by inter-governmental institu-

tions—such as the GENERAL ASSEMBLY—usually by a majority vote. Legal validity of resolutions is subject to different interpretations. This is particularly true of UN resolutions. Nations are much more likely to abide by PACTS, treaties, or CONVENTIONS they sign. According to the UN CHARTER, resolutions passed by the SECURITY COUNCIL as CHAPTER VII ENFORCEMENT MEASURES impose mandatory obligations on all member states.

right to development   *See* DECLARATION ON THE RIGHT TO DEVELOPMENT.

Rio Conference   *See* UNITED NATIONS CONFERENCE ON ENVIRONMENT AND DEVELOPMENT (UNCED).

Rio Declaration

Adopted by the UNITED NATIONS CONFERENCE ON ENVIRONMENT AND DEVELOPMENT (UNCED) on June 13, 1992, the DECLARATION is a statement of the rights and obligations of states regarding the ENVIRONMENT and the development process. It was promulgated as one of the four central "products" of the "Earth Summit" held in Rio de Janeiro; the other three being the issuance of a Plan of Action known as AGENDA 21, the STATEMENT OF FOREST PRINCIPLES, and the creation of the COMMISSION ON SUSTAINABLE DEVELOPMENT (CSD). The declaration, made up of 27 general principles, is a part of the new globalist agenda pursued by the United Nations, which became in the 1990s the leading institutional force for international environmental protection.

Advocates of the declaration had early aspirations that the Rio Conference would produce an "Earth Charter" equivalent in force to the UNIVERSAL DECLARATION OF HUMAN RIGHTS. Building on the work of the 1972 STOCKHOLM CONFERENCE ON THE HUMAN ENVIRONMENT and the 1987 BRUNDTLAND COMMISSION Report, environmentalists hoped UNCED would produce a ringing statement on international environmental law. The difficulty with the goal, however, lay in the essential conflict between protecting a global environment which would require imposing international restraints on UN member states, and preserving the fundamental UN principle of SOVEREIGNTY. On a practical level as well, the creation of an "Earth Charter" would impinge on the development programs of many poor states. Under strong pressure on both counts from LESS DEVELOPED COUNTRIES (LDCs), UNCED not only limited itself to a more prosaic "declaration" but also raised "development" concerns to the same level as "environmental" issues on the international agenda. In some of the declaration's principles, in fact, development is given priority over environmental protection. This priority was opposed strenuously by the developed nations of the North, but in the end it was accepted in order to achieve some progress on environmental matters.

The first principle proclaims that "human beings [not "nature," or the "environment"] are at the centre of concerns for SUSTAINABLE DEVELOPMENT." Principle 2 reaffirms the "sovereign right" of states to exploit their own resources and to pursue "their own environmental and developmental policies." Principles 3 and 4 make clear that the focus of the document is on the special needs of the developing countries and their right to pursue development, with the developed world having the obligation to provide assistance in the pursuit of sustainable development. In many ways the declaration provided an opportunity for the less developed countries to resurrect the agenda of the NEW INTERNATIONAL ECONOMIC ORDER (NIEO). This is affirmed in Principle 12, which calls for a "supportive and open international economic system," prohibits trade measures for environmental purposes that would constitute "arbitrary or unjustifiable discrimination" against developing states, and requires "international consensus" on environmental measures addressing transboundary concerns.

Some progress on the world's environmental agenda, however, is reflected in the declaration. Principle 10 calls for the participation of individuals at the subnational, national, and international levels of environmental policy making. Specifically, WOMEN (Principle 20), youth (Principle 21), and INDIGENOUS PEOPLES (Principle 22) are encouraged to become involved. The Rio statement also recognized the "Polluter Pays Principle" (Principle 16), which requires states to pay for not only the costs of pollution *prevention* but also damage costs from pollution itself. While this legal concept had been established in earlier limited agreements, this was the first general acceptance of it by the world community. Principle 17 calls on states to conduct environmental impact assessments for activities that could have a "significant adverse impact on the environment." Principle 18 requires states immediately to notify other states when environmental emergencies arise. Finally, the declaration recognizes the interdependence among and indivisibility of peace, development, and environmental protection.

Further Reading: Campiglio, Luigi; Laura Pineschi; Domenico Siniscalco; and Tullio Treves. *The Environment after Rio.* London: Graham and Trotman, Ltd., 1994. Sands, Philippe, ed. *Greening International Law.* New York: The New Press, 1994. Rio Declaration website: <www.un.org/documents/ga/conf151/aconf15126-lannex1.htm>.

Rome International Criminal Court Treaty Conference   *See* INTERNATIONAL CRIMINAL COURT.

Roosevelt, Eleanor (1884–1962)

Considered one of the most influential presidential spouses in American history, Eleanor Roosevelt outlived her husband Franklin Delano ROOSEVELT by 17 years, and during that time served spiritedly in a number of important public service posts. In 1962 President John F. KENNEDY appointed her to the first U.S. Commission on the Status of WOMEN, and both presidents Harry S. Truman and Kennedy made her a U.S. ambassador to the United Nations. She served as chair of the first UN COMMISSION ON HUMAN RIGHTS, which authored the UNIVERSAL DECLARATION OF HUMAN RIGHTS.

Born into a prominent New York family, Roosevelt grew up in a privileged environment. She was the niece of President Theodore Roosevelt, and in 1905 she married her distant cousin, Franklin Roosevelt. Markedly shy, she nonetheless early in life became an activist for various social causes, and continued her interest while raising five children. When in 1921 Franklin was stricken by poliomyelitis, she evinced a more determined attention to politics and worked to keep her husband engaged in public affairs. As wife of the governor of New York and then of the president of the UNITED STATES, she became uniquely visible as a first lady. She was active in women's organizations, encouraged youth movements, advocated civil rights for minorities and consumer rights for average Americans, and urged government reforms to provide sufficient housing and jobs for the poorest Americans. During the Great Depression of the 1930s her voice was particularly important. In 1933 she held the first press conference ever by a president's wife. She wrote often and on many subjects. In 1935 she began a daily column, *My Day,* which ran in wide syndication for many years, and for a while she hosted a radio program. She was well known for her wide-ranging travel throughout the country, observing and reporting on conditions among even the lowliest, giving lectures, furthering liberal causes, and publicly urging her husband to follow her lead. During World War II she served as assistant director of the Office of Civilian Defense and she traveled extensively overseas, visiting Great Britain and areas in the Pacific and the Caribbean. Always she reported back to the president.

Appointed by President Truman to the new United Nations, she served from 1945 to 1953, and then was appointed again in 1961 by President Kennedy. Mrs. Roosevelt treasured her service at the United Nations, believing that forceful labors by dedicated and talented people from throughout the world were needed to launch this new organization that had been envisaged by her late husband. She once said of the United Nations that it was "a bridge upon which we can meet and talk." Her prestige and personal qualities were key factors in developing the Universal Declaration of Human Rights. As she served, first as U.S. representative on the General Assembly THIRD COMMITTEE, and then as chair of the Commission on Human Rights, she became friends with, and was considered a leader by, some of the most significant thinkers and diplomats of the postwar period.

In early 1946 the newly formed ECONOMIC AND SOCIAL COUNCIL (ECOSOC) asked her to serve on a "nuclear" commission that was to make recommendations regarding a permanent commission on HUMAN RIGHTS. This small committee began to meet at Hunter College in New York City in spring 1946, where its first act was to elect Mrs. Roosevelt its chair. The most important recommendation forwarded by this small committee was that the proposed human rights commission consider its first task to write a bill of human rights. Mrs. Roosevelt outlined the work of this committee in an article published in the influential journal *Foreign Affairs*. In June 1946, the commission was established and Eleanor Roosevelt was unanimously elected its chair. From that moment until December 10, 1948, Mrs. Roosevelt was consumed with guiding the intricate negotiations that led to GENERAL ASSEMBLY approval of the final document. She convinced a reluctant U.S. State Department to accede to the inclusion in the DECLARATION of social and economic rights along with more traditional political and civil rights. With skilled diplomacy she encouraged and cajoled powerful individuals from a myriad of philosophical and political backgrounds to come together and agree on the final composition of the declaration.

Her success warrants more approbation when one considers the environment in which she worked. Representatives from the Western nations, the Soviet bloc, LATIN AMERICA, the developing world, and from Christian, Islamic, Hindu, Buddhist, Confucianist, and secular traditions all converged to discuss a "universal" statement on rights. And the discussion took place as the world plunged into new and difficult divisions, caused by the onset of the COLD WAR, serious divisions in South Asia as India and Pakistan gained independence, and the intractable dispute initiated with the partition of Palestine. Moreover, it fell to Mrs. Roosevelt to guide the document through a drafting committee and the Human Rights Commission, where there was serious disagreement about the type of document to recommend to the General Assembly. Several small states wanted a binding COVENANT with methods of implementation. Others, particularly among the great powers, wanted a non-binding vague declaration. And the Soviet Union wanted no document at all. Roosevelt endorsed a process that divided the commission into three working groups. She chaired the First Working Group that proceeded to draft a declaration with the persuasive "moral value" of past momentous proclamations, such as the American Declaration of Independence and the French Declaration of the Rights of Man and Citizen. The other working groups focused on drafting binding covenants and implementation procedures. Having crafted the Universal Declaration of Human Rights through this procedure, Roosevelt then shepherded it through the debate in the Third Committee of the General Assembly (where each of the 30 articles was thrashed out in detail), and before the General Assembly. In the end, the declaration passed without a negative vote. The final tally, completed early on December 10, 1948, was 48 in favor, eight abstentions (Saudi Arabia and seven nations from the Soviet bloc), and none opposed. The PRESIDENT OF THE GENERAL ASSEMBLY, Herbert Evatt, closed the session with a tribute to Eleanor Roosevelt: "It is particularly fitting that there should be present on this occasion the person who, with the assistance of many others, has played a leading role in the work, a person who has raised to greater heights even so great a name—Mrs. Roosevelt, the representative of the United States of America."

Eleanor Roosevelt continued her extraordinarily active life until her death at the age of 78, in 1962, remembering that at the age of 62 she had begun, and at the age of 64 she had completed, what she, and what many observers believe to be, as historian Mary Ann Glendon phrased it, "her greatest achievement."

See also UNITED NATIONS ASSOCIATION.

Further Reading: Cook, Blanche Wiesen. *Eleanor Roosevelt*. Vol. 2. New York: Viking, 1999. Glendon, Mary Ann. *A World Made New; Eleanor Roosevelt and the Universal Declaration of Human Rights*. New York: Random House, 2001. Roosevelt, Eleanor. *On My Own*. New York: Harper, 1958.

Roosevelt, Franklin D. (1882–1945)

Franklin Roosevelt, the 32nd president of the UNITED STATES, is the only person elected to the office four times (1933–45). Born into a family of wealth and connection in Hyde Park, New York, Roosevelt was educated at Harvard University and Columbia University School of Law. He was the fifth cousin of President Theodore Roosevelt, from whose enthusiasm for public service "FDR" developed a motivation to pursue politics and elective office. During his years at Harvard, he met, and then became engaged to, President Roosevelt's niece, Eleanor ROOSEVELT. They were married in 1905. Because of his support for Woodrow Wilson's successful 1912 presidential campaign, he was appointed assistant secretary of the navy in 1913. During World War I he was a strong advocate of military preparedness and for Wilson's internationalism. He was nominated for vice president of the United States by the Democratic Party in 1920. Sharing the ticket with James M. Cox, Roosevelt campaigned for ratification of the Versailles TREATY and the creation of the LEAGUE OF NATIONS. Following the Democrats' loss to Warren G. Harding and Calvin Coolidge, he returned to New York and a promising political future.

FDR's political fortunes were dealt a severe blow in August 1921 when he was struck with polio. It fell to his wife Eleanor to keep his name and views before the public, which she did with great skill. In 1928 he won the New York gubernatorial race, succeeding Governor Alfred E.

Smith. In 1932 he soundly defeated Republican incumbent, and former Wilson adviser, Herbert Hoover for the presidency, promising a "New Deal" in the depths of the Great Depression. During his tenure in office, Roosevelt faced not only the worst economic downturn in U.S. history but also the rising threat of European dictatorships, and then World War II.

Roosevelt became the "architect" of the United Nations. Out of the ruins of World War II it was he and his advisers—principally Cordell HULL, Leo PASVOLSKY, Edward STETTINIUS, and Sumner Welles—who crafted a new world organization that they believed suffered from few of the League's weaknesses, and it was FDR who convinced Winston CHURCHILL and Joseph STALIN to accept the United Nations as the primary vehicle for maintaining peace and security in the postwar era. FDR's central role emerged slowly, however. When Churchill broached the idea of a postwar organization during their meeting off Newfoundland in the 1941 Atlantic Conference, all that the president would agree to was "the establishment of a wider and permanent system of general security." Roosevelt entered the war an advocate of great power realism, believing former president Wilson's League had been too dependent on world public opinion and not adequately sensitive to the realities of power. Three weeks after the Japanese attack on Pearl Harbor Roosevelt and Churchill drafted the "DECLARATION BY UNITED NATIONS" laying out the new allies' war aims. Signing ceremonies were held first for the representatives of the United States, the USSR, the United Kingdom, and CHINA, followed the next day for 22 "lesser" powers committed to defeating Germany in the war. Roosevelt personally decided on the order of signatories, listing them on the basis of power differentials.

In 1942 Roosevelt assured Sumner Welles that when "the moment became ripe," he would push for a new world organization. His conception of it at the time was described best in his "FOUR POLICEMEN" PROPOSAL in which he emphasized the use of military power by the "Big Four" of the wartime Grand Alliance in order to insure postwar peace. During the course of 1943, Roosevelt shared his views of a great power dominated association of nations with Winston Churchill (a supporter of regional security arrangements), and, at the TEHERAN CONFERENCE, with Joseph Stalin. In his view the Soviet Union, Great Britain, China, and the United States would have a regional responsibility for maintaining peace, and would act together to enforce world stability, even forcibly carrying out DISARMAMENT of smaller powers. At the State Department a planning group proposed a "United Nations Authority" with a security commission consisting of the four great powers, thus incorporating Roosevelt's idea into a more general universal organization.

When the president floated his proposal in an interview in *The Saturday Evening Post* in April 1943, the public reaction was lukewarm. Moreover, there were practical problems

with the concept, since it did not provide a place in the scheme for France, did not envision how Great Britain and the USSR would disentangle their conflicting national interests in Europe, nor provide much enticement for smaller states to be part of the world organization.

While the president continued to proselytize for the Four Policemen as peacekeepers, his secretary of state, Cordell Hull, was moving slowly in another direction. Hull first mentioned to President Roosevelt in July 1942 the need for some postwar agency that could enforce the rule of law and pacific settlement in disputes. The secretary then set up a technical committee to draft plans for an international organization. This committee, largely under Leo Pasvolsky's leadership, worked until the end of the war to develop the proposals that would ultimately serve as the basis for the DUMBARTON OAKS Program and for the UN CHARTER itself. In March 1943 a draft constitution for an international organization was forwarded to Roosevelt. The proposed Charter created a general conference, a SECRETARIAT, agencies for technical services, and, most important, an executive committee consisting of the Four Policemen and a council made up of the four powers plus seven other representatives of REGIONAL ORGANIZATIONS. In a series of meetings during the spring and summer of 1943, Franklin Roosevelt informally gave his blessing to the effort to obtain British and Soviet assent to a new international organization, at least "in principle," along the lines of the draft charter.

As the allies took the offensive in 1943, concerns about maintaining cooperation among the great powers after the war were of growing importance to the president. Cordell Hull traveled to the MOSCOW CONFERENCE OF FOREIGN MINISTERS in October, hopeful that he could convince Britain, Russia, and China that cooperation in a global international organization would serve their interests after the war. Hull made the necessary concessions to achieve a Four Power DECLARATION supporting the American initiative. Following the conference, the Roosevelt administration found domestic public sentiment overwhelmingly supportive of a new institutional STRUCTURE to maintain the peace. Even many Republicans, including the party's standard-bearer in 1940, Wendell Willkie, only criticized Roosevelt for not moving fast enough to put an organization in place by the end of hostilities.

Ever in tune with shifting public opinion, the president had strong reason to push ahead with the State Department's proposals. After the Moscow Conference, he became much more directly involved in the planning for the new international organization and in the negotiation of its details. By the time the TEHERAN CONFERENCE convened in November 1943, Roosevelt's thinking about postwar arrangements had evolved to the point of combining Wilsonian organizational solutions with a hoped-for long-lasting friendship among the great powers. At Teheran FDR outlined his proposal for a worldwide assembly with an executive committee and a four-nation enforcement body. The president assured a concerned Stalin that the new organization would not be able to impose its will on its members. Stalin and his emissaries would return to this commitment during subsequent negotiations whenever proposals surfaced that would give the body some control over the great powers. In particular, Stalin would insist on an absolute VETO for the Soviet Union. Stalin, in effect, demanded a fundamental revision of the VOTING procedure from the earlier League of Nations, which had not allowed states to vote on disputes in which they were involved.

Following his return from the meeting with Soviet and British leaders, Roosevelt approved a "Plan for the Establishment of an International Organization for the Maintenance of International Peace and Security." According to the plan, not only would the new organization be responsible for international peace but also would have agencies for economic and social activities. It would also have trusteeship responsibilities, taking over the mandate system from the League of Nations, and revising it to encourage decolonization. The American government would now push for full self-determination. The future United Nations, through its TRUSTEESHIP COUNCIL, would provide the mechanism. Also included in the president's plan for the UN was a SECURITY COUNCIL, a GENERAL ASSEMBLY, a Secretariat of international civil servants, and an INTERNATIONAL COURT OF JUSTICE to replace the League's PERMANENT COURT OF INTERNATIONAL JUSTICE.

The most serious Charter issue that Roosevelt had to solve in the final months of the war was the question of voting: how to protect the traditional SOVEREIGNTY of the NATION-STATES that would be members of the world organization and yet not allow the United Nations to fall victim to the requirement of unanimity among the members which had destroyed the League. This issue was addressed in many settings by the administration, but it was at the 1944 Dumbarton Oaks Conference, and at the YALTA CONFERENCE in February 1945, that Roosevelt brought the matter to conclusion.

The U.S. government invited Russia, Britain, and China to convene at Dumbarton Oaks in Washington, D.C., in two separate sessions beginning on August 21 to thrash out the technical aspects of the new international organization. They met for five weeks, and the items still being contested were left for the three wartime leaders to resolve. While most of the American proposal put forward at the conference was adopted with little revision, Under-Secretary of State Stettinius's recommendation that parties to a dispute before the Security Council should not be allowed to vote on the matter, even if a party happened to be one of the PERMANENT MEMBERS, was not accepted. He argued that, while unanimity among the great powers was essential to the success of the new organization, if one of the powers could veto discussion of, much less action on, a dispute, the United Nations would

be as moribund as the League of Nations. The president believed that public opinion in the United States would reject an organization that appeared unlikely to work because it suffered from the League's deficiencies. The Soviets rejected the proposal, insisting that all issues before the Security Council should be subject to the unanimous agreement of the permanent members. Stalin believed this was the clear meaning of FDR's assurances at Teheran.

More surprising than the Russian rejection of the voting procedure proposed by the United States was an additional Soviet demand that the 16 Union republics of the USSR each be admitted as original members of the United Nations, in effect giving Stalin 16 votes in the General Assembly. With this arrangement unacceptable to the United States, neither issue could be resolved at the conference.

As the president prepared to travel to Yalta for a summit with Stalin and Churchill, his administration proposed a "compromise" on the voting procedure in the Security Council by limiting the requirement that a party to a dispute abstain from voting to only the questions of discussing the issue and recommending methods of pacific settlement. The unanimity rule for permanent members would still apply to decisions about enforcement where a breach of the peace had been determined. In essence, Roosevelt conceded the political necessity of the veto in order to achieve participation in the United Nations by all of the great powers. At the Yalta meeting, Stalin agreed to accept the American formulation on voting in the Security Council. On the matter of all the Soviet republics being seated as original members of the United Nations, Stalin agreed that from the 16 Union republics of the USSR only the Russian, Ukrainian, and Byelorussian republics would seek UN MEMBERSHIP. While his advisers opposed the ADMISSION of all three, Roosevelt accepted it. He needed Soviet help for the continuing war in Asia. Moreover, the United States conceivably benefited even more in terms of membership in the new organization by a decision at Yalta to allow all nations at war with Germany by March 1, 1945, to be included as original members. This resulted in the membership of several Latin American countries friendly to the United States. Roosevelt also achieved Stalin's promise to enter the war against the Japanese and to recognize the pro-American government of Jiang Jieshi (Chiang Kai-shek) in China. A pro-American China and France joined the Soviet Union, the United States, and Britain as permanent members on the Security Council. But, probably most important, when the USSR entered the American-sponsored United Nations it agreed to join an international organization that had the clear mark of an American enterprise. Sitting in the well of the House of Representatives, Roosevelt reported to the legislators upon his return: "[Yalta] spells the end of the system of unilateral action and exclusive alliances and spheres of influence and balances of power and all the other expedients which have been tried for centuries—and have failed. We propose to substitute for all of these a universal organization . . . of peace-loving nations."

The president spent the last two months of his life making plans for his address to the UNITED NATIONS CONFERENCE ON INTERNATIONAL ORGANIZATION scheduled for April 25, preparing the delegates to the conference, and fending off objections to the agreements made at Yalta. There was a concerted effort to sell the American people on the view that the United Nations marked a wholly new form of peaceful international relations in the history of world politics. There were many issues as well yet to be debated and settled at the San Francisco Conference. As late as April 9, 1945, Franklin Roosevelt told the State Department that there would be time upon his return from Warm Springs, Georgia, to make final decisions about the trusteeship of NON-SELF-GOVERNING TERRITORIES under the United Nations and other outstanding issues before the conference convened in two weeks. Three days later the architect of the United Nations died. It was a testament to his achievement that his successor, Harry S. Truman, within minutes of being sworn in as president of the United States made his first presidential decision—to go ahead with the San Francisco Conference to organize the United Nations.

See also ATLANTIC CHARTER, CAIRO DECLARATION, HISS.

Further Reading: Hoopes, Townsend, and Douglas Brinkley. *FDR and the Creation of the U.N.* New Haven, Conn.: Yale University Press, 1997. Kimball, Warren. *The Juggler.* Princeton, N.J.: Princeton University Press, 1991. ———. *Forged in War: Roosevelt, Churchill, and the Second World War.* New York: W. Morrow, 1997. Moore, John Allphin, Jr., and Jerry Pubantz. *To Create a New World? American Presidents and the United Nations.* New York: Peter Lang Publishing, 1999.

Russia   *See* RUSSIAN FEDERATION.

Russian Federation (RF) (Soviet Union, Russia, USSR)

On December 24, 1991, UN SECRETARY-GENERAL Boutros BOUTROS-GHALI received a letter from Boris Yeltsin, president of the Russian Federation, indicating that his government would take over the seat held by the Soviet Union, including its permanent MEMBERSHIP on the SECURITY COUNCIL. Yeltsin indicated that this decision was supported unanimously by members of the Commonwealth of Independent States, all former republics of the USSR. Boutros-Ghali circulated Yeltsin's letter to the members of the United Nations. No delegation objected, and without a vote or discussion in either the GENERAL ASSEMBLY or the Security Council, the Russian Federation continued the membership of one of the UN's "Big Three" founding states.

The Soviet Union was involved in all of the critical wartime meetings that forged an allied consensus on the STRUCTURE and purposes of the United Nations. It also served as one of the sponsoring governments for the 1945 San Francisco Conference that produced the UN CHARTER. Its participation in that process, however, was not that of the initiator. Led by Joseph STALIN, Soviet involvement in the crafting of the proposed world body was not based on a desire to re-create a reformed LEAGUE OF NATIONS or to establish a universal COLLECTIVE SECURITY system, but rather was undertaken to protect Soviet national interests and its freedom of action in Eastern and Central Europe. Stalin also sought to accommodate the UNITED STATES—the leading nation in the alliance essential to Russia's victory in World War II—that strongly supported the establishment of a postwar organization.

Nearly all early planning on the United Nations was conducted by the American and British governments. Both U.S. president Franklin ROOSEVELT (FDR) and British prime minister Winston CHURCHILL thought it important to engage the Soviet Union in these deliberations, but they were unable to convince Marshall Stalin to participate in early wartime meetings. They decided to present the idea of a postwar body to the Soviets as the logical continuation of allied cooperation during World War II. Roosevelt, particularly, envisioned the USSR as one of the FOUR POLICEMEN in the maintenance of future world peace. At the QUADRANT CONFERENCE in Quebec (August 1943) the two leaders decided to propose a four-power DECLARATION that included the new organization as an allied postwar commitment. The proposal was forwarded to Stalin for consideration.

The first opportunity to gauge Soviet intentions came at the MOSCOW CONFERENCE OF FOREIGN MINISTERS in late October 1943. U.S. secretary of state Cordell HULL, leader of the U.S. delegation, sought Soviet support. Only after Hull and his British counterpart agreed to open a second front from the west were the Soviets ready to consider the idea of a general international organization. Throughout the negotiations in Moscow and later, the Soviet Union focused on the implications of such a body for Soviet geopolitical concerns. Foreign Minister Vyacheslav Molotov insisted on language in the Moscow Declaration (also known as the Four Power Declaration) issued at the end of the meeting that would allow wide latitude for Soviet military operations in Eastern Europe. Hull made the necessary concessions to achieve Moscow's endorsement of a future world organization.

Roosevelt and Churchill had their first opportunity to discuss the matter with Stalin personally one month later at the TEHERAN CONFERENCE (November 27–December 1). The subject of an international organization was not on the official agenda, but Roosevelt raised the issue privately with Stalin. The president described how the United States, Soviet Union, United Kingdom, and CHINA would have sole authority to enforce the peace and prevent AGGRESSION. He also outlined the likely organs that would be part of the organization, based on U.S. and British planning to that point, including an executive council. In response to Stalin's queries, Roosevelt explained that the United States would not contribute ground troops to preserve the peace outside of the Western Hemisphere. British and Russian troops, with U.S. naval and air support, would confront crises in Europe. Stalin, worrying that the executive council might limit Soviet actions, asked FDR whether the proposed body would be able to make decisions binding on the great powers. President Roosevelt said it would not. The issue of the VETO was not discussed directly at Teheran, but the Soviet leader and his representatives returned to this commitment by FDR many times over the next two years as negotiations on the construction of the United Nations went forward.

As planning for the world organization went ahead in Western capitals, the Soviet government evinced little interest in the project. When the U.S. State Department issued an invitation on May 30, 1944, to China, Britain, and the USSR to participate in formal talks on an international organization, Moscow demurred until July 9. Finally agreeing to meet with the other governments at DUMBARTON OAKS, the Soviets indicated, however, a desire to restrict talks to the general purposes of the organization and to military and political cooperation. Moscow expressed no interest in pursuing the contemplated economic, social, and cultural functions for the body. Stalin approached the development of the future United Nations defensively, attempting to limit its ability to restrict Soviet foreign policy, or to allow intrusion by "outside" powers within its emerging buffer zone in Eastern Europe.

The Dumbarton Oaks Conference convened on August 25, 1944. While most of the American proposals concerning the institutional structure for the postwar organization were quickly accepted, the Soviet Union objected to a recommendation put forward by the United States that parties to a dispute not be allowed to vote on the issue before the SECURITY COUNCIL, even if the party happened to be a PERMANENT MEMBER. The USSR insisted that all matters be subject to the unanimous consent of the permanent members. The Soviet delegate, Andrei Gromyko, argued that this had constituted the essence of Roosevelt's assurances to Stalin at Teheran, and that the United States was now trying to change the proposed organization fundamentally. Gromyko rejected the suggested VOTING procedure and put forward a new demand that all of the Union republics of the USSR be admitted to the world body as separate members. Faced with U.S. domination in the new organization, the Soviets argued that each constituent part of the USSR, as an independent state, had a right to membership.

The Soviet proposal to gain, in effect, 16 votes in the GENERAL ASSEMBLY was completely unacceptable to the Western powers. This issue of expanded Soviet membership, along with the disagreement over voting procedure in the Security Council, remained the key challenges needing resolution in the wake of the Dumbarton Oaks meeting. Both were addressed at the YALTA CONFERENCE in February 1945. During that meeting of the three world leaders Stalin focused on the war effort and political arrangements in Eastern Europe. Only when issues related to future Polish politics and to military matters in the war with Germany were resolved to his satisfaction was the Soviet leader ready to make concessions on a postwar organization. He agreed to the American formulation put forward at Dumbarton Oaks on Security Council voting procedures. But he insisted that the price for Soviet acceptance was an American concession on multiple representation from the Soviet Union. President Roosevelt finally agreed that Byelorussia and Ukraine could be seated as original members of the body in addition to the USSR. Still, since decisions at Yalta provided that any country declaring war on the Axis powers by March 1, 1945, was to be considered an original member of the United Nations, the United States realized a substantial numerical advantage over the Soviet Union in the General Assembly should any East-West division in the new organization arise, because several pro–U.S. governments from LATIN AMERICA would be included in the original membership by such a provision.

Soviet concern about the negative impact the United Nations could have on USSR foreign policy was only slightly abated by the Yalta agreements. At the San Francisco Conference in April 1945 the Soviet delegation raised many of the same issues supposedly resolved at previous wartime meetings. U.S. president Harry S. Truman sent a special envoy to Moscow to explain that the Charter would not pass the U.S. Senate with the emendations proposed by the Soviet Union in San Francisco. Stalin backed down and directed his delegation to accept the Yalta formula. However, Stalin insisted on the veto power to keep the organization from interfering in the Soviet sphere of interest. The USSR thus attained the status of a great power together with the United States and its Western allies, while maintaining the instruments needed to protect its interests.

The ability of the new United Nations to "maintain international peace and security," as Article 1 of the Charter required, depended on continuing cooperation among the permanent members of the Security Council. But the early emergence of the COLD WAR diminished prospects for that cooperation, and thus undermined the chance for UN success. The U.S.-Soviet rivalry dominated the functioning of the Security Council most intensely, beginning with its first session in 1946, which was called to address the refusal of the USSR to remove its troops from northern Iran. During World War II both Britain and the Soviet Union had stationed troops there to guard against a Nazi seizure of oil resources; British troops had withdrawn from the country, but Stalin refused to pull out Red Army forces occupying the region. While the USSR ultimately did remove its troops unilaterally, the episode demonstrated the growing hostility between the two sides and the consequent diminution of UN effectiveness. The cold war divided UN members into competitive "East" and "West" camps, making collective action difficult, if not impossible.

From 1946 to the mid-1980s the Soviet Union wielded its veto power, just as the United States did, to keep the world body from acting against its national interests. The original 51 members of the United Nations were overwhelmingly pro-American, the bulk of them coming from Western Europe and Latin America. Soviet anger with the pro-American UN membership intensified after October 1949, when the institution refused to seat the new Chinese communist regime in the place of the delegation from the Republic of China. In protest, the Soviet PERMANENT REPRESENTATIVE boycotted future meetings of the Security Council, a fateful decision that proved disadvantageous for the USSR when the KOREAN WAR erupted in June 1950.

Particularly from 1946 to 1970, the USSR found itself in the minority on many issues to come before the council. On 51 occasions it used its veto to block the ADMISSION OF MEMBERS, fearful that its position in the already American-dominated body would only grow more precarious. Moscow objected to the admission of countries such as Austria, Italy, Ireland, and Japan until it could work out an agreement with the United States to admit pro-Soviet applicants as well. This deadlock was broken in 1955 with the admission of 16 states, but it did not diminish Soviet hostility toward an organization that it saw as a tool of American foreign policy. The USSR also used its power to block UN action on the Soviet dispatch of troops and tanks to Hungary in 1956, Czechoslovakia in 1968, and AFGHANISTAN in 1979. Both the council and the General Assembly became venues for little more than Soviet and American propaganda. Only as the new states from the former colonial areas of Africa and Asia entered the UN in the 1960s did the Soviet Union find a more congenial arena for its own foreign policy initiatives.

An early indication of the cold war's impact on the United Nations occurred on the issue of Korea. The General Assembly first considered the question of Korea at its session in 1947, with unsuccessful efforts to reestablish a unified country via elections. By 1948 two separate countries came into being, divided at the 38th parallel. When North Korean troops invaded the South, the Security Council, without Soviet participation because of its decision to boycott its meetings, recommended that member states furnish assistance to repel the attack. The Soviet Union declared the council's action illegal. Moscow refused to provide any assessed funding for the operation and supported the North Koreans during the conflict. UN PEACEKEEPING became, in the eyes of the Russians, U.S. warfare against an ally, and a demonstration of the unwelcome control of the organization by a cold war enemy.

Joseph Stalin died in the spring of 1953. A power struggle ensued in the Kremlin from which Nikita Khrushchev

emerged by 1956 as the undisputed leader of the Soviet Communist Party and state. Committed to "de-stalinization" at home and "peaceful coexistence" abroad, he jettisoned Stalin's theoretical postulates about the inevitability of war with the capitalist world, and he pursued an activist diplomatic policy meant to earn friends for the Soviet Union among the non-aligned states of the Third World. At the United Nations the USSR became a strong advocate for "general and complete DISARMAMENT" and for causes supported by developing states, such as decolonization.

Shortly after its founding the United Nations established the UN ATOMIC ENERGY COMMISSION as a forum for the negotiation of arms control agreements. At initial meetings of the commission the United States put forward the BARUCH PLAN, which recommended that the nuclear powers place their stockpiles, production facilities, and plutonium reserves under a UN inspection regime. Stalin rejected the proposal, seeing it as a poorly veiled effort by the United States to maintain its acknowledged nuclear monopoly. Negotiations in the Atomic Energy Commission in the summer of 1946 foreshadowed the general pattern of UN nuclear disarmament efforts during the cold war. The deadlock resulting from the competing interests of the United States and the Soviet Union undermined the possibility of fruitful negotiations. It also demonstrated the central role of the superpowers to any disarmament arrangement, and therefore the limited peripheral roles non-nuclear member states could play in promoting disarmament and arms control.

In August 1959 Khrushchev and U.S. president Dwight Eisenhower agreed to a new UN forum for disarmament discussions, the Ten Nation Disarmament Committee. In 1961 additional states were added to create the EIGHTEEN NATION DISARMAMENT COMMITTEE (ENDC). Within these settings, however, the Soviet government rejected any American proposal that hinted at international verification of disarmament commitments. When President Eisenhower proposed in 1955 that the two superpowers provide "open skies" to the surveillance planes of the other nation, thus allowing trust based on assurance of compliance with any disarmament TREATY, Khrushchev rejected it out of hand as "spying."

In 1960 U.S. spy planes (a U-2 surveillance craft piloted by Francis Gary Powers and an RB-47 lost over the Arctic) were shot down over Soviet territory, sending the cold war into a deep freeze. Each side proceeded to use the United Nations for bombastic speeches about the perfidy of its opponent. Khrushchev showed up at that year's UN General Assembly annual meeting, where he banged his shoe on a desk to protest Western treachery, while in the Security Council U.S. ambassador Henry Cabot Lodge accused the Russians of planting secret microphones in the U.S. embassy in Moscow.

The year 1960 also witnessed Soviet anger and retribution directed at the United Nations over its handling of the CONGO crisis. When the Congo became independent from

Belgium a complicated civil war broke out, with one side being supported by the Soviet Union, one side by Washington, and a third side trying to secede. In the confusion SEC-RETARY-GENERAL Dag HAMMARSKJÖLD tried to insert a UN presence to bring the disorder to an end. Believing the Secretary-General to be carrying out the wishes of the United States and its cold war partners, the Soviet Union demanded a reorganization of the office of Secretary-General, replacing the single secretary with a troika, whereby there would be a three-person executive with equal representation from the Western bloc, the Eastern bloc, and the neutral countries in the United Nations. The USSR also refused to pay its assessment for the peacekeeping operation, triggering a financial crisis for the United Nations.

Khrushchev's anger at the apparent tilt by Hammarskjöld in favor of the American-supported faction in the Congo reached a breaking point when the Soviet-sponsored Congolese leader, Patrice Lumumba, was assassinated after being released from UN protective custody. The Soviet delegation refused to have any further working relationship with the Secretary-General and stepped up its efforts to replace him with a troika. Hammarskjöld's 1961 death in a plane crash in a remote part of Northern Rhodesia (now Zambia) tempered Soviet promotion of the troika proposal, but it did not diminish the USSR's opposition to UN peacekeeping efforts. The Soviet refusal to pay its dues to the United Nations led to an American effort to deprive Moscow of its vote in the General Assembly under Article 19 of the UN Charter. The stalemate between the two states lasted until 1966, when the United States dropped its effort.

Perhaps the most dangerous encounter between the superpower rivals occurred during the CUBAN MISSILE CRISIS in 1962. In October of that year, U.S. intelligence discovered that the Soviet Union was placing intermediate range nuclear WEAPONS in CUBA. The Kennedy administration challenged the Soviets to remove the weapons under clear threat of military action against Cuba, and of necessity, against the Soviet Union. Khrushchev suggested using the UN Secretary-General as intermediary, but most of the tense negotiations were conducted bilaterally or through other interlocutors. By the end of October, the Russians, recognizing the strategically inferior position in which they found themselves, agreed to remove the weapons, and the United States, without admitting it was a quid pro quo, dismantled its own nuclear weapons in Turkey.

The incident seemed to have a deep impact on the rival leaders in the cold war—President Kennedy and Soviet premier Khrushchev—who, in mid-1963, agreed to sign a nuclear test ban treaty. Following the Cuban Missile Crisis, relations between the cold war adversaries never reached such dire peril again, but within the United Nations the competition continued to have an effect. Each side was interested in using the United Nations to criticize the other in its foreign adventures—the United States in Vietnam, the Sovi-

ets in Czechoslovakia. At home, the embarrassing "defeat" in Cuba, along with the detonation of an atomic device by the growingly anti-Soviet People's Republic of China, contributed to Khrushchev's downfall in 1964. His successor, Leonid Brezhnev, rejected Khrushchev's "hare-brained schemes" and sought a more business-like relationship with both the United States and the United Nations.

Brezhnev sought a relaxation of tensions with the West that later became known as "détente." Building on the 1963 Test Ban Treaty, he entered negotiations with the United States on other limited arms control agreements. As a product of those talks, on August 24, 1967, the Soviet Union and the United States submitted to the Eighteen Nation Disarmament Committee a joint draft for a multilateral NUCLEAR NON-PROLIFERATION TREATY (NPT). The NPT's intention was to halt and then reverse the spread of independent control over nuclear weapons. It established in Article IX that only states that had acquired nuclear weapons by January 1, 1967, qualified as Nuclear Weapons States (NWS). All others were considered Non-Nuclear Weapons States (NNWS) and any such state adhering to the NPT was obligated to subject its entire peaceful nuclear program to the INTERNATIONAL ATOMIC ENERGY AGENCY (IAEA) material accountancy safeguards, and to pledge only to acquire nuclear materials and equipment for peaceful purposes. Conversely, the NWS, which happened to be the five permanent members of the Security Council, pledged not to transfer nuclear weapons to any NNWS or to assist it in manufacturing or acquiring nuclear weapons (Article I); to share the benefits of the "Peaceful Atom" with any NNWS party to the treaty (Articles IV and V); and to pledge to make a "good faith" effort to end the arms race at an "early date" (Article VI).

Article VI was added at the urging of several nuclear "threshold" states that refused to sign away their nuclear futures without a commitment by the superpowers to reduce their nuclear arsenals. It was on this basis that private Soviet-American negotiations began on a Strategic Arms Limitation (SALT) agreement. A SALT agreement, including both an Anti-Ballistic Missile Treaty and a Five-Year Interim Offensive Weapons Agreement, was concluded at the 1972 Moscow Summit between U.S. president Richard Nixon and Communist Party general secretary Brezhnev. The SALT negotiations reflected a Soviet interest in direct talks with the United States outside the disarmament framework of the United Nations. It was Soviet policy to limit UN involvement, beyond the NPT, to peripheral disarmament matters, such as the completion of a MOON AGREEMENT, prohibiting militarization of that celestial body, and NUCLEAR-WEAPONS-FREE ZONES.

Leonid Brezhnev held the top post in the Soviet Union from 1964 until his death in November 1982. Much of that era, particularly after the 1972 summit, was characterized in Soviet official thinking as a time of détente, in which the two superpowers maintained military parity and sought areas of cooperation. Nonetheless, Soviet leaders did not see détente as a restriction on the country's foreign policy objectives other than in bilateral relations with the United States. In various independence and NATIONAL LIBERATION struggles, particularly in sub-Saharan Africa and Latin America, the Soviets supported leftist forces antithetical to American interests. At UN HEADQUARTERS in New York the Soviet delegation consistently endorsed initiatives from the GROUP OF 77 and other developing state CAUCUS GROUPS that criticized American policy or challenged UN Western-oriented structures and programs. The Soviet Union supported the effort to establish the NEW INTERNATIONAL ECONOMIC ORDER, the ZIONISM IS RACISM RESOLUTION, and the recognition of the Palestine Liberation Organization as the legitimate representative of the Palestinian people.

All of these actions undermined support in the United States for détente with Brezhnev's regime. It was given a fatal blow when the Soviets decided to invade Afghanistan in December 1979. Seeking to shore up a border state against Islamic fundamentalist insurgency, and to put in place a pro-Soviet regime in Kabul, Soviet troops entered Afghanistan for what was expected to be a short military operation. The United States responded with military assistance to Pakistan, Afghanistan's southern neighbor, an increased defense budget, and an effort in the UN to condemn Soviet actions. The USSR, of course, vetoed any meaningful UN action to halt its intrusion into Afghan politics. Brezhnev's calculations on the military effort that would be needed proved terribly over-optimistic. Not only did the Soviets find themselves bogged down in a lengthy war but they lost much of the goodwill with the underdeveloped world built up over a decade of diplomatic activity at the United Nations.

The costs of the Afghan war added to the growing economic woes of the Soviet Union in the early 1980s. These problems were exacerbated following Brezhnev's death, when he was succeeded by three different leaders in the space of 28 months. In March 1985 Mikhail Gorbachev became general secretary of the Communist Party of the Soviet Union and promised to introduce a "restructuring" of the Soviet economy and "new thinking" in Soviet foreign policy. In order to accomplish the former, he included in the latter a retreat from global commitments to communist regimes and an improvement in relations with the West.

It was at the United Nations, in December 1988, that Gorbachev made an important gesture toward bringing the cold war to an end. After a genial meeting on Governor's Island in New York with outgoing U.S. president Ronald Reagan, the Soviet president addressed the full General Assembly, insisting that it was now "high time to make use of the opportunities provided by this universal organization." He offered to make sizable cuts in the Soviet nuclear arsenal and implied that the days of ideological struggle in the halls of the UN were over. By the time of the Iraqi invasion of Kuwait in 1990 and the GULF WAR in 1991, Gor-

bachev's anticipation of an effective United Nations seemed prescient as Moscow and Washington cooperated within the Security Council in ways that would have astonished earlier diplomats in both countries. In 1990 Gorbachev endorsed American efforts to mold a coalition to liberate Kuwait. Regular meetings occurred between Soviet foreign minister Eduard Shevardnadze and U.S. secretary of state James Baker. As part of a unified P5 in the Security Council, the Russian delegation voted for all of the U.S.-sponsored RESOLUTIONS. In 1991, it abstained on the critical British and American resolution authorizing the use of "any means necessary" (Res. 678) against former Soviet ally Iraq.

Gorbachev's most important challenges, however, were not in international relations but rather in domestic affairs, in which his policies of *perestroika* and *glasnost* proved unsuccessful in halting the unraveling of the Soviet Union. Many critics, in fact, accused Gorbachev of contributing to the demise of the Soviet communist system by imposing ill-advised reforms. The crisis in the Soviet Union came to a head in August 1991, when a cabal of Gorbachev's ministers attempted a coup, holding Gorbachev captive in the Crimea for three days. Although the coup collapsed, it immediately led to declarations of independence by the USSR's constituent republics. Unable to knit together a loose confederation, and undermined by the Russian Republic's president, Boris Yeltsin, who undertook negotiations with his counterparts in the other republics to forge the Commonwealth of Independent States, President Gorbachev "ceased the duties of his office" on December 26. On December 31, 1991, the Soviet "hammer and sickle" was lowered for the last time from above the Kremlin in Moscow; one of the Big Three founding states of the United Nations was no more.

The initial foreign policy of the Yeltsin government continued support for Western policies at the United Nations. The Russian Federation endorsed peacekeeping efforts in Rwanda and other conflict areas. However, as nationalist and Slavophile voices were heard in the new democratic politics of Russia, Yeltsin's "Westernizing" policies came under attack at home. They were emboldened by the American decision to offer membership in the North Atlantic Treaty Organization to former East European states that had been part of the Soviet bloc. U.S. president Clinton's decision to press NATO intrusion into the fighting in BOSNIA on the side of the Muslims and Croats and against the orthodox Serbs also angered Yeltsin's critics. Nonetheless, following the successful conclusion of the DAYTON PEACE ACCORDS the Russians joined a UN-sponsored multilateral peacekeeping operation in Bosnia in 1995, and they helped end the NATO bombing of Yugoslavia in 1999 by convincing the government led by Slobodan Milosevic to withdraw its forces from Kosovo.

The nationalist movement in Russia gained further support as the breakaway Federation Republic of Chechnya achieved near independence after 1991. Faced with the success of the secessionist movement, Yeltsin ordered the Russian army into the province in December 1994. While Chechnya's capital Grozny was taken by military units, bloody resistance continued for a year, forcing the government to settle for an unobserved cease-fire. Yeltsin's government and its successor, led by Vladimir Putin, were regularly accused of HUMAN RIGHTS violations in Chechnya as they sought to destroy Islamic separatist forces. The Russian government, however, rejected any UN intervention, asserting that matters relating to Chechnya were internal affairs.

Boris Yeltsin resigned the Russian presidency at the close of the decade, to be succeeded by Putin. The new administration pursued essentially the same course in Russian-UN relations. Shortly after his ACCESSION, however, Putin faced a new challenge from Chechen insurgents when a series of deadly explosions occurred in Russia's major cities. Blaming Chechen "TERRORISM," Putin reopened the war and occupied the province. UN officials particularly were critical of Russia's human rights and refugee policies as it tried to pacify the region. In part to blunt international criticism of his Chechnya policy, Putin moved quickly to support American calls for retaliation against terrorists following September 11, 2001, attacks on the World Trade Center in New York City and the Pentagon in Washington, D.C. When hijackers commandeered four civilian airliners and crashed them into the Trade Center and other sites with a heavy loss of life, the United States sought UN support for any actions it might take in reprisal. On September 12, 2001, the Security Council unanimously adopted Resolution 1368, condemning the assault and finding it a threat to international peace and security. Russia joined in the invocation of CHAPTER VII, making the resolution's provisions mandatory on all member states. Moscow also gave its support to an American-led coalition that demanded the Taliban government of Afghanistan turn over suspected terrorist Osama bin Laden. When U.S. forces launched massive military strikes against Afghanistan in October 2001, a Russian leader, for the first time in Russian history, endorsed the deployment of American troops on the territory of the former Soviet Union, supporting the decision of Uzbekistan to let the United States use its territory as a base of operations for attacks on Afghan targets.

See also ANGOLA, ARAB-ISRAELI DISPUTE, DECLARATION BY UNITED NATIONS, GOLDBERG RESERVATION, GUATEMALA, KOREAN WAR, LIE, SECOND WORLD, SUEZ CRISIS, UNITED NATIONS CONFERENCE ON INTERNATIONAL ORGANIZATION, UNITING FOR PEACE RESOLUTION, UNIVERSAL DECLARATION OF HUMAN RIGHTS.

Further Reading: Holloway, David. The Soviet Union and the Arms Race. New Haven, Conn.: Yale University Press, 1984. Service, Robert. A History of Twentieth-Century Russia. Cambridge, Mass.: Harvard University Press, 1997. Stoessinger, John G. The United Nations and the Superpowers: China, Russia, and America. 4th ed. New York: Random House, 1977. Permanent UN Mission of the Russian Federation website: <www.un.int/russia/>.

Rwanda crisis

Over the span of 100 days in 1994, approximately 800,000 people (primarily Tutsis) were killed in the Rwandan GENOCIDE. The Rwandan crisis served as a turning point in UN PEACEKEEPING efforts and came to symbolize the political stalemate and inefficiency sometimes ascribed to the United Nations. Rwanda, a small, densely populated central African country, was a colony of Germany (until 1920) and Belgium (1920–62). Periodic ethnic conflicts between the majority Hutus (over 80 percent of the population) and the minority Tutsis created tens of thousands of Rwandan exiles after 1959. In 1990, these exiles formed the Rwandan Patriotic Front (RPF) and invaded Rwanda; a civil war ensued between the RPF (primarily Tutsi) and the Hutu-dominated government. In the Arusha Accords of 1993, the Rwandan government and RPF agreed to a cease-fire and a transitional government. At the request of both parties, the UN SECURITY COUNCIL (SC) created the UN Observer Mission Uganda-Rwanda (UNOMUR), with 81 military observers, to separate the two parties and to prevent the shipment of arms into Rwanda. During the civil war Uganda had been a supporter of the RPF.

In response to reports of HUMAN RIGHTS violations and concerns by UNOMUR about security in Rwanda, the SC unanimously passed Resolution 872 (1993), which established the UNITED NATIONS ASSISTANCE MISSION FOR RWANDA (UNAMIR). UNAMIR was composed of 2,548 military personnel (though the original proposal requested 5,500). UNAMIR's mandate was to monitor the cease-fire and the security situation under the transitional government, assist with mine clearance, help repatriate Rwandan refugees, coordinate humanitarian assistance, and oversee demilitarization procedures. Brigadier-General Romeo Dallaire (Canada) was appointed force commander. UNOMUR was integrated into UNAMIR in June 1993.

By late 1993, violence and refugee flows escalated. A Rwandan informant told Dallaire that the Interahamwe (a Hutu extremist group) had registered the location of all Tutsis, stockpiled numerous armaments for a Tutsi genocide, and planned to kill Belgian soldiers assigned to UNAMIR. In a fatal mistake, the UN DEPARTMENT OF PEACEKEEPING OPERATIONS (DPKO) did not seriously consider this information. In March 1994, the SECRETARY-GENERAL presented a progress report on UNAMIR and the deteriorating Rwandan situation to the SC. In Resolution 909 on April 5, 1994 (one day before the genocide began), the Security Council voted unanimously to extend UNAMIR's mandate by four months.

On April 6, Rwandan president Juvénal Habyarimana's plane was shot down as it landed in Kigali (the capital).

Within less than one hour, the Interahamwe set up road-blocks to prevent Tutsis from leaving Kigali. Inciting and coordinating violence through extremist Radio-Television Libre des Mille Collines (RTLM), the Interahamwe soon began to massacre Tutsis and key officials in the Rwandan transitional government. Ten Belgian soldiers were tortured and killed as they tried to protect the prime minister. Immediately after this tragedy, Belgium evacuated its troops from the country, leaving more than 2,000 Rwandans congregated at the Ecole Technique Officielle unprotected from massacre by the Interahamwe.

The remaining UNAMIR soldiers were poorly trained and poorly equipped. On April 21, in a compromise between Nigeria and CHINA, which wanted to increase UNAMIR troops, and the UNITED STATES and the United Kingdom, which wanted a complete withdrawal, the SC voted unanimously to reduce UNAMIR to 270 observers (Res. 912). As reports of violence escalated, the UN Secretary-General called for a change in UNAMIR's mandate to include ending the bloodshed. The Security Council condemned the killings, but circumvented using the term genocide by incorporating an almost direct quote from the 1948 Convention against Genocide. (Use of the word would have legally required all SC members that had ratified the CONVENTION to act.) Under continued pressure from NON-PERMANENT MEMBERS and the non-aligned caucus, on May 17, 1994, the SC increased the number of UNAMIR troops to 5,500 and imposed an arms embargo on Rwanda (Res. 918). However, few countries responded to the call for troops; over two months after Resolution 918 was adopted, UNAMIR had only 503 troops. Throughout May, the SC focused its attention on implementation of the RESOLUTION and ways to encourage a cease-fire.

On June 8, the Security Council expanded the mandate of UNAMIR to protect civilians and to provide security for humanitarian relief and urged member states to provide resources for UNAMIR (Res. 925). Despite the resolution, there was little support for UNAMIR. On June 20, France and Senegal offered to conduct a multinational operation under CHAPTER VII of the UN CHARTER to assure the security of civilians in Rwanda. By a vote of 10 in favor and five abstentions (Brazil, China, New Zealand, Nigeria, and Pak-

istan), the SC adopted Resolution 929 authorizing the French-controlled Operation Turquoise, despite concerns expressed by UNAMIR. As Operation Turquoise set up a humanitarian zone in southwest Rwanda, one million refugees (primarily Hutus who feared revenge by the RPF) flooded into Goma, Zaire, and created a humanitarian crisis. By mid-July, the RPF controlled Rwanda, declared a unilateral cease-fire, and set up a government.

On November 8, 1994, the SC established the INTERNATIONAL CRIMINAL TRIBUNAL FOR RWANDA (ICTR) to prosecute persons responsible for the genocide (Res. 955). Though overwhelmed by claims and limited by resources, jail space, investigators, and lawyers, by 1999 the tribunal had indicted over 40 individuals. In December 1994, the mandate of UNAMIR changed again to facilitate the safe and voluntary return of refugees. UNAMIR left Rwanda on April 19, 1996, and the mission was replaced by the UN Office in Rwanda charged with coordinating development, HUMAN RIGHTS, and refugee repatriation efforts.

In March 1999, the Secretary-General appointed an independent INQUIRY into UN actions in the Rwandan crisis. The report, issued in December 1999, listed several problems: the inadequacy of UNAMIR's mandate, the lack of resources and training for UNAMIR, confusion over the rules of engagement, the UN's determination to appear neutral even in a situation of genocide, member states' limited enthusiasm for peacekeeping after the SOMALIA disaster, the SC emphasis on a cease-fire in the midst of genocide, and the complications that existed from Rwanda's status as a member of the SC during the crisis. The report termed the UN's role to be an "overriding failure."

See also WAR CRIMES TRIBUNALS.

Further Reading: Adelman, Howard, and Astri Suhrke, eds. *The Rwandan Crisis from Uganda to Zaire*. New Brunswick, N.J.: Transaction Publishers, 1999. United Nations. *The United Nations and Rwanda 1993–1996*. Blue Books Series. Vol. 10. New York: United Nations, 1996. ———. *Report of the Independent Inquiry into the Actions of the United Nations during the 1994 Genocide in Rwanda*. New York: United Nations, 1999.

— *A. S. Patterson*

S

San Francisco Conference   *See* UNITED NATIONS
CONFERENCE ON INTERNATIONAL ORGANIZATION.

sanctions

Under INTERNATIONAL LAW a sanction is a penalty imposed by a NATION-STATE, a group of states, or other international entity on another actor in the international system for non-compliance with some demand made of it. Usually it is imposed in order to alter behavior that offends those imposing the sanctions. Within DOMESTIC JURISDICTION, sanctions are uniform, defined by public laws, and are enforced easily, relative to sanctions in the international community. International sanctions may range from minor forms of coercion to the use of military force. CHAPTER VII of the UN CHARTER grants the SECURITY COUNCIL the authority to carry out ENFORCEMENT MEASURES against a state that is deemed to have created a threat to or carried out a breach of the peace. The Charter, however, within the rubric of enforcement measures, distinguishes between sanctions, which are methods not employing military force, and the use of the latter.

If the Security Council imposes Chapter VII sanctions—a decision that is subject to the VETO power of the PERMANENT MEMBERS (P5)—it is mandatory that all member states apply them. Article 41 cites examples of appropriate sanctions, including "complete or partial interruption of economic relations and of rail, sea, air, postal, telegraphic, radio, and other means of communication, and the severance of diplomatic relations." But the council is not limited by this list, and it has often imposed other combinations of restraints on errant states. Usually undertaken when the pacific settlement provisions of CHAPTER VI have not been effective, when the event that occasioned their imposition has seemed too grave for traditional diplomatic methods, or when there has been disagreement among the P5 about the use of force, sanctions have allowed for the development of council consensus. When the Security Council has imposed sanctions it has created an ad hoc "SANCTIONS COMMITTEE," made up of the full council MEMBERSHIP, to monitor the sanctions' effectiveness and to recommend revisions or their abandonment. In November 2001, the council maintained eight sanctions committees, having terminated three additional ones earlier in the year.

Since 1991 mandatory UN sanctions have been imposed on Iraq, the FORMER YUGOSLAVIA, Libya, HAITI, Liberia, Rwanda, SOMALIA, UNITA forces in ANGOLA, Sudan, SIERRA LEONE, AFGHANISTAN, Eritrea, and Ethiopia. They have included arms embargoes, economic and trade sanctions, financial restrictions, and the limitation on the movement of diplomatic and state officials. Two serious difficulties, however, have arisen with imposed UN sanctions. First, their impact can be slow, minor, and not sufficiently important to the government that the United Nations is attempting to influence. This means that the objectionable behavior may continue for a lengthy period. Sanctions against Rhodesia and South Africa in the 1960s and 1970s to end secessionist policies in the first case, and APARTHEID in the second, suffered from these deficiencies. The gradual nature of sanctions works to undermine continued consensus in the Security Council as well. Second, sanctions often have adverse effects on innocent civilian populations that they were not intended to harm, as well as negatively affecting humanitarian organizations and third-party states. For example, reports of civilian suffering in Iraq following the GULF WAR due to UN sanctions engendered serious concern among Council members at the close of the century. Economic sanctions against energy producing states, and against states with traditional markets for Third World goods, have had the unintended outcome of damaging developing countries' economies.

In order to address these problems, on April 17, 2000, the Security Council established a Working Group on General Issues on Sanctions. Among the proposals for sanctions reform was the creation of "smart sanctions," described as carefully targeted penalties, with exemptions for humanitarian purposes. Freezing financial assets and the international flow of contraband owned or controlled by national elites in the countries under sanction was under consideration as a desired form of future smart sanction. An effort in this mode was attempted in 2001 with international agreement to control the sale and movement of diamonds from central Africa that were being used to finance war in Sierra Leone and the CONGO.

See also BOSNIA, COMMITTEE OF 24, HUSSEIN, IRAN HOSTAGE CRISIS, NAMIBIA, UN SECURITY COUNCIL RESOLUTION 678, UNITED STATES, UNITING FOR PEACE RESOLUTION.

Further Reading: Conlon, Paul. *United Nations Sanctions Management: A Case Study of the Iraq Sanctions Committee. 1990–1994.* Ardsley, N.Y.: Transnational Publishers, 2000. Cortright, David. *The Sanctions Decade: Assessing UN Strategies in the 1990s.* Boulder, Colo.: Lynne Rienner, 2000. Ritter, Scott. *Endgame: Solving the Iraq Problem—Once and For All.* New York: Simon and Schuster, 1999.

Sanctions Committees of the Security Council
CHAPTER VII of the UN CHARTER authorizes the SECURITY COUNCIL to impose mandatory SANCTIONS against an aggressor or any state that threatens or causes a breach of international peace. The Council has used this power on many occasions since the KOREAN WAR in 1950. Particularly after the end of the COLD WAR, the Security Council members found the use of sanctions constructive in areas of ethnic or religious conflict, and in regions of potential AGGRESSION.

In order to monitor the effectiveness and wisdom of the sanctions it has imposed, the Security Council usually establishes a sanctions committee for each occurrence. These ad hoc bodies are committees of the whole. In the autumn of 2001 there were eight such committees charged with respon-

sibility for the situation between Iraq and Kuwait (created by Security Council RESOLUTION 661 in 1990), Libya (Res. 748, 1992), SOMALIA (Res. 751, 1992), the situation in ANGOLA (Res. 864, 1993), RWANDA (Res. 918, 1994), SIERRA LEONE (Res. 1132, 1997), AFGHANISTAN (Res. 1267, 1999), and Liberia (Res. 1343, 2001).

See also GULF WAR.

Further Reading: Conlon, Paul. *United Nations Sanctions Management: A Case Study of the Iraq Sanctions Committee. 1990–1994.* Ardsley, N.Y.: Transnational Publishers, 2000.

scale of assessments
The scale of assessments lists the percentage of the UN budgets each member state must contribute in order to meet the requirements of the CHARTER's Article 17, which requires the MEMBERSHIP to pay the expenses of the organization. Members are assessed for the biennial regular UN BUDGET, the PEACEKEEPING operations budget, and the budget of international WAR CRIMES TRIBUNALS. The scale of assessments is set for a three-year period by vote of the GENERAL ASSEMBLY on the recommendations of the FIFTH COMMITTEE and the COMMITTEE ON CONTRIBUTIONS.

The "ceiling" that any member was required to pay, as of June 2001, was 22 percent of the regular budget and 27 percent of the peacekeeping budget. As the largest contributor, only the UNITED STATES was affected by these ceilings. The "floor," or lowest assessment assigned, was .001 percent and was applied to the poorest states in the United Nations.

The General Assembly established at its first session that the "capacity to pay" should be the overriding basis for setting the assessment rate. Yet, if that measure had been used without adjustment, the United States would have paid nearly 50 percent of the UN's expenses during its early years. That was politically unacceptable to the American government, and U.S. assessments never exceeded 40 percent. In 1954 the General Assembly lowered the dues of the largest contributor to no more than one-third of the regular budget. In 1973 this was reduced to 25 percent. The minimum assessment initially was .04 percent. It was lowered to .02 percent in 1973, .01 percent in 1978, and .001 percent in 1997. All assessments are made in U.S. dollars based on average rates of exchange and are determined by computing a state's gross national product over a period of time, which has varied from three to 10 years.

The use of "ceilings" and "floors" reflects a recognition that other factors than simply the "capacity to pay" (as determined by measuring a state's total national income in comparison to other states) must be considered in setting the scale of assessment. The Committee on Contributions has also taken into consideration low per capita income, giving affected states relief up to 85 percent of their assessment. Also, a state's level of debt is factored into the determination. Finally, for peacekeeping operations there are expectations that the PERMANENT MEMBERS OF THE SECURITY COUNCIL (P5) will pay for large portions of the operations, and that developing states will have no, or very limited, responsibilities. For example, for the United Nations Disengagement Observer Force (UNDOF) in the Golan Heights in the mid-1970s the P5 paid 55.28 percent of the costs, NON-PERMANENT MEMBERS from the industrialized world paid 41.97 percent, and the LEAST DEVELOPED COUNTRIES paid .054%.

The issue of paying for peacekeeping operations first arose in 1956 with the creation of the UNITED NATIONS EMERGENCY FORCE (UNEF) to separate the parties in the SUEZ CRISIS. The SECRETARY-GENERAL and the General Assembly determined that these were "expenses of the Organization," and thus all states should be assessed for them. The Soviet Union, Eastern Bloc nations, and Arab states refused to pay, arguing that the aggressors should bear the costs of the operation. The financial crisis became more severe in 1960 when the General Assembly undertook a peacekeeping effort in the CONGO. Not only the USSR but also France refused to pay its assessment, claiming that only the SECURITY COUNCIL under CHAPTER VII had the authority to order military operations, and then to require the members to pay for them. This was a crucial issue because the cost of UN involvement in the Congolese civil war was more than the entire regular budget of the world body. Even a 1962 ADVISORY OPINION by the INTERNATIONAL COURT OF JUSTICE finding these expenses to be legitimate under the terms of Article 17 could not move these members to pay their arrears, plunging the United Nations into a financial crisis from which it did not recover before the end of the century.

The UN Charter provides in Article 19 that "a Member of the United Nations which is in arrears in the payment of its financial contributions to the Organization shall have no vote in the General Assembly if the amount of its arrears equals or exceeds the amount of the contribution due from it for the preceding two full years." Following the operations in the Congo, as the UN's deficit mounted, the United States threatened to invoke Article 19 against the Soviet Union which, along with France, had compiled two years of arrears. When the USSR said it would withdraw from the United Nations if it lost its vote in the General Assembly, the United States relented. The confrontation between the U.S. and the USSR, however, was only a small part of the dilemma. Many states, not wanting to fund activities with which they did not agree, failed to pay their assessments from the 1960s onward. As 2000 began, nearly one-third of the UN membership had not paid its assessments in full for the regular budget, amounting to $244.2 million. The United States owed the most: $167.9 million, 68.7 percent of the total. When the peacekeeping and war crimes tribunal budgets were included, arrearages as of May 31 stood at $2.9 billion. On that date only 13 countries had paid all of their assessments in full.

The largest debtor at the turn of the century by far was the United States. Beginning in the 1980s, as conservative governments came to power in Washington, the United States became increasingly critical of the size of its assessment. In addition to its 25 percent share of the regular budget, Washington was paying 31 percent of the annual peacekeeping costs. As a condition for appropriating funds for past bills, Republican Congresses demanded major REFORMS at the United Nations, and a lowering of the U.S. assessment to 20 percent for the regular budget and 25 percent for peacekeeping.

Largely because of rising peacekeeping costs, American arrears were in excess of $1 billion by the end of 1999, and it was in danger of losing its vote in the General Assembly. During the Clinton administration the United States undertook a major diplomatic initiative to reduce its contribution to the United Nations. Led by its PERMANENT REPRESENTATIVE, Richard Holbrooke, and reenforced by congressional legislation known as the "Helms-Biden Agreement," the American delegation sought a reduction of its assessment to 22 percent combined with a zero growth UN budget. The U.S. Congress authorized a partial payment of $100 million in December 1999 in order to retain a vote in the Assembly, but 2000 would be decisive. On December 23, the General Assembly concluded months of negotiations by adopting its first major overhaul of UN financing in more than 20 years. It cut U.S. dues to 22 percent for the regular budget and 27 percent for peacekeeping, shifting the shortfall to developing countries with improving economies. At the last moment, however, the consensus in the Assembly nearly fell apart, because even with the expected American contribution the United Nations still faced a huge deficit for 2001. This was covered by a personal donation of $34 million from media executive Ted Turner.

See also GOLDBERG RESERVATION.

Further Reading: McDermott, Anthony. *The New Politics of Financing the UN*. Basingstoke: Macmillan, 2000. New Zealand Ministry of Foreign Trade. *United Nations Handbook*. Wellington, N.Z.: Ministry of Foreign Affairs and Trade, published annually. Simma, Bruno, ed. *The Charter of the United Nations. A Commentary*. New York: Oxford University Press, 1994. Tessitore, John, and Susan Woolfson. *A Global Agenda. Issues before the 55th General Assembly of the United Nations*. 2000–2001 ed. New York: Rowman and Littlefield, 2001.

Seabed Treaty   *See* INTERNATIONAL SEABED AUTHORITY, UNITED NATIONS CONFERENCE ON THE LAW OF THE SEA.

Second Committee of the General Assembly

The Second Committee, one of the GENERAL ASSEMBLY's six main committees, is also known as the Economic and Financial Committee (ECOFIN). Like the other five committees, it consists of representatives from every member state, each having an equal vote. It considers and drafts RESOLUTIONS on agenda items assigned to the committee by the General Assembly. Developing countries consider the Second Committee one of the most pivotal bodies in the United Nations, since it addresses questions of development and international trade and finance. The main CAUCUS GROUP in the Committee is the GROUP OF 77 (G-77) developing nations.

During the 1970s, when the demise of colonialism produced a majority of newly independent developing nations, and when the NEW INTERNATIONAL ECONOMIC ORDER (NIEO) was proposed, the Second Committee considered a lengthy list of contentious topics. Since the end of the COLD WAR and the moderation of the NIEO, controversy in the Second Committee has declined. A global consensus on economic and financial matters emerged in the mid-1990s, and differences between industrialized and developing nations were more limited, as both sought effective methods of dealing with financial problems and evenhanded representation in the international institutions addressing them. Only the injection of "rights-based" language into development programs and reports generated new concern among the developing countries on the committee. They feared that financial aid might be tied to HUMAN RIGHTS performance. In order to allay this concern, a "right to development" was included more frequently in the committee's resolutions.

The Second Committee annually addresses topics regarding trade, finance, development, debt, the international financial institutions (the BRETTON WOODS institutions), the implementation of UN Plans of Action, and the results of WORLD CONFERENCES relating to finance and development, SUSTAINABLE DEVELOPMENT, and reports from the various UN bodies, offices, and committees related to development. It also addresses regional questions from various parts of the world relating to development and finance, and to environmental issues—such as climate change, biological diversity, and DESERTIFICATION. All aspects of technical cooperation also fall within its mandate. The 55th General Assembly session (2000–01) placed 27 items on the committee's agenda, ranging from macroeconomic policy and industrial development questions to the SOVEREIGNTY of the Palestinian people over the occupied territories' natural resources. Based on this agenda, the committee approved 10 draft resolutions, including a call for the convocation of a 10-year review of the EARTH SUMMIT, to be convened in South Africa in 2002.

See also COMMITTEE SYSTEM OF THE GENERAL ASSEMBLY, COMMISSION ON SUSTAINABLE DEVELOPMENT, STRUCTURE OF THE UNITED NATIONS.

Further Reading: Second Committee website: <www.un.org/ga/55/second>. For preceding and succeeding years, substitute the GA session number in the website URL.

— *K. J. Grieb*

Second Development Decade   *See* DEVELOPMENT DECADES.

Second United Nations Conference on the Exploration and Peaceful Uses of Outer Space   *See* COMMITTEE ON THE PEACEFUL USES OF OUTER SPACE.

Second World

In the lexicon of COLD WAR development politics, second world referred to the industrialized socialist states, generally found in the Soviet bloc.

See also FIRST AND THIRD WORLDS.

Secretariat

The Secretariat is the international civil service staff that administers the day-to-day operations of the United Nations. It is one of the six PRINCIPAL ORGANS OF THE UNITED NATIONS, along with the GENERAL ASSEMBLY (GA), SECURITY COUNCIL (SC), ECONOMIC AND SOCIAL COUNCIL (ECOSOC), TRUSTEESHIP COUNCIL, and INTERNATIONAL COURT OF JUSTICE (ICJ). Provided for in Chapter XV, Articles 97–101 of the CHARTER OF THE UNITED NATIONS, the Secretariat works for the United Nations at the HEADQUARTERS in New York City and all over the world, serves other principal organs of the United Nations, and administers the programs and policies determined by these organs. The job of the Secretariat is, then, comparable, on the international stage, to the job carried out by the national bureaucracy of an individual nation. Among other functions, these international civil servants administer PEACEKEEPING operations, handle refugee problems, mediate international disputes, survey economic and social trends, prepare studies on HUMAN RIGHTS, economic development, SUSTAINABLE DEVELOPMENT, and anything else commanded by any organ of the United Nations. The Secretariat provides information to the general public about the United Nations, organizes international conferences, monitors the implementation of UN directives, interprets speeches and translates documents into the UN's official LANGUAGES, and more.

Although its main headquarters is in New York, the United Nations maintains an important presence in Geneva (UNOG), Vienna (UNOV), and Nairobi (UNON), and some related agencies are headquartered in yet other cities, such as Paris, The Hague, and Rome.

The head of the Secretariat is the SECRETARY-GENERAL, who is chosen by the General Assembly on recommendation of the Security Council. The Secretary-General is appointed for a five-year term and can be reelected. The Secretariat consists of the following offices and agencies, each headed by an UNDER SECRETARY-GENERAL, assistant secretary-general or senior official, reporting to the Secretary-General. These units are the Executive Office of the Secretary-General, the Office of Internal Oversight Services (OIOS), the Office of Legal Affairs (OLA), the Department of Political Affairs (DPA), the DEPARTMENT FOR DISARMAMENT AFFAIRS (DDA), the DEPARTMENT OF PEACEKEEPING OPERATIONS (DPKO), the OFFICE FOR THE COORDINATION OF HUMANITARIAN AFFAIRS (OCHA), the DEPARTMENT OF ECONOMIC AND SOCIAL AFFAIRS (DESA), the Department for General Assembly Affairs and Conference Services (DGAACS), the DEPARTMENT OF PUBLIC INFORMATION (DPI), and the Department of Management (DM). In April 2002 Secretary-General Kofi ANNAN added the post of ombudsman to the Secretariat and appointed the Jamaican ambassador Patricia Durrant to the position.

In 2000 there were about 8,600 men and women, under the regular BUDGET, from about 170 countries, who made up the staff of the Secretariat. There are, as well, many more employees who work for related agencies (like the WORLD HEALTH ORGANIZATION (WHO), the WORLD BANK, and several others). These are international civil servants and are not answerable to specific nations but rather to the United Nations alone. In fact employees of the Secretariat take an oath not to seek or receive instructions from any government or outside authority. According to the Charter, member states are to respect the exclusive international character and responsibilities of the members of the Secretariat and not seek to influence their activities in an improper way. Still, there have been times in the history of the United Nations when the Secretariat has been the target of suspicion and criticism by member governments. During the early days of the administration of U.S. president Dwight Eisenhower, at the height of the COLD WAR, for example, Secretary-General Trygve LIE, under pressure from Washington, allowed the Federal Bureau of Investigation (FBI) to fingerprint and question all American employees of the United Nations. The practice continued until November 1953, when the new Secretary-General, Dag HAMMARSKJÖLD, ordered the FBI to end it. But the American government, committed to removing possible communist sympathizers, established the International Organizations Employees Loyalty Board to investigate all U.S. employees at the United Nations. Among those investigated was the highly respected Ralph BUNCHE. During Hammarskjöld's term as Secretary-General, the Soviet Union displayed suspicion of the Secretariat staff, believing that under the Secretary-General, it was doing the bidding of the West. Moscow thus pressed upon the United Nations the so-called TROIKA PROPOSAL, which would have created a three-headed executive office for the Secretariat with separate appointees representing the West, the East, and the developing world.

During the 1980s and 1990s the most serious charges were that the Secretariat was too large, inefficient, and wasteful. Secretary-General Boutros BOUTROS-GHALI tried, unsuccessfully, to quiet the critics, particularly in the UNITED STATES, by freezing the budget and announcing reforms. His successor, Kofi ANNAN, presented his extensive REFORM and reorganization plans in 1997—*Renewing the United Nations*—consolidating and regrouping some 24 agencies into five divisions, and creating a new DEPUTY SECRETARY-GENERAL position to preside over the streamlined bureaucracy. When, in late 1997, the General Assembly approved the first package of proposed reforms, the savings came to about $123 million. One consequence was that the U.S. Congress finally passed an appropriation of $819 million to repay some of the $1 billion in back dues owed by the United States and withheld in part to pressure the United Nations to carry out reforms of the Secretariat bureaucracy.

Employment information about the Secretariat may be obtained via the UN's website at <www.un.org>, or by writing to the UN's Department of Public Information, New York, NY 10017.

See also STRUCTURE OF THE UNITED NATIONS, *specific Secretaries-General, specific departments and offices of the Secretariat.*

Further Reading: New Zealand Ministry of Foreign Affairs. *United Nations Handbook.* Wellington, N.Z.: Ministry of Foreign Affairs, published annually. United Nations Department of Public Information. *Basic Facts about the United Nations.* New York: United Nations Department of Public Information, published periodically.

Secretary-General

The Secretary-General is the chief administrative officer of the United Nations. Chapter XV of the UN CHARTER provides for an administrative staff for the United Nations called the SECRETARIAT. According to Article 97 of the Charter, the Secretariat is to comprise "a Secretary-General and such staff as the Organization may require." The SECURITY COUNCIL recommends the Secretary-General to the GENERAL ASSEMBLY, which then makes the appointment, typically for a five-year term.

As of 2001, there had been seven Secretaries-General: Trygve LIE of Norway (February 1946–November 1952), Dag HAMMARSKJÖLD of Sweden (April 1953–September 1961), U THANT of Burma (November 1961–December 1971), Kurt WALDHEIM of Austria (January 1972–December 1981), Javier PÉREZ DE CUÉLLAR of Peru (January 1982–December 1991), Boutros BOUTROS-GHALI of Egypt (January 1992–December 1996), and Kofi ANNAN of Ghana (January, 1997–). Each of these men came from a neutral or noncontroversial state, and each had extensive diplomatic experience prior to assuming the position of Secretary-General. Also, there was an effort to rotate the position among the different geographical regions recognized by the United Nations. Given the importance of the post, extended private negotiations and political bargaining attended the nomination and election of each successful candidate.

The Secretary-General and his staff in the Secretariat, according to Articles 100 and 101 of the Charter, are obligated to act "exclusively" as "international" civil servants, and not represent any particular nation's, or group of nations' point of view. The Secretary's international staff consists of some 8,600 men and women from about 170 countries, who conduct the day-to-day operations of the United Nations at the HEADQUARTERS in New York and at offices and centers throughout the world. The Secretary-General is chief administrator at all meetings of the General Assembly, the Security Council, the ECONOMIC AND SOCIAL COUNCIL, and the TRUSTEESHIP COUNCIL, and performs any other functions entrusted to him by those organs (Article 98). He is expected to put before the Security Council "any matter which in his opinion may threaten the maintenance of international peace and security" (Article 99), and he is responsible for the deposit of multilateral treaties completed under the auspices of the United Nations, all of which are registered with, and regularly published by the Secretariat (Article 102) in the UNITED NATIONS TREATY SERIES. Each year the Secretary-General issues a public report on the activities of the United Nations (similar to the U.S. president's "State of the Union" address and annual budget), appraising the organization's work, and outlining future priorities. The Secretary, as well, is often expected to make use of his GOOD OFFICES to effect preventive diplomacy, that is, public and private efforts to defuse an international dispute, a civil conflict, or other threat to international peace.

The Secretary-General is the UN's most highly visible representative to the world. As the position has evolved it increasingly has required of its holder a combination of taxing requirements. He must be an accomplished diplomat, a conciliator, often an activist for international causes, a liaison between aggrieved parties, and a master of public relations. The Secretary's "constituency" is particularly unwieldy, and it includes world leaders, the major powers, regional groups, NON-GOVERNMENTAL ORGANIZATIONS (NGOs), religious groups, environmental organizations, the world's media, and more. During the tensest periods of the COLD WAR, the Secretary faced the additional challenge of dealing with a dangerous worldwide competition between two heavily armed competitors, each either seeking to influence the workings of the Secretariat, or, too often, ignoring its role in international affairs.

The office has also been buffeted by controversies and grievances that surfaced as decolonization took place and UN MEMBERSHIP expanded. The Soviet Union's abortive TROIKA PROPOSAL, proposed during Secretary-General Dag Hammarskjöld's term, would have transformed fundamentally the institution of the Secretary-General from a one-person office to a three-person committee, one representing the capitalist West, another the socialist East, and one the Third World. By the 1970s, issues of NORTH-SOUTH difference began to impact the Secretary-General as much as did the cold war. For example, the growing number of poorer nations, first called the GROUP OF 77, criticized Secretary-General Kurt Waldheim for being too pro-West, particularly in his appointments to the Secretariat.

By the 1980s, the issue of REFORM OF THE UNITED NATIONS became a major concern for the Secretary-General. The administration of President Ronald Reagan in Washington was particularly critical of what it perceived as a bloated UN bureaucracy. The UNITED STATES withdrew from the UNITED NATIONS EDUCATIONAL, SCIENTIFIC, AND CULTURAL ORGANIZATION (UNESCO), rejected the LAW OF THE SEA TREATY, and endorsed a legislative proposal by Senator Nancy Kassebaum of Kansas (the Kassebaum Amendment) calling for a cut in U.S. contributions to UN agencies and a reduction in UN staff. In 1985 the president signed a congressional act lowering the American contribution to the total UN BUDGET from 25 percent to 20 percent. Relations between the Secretary-General and the United States worsened when, in 1995, Republicans gained the majority in the U.S. Senate, and Jesse Helms of North Carolina, a sharp critic of the United Nations, became chair of the powerful Senate Foreign Relations Committee. Helms was conspicuously disparaging of Secretary-General Boutros Boutros-Ghali, whose efforts at reform he characterized as insufficient. Under pressure from Helms and other conservatives in the U.S. Congress, Washington turned to the veteran diplomat Kofi Annan as its choice to replace Boutros-Ghali in 1997. Annan thus ascended to the position of Secretary-General with a mandate of sorts to bring about substantial reform of the United Nations. In his first year he presented a sweeping reform package that was largely adopted by the General Assembly in 1997. It streamlined and reorganized the United Nations, consolidated several programs, upgraded management practices, called for a zero-growth budget, and established a new post—DEPUTY SECRETARY-GENERAL—to assist in the array of duties assigned to the Secretary-General.

In the 1990s, after the cold war ended, the world witnessed an escalation of conflict within states, often marked by extreme brutality. This disturbing trend could be seen in the FORMER YUGOSLAVIA (particularly in BOSNIA and Kosovo), Rwanda, SOMALIA, and East Timor. Secretary Boutros-Ghali began to give consideration to enhancing the capability of the Secretary-General's office in addressing this ominous development. He proposed the idea of "peace enforcement" or "peace-building" as distinct from "PEACE-KEEPING." The Secretary intended this to mean that a UN force should be available to intervene in such conflicts even if not all parties to the conflict consented. The proposal was controversial, particularly in the United States. Still, by the end of Boutros-Ghali's term, the number of UN troops around the world in various hot spots had increased dramatically. His successor, Kofi Annan, essentially agreed on an enlarged UN role and set out to justify and improve such action. Annan was determined to ensure that the United Nations, when asked to undertake a peace operation, would be fully equipped to do so. He initiated three reports to forward this effort. The first, a report submitted to the General Assembly in November 1999, examined the atrocities committed against Bosnian Muslims in 1995 in the UN "safe area" of Srebrenica. The Secretary-General released the second report in December 1999. It was an independent INQUIRY conducted by Ingvar Carlsson, the former prime minister of Sweden, into the 1994 GENOCIDE in Rwanda. And the third, made public in August 2000, was a comprehensive review, composed by a distinguished international panel chaired by Lakhdar Brahimi, former foreign minister of Algeria. The BRAHIMI REPORT put forth a wide-ranging set of recommendations to advance the UN's ability to engage in peacekeeping.

During his term, Kofi Annan vigorously carried on the tradition of world diplomat. He traveled extensively throughout the world, performed the role of intermediary by extending his "good offices" in numerous long-standing disputes, sought substantive reform of the UN bureaucracy, and convened the MILLENNIUM SUMMIT, the largest gathering of high level national leaders in history. It can be said as well that he consistently materialized in the world's media, almost always in a favorable light. Crucially, his tenure may have restored the international stature of the Secretary-General at the turn of the millennium.

See also AGENDA FOR PEACE, MEDIATION, RUSSIAN FEDERATION, SPECIAL REPRESENTATIVE OF THE SECRETARY-GENERAL, STRUCTURE OF THE UNITED NATIONS, UNITED NATIONS SYSTEM, *the activities of specific Secretaries-general, particularly in the following entries:* CONGO, IRAN HOSTAGE CRISIS.

Further Reading: Boudreau, Thomas E. *Sheathing the Sword.* New York: Greenwood Press, 1991. Moore, John Allphin, Jr., and Jerry Pubantz. *To Create a New World? American Presidents and the United Nations.* New York: Peter Lang Publishers, 1999. Newman, Edward. *The UN Secretary-General from the Cold War to the New Era: A Global Peace and Security Mandate?* New York: St. Martin's, 1998. United Nations. *Report of the Secretary-General on the Work of the Organization.* General Assembly, Fifty-fifth Session. New York: United Nations, 2000.

Security Council

The Security Council (SC) is one of the six PRINCIPAL ORGANS OF THE UNITED NATIONS, as established in Article 7 of the United Nations CHARTER, and arguably its most influential one. Its primary responsibility is "to maintain or restore international peace and security" (Article 39), but it deals also with other important matters within the UNITED NATIONS SYSTEM and in the relations of the UN with the rest of world. Its composition and work is described in Chapter V of the Charter. In recent years, there have been a number of calls for the REFORM of the Security Council to reflect the new conditions characterizing world affairs since the end of the COLD WAR.

Articles 12 and 24 of the Charter identify the Security Council as the primary organ for dealing with all matters related to peace and war. Only in rare cases has the GENERAL ASSEMBLY (GA) taken over this responsibility, using the 1950 UNITING FOR PEACE RESOLUTION. The Security Council alone has the power to impose ENFORCEMENT MEASURES in accordance with CHAPTER VII. Furthermore, it can recommend actions according to CHAPTER VI and also usually authorizes PEACEKEEPING measures (CHAPTER $VI^{1}/_{2}$). All members of the United Nations, under Article 25, have accepted the obligation to carry out measures decided upon by the Security Council. Therefore, unlike RESOLUTIONS by the General Assembly, those passed by the council are legally binding under INTERNATIONAL LAW. This gives the Security Council a power unknown to other organs of the UN or indeed any international organization.

The Security Council recommends to the General Assembly the candidate for the post of SECRETARY-GENERAL as well as the ADMISSION OF MEMBERS to the United Nations. In the latter case, the Security Council's Committee on Admission of New Members—a standing committee of the council—evaluates applicants before the full council forwards a recommendation to the Assembly. The Security Council also acts in the trusteeship function for the UN in "STRATEGIC TRUST TERRITORIES" (Article 83). In connection with the INTERNATIONAL COURT OF JUSTICE (ICJ), the SC recommends terms of admission for states willing to join the Statute of the ICJ (Article 93) and elects justices to the Court together with the GA (Article 4, STATUTE OF THE INTERNATIONAL COURT OF JUSTICE). Finally, the council recommends whether members' privileges should be suspended or whether a state should be expelled according to Articles 5 and 6, respectively.

There are other specific, related functions or powers designated by the Charter to the Security Council, including: to investigate international disputes that may lead to conflict, recommend methods of adjudicating disputes, forward plans to regulate armaments, determine if a threat to the peace exists and recommend action to forestall the outbreak of violence, call on member states to apply economic SANCTIONS and other non-military measures to resist AGGRESSION, and, as noted above, take military action against an aggressor. If a complaint regarding a threat to the peace is brought before the council, it will initially recommend diplomatic efforts to

First Security Council Session, London, 1946 (UN PHOTO/MARCEL BOLOMEY)

resolve the dispute by peaceful means. The council may also investigate and attempt MEDIATION itself, or it may appoint SPECIAL REPRESENTATIVES or ask the Secretary-General to appoint such representatives or use his GOOD OFFICES to address the disagreement. The council also may send, or authorize specific countries to send, peacekeeping forces into troubled areas.

Fifteen members sit on the Security Council (Article 23). The UNITED STATES, the United Kingdom of Great Britain and Northern Ireland, France, the RUSSIAN FEDERATION (formerly the USSR), and the People's Republic of CHINA—which assumed the seat of the Republic of China (Taiwan) in October 1971—are PERMANENT MEMBERS of the council (the so-called P5) with the power to VETO decisions; 10 are NON-PERMANENT MEMBERS elected by the General Assembly. The latter group was increased in August 1965 from six original non-permanent members following AMENDMENT of Article

23. The expansion had been proposed by the General Assembly by Resolution 1991A, adopted in December 1963. The election of new non-permanent members by the General Assembly is conducted according to an equitable geographical distribution (Article 23); five members must come from Africa and Asia, two each from LATIN AMERICA and the West European and Other CAUCUS GROUPS, and one from an Eastern European country. Immediate reelection of non-permanent members is not possible (Article 23), and five new members are elected each year to serve overlapping two-year terms.

Business is conducted in accordance with the "Provisional Rules of the Security Council," provided by Article 30. VOTING is regulated by Article 27. Each member of the council has one vote; in order for a proposal to pass, it must achieve nine votes in favor (the number of votes required was raised from seven with the enlargement of the council in

1965). The Charter, however, distinguishes between procedural and substantive matters (Article 27). On SUBSTANTIVE QUESTIONS all of the P5 must support the RESOLUTION for it to pass. This is often referred to as the principle of "Great Power unanimity" or the "Veto Power." While the actual use of this power has declined steadily, many proposals fail because of the mere threat of a veto. Whether an issue is a procedural or substantive matter is itself a substantive question, thus giving the permanent members a "DOUBLE VETO" on items before the council. All five of the permanent members have exercised the veto. A permanent member may also abstain, thus officially not supporting a decision but not blocking it.

In theory, the Security Council is in continuous session at United Nations HEADQUARTERS in New York, although it has on occasion met elsewhere. It held sessions in Addis Ababa, Ethiopia, in 1972 and in Panama City, Panama, the following year. Each Security Council member state has a representative in New York at all times. On occasion, heads of state also attend meetings of the SC; for example, in January 1992, 13 heads of state or government and two ministers for foreign affairs met at a summit meeting of the council in New York, and in September 2000, at a SPECIAL SESSION of the council during the MILLENNIUM SUMMIT, heads of state replaced regular envoys to represent their countries. The SECURITY COUNCIL PRESIDENCY is occupied by the members in turn for one month, rotating according to the alphabetical order of the English name for the countries.

Sessions are supposed to be conducted openly, but once a member so requests a meeting convenes behind closed doors. Private meetings have become common practice, whereas in the UN's first years meetings were often televised. Most of the actual debates now take place in meeting rooms adjacent to the Security Council chamber and only the voting is done within the actual council room. When discussing a dispute, non-members of the Security Council may be invited to participate in the discussion (Articles 31 and 32).

As of January 2001, the Security Council had two standing committees established under Article 29: the Committee of Experts on Rules and Procedures, which provided advice on the rules of the council and other technical matters, and the aforementioned Committee on Admission of New Members. The MILITARY STAFF COMMITTEE (Article 47) was intended to help the council on military matters. Ad hoc committees also can be established. One example is the Governing Council of the United Nations Compensation Commission, which was established by Security Council Resolution 692 (1991). Such committees meet in closed session and comprise all council members. In addition, from time to time the council has created working groups, such as the Working Group on Sanctions, established by Resolution 661 (1990) following Iraq's attack on Kuwait, and the Security Council committee established pursuant to Resolution 1132 (1997) concerning SIERRA LEONE. The Security Council is also responsible for the operation of the two international WAR CRIMES TRIBUNALS—the INTERNATIONAL CRIMINAL TRIBUNAL FOR THE FORMER YUGOSLAVIA (ICTY), established by Resolution 808 (1993), and the INTERNATIONAL CRIMINAL TRIBUNAL FOR RWANDA (ICTR; Res. 955, 1994).

The post–cold war world has heard many proposals for reform of the Security Council. With UN MEMBERSHIP in 2001 at 189 countries, some observers argued that the Security Council should be enlarged from 15 members in order to be truly representative. General UN membership grew from 51 in 1945 to 113 members at the time of the 1965 enlargement of the council, but by 2001 no new seats had been added. The P5 included neither an African nor a South American state, while three European countries were represented. Thus, at the turn of the century there was a rising advocacy for expanding SC membership, including granting permanent status to countries from overlooked geographical areas. Furthermore, the former World War II "enemy states," Japan and Germany, had gained leading positions in the global community and believed themselves worthy of permanent membership on the council. Yet expansion of SC membership continued to raise issues of efficiency and effectiveness, and made chances for consensus problematic.

Nonetheless, by 2001 several proposals for reform had been put forward, ranging from the so-called quick-fix solution (that is, granting Germany and Japan permanent seats) to the idea of creating a new category of "semi-permanent membership," with 30 countries being assigned 10 seats on a rotating basis. Many reformers suggested that non-permanent membership be substantially increased.

The veto power of the P5 also has been criticized as antiquated and undemocratic. Suggested modifications range from granting the veto to new permanent members should enlargement take place to abolishing the privilege altogether. Some propose a "weighted" veto, allowing only two or three members collectively to veto any given proposal; others recommend a requirement that any veto be explained. The conducting of business behind closed doors has also been criticized.

To address concerns about representation in the Security Council, the General Assembly, in Resolution 26, passed in 1993, created the "Open-Ended Working Group of the General Assembly on the Question of Equitable Representation on and Increase in the Membership of the Security Council." All decisions regarding changing membership would necessitate a Charter amendment and therefore require a two-thirds majority of all member states; moreover, such a vote would also be subject to a veto. Thus, at the turn of the new century, the practical chances for sweeping reform were not promising.

See also AFGHANISTAN, *AGENDA FOR PEACE*, APARTHEID, APPEALS TO THE SECURITY COUNCIL, COLLECTIVE SECURITY, COLLECTIVE SELF-DEFENSE, CONGO, DUMBARTON OAKS CON-

FERENCE, EAST TIMOR DISPUTE, GULF WAR, HIV/AIDS, INDONESIA, IRAN-IRAQ WAR, KOREAN WAR, MIDDLE EAST WAR OF 1967, NAMIBIA, ROOSEVELT, SOMALIA, STRUCTURE OF THE UNITED NATIONS.

Further Reading: Bailey, Sydney D., and Sam Daws. *The Procedure of the UN Security Council.* 3d ed. New York: Oxford University Press, 1998. Bedjaoui, Mohammed. *The New World Order and the Security Council: Testing the Legality of Its Acts.* Boston: Martinus Nijhoff Publishers, 1994. Fassbender, Bodo. *UN Security Council Reform and the Right of Veto.* The Hague: Kluwer Law International, 1998. Hoffmann, Walter. *United Nations Security Council Reform and Restructuring.* Livingston, N.J.: The Center for U.N. Reform Education, 1994. Köchler, Hans. *The Voting Procedure in the United Nations Security Council: Examining a Normative Contradiction in the UN Charter and Its Consequences on International Relations.* Vienna: International Progress Organization, 1991. May, Ernest R., and Angeliki E. Laiou, eds. *The Dumbarton Oaks Conversations and the United Nations, 1944–1994.* Cambridge: Harvard University Press, 1998. Wellens, Karel C., ed. *Resolutions and Statements of the United Nations Security Council (1946–1992): A Thematic Guide.* 2d ed. Boston: Martinus Nijhoff Publishers, 1993.

— *T. J. Weiler*

Security Council presidency

The position of Security Council president is so demanding and politically sensitive that it is the only UN post that is rotated on a monthly basis, not only to assure that all members of the Security council have an opportunity to preside but also to spread the work load and the tremendous responsibility of speaking for the council and issuing presidential statements on its behalf. While the president may express his or her country's viewpoints in private "consultations," the position of president carries the responsibility of creating consensus and identifying actions that are acceptable to the member states.

The importance of the Security Council presidency stems from the way the SECURITY COUNCIL functions, for the position involves much more than merely presiding over meetings. The president functions as the leader of the council's negotiating sessions and the primary drafter of its documents. Like all other bodies of the United Nations, the Security Council bases its actions on negotiations seeking to establish a consensus on what actions are required and how they are to be carried out. There is a difference from other organs, however, in that the Security Council is a small enough body to enable it to work as a committee of the whole, and hence it conducts its negotiations as a body. For this reason, the overwhelming majority of the Security Council meetings are private, closed to the public, in order to enable the members to negotiate directly and openly with

each other. These closed negotiating sessions are called "consultations." After an initial public meeting to hear the presentations of a dispute or any other reports, the council reverts to "consultations." It is in such private sessions that RESOLUTIONS are drafted and approved. Only after reaching agreement does the council conduct another public session, at which resolutions previously written are voted on and public statements issued.

It is the responsibility of the council president to facilitate reaching agreement in the closed "consultations." This role requires that the president make proposals, explore ideas suggested by others, and in many cases prepare some of the draft versions of the final document. In addition, the Security Council issues a great many "presidential statements," which are communications short of resolutions, used to express a council consensus in a form that does not require a formal vote, often with recommendations and expressions of concern rather than direct action. These are also negotiated, and the product of repeated drafting and revisions.

See also NON-PERMANENT MEMBERS OF THE SECURITY COUNCIL, PERMANENT MEMBERS OF THE SECURITY COUNCIL.

Further Reading: Bailey, Sydney D. *The United Nations: A Concise Political Guide.* 3d ed. Lanham, Md.: Barnes and Noble, 1995. Bailey, Sydney D., and Sam Daws. *The Procedure of the UN Security Council.* 3d ed. New York: Oxford University Press, 1998.

— *K. J. Grieb*

self-determination   *See* NATIONAL LIBERATION.

Senior Management Group (SMG)

Included in his REFORM program for the United Nations—entitled *Renewing the United Nations*—UN SECRETARY-GENERAL Kofi ANNAN proposed the creation of a committee of senior UN managers to serve as the Secretary-General's cabinet. The Senior Management Group was approved in 1997 by the GENERAL ASSEMBLY. It fulfills the duties of a central policy planning body and provides strategic coherence to UN activities. Chaired by the Secretary-General, the SMG includes not only several UNDER SECRETARIES-GENERAL stationed in New York City, but also many agency heads and DIRECTORS-GENERAL headquartered in Geneva, Nairobi, Vienna, and Rome.

Members serve on the committee at the pleasure of the Secretary-General. As of February 2002, the members of Secretary Annan's cabinet were Louise FRÉCHETTE (DEPUTY SECRETARY-GENERAL), Pino Arlacchi (UN INTERNATIONAL DRUG CONTROL PROGRAMME), Carol Bellamy (UN CHILDREN'S FUND), Catherine Bertini (WORLD FOOD PROGRAMME), Joseph Connor (Department of Management), Hans Corell

(Legal Counsel), Nitin Desai (DEPARTMENT OF ECONOMIC AND SOCIAL AFFAIRS), Jayantha Dhanapala (DEPARTMENT FOR DISARMAMENT AFFAIRS), Ibrahim Gambari (Special Assignments in Africa), Jean-Marie Guéhenno (DEPARTMENT OF PEACEKEEPING OPERATIONS), Ruud Lubbers (UN HIGH COMMISSIONER FOR REFUGEES), Mark Malloch Brown (UN DEVELOPMENT PROGRAMME), Thoraya Obaid (UN POPULA-TION FUND), Jose Antonio Ocampo (ECONOMIC COMMISSION FOR LATIN AMERICA AND THE CARIBBEAN), Kenzo Oshima (OFFICE FOR THE COORDINATION OF HUMANITARIAN AFFAIRS), Olara Otunnu (Children and Armed Conflict), Vladimir Petrovsky (UN OFFICE AT GENEVA), Kieran Pren-dergast (Department of Political Affairs), Rubens Ricupero (UN CONFERENCE ON TRADE AND DEVELOPMENT), Iqbai Riza (Chef de Cabinet), Mary Robinson (UNITED NATIONS HIGH COMMISSIONER FOR HUMAN RIGHTS), Shashi Tharoor (DEPARTMENT OF PUBLIC INFORMATION), Klaus Toepfer (UN ENVIRONMENT PROGRAMME), Dileep Nair (Observer—Department of Internal Oversight Services), and Yongjian Jin (General Assembly Affairs).

Further Reading: SMG website: <www.un.org/News/ossg/sg/pages/seniorstaff.html>.

Seventh Committee   *See* FOURTH COMMITTEE.

Sierra Leone

Situated on the west coast of Africa, between Guinea and Liberia, Sierra Leone had gone relatively unnoticed in the three decades following its independence from Great Britain in 1961. It came to the public's attention because of a devastating civil war in 1991.

The Protectorate of Sierra Leone was formed in 1787 under the administration of the Sierra Leone Company as a place to repatriate former slaves. It became an official British colony in 1808, although its territorial boundaries were not settled until 1895. The expanded colony included 18 ethnic groups, the largest being the Mende.

Sierra Leone did not fight a war of independence, although there were violent revolts against British rule. In 1951, the Sierra Leone constitution was altered, opening the way for the formation of competitive political parties. In 1961, the Sierra Leone Peoples' Party (SLPP) formed the newly independent government. The first fully democratic elections were held in 1967; however, before the winning All Peoples' Congress (APC) could take office, the military staged a coup. Democratic government was not achieved until 1968 and Sierra Leone's opportunity for a peaceful transition between the SLPP and the APC was lost.

Between 1968 and 1985, APC leader Siaka Stevens consolidated control and implemented a constitutional change that entrenched a one-party system. Joseph Momoh suc-

ceeded Stevens in 1985. By the close of the 1980s, the INTER-NATIONAL MONETARY FUND (IMF) had declared Sierra Leone in a state of economic emergency and ineligible for further IMF lending. Economic disaster was met by domestic calls for a return to democratic elections. The country was further destabilized in 1991 when armed rebels attacked, initiating the civil war that ravaged Sierra Leone into the next century. The rebels, known as the Revolutionary United Front (RUF) were under the leadership of Foday Sankoh and supported by Liberian rebel cum president, Charles Taylor. As was the case in other African conflicts, such as in ANGOLA, the RUF was able to capitalize on Sierra Leone's vast resources of alluvial diamonds to fund its activities.

In 1992, dissatisfied members of the Sierra Leone army carried out a coup. Although it initially enjoyed popular support, by 1994 there were demands for a return to civilian government. In 1995, SECRETARY-GENERAL BOUTROS-GHALI appointed Mr. Berhanu Dinka as his special envoy to aid negotiations that would lead to democratic elections. Mr. Dinka worked closely with both the ORGANIZATION OF AFRICAN UNITY (OAU) and the ECONOMIC COMMUNITY OF WEST AFRICAN STATES (ECOWAS) to facilitate a return to civilian rule. Elections were held in 1996 and SLPP leader Ahmed Tejan Kabbah was elected president. However, in the spring of 1997, this time in collaboration with the RUF, the military ousted the Kabbah government despite a tentative peace agreement that had been reached at the close of 1996.

In response to the coup, the UN SECURITY COUNCIL imposed an oil and arms embargo on October 8, 1997. The embargo authorized ECOWAS to administer the SANCTIONS via its own PEACEKEEPING force, ECOMOG, comprised mostly of Nigerian troops. President Kabbah successfully regained power in the spring of 1998, and in June, the Security Council authorized the UN Observer Mission in Sierra Leone (UNOMSIL, Res. 1181). The mission mandate was to observe DISARMAMENT efforts and advise on the restructuring of the security forces. Unarmed UNOMSIL representatives also documented reports of HUMAN RIGHTS violations and ongoing atrocities committed by the combatants. Subsequently, a joint UN-ECOWAS-Sierra Leone government coordination mechanism was established for conflict management in Sierra Leone.

The RUF and the government of Sierra Leone reached a comprehensive peace accord (known as the Lomé Agreement) in July 1999. The agreement established the legal provisions for the RUF to become a political party in Sierra Leone and for its members to hold important cabinet positions within the government. At the time of the agreement the Security Council approved a peacekeeping mission in Sierra Leone (Res. 1270). The United Nations Assistance Mission in Sierra Leone (UNAMSIL) had its mandate extended in February and May 2000. In March 2001 the council extended it again and authorized the deployment of

17,500 military personnel, including 260 military observers and 60 civilian police personnel.

The main objective of UNAMSIL continued to be the provision of assistance to the government of Sierra Leone as it attempted to restore law and order throughout the country. The civil war, and the economic collapse that preceded it, had devastating effects on the Sierra Leone population. Over the course of the war, nearly 700,000 people were displaced, 75,000 died, and thousands were purposefully maimed through brutal amputations conducted by the RUF. Peace and reconciliation seemed to be in reach with the Lomé Agreement; however, the RUF failed to comply with the terms of the agreement and intermittent fighting and terrorist acts were still too common as the century turned. Parts of Sierra Leone continued to be under rebel control. As of the summer of 2001, the future for Sierra Leone was far from certain.

Further Reading: Smilie, Ian, Lansana Gberie, and Ralph Hazleton. *The Heart of the Matter: Sierra Leone, Diamonds & Human Security.* Canada: Partnership Africa, January 2000. UNOMSIL website: <www.un.org/Depts/DPKO/Missions-unomsil.htm>. UNAMSIL website: <www.un.org/dpko/unamsil/body_unamsil.htm>.

— *S. C. Rein*

Six-Day War   *See* ARAB-ISRAELI DISPUTE, MIDDLE EAST WAR OF 1967.

Sixth Committee of the General Assembly

The Sixth Committee of the GENERAL ASSEMBLY, one of its six main committees, deals with legal matters. Like all General Assembly main committees, it consists of representatives of every member state, each with an equal vote. Its function is to consider and negotiate draft RESOLUTIONS before they are placed before the full General Assembly. It works closely with the INTERNATIONAL LAW COMMISSION, a body of independent legal experts, in making recommendations to the Assembly on the progressive development of INTERNATIONAL LAW. The committee also reviews the work of the UNITED NATIONS COMMISSION ON INTERNATIONAL TRADE LAW, which is charged with developing uniform international trade law in an era of globalization.

The committee's agenda is limited, allowing it to address each item at great length. Its function is to negotiate the text of treaties and agreements, a time-consuming process. The Sixth Committee, for example, spent 30 years negotiating the definition of AGGRESSION. The committee adopts all items by unanimous consent. The agenda includes issues related to relations with the host country, the juridical immunity of states, the protection and status of diplomats and UN personnel, laws regarding TERRORISM and its defini-

tion, and international law concerning state succession. It also considers the reports of all UN bodies dealing with legal questions. At the turn of the century, the committee was also involved in several high-profile international issues, including the establishment of the INTERNATIONAL CRIMINAL COURT, and review of the UN CHARTER.

See also COMMITTEE SYSTEM OF THE GENERAL ASSEMBLY, STRUCTURE OF THE UNITED NATIONS.

Further Reading: Tessitore, John, and Susan Woolfson. *A Global Agenda. Issues before the General Assembly of the United Nations.* New York: Rowman and Littlefield, published annually. Sixth Committee website: <www.un.org/law/cod/sixth/55/sixth55.htm>. For preceding and succeeding years, substitute the GA session number in the website URL.

— *K. J. Grieb*

Social, Cultural, and Humanitarian Committee (SOCHUM)   *See* THIRD COMMITTEE.

Social Summit   *See* WORLD SUMMIT FOR SOCIAL DEVELOPMENT.

Somalia

Somalia has long been plagued by natural disasters, mainly drought. After long-time dictator Siad Barre was overthrown in 1991, political disaster struck when a civil war erupted between the different clans and factions in the country, most prominent among them the United Somali Congress/the Somali National Alliance (USC/SNA) under General Muhammed Aidid. To help ease the suffering of the population, the SECURITY COUNCIL established the UNITED NATIONS OPERATION IN SOMALIA (UNOSOM) and the accompanying military effort, the UNIFIED TASK FORCE (UNITAF) in 1992. While the deployment of the U.S.-organized and U.S.-led task force in December 1992 did much to pacify the situation and make humanitarian assistance by the United Nations and others possible (the level of malnutrition and starvation fell considerably in many areas), the needed "secure environment" could not be established. Somalia remained without a functioning and effective central government. Also, more than half of the country—the northern and northeastern part—was not covered by the mission.

In the period from March through May 1993, UNOSOM II strove to bring peace, stability, law and order to Somalia, a goal left uncompleted by UNOSOM/UNITAF. The mandate, under CHAPTER VII of the CHARTER, also included the use of ENFORCEMENT MEASURES, if necessary, and covered the whole country. The mission monitored the cease-fire, prevented new violence, and provided security at vital areas, de-arming, mine-clearing, and assisting in the repatriation of nearly 1 million refugees and the return of 1.7 million internally displaced persons. Furthermore, UNOSOM II undertook the mandate to help the Somalis rebuild a functioning economy and infrastructure and reestablish a functioning democracy with reconciled ethnic groups. Leaders of the 15 warring factions attending the Conference on National Reconciliation in Addis Ababa in March had signed an agreement pledging their support for reconciliation.

It soon became clear, however, that a number of factions—most important, that of Aidid's USC/SNA—would not abide by the agreement. Tensions mounted and in June fighting between Somalis and UN soldiers erupted. After bolstering the U.S. force, President Clinton declared that he would withdraw all American personnel by March 31, 1994.

Aidid's USC/SNA ceased hostilities against UNOSOM II on October 9, 1993, and conflict subsided. S/RES/878 extended the mandate until November 18. In a report on November 12, the SECRETARY-GENERAL (SG) underscored the positive outcome of the humanitarian relief operation, but he stressed that UNOSOM II was at a watershed, as law and order had still not been restored. By the time the mission ended in early March 1995, UN forces had suffered 147 casualties.

In February 2000, the United Nations facilitated a peace conference in Djibouti. The new Somali president, Abdiqassim Salad Hassan, was inaugurated on August 27, 2000. The country had lacked a central government since 1991. Two-thirds of the members of the new national assembly, which would reside in the provisional capital Baidoa, were sworn in. While this was an important step forward, according to David Stephen, SPECIAL REPRESENTATIVE of SECRETARY-GENERAL Kofi ANNAN, the task of rebuilding Somalia remained "formidable."

In the summer of 2000 a new call for international aid went out. Drought and flooding threatened lives in the area. Mohamed Ibrahim Egal, president of the self-declared Republic of Somaliland, also asked the United Nations to grant Somaliland a special independent status comparable to Palestine or Kosovo. Egal also sought international aid. Most of Somalia's infrastructure continued to be in a state of disintegration at the turn of the century and the country's people had been reduced to subsistence living. Among other international organizations, the FOOD AND AGRICULTURE ORGANIZATION (FAO), the UNITED NATIONS DEVELOPMENT PROGRAMME (UNDP), the UNITED NATIONS EDUCATIONAL, SCIENTIFIC AND CULTURAL ORGANIZATION (UNESCO), the UNITED NATIONS HIGH COMMISSIONER FOR REFUGEES (UNHCR), the UNITED NATIONS CHILDREN'S FUND (UNICEF), the UNITED NATIONS DEVELOPMENT FUND FOR WOMEN (UNIFEM), the WORLD HEALTH ORGANIZATION (WHO), and the WORLD FOOD PROGRAMME (WFP) were active in Somalia at the turn of the century.

See also PEACEKEEPING.

Further Reading: Hirsch, John L., and Robert B. Oakley. *Somalia and Operation Restore Hope.* Washington, D.C.: United States Institute of Peace Press, 1995. United Nations Department of Public Information. "The UN and Somalia, 1992–96," *The UN Blue Books Series.* Vol. 3. New York: United Nations Department of Public Information, 1996. UNOSOM/UNITAF website: <www.unsomalia.org>.

— *T. J. Weiler*

South   *See* NORTH-SOUTH RELATIONS.

South-West Africa Mandate   *See* NAMIBIA.

South-West Africa People's Organization (SWAPO)   *See* NAMIBIA.

Southeast Asia Treaty Organization (SEATO)

SEATO was established by the South-East Asia Collective Defense Treaty signed on September 8, 1954, in Manila. It was dissolved in 1977. As a collective defense organization for the protection of Southeast Asian countries, SEATO fell under Article 51 of the UN CHARTER: "Nothing in the present Charter shall impair the inherent right of individual or COLLECTIVE SELF-DEFENSE if an armed attack occurs against a Member."

SEATO was dominated by the non-Asian states that formed a majority of its MEMBERSHIP. U.S. secretary of state John Foster Dulles persuaded France, Great Britain, Australia, New Zealand, Pakistan, the Philippines, and Thailand to join SEATO after the defeat of the French in Indochina in order to ensure allies of American assistance in advance of any future crisis in the region. The parties to the Manila Treaty agreed to consult if any signatory felt threatened. They would act together to meet AGGRESSION if they could unanimously agree on designating an aggressor and if the threatened state agreed to action on its territory. The signatories reaffirmed their obligations under the UN Charter to resolve controversies by peaceful means, and to avoid threats or force in international relations. Measures taken under Article 4 of the Manila Treaty, the provision that calls for action in response to "aggression by means of armed attack," were to be reported at once to the UN SECURITY COUNCIL.

Protection for CAMBODIA, Laos, and South Vietnam was covered in a separate PROTOCOL, although these states were not invited to become signatories. Cambodia eventually adopted a neutralist course and withdrew from SEATO protection. The Geneva Accord of 1962 neutralizing Laos removed that state from under the TREATY's umbrella, leaving only South Vietnam unambiguously in the category of a "protocol state." The UNITED STATES government, operating from its vision of communism as a global threat and viewing U.S.-sponsored alliances for military defense as a way of bolstering its policy of containment, expressly identified SEATO as aimed at containing communism by appending to the treaty an understanding that its provisions referring to armed attack applied only to "communist aggression."

SEATO proved to have little value as a device for mobilizing its members to take effective, united action to contain communism in the region. Only two of the members—the Philippines and Thailand—were Southeast Asian states and the other members had little interest in intervening militarily in the region. The main beneficiary of SEATO among its regional members was Thailand, which gained a U.S. commitment to act in defense of the Thais. While the Bangkok-based organization proved to be militarily irrelevant, Washington used the treaty to justify unilateral American involvement in Vietnam. Under the 1964 Gulf of Tonkin Resolution, Congress gave the American president power to "repel any armed attack" against American forces and the power to protect any nation covered by SEATO that might request aid "in defense of its freedom."

See also COLD WAR.

Further Reading: Buszynski, Leszek. *SEATO, the Failure of an Alliance Strategy.* Singapore: Singapore University Press, 1983. Modelski, George. *SEATO, Six Studies.* Melbourne: F. W. Chesire for the Australian National University, 1962.
— *G. S. Silliman*

sovereignty

Sovereignty means supreme authority. In political theory it denotes the sole controlling power in a political community. In the 16th century, French thinker Jean Bodin formulated a modern explication of the term, declaring that the prince or the "sovereign" had the power to declare law. Thus, under a divine right monarchy, sovereignty resided in the person of the king. In a democracy it rests notionally with all the people; in a federal system there are in theory separate territorial areas of sovereignty (as states in the UNITED STATES). In all cases the sovereign entity is immune from all foreign JURISDICTION.

In international affairs, the idea of sovereignty contains a double claim: state autonomy in foreign affairs and non-interference by outside actors in internal matters. State sovereignty, hence, necessarily suggests the theory of "international anarchy," because there can be no higher government or enforceable law to which the state is responsible. In international affairs sovereignty consists of a constitutional independence of all states participating in diplomacy, that is, a state is not contained within a wider scheme, but stands apart and alone, absolutely with reference to domestic matters. The doctrine is recognized in the UN CHARTER,

Article 2: "The Organization is based on the principle of the sovereign equality of all its Members."

This sense of sovereignty has been central to the practice and study of international relations since the Treaty of Westphalia in 1648. It has served to identify the legitimate actors who participate in international diplomacy. Sovereignty qualifies a territorial entity to engage fully in international relations. MEMBERSHIP in the United Nations confirms such sovereignty. Accordingly, when Iraq invaded Kuwait in 1990 with the intention of absorbing the smaller country, the larger country—in the view of the SECURITY COUNCIL—had violated the victim's sovereignty, made unambiguous by its membership in the United Nations.

By the 20th century, theoretical and practical problems arose regarding the concept. Proponents of the primacy of INTERNATIONAL LAW assert that it is binding on professed sovereign states. They also argue that, since the UN Charter does not permit AGGRESSION at will, the absolute freedom of a sovereign state is a thing of the past. Moreover, sovereignty denotes the right of a state to enforce its own version of HUMAN RIGHTS, a view challenged by most Western nations, and by the United Nations UNIVERSAL DECLARATION OF HUMAN RIGHTS, which proclaims rights as universal rather than culturally or nationally determined. In 1999 SECRETARY-GENERAL Kofi ANNAN argued that those rights could not be abridged in the name of state sovereignty. Finally, the proposition that sovereignty denies any other nation or group of nations, including the United Nations, the right to interfere in a state's domestic affairs has come under increased challenge as the world community has had to deal with human tragedies in collapsing and dysfunctional states in, for example, the FORMER YUGOSLAVIA, INDONESIA, and areas of Africa. Its authorization of humanitarian intervention in SOMALIA, Rwanda, and East Timor fundamentally challenged the right of a state to control its domestic life and suggested that modern sovereignty is not without limits.

See also AGENDA FOR PEACE, BOUTROS-GHALI, BRAHIMI REPORT, CHAPTER VI ½, CHAPTER VII, COMMISSION ON SUSTAINABLE DEVELOPMENT, CONGO, ENVIRONMENT ORGANIZATION OF AFRICAN UNITY, PEACEKEEPING, RIO DECLARATION, STATEMENT OF FOREST PRINCIPLES, SUBSIDIARITY, SUSTAINABLE DEVELOPMENT, UNITED NATIONS CONFERENCE ON ENVIRONMENT AND DEVELOPMENT, UNITED NATIONS CONFERENCE ON THE HUMAN ENVIRONMENT, UNITED NATIONS CONFERENCE ON THE LAW OF THE SEA.

Soviet Union   *See* RUSSIAN FEDERATION.

Special Committee on the Implementation of the Declaration on Decolonization   *See* COMMITTEE OF 24.

Special Drawing Rights (SDRs) *See*

INTERNATIONAL MONETARY FUND.

Special Envoy *See* SPECIAL REPRESENTATIVE OF THE

SECRETARY-GENERAL.

Special Fund *See* UNITED NATIONS DEVELOPMENT

PROGRAMME.

Special Mediator *See* SPECIAL REPRESENTATIVE OF

THE SECRETARY-GENERAL.

Special Political and Decolonization Committee *See* FOURTH COMMITTEE.

special rapporteur

The word *rapporteur* derives from Old French, but its meaning can be discerned from the English word *report*. A rapporteur is a person responsible for compiling reports and presenting them to a governing body, a learned society, or a general meeting. A UN "Special Rapporteur" should be distinguished from a SPECIAL REPRESENTATIVE OF THE SECRETARY-GENERAL (SRSG), chosen by the SECRETARY-GENERAL, who acts on behalf of, or in place of, the Secretary-General. A special rapporteur receives commission from a body of the United Nations via a RESOLUTION. The appointment is typically for a set period, the special rapporteur is a servant of the body that made the appointment, and he or she is mandated to provide a comprehensive report on a specific global problem or area of concern to that body. The report is normally quite extensive and consists of an explanation of the mandates and methods of the commission; historical background; economic, social, political, and demographic information; assessment of the current situation; information received from relevant countries; reports of field or site visits; and, frequently, recommendations for UN action. Sometimes the United Nations provides these reports to affected countries for guidance. Special rapporteurs are expected to be experts in the field about which they are chosen to report and they are often well-respected academics. They are, in addition, typically multilingual individuals.

During the last two decades of the 20th century, the UN COMMISSION ON HUMAN RIGHTS most often made use of special rapporteurs. As early as 1967, the ECONOMIC AND SOCIAL COUNCIL (ECOSOC) had authorized the commission to move beyond general discussion on HUMAN RIGHTS and deliberate on violations of rights in specific countries and in specific categories. In its 1979–80 session, the commission established special procedures known as "Mechanisms," to facilitate such investigations. These procedures led to the appointment of special rapporteurs to investigate and prepare reports for the commission. Since then, the commission has appointed special rapporteurs to investigate thematic issues, such as torture, summary executions, violence against WOMEN, racial discrimination, and religious discrimination, and to examine human rights in particular countries. In 2000 there were 15 special rapporteurs covering a broad range of topics and inspecting specific countries. Some examples included special rapporteurs on conditions in Iraq, Sri Lanka, and Myanmar, on religious intolerance, and on sexual exploitation of children in specific world locales. Individual appointments have included, in 1993, that of Mr. Alejandro Artucio as special rapporteur of the Commission on Human Rights to oversee the human rights situation in Equatorial Guinea, the appointment in 1994 of Ms. Radhika Coomaraswamy as special rapporteur on violence against women, and the appointment of a special rapporteur on the human rights situation in AFGHANISTAN. In the latter case, there were three appointees from the time of the creation of the position of special rapporteur in 1984 until the turn of the century—Mr. Felix Ermacora of Austria (1984–95), Mr. Choong-Hyun Paik of the Republic of Korea (1995–98), and Mr. Kamal Hossain of Bangladesh, who served from 1998 into 2001. The periodic reports of the special rapporteurs on the situation of human rights in Afghanistan provided the most important up-to-date and substantive information for UN organs and member states as they determined their policies toward the government of Afghanistan. In the spring of 2000 the Commission on Human Rights announced that it would appoint for a period of three years a special rapporteur on the Right to Food. The new rapporteur was expected to provide full information on how the United Nations might address what the commission called "the widespread failure by States and the international community to ensure freedom from hunger and enjoyment by all of the right to food."

Despite the extraordinary service special rapporteurs provide, they have almost no UN SECRETARIAT assistance. They are unpaid volunteers with very limited funds and usually no support staff. These conditions, unfortunately, often severely restrict the benefits that could be realized from their work.

Further Reading: Tessitore, John, and Susan Woolfson. *A Global Agenda: Issues before the 55th General Assembly of the United Nations.* New York: Rowman and Littlefield Publishers, 2000. United Nations High Commissioner for Human Rights website: <www.unhchr.ch>. University of Minnesota Human Rights Library website: <www1.umn.edu/humanrts>.

Special Representative of the Secretary-General (SRSG)

The UN CHARTER gives the SECRETARY-GENERAL a broad mandate and requires of the office extensive responsibilities not only for the administration of the institution but also for the maintenance of peace and security. In order to carry out the duties of the office, Secretaries-General have appointed, on their own authority or by direction from the GENERAL ASSEMBLY or SECURITY COUNCIL, "special" or "personal" representatives. Generally, if required to do so by the RESOLUTION of one of the other PRINCIPAL ORGANS OF THE UNITED NATIONS, the appointment is made of a "Special Representative," and if it is on the Secretary-General's own authority, the appointee is titled as his or her "personal" representative. Depending on the importance and type of assignment given to the appointee, he or she may be known by various appellations, such as "Special Envoy," "Personal Adviser to the Secretary-General," "Senior United Nations Adviser," "Special Adviser," "Special Mediator," and "Special Coordinator." (It should be noted that SRSGs, appointed by the Secretary-General, have a different origin and different functions from a SPECIAL RAPPORTEUR, who typically is appointed by way of resolution from an organization of the United Nations and reports to that specific organization.)

The tradition of delegating the GOOD OFFICES function of the Secretary-General to a specially designated person dates from the partition of Palestine in 1947. At that time Secretary-General Trygve LIE appointed Swedish count Folke Bernadotte to obtain a commitment from the Jews and Arabs to the partition plan. Often the appointment made by the Secretary-General is of someone with extraordinary diplomatic or political credentials from outside the United Nations, who may be able to defuse a dangerous conflict. This was the case in the appointment of former U.S. secretary of state Cyrus Vance to seek a resolution of the conflict in BOSNIA. More usually, the Secretary-General will look inside the SECRETARIAT or to the UN diplomatic corps to find a trusted subordinate who can speak with the authority of the Secretary-General. This was the case as the crisis grew in AFGHANISTAN in the 1990s. Secretary-General Kofi ANNAN appointed Lakhdar BRAHIMI (July 1997–October 1999), and then in February 2000, Francesc Vendrell as his special envoys.

The appointment of a special representative not only reflects a need to delegate responsibility by a Secretary-General but also a desire to give an issue or area special attention and continuous UN involvement. As the United Nations entered the 21st century, there was a new penchant for the appointment of SRSGs not only in conflict regions but also in areas of THEMATIC DIPLOMACY. For example, on February 28, 2001, Secretary-General Annan appointed Adolf Ogi as his "Special Adviser" on "Sport for Development and Peace." Since 1993, special representatives have been appointed for "Children and Armed Conflicts," "the Conference on DISARMAMENT," "Gender Issues and the Advancement of WOMEN," "Information and Communication Technologies," and "Internally Displaced Persons." In June 2001, the Secretary-General had special representatives as well in Iraq,

Lebanon, the Great Lakes Region of Africa, ANGOLA, Burundi, the Central African Republic, Côte d'Ivoire, the Democratic Republic of the CONGO, Eritrea, Guinea-Bissau, Liberia, SIERRA LEONE, SOMALIA, Sudan, Western Sahara, GUATEMALA, CAMBODIA, East Timor, Myanmar, Papua New Guinea, Tajikistan, the Balkans, BOSNIA and Herzegovina, CYPRUS, Macedonia, Georgia, Kosovo, and the territories occupied by Israel.

See also ARAB-ISRAELI DISPUTE; BUNCHE, RALPH; CHAPTER VI $^1/_2$ PROVISIONS; HAMMARSKJÖLD, DAG; IRAN-IRAQ WAR; MIDDLE EAST WAR OF 1967; PÉREZ DE CUÉLLAR, JAVIER; PROVISION, UN SECURITY COUNCIL RESOLUTION 242.

Further Reading: Roberts, Adam, and Benedict Kingsbury, eds. *United Nations, Divided World: The UN's Roles in International Relations.* 2d ed. New York: Oxford University Press, 2000. Special and Personal Representatives and Envoys of the Secretary-General website: <www.un.org/News/ossg/srsg.htm>.

special sessions of the General Assembly

Article 20 of the United Nations CHARTER authorizes the GENERAL ASSEMBLY to convene special sessions "as occasion may require." These meetings of the full body meet in addition to the Assembly's annual regular sessions that convene each September, and they are to be distinguished from EMERGENCY SPECIAL SESSIONS that meet under the terms of the UNITING FOR PEACE RESOLUTION. In order for the SECRETARY-GENERAL to convoke a special session of the General Assembly, there must be a request from the SECURITY COUNCIL in the form of a RESOLUTION not subject to the VETO, from a majority of the members of the United Nations, or from a member state with the concurrence of a majority of UN members.

The earliest interpretations of Article 20 assumed that the General Assembly would call special sessions only when urgent matters required immediate consideration. Beginning with the 1974 special session on the NEW INTERNATIONAL ECONOMIC ORDER (NIEO), however, GA members found this type of meeting to be a useful way to generate public attention and action on development, humanitarian, and social issues. Principally nations from the developing world, with their working majority in the Assembly and limited individual diplomatic clout, used special sessions as a technique to create UN initiatives, such as CONVENTIONS, institutions, PROGRAMMES AND FUNDS, and public information campaigns. The frequency of special sessions and the breadth of topics expanded dramatically as the United Nations approached the end of the century.

Three General Assembly special sessions were held on DISARMAMENT (1978, 1982, 1988), and in November 2000, the Assembly decided to convene a fourth as soon as the objectives, agenda, and timing of the meeting could be decided. Following the 1974 NIEO meeting, special sessions on development issues were convened in 1975, 1980, 1986, 1990, 1999 (two sessions), and 2001. The year 2001 alone witnessed two special sessions: development and human settlements (June), and HIV/AIDS (June). A scheduled third session on children was postponed from September 2001 to 2002 in the wake of the terrorist attacks that month on New York City and Washington, D.C. The Assembly also convened sessions on Palestine (1947, 1948), NATIONAL LIBERATION in Tunisia (1961), NAMIBIA (1967, 1978, 1986), APARTHEID (1989), drugs (1990, 1998), UN financing (1963, 1978), small island developing states (1999), and WOMEN (2000).

Further Reading: Simma, Bruno, ed. *The Charter of the United Nations: A Commentary.* Oxford: Oxford University Press, 1995.

Special Session on Disarmament I–IV   *See* DISARMAMENT.

Special United Nations Fund for Economic Development (SUNFED)

Article 55 of the UN CHARTER directs the United Nations to promote "higher standards of living, full employment, and conditions of economic and social progress and development." To these ends, the GENERAL ASSEMBLY established the Special United Nations Fund for Economic Development on December 14, 1957 (Res. 1219). Member states from the Third World had been encouraged by U.S. promotion of economic development through the United Nations, beginning with the Truman administration's POINT FOUR PROGRAM, and hoped SUNFED would provide a mechanism for capital investment by the developed states in LESS DEVELOPED COUNTRIES (LDC). Prior UN development efforts had largely focused on technical assistance and the provision of experts through its EXPANDED PROGRAM OF TECHNICAL ASSISTANCE (EPTA), rather then the actual shift of significant capital for large development projects. SUNFED was meant to correct this imbalance.

The General Assembly had called for the creation of SUNFED as early as 1954 (Res. 822), citing the need to fund the construction of roads, schools, hospitals, and electric power plants. The United Nations set a target of $250 million pledged before the fund would begin operation. By 1955 contributions had been promised by the Netherlands ($7 million), Denmark ($2 million), and Norway ($1.5 million). Other pledges added to the total, but the UNITED STATES, which was an essential donor if the total were to be met, hesitated in making a large contribution. President Eisenhower had outlined in his "CHANCE FOR PEACE" SPEECH (1953) a proposal to provide savings produced by nuclear superpower DISARMAMENT for development purposes. The stalemate of

the COLD WAR, however, kept that formula from materializing. Nonetheless, in 1956, believing competition with the Soviet Union in the Third World required economic assistance from the United States, Eisenhower changed his position. He promised to make contributions equaling two-thirds of what all other nations gave, which was 40 percent of the total fund. With this commitment the Assembly went ahead with SUNFED.

Throughout its existence, LDCs demanded that the developed states contribute much larger amounts (up to 1 percent of their gross national products) to the fund than those states were willing to do. This pressure from the SOUTH was complicated further by East-West ideological disputes concerning particular SUNFED projects. Other than promoting private and public investment in the developing world, and conducting preinvestment surveys, the fund had limited impact on Third World economic conditions. SUNFED was merged with EPTA in 1965 to form the UNITED NATIONS DEVELOPMENT PROGRAMME (UNDP).

Further Reading: Stoessinger, John G. *The United Nations and the Superpowers: China, Russia, and America.* 4th ed. New York: Random House, 1977.

specialized agencies

Article 57 of the United Nations CHARTER describes specialized agencies as separately chartered, independent organizations, each dealing with a specialized or technical field, and "having wide international responsibilities . . . in economic, cultural, educational, health and related fields." Each was established to deal with a particular issue or problem that the international community identified as requiring action or regulation. Only a few of these specialized agencies were created by the GENERAL ASSEMBLY or through UN sponsored conferences. Each is governed by a Statute or TREATY that specifies its functions, duties, mandate, voting method, and organizational STRUCTURE, and each is an Inter-Governmental Organization (IGO) composed of member states. Membership in each of these organizations is determined by treaty signature, and hence the membership of each agency varies and is not identical to that of the United Nations. Specialized agencies have separate budgets, funded through members' contributions. In many cases these contributions are voluntary, although some organizations have their own methods of assessing their members that differ from those used for the regular UN BUDGET.

Since issues requiring special attention have been identified over time, the specialized agencies were created at different times and by different groups of nations. Some of the highly technical bodies, such as the UNIVERSAL POSTAL UNION, date from the previous century, while others were originally established by the LEAGUE OF NATIONS, and subsequently adopted by the United Nations. Most have been created since 1945, often urged into existence by the United Nations or by conferences it sponsored. Hence the term "specialized agency" covers a broad range of organizations conducting distinct tasks.

Articles 63 and 64 of the Charter authorize the ECO-NOMIC AND SOCIAL COUNCIL (ECOSOC) to coordinate the work of the specialized agencies. Because this must be done through "consultation" and "recommendations" to independent organizations—some with overlapping missions—supervision has proven to be difficult. Nineteen of the specialized agencies have signed formal agreements with the United Nations and report to the Economic and Social Council annually. Since each agency retains its independence, oversight is generally limited to broad issues and suggestions. An additional dozen "programmes" report to both the General Assembly and ECOSOC, so providing oversight for these groups is even more problematic.

The specialized agencies of the United Nations are:

FOOD AND AGRICULTURE ORGANIZATION OF THE UNITED NATIONS (FAO)—Rome, Italy

International Bureau of Education (IBE)—Geneva, Switzerland

International Centre for Science and High Technology (ICS)—Trieste, Italy

INTERNATIONAL CIVIL AVIATION ORGANIZATION (ICAO)—Montreal, Canada

INTERNATIONAL FUND FOR AGRICULTURAL DEVELOPMENT (IFAD)—Rome, Italy

INTERNATIONAL LABOUR ORGANIZATION (ILO)—Geneva, Switzerland

INTERNATIONAL MARITIME ORGANIZATION (IMO)—London, United Kingdom

INTERNATIONAL MONETARY FUND (IMF)—Washington, D.C., USA

INTERNATIONAL TELECOMMUNICATIONS UNION (ITU)—Geneva, Switzerland

INTERNATIONAL TRAINING CENTRE (ILO/ITC)—Turin, Italy

Multilateral Investment Guarantee Agency (MIGA)—Washington, D.C., USA

UNITED NATIONS EDUCATIONAL, SCIENTIFIC AND CULTURAL ORGANIZATION (UNESCO)—Paris, France

UNITED NATIONS INDUSTRIAL DEVELOPMENT ORGANIZATION (UNIDO)—Vienna, Austria

UNIVERSAL POSTAL UNION (UPU)—Berne, Switzerland

WORLD BANK Group—Washington, D.C., USA, including:
International Bank for Reconstruction and Development (IBRD) [World Bank]
International Development Association (IDA)
International Finance Corporation (IFC)

WORLD HEALTH ORGANIZATION (WHO)—Geneva, Switzerland

WORLD INTELLECTUAL PROPERTY ORGANIZATION (WIPO)—Geneva, Switzerland

WORLD METEOROLOGICAL ORGANIZATION (WMO)—Geneva, Switzerland

WORLD TRADE ORGANIZATION (WTO)—Geneva, Switzerland

Each specialized agency has its own mandate and mission. Collectively the work of the specialized agencies spans fields from development assistance and aid to governments and individuals to regulation in such diverse spheres as economics, trade, ENVIRONMENT, health, agriculture, and training. Some agencies consist primarily of technical experts, who, although appointed by governments, act as individual experts, while others are more political in nature and more representative of governments. Several of the agencies are simply rule-making and enforcing bodies, dealing with a narrow range of operations that entail the movement of goods or people across borders, such as the International Civil Aviation Organization, the Universal Postal Union, the International Telecommunications Union, and the International Maritime Organization. Others are designed to provide international development assistance or to deliver humanitarian aid to children and other dependent populations.

Each specialized agency has an independent governing body and structure, with a distinctive method of functioning. Usually the governing bodies are elected by general conferences of the membership. Administrators are selected by their governing boards or the full membership meetings. Decision making in the agencies often departs from the general international legal principle of one nation one vote. For example, the International Monetary Fund and World Bank both employ weighted VOTING based on contributions. In the International Labour Organization functional representation gives each nation four delegates who in turn represent government, employers, and labor organizations. These delegates cast their individual votes in plenary sessions, and on standing and technical committees. Other specialized agencies guarantee that nations important in the field addressed by the agency are always represented on the governing body. An example of this is the International Civil Aviation Organization, which specifies that the nations with the largest air carriers must hold seats. Others require general conferences to act on decisions taken by committees and governing boards. In most agencies rules or decisions can be made directly by their governing boards, though some, like the International Labour Organization, function primarily by drafting treaties that are submitted to the member states. Both ECOSOC and the General Assembly frequently endorse such treaties and urge their ratification.

Because of the expertise required to deal with specific mandates, it is in the specialized agencies that NON-GOVERNMENTAL ORGANIZATIONS exert the strongest influence, by campaigning for specific rules and by providing expertise and information that provide the basis for decisions. ECOSOC endeavors to coordinate the actions of the agencies to assure that they are complementary to each other and to the United Nations. It attempts to minimize overlapping activities, but it has no power to force the agencies to accept its recommendations. For details regarding particular functions, structure, and operations consult the individual entries for each of the specialized agencies.

See also OBSERVER STATUS, UNITED NATIONS SYSTEM.

Further Reading: Ameri, Houshang. *Politics and Process in the Specialized Agencies of the United Nations.* Aldershot, U.K.: Gowser Publishing, 1982. Boisard, M. A., and E. M. Chopsoudousky, eds. *Multilateral Diplomacy: The United Nations System at Geneva.* 2d ed. The Hague: Kluwar Law International, 1988.

— *K. J. Grieb*

Stabilization Force (SFOR)   *See* BOSNIA.

Stalin, Joseph (1879–1953)

Iosif Vissarionovich Dzhugashvili was born on December 21, 1879, to a poor peasant family in Gori, Georgia. Later known by his revolutionary pseudonym "Joseph Stalin," he rose from his humble origins in the Russian Empire to lead the communist Soviet Union through World War II and into its status as an emergent superpower. Along with American president Franklin Delano ROOSEVELT (FDR) and British prime minister Winston CHURCHILL, Stalin was one of the primary founders of the United Nations and its CHARTER.

Early in life Stalin seemed headed into the Russian Orthodox priesthood, attending the Tiflis Ecclesiastical Seminary. But his interest in the revolutionary ferment of his time and difficulties with seminary discipline led to his expulsion. Attracted to the writings of Karl Marx, he became involved with the nascent Russian workers movement by the turn of the century, and he joined Vladimir Lenin's Bolshevik faction of the Russian Social Democratic Workers Party in 1903. He became a member of the party's Central Committee and editor of its newspaper, *Pravda,* in 1912. Stalin was arrested a dozen times for revolutionary activity prior to the 1917 upheaval. With the overthrow of the tsar in March 1917 Stalin returned to Petrograd from his most recent internal exile, joining Lenin, Leon Trotsky, and a small group of Bolsheviks who overthrew the provisional government in November (by the Western calendar at the time).

Stalin had not spent much time outside of Russia prior to the Revolution. Most of his colleagues in the new Bolshevik government had been in exile in Western Europe during the preceding two decades. They were cosmopolitan, spoke Western languages, and debated the minute details of Marxist philosophy. By contrast, Stalin was parochial, and he had no special oratorical skills or political following. His talent for organization, however, would serve him well, allowing him to

defeat his rivals for power following Lenin's death in 1924. Two years earlier he had been appointed general secretary of the Central Committee, using the post to fill key bureaucratic positions with supporters and with others opposed to Trotsky, Stalin's chief competitor for leadership. Despite Lenin's admonition in his final testament that the Georgian could not be trusted to work well with other party leaders and should be removed as general secretary, Stalin managed to win the intraparty struggle for power and emerged as the uncontested leader of both the party and the state by 1929.

In the name of "socialism in one country," Stalin carried out the massive industrialization of the Soviet Union, the collectivization of agriculture, and the imposition of totalitarianism. Using the terror of the police state, he imposed centralized economic planning through "Five-Year Plans" that eliminated the vestiges of capitalism. Much of the hardship imposed by Stalin, including the purges of the 1930s that wiped out Bolshevik revolutionary veterans, the high command of the Red Army, and millions of peasants as "enemies of the people," was rationalized as the requirement of a socialist state facing inevitable future war with the imperialist capitalist states. The Soviet leader, now turned ardent Russian nationalist, saw the world divided into antagonistic ideological "camps," with the defense of the USSR dependent on the rapid development of the country and its military, the surreptitious encouragement of communist parties in capitalist states, and the pursuit of a geopolitical, rather than revolutionary, foreign policy.

The rise of Adolf Hitler in Germany in 1933 threatened Soviet security directly, and led Stalin to ease his antipathy toward the capitalist countries. He sought and achieved U.S. recognition of the Soviet state. The USSR also joined the LEAGUE OF NATIONS and Stalin directed European communist parties to form a "common front" with democratic parties in their countries in an effort to find some common defense against the German danger. As the Nazi regime progressively violated the provisions of the Versailles TREATY and moved against governments in Central and Eastern Europe, Stalin became convinced that Britain and France intended to goad Germany into a war with their communist adversary, the Soviet Union. Following the Western powers appeasement of Hitler's demands on Czechoslovakia in 1938, Stalin concluded that there was an imperialist conspiracy to destroy the socialist state by means of German AGGRESSION. Announcing that the Soviet Union would not be the country to "pull the chestnuts out of the fire" for Europe, Stalin secretly negotiated a non-aggression PACT with the Third Reich. The Molotov-Ribbentrop Agreement was signed in August 1939. Under its terms and secret PROTOCOLS, Poland would be divided between Germany and the Soviet Union, and the USSR would be allowed to occupy the Baltic states.

Stalin was a power broker and a realist. When Germany reneged on its agreement and invaded the Soviet Union in June 1941, the Soviet leader quickly forged an alliance with

Britain, and after December 8 with the UNITED STATES—not to create a new postwar global order as Churchill and Roosevelt had intimated in their 1940 ATLANTIC CHARTER, but to crush Germany and to secure the future defense of the USSR through Soviet dominance of the region. The Soviet leader declined to attend early allied summits, and his government played no role in initial planning for a postwar international organization. Only in the fall of 1943, following the August QUADRANT CONFERENCE between Churchill and Roosevelt in Quebec, was Stalin confronted by his allies with a formal proposal for such an entity.

Roosevelt and Churchill thought it important to obtain Soviet concurrence in a postwar body while the war was still underway. The incentive to join as one of Roosevelt's "FOUR POLICEMEN" in the maintenance of future world peace would be far greater while Stalin needed his Western allies. The first opportunity to gauge Soviet intentions came at the MOSCOW CONFERENCE OF FOREIGN MINISTERS in late October 1943. Only after U.S. secretary of state Cordell HULL and his British counterpart agreed to open a second front from the west was Stalin ready to consider the idea of a general international organization. Throughout the negotiations in Moscow and later, the Soviet Union focused on the implications of such a body for Soviet geopolitical concerns. Foreign Minister Vyacheslav Molotov insisted on language in the Moscow DECLARATION that would allow wide latitude for Soviet military operations in Eastern Europe.

Stalin had his first opportunity to discuss the proposed organization with Roosevelt at the TEHERAN CONFERENCE, November 27–December 1, 1943. The president described how the United States, Soviet Union, United Kingdom, and CHINA would have sole authority to enforce the peace and prevent aggression. He also outlined the likely organs that would be part of the organization, including an executive council. Stalin, apprehensive that the council might limit Soviet actions, asked FDR whether the proposed body would be able to make decisions binding on the great powers. The president said it would not. The issue of the VETO was not discussed directly at Teheran, but the Soviet leader and his representatives returned to this commitment by FDR many times over the next two years. By the end of the Moscow and Teheran meetings, however, Stalin was willing to give his support to a postwar organization.

The modalities of the new world body were developed most extensively at the DUMBARTON OAKS CONFERENCE in August and September 1944. Stalin's representatives, led by Ambassador Andrei Gromyko, accepted nearly all American proposals for the expected Charter. Only on the matter of the veto in the SECURITY COUNCIL did the Soviet delegation raise objection. The United States opposed the use of the veto by a PERMANENT MEMBER to bar the hearing of a dispute in which it was involved. Yet Stalin saw this as an essential protection to Soviet freedom of action. The matter would be left unresolved until the YALTA CONFERENCE five months later. Yalta attendees would also have to resolve a new matter raised by Gromyko at Dumbarton Oaks. The Soviet Union demanded that all 16 Union republics of the USSR be admitted as original members of the United Nations. Faced with an organization MEMBERSHIP overwhelmingly pro-American, Stalin sought to gain in effect 16 votes for the Soviet Union. Completely unacceptable to the other participants (the United States, the United Kingdom, China), the issue would be settled by Roosevelt and Stalin at Yalta.

When the final summit among Churchill, Roosevelt, and Stalin convened at Yalta in February 1945, the most important concerns for Stalin were the political and military arrangements in postwar Eastern Europe and the disposition of defeated Germany. Having lost more than 30 million Soviet citizens to German aggression in two world wars, Stalin placed his faith in control of bordering regions for the protection of the Soviet Union. Instead of seeing COLLECTIVE SECURITY embodied in the United Nations as the formula for peace in the future, Stalin sought to protect his foreign policy options from any UN limitations. Only when matters concerning the future government of Poland and the occupation of Germany were resolved was he ready to make accommodations on the world body. He reached a compromise with Roosevelt on the number of Soviet republics to be admitted—Byelorussia and Ukraine would be original members in addition to the USSR. He then conceded the position on when the veto could be used, agreeing that a permanent member could not block discussion of a dispute in which it was involved.

The Soviet Union served as a sponsor of the 1945 UNITED NATIONS CONFERENCE ON INTERNATIONAL ORGANIZATION in San Francisco. Yet, it sought significant changes in the Charter on matters supposedly resolved earlier. Stalin's delegation once again challenged the veto limitations. To convince him of America's resolve on this issue, President Harry S. Truman sent a special envoy to Moscow to explain that the Charter would not pass the U.S. Senate on the terms proposed by the Soviet Union. Stalin backed down and directed his delegation to accept the Yalta formula.

Because of the existence of the veto, the success of the new United Nations depended on continuing cooperation among the permanent members of the Security Council. This rapidly evaporated as Stalin reimposed iron-fisted control at home, subverted the provisional coalition governments in Eastern Europe, supported communist movements in Greece and Turkey, hesitated in removing Soviet troops from Iran and Austria, raided the Soviet occupation zone in East Germany for industrial resources and personnel, and declined any participation in the Marshall Plan. U.S.–Soviet cooperation turned to rivalry and COLD WAR.

Finding the Soviet Union "encircled" by the American policy of containment, and outnumbered in the United Nations, Stalin used the veto to block the ADMISSION of any new members without the addition of Soviet satellite regimes in Eastern

Europe. When Mao Zedong's revolutionary forces seized power in China in 1949, Stalin ordered a boycott of the Security Council to protest rejection of the communist regime taking the seat held by the Nationalist Chinese government. Shortly thereafter Stalin gave his approval to a North Korean invasion of South Korea, triggering a UN decision to use force to repel the attack. In June 1950, the Soviet leader found himself, by way of a surrogate, at war with the United Nations. When the Soviet delegate returned to the Security Council in order to block any further UN actions in Korea, the United States circumvented the council by pushing through the GENERAL ASSEMBLY the UNITING FOR PEACE RESOLUTION, which allowed the Assembly to make recommendations on the restoration of peace and security when the council was deadlocked by the veto. Stalin's government protested the maneuver as an unconstitutional revision of the Charter.

One of Stalin's great concerns was the nuclear monopoly of the United States after the war. He had ordered the secret and rapid development of a Soviet atomic capability, but until a Soviet arsenal could be developed, the USSR stood at a disadvantage in the cold war contest. At the United Nations, Stalin used DISARMAMENT talks to criticize American nuclear intentions and policies, and to call for large cuts in U.S. stockpiles. When the United States put forward the BARUCH PLAN in the UN ATOMIC ENERGY COMMISSION in June 1946, calling for the creation of an International Atomic Development Authority (IADA) that would own and manage all aspects of atomic energy "potentially dangerous to world security," the Soviets rejected it as a clumsy move to maintain the U.S. monopoly. The commission suspended its meetings on July 29, 1947, due to the deadlock between the United States and the Soviet Union. There would be no further serious U.S.–Soviet disarmament discussions until after Stalin's death.

Events from 1945 to 1953 in the United Nations reenforced Stalin's camp theory of international politics. He berated the institution and its first SECRETARY-GENERAL, Trygve LIE, as tools of American anti-Soviet policy. He largely responded by closing off the Soviet world behind what Churchill called an "Iron Curtain." Within the Warsaw Pact nations he insisted on Stalinist regimes, and in the Soviet Union there was a renewed effort to root out bourgeois and capitalist influences. A cult of personality, which had begun during the terror of the 1930s, returned with new enthusiasm. Stalin was praised without restraint as the near equal of Lenin in the revolutionary transformation of Russia. In the last months of his life he began laying the groundwork for another round of purges. In what was known as the "Doctors Plot" Stalin's propagandists asserted that doctors in the Kremlin were attempting to murder high communist leaders. If the scenario of the 1930s had repeated itself, these villains surely would be found to have been directed by Stalin's enemies. Fortunately for the personal and political futures of those around him, Stalin died on March 5, 1953.

See also DECLARATION BY UNITED NATIONS, KOREAN WAR.

Further Reading: Holloway, D. *Stalin and the Bomb. The Soviet Union and Atomic Energy.* New Haven, Conn.: Yale University Press, 1994. Service, Robert. *A History of Twentieth-Century Russia.* Cambridge, Mass.: Harvard University Press, 1997. Stalin, Joseph V. *Economic Problems of Socialism in the USSR.* New York: International Publishers, 1952. Tucker, Robert C. *Stalin as Revolutionary.* New York: W.W. Norton, 1973.

Standing Committees of the General Assembly

In 1946 the UN GENERAL ASSEMBLY established two standing committees to deal with the continuing financial requirements of the United Nations. They are the ADVISORY COMMITTEE ON ADMINISTRATIVE AND BUDGETARY QUESTIONS (ACABQ) and the COMMITTEE ON CONTRIBUTIONS. Both make recommendations to the Assembly via the FIFTH COMMITTEE. ACABQ has 16 members who are nominated by their governments but serve as private individuals. It advises the United Nations on financial and budgetary matters related to UN administration and programs. The committee can call upon the SECRETARY-GENERAL's office and the heads of UN PROGRAMMES AND FUNDS to meet with it and provide needed information. It evaluates and reports on the financing of PEACEKEEPING operations and international tribunals, and it carries out any other assignments given to it by the Secretary-General. It has the decision-making authority to authorize start-up expenditures on peacekeeping operations that need rapid implementation even though related budgetary matters have not yet been resolved. The Committee on Contributions determines each country's required contribution to the United Nations based on the UN's SCALE OF ASSESSMENTS, which the committee plays a key role in developing. The committee also hears appeals from states that object to the percentage of the UN BUDGET they have been asked to pay, and it makes recommendations on the application of Article 19 of the CHARTER, which allows for the removal of a state's right to vote in the General Assembly if it is sufficiently in arrears on its payments.

See also COMMITTEE SYSTEM OF THE GENERAL ASSEMBLY.

Further Reading: Fifth Committee website: <www.un.org/ga/56/fifth/>. For preceding and succeeding years, substitute the GA session number in the website URL.

State-Building   *See* AGENDA FOR PEACE.

Statement of Forest Principles

The first officially approved global consensus on forests, the Statement on Forests emanated from the 1992 UNITED NATIONS CONFERENCE ON ENVIRONMENT AND DEVELOP-

MENT (UNCED). It fell far short of the World CONVENTION on Forests that many developed states and NON-GOVERNMENTAL ORGANIZATIONS sought. Officially titled the "Non-legally binding authoritative statement of principles for a global consensus on the management, conservation and sustainable development of all types of forests," the document provided little more than voluntary guidelines.

In the 1980s global concern for the dwindling tropical rain forests and general deforestation spurred interest in establishing international standards applicable to all states. In 1987 the WORLD BANK created the International Tropical Timber Organization (ITTO), and the FOOD AND AGRICULTURE ORGANIZATION (FAO) established the Tropical Forestry Action Plan (TFAP), but neither stemmed the rapid loss of old forest stands. In July 1990 the G-7 Summit meeting in Houston endorsed the proposal by U.S. president George Bush that a forestry convention be negotiated. Supporters of the proposal hoped that UNCED would write such a document.

Opposition to a convention—which by its very existence would recognize the world's forests as part of the global commons—promptly arose from the states of the south. They saw the proposal as a threat to their right to pursue economic development, and as an effort by the developed countries to avoid dealing with greenhouse gas emissions. Led by the two largest holders of rain forests, Brazil and Indonesia, the LESS DEVELOPED COUNTRIES (LDC) blocked UNCED from approving a legally binding agreement. For these NATION-STATES, the real issue was not environmental protection but rather the preservation of SOVEREIGNTY.

The statement set forth several objectives for the world community. It called for reforestation, forest conservation, a reduction in air pollution, the introduction of prior environmental impact assessments, international cooperation, involvement of the public, and new financial resources to encourage substitution policies for current nonsustainable development forest use. These worthy goals were undercut, however, by a restatement of Principle 21 from the 1972 Stockholm Conference on the Human ENVIRONMENT that said in part, "States have . . . the sovereign right to exploit their own resources pursuant to their own environmental policies." The Forest Statement also encouraged "open and free international trade in forest products," and "condemn[ed] any measures that might restrict trade in tropical hardwoods." Taken together these provisions detached governments from any international restrictions, and they left forest protection to individual state decisions.

At best, the Statement of Forest Principles provided a minimal step toward the development of an international consensus. The COMMISSION FOR SUSTAINABLE DEVELOPMENT subsequently set up an Intergovernmental Panel on Forests that submitted a report to Earth Summit +5, the 1997 Review Session of the consequences of UNCED, which included more than 100 recommendations for forest conser-

vation and SUSTAINABLE DEVELOPMENT. The 1997 meeting then established the Intergovernmental Forum on Forests that has continued to push for an international convention on the topic.

Further Reading: *Report of the United Nations Conference on Environment and Development.* Vol. 3, A/CONF.151/26 (Vol. 3), August 12, 1992.

states at risk   *See* AGENDA FOR PEACE.

Statistical Yearbook

The United Nations Statistics Division publishes annually a *Statistical Yearbook.* This yearbook contains a useful compilation of statistics for more than 200 countries and areas of the world. It is organized into four parts: a world and regional summary, population and social statistics, economic activity, and international economic relations. The 2001 edition of the yearbook, similar to recent editions, presented more than 80 tables in the fields of demographic and social statistics, national accounts, details regarding finance, labor conditions and wages, price levels, agricultural and industrial production, developments in science and technology, and international trade and tourism. As a rule, the *Statistical Yearbook* provides a decade-long analysis of a country's economic, financial, and demographic development.

Further Reading: *Statistical Yearbook* website: <esa.un.org/unsd/pubs>.

Statute of the International Court of Justice

Acting as the guiding document for the INTERNATIONAL COURT OF JUSTICE (ICJ), the Statute of the ICJ derives directly from the Statute of the PERMANENT COURT OF INTERNATIONAL JUSTICE (PCIJ), established by RESOLUTION of the LEAGUE OF NATIONS in 1921. By this connection of the older statute with the newer one the founders of the ICJ indicated their determination to maintain a continuity in the evolution of INTERNATIONAL LAW. The Statute was drafted by a committee of jurists meeting in Washington, D.C., two weeks prior to the 1945 San Francisco Conference, and approved with minor AMENDMENTS at the time of the Charter's approval.

The Statute is considered an integral part of the UN Charter and is usually annexed to any publication of the CHARTER. It describes the organization, procedures, and JURISDICTION of the ICJ. Its 70 articles elaborate certain general principles articulated in Chapter XIV of the Charter. These articles are organized into five chapters: "Organization of the Court" (Articles 2–33), "COMPETENCE of the Court" (Articles 34–38), "Procedure" (Articles 39–64), "Advisory

Opinions" (Articles 65–68), and "AMENDMENT" (Articles 69–70). The statute can be amended by a two-thirds majority vote in the GENERAL ASSEMBLY and ratification by two-thirds of member states, including all the PERMANENT MEMBERS OF THE SECURITY COUNCIL. The only variation is that nonmembers of the United Nations who are nonetheless parties to the ICJ Statute may vote with the General Assembly on proposed amendments.

For full explication of the history, provisions, and role of the statute, refer to the entry on the International Court of Justice.

See also INTERNATIONAL COVENANT ON ECONOMIC, SOCIAL AND CULTURAL RIGHTS, *JUS COGENS*.

Stettinius, Edward R. (1900–1949)

As U.S. under secretary of state, Edward Stettinius presided over the DUMBARTON OAKS CONFERENCE in 1944. Serving as President Franklin ROOSEVELT's secretary of state, he attended and played a major role in the YALTA CONFERENCE in February 1945, and he received a presidential appointment (confirmed after Roosevelt's death by President Harry S. Truman) to become chairman of the U.S. delegation to the UNITED NATIONS CONFERENCE ON INTERNATIONAL ORGANIZATION, held in San Francisco in the spring of 1945. President Truman then appointed him to the United Nations, where he represented the UNITED STATES on the SECURITY COUNCIL from which he resigned in 1946 for health reasons.

Born in Chicago and educated at the University of Virginia, Stettinius pursued a successful career in business and industry. He worked for General Motors and in 1938, at the age of 38, became chairman of the board of directors of the US Steel Corporation. In August 1939, Roosevelt appointed him chairman of the War Resources Board. Later he worked in the new Office of Production Management and then was active in administering the wartime Lend-Lease program. The president appointed him under secretary of state in 1943 and secretary in late 1944 when Cordell HULL retired. He energetically forwarded the work for a postwar organization that had been initiated by Hull. At Dumbarton Oaks in late summer of 1944 (while he was still under secretary) he headed the American delegation and, with Sir Alexander Cadogan of the United Kingdom and Andrei A. Gromyko of the Soviet Union, formed the steering committee that directed the meetings.

With Roosevelt's encouragement he helped launch a massive campaign to gain public support for the Dumbarton Oaks proposals for a United Nations, issuing millions of copies of the proposals, comic books about them, and sending speakers around the country. As secretary he accompanied Roosevelt to the YALTA CONFERENCE in February 1945, then went to Mexico City to brief Latin American governments on the new organization. Appointed by the president as chairman of the American delegation to the San Francisco

conference that would establish the UN Charter, Stettinius proved exhaustive in cajoling the Soviet Union to stick by its earlier commitments and stay with the conference until a CHARTER had been established. He opened the conference as its temporary chairman, and then chaired the Steering and Executive Committees, the most important bodies in the conference STRUCTURE. The Steering Committee, in particular, was made up of the four sponsoring nations and decided the most important issues of policy and procedure.

The day after the conference ended Stettinius resigned. He was then appointed by President Truman to go to London as the chairman of the U.S. delegation to the meetings of the UN Preparatory Commission. He subsequently served as a member of the U.S. delegation for the first GENERAL ASSEMBLY session starting in January 1946, and he represented the country on the Security Council. He resigned from government service on June 2, 1946. When he died at an early age in 1949, SECRETARY-GENERAL Trygve LIE remarked the he would "live in history as one of the chief architects of the United Nations."

Further Reading: Campbell, Thomas M., and George C. Herring, eds. *The Diaries of Edward R. Stettinius, Jr., 1943–1946.* New York: New Viewpoints, 1975. Johnson, Walter. "Edward R. Stettinius, Jr." In *An Uncertain Tradition: American Secretaries of State in the Twentieth Century.* Edited by Norman A. Graebner. New York: McGraw-Hill, 1961. Stettinius, Edward R., Jr. *Roosevelt and the Russians; The Yalta Conference.* Edited by Walter Johnson. Westport, Conn.: Greenwood Press, 1970.

Stimson Doctrine

When Japan invaded Manchuria in 1931, sparking a war with CHINA, the world faced an act of AGGRESSION that threatened international peace. The Council of the LEAGUE OF NATIONS hesitated to use SANCTIONS, and it refused to use force, even when the Japanese undertook a military campaign to conquer all of Manchuria. The UNITED STATES, which was not a member of the League of Nations, sent an "observer" to League sessions on the crisis, and it was willing to support proposals for negotiation and conciliation, but would not support stronger actions. However, given that the Japanese invasion violated two TREATY commitments to which the United States was a party (the Nine-Power Treaty of 1922 that had endorsed the Open Door Policy in China, and the Kellogg-Briand PACT of 1928 that outlawed war), the U.S. government felt compelled to take a stand.

The result was the Hoover-Stimson Doctrine, more often called the Stimson Doctrine. It was named after its author, U.S. secretary of state Henry L. Stimson, who served under President Herbert Hoover (and later as secretary of war under Franklin ROOSEVELT). On January 3, 1932, Stimson sent a diplomatic communication officially informing the governments of China and Japan that the

United States "does not intend to recognize any situation, treaty, or agreement which may be brought about" in violation of existing treaties. In effect, the United States, unwilling to join collective enforcement action to prevent the Japanese conquest of Manchuria, declared that it would adopt a policy of non-recognition of occupations resulting from the use of force.

Japan completed its conquest and declared Manchuria to be the independent state of Manchukuo, (Manzhouguo), a Japanese protectorate. Under the League COVENANT, members were obligated to preserve "the territorial integrity and political independence" of all nations against aggression. Article 10 authorized the League Council to recommend the means, including force, to meet this obligation. Instead of taking forceful action, the League appointed an investigation commission, and adopted the Stimson Doctrine in 1932, directing its member states not to recognize Manchukuo. This of course meant that other nations did not recognize the new state as legal, but it had little effect on Japanese control of Manchuria. Tokyo responded by notifying the League that it would withdraw from League MEMBERSHIP, which it did in 1933. The League's action was deemed ineffective by many diplomats and later scholars, who argued that it represented an act of appeasement comparable to subsequent concessions to Germany. More severe critics insisted that the Manchurian crisis forecast the ultimate failure of the League and the coming of world war. Yet, nine years later President Roosevelt invoked the Stimson Doctrine to demand Japanese withdrawal from Manchuria and all of its other conquered territories. Following World War II, the juridical soundness—if not contemporary effectiveness—of the Stimson Doctrine was corroborated when several of the WAR CRIMES TRIBUNAL jurists cited the Nine-Power Treaty and the Kellogg-Briand Pact as legal bases for trying Japanese criminals in Tokyo.

Further Reading: Borg, Dorothy. *The United States and the Far Eastern Crisis of 1933–1938.* Cambridge, Mass.: Harvard University Press, 1964. Ferrell, Robert H. "Henry L. Stimson." Volume 11 of Samuel Flagg Bemis, ed. *American Secretaries of State and Their Policies.* New York: Knopf, 1958. ———. *American Diplomacy in the Great Depression: Hoover-Stimson Foreign Policy, 1929–1933.* New York: Norton, 1970. Ostrower, Gary B. *Collective Insecurity: The United States and the League of Nations during the Early Thirties.* Lewisburg, Pa.: Bucknell University Press, 1979. Schmitz, David F. *Henry L. Stimson: The First Wise Man.* Wilmington, Del.: Scholarly Resources, 2001. Stimson, Henry L., and McGeorge Bundy, *On Active Service in Peace and War.* New York: Octagon Books, 1971.

— K. J. Grieb

Stockholm Conference   *See* UNITED NATIONS CONFERENCE ON THE HUMAN ENVIRONMENT.

Strategic Trust Territories   *See* TRUSTEESHIP SYSTEM.

structure of the United Nations

The structure of the United Nations is spelled out in the initial articles of the CHARTER, and it is built around six principal organs. All other bodies are subsidiary to one of the main organs, or—as in the case of associated organizations that are independent—report to one of the six principal organs. Each of the principal organs has specific functions or responsibilities, and each organ has a different MEMBERSHIP.

The GENERAL ASSEMBLY is the most significant organ, since it is the only body in which all member states are represented, each with an equal vote. Most of the member states consequently regard the General Assembly as the focal point of the United Nations. The centrality of the General Assembly is reflected in the fact that three of the remaining five organs report to it, and in the role that the Assembly plays in electing the membership in all of the other principal organs, save for the SECRETARIAT. The General Assembly also has the power to discuss and act on any subject appropriately brought before it by any member state, and hence its powers overlap those of the other principal organs.

The General Assembly is often referred to as the "Town Meeting of the World," in which the residents of the planet are represented by their governments. Small and middle-sized nations place a great value on the equality of VOTING, which reflects the principle of the sovereign equality of states that in turn constitutes the basis of INTERNATIONAL LAW and of the UNITED NATIONS SYSTEM. The General Assembly has the power to appoint any necessary committees. It functions with six main committees, all with plenary membership, which normally provide initial consideration of most issues, and report the RESOLUTIONS they draft and adopt to the full General Assembly. The six main committees each deal with distinct topical fields.

The SECURITY COUNCIL is charged with the maintenance of international peace and security, and it is the only body whose decisions are binding on all member states of the United Nations. Action by the council requires the concurrence of the five PERMANENT MEMBERS, who were designated in the Charter and constituted the principal world powers at the time of the establishment of the organization. The permanent members are the UNITED STATES, United Kingdom, France, RUSSIAN FEDERATION (originally the Union of Soviet Socialist Republics), and the People's Republic of CHINA. The NON-PERMANENT MEMBERS are elected by the General Assembly for two-year teams, on the basis of geographical representation. Originally 11 states were members of the Security Council, but council membership increased to 15 in 1965 by Charter AMENDMENT in order to reflect the expansion of UN membership.

The ECONOMIC AND SOCIAL COUNCIL (ECOSOC), whose members are elected by the General Assembly to three-year terms according to geographical regions, oversees UN activities in the economic and social fields. While a principal organ, ECOSOC submits reports and proposals to the General Assembly for final approval. ECOSOC also receives reports and proposals from more than 15 functional and regional commissions, and it has the power to appoint committees to deal with questions before it. ECOSOC also receives reports from SPECIALIZED AGENCIES and associated organizations, and coordinates their activities. The membership of ECOSOC has been increased twice by Charter amendment, to reflect the expanding membership of the United Nations, first to 27 in 1965, and then to 54 in 1971.

The TRUSTEESHIP COUNCIL was designed to provide oversight for colonial territories being prepared for independence, with membership consisting of the administering powers, permanent members of the Security Council that did not have trust territories, and other states elected by the General Assembly. Decolonization was a principal objective of the United Nations, and this process proceeded so effectively that by the 1990s the Trusteeship Council had become obsolete. This resulted from the granting of independence to all territories placed under UN supervision, and because nearly all remaining NON-SELF-GOVERNING TERRITORIES had expressed their desire to continue in this status through referenda. Consequently, the Trusteeship Council stopped meeting in 1994.

The INTERNATIONAL COURT OF JUSTICE (ICJ) is a judicial body that the United Nations established as the successor to the PERMANENT COURT OF INTERNATIONAL JUSTICE (PCIJ). It functions as the UN legal arm but is largely independent. The Statute that describes its organization, procedures, and JURISDICTION is based on the 1922 Statute of the PCIJ. It is the only principal organ not headquartered in New York. The ICJ is based in The Hague. The Court deals only with disputes between states. It has automatic jurisdiction only over disputes between states that have signed OPTIONAL CLAUSE 36 of the Court statute granting such jurisdiction. Otherwise, cases must be brought voluntarily by the disputants. The ICJ can also issue ADVISORY OPINIONS at the request of any of the other principal organs, or the specialized agencies. Its 15 members are independent jurists elected by the General Assembly and the Security Council, each serving a nine-year term. Five are elected every three years with due regard for geographical representation. No two judges may be from the same country.

The SECRETARIAT is the most complex of the principal organs and exists to assist and facilitate the functioning of the other organs and to carry out their decisions. The Secretariat is headed by the UN's principal officer, the SECRETARY-GENERAL, who is elected for a five-year term by the General Assembly, with the concurrence of the Security Council. The Secretariat is composed of international civil servants and appointed officials, selected from the member states to reflect the geographical distribution of the membership, but they function as individuals without national allegiance. The Secretariat administers the BUDGET, performs all necessary administrative functions, and provides staff, translators, secretaries, and other officials needed by each of the principal organs and by conferences convened by the United Nations. It also maintains the UN's physical facilities.

Among the Secretariat's most important duties are drafting the budget, arranging the agendas of each of the UN bodies and organs, and preparing the reports that constitute the basis of discussion on each of the agenda topics. The Secretariat provides expert advice at the meetings of all bodies, supervises all ongoing operations resulting from decisions by those bodies between sessions, and suggests new programs.

The Secretariat is organized into offices reflecting the functions and duties of each of the principal organs. There are departments dealing with Political Affairs, Economic and Social Affairs, DISARMAMENT Affairs, and Legal Affairs. The Department of General Assembly Affairs and Conference Services provides staffing for all conferences called by any of the UN organs, as well as for the annual General Assembly session. The DEPARTMENT OF PEACEKEEPING OPERATIONS plays a particularly important role, since it is charged with staffing and conducting all PEACEKEEPING operations established by the Security Council. There are also functional departments, carrying out internal oversight, management, and security, as well as staffing the offices at all UN locations. Informing the people of the world of the organization's activities and publicizing its endeavors is the responsibility of the DEPARTMENT OF PUBLIC INFORMATION, which prepares news releases, announcements. informational booklets, and publications, and conducts daily news conferences for the world's media at the New York HEADQUARTERS. The OFFICE FOR THE COORDINATION OF HUMANITARIAN AFFAIRS (OCHA) was established during the 1990s as the importance of these functions grew. In addition, there is an entire range of specialized offices dealing with particular issues such as drug control and crime prevention.

The United Nations maintains several offices in all regions of the world, though the largest after the headquarters in New York are those in Geneva, Nairobi, and Vienna, which also serve as the headquarters of several UN bodies. All of the principal organs, except for the International Court of Justice, are based at the New York headquarters. Several also hold meetings at alternate locations. For example, the Security Council and the General Assembly at times have held special meetings outside of New York City, and ECOSOC alternates its meetings between New York and Geneva.

See also ADMINISTRATIVE COMMITTEE ON COORDINATION, ADVISORY COMMITTEE ON ADMINISTRATIVE AND BUDGETARY QUESTIONS, COMMITTEE ON CONTRIBUTIONS, COMMITTEE SYSTEM OF THE GENERAL ASSEMBLY, DEPUTY SECRETARY-GEN-

ERAL, DUMBARTON OAKS CONFERENCE, FOUR POLICEMEN PROPOSAL, TEHERAN CONFERENCE, TRUSTEESHIP SYSTEM, YALTA CONFERENCE.

Further Reading: Russell, Ruth B. *A History of the United Nations Charter: The Role of the United States, 1940–1945.* Washington, D.C.: Brookings Institution, 1958. United Nations Department of Public Information. *Basic Facts about the United Nations.* New York: United Nations Department of Public Information, issued periodically. ———. *Everyone's United Nations: A Handbook of the Work of the United Nations.* New York: United Nations Department of Public Information, issued periodically.

— *K. J. Grieb*

subsidiarity

Subsidiarity is a concept and model of governance that is most readily related to supranational organizations. It is a principle that originated in papal opposition to state intervention in church affairs and is now employed by the European Union (EU). Subsidiarity conceives of an organizational model in which lower levels of governance are not denied their policy-making and implementation COMPETENCIES, provided they are capable of carrying out their assigned tasks. Responsibility for governance is posited at the lowest level commensurate with that level's ability to effectively and efficiently perform assignments. In the case of the European Union, subsidiarity assigns multilateral organizational tasks only when those tasks, because of scale or scope of effect, cannot be disposed of by member states.

Subsidiarity addresses more than relations between different levels of government; the concept is expansive and includes also relationships with and between sovereignty-free actors, civil society, and regional and transregional organizations such as SPECIALIZED AGENCIES that work closely with NON-GOVERNMENTAL ORGANIZATIONS as well as the United Nations. Subsidiarity is a concept related to the United Nations by scholars who see in it the promise of an empowered international organization. The ideas of burden-sharing and devolution of governing tasks embedded in the principle are identified as means of protecting the United Nations from overload and of lowering the locus of decision making as close as possible to the level where the costs and benefits of decisions are most immediately experienced. SECRETARY-GENERAL Kofi ANNAN's initiative to create a "GLOBAL COMPACT" with multinational corporations reflected this trend. United Nations REFORM based on the subsidiarity model is implied in Chapter VIII of the organization's CHARTER.

Further Reading: Knight, W. Andy. *A Changing United Nations: Multilateral Evolution and the Quest for Global Governance.* Houndsmill, England: Macmillan Press, 2000. Peou,

Sorpong. "The Subsidiarity Model of Global Governance in the UN-ASEAN Context." In *Global Governance: A Review of Multilateralism and International Organizations* 4, no. 4 (October–December 1998): 439–60.

— *S. F. McMahon*

Substantial New Programme of Action (SNPA)

The First United Nations Conference on the Least Developed Countries (UNLDC-I) in Paris in 1981 adopted the Substantial New Programme of Action in an effort to halt the decline in the LEAST DEVELOPED COUNTRIES' (LDCs') standards of living that had been occurring for more than a decade. Neither earlier efforts by the UNITED NATIONS CONFERENCE ON TRADE AND DEVELOPMENT (UNCTAD) nor the passage in 1974 of the NEW INTERNATIONAL ECONOMIC ORDER had produced an improvement in the economic conditions of the world's poorest countries. Nor had these efforts generated an increase in donor assistance from the developed states, essential for capital investment in LDC DEVELOPMENT projects. In 1978 UNCTAD established an Intergovernmental Group on the LDC, which drafted the SNPA as a new approach to the problem.

Launched as part of the UN's Third DEVELOPMENT DECADE and its New International Development Strategy (NIDS), SNPA urged a transformation of LDC economies, enabling these states to provide minimum necessary levels of nutrition, housing, education, and jobs. It encouraged the creation of LDC programs to mitigate the impact of external shocks to the economy, including those from natural disasters. It also called for the identification of major investment opportunities in the least developed countries. These advances could be accomplished, in the unanimous view of UNLDC-I participants, by LDC governments instituting economic liberalization, ending corruption, and providing greater transparency and consistency in economic policies. The program set an annual gross domestic product (GDP) overall growth rate of 7.2 percent, with a 4 percent rate in agriculture. It called for manufacturing to grow by 9 percent. SNPA also encouraged donor states to increase aid to 0.15 percent of their GDP. This target was far below the 1 percent of GDP sought by earlier UNCTAD and developing state pronouncements, but still beyond what most industrialized states had provided.

SNPA had negligible impact on LDC economies in the 1980s. Actual growth in these states averaged 2.2 percent, with negative growth rates in some states. "Donor fatigue" reduced contributions to the LDC, even from Nordic states that traditionally had met international targets for Official Development Assistance (ODA). Exports also fell from the least developed states, amounting to 0.3 percent of world exports in 1988, down from 1.4 percent in 1960. The global recession in the early 1980s had a particularly hard impact on LDC, drying up both capital inflows and markets for their products. These developments resulted in increasing debt burdens and, therefore, interest payments. With these setbacks governments in the least developed countries were decreasingly able to meet the basic needs of their populations, requiring higher levels of international humanitarian assistance. Even compared to LESS DEVELOPED COUNTRIES and upper-income developing countries, the LDCs declined in all areas of per capita measurement. The worsening circumstance of the LDC led the GENERAL ASSEMBLY to call for the 1991 convocation of the Second World Conference on LDC, in hopes of revitalizing or reforming the SNPA.

See also UNITED NATIONS CONFERENCE ON THE LEAST DEVELOPED COUNTRIES, WORLD CONFERENCES.

Substantive Question   *See* DOUBLE VETO.

Suez crisis

The Suez crisis occurred between July and November of 1956 but grew out of a longer history that is connected to Egypt's experience with colonialism. Four years after helping to depose King Farouk of Egypt, Gamal Abdul NASSER nationalized the Suez Canal Company on July 26, 1956. Nasser announced that canal dues would be used by Egypt to finance construction of the Aswan High Dam, a project for which he was unable to obtain American funding.

Egypt's former colonial masters Britain and France—owners of the majority of the company's shares—objected to the nationalization of the Canal Company. They undertook private discussions to consider an invasion of Egypt. When Britain and France failed to secure American support for their planned attack, collusion between Britain, France, and Israel produced a secret arrangement that called for an invasion of Egypt by the latter and a reaction from the imperial powers that would involve the stationing of an Anglo-French contingent of troops in the Canal Zone ostensibly to restore order, effectively wresting control of the canal from Egypt. Israel colluded with France and Britain because since 1948 Egyptian officials, in opposition to Israel's dismantling and disruption of Palestinian society, had not permitted Israeli ships to use the canal.

Israel invaded Egypt on October 29, 1956, and forces of the former imperial powers landed at Port Said and Port Faud on November 5 and 6. This AGGRESSION was rebuked by the U.S. administration, the international community, and the United Nations and resulted in the almost immediate suspension of the Anglo-French operation with the delayed extrication of Israeli forces following in March 1957. The UNITED NATIONS EMERGENCY FORCE (UNEF) was positioned in the Suez area prior to the cessation of the Israeli occupation at the behest of Lester B. PEARSON, Canada's ambassador to the United Nations and the former president of the GEN-ERAL ASSEMBLY. It is worth noting that with this crisis UNEF initiated the UN practice of PEACEKEEPING.

The tripartite aggression against Egypt resulted in two UN SECURITY COUNCIL resolutions and one General Assembly RESOLUTION. One week after their invasion the French and British delegations to the UN lodged a complaint that produced Security Council Resolution 118 by unanimous vote. On October 31 the Egyptian delegation leveled a complaint against France and Britain that resulted in Security Council Resolution 119 by a vote of 7 in favor, 2 in opposition (France and the United Kingdom), and 2 abstentions (Australia and Belgium). Neither resolution was particularly robust. The Anglo-French complaint resulted in a Security Council DECLARATION of agreement pertaining, most importantly, to free and open transit through the canal and respect of Egyptian SOVEREIGNTY. The Egyptian initiative produced a call for an emergency session of the General Assembly on the issue of the Suez Canal. The General Assembly resolution that came out of the EMERGENCY SPECIAL SESSION urged a cease-fire, the withdrawal of invading forces, and the reopening of the Suez Canal. The U.S.-sponsored General Assembly resolution was passed by a vote of 64 in favor and 5 opposed (Australia, New Zealand, Britain, France, and Israel) with 6 abstentions.

The Suez crisis was SECRETARY-GENERAL HAMMARSKJÖLD'S greatest hour. Hammarskjöld's initiatives prompted the UN to condemn the tripartite invasion (this condemnation was to become a powerful tool deployed by the UN to end the hostilities) and enabled the United Nations to assemble the first force of "BLUE HELMETS," that is, peacekeepers. Hammarskjöld organized this emergency force with the assistance of Ralph BUNCHE, the Secretary-General's chief mediator for the Middle East at the time.

See also ARAB-ISRAELI DISPUTE.

Further Reading: Meisler, Stanley. *United Nations: The First Fifty Years.* New York: Atlantic Monthly Press, 1995. Miller, Richard. *Dag Hammarskjold and Crisis Diplomacy.* New York: Oceana Publications, 1961. Thant, U. *View from the UN.* Garden City, N.Y.: Doubleday, 1978.

— S. F. McMahon

suspension and expulsion of members

Chapter II of the UN Charter describes the requirements for MEMBERSHIP in the United Nations. It also provides a procedure by which the world organization may suspend "the rights and privileges" of its members (Article 5), or even expel a member state, "which has persistently violated" the principles contained in the CHARTER. Given the intent of the United Nations to be a "universal" international organization, these actions are of the most serious nature, not only for the state involved but also for the United Nations. While there have been many efforts mounted to use Articles 5 and

6 against selected members, no state has ever been formally suspended or expelled.

The United Nations may, but is not required to, suspend a member's exercise of its rights in the world body if the SECURITY COUNCIL has taken some "preventive or enforcement action" against it. The GENERAL ASSEMBLY (GA) has the power to suspend the member upon the recommendation of the council. Because of the seriousness of suspension, and because the language of Article 5 clearly associates suspension with the council's CHAPTER VII powers, this matter, like expulsion, is considered an "IMPORTANT QUESTION," subject to the veto and requiring a two-thirds vote in the Assembly. These high hurdles have made it very difficult, even when there is strong support for suspension, formally to move a RESOLUTION beyond the discussion stage in the Security Council. The VOTING procedure guarantees that no PERMANENT MEMBER OF THE SECURITY COUNCIL (P5), nor any state supported by one of the P5, can be suspended or expelled. Furthermore, should a suspension be imposed, it is the prerogative of the Security Council to lift it at any time. A special form of limited suspension, however, does exist under Article 19 of the Charter that is far more likely to be exercised. That provision automatically suspends the vote in the General Assembly of a member that is in arrears equaling two full years on its required contributions to the UN BUDGET. In the 1960s the Soviet Union and France were threatened with the imposition of this article, and in 1999 the UNITED STATES had to make a partial payment of $100 million to avoid losing its vote.

Expulsion follows the same procedure as suspension. The closest the United Nations has come to exercising Article 6 occurred in 1992, following the breakup of the FORMER YUGOSLAVIA. While several of the seceding parts of Yugoslavia were immediately admitted as new members of the United Nations, the Security Council decided that the remaining "Yugoslavia" (Serbia and Montenegro) could not assume the seat of the defunct Socialist Federal Republic of Yugoslavia. The Council held that the government in Belgrade would have to apply for UN membership, and in the interim could not exercise its privileges in the General Assembly. That circumstance remained in place until 2000, when a new Yugoslav government replaced the regime of Slobodan Milosevic, an indicted war criminal.

Majorities in the General Assembly and in other UN bodies, faced with the difficulties of implementing Articles 5 and 6 procedures, have found informal ways to "suspend" the participation of states that they believe have violated UN principles. Israel and South Africa, which both faced formal requests for suspension or expulsion, were regular targets of these more practical measures beginning in the 1950s. One method has been to challenge the credentials of the representatives sent to New York by their governments. This was done to the South African delegation in 1974 and the Israeli delegation in 1982, effectively excluding them from participation in GA debate and voting. Following the overthrow of the Hungarian government in 1956, the General Assembly refused to seat the new regime's representatives for the next six years. Another technique has been to exclude a state from some subsidiary body, SPECIALIZED AGENCY, or CAUCUS GROUP. This drastically limits the influence a state may have in the UNITED NATIONS SYSTEM. Again, Israel and South Africa, but so too Spain and Portugal have been subjected to this stratagem. Israel, for example, achieved membership in the West European and Other States CAUCUS GROUP only in 2000.

See also APARTHEID, ORGANIZATION OF AFRICAN UNITY.

Further Reading: Simma, Bruno, ed. *The Charter of the United Nations. A Commentary.* New York: Oxford University Press, 1994.

sustainable development

In 1987 the WORLD COMMISSION ON ENVIRONMENT AND DEVELOPMENT (WCED) issued its report, *Our Common Future,* in which for the first time, a United Nations body officially endorsed "sustainable development." The commission defined it as "development that meets the needs of the present without compromising the ability of future generations to meet their own needs." A concept meant to balance the competing interests of DEVELOPMENT and environmental protection, sustainable development became the standard for all subsequent UN efforts in both areas. All future UN conferences, SPECIAL SESSIONS, and diplomatic undertakings focused on how to give life and meaning to the formulation. The United Nations also created new agencies and reformed old ones to enshrine it as a central responsibility of national governments and international organizations.

During the 15 years leading up to the WCED's report, sustainable development emerged as a vague but important compromise between the developed countries that were interested in global environmental protection and LESS DEVELOPED COUNTRIES (LDCs) that worried about limitations environmental restrictions might place on their development policies. Beginning with the 1972 Stockholm Conference on the Human Environment (UNCHE), the United Nations opened a new arena of THEMATIC DIPLOMACY, staking out a critical role in environmental affairs. The focus of the Stockholm meeting on preserving "nature," and its encouragement of the world community to protect the global commons, however, raised serious concerns among LDCs that international environmental efforts would be undertaken at their expense. Despite the Stockholm DECLARATION and Plan of Action recognizing the fundamental principle of SOVEREIGNTY and the right of states to control their own natural resources, both documents established concepts of state responsibility for environmental protection. Among other obligations the conference established the

"Polluter Pays Principle" (PPP), and the "Precautionary Approach" for all states. PPP obligated states to pay for pollution prevention. As a corollary, the conference asserted that states were responsible for pollution caused by their activities that extended beyond their borders. The second principle required states, even when science had not yet fully proven the damaging environmental effects of various development activities, to take precautionary measures to avoid degrading the ENVIRONMENT. To spearhead the UN's environmental efforts, the UNCHE called on the GENERAL ASSEMBLY to create a new institutional structure. In response, the Assembly established the UNITED NATIONS ENVIRONMENT PROGRAMME (UNEP).

The environmental effort by the United Nations quickly became a contentious focus of NORTH-SOUTH relations. Two issues emerged: the inherent conflict between global obligations and a NATION-STATE's sovereign authority over domestic resources, and the suggested restrictions on poor countries' efforts to pursue traditional methods of industrialization and modernization. The disagreement between the developed and developing nations stymied the UN's efforts. On the 10th anniversary of the Stockholm conference a meeting of 70 governments in Nairobi called on the United Nations to revitalize its environmental efforts and to find a solution to these issues. As a result, the General Assembly and the SECRETARY-GENERAL convened the World Commission on Environment and Development, which took four years to complete its work.

As early as 1971, a group of experts meeting in Founex, Switzerland, had noted the interconnections between development and the environment. Many NON-GOVERNMENTAL ORGANIZATIONS (NGOs) during the 1970s also promoted policies that would make the two mutually supportive. It was the WCED, however, after holding public hearings and interviewing thousands of individuals, that concluded further progress could only be made on the basis of recognizing the legitimate claims of both camps. In *Our Common Future* the commission encouraged the world community to develop legally binding rights and obligations for states in relation to the environment and sustainable development. It called for an international conference on the latter, recommended the creation of a powerful UN commission on the environment and sustainable development, and even encouraged the appointment of a high commissioner who would implement a system of monitoring and investigation.

General Assembly Resolution 228 (December 22, 1989) authorized the convocation of what became the largest United Nations conference in history. Meeting in Rio de Janeiro, Brazil, in June 1982, the UNITED NATIONS CONFERENCE ON ENVIRONMENT AND DEVELOPMENT (UNCED)— also known as the Earth Summit—attracted nearly 30,000 people to its sessions or to the accompanying global forum. It approved three cornerstones of the sustainable develop-

ment principle: the RIO DECLARATION, AGENDA 21, and the COMMISSION ON SUSTAINABLE DEVELOPMENT (CSD). The declaration, while not legally binding, committed the participating governments to 27 principles that reflected the existing consensus on sustainable development. The first principle proclaimed that "human beings are at the centre of concerns for sustainable development," shifting the emphasis away from "nature," and the "environment." It recognized both the obligation to environmental protection and the right to development. It called upon developed states to increase aid to poor nations to support the latter's efforts to meet the goals of the declaration. Agenda 21 laid out a lengthy plan of action for states and international organizations in the 21st century. It called for the protection of the world's oceans, atmosphere, forests, mountains, climate, fish stocks and all marine life, and an effort to slow or end DESERTIFICATION, pollution, poverty, and overpopulation, and a massive increase in aid to developing countries. The agenda identified many United Nations agencies including UNEP, the UNITED NATIONS DEVELOPMENT PROGRAMME (UNDP), the WORLD BANK, and the UNITED NATIONS CONFERENCE ON TRADE AND DEVELOPMENT (UNCTAD) as actors with central responsibility for making sustainable development a reality. The most lasting product of UNCED's work was the recommendation that the General Assembly create a permanent commission to oversee the implementation of Agenda 21. The Assembly acted on the proposal in 1993, establishing the Commission on Sustainable Development as a functional body of the ECONOMIC AND SOCIAL COUNCIL (ECOSOC).

It was in the documents of UNCED and the subsequent work of CSD that much of the meaning of sustainable development emerged. Sustainable development recognized the right of all states to sustained growth as long as it did not diminish the living standards of future generations. Thus, while recognizing intergenerational equity as a fundamental principle, it encouraged continuing modernization in the less developed world. For the first time the United Nations accepted a "right to development," albeit within protective environmental parameters. Furthermore, all of the UN initiatives to promote sustainable development encouraged broad participation by NGOs, individuals, subnational JURISDICTIONS, business, labor, and the intellectual community. While the UN reasserted sovereignty as an element of sustainable development, it sought to democratize diplomacy and remove the effort from the sole purview of national governments.

The effort to broaden participation in sustainable development reached a new plateau in January 1999 when Secretary-General Kofi ANNAN proposed a GLOBAL COMPACT between the United Nations and multinational corporations to protect HUMAN RIGHTS, international labor standards, and the global environment. Speaking to the World Economic Forum in Davos, Switzerland, Annan urged corporations to work directly with the world body, bypassing national governments, to fulfill the environmental principles established in the Rio Declaration. In particular, he called upon those companies joining the compact to support sustainable development's precautionary approach to environmental challenges, and to undertake greater diffusion of environmentally friendly technologies to the developing world. Within a year more than 50 transnational corporations had signed the compact.

Secretary-General Annan wrote in 1998 that the United Nations was "focusing on the importance of sustainability—on sustainable development—in all aspects of [its] work, [even] including peace and security." At the epicenter of the effort were six UN-related agencies: CSD, the World Bank, UNCTAD, UNDP, the UNITED NATIONS CENTRE FOR HUMAN SETTLEMENTS (Habitat), and the WORLD TRADE ORGANIZATION (WTO). The CSD did the preparatory work for the General Assembly's special session, Earth Summit +5, held in 1997, which in turn directed the commission to review all major areas of Agenda 21 for global progress, and to develop "ISD"s, Indicators of Sustainable Development. The World Bank through its GLOBAL ENVIRONMENT FACILITY (GEF), the WTO, and UNCTAD took on primary responsibility for enhancing financial and trade assistance to the developing world in order to help states reach self-sustaining development. As part of that effort UNCTAD decided to make sustainable development the central theme of its third UNITED NATIONS CONFERENCE ON THE LEAST DEVELOPED COUNTRIES (LDC-III) in 2001. At the national and subnational levels the UNDP and Habitat assisted with capacity building and infrastructure necessary for a social and economic order able to maintain sustainable development. The former launched a "Sustainable Development Network" (SDN) to foster dialogue among citizens and policy makers, and to provide the latest technical information related to the topic. Beyond these six entities, nearly all UN bodies contributed to the evolution of the sustainable development doctrine. Even relatively independent agencies such as the WORLD HEALTH ORGANIZATION (WHO) undertook to promote the idea. After Gro Harlem BRUNDTLAND, the former chair of the World Commission on Environment and Development, which had first formulated the concept, took over as DIRECTOR-GENERAL of WHO in July 1998, the organization restructured to make "Sustainable Development and Healthy Environment" one of its primary "clusters" of activity.

The WHO experience along with the Global Compact demonstrated that by the turn of the century sustainable development had metamorphosed from solely a development and environmental construct. It has been adapted to other areas of UN concern. UNEP executive director Klaus Toepfer told the world community in July 2000 that "the most toxic element in the environment is poverty." Toepfer and other UN officials began talking about "Sustainable Human Development (SHD)," reinforcing Secretary-General Annan's assertion that the core mission of the United Nations by the end of the 1990s was "promoting human security." While his predecessor, Boutros BOUTROS-GHALI, had first suggested the idea of SHD in AN AGENDA FOR DEVELOPMENT (1994), Annan's reinvigoration of the world body incorporated a merger of "sustainable development" with "human development," thus opening a new chapter in the evolution of the concept first declared in 1987.

See also UNITED NATIONS CONFERENCE ON THE HUMAN ENVIRONMENT.

Further Reading: Grubbs, Michael, Matthias Koch, Koy Thomson, Abby Manson, and Francis Sullivan. *The 'Earth Summit' Agreements: A Guide and Assessment.* London: Earthscan Publications, 1993. Sands, Philippe, ed. *Greening International Law.* New York: The New Press, 1994. Tessitore, John, and Susan Woolfson. *A Global Agenda. Issues before the 54th General Assembly of the United Nations.* New York: Rowman and Littlefield, Publishers, 1999. Werksman, Jacob. *Greening International Institutions.* London: Earthscan Publications, 1996.

sustainable human development   *See* AGENDA FOR DEVELOPMENT.

T

Teheran Conference

The Teheran Conference was the first Allied summit conference during World War II (November 27–December 1, 1943) at which ROOSEVELT, CHURCHILL, and STALIN met together. Joseph Stalin confirmed that the USSR would enter the war against Japan once Germany had been defeated. Roosevelt and Churchill then announced their decision that the Normandy landings would be launched in May 1944. Other issues discussed included the future of Poland, the postwar division of Germany, and support for Tito and the partisans in Yugoslavia. In contrast to the recent MOSCOW FOREIGN MINISTERS' CONFERENCE (October 1943), the subject of an international organization was not a major concern and did not appear on the agenda of any of the plenary sessions.

Nevertheless, in an effort to establish personal rapport with Stalin, Roosevelt twice privately discussed his views on international organization with him. Churchill was not included in these conversations, although he was familiar with their substance since he had conferred with FDR at the QUEBEC CONFERENCE in August. Roosevelt's plan drew heavily on the ideas of Sumner Welles. He described a three-part structure consisting of an assembly of all the United Nations that would discuss major world problems but lack the authority to act. Next, an executive committee composed of the Big Four and six regional representatives would deal with social and economic issues. Finally, the FOUR POLICEMEN (UNITED STATES, Soviet Union, United Kingdom, CHINA) would have sole authority to enforce the peace and prevent AGGRESSION. In response to Stalin's queries, Roosevelt indicated that the United States would not contribute ground troops to preserve the peace outside of the Western Hemisphere. British and Russian troops, with U.S. naval and air support, would confront crises in Europe. Neither Roosevelt nor Stalin commented on how they would proceed if one of the Four Policemen committed aggression.

The later issue of the VETO was still inchoate at Teheran since both Stalin and the U.S. Senate supported an absolute veto on the use of armed force. Stalin, also worrying that the executive committee might limit Soviet actions, asked FDR at Teheran whether the proposed body would be able to make decisions binding on the Great Powers. President Roosevelt said it could not. The Soviet leader and his representatives returned to this commitment by FDR many times over the next two years as negotiations on the construction of the United Nations went forward. Roosevelt's main objective, which he felt he had achieved, was to commit Stalin to his quest for a postwar organization to preserve peace. At the close of the conference, however, the three statesmen drew up a DECLARATION that was purposefully vague in its commitment to a postwar world in which all nations, large and small, would be welcomed "into a world family of Democratic Nations."

297

Further Reading: Divine, Robert A. *Second Chance: The Triumph of Internationalism in America during World War II.* New York: Atheneum, 1967. Eubank, Keith. *Summit at Teheran.* New York: Morrow, 1985. Hoopes, Townsend, and Douglas Brinkley. *FDR and the Creation of the U.N.* New Haven, Conn: Yale University Press, 1997.

— *E. M. Clauss*

terrorism

The issue of terrorism was brought before the United Nations GENERAL ASSEMBLY (GA) in 1972, after a Palestinian group massacred Israeli athletes at the Munich Olympics. Sporadically since that time, the United Nations has worked on measures to combat the global problem. In the 1970s, the ad hoc committee tasked with generating consensus for action on the issue was deadlocked in a struggle to define the term "terrorism."

After a decade of effort, the committee reported that the issue was "too politically difficult" to define, making consensus on appropriate actions in response not possible. The problem in the General Assembly lay in differentiating between the legitimate struggles of peoples under colonial rule, alien domination, or foreign occupation on the one hand, and terrorism on the other hand. Many member states had experienced struggles for self-determination and NATIONAL LIBERATION and were consequently reluctant to create law that might characterize the methods of such struggles as terrorism.

The General Assembly's SIXTH COMMITTEE realized a greater degree of success in generating legal responses to this issue. By the end of the 20th century, 11 legal documents had been drafted. Each draft TREATY dealt with a specific aspect of terrorism, since a focused approach to a particular issue was easier to make operational than general anti-terrorism legislation. Earlier treaties involved attacks on civil aviation, making aerial hijacking an international crime. Two treaties at the close of the century focused on the threat of nuclear terrorism, and on efforts to restrict financial support for terrorist acts. In the case of the latter, the Convention for the Suppression of the Financing of Terrorism adopted by the General Assembly on December 9, 1999, made it an offense to provide or collect funds for terrorist acts.

Terrorism appeared on the agenda of several other UN organs, with less clarity or successful action. Consensus that terrorism constituted a violation of HUMAN RIGHTS made the topic an agenda item in the GA THIRD COMMITTEE, as well as the ECONOMIC AND SOCIAL COUNCIL (ECOSOC), and several of its subunits, particularly the COMMISSION ON HUMAN RIGHTS. On November 1, 1997, the SECRETARIAT created the OFFICE FOR DRUG CONTROL AND CRIME PREVENTION (ODCCP). Located in Vienna, the office maintained the Centre for International Crime Prevention (CICP), which was charged with combating terrorism. In its 1998–99 BUDGET the United Nations allocated $7.7 million to CICP's activities, with 29 percent coming from voluntary contributions.

On November 26, 1997, the GA Third Committee denounced terrorism. The committee drafted a RESOLUTION that condemned violations of the rights to life, liberty, and security, as well as terrorism in general. Provisions of this resolution, approved by a recorded vote of 97 in favor to none against, with 57 abstentions, called on states to take all necessary and effective measures to prevent, combat, and eliminate terrorism. It also urged the international community to enhance regional and international cooperation for fighting against terrorism and to condemn incitement of ethnic hatred, violence, and terrorism. The resolution carried no method of enforcement, and thus was similar to most actions taken by the UN on this issue, simply issuing a call for cooperation, condemning terrorist acts, but recommending no further action or obligation.

Using the General Assembly Plenary Declaration in 1994, which stated that acts of terrorism could also threaten international peace and security, the SECURITY COUNCIL (SC) became more involved in the struggle to deal with this issue. Unanimously adopting Resolution 1269 (1999), the council stressed the vital role of the United Nations in strengthening international cooperation in combating terrorism, and emphasized the importance of enhanced coordination among states, and among international and regional organizations. It called upon all states to take steps to cooperate with each other through bilateral and multilateral agreements and arrangements, prevent and suppress terrorist acts, protect their nationals and other persons against terrorist attacks, and bring to justice the perpetrators of such acts. The Security Council continued to advocate exchanging information in accordance with international and domestic law, cooperating on administrative and judicial matters to prevent the commission of terrorist acts, and using all lawful means to prevent and suppress the preparation and financing of any such acts in member states' territories.

In other resolutions passed in the 1990s, the council called on all states to deny safe havens for those who planned, financed, or committed terrorist acts by ensuring their apprehension and prosecution or extradition. These resolutions also stressed that, before granting refugee status, states should take appropriate measures in conformity with national and INTERNATIONAL LAW, including international standards of human rights, to ensure that the asylum-seeker had not participated in terrorist acts.

Until September 2001, the Security Council was careful not to take actions on this issue that would replace the General Assembly's efforts. The council sought to complement the larger organ's decisions on the basis of its own COMPETENCE within the CHARTER. Noting that the degree of sophistication of terrorist acts and the increasingly globalized nature of those acts were new trends, and that the extensive international networks of organized criminals were creating an infrastructure of "catastrophic terrorism," the Security Council resolved that terrorism posed a serious threat to international peace and security, making it an issue that needed council action as well as that of the General Assembly and the Economic and Social Council. At the beginning of the 21st century, however, the GA Sixth Committee remained the primary source of legal action concerning terrorism taken by the United Nations.

On September 11, 2001, the day scheduled for the opening of the General Assembly's 56th session, terrorists seized control of four U.S. civilian airliners. They crashed two of them into the World Trade Center towers in New York City, bringing both towers to the ground and killing approximately 3,000 people. The third plane crashed into the Pentagon in Northern Virginia after circling major government sites in Washington, D.C. The devastation to the U.S. military headquarters also took a heavy toll of life. Passengers on the fourth airliner struggled with the hijackers, and the plane crashed in western Pennsylvania with the loss of all aboard. President George W. Bush declared the events "acts of war," and made harsh demands on the Taliban government in AFGHANISTAN, believing that the regime was harboring Osama bin Laden, reputedly the mastermind behind the terrorist attack.

The UNITED STATES also sought UN support for any actions it might take in reprisal. On September 12 the Security Council unanimously adopted Resolution 1368. Council members departed from tradition and stood during its adoption. In the text, the council held that any act of international terrorism was a threat to international peace and security. It specifically noted in the resolution that the Council remained "seized" with the matter. This meant that it now had taken primary responsibility under the UN Charter for the terrorism issue. This reflected an important shift from past policy. The General Assembly, once it convened on the 13th, followed with a condemnation of the attack. The Security Council also passed Resolution 1373 on September 28, calling on all states to "prevent and suppress the financing of terrorist acts." Council members invoked CHAPTER VII, making the resolution's provisions mandatory on all member states. The Security Council decided that all states should criminalize the provision or collection of funds for such acts. It also called on states to freeze the assets of suspected terrorist groups. It decided that states should prohibit their nationals or organizations from making FUNDS and financial assets available to potential terrorists. They were also required by the resolution to deny safe haven to those who finance, plan, support, or commit terrorist acts. Additionally, the council decided that states should afford one another the greatest measure of assistance for criminal investigations or criminal proceedings relating to these activities. Resolution 1373 established a Security Council Counter-Terrorism Committee. Made up of all council members, the committee was directed to monitor implementation of the resolution and to draft measures to assure its enforcement.

See also INTERNATIONAL CRIMINAL COURT, THEMATIC DIPLOMACY.

Further Reading: Combs, Cindy C., and Martin Slann. *Encyclopedia of Terrorism.* New York: Facts On File, 2001. Lopez, George A. "Terrorism and World Order." *Annual Editions: Violence and Terrorism.* Guilford, Conn.: Dushkin Publishers, 1993. Tessitore, John, and Susan Woolfson. *A Global Agenda: Issues before the 53rd General Assembly of the United Nations.* New York: United Nations Association of the United States of America, 1999. Tucker, David. "Responding to Terrorism." *21 Debated Issues in World Politics.* Upper Saddle River, N.J.: Prentice Hall, 2000.

— *C. C. Combs*

Thant, U (1909–1974)

U Thant was the third person to hold the position of SECRETARY-GENERAL. He began serving following the death of Dag HAMMARSKJÖLD in 1961, and he continued in the post until 1971. Thant was born in 1909 in Pantanaw, Burma (now Myanmar). He was educated at the University of Rangoon (Yangôn) and then the Arts and Science University, where he met future Burmese prime minister U Nu. When Thant's father died in 1928, the young student left school prior to graduation in order to assume responsibilities in his hometown of Pantanaw, where he became a teacher and then, in 1931, headmaster at his alma mater, the National High School. Before the outbreak of World War II, he was active in a number of educational activities within Burma. In 1942, while Japan occupied the country, he served briefly as secretary of a committee authorized to reorganize Burmese education. He then returned to the position of headmaster, and, after the war, U Nu and leaders of the Anti-Fascist People's Freedom League recruited him for government service. He became the government's press director in 1947, director of broadcasting in 1948, and secretary of the Ministry of Information in 1949. By 1953 he had been promoted to secretary for projects in the office of the prime minister and then in 1955 to executive secretary of Burma's Economic and Social Board.

He went to the UN GENERAL ASSEMBLY (GA) in 1952 as an alternate member of the Burmese delegation, and he returned in 1957 to serve as ambassador, his position when he replaced Hammarskjöld following the latter's untimely death in 1961. Thant was an active ambassador, serving in 1959 as one of the vice-presidents of the GA 14th Session, and, in 1961, as chair of the UN Congo Conciliation Commission and chair of the Committee on a UN Capital Development Fund. Following the death of Hammarskjöld, the UNITED STATES and the Soviet Union, unable to agree on a permanent successor, finally compromised by agreeing to

Secretary-General U Thant (UN PHOTO/Y. NAGATA)

accept Thant as acting Secretary-General to complete Hammarskjöld's unexpired term, and the General Assembly accordingly appointed him unanimously to that interim title on November 3, 1961. Thant proved acceptable enough to the COLD WAR competitors to receive their endorsement for a full term, to which he was appointed, again by unanimous GA vote, on November 30, 1962. He succeeded yet again with a unanimous SECURITY COUNCIL recommendation and appointment by the General Assembly in December 1966, completing his second term on December 31, 1971.

Like his predecessors Trygve LIE and Hammarskjöld, Thant took seriously the injunction framed in Article 99 of the UN CHARTER that gave the Secretary-General certain express powers and implied additional authority. At the same time, he had to deal with the specific interests, grievances, and challenges to his authority from the great powers. France, for example, unhappy that Thant neither spoke nor read French, opposed a stronger United Nations; Thant argued in favor of it, but he had to be sensitive to the views of a PERMANENT MEMBER of the Security Council. Others, particularly in the West, were wary of the Secretary-General's reputation for being strictly neutral, and his support while a Burmese diplomat of UN membership for the Chinese government in Beijing; once he became Secretary-General, he found himself constrained not to voice an opinion on the Chinese issue. His

tenure was also complicated by cold war tensions, as can be seen in his efforts to resolve the U.S.–Cuban crisis in 1962 (see below), and his frustrations in failing to play a role in mediating the Vietnam War. A devout Buddhist who sought to apply the principles of detachment to international diplomacy, Thant, in appearance and practice, inclined toward neutralism. He could be critical of both the East and the West when he believed their national purposes and actions threatened international comity.

There were times during his tenure when Thant played an important part in critical international events. Once such moment was in 1962 when the U.S. ambassador to the United Nations, Adlai Stevenson, privately sounded out the Secretary-General as a possible intermediary during the CUBAN MISSILE CRISIS; and Nikita Khrushchev even publicly suggested that Thant serve as the principal mediator to resolve the dispute. But, in the end, the United Nations played a secondary role in ending the standoff. During his first term, the Secretary-General was involved in the transfer of Irian Jaya (Western New Guinea) to INDONESIA in 1962, a resolution of the civil war in the CONGO in 1963, and the establishment of a PEACEKEEPING force on Cyprus in 1964. But he faced many frustrations, including, as noted above the inability of the Secretary-General's office to play any effective role in pursuing a settlement of the war in Vietnam, which raged throughout his term. In 1964 he recommended that the General Assembly temporarily cease VOTING on any issue in order to avoid a showdown over the Soviet Union's refusal to pay for previous PEACEKEEPING operations. In 1965, however, following the outbreak of hostilities between India and Pakistan over their ongoing territorial disputes, the United Nations declared a cease-fire, and Thant, on his own authority, created a new peacekeeping operation—the UNITED NATIONS INDIA-PAKISTAN OBSERVATION MISSION (UNIPOM).

The action for which the Secretary-General received perhaps most criticism occurred in spring 1967, when Egyptian president Gamal Abdul NASSER insisted that Thant withdraw UN peacekeepers from the Sinai and the Gaza Strip, where they had been since the armistice of 1956. The Secretary-General, believing the lives of UN troops were in danger and also committed to the sovereign right of Egypt to demand removal of outside forces from her land, withdrew the UN forces. Nasser closed the Gulf of Aqaba. Israel set in motion a preemptive strike, and by June of that year a new Israeli-Arab war broke out, resulting in Israeli occupation of the Sinai, as well as the Gaza Strip, the West Bank of the Jordan River, East Jerusalem, and the Golan Heights. Critics believed that the vacuum left when the UN withdrew paved the way for the territorial disruptions of the Middle East, which international diplomacy tried to resolve for the next decades.

During Thant's years in New York, the United Nations substantially increased its involvement in social and economic development in the Third World, now representing a majority of member states in the world organization, but he could not find a solution to the growing problem of financing UN operations. Thant retired on January 1, 1972, and he continued to live in New York, where he died of cancer in November 1974. When, the next month, his remains were returned to Rangoon, students there absconded with the body and buried it in a hastily built mausoleum at the Arts and Science University. The police removed the body by force and buried it in a private and sealed tomb. Riots followed, and the military regime declared martial law. Thant's life of educational reform, diplomacy, and peace-seeking hardly warranted this chaotic finale. He was in fact a man of sensitivity and learning, as well as a committed diplomat. He wrote, in Burmese, books on the history of cities, the LEAGUE OF NATIONS, education in Burma, and three volumes of the post–World War II history of his country.

See also MIDDLE EAST WAR OF 1967.

Further Reading: Cordier, Andrew, and Wilder Foote, eds. *Public Papers of the Secretaries-General of the United Nations.* New York: Columbia University Press, 1969–1977. Nassif, Ramses. *U Thant in New York, 1961–1971: A Portrait of the Third Secretary-General.* London: Hurst, 1988. Thant, U. *Portfolio for Peace: Excerpts from the Writings and Speeches of U Thant, Secretary-General of the United Nations.* New York: United Nations, 1971. ———. *View from the UN.* Garden City, N.Y.: Doubleday, 1978.

thematic diplomacy

Initially conceived by wartime leaders as an organization to preserve international peace and security, the United Nations developed a much broader mandate in the decades following the 1945 adoption of its CHARTER. The founding document itself committed the world body to international cooperation "in solving international problems of an economic, social, cultural, or humanitarian character, and in promoting and encouraging respect for HUMAN RIGHTS and for fundamental freedoms for all" (Article 1). Pressed by the UNITED STATES and delegations from the newly liberated parts of the world, the Charter's authors also laid upon the organization responsibilities for DISARMAMENT, decolonization, and the development of INTERNATIONAL LAW. As the COLD WAR emerged in the late 1940s and UN activities shifted from the deadlocked SECURITY COUNCIL, with its primary duty under CHAPTER VII to maintain world peace, to the GENERAL ASSEMBLY, these thematic areas and others emerged as important arenas for global cooperation. Rising UN MEMBERSHIP, largely from the underdeveloped world, added impetus to the UN's preoccupation with the global challenges to human development and well-being. Often characterized as the "Other UN," which addressed "soft," or "functional" areas of international affairs, the thematic approach to solving worldwide prob-

lems of a social, environmental, or financial nature became the overarching framework for all UN activity by the end of the 20th century.

Many areas of functional human cooperation on the international level already were being addressed by intergovernmental organizations (IGOs) when the United Nations was founded. The Charter contemplated bringing those efforts within the UNITED NATIONS SYSTEM through the device of SPECIALIZED AGENCIES—formal agreements with IGOs such as the INTERNATIONAL LABOUR ORGANIZATION, the UNIVERSAL POSTAL UNION, and other existing bodies— that would then work in cooperative, but autonomous, fashion to solve global human problems. Among the principal UN organs, the ECONOMIC AND SOCIAL COUNCIL was given the broadest authority to address these issues. However, beginning with the adoption of the UNIVERSAL DECLARATION OF HUMAN RIGHTS in 1948, the United Nations as a whole successively took on new organizational initiatives.

By 2002 the United Nations was pursuing many areas of thematic diplomacy, but 10 topics of international cooperation predominated. They were the ENVIRONMENT, WOMEN, DISARMAMENT, SUSTAINABLE DEVELOPMENT, globalization, HUMAN RIGHTS, PEACEKEEPING, poverty eradication especially in Africa, population, and international law. Other thematic issues included democratization, human settlements, disease, migration, and the information revolution. Each originated as a focus of UN attention at a particular point in the history of the organization. Concern for the environment, for example, could be dated from the 1972 UNITED NATIONS CONFERENCE ON THE HUMAN ENVIRONMENT (UNCHE). Each developed through the adoption of DECLARATIONS, CONVENTIONS, and UN RESOLUTIONS. In the field of human rights, the 1948 Universal Declaration laid out the principles to which the world community committed itself. They were subsequently codified in two international COVENANTS in 1966. In the areas of disarmament, sustainable development, and peacekeeping, UN efforts created evolving definitions and international standards of behavior for NATION-STATES and their leaders. In all of these areas, WORLD CONFERENCES, preparatory meetings, implementing PROGRAMMES AND FUNDS, and intense multilateral negotiations were used to solve perceived problems.

While the United Nations is an organization made up of sovereign states, thematic diplomacy brought many non-state actors into UN-sponsored negotiations and activities. NON-GOVERNMENTAL ORGANIZATIONS, in particular, were welcomed into the deliberations of world conferences such as the EARTH SUMMIT (1992), the four women's conferences (1980–2000), and the Conference to Combat Racial Discrimination (2001). They also increasingly were asked to participate in substantive negotiations, serving on agencies such as the JOINT UNITED NATIONS PROGRAMME ON HIV/AIDS, or to help in the implementation of UN initiatives. The pursuit of partnerships with private enterprises, research groups, and humanitarian organizations became a regular feature of UN diplomacy in the 1990s. As an example, in the effort to ameliorate problems flowing from rapid globalization, SECRETARY-GENERAL Kofi ANNAN launched the GLOBAL COMPACT program in 1999. Meant to gain the commitment of the private sector to UN social and economic goals, the Global Compact established formal relations with multinational corporations, totaling more than 1,000 partners in 2002, and added a new sector of international actors to the UN community. Going beyond the 189 governments that were UN members at the time of the MILLENNIUM SUMMIT in 2000, the United Nations recognized an emerging "international civil society" that needed to be engaged in UN activities. Thematic diplomacy opened an avenue for the "democratization" of the United Nations, giving enhanced meaning to the opening words of the UN Charter Preamble, "We the Peoples of the United Nations."

See also AGENDA 21, CHAPTER VI $^1/_2$, CLIMATE CHANGE, DEPARTMENT OF ECONOMIC AND SOCIAL AFFAIRS, FRÉCHETTE, SPECIAL RAPPORTEUR, SPECIAL REPRESENTATIVE OF THE SECRETARY-GENERAL, TERRORISM, WORLD CONFERENCES ON WOMEN, WORLD SUMMIT FOR SOCIAL DEVELOPMENT.

Further Reading: Bastos, Cristiana. *Global Responses to AIDS: Science in Emergency.* Bloomington: Indiana University Press, 1999. Chopra, Jarat, "United Nations Peace-Maintenance." *The United Nations at Work.* Edited by Martin Ira Glassner. Westport, Conn.: Praeger Publishers, 1998. Meisler, Stanley. *United Nations: The First Fifty Years.* New York: Atlantic Monthly Press, 1995. Mingst, Karen, and Margaret Karns. *The United Nations in the Post–Cold War Era, Dilemmas in World Politics.* Boulder, Colo.: Westview Press, 2000. Muldoon, James P., JoAnn Fagot Aviel, Richard Reitano, and Earl Sullivan. *Multilateral Diplomacy and the United Nations Today.* Boulder, Colo.: Westview Press, 1999. United Nation Department of Public Information. *The United Nations and the Advancement of Women, 1945–1996.* New York: United Nations Department of Public Information, 1996. Global issues on the UN agenda website: <www.un.org/partners/ civil_society/agenda.htm>.

Third Committee of the General Assembly

The Third Committee of the GENERAL ASSEMBLY, one of its six main committees, is also known as the Social, Humanitarian, and Cultural Committee (SOCHUM). Like all GA main committees, it consists of representatives of every member state, each having an equal vote. Its function is to consider and negotiate agreement on draft RESOLUTIONS before they are placed before the full General Assembly.

The Third Committee has a broad mandate, and consequently a lengthy agenda. It usually considers and adopts more resolutions than any of the other GA committees. Topics considered each year include HUMAN RIGHTS, education,

health and health care, social development, crime, drug trafficking, traditional and customary practices, the role of WOMEN, children, minority groups, racism, religious freedoms, refugees and internally displaced persons, INDIGENOUS PEOPLES, and the movement of people between nations. It also addresses all items relating to the operation of UN human rights offices.

The inclusion of human rights topics on the Third Committee agenda proves to be the most contentious. Committee members discuss human rights violations in particular countries and usually draft six to 12 resolutions criticizing specific governments. The country being criticized, and often its allies, inevitably resists acknowledging these resolutions. However, the committee's purpose is served if world public opinion is brought to bear on the offending state.

See also COMMITTEE SYSTEM OF THE GENERAL ASSEMBLY, STRUCTURE OF THE UNITED NATIONS, TERRORISM.

Further Reading: Third Committee (55th General Assembly Session) website: <www.un.org/ga/55/third/>. For preceding and succeeding years, substitute the GA session number in the website URL.

— *K. J. Grieb*

Third Development Decade   *See* DEVELOPMENT DECADES.

Third World   *See* FIRST AND THIRD WORLDS.

Thornburgh Report   *See* REFORM OF THE UNITED NATIONS.

torture   *See* CONVENTION AGAINST TORTURE AND OTHER CRUEL, INHUMAN OR DEGRADING TREATMENT OR PUNISHMENT.

treaty

Article 2 of the Vienna CONVENTION on the Law of Treaties, signed in 1969, defines a treaty as "an international agreement concluded between states in written form and governed by INTERNATIONAL LAW."

The development of formal relations between and among nations, empires, and peoples has characterized human activity since the millennia before the common era. The word *treaty,* which commonly designates such relations in our own day, derives from Latin. Its modern meaning surfaced in the 17th century as a term to indicate a discussion or terms of negotiation. From this early beginning it came to mean an agreement or contract between individuals or states, formally concluded and usually ratified by an official government agency, and relating to peace, alliance, commerce, or any other state-state relationship. Treaties, like PACTS, tend to oblige their members to compliance more than do DECLARATIONS or RESOLUTIONS. That is because a treaty is a contract between the parties that is binding on them under the legal principle of *pacta sunt servanda* (promises are to be kept). Treaty obligations are expected to be honored by successor states, unless, *in rebus sic stantibus* (things staying as they are), conditions have so fundamentally changed that the state believes it is no longer bound by the treaty's terms. Generally, treaties fall into two categories: "Law-making" treaties and "treaty-contracts." The former are intended to have universal application in the international community, and the latter establish obligations only among the parties to the document.

Article 102 of the UN CHARTER requires member states to register "as soon as possible" all treaties with the SECRETARIAT, which in turn must publish the agreement. This requirement is a continuation of the practice established by the LEAGUE OF NATIONS and is meant to eliminate the likelihood of "secret" treaties between states.

Treaty of Bangkok   *See* NUCLEAR-WEAPONS-FREE ZONES.

Treaty of Pelindaba   *See* NUCLEAR-WEAPONS-FREE ZONES.

Treaty of Rarotonga   *See* NUCLEAR-WEAPONS-FREE ZONES.

Treaty of Tlatleloco

The Treaty for the Prohibition of Nuclear Weapons in LATIN AMERICA and the Caribbean of 1967, more commonly called the Treaty of Tlatleloco, after the site of the Mexican Foreign Ministry building where it was signed, constituted the initial regional NUCLEAR-WEAPONS-FREE ZONE treaty. It was the first TREATY declaring a populated continent, and hemispheric region, to be out of bounds for nuclear weapons. Only the ANTARCTIC TREATY preceded it, but that accord dealt with a continent that was uninhabited. The Treaty of Tlatleloco set a precedent and served as a model for later nuclear free zone treaties. It also was one of the initial accords in the effort to prevent nuclear proliferation; it was signed in advance of the NUCLEAR NON-PROLIFERATION TREATY of 1968, although coming after the Partial Test Ban Treaty (1963).

Parties to the treaty renounced the "manufacture, production or acquisition by any means whatsoever of nuclear weapons," as well as the storage, installation, or deployment of such weapons. They pledged to refrain from "the testing, use, manufacture, production, possession, or control of any nuclear weapon," although the treaty expressly allowed testing for "peaceful purposes." The parties also pledged to place their nuclear programs and facilities under the INTERNATIONAL ATOMIC ENERGY AGENCY (IAEA) safeguards, which required inspections. The treaty created the Agency for the Prohibition of Nuclear Weapons in Latin America to hold consultations, receive annual reports by the signatories, and settle disputes. Additional PROTOCOLS were added requiring signatories to renounce the positioning of nuclear weapons in NON-SELF-GOVERNING TERRITORIES in the region, and to refrain from threatening to use nuclear weapons against any signatory.

All Latin American nations signed the treaty, although there were some initial difficulties stemming from the long-standing military and political rivalry between Brazil and Argentina. These two nations filed reservations, each fearing that the other would develop nuclear weapons. This dispute ended in the 1990s, when both agreed to act simultaneously to accept all provisions of the treaty. CUBA signed but never ratified the treaty, contending that it was threatened by the American economic boycott and could not accept the limits of the treaty until U.S. hostility ended. By the turn of the century Cuba remained the only nation within the treaty zone that had not ratified the agreement. All five of the Nuclear Weapons States (UNITED STATES, RUSSIAN FEDERATION, France, United Kingdom, and the Peoples Republic of CHINA) signed the accord.

See also DISARMAMENT.

Further Reading: Garcia Robles, Alfonso. *El Tratado de Tlatleloco*. Mexico: El Collegio de Mexico, 1967. United Nations Department of Public Information. *The United Nations and Nuclear Non-Proliferation*. Volume 3 of the United Nations Bluebook Series. New York: United Nations Department of Public Information, 1995. UN Disarmament Treaty website: <domino.un.org/TreatyStatus.nsf>.

— *K. J. Grieb*

Troika Proposal

On September 23, 1960, in a speech to the UN GENERAL ASSEMBLY, Soviet premier Nikita Khrushchev demanded the resignation of SECRETARY-GENERAL Dag HAMMARSKJÖLD for abuse of office and urged amendment of the UN CHARTER, creating a three-person "executive agency" to replace the post of Secretary-General. The Soviet Union was deeply upset with Hammarskjöld's active leadership of UN involvement in the Congolese civil war—an involvement that largely supported Western-backed forces in opposition to the Soviet-favored contingents of Prime Minister Patrice Lumumba. Khrushchev argued that only a SECRETARIAT headed by representatives of "the Western powers, socialist states, and neutralist countries" could garner the universal confidence of the UN MEMBERSHIP. Seen at the time as a Soviet effort to gut the powers of the Secretary-General and to insert an additional Soviet "VETO" on UN PEACEKEEPING operations, the Troika proposal was defeated by a General Assembly vote of 83 to 11 to 5.

Hammarskjöld refused to accept Khrushchev's invitation to "resign in a chivalrous manner." Coupled with the Assembly vote, the matter seemed moot by the end of the year. But the assassination of Lumumba in February 1961 resurrected Soviet anger with the Secretary-General. The USSR demanded his removal from office on the charge of being an "accomplice and organizer" of Lumumba's death. The Soviet Union refused to recognize him any longer as Secretary-General or to have a continuing relationship with him, and the Russians demanded that the Troika principle be expanded throughout the Secretariat. Asserting there were "no neutral men," the Soviets pushed for more representatives of the socialist and non-aligned camps at the highest levels of the UN bureaucracy. Change was blocked, however, by continuing U.S. support for Hammarskjöld and the existing Secretariat STRUCTURE.

The Secretary-General's death in an airplane crash in central Africa on September 18, 1961, brought the Troika issue to a head. The UNITED STATES pressed for the quick appointment of a single person as acting Secretary-General. The Soviet government suggested several versions of its troika proposal as a substitute, creating a deadlock on the appointment of a replacement for Hammarskjöld. Not until November 1 was the impasse broken with the appointment of U THANT of Burma (Myanmar) to complete Hammarskjöld's term, reflecting a willingness of the Soviet delegation to "postpone" the Troika issue until the deceased Secretary-General's term would have naturally expired in April 1963. By April, however, the USSR was no longer interested in pressing its proposal and joined in a unanimous SECURITY COUNCIL recommendation to seat Thant as the permanent Secretary-General. The intervening CUBAN MISSILE CRISIS, in which Thant played a mediating role, apparently contributed to growing Soviet trust. The inability to build much support in the LESS DEVELOPED COUNTRIES for the proposal also dissuaded Khrushchev from pursuing the matter. Finally, the desire to seek a more conciliatory relationship with the United States after the fall confrontation in the Caribbean mitigated against a new Soviet-sponsored initiative that was bound to raise tensions. The outcome was the continuation of the post of Secretary-General as described in the Charter.

See also COLD WAR, CONGO.

Further Reading: Nicholas, H. G. *The United Nations as a Political Institution.* 5th ed. Oxford: Oxford University Press, 1975. Stoessinger, John G. *The United Nations and the Super-powers: China, Russia, and America.* 4th ed. New York: Random House, 1977.

Trusteeship Council

In 1994 the Trusteeship Council became the first PRINCIPAL ORGAN OF THE UNITED NATIONS to cease operation. This was the result not of failure but of success in the completion of its mission assigned by the UN CHARTER. During the previous half century the Council presided over the NATIONAL LIBERATION of 11 trust territories, and contributed to the general process of decolonization that followed World War II.

The Trusteeship Council was the central institution of the United Nations' TRUSTEESHIP SYSTEM established at the 1945 San Francisco Conference. Chapter XIII (Articles 86–91) of the Charter established its MEMBERSHIP, powers, and procedures. Its members included those states administering trust territories, the remaining PERMANENT MEMBERS of the SECURITY COUNCIL that did not administer any territories in the system, and sufficient elected member states to assure an equal number of administering and non-administering governments on the Council. Under this complicated formula the Trusteeship Council reached a membership of 14 during its active life. By the late 1960s, however, rapid decolonization had reduced the membership to the UNITED STATES (administrator of the Pacific Islands Strategic Trust), and the four other Security Council permanent members.

The Trusteeship Council was empowered to conduct studies and make recommendations concerning specific trust territories. It could receive and deliberate on petitions from individuals and groups living in trust areas. Annually it received hundreds of such petitions. This led to regular debates on the policies of administering states and the public airing of grievances. Additionally the Council sent inspection missions, each consisting of four persons (two appointed by the administering states and two by the non-administering members), to the trust territories. The missions could interview inhabitants, collect information, and make a report to the Council. The Council, in turn, made annual reports to the GENERAL ASSEMBLY's FOURTH COMMITTEE regarding conditions in the non-strategic territories. Reports on strategic trusts were sent to the Security Council. The Charter also authorized the Council to administer a detailed questionnaire to the administering states. All of this public attention within the UN STRUCTURE had the effect of encouraging administering states to promote independence at the earliest date.

The first trust territory to gain independence was British Togoland, when London merged it with Gold Coast to create the state of Ghana in 1957. The United Kingdom relinquished its authority over part of Cameroons in 1961, merging it with Nigeria. In 1962 Belgium ended its control of Ruanda–Urundi. The independent states of Rwanda and Burundi emerged from the territory. France freed its parts of

Togoland and Cameroons in 1960, creating Togo and Cameroon, respectively. Italy ended its administration of Somaliland in 1960, and its territory was merged with British Somaliland to form SOMALIA. New Zealand freed Western Samoa in 1962. Australia granted independence to Nauru in 1968 and to Papua New Guinea in 1975. Australia's 1975 decision left the United States as the only administering authority. Its Pacific holdings included the Federated States of Micronesia, the Marshall Islands, and Palau. The first two approved a "free association" with the United States in 1986 that allowed for complete domestic autonomy, and Palau gained independence following a plebiscite in 1994.

The Council amended its rules of procedure following Palau's independence to call meetings only as needed. By now the Council had nothing to do; its UN mandate was completed. SECRETARY-GENERAL BOUTROS-GHALI recommended that the General Assembly abolish it in accordance with Article 108 of the Charter. But his successor, Kofi ANNAN, encouraged its resurrection in his 1997 REFORM proposal, *RENEWING THE UNITED NATIONS*. He suggested that the Trusteeship Council "be reconstituted as the forum through which member states exercise their collective trusteeship for the integrity of the global ENVIRONMENT and common areas such as the oceans, atmosphere and outer space." In December 1997, the General Assembly approved most of Annan's reform proposals, but it did not reorganize the Trusteeship Council. Instead, it called upon the Secretary-General to present to it "a new concept of trusteeship." A task force was established to consider future options. Again in 1999 the General Assembly urged further study of Annan's proposal, but the Assembly gave no indication that it intended to alter the mission of the Council.

See also UNITED NATIONS SYSTEM.

Further Reading: New Zealand Ministry of Foreign Affairs. *United Nations Handbook 2000.* Wellington, N.Z.: Ministry of Foreign Affairs and Trade, published annually.

Trusteeship System

The founding members of the United Nations established in the CHARTER an international trusteeship system "for the administration and supervision" of colonial territories until self-determination could be achieved by their populations. It was the "successor" to the mandate system of the LEAGUE OF NATIONS established at Versailles in 1919. It was a compromise between American desires for an end to colonial empires and the interests of the wartime Allies of the UNITED STATES, particularly those of the United Kingdom and France, who wanted unfettered control of their non-European possessions. Administered by the TRUSTEESHIP COUNCIL, one of the six PRINCIPAL ORGANS OF THE UNITED NATIONS, the trusteeship system not only presided over the liberation of the non-self-governing territories within its JURISDICTION but also encouraged the successful process of decolonization after World War II.

U.S. State Department planning for a postwar international organization included provision for the replacement of the mandate system. Both President ROOSEVELT and President Truman believed in Woodrow Wilson's philosophy of "self-determination," and were willing to use the "procedure and method" of the United Nations to meet the increasing demands for national freedom at the end of the war. At the 1945 YALTA CONFERENCE President Roosevelt reached an uneasy agreement with British prime minister Winston CHURCHILL and Soviet leader Joseph STALIN on the major elements of the UN trusteeship system. Churchill, who had earlier opposed any intrusion into British imperial affairs by the world community—saying he "had not become the King's First Minister in order to preside over the liquidation of the British empire"—accepted at Yalta a limited and largely voluntary trusteeship arrangement. Three types of territories would be placed under UN supervision: territories then under the League's mandate system, colonial holdings of the defeated powers, and areas voluntarily placed in the system by administering powers.

Following the Yalta meeting, differences in Washington between the State Department and the War Department arose over the role the United Nations should play in supervising Japanese Pacific islands recently captured by the United States. The military argued that these U.S. possessions were critical to future American security and should not be placed in the new trusteeship system, while Secretary of State Cordell HULL believed the United States could not maintain its credibility on the issue if it prohibited UN involvement. An Interdepartmental Committee on Dependent Areas reconciled the differences by proposing to the president that trusteeship areas should be divided between "strategic" and "non-strategic" territories, limiting the role of the proposed UN Trusteeship Council in those defined as strategic. Roosevelt and his successor accepted the idea and it became part of the final Charter provisions at the San Francisco Conference in April 1945.

When the UNITED NATIONS CONFERENCE ON INTERNATIONAL ORGANIZATION convened in San Francisco, the great power proposal on trusteeship, which essentially followed the American outline, found serious opposition from states that formerly had been colonies or mandate territories—the Philippines, Iraq, Egypt, Syria, and Argentina. They sought a mandatory system that would include all colonial holdings. While their demand was rejected, they were mollified with the inclusion directly in the Charter of a "Declaration Regarding Non-Self-Governing Territories" (Chapter XI). The DECLARATION committed the United Nations "to promote to the utmost . . . the well-being of the inhabitants of these territories, . . . to develop self-government, . . . to take due account of the political aspirations of the peoples, and to assist them in the progressive development of their free political institutions." In other words, the United Nations made a fundamental commitment to ending the 500-year-old phenomenon of colonialism.

Chapter XII of the Charter established the trusteeship system essentially along the lines developed by the United States. Territories were placed in the system and under the supervision of the Trusteeship Council by voluntary agreement between the United Nations and the administering authority (Articles 79 and 80). By the mid-1950s, the UN had agreements with seven administering states controlling 11 territories. All League of Nations mandate regions were included in this group, except for South-West Africa. Its mandate administrator, the Republic of South Africa, refused to participate. Article 81 recognized the distinction between strategic and non-strategic areas, allowing the administering state to decide where each classification applied. All Trusteeship Council activities related to strategic areas were subject to review by the SECURITY COUNCIL, where the United States retained the VETO. The Trusteeship Council's supervision of non-strategic territories was to be reviewed by the GENERAL ASSEMBLY.

Under the terms of the Charter's Chapter XIII the Trusteeship Council had the authority to conduct studies and make recommendations concerning specific trust territories. It could receive and deliberate on petitions from individuals and groups living in trust areas. It made annual reports to the General Assembly's FOURTH COMMITTEE on conditions in the territories based on information gathered in detailed questionnaires it required administering states to complete, and on Council missions that visited each trust area, interviewing representative groups of the inhabitants.

The first trust territory to gain independence was British Togoland, when London merged it with Gold Coast to create the state of Ghana in 1957. Over the next 18 years, all of the remaining areas, with the exception of the American strategic Pacific island trusts were liberated. The Belgians gave up their control over Rwanda and Burundi, in 1962. France freed its part of Togoland in 1960, creating an independent Togo. Italy ended its administration of Somaliland in 1960, and its territory was merged with British Somaliland to form SOMALIA. Australia granted independence to Nauru in 1968 and to Papua New Guinea in 1975. Australia's 1975 decision left the United States as the only administering authority. Its Pacific holdings included the Federated States of Micronesia and the Marshall Islands, both of which approved in 1986 elections a "free association" with the United States that allowed for complete domestic autonomy. They also included Palau, which gained independence following a plebiscite in 1994, and became the 185th member of the United Nations in 1995. With Palau's independence, the trusteeship system accomplished the goal of the UN's founders. With no further business to conduct, the Trusteeship Council became the first principal organ of the UN to cease operation.

See also BUNCHE, CAIRO DECLARATION, NAMIBIA, NATIONAL LIBERATION, STRUCTURE OF THE UNITED NATIONS.

Further Reading: Bennett, A. LeRoy. *International Organizations: Principles and Issues.* 4th ed. Englewood Cliffs, N.J.: Prentice Hall, 1988. Riggs, Robert E., and Jack C. Plano. *The United Nations. International Organization and World Politics.* Pacific Grove, Calif.: Brooks/Cole Publishing Co., 1988. Russell, Ruth B. *A History of the United Nations Charter: The Role of the United States, 1940–1945.* Washington, D.C.: Brookings Institution, 1958.

U

Under Secretary-General (USG)

The UN SECRETARIAT is divided into administrative offices and departments, each with responsibilities to support the work of related UN bodies and to develop policy initiatives in its particular area of UN activity. Each of these Secretariat divisions is headed by an Under Secretary-General, who is directly accountable to the SECRETARY-GENERAL. The appointment of these international civil servants is solely the responsibility of the Secretary-General, guided technically by Articles 100 and 101 of the UN CHARTER, which require the appointment of individuals with "the highest standards of efficiency, COMPETENCE and integrity," and with due regard for "as wide a geographical basis as possible."

In practice, USGs make up a "political senior level" within the Secretariat, with positions often assigned to nationals from the great powers. An informal agreement made among the PERMANENT MEMBERS OF THE SECURITY COUNCIL shortly after the UN's formation led to the holding of these posts for specific states in order to assure their representation in the inner circle of advisers around the Secretary-General. This practice was also seen as a legitimate balance to the expected appointment of Secretaries-General from small, neutral states. During most of the COLD WAR, the DEPARTMENT OF POLITICAL AFFAIRS was headed by a Soviet diplomat, and influential Americans, like Ralph BUNCHE, served as Under Secretary-General for Special Political Affairs or as USG for other critical departments. So, too, French, British, and Chinese officials regularly held USG positions. The close of the cold war and the expansion of UN MEMBERSHIP and Secretariat size, however, led to less concern about balancing great power interests at this level. Geographical distribution, and particularly representation from the developing world, were urged on the Secretary-General as paramount criteria in the appointment process. By the beginning of the new millennium, the USGs made up a major portion of Secretary-General Kofi Annan's SENIOR MANAGEMENT GROUP (SMG), serving along with the DEPUTY SECRETARY-GENERAL and administrators of key UN programs and SPECIALIZED AGENCIES, and came from countries such as Sri Lanka, Japan, and India in addition to the great power states. The position had also become a possible route to appointment as UN Secretary-General. As of 2002, two Secretaries-General had served formerly in USG posts: Javier PÉREZ DE CUÉLLAR, and Kofi ANNAN.

See also DEPARTMENT FOR DISARMAMENT AFFAIRS, DEPARTMENT OF ECONOMIC AND SOCIAL AFFAIRS, DEPARTMENT OF PEACEKEEPING OPERATIONS, DEPARTMENT OF PUBLIC INFORMATION, INTER-AGENCY COMMITTEE ON SUSTAINABLE DEVELOPMENT, UNITED NATIONS FRAMEWORK CONVENTION ON CLIMATE CHANGE, URQUHART.

Further Reading: SMG website: <www.un.org/News/ossg/sg/pages/seniorstaff.html>.

Unified Task Force (UNITAF)

On December 3, 1992, with the situation in SOMALIA deteriorating, the UN SECURITY COUNCIL unanimously authorized the formation of the Unified Task Force (Res. 794). It called upon member states to provide military forces, or contributions in cash or materiel. UNITAF was equipped with a mandate under CHAPTER VII of the CHARTER to establish a safe environment in Somalia for the humanitarian assistance that was at that time conducted by the UNITED NATIONS OPERATION IN SOMALIA (UNOSOM). Welcoming the offer of the UNITED STATES to create the needed security and assume overall command of the operation, members were authorized to use "all necessary means" to restore order.

On December 9, the task force established a beachhead and soon seized control of Baledogle airfield and later the city of Baidoa. Following a four-stage plan, key air and sea installations and food distribution points were secured. UNITAF then provided open, free, and secure passages for relief convoys and organizations to deliver humanitarian assistance.

Troop numbers rose to 37,000, with 28,000 of those being U.S. personnel (Operation "Restore Hope") and the rest coming from Australia, Belgium, Botswana, Canada, Egypt, France, Germany, Greece, India, Italy, Kuwait, Morocco, New Zealand, Nigeria, Norway, Pakistan, Saudi Arabia, Sweden, Tunisia, Turkey, the United Arab Emirates, the United Kingdom, and Zimbabwe. Forces deployed in southern and central Somalia, covering approximately 40 percent of the country. The presence of UNITAF had a moderately positive impact on the overall situation in Somalia, making effective humanitarian assistance possible. However, it failed to achieve its main goal, establishing a secure environment. Several military personnel died during its operations, including 18 U.S. peacekeepers just prior to its dissolution in May 1993.

On March 3 1993, SECRETARY-GENERAL BOUTROS-GHALI recommended that the Unified Task Force be withdrawn to be replaced by a new UN operation in Somalia, UNOSOM II. In May the Security Council accepted the Secretary-General's recommendation (Res. 814). UNOSOM II became the first United Nations PEACEKEEPING operation authorized under Chapter VII's enforcement articles.

See also CHAPTER VI $^1/_2$ PROVISIONS.

Further Reading: Hirsch, John L., and Robert B. Oakley. *Somalia and Operation Restore Hope.* Washington, D.C.: United States Institute of Peace Press, 1995. United Nations Department of Public Information. "The UN and Somalia, 1992–96." *The UN Blue Books Series.* Vol. 8. New York: United Nations Department of Public Information, 1996. UNOSOM website: <www.un.org/Depts/DPKO/Missions/unosomi.htm>.

— *T. J. Weiler*

Union of Soviet Socialist Republics   *See*

RUSSIAN FEDERATION.

United Nations Administrative Tribunal   *See*

ADMINISTRATIVE TRIBUNALS.

United Nations Advance Mission in Cambodia (UNAMIC)

Authorized by the UN SECURITY COUNCIL immediately prior to the adoption of the 1991 Paris Agreements, the United Nations Advance Mission in CAMBODIA became operational in November with a staff of 1,504 military and civilian personnel. Its objectives were to assist the four factions of the Cambodian civil war to maintain the cease-fire agreed to in June and to lay the foundation for a more elaborate UN PEACEKEEPING operation projected for 1992. UNAMIC facilitated communications between the military headquarters of the Cambodian parties, monitored cease-fire violations, and conducted a mine-clearance training program. UNAMIC terminated in 1992 when the UNITED NATIONS TRANSITIONAL AUTHORITY IN CAMBODIA became operational.

Further Reading: UNAMIC website: <www.un.org/Depts/dpko/dpko/co_mission/unamic.htm>.

— *G. S. Silliman*

United Nations Angola Verification Mission (UNAVEM I, II, III)

The United Nations undertook several missions in ANGOLA. The first verification mission (UNAVEM I) was initiated in 1988 as the result of a complex international negotiation that mandated the withdrawal of Cuban troops from Angola and recognized the independence of NAMIBIA. Established by SECURITY COUNCIL RESOLUTION 626, UNAVEM I provided a military observer group to verify the withdrawal of 50,000 Cuban troops from Angolan soil. The mission was concluded successfully in May 1991 and UNAVEM I was judged to be successful example of a UN PEACEKEEPING mission.

Following the completion of UNAVEM I, the government of Angola requested that the United Nations participate in another verification mission. In this case, UNAVEM II was initiated to verify the implementation of peace agreements between two warring groups: Movimento Popular de Libertação de Angola (MPLA) and União Nacional para a Independência Total de Angola (UNITA). Security Council Resolution 696 (1991) directed UNAVEM II to verify the cease-fire and monitor the neutrality of the Angolan police service for 17 months. By March 1992, again at the request of the government of Angola, UNAVEM II's mandate was extended (SC Res. 747) to include observation of the general elections scheduled for the fall of 1992. The UNITED NATIONS DEVELOPMENT PROGRAMME provided technical consultation for the elections.

Although the elections were judged to have been generally fair and free by international election observers, Jonas Savimbi's UNITA alleged electoral fraud and rejected the election results. On January 21, 1993, SECRETARY-GENERAL BOUTROS-GHALI reported that the country had returned to a state of civil war. Security Council Resolution 804 extended the mandate of UNAVEM II, but the Secretary-General soon decided to decrease the strength of the mission given the deteriorating security conditions in Angola. UNAVEM II was subsequently extended by Resolutions 864, 952, and 966. The mission monitored the early implementation of the Lusaka Protocol (effective November 22, 1994).

The Secretary-General recommended the establishment of UNAVEM III in February 1995. Authorized by Security Council Resolution 976, UNAVEM III assisted the government of Angola and UNITA in restoring peace and achieving national reconciliation. UNAVEM III had a maximum strength of 7,000 troops and military support personnel. It officially ended on June 30, 1997, as the Security Council authorized an observer mission (United Nations Observer Mission in Angola—MONUA) beginning July 1, 1997 (Res. 1118). However, at the close of UNAVEM III's term, it was clear that progress toward peace was being thwarted by the failure of UNITA to adhere to the elements of the peace accords and the Lusaka Protocol.

The mandate for MONUA was to aid the implementation of the Lusaka Protocol by continuing to verify the neutrality of the Angola national police force, monitor the collection and destruction of WEAPONS, and oversee the security of UNITA leaders. The Security Council originally anticipated that the mission would be completed by February 1998. However, as the security situation continued to deteriorate within Angola, the mission was extended several times until February 26, 1999. During the last week of 1998 rebel forces shot down two MONUA airplanes, killing more than 20 passengers and crew. When UN officials were denied access to the crash site, the Security Council condemned the rebel actions, "deplored the incomprehensible lack of cooperation," and ordered all UN workers out of the country. In February the Security Council endorsed the recommendations of the Secretary-General to terminate the mission.

See also PÉREZ DE CUÉLLAR, JAVIER.

Further Reading: Hare, Paul J. *Angola's Last Best Chance of Peace: An Insider's Account of the Peace Process.* Washington, D.C.: United States Institute of Peace Press, 1998. MONUA website: <www.un.org/Depts/DPKO/Missions/Monua/monuabl.htm>. UNAVEM website: <www.un.org/Depts/ dpko/dpko/co_mission/unavem_p.htm>.

— *S. C. Rein*

United Nations Assistance Mission for Rwanda (UNAMIR)   *See* RWANDA CRISIS.

United Nations Assistance Mission in Sierra Leone (UNAMSIL)   *See* SIERRA LEONE.

United Nations Association (UNA)

The World Federation of UN Associations (WFUNA), an international NON-GOVERNMENTAL ORGANIZATION (NGO), was founded in Luxembourg, on August 2, 1946. Its headquarters is in the Palais des Nations in Geneva. Beginning with 12 founding NATION-STATES, its MEMBERSHIP by 2001 had grown to include affiliated organizations in over 100 nations, including three UNAs in states not members of the United Nations: British Virgin Islands, Gibraltar, and Switzerland. Nationally based UNAs are linked at the international level through the WFUNA. Each national UNA is a nonprofit, nonpartisan organization committed to encouraging its national government's participation in the UNITED NATIONS SYSTEM and to strengthening the system.

UNAs serve as a link between the United Nations and the citizens of their member states. They are typically subdivided into regional and local chapters. UNAs are made up of dues-paying members; they disseminate information about the United Nations, provide educational tools regarding the organization, publish newsletters, do public research and substantive policy analyses, and encourage ongoing dialogue among their nationals regarding UN activities.

One of the most active original participants in the WFUNA was Eleanor ROOSEVELT. Mrs. Roosevelt was leader of the American Association for the United Nations (AAUN), a citizen-based group initiated in 1943 with the objective of educating Americans about the new United Nations and about global issues. The AAUN merged in 1964 with the U.S. Committee for the United Nations, bringing almost 140 regional organizations into the UNA–USA, which in turn is part of the larger WFUNA network of national UNAs. The UNA–USA's national headquarters is in New York City, near the United Nations.

Mrs. Roosevelt's leadership role in the adoption of the UNIVERSAL DECLARATION OF HUMAN RIGHTS in 1948 proved important to the WFUNA and its members. The WFUNA has organized international seminars on the teaching of HUMAN RIGHTS, and for many years the proposal for creating a position of UN HIGH COMMISSIONER FOR HUMAN RIGHTS was a major agenda item for the WFUNA and its members.

WFUNA has CONSULTATIVE STATUS with the ECONOMIC AND SOCIAL COUNCIL (ECOSOC), the UN CHILDREN'S FUND (UNICEF), the WORLD HEALTH ORGANIZATION (WHO), the WORLD METEOROLOGICAL ORGANIZATION (WMO), the FOOD

AND AGRICULTURE ORGANIZATION (FAO), the INTERNATIONAL LABOUR ORGANIZATION (ILO) and other parts of the UN system. Its main organs are a Plenary Assembly that holds sessions every year, a SECRETARIAT in Geneva, and an office at UN HEADQUARTERS in New York City.

Several prominent leaders have served as president of the WFUNA, including Czechoslovakian national leader Jan Masaryk, who was the first president, from 1946 to 1947, and former SECRETARY-GENERAL U THANT, president in 1973–74. In 2001, the president was Hashim Abdul of India, who was serving his second term.

Further Reading: New Zealand Ministry of Foreign Affairs. *United Nations Handbook.* Wellington, N.Z.: Ministry of Foreign Affairs and Trade, published annually. WFUNA website: <www.wfuna.org>. UNA-USA Website: <www.unausa.org>.

United Nations Atomic Energy Commission (UNAEC)   *See* DISARMAMENT.

United Nations Centre for Human Settlements (UNCHS-Habitat)

UNCHS was established by the GENERAL ASSEMBLY in October 1978 as the lead agency in the UNITED NATIONS SYSTEM for coordinating activities in the field of human settlements. Its mission is to promote sustainable human settlements development and adequate shelter for all. It seeks to fulfill its mandate by developing policies, enhancing capacity-building, providing knowledge creation and strengthening the relationship between governments and civil society. Habitat works with governments, local officials, NON-GOVERNMENTAL ORGANIZATIONS (NGOs), the private sector, and with other bilateral support groups. In 2001 it had well over 200 projects underway around the world. It was particularly concerned with urban management, housing, basic services, and infrastructure improvements. Its work is all the more important considering that UN estimates predict that by 2025 more than 60 percent of the world's people will live in urban areas, creating enormous strains on prospective sources of services, housing, and health facilities.

The General Assembly authorized Habitat to be the central agency for implementing the Habitat Agenda, derived from a DECLARATION and Global Plan of Action adopted at the second UN Conference on Human Settlements held in Istanbul, Turkey, in June 1996. Attended by representatives from 171 countries, mayors from over 500 cities, numerous community groups, and over 2000 NGOs, the Conference's main themes were "adequate shelter for all" and "sustainable human settlements in an urbanizing world."

Habitat is governed by the 58-member COMMISSION ON HUMAN SETTLEMENTS, established by the General Assembly in December 1977. UNCHS is headquartered in Nairobi,

Kenya, and in 2001 its executive director was Anna Kajumulo Tibaijuka.

See also PROGRAMMES AND FUNDS, SUSTAINABLE DEVELOPMENT.

Further Reading: Leckie, Scott. *Towards an International Convention on Housing Rights: Options at Habitat II.* Washington, D.C.: American Society of International Law, 1994. United Nations Conference on Human Settlements. *The City Summit: Habitat II, United Nations Conference on Human Settlements, Istanbul, Turkey, 3–14 June 1996.* New York: United Nations Department of Public Information, 1995. Habitat website: <www.unchs.org>.

United Nations Centre for International Crime Prevention   *See* OFFICE FOR DRUG CONTROL AND CRIME PREVENTION.

United Nations Charter   *See* CHARTER OF THE UNITED NATIONS.

United Nations Children's Fund (UNICEF)

Among the most visible and popular of UN-affiliated bodies—and the only one to deal exclusively with children's issues—the United Nations Children's Fund, or UNICEF as it is most generally known, is widely recognized for its sales of greeting cards during the holiday season at the end of each year. Proceeds from these card sales supplement UNICEF's BUDGET, which depends solely on voluntary contributions.

By a RESOLUTION passed in 1946, the GENERAL ASSEMBLY (GA) set up the UN International Children's Emergency Fund as a temporary agency to provide urgent assistance to children in countries ravaged by the recent war. In 1953 the Assembly, by resolution, extended its mandate indefinitely, making the organization permanent. UNICEF is charged with assisting children and adolescents throughout the world, particularly in devastated areas and in developing countries. Its concerns include child health care, malnutrition, disease, illiteracy, welfare services, and related challenges. It is particularly concerned with the well-being of girls. For its work UNICEF received the Nobel Peace Prize in 1965.

Although its name changed in 1953 to the UN Children's Fund to denote its permanent nature, it kept the widely familiar acronym UNICEF. Retaining semiautonomous status, UNICEF reports regularly to the ECONOMIC AND SOCIAL COUNCIL (ECOSOC) and to the General Assembly. Its main headquarters, UNICEF House, is in New York City, but in 2001 it also had eight regional offices and 125 country offices.

UNICEF is governed by a 36-member Executive Board that determines policies, reviews programs, and approves budgets. ECOSOC elects the board members for three-year terms according to an equitable regional allocation of seats. The board elects its own officers—called the Bureau—during the first regular session of each calendar year. There are five officers (a president and four vice presidents) representing the five regional groups of the United Nations. Officers are elected for a one-year term. Board sessions are held at UN HEADQUARTERS in New York. The Office of the Secretary of the Executive Board (OSEB), a staff organization, maintains year-round contact with the full board and with the UNICEF SECRETARIAT, organizes the business of all board sessions, provides editorial and technical assistance to the board, and works closely with the UN Secretariat on all matters related to UNICEF's mission.

In 2001, the executive director of UNICEF was Carol Bellamy of the UNITED STATES. The organization could count about 37 national committees for UNICEF—NON-GOVERN-MENTAL ORGANIZATIONS (NGO) mostly in developed nations that offered public support. It had a professional staff of about 6,000, more than 85 percent located in over 200 field sites serving some 160 countries. In 1999 UNICEF's total expenditures amounted to a little more than $1 billion, of which 91 percent was spent on programs, the remainder on administrative and management affairs. About 60 percent of the organization's funds came from contributions of governments; 40 percent from direct fund-raising and the sale of greeting cards.

During the 1980s UNICEF participated in a joint program with the WORLD HEALTH ORGANIZATION (WHO) to raise global immunization coverage in order to combat polio, tetanus, measles, whooping cough, diphtheria, and tuberculosis. According to UN appraisals, the effort saved the lives of three million children every year. Also, UNICEF has worked jointly with the UNITED NATIONS EDUCATIONAL, SCIENTIFIC AND CULTURAL ORGANIZATION (UNESCO) to help train teachers and provide free, compulsory, primary education. The organization has been particularly interested in improving schooling opportunities for girls. In 1997 it earmarked 14 percent of its program budget (over $100 million) to education and early childhood care. UNICEF has been the lead agency in promoting the DECLARATION ON THE RIGHTS OF THE CHILD, adopted by the General Assembly in 1959, and affirming the need for special protection, opportunities, and health for the world's youngest inhabitants. In 1989 the General Assembly installed these rights in the binding CONVENTION ON THE RIGHTS OF THE CHILD that by 2001 had achieved almost universal ratification. In 1990, due in large part to the labors of UNICEF, more than 150 countries attended the WORLD SUMMIT FOR CHILDREN (WSC) in New York. The summit recognized that the rights of the young should claim "first call" on nations' resources. Following the summit, its objectives were written into many countries'

policies and plans. Remembering its original function, UNICEF also has continued to provide relief and assistance in emergencies. The organization has, for example, tried to meet the needs of children harmed by warfare and civil strife. During the 1990s, conflicts caused an estimated one million children to be orphaned or separated from their families. An additional 12 million were made homeless. UNICEF sought to provide these child victims with food, safe water, medicine, shelter, trauma counseling, and help locating extended families.

Although several factors account for progress discerned in the life of children by the 21st century, UNICEF could take considerable satisfaction for its half century's contributions to these improvements. While severe challenges for children remained, particularly in poor areas plagued by civil war and dysfunctional civil authority, advances could be cited in arresting under-five mortality rates worldwide, enhancing child nutrition, increasing school attendance and literacy rates, and combating dangerous childhood diseases. In late August 2001, the International Food Institute in Washington, D.C., funded by the United Nations and the

UNICEF in Somalia, 1992 (UN PHOTO 159358/M. GRANT)

WORLD BANK, reported that, worldwide, child malnutrition had decreased significantly since the mid-1960s. The report anticipated that by the year 2020 all child malnutrition would be eliminated in LATIN AMERICA, that CHINA could expect to reduce the number of undernourished children by half, and that India would also see improvements (although one-third of the total of poorly fed children will be in India). Only Sub-Saharan Africa appeared in the report to lack progress. Here, one-third of all children were malnourished.

See also ADMINISTRATIVE COMMITTEE ON COORDINATION, DESERTIFICATION, HUMAN RIGHTS, SOMALIA, UNITED NATIONS POPULATION FUND, SPECIALIZED AGENCIES.

Further Reading: United Nations Department of Public Information. *Basic Facts about the United Nations.* New York: United Nations Department of Public Information, published periodically. Beigbeder, Yves. *New Challenges for UNICEF: Children, Women, and Human Rights.* New York: Palgrave, 2001. New Zealand Ministry of Foreign Affairs. *United Nations Handbook.* Wellington, N.Z.: Ministry of Foreign Affairs and Trade, published annually. UNICEF website: <www.unicef.org>.

UN Chronicle

The *UN Chronicle* is the flagship publication of the United Nations. Published and made available by the DEPARTMENT OF PUBLIC INFORMATION, the *Chronicle* appears quarterly. All important activities of UN bodies and associated PRO-GRAMMES AND FUNDS and SPECIALIZED AGENCIES are covered. The *Chronicle* also carries special features on world problems and UN responses to them.

United Nations Civilian Police Mission in Haiti (MIPONUH)

The UN SECURITY COUNCIL created the Civilian Police Mission to Haiti on November 28, 1997 (Res. 1141) for the purpose of assisting the Haitian government with the professionalization of the Haitian National Police (HNP). It was the first PEACEKEEPING operation in UN history to include police development explicitly in its mandate. It also was the first UN operation in HAITI to have no military component, succeeding two peacekeeping efforts—UNMIH (UN Mission in Haiti) and UNSMIH (UN Support Mission in Haiti)—both of which depended on large multilateral military contingents.

A total of 300 police and instructors from Argentina, Benin, Canada, France, India, Mali, Niger, Senegal, Togo, Tunisia, and the UNITED STATES, under the leadership of the SPECIAL REPRESENTATIVE OF THE SECRETARY-GENERAL, Alfredo Lopes Cabral (Guinea-Bissau), remained in Haiti until March 15, 2000. The Mission was often criticized for employing underqualified personnel, who failed to take

seriously the assignment of training a nonpolitical Haitian police force. Beginning in late 1999, Haitian police attacks on opponents of the regime and police violence escalated. MIPONUH's effectiveness also was greatly diminished by the lack of financial support. During its mandate, no contributions were made to the Voluntary Trust fund established for its maintenance. In the spring of 2000, the U.S. Congress cut off all financial support for the effort. Faced with no funds to continue, MIPONUH was replaced with the International Civilian Support Mission in Haiti (MICAH) on March 16. MICAH had no police, military, or enforcement capability. Its assignment was a purely political one, namely, to encourage the development of democratic institutions and process.

See also INTERNATIONAL CIVILIAN MISSION TO HAITI.

Further Reading: Holm, Tor Tanke, and Espen Barth Eide, eds. *Peacebuilding and Police Reform.* London: Frank Cass, 2000. Tessitore, John, and Susan Woolfson, eds. *A Global Agenda. Issues before the 55th General Assembly of the United Nations.* New York: Rowman and Littlefield, 2000. MIPONUH website: <www.un.org/Depts/dpko/dpko/co_mission/miponuh.htm>.

United Nations Command in Korea (UNCF)

See KOREAN WAR.

United Nations Commission for Indonesia (UNCI)

The 1945–49 conflict between the Netherlands and Indonesian nationalists was one of the first colonial disputes to elicit extensive UN involvement. The UN mission, conducted from 1947 to 1951, was structured around the GOOD OFFICES Committee and its eventual replacement, which was the United Nations Commission for Indonesia.

After the first Dutch "police action" of July 1947, Australia and India brought the "Indonesian question" before the SECURITY COUNCIL. Australia was subsequently nominated by INDONESIA to the Good Offices Committee that the Security Council established in August 1947 to facilitate a resolution of the conflict. Belgium was the representative for the Netherlands on the Good Office Committee and the UNITED STATES accepted the third seat. The Security Council authorized UNCI in January 1949 as part of its continuing effort to achieve a settlement between the Netherlands and Indonesia after the arrangements stipulated by the Renville Agreement collapsed under a second Dutch military action in late 1948.

UN military observers associated with the Good Offices Committee and UNCI arranged cease-fires in the field, maintained a small truce observation team, and assisted with the negotiations between the parties. The UN mission also observed the repatriation of Dutch forces after the recognition of Indonesian independence in 1949.

United Nations operations in Indonesia in the 1940s represent one of several early experiments with a non-fighting military presence. UNCI, however, is not included in official lists of PEACEKEEPING operations as it was not organized and administered by the UN SECRETARIAT.

Further Reading: White, N.D. *Keeping the Peace: The United Nations and the Maintenance of International Peace and Security.* New York: Manchester University Press, 1993.

— *G. S. Silliman*

United Nations Commission on International Trade Law (UNCITRAL)

On December 12, 2000, in Resolution 151, the UN GENERAL ASSEMBLY expressed its "concern" that organs of the UNITED NATIONS SYSTEM had not coordinated effectively their work in the field of international trade law with the UN commission created in 1966 as the UN's "core legal body" in this area. At the time of its creation the Assembly mandated UNCITRAL, headquartered in Vienna, to harmonize national trade laws, draft model laws and CONVENTIONS on international trade law, and encourage conformity among states to common standards, leading to one worldwide commercial law. With accelerated globalization at the end of the century, the General Assembly's RESOLUTION reflected an effort by the United Nations to play a more active role in reducing or removing obstacles to the free flow of international trade.

The commission has 36 members, increased from 29 in 1973, elected by the General Assembly under a formula for appropriate geographical representation. Nine members are elected from Africa, seven from Asia, five from Eastern Europe, six from LATIN AMERICA and the Caribbean, and nine from the Western European and Other States Group. Members serve six-year terms with half of the MEMBERSHIP elected every three years. The members meet annually, alternating every year between UN HEADQUARTERS in New York City and Vienna. The commission's work is done in three working groups—Electronic Commerce, ARBITRATION, and International Contract Practices—with each meeting several times a year. In addition to its membership, all interested states and international organizations may send representatives to its meetings and may participate in UNCITRAL's discussions. The commission is serviced by a SECRETARIAT provided by the International Trade Law Branch of the UN's OFFICE OF LEGAL AFFAIRS. The commission annually submits its reports and recommendations to the SIXTH COMMITTEE of the General Assembly.

UNCITRAL's achievements include the Vienna Convention on Contracts for the International Sale of Goods (1980), its formulation of uniform arbitration rules, the 1978 UN Convention on the Carriage of Goods by Sea, and the 1988 UN Convention on International Bills of Exchange and International Promissory Notes. The General Assembly has regularly urged states to adopt these international PACTS, as well as to accept the commission's proposed uniform "Model Rules," "Provisions," and "Model Laws." The most important of these have been its 1993 Model Law on Procurement of Goods and Construction, 1976 UNCITRAL Arbitration Rules, 1985 Model Law on International Commercial Arbitration, and 1982 Provisions for a Unit of Account. As the new century began, UNCITRAL focused on establishing rules for privately financed infrastructure projects, electronic signatures, and integrating developing nations into the international trade system. UNCITRAL also publishes a *Yearbook* to keep professionals in the field informed, conducts symposia in Vienna on international trade law, and provides an internship program for young lawyers in the field.

Further Reading: Tessitore, John, and Susan Woolfson. *A Global Agenda: Issues before the 55th General Assembly of the United Nations.* New York: Rowman and Littlefield, 2000. New Zealand Ministry of Foreign Affairs. *United Nations Handbook.* Wellington, N.Z. Ministry of Foreign Affairs and Trade, published annually. *Yearbook of the United Nations.* Special Edition, UN Fiftieth Anniversary, 1945–1995. The Hague: Martinus Nijhoff Publishers, 1995. UNCITRAL website: <www.uncitral.org>.

United Nations Conference on Environment and Development (UNCED)

Better known as the "Earth Summit," the United Nations Conference on Environment and Development took place June 3–14, 1992, in Rio de Janeiro, Brazil. It was the largest international conference held to that time. A total of 178 national delegations and two-thirds of the world's heads of state attended. More than 1,400 NON-GOVERNMENTAL ORGANIZATIONS (NGOs) were accredited to UNCED. The NGOs, with UN blessing, also staged a Global Forum in tandem with the conference that attracted 30,000 participants. UNCED produced three important international agreements—the RIO DECLARATION, AGENDA 21, and the STATEMENT OF FOREST PRINCIPLES—and served as the venue for the signing of the FRAMEWORK CONVENTION ON CLIMATE CHANGE (UNFCCC) and the Convention on Biological Diversity (CBD). Led by Canadian Maurice F. Strong, who had also served as SECRETARY-GENERAL of the Stockholm Conference on the Human Environment 20 years earlier, the Rio meeting attempted to bridge the gap between developed and developing states on environmental issues. It did this in part by urging the GENERAL ASSEMBLY to create new institutional and financial mechanisms to ensure sufficient attention and resources for achieving SUSTAINABLE DEVELOPMENT.

Signing the Earth Pledge (UN PHOTO 180303/M. TZOVARAS)

The WORLD COMMISSION ON ENVIRONMENT AND DEVEL-OPMENT (WCED) first proposed in 1987 the convocation of an international conference to delineate the interconnections between ENVIRONMENT and development. The General Assembly endorsed the WCED's initiative and set the parameters for the conference in Resolution 228, December 22, 1989. The RESOLUTION called for the conference to recommend "strategies . . . to halt and reverse environmental degradation in the context of increased . . . efforts to promote sustainable and environmentally sound development in all countries." The Assembly advocated broad participation by non-governmental groups. As a result, the Rio Conference witnessed the involvement of many private groups that normally had not been involved in UN environmental activities. As one example, international businesses paid for nearly half the costs of the conference SECRETARIAT.

A series of preparatory meetings (known as PrepCom) were held prior to the scheduled opening of UNCED in June 1992. At the first PrepCom session in New York Secretary-General Strong put forward an ambitious agenda for the conference, calling for an "Earth Charter" that would spell out

clear, internationally accepted principles on the environment, and a detailed Plan of Action. PrepCom members also decided to urge negotiators of the CONVENTIONS on climate change and biodiversity to complete their work so that both agreements could be opened for signature at the conference. Additionally, Strong and his colleagues encouraged the extensive involvement of the NGO community not only in the preparation for the Rio meeting but also in the environmental programs of their individual states. The organizers hoped and planned for a conference that would capture media and popular attention.

During later PrepCom meetings, however, it became clear that the divisions between the developed states and the LESS DEVELOPED COUNTRIES (LDCs) were so deep that no grand consensus could be achieved. The nations of Europe and North America, in particular, sought binding global commitments to protect the environment from dangerous development policies. The destruction of the rain forests through land clearing policies in developing states, the indiscriminate use of fossil fuel technologies as poor countries pursued development, and the pollution of significant bodies of water with toxic effluents particularly troubled the industrialized powers. States in the developing world saw the efforts by the North to impose international environmental restrictions on their development strategies to be a violation of SOVEREIGNTY and an effort to limit their pursuit of the same development policies used by the industrialized states in the past. Working in close cooperation through the G-77 CAUCUS GROUP, the LDCs formulated a consensus position to protect their development policies from environmental limitation. They also sought to obtain a commitment from the rich states to give additional aid for any new costs arising from imposed environmental requirements. They were largely successful both in the PrepCom meetings and the final conference in giving development an equal status with environmental protection and limiting the conference's final documents to statements of aspiration, with little direct obligation for the participating states. They were not able, however, to attract significant sums from the donor states. Led by the UNITED STATES, which remained largely hostile to the UNCED negotiations, major powers refused to go much beyond their current financial commitments.

The Rio Declaration contained 26 broad principles that outlined the general obligations and rights of states regarding the environment and the development process. It reflected the many uneasy compromises that emerged between the developing and developed worlds at the conference. In the opening principle, the DECLARATION proclaimed that "human beings are at the centre of concerns for sustainable development." This discouraged environmental activists because it seemed to demote the preservation of "nature" and the "environment" as the primary interests of the world community. It also gave a strong rationale for the defense of development policies in the poor states, even if those policies hurt the environment. This concern was reinforced in Principle 2, which recognized the sovereign right of states to exploit their natural resources. For the first time an international document recognized the right to development (Principle 3). The declaration gave support, however, to the development of international environmental law and standards. It recognized the "Polluter Pays Principle" (PPP) in Principle 16, which required states to pay not only for pollution prevention on their territory but also for damage costs from pollution. It reaffirmed the idea first asserted in Principle 21 of the 1972 Stockholm Declaration that states are accountable for practices that injure the environment beyond their borders. The Rio Declaration called on governments to conduct environmental impact assessments before undertaking possibly hazardous development activities. States were also required to notify other countries when environmental emergencies arose.

The details of how to implement the broad guidelines of the declaration were left to Agenda 21, an 800-page document filled with more than 1,000 specific recommendations to achieve a "comprehensive plan for global action in all areas of sustainable development." Its 40 chapters and 115 program areas outlined the environmental/development challenge, set international and national objectives, and provided programmatic suggestions on how to fulfill the objectives. The areas for action included world trade, poverty eradication, population, cities, atmospheric pollution, deforestation, drought, DESERTIFICATION, marine resources and management, waste management, agriculture, biodiversity, and the transfer of technology. The Plan of Action called for the broad involvement of national and subnational groups, ordinary citizens, NGOs, business and labor, INDIGENOUS PEOPLES, youth, WOMEN, and the scientific/intellectual community in the implementation of its recommendations. It also directed key UN bodies to make sustainable development a central part of their responsibilities (Chapter 38). In particular, it identified the UNITED NATIONS ENVIRONMENT PROGRAMME (UNEP), the UNITED NATIONS DEVELOPMENT PROGRAMME (UNDP), the WORLD BANK, the UNITED NATIONS CONFERENCE ON TRADE AND DEVELOPMENT (UNCTAD), the GLOBAL ENVIRONMENT FACILITY (GEF), the INTERNATIONAL DEVELOPMENT ASSOCIATION (IDA), and REGIONAL DEVELOPMENT BANKS as the central agencies for future UN activity.

To ensure continuing public and governmental attention to the problems of environment and development, Agenda 21 urged the GENERAL ASSEMBLY to create a new functional commission under the auspices of the ECONOMIC AND SOCIAL COUNCIL (ECOSOC). In 1993 the Assembly responded by establishing the COMMISSION ON SUSTAINABLE DEVELOPMENT (CSD), and charged it with reviewing progress on the agenda and making recommendations for implementing it. The developing states hoped the new UN body could be used to encourage greater financial aid from the donor states. To implement all of the recommendations in Agenda 21 the conference secretariat estimated that $125 billion in foreign assistance would be needed, nearly 10 times the 1992 levels of global aid. Poor states argued for a new "Green Fund" with assets coming from the developed world. When it became clear that the rich nations were not going to give any significant new funds to implement Agenda 21, the conference fell back on using the World Bank's Global Environment Facility as an interim mechanism.

UNCED also issued a "non-legally binding authoritative statement of principles for a global consensus on the management, conservation and sustainable development of all types of forests." The document fell far short of the World Convention on Forests that developed states and NGOs sought. They had become concerned in the 1980s by reports of significant damage to the rain forests and to tropical stands of timber as the result of land clearing, the sale of mahogany and other precious lumber, and development practices that threatened this part of the global commons. Resistance to international restrictions on the use of forests, however, quickly arose from developing countries. Brazil and INDONESIA, states with a large percentage of the world's forests, led the opposition. With no possibility of reaching an agreement between developing and developed states, the Statement of Forest Principles could be little more than a list of voluntary guidelines. It called for reforestation, conservation, and new financial resources to protect the forests, but the document recognized the right of states to use their forests as they wished.

The signing of the climate change CONVENTION by 153 nations and the European Union (EU), and the biodiversity convention by the EU and 155 countries during the Rio Conference, helped to offset the passage of relatively weak final documents. The global media coverage also made UNCED a critical moment in the UN effort to create an era of international environmental governance. The conference provided the impetus for many national governments to establish domestic environmental programs and agencies. As a consequence of the Rio meeting, the General Assembly subsequently committed its members to the negotiation of a convention to combat desertification, future conferences on the sustainable development of small island states and the protection of migratory fish stocks, the establishment of the WORLD DAY FOR WATER, and the endorsement of new UNDP programs in capacity building, in addition to its creation of the CSD.

Further Reading: Elliott, Lorraine. *The Global Politics of the Environment*. New York: New York University Press, 1998. Grubb, Michael, Matthias Koch, Koy Thomson, Abby Manson, and Francis Sullivan. *The 'Earth Summit' Agreements: A Guide and Assessment*. London: Earthscan Publications, 1993. Halpern, Shanna. *The United Nations Conference on Environment and Development: Process and Documentation*. Providence, R.I.: Academic Council on the United Nations System, 1993.

United Nations Conference on International Organization (UNCIO) (San Francisco Conference)

The United Nations Conference on International Organization convened in San Francisco on April 25, 1945, as the culminating event in a series of wartime allied meetings that negotiated, drafted, and adopted the CHARTER OF THE UNITED NATIONS, giving birth to the world organization. Sponsored by the UNITED STATES, the Soviet Union, the United Kingdom, and CHINA, the conference invited as participants the "peace-loving nations" that had declared war on the Axis powers by March 1, 1945. The purpose of the UNCIO was to consider the proposals drafted at the DUMB-ARTON OAKS CONFERENCE the previous fall. The meeting concluded its work on June 26 with 50 "original members" signing the Charter. Poland, not in attendance because of the ongoing dispute between the Soviet Union and the Western

powers over the makeup of its government, signed the document at a later date as the 51st member.

While the Big Three—the United States, the Soviet Union, and Great Britain—already had crafted many of the important decisions about the workings of the new United Nations, the participation of many other nations, with their own interests, made the San Francisco Conference a complex exercise in multilateral diplomacy. The great powers often were required to make meaningful alterations in the proposed Charter in order to achieve the necessary votes for passage of its provisions. At the opening session even the question of who could participate in the deliberations did not escape intense debate. Latin American nations (21 of the participating 50 states) pressed for the inclusion of Argentina in the conference, which both the United States and the Soviet Union opposed because of the Argentine government's friendly relations with the Axis powers during the war. The proposal to seat Argentina led to an angry counterrequest from Soviet foreign minister Vyacheslav I. Molotov that the Russian-backed Lublin government in Poland also be invited to participate, even though that government was not recognized by any Western state. He also reopened the matter of Byelorussia's and Ukraine's participation. Both were to be admitted to the United Nations under the terms of the Yalta agreement, but neither had been invited by Washington to San Francisco. After five days of argument, Byelorussia, Ukraine, and Argentina were invited to the conference; Poland was not.

Plenary sessions of the UNCIO were chaired on a rotating basis by the heads of the sponsoring countries' delegations—Secretary of State Edward STETTINIUS (U.S.), Molotov (USSR), Foreign Minister Anthony EDEN (U.K.), and Premier T.V. Soong (China). Stettinius opened the conference as its temporary chairman, and he then chaired the Steering and Executive Committees, the most important bodies in the conference STRUCTURE. The Steering Committee, made up of the four sponsoring nations, decided important issues of policy and procedure. On June 27 it decided that the proposals of the Dumbarton Oaks Conference (August–October 1944) and the supplementary decisions made at the YALTA CONFERENCE (February 1945) would serve as the agenda for the meeting. It also decided that decisions in all of the working bodies dealing with the Charter draft must be made by a two-thirds majority. In so doing, the Steering Committee set aside the traditional rule of unanimity that had applied in diplomacy among sovereign states and had been the guiding principle during the drafting of the COVENANT of the LEAGUE OF NATIONS. An Executive Committee provided broader representation in the inner circle of powerful states. Ten additional states served with the sponsoring governments. The committee made recommendations to the Steering Committee on critical and contentious issues. These structural and VOTING arrangements created a system of "parliamentary diplomacy" that gave smaller states a substantive role in the decision process.

The final drafting of the Charter was the responsibility of the Coordination Committee, chaired by Leo PASVOLSKY, a U.S. States Department official. Recommended LANGUAGE for the Charter flowed into the Coordination Committee from four conference commissions and 12 technical committees. Each of these bodies had an elected chairman and rapporteur, and each was serviced by the conference SECRETARIAT, headed by UNCIO SECRETARY-GENERAL Alger HISS. It was in these committees and commissions that hundreds of new proposals and amendments to the Dumbarton Oaks provisions were made. Among their contributions were the ECONOMIC AND SOCIAL COUNCIL (ECOSOC) and the TRUSTEESHIP COUNCIL, neither of which had been proposed as PRINCIPAL ORGANS for the United Nations in the Dumbarton Oaks negotiations.

The success of the conference turned on the resolution of several remaining contentious issues. The most serious were matters related to the enforcement organ of the United Nations, the SECURITY COUNCIL. An evolution of President Franklin ROOSEVELT'S FOUR POLICEMEN concept, the proposed Security Council was made up of five PERMANENT MEMBERS and six NON-PERMANENT MEMBERS, and was authorized to impose mandatory ENFORCEMENT MEASURES against an aggressor. Several proposals were put forward at San Francisco to assure that the non-permanent seats were filled by states from certain regions of the world, or by states capable of contributing to international peace and security. Middle powers particularly emphasized this last point. Canada sponsored a proposal to hold seats on the Council only for states with the means to carry out enforcement responsibilities. India recommended that only states representing a significant proportion of the world's population be elected to the Security Council. Latin American representatives sought a greater role for states from the Western Hemisphere from the outset. This advocacy generated an effort, led by EL SALVADOR and Brazil, to have LATIN AMERICA guaranteed representation. El Salvador recommended the addition of members to the Council, which would have raised its

Signing ceremony for the UN Charter, San Francisco (UN/DPI PHOTO)

original MEMBERSHIP from 11 to 15. While the proposal gained support from small states in other regions, Brazil determined instead to seek a permanent seat on the Security Council for one Latin American country.

The sponsoring powers marshaled the votes to defeat all of these proposals, successfully arguing that any attempt to alter the Council's proposed composition would upset arduously worked out settlements and delay the establishment of the United Nations. They let it be known that any major change in the composition, powers, or responsibilities of the Council would mean the end of great power support for the organization. After intense negotiations among the four powers, the Steering Committee proposed language on the qualifications for election to the Council that mollified some of the delegations. According to the draft, non-permanent members would be elected by the GENERAL ASSEMBLY "with due regard being specially paid, in the first instance to the contribution of Members of the United Nations to the maintenance of international peace and security and to the other purposes of the Organization, and also to equitable geographical distribution."

Separate from the matter of Council membership, the UNCIO was embroiled in the ongoing debate about the VETO retained by the permanent members. Early in the conference, the Soviet delegation resurrected Stalin's persistent demand for an absolute veto on all matters before the Council. The USSR had made this a condition of its participation in the United Nations on earlier occasions, but at Yalta Joseph STALIN had agreed that procedural matters could be decided by an affirmative vote of seven Council members, the veto not being allowed. He had also accepted the American position that when permanent members were parties to a dispute, they could not veto a discussion of the dispute. To convince Stalin of America's resolve on this issue, President Truman sent a special envoy to Moscow to explain that the Charter would not pass the U.S. Senate on the terms proposed by the Soviet Union. Stalin backed down and directed his delegation to accept the Yalta formula.

The veto issue highlighted a general concern of smaller states at the conference—that the predominance of the great powers' control over peace and security issues would denigrate their role within the organization, diminish the COMPETENCE of the General Assembly, and demote other purposes for the United Nations dear to weaker powers. For Latin American states, in particular, there was a concern that the use of the veto could limit the region's ability to deal with hemispheric threats. A lengthy history of regional cooperation in the Pan American Union had created nervousness among the region's leaders, and led them to seek a major role for REGIONAL ORGANIZATIONS on security matters, and greater autonomy from Security Council intervention. The American delegation, however, feared that public support and U.S. Senate support would be lost if the Security Council was not given absolute authority to address all threats to the peace. Facing an impasse, the United States orchestrated a compromise that recognized the authority of "regional arrangements" to manage local or regional affairs, provided that their activities were "consistent with the Purposes and Principles of the United Nations" (Chapter VIII, Article 52). Additionally, under Article 51 states were permitted to undertake "COLLECTIVE SELF-DEFENSE" until the Security Council had taken sufficient steps to restore peace. The new wording in the Charter, however, limited this grant of autonomy by asserting the right of the Council to investigate and take action on any threat to the peace. Additionally, it allowed any state to bring any dispute directly to the Council.

Also in response to small state concerns, the competence of the General Assembly was expanded during the San Francisco negotiations. It was given control of the UN BUDGET. The conference likewise agreed that the Assembly could discuss any issue, including security concerns and threats to the peace, at least until the Security Council was "seized" with the issue. Furthermore, the SECRETARY-GENERAL, elected by the General Assembly, would be able to bring any matter that he believed threatened international peace and security to the attention of the Council (Article 99).

States from Latin America, Africa, and Asia envisioned an institution of universal membership with extensive activities in the economic, cultural, and HUMAN RIGHTS domains, beyond the initial security concerns of the great powers. In particular, they pressed for a UN role in the achievement of "independence" for existing colonial possessions. President Truman was also deeply concerned about the projected duties of the United Nations in the newly liberated territories of the enemy states and in the old colonial empires of the European powers. On this matter he found British prime minister Winston CHURCHILL adamant in opposing any structure that might endanger the British Empire. So too the French delegation opposed Charter provisions that might limit France's policies in Indochina and Africa. During the Yalta meeting, where trusteeship was not on the formal agenda, the Americans had come up with a formulation that was acceptable to the British by limiting the JURISDICTION of the UN's TRUSTEESHIP SYSTEM to territories still held under the League's mandate system, territories detached from the enemy states during World War II, and "territories voluntarily placed under the system by states responsible for their administration." This solution, however, led to the unintended consequence of raising concerns by Syria and other former mandate regions that were independent states in the spring of 1945. The formulation could be interpreted to allow renewed administration by outside powers. Article 78 was added to make this impossible.

The more serious trusteeship challenge came from those states at San Francisco that wanted a Charter commitment to full independence and decolonization. Led by Carlos Romulo of the Philippines delegation, small states urged much stronger commitments in policy and structure on the question of ending imperial control. In the lengthy negotiations that ensued the British and French made clear that no reference to "independence" would be allowed in the Charter. The sponsoring powers, however, did accept a commitment to "self-government," and took the unusual step of allowing the placement of a "DECLARATION Regarding NON-SELF-GOVERNING TERRITORIES" into the Charter text (Chapter XI). The declaration called upon administering states "to assist [these territories] in the progressive development of their free political institutions."

Even the United States, which generally supported a trusteeship system dedicated to ending colonial control, sought and obtained a limitation of the TRUSTEESHIP COUNCIL's authority when it came to STRATEGIC TRUST TERRITORIES. As the U.S. armed forces liberated important Pacific islands from Japanese control toward the end of the war, the military expressed concern with plans to have the United Nations take these holdings into the trusteeship system. Shortly before his death, President Franklin ROOSEVELT approved dividing designated trusteeship areas into "strategic" and "non-strategic" territories, and limiting the role of the Trusteeship Council in the former areas. This was accomplished in Articles 82 and 83, which allowed administering states to declare specific areas as "strategic" territories, and then made those areas subject to the Security Council, where the United States had the veto.

Before convening in San Francisco, Latin American governments had met with a delegation from the United States in Mexico City. There they had endorsed an enlarged role for the United Nations in social, economic, and human rights cooperation. At the conference they were joined by other states on the Economic and Social Co-operation Committee in passing broadened objectives for the United Nations in these areas. The committee recommended that the new organization promote "universal respect for, and observance of, human rights and fundamental freedoms for all without distinction as to race, sex, language or religion." American planners earlier had pushed for Charter provisions on human rights, but these had been rebuffed by the other participants at Dumbarton Oaks. At San Francisco there were many proposals to incorporate the "protection" of human rights into the Charter obligations of the organization. There was also much discussion, covered by the media, of establishing in the Charter a COMMISSION ON HUMAN RIGHTS. Time constraints made the drafting of a bill of human rights for Charter inclusion impossible. However, a desire to meet public expectations for action in this area after the horrors of the Holocaust, and strong endorsement from a majority of the delegations, persuaded the sponsoring powers to agree to Article 68, authorizing the Economic and Social Council to set up commissions "in the fields of economic and social activities and for the promotion of human rights." Thus a consequence of the deliberations in San Francisco was that ECOSOC, in February 1946, established the Commission on Human Rights, which proceeded under the leadership of Eleanor Roosevelt to draft the UNIVERSAL DECLARATION OF HUMAN RIGHTS.

Two months to the day after the conference opened the delegates to UNCIO adopted the Charter on June 25. The minutes of the session recorded that "at this point, the delegates and the entire audience rose and cheered." The following day President Truman addressed the closing session and congratulated the delegates on fulfilling their roles as, what he described two months earlier, "architects of a better world . . . a new world in which the eternal dignity of man is respected."

See also ACHESON, DEAN; DOUBLE VETO; PEARSON, LESTER; REGIONAL ORGANIZATIONS.

Further Reading: Krasno, Jean E. *The Founding of the United Nations. International Cooperation as an Evolutionary Process.* New Haven, Conn.: Academic Council on the United Nations System, 2001. Moore, John Allphin, Jr., and Jerry Pubantz. *To Create a New World? American Presidents and the United Nations.* New York: Peter Lang Publishing, 1999. Russell, Ruth B. *A History of the United Nations Charter: The Role of the United States, 1940–1945.* Washington, D.C.: Brookings Institution, 1958. Simma, Bruno, ed. *The Charter of the United Nations: A Commentary.* New York: Oxford University Press, 1994.

United Nations Conference on the Human Environment (UNCHE)

Opening a new chapter in the THEMATIC DIPLOMACY of the United Nations, the Conference on the Human Environment took place June 5–16, 1972, in Stockholm, Sweden. The Stockholm Conference marked the beginning of the globalization of environmental politics and law, which were then legitimized over the next 30 years by the adoption of new international agreements and the establishment of several UN bodies committed to promoting environmental progress. UNCHE produced the "Stockholm Declaration," 26 principles meant to suggest the environmental obligations and duties of states. There was also a Plan of Action with 109 recommendations, and a proposal that the United Nations establish a new environmental agency to guide the world effort, which led to the creation of the UNITED NATIONS ENVIRONMENT PROGRAMME (UNEP).

In the 1960s private environmental groups were the primary advocates for world action on growing environmental problems. However, by 1968 several major powers, most Western European nations, and some developing countries were urging coordinated action. At the 1968 Glassboro Summit between Soviet and American leaders, President Lyndon Johnson proposed an international meeting on environmental matters as an opportunity for East-West cooperation. On May 20 of that year the Swedish PERMANENT REPRESENTA-

TIVE to the United Nations wrote to the SECRETARY-GENERAL proposing a conference on the human ENVIRONMENT, and his government offered to host the meeting. The convocation in September of a "Biosphere Conference" by the UNITED NATIONS EDUCATIONAL, SCIENTIFIC AND CULTURAL ORGANIZATION (UNESCO) added momentum to the initiative. On December 3, 1968, the GENERAL ASSEMBLY adopted Resolution 2398 authorizing the conference and establishing a lengthy preparatory process.

At Stockholm, to an unprecedented extent, NON-GOVERNMENTAL ORGANIZATIONS (NGOs) were involved in the preparation and activities of a UN conference. More than 400 groups were accredited to the meeting. They were allowed to present statements to the conference and to lobby delegations. They played a critical role in encouraging public support for the effort and provided important expertise related to the environment. NGOs also sponsored a parallel forum while the UN gathering was in session, setting a precedent followed at all future UN thematic conferences. UNCHE secretary-general Maurice Strong, a Canadian, believed NGO participation to be critical not only to the success of the conference but also to the implementation of its initiatives. In its final report the conference called upon not only states but also "citizens and communities, . . . enterprises and institutions at every level [and] . . . [g]overnments and peoples to exert common efforts for the preservation and improvement of the human environment."

The meeting itself, held in the Royal Opera House of Stockholm, attracted 114 governments from all regions of the globe. Only the Soviet Union and its East European allies refused to participate because the conference did not invite the German Democratic Republic, thus avoiding implicit diplomatic recognition. NATION-STATES at UNCHE were unwilling to draft a legally binding document, given the suspicion by developing states that the protection of the global environment might occur at the expense of their modernization activities. Consequently, the final DECLARATION embodied a statement of the existing consensus on the topic. It attempted to strike a balance between the interests of the developed and developing states, and to protect the environment while defending the principle of state SOVEREIGNTY. Over the next two decades, however, the Stockholm Declaration took on increasing political and moral authority, with its provisions often cited in important international documents and agreements.

The declaration's first principle acknowledged that "man has a fundamental right to freedom, equality and adequate conditions of life, in an environment of a quality that permits a life of dignity and well-being." The document also recognized the importance of the natural world in which human beings live. Principle 4 noted the "special responsibility to safeguard and wisely manage the heritage of wildlife and its habitat." For the first time, a UN document recognized the connection between development and environ-

ment (Principle 8), and asserted the principle of "additionality," calling upon the developed world to increase financial assistance to poor countries because of the "additional" costs associated with environmental recommendations made by the conference (Principle 9). Most important, Principle 21 asserted that "States have . . . a sovereign right to exploit their own resources pursuant to their own environmental policies . . . [States have] the responsibility to ensure that activities within their jurisdiction or control do not cause damage to the environment of other States, or of areas beyond the limits of national jurisdiction." Principle 21 soon became "hard" INTERNATIONAL LAW, cited regularly in subsequent international agreements such as the RIO DECLARATION, the STATEMENT OF FOREST PRINCIPLES, and the CONVENTION ON BIOLOGICAL DIVERSITY (CBD), all approved 20 years after Stockholm at the Earth Summit. The principle also highlighted the tension between a government's sovereign authority over its own territory and the global concern about the transboundary environmental impact of a state's domestic activities. This tension went unresolved at Stockholm and remained a central issue in future UN negotiations on environmental matters.

See also COMMITTEE OF INTERNATIONAL DEVELOPMENT INSTITUTIONS ON THE ENVIRONMENT, STATEMENT OF FOREST PRINCIPLES, WORLD COMMISSION ON ENVIRONMENT AND DEVELOPMENT.

Further Reading: Caldwell, Lynton Keith. *International Environmental Policy, Emergence and Dimensions.* Durham, N.C.: Duke University Policy Studies, 1984. Campiglio, Luigi, Laura Pineschi, Domenico Siniscalco, and Tullio Treves. *The Environment after Rio.* London: Graham and Trotman, 1994. Elliott, Lorraine. *The Global Politics of the Environment.* New York: New York University Press, 1998.

United Nations Conference on the Law of the Sea (UNCLOS)

For roughly 350 years, the concept of "freedom of the seas" served as the guiding principle for law of the sea (LOS). This concept safeguarded the rights of seafaring states to use the oceans while limiting the JURISDICTION of states over all but a narrow strip adjacent to their coastlines. By the mid-20th century, various pressures on the oceans brought about several challenges to this long-standing custom. Specifically, concerns over exploitation of global fish stocks by expanded distant fishing fleets, the realization that offshore areas contained significant supplies of natural resources (especially oil and natural gas), increased potential for environmental damage to the marine ENVIRONMENT from various sources (especially increased oil tanker traffic), and the superpower rivalry at sea in the post–World War II era all contributed to the realization that there was a need for modification of existing law of the sea.

The first substantive action that served as an impetus to a revision of LOS was the so-called Truman Proclamation issued by the U.S. president in 1945 by which the UNITED STATES declared jurisdiction over all natural resources of its continental shelf outward to 200 nautical miles. Several Latin American states quickly followed this action by declaring similar jurisdictional zones off their coasts. This so-called enclosure movement expanded with more states claiming often conflicting jurisdictional zones adjacent to their coastlines. By the mid-1950s, the situation had become so serious that the GENERAL ASSEMBLY summoned a conference to develop a CONVENTION on LOS. The first UN Conference on the Law of the Sea (UNCLOS), attended by 86 states, was held in Geneva in 1958. Through four conventions (Territorial Sea and the Contiguous Zone, Continental Shelf, High Seas, and Fishing and Conservation of the Living Resources of the High Seas), much of the existing LOS was codified. These conventions entered into force between 1962 and 1966. A second UNCLOS was convened in 1960 in order to address several ambiguous points concerning the continental shelf and the territorial sea. This conference was unable to produce any substantive changes or additions in the conventions and was generally viewed as a failure by most of the 87 attending states.

One of the more distinctive provisions to emerge from the first UNCLOS was Article 3 of the Convention on the High Seas, which addressed the rights of landlocked states for access to the oceans. The 1965 UN Convention on Transit Trade of Landlocked States further developed this concept. However, very few transit states ratified the convention, thus leaving the issue unresolved and a matter for further consideration at later UNCLOS conferences.

Although the first two UNCLOS did much to clarify international maritime issues and regulations, the potential for future conflicts and disagreements over certain issues remained. A particularly controversial and complex issue was that of deep seabed mining. The presence of vast quantities of mineral nodules throughout the deep ocean area presented potentially contentious questions about their exploitation. In order to avert any serious confrontations over this issue, Dr. Arvid Pardo, Malta's ambassador to the United Nations, called for a DECLARATION in the General Assembly concerning the deep seabed. In December 1967, the General Assembly established an ad hoc committee known as the Seabed Committee to deal with the "peaceful uses of the seabed and ocean floor beyond the limits of national jurisdiction." This committee, enlarged in 1969, worked for three years to produce a declaration of principles on the common heritage of the seabed that was adopted by the General Assembly in 1970. At this time an additional resolution was passed authorizing a third UNCLOS (UNCLOS III).

UNCLOS III officially opened in December 1973 and the working sessions commenced in June 1974. Prior to the opening, the Seabed Committee developed a comprehensive list of 92 subjects to be addressed at the conference. The goal, as would eventually be set forth in the preamble of the convention, was to "settle all issues relating to the law of the sea . . . for all peoples of the world." Specific objectives included: "the establishment of a legal order for the seas, promotion of the peaceful uses of the seas, the equitable and efficient utilization of their resources, the conservation of their living resources, and the study, protection and preservation of the marine environment." Special concern was given to "the interests and needs of developing countries, whether coastal or landlocked." Thus, the conference began with an ambitious set of objectives, and, to ensure that they would be accomplished, two important provisos were set forth at the start. First, the goal was to produce a single, all encompassing convention, not a series of conventions. Second, no VOTING on substantive issues would be taken until "all efforts at consensus had been exhausted." Thus there was to be no vote until there was consensus on the entire convention.

The conference actually consisted of a series of 14 meetings that took place between 1974 and 1982, most in New York and Geneva. More than 150 delegations were in attendance, making UNCLOS III the largest international conference in history up to that time. The conference was divided into three main committees. The First Committee dealt with an international regime on the seabed beyond the limits of national jurisdiction, the Second Committee handled traditional LOS matters as well as the new concept known as the Exclusive Economic Zone (EEZ), while the Third Committee dealt with marine scientific research issues, the preservation of the marine environment, and the transfer of marine technology from the developed states to the less developed world. The conference was shaped in large part by the politics of the time, with states breaking into various blocks based upon regional groupings, issues, development/economic wealth status, and COLD WAR affiliations. Two main groups emerged. The first was made up of the traditional maritime states that were concerned with preserving freedom of the seas and economic exploitation rights of marine resources, including those of the seabed. The other, known as the GROUP OF 77, was comprised of developing states that supported the enclosure concept of expanded national jurisdictional zones and the equitable distribution of marine resources. A third group that was prominent during the conference was the landlocked states, whose primary concern was not to be left out of any LOS arrangement. This last group would actually obtain an entire section of the convention (Part X) devoted to their rights regarding access to the oceans.

The final meeting of UNCLOS III was held at Montego Bay, Jamaica, in 1982. The UN Convention on the LOS that consisted of 17 parts, containing 320 articles and nine annexes, was issued for signature that December. It was truly an all-encompassing, comprehensive TREATY described as the most significant legal instrument of the 20th century concerning the world's oceans. Although dealing with a multitude of issues, the most significant elements of the convention were the establishment of a 12-nautical-mile territorial sea zone (Part II) in which states exercised SOVEREIGNTY while allowing others the right of innocent passage, the creation, in Part V, of a 200-nautical-mile Exclusive Economic Zone extending out from a state's coastline, where the state has legal ownership and management responsibility over all marine resources, economic activity, marine scientific research, and environmental protection efforts. All other states have, according to the same provision, complete freedom of navigation within the EEZ. Of all the stipulations within the convention, those establishing national maritime jurisdictional zones are perhaps the most revolutionary to international LOS. Through the creation of these zones, fully one-third of the ocean's territory falls under some form of national control. This is a major change from the period prior to UNCLOS III when states exercised control over, at most, a three-mile strip outward from their coastline.

The convention also defined the high seas (Part VII) and continental shelf (Part VI) areas and spelled out the rights and responsibilities of states within and over these areas. Other important elements of the convention included a set of rules governing navigation through international straits (Part III), and archipelagic waters (Part IV). Included as well was a regime on islands and semi-enclosed seas (Part IX). Parts XII, XIII and XIV dealt with the protection and preservation of the marine environment, marine scientific research, and the development and transfer of marine technology, respectively. The settlement of maritime disputes (Part XV) was provided for through referral to the INTERNATIONAL COURT OF JUSTICE (ICJ), ARBITRATION, or CONCILIATION. To facilitate further the resolving of disputes, an international tribunal for the LOS was established in 1996 and consists of 21 elected judges who meet in Hamburg, Germany.

Two additional bodies have been created under the auspices of the convention. The INTERNATIONAL SEABED AUTHORITY (ISA), established in 1994, is charged with overseeing the organization and control of activities in the international seabed area beyond the limits of national jurisdiction, and particularly with a view to administering the mineral resources of this area. This body stems from the Agreement on the Implementation of Part XI of the convention that was adopted in 1994 (entering into force in July 1996) after several industrialized states expressed concern over the provisions within Part XI dealing with deep seabed mining. Through the establishment of what is called a "Pioneer Investor Protection" regime, states and companies already having investments in deep seabed mining operations are guaranteed certain rights over their existing mining sites. The ISA is located in Kingston, Jamaica, and it consists of an Assembly, Council, and SECRETARIAT. The other special body is the Commission on the Limits of the Continental Shelf, which was established in 1997 and consists of 21 elected members who meet at the UN HEADQUARTERS. This body is charged with making recommendations concerning states claiming that their continental shelf extends beyond the recognized 200-nautical-mile limit. The Division for Ocean Affairs and the LOS (DOALOS) of the OFFICE OF LEGAL AFFAIRS (OLA) of the United Nations serves as the secretariat of the UN Convention on the LOS.

The most recent related instrument was added under the convention in August 1995 and dealt with the issue of migratory fish stocks, an issue that has proven to be the source of several disputes among signatory states. The Agreement for the Implementation of the Provisions of the UNCLOS of 10 December 1982 Relating to the Conservation and Management of Straddling Fish Stocks and Highly Migratory Fish Stocks attempts to deal with this matter in the hopes of heading off future disagreements. Although 59 states have signed the agreement, only 25 of the required 30 have ratified it and thus it had not been officially authorized as of the end of 2000.

However, the UN Convention on the LOS entered into force in November 1994 when the requisite 60th state ratified. As of June 2000, 133 states had ratified the convention and it had become internationally recognized, even by most of those states that had not yet ratified or even signed it. Thus, it became the basis for all current and future actions involving the law of the seas.

Further Reading: Brown, E.D. *The International Law of the Sea.* Two Volumes. Aldershot, U.K.: Dartmouth, 1994. Degenhardt, Henry W. *Maritime Affairs—A World Handbook: A Reference Guide to Maritime Organizations, Conventions, and Disputes and to the International Politics of the Sea.* Harlow, U.K.: Longman, 1985. Glassner, Martin Ira. *Neptune's Domain: A Political Geography of the Sea.* Boston: Unwin Hyman, 1990. Miles, Edward L. *Global Ocean Politics: The Decision Process at the Third United Nations Conference on the Law of the Sea, 1973–1982.* The Hague: Martinus Nijhoff Publishers, 1998.

— *M. S. Lindberg*

United Nations Conferences on the Least Developed Countries (UNLDC-I, II, III)

Between 1980 and 2001 The UN GENERAL ASSEMBLY convened three WORLD CONFERENCES on the plight of LEAST DEVELOPED COUNTRIES (LDC), acknowledging at each meeting that the many international efforts to lift these impoverished NATION-STATES out of the depths of underdevelopment had largely failed. Conference DECLARATIONS noted that "LDCs as a whole remained marginalized in the world economy," with their per capita incomes in many cases falling, even in absolute terms. Yet each conference developed a Plan of Action to encourage new types of aid from the developed world, and to bring about economic reforms in the LDC that would make these states more competitive in world trade, and more efficient at home.

The first UN conference on the least developed countries occurred in Paris in 1981. It was the product of a long effort by the UNITED NATIONS CONFERENCE ON TRADE AND DEVELOPMENT (UNCTAD) to bring world attention to the states in the developing world that did not seem capable of raising their standard of living. At its first session in 1964 UNCTAD called for special attention to the "LESS DEVELOPED COUNTRIES" among the developing states. The organization created a typology after 1964 that brought about a definition of "least developed countries" in 1971. As growth rates in those states fell during the 1970s, despite the impact of the Second UN DEVELOPMENT DECADE, UNCTAD set up an "Intergovernmental Group on the LDC" that pushed for a new development strategy and an international conference to endorse it.

The 1981 conference adopted the Intergovernmental Group's "SUBSTANTIAL NEW PROGRAMME OF ACTION" (SNPA), which called for decentralization of LDCs' economies, political democratization, and financial transparency at both the national and the international levels. It encouraged far greater contributions of aid and trade preferences by the states of the industrialized North. When UNLDC-II convened nine years later in Paris, there was little evidence that SNPA had halted the slide into extreme poverty. Even compared to less developed countries and upper-income developing countries, the LDCs had declined in all areas of per capita measurement. They had also taken on huge debt burdens that eliminated resources for investment, and they had discouraged foreign direct investment as well. The 150 governments attending the second world conference approved the Paris declaration. It established as its basic principle "shared responsibility and strengthened partnership" between LDC and all other groups—developed states, NON-GOVERNMENTAL ORGANIZATIONS, other developing states, international financial institutions, and the private sector. The conference charged UNCTAD with the implementation of its recommendations, and called upon the WORLD BANK and the UNITED NATIONS DEVELOPMENT PROGRAMME to monitor and encourage country-level efforts to enhance economic vitality.

While economic conditions did not improve noticeably in the least developed states during the 1990s (only one LDC—Botswana—"graduated" from the official list of 49 nations in this category), there were signs that the UN's attention had generated new international and domestic efforts to solve their problems. There was a new interest by lending states and institutions in debt relief, as evidenced by the creation of the Heavily Indebted Poor Country Initiative. An increasing share of multilateral aid flowed to the LDC. The WORLD TRADE ORGANIZATION (WTO) established a special committee and then a Plan of Action to address LDC problems. More trade concessions were granted under the General System of Preferences. Importantly, 33 least developed countries of the 49 undertook economic liberalization and structural reform in their own societies. Nonetheless, between 1990 and 1998 gross domestic product (GDP) grew by only 3.2 percent as compared to 3.4 percent for other developing countries, much of that growth explained by one state's progress, namely, Bangladesh.

It is in this context that SECRETARY-GENERAL Kofi ANNAN opened the Third United Nations Conference on the Least Developed Countries on May 14, 2001, in Brussels, hosted by the European Union. Charged with developing "measures for the SUSTAINABLE DEVELOPMENT of the least developed countries and their progressive integration into the world economy," the conference produced a final declaration and a lengthy Plan of Action. Continuing the commitment to "shared responsibility," the signatories set a goal of 0.15–0.20 percent of developed states' GDP in official development assistance. As of 1998, only five states had achieved that target: Denmark, the Netherlands, Sweden, Norway, and Luxembourg. The conference recognized the "right to development" as one of the "internationally recognized HUMAN RIGHTS." It set as its objectives the halving of the proportion of people living in extreme poverty and suffering from hunger by 2015, the increase in LDC growth rates to 7 percent per annum (with a rate of investment to GDP of 25 percent), the encouragement of public-private cooperation among North-South and South-South countries. Priority issues to be addressed, according to the conference report, included poverty eradication, gender equality, national governance, the environmental goals established in the RIO DECLARATION of the Earth Summit, and the need to reduce HIV infection rates by 25 percent in the most affected countries. Finally, the conference called for the ACCESSION of the least developed states to the World Trade Organization, with the goal of creating "duty-free and quota-free market access for LDC's products in the markets of developed countries."

Further Reading: Secretary-General of UNCTAD. *The Least Developed Countries. 2000 Report.* New York: United Nations, 2000. LDC website: <www.unctad.org/en/subsites/ldcs/ldc11.htm>. UNLDC-III website: <www.unctad.org/en/subsites/ldcs/3-review.htm>.

United Nations Conference on Trade and Development (UNCTAD)

The United Nations Conference on Trade and Development is part of the UNITED NATIONS SYSTEM. A total of 190 nations were members of UNCTAD in the year 2000, including Switzerland and the Holy See, two political entities not members of the United Nations itself. UNCTAD's mission has been to ameliorate the problems of economic underdevelopment

Nelson Mandela and King Hussein at UNCTAD 9 (UN/DPI Photo by John Isaac, Copyright United Nations)

of countries in the global SOUTH by negotiation with the industrialized nations of the North, particularly on issues related to trade.

UNCTAD assists governments, government agencies, and NON-GOVERNMENTAL ORGANIZATIONS in understanding and dealing with foreign direct investment, the connection between foreign investment, trade, technology, and development, and problems related to economic globalization. It carries the task of ensuring the integration of all countries in global trade, and it attempts to assist developing countries in attracting investors by way of reliable, transparent, and comparable financial information at the corporate level. The organization's data is provided in UNCTAD's *Commission on Investment, Technology and Related Financial Issues,* and it disseminates information in its *Division on Investment Technology and Enterprise Development.* It has also undertaken extensive responsibilities for the implementation of the United Nations's SUSTAINABLE DEVELOPMENT program in the developing world.

UNCTAD's first meeting was held in Geneva from March 23 to June 16, 1964. The ECONOMIC AND SOCIAL COUNCIL (ECOSOC) had called for the meeting in August 1962. Such action had been urged by the GENERAL ASSEMBLY, where by 1960 Third World nations held the balance of power. The 1961 RESOLUTION entitled "International Trade as the Primary Instrument for Economic Development" (introduced by Argentina and 16 other Latin American, African, and Asian nations) called on the SECRETARY-GENERAL to survey all UN members on the advisability of holding a conference on international trade. The resolution was approved in the ECOSOC Second Committee by a vote of 45 to 36, with 10 abstentions.

The first initiative for such a conference had come from outside the UN system. The NON-ALIGNED MOVEMENT, a group that began with a conference of Asian and African nations held in Bandung, Indonesia, in 1955, first proposed the idea of a trade conference for development during its 1962 Cairo conference, where 31 nations, now also including Bolivia, Brazil, and Mexico, participated. The Cairo participants proposed that RAÚL PREBISCH serve as secretary-general, and an Egyptian, El Kaissouni, as president of the contemplated conference.

At the same time, the leaders of the nations of the industrialized West were beginning to regard the ability of the so-called developing nations to progress economically to be a matter of concern to their own economies. U.S. president John F. KENNEDY called for the 1960s to be declared the DEVELOPMENT DECADE and the United Nations officially designated it as such.

The first meeting of UNCTAD was expected to be only a conference, but at that meeting delegates recommended making it a permanent organization in the United Nations system, with Prebisch serving as the first secretary-general. The General Assembly established UNCTAD's headquarters at Geneva. Subsequent meetings were held quadrennially, with the next three occurring in nations of the global South—New Delhi, Santiago, and Nairobi.

Prebisch, in contrast to other heads of UN organs, was an active advocate of the interests of the developing nations of the South. The major initiatives undertaken during his tenure included the creation of commodity agreements and the establishment of a General System of Preferences (GSP). Other early concerns included the problems of landlocked nations, shipping regulation, transfer of technology, and cooperation among debtor nations.

Commodity agreements are arrangements among producing nations, sometimes including consuming nations, to cooperate in the marketing of raw materials. The objective of these agreements was to stabilize prices. Two types of mechanisms were employed to accomplish this goal. One was by establishing a fund among producers that would enter the market to buy or sell the product if the prices varied from a preestablished range. This procedure proved successful with tin prices until the early 1970s when world inflation rendered the fund's resources inadequate for the task. An alternate approach was for the member producing nations to establish marketing quotas that would limit the amount of a given product in world trade, thus preventing competition that would result in prices that otherwise often fell below the cost of production. This had been successful in the preexisting sugar and coffee agreements and for OPEC (the Organization of Petroleum Exporting Countries). The UNCTAD SECRETARIAT promoted the establishment of additional commodity agreements and a Common Fund that would support price stabilizing activities. The issue came to a head at the Nairobi meetings in 1976 when Henry Kissinger made a special trip to express U.S. opposition to commodity agreements and to the establishment of the Common Fund. The proposal failed at that time, but a Common Fund was created in 1989. By the 1990s there were no existing commodity agreements that sought to regulate prices. There were, however, several international commodity groups dedicated to improvement of the technology of production, to sharing information about markets and to other forms of cooperation with projects supported through the Common Fund. UNCTAD was successful in achieving acceptance of the preferences for export products in the markets of nations of the industrialized North, but this was accomplished through the implementation of GSPs by individual nations rather than as a unified system. The decline in overall tariff levels meant that this measure created less than the expected tariff differentials.

Although the initial thrust of UNCTAD was undermined by the success of neoliberal policies of open economies gaining acceptance worldwide, the relative decline of developing countries' economies during the 1990s revived interest in the role of the organization. In 1996, at UNCTAD 9, held in Midrand, South Africa, the organization adopted changes in its structure that focused its work, streamlined its relationship with member governments, reduced its staff and improved its link with civil society and other international organizations. UNCTAD's present mission includes pursuing economic development through trade, finance technology, investment, and sustainable development, and helping developing nations deal with the challenges presented by economic globalization. Issues of particular importance include the plight of least developed, landlocked, and island countries, development of Africa, poverty alleviation, the empowerment of WOMEN, and economic cooperation among developing nations. UNCTAD X was held in February 2000 in Bangkok, where, in his concluding remarks, Secretary-General Rubens Ricupero reaffirmed the continuing need for UNCTAD.

See also GROUP OF 77, NEW INTERNATIONAL ECONOMIC ORDER, SUSTAINABLE DEVELOPMENT, UNITED NATIONS CONFERENCE ON ENVIRONMENT AND DEVELOPMENT.

Further Reading: United Nations Conference on Trade and Development. *The History of UNCTAD: 1964–1984.* New York: United Nations, 1985. UNCTAD website: <www.unctad.org/en/enhome.htm>.

— *M. W. Bray*

United Nations Day

The most important day on the United Nations calendar, October 24 marks the anniversary of the entry into force of the United Nations CHARTER in 1945. United Nations Day has been observed since 1948. It is usually celebrated around the world with exhibits, school events, lectures, meetings, and debates.

United Nations Day for Women's Rights and International Peace

The United Nations began observing this day on March 8, 1975—the International Women's Year. In 1977 the General Assembly invited states to declare a national day for WOMEN, and to create nondiscriminatory conditions for women in their societies.

United Nations Decade for Women
(1976–1985)

In December of 1975, the UN GENERAL ASSEMBLY declared the United Nations Decade for Women. The UN focus on WOMEN was triggered by two important factors: first, the growing visibility and demands of the international women's movement, which argued that women be recognized in the international system; and second, the realization that women in developing countries might very well be the key to solving international problems such as population growth, hunger, and poverty. The purpose of the Decade was to encourage governments, NON-GOVERNMENTAL ORGANIZATIONS (NGOs), and various units of the United Nations to focus on the needs of women. In particular, the Decade pressed for the implementation of the World Plan of Action passed at the United Nations WORLD CONFERENCES ON WOMEN held in Mexico in mid-1975. The main themes of the Decade were equality, development, and peace with an emphasis on education, health, and employment for women.

The United Nations Decade for Women provided the impetus for several major women's conferences: at Copenhagen in 1980, Nairobi in 1985, and Beijing in 1995. The Decade also launched a massive research effort, including the gathering of explicit statistics regarding women. Before the Decade, separate statistics on men and women were practically nonexistent. While the outcomes of the work of the United Nations during the decade met with mixed reviews, many UN officials and women's groups agreed with the words of Leticia R. Shahani, the SECRETARY-GENERAL of the NAIROBI CONFERENCE on Women, that "the Decade has caused the invisible majority of humankind—the women—to be more visible on the global scene."

See also CONVENTION ON THE POLITICAL RIGHTS OF WOMEN, UNITED NATIONS DEVELOPMENT FUND FOR WOMEN, WORLD CONFERENCES ON WOMEN.

Further Reading: Pietilla, Hilkka, and Jeanne Vickers. *Making Women Matter: The Role of the United Nations.* 3d ed. London: Zed Books, 1996. Website: <www.un.org/ecosocdev/geninfo/women>.

— *K. J. Vogel*

United Nations Development Fund for Women (UNIFEM)

In 1976, a voluntary fund for the UNITED NATIONS DECADE FOR WOMEN was created to help assist women's development projects. In 1985, the fund officially became a separate agency in autonomous association with the UNITED NATIONS DEVELOPMENT PROGRAMME (UNDP).

According to GENERAL ASSEMBLY Resolution 125, UNIFEM had three purposes: (1) to support innovative development projects benefiting WOMEN; (2) to serve as a catalyst for encouraging the inclusion of women in decision-making processes associated with mainstream development activities; and (3) to serve as a liaison for women in the United Nations's overall system of development cooperation. Since the mid-1990s, UNIFEM has adopted a new program strategy emphasizing what it calls an "ABC approach: Advocacy, Brokering, and Capacity." The aim of this strategy was to strengthen women's economic capacity as entrepreneurs and producers, seek governance and leadership roles for women, and advocate for women's HUMAN RIGHTS.

UNIFEM supports many projects promoting the political, social, and economic empowerment of women within three developing regions of the world: Africa, Asia and the Pacific, and LATIN AMERICA and the Caribbean. These projects range from small grass-roots enterprises that improve working conditions for women to widespread public education campaigns about AIDS and preventing violence against women. Since 1978, UNIFEM has funded projects in more than 100 developing countries with an average cost of $130,000 per project. Since the Fourth WORLD CONFERENCE ON WOMEN, held in Beijing in 1995, UNIFEM has been engaged in urging implementation of the Beijing Platform for Action, which was designed to enhance the empowerment of women in all issues concerning their lives.

The primary source for UNIFEM's income is voluntary contributions from UN member states. Some additional funding comes from UNIFEM's national committees, other international women's organizations, foundations, corporations, and private citizens. Member states with consistently high donations to UNIFEM include the Netherlands, Norway, Canada, and the UNITED STATES.

See also CONVENTION ON THE POLITICAL RIGHTS OF WOMEN, UNITED NATIONS DECADE FOR WOMEN.

Further Reading: Pietilla, Hilkka, and Jeanne Vickers, *Making Women Matter: The Role of the United Nations.* London: Zed Books, 1996.

— *K. J. Vogel*

United Nations Development Programme (UNDP)

The GENERAL ASSEMBLY established the United Nations Development Programme in 1965 to provide technical assistance to developing countries. UNDP HEADQUARTERS is in New York City. As a "programme" of the United Nations, UNDP reports to the General Assembly and is open to all UN member states. It is headed by an administrator who is responsible to a 36-nation Executive Board that represents all major regions and both donor and program countries. The board reports to the General Assembly annually, and it is funded by voluntary contributions from member states.

The UNDP's overall objective is to ensure peace through DEVELOPMENT. It defines development as capacity building through technical assistance in areas ranging from transportation to political and social infrastructure. The three overarching goals of UNDP are to strengthen international cooperation for SUSTAINABLE DEVELOPMENT and to serve as a major substantive resource on how to achieve it, help the UN family become a unified and powerful force for sustainable human development, and focus its strengths and assets in order to make the maximum contribution to sustainable human development in countries it serves.

By the year 2000 UNDP had become the UN program with the largest BUDGET and was the largest multilateral source for grants for sustainable human development. It coordinated most of the technical assistance provided by the UNITED NATIONS SYSTEM, and it provided research and data collection published in the form of statistics and reports. Initially, technical assistance included projects to ensure sufficient supplies of safe drinking water, logistical support for the WORLD HEALTH ORGANIZATION's (WHO) immunization campaigns, and technical support for the construction of durable national and international infrastructure. From exclusively providing technical assistance for long-term goals, the mission statement of UNDP was expanded in the early 1990s to encompass humanitarian assistance and social development. Subsequently, UNDP became increasingly active in diverse fields. In 1991 UNDP established a solar power–based energy supply system in Kiribati and a natural disaster management system in Nepal for securing water supplies. In 1993, UNDP supported the election preparations in CAMBODIA. The 1992 UNITED NATIONS CONFERENCE ON ENVIRONMENT AND DEVELOPMENT (UNCED) dramatically expanded the goals and activities of the UN Development Programme. The Conference's AGENDA 21 called for UNDP to join with the UNITED NATIONS ENVIRONMENT PROGRAMME (UNEP), the WORLD BANK, the UNITED NATIONS CONFERENCE ON TRADE AND DEVELOPMENT (UNCTAD), the GLOBAL ENVIRONMENTAL FACILITY (GEF), the INTERNATIONAL DEVELOPMENT ASSOCIATION (IDA), and regional development banks to carry out more than 1,000 specific recommendations.

The new UNDP of the 1990s coordinated multilateral and bilateral assistance and collaborated with civil society groups, the private sector, and bilateral agencies to help bring a wide range of resources to bear on development. Its guiding principles included guaranteeing national control of development goals, strategies, policies, and programs at all levels, stressing national execution and reliance on local knowledge and institutions, and building on lessons learned and best practices in order to ensure that past experience guided future programming. UNDP made every effort to assure that program designs were results-oriented and encouraged the measurement and evaluation of the impact of its programs. UNDP continued to support technical and other economic cooperation among developing countries.

In order to attain the larger goal of sustainable human development, UNDP focuses on poverty eradication, good governance, public resource management, environmental resources, and food security. To promote poverty eradication UNDP strives to empower the poor through access to productive assets, such as skills, micro-credit, jobs, legal rights for WOMEN and minorities, information, land, energy services, and medium-scale enterprise development. It tries to advance good governance by encouraging democratization, the political empowerment of the poor, and the strengthening of civil society organizations. Environmental resources and food security are targeted through a regime of sustainable policies for management of resources in energy, agriculture, and fishery practices. Contributions to improve public resource management include debt management, the mobilization of external resources, and the "roundtable process," which brings together governments that receive assistance and the donor community. A majority of LESS DEVELOPED COUNTRIES (LDCs) has a roundtable process with their donors, and the UNDP organizes those meetings.

In its efforts to eliminate duplication in UN work, UNDP manages a number of associated funded projects. Among them are the Special Unit/Technical Cooperation among Developing Countries (SU/TCDC) and the UNITED NATIONS VOLUNTEERS (UNV). SU/TCDC promotes cooperation as a strategy to involve developing countries in all aspects of the world economy, and UNV is the only component of the UN system employing volunteers. UNV was established in 1970 and contracts mid-career women and men from all countries for assignments in developing countries. Other associated funds include the UNITED NATIONS DEVELOPMENT FUND FOR WOMEN (UNIFEM), the United Nations Capital Development Fund (UNCDF), the United Nations Fund for Science and Technology for Development (UNFSDT), the United Nations Revolving Fund for Natural Resources (UNRFNRE), and the United Nations Sudano-Sahelian Office (UNSO). UNIFEM provides technical support for alleviating the daily workload of women. One example is the funding of the construction of wood stoves, domestically produced from locally available material, which consume less wood. Another simple but practical innovation of UNIFEM is the provision of wheelbarrows to women, allowing them one trip instead of several to bring back a family's needed water supply from a distant source. Since the FOURTH WORLD CONFERENCE ON WOMEN in Beijing in 1995, UNIFEM has vigorously supported implementation of the Beijing Platform for Action. UNIFEM has worked in three program areas to transform development into an equitable process: strengthening women's economic capacity as entrepreneurs and producers; engendering governance and leadership that increase women's participation in decision-making processes; and promoting HUMAN RIGHTS initiatives to eliminate all forms of violence against women. UNCDF provides credit for the poor in LEAST DEVELOPED COUNTRIES and encourages sustainable uses of natural resources through its local development projects. The United Nations created UNSO in 1973 to spearhead efforts to reverse the spread of DESERTIFICATION and achieve food self-sufficiency in West African countries. As the new millennium began, UNSO's efforts were not limited to West Africa but targeted all areas facing desertification and drought.

UNDP has formed partnerships with other UN program, and SPECIALIZED AGENCIES to address specific issues, such as HIV/AIDS and environmental degradation. UNDP was one of the implementing agencies of the Global Programme to Combat HIV/AIDS, which strives to alleviate the effects of the AIDS epidemic. It also implemented programs funded by the GLOBAL ENVIRONMENT FACILITY (GEF)—founded in 1991—to be in place for the Earth Summit in Rio de Janeiro in 1992. GEF provides funding for countries to translate global concerns into national action in order to prevent ozone depletion, global warming, damage to biodiversity, and pollution of international waters.

UNDP plans, implements, and assesses its work at its headquarters in New York and through its worldwide network of some 132 offices, in over 170 countries and territories. About 90 percent of UNDP's resources—derived primarily from volunteer contributions—go to about 66 nations with close to 90 percent of the world's poorest people. More than 80 percent of UNDP staff is assigned to local offices in developing countries. The offices work closely with the national governments and civil societies of these countries and often function as the local contact and coordination office for the entire United Nations System. UNDP prepares publications, such as the annual *Human Development Report* (published since 1990) and the journal *Cooperation South*. The *Human Development Report* compiles statistics based on comparative country data in order to provide information on specific countries as well as on world and regional trends. The report includes numerous articles that analyze the statistical data with a different focus each year.

See also COMMITTEE OF INTERNATIONAL DEVELOPMENT INSTITUTIONS ON THE ENVIRONMENT, INTER-AGENCY COMMITTEE ON SUSTAINABLE DEVELOPMENT, JOINT UNITED NATIONS PROGRAMME ON HIV/AIDS, UNITED NATIONS OFFICE OF PROJECT SERVICES.

Further Reading: United Nations Development Programme. *Donor Organizations and Participatory Development.* New York: United Nations Development Programme, 1995. *UNDP Newsletter, Human Development Reports.* UNDP website: <www.undp.org/>.

— *A. S. Hansen*

United Nations Educational, Scientific and Cultural Organization (UNESCO)

The United Nations Educational, Scientific and Cultural Organization is a SPECIALIZED AGENCY created on November

1945 by 37 nations participating in the London conference convened for this purpose. The UNESCO constitution, signed on November 16, 1945, dedicated the agency to strengthening peace and security "by promoting collaboration among nations through education, science and culture in order to further universal respect for justice, for the rule of law and for . . . HUMAN RIGHTS and fundamental freedoms." Its HEADQUARTERS was established in Paris from where the organization oversaw the establishment of more than 70 regional offices worldwide. The organization grew in MEMBERSHIP from 20 states in 1950 to 188 in 2000. The membership total has fluctuated, however, because of charges that UNESCO has taken ideological positions despite its largely nonpolitical mission. Ten nations, including the UNITED STATES, the United Kingdom, Portugal, and South Africa, at various times have withdrawn from UNESCO, most of them reestablishing their ties after several years of non-participation.

UNESCO's principal functions are to facilitate technical cooperation, provide experts, and create common international standards in the areas of educational opportunity, science dedicated to the service of development, and the protection of cultural heritage and creativity. Under its auspices a significant number of international CONVENTIONS have been adopted to accomplish these goals. Among the more important have been the Universal Copyright Convention (1952), the Convention against Discrimination in Education (1960), and the Convention concerning the Protection of World Cultural and Natural Heritage (1972). Efforts to implement these PACTS have often brought UNESCO into conflict with governments that defy international standards in the name of SOVEREIGNTY and cultural independence.

The UN Educational, Scientific and Cultural Organization has three primary organs: the General Conference, the Executive Board, and the SECRETARIAT. The General Conference is the supreme governing body of the organization, meets biennially, and is made up of the total membership. Its 31st regular session met in October 2001. The conference sets the BUDGET, approves agency activities, and oversees the work of many subsidiary commissions and committees. It also elects the Executive Board, composed of 58 member states. The board meets twice a year and serves as the administrative council to implement the conference's decisions. Its membership is selected from geographical groupings meant to assure broad representation. The daily operation of UNESCO is directed by a Secretariat divided into five policy bureaus: Education, Natural Sciences, Social and Human Sciences, Culture, and Communication and Information. The Secretariat is headed by a DIRECTOR-GENERAL who is elected by the General Conference to a six-year term. In 1999 Koichiro Matsuura of Japan became the director-general. He directed a staff of more than 2,100 personnel with nearly one-third working at regional offices around the world.

The Secretariat also coordinates relations with hundreds of NON-GOVERNMENTAL ORGANIZATIONS (344 in 2001) that have official relations with UNESCO. In addition, all member states have national commissions that maintain ties to the Paris headquarters. Since 1945 more than 100 advisory and consultative bodies have been established by UNESCO that cooperate with the Secretariat on UNESCO-sponsored projects. Among them are the Intergovernmental Oceanographic Commission, the International Commission on Education and Learning in the 21st Century—chaired in the 1990s by Jacques Delors, the former chairman of the European Union Commission—and the World Commission on Culture and Development, headed from 1992 to 1999 by former UN SECRETARY-GENERAL Javier PÉREZ DE CUÉLLAR.

At the close of the 20th century UNESCO took a special interest in the science of genetics. In 1997 its members adopted the Universal DECLARATION on the Human Genome and Human Rights, the first international statement on the ethics of genetic research. It also renewed its concern over the loss of cultural sites identified on its *World Heritage List.* For example, in 2001 it unsuccessfully joined in the international campaign to preserve religious sites in AFGHANISTAN from destruction by that country's ardent Islamic government. It also launched a cultural awareness campaign in conjunction with the 30th anniversary of the Convention on the Means of Prohibiting and Preventing the Illicit Import, Export, and Transfer of Ownership of Cultural Property. UNESCO joined with Interpol in the effort to find better ways to enforce the convention. As part of the campaign, the organization's governing board approved an International Code of Ethics for Dealers in Cultural Property. Through its Inter-governmental Informatics Programme UNESCO also promoted the rapid integration of developing countries into the global network of electronic information flow, providing media and technology experts, as well as disseminating recommendations on legal and ethical issues related to cyberspace.

See also ENVIRONMENT, EXPANDED PROGRAM OF TECHNICAL ASSISTANCE, GROUP OF 77, INTER-AGENCY COMMITTEE ON SUSTAINABLE DEVELOPMENT, JOINT UNITED NATIONS PROGRAMME ON HIV/AIDS, REFORM OF THE UNITED NATIONS, UNITED NATIONS CONFERENCE ON THE HUMAN ENVIRONMENT, UNITED NATIONS UNIVERSITY.

Further Reading: Imber, Mark. *The USA, ILO, UNESCO, and IAEA: Politicization and Withdrawal in the Specialized Agencies.* London: Macmillan, 1989. Wells, Clare. *The UN, UNESCO and the Politics of Knowledge.* London: Macmillan, 1987. United Nations Department of Public Information. *Basic Facts about the United Nations.* New York: United Nations Department of Public Information, published periodically. UNESCO website: <www.unesco.org>.

United Nations Emergency Force (UNEF)

The unending and unresolved ARAB-ISRAELI DISPUTE has resulted in major wars in the Middle East. On July 26, 1956, Egyptian president Gamal Abdel Nasser nationalized the Suez Canal. Israel invaded the Sinai Peninsula at the end of October. France and Great Britain landed forces, effectively joining the Israelis, and bombarded Egyptian positions. The issue surfaced rapidly in the UN SECURITY COUNCIL, where tension between the annoyed UNITED STATES and its erstwhile wartime allies Britain and France became obvious. A key result was the establishment of the UN's first full-fledged PEACEKEEPING operation, the United Nations Emergency Force. On November 5, 1956, the GENERAL ASSEMBLY (GA), with U.S. concurrence, established UNEF to monitor a cease-fire that, by consequent UN intervention, ended the conflict. On November 17 the cease-fire mandated by the United Nations went into effect under the world organization's supervision. The placement of the Emergency Force along the Sinai was contingent, as would be the case of all early UN peacekeeping efforts, on approval by the sovereign state involved, in this case Egypt. UNEF patrolled the border and monitored the cease-fire until 1967.

In the spring of 1967, Egyptian incursions in the Gaza Strip and Sharm al-Sheik, plus moves by other Arab states, convinced the Israelis that an attack was imminent. Of particular moment was Nasser's insistence that the UN "BLUE HELMETS" that is, the trip-wire UNEF group, be removed in order to open the Sinai for any projected attack. SECRETARY-GENERAL U THANT, shocking many world leaders, conceded to the demand, and he withdrew UNEF. With the buffer zone gone, Israelis (and Arabs) proceeded to launch the MIDDLE EAST WAR OF 1967, resulting in Israeli victory and the occupation of the West Bank, Gaza, East Jerusalem, the Golan Heights, and the Sinai Peninsula. The triumph of the Israelis inaugurated the territorial crisis that plagued the Middle East from 1967 to the turn of the century.

See also BUNCHE, RALPH; EDEN, ANTHONY; PEARSON, LESTER; SUEZ CRISIS; UNITED NATIONS TRUCE SUPERVISION ORGANIZATION; UNITING FOR PEACE RESOLUTION.

Further Reading: Meisler, Stanley. *United Nations; The First Fifty Years.* New York: Atlantic Monthly Press, 1995. Moore, John Allphin and Jerry Pubantz. *To Create a New World? American Presidents and the United Nations.* New York: Peter Lang Publishers, 1999.

United Nations Environment Programme (UNEP)

The United Nations lead organization on environmental affairs, the UN Environment Programme (UNEP) has as its mission "to provide leadership and encourage partnership in caring for the ENVIRONMENT by inspiring, informing and enabling nations and peoples to improve their quality of life without compromising that of future generations." Unlike most other UN bodies, UNEP is headquartered neither in New York City nor in Geneva. It shares the United Nations Office complex (UNON) in Nairobi, Kenya, with the United Nations Centre for Human Settlements (HABITAT/UNCHS). The programme is administered by an executive director and a deputy. (In 1998 Klaus Töpfer of Germany and Shafqat Kakakhel of Pakistan were appointed to these posts, respectively.) They oversee a significant number of departments, UNEP programs, and initiatives in many nations around the world. The policy-making body is the Governing Council, made up of 58 states, that meets biennially and in special sessions in alternate years, and reports to the GENERAL ASSEMBLY (GA) through the ECONOMIC AND SOCIAL COUNCIL (ECOSOC). The executive director, who is nominated by the UN SECRETARY-GENERAL and chosen by the General Assembly, reports to the Governing Council, alerts the council to UN planning proposals dealing with the environment, implements the council's decisions, and advises other UN bodies on environmental affairs.

Created by General Assembly Resolution 2997 (XXVII), December 15, 1972, in response to the recommendation of the UNITED NATIONS CONFERENCE ON THE HUMAN ENVIRONMENT (UNCHE), UNEP began its work with limited expectations from the world community. While the major industrial powers encouraged the creation of a UN STRUCTURE to coordinate environmental activities, they feared paying for a massive new bureaucracy. LESS DEVELOPED COUNTRIES (LDC) were concerned that a new SPECIALIZED AGENCY would create international pressures to limit their development programs. The result was a "programme," not an "agency," with its structure and duties carefully laid out in the authorizing RESOLUTION. A Voluntary Fund was also established to pay for most of the program's expenses. The dependence on contributions and the decision to locate its operations in Nairobi to assuage the less developed world's unease limited the likelihood that UNEP would be a major actor in world affairs.

However, the appointment of Maurice Strong of Canada, who had chaired UNCHE in Stockholm, assured a powerful advocate for UNEP in its formative period. He was succeeded in 1976 by Mostapha Tolba (Egypt) who served four terms as executive director. Tolba's long tenure gave the organization stability, and his effective leadership led to a broad expansion of UNEP's activities. He was also successful in obtaining significant contributions to the Voluntary Fund from the UNITED STATES, Japan, the USSR, Sweden, the Federal Republic of Germany, and the United Kingdom. Another Canadian, Elizabeth Dowdswell, succeeded Tolba in 1993.

The General Assembly elects members to UNEP's Governing Council on a regional basis for four-year terms. Sixteen seats are allocated to African states, 13 to Asia, six to Eastern Europe, 10 to Latin American states, and 13 to Western European and Other states. In turn, the council elects a Bureau with a president, three vice presidents, and a rappor-

teur. Since a majority of seats are held by developing states, the SOUTH has become less concerned that UNEP will unduly serve rich nations' environmental interests. Increasingly, developing states have encouraged UNEP programs on their territories and in their regions. At its 19th session in January and February 1997 the Governing Council approved the Nairobi Declaration, which launched a new era of activism for UNEP. Responding to the momentum established by the 1992 UNITED NATIONS CONFERENCE ON THE ENVIRONMENT AND DEVELOPMENT (UNCED), the Nairobi Declaration committed a "revitalized" United Nations Environment Programme to fulfilling its obligations under AGENDA 21, passed by the Earth Summit. The council declared UNEP the "principal United Nations body in the field of environment." It set a global agenda, which included developing international environmental law aimed at SUSTAINABLE DEVELOPMENT, monitoring state compliance with environmental agreements and principles, serving as a link between the scientific community and policy makers, and strengthening its role as the Implementing Agency of the GLOBAL ENVIRONMENT FACILITY (GEF).

The Governing Council has two subordinate organs: the Committee of Permanent Representatives (CPR) and the High Level Committee of Ministers and Officials (HLCOMO). Usually made up of diplomats serving at national embassies and missions in Nairobi, the CPR meets quarterly, prepares draft decisions for consideration by the Governing Council, reviews reports from the SECRETARIAT, and considers the draft BUDGET. The HLCOMO advises the executive director on emerging environmental issues in order to enable the United Nations Environment Programme to respond in a timely manner. It also supports the executive director in the effort to raise adequate financial resources.

The Secretariat provides extensive environmental information and communication to governments and NON-GOVERNMENTAL ORGANIZATIONS (NGOs). It operates several functional programs, including ones on "Technology, Industry and Economics," "Environmental Information, Assessment and Early Warning," "Environmental Policy and Law," "Environmental Policy Implementation," and "Regional Cooperation and Representation." The last of these is serviced by UNEP offices in Africa, Asia, Europe, Latin and North America, and the Caribbean. UNEP also provides the Secretariat for several international environmental CONVENTIONS, including the MONTREAL PROTOCOL, the CONVENTION ON BIOLOGICAL DIVERSITY, the BASEL CONVENTION, the CONVENTION ON INTERNATIONAL TRADE IN ENDANGERED SPECIES OF WILD FAUNA AND FLORA (CITES), and the CONVENTION ON THE CONSERVATION OF MIGRATORY SPECIES OF WILD ANIMALS (CMS). It also provides secretariats for conventions on climate change, DESERTIFICATION, and regional seas.

The success of UNEP can be credited in significant part to its development of scientific and technical expertise which it employs in a number of successful monitoring and information-sharing programs. Nearly one-fifth of its annual budget is directed toward environmental assessment. UNEP coordinates or sponsors seven critical environmental network programs. (1) *Earthwatch* serves as a coordinating agency for UN system-wide environmental activities. It maintains partnerships with more than 50 UN organs. It also identifies possibilities for cooperation among UN bodies, the scientific community, and NGOs. (2) The Infoterra network is an information exchange system that operates through centers in more than 170 states. Each center provides a national environmental information service. The Infoterra secretariat is located in Nairobi and provides technical services, training manuals, and capacity-building materials. (3) The *Global Environmental Outlook* (GEO) provides a global network of regional multidisciplinary institutes that conduct assessments and forecasts necessary for sustainable development. The collaborating centers use new methodologies, such as modeling, scenario development, and policy debates, to assess the state of the environment in any given region or state. (4) UNEP's *Global Resource Information Database* (GRID) gathers information through a network of more than a dozen focal points around the world on the atmosphere, oceans, climate, transboundary pollution, and renewable resources. Employing the efforts of more than 30,000 scientists, GRID provides a comprehensive database for further research and for policy action in the more than 140 nations with which UNEP works on the project. (5) To provide data to both GRID and Earthwatch, UNEP operates GEMS, the *Global Environment Monitoring System* through 25 sites around the world. (6) The *Environment and Natural Resources Information Networking* (ENRIN) program is administered by UNEP's Environmental Information Networking Unit. ENRIN promotes national and subregional capacities in data and information management in the effort to address issues raised by Agenda 21. It focuses on the developing countries and economies in transition (EIT) in Eastern Europe and provides technical assistance to both national governments and intergovernmental regional organizations. UNEP has appointed regional coordinators to facilitate the work of ENRIN. (7) Finally, the Environment Programme's *Industry and Environment Office* in Paris promotes environmentally sound business practices through cooperation with international businesses.

In the 1970s the United Nations Environment Programme was effectively the only UN organ focused on environmental matters. It became the catalyst and energizer for an international movement that gained public attention and support throughout the decade. From the beginning it sought to form partnerships with other international bodies whose mandate affected the global environment. In 1980 it reached agreement with the WORLD BANK, several REGIONAL DEVELOPMENT BANKS and the UNITED NATIONS DEVELOPMENT PROGRAMME (UNDP) on the formation of the COM-

MITTEE OF INTERNATIONAL DEVELOPMENT INSTITUTIONS ON THE ENVIRONMENT (CIDIE). This set the pattern by which UNEP assured its continued relevance to international environmental affairs. UNEP also carved out areas of expertise and primary concern. Early efforts to protect the world's oceans resulted in a number of regional seas agreements. Nine were signed in the 1970s, beginning with an agreement among countries bordering the Mediterranean. This was followed in the 1980s with six more agreements, together covering many of the regional seas of the world. UNEP officials focused much of their work on organizing the international bargaining process and promoting new ideas for international environmental cooperation. It became an important negotiator in moving the world community toward pollution control, protection of the ozone layer, regulation of transboundary shipments of hazardous wastes, and the protection of biodiversity.

At its fourth session in 1976 the Governing Council adopted a resolution on "Environment and Development," recognizing the link between the global ecological system and development policies in the poorer states of the world. UNEP, thus, was well positioned to take a leading role in the promotion of sustainable development, which became the controlling concept in UN thinking following the Earth Summit in 1992. The concept of sustainable development itself had first evolved from the findings of the 1983 WORLD COMMISSION ON ENVIRONMENT AND DEVELOPMENT (WCED), which in turn had been established by the United Nations at UNEP urging. The 1992 meeting in Rio de Janeiro created the COMMISSION ON SUSTAINABLE DEVELOPMENT (CSD) to monitor progress on its recommendations. The CSD, however, has not emerged as a challenger to UNEP's preeminence in framing the environmental debate, providing authoritative expertise, and initiating new international agreements.

In cooperation with the WORLD METEOROLOGICAL ORGANIZATION (WMO), in the late 1980s UNEP launched two important initiatives. The first was the creation of the INTERGOVERNMENTAL PANEL ON CLIMATE CHANGE (IPCC), which made its first assessment report in August 1990. The work of the panel led to the UNITED NATIONS FRAMEWORK CONVENTION ON CLIMATE CHANGE (UNFCCC), shepherded through the negotiation process by UNEP, and signed at UNCED in 1992. The second was the promotion of a World Climate Conference that convened in November 1990, setting the stage for several climate agreements during the decade. The conference called worldwide attention to the problem of global warming and the need to limit carbon dioxide emissions. UNEP also oversaw the negotiation of the Convention on Biological Diversity, which was opened for signature at the 1992 Earth Summit.

Since its inception the United Nations Environment Programme has concerned itself with the movement of hazardous chemicals. In 1976 it established the International

Register for Potentially Toxic Chemicals (IRPTC), and eight years later created a Provisional Notification Scheme for Banned and Severely Restricted Chemicals. Its work in this area soon led to world experts referencing these substances as "UNEP's Chemicals." UNEP's efforts led to the "London Guidelines" for the exchange of information on chemicals in international trade in 1987, and the subsequent 1989 "Amended London Guidelines." Throughout the period UNEP worked closely with the FOOD AND AGRICULTURE ORGANIZATION (FAO) to develop a code of conduct on the distribution and use of dangerous pesticides.

Chapter 38 of the Earth Summit's Agenda 21 stipulated UNEP as the principal body in the UNITED NATIONS SYSTEM for environmental affairs. Its extensive history of activity assured it no peer in the world community. Agenda 21 assigned it the tasks of developing international environmental law, dealing with environmental emergencies, providing legal and technical advice to governments, and coordinating activities authorized by different international environmental conventions. This mandate led to UNEP's Programme for the Development and Periodic Review of Environmental Law, a new Programme of Action for the Protection of the Marine Environment, and a cooperative Sustainable Cities Programme with habitat. The last of these provided urban environmental planning, and capacity building in local communities. With limited funds but increasing authority the United Nations Environment Programme entered the new century with a broad agenda meant to maintain international momentum toward the protection of the global ecological commons while supporting sustainable development for future generations.

See also VIENNA CONVENTION FOR THE PROTECTION OF THE OZONE LAYER.

Further Reading: Imber, Mark. *Environment, Security and U.N. Reform.* New York: St. Martin's, 1994. Victor, David G., Kal Raustiala, Eugene B. Skolnikoff. *The Implementation and Effectiveness of International Environmental Commitments: Theory and Practice.* Cambridge, Mass.: MIT Press, 1998. Young, Oran B. *International Governance: Protecting the Environment in a Stateless Society.* Ithaca, N.Y.: Cornell University Press, 1994. UNEP website: <www.unep.org>.

UN flag

The UN GENERAL ASSEMBLY adopted a flag for the world organization on October 20, 1947. The flag's background is light blue with the emblem of the United Nations centered in white. The proportions of the flag may be 2:3 (height to fly width), 3:5, or the proportions of the national flag of any country in which the UN flag is flown. The emblem, which is half the height (hoist) of the flag, was approved on December 7, 1946. As adopted by the General Assembly on the recommendation of the SIXTH COMMITTEE, the design is "a map

of the world representing an azimuthal equidistant projection centered on the North Pole, inscribed in a wreath consisting of crossed conventionalized branches of the olive tree, in gold on a field of smoke-blue with all water areas in white. The projection of the map extends to 60 degrees south latitude, and includes five concentric circles."

The five inhabited continents of the world are depicted in the flag's emblem. By picturing the world from the North Pole, no part of the globe is given greater spatial representation to the detriment of other areas. The surrounding olive branches symbolize the UN's commitment to world peace. SECRETARY-GENERAL Trygve LIE issued the Flag Code and Regulations in December 1947 to govern the flag's display and use. The code was amended in 1952 and 1967 to permit individuals and other organizations to demonstrate their support for the United Nations by flying it, or replicating it on other objects.

Further Reading: Abelson, Nathaniel. "Official Symbols of the United Nations." *Flag Bulletin* 34, no. 4 (July–August 1995): 142–52. De Henseler, Max. *The United Nations Emblem and Flag.* Addis Ababa: Mimeo, 1972. Macalister-Smith, Peter. "The United Nations Emblem and Flag." *Nordic Journal of International Law* 55, no. 35 (1986): 262–65.

United Nations Force in Cyprus (UNFICYP)

See CYPRUS DISPUTE.

United Nations Framework Convention on Climate Change (UNFCCC)

The United Nations opened the Framework Convention on Climate Change for signature at the 1992 UNITED NATIONS CONFERENCE ON ENVIRONMENT AND DEVELOPMENT. By 2001 more than 170 nations had signed the agreement, committing themselves to sweeping changes in national policy to protect the atmosphere and slow global warming. The CONVENTION set as its objective stabilizing greenhouse gases (GHGs) in the atmosphere "at a level that would prevent dangerous anthropogenic interference with the climate system." Article 3 of the convention called upon developed countries to "take the lead in combating climate change and the adverse effects thereof." Developed state signatories committed to take steps to return their GHG emissions to 1990 levels by the year 2000. The convention recognized the special problems of LESS DEVELOPED COUNTRIES (LDC) that might have to carry a "disproportionate and abnormal burden" if they had to meet the same standards as the developed states, and, consequently, established that LDC environmental responsibilities would have to be "integrated into national development programmes."

The successful conclusion of a climate TREATY came at the end of a lengthy negotiation process begun by the

WORLD METEOROLOGICAL ORGANIZATION (WMO) and the UNITED NATIONS ENVIRONMENT PROGRAMME (UNEP) in 1988, when the two organizations created the INTERGOVERN-MENTAL PANEL ON CLIMATE CHANGE (IPCC), a multinational committee of scientists and policy experts brought together to provide detailed data on global climate trends. The IPCC, in its *First Assessment Report* in 1990, called for a world convention as soon as possible. Coupled with a GENERAL ASSEM-BLY RESOLUTION (Res. 228) on December 22, 1989, calling for UNCED to devise "strategies and measures to halt and reverse environmental degradation," the IPCC report led to a fast-track negotiation of the terms of the convention. At the Second World Climate Conference in 1990, the Alliance of Small Island States (AOSIS) vigorously pressed for action before global warming led to rising ocean levels threatening their economic development. The General Assembly established the Intergovernmental Negotiating Committee (INC) in 1991 to direct the drafting of the convention.

The convention, which went into force on March 21, 1994, required national inventory reports on greenhouse gases, implementation of national and regional plans to mitigate climate change, the promotion of international cooperation on the transfer of technology, and the provision of additional financial resources from the developed world to the developing countries to assist in meeting the terms of the agreement. Article 7 established the Conference of the Parties (COP) as the supreme body of the convention. Made up of the signatories, COP met annually to assess progress on the convention's guidelines and to promote further progress on climate change measures. At its first meeting (COP-I), held in Berlin in 1995, the conference launched the talks that led to the adoption of the 1997 KYOTO PROTOCOL, which in turn established specific national limits on a group of GHGs to be achieved by 2008–12. In particular, meetings of COP focused attention on the deleterious effects of three greenhouse gases: carbon dioxide (CO_2). methane (CH_4), and nitrous oxide (N_2O). The convention created a SECRE-TARIAT, which since 1996 has been located in Bonn, Germany, at the invitation of the German government. Its head, the executive secretary, is appointed by the SECRETARY-GEN-ERAL of the United Nations in consultation with the COP and holds the rank of assistant secretary-general. The executive secretary reports to the Secretary-General through the UNDER SECRETARY-GENERAL heading the DEPARTMENT OF MANAGEMENT on administrative and financial matters, and through the Under Secretary-General heading the DEPART-MENT FOR ECONOMIC AND SOCIAL AFFAIRS on other matters. As of 2001, Michael Zammit Cutajar (Malta), had headed the organization since it was created in 1991. The convention called for a "financial mechanism," with funds supplied through voluntary contributions, to transfer resources to the developing states. The mechanism has been operated by the GLOBAL ENVIRONMENT FACILITY (GEF) since the convention went into force.

Because the major reductions in greenhouse gases contemplated by the convention were to come from reduced emissions in the developed states, the success of the PACT depended on the commitment of industrialized nations to live up to its terms. The strongest supporters in this group proved to be the members of the European Union. The UNITED STATES, while it had reservations, embraced the convention and the subsequent Kyoto Protocol during the Clinton administration. However, President Clinton's successor, George W. Bush, indicated that the U.S. government would not support the contemplated reductions. Secretary-General Kofi ANNAN, in a speech at Tufts University on May 20, 2001, called President Bush's decision a "grievous setback" that may undercut the "hard-won global gains in combating climate change" since the signing of the UNFCCC.

See also ENVIRONMENT.

Further Reading: Elliott, Lorraine. *The Global Politics of the Environment.* New York: New York University Press, 1998. Grubbs, Michael, Matthias Koch, Koy Thomson, Abby Manson, and Francis Sullivan. *The 'Earth Summit' Agreements: A Guide and Assessment.* London: Earthscan Publications, 1993. Halpern, Shanna. *The United Nations Conference on Environment and Development: Process and Documentation.* Providence, R.I.: Academic Council on the United Nations System, 1993. Young, Oran B. *International Governance. Protecting the Environment in a Stateless Society.* Ithaca, N.Y.: Cornell University Press, 1994. UNFCCC website: <www.unfccc.de/>.

United Nations Headquarters   *See*
HEADQUARTERS OF THE UNITED NATIONS.

United Nations High Commissioner for Human Rights (UNHCHR)

The GENERAL ASSEMBLY created the post of United Nations High Commissioner for Human Rights in 1993, in response to the Vienna DECLARATION and the Program of Action of the WORLD CONFERENCE ON HUMAN RIGHTS. The conference, attended by 177 nations, reviewed, for the first time in 25 years, UN actions in promoting HUMAN RIGHTS. The Assembly charged the Office of the UN High Commissioner with the advocacy of human rights throughout the UNITED NATIONS SYSTEM, and with the promotion of all civil, political, economic, social, and cultural rights. It was also authorized to coordinate all UN programs, agencies, and offices involved in the field of human rights.

As the focal point for all UN human rights activities, UNHCHR serves as the SECRETARIAT for all TREATY bodies relating to human rights, and compiles reports for the various bodies monitoring compliance with human rights

COVENANTS and agreements. It also manages the CENTRE FOR HUMAN RIGHTS in Geneva, which conducts studies and provides recommendations, information, and analysis to all UN organs dealing with human rights issues. As a relatively new office, the post of High Commissioner has expanded the visibility of human rights issues before all the organs and bodies comprising the UN system, and assured more regular review of governmental actions relating to human rights. It has also systemized human rights reporting.

SECRETARY-GENERAL Kofi ANNAN's appointment of Mary Robinson, the former president of Ireland, as the High Commissioner for Human Rights in 1997 brought new attention to the office. Her trip to the war-torn province of Chechnya led to the first debate in UN history on the human rights violations by a PERMANENT MEMBER OF THE SECURITY COUNCIL. Robinson's fact-finding tour of Kosovo and other areas where rights violations had occurred generated increased support for universal JURISDICTION over suspected war criminals. At the time of the MILLENNIUM SUMMIT in September 2000, the Secretary-General gave special significance to the work of UNHCHR in the defense of personal rights.

See also PROGRAMMES AND FUNDS.

Further Reading: Dias, Clarence J. "The United Nations World Conference on Human Rights: Evaluation, Monitoring, and Review." *United Nations-sponsored World Conferences: Focus on Impact and Follow-up.* Edited by Michael G. Schechter. Tokyo: United Nations University, 2001. UNHCHR website: <www.unhchr.ch>.

— *K. J. Grieb*

United Nations High Commissioner for Refugees (UNHCR)

Refugees, from both natural and human-made disasters, have long constituted a major concern of the international system and of the United Nations. The refugee problem increased during the post–COLD WAR era, when civil wars and ethnic and religious conflicts drove a rising number of civilians from their homes, resulting in large-scale movements of peoples and in forced emigration. In 1998 alone there were more than 27 million people made homeless by natural or man-made disasters. This number was equivalent to one out of every 220 of the world's inhabitants.

The 1948 ARAB-ISRAELI war produced huge flows of Palestinian refugees, numbering nearly 700,000 individuals.

Cambodians returning from refugee camps in Thailand (UN PHOTO 159457/P.S. SUDHAKARAN)

Thus in its earliest days the United Nations was confronted with a vast refugee problem. On November 19, 1948, the GENERAL ASSEMBLY created the UN Relief for Palestine Refugees (UNRPR), sought $25 million in voluntary contributions for it, and gave the effort nine months to assist the refugees. In 1949 the Assembly established the post of High Commissioner for Refugees as a response to the broader problem of refugees around the world, and the office began functioning in 1951.

Initially the High Commissioner for Refugees was a non-operational office, but its mandate was expanded in 1952, empowering it to solicit funds and to assist refugees directly. Its mandate included helping displaced persons within the borders of their own country, who, through no fault of their own, had lost their homes to disaster or catastrophe. Both types of victims were covered in the comprehensive term "persons of concern." By 2001, the UNHCR was assisting more than 30 million refugees. Its principal functions were to provide protection for refugees and displaced persons, assure that their HUMAN RIGHTS were protected, and seek enduring solutions to their plight while furnishing them with temporary assistance. In all cases it sought to secure the voluntary repatriation of the refugees to their home country or area, and to provide them with the means to restart their lives. If this proved impossible, the UNHCR assisted with the integration of refugees into their host country. By the late 1990s, the Office of the High Commissioner for Refugees numbered more than 5,000 personnel, and it maintained offices in 122 countries, reflecting the breadth of its work. This meant that the High Commissioner had one staff member to assist 4,515 people in need.

As of 2001, a 50-member Executive Committee oversaw the Office of the High Commissioner, meeting annually to determine general policies. The members of the committee are elected by the ECONOMIC AND SOCIAL COUNCIL with due regard for geographical distribution of the UN MEMBERSHIP. About 95 percent of the agency's $1 billion operating budget in 2001 came from 15 major donor nations. Voluntary contributions are used to provide assistance in the field, with administrative costs met through a small portion of the regular UN BUDGET. The Office of the High Commissioner works in partnership with more than 400 NON-GOVERNMENTAL ORGANIZATIONS to assist persons in need by providing basic temporary shelter, food, and health care. The UNHCR has increasingly worked in cooperation with PEACEKEEPING operations, providing assistance to the civilians affected by conflicts. This latter undertaking has important implications, since troops on peacekeeping missions at the turn of the century were more and more called upon to protect the delivery of humanitarian assistance, adding a new responsibility to their missions.

In addition to providing assistance, the Office of the High Commissioner has primary responsibility for providing and promoting international protection of persons dispossessed of their homes. This protection is guaranteed and codified by the CONVENTION RELATING TO THE STATUS OF REFUGEES of 1951, and its 1967 Optional PROTOCOL, which extended the rights accorded to refugees, guaranteeing them access to local government offices and standard protections accorded to citizens of the host country. By 1997, 134 states were parties to these agreements. In recognition of the significance, and the strictly humanitarian and nonpolitical nature of its work, the Office of the High Commissioner for Refugees has twice been awarded the Nobel Peace Prize, in 1954 and 1981.

See also MILLENNIUM SUMMIT, ORGANIZATION OF AFRICAN UNITY, PROGRAMMES AND FUNDS, SOMALIA.

Further Reading: Nicholson, Frances, and Patrick Twomey, eds. *Refugee Rights and Realities: Evolving International Concepts and Regimes.* Cambridge: Cambridge University Press, 1999. United Nations High Commissioner for Refugees. *State of the World's Refugees.* New York: United Nations, issued every two years. UNHCR website: <www.unhcr.ch>.

— *K. J. Grieb*

United Nations India-Pakistan Observation Mission (UNIPOM)

During the summer of 1965 hostilities broke out between India and Pakistan over the disputed state of Jammu and KASHMIR. The two powers had fought over the region in 1949, leading to the deployment of the UNITED NATIONS MILITARY OBSERVER GROUP IN INDIA AND PAKISTAN (UNMOGIP) to supervise an uneasy cease-fire. The resumption of fighting led to a SECURITY COUNCIL resolution on September 6, 1965, asking the UN SECRETARY-GENERAL to intervene diplomatically in order to restore the cease-fire. The conflict quickly spread beyond Jammu and Kashmir to the international border between Pakistan and India, prompting Security Council RESOLUTION 211 demanding a halt in hostilities and a return of military forces to the positions that they held on August 5. Secretary-General U THANT, on his own authority, decided to establish an adjunct mission to UNMOGIP for the purpose of supervising the called-for cease-fire outside of Jammu and Kashmir. The United Nations India-Pakistan Observation Mission was staffed with 96 observers from 10 nations who had no authority to enforce the cease-fire, but they were charged with persuading local commanders to honor it.

As the product of negotiations between India and Pakistan mediated by the USSR, the two sides announced on January 10, 1966, the Tashkent Agreement, which committed the parties to the withdrawal of forces to the lines requested earlier by the Security Council. UNIPOM provided GOOD OFFICES for the withdrawal process from the border of Kashmir to the Arabian Sea. The mission was terminated on March 22, 1966, having cost the United Nations $1,713,280 and no fatalities.

See also DEPARTMENT OF PEACEKEEPING OPERATIONS, PEACEKEEPING.

Further Reading: United Nations Department of Public Information. *The Blue Helmets: A Review of United Nations Peace-Keeping.* 3d ed. New York: United Nations Department of Public Information, 1996. UNIPOM website: <www.un.org/Depts/dpko/dpko/co_mission/unipom.htm>.

United Nations Industrial Development Organization (UNIDO)

Created by the UN GENERAL ASSEMBLY in 1966, the 169-member (as of November 2001) United Nations Industrial Development Organization assists with the development of industry in developing countries and states with economies in transition. Headquartered in Vienna, UNIDO provides information, skills, and technology to its members in order to promote industrialization that will be economically sound and environmentally friendly. It is also one of four implementing agencies of the MONTREAL PROTOCOL, which phases out the use of ozone-depleting substances. UNIDO maintains field offices in 36 nations and investment and technology promotion offices in 12.

UNIDO became a SPECIALIZED AGENCY in the UNITED NATIONS SYSTEM in 1985. Led by a DIRECTOR-GENERAL— Carlos Magariños from Argentina was first appointed in 1997 and recommended for a second term of four years in June 2001—UNIDO employs more than 350 staff in Vienna and another 100 in the field. It also contracts with more than 1,500 experts on a regular basis for specific projects. The director-general reports to the General Conference of the MEMBERSHIP, which meets every two years in order to set policy, approve the BUDGET ($132.9 million in 2000–01), and elect representatives to the 53-member Industrial Development Board and the 27-member Programme and Budget Committee. The Industrial Development Board conducts the business of the organization between meetings of the General Conference. UNIDO is funded by assessed contributions from its members, allocations from the UNITED NATIONS DEVELOPMENT PROGRAMME, the Common Fund for Commodities, and the Multilateral Fund for the Implementation of the Montreal Protocol.

In 1997 the board and the General Conference approved a sweeping revision of UNIDO's work when it endorsed the *Business Plan for the Future Role and Function of UNIDO.* The *Business Plan* clustered the organization's work into two "tracks": strengthening industrial capacities, and producing "cleaner and sustainable industrial development." Both areas were to be focused primarily on the LEAST DEVELOPED COUNTRIES (LDC), especially on the agricultural industries of Africa. The plan emphasized cooperation with the private sector, the provision of comprehensive UNIDO services, and the integration of WOMEN in industrial development. It also

called for a streamlining of UNIDO's STRUCTURE, following in the general trend toward efficiency and REFORM throughout the UNITED NATIONS SYSTEM. Under the plan in 2001, UNIDO had developed 44 programs in technical cooperation costing $65 million. A total of 55 percent of that amount was allocated to sub-Saharan Africa.

Defining itself as a "global forum" on industrialization, UNIDO produces a number of public reports and publications. It provides databases covering industrial statistics, the business environment, finance, and energy. Annually it publishes the *World Industrial Development Report.* It also maintains "UNIDO Exchange," a business intelligence network.

See also ADMINISTRATIVE COMMITTEE ON COORDINATION, GROUP OF 77, INTERNATIONAL TRADE CENTRE, JOINT INSPECTIONS UNIT.

Further Reading: New Zealand Ministry of Foreign Affairs. *United Nations Handbook.* Wellington, N.Z.: Ministry of Foreign Affairs and Trade, published annually. UNIDO website: <www.unido.org>.

United Nations Institute for Disarmament Research (UNIDIR)

UNIDIR began operations in 1980 as a result of recommendations made by the SPECIAL SESSION ON DISARMAMENT in 1978, and it was approved by the UN GENERAL ASSEMBLY on December 13, 1982, as "an autonomous institution within the framework of the United Nations." The institute's small permanent staff is located in Geneva, Switzerland. Funded by voluntary contributions and the regular UN BUDGET, UNIDIR implements its program through short-term project contracts with experts and research organizations in the field of DISARMAMENT and arms control. The agency's purpose is to provide the international community with data and analyses on problems related to the arms race, particularly in the nuclear field, and international security. It also promotes and assists ongoing disarmament negotiations.

The director of UNIDIR is appointed by the UN SECRETARY-GENERAL. In 1997, Pamela Lewis from the United Kingdom was appointed to the post. The Secretary-General's Advisory Board on Disarmament Matters serves as UNIDIR's Board of Directors. The Advisory Board was originally appointed by Secretary-General Kurt WALDHEIM, and permanently established by the General Assembly in 1983. The board's 20 members authorize UNIDIR's program, and report annually to the General Assembly.

As the new millennium began, UNIDIR undertook projects on the costs of disarmament, tactical nuclear weapons, strengthening the role of REGIONAL ORGANIZATIONS in arms control TREATY implementation, the illicit traffic in small arms, and information technology warfare. It also sponsored meetings of experts, government representatives, and international organization personnel on such varied topics as

NUCLEAR-WEAPONS-FREE ZONES in the Next Century, Biological Warfare and Disarmament, the U.S. Missile Defense Proposal, and the Uses of Commercial Satellite Technology in the Middle East. Its most pressing agenda item in 2001, however, was the revitalization of the CONFERENCE ON DISARMAMENT (CD) as the premier negotiating forum on the topic. Growing out of a UNIDIR meeting of more than 100 participants from 60 countries in November 2000, the institute promoted a number of REFORMS in the conference's structure and process. It suggested an end to the consensus rule at least on procedural matters, the inclusion of all UN member states, an expanded role for NON-GOVERNMENTAL ORGANIZATIONS in the CD, and the development of a new mandate for the conference, including a new emphasis on preventing an arms race in outer space.

To promote regional cooperation in disarmament studies UNIDIR maintains a Visiting Fellowship Program that brings to Geneva four researchers from different countries in the same region to work together for four to six months. The fellows work on problems of regional arms control and their work is used as the basis for policy discussions. UNIDIR also publishes the quarterly journal *Disarmament Forum* for scholars, policy makers and interested individuals, with each issue focused on a single topic.

See also PROGRAMMES AND FUNDS.

Further Reading: UNIDIR website: <www.unog.ch/unidir>.

United Nations Institute for Training and Research (UNITAR)

UNITAR, created in 1965, is an autonomous body within the UNITED NATIONS SYSTEM. Its mandate is to improve and aid the effectiveness of the United Nations by way of training and research. It organizes training programs annually for thousands of participants. Targeted audiences include diplomats assigned to the United Nations and individuals from Third World nations interested in assignments with UN bodies SPECIALIZED AGENCIES, or in the civil service of their own countries that might be related to UN work. UNITAR offers training and research in a variety of topics, including social and economic development, peacemaking, information and communications technologies, environmental law, and environmental management.

The institute's main HEADQUARTERS is at the Palais des Nations in Geneva. There is also an active office in New York that conducts training programs at the rate of about two or three every month for delegates working at UN headquarters there. The governing body of UNITAR is its 21 member Board of Trustees, appointed by the UN SECRETARY-GENERAL, who serves as an ex officio member of the board. In 2001 the executive director was Marcel A. Boisard from Switzerland.

Further Reading: UNITAR website: <www.unitar.org>.

United Nations Interim Administration Mission for Kosovo (UNMIK)

Following the secession of BOSNIA from Yugoslavia through civil war and the 1995 DAYTON PEACE ACCORDS, the president of the remaining Federal Republic, Slobodan Milosevic, moved to crush the ethnic Albanian drive for independence in Kosovo. Fighting between Yugoslavia's army and the Kosovo Liberation Army (KLA) reached fever pitch in 1999 with thousands of Kosovar refugees forced to flee to the Albanian mountains and to Macedonia. When a peace proposal (arranged by Richard Holbrooke, U.S. PERMANENT REPRESENTATIVE to the United Nations) could not be negotiated between the two sides, the North Atlantic Treaty Organization (NATO) bombed Yugoslav targets in both Kosovo and Serbia. Milosevic accepted a UN-approved peace agreement on June 3, 1999. By then, according to the UN HIGH COMMISSIONER FOR REFUGEES, at least 850,000 people had been displaced from their homes in Kosovo. One week later the SECURITY COUNCIL adopted RESOLUTION 1244 directing the SECRETARY-GENERAL to establish an interim administration in Kosovo—UNMIK—that would provide civilian administration in the province and move Kosovo toward self-governance.

UNMIK's task was particularly difficult since it was charged with developing Kosovar autonomy, yet maintaining Kosovo as an integral part of Yugoslavia. The Belgrade government opposed the UN's and NATO's presence within Yugoslavia, and the KLA hoped to limit the duration of foreign intervention, desiring ultimately to create an independent Kosovar state. Under the adroit leadership of the SPECIAL REPRESENTATIVE OF THE SECRETARY-GENERAL, Dr. Bernard Kouchner of France, UNMIK moved quickly to provide humanitarian assistance and basic governmental and social services. UNMIK administrators reestablished education, postal and communication services, health care, banking, and law and order institutions. The mission also introduced a democratization process that achieved the electoral registration of voting age citizens and the completion of successful municipal elections in October 2000.

UNMIK's performance in Kosovo was an example of relatively successful NATION-BUILDING by the United Nations. Kouchner's approach to restoring normalized civilian society included the creation of the Joint Interim Administrative STRUCTURE (JIAS). At every level of Kosovar life UN administrators worked with representatives from the various communities in the province, sharing the decision-making process on nearly all matters. The October 2000 elections selected 30 municipal assemblies that took responsibility, under the supervision of UN staff, for day-to-day services. At the regional level 20 administrative departments were created, each operated by UN personnel and local officials reflective of Kosovo's diversity. The province as a whole was subject to the 36-member Kosovo

Transitional Council (KTC). The KTC reflected an effort at building tolerance among the many ethnic and religious communities. In May 2001 the council approved a "Constitutional Framework for Kosovo." The KTC held its last meeting in October 2001, as the province prepared for comprehensive elections on November 17. Following his resignation in January 2001, Kouchner's policies were continued by his successor, Hans Haekkerup, the former defense minister of Denmark.

When UNMIK entered Kosovo, there was skepticism that a UN PEACEKEEPING operation could be successful in overcoming ethnic Serb-Albanian animosity. Fearful of KLA retribution, and faced with sporadic bloody reprisals, almost immediately upon the cessation of NATO bombing in 1999, Serbs began a mass exodus. This emboldened KLA leaders, who rapidly sought to impose independent control on the province. To insure UNMIK authority, NATO forces under UN mandate were dispatched as the Kosovo Force (KFOR). Troops provided security for the civilian populace, and, more important, began the disarming and demilitarization of the KLA. UNMIK assisted this effort by establishing the Kosovo Protection Corps that attracted KLA manpower to the tasks of providing emergency and reconstruction services. Some of KFOR's duties were then transferred to the UNMIK police and to the newly created Kosovo Police Service. The election of President Vojislav Kostunica in Yugoslavia, replacing the indicted war criminal Milosevic and returning democratic politics to the republic, also contributed to the pacification of Kosovo. By the close of 2001, two and a half years after intervention by the United Nations and at great cost to the international community ($207.4 million for 2000–01), relative stability and a working civil society had been restored to Kosovo. Hans Haekkerup stepped down as head of UNMIK in January 2002 and was replaced by senior German diplomat Michael Steiner.

See also FORMER YUGOSLAVIA, UNITED NATIONS VOLUNTEERS.

Further Reading: Schnabel, Albrecht, and Ramesh Thakur, eds. *Kosovo and the Challenge of Humanitarian Intervention.* New York: United Nations University, 2000. UNMIK website: <www.un.org/peace/kosovo/pages/kosovo12.htm>.

United Nations Interim Force in Lebanon (UNIFIL)

Established by the SECURITY COUNCIL (SC) on March 19, 1978, UNIFIL was sent to the Middle East to confirm withdrawal of Israeli forces that had invaded southern Lebanon in mid March in response to an earlier Palestinian commando attack, restore international peace and security in the area, and assist the Lebanese government in returning its effective authority to its southern region. The force, still in that country in 2002, seemed less and less "interim" as

troubled Lebanon remained embedded in the ARAB-ISRAELI DISPUTE, the longest ongoing challenge to the United Nations.

Lebanon had been joined with Syria as a single political unit in the Ottoman Empire. But after the defeat and collapse of the empire in World War I, France gained a LEAGUE OF NATIONS mandate over both Lebanon and Syria and divided them into separate administrations, detaching predominantly Muslim Syria from multireligious Lebanon, where the majority Maronite Christians became the dominant influence. Lebanon achieved independence at the conclusion of World War II and established a government that tried to provide equitable representation among the often bickering religious groups. It became an original member of the United Nations on October 24, 1945. But with competing Maronite Christians, Sunni Muslims, Shiite Muslims, and Druze (a religious faith incorporating aspects of Islam and Gnosticism), the country began a cycle of civil wars in the late 1950s.

By the early 1970s the delicate balance among Lebanese ethnic and religious groups was badly disrupted by a new wave of Palestinian refugees. Driven out of Jordan by King Hussein in 1970, they joined Palestinians who had come to Lebanon after 1948 and others who had arrived after the MIDDLE EAST WAR OF 1967. Between March 1975 and November 1976 an estimated 40,000 Lebanese were killed in civil strife, which only ended when a Syrian force intervened. Subsequently, Palestinian guerrillas living in Lebanon began to stage raids on Israel to the immediate south, dragging Lebanon into the wider regional conflict. On March 11, 1978, commandos, in a daring cross boundary attack, killed and wounded many Israelis. On March 14 Israeli forces invaded Lebanon and within days occupied the southern part of the country except for Tyre (the famous ancient city of Phoenicia). Beirut appealed to the Security Council, insisting that it had no connection with the Palestinian raid and protesting the invasion. On March 19 the Council adopted two RESOLUTIONS, 425 and 426, calling on Israel to halt its military action and withdraw its forces and establishing the UN Interim Force in Lebanon, and providing it with operational guidelines.

In June 1978, Israel withdrew. But, because of the activities of the various, virtually autonomous, militias in the country, and because of conflict between Syrian forces and Christians, as well as Israeli air raids in the Beirut region, the central government appeared powerless. Under such circumstances, UNIFIL's directive to restore peace and security and to assure the return of legitimate and effective Lebanese government control in the south seemed unattainable. Then, on June 6, 1982, Israel invaded again, this time driving all the way to Beirut. The following three years witnessed a massacre by Israeli-allied Christian forces in Palestinian refugee camps in a Beirut suburb, the short-lived intrusion of a multinational force from the UNITED STATES, the United Kingdom, France, and Italy, and the departure of the Pales-

UNIFIL, 1980 (UN Photo/J.K. Isaac)

tine Liberation Organization (PLO), whose center of operations had been in Lebanon's capital. UNIFIL found itself behind Israeli lines and limited to providing humanitarian assistance. In 1985 Israel withdrew partially, but continued its presence in southern Lebanon, where the Israel Defense Forces (IDF) and an allied Lebanese de facto force (DFF— the "South Lebanon Army") took control. Resolution 425's mandate remained unfulfilled and UNIFIL remained in Lebanon.

Finally, in April 2000, the Israeli government of Prime Minister Ehud Barak notified SECRETARY-GENERAL Kofi ANNAN of its intention to withdraw all forces from Lebanon by July "in full accordance with Security Council Resolutions 425 and 426." To help expedite the withdrawal, Annan sent a SPECIAL ENVOY, Terje Roed-Larsen of Norway, the force commander of UNIFIL, and a team of experts to meet with the governments of Israel and Lebanon, other concerned states in the region, the League of Arab States, and the PLO. Withdrawal began on May 16, earlier than anticipated, and in the midst of hostile fire. Within days large crowds entered the area formerly under occupation. Many members of the de facto Lebanese forces retreated

with the Israelis. By June 16 the Secretary-General was able to report to the Security Council that withdrawal had been completed in compliance with Resolution 425; on July 20 he reported that all guns had fallen silent. By late August the formerly occupied territory participated for the first time since 1972 in a parliamentary election, and by January 2001, according to the Secretary-General, about 1,600 former members of the de facto forces, and their families, had returned to Lebanon.

But challenges lingered. Mine clearance was an acute problem. Numerous minor violations of the line of withdrawal (the so-called Blue Line) took place on both sides. On October 7, 2000, Israeli troops opened fire on a crowd trying to cross the Israeli border fence, and that same day the Islamic guerrilla group Hizbollah breached the cease-fire by launching an attack across the Blue Line and taking three Israeli soldiers prisoner. The UN hope for "peace and security" in Lebanon was still problematic. Well into late 2001 the Lebanese central government in Beirut continued to take the position that as long as there was no comprehensive peace with Israel, its army would not act as a border guard in the south. As a consequence, Hizbollah was left to control the area, and Resolution 425's insistence on the return of Lebanese government administration was frustrated. For all of these reasons, Secretary-General Annan recommended to the Security Council that UNIFIL remain in Lebanon, admitting that the role of the force had become more of an observer mission than a PEACEKEEPING one. The Council consistently responded positively to these recommendations. On July 31, 2001, it extended UNIFIL's mission to at least January 22, 2002.

As of late 2001, UNIFIL had been in Lebanon for more than 23 years. Headquartered at Naqoura in southern Lebanon, its force strength had varied over that time but was about 4,500 in summer 2001, supplemented by more than 500 international and local civilian staff and 50 military observers from the UNITED NATIONS TRUCE SUPERVISION ORGANIZATION—the first UN peacekeeping operation set up in the Middle East. Personnel for UNIFIL came from Fiji, Finland, France, Ghana, INDIA, Ireland, Italy, Poland, and Ukraine. As of August 2, 2001, the force had suffered 243 fatalities.

See also MIDDLE EAST WAR OF 1973.

Further Reading: Collelo, Thomas, ed. *Lebanon: A Country Study.* 3d ed. Washington, D.C.: U.S. Government Printing Office, 1989. New Zealand Ministry of Foreign Affairs. *United Nations Handbook.* Wellington, N.Z.: Ministry of Foreign Affairs and Trade, published annually. UNIFIL website: <www.un.org/Depts/DPKO/Missions/unifil>.

United Nations International Drug Control Programme (UNDCP)   *See* OFFICE FOR DRUG

CONTROL AND CRIME PREVENTION.

United Nations Interregional Crime and Justice Research Institute (UNICRI)

The ECONOMIC AND SOCIAL COUNCIL (ECOSOC), by RESOLUTION 1086 B in 1968, established the United Nations Social Defence Research Institute (UNSDRI), the predecessor to UNICRI. ECOSOC simultaneously asked the SECRETARY-GENERAL to strengthen UN efforts to prevent and control juvenile delinquency and adult crime. Secretary-General U THANT formally inaugurated UNSDRI on April 29, 1969. Originally UNSDRI conducted international comparative research to support the UN Crime Prevention and Criminal Justice Programme. As MEMBERSHIP in the United Nations grew, bringing more and more developing countries into the organization, the challenges to UNSDRI also grew and became more multifaceted. As a consequence, ECOSOC in 1989 reconstituted UNSDRI as the United Nations Interregional Crime and Justice Research Institute.

Article II of its statute (established in ECOSOC Resolution 1989/56) details UNICRI's objectives and functions,

which include research, training, field activities, and the collection, exchange, and dissemination of information to improve crime prevention and control. The institute is expected to collaborate with countries concerned and support field activities to create reliable bases of knowledge and information on social problems regarding juvenile delinquency and adult crime, with special concern directed at the transnational forms of these problems. Other duties include developing strategies and policies to aid in the prevention and control of crime. In 2001 the institute was engaged in several ongoing projects, including a Global Programme against Trafficking in Human Beings, a Global Programme against Corruption, a Global Study on Illegal Drug Markets, a Drug Abuse Comprehensive Project, an International Crime Victim Survey, and an International Business Crime Survey.

In 2001 UNICRI's headquarters was in Rome, where UNSDRI had been located. Eventually, however, in accordance with a 1995 agreement with the Italian government, the institute was scheduled to move to Turin. UNICRI is funded by voluntary contributions, made by governments, international organizations, and public or private institutions. In 2001 it had a staff of about 20, made use of expert consultants, and was governed by a Board of Trustees. The board was composed of seven members selected by the UN Commission on Crime Prevention and Criminal Justice. ECOSOC endorses the selections. Board members are chosen according to equitable geographical distribution and are expected to be experts in the field of crime prevention. They serve for five-year terms and are eligible for one reappointment term. The Board of Trustees determines the BUDGET, approves the work program, and formulates all guidelines for UNICRI.

See also PROGRAMMES AND FUNDS.

Further Reading: UNICRI website: <www.unicri.it>.

United Nations Iraq-Kuwait Observation Mission (UNIKOM)   *See* GULF WAR.

United Nations Library   *See* DAG HAMMARSKJÖLD

LIBRARY.

United Nations Military Observer Group in India and Pakistan (UNMOGIP)

The 1947 partition plan for the Indian subcontinent allowed the state of Jammu and KASHMIR to join either Pakistan or India. Following its ACCESSION to India, an act disputed by Pakistan, fighting broke out between India and Pakistan. In January 1948 the UN SECURITY COUNCIL appointed the

United Nations Commission for India and Pakistan (UNCIP) to conduct an INQUIRY and to provide MEDIATION between the parties. UNCIP proposed, among other items, the deployment of UN observers to monitor a cease-fire. Accepted by both sides. UNMOGIP observers arrived in January 1949. The UN mission remained in place through the remainder of the century, and it continued operations as of January 2002, making it one of the longest peace operations in UN history.

UNMOGIP observers were directed to investigate and report violations of the cease-fire but not to interfere with Indian or Pakistani military operations. During its first 15 years of operation, UNMOGIP employed between 35 and 67 observers. This number grew in 1965 when hostilities broke out between the two nations. It was augmented with the creation of the UNITED NATIONS INDIA-PAKISTAN OBSERVER MISSION (UNIPOM), an adjunct operation outside of Jammu and Kashmir. Following the restoration of the cease-fire and the withdrawal of forces in 1966, UNMOGIP continued its responsibilities until yet another outbreak of war in 1971.

Rising tensions between India and Pakistan in 1971, and a secessionist movement in East Pakistan led UN SECRETARY-GENERAL U THANT to invoke his powers under Article 99 of the CHARTER to convene the Security Council to consider the impending conflict on the subcontinent. Due to a deadlock among the PERMANENT MEMBERS, a Council majority invoked the UNITING FOR PEACE RESOLUTION to convene an EMERGENCY SPECIAL SESSION OF THE GENERAL ASSEMBLY. On December 7 the Assembly adopted RESOLUTION 2793 demanding a cease-fire, which was honored by both sides on December 17. Subsequently, the Security Council authorized UNMOGIP to monitor the established cease-fire line.

Over the next three decades Pakistan regularly reported to UNMOGIP "violations" by India. The Indian government, however, took the position that UNMOGIP's mandate had lapsed with the 1971 war. In July 1972 the two sides agreed to a line of control in Jammu and Kashmir, roughly corresponding to the cease-fire line established in 1949. With this agreement India opposed the continuation of the UN mission. Succeeding Secretaries-General, nonetheless, took the position that only the Security Council could terminate the operation, which it had not done by the end of 2001. As of August 31 of that year, UNMOGIP had cost the United Nations approximately $100 million, paid out of the UN regular BUDGET. It had a force of 45 military observers, 24 international civilian personnel, and 42 local civilian staff. Its commander, Major-General Hermann K. Loidolt from Austria, oversaw personnel from his home country and from Belgium, Chile, Denmark, Finland, Italy, South Korea, Sweden, and Uruguay.

See also DEPARTMENT OF PEACEKEEPING OPERATIONS, PEACEKEEPING.

Further Reading: United Nations Department of Public Information. *The Blue Helmets: A Review of United Nations Peace-Keeping.* 3d ed. New York: United Nations Department of Public Information, 1996. UNMOGIP website: <www.un.org/Depts/DPKO/Missions/unmogip/body_unmogip.htm>.

United Nations Mission in Bosnia and Herzegovina (UNMIBH)

The DAYTON PEACE ACCORDS, which ended the fighting in BOSNIA and Herzegovina, were signed in Paris on December 14, 1995. The three Balkan states that were signatories to the agreement—the Republic of Bosnia and Herzegovina, the Federal Republic of Yugoslavia, and the Republic of Croatia—called for the establishment of a UN International Police Task Force (IPTF) to be deployed throughout the conflict area. The SECURITY COUNCIL responded on December 21 in Resolution 1035 with the creation of IPTF and a UN civilian office headquartered in Sarajevo and headed by a SPECIAL REPRESENTATIVE OF THE SECRETARY-GENERAL (SRSG). Together they became known as UNMIBH, which had its mandate renewed annually through the summer of 2002.

Following its creation in 1995 the United Nations Mission in Bosnia and Herzegovina took on a wide range of responsibilities, coordinating UN humanitarian and relief activities, HUMAN RIGHTS enforcement, demining, elections, and rebuilding Bosnian infrastructure. It oversaw the replacement of the UNITED NATIONS PROTECTION FORCE (UNPROFOR) with a civilian administration of the Dayton Accords. UNMIBH worked closely with the North Atlantic Treaty Organization (NATO) in the deployment of the multinational IFOR (Implementation Force) in order to assure security under the terms of the peace agreement. It established regional and district headquarters in Bihac, Banja Luka, Doboj, Mostar, Sarajevo, Tuzla, and Brcko, which gave UNMIBH nationwide capabilities to coordinate the efforts of all international organizations operating in the country.

In 1996 the Security Council charged UNMIBH with "investigating or assisting with investigations into human rights abuses by law enforcement personnel." The mission set up a human rights office for this purpose. It also created the Judicial System Assessment Program (JSAP) to monitor the Bosnian court system, the Civil Affairs Office to work with local elected officials, and an administrative office to work with the UN MISSION OF OBSERVERS IN PREVLAKA (UNMOP) and other UN agencies in order to assure efficiency and human rights compliance. Originally authorized to have 1,721 civilian police, UNMIBH grew to more than 2,000 personnel by the fall of 2001 due to its enhanced duties under Security Council RESOLUTIONS. A total of 44 nations participated in the mission's work, including recruits from all five of the PERMANENT MEMBERS of the Council. Its estimated BUDGET for 2001–02 was $144.7 million.

See also DEPARTMENT OF PEACEKEEPING OPERATIONS, FORMER YUGOSLAVIA.

Further Reading: Holm, Tor Tanke, and Espen Barth Eide. *Peacebuilding and Police Reform.* London: Frank Cass, 2000. Rogel, Carole. *The Breakup of Yugoslavia and the War in Bosnia.* Westport, Conn.: Greenwood Press, 1998. UNMIBH website: <www.un.org/Depts/DPKO/Missions/unmibh/>.

United Nations Mission in East Timor (UNAMET)

The UN SECURITY COUNCIL established the United Nations Mission in East Timor on June 11, 1999, to carry out the referendum agreed to by INDONESIA and Portugal in May 1999 on whether the East Timorese people desired autonomy for East Timor within the Republic of Indonesia. The agreement stipulated that UNAMET would also oversee a transition period pending implementation of the decision of the East Timorese people. The Security Council authorized a multinational force (INTERFET) in September to restore peace and security in East Timor, and to protect UNAMET when violence broke out after the popular consultation. UNAMET was replaced by the UNITED NATIONS TRANSITIONAL ADMINISTRATION IN EAST TIMOR (UNTAET) in October 1999. UN operations came to an end on May 31, 2002, when East Timor achieved full independence and applied the next day for MEMBERSHIP in the United Nations.

See also EAST TIMOR DISPUTE.

— *G. S. Silliman*

United Nations Mission of Observers in Prevlaka (UNMOP)   *See* FORMER YUGOSLAVIA.

United Nations Monetary and Financial Conference   *See* BRETTON WOODS.

United Nations Observer Mission for the Verification of Elections in Nicaragua (ONUVEN)

United Nations efforts to resolve serious conflicts in Central America represented, for the most part, a model of successful international intercession. For example, protracted conflicts in Central America during the 1970s and 1980s were resolved by the early 1990s through UN intervention. In 1989, in Nicaragua, a peace effort led to the voluntary demobilization of the resistance Contra group, which turned in its WEAPONS to a UN PEACEKEEPING force. In 1990, the United Nations Observation Mission for the Verification of Elections in Nicaragua (ONUVEN) monitored elections, the first observed elections ever administered by the United Nations in an independent country. The success of ONUVEN pro-

vided the environment for the ultimate voluntary demobilization of forces who had fought a brutal civil war in the country. By July 1990, more than 20,000 Contras had relinquished their arms to UN observers. The United Nations Observer Group in Central America (ONUCA), deployed in all five countries in Central America to verify termination of civil strife, remained in Nicaragua until 1992, after which a regularized practice of elections characterized the country.

See also DEPARTMENT OF PEACEKEEPING OPERATIONS, LATIN AMERICA.

United Nations Observer Mission in Angola (MONUA)   *See* UNITED NATIONS ANGOLA VERIFICATION MISSION.

United Nations Observer Mission in El Salvador (ONUSAL)

In May 1991, the UN SECURITY COUNCIL authorized the creation of the UN Observer Mission in El Salvador. ONUSAL helped ensure the successful implementation of several peace agreements between the Salvadoran government and the Frente Faribundo Martí para la Liberación Nacional (FMLN). It stationed observers throughout the country to verify a cease-fire in the decade-long civil war, to certify national elections, and to assist in the REFORM of the armed forces and police. During its four years of service in EL SALVADOR, ONUSAL reached a force size of more than 1,000 personnel and cost the United Nations in excess of $107 million.

In the wake of a final peace agreement between the warring parties in early 1992, the Observer Mission was expanded, and its work divided into a HUMAN RIGHTS Division, a Military Division, a Police Division, and an Electoral Division. The Human Rights Division worked closely with Salvadoran NON-GOVERNMENTAL ORGANIZATIONS to enhance civil support for human rights standards. The military component consisted of officers from Canada, Ecuador, Brazil, Spain, and Venezuela. It oversaw the redeployment of El Salvador's armed forces, the clearing of 425 minefields, and the cease-fire process. The Police Division replaced the old public security system with a professional police force. The division also located illegal arms caches and conducted criminal inquiries. ONUSAL's Election Division monitored the March 1994 elections for president, parliament, and municipal government. Once the elections were completed successfully the Observer Mission began a gradual withdrawal. It was replaced, beginning on April 30, 1995, by the United Nations Mission in El Salvador (MINUSAL)—a small group of civilian personnel to provide GOOD OFFICES for further implementation of the peace agreements.

Further Reading: ONUSAL website: <www.un.org/Depts/dpko/dpko/co_mission/onusal.htm>.

United Nations Observer Mission in Sierra Leone (UNOMSIL)   *See* SIERRA LEONE.

United Nations Office for Project Services (UNOPS)

The GENERAL ASSEMBLY created the United Nations Office for Project Services in 1995 to provide management for United Nations PROGRAMMES AND FUNDS, and projects as well as for activities undertaken by contracting governments in a variety of areas. Unique among UN agencies, UNOPS is not part of any United Nations functional sector, must raise its own revenues by marketing its services, and provides no funding to its clients and partners. UN bodies and member states are not required to use the services of UNOPS, and therefore the Office for Project Services must operate according to a business model, keeping costs low and providing quality services at a competitive price.

UNOPS is the outgrowth of the Division for Project Execution in the UNITED NATIONS DEVELOPMENT PROGRAMME (UNDP), which had first been charged with implementing UNDP activities in 1973. By 1988, the division had become the Office for Project Services, and was delivering $200 million annually in administrative services for UNDP and several other agencies, including the WORLD BANK. With the General Assembly's action in 1995 UNOPS expanded the availability of its services to all UN organs and to individual countries. By 1998 it had revenues of $48.2 million, and implemented projects in 146 countries. Its administrative oversight extended to humanitarian relief, development, ENVIRONMENT, HUMAN RIGHTS, mine clearing, loan distribution, and waterway and infrastructure projects.

The Executive Board of UNDP/UNFPA (United Nations Development Programme/UNITED NATIONS POPULATION FUND) governs UNOPS and sets overall policy. The Management Coordination Committee and UNOP's executive director are responsible for the management of UNOPS under the guidance of the UN SECRETARY-GENERAL. In 2001 the agency maintained offices at UN HEADQUARTERS in New York, and in Tokyo, Geneva, Nairobi, Copenhagen, Rome, Abidjan, Kuala Lumpur, and San Salvador. Within each nation where UNOPS managed a project, a resident coordinator had responsibility for implementing the agency's operation.

The United Nations Development Programme has been UNOP's largest client. Under a 1997 agreement between the two agencies, UNOPS delivered over $2 billion in services to UNDP projects. It also counts among its clients the various REGIONAL ECONOMIC COMMISSIONS of the United Nations, the FOOD AND AGRICULTURE ORGANIZATION (FAO), the European Union (EU), the UNITED NATIONS EDUCATIONAL, SCIENTIFIC AND CULTURAL ORGANIZATION (UNESCO), the WORLD HEALTH ORGANIZATION (WHO), the WORLD INTELLECTUAL PROPERTY ORGANIZATION (WIPO), the WORLD METEOROLOGICAL ORGANIZATION (WMO), the INTERNATIONAL LABOUR ORGANIZATION (ILO), and the INTERNATIONAL ATOMIC ENERGY ORGANIZATION (IAEA). Through its Rehabilitation and Social Sustainability Division (RESS) in Geneva, UNOPS provided $440 million in post-conflict reconstruction aid by the end of the century to countries such as AFGHANISTAN, BOSNIA, SOMALIA, Tajikistan, and Ukraine. As the manager of major projects UNOPS also subcontracts elements of the provided services to local governmental bodies and private firms, as well as to universities, research laboratories, and training institutes around the world.

Among its more visible activities in 2001 was its provision of "de-mining" services for the UNITED NATIONS SYSTEM. It recruited the personnel, assembled the technical resources, procured the equipment, and provided technical support for specific efforts to remove LAND MINES and other detonation devices in countries that had recently experienced conflict. It was responsible for mine clearing in northern Iraq under an agreement with the UN Office of the Iraq Programme (UNOIP), and in Kosovo, Mozambique, Somalia, CAMBODIA, Azerbaijan, Bosnia, Nicaragua, Croatia, and Eritrea.

In many LESS DEVELOPED COUNTRIES (LDC) UNOPS contracted to reconstruct national infrastructure. In Afghanistan UNOPS oversaw the repair of 2,000 miles of canals and the rebuilding of irrigation systems. In Ecuador it managed the rebuilding of 56 schools destroyed by tropical storms. In Albania it worked with local contractors to build health facilities and sewer systems. It also administered many of the loans to these states from international lending agencies and provided administrative services in waterway projects for the UNITED NATIONS ENVIRONMENT PROGRAMME (UNEP)—its most significant contribution being to the Danube River Project, meant to implement the Danube River Protection CONVENTION signed in 1998.

Further Reading: Dijkzeul, Dennis. *Reforming for Results in the UN System: A Study of UNOPS.* New York: St. Martin's, 2000. UNOPS website: <www.unops.org>.

United Nations Office in Geneva   *See* GENEVA HEADQUARTERS OF THE UNITED NATIONS.

United Nations Office of Public Information (OPI)   *See* DEPARTMENT OF PUBLIC INFORMATION.

United Nations Operation in Mozambique (ONUMOZ)

From December 1992 until December 1994 the United Nations Operation in Mozambique acted to effect PEACEKEEPING and to monitor the country's first free parliamentary and presidential elections.

Mozambique, on the southeast coast of Africa, was a colony of Portugal from the early 16th century until 1975. One year following a revolution in 1974 that overthrew the harshly colonial government in Lisbon, Portugal conceded independence to its former colony. Many Portuguese settlers returned to Portugal, leaving Mozambique deficient in administrative expertise and needing infrastructure and social support. A Marxist government, headed by Samora Michel of the Frelimo Party, took over. Shortly thereafter a conflict between the new government and neighboring Rhodesia plunged the country into further turmoil. Rhodesia became independent in 1980, changed its name to Zimbabwe, and relations with Mozambique improved. But another hostile force, the revolutionary Renamo—the Mozambique National Resistance Movement—rebelled against Michel's government. Results for the country were ruinous. In 1986 Michel died, to be replaced by Joachím Alberto Chissanó. In 1987 a UN relief effort began. In 1989 Mozambique and South Africa signed a cooperation agreement, effectively cutting off aid to Renamo. On October 4, 1992, President Chissanó and Renamo leader Alfonso Dhlakama signed a cease-fire agreement. SECURITY COUNCIL Resolution 797 of December 16, 1992, established ONUMOZ to help implement this accord.

ONUMOZ's mandate was to facilitate with impartiality the implementation of the agreement, monitor the cease-fire, coordinate the separation and demobilization of opposing forces, supervise the disbanding of private and irregular armed groups, and provide help in revitalizing infrastructure and delivering humanitarian assistance, particularly to the huge number of refugees and displaced persons. Finally, ONUMOZ was authorized to supervise and monitor the presidential and legislative elections in October 1994. For the two years of the operation, ONUMOZ deployed almost 7,000 troops, 354 military observers, 1,144 civilian police, and about 900 electoral observers. There were an additional 861 international and local staff that worked with ONUMOZ. Expenditures for the two-year operation approached $490 million.

Although the task was daunting and the problems taxing, the UN operation performed with diligence and professionalism. A very high proportion of the estimated number of eligible voters participated in the elections, which UN observers declared "free and fair." Chissanó won the presidency with about 53 percent of the votes and the Renamo candidate garnered about 34 percent. Frelimo gained a plurality of 44 percent of the vote in the legislature. By RESOLUTION 960 on November 21, 1994, the Security Council endorsed the results of the election. When the new government was installed and the president inaugurated in early December 1994, ONUMOZ's surprisingly successful mandate was fulfilled. The mission was formally concluded at the end of January 1995.

See also DEPARTMENT OF PEACEKEEPING OPERATIONS.

Further Reading: Berman, Eric. *Managing Arms in Peace Processes: Mozambique.* New York: United Nations Institute for Disarmament Research, 1996. Ciment, James. *Angola and Mozambique: Postcolonial Wars in Southern Africa.* New York: Facts On File, 1997. ONUMOZ website: <www.un.org/ Depts/DPKO/Missions/onumoz>.

United Nations Operation in Somalia (UNOSOM I, II)

The United Nations Operation in Somalia came into being as a result of Security Council RESOLUTION 751 on April 24, 1992. It was intended to facilitate humanitarian assistance in the complex emergency then going on in SOMALIA, where 1.5 million inhabitants were at the brink of starvation. Famine brought about by drought and civil war further endangered another 3.5 million people. SECRETARY-GENERAL Boutros BOUTROS-GHALI appointed Mr. Mohamed Sahnoun of Algeria as SPECIAL REPRESENTATIVE to Somalia and, after the major parties had agreed to the appointment on June 23, 50 unarmed but uniformed UN military observers from Austria, Bangladesh, Czechoslovakia, Egypt, Fiji, Finland, INDONESIA, Jordan, Morocco, and Zimbabwe were sent to Mogadishu under the leadership of Brigadier General Imtiaz Shaheen of Pakistan.

Meanwhile, efforts to consult and negotiate with the warring factions in Somalia continued. In August 1992, backed by S/RES/767, the observer force was increased to approximately 3,500. The mission monitored the cease-fire in Mogadishu and provided safe passage for relief convoys from the capital to distribution sites in the center and south of the country. With the situation deteriorating, however, Secretary-General Boutros-Ghali called for further international action. Responding to the Secretary-General's request, U.S. president George Bush urged the SECURITY COUNCIL to invoke CHAPTER VII of the CHARTER. On December 3 the Council passed Resolution 794, officially finding the circumstances in Somalia to be a threat to international peace and security. The RESOLUTION endorsed the offer by the UNITED STATES to put together an international force to protect humanitarian relief. For the first time the United Nations subcontracted out a PEACEKEEPING operation. While the Security Council had given the mandate, a primarily American-led UNIFIED TASK FORCE (UNITAF) conducted the operation, which was to work in coordination with UNOSOM to provide the needed safe environment.

Even though these efforts improved the overall situation in Somalia, the goal of achieving a secure environment for humanitarian assistance was not achieved. Therefore, in early 1993 the Security Council decided to set up a new mission. The mandate of UNOSOM II also was established under Chapter VII with S/RES/814 on March 26, 1993. The mission was destined to take over where both UNOSOM I and UNITAF had failed. The 28,000 military and police personnel were to restore peace, stability, and law and order in war-ridden Somalia. To that end, their responsibilities included DISARMAMENT of local factions, providing security at vital points of infrastructure and where UN agencies and NON-GOVERNMENTAL ORGANIZATIONS (NGOs) were working in Somalia, de-mining, and assisting in repatriation efforts. Furthermore, they were to monitor the cease-fire and prevent renewed violence. Finally, UNOSOM II was tasked with helping the Somali people rebuild a working economy, infrastructure, and social and political life, in essence with re-creating a viable and reconciled state. Therefore, unlike UNITAF and UNOSOM I, its mandate covered the whole country. When UNOSOM II took over under the command of Lieutenant General Cervik Bir of Turkey in May 1993, the country was still not secure.

After several violent attacks, which, among other tragic consequences, led to the deaths of 25 Pakistani soldiers in June 1993, the situation deteriorated further. The Security Council passed Resolution 837 on June 8, condemning the attacks, and it was backed in this by several Somali parties. General Muhammed Aidid's USC/SNA however, the strongest faction in the conflict, continued its attacks on UN personnel. U.S. Special Forces (Rangers and the Quick Reaction Force) were brought to Mogadishu in fall 1993 to capture Aidid. In an ill-fated operation in October, 18 U.S. soldiers were killed when two helicopters were shot down. The United States sent a joint task force to Somalia, reinforcing the Quick Reaction Force, while at the same time announcing American withdrawal from Somalia by the end of March 1994. After a unilateral DECLARATION of hostilities from USC/SNA on October 9, 1993, and after the mandate had been extended twice by S/RES/878 and 886, the Security Council revised UNOSOM II's mandate in February 1994. It gradually reduced force levels to 22,000 and prohibited the use of coercive measures. UNOSOM II left in early March 1995. A total of 147 casualties, four of them civilian staff, were sustained during the two years of the mission.

See also CHAPTER VI$^1/_2$, ORGANIZATION OF AFRICAN UNITY.

Further Reading: Hirsch, John L., and Robert B. Oakley. *Somalia and Operation Restore Hope.* Washington, D.C.: United States Institute of Peace Press, 1995. United Nations Department of Public Information. "The UN and Somalia, 1992–96." *The UN Blue Books Series.* Vol. 8. New York: United Nations Department of Public Information, 1996. ———. *The Blue Helmets: A Review of United Nations Peace-Keeping.* 3d ed. New York: Department of Public Information, 1996.

— *T. J. Weiler*

United Nations Organization Mission in the Democratic Republic of the Congo (MONUC) *See* CONGO.

United Nations Population Fund (UNFPA)

The UN SECRETARY-GENERAL established the United Nations Population Fund in 1969 pursuant to a 1966 General Assembly RESOLUTION. It is a subsidiary organ of the GENERAL ASSEMBLY, and it exists to assist national governments and the international community with the development of population policies and reproductive services. Its primary responsibilities are to carry out the recommendations of the 1994 INTERNATIONAL CONFERENCE ON POPULATION AND DEVELOPMENT (ICPD) and to assist in achieving the benchmark targets set by ICPD+5, approved at the 1999 SPECIAL SESSION OF THE GENERAL ASSEMBLY. By the turn of the century UNFPA had become the largest internationally funded population assistance program to the developing world and to nations with economies in transition. One-fourth of all international population assistance was being channeled through UNFPA.

The Executive Board of the UNITED NATIONS DEVELOPMENT PROGRAMME also serves as the board for UNFPA, but the Population FUND has its own executive director. From 1987 to 2000 Dr. Nafis Sadik of Pakistan headed UNFPA. She was succeeded on January 1, 2001, by UN UNDER SECRETARY-GENERAL Thoraya Ahmed Obaid from Saudi Arabia, who became the first Saudi Arabian national to head a UN agency. Her offices were at UNFPA HEADQUARTERS in New York City, from where the executive director oversaw a staff of more than 900 personnel. The agency is completely funded by voluntary contributions, amounting to more than $250 million annually. More than 90 nations regularly contribute to UNFPA's BUDGET.

At the millennium, UNFPA had three main areas of work: achieving universal access to reproductive health services by 2015, supporting population and development projects, and promoting awareness of the connections between population policy and development. It gave critical attention to the empowerment of WOMEN and the achievement of gender equality, focusing on the education of women and girls. The agency also worked closely with the JOINT UNITED NATIONS PROGRAMME ON HIV/AIDS (UNAIDS). It also encouraged cooperative ventures with other bodies in the UNITED NATIONS SYSTEM, NON-GOVERNMENTAL ORGANIZATIONS, REGIONAL DEVELOPMENT BANKS, and the private sector. All of its in-country projects, however, were offered only at the national government's request.

See also SENIOR MANAGEMENT GROUP, UNITED NATIONS OFFICE FOR PROJECT SERVICES.

Further Reading: UNFPA website: <www.unfpa.org>.

United Nations Preventive Deployment Force in the Former Yugoslav Republic of Macedonia (UNPREDEP)

The UN Preventive Deployment Force in Macedonia was the first mission in UN PEACEKEEPING history to have a preventive mandate. The mandate derived from several SECURITY COUNCIL recommendations dating from 1992 that dealt with the disintegrating situation in the FORMER YUGOSLAVIA. Macedonia, sometimes known by the acronym FYROM (Former Yugoslav Republic of Macedonia) had been one of the republics in the Yugoslav federation. It declared independence in 1991. Because of Greek opposition, full diplomatic recognition of independence was delayed until 1995.

In February 1992 the Security Council created the UNITED NATIONS PROTECTION FORCE (UNPROFOR) to bring peace and security to Yugoslavia and to encourage negotiation of a comprehensive settlement of the crisis there. On March 31, 1995, the Council replaced UNPROFOR with three separate peacekeeping operations. Security Council Resolution 983 instituted UNPREDEP as the operation for Macedonia. Its mandate included the responsibilities originally given to UNPROFOR, and also intended to conform to a innovative UN procedure called by SECRETARY-GENERAL Boutros BOUTROS-GHALI "PREVENTIVE DIPLOMACY." The Secretary-General outlined his thoughts in "An Agenda for Preventive Diplomacy: Theory and Practice," presented to an International Workshop in the Macedonian capital of Skopje on October 16–19, 1996.

UNPREDEP's mandate continued until February 28, 1999, when it failed to receive a renewal as China VETOED a draft six-month extension in the Security Council. From March 31, 1995, until February 28, 1999, the force had worked to deter outbreaks of violence, monitored border areas, and reported any activities that might pose a threat to Macedonia, including the importation into the country of illicit arms. Its troop strength as of February 1999 was 1,110 personnel, including 1,049 troops, 35 military observers, and 26 civilian police. Personnel had come from 50 different nationalities, and two mechanized infantry battalions included a Nordic force and a U.S. task force.

By early 2001, Macedonia faced an insurrection from a liberation force of ethnic Albanians. While about two-thirds of Macedonia's population of two million are ethnic Macedonian Slavs who are Orthodox Christians, between a third and 40 percent are ethnic Albanians and Muslims. The Albanians complained about their lower status in Macedonian law and social practice, and from their numbers came the rebels. By the summer of 2001, a combined European Union (EU)–NATO (North Atlantic Treaty Organization) diplomatic effort sought a tentative peace agreement. As a consequence of this tutelage, by early fall, Macedonian and Albanian political parties had negotiated constitutional changes benefiting the Albanian minority, and calling on the insurrectionists to cease the uprising. As of October 2001, EU security chief Javier Solana could report that most outstanding issues between the main Macedonian Slav and ethnic Albanian political parties had been resolved.

See also DEPARTMENT OF PEACEKEEPING OPERATIONS.

Further Reading: Williams, Abiodun. *Preventing War: The United Nations and Macedonia.* Lanham, Md.: Rowman and Littlefield, 2000. UNPREDEP website: <www.un.org/Depts/DPKO/Missions/unpred>.

United Nations Protection Force (UNPROFOR)   *See* FORMER YUGOSLAVIA.

United Nations Relief and Rehabilitation Administration (UNRRA)

In 1943, in the midst of World War II, UNRRA came into existence. It was formed by concerned nations to provide aid to areas liberated from the Axis powers. At the high point of its existence it had 52 participating nations, each contributing funds to its BUDGET equaling 2 percent of the national income of each participant. Almost $4 billion was raised and spent on a number of emergency aid measures, including the provision of medicine and food, restoration of public services, and reenergizing of industrial and agricultural production in those countries that had been attacked and occupied by Axis powers. Chief beneficiaries of aid from UNRRA included CHINA, Czechoslovakia, Greece, Italy, Poland, the Ukraine, and Yugoslavia. UNRRA arranged for the repatriation of some 7 million refugees to countries of origin. It also operated relief camps for about one million displaced persons who were unwilling to be sent back to their areas of origin. The UNITED STATES contributed more than half the funds for UNRRA as well as the three DIRECTORS-GENERAL who administered the program—Herbert H. Lehman, Fiorello La Guardia, and General Lowell Rooks. UNRRA ended its operations in Europe in June 1947, and in China in March 1949. After that its functions were transferred to other UN institutions, mainly the International Refugee Organization, the UNITED NATIONS CHILDREN'S FUND (UNICEF), and the FOOD AND AGRICULTURE ORGANIZATION (FAO).

See also PEARSON, LESTER.

United Nations Relief and Works Agency for Palestine Refugees in the Near East (UNRWA)

The GENERAL ASSEMBLY (GA), by RESOLUTION 302 of December 8, 1949, established the United Nations Relief and Works Agency to provide direct relief to Palestinians displaced by the ARAB-ISRAELI conflict of 1948. The agency began operations on May 1, 1950, inheriting the refugee registration records compiled by predecessor agencies—the United Nations Relief for Palestine Refugees, the American Friends Service Committee, and the International Committee of the Red Cross (ICRC)—that had moved quickly to offer emergency assistance with the outbreak of fighting.

UNRWA became unique among UN agencies in that its commitment remained to one group of refugees only. Intended as a temporary SPECIALIZED AGENCY to aid 750,000 refugees in the Middle East, UNRWA's mandate has been renewed every three years since 1949 by the General Assembly. By the turn of the century it served more than three and a half million Palestinians.

After the United Kingdom relinquished its mandate in Palestine to the United Nations on May 14, 1948, the Jewish Agency proclaimed the State of Israel. Arabs living in Palestine (that is, "Palestinians") rejected what they believed to be an unjust intrusion into their land and, joined by neighbouring Arab states, began hostilities against Israel. By the time that the SECURITY COUNCIL established a truce and a cease-fire line—that became a de facto boundary line of Israel—about three-quarters of a million Arabs in the area had lost their homes and livelihoods or left their homes to reside in

refugee camps in surrounding countries. UNRWA became the major UN source of assistance and stability for these Palestinians, providing health, education, relief, and social services.

Following the MIDDLE EAST WAR OF 1967, the GA, by Resolution 2252, temporarily expanded the agency's mandate to extend emergency humanitarian assistance to persons other than Palestinians affected by the war. The civil war in Lebanon, the intifada (Palestinian uprising) in the late 1980s, and the GULF WAR of 1991 resulted in the displacement of an additional 300,000 refugees into UNRWA's area of administration. After the 1993 accords between Israel and the Palestine Liberation Organization, UNRWA initiated a Peace Implementation Programme intended to upgrade infrastructure, improve employment opportunities, and enhance living conditions among refugees. UNRWA also began close cooperation with the Palestinian Authority.

Palestinian refugees in Gaza Strip (UNITED NATIONS)

UNRWA defines a Palestinian refugee as one whose "normal place of residence was Palestine during the period 1 June 1946 to 15 May 1948 and who lost both home and means of livelihood as a result of the 1948 conflict," and descendants of fathers fulfilling that definition. By 2001 about 3.8 million Palestinians qualified under this needs-based definition and, thus, were registered with UNRWA. Its work has been in five geographic fields of operation—the Gaza Strip, the West Bank, and with the governments of Jordan, Lebanon, and Syria. It has field offices in Gaza City, Jerusalem, Amman, Beirut, and Damascus.

At the turn of the century, the agency operated about 650 elementary and preparatory schools with close to one-half million students, eight vocational training centers with more than 6,000 students, and about 125 health centers receiving some 7.5 million patient visits. It had an international staff of more than 100 personnel and employed about 22,000 civilian staff from the area, mostly Palestinians. Its budget depended overwhelmingly on voluntary contributions of donor states (although financing for all international staff positions came from the regular BUDGET OF THE UNITED NATIONS). Traditionally the UNITED STATES has been the largest donor, followed by the European Union and the United Kingdom. Scandinavian countries, Canada, and the Netherlands are other major benefactors, whose contributions relative to population and gross domestic product have often been the highest. The 2001 budget was $311 million. About 54 percent was spent on education programs, 18 percent on health services, and 10 percent on social services and relief. By the summer of 2001, however, UNRWA faced a financial crisis with a budget deficit of $58 million. Unless new funds were found quickly, the agency expected to run out of cash within several months. Without an increase in giving by the major donors UNRWA would have to suspend many of its programs.

The agency's chief officer is a commissioner-general, appointed by the SECRETARY-GENERAL following consultation with the Advisory Commission. The commissioner—Peter Hansen of Denmark in 2001—is the only head of a UN body that reports directly to the General Assembly. The Advisory Commission, consisting of Belgium, Egypt, France, Japan, Jordan, Lebanon, Syria, Turkey, the United Kingdom, and the UNITED STATES, meets annually to review the agency's programs and activities. UNRWA's HEADQUARTERS from 1950 to 1978 was in Beirut, then moved to Vienna, and, to underscore the UN's commitment to Middle East peace, relocated to Gaza City and Amman in 1996.

See also BUNCHE, RALPH; PROGRAMMES AND FUNDS; UNITED NATIONS INTERIM FORCE IN LEBANON; UNITED NATIONS HIGH COMMISSIONER FOR REFUGEES.

Further Reading: New Zealand Ministry of Foreign Affairs. *United Nations Handbook.* Wellington, N.Z.: Ministry of Foreign Affairs and Trade, published annually. UNRWA website: <www.un.org/unrwa>.

United Nations Research Institute for Social Development (UNRISD)

Established in 1963 at the initiative of the UN SECRETARY-GENERAL's office, UNRISD has a mandate "to conduct research into problems and policies of social development and relationships between various types of social development and economic development during different phases of economic growth." Although an autonomous agency, the research institute is considered a UN affiliate, and its studies and research are intended to help the work of the UN SECRETARIAT in carrying out its various mandates in the areas of economic and social development. It focuses its research on the social, environmental, and grassroots impact of development and globalization, particularly on poorer countries. Also, the institute seeks to understand—and aid in the encouragement of—gender equality, use of new tools of information technology, and governmental REFORM in development strategies. The institute provides publications and policy briefs, and holds conferences. Its research programs include: Civil Society and Social Movements, Democracy and HUMAN RIGHTS, Identities Conflict and Cohesion, and Business Responsibility for SUSTAINABLE DEVELOPMENT. UN organs, other international agencies, NON-GOVERNMENTAL ORGANIZATIONS (NGO), governments and grassroots organizations may solicit advice from the institute.

UNRISD meets in UN HEADQUARTERS in Geneva (Palais des Nations). It is governed by a board of 11 members and has a staff of about 30, headed by its director, who in 2001 was Thandika Mkandawire, of Sweden. It is funded only by voluntary contributions. For the fiscal year 1998–99, contributors were the states of Denmark, Finland, France, Mexico, Netherlands, Norway, Sweden, Switzerland, and the United Kingdom, plus the Rockefeller Foundation and a few UN agencies and other multilateral organizations.

Further Reading: UNRISD website: <www.unrisd.org>.

UN Security Council Resolution 242

United Nations SECURITY COUNCIL Resolution 242 was adopted unanimously on November 22, 1967, following the cessation of the MIDDLE EAST WAR OF 1967 or *al naksa* (June 5–10). The RESOLUTION was precipitated by Israel's June 5, 1967, attack on Egypt, Iraq, Jordan, and Syria, in which Israeli forces seized Egyptian territory in the Sinai Peninsula, Syrian territory in the Golan Heights, and the remainder of the land designated by the 1947 UN partition plan for Palestine as the space for the Arab state.

Security Council Resolution 242 constituted the most significant, albeit belated, UN response to the 1967 war. During and immediately after the war the Security Council contributed little to the settlement of the ARAB-ISRAELI conflict; opposition characterized the relations between the

UNITED STATES and the Soviet Union and these antagonisms were reflected in the vetoing of resolutions each power put before the Council.

Political machinations in the Security Council and GENERAL ASSEMBLY delayed the adoption of any significant resolutions until Great Britain proposed 242 on November 16. The important facets of Resolution 242 are: its emphasis on the inadmissibility of acquiring territory by war and the need for a just and lasting regional peace, its suggestion that Israel's armed forces be withdrawn from territories occupied in the June conflict, and its further affirmation of the necessity of regional demilitarized zones and a just solution to the "refugee problem." The inadmissibility of acquiring territory by means of war and the requirement of a just and lasting peace reaffirmed basic tenets of the UN CHARTER. The suggestion that Israel withdraw from occupied territory remained salient in subsequent negotiations between Israel and the Palestinian National Authority as each demonstrated differing interpretations of the resolution's clause (Palestinian negotiators argued that Israel must extricate itself from *all* of the Gaza Strip and the West Bank while Israeli representatives contended that Israel must vacate only selected portions of the occupied territory). The necessity of regional demilitarized zones recalls the stationing of UN peacekeepers in the Sinai (removed at Gamal Abdul NASSER's insistence in 1956) and whose absence may have exacerbated regional tensions before Israel's attack.

The affirmation of the necessity of a just solution to the refugee problem is the most problematic clause of the resolution. Resolution 242 nowhere mentions Palestinians, those people made refugees by the war and who came under Israeli military occupation at its close. Instead the resolution refers to anonymous "refugees." This clause of Resolution 242 appears to deny Palestinians their national rights in direct contravention of the 1947 UN Partition Plan for Palestine, which called for national self-determination for both peoples of mandate Palestine.

SECRETARY-GENERAL U THANT and UNDER SECRETARY-GENERAL for Political Affairs Ralph BUNCHE helped nurture the development of 242 and the former appointed Gunnar Jarring as his SPECIAL REPRESENTATIVE to the Middle East following its adoption.

Further Reading: Said, Edward. *The Politics of Dispossession: The Struggle for Palestinian Self-Determination, 1969–1994.* New York: Vintage Books, 1995. Thant, U. *View from the UN.* Garden City, N.Y.: Doubleday, 1978.

— S. F. McMahon

UN Security Council Resolution 338

UN SECURITY COUNCIL Resolution 338 was passed on October 22, 1973, two days before a cease-fire between Israel and Egypt halted fighting in Egypt's Sinai Desert. Resolution 338

was adopted by a vote of 14 in favor with none opposed. The resolution served as the response by the United Nations to the war Israeli Jews call the Yom Kippur War and the Arabic-speaking peoples in the Middle East identify as the October or Ramadan War.

On October 6, 1973, forces from Egypt and Syria entered territory that had been occupied by Israel since the conclusion of the MIDDLE EAST WAR OF 1967 (territory Israel was instructed to vacate by UN SECURITY COUNCIL RESOLUTION 242). Successful Egyptian and Syrian advances were aided by a Soviet airlift, which produced similar American assistance to Israel. On October 24, 1973, a second UN cease-fire (the first being approved on October 22 but not implemented) ended the fighting and the threat of wider superpower involvement in the conflict. UN Security Council Resolution 338 secured this second UN cease-fire.

Resolution 338 is notable because it called upon the parties to the conflict of 1973 to implement UN Security Council Resolution 242 in its entirety while also affirming that direct negotiations between the conflict's belligerents should start. While this latter directive was seen to be paternalistic, it was notable that 338 contained instruction from the Security Council that the members of the region should initiate a conversation aimed at securing a just and lasting peace. Despite myriad problems, UN Security Council Resolution 338 was regularly affirmed, along with Resolution 242, as a basic foundational tenet of ongoing Israeli-Palestinian negotiations.

Resolution 338 is of derivative importance; its significance comes from its call to implement Resolution 242. It reaffirmed 242 but did not provide for any means of implementing itself, or by extension the reaffirmed RESOLUTION. More problematic is the fact that, because Resolution 338 made a blanket reference to Resolution 242, it failed to correct the problems associated with the earlier resolution. For example, it did not clarify the military withdrawal clause of 242 which later would be differentially interpreted in ongoing Israeli-Palestinian negotiations. Similarly, Resolution 338 did not mention the Palestinians and, by extension, did not name the people who were refugees and forced to endure Israeli military occupation. This omission perpetuated the denial of Palestinian national rights in contravention of the 1947 UN Partition Plan for Palestine that first appeared in Resolution 242.

Following the war of 1973 and the imposition of the cease-fire, a second UNITED NATIONS EMERGENCY FORCE was positioned—at the instruction of the Security Council—in the Sinai Desert. Peacekeepers were also stationed in the Golan Heights.

See also ARAB-ISRAELI DISPUTE.

Further Reading: Bickerton, Ian, and Carla Klausner. *A Concise History of the Arab-Israeli Conflict.* 2d ed. Englewood Cliffs, N.J.: Prentice Hall, 1995. Laqueur, Walter, and Barry

Rubin. *The Israel-Arab Reader: A Documentary History of the Middle East Conflict.* New York: Penguin Books, 2000. Said, Edward. *The Politics of Dispossession: The Struggle for Palestinian Self-Determination, 1969–1994.* New York: Vintage Books, 1995.

— *S. F. McMahon*

UN Security Council Resolution 598 *See* IRAN-IRAQ WAR.

UN Security Council Resolution 678

The SECURITY COUNCIL passed Resolution 678 on November 29, 1990. The RESOLUTION was adopted by a vote of 12 in favor and 2 opposed (CUBA and Yemen) with one abstention (CHINA). The UNITED STATES opposed the August 2, 1990, Iraqi invasion of Kuwait and was the chief proponent of the resolution.

Resolution 678 recalled and reaffirmed several resolutions pertaining to the Iraqi invasion. Included among these were Resolutions 660 and 661. Resolution 660 of August 2, 1990, condemned the Iraqi invasion and demanded that Iraq withdraw immediately and unconditionally. Resolution 661 was passed on August 6, 1990. This resolution imposed SANCTIONS on Iraq; the short 17 weeks between the passage of Resolutions 661 and 678 did not, however, provide enough time for the sanctions to take effect. They prohibited Iraq from importing commodities that would allow it to build WEAPONS OF MASS DESTRUCTION as well as more banal items such as ashtrays, doorknobs, and paper clips.

Resolution 678 set January 15, 1991, as the deadline for full Iraqi implementation of Resolution 660 and all subsequent relevant resolutions. Anticipating Iraqi noncompliance, Resolution 678 authorized member states cooperating with the government of Kuwait to "use all necessary means to uphold and implement resolution 660." Resolution 678 requested that all states provide appropriate support for actions undertaken in accordance with this authorization.

Following Iraq's invasion of Kuwait, a U.S.-led coalition assembled military forces in the Gulf region. This operation became known as Desert Shield. When Iraq did not withdraw from Kuwait by January 15, a military campaign was initiated in accordance with the "use of all necessary means to uphold and implement resolution 660." To remove Iraqi forces forcibly from Kuwait, the coalition began an aerial bombardment. Following the air campaign, the allies launched a land incursion into Kuwait. Together, the air and land campaigns were known as Desert Storm and Desert Sabre. The commander of the coalition forces that drove Iraqi forces from Kuwait was U.S. general Norman Schwarzkopf.

The implementation of Resolution 678 raised two salient issues. First, the war against Iraq reestablished the United Nations as an important agent for international peace and security at the end of the COLD WAR. Second, it highlighted the importance of economic and environmental warfare in the evolving world system. Before retreating, Iraqi troops set fire to 640 Kuwaiti oil wells. This destroyed Kuwaiti oil resources—Kuwait's primary export and source of foreign currency. It also created an environmental disaster that transcended state boundaries.

See also ENFORCEMENT MEASURES; GULF WAR, HUSSEIN, SADDAM; PÉREZ DE CUÉLLAR, JAVIER.

Further Reading: Hiro, D. *Desert Shield to Desert Storm: The Second Gulf War.* London: Paladin, 1992. Sifry, Micah L., and Christopher Cerf. *The Gulf War Reader: History, Documents, Opinions.* New York: Times Books, 1991.

— *S. F. McMahon*

UN Security Council Resolution 751 *See* SOMALIA.

UN Security Council Resolution 1368 *See* APPENDIX F, TERRORISM.

United Nations Security Force (UNSF)

UNSF was created to effect a cease-fire between the Netherlands and INDONESIA and to support the UNITED NATIONS TEMPORARY EXECUTIVE AUTHORITY (UNTEA) in its administration of West New Guinea (West Irian) in 1962–63. The governments of the Netherlands and Indonesia paid the full cost of the operation in equal shares. This was the last PEACEKEEPING force acting under GENERAL ASSEMBLY authorization.

— *G. S. Silliman*

United Nations Special Commission on Iraq (UNSCOM) *See* GULF WAR.

United Nations Special Mission to Afghanistan (UNSMA) *See* AFGHANISTAN.

United Nations System

The full range of UN organizations, functions, PROGRAMMES AND FUNDS, SPECIALIZED AGENCIES, and international bodies related to the United Nations is subsumed under the heading United Nations System. Sometimes called the "UN Family of Organizations," the system's STRUCTURE is shown in the accompanying graphic presentation. Although there are

The United Nations System, January 2001
Principal Organs of the United Nations

International Court of Justice	Security Council	General Assembly	Economic and Social Council	Trusteeship Council	Secretariat

Military Staff Committee
Standing Committees
Ad hoc Bodies
International Criminal
   Tribunal for the Former
   Yugoslavia
International Criminal
   Tribunal for Rwanda
Un Monitoring,
   Verification and Inspection
   Commission (Iraq)
Peacekeeping Missions

Six Main Committees
Sessional Committees
Standing Committees
Subsidiary Organs

Other UN Entities
UN High Commissioner
   for Human Rights
UN Centre for Human
   Settlements
UN Office for Project Services

Office of the Secretary-General
Offices and Departments:
   International Oversight Services
   Legal Services
   Political Affairs
   Disarmament Affairs
   Peacekeeping Operations
   Coordination of Humanitarian Affairs
   Economic and Social Affairs
   General Assembly Affairs and
      Conference Services
   Public Information
   Management
   Iraqi Programme
   United Nations Security Coordination
   Drug Control and Crime Prevention
UN Office at Geneva
UN Office at Vienna
UN Office at Nairobi

Research and Training Institutes
International Research and
   Training Institute for the
   Advancement of Women
UN Interregional Crime and
   Justice Research Institute
UN Institute for Training and
   Research
UN Research Institute for Social
   Development
UN Institute for
   Disarmament Research

Programmes and Funds
UN Conference on Trade and
   Development
   – International Trade Centre
UN Drug Control Programme
UN Environment Programme
UN Development Programme
   – UN Development Fund
     for Women
   – UN Volunteers
UN Population Fund
UN High Commissioner for
   Refugees
UN Children's Fund
World Food Programme
UN Relief and Works
   Agency for Palestine
   Refugees in the Near East

Functional Commissions
Comm. for Social Development
Comm. on Human Rights
Comm. on Narcotic Drugs
Comm. on Crime Prevention and
   Criminal Justice
Comm. on Science and Technology
   for Development
Comm. on Sustainable Development
Comm. on the Status of Women
Comm. on Population and Development
Statistical Commission

Specialized Agencies
International Labour Org.
Food and Agriculture Org.
UN Educational, Scientific and
   Cultural Org.
World Health Org.
World Bank Group
International Monetary Fund
International Civil Aviation Org.
International Maritime Org.
International
   Telecommunications Union
Universal Postal Union
World Meteorological Org.
World Intellectual Property Org.
International Fund for
   Agricultural Development
UN Industrial Development
   Org.

Related Organizations
International Atomic Energy
   Agency
World Trade Organization
Comprehensive Nuclear
   Test-Ban Treaty Organization
Organization for the
   Prohibition of Chemical
   Weapons
World Tourism Organization

Regional Commissions
Economic Commission for Africa
Economic Commission for Europe
Economic Commission for Latin
   America and the Caribbean
Economic and Social Commission for
   Asia and the Pacific
Economic and Social Commission for
   Western Asia

Ad hoc and Other Committees
Expert and Standing Committees

organizations in the system that act independently, communication within the system is usually directed upwardly to the top of an organizational arrangement featuring the six PRINCIPAL ORGANS OF THE UNITED NATIONS. Of the six organs, four—the GENERAL ASSEMBLY, the SECURITY COUNCIL, the ECONOMIC AND SOCIAL COUNCIL, and the SECRETARIAT—are the chief conduits for the full system. The UN SECRETARY-GENERAL maintains effective control over the system through the ADMINISTRATIVE COMMITTEE ON COORDINATION (renamed in 2002 the UN System Chief Executives Board for Coordination) which has as its members the heads of all important bodies and agencies.

See also ADMINISTRATIVE TRIBUNALS, ANNAN, CHINA, DECLARATION, HIV/AIDS, HUMAN RIGHTS, INTER-AGENCY COMMITTEE ON SUSTAINABLE DEVELOPMENT, NON-ALIGNED MOVEMENT, REFORM OF THE UNITED NATIONS, REGIONAL DEVELOPMENT BANKS, REGIONAL ORGANIZATIONS, UNITED NATIONS COMMISSION ON INTERNATIONAL TRADE LAW, UNITED NATIONS DEVELOPMENT PROGRAMME, UNITED NATIONS ENVIRONMENT PROGRAMME, UNITED NATIONS HIGH COMMISSIONER FOR HUMAN RIGHTS, UNITED NATIONS OFFICE FOR PROJECT SERVICES.

Further Reading: Boisard, M.A., and E.M. Chopsoudousky, eds. *Multilateral Diplomacy: The United Nations System at Geneva.* 2d ed. The Hague: Kluwer Law International, 1988. Publications of the UN Department of Public Information. UN website: <www.un.org>. United Nations website locator: <www.unsystem.org>.

UN System Chief Executives Board for Coordination   *See* ADMINISTRATIVE COMMITTEE ON COORDINATION.

United Nations Temporary Commission on Korea (UNTCOK)   *See* KOREAN WAR.

United Nations Temporary Executive Authority (UNTEA)

Initiated by UN SECRETARY-GENERAL U THANT, UNTEA facilitated the 1962–63 transfer of authority over West New Guinea (West Irian) from the Netherlands to INDONESIA.

— G. S. Silliman

United Nations Transitional Administration in East Timor (UNTAET)

The UN SECURITY COUNCIL established UNTAET on October 25, 1999, through RESOLUTION 1272 to administer East Timor during its transition to independence from Indonesian

rule. UNTAET was charged with maintaining law and order, establishing an effective administration for East Timor, coordinating the delivery of humanitarian assistance, enhancing Timorese capacity for self-government, and establishing the conditions for SUSTAINABLE DEVELOPMENT.

As of January 1, 2001, UNTAET commanded 7,765 military and 1,398 civilian police contributed by 47 nations including all five of the PERMANENT MEMBERS of the Security Council. The UN PEACEKEEPING effort was financed through an annual UN BUDGET of $563 million. During its first 18 months of operation the transitional administration suffered 15 fatalities, partly as a product of clashes with militia operating out of West Timor, who were committed to keeping East Timor under Indonesian control. Among its most important actions, UNTAET endorsed the creation of a Truth and Reconciliation Commission to provide a historical record of HUMAN RIGHTS violations between 1974 and 1999, and monitored elections in August 2001 for the formation of an 88-member constituent assembly to draft a constitution for East Timor. UNTAET transferred authority to an independent East Timorese government on May 31, 2002.

See also EAST TIMOR DISPUTE, INDONESIA, UNITED NATIONS MISSION IN EAST TIMOR.

Further Reading: UNTAET website: <www.un.org/peace/etimor/etimor.htm>.

United Nations Transition Assistance Group (UNTAG)   *See* NAMIBIA.

United Nations Transitional Authority in Cambodia (UNTAC)

Approved in February 1992 by the UN SECURITY COUNCIL to ensure implementation of the Paris Agreements of 1991, UNTAC was charged with responsibilities far beyond those of any previous PEACEKEEPING operation. UNTAC's mandate was to exercise "all necessary powers" over all aspects of the comprehensive settlement of the Cambodian civil war, including civil administration, military functions, HUMAN RIGHTS, and elections. Beginning in July 1992 it took over the administration of Cambodian foreign affairs, defense, and finances. UNTAC had the monumental task of preserving order, demobilizing the armed forces of four Cambodian factions, repatriating some 3,700 refugees, planning for the social and economic rehabilitation of CAMBODIA, conducting elections, and providing transitional governance until an elected government could assume control. It grew to become the largest peacekeeping operation since the CONGO operation in 1961, with about 16,000 troops, 3,600 police monitors, and 2,150 civilian administrators. UNTAC's mandate came to an end in September 1993 when the Constituent Assembly elected under UN supervision adopted a new

Cambodian constitution. The last UN military forces withdrew in November.

UNTAC's role in the resettlement of displaced Cambodians and in conducting the elections of May 1993 is generally viewed as a success. On the other hand, civil administration, the military mandate, and human rights are commonly evaluated as either suffering from shortcomings or as outright failures. The mission suffered 78 fatalities during its 19-month tenure. UNTAC and its predecessor, the UNITED NATIONS ADVANCE MISSION IN CAMBODIA (October 1991–March 1992), cost the United Nations officially more than $1.6 billion.

See also UNITED NATIONS VOLUNTEERS.

Further Reading: Doyle, Michael W. *Peacekeeping in Cambodia: UNTAC's Civil Mandate.* Boulder, Colo.: Lynne Rienner Publishers, 1995. Thayer, Carlyle A. "The UN Transitional Authority in Cambodia." *A Crisis of Expectations: UN Peacekeeping in the 1990s.* Edited by Ramesh Thakur and Carlyle A. Thayer. Boulder, Colo.: Westview, 1995. UNTAC website: <www.un.org/Depts/dpko/dpko/co_mission/untac.htm>.

— *G. S. Silliman*

United Nations Treaty Series

The UN CHARTER, Article 102, requires member states to deposit treaties and agreements with the SECRETARIAT. They are then published in the *United Nations Treaty Series.* No state may invoke a treaty before any UN organ that has not been registered.

Further Reading: UN Treaty Series website: <http://untreaty.un.org>.

United Nations Truce Supervision Organization (UNTSO)

Although the UN CHARTER does not expressly authorize PEACEKEEPING operations, the United Nations initiated such activities in 1948 by creating the United Nations Truce Supervision Organization in the Middle East. This occurred after the United Kingdom ended its mandate over Palestine on May 14, 1948, and the Jewish Agency announced the establishment of the State of Israel. A year earlier, the GENERAL ASSEMBLY (GA) had endorsed a proposal offered by the UN Special Committee on Palestine to divide the territory into a Jewish state and an Arab state, with Jerusalem attaining international status. Palestinian Arabs and the Arab states did not accept the plan, and when the State of Israel was proclaimed hostilities broke out, beginning the ARAB-ISRAELI DISPUTE.

SECURITY COUNCIL Resolution 50 of May 29, 1948, stipulated the truce that brought about a pause in the hostilities. It called for a UN mediator, appointed by the General Assembly. UNTSO, created by the same RESOLUTION, was designed to serve as a military observer force to assist the mediator in supervising the truce and maintaining the cease-fire then in place. The UN Truce Supervision Organization arrived in the Middle East in June 1948 and remained there to oversee elusive armistice agreements between Israel and its Arab neighbors. Eventually its operations extended to five States—Israel, Egypt, Jordan, Lebanon, and Syria. It worked with the first UN mediator, Count Folke BERNADOTTE, who was assassinated by extremists on September 17, 1948, in Jerusalem. Earlier, on July 6, 1948, Commandant René de Labarrière, a military observer from France serving in UNTSO, became the first UN peacekeeper in history to die in the line of duty. His jeep hit a mine in the Afoula area of Palestine.

UNTSO continued to function into the new century and to adjust to new demands. It continued to monitor cease-fires and supervise armistice agreements, but it also tried to prevent isolated incidents from spiraling into more serious conflicts, acted as a liaison for hostile parties, and supported additional peacekeeping efforts in the Middle East, often providing personnel for these undertakings on short notice. It cooperated with other UN operations, particularly those established after the MIDDLE EAST WAR OF 1967. Its activities tended to be subsumed under the UNITED NATIONS EMERGENCY FORCE (UNEF, dissolved in 1979), the United Nations Disengagement Observer Force (UNDOF) in the Golan Heights, and the UNITED NATIONS INTERIM FORCE IN LEBANON (UNIFIL). UNTSO cooperated with and assisted each of these other organizations. In the case of UNIFIL it acted as a separate entity, but it became an integral part of UNDOF.

As of mid 2001, UNTSO had 140 military observers from 21 countries, assisted by 107 international civilian staff and 113 local personnel. Since 1948 it had suffered 38 fatalities. Its financing came from the regular UN BUDGET and was $22.8 million in 2001. It was headquartered in Government House in Jerusalem, and its chief of staff in 2001 was Major-General Franco Ganguzza of Italy.

See also BUNCHE, RALPH, MIDDLE EAST WAR OF 1973, SUEZ CRISIS, UN SECURITY COUNCIL RESOLUTION 242, UN SECURITY COUNCIL RESOLUTION 338.

Further Reading: New Zealand Ministry of Foreign Affairs. *United Nations Handbook.* Wellington: N.Z.: Ministry of Foreign Affairs and Trade, published annually. UNTSO website: <www.un.org/Depts/DPKO/Missions/untso>.

United Nations University (UNU)

The United Nations University is a United Nations "programme," which means that it was created by and reports annually to the GENERAL ASSEMBLY of the United Nations. UNU is funded by voluntary contributions and its headquarters is in Tokyo, Japan. According to the General Assembly decision of December 1972 to establish it, the UNU was to consist of a system of academic institutions, which worked closely with UNESCO (UNITED NATIONS EDUCATIONAL, SCIENTIFIC AND CULTURAL ORGANIZATION) and UNITAR (UNITED NATIONS INSTITUTE FOR TRAINING AND RESEARCH). After the adoption of its CHARTER in 1973, the university commenced operations in 1975, providing a research facility for all UN member states to build networks, exchange research findings, and cooperate on research projects. UNU is not an educational institution that offers courses. However, scholarships, lecture series, and a library are available to researchers within a wide range of fields, such as ENVIRONMENT, development, and poverty reduction. In Tokyo, at the Institute of Advanced Studies, a project to establish a "Universal Networking Language" (UNL) aims to develop a multilingual system that will ensure unlimited possibilities for information flow, e-business, and the enhancement of education and public services, "to peoples of all nations."

The university has research and training centers and programs (RTC/Ps) around the world, such as UNU World Institute for Development Economics Research (UNU/WIDER) in Helsinki, Finland, established in 1985; UNU Programme for Biotechnology for LATIN AMERICA and the Caribbean (UNU/BIOLAC) in Caracas, Venezuela, established in 1988; UNU Institute for Natural Resources in Africa (UNU/INRA) in Legon, Ghana, established in 1990; UNU Institute for New Technologies (UNU/TECH) in Maastricht, the Netherlands, established in 1990; UNU International Institute for Software Technology (UNU/IIST) in Macau, established in 1992; UNU International Leadership Academy (UNU/ILA) in Amman, Jordan, established in 1995; and UNU International Network on Water, Environment, and Health (UNU/INWEH) in Ontario, Canada, established in 1996.

The operations of the university are supervised by the UNU Council, consisting of 28 members. The UN SECRETARY-GENERAL and the DIRECTOR-GENERAL of UNESCO appoint 24 members to six-year terms. The Secretary-General, the director-general, the executive director of UNITAR, and the rector of the university serve ex officio. The rector appointed in 1997 for a five-year period was Professor Hans J. A. Van Ginkel from the Netherlands.

Further Reading: UNU website: <www.unu.edu>.

— A. S. Hansen

United Nations Verification Mission in Guatemala (MINUGUA)   See GUATEMALA.

United Nations Volunteers (UNV)

As the new millennium began, the far-flung reaches of the world found more than 3,000 volunteers working for the United Nations in PEACEKEEPING operations, development projects, humanitarian assistance programs, and health and education activities. They were part of the United Nations Volunteer Programme created by the GENERAL ASSEMBLY in 1970. Volunteers are recruited regularly from more than 140 nations, with the majority coming from the developing world. They serve in more than 130 nations, providing skilled service in agriculture, HUMAN RIGHTS, engineering, health, natural and social sciences, and education. UNV gives special emphasis to recruiting youth and providing skilled assistance to youth programs. The programme is financed through its parent body, the UNITED NATIONS DEVELOPMENT PROGRAMME, and through the Special Voluntary Fund (SVF), also established in 1970. More than 60 nations have contributed to the fund. Depending on the project in which the volunteers are involved, funding also comes from the SPECIALIZED AGENCY or UN body sponsoring it. As of 2001 the UNV annual BUDGET was more than $17 million.

With headquarters in Bonn, Germany, UNV added election monitoring and support to its responsibilities in 1992. Its largest contingent for this purpose served in CAMBODIA as part of UNTAC (UN Transitional Authority in Cambodia). UNV also assisted with South Africa's first all race elections in 1994, and it provided election supervisors for the 1996 elections in BOSNIA and Herzegovina. Other electoral service has occurred in Uganda, Mozambique, East Timor, the Central African Republic, and GUATEMALA. As part of peacekeeping operations, UN volunteers served as public affairs officers with the UN operation in Kosovo (UNMIK). The largest number of volunteers, as of May 2001, was in East Timor (499), followed by the FORMER YUGOSLAVIA with 263.

In his Millennium Report, SECRETARY-GENERAL Kofi ANNAN gave UNV the new assignment of coordinating a coalition of UN bodies and outside groups to administer the UN's Information Technology Service (UNITeS). UNV launched the service in November 2000. Sharing in Annan's hope to engage private entrepreneurs and corporations in the work of the United Nations, UNV in early 2001 signed its first contract with a private corporation to provide volunteers for Jamaica, Lesotho, and Uzbekistan.

Further Reading: UNV website: <www.unv.org>.

United Nations Yemen Observation Mission (UNYOM)

Civil war broke out in Yemen in September 1962 between republican forces and the royal government. International concern was heightened when Saudi Arabia began providing aid to the Yemeni Royal Family, and Egypt (then known as the United Arab Republic) sent troops to defend the rebel government that had displaced the former regime. Diplomacy by UN SECRETARY-GENERAL U THANT led to an agreement in April 1963 that required Saudi Arabia to end its aid and Egypt to withdraw its forces. A 20-kilometer demilitarized zone on each side of the border between Yemen and Saudi Arabia was established. On June 11 the SECURITY COUNCIL authorized the creation of UNYOM to patrol the zone. Egypt and Saudi Arabia agreed to pay the costs of the mission.

The original authorization for the mission was for two months. Continuing tensions, however, led to a number of extensions of UNYOM's mandate. After November 1963, command of the force was placed under Pier P. Spenelli, U Thant's SPECIAL REPRESENTATIVE. Spenelli headed a small force of approximately 200 personnel. UNYOM set up checkpoints along the border and created reconnaissance units throughout Yemen. In his reports to the Security Council throughout 1963 and 1964, Secretary-General Thant expressed frustration that UNYOM had not been able to bring about a disengagement of the warring sides, nor to move the political conflict toward resolution. The mission ended on September 4, 1964, following decisions in both Cairo and Riyadh to end Egyptian and Saudi Arabian funding.

See also PEACEKEEPING.

Further Reading: United Nations Department of Public Information. *The Blue Helmets: A Review of United Nations Peace-keeping.* 2d ed. New York: United Nations Department of Public Information, 1990.

United States

U.S. president Franklin D. ROOSEVELT named the United Nations and led the process that culminated in its establishment in 1945. Meeting with World War II ally British prime minister Winston CHURCHILL, FDR issued the "ATLANTIC CHARTER" on August 14, 1941, calling for postwar economic collaboration to prevent another worldwide economic crisis such as the one that followed the crash of 1929 and led to the rise of militarist states in Japan and Germany. The United States also supported the creation of a postwar system for the preservation of international peace and security, which the LEAGUE OF NATIONS had failed to ensure. In January 1942 the United States signed a DECLARATION of 26 united nations announcing their plans to proceed to design such an organization. In February 1945, at the YALTA CONFERENCE, Soviet leader Joseph STALIN, Prime Minister Churchill, and President Roosevelt negotiated their design for the postwar order, which would include a United Nations with universal MEMBERSHIP, but with permanent great power members of the SECURITY COUNCIL (SC). The Security Council would have a "consensus" rule among the PERMANENT MEMBERS, creating a de facto VETO. The United States hosted the TREATY signing conference in April 1945 in San Francisco establishing the United Nations, and the U.S. Senate ratified the treaty in July, making the United States the first signatory to ratify the treaty, and the first founding member to join the ranks of the permanent five (P5) members of the Security Council. Initially, the United States paid 30 percent of the UN operating BUDGET.

Secretary of State Madeleine Albright addresses UN delegates, 2000 (UN/DPI PHOTO BY ESKINDER DEBEBE)

The United States became home to the permanent HEADQUARTERS OF THE UNITED NATIONS when the Rockefeller family donated land in Manhattan, New York, expressly for that purpose. Ground was broken in 1948 for the construction of UN facilities. The Security Council, GENERAL ASSEMBLY (GA), and ECONOMIC AND SOCIAL COUNCIL (ECOSOC) meet there, and a majority of the permanent SECRETARIAT is located in New York City as well.

U.S. foreign policy at the United Nations has reflected and paralleled its larger goals in the international environment. During the COLD WAR the United States was successful in pursuing its policy of containing communism through the UN, especially the Security Council. For example, the USSR'S refusal to pull its troops out of Iran (as previously agreed with the British, who had also placed troops in Iran during WWII to stymie Nazi efforts to control oil fields there) triggered an emergency session in January 1946 of the fledgling Security Council, and shed unwanted attention on the Soviet policy, forcing the Soviet Union to withdraw its troops. In 1950, the United States obtained the first use of a UNITING FOR PEACE RESOLUTION approving the military response taken by the United States on behalf of the Republic of Korea. The USSR ambassador had been boycotting SC sessions in protest of the failure to seat the People's Republic of CHINA (PRC) as the sole legitimate representative of the Chinese people. Even though the Soviets vetoed any further action at subsequent Security Council sessions, the United States successfully obtained the General Assembly's approval of the multilateral force later assembled under U.S. leadership to roll back North Korean troops and restore the 38th parallel line of demarcation on the Korean Peninsula. During the French, and later the American, involvement in the Vietnam conflict, the United States blocked Security Council action on that civil war and external state intervention. Despite cold war tensions, the United States and the USSR did collaborate on crisis management through the UN, as demonstrated in the 1956 SUEZ CRISIS, when the Americans and Soviets denounced the AGGRESSION against Egypt by the United Kingdom, France, and Israel. The United States and the USSR sponsored a RESOLUTION in the General Assembly demanding a cease-fire of hostilities. The UN was not the central stage in which the 1962 CUBAN MISSILE CRISIS played out, but the subsequent onset of U.S.–Soviet arms control efforts was reflected in multilateral arms control and non-proliferation efforts undertaken at the UN (and supported by the Americans and Soviets) that culminated in the NUCLEAR NON-PROLIFERATION TREATY (NPT) and the COMPREHENSIVE TEST BAN TREATY (CTBT).

The 1973 crisis triggered by the surprise Arab attack on Israel included a prominent role for the United Nations. After the Israel Defense Forces turned back Egyptian and Syrian troops, the Soviet Union threatened to intervene in support of the Egyptians. U.S. president Richard Nixon, facing the possibility of having to intervene on behalf of Israel, ordered American troops worldwide onto alert. The two superpowers were able to back away from the brink of confrontation by joining in a Security Council resolution calling for a cease-fire. The Americans prevailed on the Israelis to join the cease-fire, and U.S. and Soviet forces then stood down from alert. In December 1973 the United States and Soviet Union co-chaired a conference in Geneva sponsored by the UN to explore prospects for an Arab-Israeli peace. That peace process never found a place in the UN, and the role of peace broker was assumed exclusively by the United States. Also in the Middle East in 1979, when the American embassy in Tehran, Iran, was occupied and its diplomats were held hostage, the United States received support in the SC and GA for actions that included condemnation of Iran's violation of diplomatic immunity and imposition of economic SANCTIONS on Iran.

As the cold war drew to an end with the impending collapse of the USSR, the United States and Soviet delegations at the UN collaborated in managing the crisis triggered by Iraq's invasion of Kuwait in August 1990. The Americans and British sponsored SC Resolution 678, authorizing the use of "all necessary means" to restore Kuwait's SOVEREIGNTY, that was passed with Soviet approval (and an abstention by the PRC) in December. The U.S. Congress approved use of force against Iraq in January 1991, and Kuwait was liberated by March. Subsequently, the United States and co-sponsor Great Britain clashed with fellow permanent SC members France, China, and Russia over continued imposition of sanctions against Iraq, and the companion issue of the inspection and dismantling of Iraq's infrastructure for the manufacture of WEAPONS OF MASS DESTRUCTION (WMD).

In 1994, the U.S. Congress voted to withhold payment of the U.S. share of UN dues, and it refused to pay current accumulated arrearages (despite the fact that its dues had already been reduced to 25 percent in 1972 by way of an American request to the United Nations). U.S. president George Bush, himself a former U.S. ambassador to the United Nations, had actively engaged the United Nations in his administration's multilateral efforts (1990–91) to liberate Kuwait. Both Bush and his successor, William J. Clinton, were strong advocates of reforming the UN to make it a more efficient and effective forum for the international management of peace and conflict issues in the new millennium. President Bush had even declared the onset of a "new world order" in which Americans and Soviets and other states would collaborate through the UN to address crises like the invasion of Kuwait. In 1994, however, a Congress much less friendly to the United Nations than its predecessors took office. Since Ronald Reagan's presidency (1981–89), a growing number of members of Congress had adopted a position critical of the UN for its alleged inefficiency and some members were overtly hostile to a UN-led "new world order."

Beginning in the U.S. House of Representatives under Speaker Newt Gingrich, the Congress voted to withhold dues in order to pressure the United Nations to pursue a balanced BUDGET and to reduce the size of the Secretariat. In 1994, Congress voted to freeze payments on dues, peacekeeping ASSESSMENTS, and restrict presidential discretion to commit U.S. troops to UN PEACEKEEPING operations. In 1995, the United States refused to approve a second term for incumbent SECRETARY-GENERAL BOUTROS-GHALI, supporting instead promotion of Kofi ANNAN of Ghana to that position. In 1999, U.S. ambassador to the UN Richard Holbrooke and (former U.S. envoy to the UN) Secretary of State Madeleine Albright worked to reduce the schism between the U.S. Congress and the UN. Ambassador Holbrooke invited the U.S. Senate Foreign Relations Committee chairman Jesse Helms to address the Security Council. Senator Helms returned the favor, inviting a UN delegation to visit the Senate. The U.S. arrearage in dues (approaching $1.8 billion) remained unresolved at the end of 2000, but with the international crisis resulting from the terrorist attacks occurring on September 11, 2001, the U.S. Congress quickly approved the remaining negotiated payment of $582 million.

Despite frequent criticism of the UN for its large bureaucracy and the many difficulties involved in peace-making and peacekeeping in the growing number of intra-state conflicts, American public opinion of the United Nations remained positive at the beginning of the 21st century, as did public support for a continued U.S. leadership role at the

UN. The U.S. government maintained its position on the REFORM and restructuring challenges facing the United Nations, consistently supporting expansion of the permanent SC membership to include Japan and Germany. Both the U.S. government and the American public did not support, however, the concept of a peacekeeping force under the direct authority of the United Nations.

On September 11, 2001, terrorists seized control of four U.S. civilian airliners, crashing two of them into the World Trade Center towers in New York City, bringing both towers to the ground and killing approximately 3,000 people. The third plane crashed into the Pentagon in Northern Virginia after circling major government sites in Washington, D.C. The fourth airliner crashed in western Pennsylvania with the loss of all onboard. President George W. Bush declared the events "acts of war," and made harsh demands on the Taliban government in AFGHANISTAN, believing that the regime was harboring Osama bin Laden, reputedly the mastermind behind the terrorist attack. The United States sought UN support for any actions it might take in reprisal.

On September 12 the Security Council unanimously adopted Resolution 1368. The council held that any act of international TERRORISM was a threat to international peace and security. The General Assembly, once it convened on the 13th, followed with a condemnation of the attack. The council also passed Resolution 1373 on September 28, calling on all states to "prevent and suppress the financing of terrorist acts." Council members invoked CHAPTER VII, making the resolution's provisions mandatory on all member states. At American urging, the Security Council decided that all states should criminalize the provision or collection of funds for such acts. It also called on states to freeze the assets of suspected terrorist groups. It affirmed that states should prohibit their nationals or organizations from making funds and financial assets available to potential terrorists. They were also required by the resolution to deny safe haven to those who finance, plan, support, or commit terrorist acts. Resolution 1373 established a Security Council Counter-Terrorism Committee.

The United States issued an ultimatum to the Taliban demanding the extradition of bin Laden and his senior associates, the closing of his training bases in Afghanistan, and the stationing of U.S. personnel on Afghan territory to investigate and destroy terrorist camps. The Bush administration organized a large coalition in support of its demands, including Afghanistan's neighboring states of Pakistan and Uzbekistan. The North Atlantic Treaty Organization declared the attack on the United States an act requiring COLLECTIVE SELF-DEFENSE. On October 7, 2001, the United States and Great Britain launched intensive air attacks on major cities, military targets, and training areas inside Afghanistan. Faced with a growing refugee and humanitarian crisis, and with calls from UN officials, among others, to assist innocent Afghan victims of the attack, the U.S. administration made airdrops of food rations and offered to assist with humanitarian relief. Also recognizing the need to assure stability in Afghanistan if the Taliban was driven from power, President Bush lent support to future UN efforts at NATION-BUILDING in Afghanistan, reversing the position of the administration on this aspect of contemporary UN PEACEKEEPING activities.

See also DECLARATION BY UNITED NATIONS, GULF WAR, TEHERAN CONFERENCE, UNITED NATIONS CONFERENCE ON INTERNATIONAL ORGANIZATION.

Further Reading: Bertrand, Maurice. *The United Nations: Past, Present And Future.* The Hague: Martinus Nijhoff Publishers, 1997. Moore, John Allphin, Jr., and Jerry Pubantz. *To Create a New World: American Presidents and the United Nations.* New York: Peter Lang Publishers, 1999. Muldoon, James P., JoAnn Fagot Aviel, Richard Reitano, and Earl Sullivan. *Multilateral Diplomacy and the United Nations Today.* Boulder, Colo.: Westview Press, 1999. Ostrower, Gary B. *The United Nations and the United States.* New York: Twayne Publishers, 1998. Schulzinger, Robert D. *American Diplomacy in the Twentieth Century.* 3d ed. New York: Oxford University Press, 1998.

— D. M. Schlagheck

Uniting for Peace Resolution

On November 3, 1950, the United Nations GENERAL ASSEMBLY (GA) approved the Uniting for Peace Resolution, giving the Assembly the authority to discuss a threat to the peace, a breach of the peace, or an act of AGGRESSION, and to make recommendations for collective measures whenever "the SECURITY COUNCIL, because of lack of unanimity of the PERMANENT MEMBERS, fails to exercise its primary responsibility for the maintenance of international peace and security." Passed in the midst of the KOREAN WAR, this decision provided a mechanism to circumvent the anticipated use of the VETO—at the time by the Soviet Union, later by other permanent members—to ensure the UN's ability to undertake action to restore the peace. The RESOLUTION amounted to an informal AMENDMENT of the CHARTER, shifting authority for ENFORCEMENT MEASURES from the exclusive control of the Security Council and allowing the Assembly to provide legal authority for "the use of armed force when necessary." The resolution allowed for EMERGENCY SPECIAL SESSIONS of the General Assembly to consider recommendations within 24 hours of a request by any seven members of the Security Council (nine members after the Charter revisions of 1965). The emergency special session could also be convened at the request of a majority of the Assembly's members. The resolution established a Peace Observation Committee and a Collective Measures Committee, and it called on all states to designate and train troops to be on call by either the General Assembly or the Security Council.

When North Korea invaded the South in June 1950, U.S. president Harry S. Truman took immediate action, calling for an emergency meeting of the UN Security Council. A UN resolution of June 27 provided for military SANCTIONS against North Korea and called on member states to assist the Republic of Korea. The Security Council was able to act decisively because the Soviet ambassador was boycotting council meetings at the time, protesting the seating of the Nationalist Government as the representative of CHINA. His absence meant the Soviet veto was not an obstacle to action.

Anticipating a Security Council deadlock once the Soviets returned to the table, which would make council actions under CHAPTER VII in Korea and in future COLD WAR conflicts nearly impossible, the American delegation shepherded through the GA COMMITTEE SYSTEM the draft resolution. The USSR argued that it violated Article 12 of the Charter, which prohibits the General Assembly from making any recommendations concerning a dispute while the Security Council is deliberating on the matter. With its large working majority in the body, however, the UNITED STATES easily secured passage of the measure with 52 states VOTING in favor, five (all from the Soviet bloc) voting against, and two abstentions. In subsequent years the call for troops and the committee system created by the resolution would prove moribund. But the convocation of emergency special sessions would become an accepted procedure.

Ironically, it was the USSR that first employed the resolution's provisions, joining with Yugoslavia to call for an emergency GA session in 1956 on the SUEZ CRISIS. The United Kingdom and France had vetoed Security Council measures to end their invasion of the canal region. The General Assembly did what a majority in the Security Council could not do. It passed a resolution calling for an immediate ceasefire and the withdrawal of forces from the area. It also directed SECRETARY-GENERAL Dag HAMMARSKJÖLD to report within 48 hours on the preparation and dispatch of a UNITED NATIONS EMERGENCY FORCE (UNEF) to separate the parties. The end of the crisis and the apparent effectiveness of the UN's first PEACEKEEPING operation seemed to demonstrate the worth of the resolution. The Soviet Union also succeeded in bringing about an emergency special session on the Middle East when war broke out in 1967.

In 1956 a second emergency special session convened to consider the Hungarian crisis and the Soviet invasion of that country. Unfortunately, the session demonstrated one of the two most serious weaknesses of the Uniting for Peace Resolution. In this case the offender was one of the two superpowers. It quickly became clear that there was nothing the General Assembly might do to force the Soviets to change course. A similar impasse occurred in January 1980, when the Assembly held its 10th emergency session, this time to consider the Soviet invasion of AFGHANISTAN. By a vote of 104 to 18 to 18, the Assembly "deplored" the invasion, called upon the USSR to withdraw, and urged the Security Council to find ways to implement the Assembly's resolution. But UN action had little discernible impact on Soviet foreign policy.

Recommendations by the Assembly on matters originally thought to be within the sole JURISDICTION of the Security Council also raised constitutional concerns for some UN members, making them unwilling to pay for or support UN actions that flowed from those recommendations. Following the fourth emergency special session (1960) on the CONGO, both Russia and France refused to pay their assessments for peacekeeping operations. These rebuffs led to a financial crisis that brought the world body to the verge of bankruptcy. The Congolese experience made the procedure far less appealing to UN members. The resolution was not invoked again until 1980.

Despite its limitations, the Uniting for Peace Resolution effectively altered the relative roles of the Security Council and the General Assembly. Cold war politics undercut the ability of the council to carry out its functions as the primary organ responsible for maintaining peace. By "stretching" the Charter, the resolution opened up an opportunity for the Assembly to fill this role when conflict between Washington and Moscow threatened to make the United Nations helpless. Thus, the Uniting for Peace innovation represented part of a general shift in UN activity during the cold war from the council to the larger body, where simple majorities, and, importantly, the absence of the veto, made action possible.

Further Reading: Plano, Jack C., and Robert E. Riggs. *Forging World Order: The Politics of International Organization*. New York: Macmillan, 1967. Simma, Bruno, ed. *The Charter of the United Nations: A Commentary.* New York: Oxford University Press, 1994.

Universal Children's Day
Celebrated on November 20 annually, the day marks the anniversary of the GENERAL ASSEMBLY's adoption of the DECLARATION OF THE RIGHTS OF THE CHILD in 1959 and the CONVENTION on the Rights of the Child in 1989.

Universal Declaration of Human Rights
The Universal Declaration of Human Rights, adopted by the GENERAL ASSEMBLY on December 10, 1948, is the basis of global efforts to promote and protect HUMAN RIGHTS. The DECLARATION serves as the foundation on which all other global human rights instruments are built. While the UN CHARTER did not define "human rights," it was the first global instrument to use the term, and its signatories were the first to pledge to promote human rights at the international level. According to its preamble, the declaration is designed to set "a common standard of achievement for all peoples and all nations, to the end that every individual and

every organ of society, keeping this Declaration constantly in mind, shall strive by teaching and education to promote respect for these rights and freedoms and by progressive measures, national and international, to secure their universal and effective recognition and observance, both among the peoples of Member States themselves and among the peoples of territories under their JURISDICTION."

The declaration stresses the "inherent dignity" of the individual, the principle of equality, and the three interrelated fundamental rights of life, liberty, and security of the person. It pledges such basic rights as equality before the law, freedom of movement and residence, civil liberties, including freedom from cruel, inhuman, or degrading treatment or punishment, and freedom of thought, conscience, expression, and religion, and access to judicial processes and the rule of law. It guarantees everyone the right to own property. It also guarantees the right to vote and participate in the political process, the right to an education, an adequate standard of living, and health protection. By acknowledging that minimal social standards of life are among the human rights

of all, the declaration goes beyond traditional Western notions of individual rights, and it incorporates the societal perspective promoted by states in Africa, Asia, and LATIN AMERICA. It recognizes the need for social order, and it stipulates that individuals also have duties, which impose certain limitations on the exercise of their freedoms. Since those limitations are determined by national law, the declaration accepts the principle that states can limit these rights, provided that such laws are "solely for the purpose of securing due recognition and respect for the rights" of others, and establish "the just requirements of morality, public order and the general welfare in a democratic society." The Universal Declaration set the direction for all subsequent agreements in the field of human rights.

Despite its fundamental nature, reaching agreement on the Universal Declaration proved difficult because of sharply differing views regarding what constituted a human right. The 1945 San Francisco Conference decided not to define human rights in the CHARTER in order to avoid a lengthy debate that would delay the launching of the United

Eleanor Roosevelt, Chair, Commission on Human Rights (UN PHOTO 23783)

Nations. It was understood at the conference that a document would be drafted at a later date. At its initial session, the newly formed COMMISSION ON HUMAN RIGHTS established a small drafting group to prepare a document on human rights. Eleanor Roosevelt, the widow of U.S. president Franklin D. ROOSEVELT, chaired both the full commission and the drafting committee. Mrs. Roosevelt played a central role in the evolution of the document, along with John Humphrey of Canada, the first director of the SECRETARIAT's Division of Human Rights, Charles Malik, the rapporteur of the commission, and René Cassin, the commission's second vice-president. Throughout the drafting, the Soviet Union and its Eastern European allies resisted the idea of an international bill of rights, or any binding agreement. Even at a time when UN MEMBERSHIP was small, reaching agreement on the declaration proved difficult. International tensions resulting from the partition of Palestine and the onset of the COLD WAR threatened division rather than diplomacy in discussions of such a document. The commission went through several drafts before recommending one to the GA THIRD COMMITTEE, where the declaration was discussed article by article and where numerous separate votes were taken on various articles. Remarkably, the declaration, as it had been penned by the drafting committee and approved by the Human Rights Commission, survived relatively intact. Charles Malik, chair of the Third Committee, then submitted the declaration to the General Assembly on the evening of December 9, 1948, describing it as a "composite synthesis" of all existing rights traditions. Nothing like this had ever occurred before. Just before midnight, at the Palais de Chaillot in Paris, the roll call tally began. The final vote was 48 in favor, eight abstentions, and none opposed.

The General Assembly declared it to be the responsibility of all member states to respect the rights described in the document. Unlike a TREATY, COVENANT, or CONVENTION, a declaration is not legally binding. Thus, once the General Assembly approved, the Declaration of Human Rights did not require ratification by the various states. Rather, it set standards for governments, which were subject to review by the international community through UN bodies. Nevertheless, it, like the Charter and the STATUTE OF THE INTERNATIONAL COURT OF JUSTICE, was considered a basic agreement of the United Nations. States joining the United Nations since its adoption were required to accept its principles. As the framers of the declaration discerned, this document was something new in international affairs. Its concise 30 articles, declaring that rights belonged to everyone, represented a fusion of rights ideas from the older Western tradition of political and civil liberty and the more recent concern with social and economic needs. As Frenchman René Cassin noted at the time, while national jurisdiction over the treatment of citizens remained, "it will no longer be exclusive." Largely through the efforts of Hansa Mehta, India's representative on the Human Rights Commission, the document, as specifically indicated in Article 1, expressly included WOMEN as well as men. The words "All human beings" also replaced the more traditional "all men" in the document. Finally, by virtue of the fortuitous phrasing of the commission's subcommittee on style, headed by Cassin, the title of the document was officially changed to the "Universal" rather than "International" Declaration of Rights. That is, it was morally binding on everyone, not just on governments who approved it.

All subsequent human rights instruments were based on the Universal Declaration. It is part of the "International Bill of Human Rights," together with the much more specific INTERNATIONAL COVENANT ON CIVIL AND POLITICAL RIGHTS (ICCPR) and the INTERNATIONAL COVENANT ON ECONOMIC, SOCIAL, AND CULTURAL RIGHTS (ICESCR), which the General Assembly adopted in 1966, and which took some 10 additional years to gain sufficient ratifications to go into effect. The covenants defined rights more precisely, and added new rights. They also strengthened the declaration since, as covenants, they were legally binding for those states that signed them.

See also DECLARATION BY UNITED NATIONS, DECLARATION ON THE GRANTING OF INDEPENDENCE TO COLONIAL COUNTRIES AND PEOPLES, SOVEREIGNTY.

Further Reading: Glendon, Mary Ann. *A World Made New. Eleanor Roosevelt and the Universal Declaration of Human Rights.* New York: Random House, 2001. Malik, Habib C. *The Challenge of Human Rights: Charles Malik and the Universal Declaration.* Oxford: Center for Lebanese Studies, 2000. Morsink, Johannes. *The Universal Declaration of Human Rights: Origins, Drafting and Intent.* Philadelphia: University of Pennsylvania Press, 1999. Power, Samantha, and Graham Allison, eds. *Realizing Human Rights: Movement from Inspiration to Impact.* New York: St. Martin's, 2000.

— *K. J. Grieb*

Universal Postal Union (UPU)

Established by the Berne Treaty of 1874, the Universal Postal Union became a UN SPECIALIZED AGENCY in 1948. Its headquarters is in Berne, Switzerland. In 1964, the Universal Postal Congress in Vienna adopted the current constitution of the UPU, which has been amended on several occasions since. According to Article I of its constitution, the union is to "secure the organization and improvement of the postal services and to promote in this sphere the development of international collaboration and undertake, as far as possible, technical assistance in postal matters requested by member countries." The UPU is the primary international organization to provide communication and cooperation among postal services. Those NATION-STATES having adopted the constitution comprise a single, worldwide, postal territory. At the turn of the century there were 189 members.

Every five years the UPU convenes a congress, with plenipotentiary representatives from all member states, to update its procedures, pass legislation, set a budget, and elect its Council of Administrators, who carry on the work of the UPU between congresses. On its legislative agenda are weight and size limits for mailed items, the conditions of acceptance for postal materials, and recommendations on postage rates. There are 40 members on the Council of Administrators plus an additional member representing the host country of the quinquennial congress, who serves as chair. The union chooses the council on the basis of equitable regional distribution, and its members are limited to two consecutive terms. In addition to the plenary Congress and the Council of Administrators, there is also a Postal Operations Council—which has 40 elected members and acts as a technical operations body, revises details of the UPU's regulations, and is responsible for keeping the UPU up-to-date technologically—and an International Bureau, which is the permanent SECRETARIAT of the UPU and the main liaison with other organizations.

See also ADMINISTRATIVE COMMITTEE ON COORDINATION, ADMINISTRATIVE TRIBUNALS, EXPANDED PROGRAM OF TECHNICAL ASSISTANCE.

Further Reading: UPU website: <www.upu.int>.

Urquhart, Brian (1919–)

Among the most visible and articulate commentators on the United Nations, Sir Brian Urquhart became a central figure during the latter 20th century whenever and wherever UN discussions arose. Born in the United Kingdom in 1919, he attended Westminster School and Christ Church, Oxford, before serving in the British army and military intelligence in World War II. He was personal assistant to Gladwyn Jebb, who worked on the UN preparatory commission in London. He then became personal assistant to Trygve LIE, the first SECRETARY-GENERAL. From 1954 to 1971 he served under Ralph BUNCHE in a number of capacities, and he was involved in conferences on the peaceful uses of atomic energy and on the CONGO crisis of the early 1960s. He also participated in UN PEACEKEEPING activities in CYPRUS, KASHMIR, and the Middle East. Afterward he served as UNDER SECRETARY-GENERAL for Special Political Affairs, working on assignments in Lebanon, Israel and Palestine, NAMIBIA, and elsewhere. He retired from the SECRETARIAT in 1986 and began an active writing career. He published major biographies of Dag HAMMARSKJÖLD (1972) and Ralph Bunche (1993), studies of decolonization (1989) and the relationship of the United Nations with INTERNATIONAL LAW (1986), an extensive autobiography (1987), and, with Erskine Childers, a number of monographs for the Dag Hammarskjöld Foundation in Uppsala, Sweden, dealing with REFORM and revitalization of the United Nations. From the early 1990s his essays and book reviews appeared regularly in the *New York Review of Books*.

Further Reading: Urquhart, Brian. *A Life in Peace and War.* New York: Harper and Row, 1987.

V

Vance-Owen Plan *See* BOSNIA.

veto

A special power given only to the permanent five powers (P5) of the SECURITY COUNCIL—the People's Republic of CHINA, France, Russia, the United Kingdom, and the UNITED STATES OF AMERICA—is the veto over resolutions being considered by the council. In order to pass, according to Article 27 (3) of the UN CHARTER, a RESOLUTION requires nine votes in favor with none of the P5 being opposed. Article 27 (2) stipulates that the veto, however, does not apply in the case of a procedural matter, but only on SUBSTANTIVE QUESTIONS. Whether a matter is procedural or substantive is itself a substantive question and, therefore, subject to the veto. While used only sparingly since the 1940s, the DOUBLE VETO allows a permanent member to block even the decision to qualify a matter as procedural. The veto recognizes the critical importance and power of the PERMANENT MEMBERS of the council, at the expense in some cases of the UN's ability to act in a timely manner to meet threats to the peace. It has been used not only to block resolutions but also to thwart nominations for SECRETARY-GENERAL (43 cases) and to impede the ADMISSION of new members (59 vetoes).

The current VOTING arrangement that guides the Security Council was developed at the meetings of the victors of World War II during the DUMBARTON OAKS conference (1944) and the YALTA CONFERENCE (1945). The Soviet Union from the very beginning demanded a veto for each of the major powers. During the wartime negotiations with the United States, Joseph STALIN insisted on guarantees that the new organization could not take action concerning international peace and security without Russia's agreement.

Despite prior allied agreements on the voting procedure, the meaning of the Charter provisions concerning the veto was a matter of serious contention among the permanent members in the early years of the United Nations. The Soviet Union argued that Article 27 (3) demanded a positive vote cast by all of the P5 for a resolution to pass. In this case, if any of the P5 were to abstain or not participate, a resolution would fail. On this basis the Soviet delegation protested Security Council actions at the commencement of the KOREAN WAR, since it was then boycotting council meetings. Fearing deadlock, Great Britain and the United States proposed, and the Security Council president ruled, that an abstention or no vote at all by a permanent member did not constitute a veto. This meant that a decision could be taken without the positive backing of one of the P5. This would also be true if a permanent member were a party to a dispute, since the Charter requires it to abstain from voting in that case [Article 27 (3)].

In recent years, the actual use of the veto has declined. The P5, more and more in closed negotiations, use the threat of the veto, thereby forcing others to withdraw their proposals. This strategy has been described as a "closet veto." Also, a permanent member can convince six or more other mem-

Changing Patterns in the Use of the Veto in the Security Council
Table shows number of times veto was cast, by country[1]
Information prepared by Solange Habib, Senior Research Assistant,
UN Security Council – Office of the Assistant Secretary General

Period	China*	France	Britain	U.S.	USSR/Russia	Total
Total	4–5	18	32	73	120	248
2001	–	–	–	1	–	1
2000	–	–	–	–	–	0
1999	1	–	–	–	–	1
1998	–	–	–	–	–	0
1997	1	–	–	2	–	3
1996	–	–	–	–	–	0
1986–95	–	3	8	24	2	37
1976–85	–	9	11	34	6	60
1966–75	2	2	10	12	7	33
1956–65	–	2	3	–	26	31
1946–55	(1*)	2	–	–	79	82

Source: Global Policy Forum

* *Between 1946 and 1971, the Chinese seat on the Security Council was occupied by the Republic of China, which used the veto only once (to block Mongolia's application for membership in 1955). The first veto exercised by the present occupant, the People's Republic of China, was therefore not until August 25, 1972.*

[1] Only a minority of vetoes have been cast in cases where vital international security issues were at stake. 59 vetoes have been cast to block admission of member states. Additionally, 43 vetoes have been used to block nominees for Secretary-General, although these vetoes were cast during closed sessions of the council and are not included in the table above.

bers to abstain or oppose a decision, and thereby block an action without casting a negative vote.

Within the context of REFORM OF THE UNITED NATIONS, especially of the Security Council, most of the countries that do not have the veto criticize its use by the permanent powers. While some call for the veto to be abolished completely, others, contemplating enlargement of the council, recommend extending the power to other states or regions. Some scholars and politicians argue that a veto should only be allowed in certain, limited cases, such as those occurring within the context of CHAPTER VII; others ask that a veto, if cast, be announced and justified. Other plans call for a formula of a "concurrent veto," requiring two or three of the P5 acting together to block a resolution. Finally, sometimes suggested is a weighted voting system to replace the veto altogether. As all proposals needing an AMENDMENT of the Charter, these initiatives are themselves subject to a veto (Article 108), meaning that no alternative to the current voting system can be created against the will of any one of the five permanent members.

See also TEHERAN CONFERENCE, UNITED STATES OF AMERICA, *references to the use of the veto in the following entries:* AFGHANISTAN, BOUTROS-GHALI, COLD WAR, LIE, MIDDLE EAST WAR OF 1967, UN SECURITY COUNCIL RESOLUTION 242, UNITING FOR PEACE RESOLUTION, WALDHEIM.

Further Reading: Fassbender, Bodo. *UN Security Council Reform and the Right of Veto.* The Hague: Kluwer Law International, 1998. May, Ernest R., and Angeliki E. Laiou, eds. *The Dumbarton Oaks Conversations and the United Nations, 1944–1994.* Cambridge, Mass.: Harvard University Press, 1998.

— *T. J. Weiler*

Vice President of the General Assembly   *See*
GENERAL COMMITTEE.

Vienna Convention for the Protection of the Ozone Layer
On March 22, 1985, the Vienna Convention for the Protection of the Ozone Layer—negotiated over four years from the time a working group designated by the UNITED NATIONS ENVIRONMENT PROGRAMME (UNEP) first began to prepare a global framework—opened for signature. A total of 20 nations signed at Vienna and others followed in subsequent years. The CONVENTION entered into force September 22, 1988, and by 2001 it counted 177 parties. The convention is open to not only all states but also (according to Article 13) to regional economic integration organizations.

Ozone can be found in two areas: near the ground where it is too plentiful and causes smog pollution, and in the stratosphere, where there may not be enough. In the upper atmosphere, ozone absorbs the sun's ultraviolet radiation. Thus, if it is depleted, humans and other living things are exposed to more dangerous levels of radiation. Consequences can include increased cases of skin cancer, eye problems, and damage to plants and animals. In 1974, scientists began to discern that a group of chemicals, called chlorofluorocarbons (CFCs), was particularly aggressive in depleting ozone in the upper atmosphere. CFCs, unfortunately, are emitted from air conditioners, refrigerators, aerosol cans, fire extinguishers, industrial solvents, and other devices that have become part of modern life.

UNEP led in the negotiating of, and now administers, the Vienna Convention as well as the MONTREAL PROTOCOL (1987; entered into force January 1, 1989) and amendments to it negotiated at London in 1990 and Copenhagen in 1992. Under the terms of these agreements, developed countries have worked to ban the production and sale of CFCs and have agreed to schedules to phase out other substances that emit CFCs. Scientists working with a joint UNEP–WORLD METEOROLOGICAL ORGANIZATION (WMO) assessment regime have at periodic meetings confirmed the danger of ozone depletion and suggested the value of the international agreements.

The SECRETARIAT for the Vienna Convention and the Montreal PROTOCOL is headquartered in Nairobi, Kenya.

See also ENVIRONMENT, KYOTO PROTOCOL.

Further Reading: Jones, Laura, ed. *Global Warming: The Science and the Politics.* Vancouver: Fraser Institute, 1997. Vienna Convention website: <www.unep.org/ozone/vienna>.

Vienna Declaration *See* WORLD CONFERENCE ON HUMAN RIGHTS.

Volcker-Ogata Report *See* REFORM OF THE UNITED NATIONS.

Voluntary Fund for the United Nations Decade for Women *See* UNITED NATIONS DEVELOPMENT FUND FOR WOMEN.

Voluntary Programs Budget *See* BUDGET OF THE UNITED NATIONS.

voting
The UN CHARTER establishes a system of parliamentary diplomacy, in that decisions are taken by votes of the MEMBERSHIP on RESOLUTIONS that have been debated and revised in committees and plenary sessions. Under this system, unanimity is not required as it is in TREATY negotiations and other diplomatic activities directly between states. The process of decision making differs among the organs of the United Nations. For example, procedures for voting in the TRUSTEESHIP COUNCIL (Article 89 of the UN CHARTER) and in the ECONOMIC AND SOCIAL COUNCIL (Article 67) are more straightforward than in the GENERAL ASSEMBLY (GA) and the SECURITY COUNCIL (SC). In the former two organs each member has one vote and decisions are made by a simple majority of those members present and voting. There is no two-thirds vote requirement for certain categories of questions as in the General Assembly, no weighting of voting as, for example, in the WORLD BANK group, and no particular nations have specific voting privileges, such as the VETO accorded to the PERMANENT MEMBERS (P5) of the Security Council. The most difficult voting threshold established by the Charter is for AMENDMENTS to the document. According to Article 108, this requires a vote of two-thirds in the General Assembly and ratification by two-thirds of the UN's members, including all the permanent members of the Security Council. There are also procedures to assure that a country does not lose its vote when its representative serves in a parliamentary position. The president of the Economic and Social Council (ECOSOC), for example, has no vote but may delegate the vote to another member of his or her delegation. A majority is required to pass any ECOSOC decision. This rule makes it easier to achieve the required 28 votes if all 54 members are present and voting.

Unlike the three councils (SC, ECOSOC, and Trusteeship Council), which have limited membership, the General Assembly, fully representing the principle of equal SOVEREIGNTY, is composed of all NATION-STATES that are members of the United Nations. Each has one vote, and each may participate in all decisions and all voting of the Assembly. All drafts of the UN Charter leading up to its approval in San Francisco on June 26, 1945, committed the new organization to the principle of one-state-one-vote in the General Assembly. However, involved discussions took place regarding the exact majorities required. For example, the Dominican Republic proposed that the vote on IMPORTANT QUESTIONS be greater than two-thirds, Mexico suggested three-fourths, and Chile sought unanimity, particularly on questions relating to military action. It is Article 18 of the Charter that details voting practice in the General Assembly. The Article's three paragraphs (1) accord each member one equal vote, (2) establish that specific important questions require a two-thirds majority of the members present and voting, and (3) allow the General Assembly, by simple majority vote, to determine any other questions ("including the determination of additional categories of questions") that must be decided by a two-thirds majority. The provisions of Article 18 were extensively debated at the San Francisco Conference. Delegates entertained several additional suggestions for inclusion in the Important Questions category of paragraph 2 before settling on the extant language. Article 18's third paragraph, allowing a GA simple majority to determine other issues to be approved by a two-thirds vote, however, was adopted almost verbatim from the DUMBARTON OAKS proposals of 1944.

The main committees of the General Assembly, also composed of all UN members, decide all issues by a simple majority vote; there is no two-thirds requirement on specific or determined issues, as in the GA plenary (consequently, a GA committee, by simple majority, could forward a recommendation that is unable to obtain a necessary plenary vote of two-thirds). Also, it should be noted that a member may lose the right to vote through SUSPENSION (Article 4), EXPULSION (Article 5), or being in arrears in its financial contributions for two years (Article 19).

The distinction in Article 18 between "important questions" and "other questions" refers to those issues specified in the second paragraph, which are "important," and those referenced in the third paragraph, which are "other." Thus a two-thirds vote of those present and voting *must* be garnered on important questions specifically listed in paragraph 2: matters regarding international peace and security, electing NON-PERMANENT MEMBERS to the Security Council and all members of ECOSOC and the Trusteeship Council, the ADMISSION OF MEMBERS to the United Nations, issues relating to the operation of the TRUSTEESHIP SYSTEM, a member's expulsion or suspension, and budgetary questions. In addition, the GA's Rules of Procedure require a two-thirds vote in order to reconsider proposals that have been adopted or rejected, and in order to add items to the supplementary list or the agenda of an EMERGENCY SPECIAL SESSION. Rule 84 of the Rules of Procedure provides that amendments to proposals relating to Important Questions require a two-thirds vote.

Using the third paragraph of Article 18, the General Assembly has, over the years, determined by a simple majority vote that a question was "important," and required a two-thirds vote of those present and voting. There are numerous examples of such GA action, including consideration of new Trusteeship Agreements, questions on the disposal of former Italian colonies, questions regarding racial conflict in South Africa, the question of South-West Africa, and many more. One of the most notable was the use of the third paragraph to make the question of Chinese representation in the United Nations an important question. From 1961 on the UNITED STATES used this provision of the Charter to make any change in Chinese representation an important question. In this way, Washington was able to flout supporters of the People's Republic of CHINA (PRC) who sought to oust the U.S.-supported republican government on Taiwan as the official Chinese representative (and permanent member to the Security Council). There were, then, always two votes on this volatile issue, one on the important question resolution, which required only a majority vote, and a second on

whether or not to seat Beijing, which required the more difficult two-thirds super majority. Until 1971, the procedural technique had allowed the United States to deny membership to the PRC. Then, on October 25, 1971, the vote on the important question resolution regarding Chinese representation lost for the first time, 59–55, with 15 abstaining, and on the next vote, the General Assembly removed Taiwan and seated Beijing as the official Chinese representative in the United Nations.

The GA's Rules of Procedure define the Charter's words "members present and voting" as "members casting an affirmative or negative vote. Members that abstain from voting are considered as not voting." That is, less than a majority of the total membership can make decisions. The rules also speak to the definition of a "quorum." At least one-third of the members of the General Assembly must be in attendance to open a meeting and to begin debate. But decisions may be taken only when a majority of the full body is present.

Rule 87 of the GA's Rules of Procedure provides that voting shall normally be made "by show of hands or by standing but any representative may request a roll-call." Since 1976 voting has been possible by mechanical means, with votes registered instantly on illuminated boards easily visible in the General Assembly Hall and in GA committee meeting halls. Elections typically require a secret ballot.

The overwhelming majority of GA decisions have been made by a margin of two-thirds or more of those voting. Many have been adopted without a vote or by acclamation (such as in the cases of the admittance of new members and, in 2001, the reelection of SECRETARY-GENERAL Kofi ANNAN) demonstrating that the practice of seeking consensus is more widespread in the General Assembly than often thought.

Voting in the Security Council is unique in large part because of the veto privilege accorded to the permanent members. Article 27 explains voting procedures in the Security Council. Each of the 15 members has one vote. Decisions on "procedural" matters are to be made by an affirmative vote of nine members. All other matters must be made by nine votes with the concurrence of all the permanent members. Some small and medium sized states opposed the advantage granted permanent members, but they eventually accepted when the sponsoring governments made it clear that such voting procedures were a non-negotiable condition for forming the new organization. Indeed, the United States, the United Kingdom, and the Soviet Union insisted on the veto. None would have joined the United Nations without it.

The veto, however, applies only in the Security Council. Although all P5 nations have been members of the Trusteeship Council, the INTERNATIONAL COURT OF JUSTICE (ICJ), and, with the exception of China, have always sat on the Economic and Social Council, their vote carries no more weight nor special character than other members in those bodies. The only other "weighted" voting advantage those states, or any others, might have are found in the financial institutions of the UNITED NATIONS SYSTEM. The BRETTON WOODS organs, specifically the World Bank, the INTERNATIONAL MONETARY FUND, the INTERNATIONAL FINANCE CORPORATION, and the INTERNATIONAL DEVELOPMENT ASSOCIATION, grant voting power on the basis of financial contributions to the assets of these facilities. The consequence is that the United States has on average nearly one-fifth of the vote in these institutions.

The DUMBARTON OAKS proposals of 1944 had no provisions on voting procedure for the Security Council. The United Kingdom held the view that a party to a dispute, even if a permanent member, must abstain from voting on the issues of the dispute. The Soviet Union held the opposite position, insisting that the rule of unanimity among the permanent members (thus the veto) should obtain in all matters. The U.S. Department of State then proposed a compromise that became the basis of the so-called Yalta Formula, agreed to at the Big Power meeting in the Crimea in February 1945. By this formula, the veto would not apply to "procedural matters," a party to a dispute would not vote in matters in which peaceful adjustment of disputes was involved (under CHAPTER VI and under paragraph 3 of Article 52), but great power unanimity would be required in ENFORCEMENT MEASURES, even if one of the permanent members were a party to the dispute. This became the accepted, if hazy, interpretation of the third paragraph of Article 27.

Article 27 offers no clear definition of "procedural matters." Nor is there an enumeration of such matters comparable to the specific designation of "Important Questions" for the General Assembly as contained in Article 18. In practice, certain questions have been decided by the Security Council by a majority of nine, without the necessary concurrence of the P5. Examples include determining the agenda, placing an item on the agenda, and determining the order of the agenda's items; suspension of a meeting; conduct of business; and inviting a state to participate in Security Council proceedings if that state's interests are affected. Other, more sensitive, matters have been considered non-procedural and thus susceptible to veto. Examples are: the admission of new members, the suspension of membership rights, the expulsion of members, the execution of opinions by the International Court of Justice, and recommending the appointment of the Secretary-General. Moreover, the practice within the Security Council has been to allow a decision as to whether a matter was substantive or procedural to be itself a SUBSTANTIVE QUESTION and hence subject to veto. By this "DOUBLE VETO" process there can be one vote to decide whether a matter is substantive or procedural and a second on the issue itself. In this way, a permanent member can veto almost anything it chooses. There is also the so-called hidden veto, used by the United States in the first decades of the United Nations,

in which, by obtaining sufficient votes against a resolution it opposes, a P5 member is not compelled to cast a single veto.

The word *veto* does not appear in Article 27. Rather, "the concurring votes of the permanent members" are required for all non-procedural matters. The requirement of concurrence has led, in practice, to allowing for abstentions by permanent members. In 1946 the Soviet Union exercised the first abstention and, since that time, abstentions have been interpreted as not preventing a non-procedural decision by the Security Council. The interpretation gains some force from the fact that, for the General Assembly, Article 18 of the Charter specifically refers to members "present and voting," while such a phrase is missing from Article 27. Abstention thus complies with the unanimity principle, which is challenged only by an overt veto. Otherwise, consent is accorded "in disguise." The People's Republic of China has been the most frequent abstainer among the P5, and in each instance the abstention has been interpreted (and intended by the PRC) as concurrence.

Early in UN history the General Assembly made two requests to the International Court of Justice for ADVISORY OPINIONS on vetoes exercised on membership questions. In the first case the GA asked the Court whether a permanent member could justify a veto against the admission of a new member on any grounds other than those expressly detailed in Article 4 of the Charter. The Soviet Union, conceding the qualifications of Finland and Italy, had nonetheless voted against their admission. The ICJ's majority opinion, made in 1948, found Moscow's veto unjustified, but the opinion had no impact on Soviet behavior. Ultimately, compromises in the Security Council resulted in admitting a number of new states from both the West and the East blocs. A second GA request to the Court asked for an opinion as to whether or not the General Assembly could admit a new member in the absence of a Security Council recommendation. In 1950 the Court said no. The result of the two opinions was to solidify the authority of the P5 and the veto.

The consequence of the presence of the veto, as John Stoessinger has noted, has led the Security Council away from the notion of majority, or democratic, rule toward the practice of consensus. What this requires is serious diplomacy in order for the Security Council to function properly. Indeed, observing voting in all organs of the United Nations, one can discern a movement to consensus and away from narrow majoritarianism.

See also COLD WAR, COMMITTEE SYSTEM OF THE GENERAL ASSEMBLY, GOLDBERG RESERVATION, KOREAN WAR, SCALE OF ASSESSMENTS, STRUCTURE OF THE UNITED NATIONS, UNITING FOR PEACE RESOLUTION.

Further Reading: Köchler, Hans. *The Voting Procedure in the United Nations Security Council: Examining a Normative Con-*

tradiction in the UN Charter and Its Consequences on International Relations. Vienna: International Progress Organization, 1991. Moore, John Allphin, Jr., and Jerry Pubantz. *To Create a New World? American Presidents and the United Nations.* New York: Peter Lang, 1999. Nicholas, H. G. *The United Nations as a Political Institution.* 5th ed. Oxford: Oxford University Press, 1975. Simma, Bruno, ed. *The Charter of the United Nations; A Commentary.* Oxford: Oxford University Press, 1994.

Waldheim, Kurt (1918–)

The fourth SECRETARY-GENERAL was born in Sankt Andrä-Wördern, Austria, near Vienna, in 1918. He served as a volunteer in the Austrian army from 1936 to 1937, and, following the Anschluss that merged Germany and Austria, was conscripted into the German army. He served on the Russian front until he was wounded in 1941. Although he later claimed to have spent the remainder of the war studying law, documents uncovered in 1986 indicated that he had been a German army staff officer in the Balkans from about 1942 to the end of the war. He received a doctorate of jurisprudence from the University of Vienna in 1944. He also graduated from the Vienna Consular Academy, and in 1945 he joined the Austrian diplomatic service. From 1948 to 1951 he was assigned to Paris where he served as first secretary of the legation. He returned to Vienna and headed the personnel department of the Ministry of Foreign Affairs until 1955 when he became permanent observer for Austria to the United Nations. Later that same year, when Austria was admitted to the world organization, he became head of the mission. He then served as minister and ambassador to Canada (1956–60), head of the Ministry's Political Department (1960–62), and DIRECTOR-GENERAL for political affairs (1962–64). He became permanent Austrian representative to the United Nations in 1964, left New York for a two-year stint as his nation's foreign minister (1968–70), and then returned to the United Nations, where he was again PERMANENT REPRESENTATIVE until he succeeded U THANT.

Waldheim was the first candidate for Secretary-General openly to seek the post, which he did on three occasions. He began his term in January 1972, after having been recommended by the SECURITY COUNCIL and appointed by the GENERAL ASSEMBLY in December 1971. Reelected in 1976, despite opposition from some Third World countries, Waldheim served until 1981, when he unsuccessfully sought a third term, being blocked by a VETO from the Chinese. His recurrent difficulties with Third World nations reflected a tense shift of sentiment in the United Nations as relations between the so-called Northern countries and the more numerous, poorer Southern nations soured. New, former colonialized UN members became dissatisfied that Waldheim did not accelerate the recruitment and appointment of Third World nationals to the SECRETARIAT. In 1974, contrary to the strong opposition of the UNITED STATES, the General Assembly invited Palestinian leader Yasser Arafat to address the body and granted the Palestine Liberation Organization OBSERVER STATUS. That same year developing nations overwhelmingly pressed through the General Assembly the Charter of Economic Rights and Duties of States, calling for the nationalization and expropriation of foreign property. Many in the Third World agreed with the critical views of Algerian president Houari Boumédienne that Waldheim, sensitive to Western powers' preferences, had sought to sidetrack the drive toward the so-called NEW INTERNATIONAL ECONOMIC ORDER (NIEO). The next year, the General Assembly passed a RESOLUTION equating ZIONISM with "racism." These events of the middle 1970s led the Secretary-General to conclude that NORTH-SOUTH RELATIONS in the United Nations had reached an all-time low.

Waldheim attempted to transcend these difficult strains, and in so doing he traveled extensively, visiting areas of special concern to the United Nations, including South Africa, Cyprus, the Middle East, the Indian Subcontinent, and the Sudan and Sahelian areas of Africa. His administration was constantly engaged in trying to resolve, or help resolve, major international problems, including the 1971 India-Pakistan dispute, the MIDDLE EAST WAR OF 1973, the Vietnamese invasion of CAMBODIA, the decade-long IRAN-IRAQ WAR, and the ripple effects of the Iranian Revolution of 1979. Waldheim also oversaw large relief efforts in Bangladesh, Cambodia, Nicaragua, and GUATEMALA, and PEACEKEEPING operations in Cyprus, the two Yemens, ANGOLA, and Guinea, as well as in the Middle East. He opened and addressed a number of international conferences convened under the auspices of the United Nations, including the third session of the UNITED NATIONS CONFERENCE ON TRADE AND DEVELOPMENT (in Santiago, 1972), the UNITED NATIONS CONFERENCE ON THE HUMAN ENVIRONMENT (in Stockholm, 1972), the third UNITED NATIONS CONFERENCE ON THE LAW OF THE SEA (in Caracas, 1974), the WORLD POPULATION CONFERENCE (in Bucharest, 1974), and the WORLD FOOD SUMMIT (in Rome, 1974). His efforts to effect withdrawal of various forces from occupied areas proved less successful, including those efforts to convince the Vietnamese to leave Cambodia, Israelis to withdraw from occupied territories, South Africa to leave NAMIBIA, and the Soviet Union to remove itself from AFGHANISTAN.

He also became a point person in efforts to gain the release of American hostages held by the revolutionary Iranian government from November 1979 to January 1981 (See IRAN HOSTAGE CRISIS). He met privately in New York with U.S. secretary of state Cyrus Vance, who wanted the Secretary-General to be the intermediary to deliver the hostages back to the country. When Security Council Resolution 457 (December 4, 1979) demanded release of the hostages and the use of the Secretary-General's GOOD OFFICES to carry out the resolution, Waldheim set out for Tehran on a visit he described as a "nightmare." He returned in early 1980 empty-handed, once again frustrated in a spirited attempt to resolve an international crisis.

Waldheim left office in 1981, but he remained active in Austrian politics. He had failed in an attempt to gain the presidency of his country in 1971, but he proved successful in 1986, winning a six-year term. His candidacy, however, became controversial in the international arena when documents surfaced revealing in more detail his wartime service with the German army, showing that he had been an interpreter and intelligence officer for the Germans who were engaged in reprisals against Yugoslav partisans and civilians,

Secretary-General Kurt Waldheim (UN PHOTO/Y. NAGATA)

as well as being responsible for sending much of the Jewish population of Salonika, Greece, to concentration camps. Waldheim admitted his earlier lack of candor but denied knowledge or participation in wartime atrocities. An international investigation cleared him of complicity, but his reputation, severely tarnished, hurt his presidency, and he did not run for reelection in 1992.

Further Reading: Finger, Seymour Maxwell, and Arnold A. Saltzman. *Bending with the Winds: Kurt Waldheim and the United Nations.* New York: Praeger, 1990. Hazzard, Shirley. *Countenance of Truth: The United Nations and the Waldheim Case.* New York: Viking, 1990. Waldheim, Kurt. *In the Eye of the Storm: A Memoir.* Bethesda, Md.: Adler and Adler, 1986.

War Crimes Tribunal for the Former Yugoslavia   *See* INTERNATIONAL CRIMINAL TRIBUNAL FOR THE FORMER YUGOSLAVIA (ICTY); *see also* FORMER YUGOSLAVIA, WAR CRIMES TRIBUNALS.

war crimes tribunals

The 20th century witnessed a growth in the principle of individual criminal responsibility for what previously had been considered acts of state. Formerly, public leaders could cite their role as political figures and have little fear that they would face legal prosecution for their acts. But beginning in World War I, massive atrocities associated with war compelled the world to begin asserting universal JURISDICTION over these kinds of crimes and to put the perpetrators on trial. The Versailles Peace TREATY of 1919 that ended World War I called for Kaiser Wilhelm II, the German monarch, to be prosecuted for starting the war. The kaiser escaped to the Netherlands but the victorious powers insisted that the Germans put their own war criminals on trial. By the resultant Leipzig trials, considered a sham by some legal critics, no Germans suffered major punishment for such crimes. Also during World War I, the Turks committed atrocities against Armenian peoples amounting to what later would be charged as GENOCIDE (a term developed during World War II by the French philosopher Raphael Lemkin).

Following World War II, the allies successfully tried the German and Japanese leadership for war crimes. The tribunals at Nuremberg and Tokyo included a new charge—"crimes against humanity." For the first time, the international community asserted that an individual leader could be tried in an international court for crimes committed against the domestic population. (Previously, such a prosecution was considered an infringement on national SOVEREIGNTY.) At Nuremberg, the four victorious powers—the UNITED STATES, the United Kingdom, France, and the Soviet Union—served as judges. At Tokyo, there were 11 judges, including two from the newly decolonized India and the Philippines. The highest leaders under indictment received the death penalty from both tribunals. Each court cooperated with the United Nations War Crimes Commission, but the trials were military rather than UN trials.

In one of its first actions, the UN GENERAL ASSEMBLY, in two RESOLUTIONS passed in 1946, affirmed the principles of INTERNATIONAL LAW recognized by the Nuremberg Tribunal, and declared that genocide was "a crime under international law." Subsequently, the international community, within the framework of the United Nations, adopted numerous HUMAN RIGHTS instruments that underscored the developing concern with war crimes. Among the most notable of these agreements were the UNIVERSAL DECLARATION OF HUMAN RIGHTS (1948), the CONVENTION ON THE PREVENTION AND PUNISHMENT OF THE CRIME OF GENOCIDE (1948), and the CONVENTION AGAINST TORTURE AND OTHER INHUMAN OR DEGRADING TREATMENT OR PUNISHMENT (1984). Using these CONVENTIONS and the Nuremberg precedents, the UN SECURITY COUNCIL, by Resolution 827 in 1993, created the INTERNATIONAL CRIMINAL TRIBUNAL FOR THE FORMER YUGOSLAVIA (ICTY), seated in The Hague. In 1994, the Security Council followed the same precedents in Resolution 955, creating the INTERNATIONAL CRIMINAL TRIBUNAL FOR RWANDA, located in Arusha, Tanzania. As of 2001, these ad hoc tribunals had jurisdiction only to try cases directly relating to the civil wars within their respective countries. Unlike at Nuremberg and Tokyo, these tribunals were held under the direct auspices of the United Nations, and neither tribunal had a provision for capital punishment. The ICTY became more visible to the world after democratic elections in Yugoslavia in the fall of 2000 ousted Serb strongman Slobodan Milosevic from office, and international prosecutors began a serious effort to bring him to trial. By June 2001, Milosevic, earlier indicted for war crimes violations, had been arrested and was in custody at the Tribunal in The Hague (although others indicted, including Bosnian Serb leaders Radovan Karadzic and Ratko Mladic, remained at large). By the time of Milosevic's arrest, the Tribunal had publicly indicted 98 individuals, detained 36, and conducted 14 trials. Of those found guilty, Tihomir Blaskic (a former general in the Croatian Defense Council) received the most severe sentence. The ICTY sentenced him to 45 years' imprisonment for three counts of crimes against humanity, six counts of grave breaches of the Geneva Conventions, and 10 counts of violations of the laws or customs of war.

In 1998, the international community concluded negotiations on the Rome Statute of the International Criminal Court, which would create a permanent INTERNATIONAL CRIMINAL COURT. The statute then opened for signature and achieved sufficient ratification by April 11, 2002, to go into effect on the following July 1.

See also SCALE OF ASSESSMENTS.

Further Reading: Bass, Gary Jonathan. *Stay the Hand of Vengeance: The Politics of War Crimes Tribunals*. Princeton, N.J.: Princeton University Press, 2000. Cooper, Belinda, ed. *War Crimes: The Legacy of Nuremberg*. New York: TV Books, 1999. Neier, Aryeh. *War Crimes: Brutality, Genocide, Terror, and the Struggle for Justice*. New York: Times Books, 1998.

— *D. J. Becker*

weapons

Article 11 of the UN CHARTER authorizes the GENERAL ASSEMBLY (GA) to "consider the general principles . . . governing DISARMAMENT and the regulation of armaments." The Assembly may make recommendations based on those principles, but the Charter (Article 26) charges the SECURITY COUNCIL with the responsibility for "formulating . . . plans to be submitted to the Members of the United Nations for the establishment of a system for the regulation of armaments." The Charter does not go as far as the COVENANT of the LEAGUE OF NATIONS did in calling for a "reduction of armaments," but its provisions reflected a continuing concern in the 20th century with the threat to international peace and security posed by NATION-STATES maintaining huge armament stockpiles, and by the technological development of many new weapons systems. During the COLD WAR the UN's preoccupation was with WEAPONS OF MASS DESTRUCTION (WMD) owned by the major powers of the world. However, by the turn of the millennium, a virtually unlimited supply of even the most modern weapons in the hands of large and small states, ethnic groups, and terrorist organizations meant that all wars held the potential to endanger the lives of millions. A total 46 of the 49 conflicts waged during the 1990s were fought mainly with small arms, killing nearly 4 million people. Faced with an estimated 500 million small arms in circulation worldwide, and new types of WMD, the United Nations turned its attention to a broader weapons agenda as the new century began.

The General Assembly's duties in the field of arms regulation have been delegated to various committees and subsidiary bodies. Over time these organs, along with the SECRETARIAT's DEPARTMENT OF DISARMAMENT AFFAIRS, have delineated the types of weapons systems causing most unease to the world community. The CONFERENCE ON DISARMAMENT (CD), established in 1979, categorized the critical weapons systems as nuclear weapons, CHEMICAL WEAPONS (CW), other weapons of mass destruction, such as biological agents, and conventional weapons. This last category came to include in the 1990s LAND MINES, small arms (defined as weapons for personal use), and light weapons (designed for use by several persons working as a team). The General Assembly's SPECIAL SESSIONS ON DISARMAMENT also added arms transfers (both open military aid from one country to another and clandestine arms sales) to the list of weapons concerns. The horizontal proliferation of weapons by these methods threatened not only to increase the number and ferocity of local conflicts but also to endanger UN peacekeepers in the many operations underway at the end of the century.

In the wake of the American use of nuclear weapons against Japan in August 1945 and the commencement of the cold war soon after, the UN's initial efforts to control weapons systems focused on atomic bombs. The establishment in 1946 of the ATOMIC ENERGY COMMISSION initiated a permanent UN effort to limit the growth of nuclear arsenals. Despite its efforts, however, by 1970 the "nuclear club" had grown to five states: the UNITED STATES, the Soviet Union, France, CHINA, and the United Kingdom. U.S. and Soviet nuclear stockpiles accounted for nearly 98 percent of all nuclear warheads, largely mounted on intercontinental missiles (the United States had 1,054 of these; the USSR 1,290), or submarine-launched ballistic missiles (the United States had 656; the USSR had 30). Many of these delivery systems were capable of carrying multiple warheads, all of which were much larger in megatonnage than those dropped at Hiroshima and Nagasaki. Perhaps the most dangerous encounter between the superpower rivals occurred during the CUBAN MISSILE CRISIS in 1962. In October of that year,

U.S. intelligence discovered that the Soviet Union had placed intermediate-range nuclear weapons in CUBA. The Kennedy administration challenged the Soviets to remove the weapons under clear threat of military action against the Soviet Union. The United States imposed a naval quarantine on Cuba in hopes of forcing the Soviets to withdraw the missiles. Meanwhile, urgent secret negotiations transpired at UN HEADQUARTERS and in Washington to defuse the possibility of a nuclear exchange. By the end of October, the Russians agreed to remove the weapons, and the United States, in response, was poised to dismantle its own nuclear weapons in Turkey.

Beyond the nuclear weapon states, there were several "threshold states" that appeared to be technologically capable, and possibly willing, to develop these most destructive of weapons. Motivated by the belief that the possession of nuclear weapons could bestow great power status, provide effective deterrence, or tilt the balance of power favorably in a contest with an adversary, Israel, Brazil, South Africa, India, and Pakistan were reported in the 1970s to be on the verge of developing nuclear capabilities. To halt proliferation and to pressure the superpowers into cutting their arsenals the United Nations approved the NUCLEAR NON-PROLIFERATION TREATY in 1968, convened three Special Sessions on Disarmament, and concentrated the work of the General Assembly's FIRST COMMITTEE on this problem.

Chemical weapons are a much older form of WMD than nuclear weapons. Their first modern use was in World War I. General revulsion with the suffering they produced in that conflict led to the 1925 Geneva Protocol on Gas Warfare, which sought to ban them in future conflicts. The PROTOCOL, however, only prohibited their use, not their production or possession. During the cold war several states produced weapons that fell within this category. In 1969, the United Nations defined chemical warfare agents as "chemical substances, whether gaseous, liquid or solid, which might be employed because of their direct toxic effects on man, animals and plants." Not only the toxic chemicals but also the equipment for their dispersal was classified as a chemical weapon. The major types of chemical weapons included tear gas and other irritants, poisons that blocked the blood's oxygen-carrying capacity, blistering agents such as mustard gas, chemicals like sarin and VX that destroyed the brain's or the nervous system's ability to function, and asphyxiation weapons such as phosgene and chlorine. In recent years, the Iraqi government used CW agents against Iraqi Kurds (in Halabja in 1988) and against Iran during the IRAN-IRAQ WAR. Also, the chemical Sarin was used in a terrorist attack in the Tokyo subway in 1995.

On November 30, 1992, the GENERAL ASSEMBLY adopted the "Convention on the Prohibition of the Development, Production, Stockpiling and Use of Chemical Weapons and on their Destruction." As of July 2001, 143 states had become or were in the process of becoming parties to the

CONVENTION. It was the first international DISARMAMENT agreement that set as its goal eliminating an entire category of WMDs. To enforce its provisions the convention established the ORGANIZATION FOR THE PROHIBITION OF CHEMICAL WEAPONS (OPCW) with the authority to conduct surprise inspections. The dual use nature of chemicals and the ease of their production, however, made the exclusion of chemical weapons from the world's arsenals nearly impossible.

Biological weapons (BW) are living organisms, most commonly bacteria and viruses, deliberately disseminated to cause death or disease in humans, animals, or plants. Biological weapons are considered weapons of mass destruction because they have the potential to destroy life equaled only by nuclear weapons. They can also be used for much smaller effect and in clandestine operations. Despite the concern about BW TERRORISM in recent years, the power of governments to build, maintain, and hide offensive BW programs still constituted the most serious biological weapons threat to international peace and security. Accelerated advances in the biological sciences added to the risk that such expertise could be misused.

The 1925 Geneva Protocol prohibited the use of biological weapons in warfare. The 1972 CONVENTION ON THE PROHIBITION OF THE DEVELOPMENT, PRODUCTION AND STOCKPILING OF BACTERIOLOGICAL (BIOLOGICAL) AND TOXIN WEAPONS AND ON THEIR DESTRUCTION (BWC) went further by prohibiting their development and possession. The UN SECRETARY-GENERAL has the authority to investigate the alleged use of biological weapons, ascertain facts regarding such alleged use, and report the findings to member states. A number of countries violated their obligations under the BWC by initiating or continuing to develop and produce biological weapons following the convention's entry into force. The Soviet Union maintained a secret BW program; South Africa produced biological weapons in the 1980s and 1990s, and Iraq, while a signatory of the BWC, developed an offensive biological program in the 1980s.

Conventional weapons also continued to be a concern for the United Nations. Expanded use of land mines and small arms caused particular anxiety. As of 2001, there were between 60 and 110 million land mines deployed in over 60 countries around the world. Some of the most heavily mine-affected states included AFGHANISTAN, BOSNIA, and CAMBODIA. Land mines as a class of weapons do not distinguish between combat forces and civilians. In fact, 80 to 90 percent of victims of land mines have been civilians. Furthermore, they continue to kill and maim long after emplacement, well after hostilities have ended. These devastating effects prompted the United Nations to support numerous mine-clearing projects. The UN Mine Action Service was involved in de-mining activities in states such as Azerbaijan, Cambodia, and Lebanon. The UNITED NATIONS OFFICE OF PROJECT SERVICES also provided extensive de-mining services in states

where UN PEACEKEEPING operations were underway. In 1997 the United Nations opened for signature the CONVENTION ON THE PROHIBITION OF THE USE, STOCKPILING, PRODUCTION AND TRANSFER OF ANTI-PERSONNEL MINES AND THEIR DESTRUCTION. The inexpensive nature of land mines, and their relatively simple technology, however, made these weapons extremely attractive to rebel, ethnic, and religious forces fighting in the developing world.

Conflicts in the post–cold war era have been fought almost exclusively with light or small arms. Their victims have been combatants and non-combatants alike. Among the latter group has been an extraordinarily high percentage of WOMEN and children. Clandestine arms brokers found these types of weapons the easiest to sell and deploy, exacerbating international efforts to limit their numbers. The disintegration of states and the weakening of central control over national arsenals also produced a huge dispersion of these armaments. In 2001 the United Nations convened a WORLD CONFERENCE to address this type of weapon, but participating states could not arrive at a consensus on how to cut small arms quantities or how to regulate their movement.

Further Reading: Bader, William. *The United States and the Spread of Nuclear Weapons.* New York: Pegasus, 1968. Cameron, Maxwell A., Robert J. Lawson, and Brian W. Tomlin. *To Walk without Fear: The Global Movement to Ban Landmines.* Toronto: Oxford University Press, 1998. Herken, Gregg. *The Winning Weapon: The Atomic Bomb in the Cold War, 1945–1950.* New York: Vintage Books, 1980. Holloway, David. *The Soviet Union and the Arms Race.* New Haven, Conn.: Yale University Press, 1984. Tucker, Jonathan B., ed. *The Chemical Weapons Convention: Implementation Challenges and Solutions.* Monterey, Calif.: Monterey Institute of International Studies' Center for Nonproliferation Studies, 2001. ———. *Toxic Terror: Assessing Terrorist Use of Chemical and Biological Weapons.* Cambridge, Mass.: MIT Press, 2000.

weapons of mass destruction (WMD)

WEAPONS of mass destruction have threatened mankind since the beginning of the 20th century. Nuclear, biological, and CHEMICAL WEAPONS (also referred to as NBC-weapons) are classified as WMD, because they enable their users to kill large numbers of people in a very short period. With the close of the COLD WAR, the world community worried that "States of Concern" or terrorist groups might use such weapons. These fears were confirmed by Iraq's use of chemical weapons against its Kurdish population in the 1980s, and by a terrorist attack, using Sarin gas, in the Tokyo subway in 1995.

BIOLOGICAL WEAPONS (BW) were the first WMD to be used in warfare, when, during the Middle Ages, carcasses of animals or corpses of people having died of diseases were catapulted into enemy-held fortresses. The development of man-made weapons of this kind began in the 1930s. The infamous "Unit 731" of the Imperial Japanese army experimented with different diseases, including the plague. In the late 1930s, Japanese invaders dropped specially bred plague-infected rats and fleas that carried the disease over a small village in China, killing approximately 500 people. The Japanese also conducted tests with humans on a large scale. However, there were serious logistical problems due to the lack of an effective method of deployment, and such weapons were not used in World War II. Research in this field began anew and biological weapons were developed as a potential munition during the cold war. While the UNITED STATES stopped its program in 1970, the USSR expanded its capabilities. BW are also known as the "poor man's atom bomb" since they are easy and cheap to develop and employ. As of the turn of the century, however, biological weapons had never been used in combat.

On two occasions international treaties sought to eliminate biological weapons from military arsenals. The 1925 Geneva PROTOCOL prohibited the use of biological weapons in warfare. The 1972 CONVENTION ON THE PROHIBITION OF THE DEVELOPMENT, PRODUCTION AND STOCKPILING OF BACTERIOLOGICAL (BIOLOGICAL) AND TOXIN WEAPONS AND ON THEIR DESTRUCTION (BWC) went further by prohibiting their development and possession. Under the BWC, the UN SECRETARY-GENERAL has the authority to investigate the alleged use of biological weapons, ascertain facts regarding such alleged use, and report his findings to the member states. Nonetheless, a number of countries violated their TREATY obligations by initiating or continuing to develop and produce these types of weapons. For example, Iraq, while a signatory of the BWC, developed an offensive biological program in the 1980s. In 1991, following the GULF WAR, the UN SECURITY COUNCIL required Baghdad to accept the unconditional destruction of its biological weapons and all components of its BW program. Despite years of inspections and extensive evidence and documentation of Iraq's BW program, its complete destruction could not be confirmed.

Chemical Weapons (CW) were developed at the beginning of the 20th century and used for the first time in 1915. Thousands were killed and maimed during the so-called Gas War on the Western Front in World War I. More recently, the Iraqi government used CW in its war with Iran and against the Kurdish minority inside Iraq. On November 30, 1992, the GENERAL ASSEMBLY adopted the "Convention on the Prohibition of the Development, Production, Stockpiling and Use of Chemical Weapons and on Their Destruction" (Res. 39). The Chemical Weapons Convention (CWC) entered into force in 1997. The CONVENTION was the first international DISARMAMENT agreement with the purpose of eliminating an entire category of WMDs. It prohibited the development, acquisition, production, stockpiling, and use of chemical weapons. States were required to destroy all chemical weapons and production facilities. Given the relative simplicity of producing chemical agents, however, the danger remained that states and terrorist groups could produce, conceal, and use these dangerous weapons.

Nuclear weapons research occurred in Germany and the United States during World War II. Only twice in history have such weapons been used: in August 1945, at the conclusion of World War II, when the United States dropped two atomic bombs on Japan, one over Hiroshima and a second over Nagasaki. Japan surrendered later that month, but almost immediately after the war a nuclear arms race developed between the United States and the USSR, with each side developing huge arsenals of strategic and tactical nuclear weapons. Other states to join the "nuclear club" were the United Kingdom, France, CHINA, and India. In 1998, Pakistan successfully tested a nuclear device. In an effort to limit the threat of nuclear weapons, the United Nations, beginning in the 1940s, undertook a complex array of disarmament initiatives. It created negotiating forums like the UNITED NATIONS ATOMIC ENERGY COMMISSION, the EIGHTEEN NATION DISARMAMENT COMMITTEE, and the CONFERENCE ON DISARMAMENT. It held SPECIAL SESSIONS on disarmament and focused world attention on the varied aspects of the nuclear problem: proliferation, regional arms races, weapons testing, deployment of nuclear devices in outer space, and arms technology transfers.

According to Part III of the Facultative Protocol No. I to the Geneva Conventions, parties to a conflict are not free in the kind of weapons they may employ. Weapons or methods of war that are likely to have long-lasting and severe negative effects on the ENVIRONMENT or induce unnecessary suffering are forbidden under INTERNATIONAL LAW and are expressly outlawed in Article 23 of The Hague Convention respecting the Laws and Customs of War (1907). Moreover, developing treaty law proscribes the use, possession, or deployment of many types of weapons of mass destruction. In addition to the agreements cited above, treaties dealing with WMDs include the NUCLEAR NON-PROLIFERATION TREATY (NPT), the COMPREHENSIVE NUCLEAR TEST BAN TREATY (CTBT), the TREATY OF TLATLELOCO, the Partial Test Ban Treaty, the Strategic Arms Limitation Treaty, and the MOON TREATY.

Further Reading: Cirincione, Joseph, ed. *Repairing the Regime: Preventing the Spread of Weapons of Mass Destruction.* New York: Routledge, 2000. Clark, William, Jr., and Ryukichi Imai, eds. *Next Steps in Arms Control and Non-Proliferation: Report of the U.S.-Japan Study Group on Arms Control and Non-Proliferation after the Cold War.* Washington, D.C.: Carnegie Endowment for Peace, 1997. Rauf, Tariq, Mary Beth Nikitin, and Jenni Rissanen. *Inventory of International Nonproliferation Organizations and Regimes, 2000 Edition.* Monterey, Calif.: Program for Nonproliferation Studies, Monterey Institute of International Studies, 1993.

— *T. J. Weiler*

weighted voting   *See* VOTING.

women

In 1945, the CHARTER OF THE UNITED NATIONS became the first international document in history to acknowledge the role of women in the world and to accentuate gender equality as a fundamental human right. Over the ensuing decades the United Nations engaged in a multifaceted approach to advance the status of women. Four key strategies were critical in this work. These included the promotion of legal standards through binding UN CONVENTIONS or treaties that addressed women's HUMAN RIGHTS, the mobilization of public opinion through WORLD CONFERENCES and public forums, the enhancement of research about women, and the provision of assistance for women in areas such as health, education, development, and environmental safety.

The United Nations created several legal instruments intended to enhance the status of women. These documents addressed a number of issues, including prostitution in the Convention for the Suppression of the Traffic in Persons and of the Exploitation of the Prostitution of Others, equal pay for work of equal value in the INTERNATIONAL LABOUR ORGANIZATION (ILO) Convention on Equal Remuneration, the ability to vote and hold public office in the CONVENTION ON THE POLITICAL RIGHTS OF WOMEN, the right of consent to marriage in the Convention on Consent to Marriage, Minimum Age for Marriage and Registration for Marriages, the right to equal education in the UNITED NATIONS EDUCATIONAL, SCIENTIFIC AND CULTURAL ORGANIZATION (UNESCO), the Convention against Discrimination in Education, and the elimination of all forms of discrimination against women as provided in the UN CONVENTION ON THE ELIMINATION OF ALL FORMS OF DISCRIMINATION AGAINST WOMEN (CEDAW).

Beginning with the UN DECADE FOR WOMEN (1976–85), the United Nations directed media attention toward the conditions of women around the world. The United Nations hosted four major WORLD CONFERENCES ON WOMEN (Mexico City, 1975; Copenhagen, 1980; Nairobi, 1985; and Beijing, 1995) to outline the challenges to gender equality and the actions needed to remove these barriers. These conferences served to mobilize public opinion and raise awareness about the conditions of women and girls around the world. Other UN conferences, such as the 1993 WORLD CONFERENCE ON HUMAN RIGHTS and the 1995 WORLD SOCIAL SUMMIT in Copenhagen, emphasized the critical needs and roles of women in their societies. The United Nations also collected statistics on women. Few countries kept separate records on women or even attempted any statistical analysis of women's lives and work. Since the late 1970s, the United Nations Statistical Office, the UN INTERNATIONAL RESEARCH AND TRAINING INSTITUTE FOR THE ADVANCEMENT OF WOMEN (INSTRAW), and the ILO have been helpful in creating methodologies appropriate for the study of women. Two key studies, *The World's Women 1970–1990* and *The World's Women 1995*, provided data and analysis on women's experiences around the globe. These studies often highlighted the effects of long-term inequalities and encouraged governments as well as the United Nations to take action to prevent them. In the 1990s, UN advocacy for women fostered training programs and development projects all aimed at raising awareness and improving women's lives.

The United Nations has also been instrumental in providing assistance to women in areas such as health, education, and the ENVIRONMENT. Several initiatives are worthy of note. The UNITED NATIONS CHILDREN'S FUND (UNICEF), the WORLD FOOD PROGRAMME (WFP), and the WORLD HEALTH ORGANIZATION (WHO) provide assistance to women and girls in more than 100 countries around the world. The UNITED NATIONS DEVELOPMENT FUND FOR WOMEN (UNIFEM), in conjunction with the UNITED NATIONS DEVELOPMENT PROGRAMME (UNDP), gives direct financial and technical support to development projects for women in developing countries, and the World Health Organization's Global Action for AIDS has directed international attention to the effects of AIDS on women and girls.

Although women have found voice and recognition through the work of the United Nations, they have not always been represented equally in the institutional STRUCTURE or the UN's decision-making bodies. Studies of the bureaucracy, professional ranks, and operation of SPECIALIZED AGENCIES have found that women are hired in lower numbers than men and are often underrepresented in the highest levels of the UNITED NATIONS SYSTEM. In 1994 the United Nations set a goal of complete gender equality by the year 2000 within the organization. As of March 2000, 38.9 percent of professional and higher level staff were women. In other categories the percentage was often lower. At the existing rate of change in 2000, the UN goal of absolute parity would be reached in 2012.

At the turn of the century, women tended to be concentrated in gender-traditional, junior-level positions and in subagencies designed to handle women's issues. For example, only two women had ever chaired the SECURITY COUNCIL (Ambassador Jeanne Martin Cisse of Guinea, who served as her country's UN ambassador from 1972 to 1976, and U.S. secretary of state Madeleine Albright, who served a term as SECURITY COUNCIL PRESIDENT in 1996). At the same time, groundbreaking appointments were made in the 1980s and 1990s. The first woman elected to the bench of the INTERNATIONAL COURT OF JUSTICE was Rosalyn Higgins of the United Kingdom in 1995. Nafis Sadik of Pakistan became the first woman to head a major UN program—UNITED NATIONS POPULATION FUND (UNFPA)—in April 1987. Margaret Joan Anstee of the United Kingdom became the first woman to head a PEACEKEEPING mission (UNITED NATIONS ANGOLA VERIFICATION MISSION, UNAVEM) and to be appointed a SPE-

Percentage of Women in UN Secretariat Senior Posts, 1996–1999

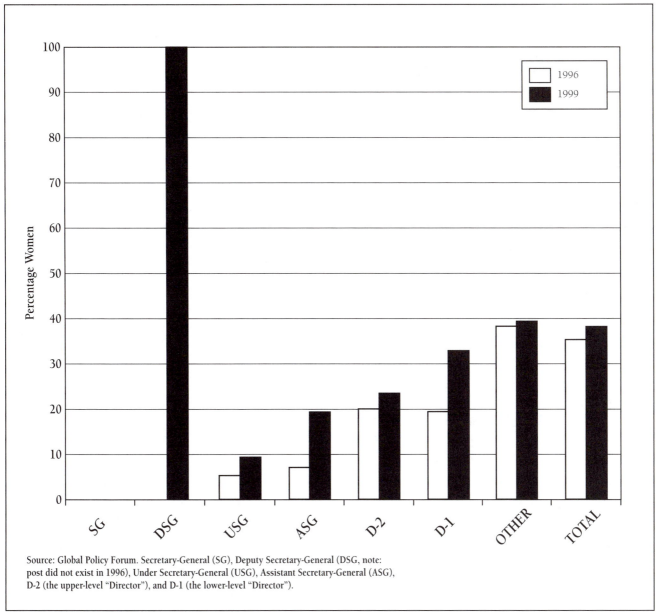

Source: Global Policy Forum. Secretary-General (SG), Deputy Secretary-General (DSG, note:
post did not exist in 1996), Under Secretary-General (USG), Assistant Secretary-General (ASG),
D-2 (the upper-level "Director"), and D-1 (the lower-level "Director").

CIAL REPRESENTATIVE OF THE SECRETARY-GENERAL (to ANGOLA). In September 1997, former Irish president Mary Robinson was appointed to the highly visible position of UN HIGH COMMISSIONER FOR HUMAN RIGHTS. On March 2, 1998, Louise FRÉCHETTE became the first DEPUTY SECRETARY-GENERAL of the United Nations. The post had been created in December 1997 as part of the REFORM package put forward by SECRETARY-GENERAL Kofi ANNAN. Fréchette's duties included serving as the Secretary-General's primary adviser, promoting the reform process, coordinating UN agencies, and representing the Secretary-General at conferences and official functions. With her appointment, Fréchette became the highest-ranking woman within the institution in UN history. And in April, 2002, Secretary-General Annan appointed Patricia Durrant of Jamaica to the new post of UN ombudsman. But within individual UN MISSIONS, progress was slower. Fewer women than men served in national delegations at high diplomatic ranks at the turn of the century.

In the 1990s, the United Nations began addressing sexual harassment policies and problems of gendered promotion criteria. These changes came about as a result of organized activities of UN workers, pressure from international leaders to make changes, appointments of women to prominent diplomatic positions by concerned states, and lobbying by

NON-GOVERNMENTAL ORGANIZATIONS (NGOs) interested in women's rights in the workplace. Still, as Secretary-General Annan pointed out in 1998, the United Nations had much work to do for "if we are convinced of all these things in relation to all the societies we are trying to help in this world, then how can we fail to apply this conviction to our own society in our own house?"

See also ADMINISTRATIVE COMMITTEE ON COORDINATION, AFGHANISTAN, AGENDA 21, BEIJING +5, BRUNDTLAND, COMMISSION ON HUMAN RIGHTS, COMMISSION ON THE STATUS OF WOMEN, DEPARTMENT OF ECONOMIC AND SOCIAL AFFAIRS, DECLARATION ON THE ELIMINATION OF VIOLENCE AGAINST WOMEN, ECONOMIC AND SOCIAL COUNCIL, HIV/AIDS, INTERNATIONAL COVENANT ON CIVIL AND POLITICAL RIGHTS, INTERNATIONAL COVENANT ON ECONOMIC, SOCIAL AND CULTURAL RIGHTS, INTERNATIONAL DAY FOR THE ELIMINATION OF VIOLENCE AGAINST WOMEN, INTERNATIONAL LAW, MILLENNIUM SUMMIT, RIO DECLARATION, ROOSEVELT, ELEANOR, SPECIAL RAPPORTEUR, THIRD COMMITTEE OF THE GENERAL ASSEMBLY, UNITED NATIONS DAY FOR WOMEN'S RIGHTS AND INTERNATIONAL PEACE, UNIVERSAL DECLARATION OF HUMAN RIGHTS.

Further Reading: Beigbeder, Yves. *New Challenges for UNICEF: Children, Women, and Human Rights.* New York: Palgrave, 2001. D'Amico, Francine. "Women Workers in the United Nations: From Margin to Mainstream?" In Meyer, Mary K., and Elisabeth Prügl. *Gender Politics in Global Governance.* Lanham, Md: Rowman and Littlefield, 1999. Pietilla, Hilkka, and Jeanne Vickers. *Making Women Matter: The Role of the United Nations.* London: Zed Books, 1996. United Nations Department of Public Information. *The United Nations and the Advancement of Women, 1945–1996.* New York: United Nations Department of Public Information, 1996. UN Women Watch website: http://www.un. org/womenwatch/. UN DPI "Women" website: <www.un.org/ecosocdev/geninfo/women>.

— *K. J. Vogel*

working languages of the United Nations   *See* LANGUAGES, UNITED NATIONS OFFICIAL AND WORKING.

World AIDS Day

The GENERAL ASSEMBLY established the day in 1988. It is commemorated on December 1 annually. The WORLD HEALTH ORGANIZATION had earlier created an observance on that day.

World Bank

The World Bank is a group of five financial institutions with headquarters in Washington, D.C. These institutions include the International Bank for Reconstruction and Development (IBRD)—the original "World Bank"—the International Finance Corporation (IFC), the International Development Association (IDA), the Multilateral Investment Guarantee Agency (MIGA), and the International Centre for Settlement of Investment Disputes (ICSID).

The International Bank for Reconstruction and Development was created at the BRETTON WOODS Conference in 1944. It began operations in 1946 with a mandate to aid the reconstruction of nations ravaged by World War II and to further the flow of capital around the world. The IBRD and the other institutions in the World Bank Group often find themselves working in close cooperation with the INTERNATIONAL MONETARY FUND (IMF). These entities, all headquartered in Washington, D.C., along with the WORLD TRADE ORGANIZATION (WTO), are the primary international monetary and financial institutions in the global financial framework initiated after World War II.

At the conclusion of the war, diplomats and political leaders, along with financiers and economists, determined to elude the financial and economic policies of economic nationalism that they thought had helped bring on the interwar challenges of economic ruin, international collapse, and world war. Starting at Bretton Woods, these leaders created institutions to encourage freer trade in goods, money, and people, international rules to effect economic liberalization, transparency in economic and financial dealings, the ability to locate and rectify sudden economic troubles in specific areas of the world, and mechanisms to provide necessary capital assistance to nations requiring development financing. As the world's economy grew substantially during the later 20th century, these efforts appeared to be remarkably successful. However, during the 1990s, the World Bank, the IMF, and the WTO became controversial and were seen by some as promoters of a development called "globalization" that, detractors charged, benefited only large corporations in the richest capitalist nations at the expense of Third World countries, laboring people, distinctive native cultures, and the ENVIRONMENT. Critics also insisted that self-interested bankers and financiers, not representatives democratically selected by governments, made the key decisions of the World Bank, the IMF, and the WTO.

The World Bank has, since its origin in 1944, expanded its activities in ways that have made it even more important while also increasingly controversial. From the initial objective of restoring war-devastated nations, the World Bank Group has broadened its goals to include reducing poverty worldwide, strengthening the economies of poor nations, improving living standards, and promoting economic growth and development. The IBRD is analogous to a global financial cooperative. That is, it is effectively owned by its member countries. Its 183 member states (as of 2001) hold shares in the bank the amount of which is determined by the size of the country's economy relative to the world's economy. Thus, although all members of the Bank are represented on the Board of Executive Directors in Washington (and developing nations together could count close to half of the votes in 2001), at the turn of the century the richest nations (the Group of 7: UNITED STATES, United Kingdom, France, Germany, Japan, Italy, and Canada) accounted for about 45 percent of the shares, and thus had a considerable influence over the bank's policies. The United States, with 17 percent of the shares, held a power of VETO over any changes in the bank's articles or policies, since by the 1944 Articles of Agreement, 85 percent of the shares are needed to effect such changes.

The bank does not make grants. It lends money to countries, almost always developing countries who need capital, technical assistance, and sometimes financial and economic policy advice. The loans are repaid. There are two types of lending characteristic of the bank. The first is for developing countries that have an ability to pay market interest rates for the loans. The money for these loans comes from investors around the world who buy bonds issued by the bank. A second type of loan goes to the neediest countries, which are unable to pay market interest rates. Because the bank cannot issue bonds to raise money for these loans, lending is done by way of the affiliate International Development Association (IDA), the World Bank Group's "concessional" lending body. The IDA's Articles of Agreement became effective in 1960. It shares the same staff as the IBRD, the same HEADQUARTERS, reports to the same president (James D. Wolfensohn in 2002), uses the same financial standards in evaluating projects, and, in 2001, had 161 members. The IDA, taking advantage of some 30 countries that provide money needed to extend "credits" to the poorest borrowers, makes loans free of interest. These loans carry a very low administrative charge (.75 percent annually in 2001), are very long term, and include 10 years grace.

The International Finance Corporation (IFC), established in 1956, is the largest multilateral source of loan and equity financing for private sector projects in the developing world. It is particularly engaged in promoting sustainable private sector development. In 2001 the IFC had a MEMBERSHIP of 175 nations, all of whom must be members of the IBRD. IFC members appoint representatives to a Board of Governors that can delegate powers to a Board of Directors, composed of the IBRD's executive directors. The organization's president is the same as that for the IBRD, although it has its own Articles of Agreement.

Created in 1988, the Multilateral Investment Guarantee Agency (MIGA) promotes foreign direct investment into emerging economies to reduce poverty and seek improvement of life in poorer areas of the world. MIGA offers political risk insurance to investors and lenders in order to attract investment in developing countries. In 2001, MIGA had a membership of 154. Membership is open to all World Bank members. It is administered by a Council of Governors and receives some of its operating capital from the IBRD.

In 1966, the International Centre for Settlement of Investment Disputes was established under the Convention on the Settlement of Investment Disputes between States and Nationals of Other States. ICSID is an autonomous international organization with close links to the World Bank. By use of ARBITRATION procedures, it assists in MEDIATION or CONCILIATION when investment disputes arise between private foreign investors and governments. World Bank national representatives typically sit as ex-officio members of ICSID's Administrative Council and the bank finances the ICSID SECRETARIAT, although costs of specific mediations are borne by the involved parties.

Altogether, the World Bank Group is one of the largest sources of development assistance in the world. In 2001 it provided more than $17 billion in loans and was involved in more than 100 developing economies. Since its education funding began in 1963, through 2000 it provided more than $30 billion in loans and credits and, as of 2001, was financing 164 educational projects in 82 countries. The Bank is also a co-sponsor of the JOINT UNITED NATIONS PROGRAMME ON HIV/AIDS (UNAIDS), having committed by 2001 more than $1.7 billion to combating the spread of the disease. Finally, by the turn of the century, the bank was providing an average of $1.3 billion in new lending every year for health, nutrition, and population projects in developing countries.

Although critics continued to fault the World Bank for ignoring challenges such as the environment, distinctive native cultures, the role of civil society, and more, others found by the turn of the century that the bank had added too much to its mandate. From reconstruction efforts in the Balkans to educational programs for young girls in Islamic countries to the struggle against AIDS, the mission of the bank, former managing director Jessica Einhorn warned, had become unwieldy. The World Bank, it seemed to contrary perspectives, was either doing too much or not enough.

See also ADMINISTRATIVE COMMITTEE ON COORDINATION, ADMINISTRATIVE TRIBUNALS, CHINA, COMMITTEE OF INTERNATIONAL DEVELOPMENT INSTITUTIONS ON THE ENVIRONMENT, GLOBAL ENVIRONMENT FACILITY, MULTILATERAL DEVELOPMENT BANKS, NEW INTERNATIONAL ECONOMIC ORDER, NORTH-SOUTH RELATIONS, RIO DECLARATION, SPECIALIZED AGENCIES, SUSTAINABLE DEVELOPMENT, UNITED NATIONS CONFERENCE ON TRADE AND DEVELOPMENT, UNITED NATIONS DEVELOPMENT PROGRAMME.

Further Reading: Einhorn, Jessica. "The World Bank's Mission Creep." *Foreign Affairs* (September–October 2001): 22–35. Micklethwait, John, and Adrian Wooldridge. *Future Perfect: The Challenge and Hidden Promise of Globalization.* New York: Crown Publishers, 2000. O'Brien, Robert, et al. *Contesting Global Governance: Multilateral Institutions and Global Movements.* New York: Cambridge University Press, 2000. World Bank website: <www.worldbank.org>.

World Banking Group   *See* WORLD BANK.

World Commission on Environment and Development (WCED)

Created by the GENERAL ASSEMBLY in 1983 (Res. 38/161) to reinvigorate the global effort at environmental protection, the World Commission on Environment and Development was also known as the Brundtland Commission. The SECRETARY-GENERAL, Javier PÉREZ DE CUÉLLAR, appointed Norwegian prime minister Gro Harlem BRUNDTLAND as the commission's chairperson. He charged the commission with establishing "a global agenda for change." The Secretary-General was responding to the recommendations of a 1982 meeting of 70 government representatives in Nairobi on the 10th anniversary of THE UNITED NATIONS CONFERENCE ON THE HUMAN ENVIRONMENT, which had been held in Stockholm. The diplomats at Nairobi had expressed disappointment with the limited progress since the Stockholm gathering and urged the United Nations to undertake a new effort at environmental policy making.

Under Dr. Brundtland's leadership the commission formulated one of the world's more enduring conceptualizations. It struck a balance between the ENVIRONMENT and development. It called for SUSTAINABLE DEVELOPMENT, defined as "development that meets the needs of the present without compromising the ability of future generations to meet their own needs." The idea of sustainable development became the bedrock for all future UN efforts to address global environmental challenges. While imprecisely defined, the idea of "sustainable development" appealed to political leaders in states with environmental concerns because it seemed to put a natural limit on economic development strategies. For developing countries it officially recognized for the first time the legitimate competing claim to development even when environmental degradation might occur. On a substantive level the WCED's promotion of sustainable development introduced the idea of intergenerational equity as a standard for national and international development and environmental activities.

Dr. Brundtland and her vice chairman, Dr. Mansour Khalid, of Sudan, appointed the other members of the commission, who came from 21 nations evenly balanced between developed and developing states. The commission members, however, served as individuals and did not represent their national governments. Ms. Brundtland also appointed a panel of experts to prepare a compendium of international environmental legal principles. The commission held open hearings on the problems presented by the apparent conflicts between development and preservation of the global environment. Between March 1985 and February 1987, the commission and its staff interviewed thousands of individuals and organizations in the preparation of its recommendations.

The commission's final report in 1987, entitled *Our Common Future,* proved to be one of the most widely read and influential UN publications. The report recognized direct links among a nation's economy, social system, and environment. It noted that only meaningful economic growth could give a country the ability to provide environmental protection. It argued that concepts of economic growth had to be broadened to include noneconomic variables such as health, education, population growth, and the preservation of water, air, and natural beauty. The report called on governments to integrate environmental considerations into their development planning. It urged international financial institutions, particularly the WORLD BANK, to provide assistance for sustainable development projects. The commission also recommended that the world community negotiate an international CONVENTION on the rights and duties of states in terms of sustainable development, and it called upon the United Nations to convene an international conference on the subject.

In response to *Our Common Future* the General Assembly, in its 44th session (1989), authorized the calling of the UNITED NATIONS CONFERENCE ON ENVIRONMENT AND DEVELOPMENT (UNCED), later known as the Earth Summit. The Assembly endorsed the WCED's recommendations and called on the planned conference to draft an appropriate CONVENTION. In 1990 the World Bank set up the GLOBAL ENVIRONMENT FACILITY (GEF) to meet the Brundtland Commission's concerns about insufficient international financing of environmentally friendly development projects. The bank provided $1.4 billion in initial funding for projects focused on biodiversity, global warming, ocean pollution, and ozone depletion. At the national level many governments seized upon the idea of sustainable development to reorder their environmental and development policies and institutions.

See also UNITED NATIONS ENVIRONMENT PROGRAMME.

Further Reading: Sands, Philippe, ed. *Greening International Law.* New Youk: The New Press, 1994. World Commission on Environment and Development. *Our Common Future.* New York: Oxford University Press, 1987.

World Conference on Human Rights

A total of 7,000 participants, including 171 state representatives, academics, TREATY bodies, national institutions, and representatives of more than 800 NON-GOVERNMENTAL ORGANIZATIONS (two-thirds of them at the grassroots level) gathered in Vienna for the second WORLD CONFERENCE on Human Rights, June 14–25, 1993, in order to review and debate the status of HUMAN RIGHTS implementation around the world. The first such meeting took place in Tehran in 1968. The conference marked the beginning of a renewed effort to strengthen and implement further the body of human rights instruments that had been constructed on the foundation of the UNIVERSAL DECLARATION OF HUMAN RIGHTS since 1948.

The 1993 conference was the result of a 1989 RESOLUTION by the UN GENERAL ASSEMBLY. The conference was intended to identify obstacles to the elaboration of human rights and ways those obstacles might be overcome. The conference agenda included examination of the links connecting development, democracy, and economic, social, cultural, civil, and political rights. It also included the evaluation of the effectiveness of UN methods and mechanisms to ensure adequate financing and other resources for UN human rights activities.

The final document in Vienna, endorsed by the 48th session of the General Assembly in Resolution 121 of 1993, reaffirmed the principles established in the field of human rights in the previous 45 years, and, in a sweeping DECLARATION, affirmed the principle that "all human rights are universal," and that "it is the duty of states, regardless of their political, economic and cultural systems, to promote and protect all human rights and fundamental freedoms." The Vienna Declaration and Program of Action further expressed support for the creation of new mechanisms to strengthen the activities of the United Nations in the field of human rights. The declaration recommended the establishment of a SPECIAL RAPPORTEUR on Violence against WOMEN, the universal ratification of the Convention on the Rights of the Child by the year 1995, and the proclamation by the General Assembly of an international decade of the world's INDIGENOUS PEOPLES. The declaration also called for the General Assembly to establish a HIGH COMMISSIONER FOR HUMAN RIGHTS. Subsequently, three of these recommendations were carried out. The post of the High Commissioner for Human Rights was established on December 20, 1993, the International Decade of the World's Indigenous People was launched on December 9, 1994, and the post of the Special Rapporteur on Violence against Women was established. Only the call for universal ratification of the Convention on the Rights of the Child remained unfulfilled by the end of 2001.

Further Reading: Dias, Clarence J. "The United Nations World Conference on Human Rights: Evaluation, Monitoring, and Review." *United Nations-sponsored World Conferences: Focus on Impact and Follow-up.* Edited by Michael G. Schechter. Tokyo: United Nations University, 2001. Reilly, Niamh, ed. *Testimonies of the Global Tribunal on Violations of Women's Human Rights at the United Nations World Conference on Human Rights, Vienna, June 1993.* New Brunswick, N.J.: Center for Women's Global Leadership, 1994. United Nations. *Report of the World Conference on Human Rights [Vienna, 14–25 June 1993].* New York: United Nations, 1993. World Conference on Human Rights. *World Conference on Human Rights, Vienna, June 1993: The Contributions of NGOs:*

Reports and Documents. Vienna: Manzsche Verlags und Universitätsbuchhandlung, 1994. UNHCR website: <www.unhchr.ch>.

— I. Kebreau

world conferences

World conferences are UN-sponsored international meetings often attended by thousands of individuals, representing themselves, governments, international organizations, UN bodies, media, NON-GOVERNMENTAL ORGANIZATIONS (NGOs), and the international scientific and technical community. While nothing in the UN CHARTER specifically authorizes the United Nations to convene these conferences, the world body has used the directive in the Charter's Preamble, calling upon it to be the "centre for harmonizing the actions of nations," as the basis for its sponsorship. Held at UN HEADQUARTERS, other UN venues, and in cities around the world, these international meetings grew in number, size, and authoritative character during the last third of the 20th century. The first UN-sponsored world conference was held in Havana, CUBA, in 1947–48 and focused on "Trade and Employment." These early gatherings, prior to the 1960s, were relatively small, sporadic sessions. The convocation of the UNITED NATIONS CONFERENCE ON TRADE AND DEVELOPMENT (UNCTAD) in 1964 in Geneva was the first to garner worldwide attention, and to lead to the formation of a formal UN organ, also known as UNCTAD. Subsequent UNCTAD meetings were held quadrennially, with the next three occurring in nations of the global SOUTH—New Delhi, Santiago, and Nairobi. Beginning with the 1972 Stockholm Conference on the Human Environment, UN world conferences attracted the involvement of private international interest groups. More than 400 groups were accredited to the Stockholm meeting. They were allowed to present statements to the conference and to lobby delegations. They played a critical role in encouraging public support for the conference's aims and in providing important expertise related to the ENVIRONMENT. NGOs also sponsored a parallel forum while the UN gathering was in session, setting a precedent followed at all future UN thematic conferences.

UN-sponsored world conferences have often served as defining events in the development of international legal regimes and global policies. Since the late 1980s, the United Nations has used world conferences with increasing frequency to focus world attention on the problems and opportunities associated with HUMAN RIGHTS, environment, WOMEN and development, human settlements, racism, ozone depletion, natural disasters, education, DISARMAMENT, children, population policy, DESERTIFICATION, social issues, and SUSTAINABLE DEVELOPMENT. Each conference in the 1990s was accompanied by a parallel "people's forum," which allowed private groups to present their views and attempt to mold public opinion. In some cases, NGOs were authorized by the sponsoring UN body to participate actively in the sessions and planning groups of the conference. A total of 47,000 people attended the 1992 Earth Summit in Rio de Janeiro, 50,000 attended the FOURTH WORLD CONFERENCE ON WOMEN in Beijing in 1995, and 30,000 were accredited to the 1996 Istanbul Second World Conference on Human Settlements (HABITAT II). Heads of state and of government began active participation in the sessions of world conferences starting with the 1990 WORLD SUMMIT FOR CHILDREN held in New York City.

The extraordinary costs associated with convening the world community to address an important international issue, and the usual outcome of world meetings in the form of vague consensual statements, have produced serious debate among supporters and critics of the world conference process. The bill to the United Nations for meetings in the 1990s generally ranged from $1.8 to $3.4 million. The most expensive was the UNITED NATIONS CONFERENCE ON ENVIRONMENT AND DEVELOPMENT, which cost more than $10 million. These expenditures did not include expenses paid by the nations that hosted the conference, expenses that often rivaled UN outlays. Conference opponents argued that the money would have been better spent ameliorating the problems rather than talking about them. Critics also contended that the meetings were often duplications of efforts then being undertaken by SPECIALIZED AGENCIES or private groups, diverted world attention from more serious problems, produced diplomatic compromises with little in the way of concrete commitments of resources, and "politicized" issues that required humanitarian or scientific responses.

Defenders of the world conference phenomenon, including a significant number of states in the developing world, saw the meetings as opportunities to mobilize national, local, and non-governmental activities to solve major global problems, create international standards that powerful states would find difficult to ignore, serve as fertile ground for the creation of new ideas and strategies, and cut through UN bureaucracy and world lethargy. As the new century began, there was little indication that the momentum for convening world conferences had slackened. SECRETARY-GENERAL Kofi ANNAN himself was an advocate of more world meetings, conceiving and convening the MILLENNIUM SUMMIT in the fall of 2000. States vied for the right to host future sessions. As an example, South Africa committed to host two world conferences in 2001–02: the World Conference against Racism, Racial Discrimination, Xenophobia and Related Intolerance (August 31–September 7, 2001) in Durban, and the World Summit on Sustainable Development (September 2–11, 2002) in Johannesburg. In addition to the South African meetings, the United Nations sponsored seven world conferences between 1999 and 2002.

See also BEIJING +5, DECLARATION, GENERAL AGREEMENT ON TARIFFS AND TRADE, UNITED NATIONS CONFERENCE ON THE LAW OF THE SEA, WORLD CONFERENCE ON HUMAN RIGHTS, WORLD CONFERENCES ON WOMEN, WORLD CONFERENCES TO COMBAT RACISM AND RACIAL DISCRIMINATION.

Further Reading: Schechter, Michael G. *United Nations-sponsored World Conferences. Focus on Impact and Follow-up.* Tokyo: United Nations University Press, 2001. United Nations Department of Public Information. *UN Briefing Papers: The World Conferences, Developing Priorities for the 21st Century.* New York: United Nations Department of Public Information, 1997.

World Conferences on Women

By the turn of the new century, the United Nations had sponsored four world conferences on women (Mexico City, 1975; Copenhagen, 1980; Nairobi, 1985; and Beijing, 1995). These conferences were an outgrowth of the International Women's Year and the UNITED NATIONS DECADE FOR WOMEN (1976–85) that encouraged governments, NON-GOVERNMENTAL ORGANIZATIONS (NGOs), and UN units to focus on women's conditions in various parts of the world.

Delegations from 133 governments took part in the first WORLD CONFERENCE on WOMEN held in Mexico City, where they debated and then adopted a World Plan of Action for addressing issues of equality, DEVELOPMENT, and peace. Delegates also proposed that a second world conference be held at the mid-point of the UN designated "Decade for Women." A notable consequence of this first world conference was the 1979 GENERAL ASSEMBLY vote establishing the CONVENTION ON THE ELIMINATION OF ALL FORMS OF DISCRIMINATION AGAINST WOMEN (CEDAW).

The next World Conference on Women, held in Copenhagen in 1980, represented a mid-decade review of the progress on the World Plan of Action passed in Mexico City. More than 145 governments participated with nearly 8,000 women attending the concurrent NGO Forum. Although high hopes existed for progress at the conference, much of this optimism was dashed in ensuing political debates. Representatives of the developing SOUTH accused countries of the North of economic and political neo-colonialism. Meanwhile, other RESOLUTIONS passed by the conference condemned governments for authoritarianism or APARTHEID. Despite these conflicts, a redefined Plan of Action for the second part of the decade was adopted. This document focused on problems of employment, health, and education for women. A Third World conference was proposed for the end of the Decade for Women in 1985.

The third World Conference, held in Nairobi in 1985, assessed the remaining obstacles to gender equality and the actions required to address them. Strategies were devised to accelerate fulfillment of women's rights issues during the last 15 years of the century. The focus once again was given to themes of equality, peace, and development. The final document of the conference, known as the "Nairobi Forward-Looking Strategies for the Advancement of Women," called for new efforts to recognize that women and children are often the hardest hit by poverty, drought, armed conflict, family violence, and marginalization caused by refugee, migrant, or ethnic minority status. According to the United Nations, approximately 120 governments in the last 10 years of the century reported progress in meeting the targets established at this conference.

In 1995, a fourth World Conference on Women was held in Beijing. Representatives of 189 governments attended the meeting, and a new five-year global action plan affirming the themes of equality, peace, and development was adopted. The Beijing Declaration and Platform for Action built on earlier commitments made by the United Nations and identified 12 critical areas of concern for women's advancement and empowerment, including poverty, education and training, health, violence, armed conflict, economy, decision making, institutional mechanisms, HUMAN RIGHTS, media, ENVIRONMENT, and the girl child. Five years after Beijing, the SPECIAL SESSION held in June 2000, known as BEIJING +5, gave government representatives and NGOs an opportunity to assess progress on the platform.

See also ADMINISTRATIVE COMMITTEE ON COORDINATION, UNITED NATIONS DEVELOPMENT FUND FOR WOMEN.

Further Reading: "United Nations Decade for Women 1976–1985: Really Only a Beginning. Mexico to Copenhagen, to Nairobi: An Irresistible Momentum. . ." *UN Chronicle* 22, no. 7 (July–August 1985): ii–xxiv. "Women's Conference Adopts 'Beijing Declaration and Platform for Action." *UN Chronicle* 32, no. 4 (December 1995): 25–31. Pietilla, Hilkka, and Jeanne Vickers, *Making Women Matter: The Role of the United Nations.* London: Zed Books, 1996. Beijing +5 website: <www.un.org/womenwatch/followup/beijing5>.

— *K. J. Vogel*

World Conferences to Combat Racism and Racial Discrimination (WCAR)

On November 2, 1972, the UN GENERAL ASSEMBLY designated the 10-year period 1973–82 as the Decade for Action to Combat Racism and Racial Discrimination. Subsequently, the United Nations proclaimed two more Decades for Action (1983–92 and 1993–2002) in order to attain the goal of "vigorous and continued mobilization against racism and racial discrimination in all its forms." The program of action for the first decade was structured around a worldwide education campaign and measures to be taken to implement UN instruments promoting the elimination of racial discrimination. The First WORLD CONFERENCE to Combat Racism and Racial Discrimination was held in Geneva in 1978. The goal of the conference was to assess the aims of the first decade.

As such, the DECLARATION and Programme of Action of the conference reaffirmed the inherent callousness of racism and the threat it posed to friendly relations among peoples and nations. The declaration specifically condemned APARTHEID and recommended that efforts to combat racism include measures aimed at improving the living conditions of men and WOMEN.

The Second World Conference to Combat Racism and Racial Discrimination occurred in Geneva in August 1983. It reviewed and assessed the activities undertaken during the first decade. In addition to calling for measures against all ideologies and practices based on racial or ethnic exclusiveness or intolerance, the conference noted the double discrimination often encountered by women. Examples of "ideological" hatred cited in the Final Document included terror and the systematic denial of rights endorsed by such political movements as nazism and fascism. The conference declaration also urged protection of the rights of refugees, immigrants, and migrant workers and welcomed the establishment of the United Nations Working Group on Indigenous Populations.

The Third World Conference against Racism, Racial Discrimination, Xenophobia and Related Intolerance was held in Durban, South Africa, from August 31 to September 7, 2001. The conference intended to flesh out a broadened view of racism, recognizing that all societies in the world are affected and hindered by discrimination. But divisiveness beset the preparatory process of drafting a document for discussion and continued divisions exacerbated tensions during the conference. Little unity could be found among the official delegates, NON-GOVERNMENTAL ORGANIZATIONS (NGOs), and the "unofficial" caucuses participating in the conference. The major disagreements were evident during the preparatory period. Two Working Groups—one on the declaration and the other on the Programme of Action—were divided further into four informal groups entitled Middle East questions, issues of the legacy of the past, the grounds of racism, and lists of victims of racism.

The UNITED STATES resisted participation in the conference because the draft declaration condemned ZIONISM as a form of racism, reviving an anti-Israeli position that the United Nations had endorsed in 1974 but rejected in the early 1990s. Thus Washington sent a downgraded delegation (crucially, minus Secretary of State Colin Powell) to the opening sessions, then withdrew completely to show its distaste with the course of the conference. There was also acrimony over the extent to which the conference should insist on reparations for the pre–20th century slave trade. European representatives wanted to relay the message that the West was aware of its historical responsibility for the slave trade and its resulting poverty and inequality, especially in Africa. The European Union demonstrated that it was prepared to continue work to improve conditions among Third World countries that legitimately could claim the primary injury. European states, however, were not willing to accept NGO proposals for direct payments to the victims of racism.

Thousands of non-governmental organizations participated in the parallel NGO Forum in Durban. The NGO declaration contained more radical language than the official UN document. It condemned contemporary racist exploitation of groups such as the Palestinians, the Dalits (the "untouchables") in India, and present-day slaves in Mauritania and elsewhere. It further called for direct financial reparations to be paid to the victims of racism, and accused globalization of causing ongoing racial inequality. Despite their seeming unity, 77 NGOs from 37 countries in Europe, North America, and Southeast Asia, as well as five prominent HUMAN RIGHTS groups, rejected the NGO Declaration and Plan of Action. Nonetheless, both documents were included in the final conference declaration, together with the Youth Summit Declaration.

Complicating the work of the conference were the simultaneous demonstrations by local citizens and groups. The unofficial "pavement conference" attended by 20,000 poor people from South Africa turned into the largest political protest in the country since the demise of apartheid. The protesters' message was clear: landlessness equals racism.

More than 50 informal negotiations were held during the run of the conference, and consensus on most sensitive issues was reached only in general terms during the final hours. Due to the divisive nature of the issues involved, a number of delegations made known their reservations or disassociations on certain issues, including those relating to the Middle East and to the legacy of the past. The Conference adopted a Declaration and Programme of Action that committed member states to undertake a wide range of measures to combat racism and discrimination at the international, regional, and national levels. The conference denounced slavery and colonialism and recommended remedies based on a "developmental partnership," such as the "promotion of foreign direct investment and market access." African leaders acquiesced in this formulation.

On the Middle East question, the conference called for an end to violence and encouraged cooperation between Israel and the Palestinian people and among others involved. The final declaration recognized the inalienable right of the Palestinian people to self-determination and to the establishment of an independent state. On the question of slavery, the conference acknowledged and regretted the massive human suffering and the tragic plight of millions of people resulting from slavery, the slave trade, apartheid, colonialism, and GENOCIDE. The conference asserted that slavery and the slave trade were crimes against humanity. Thus, due to the painstaking diplomatic efforts of the South African delegation and the European Union, the most contentious issues facing the conference were

resolved and the language accepted by consensus in the final declaration, without "ZIONISM" and "racism" being coupled, and without a provision for compensation for past practices of slavery. The relevant words were the following: "We recall that the Holocaust must never be forgotten. . . . We recognize the inalienable right of the Palestinian people to self-determination and to the establishment of an independent state, and we recognize the right to security for all states in the region, including Israel. . . . We acknowledge that slavery and the slave trade, including the trans-Atlantic slave trade, were appalling tragedies in the history of humanity . . . and further acknowledge that slavery and the slave trade are a crime against humanity and should always have been so."

Additionally, the conference acknowledged the contribution of slavery, the slave trade, and other historic injustices to poverty, underdevelopment, marginalization, social exclusion, economic disparities, and instability and insecurity, particularly in developing countries. It recognized the need to develop a new partnership in the areas of debt relief, poverty eradication, the building and strengthening of democratic institutions, and the promotion of foreign direct investment and market access. Because delegates were unable to reach an agreement on the question of victims of racism, the conference agreed on a self-evident text that defined the victims of racism, racial discrimination, xenophobia, and related intolerance as "individuals or groups of individuals who are or who have been affected by or subjected to or targets of those scourges." The conference recognized that discrimination derived from several sources, including race, color, ancestors, national or ethnic origins, language, sex, religion, political or other opinion, social origin, property, and birth or other status. Mary Robinson, the Secretary-General of the conference, noting the divisiveness of the meeting, heralded the Durban meeting as a beginning and not an end in urging: "There must be follow-ups."

Further Reading: Gle-Ahanhanzo. *Report by the Special Rapporteur on Contemporary Forms of Racial Discrimination, Xenophobia and Related Intolerance.* UN Document CN.4/1997/71. January 16, 1997. WCAR website: <www.un.org/WCAR>.

— *I. Kebreau*

World Court   *See* INTERNATIONAL COURT OF JUSTICE, PERMANENT COURT OF INTERNATIONAL JUSTICE.

World Day for Water

Observed annually on March 22, the day is intended to promote awareness of the importance of water resources to economic development.

World Day to Combat Desertification and Drought

Celebrated on June 17 annually, this day marks the anniversary of the adoption of the United Nations CONVENTION TO COMBAT DESERTIFICATION in 1994.

World Development Information Day

The GENERAL ASSEMBLY intentionally chose to make this annual observance coincide with UNITED NATIONS DAY, October 24. That date in 1970 was also the adoption date of the International development Strategy for the Second United Nations DEVELOPMENT DECADE. The General Assembly in 1972 instituted World Development Information Day to draw world public attention to development problems and cooperative ways to solve them.

World Economic and Social Survey

The *Survey* is the annual publication of the UN Secretariat's DEPARTMENT OF ECONOMIC AND SOCIAL AFFAIRS (DESA). Its Division for Development Policy Analysis produces the compendium to complement its semi-annual short-term economic forecasts for regions and major economies in the world. The *Survey* analyzes topical global economic issues and current developments in the world economy. It provides UN forecasts on world trade and discusses net transfers of financial resources of developing countries. It includes extensive statistical tables on macroeconomic and trade trends.

World Environment Day

Celebrated annually on June 5, the day marks the anniversary of the opening session of the UNITED NATIONS CONFERENCE ON THE HUMAN ENVIRONMENT (Stockholm, 1972), which led to the establishment of the UNITED NATIONS ENVIRONMENT PROGRAMME (UNEP).

World Federation of United Nations Associations   *See* UNITED NATIONS ASSOCIATION.

World Food Day

Celebrated on October 16 annually, the day was proclaimed by the FOOD AND AGRICULTURE ORGANIZATION (FAO) in 1979. The day marks the date of FAO's founding in 1945.

World Food Programme (WFP)

The World Food Programme began operations in 1962 as a product of decisions taken in 1961 by the UN GENERAL ASSEMBLY and the FOOD AND AGRICULTURE ORGANIZATION (FAO). As the food distribution agency of the UNITED NATIONS SYSTEM, WFP is the largest international food aid provider in the world. At the close of the century it expended each year in excess of $1 billion, supporting a field staff of more than 5,000 who annually distributed more than 3.4 million tons of food. Its services include food deliveries to people in emergency circumstances—natural or man-made—to poor people in developing countries, communities where the food assistance will help with economic development projects, and "internally displaced persons" (IDPs) who are refugees from internecine conflict.

In 1994 the World Food Programme became the first UN agency to draft a mission statement to guide its work. According to that statement, the WFP uses its food to meet emergency needs, support economic and social development, and provides logistical support necessary for the delivery of food. The agency also is committed to putting the issue of hunger at the center of the international agenda. WFP works most closely with the Food and Agriculture Organization and the INTERNATIONAL FUND FOR AGRICULTURAL DEVELOPMENT (IFAD), but it also conducts many projects with the UNITED NATIONS DEVELOPMENT PROGRAMME, the WORLD BANK, the UN HIGH COMMISSIONER FOR REFUGEES, the UNITED NATIONS CHILDREN'S FUND (UNICEF), the WORLD HEALTH ORGANIZATION, the INTERNATIONAL LABOUR ORGANIZATION, and the UNITED NATIONS EDUCATIONAL, SCIENTIFIC AND CULTURAL ORGANIZATION. It also has working agreements with several international NON-GOVERNMENTAL ORGANIZATIONS, including Catholic Relief Services, Save the Children, CARE, World Vision International, and Food for the Hungry.

In 1990 two-thirds of all WFP food aid went for development projects, attempting to make individuals self-reliant. By the end of the decade, however, 80 percent of food distributed went for the humanitarian relief of people in crisis. In 2000 the World Food Programme fed 83 million people in 83 countries. In LATIN AMERICA it operated a food program for several hundred thousand IDPs who were displaced by civil war in Colombia. In Central Asia, WFP provided extensive aid in AFGHANISTAN, and continued to do so even as the country came under military attack following the 2001 terrorist attacks on the UNITED STATES. It focused much of the relief aid on vulnerable populations such as WOMEN and children, and it provided food to ex-combatant soldiers in civil conflicts. For example, in Sudan during the 1990s WFP was one of two lead organizations—the other was UNICEF—for Operation Sudan Lifeline, an effort to save more than one million people from famine.

The executive director of the World Food Programme is appointed for a five-year term jointly by the FAO DIRECTOR-GENERAL and the UN SECRETARY-GENERAL. Directed in 2001 by Catherine Bertini of the United States, the WFP is governed by a 36-member Executive Board, half elected by the

UN ECONOMIC AND SOCIAL COUNCIL (ECOSOC) and half by the Food and Agriculture Organization to reelectable three-year terms. The board reports to ECOSOC and to the FAO Council yearly. WFP's headquarters is in Rome, Italy.

The organization is funded and receives food supplies from donor nations on a voluntary basis. At the turn of the century more than 60 nations supported WFP's projects. In 2000, the United States was the largest donor ($796 million), Japan was second in donations ($260 million), and the European Union third ($118 million).

See also ADMINISTRATIVE COMMITTEE ON COORDINATION, DESERTIFICATION, PROGRAMMES AND FUNDS, SOMALIA.

Further Reading: Shaw, D. John, and Sir Hans W. Singer. "A Note on Some UN Achievements with Special Reference to the World Food Programme." *The United Nations at Work.* Edited by Martin Ira Glassner. Westport, Conn. Praeger Publishers, 1998, 186–211. United Nations Department of Public Information. *Basic Facts about the United Nations.* New York: United Nations Department of Public Information, published periodically. WFP website: <www.wfp.org>.

World Food Summit   *See* FOOD AND AGRICULTURE ORGANIZATION.

World Habitat Day
Celebrated on the first Monday of October each year, the day marks the anniversary of the first United Nations Conference on Human Settlements, held in Vancouver, Canada, in 1976.

World Health Day
Celebrated on April 7 annually, World Health Day marks the anniversary of the entry into force of the constitution of the WORLD HEALTH ORGANIZATION. On April 7, 1948, the required 26th nation ratified the document.

World Health Organization (WHO)
At the 1945 founding conference of the United Nations in San Francisco, CHINA and Brazil proposed that an international health organization be made a part of the UN. Because of the broad support for the recommendation, the new ECONOMIC AND SOCIAL COUNCIL (ECOSOC) organized an International Health Conference in 1947, at which 61 nations adopted the constitution of the World Health Organization. It came into existence on April 7, 1948, when the 26th state ratified the constitution, making that date in April henceforth celebrated by the UNITED NATIONS SYSTEM as World Health Day. WHO became a UN SPECIALIZED AGENCY on July 10, 1948. It subsumed within its orga-

nizational STRUCTURE the activities of two earlier international organizations dedicated to global health efforts: the International Office of Public Hygiene founded in Paris in 1907, and the LEAGUE OF NATIONS Health Organization created in 1920.

According to WHO's constitution, the goal of the organization is "the attainment by all peoples of the highest possible level of health," which it defines as "a state of complete physical, mental and social well-being and not merely the absence of disease or infirmity." Given this broad mandate, the World Health Organization has developed more than 50 programs related to research, humanitarian health assistance, health education, medical cooperation, clinical technology, and conference organization related to worldwide health problems, as well as worldwide programs to eradicate disease. Its headquarters is in Geneva, where more than one-third of its 3,600 personnel work. It also maintains six regional conferences and offices for its member states. These are in Washington, Copenhagen, Brazzaville (CONGO), New Delhi, Manila, and Alexandria (Egypt). While it provides only limited field services, it works in alliance with "collaborating centres," governments, NON-GOVERNMENTAL ORGANIZATIONS, businesses, medical communities, and philanthropic foundations to achieve its goals. In 1980 WHO achieved its greatest accomplishment with the announcement of the eradication of smallpox. At the turn of the century it had refocused its efforts to fight HIV/AIDS, tobacco use, malaria, and childhood diseases that could be halted by the universal use of vaccines. In February 2002, WHO joined with the ORGANIZATION OF AFRICAN UNITY, the FOOD AND AGRICULTURE ORGANIZATION, and the INTERNATIONAL ATOMIC ENERGY AGENCY in a campaign to eradicate the tsetse fly from Africa. The organizations planned to introduce millions of sterilized male flies into infected regions, hoping to eliminate the fly population, and its consequent threat to local human communities.

The plenary body of the World Health Organization is the World Health Assembly that meets annually, usually in May. Only five times has it met outside of Geneva. The World Health Assembly, made up of the full MEMBERSHIP (191 states as of July 2001), approves the BUDGET (approximately $1 billion in 2001) and program of the organization. It also appoints the DIRECTOR-GENERAL to a five-year term on the recommendation of the Executive Board. The board is made up of 32 individuals appointed for their expertise in the field of international and public health. They are appointed to three-year terms by member states elected to make appointment of one of their nationals at the annual World Health Assembly meeting. Each annual meeting makes appointments to the board on a rotating basis of 12:10:10. The board meets twice yearly, in January and immediately following the World Health Assembly meeting. It is charged with implementing the World Health Assembly's RESOLUTIONS, preparing the agenda for the organization, and nominating the director-general.

In 1998, the World Health Assembly elected Dr. Gro Harlem BRUNDTLAND as the director-general to succeed Dr. Hiroshi Nakajima, who had served two terms. It was hoped that Dr. Brundtland—a doctor, graduate of advanced studies in public health at Harvard University, former prime minister of Norway, and head of the WORLD COMMISSION ON ENVIRONMENT AND DEVELOPMENT—could bring new vitality to the organization. In her past work she had coined the term "SUSTAINABLE DEVELOPMENT," which had become a cornerstone of all UN DEVELOPMENT efforts, and she had emerged as one of the most active and visible WOMEN in the UN system. Dr. Brundtland immediately reorganized WHO, bringing in a new senior management team as her "cabinet," and placing WHO's programs in policy clusters under the direction of cabinet officers. She shifted the focus away from support services in emergency or chronic health situations in poor countries toward the development of global core programs meant to create worldwide responses to health problems. With these efforts she brought new attention and resources to the organization. This was reflected in the first-ever address by a UN SECRETARY-GENERAL to the annual World Health Assembly meeting. Kofi ANNAN spoke to the May 2001 session, lauding WHO for its initiatives, and calling upon it to join in a Global Alliance on Health, and particularly in the fight against AIDS in Africa.

Beginning in 1999, WHO launched two initiatives that reflected Dr. Brundtland's desire to inject WHO into larger social debates that will affect the health of many future generations. The World Health Assembly that year unanimously endorsed a resolution calling for the negotiation of a Framework Convention on Tobacco Control (FCTC). The CONVENTION would bolster WHO's Tobacco Free Initiative by imposing a worldwide ban on tobacco advertising and promotion, increasing taxes on cigarettes, and fostering education programs aimed at youth. WHO also created a Global Programme on Evidence for Health Policy, which for the first time created an index on the performance of national health systems. Through the index WHO hoped to identify the policies and factors that would assure "good" health for the population, a responsiveness in the health system to popular expectations, and systems that were "fair" in their distribution of medical services and costs. As a result of the first index survey, WHO identified France as having the "best" health system, followed by Italy, Spain, Oman, Austria, and Japan. The "worst" were found in sub-Saharan Africa. The index allowed WHO to make general recommendations to states on methods to improve their systems, including the recommendation in 2001 that national governments assure that medical insurance programs were available to all citizens.

See also ADMINISTRATIVE COMMITTEE ON COORDINATION, APARTHEID, EXPANDED PROGRAM OF TECHNICAL ASSISTANCE, JOINT UNITED NATIONS PROGRAMME ON HIV/AIDS, KIM IL-SUNG, ORGANIZATION OF AFRICAN UNITY, SOMALIA, UNITED NATIONS OFFICE FOR PROJECT SERVICES.

Further Reading: Eco'Diagnostic, Geneva. *International Geneva Yearbook, 2000–2001.* Vol 14. Geneva: United Nations, 2000. Tessitore, John, and Susan Woolfson. *A Global Agenda. Issues before the 55th General Assembly of the United Nations.* New York: Rowman and Littlefield, 2000. World Health Organization. *Handbook of Resolutions and Decisions of the World Health Assembly and the Executive Board.* Geneva: World Health Organization, published annually. WHO website: <www.who.int>.

World Intellectual Property Organization (WIPO)

In 1967, in Stockholm, a CONVENTION was signed creating the World Intellectual Property Organization. The convention came into force on December 17, 1974, and by RESOLUTION 3346, the GENERAL ASSEMBLY unanimously made WIPO a SPECIALIZED AGENCY of the United Nations. Among the 16 specialized agencies that were part of the UNITED NATIONS SYSTEM by 2001, WIPO was the UN-related organization dedicated to promoting the use and security of intellectual property throughout the world. It sought cooperation among NATION-STATES to protect patents, copyrights, and intellectual property generally.

WIPO's ancestry dates to the late 19th century. In 1883 the Paris Convention for the Protection of Industrial Property became the first international TREATY designed to protect industrial property rights. The Paris convention entered into force in 1884 with 14 members. In 1886, copyright protection became part of INTERNATIONAL LAW with the Berne Convention for the Protection of Literary and Artistic Works. In 1893, the international bureaus set up to govern both the Paris and Berne instruments merged into the United International Bureaux for the Protection of Intellectual Property (the French acronym being BIRPI), based in Berne, Switzerland. This organization was the immediate predecessor to the World Intellectual Property Organization. In 1960, BIRPI relocated to Geneva. In 1970 BIRPI, by virtue of the Convention Establishing the World Intellectual Property Organization, became WIPO. When the convention entered into force in 1974, WIPO then became a specialized agency to administer intellectual property matters recognized by UN member states. In 1996 WIPO entered into a cooperative agreement with the WORLD TRADE ORGANIZATION (WTO), expanding the importance and protection possibilities for intellectual property worldwide.

The WIPO seeks collaboration among its 177 member states (as of 2001) to assure global cooperation in protecting all intellectual property, by which is meant industrial property such as inventions, trademarks, and industrial designs, and copyright of literary, musical, artistic, photographic, and audiovisual creations. It encourages the composing of international agreements to promote the safeguarding of new forms of intellectual property occasioned by developments in patent law and digital and Internet advances. WIPO also encourages developing countries to make use of innovative intellectual property progress, and to acquire foreign technology and skills to take full advantage of new forms of scientific, technological, and artistic developments. It provides advice, training, and published documents regarding all facets in the field of intellectual property rights and progress. By the turn of the century the organization administered 23 treaties (16 regarding industrial property and six pertaining to copyright law). A total of 181 NON-GOVERNMENTAL ORGANIZATIONS had OBSERVER STATUS with the organization in 2001.

WIPO has three governing bodies: a General Assembly, composed of all member states, which meets every two years; the Conference, also made up of all members, which meets as well every two years; and a smaller Coordination Committee (68 members in 2001), which convenes annually. These governing bodies establish the program for WIPO and approve the BUDGET. In 2001 the DIRECTOR-GENERAL of WIPO was Dr. Kamil Idris from Sudan, whose office was at the HEADQUARTERS in Geneva. A SECRETARIAT of 817 staff members administered the work of WIPO, and the BUDGET in 2001 was 410 million Swiss francs.

See also ADMINISTRATIVE COMMITTEE ON COORDINATION, CONSULTATIVE STATUS.

Further Reading: Eco'Diagnostic, Geneva. *International Geneva Yearbook.* Geneva: United Nations, published annually. WIPO website: <www.wipo.org>.

World Meteorological Day

Celebrated on March 23 annually, World Meteorological Day marks the anniversary of the opening of operations by the WORLD METEOROLOGICAL ORGANIZATION (WMO) in 1950. The WMO had been created by the adoption of the World Meteorological CONVENTION in 1947.

World Meteorological Organization (WMO)

The World Meteorological Organization is the successor to the International Meteorological Organization (IMO), and was created by the World Meteorological CONVENTION as adopted by IMO in 1947. It came into being on March 23, 1950, that day in March now celebrated by the UNITED NATIONS SYSTEM as WORLD METEOROLOGICAL DAY. In 1952, the WMO became a SPECIALIZED AGENCY of the United Nations. The organization has more than 180 members and has its headquarters in Geneva.

The WMO facilitates international cooperation in meteorological and hydrological observations, the exchange of important information about the weather and climate, the creation of standardized methods for observing and reporting atmospheric data, and the application of environmental information to development. In October 1999, the WMO adopted a Universal DECLARATION, committing the organization to a long-term plan through 2005. The plan's objectives commit the agency to providing leadership in climate change monitoring, to contributing to environmentally SUSTAINABLE DEVELOPMENT in all countries, and to helping arrest "degradation of the atmosphere . . . and marine ENVIRONMENTS."

The policy-making body of WMO is the World Meteorological Congress, which meets every four years. The 14th congress is scheduled to meet in May 2003. A total of 36 members serve on the agency's Executive Council, which implements the Congress's RESOLUTIONS and regulations. WMO has six regional associations (Africa, Asia, South America, North and Central America, South-West Pacific, and Europe) that also meet every four years to coordinate activities within their regions. It has eight technical commissions as well for different functional areas of its activities.

Headed by a secretary-general, who directs a staff of more than 200, the WMO administers several global programs and works with other specialized agencies and UN bodies to focus attention on serious climatological problems. It serves on the INTER-AGENCY COMMITTEE ON SUSTAINABLE DEVELOPMENT of the UN SYSTEM CHIEF EXECUTIVES BOARD FOR COORDINATION, chaired by the UN SECRETARY-GENERAL. WMO's largest program is World Weather Watch (WWW), which provides up-to-the-minute weather information from all parts of the world. In addition to linking all national weather services, WWW gathers information from four polar-orbiting and five geostationary satellites. Its World Climate Programme (WCP), however, has been its most important effort, promoting international policy on critical climate change issues, transboundary pollution, and ozone degradation. It was created in 1979, following the First World Climate Conference, with the purpose of using climate information to improve the understanding of climate processes, and to use that understanding to warn governments of impending climate changes. Subsequently, the WMO was joined in its sponsorship of WCP by the UNITED NATIONS ENVIRONMENT PROGRAMME (UNEP), the Inter-governmental Commission of UNESCO, and the International Council for Science.

Based on the data from WCP, the World Meteorological Organization joined with UNEP to establish the INTERGOVERNMENTAL PANEL ON CLIMATE CHANGE (IPCC) in 1988. The panel, in turn, produced the data and momentum that led to the signing of the UNITED NATIONS FRAMEWORK CONVENTION ON CLIMATE CHANGE at the 1992 Earth Summit in Rio de Janeiro. WMO's research also contributed to the drafting of the VIENNA CONVENTION and MONTREAL PROTOCOL on the Ozone Layer. It maintains in Geneva a Commission for Climatology to promote activities relating climate to human well-being and sustainable development.

The WMO also has assisted UN activities in drought-prone areas of Africa, providing scientific information on DESERTIFICATION. It was involved in the negotiation of the CONVENTION TO COMBAT DESERTIFICATION, opened for signature in October 1994. Closely connected to its work in this area is the WMO-maintained Hydrology and Water Resources Programme, which implements its activities through WMO offices in Bujumbura, Burundi, and Lagos, Nigeria.

See also EXPANDED PROGRAM OF TECHNICAL ASSISTANCE, UNITED NATIONS CONFERENCE ON ENVIRONMENT AND DEVELOPMENT, UNITED NATIONS OFFICE FOR PROJECT SERVICES.

Further Reading: New Zealand Ministry of Foreign Affairs. *United Nations Handbook 2000.* Wellington, N.Z.: Ministry of Foreign Affairs and Trade, published annually. WMO website: <www.wmo.ch/>.

World Population Conference   *See*
INTERNATIONAL CONFERENCE ON POPULATION AND DEVELOPMENT.

World Population Day
Celebrated on July 11 annually, this observance is an outgrowth of the Day of Five Billion on July 11, 1987. It was estimated that world population surpassed that number on that date. In 2000, world population stood at 6.06 billion and was growing by 78 million a year.

World Refugee Day
Celebrated on June 20 annually, the day marks the anniversary of the 1951 CONVENTION RELATING TO THE STATUS OF REFUGEES.

World Summit for Children (WSC)   *See* UNITED
NATIONS CHILDREN'S FUND.

World Summit for Social Development (WSSD)
The World Summit for Social Development convened in Copenhagen, March 6–12, 1995. Informally known as "The Social Summit," the conference attracted 186 state participants, 117 of them represented by either the head of state or government, the largest gathering to date of world leaders. A total 811 NON-GOVERNMENTAL ORGANIZATIONS

(NGOs) were also accredited to the conference proceedings, with additional NGOs holding a parallel NGO Forum. The WSSD served as a collective summation of previous WORLD CONFERENCES on different aspects of social life—conferences on WOMEN, children, INDIGENOUS PEOPLES, HUMAN RIGHTS, and SUSTAINABLE DEVELOPMENT. The Social Summit focused on the eradication of poverty, the expansion of productive employment, the concomitant reduction in unemployment, and the promotion of social integration as the key elements in a "people-centered" development process. The World Conference concluded with the approval of the Copenhagen Declaration on Social Development and a Programme of Action.

The Copenhagen Declaration proclaimed social development as the highest priority in international and national policy making and implementation. To achieve that development the DECLARATION made 10 commitments on behalf of the international community, and then outlined specific recommendations each nation and international organization should take to achieve them. They were: (1) to create an economic, political, and social environment that will make social development possible, (2) to eradicate absolute poverty by a target date in each country, (3) to promote full employment as a priority issue at the national and international levels, (4) to promote social integration by protecting human rights and by respect for diversity, (5) to achieve equality and equity between men and women, (6) to achieve universal access to health care and education, (7) to accelerate development in the LEAST DEVELOPED COUNTRIES, especially in Africa, (8) to include social development goals in structural adjustment programs, (9) to allocate more resources for social development, and (10) to strengthen local, national, and international cooperation on behalf of social development. Subsequent to the conference specific indicators were developed to measure progress on each of these commitments, and a follow-up SPECIAL SESSION OF THE GENERAL ASSEMBLY was convened at GENEVA HEADQUARTERS in June 2000 to assess the level of fulfillment that had occurred. The Copenhagen +5 Social Summit Special Session determined that the eradication of poverty should be given new emphasis and set a goal of halving the number of the world's poor people by 2015.

The Copenhagen Plan of Action named the UNITED NATIONS DEVELOPMENT PROGRAMME as the lead organization in mobilizing the UNITED NATIONS SYSTEM to carry out the conference's recommendations. Assessment of progress made on the 10 commitments was assigned to the COMMISSION FOR SOCIAL DEVELOPMENT (CSocD). Founded in 1946, the commission established a thematic agenda for its work based on the Copenhagen Programme for Action—the eradication of poverty (1996), productive employment (1997), promotion of social integration (1998), social services (1999), contributions made by the commission (2000), social protection and vulnerability during globalization, the role of volunteerism (2001), and the integration of social and economic policy (2002). At its 39th session in February 2001, the commission agreed on a multiyear program of work through 2006, continuing its thematic approach. Under the leadership of the UN's ADMINISTRATIVE COMMITTEE FOR COORDINATION, a number of Inter-Agency Task Forces were also established to assure integrated efforts to achieve the conference's goals.

Further Reading: Paul, James. *Incorporating Human Rights into the Work of the World Summit for Social Development.* Washington, D.C.: American Society of International Law, 1995. United Nations Department of Public Information. *UN Briefing Papers: The World Conferences, Developing Priorities for the 21st Century.* New York: United Nations Department of Public Information, 1997. United Nations Development Programme. *Progress against Poverty: A Report on Activities since Copenhagen.* New York: United Nations Development Programme, 1996.

World Tourism Day

Celebrated annually on September 27, World Tourism Day notes the anniversary of the formation of the WORLD TOURISM ORGANIZATION in 1970.

World Tourism Organization (WTO)

The World Tourism Organization succeeded several international non-governmental tourism agencies dating back to 1925 when it became in 1976 the executing body for the UNITED NATIONS DEVELOPMENT PROGRAMME in the promotion of world tourism. A formal agreement of cooperation with the United Nations was signed the following year. Headquartered in Madrid, the organization had 139 member countries in 2001 and 350 affiliate members representing local governments, tourism associations, and private companies. By encouraging tourism the WTO stimulates economic development and employment. It carries out its work through six regional commissions focused on Africa, the Americas, East Asia and the Pacific, Europe, the Middle East, and South Asia.

The inter-governmental organization is governed by a General Assembly that meets every two years to approve the BUDGET and the agency's program, and to elect its secretary-general, who serves a four-year term. Between sessions of the assembly a 26-member Executive Board guides the WTO. The budget for 2000–01 was $19.5 million, 90 percent of it coming from MEMBERSHIP dues. The tourism body uses its resources, among other things, to promote regional tourism projects. In the 1990s two of the more important projects were "The Silk Road" and "The Slave Route" cultural initiatives. Begun in 1994, the Silk Road project promoted tourism along the route taken by Marco Polo to CHINA. "The Slave Route" encouraged tourism to West African states.

In 2001 the organization undertook an internal revitalization program. Among other actions it established a Committee on World Tourism Ethics, and it began development of a code of conduct for tourism organizations and member states in light of international TERRORISM.

See also ADMINISTRATIVE COMMITTEE ON COORDINATION, WORLD TOURISM DAY.

Further Reading: WTO website: <www.world-tourism.org>.

World Trade Organization (WTO)

With its HEADQUARTERS in Geneva, the World Trade Organization is the member-directed institution that administers the rules governing world trade. These rules are designed to help trade flow smoothly, fairly, freely, and predictably. The WTO was created in 1995 as the result of the Uruguay Round of Multilateral Trade Negotiations to give the GENERAL AGREEMENT ON TARIFFS AND TRADE (GATT) the needed institutional support for what was becoming an increasingly complicated system of trade rules. At that time, the WTO took its place with the INTERNATIONAL MONETARY FUND (IMF) and the INTERNATIONAL BANK FOR RECONSTRUCTION AND DEVELOPMENT (WORLD BANK) to complete the BRETTON WOODS troika of international institutions overseeing the international economy. Increased world trade since 1945, which has been facilitated by the establishment of international rules under the WTO and its predecessor the GATT, has been one of the main engines of economic DEVELOPMENT and has contributed greatly to the improvement in income and the reduction of poverty around the world.

A DIRECTOR-GENERAL heads the WTO. The incumbent in 2001 was Michael Moore, the former New Zealand prime minister and trade minister. He was scheduled to be replaced in September 2002 by Supachai Panitchpakdi, the former Thai deputy prime minister, who would serve out the remainder of Moore's six-year term. This unusual term-sharing arrangement was necessary to resolve an impasse over the appointment of the WTO's head between the UNITED STATES and an Asian bloc of countries led by Japan.

The Ministerial Conference, which is made up of trade ministers or equivalents from member countries and meets at least once every two years as it did in 1999 in Seattle, is the WTO's supreme decision-making body. It sets the organization's strategic direction. The World Trade Organization also has a General Council made up of ambassadors and heads of delegation in Geneva, which meets regularly to make the necessary day-to-day decisions. The General Council also meets as the Trade Policy Review Body and the Dispute Settlement Body (DSB). The Goods Council, Services Council, and Intellectual Property (TRIPS) Council report to the General Council. There are also specialized committees, working groups, and working parties set up to deal with special issues.

The WTO has six main functions: (1) administering WTO trade agreements, (2) providing a forum for trade negotiations, (3) handling trade disputes, (4) monitoring national trade policies, (5) providing technical assistance and training for developing countries on trade policy, and (6) cooperating with other international organizations on trade issues.

Over a series of eight rounds of trade negotiations under the GATT, a complex web of some 60 agreements governing world trade grew up. The GATT itself, with annexes covering specific sectors such as agriculture and textiles, and specific issues such as state trading, product standards, subsidies and anti-dumping, became the umbrella agreement mandating non-discrimination for trade in goods. A General Agreement on Trade in Services (GATS), which contained both a framework and specific commitments for opening up service sectors to foreign competition, did the same for services. An Agreement on Trade-Related Aspects of Intellectual Property Rights provided protection to "intellectual property" such as patents, copyrights, trademarks, and trade secrets when trade was involved. Finally, a strengthened Dispute Settlement Understanding accord established procedures for resolving trade disputes through panels and appeals without resort to unilateral actions. The creation of the Dispute Settlement Board to adjudicate trade complaints among members was the greatest single accomplishment of the Uruguay Round, and the most important advancement over the previous GATT dispute resolution process. It had been so successful that everyone from HUMAN RIGHTS activists to environmentalists have sought access to it for their own purposes.

There were more than 140 countries as of early 2001 that were members of the WTO and bound by its agreements, accounting for more than 90 percent of world trade. The number continued to grow with important countries like CHINA, Russia, Saudi Arabia, and Taiwan negotiating to join.

The impact of the WTO on the world economy at the turn of the century was extraordinary, given that the organization had, in 2001, a staff of barely 500 and a frugal BUDGET of slightly more than $76 million. By comparison, the IMF spent as much on travel alone during the same period.

As the 20th century concluded, the world trading system epitomized by the WTO came under heavy criticism by protest groups opposed to globalization, and by labor and environmental groups worried that trade was undermining labor standards and the ENVIRONMENT. The large demonstrations that disrupted the ill-fated Third WTO Ministerial held in Seattle in late 1999 received worldwide media coverage and underlined the popular resistance to trade liberalization that governments would have to address to make further progress.

The planned new round of multilateral trade negotiations that was supposed to be launched at Seattle never occurred. The main reasons for this failure were: disagreements between the United States, the European Union, and Japan over agriculture; dissatisfaction among developing countries over the implementation of the previous Uruguay Round WTO agreements; and the potential use of trade SANCTIONS to enforce labor standards. The protests at Seattle, creating a tense and often acrimonious atmosphere, exacerbated these disagreements.

Even though a new formal round was not launched, specific sectoral negotiations in agriculture and services that were already mandated in the Uruguay Round agreements got underway early in 2000. However, it proved to be difficult to bring these sectoral negotiations to a successful conclusion by themselves. Consequently, some member states expressed interest in renewed efforts at the next WTO Ministerial in Qatar in November 2001 to launch another global round of trade negotiations.

See also SUSTAINABLE DEVELOPMENT.

Further Reading: Grady, Patrick, and Kathleen Macmillan, *Seattle and Beyond: The WTO Millennium Round.* Ottawa, Canada: Global Economics Ltd., 1999. Schott, Jeffrey J., ed. *The WTO after Seattle.* Washington, D.C.: Institute for International Economics, 2000.

— *P. M. Grady*

World Youth Forums *See* DEPARTMENT OF ECONOMIC AND SOCIAL AFFAIRS.

X, Y, Z

xenophobia   *See* WORLD CONFERENCES TO COMBAT RACISM AND RACIAL DISCRIMINATION

Yalta Conference

The Yalta Conference was one of a series of summits held during World War II to allow the leaders of the Allied powers to coordinate strategy. Held in secret in the Russian Crimea, February 4–11, 1945, the conference brought together the so-called Big Three leaders, Franklin D. ROOSEVELT of the UNITED STATES, Winston CHURCHILL of the United Kingdom, and Marshal Joseph STALIN of the Union of Soviet Socialist Republics. The three leaders met daily, often with only translators present, to plan the final stages of the war.

While several important decisions were made at Yalta regarding the planned international organization to be called the United Nations, the focus of the summit was on the conduct of the war, rather than the postwar era or the United Nations. The wartime relationship among the Big Three powers was strained. Roosevelt, Churchill, and Stalin had little in common except that each of their countries had been attacked by the Axis powers. Prior to the Yalta Conference Stalin had not even agreed to enter the war against Japan, since officially the USSR was neutral in the East Asian theater of the world conflict. European questions, such as the administration and control of Eastern Europe (particularly in Poland), details regarding the occupation of Germany, and the issue of Russian entry into the conflict with Japan after Germany was defeated were the primary concerns of all three leaders.

Prior to Yalta, several steps regarding the United Nations had been taken, but many details remained to be negotiated. Indeed, Stalin had not agreed that the USSR would join the United Nations. The idea of an international organization to maintain international peace and security had evolved over time, in part as a means to assure the continuation of wartime cooperation. The first commitment to the concept of such an organization was made at the MOSCOW CONFERENCE OF FOREIGN MINISTERS in 1943. Further negotiations at DUMBARTON OAKS during the summer and fall of 1944 had allowed the Big Four (the Big Three plus CHINA) to agree on an outline of the STRUCTURE of the organization, and to adopt the name—United Nations—used by the wartime alliance.

At Yalta several key agreements were reached regarding the UN, its structure, and MEMBERSHIP. Additionally, the Big Three set the date of the San Francisco Conference. The details were negotiated in several separate conversations, interspersed with discussions of other issues regarding the war. It was at Yalta that the leaders decided that the United Nations would include an INTERNATIONAL COURT OF JUSTICE to adjudicate disputes between states, and that a TRUSTEESHIP SYSTEM would be created to succeed the LEAGUE OF NATIONS mandate system and would administer the same territories.

At Yalta the Big Three agreed on a definition of the term "peace-loving" nations that would determine which nations gained original membership in the new organization. Stalin had insisted that only nations currently at war with the Axis be admitted as founding members. Roosevelt, responding to Latin American nations, secured Stalin's agreement that nations that had not yet entered the war could have a few more weeks to decide, thereby allowing latecomers Argentina and Chile to become founding members of the United Nations, creating a united Latin American bloc in the new organization. The formula was that a "peace-loving" nation was one that declared war on the Axis before March 1, 1945.

Significantly, a dispute regarding the VOTING power of the Big Three was also resolved. At Dumbarton Oaks, Stalin had sought votes for each of the 16 Soviet republics, contending that the nations of the British Empire gave the United Kingdom control of multiple votes. At Yalta, Roosevelt empathized with Stalin's concerns, but insisted that in order to secure congressional agreement to each Soviet republic having a separate vote, he would need votes for each of the 48 states. Stalin backed down, but insisted that in view of the huge wartime destruction in the Ukraine and Byelorussia, those states must become members. Roosevelt agreed, regarding this as a minor matter, since he counted on the support of the European and Latin American nations to give the United States an effective voting majority. In addition, at Yalta, Stalin finally acceded to some restrictions on the VETO power of the PERMANENT MEMBERS OF THE SECURITY COUNCIL, retreating from his previous insistence on an absolute veto over all matters. He agreed that the veto would not apply to procedural matters and could not be invoked by a state that was a party to a dispute under consideration.

Thus, the final details regarding the organization and membership of the United Nations were settled at Yalta, which concluded the series of great power negotiations regarding the proposed international organization. Most important, at Yalta the Soviet Union committed itself to joining the United Nations.

See also CAIRO DECLARATION, TEHERAN CONFERENCE.

Further Reading: Bennett, Edward M. *Franklin D. Roosevelt and the Search for Victory: American-Soviet Relations, 1939–1945.* Wilmington, Del.: Scholarly Resources, 1990. Buhite, Russell D. *Decisions at Yalta: An Appraisal of Summit Diplomacy.* Wilmington, Del.: Scholarly Resources, 1986.

Hoopes, Townsend, and Douglas Brinkley. *FDR and the Creation of the U.N.* New Haven, Conn.: Yale University Press, 1997. Kimball, Warren. *The Juggler.* Princeton, N.J.: Princeton University Press, 1991.

— *K. J. Grieb*

Yom Kippur War   *See* ARAB-ISRAELI DISPUTE.

Yugoslavia, former   *See* FORMER YUGOSLAVIA.

Zaire   *See* CONGO.

Zionism   *See* ARAB-ISRAELI DISPUTE.

Zionism Is Racism Resolution

The RESOLUTION that proclaimed Zionism a form of racism and racial discrimination is entitled 3379 (XXX), *Elimination of All Forms of Racial Discrimination,* and it was adopted by the United Nations GENERAL ASSEMBLY on November 10, 1975. The resolution received support from states such as Algeria, Brazil, Iraq, Mexico, Morocco, Ukraine, and the USSR, and it was opposed by states such as Australia, Canada, Israel, Norway, and the UNITED STATES. The resolution, adopted by a vote of 72 in favor, 35 opposed, with 32 abstentions and 3 absences, condemned the unholy alliance between South African racism and Zionism, took note that the DECLARATION of Mexico stated that a prerequisite for international peace required the elimination of Zionism, and also took note that the racist regimes in Rhodesia (Zimbabwe), South Africa, and occupied Palestine had a common imperialist origin. The General Assembly revoked the resolution in December 1991.

See also ARAB-ISRAELI DISPUTE.

Further Reading: Manor, Y. *To Right a Wrong.* New York: Shengold Publishers, 1997. Said, Edward. *The Question of Palestine.* New York: Vintage Books, 1980. United Nations. A/RES/3379 (XXX) *Elimination of All Forms of Racial Discrimination.* General Assembly Plenary meeting, November 10, 1975.

— *S. F. McMahon*

APPENDIX A
Charter of the United Nations

Preamble

WE THE PEOPLES OF THE UNITED NATIONS DETERMINED

to save succeeding generations from the scourge of war, which twice in our lifetime has brought untold sorrow to mankind, and

to reaffirm faith in fundamental human rights, in the dignity and worth of the human person, in the equal rights of men and women and of nations large and small, and

to establish conditions under which justice and respect for the obligations arising from treaties and other sources of international law can be maintained, and

to promote social progress and better standards of life in larger freedom,

AND FOR THESE ENDS

to practice tolerance and live together in peace with one another as good neighbours, and

to unite our strength to maintain international peace and security, and

to ensure, by the acceptance of principles and the institution of methods, that armed force shall not be used, save in the common interest, and

to employ international machinery for the promotion of the economic and social advancement of all peoples,

HAVE RESOLVED TO COMBINE OUR EFFORTS TO ACCOMPLISH THESE AIMS

Accordingly, our respective Governments, through representatives assembled in the city of San Francisco, who have exhibited their full powers found to be in good and due form, have agreed to the present Charter of the United Nations and do hereby establish an international organization to be known as the United Nations.

Chapter I: Purposes and Principles

Article 1

The Purposes of the United Nations are:

1. To maintain international peace and security, and to that end: to take effective collective measures for the prevention and removal of threats to the peace, and for the suppression of acts of aggression or other breaches of the peace, and to bring about by peaceful means, and in conformity with the principles of justice and international law, adjustment or settlement of international disputes or situations which might lead to a breach of the peace;
2. To develop friendly relations among nations based on respect for the principle of equal rights and self-determination of peoples, and to take other appropriate measures to strengthen universal peace;
3. To achieve international co-operation in solving international problems of an economic, social, cultural, or humanitarian character, and in promoting and encouraging respect for human rights and for fundamental freedoms for all without distinction as to race, sex, language, or religion; and
4. To be a centre for harmonizing the actions of nations in the attainment of these common ends.

Article 2

The Organization and its Members, in pursuit of the Purposes stated in Article 1, shall act in accordance with the following Principles.

1. The Organization is based on the principle of the sovereign equality of all its Members.
2. All Members, in order to ensure to all of them the rights and benefits resulting from membership, shall fulfil in good faith the obligations assumed by them in accordance with the present Charter.
3. All Members shall settle their international disputes by peaceful means in such a manner that international peace and security, and justice, are not endangered.
4. All Members shall refrain in their international relations from the threat or use of force against the territorial integrity or political independence of any state,

or in any other manner inconsistent with the Purposes of the United Nations.

5. All Members shall give the United Nations every assistance in any action it takes in accordance with the present Charter, and shall refrain from giving assistance to any state against which the United Nations is taking preventive or enforcement action.

6. The Organization shall ensure that states which are not Members of the United Nations act in accordance with these Principles so far as may be necessary for the maintenance of international peace and security.

7. Nothing contained in the present Charter shall authorize the United Nations to intervene in matters which are essentially within the domestic jurisdiction of any state or shall require the Members to submit such matters to settlement under the present Charter; but this principle shall not prejudice the application of enforcement measures under Chapter VII.

Chapter II: Membership

Article 3

The original Members of the United Nations shall be the states which, having participated in the United Nations Conference on International Organization at San Francisco, or having previously signed the Declaration by United Nations of 1 January 1942, sign the present Charter and ratify it in accordance with Article 110.

Article 4

1. Membership in the United Nations is open to all peace-loving states which accept the obligations contained in the present Charter and, in the judgment of the Organization, are able and willing to carry out these obligations.

2. The admission of any such state to membership in the Nations will be effected by a decision of the General Assembly upon the recommendation of the Security Council.

Article 5

A Member of the United Nations against which preventive or enforcement action has been taken by the Security Council may be suspended from the exercise of the rights and privileges of membership by the General Assembly upon the recommendation of the Security Council. The exercise of these rights and privileges may be restored by the Security Council.

Article 6

A Member of the United Nations which has persistently violated the Principles contained in the present Charter may be expelled from the Organization by the General Assembly upon the recommendation of the Security Council.

Chapter III: Organs

Article 7

1. There are established as the principal organs of the United Nations: a General Assembly, a Security Council, an Economic and Social Council, a Trusteeship Council, an International Court of Justice, and a Secretariat.

2. Such subsidiary organs as may be found necessary may be established in accordance with the present Charter.

Article 8

The United Nations shall place no restrictions on the eligibility of men and women to participate in any capacity and under conditions of equality in its principal and subsidiary organs.

Chapter IV: The General Assembly

COMPOSITION

Article 9

1. The General Assembly shall consist of all the Members of the United Nations.

2. Each Member shall have not more than five representatives in the General Assembly.

FUNCTIONS AND POWERS

Article 10

The General Assembly may discuss any questions or any matters within the scope of the present Charter or relating to the powers and functions of any organs provided for in the present Charter, and, except as provided in Article 12, may make recommendations to the Members of the United Nations or to the Security Council or to both on any such questions or matters.

Article 11

1. The General Assembly may consider the general principles of co-operation in the maintenance of international peace and security, including the principles governing disarmament and the regulation of armaments, and may make recommendations with regard to such principles to the Members or to the Security Council or to both.

2. The General Assembly may discuss any questions relating to the maintenance of international peace and security brought before it by any Member of the United Nations, or by the Security Council, or by a state which is not a Member of the United Nations in accordance with Article 35, paragraph 2, and, except as provided in Article 12, may make recommendations with regard to any such questions to the state or

states concerned or to the Security Council or to both. Any such question on which action is necessary shall be referred to the Security Council by the General Assembly either before or after discussion.

3. The General Assembly may call the attention of the Security Council to situations which are likely to endanger international peace and security.

4. The powers of the General Assembly set forth in this Article shall not limit the general scope of Article 10.

Article 12

1. While the Security Council is exercising in respect of any dispute or situation the functions assigned to it in the present Charter, the General Assembly shall not make any recommendation with regard to that dispute or situation unless the Security Council so requests.

2. The Secretary-General, with the consent of the Security Council, shall notify the General Assembly at each session of any matters relative to the maintenance of international peace and security which are being dealt with by the Security Council and similarly notify the General Assembly, or the Members of the United Nations if the General Assembly is not in session, immediately the Security Council ceases to deal with such matters.

Article 13

1. The General Assembly shall initiate studies and make recommendations for the purpose of:
   a. promoting international co-operation in the political field and encouraging the progressive development of international law and its codification;
   b. promoting international co-operation in the economic, social, cultural, educational, and health fields, and assisting in the realization of human rights and fundamental freedoms for all without distinction as to race, sex, language, or religion.

2. The further responsibilities, functions and powers of the General Assembly with respect to matters mentioned in paragraph 1(b) above are set forth in Chapters IX and X.

Article 14

Subject to the provisions of Article 12, the General Assembly may recommend measures for the peaceful adjustment of any situation, regardless of origin, which it deems likely to impair the general welfare or friendly relations among nations, including situations resulting from a violation of the provisions of the present Charter setting forth the Purposes and Principles of the United Nations.

Article 15

1. The General Assembly shall receive and consider annual and special reports from the Security Council;

these reports shall include an account of the measures that the Security Council has decided upon or taken to maintain international peace and security.

2. The General Assembly shall receive and consider reports from the other organs of the United Nations.

Article 16

The General Assembly shall perform such functions with respect to the international trusteeship system as are assigned to it under Chapters XII and XIII, including the approval of the trusteeship agreements for areas not designated as strategic.

Article 17

1. The General Assembly shall consider and approve the budget of the Organization.

2. The expenses of the Organization shall be borne by the Members as apportioned by the General Assembly.

3. The Assembly shall consider and approve any financial and budgetary arrangements with specialized agencies referred to in Article 57 and shall examine the administrative budgets of such specialized agencies with a view to making recommendations to the agencies concerned.

VOTING

Article 18

1. Each member of the General Assembly shall have one vote.

2. Decisions of the General Assembly on important questions shall be made by a two-thirds majority of the members present and voting. These questions shall include: recommendations with respect to the maintenance of international peace and security, the election of the non-permanent members of the Security Council, the election of the members of the Economic and Social Council, the election of members of the Trusteeship Council in accordance with paragraph 1 of Article 86, the admission of new Members to the United Nations, the suspension of the rights and privileges of membership, the expulsion of Members, questions relating to the operation of the trusteeship system, and budgetary questions.

3. Decisions on other questions, including the determination of additional categories of questions to be decided by a two-thirds majority, shall be made by a majority of the members present and voting.

Article 19

A Member of the United Nations which is in arrears in the payment of its financial contributions to the Organization shall have no vote in the General Assembly if the amount of its arrears equals or exceeds the amount of the contributions due from it for the preceding two full years. The General

Assembly may, nevertheless, permit such a Member to vote if it is satisfied that the failure to pay is due to conditions beyond the control of the Member.

PROCEDURE

Article 20

The General Assembly shall meet in regular annual sessions and in such special sessions as occasion may require. Special sessions shall be convoked by the Secretary-General at the request of the Security Council or of a majority of the Members of the United Nations.

Article 21

The General Assembly shall adopt its own rules of procedure. It shall elect its President for each session.

Article 22

The General Assembly may establish such subsidiary organs as it deems necessary for the performance of its functions.

Chapter V: The Security Council

COMPOSITION

Article 23

1. The Security Council shall consist of fifteen Members of the United Nations. The Republic of China, France, the Union of Soviet Socialist Republics, the United Kingdom of Great Britain and Northern Ireland, and the United States of America shall be permanent members of the Security Council. The General Assembly shall elect ten other Members of the United Nations to be non-permanent members of the Security Council, due regard being specially paid, in the first instance to the contribution of Members of the United Nations to the maintenance of international peace and security and to the other purposes of the Organization, and also to equitable geographical distribution.
2. The non-permanent members of the Security Council shall be elected for a term of two years. In the first election of the non-permanent members after the increase of the membership of the Security Council from eleven to fifteen, two of the four additional members shall be chosen for a term of one year. A retiring member shall not be eligible for immediate re-election.
3. Each member of the Security Council shall have one representative.

FUNCTIONS AND POWERS

Article 24

1. In order to ensure prompt and effective action by the United Nations, its Members confer on the Security Council primary responsibility for the maintenance of international peace and security, and agree that in carrying out its duties under this responsibility the Security Council acts on their behalf.
2. In discharging these duties the Security Council shall act in accordance with the Purposes and Principles of the United Nations. The specific powers granted to the Security Council for the discharge of these duties are laid down in Chapters VI, VII, VIII, and XII.
3. The Security Council shall submit annual and, when necessary, special reports to the General Assembly for its consideration.

Article 25

The Members of the United Nations agree to accept and carry out the decisions of the Security Council in accordance with the present Charter.

Article 26

In order to promote the establishment and maintenance of international peace and security with the least diversion for armaments of the world's human and economic resources, the Security Council shall be responsible for formulating, with the assistance of the Military Staff Committee referred to in Article 47, plans to be submitted to the Members of the United Nations for the establishment of a system for the regulation of armaments.

VOTING

Article 27

1. Each member of the Security Council shall have one vote.
2. Decisions of the Security Council on procedural matters shall be made by an affirmative vote of nine members.
3. Decisions of the Security Council on all other matters shall be made by an affirmative vote of nine members including the concurring votes of the permanent members; provided that, in decisions under Chapter VI, and under paragraph 3 of Article 52, a party to a dispute shall abstain from voting.

PROCEDURE

Article 28

1. The Security Council shall be so organized as to be able to function continuously. Each member of the Security Council shall for this purpose be represented at all times at the seat of the Organization.
2. The Security Council shall hold meetings at which each of its members may, if it so desires, be represented by a member of the government or by some other specially designated representative.
3. The Security Council may hold meetings at such places other than the seat of the Organization as in its judgment will best facilitate its work.

Article 29

The Security Council may establish such subsidiary organs as it deems necessary for the performance of its functions.

Article 30

The Security Council shall adopt its own rules of procedure, including the method of selecting its President.

Article 31

Any Member of the United Nations which is not a member of the Security Council may participate, without vote, in the discussion of any question brought before the Security Council whenever the latter considers that the interests of that Member are specially affected.

Article 32

Any Member of the United Nations which is not a member of the Security Council or any state which is not a Member of the United Nations, if it is a party to a dispute under consideration by the Security Council, shall be invited to participate, without vote, in the discussion relating to the dispute. The Security Council shall lay down such conditions as it deems just for the participation of a state which is not a Member of the United Nations.

Chapter VI: Pacific Settlement of Disputes

Article 33

1. The parties to any dispute, the continuance of which is likely to endanger the maintenance of international peace and security, shall, first of all, seek a solution by negotiation, enquiry, mediation, conciliation, arbitration, judicial settlement, resort to regional agencies or arrangements, or other peaceful means of their own choice.
2. The Security Council shall, when it deems necessary, call upon the parties to settle their dispute by such means.

Article 34

The Security Council may investigate any dispute, or any situation which might lead to international friction or give rise to a dispute, in order to determine whether the continuance of the dispute or situation is likely to endanger the maintenance of international peace and security.

Article 35

1. Any Member of the United Nations may bring any dispute, or any situation of the nature referred to in Article 34, to the attention of the Security Council or of the General Assembly.
2. A state which is not a Member of the United Nations may bring to the attention of the Security Council or of the General Assembly any dispute to which it is a party if it accepts in advance, for the purposes of the dispute, the obligations of pacific settlement provided in the present Charter.
3. The proceedings of the General Assembly in respect of matters brought to its attention under this Article will be subject to the provisions of Articles 11 and 12.

Article 36

1. The Security Council may, at any stage of a dispute of the nature referred to in Article 33 or of a situation of like nature, recommend appropriate procedures or methods of adjustment.
2. The Security Council should take into consideration any procedures for the settlement of the dispute which have already been adopted by the parties.
3. In making recommendations under this Article the Security Council should also take into consideration that legal disputes should as a general rule be referred by the parties to the International Court of Justice in accordance with the provisions of the Statute of the Court.

Article 37

1. Should the parties to a dispute of the nature referred to in Article 33 fail to settle it by the means indicated in that Article, they shall refer it to the Security Council.
2. If the Security Council deems that the continuance of the dispute is in fact likely to endanger the maintenance of international peace and security, it shall decide whether to take action under Article 36 or to recommend such terms of settlement as it may consider appropriate.

Article 38

Without prejudice to the provisions of Articles 33 to 37, the Security Council may, if all the parties to any dispute so request, make recommendations to the parties with a view to a pacific settlement of the dispute.

Chapter VII: Action with Respect to Threats to the Peace, Breaches of the Peace, and Acts of Aggression

Article 39

The Security Council shall determine the existence of any threat to the peace, breach of the peace, or act of aggression and shall make recommendations, or decide what measures shall be taken in accordance with Articles 41 and 42, to maintain or restore international peace and security.

Article 40

In order to prevent an aggravation of the situation, the Security Council may, before making the recommendations or deciding upon the measures provided for in Article 39, call upon the parties concerned to comply with such provisional measures as it deems necessary or desirable. Such provisional measures shall be without prejudice to the rights, claims, or position of the parties concerned. The Security Council shall duly take account of failure to comply with such provisional measures.

Article 41

The Security Council may decide what measures not involving the use of armed force are to be employed to give effect to its decisions, and it may call upon the Members of the United Nations to apply such measures. These may include complete or partial interruption of economic relations and of rail, sea, air, postal, telegraphic, radio, and other means of communication, and the severance of diplomatic relations.

Article 42

Should the Security Council consider that measures provided for in Article 41 would be inadequate or have proved to be inadequate, it may take such action by air, sea, or land forces as may be necessary to maintain or restore international peace and security. Such action may include demonstrations, blockade, and other operations by air, sea, or land forces of Members of the United Nations.

Article 43

1. All Members of the United Nations, in order to contribute to the maintenance of international peace and security, undertake to make available to the Security Council, on its and in accordance with a special agreement or agreements, armed forces, assistance, and facilities, including rights of passage, necessary for the purpose of maintaining international peace and security.
2. Such agreement or agreements shall govern the numbers and types of forces, their degree of readiness and general location, and the nature of the facilities and assistance to be provided.
3. The agreement or agreements shall be negotiated as soon as possible on the initiative of the Security Council. They shall be concluded between the Security Council and Members or between the Security Council and groups of Members and shall be subject to ratification by the signatory states in accordance with their respective constitutional processes.

Article 44

When the Security Council has decided to use force it shall, before calling upon a Member not represented on it to provide armed forces in fulfilment of the obligations assumed under Article 43, invite that Member, if the Member so desires, to participate in the decisions of the Security Council concerning the employment of contingents of that Member's armed forces.

Article 45

In order to enable the Nations to take urgent military measures, Members shall hold immediately available national air-force contingents for combined international enforcement action. The strength and degree of readiness of these contingents and plans for their combined action shall be determined, within the limits laid down in the special agreement or agreements referred to in Article 43, by the Security Council with the assistance of the Military Staff Committee.

Article 46

Plans for the application of armed force shall be made by the Security Council with the assistance of the Military Staff Committee.

Article 47

1. There shall be established a Military Staff Committee to advise and assist the Security Council on questions relating to the Security Council's military requirements for the maintenance of international peace and security, the employment and command of forces placed at its disposal, the regulation of armaments, and possible disarmament.
2. The Military Staff Committee shall consist of the Chiefs of Staff of the permanent members of the Security Council or their representatives. Any Member of the United Nations not permanently represented on the Committee shall be invited by the Committee to be associated with it when the efficient discharge of the Committee's responsibilities requires the participation of that Member in its work.
3. The Military Staff Committee shall be responsible under the Security Council for the strategic direction of any armed forces placed at the disposal of the Security Council. Questions relating to the command of such forces shall be worked out subsequently.
4. The Military Staff Committee, with the authorization of the Security Council after consultation with appropriate regional agencies, may establish sub-committees.

Article 48

1. The action required to carry out the decisions of the Security Council for the maintenance of international peace and security shall be taken by all the Members of the United Nations or by some of them, as the Security Council may determine.
2. Such decisions shall be carried out by the Members of the United Nations directly and through their action in the appropriate international agencies of which they are members.

Article 49

The Members of the United Nations shall join in affording mutual assistance in carrying out the measures decided upon by the Security Council.

Article 50

If preventive or enforcement measures against any state are taken by the Security Council, any other state, whether a Member of the United Nations or not, which finds itself confronted with special economic problems arising from the carrying out of those measures shall have the right to consult the Security Council with regard to a solution of those problems.

Article 51

Nothing in the present Charter shall impair the inherent right of individual or collective self-defence if an armed attack occurs against a Member of the United Nations, until the Security Council has taken measures necessary to maintain international peace and security. Measures taken by Members in the exercise of this right of self-defence shall be immediately reported to the Security Council and shall not in any way affect the authority and responsibility of the Security Council under the present Charter to take at any time such action as it deems necessary in order to maintain or restore international peace and security.

Chapter VIII: Regional Arrangements

Article 52

1. Nothing in the present Charter precludes the existence of regional arrangements or agencies for dealing with such matters relating to the maintenance of international peace and security as are appropriate for regional action, provided that such arrangements or agencies and their activities are consistent with the Purposes and Principles of the United Nations.
2. The Members of the United Nations entering into such arrangements or constituting such agencies shall make every effort to achieve pacific settlement of local disputes through such regional arrangements or by such regional agencies before referring them to the Security Council.
3. The Security Council shall encourage the development of pacific settlement of local disputes through such regional arrangements or by such regional agencies either on the initiative of the states concerned or by reference from the Security Council.
4. This Article in no way impairs the application of Articles 34 and 35.

Article 53

1. The Security Council shall, where appropriate, utilize such regional arrangements or agencies for enforce-

ment action under its authority. But no enforcement action shall be taken under regional arrangements or by regional agencies without the authorization of the Security Council, with the exception of measures against any enemy state, as defined in paragraph 2 of this Article, provided for pursuant to Article 107 or in regional arrangements directed against renewal of aggressive policy on the part of any such state, until such time as the Organization may, on request of the Governments concerned, be charged with the responsibility for preventing further aggression by such a state.
2. The term enemy state as used in paragraph 1 of this Article applies to any state which during the Second World War has been an enemy of any signatory of the present Charter.

Article 54

The Security Council shall at all times be kept fully informed of activities undertaken or in contemplation under regional arrangements or by regional agencies for the maintenance of international peace and security.

Chapter IX: International Economic and Social Co-operation

Article 55

With a view to the creation of conditions of stability and well-being which are necessary for peaceful and friendly relations among nations based on respect for the principle of equal rights and self-determination of peoples, the United Nations shall promote:
  a. higher standards of living, full employment, and conditions of economic and social progress and development;
  b. solutions of international economic, social, health, and related problems; and international cultural and educational co-operation; and
  c. universal respect for, and observance of, human rights and fundamental freedoms for all without distinction as to race, sex, language, or religion.

Article 56

All Members pledge themselves to take joint and separate action in co-operation with the Organization for the achievement of the purposes set forth in Article 55.

Article 57

1. The various specialized agencies, established by intergovernmental agreement and having wide international responsibilities, as defined in their basic instruments, in economic, social, cultural, educational, health, and related fields, shall be brought into

relationship with the United Nations in accordance with the provisions of Article 63.

2. Such agencies thus brought into relationship with the United Nations are hereinafter referred to as specialized agencies.

Article 58

The Organization shall make recommendations for the co-ordination of the policies and activities of the specialized agencies.

Article 59

The Organization shall, where appropriate, initiate negotiations among the states concerned for the creation of any new specialized agencies required for the accomplishment of the purposes set forth in Article 55.

Article 60

Responsibility for the discharge of the functions of the Organization set forth in this Chapter shall be vested in the General Assembly and, under the authority of the General Assembly, in the Economic and Social Council, which shall have for this purpose the powers set forth in Chapter X.

Chapter X: The Economic and Social Council

COMPOSITION

Article 61

1. The Economic and Social Council shall consist of fifty-four Members of the United Nations elected by the General Assembly.

2. Subject to the provisions of paragraph 3, eighteen members of the Economic and Social Council shall be elected each year for a term of three years. A retiring member shall be eligible for immediate re-election.

3. At the first election after the increase in the membership of the Economic and Social Council from twenty-seven to fifty-four members, in addition to the members elected in place of the nine members whose term of office expires at the end of that year, twenty-seven additional members shall be elected. Of these twenty-seven additional members, the term of office of nine members so elected shall expire at the end of one year, and of nine other members at the end of two years, in accordance with arrangements made by the General Assembly.

4. Each member of the Economic and Social Council shall have one representative.

FUNCTIONS AND POWERS

Article 62

1. The Economic and Social Council may make or initiate studies and reports with respect to international economic, social, cultural, educational, health, and related matters and may make recommendations with respect to any such matters to the General Assembly, to the Members of the United Nations, and to the specialized agencies concerned.

2. It may make recommendations for the purpose of promoting respect for, and observance of, human rights and fundamental freedoms for all.

3. It may prepare draft conventions for submission to the General Assembly, with respect to matters falling within its competence.

4. It may call, in accordance with the rules prescribed by the United Nations, international conferences on matters falling within its competence.

Article 63

1. The Economic and Social Council may enter into agreements with any of the agencies referred to in Article 57, defining the terms on which the agency concerned shall be brought into relationship with the United Nations. Such agreements shall be subject to approval by the General Assembly.

2. It may co-ordinate the activities of the specialized agencies through consultation with and recommendations to such agencies and through recommendations to the General Assembly and to the Members of the United Nations.

Article 64

1. The Economic and Social Council may take appropriate steps to obtain regular reports from the specialized agencies. may make arrangements with the Members of the United Nations and with the specialized agencies to obtain reports on the steps taken to give effect to its own recommendations and to recommendations on matters falling within its competence made by the General Assembly.

2. It may communicate its observations on these reports to the General Assembly.

Article 65

The Economic and Social Council may furnish information to the Security Council and shall assist the Security Council upon its request.

Article 66

1. The Economic and Social Council shall perform such functions as fall within its competence in connexion with the carrying out of the recommendations of the General Assembly.

2. It may, with the approval of the General Assembly, perform services at the request of Members of the United Nations and at the request of specialized agencies.

3. It shall perform such other functions as are specified elsewhere in the present Charter or as may be assigned to it by the General Assembly.

VOTING

Article 67

1. Each member of the Economic and Social Council shall have one vote.
2. Decisions of the Economic and Social Council shall be made by a majority of the members present and voting.

PROCEDURE

Article 68

The Economic and Social Council shall set up commissions in economic and social fields and for the promotion of human rights, and such other commissions as may be required for the performance of its functions.

Article 69

The Economic and Social Council shall invite any Member of the United Nations to participate, without vote, in its deliberations on any matter of particular concern to that Member.

Article 70

The Economic and Social Council may make arrangements for representatives of the specialized agencies to participate, without vote, in its deliberations and in those of the commissions established by it, and for its representatives to participate in the deliberations of the specialized agencies.

Article 71

The Economic and Social Council may make suitable arrangements for consultation with non-governmental organizations which are concerned with matters within its competence. Such arrangements may be made with international organizations and, where appropriate, with national organizations after consultation with the Member of the United Nations concerned.

Article 72

1. The Economic and Social Council shall adopt its own rules of procedure, including the method of selecting its President.
2. The Economic and Social Council shall meet as required in accordance with its rules, which shall include provision for the convening of meetings on the request of a majority of its members.

Chapter XI: Declaration Regarding Non-Self-Governing Territories

Article 73

Members of the United Nations which have or assume responsibilities for the administration of territories whose peoples have not yet attained a full measure of self-government recognize the principle that the interests of the inhabitants of these territories are paramount, and accept as a sacred trust the obligation to promote to the utmost, within the system of international peace and security established by the present Charter, the well-being of the inhabitants of these territories, and, to this end:

a. to ensure, with due respect for the culture of the peoples concerned, their political, economic, social, and educational advancement, their just treatment, and their protection against abuses;

b. to develop self-government, to take due account of the political aspirations of the peoples, and to assist them in the progressive development of their free political institutions, according to the particular circumstances of each territory and its peoples and their varying stages of advancement;

c. to further international peace and security;

d. to promote constructive measures of development, to encourage research, and to co-operate with one another and, when and where appropriate, with specialized international bodies with a view to the practical achievement of the social, economic, and scientific purposes set forth in this Article; and

e. to transmit regularly to the Secretary-General for information purposes, subject to such limitation as security and constitutional considerations may require, statistical and other information of a technical nature relating to economic, social, and educational conditions in the territories for which they are respectively responsible other than those territories to which Chapters XII and XIII apply.

Article 74

Members of the United Nations also agree that their policy in respect of the territories to which this Chapter applies, no less than in respect of their metropolitan areas, must be based on the general principle of goodneighbourliness, due account being taken of the interests and well-being of the rest of the world, in social, economic, and commercial matters.

Chapter XII: International Trusteeship System

Article 75

The United Nations shall establish under its authority an international trusteeship system for the administration and supervision of such territories as may be placed thereunder by subsequent individual agreements. These territories are hereinafter referred to as trust territories.

Article 76

The basic objectives of the trusteeship system, in accordance with the Purposes of the United Nations laid down in Article 1 of the present Charter, shall be:

a. to further international peace and security;

b. to promote the political, economic, social, and educational advancement of the inhabitants of the trust territories, and their progressive development towards self-government or independence as may be appropriate to the particular circumstances of each territory and its peoples and the freely expressed wishes of the peoples concerned, and as may be provided by the terms of each trusteeship agreement;

c. to encourage respect for human rights and for fundamental freedoms for all without distinction as to race, sex, language, or religion, and to encourage recognition of the interdependence of the peoples of the world; and

d. to ensure equal treatment in social, economic, and commercial matters for all Members of the United Nations and their Nationals, and also equal treatment for the latter in the administration of justice, without prejudice to the attainment of the foregoing objectives and subject to the provisions of Article 80.

Article 77

1. The trusteeship system shall apply to such territories in the following categories as may be placed thereunder by means of trusteeship agreements:

    a. territories now held under mandate;

    b. territories which may be detached from enemy states as a result of the Second World War; and

    c. territories voluntarily placed under the system by states responsible for their administration.

2. It will be a matter for subsequent agreement as to which territories in the foregoing categories will be brought under the trusteeship system and upon what terms.

Article 78

The trusteeship system shall not apply to territories which have become Members of the United Nations, relationship among which shall be based on respect for the principle of sovereign equality.

Article 79

The terms of trusteeship for each territory to be placed under the trusteeship system, including any alteration or amendment, shall be agreed upon by the states directly concerned, including the mandatory power in the case of territories held under mandate by a Member of the United Nations, and shall be approved as provided for in Articles 83 and 85.

Article 80

1. Except as may be agreed upon in individual trusteeship agreements, made under Articles 77, 79, and 81, placing each territory under the trusteeship system, and until such agreements have been concluded, nothing in this Chapter shall be construed in or of itself to alter in any manner the rights whatsoever of any states or any peoples or the terms of existing international instruments to which Members of the United Nations may respectively be parties.

2. Paragraph 1 of this Article shall not be interpreted as giving grounds for delay or postponement of the negotiation and conclusion of agreements for placing mandated and other territories under the trusteeship system as provided for in Article 77.

Article 81

The trusteeship agreement shall in each case include the terms under which the trust territory will be administered and designate the authority which will exercise the administration of the trust territory. Such authority, hereinafter called the administering authority, may be one or more states or the Organization itself.

Article 82

There may be designated, in any trusteeship agreement, a strategic area or areas which may include part or all of the trust territory to which the agreement applies, without prejudice to any special agreement or agreements made under Article 43.

Article 83

1. All functions of the United Nations relating to strategic areas, including the approval of the terms of the trusteeship agreements and of their alteration or amendment, shall be exercised by the Security Council.

2. The basic objectives set forth in Article 76 shall be applicable to the people of each strategic area.

3. The Security Council shall, subject to the provisions of the trusteeship agreements and without prejudice to security considerations, avail itself of the assistance of the Trusteeship Council to perform those functions of the United Nations under the trusteeship system relating to political, economic, social, and educational matters in the strategic areas.

Article 84

It shall be the duty of the administering authority to ensure that the trust territory shall play its part in the maintenance of international peace and security. To this end the administering authority may make use of volunteer forces, facilities, and assistance from the trust territory in carrying out the obligations towards the Security Council undertaken in this regard by the administering authority, as well as for local defence and the maintenance of law and order within the trust territory.

Article 85

1. The functions of the United Nations with regard to trusteeship agreements for all areas not designated as

strategic, including the approval of the terms of the trusteeship agreements and of their alteration or amendment, shall be exercised by the General Assembly.

2. The Trusteeship Council, operating under the authority of the General Assembly, shall assist the General Assembly in carrying out these functions.

Chapter XIII: The Trusteeship Council

COMPOSITION

Article 86

1. The Trusteeship Council shall consist of the following Members of the United Nations:
   a. those Members administering trust territories;
   b. such of those Members mentioned by name in Article 23 as are not administering trust territories; and
   c. as many other Members elected for three-year terms by the General Assembly as may be necessary to ensure that the total number of members of the Trusteeship Council is equally divided between those Members of the United Nations which administer trust territories and those which do not.
2. Each member of the Trusteeship Council shall designate one specially qualified person to represent it therein.

FUNCTIONS AND POWERS

Article 87

The General Assembly and, under its authority, the Trusteeship Council, in carrying out their functions, may:
   a. consider reports submitted by the administering authority;
   b. accept petitions and examine them in consultation with the administering authority;
   c. provide for periodic visits to the respective trust territories at times agreed upon with the administering authority; and
   d. take these and other actions in conformity with the terms of the trusteeship agreements.

Article 88

The Trusteeship Council shall formulate a questionnaire on the political, economic, social, and educational advancement of the inhabitants of each trust territory, and the administering authority for each trust territory within the competence of the General Assembly shall make an annual report to the General Assembly upon the basis of such questionnaire.

VOTING

Article 89

1. Each member of the Trusteeship Council shall have one vote.

2. Decisions of the Trusteeship Council shall be made by a majority of the members present and voting.

PROCEDURE

Article 90

1. The Trusteeship Council shall adopt its own rules of procedure, including the method of selecting its President.
2. The Trusteeship Council shall meet as required in accordance with its rules, which shall include provision for the convening of meetings on the request of a majority of its members.

Article 91

The Trusteeship Council shall, when appropriate, avail itself of the assistance of the Economic and Social Council and of the specialized agencies in regard to matters with which they are respectively concerned.

Chapter XIV: The International Court of Justice

Article 92

The International Court of Justice shall be the principal judicial organ of the United Nations. It shall function in accordance with the annexed Statute, which is based upon the Statute of the Permanent Court of International Justice and forms an integral part of the present Charter.

Article 93

1. All Members of the United Nations are ipso facto parties to the Statute of the International Court of Justice.
2. A state which is not a member of the United Nations may become a party to the Statute of the International Court of Justice on conditions to be determined in each case by the General Assembly upon the recommendation of the Security Council.

Article 94

1. Each Member of the United Nations undertakes to comply with the decision of the International Court of Justice in any case to which it is a party.
2. If any party to a case fails to perform the obligations incumbent upon it under a judgment rendered by the Court, the other party may have recourse to the Security Council, which may, if it deems necessary, make recommendations or decide upon measures to be taken to give effect to the judgment.

Article 95

Nothing in the present Charter shall prevent Members of the United Nations from entrusting the solution of their differences to other tribunals by virtue of agreements already in existence or which may be concluded in the future.

Article 96

1. The General Assembly or the Security Council may request the International Court of Justice to give an advisory opinion on any legal question.
2. Other organs of the United Nations and specialized agencies, which may at any time be so authorized by the General Assembly, may also request advisory opinions of the Court on legal questions arising within the scope of their activities.

Chapter XV: The Secretariat

Article 97

The Secretariat shall comprise a Secretary-General and such staff as the Organization may require. The Secretary-General shall be appointed by the General Assembly upon the recommendation of the Security Council. He shall be the chief administrative officer of the Organization.

Article 98

The Secretary-General shall act in that capacity in all meetings of the General Assembly, of the Security Council, of the Economic and Social Council, and of the Trusteeship Council, and shall perform such other functions as are entrusted to him by these organs. The Secretary-General shall make an annual report to the General Assembly on the work of the Organization.

Article 99

The Secretary-General may bring to the attention of the Security Council any matter which in his opinion may threaten the maintenance of international peace and security.

Article 100

1. In the performance of their duties the Secretary-General and the staff shall not seek or receive instructions from any government or from any other authority external to the Organization. They shall refrain from any action which might reflect on their position as international officials responsible only to the Organization.
2. Each Member of the United Nations undertakes to respect the exclusively international character of the responsibilities of the Secretary-General and the staff and not to seek to influence them in the discharge of their responsibilities.

Article 101

1. The staff shall be appointed by the Secretary-General under regulations established by the General Assembly.
2. Appropriate staffs shall be permanently assigned to the Economic and Social Council, the Trusteeship Council, and, as required, to other organs of the United Nations. These staffs shall form a part of the Secretariat.

3. The paramount consideration in the employment of the staff and in the determination of the conditions of service shall be the necessity of securing the highest standards of efficiency, competence, and integrity. Due regard shall be paid to the importance of recruiting the staff on as wide a geographical basis as possible.

Chapter XVI: Miscellaneous Provisions

Article 102

1. Every treaty and every international agreement entered into by any Member of the United Nations after the present Charter comes into force shall as soon as possible be registered with the Secretariat and published by it.
2. No party to any such treaty or international agreement which has not been registered in accordance with the provisions of paragraph 1 of this Article may invoke that treaty or agreement before any organ of the United Nations.

Article 103

In the event of a conflict between the obligations of the Members of the United Nations under the present Charter and their obligations under any other international agreement, their obligations under the present Charter shall prevail.

Article 104

The Organization shall enjoy in the territory of each of its Members such legal capacity as may be necessary for the exercise of its functions and the fulfilment of its purposes.

Article 105

1. The Organization shall enjoy in the territory of each of its Members such privileges and immunities as are necessary for the fulfilment of its purposes.
2. Representatives of the Members of the United Nations and officials of the Organization shall similarly enjoy such privileges and immunities as are necessary for the independent exercise of their functions in connexion with the Organization.
3. The General Assembly may make recommendations with a view to determining the details of the application of paragraphs 1 and 2 of this Article or may propose conventions to the Members of the United Nations for this purpose.

Chapter XVII: Transitional Security Arrangements

Article 106

Pending the coming into force of such special agreements referred to in Article 43 as in the opinion of the Security

Council enable it to begin the exercise of its responsibilities under Article 42, the parties to the Four-Nation Declaration, signed at Moscow, 30 October 1943, and France, shall, in accordance with the provisions of paragraph 5 of that Declaration, consult with one another and as occasion requires with other Members of the United Nations with a view to such joint action on behalf of the Organization as may be necessary for the purpose of maintaining international peace and security.

Article 107

Nothing in the present Charter shall invalidate or preclude action, in relation to any state which during the Second World War has been an enemy of any signatory to the present Charter, taken or authorized as a result of that war by the Governments having responsibility for such action.

Chapter XVIII: Amendments

Article 108

Amendments to the present Charter shall come into force for all Members of the United Nations when they have been adopted by a vote of two-thirds of the members of the General Assembly and ratified in accordance with their respective constitutional processes by two-thirds of the Members of the United Nations, including all the permanent members of the Security Council.

Article 109

1. A General Conference of the Members of the United Nations for the purpose of reviewing the present Charter may be held at a date and place to be fixed by a two-thirds vote of the members of the General Assembly and by a vote of any nine members of the Security Council. Each Member of the United Nations shall have one vote in the conference.
2. Any alteration of the present Charter recommended by a two-thirds vote of the conference shall take effect when ratified in accordance with their respective constitutional processes by two-thirds of the Members of the United Nations including the permanent members of the Security Council.
3. If such a conference has not been held before the tenth annual session of the General Assembly following the coming into force of the present Charter, the proposal to call such a conference shall be placed on the agenda of that session of the General Assembly, and the conference shall be held if so decided by a majority vote of the members of the General Assembly and by a vote of any seven members of the Security Council.

Chapter XIX: Ratification and Signature

Article 110

1. The present Charter shall be ratified by the signatory states in accordance with their respective constitutional processes.
2. The ratifications shall be deposited with the Government of the United States of America, which shall notify all the signatory states of each deposit as well as the Secretary-General of the Organization when he has been appointed.
3. The present Charter shall come into force upon the deposit of ratifications by the Republic of China, France, the Union of Soviet Socialist Republics, the United Kingdom of Great Britain and Northern Ireland, and the United States of America, and by a majority of the other signatory states. A protocol of the ratifications deposited shall thereupon be drawn up by the Government of the United States of America which shall communicate copies thereof to all the signatory states.
4. The states signatory to the present Charter which ratify it after it has come into force will become original Members of the United Nations on the date of the deposit of their respective ratifications.

Article 111

The present Charter, of which the Chinese, French, Russian, English, and Spanish texts are equally authentic, shall remain deposited in the archives of the Government of the United States of America. Duly certified copies thereof shall be transmitted by that Government to the Governments of the other signatory states.

IN FAITH WHEREOF the representatives of the Governments of the United Nations have signed the present Charter.

DONE at the city of San Francisco the twenty-sixth day of June, one thousand nine hundred and forty-five.

APPENDIX B

Universal Declaration of Human Rights

Preamble

Whereas recognition of the inherent dignity and of the equal and inalienable rights of all members of the human family is the foundation of freedom, justice and peace in the world,

Whereas disregard and contempt for human rights have resulted in barbarous acts which have outraged the conscience of mankind, and the advent of a world in which human beings shall enjoy freedom of speech and belief and freedom from fear and want has been proclaimed as the highest aspiration of the common people,

Whereas it is essential, if man is not to be compelled to have recourse, as a last resort, to rebellion against tyranny and oppression, that human rights should be protected by the rule of law,

Whereas it is essential to promote the development of friendly relations between nations,

Whereas the peoples of the United Nations have in the Charter reaffirmed their faith in fundamental human rights, in the dignity and worth of the human person and in the equal rights of men and women and have determined to promote social progress and better standards of life in larger freedom,

Whereas Member States have pledged themselves to achieve, in co-operation with the United Nations, the promotion of universal respect for and observance of human rights and fundamental freedoms,

Whereas a common understanding of these rights and freedoms is of the greatest importance for the full realization of this pledge,

Now, Therefore THE GENERAL ASSEMBLY proclaims THIS UNIVERSAL DECLARATION OF HUMAN RIGHTS as a common standard of achievement for all peoples and all nations, to the end that every individual and every organ of society, keeping this Declaration constantly in mind, shall strive by teaching and education to promote respect for these rights and freedoms and by progressive measures, national and international, to secure their universal and effective recognition and observance, both among the peoples of Member States themselves and among the peoples of territories under their jurisdiction.

Article 1

All human beings are born free and equal in dignity and rights. They are endowed with reason and conscience and should act towards one another in a spirit of brotherhood.

Article 2

Everyone is entitled to all the rights and freedoms set forth in this Declaration, without distinction of any kind, such as race, colour, sex, language, religion, political or other opinion, national or social origin, property, birth or other status. Furthermore, no distinction shall be made on the basis of the political, jurisdictional or international status of the country or territory to which a person belongs, whether it be independent, trust, non-self-governing or under any other limitation of sovereignty.

Article 3

Everyone has the right to life, liberty and security of person.

Article 4

No one shall be held in slavery or servitude; slavery and the slave trade shall be prohibited in all their forms.

Article 5

No one shall be subjected to torture or to cruel, inhuman or degrading treatment or punishment.

Article 6

Everyone has the right to recognition everywhere as a person before the law.

Article 7

All are equal before the law and are entitled without any discrimination to equal protection of the law. All are entitled to equal protection against any discrimination in violation of this Declaration and against any incitement to such discrimination.

Article 8

Everyone has the right to an effective remedy by the competent national tribunals for acts violating the fundamental rights granted him by the constitution or by law.

Article 9

No one shall be subjected to arbitrary arrest, detention or exile.

Article 10

Everyone is entitled in full equality to a fair and public hearing by an independent and impartial tribunal, in the determination of his rights and obligations and of any criminal charge against him.

Article 11

(1) Everyone charged with a penal offence has the right to be presumed innocent until proved guilty according to law in a public trial at which he has had all the guarantees necessary for his defence.

(2) No one shall be held guilty of any penal offence on account of any act or omission which did not constitute a penal offence, under national or international law, at the time when it was committed. Nor shall a heavier penalty be imposed than the one that was applicable at the time the penal offence was committed.

Article 12

No one shall be subjected to arbitrary interference with his privacy, family, home or correspondence, nor to attacks upon his honour and reputation. Everyone has the right to the protection of the law against such interference or attacks.

Article 13

(1) Everyone has the right to freedom of movement and residence within the borders of each state.

(2) Everyone has the right to leave any country, including his own, and to return to his country.

Article 14

(1) Everyone has the right to seek and to enjoy in other countries asylum from persecution.

(2) This right may not be invoked in the case of prosecutions genuinely arising from non-political crimes or from acts contrary to the purposes and principles of the United Nations.

Article 15

(1) Everyone has the right to a nationality.

(2) No one shall be arbitrarily deprived of his nationality nor denied the right to change his nationality.

Article 16

(1) Men and women of full age, without any limitation due to race, nationality or religion, have the right to marry and to found a family. They are entitled to equal rights as to marriage, during marriage and at its dissolution.

(2) Marriage shall be entered into only with the free and full consent of the intending spouses.

(3) The family is the natural and fundamental group unit of society and is entitled to protection by society and the State.

Article 17

(1) Everyone has the right to own property alone as well as in association with others.

(2) No one shall be arbitrarily deprived of his property.

Article 18

Everyone has the right to freedom of thought, conscience and religion; this right includes freedom to change his religion or belief, and freedom, either alone or in community with others and in public or private, to manifest his religion or belief in teaching, practice, worship and observance.

Article 19

Everyone has the right to freedom of opinion and expression; this right includes freedom to hold opinions without interference and to seek, receive and impart information and ideas through any media and regardless of frontiers.

Article 20

(1) Everyone has the right to freedom of peaceful assembly and association.

(2) No one may be compelled to belong to an association.

Article 21

(1) Everyone has the right to take part in the government of his country, directly or through freely chosen representatives.
(2) Everyone has the right of equal access to public service in his country.
(3) The will of the people shall be the basis of the authority of government; this will shall be expressed in periodic and genuine elections which shall be by universal and equal suffrage and shall be held by secret vote or by equivalent free voting procedures.

Article 22

Everyone, as a member of society, has the right to social security and is entitled to realization, through national effort and international co-operation and in accordance with the organization and resources of each State, of the economic, social and cultural rights indispensable for his dignity and the free development of his personality.

Article 23

(1) Everyone has the right to work, to free choice of employment, to just and favourable conditions of work and to protection against unemployment.
(2) Everyone, without any discrimination, has the right to equal pay for equal work.
(3) Everyone who works has the right to just and favourable remuneration ensuring for himself and his family an existence worthy of human dignity, and supplemented, if necessary, by other means of social protection.
(4) Everyone has the right to form and to join trade unions for the protection of his interests.

Article 24

Everyone has the right to rest and leisure, including reasonable limitation of working hours and periodic holidays with pay.

Article 25

(1) Everyone has the right to a standard of living adequate for the health and well-being of himself and of his family, including food, clothing, housing and medical care and necessary social services, and the right to security in the event of unemployment, sickness, disability, widowhood, old age or other lack of livelihood in circumstances beyond his control.
(2) Motherhood and childhood are entitled to special care and assistance. All children, whether born in or out of wedlock, shall enjoy the same social protection.

Article 26

(1) Everyone has the right to education. Education shall be free, at least in the elementary and fundamental stages. Elementary education shall be compulsory. Technical and professional education shall be made generally available and higher education shall be equally accessible to all on the basis of merit.
(2) Education shall be directed to the full development of the human personality and to the strengthening of respect for human rights and fundamental freedoms. It shall promote understanding, tolerance and friendship among all nations, racial or religious groups, and shall further the activities of the United Nations for the maintenance of peace.
(3) Parents have a prior right to choose the kind of education that shall be given to their children.

Article 27

(1) Everyone has the right freely to participate in the cultural life of the community, to enjoy the arts and to share in scientific advancement and its benefits.
(2) Everyone has the right to the protection of the moral and material interests resulting from any scientific, literary or artistic production of which he is the author.

Article 28

Everyone is entitled to a social and international order in which the rights and freedoms set forth in this Declaration can be fully realized.

Article 29

(1) Everyone has duties to the community in which alone the free and full development of his personality is possible.
(2) In the exercise of his rights and freedoms, everyone shall be subject only to such limitations as are determined by law solely for the purpose of securing due recognition and respect for the rights and freedoms of others and of meeting the just requirements of morality, public order and the general welfare in a democratic society.

(3) These rights and freedoms may in no case be exercised contrary to the purposes and principles of the United Nations.

Article 30

Nothing in this Declaration may be interpreted as implying for any State, group or person any right to engage in any activity or to perform any act aimed at the destruction of any of the rights and freedoms set forth herein.

APPENDIX C
United Nations Member States June 2002

Member	Date of Admission
Afghanistan	November 19, 1946
Albania	December 14, 1955
Algeria	October 8, 1962
Andorra	July 28, 1993
Angola	December 1, 1976
Antigua and Barbuda	November 11, 1981
Argentina	October 24, 1945
Armenia	March 2, 1992
Australia	November 17, 1945
Austria	December 14, 1955
Azerbaijan	March 9, 1992
Bahamas	September 18, 1973
Bahrain	September 21, 1971
Bangladesh	September 17, 1974
Barbados	December 9, 1966
Belarus	October 24, 1945
Belgium	December 27, 1945
Belize	September 25, 1981
Benin	September 20, 1960
Bhutan	September 21, 1971
Bolivia	November 14, 1945
Bosnia and Herzegovina	May 22, 1992
Botswana	October 17, 1966
Brazil	October 24, 1945
Brunei Darussalam	September 21, 1984
Bulgaria	December 14, 1955
Burkina Faso	September 20, 1960
Burundi	September 18, 1962
Cambodia	December 14, 1955
Cameroon	September 20, 1960
Canada	November 9, 1945
Cape Verde	September 16, 1975
Central African Republic	September 20, 1960
Chad	September 20, 1960
Chile	October 24, 1945
China	October 24, 1945
Colombia	November 5, 1945
Comoros	November 12, 1975
Congo	September 20, 1960
Costa Rica	November 2, 1945
Côte d'Ivoire	September 20, 1960
Croatia	May 22, 1992
Cuba	October 24, 1945
Cyprus	September 20, 1960
Czech Republic	January 19, 1993[1]
Democratic Republic of the Congo	September 20, 1960
Denmark	October 24, 1945
Djibouti	September 20, 1977
Dominica	December 18, 1978
Dominican Republic	October 24, 1945
Ecuador	December 21, 1945
Egypt	October 24, 1945
El Salvador	October 24, 1945
Equatorial Guinea	November 12, 1968
Eritrea	May 28, 1993
Estonia	September 17, 1991
Ethiopia	November 13, 1945
Fiji	October 13, 1970
Finland	December 14, 1955
France	October 24, 1945
Gabon	September 20, 1960
Gambia	September 21, 1965
Georgia	July 31, 1992
Germany	September 18, 1973[2]
Ghana	March 8, 1957
Greece	October 25, 1945

---

[1] The Czech Republic is one of two successor states to Czechoslovakia which was an original member of the United Nations. Czechoslovakia ceased to exist on December 31, 1992. The other successor state is the Slovak Federal Republic, which was also admitted to the United Nations.

[2] On September 18, 1973, both the Federal Republic of Germany (FRG) and the German Democratic Republic (GDR) were admitted to UN membership. The absorption of the GDR by the FRG in 1990 united the two entities into one state.

Grenada	September 17, 1974	Nauru	September 14, 1999
Guatemala	November 21, 1945	Nepal	December 14, 1955
Guinea	December 12, 1958	Netherlands	December 10, 1945
Guinea-Bissau	September 17, 1974	New Zealand	October 24, 1945
Guyana	September 20, 1966	Nicaragua	October 24, 1945
Haiti	October 24, 1945	Niger	September 20, 1960
Honduras	December 17, 1945	Nigeria	October 7, 1960
Hungary	December 14, 1955	Norway	November 27, 1945
Iceland	November 19, 1946	Oman	October 7, 1971
India	October 30, 1945	Pakistan	September 30, 1947
Indonesia	September 28, 1950	Palau	December 15, 1994
Iran	October 24, 1945	Panama	November 13, 1945
Iraq	December 21, 1945	Papua New Guinea	October 10, 1975
Ireland	December 14, 1955	Paraguay	October 24, 1945
Israel	May 11, 1949	Peru	October 31, 1945
Italy	December 14, 1955	Philippines	October 24, 1945
Jamaica	September 18, 1962	Poland	October 24, 1945
Japan	December 18, 1956	Portugal	December 14, 1955
Jordan	December 14, 1955	Qatar	September 21, 1971
Kazakhstan	March 2, 1992	Romania	December 14, 1955
Kenya	December 16, 1963	Russian Federation	October 24, 1945[3]
Kiribati	September 14, 1999	Rwanda	September 18, 1962
Korea, North	September 17, 1991	Saint Kitts and Nevis	September 23, 1983
Korea, South	September 17, 1991	Saint Lucia	September 18, 1979
Kuwait	May 14, 1963	Saint Vincent and the Grenadines	September 16, 1980
Kyrgyzstan	March 2, 1992	Samoa	December 15, 1976
Laos	December 14, 1955	San Marino	March 2, 1992
Latvia	September 17, 1991	São Tomé and Príncipe	September 16, 1975
Lebanon	October 24, 1945	Saudi Arabia	October 24, 1945
Lesotho	October 17, 1966	Senegal	September 28, 1960
Liberia	November 2, 1945	Seychelles	September 21, 1976
Libya	December 14, 1955	Sierra Leone	September 27, 1961
Liechtenstein	September 18, 1990	Singapore	September 21, 1965
Lithuania	September 17, 1991	Slovakia	January 19, 1993[4]
Luxembourg	October 24, 1945	Slovenia	May 22, 1992
Macedonia	April 8, 1993	Solomon Islands	September 19, 1978
Madagascar	September 20, 1960	Somalia	September 20, 1960
Malawi	December 1, 1964	South Africa	November 7, 1945
Malaysia	September 17, 1957	Spain	December 14, 1955
Maldives	September 21, 1965	Sri Lanka	December 14, 1955
Mali	September 28, 1960	Sudan	November 12, 1956
Malta	December 1, 1964	Suriname	December 4, 1975
Marshall Islands	September 17, 1991	Swaziland	September 24, 1968
Mauritania	October 7, 1961	Sweden	November 19, 1946
Mauritius	April 24, 1968		
Mexico	November 7, 1945		
Micronesia	September 17, 1991		
Moldova	March 2, 1992		
Monaco	May 28, 1993		
Mongolia	October 27, 1961		
Morocco	November 12, 1956		
Mozambique	September 16, 1975		
Myanmar	April 19, 1948		
Namibia	April 23, 1990		

---

[3] On December 24, 1991, the Russian Federation took over the seat of the Union of Soviet Socialist Republics (USSR) in all of the organs of the United Nations. The USSR had ceased to exist.

[4] The Slovak Federal Republic is one of two successor states to Czechoslovakia which was an original member of the United Nations. Czechoslovakia ceased to exist on December 31, 1992. The other successor state is the Czech Republic, which was also admitted to the United Nations.

Syria	October 24, 1945	United Arab Emirates	December 9, 1971
Tajikistan	March 2, 1992	United Kingdom	October 24, 1945
Tanzania	December 14, 1961[5]	United States of America	October 24, 1945
Thailand	December 16, 1946	Uruguay	December 18, 1945
Togo	September 20, 1960	Uzbekistan	March 2, 1992
Tonga	September 14, 1999	Vanuatu	September 15, 1981
Trinidad and Tobago	September 18, 1962	Venezuela	November 15, 1945
Tunisia	November 12, 1956	Vietnam	September 20, 1971
Turkey	October 24, 1945	Yemen	September 30, 1947[6]
Turkmenistan	March 2, 1992	Yugoslavia	October 24, 1945[7]
Tuvalu	September 5, 2000	Zambia	December 1, 1964
Uganda	October 25, 1962	Zimbabwe	August 25, 1980
Ukraine	October 24, 1945		

[5] Tanganyika became a member of the United Nations on December 14, 1961. Its union with Zanzibar, which had been a member of the UN as well, on April 26, 1964, led to the change of the name of the country to the United Republic of Tanzania.

[6] On May 22, 1990, Yemen merged with Democratic Yemen, which was also a member state of the United Nations. Since then the two entities have been represented as one member with the name of Yemen.

[7] The Federal Republic of Yugoslavia, the successor state to the founding member state, was admitted as a member of the United Nations by General Assembly resolution A/RES/55/12 on November 1, 2000.

APPENDIX D

Secretaries-General of the United Nations

	National Origin	Tenure	Personal Dates
Trygve Lie	Norway	1945–1953	July 16, 1896–December 30, 1968
Dag Hammarskjöld	Sweden	1953–1961	July 29, 1905–September 18, 1961
U Thant	Burma	1961–1971	Jan. 22, 1909–November 25, 1974
Kurt Waldheim	Austria	1972–1981	December 21, 1918–
Javier Pérez de Cuéllar	Peru	1982–1991	January 19, 1920–
Boutros Boutros-Ghali	Egypt	1992–1996	November 14, 1922–
Kofi Annan	Ghana	1997–	April 8, 1938–

APPENDIX E

Statute of the International Court of Justice

Article 1

The International Court of Justice established by the Charter of the United Nations as the principal judicial organ of the United Nations shall be constituted and shall function in accordance with the provision of the present Statute.

Chapter I: Organization of the Court

Article 2

The Court shall be composed of a body of independent judges, elected regardless of their nationality from among persons of high moral character, who possess the qualifications required in their respective countries for appointment to the highest judicial offices, or are jurisconsults of recognized competence in international law.

Article 3

1. The Court shall consist of fifteen members, no two of whom may be nationals of the same state.
2. A person who for the purposes of membership in the Court could be regarded as a national of more than one state shall be deemed to be a national of the one in which he ordinarily exercises civil and political rights.

Article 4

1. The members of the Court shall be elected by the General Assembly and by the Security Council from a list of persons nominated by the national groups in the Permanent Court of Arbitration, in accordance with the following provisions.
2. In the case of Members of the United Nations not represented in the Permanent Court of Arbitration, candidates shall be nominated by national groups appointed for this purpose by their governments under the same conditions as those prescribed for members of the Permanent Court of Arbitration by Article 44 of the Convention of The Hague of 1907 for the pacific settlement of international disputes.

3. The conditions under which a state which is a party to the present Statute but is not a Member of the United Nations may participate in electing the members of the Court shall, in the absence of a special agreement, be laid down by the General Assembly upon recommendation of the Security Council.

Article 5

1. At least three months before the date of the election, the Secretary-General of the United Nations shall address a written request to the members of the Permanent Court of Arbitration belonging to the states which are parties to the present Statute, and to the members of the national groups appointed under Article 4, paragraph 2, inviting them to undertake, within a given time, by national groups, the nomination of persons in a position to accept the duties of a member of the Court.
2. No group may nominate more than four persons, not more than two of whom shall be of their own nationality. In no case may the number of candidates nominated by a group be more than double the number of seats to be filled.

Article 6

Before making these nominations, each national group is recommended to consult its highest court of justice, its legal faculties and schools of law, and its national academies and national sections of international academies devoted to the study of law.

Article 7

1. The Secretary-General shall prepare a list in alphabetical order of all the persons thus nominated. Save as provided in Article 12, paragraph 2, these shall be the only persons eligible.
2. The Secretary-General shall submit this list to the General Assembly and to the Security Council.

Article 8

The General Assembly and the Security Council shall proceed independently of one another to elect the members of the Court.

Article 9

At every election, the electors shall bear in mind not only that the persons to be elected should individually possess the qualifications required, but also that in the body as a whole the representation of the main forms of civilization and of the principal legal systems of the world should be assured.

Article 10

1. Those candidates who obtain an absolute majority of votes in the General Assembly and in the Security Council shall be considered as elected.
2. Any vote of the Security Council, whether for the election of judges or for the appointment of members of the conference envisaged in Article 12, shall be taken without any distinction between permanent and non-permanent members of the Security Council.
3. In the event of more than one national of the same state obtaining an absolute majority of the votes both of the General Assembly and of the Security Council, the eldest of these only shall be considered as elected.

Article 11

If, after the first meeting held for the purpose of the election, one or more seats remain to be filled, a second and, if necessary, a third meeting shall take place.

Article 12

1. If, after the third meeting, one or more seats still remain unfilled, a joint conference consisting of six members, three appointed by the General Assembly and three by the Security Council, may be formed at any time at the request of either the General Assembly or the Security Council, for the purpose of choosing by the vote of an absolute majority one name for each seat still vacant, to submit to the General Assembly and the Security Council for their respective acceptance.
2. If the joint conference is unanimously agreed upon any person who fulfills the required conditions, he may be included in its list, even though he was not included in the list of nominations referred to in Article 7.
3. If the joint conference is satisfied that it will not be successful in procuring an election, those members of the Court who have already been elected shall, within a period to be fixed by the Security Council, proceed to fill the vacant seats by selection from among those candidates who have obtained votes either in the General Assembly or in the Security Council.

4. In the event of an equality of votes among the judges, the eldest judge shall have a casting vote.

Article 13

1. The members of the Court shall be elected for nine years and may be re-elected; provided, however, that of the judges elected at the first election, the terms of five judges shall expire at the end of three years and the terms of five more judges shall expire at the end of six years.
2. The judges whose terms are to expire at the end of the above-mentioned initial periods of three and six years shall be chosen by lot to be drawn by the Secretary-General immediately after the first election has been completed.
3. The members of the Court shall continue to discharge their duties until their places have been filled. Though replaced, they shall finish any cases which they may have begun.
4. In the case of the resignation of a member of the Court, the resignation shall be addressed to the President of the Court for transmission to the Secretary-General. This last notification makes the place vacant.

Article 14

Vacancies shall be filled by the same method as that laid down for the first election subject to the following provision: the Secretary-General shall, within one month of the occurrence of the vacancy, proceed to issue the invitations provided for in Article 5, and the date of the election shall be fixed by the Security Council.

Article 15

A member of the Court elected to replace a member whose term of office has not expired shall hold office for the remainder of his predecessor's term.

Article 16

1. No member of the Court may exercise any political or administrative function, or engage in any other occupation of a professional nature.
2. Any doubt on this point shall be settled by the decision of the Court.

Article 17

1. No member of the Court may act as agent, counsel, or advocate in any case.
2. No member may participate in the decision of any case in which he has previously taken part as agent, counsel, or advocate for one of the parties, or as a member of a national or international court, or of a commission of enquiry, or in any other capacity.
3. Any doubt on this point shall be settled by the decision of the Court.

Article 18

1. No member of the Court can be dismissed unless, in the unanimous opinion of the other members, he has ceased to fulfill the required conditions.
2. Formal notification thereof shall be made to the Secretary-General by the Registrar.
3. This notification makes the place vacant.

Article 19

The members of the Court, when engaged on the business of the Court, shall enjoy diplomatic privileges and immunities.

Article 20

Every member of the Court shall, before taking up his duties, make a solemn declaration in open court that he will exercise his powers impartially and conscientiously.

Article 21

1. The Court shall elect its President and Vice-President for three years; they may be re-elected.
2. The Court shall appoint its Registrar and may provide for the appointment of such other officers as may be necessary.

Article 22

1. The seat of the Court shall be established at The Hague. This, however, shall not prevent the Court from sitting and exercising its functions elsewhere whenever the Court considers it desirable.
2. The President and the Registrar shall reside at the seat of the Court.

Article 23

1. The Court shall remain permanently in session, except during the judicial vacations, the dates and duration of which shall be fixed by the Court.
2. Members of the Court are entitled to periodic leave, the dates and duration of which shall be fixed by the Court, having in mind the distance between The Hague and the home of each judge.
3. Members of the Court shall be bound, unless they are on leave or prevented from attending by illness or other serious reasons duly explained to the President, to hold themselves permanently at the disposal of the Court.

Article 24

1. If, for some special reason, a member of the Court considers that he should not take part in the decision of a particular case, he shall so inform the President.
2. If the President considers that for some special reason one of the members of the Court should not sit in a particular case, he shall give him notice accordingly.

3. If in any such case the member Court and the President disagree, the matter shall be settled by the decision of the Court.

Article 25

1. The full Court shall sit except when it is expressly provided otherwise in the present Statute.
2. Subject to the condition that the number of judges available to constitute the Court is not thereby reduced below eleven, the Rules of the Court may provide for allowing one or more judges, according to circumstances and in rotation, to be dispensed from sitting.
3. A quorum of nine judges shall suffice to constitute the Court.

Article 26

1. The Court may from time to time form one or more chambers, composed of three or more judges as the Court may determine, for dealing with particular categories of cases; for example, labour cases and cases relating to transit and communications.
2. The Court may at any time form a chamber for dealing with a particular case. The number of judges to constitute such a chamber shall be determined by the Court with the approval of the parties.
3. Cases shall be heard and determined by the chambers provided for in this article if the parties so request.

Article 27

A judgment given by any of the chambers provided for in Articles 26 and 29 shall be considered as rendered by the Court.

Article 28

The chambers provided for in Articles 26 and 29 may, with the consent of the parties, sit and exercise their functions elsewhere than at The Hague.

Article 29

With a view to the speedy dispatch of business, the Court shall form annually a chamber composed of five judges which, at the request of the parties, may hear and determine cases by summary procedure. In addition, two judges shall be selected for the purpose of replacing judges who find it impossible to sit.

Article 30

1. The Court shall frame rules for carrying out its functions. In particular, it shall lay down rules of procedure.
2. The Rules of the Court may provide for assessors to sit with the Court or with any of its chambers, without the right to vote.

Article 31

1. Judges of the nationality of each of the parties shall retain their right to sit in the case before the Court.

2. If the Court includes upon the Bench a judge of the nationality of one of the parties, any other party may choose a person to sit as judge. Such person shall be chosen preferably from among those persons who have been nominated as candidates as provided in Articles 4 and 5.

3. If the Court includes upon the Bench no judge of the nationality of the parties, each of these parties may proceed to choose a judge as provided in paragraph 2 of this Article.

4. The provisions of this Article shall apply to the case of Articles 26 and 29. In such cases, the President shall request one or, if necessary, two of the members of the Court forming the chamber to give place to the members of the Court of the nationality of the parties concerned, and, failing such, or if they are unable to be present, to the judges specially chosen by the parties.

5. Should there be several parties in the same interest, they shall, for the purpose of the preceding provisions, be reckoned as one party only. Any doubt upon this point shall be settled by the decision of the Court.

6. Judges chosen as laid down in paragraphs 2, 3, and 4 of this Article shall fulfil the conditions required by Articles 2, 17 (paragraph 2), 20, and 24 of the present Statute. They shall take part in the decision on terms of complete equality with their colleagues.

Article 32

1. Each member of the Court shall receive an annual salary.

2. The President shall receive a special annual allowance.

3. The Vice-President shall receive a special allowance for every day on which he acts as President.

4. The judges chosen under Article 31, other than members of the Court, shall receive compensation for each day on which they exercise their functions.

5. These salaries, allowances, and compensation shall be fixed by the General Assembly. They may not be decreased during the term of office.

6. The salary of the Registrar shall be fixed by the General Assembly on the proposal of the Court.

7. Regulations made by the General Assembly shall fix the conditions under which retirement pensions may be given to members of the Court and to the Registrar, and the conditions under which members of the Court and the Registrar shall have their travelling expenses refunded.

8. The above salaries, allowances, and compensation shall be free of all taxation.

Article 33

The expenses of the Court shall be borne by the United Nations in such a manner as shall be decided by the General Assembly.

Chapter II: Competence of the Court

Article 34

1. Only states may be parties in cases before the Court.

2. The Court, subject to and in conformity with its Rules, may request of public international organizations information relevant to cases before it, and shall receive such information presented by such organizations on their own initiative.

3. Whenever the construction of the constituent instrument of a public international organization or of an international convention adopted thereunder is in question in a case before the Court, the Registrar shall so notify the public international organization concerned and shall communicate to it copies of all the written proceedings.

Article 35

1. The Court shall be open to the states parties to the present Statute.

2. The conditions under which the Court shall be open to other states shall, subject to the special provisions contained in treaties in force, be laid down by the Security Council, but in no case shall such conditions place the parties in a position of inequality before the Court.

3. When a state which is not a Member of the United Nations is a party to a case, the Court shall fix the amount which that party is to contribute towards the expenses of the Court. This provision shall not apply if such state is bearing a share of the expenses of the Court.

Article 36

1. The jurisdiction of the Court comprises all cases which the parties refer to it and all matters specially provided for in the Charter of the United Nations or in treaties and conventions in force.

2. The states parties to the present Statute may at any time declare that they recognize as compulsory ipso facto and without special agreement, in relation to any other state accepting the same obligation, the jurisdiction of the Court in all legal disputes concerning:

   a. the interpretation of a treaty;

   b. any question of international law;

   c. the existence of any fact which, if established, would constitute a breach of an international obligation;

d. the nature or extent of the reparation to be made for the breach of an international obligation.

3. The declarations referred to above may be made unconditionally or on condition of reciprocity on the part of several or certain states, or for a certain time.

4. Such declarations shall be deposited with the Secretary-General of the United Nations, who shall transmit copies thereof to the parties to the Statute and to the Registrar of the Court.

5. Declarations made under Article 36 of the Statute of the Permanent Court of International Justice and which are still in force shall be deemed, as between the parties to the present Statute, to be acceptances of the compulsory jurisdiction of the International Court of Justice for the period which they still have to run and in accordance with their terms.

6. In the event of a dispute as to whether the Court has jurisdiction, the matter shall be settled by the decision of the Court.

Article 37

Whenever a treaty or convention in force provides for reference of a matter to a tribunal to have been instituted by the League of Nations, or to the Permanent Court of International Justice, the matter shall, as between the parties to the present Statute, be referred to the International Court of Justice.

Article 38

1. The Court, whose function is to decide in accordance with international law such disputes as are submitted to it, shall apply:
   a. international conventions, whether general or particular, establishing rules expressly recognized by the contesting states;
   b. international custom, as evidence of a general practice accepted as law;
   c. the general principles of law recognized by civilized nations;
   d. subject to the provisions of Article 59, judicial decisions and the teachings of the most highly qualified publicists of the various nations, as subsidiary means for the determination of rules of law.

2. This provision shall not prejudice the power of the Court to decide a case ex aequo et bono, if the parties agree thereto.

Chapter III: Procedure

Article 39

1. The official languages of the Court shall be French and English. If the parties agree that the case shall be conducted in French, the judgment shall be delivered in French. If the parties agree that the case shall be conducted in English, the judgment shall be delivered in English.

2. In the absence of an agreement as to which language shall be employed, each party may, in the pleadings, use the language which it prefers; the decision of the Court shall be given in French and English. In this case the Court shall at the same time determine which of the two texts shall be considered as authoritative.

3. The Court shall, at the request of any party, authorize a language other than French or English to be used by that party.

Article 40

1. Cases are brought before the Court, as the case may be, either by the notification of the special agreement or by a written application addressed to the Registrar. In either case the subject of the dispute and the parties shall be indicated.

2. The Registrar shall forthwith communicate the application to all concerned.

3. He shall also notify the Members of the United Nations through the Secretary-General, and also any other states entitled to appear before the Court.

Article 41

1. The Court shall have the power to indicate, if it considers that circumstances so require, any provisional measures which ought to be taken to preserve the respective rights of either party.

2. Pending the final decision, notice of the measures suggested shall forthwith be given to the parties and to the Security Council.

Article 42

1. The parties shall be represented by agents.

2. They may have the assistance of counsel or advocates before the Court.

3. The agents, counsel, and advocates of parties before the Court shall enjoy the privileges and immunities necessary to the independent exercise of their duties.

Article 43

1. The procedure shall consist of two parts: written and oral.

2. The written proceedings shall consist of the communication to the Court and to the parties of memorials, counter-memorials and, if necessary, replies; also all papers and documents in support.

3. These communications shall be made through the Registrar, in the order and within the time fixed by the Court.

4. A certified copy of every document produced by one party shall be communicated to the other party.

5. The oral proceedings shall consist of the hearing by the Court of witnesses, experts, agents, counsel, and advocates.

Article 44

1. For the service of all notices upon persons other than the agents, counsel, and advocates, the Court shall apply direct to the government of the state upon whose territory the notice has to be served.
2. The same provision shall apply whenever steps are to be taken to procure evidence on the spot.

Article 45

The hearing shall be under the control of the President or, if he is unable to preside, of the Vice-President; if neither is able to preside, the senior judge present shall preside.

Article 46

The hearing in Court shall be public, unless the Court shall decide otherwise, or unless the parties demand that the public be not admitted.

Article 47

1. Minutes shall be made at each hearing and signed by the Registrar and the President.
2. These minutes alone shall be authentic.

Article 48

The Court shall make orders for the conduct of the case, shall decide the form and time in which each party must conclude its arguments, and make all arrangements connected with the taking of evidence.

Article 49

The Court may, even before the hearing begins, call upon the agents to produce any document or to supply any explanations. Formal note shall be taken of any refusal.

Article 50

The Court may, at any time, entrust any individual, body, bureau, commission, or other organization that it may select, with the task of carrying out an enquiry or giving an expert opinion.

Article 51

During the hearing any relevant questions are to be put to the witnesses and experts under the conditions laid down by the Court in the rules of procedure referred to in Article 30.

Article 52

After the Court has received the proofs and evidence within the time specified for the purpose, it may refuse to accept any further oral or written evidence that one party may desire to present unless the other side consents.

Article 53

1. Whenever one of the parties does not appear before the Court, or fails to defend its case, the other party may call upon the Court to decide in favour of its claim.
2. The Court must, before doing so, satisfy itself, not only that it has jurisdiction in accordance with Articles 36 and 37, but also that the claim is well founded in fact and law.

Article 54

1. When, subject to the control of the Court, the agents, counsel, and advocates have completed their presentation of the case, the President shall declare the hearing closed.
2. The Court shall withdraw to consider the judgment.
3. The deliberations of the Court shall take place in private and remain secret.

Article 55

1. All questions shall be decided by a majority of the judges present.
2. In the event of an equality of votes, the President or the judge who acts in his place shall have a casting vote.

Article 56

1. The judgment shall state the reasons on which it is based.
2. It shall contain the names of the judges who have taken part in the decision.

Article 57

If the judgment does not represent in whole or in part the unanimous opinion of the judges, any judge shall be entitled to deliver a separate opinion.

Article 58

The judgment shall be signed by the President and by the Registrar. It shall be read in open court, due notice having been given to the agents.

Article 59

The decision of the Court has no binding force except between the parties and in respect of that particular case.

Article 60

The judgment is final and without appeal. In the event of dispute as to the meaning or scope of the judgment, the Court shall construe it upon the request of any party.

Article 61

1. An application for revision of a judgment may be made only when it is based upon the discovery of some fact of such a nature as to be a decisive factor, which fact was, when the judgment was given,

unknown to the Court and also to the party claiming revision, always provided that such ignorance was not due to negligence.

2. The proceedings for revision shall be opened by a judgment of the Court expressly recording the existence of the new fact, recognizing that it has such a character as to lay the case open to revision, and declaring the application admissible on this ground.

3. The Court may require previous compliance with the terms of the judgment before it admits proceedings in revision.

4. The application for revision must be made at latest within six months of the discovery of the new fact.

5. No application for revision may be made after the lapse of ten years from the date of the judgment.

Article 62

1. Should a state consider that it has an interest of a legal nature which may be affected by the decision in the case, it may submit a request to the Court to be permitted to intervene.

2. It shall be for the Court to decide upon this request.

Article 63

1. Whenever the construction of a convention to which states other than those concerned in the case are parties is in question, the Registrar shall notify all such states forthwith.

2. Every state so notified has the right to intervene in the proceedings; but if it uses this right, the construction given by the judgment will be equally binding upon it.

Article 64

Unless otherwise decided by the Court, each party shall bear its own costs.

Chapter IV: Advisory Opinions

Article 65

1. The Court may give an advisory opinion on any legal question at the request of whatever body may be authorized by or in accordance with the Charter of the United Nations to make such a request.

2. Questions upon which the advisory opinion of the Court is asked shall be laid before the Court by means of a written request containing an exact statement of the question upon which an opinion is required, and accompanied by all documents likely to throw light upon the question.

Article 66

1. The Registrar shall forthwith give notice of the request for an advisory opinion to all states entitled to appear before the Court.

2. The Registrar shall also, by means of a special and direct communication, notify any state entitled to appear before the Court or international organization considered by the Court, or, should it not be sitting, by the President, as likely to be able to furnish information on the question, that the Court will be prepared to receive, within a time limit to be fixed by the President, written statements, or to hear, at a public sitting to be held for the purpose, oral statements relating to the question.

3. Should any such state entitled to appear before the Court have failed to receive the special communication referred to in paragraph 2 of this Article, such state may express a desire to submit a written statement or to be heard; and the Court will decide.

4. States and organizations having presented written or oral statements or both shall be permitted to comment on the statements made by other states or organizations in the form, to the extent, and within the time limits which the Court, or, should it not be sitting, the President, shall decide in each particular case. Accordingly, the Registrar shall in due time communicate any such written statements to states and organizations having submitted similar statements.

Article 67

The Court shall deliver its advisory opinions in open court, notice having been given to the Secretary-General and to the representatives of Members of the United Nations, of other states and of international organizations immediately concerned.

Article 68

In the exercise of its advisory functions the Court shall further be guided by the provisions of the present Statute which apply in contentious cases to the extent to which it recognizes them to be applicable.

Chapter V: Amendment

Article 69

Amendments to the present Statute shall be effected by the same procedure as is provided by the Charter of the United Nations for amendments to that Charter, subject however to any provisions which the General Assembly upon recommendation of the Security Council may adopt concerning the participation of states which are parties to the present Statute but are not Members of the United Nations.

Article 70

The Court shall have power to propose such amendments to the present Statute as it may deem necessary, through written communications to the Secretary-General, for consideration in conformity with the provisions of Article 69.

APPENDIX F

Important United Nations Resolutions

Uniting for Peace Resolution General Assembly 377 (V)

(Faced with the use of the VETO in the SECURITY COUNCIL by the SOVIET UNION during the early stages of the KOREAN WAR, the UNITED STATES successfully sponsored in the GENERAL ASSEMBLY the UNITING FOR PEACE RESOLUTION, which allowed the members to "discuss" threats to the peace and "recommend" UN action when the Security Council was deadlocked.)

The General Assembly,

Recognizing that the first two stated Purposes of the United Nations are:

"To maintain international peace and security, and to that end: to take effective collective measures for the prevention and removal of threats to the peace, and for the suppression of acts of aggression or other breaches of the peace, and to bring about by peaceful means, and in conformity with the principles of justice and international law, adjustment or settlement of international disputes or situations which might lead to a breach of the peace", and

"To develop friendly relations among nations based on respect for the principle of equal rights and self determination of peoples, and to take other appropriate measures to strengthen universal peace",

Reaffirming that it remains the primary duty of all Members of the United Nations, when involved in an international dispute, to seek settlement of such a dispute by peaceful means through the procedures laid down in Chapter VI of the Charter, and recalling the successful achievements of the United Nations in this regard on a number of previous occasions,

Finding that international tension exists on a dangerous scale,

Recalling its resolution 290 (IV) entitled "Essentials of peace", which states that disregard of the Principles of the Charter of the United Nations is primarily responsible for the continuance of international tension and desiring to contribute further to the objectives of that resolution,

Reaffirming the importance of the exercise by the Security Council of its primary responsibility for the maintenance of international peace and security, and the duty of the permanent members to seek unanimity and to exercise restraint in the use of the veto,

Reaffirming that the initiative in negotiating the agreements for armed forces provided for in Article 43 of the Charter belongs to the Security Council, and desiring to ensure that, pending the conclusion of such agreements, the United Nations has at its disposal means for maintaining international peace and security,

Conscious that failure of the Security Council to discharge its responsibilities on behalf of all the Member States, particularly those responsibilities referred to in the two preceding paragraphs, does not relieve Member States of their obligations or the United Nations of its responsibility under the Charter to maintain international peace and security,

Recognizing in particular that such failure does not deprive the General Assembly of its rights or relieve it of its responsibilities under the Charter in regard to the maintenance of international peace and security,

Recognizing that discharge by the General Assembly of its responsibilities in these respects calls for possibilities of observation which would ascertain the facts and expose aggressors; for the existence of armed forces which could be used collectively; and for the possibility of timely recommendation by the General Assembly to Members of the United Nations for collective action which, to be effective, should be prompt,

A

1. *Resolves* that if the Security Council, because of lack of unanimity of the permanent members, fails to exercise its primary responsibility for the maintenance of international

peace and security in any case where there appears to be a threat to the peace, breach of the peace, or act of aggression, the General Assembly shall consider the matter immediately with a view to making appropriate recommendations to Members for collective measures, including in the case of a breach of the peace or act of aggression the use of armed force when necessary, to maintain or restore international peace and security. If not in session at the time, the General Assembly may meet in emergency special session within twenty-four hours of the request therefor. Such emergency special session shall be called if requested by the Security Council on the vote of any seven members, or by a majority of the Members of the United Nations;

2. *Adopts* for this purpose the amendments to its rules of procedure set forth in the annex to the present resolution;

B

3. *Establishes* a Peace Observation Commission which, for the calendar years 1951 and 1952, shall be composed of fourteen Members, namely: China, Colombia, Czechoslovakia, France, India, Iraq, Israel, New Zealand, Pakistan, Sweden, the Union of Soviet Socialist Republics, the United Kingdom of Great Britain and Northern Ireland, the United States of America and Uruguay, and which could observe and report on the situation in any area where there exists international tension the continuance of which is likely to endanger the maintenance of international peace and security. Upon the invitation or with the consent of the State into whose territory the Commission would go, the General Assembly, or the Interim Committee when the Assembly is not in session, may utilize the Commission if the Security Council is not exercising the functions assigned to it by the Charter with respect to the matter in question. Decisions to utilize the Commission shall be made on the affirmative vote of two-thirds of the members present and voting. The Security Council may also utilize the Commission in accordance with its authority under the Charter;

4. *Decides* that the Commission shall have authority in its discretion to appoint sub-commissions and to utilize the services of observers to assist it in the performance of its functions;

5. *Recommends* to all governments and authorities that they co-operate with the Commission and assist it in the performance of its functions;

6. *Requests* the Secretary-General to provide the necessary staff and facilities, utilizing, where directed by the Commission, the United Nations Panel of Field Observers envisaged in General Assembly resolution 297 B (IV);

C

7. *Invites* each Member of the United Nations to survey its resources in order to determine the nature and scope of the assistance it may be in a position to render in support of any recommendations of the Security Council or of the General Assembly for the restoration of international peace and security;

8. *Recommends* to the States Members of the United Nations that each Member maintain within its national armed forces elements so trained, organized and equipped that they could promptly be made available, in accordance with its constitutional processes, for service as a United Nations unit or units, upon recommendation by the Security Council or the General Assembly, without prejudice to the use of such elements in exercise of the right of individual or collective self-defence recognized in Article 51 of the Charter;

9. *Invites* the Members of the United Nations to inform the Collective Measures Committee provided for in paragraph 11 as soon as possible of the measures taken in implementation of the preceding paragraph;

10. *Requests* the Secretary-General to appoint, with the approval of the Committee provided for in paragraph 11, a panel of military experts who could be made available, on request, to Member States wishing to obtain technical advice regarding the organization, training, and equipment for prompt service as United Nations units of the elements referred to in paragraph 8;

D

11. *Establishes* a Collective Measures Committee consisting of fourteen Members, namely: Australia, Belgium, Brazil, Burma, Canada, Egypt, France, Mexico, Philippines, Turkey, the United Kingdom of Great Britain and Northern Ireland, the United States of America, Venezuela and Yugoslavia, and directs the Committee, in consultation with the Secretary-General and with such Member States as the Committee finds appropriate, to study and make a report to the Security Council and the General Assembly, not later than 1 September 1951, on methods, including those in section C of the present resolution, which might be used to maintain and strengthen international peace and security in accordance with the Purposes and Principles of the Charter, taking account of collective self-defence and regional arrangements (Articles 51 and 52 of the Charter);

12. *Recommends* to all Member States that they co-operate with the Committee and assist it in the performance of its functions;

13. *Requests* the Secretary-General to furnish the staff and facilities necessary for the effective accomplishment of the purposes set forth in sections C and D of the present resolution;

E

14. *Is fully conscious* that, in adopting the proposals set forth above, enduring peace will not be secured solely by collective security arrangements against breaches of international peace and acts of aggression, but that a genuine and lasting peace depends also upon the observance of all the Principles and Purposes established in the Charter of the

United Nations, upon the implementation of the resolutions of the Security Council, the General Assembly and other principal organs of the United Nations intended to achieve the maintenance of international peace and security, and especially upon respect for and observance of human rights and fundamental freedoms for all and on the establishment and maintenance of conditions of economic and social well-being in all countries; and accordingly

15. *Urges* Member States to respect fully, and to intensify, joint action, in co-operation with the United Nations, to develop and stimulate universal respect for and observance of human rights and fundamental freedoms, and to intensify individual and collective efforts to achieve conditions of economic stability and social progress, particularly through the development of under-developed countries and areas.

Annex

The rules of procedure of the General Assembly are amended in the following respects:

1. The present text of rule 8 shall become paragraph (*a*) of that rule, and a new paragraph (*b*) shall be added to read as follows:

"Emergency special sessions pursuant to resolution 377 A (V) shall be convened within twenty-four hours of the receipt by the Secretary-General of a request for such a session from the Security Council, on the vote of any seven members thereof, or of a request from a majority of the Members of the United Nations expressed by vote in the Interim Committee or otherwise, or of the concurrence of a majority of Members as provided in rule 9."

2. The present text of rule 9 shall become paragraph (*a*) of that rule and a new paragraph (*b*) shall be added to read as follows:

"This rule shall apply also to a request by any Member for an emergency special session pursuant to resolution 377 A (V), In such a case the Secretary-General shall communicate with other Members by the most expeditious means of communication available."

3. Rule 10 is amended by adding at the end thereof the following:

"...In the case of an emergency special session convened pursuant to rule 8 (*b*), the Secretary-General shall notify the Members of the United Nations at least twelve hours in advance of the opening of the session."

4. Rule 16 is amended by adding at the end thereof the following:

"...The provisional agenda of an emergency special session shall be communicated to the Members of the United Nations simultaneously with the communication summoning the session."

5. Rule 19 is amended by adding at the end thereof the following:

"...During an emergency special session additional items concerning the matters dealt with in resolution 377 A (V)

may be added to the agenda by a two-thirds majority of the Members present and voting."

6. There is added a new rule to precede rule 65 to read as follows:

"Notwithstanding the provisions of any other rule and unless the General Assembly decides otherwise, the Assembly, in case of an emergency special session, shall convene in plenary session only and proceed directly to consider the item proposed for consideration in the request for the holding of the session, without previous reference to the General Committee or to any other Committee; the President and Vice-Presidents for such emergency special sessions shall be, respectively, the Chairman of those delegations from which were elected the President and Vice-Presidents of the previous session."

302nd plenary meeting, 3 November 1950.

Declaration on the Establishment of a New International Economic Order Resolution 3202 (S-VI)

(Initiated and promoted by the GROUP OF 77 in the UNITED NATIONS CONFERENCE ON TRADE AND DEVELOPMENT and in other UN bodies, the New International Economic Order represented a challenge and alternative to the BRETTON WOODS AGREEMENT put in place at the end of World War II. The NIEO represented an effort particularly by LESS DEVELOPED COUNTRIES to establish a "fairer" trade regime than the "free trade" system then in existence.)

We, the Members of the United Nations,

Having convened a special session of the General Assembly to study for the first time the problems of raw materials and development, devoted to the consideration of the most important economic problems facing the world community,

Bearing in mind the spirit, purposes and principles of the Charter of the United Nations to promote the economic advancement and social progress of all peoples,

Solemnly proclaim our united determination to work urgently for *the establishment of a new international economic order* based on equity, sovereign equality, interdependence, common interest and co-operation among all States, irrespective of their economic and social systems which shall correct inequalities and redress existing injustices, make it possible to eliminate the widening gap between the developed and the developing countries and ensure steadily accelerating economic and social development and peace and justice for present and future generations, and, to that end, declare:

1. The greatest and most significant achievement during the last decades has been the independence from colonial and alien domination of a large number of peoples and nations which has enabled them to become members of the

community of free peoples. Technological progress has also been made in all spheres of economic activities in the last three decades, thus providing a solid potential for improving the well-being of all peoples. However, the remaining vestiges of alien and colonial domination, foreign occupation, racial discrimination, *apartheid* and neo-colonialism in all its forms continue to be among the greatest obstacles to the full emancipation and progress of the developing countries and all the peoples involved. The benefits of technological progress are not shared equitably by all members of the international community. The developing countries which constitute 70 percent of the world's population account for only 30 percent of the world's income. It has proved impossible to achieve an even and balanced development of the international community under the existing international economic order. The gap between the developed and the developing countries continues to widen in a system which was established at a time when most of the developing countries did not even exist as independent States and which perpetuates inequality.

2. The present international economic order is in direct conflict with current developments in international political and economic relations. Since 1970, the world economy has experienced a series of grave crises which have had severe repercussions, especially on the developing countries because of their generally greater vulnerability to external economic impulses. The developing world has become a powerful factor that makes its influence felt in all fields of international activity. These irreversible changes in the relationship of forces in the world necessitate the active, full and equal participation of the developing countries in the formulation and application of all decisions that concern the international community.

3. All these changes have thrust into prominence the reality of interdependence of all the members of the world community. Current events have brought into sharp focus the realization that the interests of the developed countries and those of the developing countries can no longer be isolated from each other, that there is a close interrelationship between the prosperity of the developed countries and the growth and development of the developing countries, and that the prosperity of the international community as a whole depends upon the prosperity of its constituent parts. International co-operation for development is the shared goal and common duty of all countries. Thus the political, economic and social well-being of present and future generations depends more than ever on co-operation between all the members of the international community on the basis of sovereign equality and the removal of the disequilibrium that exists between them.

4. The new international economic order should be founded on full respect for the following principles:

(a) Sovereign equality of States, self-determination of all Peoples, inadmissibility of the acquisition of territories by force, territorial integrity and non-interference in the internal affairs of other States;

(b) The broadest co-operation of all the States members of the international community, based on equity, whereby the prevailing disparities in the world may be banished and prosperity secured for all;

(c) Full and effective participation on the basis of equality of all countries in the solving of world economic problems in the common interest of all countries, bearing in mind the necessity to ensure the accelerated development of all the developing countries while devoting particular attention to the adoption of special measures in favour of the least developed, land-locked and island developing countries as well as those developing countries most seriously affected by economic crises and natural calamities, without losing sight of the interests of other developing countries;

(d) The right of each country to adopt the economic and social system that it deems the most appropriate for its own development and not to be subjected to discrimination of any kind as a result;

(e) Full permanent sovereignty of each State over its natural resources and all economic activities. In order to safeguard these resources, each State is entitled to exercise effective control over them and their exploitation with means suitable to its own situation, including the right to nationalization or transfer of ownership to its nationals, this right being an expression of the full permanent sovereignty of the State. No State may be subjected to economic, political or any other type of coercion to prevent the free and full exercise of this inalienable right;

(f) The right of all States, territories and peoples under foreign occupation, alien and colonial domination or *apartheid* to restitution and full compensation for the exploitation and depletion of, and damages to, the natural resources and all other resources of those States, territories and peoples;

(g) Regulation and supervision of the activities of transnational corporations by taking measures in the interest of the national economies of the countries where such transnational corporations operate on the basis of the full sovereignty of those countries;

(h) The right of the developing countries and the peoples of territories under colonial and racial domination and foreign occupation to achieve their liberation and to regain effective control over their natural resources and economic activities;

(i) The extending of assistance to developing countries, peoples and territories which are under colonial and alien domination, foreign occupation, racial discrimination or *apartheid* or are subjected to economic, political or any other type of coercive measures to obtain from them the subordination of the exercise of their sovereign rights and to secure from them advantages of any kind, and to neo-colonialism in all its forms, and which have established or are endeavouring to establish effective control over their natural resources and economic activities that have been or are still under foreign control;

(j) Just and equitable relationship between the prices of raw materials, primary commodities, manufactured and semi-manufactured goods exported by developing countries and the prices of raw materials, primary commodities, manufactures, capital goods and equipment imported by them with the aim of bringing about sustained improvement in their unsatisfactory terms of trade and the expansion of the world economy;

(k) Extension of active assistance to developing countries by the whole international community, free of any political or military conditions;

(l) Ensuring that one of the main aims of the reformed international monetary system shall be the promotion of the development of the developing countries and the adequate flow of real resources to them;

(m) Improving the competitiveness of natural materials facing competition from synthetic substitutes;

(n) Preferential and non-reciprocal treatment for developing countries, wherever feasible, in all fields of international economic co-operation whenever possible;

(o) Securing favourable conditions for the transfer of financial resources to developing countries;

(p) Giving to the developing countries access to the achievements of modern science and technology, and promoting the transfer of technology and the creation of indigenous technology for the benefit of the developing countries in forms and in accordance with procedures which are suited to their economies;

(q) The need for all States to put an end to the waste of natural resources, including food products;

(r) The need for developing countries to concentrate all their resources for the cause of development;

(s) The strengthening, through individual and collective actions, of mutual economic, trade, financial and technical co-operation among the developing countries, mainly on a preferential basis;

(t) Facilitating the role which producers' associations may play within the framework of international co-operation and, in pursuance of their aims, *inter alia* assisting in the promotion of sustained growth of the world economy and accelerating the development of developing countries.

5. The unanimous adoption of the International Development Strategy for the Second United Nations Development Decade was an important step in the promotion of international economic co-operation on a just and equitable basis. The accelerated implementation of obligations and commitments assumed by the international community within the framework of the Strategy, particularly those concerning imperative development needs of developing countries, would contribute significantly to the fulfilment of the aims and objectives of the present Declaration.

6. The United Nations as a universal organization should be capable of dealing with problems of international economic co-operation in a comprehensive manner and ensuring equally the interests of all countries. It must have an even greater role in the establishment of a new international economic order. The Charter of Economic Rights and Duties of States, for the preparation of which the present Declaration will provide an additional source of inspiration, will constitute a significant contribution in this respect. All the States Members of the United Nations are therefore called upon to exert maximum efforts with a view to securing the implementation of the present Declaration, which is one of the principal guarantees for the creation of better conditions for all peoples to reach a life worthy of human dignity.

7. The present Declaration on the Establishment of a New International Economic Order shall be one of the most important bases of economic relations between all peoples and all nations.

Adopted unanimously by the General Assembly
1 May 1974

Security Council Resolution 242

(UN SECURITY COUNCIL RESOLUTION 242 was adopted unanimously on November 22, 1967, following the cessation of the MIDDLE EAST WAR OF 1967 [June 5–10]. The RESOLUTION was precipitated by Israel's June 5, 1967, attack on EGYPT, Iraq, Jordan, and Syria in which Israeli forces seized Egyptian territory in the Sinai peninsula, Syrian territory in the Golan Heights, and the remainder of the land designated by the 1947 UN partition plan for Palestine as the space for the Arab state. Resolution 242 was the most significant, albeit belated, UN response to the 1967 war.)

The Security Council,

Expressing its continuing concern with the grave situation in the Middle East,

Emphasizing the inadmissibility of the acquisition of territory by war and the need to work for a just and lasting peace in which every State in the area can live in security,

Emphasizing further that all Member States in their acceptance of the Charter of the United Nations have undertaken a commitment to act in accordance with Article 2 of the Charter,

1. *Affirms* that the fulfilment of Charter principles requires the establishment of a just and lasting peace in the Middle East which should include the application of both the following principles:

(i) Withdrawal of Israel armed forces from territories occupied in the recent conflict;

(ii) Termination of all claims or states of belligerency and respect for and acknowledgement of the sovereignty, territorial integrity and political independence of every State in the area and their right to live in peace within secure and recognized boundaries free from threats or acts of force;

2. *Affirms further* the necessity

(a) For guaranteeing freedom of navigation through international waterways in the area;

(b) For achieving a just settlement of the refugee problem;

(c) For guaranteeing the territorial inviolability and political independence of every State in the area, through measures including the establishment of demilitarized zones;

3. *Requests* the Secretary-General to designate a Special Representative to proceed to the Middle East to establish and maintain contacts with the States concerned in order to promote agreement and assist efforts to achieve a peaceful and accepted settlement in accordance with the provisions and principles in this resolution;

4. *Requests* the Secretary-General to report to the Security Council on the progress of the efforts of the Special Representative as soon as possible.

Adopted unanimously at the 1382nd meeting.

Security Council Resolution 598

(In the first UN SECURITY COUNCIL Resolution on the MIDDLE EAST jointly sponsored by the UNITED STATES and the USSR, the Council called upon Iran and Iraq to accept a cease-fire in the seven-year war between them. The Council took the unusual step of threatening to take "further steps to ensure compliance" if either of the parties refused to accept RESOLUTION 598.)

The Security Council,

Reaffirming its resolution 582 (1986),

Deeply concerned that, despite its calls for a cease-fire, the conflict between the Islamic Republic of Iran and Iraq continues unabated, with further heavy loss of human life and material destruction,

Deploring the initiation and continuation of the conflict,

Deploring also the bombing of purely civilian population centres, attacks on neutral shipping or civilian aircraft, the violation of international humanitarian law and other laws of armed conflict, and, in particular, the use of chemical weapons contrary to obligations under the 1925 Geneva Protocol,

Deeply concerned that further escalation and widening of the conflict may take place,

Determined to bring to an end all military actions between Iran and Iraq,

Convinced that a comprehensive, just, honourable and durable settlement should be achieved between Iran and Iraq,

Recalling the provisions of the Charter of the United Nations, and in particular the obligation of all Member States to settle their international disputes by peaceful means in such a manner that international peace and security and justice are not endangered,

Determining that there exists a breach of the peace as regards the conflict between Iran and Iraq,

Acting under Articles 39 and 40 of the Charter,

1. *Demands* that, as a first step towards a negotiated settlement, the Islamic Republic of Iran and Iraq observe an immediate cease-fire, discontinue all military actions on land, at sea and in the air, and withdraw all forces to the internationally recognized boundaries without delay;

2. *Requests* the Secretary-General to dispatch a team of United Nations observers to verify, confirm and supervise the cease-fire and withdrawal and further requests the Secretary-General to make the necessary arrangements in consultation with the Parties and to submit a report thereon to the Security Council;

3. *Urges* that prisoners-of-war be released and repatriated without delay after the cessation of active hostilities in accordance with the Third Geneva Convention of 12 August 1949:

4. *Calls upon* Iran and Iraq to co-operate with the Secretary-General in implementing this resolution and in mediation efforts to achieve a comprehensive, just and honourable settlement, acceptable to both sides, of all outstanding issues, in accordance with the principles contained in the Charter of the United Nations;

5. *Calls upon* all other States to exercise the utmost restraint and to refrain from any act which may lead to further escalation and widening of the conflict, and thus to facilitate the implementation of the present resolution;

6. *Requests* the Secretary-General to explore, in consultation with Iran and Iraq, the question of entrusting an impartial body with inquiring into responsibility for the conflict and to report to the Council as soon as possible;

7. *Recognizes* the magnitude of the damage inflicted during the conflict and the need for reconstruction efforts, with appropriate international assistance, once the conflict is ended and, in this regard, requests the Secretary-General to assign a team of experts to study the question of reconstruction and to report to the Council;

8. *Further requests* the Secretary-General to examine, in consultation with Iran and Iraq and with other States of the region, measures to enhance the security and stability of the region;

9. *Requests* the Secretary-General to keep the Council informed on the implementation of this resolution;

10. *Decides* to meet again as necessary to consider further steps to ensure compliance with this resolution.

Adopted unanimously by the Security Council on 20 July 1987

Security Council Resolution 678

(Invoking the enforcement provisions of CHAPTER VII for only the second time in its history, the SECURITY COUNCIL authorized member states "to use all necessary means" in the liberation of Kuwait from Iraqi occupation. The RESOLUTION provided the legal basis for the military operations subsequently conducted by a coalition of states led by the UNITED STATES.)

The Security Council,

Recalling and reaffirming its resolutions 660 (1990) of 2 August 1990, 661 (1990) of 6 August 1990, 662 (1990) of 9 August 1990, 664 (1990) of 18 August 1990, 665 (1990) of 25 August 1990, 666 (1990) of 13 September 1990, 667 (1990) of 16 September 1990, 669 (1990) of 24 September 1990, 670 (1990) of 25 September 1990, 674 (1990) of 29 October 1990 and 677 (1990) of 28 November 1990,

Noting that, despite all efforts by the United Nations, Iraq refuses to comply with its obligation to implement resolution 660 (1990) and the above-mentioned subsequent relevant resolutions in flagrant contempt of the Security Council,

Mindful of its duties and responsibilities under the Charter of the United Nations for the maintenance and preservation of international peace and security,

Determined to secure full compliance with its decisions,

Acting under Chapter VII of the Charter,

1. *Demands* that Iraq comply fully with resolution 660 (1990) and all subsequent relevant resolutions, and decides, while maintaining all its decisions, to allow Iraq one final opportunity, as a pause of goodwill, to do so;

2. *Authorizes* Member States co-operating with the Government of Kuwait, unless Iraq on or before 15 January 1991 fully implements, as set forth in paragraph 1 above, the above-mentioned resolutions, to use all necessary means to uphold and implement resolution 660 (1990) and all subsequent relevant resolutions and to restore international peace and security in the area;

3. *Requests* all States to provide appropriate support for the actions undertaken in pursuance of paragraph 2 above;

4. *Requests* the States concerned to keep the Security Council regularly informed on the progress of actions undertaken pursuant to paragraphs 2 and 3 above;

5. *Decides* to remain seized of the matter.

Adopted at the 2963rd meeting by 12 votes to 2 (Cuba and Yemen), with one abstention (China). 29 November 1990

UN Security Council Resolution 1368

(The SECURITY COUNCIL unanimously adopted RESOLUTION 1368 on September 12, 2001, one day after terrorists killed thousands of people by crashing civilian jetliners into both towers of the World Trade Center in New York City and into the Pentagon near Washington, D.C. Another commandeered airplane crashed in Pennsylvania. Council members departed from tradition and stood to adopt Resolution 1368. In the text, the Council held that any act of international TERRORISM was a threat to international peace and security.)

The Security Council,

Reaffirming the principles and purposes of the Charter of the United Nations,

Determined to combat by all means threats to international peace and security caused by terrorist acts,

Recognizing the inherent right of individual or collective self-defence in accordance with the Charter,

1. *Unequivocally condemns* in the strongest terms the horrifying terrorist attacks which took place on 11 September 2001 in New York, Washington (D.C.) and Pennsylvania and regards such acts, like any act of international terrorism, as a threat to international peace and security;

2. *Expresses* its deepest sympathy and condolences to the victims and their families and to the People and Government of the United States of America;

3. *Calls on* all States to work together urgently to bring to justice the perpetrators, organizers and sponsors of these terrorist attacks and stresses that those responsible for aiding, supporting or harbouring the perpetrators, organizers and sponsors of these acts will be held accountable;

4. *Calls also on* the international community to redouble their efforts to prevent and suppress terrorist acts including by increased cooperation and full implementation of the relevant international anti-terrorist conventions and Security Council resolutions, in particular resolution 1269 of 19 October 1999;

5. *Expresses* its readiness to take all necessary steps to respond to the terrorist attacks of 11 September 2001, and to combat all forms of terrorism, in accordance with its responsibilities under the Charter of the United Nations;

6. *Decides to* remain seized of the matter.

Adopted unanimously at the 4370th meeting.

List of Conventions, Declarations, and Other Instruments Contained in General Assembly Resolutions

NOTE: This list is an update (August 28, 2001) of the latest printed version contained in A/50/49 (Official Records of the GENERAL ASSEMBLY, 50th session, Supplement No. 49), Annex II.

Title of Instrument / Date of Resolution	Resolution Number
Agenda for Development (20 June 1997)	A/RES/51/240
Agreement between the United Nations and the Carnegie Foundation concerning the Use of the Premises of the Peace Palace at The Hague (11 Dec. 1946) and Supplementary Agreement (22 Dec. 1971)	A/RES/84(I) A/RES/2902 (XXVI)
Agreement between the United Nations and the International Fund for Agricultural Development (15 Dec. 1977)	A/RES/32/107
Agreement between the United Nations and the United Nations Industrial Development Organization (17 Dec. 1985)	A/RES/40/180
Agreement between the United Nations and the United States of America regarding the Headquarters of the United Nations (31 Oct. 1947)	A/RES/169 (II)
Agreement between the United Nations and the World Intellectual Property Organization (17 Dec. 1974)	A/RES/3346 (XXIX)
Agreement concerning the Relationship between the United Nations and the International Seabed Authority (26 Nov. 1997)	A/RES/52/27
Agreement Governing the Activities of States on the Moon and Other Celestial Bodies (5 Dec. 1979)	A/RES/34/68
Agreement on Cooperation and Relationship between the United Nations and the International Tribunal for the Law of the Sea (8 Sept. 1998)	A/RES/52/251
Agreement on Cooperation and Relationships between the United Nations and the World Tourism Organization (19 Dec. 1977)	A/RES/32/156
Agreement on the Rescue of Astronauts, the Return of Astronauts and the Return of Objects Launched into Outer Space (19 Dec. 1967)	A/RES/2345 (XXII)
Agreement relating to the Implementation of Part XI of the United Nations Convention on the Law of the Sea (28 July 1994)	A/RES/48/263
Agreement to Regulate the Relationship between the United Nations and the Preparatory Commission for the Comprehensive Nuclear-Test-Ban Treaty Organization (30 June 2000)	A/RES/54/280
Articles on Nationality of Natural Persons in Relation to the Succession of States (12 Dec. 2000)	A/RES/55/153
Basic Principles for the Treatment of Prisoners (14 Dec. 1990)	A/RES/45/111
Body of Principles for the Protection of All Persons under Any Form of Detention or Imprisonment (9 Dec. 1988)	A/RES/43/173
Charter of Economic Rights and Duties of States (12 Dec. 1974)	A/RES/3281 (XXIX)
Charter of Rights for Migrant Workers in Southern Africa (20 Dec. 1978)	A/RES/33/162
Code of Conduct for Law Enforcement Officials (17 Dec. 1979)	A/RES/34/169
Convention against Torture and Other Cruel, Inhuman or Degrading Treatment or Punishment (10 Dec. 1984)	A/RES/39/46
Convention for the Suppression of the Traffic in Persons and of the Exploitation of the Prostitution of Others (2 Dec. 1949)	A/RES/317 (IV)
Convention on Consent to Marriage, Minimum Age for Marriage and Registration of Marriages (7 Nov. 1962) and Recommendation (1 Nov. 1965)	A/RES/1763 A (XVII) A/RES/2018 (XX)
Convention on International Liability for Damage Caused by Space Objects (29 Nov. 1971)	A/RES/2777 (XXVI)
Convention on Registration of Objects Launched into Outer Space (12 Nov. 1974)	A/RES/3235 (XXIX)
Convention on Special Missions and Optional Protocol concerning the Compulsory Settlement of Disputes (8 Dec. 1969)	A/RES/2530 (XXIV)
Convention on the Elimination of All Forms of Discrimination against Women (18 Dec. 1979)	A/RES/34/180
Convention on the International Right of Correction (16 Dec. 1952)	A/RES/630 (VII)
Convention on the Law of the Non-Navigational Uses of International Watercourses (21 May 1997)	A/RES/51/229
Convention on the Nationality of Married Women (29 Jan. 1957)	A/RES/1040 (XI)
Convention on the Non-Applicability of Statutory Limitations to War Crimes and Crimes against Humanity (26 Nov. 1968)	A/RES/2391 (XXIII)

Convention on the Political Rights of Women (20 Dec. 1952)	A/RES/640 (VII)
Convention on the Prevention and Punishment of Crimes against Internationally Protected Persons, including Diplomatic Agents (14 Dec. 1973)	A/RES/3166 (XXVIII)
Convention on the Prevention and Punishment of the Crime of Genocide (9 Dec. 1948)	A/RES/260 A (III)
Convention on the Privileges and Immunities of the Specialized Agencies (21 Nov. 1947)	A/RES/179 (II)
Convention on the Privileges and Immunities of the United Nations (13 Feb. 1946)	A/RES/22 A (I)
Convention on the Prohibition of Military or Any Other Hostile Use of Environmental Modification Techniques (10 Dec. 1976)	A/RES/31/72
Convention on the Prohibition of the Development, Production and Stockpiling of Bacteriological (Biological) and Toxin Weapons and on Their Destruction (16 Dec. 1971)	A/RES/2826 (XXVI)
Convention on the Rights of the Child (20 Nov. 1989)	A/RES/44/25
Convention on the Safety of United Nations and Associated Personnel (9 Dec. 1994)	A/RES/49/59
Declaration and Programme of Action on a Culture of Peace (13 Sept. 1999)	A/RES/53/243
Declaration and State of Progress and Initiatives for the Future Implementation of the Programme of Action for the Sustainable Development of Small Island Developing States (28 Sept. 1999)	A/RES/S-22/2
Declaration in Commemoration of the Fiftieth Anniversary of the End of the Second World War (18 Oct. 1995)	A/RES/50/5
Declaration of Basic Principles of Justice for Victims of Crime and Abuse of Power (29 Nov. 1985)	A/RES/40/34
Declaration of Commitment on HIV/AIDS (27 June 2001)	A/RES/S-26/2
Declaration of Legal Principles Governing the Activities of States in the Exploration and Use of Outer Space (13 Dec. 1963)	A/RES/1962 (XVIII)
Declaration of Principles Governing the Seabed and the Ocean Floor, and the Subsoil Thereof, beyond the Limits of National Jurisdiction (17 Dec. 1970)	A/RES/2749 (XXV)
Declaration of the Indian Ocean as a Zone of Peace (16 Dec. 1971)	A/RES/2832 (XXVI)
Declaration of the 1980s as the Second Disarmament Decade (3 Dec. 1980)	A/RES/35/46
Declaration of the 1990s as the Third Disarmament Decade (4 Dec. 1990)	A/RES/45/62 A
Declaration of the Rights of the Child (20 Nov. 1959)	A/RES/1386 (XIV)
Declaration on Apartheid and Its Destructive Consequences in Southern Africa (14 Dec. 1989)	A/RES/S-16/1
Declaration on Fact-finding by the United Nations in the Field of the Maintenance of International Peace and Security (9 Dec. 1991)	A/RES/46/59
Declaration on International Cooperation for Disarmament (11 Dec. 1979)	A/RES/34/88
Declaration on International Cooperation in the Exploration and Use of Outer Space for the Benefit and in the Interest of all States, Taking into Particular Account the Needs of Developing Countries (13 Dec. 1996)	A/RES/51/122
Declaration on International Economic Cooperation, in Particular the Revitalization of Economic Growth and Development of the Developing Countries (1 May 1990)	A/RES/S-18/3
Declaration on Measures to Eliminate International Terrorism (9 Dec. 1994)	A/RES/49/60
Declaration on Namibia (3 May 1978)	A/RES/S-9/2
Declaration on Principles of International Law concerning Friendly Relations and Cooperation among States in accordance with the Charter of the United Nations (24 Oct. 1970)	A/RES/2625 (XXV)
Declaration on Social and Legal Principles relating to the Protection and Welfare of Children, with Special Reference to Foster Placement and Adoption Nationally and Internationally (3 Dec. 1986)	A/RES/41/85
Declaration on Social Progress and Development (11 Dec. 1969)	A/RES/2542 (XXIV)
Declaration on South Africa (12 Dec. 1979)	A/RES/34/93 O
Declaration on Territorial Asylum (14 Dec. 1967)	A/RES/231 2 (XXII)
Declaration on the Control of Drug Trafficking and Drug Abuse (14 Dec. 1984)	A/RES/39/142
Declaration on the Critical Economic Situation in Africa (3 Dec. 1984)	A/RES/39/29
Declaration on the Deepening and Consolidation of International Detente (19 Dec. 1977)	A/RES/32/155
Declaration on the Elimination of All Forms of Intolerance and of Discrimination Based on Religion or Belief (25 Nov. 1981)	A/RES/36/55
Declaration on the Elimination of Discrimination against Women (7 Nov. 1967)	A/RES/2263 (XXII)
Declaration on the Elimination of Violence against Women (20 Dec. 1993)	A/RES/48/104

Declaration on the Enhancement of Cooperation between the United Nations and Regional
　　Arrangements or Agencies in the Maintenance of International Peace and Security (9 Dec. 1994)　　A/RES/49/57
Declaration on the Enhancement of the Effectiveness of the Principle of Refraining from the
　　Threat or Use of Force in International Relations (18 Nov. 1987)　　A/RES/42/22
Declaration on the Establishment of a New International Economic Order (1 May 1974)　　A/RES/3201 (S-VI)
Declaration on the Granting of Independence to Colonial Countries and Peoples (14 Dec. 1960)　　A/RES/1514 (XV)
Declaration on the Guiding Principles of Drug Demand Reduction (10 June 1998)　　A/RES/S-20/3
Declaration on the Human Rights of Individuals Who are not Nationals of the Country in Which
　　They Live (13 Dec. 1985)　　A/RES/40/144
Declaration on the Inadmissibility of Intervention and Interference in the Internal Affairs of
　　States (9 Dec. 1981)　　A/RES/36/103
Declaration on the Inadmissibility of Intervention in the Domestic Affairs of States and the
　　Protection of Their Independence and Sovereignty (21 Dec. 1965)　　A/RES/2131 (XX)
Declaration on the Occasion of the Fiftieth Anniversary of the United Nations (24 Oct. 1995)　　A/RES/50/6
Declaration on the Occasion of the Fiftieth Anniversary of United Nations Peacekeeping
　　(6 Oct. 1998)　　A/RES/53/2
Declaration on the Occasion of the Twenty-fifth Anniversary of the United Nations (24 Oct. 1970)　　A/RES/2627 (XXV)
Declaration on the Participation of Women in Promoting International Peace and Cooperation
　　(3 Dec. 1982)　　A/RES/37/63
Declaration on the Preparation of Societies for Life in Peace (15 Dec. 1978)　　A/RES/33/73
Declaration on the Prevention and Removal of Disputes and Situations Which May Threaten
　　International Peace and Security and on the Role of the United Nations in this Field (5 Dec. 1988)　　A/RES/43/51
Declaration on the Prevention of Nuclear Catastrophe (9 Dec. 1981)　　A/RES/36/100
Declaration on the Prohibition of the Use of Nuclear and Thermonuclear Weapons (24 Nov. 1961)　　A/RES/1653 (XVI)
Declaration on the Promotion of the Ideals of Peace, Mutual Respect and Understanding
　　between Peoples (7 Dec. 1965)　　A/RES/2037 (XX)
Declaration on the Protection of All Persons from Being Subjected to Torture and Other Cruel,
　　Inhuman or Degrading Treatment or Punishment (9 Dec. 1975)　　A/RES/3452 (XXX)
Declaration on the Protection of All Persons from Enforced Disappearance (18 Dec. 1992)　　A/RES/47/133
Declaration on the Protection of Women and Children in Emergency and Armed Conflict
　　(14 Dec. 1974)　　A/RES/3318 (XXIX)
Declaration on the Right and Responsibility of Individuals, Groups and Organs of Society to
　　Promote and Protect Universally Recognized Human Rights and Fundamental Freedoms
　　(9 Dec. 1998)　　A/RES/53/144
Declaration on the Right of Peoples to Peace (12 Nov. 1984)　　A/RES/39/11
Declaration on the Right to Development (4 Dec. 1986)　　A/RES/41/128
Declaration on the Rights of Disabled Persons (9 Dec. 1975)　　A/RES/3447 (XXX)
Declaration on the Rights of Mentally Retarded Persons (20 Dec. 1971)　　A/RES/2856 (XXVI)
Declaration on the Rights of Persons Belonging to National or Ethnic, Religious and Linguistic
　　Minorities (18 Dec. 1992)　　A/RES/47/135
Declaration on the Strengthening of International Security (16 Dec. 1970)　　A/RES/2734 (XXV)
Declaration on the Use of Scientific and Technological Progress in the Interests of Peace and for
　　the Benefit of Mankind (10 Nov. 1975)　　A/RES/3384 (XXX)
Declaration to Supplement the 1994 Declaration on Measures to Eliminate International
　　Terrorism (17 Dec. 1996)　　A/RES/51/210
Definition of Aggression (14 Dec. 1974)　　A/RES/3314 (XXIX)
Environmental Perspective to the Year 2000 and Beyond (11 Dec. 1987)　　A/RES/42/186
Guidelines for the Regulation of Computerized Data Files (14 Dec. 1990)　　A/RES/45/95
International Agreement for the Establishment of the University for Peace and Charter of the
　　University for Peace (5 Dec. 1980)　　A/RES/35/55
International Code of Conduct for Public Officials (12 Dec. 1996)　　A/RES/51/59
International Convention against Apartheid in Sports (10 Dec. 1985)　　A/RES/40/64 G
International Convention against the Recruitment, Use, Financing and Training of Mercenaries
　　(4 Dec. 1989)　　A/RES/44/34

International Convention against the Taking of Hostages (17 Dec. 1979)   A/RES/34/146
International Convention for the Suppression of Terrorist Bombings (15 Dec. 1997)   A/RES/52/164
International Convention for the Suppression of the Financing of Terrorism (9 Dec. 1999)   A/RES/54/109
International Convention on the Elimination of All Forms of Racial Discrimination (21 Dec. 1965)   A/RES/2106 A (XX)
International Convention on the Protection of the Rights of All Migrant Workers and Members of
    Their Families (18 Dec. 1990)   A/RES/45/158
International Convention on the Suppression and Punishment of the Crime of Apartheid
    (30 Nov. 1973)   A/RES/3068 (XXVIII)
International Covenant on Civil and Political Rights and Optional Protocol (16 Dec. 1966)   A/RES/2200 A (XXI)
International Covenant on Civil and Political Rights: Second Optional Protocol Aiming at the
    Abolition of the Death Penalty (15 Dec. 1989)   A/RES/44/128
International Covenant on Economic, Social and Cultural Rights (16 Dec. 1966)   A/RES/2200 A (XXI)
International Declaration against Apartheid in Sports (14 Dec. 1977)   A/RES/32/105 M
International Development Strategy for the Fourth United Nations Development Decade
    (21 Dec. 1990)   A/RES/45/199
International Development Strategy for the Second United Nations Development Decade
    (24 Oct. 1970)   A/RES/2626 (XXV)
International Development Strategy for the Third United Nations Development Decade
    (5 Dec. 1980)   A/RES/35/56
Manila Declaration on the Peaceful Settlement of International Disputes (15 Nov. 1982)   A/RES/37/10
Model Law on Cross-Border Insolvency (15 Dec. 1997)   A/RES/52/158
Model Law on Electronic Commerce (16 Dec. 1996)   A/RES/51/162
Model Strategies and Practical Measures on the Elimination of Violence against Women in
    the Field of Crime Prevention and Criminal Justice (12 Dec. 1997)   A/RES/52/86
Model Treaty on Extradition (14 Dec. 1990)   A/RES/45/116
Model Treaty on Mutual Assistance in Criminal Matters and Optional Protocol concerning the
    Proceeds of Crime (14 Dec. 1990)   A/RES/45/117
Model Treaty on the Transfer of Proceedings in Criminal Matters (14 Dec. 1990)   A/RES/45/118
Model Treaty on the Transfer of Supervision of Offenders Conditionally Sentenced or Conditionally
    Released (14 Dec. 1990)   A/RES/45/119
Optional Protocol to the Convention on the Elimination of All Forms of Discrimination against
    Women (6 Oct. 1999)   A/RES/54/4
Optional Protocols to the Convention on the Rights of the Child, on the Involvement of Children in
    Armed Conflict and on the Sale of Children, Child Prostitution and Child Pornography
    (16 May 2000)   A/RES/54/263
Principles and Guidelines for International Negotiations (8 Dec. 1998)   A/RES/53/101
Principles for the Protection of Persons with Mental Illness and for the Improvement of Mental
    Health Care (17 Dec. 1991)   A/RES/46/119
Principles Governing the Use by States of Artificial Earth Satellites for International Direct
    Television Broadcasting (10 Dec. 1982)   A/RES/37/92
Principles of International Cooperation in the Detection, Arrest, Extradition and Punishment of
    Persons Guilty of War Crimes and Crimes against Humanity (3 Dec. 1973)   A/RES/3074 (XXVIII)
Principles of Medical Ethics relevant to the Role of Health Personnel, particularly Physicians, in
    the Protection of Prisoners and Detainees against Torture and Other Cruel, Inhuman or
    Degrading Treatment or Punishment (18 Dec. 1982)   A/RES/37/194
Principles relating to Remote Sensing of the Earth from Outer Space (3 Dec. 1986)   A/RES/41/65
Principles relating to the Status of National Institutions for the Promotion and Protection of
    Human Rights (Paris Principles) (20 Dec. 1993)   A/RES/48/134
Principles relevant to the Use of Nuclear Power Sources in Outer Space (14 Dec. 1992)   A/RES/47/68
Principles that should Govern Further Actions of States in the Field of the Freezing and Reduction
    of Military Budgets (15 Dec. 1989)   A/RES/44/114 A
Principles which should Guide Members in Determining Whether or Not an Obligation Exists to
    Transmit the Information Called for under Article 73 e of the Charter (15 Dec. 1960)   A/RES/1541 (XV)
Proclamation on Aging (16 Oct. 1992)   A/RES/47/5

Protocol against the Illicit Manufacturing of and Trafficking in Firearms, Their Parts and Components and Ammunition, supplementing the United Nations Convention against Transnational Organized Crime (31 May 2001) — A/RES/55/255

Protocol against the Smuggling of Migrants by Land, Sea and Air, supplementing the United Nations Convention against Transnational Organized Crime (15 Nov. 2000) — A/RES/55/25 (Annex III)

Protocol Amending the Agreements, Conventions and Protocols on Narcotic Drugs (9 Nov. 1946) — A/RES/54 (I)

Protocol Bringing under International Control Drugs outside the Scope of the Convention of 13 July 1931 for Limiting the Manufacture and Regulating the Distribution of Narcotic Drugs (8 Oct. 1948) — A/RES/211 (III)

Protocol to Prevent, Suppress and Punish Trafficking in Persons, Especially Women and Children, supplementing the United Nations Convention against Transnational Organized Crime (15 Nov. 2000) — A/RES/55/25 (Annex II)

Standard Rules on the Equalization of Opportunities for Persons with Disabilities (20 Dec. 1993) — A/RES/48/96

Statement of Principles and Programme of Action of the United Nations Crime Prevention and Criminal Justice Programme (18 Dec. 1991) — A/RES/46/152

Statute of the Office of the United Nations High Commissioner for Refugees (14 Dec. 1950) — A/RES/428 (V)

Statute of the United Nations System Staff College in Turin, Italy (12 July 2001) — A/RES/55/278

Treaty on Principles Governing the Activities of States in the Exploration and Use of Outer Space, including the Moon and Other Celestial Bodies (19 Dec. 1966) — A/RES/2222 (XXI)

Treaty on the Non-Proliferation of Nuclear Weapons (12 June 1968) — A/RES/2373 (XXII)

Treaty on the Prohibition of the Emplacement of Nuclear Weapons and Other Weapons of Mass Destruction on the Seabed and the Ocean Floor and in the Subsoil Thereof (7 Dec. 1970) — A/RES/2660 (XXV)

United Nations Convention on Independent Guarantees and Stand-by Letters of Credit (11 Dec. 1995) — A/RES/50/48

United Nations Convention on International Bills of Exchange and International Promissory Notes (9 Dec. 1988) — A/RES/43/165

United Nations Convention against Transnational Organized Crime (15 Nov. 2000) — A/RES/55/25

United Nations Declaration against Corruption and Bribery in International Commercial Transactions (16 Dec. 1996) — A/RES/51/191

United Nations Declaration on Crime and Public Security (12 Dec. 1996) — A/RES/51/60

United Nations Declaration on the Elimination of All Forms of Racial Discrimination (20 Nov. 1963) — A/RES/1904 (XVIII)

United Nations Guidelines for the Prevention of Juvenile Delinquency (The Riyadh Guidelines) (14 Dec. 1990) — A/RES/45/112

United Nations Millennium Declaration (8 Sept. 2000) — A/RES/55/2

United Nations Model Rules for the Conciliation of Disputes between States (11 Dec. 1995) — A/RES/50/50

United Nations New Agenda for the Development of Africa in the 1990s (18 Dec. 1991) — A/RES/46/151

United Nations Principles for Older Persons (16 Dec. 1991) — A/RES/46/91

United Nations Rules for the Protection of Juveniles Deprived of Their Liberty (14 Dec. 1990) — A/RES/45/113

United Nations Standard Minimum Rules for Non-Custodial Measures (The Tokyo Rules) (14 Dec. 1990) — A/RES/45/110

United Nations Standard Minimum Rules for the Administration of Juvenile Justice (The Beijing Rules) (29 Nov. 1985) — A/RES/40/33

Universal Declaration of Human Rights (10 Dec. 1948) — A/RES/217 A (III)

Vienna Declaration on Crime and Justice: Meeting the Challenges of the Twenty-first Century (4 Dec. 2000) — A/RES/55/59

World Charter for Nature (28 Oct. 1982) — A/RES/37/7

APPENDIX G
United Nations Chronology

1941

June 12   Inter-Allied DECLARATION signed in London "to work together, with other free peoples, both in war and in peace."

August 14   U.S. president Franklin Delano ROOSEVELT and British prime minister Winston CHURCHILL issue the ATLANTIC CHARTER

1942

January 1   Twenty-six nations issue the "DECLARATION BY UNITED NATIONS"

1943

May 18–June 3   United Nations Conference on Food and Agriculture convenes in Hot Springs, Virginia

October 30   MOSCOW CONFERENCE OF FOREIGN MINISTERS meets and CHINA, the USSR, the UNITED STATES, and the United Kingdom agree on the need for a postwar international organization

November 9   44 nations sign agreement establishing the UNITED NATIONS RELIEF AND REHABILITATION ADMINISTRATION (UNRRA), the UN's first formal agency

November 23–26   CAIRO CONFERENCE convenes

November 27–December 1   TEHERAN CONFERENCE convenes

December 3–7   CAIRO CONFERENCE reconvenes

1944

May 30   UNITED STATES issues invitations to Great Britain, CHINA, and the Soviet Union to participate in the DUMBARTON OAKS CONFERENCE

July 1–22   United Nations Monetary and Financial Conference convenes at BRETTON WOODS, New Hampshire

August 21–October 7   DUMBARTON OAKS CONFERENCE convenes

November 1–December 7   International Civil Aviation Conference convenes in Chicago

1945

January 30–February 2   Prime Minister CHURCHILL and President ROOSEVELT meet in Malta in preparation for the YALTA CONFERENCE

February 4–11   YALTA CONFERENCE convenes. Big Three agree on voting formula for the SECURITY COUNCIL

February 11   Western Hemispheric states meet at the Chapultepec Palace in Mexico City for the Inter-American Conference on War and Peace Problems to discuss the role of REGIONAL ORGANIZATIONS in the proposed United Nations

February 21–March 8   Central and South American republics, except Argentina, meet and agree to DUMBARTON OAKS Proposals

April 9–20   Jurists from 44 nations draft STATUTE OF THE INTERNATIONAL COURT OF JUSTICE

April 25–June 25   UNITED NATIONS CONFERENCE ON INTERNATIONAL ORGANIZATION convenes in San Francisco

June 26   The United Nations CHARTER is signed at the San Francisco Conference

July 6   Nicaragua is the first state to ratify the UN CHARTER

August 8   UNITED STATES is the first state to deposit its ratification of the CHARTER

August 15   INTERNATIONAL CIVIL AVIATION ORGANIZATION (ICAO) comes into being

October 16   Quebec Conference of 44 nations creates the FOOD AND AGRICULTURE ORGANIZATION (FAO)

October 24   The United Nations CHARTER comes into force

November 16 The London Conference of 37 nations adopts the constitution of the UNITED NATIONS EDUCATIONAL, SCIENTIFIC AND CULTURAL ORGANIZATION (UNESCO)

December 16 USSR, U.S., U.K. foreign ministers agree to creation of UN COMMISSION ON ATOMIC ENERGY

December 27 29 nations sign the Articles of Agreement establishing the INTERNATIONAL MONETARY FUND (IMF) and the WORLD BANK (International Bank of Reconstruction and Development—IBRD)

1946

January 10–February 14 First session of the GENERAL ASSEMBLY meets in London

January 17 SECURITY COUNCIL holds its first meeting in London

January 19 SECURITY COUNCIL takes up the presence of Soviet troops in Iran as its first dispute resolution deliberation

January 23–February 18 ECONOMIC AND SOCIAL COUNCIL holds its first meeting

January 24 GENERAL ASSEMBLY passes its first RESOLUTION, which establishes the ATOMIC ENERGY COMMISSION

January 31 The judges of the PERMANENT COURT OF INTERNATIONAL JUSTICE resign

February 1 Trygve LIE becomes the first SECRETARY-GENERAL

February 4 MILITARY STAFF COMMITTEE meets for the first time

February 6 First Justice elected to the INTERNATIONAL COURT OF JUSTICE

February 13 GENERAL ASSEMBLY adopts the CONVENTION on the Privileges and Immunities of the United Nations

February 14 GENERAL ASSEMBLY establishes interim UN HEADQUARTERS in New York City

February 16 ECONOMIC AND SOCIAL COUNCIL creates COMMISSION ON HUMAN RIGHTS and COMMISSION ON NARCOTIC DRUGS

February 16 USSR casts the first SECURITY COUNCIL VETO

March 21 Temporary UN HEADQUARTERS are established at Hunter College in New York City

April 3 INTERNATIONAL COURT OF JUSTICE meets for the first time

April 8–18 LEAGUE OF NATIONS is abolished

June 14 UNITED STATES submits the BARUCH PLAN to the UNITED NATIONS ATOMIC ENERGY COMMISSION

June 21 ECONOMIC AND SOCIAL COUNCIL creates the COMMISSION ON THE STATUS OF WOMEN (CSW)

June 21 ECONOMIC AND SOCIAL COUNCIL adopts "CONSULTATIVE STATUS" for NON-GOVERNMENTAL ORGANIZATIONS

June 26 France casts its first VETO

August 2 In Luxembourg, twelve NATION-STATES found the WORLD FEDERATION OF UNITED NATIONS ASSOCIATIONS (WFUNA)

August 16 UN moves its HEADQUARTERS to Lake Success, New York

September 21 GENERAL ASSEMBLY creates the ADMINISTRATIVE COMMITTEE ON COORDINATION (ACC)

October 3 ECONOMIC AND SOCIAL COUNCIL creates the POPULATION COMMISSION

October 24 GENERAL ASSEMBLY officially designates "UNITED NATIONS DAY"

December 7 GENERAL ASSEMBLY adopts the UN Emblem

December 11 GENERAL ASSEMBLY establishes the UNITED NATIONS INTERNATIONAL CHILDREN'S EMERGENCY FUND (UNICEF)

December 11 United Nations and the Carnegie Foundation agree on terms for the UN's use of the Peace Palace in The Hague

December 13 GENERAL ASSEMBLY approves eight TRUSTEESHIP agreements

December 14 GENERAL ASSEMBLY approves New York City as the permanent HEADQUARTERS of the United Nations

December 14 GENERAL ASSEMBLY approves SPECIALIZED AGENCY agreements with the INTERNATIONAL LABOUR ORGANIZATION (ILO), the UN FOOD AND AGRICULTURE ORGANIZATION (FAO), the UN EDUCATIONAL, SCIENTIFIC AND CULTURAL ORGANIZATION (UNESCO), and the INTERNATIONAL CIVIL AVIATION ORGANIZATION (ICAO)

1947

January 27–February 10 First session of the COMMISSION ON HUMAN RIGHTS meets

February 10–24 First session of the COMMISSION ON THE STATUS OF WOMEN meets

March 26–April 28 TRUSTEESHIP COUNCIL holds its first meeting

March 28 ECONOMIC AND SOCIAL COUNCIL establishes ECONOMIC COMMISSION FOR EUROPE and the ECONOMIC COMMISSION FOR ASIA AND THE FAR EAST

April 28–May 15 GENERAL ASSEMBLY holds its first SPECIAL SESSION—on Palestine

May 15 GENERAL ASSEMBLY establishes Special Committee on Palestine

July 24–August 8 First session of the COMMISSION ON NARCOTIC DRUGS meets

August 31 Special Committee on Palestine recommends partition

October 20 GENERAL ASSEMBLY adopts the UN FLAG

October 30 Trading nations adopt the GENERAL AGREEMENT ON TARIFFS AND TRADE

November 14   GENERAL ASSEMBLY establishes Temporary Commission on Korea

November 15   GENERAL ASSEMBLY approves the WORLD BANK and the INTERNATIONAL MONETARY FUND

November 21   GENERAL ASSEMBLY establishes the INTERNATIONAL LAW COMMISSION

November 29   GENERAL ASSEMBLY approves Palestine partition plan

1948

February 25   ECONOMIC AND SOCIAL COUNCIL establishes the ECONOMIC COMMISSION FOR LATIN AMERICA (ECLA)

May 2   ORGANIZATION OF AMERICAN STATES (OAS) approves the American DECLARATION on the Rights and Duties of Man

May 14   United Kingdom relinquishes mandate in Palestine; state of Israel declares independence

May 29   UN establishes UN TRUCE SUPERVISION ORGANIZATION (UNTSO), first observer mission

June 17   INTERNATIONAL LAW COMMISSION (ILC) convenes its first meeting

July 6   Commandant René de Labarrière, a military observer from France serving in the UNITED NATIONS TRUCE SUPERVISION ORGANIZATION (UNTSO) becomes the first UN peacekeeper in history to die in the line of duty

July 10   WORLD HEALTH ORGANIZATION (WHO) becomes a SPECIALIZED AGENCY of the United Nations

September 17   Assassin kills UN SPECIAL REPRESENTATIVE to Palestine Folke BERNADOTTE

October 16   GENERAL ASSEMBLY grants OBSERVER STATUS to the ORGANIZATION OF AMERICAN STATES

November 19   GENERAL ASSEMBLY creates the UN Relief for Palestine Refugees Agency

December 9   GENERAL ASSEMBLY approves the CONVENTION on GENOCIDE

December 10   GENERAL ASSEMBLY adopts the UNIVERSAL DECLARATION OF HUMAN RIGHTS

1949

January 7   Ralph BUNCHE achieves cease-fire in the Arab-Israeli War

April 9   INTERNATIONAL COURT OF JUSTICE finds against Albania in *Corfu Channel Case*, its first decision handed down

May 11   GENERAL ASSEMBLY admits Israel to UN MEMBERSHIP

August 15   ECONOMIC AND SOCIAL COUNCIL recommends the creation of the EXPANDED PROGRAM OF TECHNICAL ASSISTANCE (EPTA)

September 14   Construction of UN HEADQUARTERS begins in New York City

October 24   Officials lay cornerstone for UN HEADQUARTERS in New York City

December 8   GENERAL ASSEMBLY establishes the UNITED NATIONS RELIEF AND WORKS AGENCY FOR PALESTINIAN REFUGEES IN THE NEAR EAST (UNRWA)

1950

May 1   UNITED NATIONS RELIEF AND WORKS AGENCY FOR PALESTINIAN REFUGEES IN THE NEAR EAST (UNRWA) begins operations

June 27   SECURITY COUNCIL calls upon member states to assist South Korea to repel invasion from the North

November 1   GENERAL ASSEMBLY grants OBSERVER STATUS to the League of Arab States

November 3   GENERAL ASSEMBLY approves UNITING FOR PEACE RESOLUTION

December 14   GENERAL ASSEMBLY adopts the Statute of the Office of the UNITED NATIONS HIGH COMMISSIONER FOR REFUGEES (UNHCR)

December 14   GENERAL ASSEMBLY adopts the CONVENTION RELATING TO THE STATUS OF REFUGEES

1951

January 1   Office of the UNITED NATIONS HIGH COMMISSIONER FOR REFUGEES begins operation

January 12   GENOCIDE Convention enters into force

February 1   GENERAL ASSEMBLY declares CHINA an aggressor in the KOREAN WAR

March 28   United Nations reaches agreement with the UNITED STATES allowing it to issue and use its own stamps

March 30   SECURITY COUNCIL appoints Frank P. Graham UN SPECIAL REPRESENTATIVE for KASHMIR

May 18   GENERAL ASSEMBLY recommends embargo against North Korea and CHINA

July 2–25   UN Conference on the Status of Refugees and Stateless Persons convenes

July 10   Cease-fire talks begin in the KOREAN WAR

July 25   Nations sign the CONVENTION RELATING TO THE STATUS OF REFUGEES

October 24   United Nations issues stamps for the first time

December 20   GENERAL ASSEMBLY approves the WORLD METEOROLOGICAL ORGANIZATION (WMO) as a SPECIALIZED AGENCY

1952

January 11 GENERAL ASSEMBLY replaces the ATOMIC ENERGY COMMISSION with the DISARMAMENT COMMISSION

February 1 GENERAL ASSEMBLY adopts RESOLUTIONS describing the requirements a state must meet to be in accordance with the MEMBERSHIP criteria stipulated in Article 4 of the CHARTER

February 27 United Nations formally inaugurates HEAD-QUARTERS building in New York City

November 10 Trygve LIE submits his resignation as SECRE-TARY-GENERAL

December 20 GENERAL ASSEMBLY approves the CONVEN-TION ON POLITICAL RIGHTS OF WOMEN

1953

March 13 USSR VETOES the nomination of Lester PEARSON to succeed Trygve LIE as UN SECRETARY-GENERAL

March 31 SECURITY COUNCIL meets and nominates Dag HAMMARSKJÖLD to be UN SECRETARY-GENERAL without his knowledge

April 10 GENERAL ASSEMBLY appoints Dag HAMMARSKJÖLD of Sweden as the UN's second SECRETARY-GENERAL

July 27 UN Command signs Armistice Agreement with Chinese–North Korean Command

July 30 UN forces withdraw from the demilitarized zone in Korea

October 6 UNITED NATIONS CHILDREN'S FUND becomes permanent agency, retains "emergency" acronym UNICEF

December 8 U.S. president Eisenhower delivers "ATOMS FOR PEACE" speech to the GENERAL ASSEMBLY

1954

April 22 CONVENTION ON THE STATUS OF REFUGEES enters into force

July 7 CONVENTION ON THE POLITICAL RIGHTS OF WOMEN enters into force

July 13 INTERNATIONAL COURT OF JUSTICE issues advisory opinion endorsing UN ADMINISTRATIVE TRIBUNAL awards to fired UN SECRETARIAT members

Autumn UN HIGH COMMISSIONER FOR REFUGEES receives Nobel Peace Prize

August 31–September 10 World POPULATION Conference convenes

September 8 SOUTHEAST ASIAN TREATY ORGANIZATION (SEATO) comes into being

December 4 GENERAL ASSEMBLY approves the Statute of the INTERNATIONAL ATOMIC ENERGY AGENCY (IAEA)

1955

July 1 U.S. president Eisenhower makes "Open Skies" PRO-POSAL

August 8–20 International Conference on the Peaceful Uses of Atomic Energy convenes

November 3 GENERAL ASSEMBLY approves the charter of the INTERNATIONAL FINANCE CORPORATION

1956

July 24 INTERNATIONAL FINANCE CORPORATION begins operation

July 26 Egyptian president Gamal Abdul NASSER national-izes the Suez Canal

October 13 SECURITY COUNCIL approves six principles for the settlement of the SUEZ CRISIS

October 23 The Conference of Signatories approves the Statute of the INTERNATIONAL ATOMIC ENERGY AGENCY (IAEA)

October 28 SECURITY COUNCIL takes up the Hungarian crisis

October 29 Israel invades Egypt

October 30 France and the United Kingdom cast their first vetoes in the SECURITY COUNCIL, blocking RESOLUTION calling upon them and Israel to refrain from the use of force in the SUEZ CRISIS

October 31 France and the United Kingdom invade EGYPT

November 1–10 GENERAL ASSEMBLY convenes its first EMERGENCY SPECIAL SESSION, and takes up the SUEZ CRI-SIS

November 5 GENERAL ASSEMBLY creates UNITED NATIONS EMERGENCY FORCE (UNEF), first UN PEACEKEEPING mis-sion

1957

January 24 SECURITY COUNCIL calls for plebiscite in KASH-MIR

February 20 GENERAL ASSEMBLY approves the CONVEN-TION on the Nationality of Married WOMEN

March 1 Israeli government announces that it will with-draw from the Suez Canal area, to be replaced by UN peacekeepers

July 29 Statute of the INTERNATIONAL ATOMIC ENERGY AGENCY (IAEA) enters into force

November 19 MEMBERSHIP of the UN DISARMAMENT COM-MISSION increases from 11 to 25

December 14 GENERAL ASSEMBLY establishes the SPECIAL UNITED NATIONS FUND FOR ECONOMIC DEVELOPMENT (SUNFED)

1958

April 29   ECONOMIC AND SOCIAL COUNCIL establishes the ECONOMIC COMMISSION FOR AFRICA (ECA)

June 11   SECURITY COUNCIL establishes the United Nations Observer Group in Lebanon (UNOGIL)

August 8–21   GENERAL ASSEMBLY convenes an EMERGENCY SPECIAL SESSION on the crisis in Lebanon and Jordan

November 4   MEMBERSHIP of the UN DISARMAMENT COMMISSION expands to include all UN member states

December 9   United Nations Observer Group in Lebanon (UNOGIL) ceases operations

1959

January 1   SPECIAL UNITED NATIONS FUND FOR ECONOMIC DEVELOPMENT (SUNFED) comes into being

March 13   GENERAL ASSEMBLY terminates the French TRUSTEESHIP over Cameroon

November 20   GENERAL ASSEMBLY adopts the DECLARATION ON THE RIGHTS OF THE CHILD

December 1   Twelve nations sign the ANTARCTIC TREATY

December 12   GENERAL ASSEMBLY creates the COMMITTEE ON PEACEFUL USES OF OUTER SPACE (COPUOS)

1960

March 17–April 26   Second LAW OF THE SEA Conference convenes

May 23–June 24   UN Tin Conference convenes

July 12   Congolese leaders and Belgium request the dispatch of UN troops to the CONGO to restore order

July 13   SECRETARY-GENERAL HAMMARSKJÖLD employs Article 99 of the UN CHARTER to convene the SECURITY COUNCIL on the CONGO crisis

July 14   SECURITY COUNCIL establishes PEACEKEEPING mission to the CONGO

August 1   UNITED NATIONS OPERATION IN THE CONGO (ONUC) arrives in the country

September 17–19   GENERAL ASSEMBLY meets in EMERGENCY SPECIAL SESSION on the CONGO crisis

September 20   UN admits 17 new members, 16 from AFRICA—largest number admitted to date in one year

September 22   Soviet premier Nikita Khrushchev makes "TROIKA PROPOSAL," proposes replacement of the post of SECRETARY-GENERAL with a three-person committee

November 8   INTERNATIONAL DEVELOPMENT ASSOCIATION (IDA) begins operation

December 14   GENERAL ASSEMBLY adopts the DECLARATION ON THE GRANTING OF INDEPENDENCE TO COLONIAL COUNTRIES AND PEOPLES

1961

February 15   SECRETARY-GENERAL HAMMARSKJÖLD expands the mission of the United Nations forces in the CONGO

February 21   SECURITY COUNCIL authorizes the use of force in order to prevent civil war in the CONGO

June 23   ANTARCTIC TREATY enters into force

September 18   SECRETARY-GENERAL HAMMARSKJÖLD dies in an airplane crash while on a mission to the CONGO

November 3   GENERAL ASSEMBLY appoints U THANT Acting SECRETARY-GENERAL in the wake of HAMMARSKJÖLD's death

1962

May 1   UNITED NATIONS TEMPORARY EXECUTIVE AUTHORITY transfers full administrative control over West New Guinea to INDONESIA

May 25   The Soviet Union and the UNITED STATES place "Measures to Prevent Further Dissemination of Nuclear Weapons" on the agenda of the EIGHTEEN NATION DISARMAMENT COMMITTEE (ENDC)

July 20   INTERNATIONAL COURT OF JUSTICE issues advisory opinion that PEACEKEEPING costs are "expenses of the organization" to be paid by the regular BUDGET

October 23–25   SECURITY COUNCIL conducts debate on the CUBAN MISSILE CRISIS

November 3   GENERAL ASSEMBLY appoints U THANT to a full term as SECRETARY-GENERAL

November 30   U THANT elected SECRETARY-GENERAL for a term ending on November 3, 1966

1963

May 14–June 17   GENERAL ASSEMBLY convenes SPECIAL SESSION on the financial problems of the United Nations

June 11   SECURITY COUNCIL authorizes the creation of the UNITED NATIONS YEMEN OBSERVER MISSION (UNYOM)

August 7   SECURITY COUNCIL calls for a voluntary arms embargo against South Africa

November 20   GENERAL ASSEMBLY adopts the United Nations DECLARATION on the Elimination of All Forms of Racial Discrimination

December 17   GENERAL ASSEMBLY recommends increasing SECURITY COUNCIL MEMBERSHIP from 11 to 15 and ECONOMIC AND SOCIAL COUNCIL membership from 18 to 25

1964

March 4   SECURITY COUNCIL approves a PEACEKEEPING mission to Cyprus (UNFICYP)

March 23–June 15   First UNITED NATIONS CONFERENCE ON TRADE AND DEVELOPMENT (UNCTAD) convenes

March 27   UNITED NATIONS FORCE IN CYPRUS (UNFICYP) begins operations

June 30   UN Operations in the CONGO (UNOC) end after four years

September 4   UNITED NATIONS YEMEN OBSERVER MISSION (UNYOM) ends

December 1–23   "No-Vote" session of the GENERAL ASSEMBLY convenes with all business conducted in plenary session in order to avoid invocation of the CHARTER's Article 19

December 30   GENERAL ASSEMBLY establishes the UNITED NATIONS CONFERENCE ON TRADE AND DEVELOPMENT (UNCTAD) as a body of the United Nations

1965

January 21   INDONESIA withdraws from MEMBERSHIP in the United Nations

August 16   UNITED STATES gives up its effort to deny the SOVIET UNION a vote in the GENERAL ASSEMBLY under Article 19 of the UN CHARTER

August 31   Amendments to Articles 23, 27, and 61 of the UN CHARTER, enlarging the MEMBERSHIP of the ECONOMIC AND SOCIAL COUNCIL from 18 to 27, and the SECURITY COUNCIL from 11 to 15 (with a VOTING majority raised from seven to nine) enter into force

November 11   GENERAL ASSEMBLY grants OBSERVER STATUS to the ORGANIZATION OF AFRICAN UNITY

November 20   SECURITY COUNCIL applies mandatory SANCTIONS for the first time (on Rhodesia)

November 22   GENERAL ASSEMBLY establishes the UNITED NATIONS DEVELOPMENT PROGRAMME (UNDP)

December 10   UNICEF wins Nobel Peace Prize

December 20   GENERAL ASSEMBLY approves the DECLARATION ON THE RIGHTS OF THE CHILD

December 21   GENERAL ASSEMBLY adopts the International CONVENTION on the Elimination of All Forms of Racial Discrimination

1966

March 22   United Nations terminates the operations of the UN INDIA-PAKISTAN OBSERVATION MISSION (UNIPOM)

September 19   INDONESIA restores its MEMBERSHIP in the United Nations

October 27   GENERAL ASSEMBLY ends South Africa's mandate over South-West AFRICA

December 16   SECURITY COUNCIL imposes mandatory SANCTIONS against Rhodesia

December 16   GENERAL ASSEMBLY adopts the INTERNATIONAL COVENANT ON CIVIL AND POLITICAL RIGHTS, and the INTERNATIONAL COVENANT ON ECONOMIC, SOCIAL AND CULTURAL RIGHTS

December 17   GENERAL ASSEMBLY creates the UNITED NATIONS COMMISSION ON INTERNATIONAL TRADE LAW (UNCITRAL) as the "core legal body" in its field

1967

May 18   United Arab Republic requests the immediate withdrawal of the UNITED NATIONS EMERGENCY FORCE (UNEF) from Egypt

May 19   SECRETARY-GENERAL U THANT withdraws UNEF from Suez Canal Zone

June 5   MIDDLE EAST WAR OF 1967 commences

June 10   Parties halt fighting in the MIDDLE EAST WAR OF 1967

July 9   SECURITY COUNCIL establishes UNITED NATIONS TRUCE SUPERVISION ORGANIZATION (UNTSO) to monitor cease-fire along the Suez Canal

November 7   GENERAL ASSEMBLY adopts the DECLARATION on the Elimination of Discrimination against WOMEN

November 22   SECURITY COUNCIL adopts RESOLUTION 242 following 1967 MIDDLE EAST WAR

1968

January 31   MEMBERSHIP of the TRUSTEESHIP COUNCIL no longer conforms to the requirements of the UN CHARTER because of the achievement of independence by Nauru

February 1–March 29   Second UNITED NATIONS CONFERENCE ON TRADE AND DEVELOPMENT (UNCTAD) convenes in New Delhi

May 27   SECURITY COUNCIL imposes comprehensive mandatory economic SANCTIONS against Southern Rhodesia

June 12   GENERAL ASSEMBLY approves the NUCLEAR NONPROLIFERATION TREATY (NPT)

November 26   GENERAL ASSEMBLY adopts the CONVENTION on the Non-Applicability of Statutory Limitations to War Crimes and Crimes against Humanity

1969

January 4   International CONVENTION on the Elimination of All Forms of Racial Discrimination comes into force

April 9–May 22   UN Conference on the Law of TREATIES adopts the International CONVENTION on the Law of Treaties

April 29   United Nations Social Defence Research Institute (UNSDRI), predecessor to the UNITED NATIONS INTERREGIONAL CRIME AND JUSTICE RESEARCH INSTITUTE (UNICRI) begins operations

July 3   SECURITY COUNCIL unanimously censures Israel for declaring Jerusalem its permanent and indivisible capital

Autumn   INTERNATIONAL LABOUR ORGANIZATION (ILO) wins Nobel Peace Prize

1970

May 12   SECURITY COUNCIL demands the withdrawal of Israeli forces from Lebanon

October 24   GENERAL ASSEMBLY adopts the DECLARATION on Principles of INTERNATIONAL LAW concerning Friendly Relations and Cooperation among States in accordance with the CHARTER OF THE UNITED NATIONS

December 17   GENERAL ASSEMBLY adopts the DECLARATION of Principles Governing the Seabed and Ocean Floor

1971

July 21   INTERNATIONAL COURT OF JUSTICE (ICJ) issues advisory opinion holding South Africa's control of NAMIBIA to be illegal

October 25   GENERAL ASSEMBLY seats the representatives of the People's Republic of CHINA

December 7   GENERAL ASSEMBLY adopts RESOLUTION 2793 demanding a cease-fire in the war between India and Pakistan

December 9   Ralph BUNCHE dies

December 14   GENERAL ASSEMBLY establishes the Office of Disaster Relief Coordinator (UNDRO)

December 16   GENERAL ASSEMBLY adopts the BIOLOGICAL WEAPONS CONVENTION (BWC)

December 16   GENERAL ASSEMBLY adopts a DECLARATION on the Indian Ocean as a zone of peace

December 17   India and Pakistan accept the cease-fire proposed by the GENERAL ASSEMBLY

December 20   GENERAL ASSEMBLY recommends amendment to Article 61 of the CHARTER, enlarging the ECONOMIC AND SOCIAL COUNCIL (ECOSOC) from 27 to 54 members

December 20   GENERAL ASSEMBLY adopts the DECLARATION on the Rights of Mentally Retarded Persons

1972

January 1   Kurt WALDHEIM becomes fourth SECRETARY-GENERAL of the United Nations

January 28–February 4   SECURITY COUNCIL meets for the first time away from UN HEADQUARTERS, in Addis Ababa, Ethiopia

April 13-May 21   Third UNITED NATIONS CONFERENCE ON TRADE AND DEVELOPMENT (UNCTAD) convenes in Santiago, Chile

June 5–16   UNITED NATIONS CONFERENCE ON THE HUMAN ENVIRONMENT (UNCHE) convenes in Stockholm, Sweden

November 2   GENERAL ASSEMBLY designates 1973–1982 as the Decade for Action to Combat Racism and Racial Discrimination

December 1   GENERAL ASSEMBLY establishes the UNITED NATIONS UNIVERSITY (UNU)

1973

March 3   80 nations sign the CONVENTION ON INTERNATIONAL TRADE IN ENDANGERED SPECIES OF WILD FAUNA AND FLORA (CITES)

September 24   Amendment to UN CHARTER's Article 61 expanding the MEMBERSHIP of the ECONOMIC AND SOCIAL COUNCIL (ECOSOC) from 27 to 54 comes into force

October 2   UNITED NATIONS ENVIRONMENT PROGRAMME (UNEP) opens its office in Nairobi, Kenya

October 22   SECURITY COUNCIL adopts RESOLUTION 338 following MIDDLE EAST WAR OF 1973

October 28   UNITED NATIONS TRUCE SUPERVISION ORGANIZATION (UNTSO) oversees first direct talks between Israeli and Egyptian officials in the Sinai

December 18   GENERAL ASSEMBLY adds Chinese and Arabic to the official LANGUAGES of the United Nations

1974

May 1   GENERAL ASSEMBLY adopts the DECLARATION on the Establishment of a NEW INTERNATIONAL ECONOMIC ORDER (NIEO)

August 19–30   World Population Conference convenes in Bucharest

November 11   GENERAL ASSEMBLY grants OBSERVER STATUS to the European Economic Community

November 13   GENERAL ASSEMBLY recognizes the Palestine Liberation Organization as the "sole legitimate representative of the Palestinian people"

November 22 GENERAL ASSEMBLY grants UN OBSERVER STATUS to the Palestine Liberation Organization

December 12 GENERAL ASSEMBLY adopts the CHARTER ON THE ECONOMIC RIGHTS AND DUTIES OF STATES

December 14 GENERAL ASSEMBLY approves a definition of AGGRESSION

December 17 GENERAL ASSEMBLY creates the UN World Food Council (WFC)

December 17 GENERAL ASSEMBLY approves agreement establishing WORLD INTELLECTUAL PROPERTY ORGANIZATION as a SPECIALIZED AGENCY

1975

January 20 UNITED NATIONS UNIVERSITY opens in Tokyo

March 17–28 COMMISSION ON TRANSNATIONAL CORPORATIONS meets for the first time

March 26 CONVENTION ON THE PROHIBITION OF BACTERIOLOGICAL (BIOLOGICAL) WEAPONS enters into force

May 19–30 INTERNATIONAL CIVIL SERVICE COMMISSION meets for the first time

June 19–July 2 First United Nations Conference on WOMEN meets in Mexico City

June 23–28 UN World Food Council meets for the first time

July 1 CONVENTION ON INTERNATIONAL TRADE IN ENDANGERED SPECIES OF WILD FAUNA AND FLORA (CITES) enters into force

November 10 GENERAL ASSEMBLY adopts "ZIONISM IS RACISM" RESOLUTION

November 10 GENERAL ASSEMBLY grants OBSERVER STATUS to the Organization of the Islamic Conference

December 9 GENERAL ASSEMBLY adopts the DECLARATION on Torture and Other Cruel, Inhuman or Degrading Treatment

December 9 GENERAL ASSEMBLY adopts the DECLARATION on the Rights of Disabled Persons

1976

January 3 INTERNATIONAL COVENANT ON ECONOMIC, SOCIAL AND CULTURAL RIGHTS enters into force

March 23 INTERNATIONAL COVENANT ON CIVIL AND POLITICAL RIGHTS enters into force

May 3–28 Fourth UNITED NATIONS CONFERENCE ON TRADE AND DEVELOPMENT (UNCTAD) convenes in Nairobi, Kenya

October 18 GENERAL ASSEMBLY grants OBSERVER STATUS to the Commonwealth SECRETARIAT

1977

August 22–26 WORLD CONFERENCE against APARTHEID convenes in Lagos, Nigeria

August 29–September 9 UN Conference on DESERTIFICATION convenes in Nairobi

November 4 SECURITY COUNCIL imposes mandatory arms embargo against South Africa

December 15 GENERAL ASSEMBLY approves the designation of the INTERNATIONAL FUND FOR AGRICULTURAL DEVELOPMENT (IFAD) as a SPECIALIZED AGENCY

December 19 GENERAL ASSEMBLY approves a formal agreement of cooperation with the WORLD TOURISM ORGANIZATION (WTO/OMT)

1978

March 19 SECURITY COUNCIL establishes the UNITED NATIONS INTERIM FORCE IN LEBANON (UNIFIL)

May 23–July 1 First SPECIAL SESSION ON DISARMAMENT convenes

August 14–26 WORLD CONFERENCE TO COMBAT RACISM AND RACIAL DISCRIMINATION convenes

October 9–13 DISARMAMENT COMMISSION meets for the first time

December 19 GENERAL ASSEMBLY suspends the operations of the SPECIAL UNITED NATIONS FUND FOR ECONOMIC DEVELOPMENT (SUNFED)

1979

March 26 Egypt and Israel sign the Framework for Peace and a peace TREATY at the White House in Washington, D.C.

November 4 Iranian militants occupy the U.S. embassy in Tehran, Iran

December 4 SECURITY COUNCIL demands the release of Americans held in Iran

December 15 INTERNATIONAL COURT OF JUSTICE (ICJ) orders the government of Iran to release all American nationals held in Iran and that neither government undertake any action that would aggravate tensions

December 17 GENERAL ASSEMBLY adopts the International CONVENTION against the Taking of Hostages

December 18 GENERAL ASSEMBLY adopts the CONVENTION ON THE ELIMINATION OF ALL FORMS OF DISCRIMINATION AGAINST WOMEN

December 18 MOON AGREEMENT opens for signature

December 27 Soviet Union invades AFGHANISTAN

1980

May 8   WORLD HEALTH ORGANIZATION (WHO) declares smallpox eradicated

May 24   The INTERNATIONAL COURT OF JUSTICE (ICJ) finds in favor of the UNITED STATES and against Iran in the IRAN HOSTAGE CRISIS

October 1   UNITED NATIONS INSTITUTE FOR DISARMAMENT RESEARCH (UNIDIR) begins operation

October 10   GENERAL ASSEMBLY grants OBSERVER STATUS to the Asian-African Legal Consultative Committee

1981

September 1–14   UNITED NATIONS CONFERENCE ON THE LEAST DEVELOPED COUNTRIES meets in Paris and adopts "SUBSTANTIAL NEW PROGRAMME OF ACTION"

September 3–14   GENERAL ASSEMBLY convenes EMERGENCY SPECIAL SESSION on NAMIBIA

October 14   UN HIGH COMMISSIONER FOR REFUGEES wins Nobel Peace Prize

November 25   GENERAL ASSEMBLY adopts DECLARATION on the Elimination of All Forms of Intolerance and Discrimination Based on Religion or Belief

December 14   GENERAL ASSEMBLY declares the RIGHT TO DEVELOPMENT to be an inalienable right

December 15   GENERAL ASSEMBLY appoints Javier PÉREZ DE CUÉLLAR of Peru SECRETARY-GENERAL

1982

April 16   State parties to the CONVENTION ON THE ELIMINATION OF ALL FORMS OF DISCRIMINATION AGAINST WOMEN establish Committee of the same name.

June 6   Israel invades Lebanon; SECURITY COUNCIL responds with a demand for complete and unconditional withdrawal (Res. 509)

October 28   GENERAL ASSEMBLY adopts the World Charter for Nature

December 3   GENERAL ASSEMBLY adopts the DECLARATION on the Participation of WOMEN in Promoting International Peace and Security

December 10   117 nations sign UN CONVENTION on the LAW OF THE SEA

December 13   GENERAL ASSEMBLY approves the UNITED NATIONS INSTITUTE FOR DISARMAMENT RESEARCH (UNIDIR) as an autonomous institution within the UN framework

1983

August 1–12   Second WORLD CONFERENCE TO COMBAT RACISM AND RACIAL DISCRIMINATION convenes in Geneva

August 11   INTERNATIONAL RESEARCH AND TRAINING INSTITUTE FOR THE ADVANCEMENT OF WOMEN (INSTRAW) opens its permanent headquarters in Santo Domingo, Dominican Republic

November 1   CONVENTION ON THE CONSERVATION OF MIGRATORY SPECIES OF WILD ANIMALS enters into force

1984

April 6   UNITED STATES withdraws from the COMPULSORY JURISDICTION of the INTERNATIONAL COURT OF JUSTICE in cases involving Central America for a period of two years

May 10   INTERNATIONAL COURT OF JUSTICE calls on the UNITED STATES to desist in the mining of Nicaraguan ports

July 11   MOON AGREEMENT enters into force

December 3   GENERAL ASSEMBLY adopts DECLARATION on the Critical Economic Situation in Africa

December 10   GENERAL ASSEMBLY adopts the CONVENTION AGAINST TORTURE AND OTHER CRUEL, INHUMAN OR DEGRADING TREATMENT OR PUNISHMENT

December 11   United Nations publishes first *World Survey on the Role of WOMEN in DEVELOPMENT*

December 14   GENERAL ASSEMBLY adopts the DECLARATION on the Control of Drug Trafficking and Drug Abuse

December 14   Voluntary fund for the UN Decade for WOMEN becomes the UNITED NATIONS DEVELOPMENT FUND FOR WOMEN (UNIFEM), a separate entity in association with the UNITED NATIONS DEVELOPMENT PROGRAMME (UNDP)

December 17   SECRETARY-GENERAL creates the Office of Emergency Operations in Africa (OEOA) to coordinate all UN activities on the continent

1985

January 18   UNITED STATES informs the INTERNATIONAL COURT OF JUSTICE that it intends not to participate in the case brought against it by Nicaragua

February 4   CONVENTION AGAINST TORTURE is signed and enters into force on the same day

February 26   SECRETARY-GENERAL appoints a Coordinator for the Improvement of the Status of WOMEN in the SECRETARIAT, and establishes a committee for that purpose

March 22   20 nations sign the VIENNA CONVENTION FOR THE PROTECTION OF THE OZONE LAYER

April 9   GENERAL ASSEMBLY adopts the Statute of the INTER-NATIONAL RESEARCH AND TRAINING INSTITUTE FOR THE ADVANCEMENT OF WOMEN (INSTRAW)

July 15–27   Third United Nations Conference on WOMEN convenes in Nairobi, Kenya

December 17   GENERAL ASSEMBLY approves the designation of the UNITED NATIONS INDUSTRIAL DEVELOPMENT ORGANIZATION (UNIDO) as a SPECIALIZED AGENCY

December 18   GENERAL ASSEMBLY creates the Group of 18 to consider and make recommendations on the REFORM of UN administrative and financial operations

December 27   Terrorists bomb Rome and Vienna airports

1986

January 31   UNDER SECRETARY-GENERAL for Special Affairs Brian E. URQUHART leaves office after 41 years of service to the United Nations

February 24   SECURITY COUNCIL agrees on a cease-fire ultimatum to both sides in the IRAN-IRAQ WAR

June 27   INTERNATIONAL COURT OF JUSTICE in the *Nicaragua v. United States Case* rules that the UNITED STATES has violated customary INTERNATIONAL LAW

August 18   Group of 18 makes 71 recommendations to the SECRETARY-GENERAL on REFORM of the United Nations

October 10   GENERAL ASSEMBLY appoints Javier PÉREZ DE CUÉLLAR to a second term as SECRETARY-GENERAL

December 4   GENERAL ASSEMBLY adopts the DECLARATION ON THE RIGHT TO DEVELOPMENT

1987

April 20   Nafis Sadik of Pakistan becomes the first woman to head a major UN program—UNITED NATIONS POPULATION FUND (UNFPA)

May 14   SECURITY COUNCIL condemns the use of CHEMICAL WEAPONS by Iran and Iraq in violation of the Geneva PROTOCOL of 1925

June 26   CONVENTION on Torture enters into force

July 11   United Nations notes the birth of the five billionth person on Earth

July 20   SECURITY COUNCIL calls for and specifies conditions for a cease-fire in the IRAN-IRAQ WAR

August 7   Presidents of five Central American states sign GUATEMALA Agreement for the establishment of peace in the region

October 19   Gro Harlem BRUNDTLAND presents the report of the WORLD COMMISSION ON ENVIRONMENT AND DEVELOPMENT, *Our Common Future,* to the GENERAL ASSEMBLY

1988

February 17   The head of the UN TRUCE SUPERVISION ORGANIZATION, Lieutenant Colonel William Higgins, is abducted in Lebanon

March 11   UNITED STATES informs the United Nations that it will close the Palestine Liberation Organization Mission in New York under the U.S. Anti-TERRORISM Act

April 26   INTERNATIONAL COURT OF JUSTICE rules that the UNITED STATES is obligated to arbitrate the closing of the Palestine Liberation Organization Mission under the 1947 HEADQUARTERS Agreement

May 31–June 26   Third SPECIAL SESSION of the GENERAL ASSEMBLY on DISARMAMENT convenes but is unable to reach consensus on a Final Document

July 30   Common Fund for Commodities enters into force, providing capital to finance buffer stocks of commodities in price stabilization plan

August 2–5   Four-nation (UNITED STATES, ANGOLA, CUBA, South Africa) conference reaches agreement on the withdrawal of South Africa from NAMIBIA

August 9   SECURITY COUNCIL creates the UN Iran-Iraq Military Observer Group (UNIIMOG) to monitor the border between the two countries

August 20   UN-sponsored cease-fire in the IRAN-IRAQ WAR goes into effect

September 22   VIENNA CONVENTION FOR THE PROTECTION OF THE OZONE LAYER enters into force

September 29   UN Peacekeepers win Nobel Peace Prize

November 15   GENERAL ASSEMBLY SPECIAL SESSION decides that the UNITED NATIONS SYSTEM will refer to the Palestine Liberation Organization as "Palestine"

November 27   U.S. secretary of state George Shultz announces that his government will not grant a visa to Yasser Arafat to address the GENERAL ASSEMBLY in New York

December 13–15   GENERAL ASSEMBLY convenes in Geneva to debate the question of Palestine

December 22   SECURITY COUNCIL creates the UNITED NATIONS ANGOLA VERIFICATION MISSION (UNAVEM)

1989

January 1   MONTREAL PROTOCOL ON SUBSTANCES THAT DEPLETE THE OZONE LAYER enters into force

February 16   SECURITY COUNCIL authorizes UNITED NATIONS TRANSITION ASSISTANCE GROUP (UNTAG) to begin operations in NAMIBIA

March 20–22   UN Conference approves BASEL CONVENTION ON THE CONTROL OF TRANSBOUNDARY MOVEMENTS OF HAZARDOUS WASTES AND THEIR DISPOSAL

July 27 SECURITY COUNCIL creates UN OBSERVER MISSION FOR THE VERIFICATION OF ELECTIONS IN NICARAGUA (ONUVEN)

November 20 GENERAL ASSEMBLY adopts the CONVENTION on the Rights of the Child

November 22 GENERAL ASSEMBLY adopts 12 RESOLUTIONS penalizing South Africa for APARTHEID

December 15 GENERAL ASSEMBLY adopts the Second PROTOCOL of the INTERNATIONAL COVENANT ON CIVIL AND POLITICAL RIGHTS, aiming at the abolition of the death penalty

1990

March 5–9 WORLD CONFERENCE for Education for All convenes in Jomtien, Thailand

August 2 Iraq invades Kuwait

August 2 SECURITY COUNCIL RESOLUTION 660 condemns the Iraqi invasion of Kuwait and demands immediate and unconditional withdrawal

August 6 SECURITY COUNCIL RESOLUTION 661 imposes mandatory SANCTIONS on Iraq

September 2 CONVENTION on the Rights of the Child enters into force

September 29–30 World Summit for Children convenes

November 29 SECURITY COUNCIL approves RESOLUTION 678 authorizing states "to use all necessary means" in the liberation of Kuwait from Iraqi occupation, sets January 15, 1991, as the deadline for Iraqi implementation of Security Council RESOLUTIONS

December 16 GENERAL ASSEMBLY adopts the Model TREATY on Extradition

December 21 GENERAL ASSEMBLY establishes targets for the employment of WOMEN in the UN SECRETARIAT by 1995: 35 percent in professional posts, 25 percent in senior posts

1991

January 12–13 SECRETARY-GENERAL PÉREZ DE CUÉLLAR visits Iraq in order to urge President Saddam HUSSEIN to comply with all SECURITY COUNCIL RESOLUTIONS

January 16 34-nation coalition undertakes seven-week GULF WAR to drive Iraqi troops from Kuwait

February 23 UN ground forces begin operations in the GULF WAR

February 27 UN forces liberate Kuwait City

February 27 Iraq agrees to comply with all SECURITY COUNCIL RESOLUTIONS

April 6 GULF WAR ends with Iraqi acceptance of SECURITY COUNCIL conditions for a cease-fire

May 14–22 First UN nuclear inspection team does its work in Iraq

May 20 SECURITY COUNCIL establishes UNITED NATIONS OBSERVER MISSION IN EL SALVADOR (ONUSAL)

May 31 United Nations achieves a cease-fire in the 16-year Angolan civil war

June 9–15 First UN CHEMICAL WEAPONS inspection team does its work in Iraq

June 17 South African Parliament repeals the legal basis for APARTHEID

July 11 Second Optional PROTOCOL of the INTERNATIONAL COVENANT ON CIVIL AND POLITICAL RIGHTS enters into force

August 2–8 First UN BIOLOGICAL WEAPONS inspection team does its work in Iraq

August 16 UNITED NATIONS HIGH COMMISSIONER FOR REFUGEES and South Africa sign an agreement on the return of exiles and refugees to South Africa under UN supervision

September 17 GENERAL ASSEMBLY admits both North and South Korea to UN MEMBERSHIP, also admits three former republics of the Soviet Union: Latvia, Lithuania, and Estonia

September 27 Foreign Ministers of the five PERMANENT MEMBERS OF THE SECURITY COUNCIL issue a statement recognizing the central role of the United Nations in international affairs, pledging to support preventive diplomacy, and supporting increased UN PEACEKEEPING efforts

October 16 SECURITY COUNCIL establishes UNITED NATIONS ADVANCE MISSION IN CAMBODIA (UNAMIC)

December 16 GENERAL ASSEMBLY revokes "ZIONISM IS RACISM" RESOLUTION

December 24 Soviet Union, one of the founding members of the United Nations, ceases to exist

December 24 President Boris Yeltsin informs the UN SECRETARY-GENERAL that the RUSSIAN FEDERATION will take the seat of the former Soviet Union with the concurrence of the USSR republics

December 31 Through the GOOD OFFICES of the SECRETARY-GENERAL, the United Nations achieves a cease-fire in 12-year civil war in EL SALVADOR

1992

January 1 Boutros BOUTROS-GHALI assumes the post of UN SECRETARY-GENERAL

January 31 First SECURITY COUNCIL heads of state summit convenes in New York City

February 7 Margaret Joan Anstee of the United Kingdom becomes the first woman to head a PEACEKEEPING mission (UNITED NATIONS ANGOLA VERIFICATION MISSION,

UNAVEM) and to be appointed a SPECIAL REPRESENTA-TIVE OF THE SECRETARY-GENERAL (to ANGOLA)

March 2   Seven former republics of the Soviet Union gain MEMBERSHIP in the United Nations

March 8   SECRETARY-GENERAL announces a plan to improve the status of WOMEN in the SECRETARIAT from 1995 to 2000

May 5   BASEL CONVENTION ON THE CONTROL OF TRANS-BOUNDARY MOVEMENTS OF HAZARDOUS WASTES AND THEIR DISPOSAL enters into force

May 6   Mujahadeen forces establish an interim government in AFGHANISTAN, which is subsequently accepted as Afghanistan's representative in the United Nations

June 3–14   UNITED NATIONS CONFERENCE ON ENVIRON-MENT AND DEVELOPMENT (UNCED, Earth Summit) con-venes in Rio de Janeiro

June 4   UN FRAMEWORK CONVENTION ON CLIMATE CHANGE (UNFCCC) is opened for signature

June 5   CONVENTION ON BIOLOGICAL DIVERSITY is opened for signature

June 17   SECRETARY-GENERAL Boutros BOUTROS-GHALI issues AN AGENDA FOR PEACE

July 31   Georgia achieves MEMBERSHIP in the United Nations, the last of the former Soviet republics to do so

November 30   GENERAL ASSEMBLY adopts the CHEMICAL WEAPONS Convention

December 3   SECURITY COUNCIL passes RESOLUTION 794, finding the circumstances in SOMALIA to be a threat to international peace and security, approves the formation of the UNIFIED TASK FORCE (UNITAF)

December 16   SECURITY COUNCIL establishes the UNITED NATIONS OPERATION IN MOZAMBIQUE (ONUMOZ)

December 31   Czechoslovakia, one of the original members of the United Nations, ceases to exist

1993

January 13   CHEMICAL WEAPONS CONVENTION is opened for signature

February 12   United Nations establishes the COMMISSION ON SUSTAINABLE DEVELOPMENT (CSD)

March 23–25   INTER-AGENCY COMMITTEE ON SUSTAINABLE DEVELOPMENT (IACSD) holds its first meeting

June 14–25   WORLD CONFERENCE ON HUMAN RIGHTS con-venes in Vienna

July 3   Representatives of the United Nations and HAITI agree to the Governors Island Accord

July 27   ECONOMIC AND SOCIAL COUNCIL merges the INTERNATIONAL RESEARCH AND TRAINING INSTITUTE FOR THE ADVANCEMENT OF WOMEN (INSTRAW) and the UNITED NATIONS DEVELOPMENT FUND FOR WOMEN (UNIFEM) into a single program

December 20   GENERAL ASSEMBLY creates the Office of UN HIGH COMMISSIONER FOR HUMAN RIGHTS (UNHCHR)

December 20   GENERAL ASSEMBLY adopts the DECLARATION ON THE ELIMINATION OF VIOLENCE AGAINST WOMEN

1994

March 11   UN COMMISSION ON HUMAN RIGHTS (CHR) appoints a SPECIAL RAPPORTEUR on gender-based violence

April 6   Presidents of Rwanda and Burundi killed in down-ing of their aircraft, GENOCIDE of Tutsis in Rwanda begins

April 25–May 6   WORLD CONFERENCE on the SUSTAINABLE DEVELOPMENT of Small Island Developing States con-venes in Bridgetown, Barbados

May 6   SECRETARY-GENERAL BOUTROS-GHALI issues "AN AGENDA FOR DEVELOPMENT"

May 10   South African voters elect Nelson Mandela the country's first black president

May 24   SECURITY COUNCIL terminates the arms embargo against South Africa

September 5–13   INTERNATIONAL CONFERENCE ON POPU-LATION AND DEVELOPMENT convenes and issues the Cairo PROGRAMME for Action

October 14   The CONVENTION TO COMBAT DESERTIFICA-TION is opened for signature in Paris

November 16   CONVENTION on the LAW OF THE SEA enters into force

December 9   GENERAL ASSEMBLY adopts the DECLARATION on Measures to Eliminate International TERRORISM

December 9   GENERAL ASSEMBLY launches the International Decade of the World's INDIGENOUS PEOPLES

1995

January 1   The WORLD TRADE ORGANIZATION becomes the successor body to the GENERAL AGREEMENT ON TARIFFS AND TRADE

March 6–12   WORLD SUMMIT FOR SOCIAL DEVELOPMENT convenes in Copenhagen

July 12   Rosalyn Higgins is elected the first woman judge to the INTERNATIONAL COURT OF JUSTICE (ICJ)

September 4–15   FOURTH WORLD CONFERENCE ON WOMEN convenes in Beijing

September 17   Haitian military officers agree to relinquish power to a civilian government that will be assisted by the United Nations Support Mission in HAITI (UNSMIH)

December 4   Agreement for the Implementation of the Provisions of the United Nations CONVENTION on the LAW OF THE SEA Relating to the Conservation and Man-agement of Straddling Fish Stocks and Highly Migratory Fish Stocks is opened for signature

December 14   Parties sign the DAYTON PEACE ACCORDS in Paris

1996

April 27–May 11   UNITED NATIONS CONFERENCE ON TRADE AND DEVELOPMENT IX convenes in Midrand, South Africa

June 3–14   United Nations Conference on Human Settlements II convenes in Istanbul

September 24   COMPREHENSIVE NUCLEAR TEST BAN TREATY (CTBT) opens for signature

December 16   GENERAL ASSEMBLY adopts the Model Law on Electronic Commerce

December 17   SECURITY COUNCIL nominates Kofi ANNAN of Ghana to be the seventh SECRETARY-GENERAL of the United Nations

December 26   The CONVENTION TO COMBAT DESERTIFICATION (CCD) enters into force

1997

January 1   Kofi ANNAN becomes the SECRETARY-GENERAL of the United Nations

April 24–25, July 15, November 13   Tenth EMERGENCY SPECIAL SESSION OF THE GENERAL ASSEMBLY convenes to consider occupied East Jerusalem and the occupied territories

April 29   CHEMICAL WEAPONS CONVENTION enters into force

June 20   GENERAL ASSEMBLY adopts the AGENDA FOR DEVELOPMENT

June 23–27   EARTH SUMMIT +5 convenes at UN HEADQUARTERS

June 30   UNITED NATIONS ANGOLA VERIFICATION MISSION III (UNAVEM) terminates its operations

July 1   UNITED NATIONS OBSERVER MISSION IN ANGOLA (MONUA) commences operations

July 16   UN SECRETARY-GENERAL issues *Renewing the United Nations: A Programme for Reform*

July 25   ECONOMIC AND SOCIAL COUNCIL establishes the Intergovernmental Forum on Forests

November 1   UN SECRETARIAT creates the OFFICE FOR DRUG CONTROL AND CRIME PREVENTION (ODCCP)

December 3   CONVENTION on the Prohibition of the Use, Stockpiling, Production and Transfer of Anti-Personnel Mines and Their Destruction is opened for signature

December 11   Parties to the UNITED NATIONS FRAMEWORK CONVENTION ON CLIMATE CHANGE (UNFCCC) adopt the KYOTO PROTOCOL

December 15   GENERAL ASSEMBLY adopts the International CONVENTION for the Suppression of Terrorist Bombings

December 15   GENERAL ASSEMBLY establishes the dates (June 15–July 17, 1998) for the Rome Conference to create an INTERNATIONAL CRIMINAL COURT (ICC)

1998

February 22   SECRETARY-GENERAL Kofi ANNAN achieves a Memorandum of Understanding in which Iraq accepts all previous SECURITY COUNCIL RESOLUTIONS

June 10   GENERAL ASSEMBLY adopts the DECLARATION on the Guiding Principles of Drug Demand Reduction

June 15–July 28   UN Diplomatic Conference of Plenipotentiaries on the Establishment of an INTERNATIONAL CRIMINAL COURT (ICC) convenes in Rome

June 18   INTERNATIONAL LABOUR ORGANIZATION (ILO) adopts the "DECLARATION on Fundamental Principles and Rights at Work and its Follow-up"

June 22–24   Vienna +5 Global Forum (Five-Year Review Conference of the WORLD CONFERENCE ON HUMAN RIGHTS) convenes in Ottawa

July 17   Negotiating parties adopt the Rome Statute for the INTERNATIONAL CRIMINAL COURT (ICC)

December 8   GENERAL ASSEMBLY adopts Principles and Guidelines for International Negotiations

December 9   GENERAL ASSEMBLY adopts the DECLARATION on the Rights and Responsibility of Individuals, Groups and Organs of Society to Promote and Protect Universally Recognized HUMAN RIGHTS and Fundamental Freedoms

1999

January 31   UN SECRETARY-GENERAL Kofi ANNAN proposes the GLOBAL COMPACT program at the World Economic Forum in Davos, Switzerland

February 2   Senegal becomes the first country to ratify the Rome Statute on the INTERNATIONAL CRIMINAL COURT

February 28   Mandate for the UNITED NATIONS PREVENTIVE DEPLOYMENT FORCE IN THE FORMER YUGOSLAV REPUBLIC OF MACEDONIA (UNPREDEP) ends

March 25   North Atlantic Treaty Organization bombs Yugoslavia in an effort to enforce UN RESOLUTIONS and force the Yugoslav army out of Kosovo

June 3   Yugoslavia accepts UN peace terms in Kosovo

June 10   SECURITY COUNCIL establishes the UNITED NATIONS INTERIM ADMINISTRATION MISSION FOR KOSOVO (UNMIK)

June 11   SECURITY COUNCIL establishes the UNITED NATIONS MISSION IN EAST TIMOR (UNAMET)

June 30–July 2   SPECIAL SESSION OF THE GENERAL ASSEMBLY to review the implementation of the ICPD (INTERNATIONAL CONFERENCE ON POPULATION AND DEVELOPMENT) Plan of Action convenes in New York

October 13   U.S. Senate rejects ratification of the COMPREHENSIVE TEST BAN TREATY

October 15 SECURITY COUNCIL bans non-humanitarian flights and freezes Taliban assets until Osama bin Laden is extradited

December 9 GENERAL ASSEMBLY adopts the International CONVENTION for the Suppression of the Financing of TERRORISM

2000

April 17 SECURITY COUNCIL establishes a Working Group on General Issues on SANCTIONS

May 16 GENERAL ASSEMBLY adopts Optional PROTOCOLS to the CONVENTION on the Rights of the Child on the Involvement of Children in Armed Conflict and on the Sale of Children, Child Prostitution and Child Pornography

June 5–9 SPECIAL SESSION OF THE GENERAL ASSEMBLY to appraise the progress achieved in the implementation of the Nairobi Forward-looking Strategies for the Advancement of Women and the Plan of Action convenes in New York

June 26–30 SPECIAL SESSION OF THE GENERAL ASSEMBLY on the implementation of the outcome of the WORLD SUMMIT FOR SOCIAL DEVELOPMENT convenes in New York

July 26 Operational phase of the GLOBAL COMPACT begins

August 23 Panel on United Nations Peace Operations publishes the BRAHIMI REPORT

September 6–8 150 heads of state gather in New York City for the MILLENNIUM SUMMIT

September 8 GENERAL ASSEMBLY adopts the United Nations Millennium DECLARATION

November 15 GENERAL ASSEMBLY adopts the PROTOCOL against the Smuggling of Migrants by Land, Sea, and Air

November 15 GENERAL ASSEMBLY adopts the PROTOCOL to Prevent, Suppress and Punish Trafficking in Persons, Especially WOMEN and Children

November 15 GENERAL ASSEMBLY adopts the United Nations CONVENTION against Transnational Organized Crime

December 4 GENERAL ASSEMBLY adopts the Vienna DECLARATION on Crime and Justice

2001

May 14 Third UNITED NATIONS CONFERENCE ON THE LEAST DEVELOPED COUNTRIES convenes

May 31 GENERAL ASSEMBLY adopts the PROTOCOL against Illicit Manufacturing of and Trafficking in Firearms

June 27 GENERAL ASSEMBLY adopts the DECLARATION of Commitment on HIV/AIDS

June 27 SECURITY COUNCIL unanimously nominates Kofi ANNAN for a second term as UN SECRETARY-GENERAL

June 29 GENERAL ASSEMBLY elects by acclamation Kofi ANNAN to a second term as SECRETARY-GENERAL

July 12 GENERAL ASSEMBLY adopts the Statute of the UNITED NATIONS SYSTEM Staff College

August 31–September 7 WORLD CONFERENCE AGAINST RACISM, RACIAL DISCRIMINATION, Xenophobia and Related Intolerance convenes in Durban, South Africa

September 11 Terrorists seize control of four U.S. civilian airliners and crash three of them into the World Trade Center in New York City and the Pentagon in Northern Virginia

September 11 United Nations postpones opening of the 56th session of the GENERAL ASSEMBLY due to the terrorist attacks on New York City

September 12 SECURITY COUNCIL condemns terrorist attacks on U.S. sites and asserts it "regards such acts, like any act of international TERRORISM, as a threat to international peace and security" (UN SECURITY COUNCIL RESOLUTION 1368)

September 13 GENERAL ASSEMBLY condemns terrorist attacks on the UNITED STATES

September 28 SECURITY COUNCIL invokes CHAPTER VII of the UN CHARTER and adopts RESOLUTION 1373 requiring states to prevent the financing of terrorist groups and to freeze terrorist assets within their borders

October 7 Coalition led by the UNITED STATES launches military retaliation against the Taliban government in AFGHANISTAN in response to terrorist attacks on New York City and Washington, D.C.

October 12 United Nations and SECRETARY-GENERAL Kofi ANNAN receive the Nobel Peace Prize

2002

January 22 SECURITY COUNCIL confirms Michael Steiner as the new head of the UNITED NATIONS INTERIM ADMINISTRATION MISSION FOR KOSOVO (UNMIK), replacing Hans Haekkerup

March 3 Swiss voters approve Switzerland's application for UN MEMBERSHIP

March 12 SECURITY COUNCIL condemns violence in the Middle East and affirms its "vision of a region where two states, Israel and Palestine, live side by side within secure and recognized borders."

April 8–12 Second WORLD CONFERENCE on Ageing convenes in Madrid, Spain

April 11 Rome TREATY establishing the INTERNATIONAL CRIMINAL COURT achieves the necessary 60 ratifications to enter into force

April 19 SECRETARY-GENERAL Kofi ANNAN asks the SECU-RITY COUNCIL to authorize a multinational PEACEKEEPING force for the Middle East

April 26 SECRETARY-GENERAL Kofi ANNAN appoints Patricia Durrant the UN's first ombudsman.

May 20 East Timor becomes an independent state and requests admission to the United Nations

July 1 INTERNATIONAL CRIMINAL COURT comes into existence

APPENDIX H
Important United Nations Websites

Administrative Committee on Coordination (ACC)
http://acc.unsystem.org/

ACC Network on Rural Development and Food Security
http://www.accnetwork.net/

ACC Subcommittee on Drug Control
http://acc.unsystem.org/-subsidiary.bodies/accsdc.htm
http://acc.unsystem.org/-subsidiary.bodies/accsdc.htm

ACC Subcommittee on Nutrition
http://acc.unsystem.org/scn/

ACC Subcommittee on Oceans and Coastal Areas
http://acc.unsystem.org/-subsidiary.bodies/accsoca.htm

ACC Subcommittee on Statistical Activities
http://http://acc.unsystem.org/-subsidiary.bodies/accssa.htm

ACC Subcommittee on Water Resources
http://acc.unsystem.org/-subsidiary.bodies/accswr.htm

ACC Subsidiary Bodies
http://acc.unsystem.org/-subsidiary.bodies/

Basel Convention on the Control of Transboundary Movements of Hazardous Wastes and Their Disposal
http://www.basel.int/

Beijing +5 Special Session
http://www.un.org/womenwatch/followup/beijing5/about.htm

Centre for International Crime Prevention
http://www.odccp.org/

Commission for Social Development (CSocD)
http://www.un.org/esa/socdev/csd/index.html

Commission on Crime Prevention and Criminal Justice (CCPCJ)
http://www.uncjin.org

Commission on Sustainable Development (CSD)
http://www.un.org/esa/sustdev/index.html

Commission on the Status of Women (CSW)
http://www.un.org/womenwatch/daw/csw

Committee of Experts on the Transport of Dangerous Goods
http://www.unece.org/trans/danger/danger.htm

Committee on the Peaceful Uses of Outer Space (COPUOS)
http://www.oosa.unvienna.org/COPUOS

Comprehensive Test Ban Treaty Organization (CTBTO)
http://www.ctbto.org/

Consultative Committee on Administrative Questions (CCAQ)
http://accsubs.unsystem.org/-subsidiary.bodies/ccaq/

Consultative Committee on Administrative Questions (Financial and Budgetary Questions) (CCAQ(FB))
http://acc.unsystem.org/-subsidiary.bodies/ccaqfb.htm

Consultative Committee on Administrative Questions (Personnel and General Administrative Questions) (CCAQ(PER))
http://accsubs.unsystem.org/ccaqper/

Consultative Committee on Programme and Operational Questions (CCPOQ)
http://accsubs.unsystem.org/ccpoq/

Convention on Biological Diversity (CBD)
http://www.biodiv.org/

Convention on International Trade in Endangered Species of Wild Fauna and Flora (CITES)
http://www.cites.org

Convention on the Conservation of Migratory Species of Wild Animals (CMS)
http://www.wcmc.org.uk/cms

Dag Hammarskjöld Library
http://www.un.org/Depts/dhl/services.htm

Declaration on the Elimination of Violence against Women
http://www.unhchr.ch/women/focus-violence.html

Department for Disarmament Affairs (DDA)
http://www.un.org/Depts/dda/dda.htm

Department of Economic and Social Affairs (DESA)
http://www.un.org/esa

Department of Public Information "Women" Website
www.un.org/ecosocdev/geninfo/women

Disarmament Notes
http://www.un.org/Depts/dda/DDAHome.htm

Economic and Social Commission for Asia and the Pacific (ESCAP)
http://www.unescap.org/

Economic and Social Commission for Western Asia (ESCWA)
http://www.escwa.org.lb/

Economic and Social Council (ECOSOC)
http://www.un.org/esa/coordination/ecosoc/

Economic Commission for Africa (ECA)
http://www.uneca.org/

Economic Commission for Europe (ECE)
http://www.unece.org/

Economic Commission for Latin America and the Caribbean (ECLAC)
http://www.eclac.cl/indexl.html

Fifth Committee of the General Assembly
http://www.un.org/ga/fifth/

Fifty-fifth Session of the General Assembly*
http://www.un.org/ga/55/

First Committee of the General Assembly
http://www.un.org/ga/first/

Food and Agriculture Organization (FAO)
http://www.fao.org/

Fourth Committee of the General Assembly
http://www.un.org/ga/fourth/

General Assembly
http://www.un.org/ga/

Geneva Headquarters of the United Nations
http://www.genevabriefingbook.com/chapters/palais

Global Compact
http://www.unglobalcompact.org/

Global Environment Facility (GEF)
http://www.gefweb.org/

Global Issues on the UN Agenda
http://www.un.org/partners/civil_society/agenda.htm

Group of 77
http://www.g77.org/

Habitat
http://www.unchs.org

Hague Academy of International Law
http://www.hagueacademy.nl/Eng

Indigenous Peoples
http://www.unhchr.ch/indigenous/ind

Information Systems Coordination Committee (ISCC)
http://acc.unsystem.org/iscc/

Inter-Agency Committee on Sustainable Development (IACSD)
http://acc.unsystem.org/-subsidiary.bodies/iacsd.htm

Inter-Agency Committee on Women and Gender Equality (IACWGE)
http://acc.unsystem.org/-subsidiary.bodies/iacwge.htm

Inter-Agency Procurement Services Office (IAPSO)
http://www.iapso.org/

Intergovernmental Panel on Climate Change (IPCC)
http://www.ipcc.ch/

International Atomic Energy Agency (IAEA)
http://www.iaea.int/

International Bank for Reconstruction and Development (IBRD)
http://www.worldbank.org/html/extdr/backgrd/ibrd/

International Bureau of Education (IBE)
http://www.ibe.unesco.org/

International Campaign to Ban Landmines (ICBL)
http://www.icbl.org/

International Centre for Science and High Technology (ICS)
http://www.ics.trieste.it/

International Centre for Settlement of Investment Disputes (ICSID)
http://www.worldbank.org/icsid/

International Civil Aviation Organization (ICAO)
http://www.icao.int/

International Civil Service Commission (ICSC)
http://www.un.org/Depts/icsc/index.html

---

* For preceding and succeeding years, substitute the GA session number in the website URL.

International Civilian Mission in Haiti (MICIVIH)
http://www.un.org/rights/micivih/first.htm

International Computing Centre (ICC)
http://www.unicc.org/

International Conference on Population and Development (ICPD)
http://www.unfpa.org/icpd/index.htm

International Court of Justice (ICJ)
http://www.icj-cij.org/icj

International Criminal Court (ICC)
http://www.un.org/law/icc/

International Criminal Tribunal for Rwanda (ICTR)
http://www.ictr.org/

International Criminal Tribunal for the Former Yugoslavia
http://www.un.org/icty/

International Development Association (IDA)
http://www.worldbank.org/ida/

International Finance Corporation (IFC)
http://www.ifc.org/

International Fund for Agricultural Development (IFAD)
http://www.ifad.org/

International Institute for Educational Planning (IIEP)
http://www.unesco.org/iiep/

International Institute on Aging (INIA)
http://www.inia.org.mt/

International Labour Organization (ILO)
http://www.ilo.org/

International Law
http://www.un.org/law/

International Law Commission (ILC)
http://www.un.org/law/ilc/index.htm

International Maritime Organization (IMO)
http://www.imo.org/

International Monetary Fund (IMF)
http://www.imf.org/

International Research and Training Institute for the Advancement of Women (INSTRAW)
http://www.un-instraw.org

International Seabed Authority
http://www.isa.org.jm

International Telecommunications Union (ITU)
http://www.itu.int/

International Trade Centre UNCTAD/WTO (ITC)
http://www.intracen.org/

International Training Centre of the ILO (ITC/ILO)
http://www.itcilo.it/

Joint Inspection Unit (JIU)
http://www.unsystem.org/jiu/

Joint Inter-Agency Meeting on Computer-Assisted Translation and Terminology (JIAMCATT)
http://jiamcatt.unsystem.org/english/jiamcate.htm

Joint United Nations Information Committee (JUNIC)
http://acc.unsystem.org/-subsidiary.bodies/junic.htm

Joint United Nations Programme on HIV/AIDS (UNAIDS)
http://www.unaids.org

Kyoto Protocol
http://www.unfccc.de/resource/convkp.html

Least Developed Countries Home Page (LDCs)
http://www.unctad.org/en/subsites/ldcs/ldc11.htm

Millennium Report of the Secretary-General
http://www.un.org/millennium/sg/report/index.html

Multilateral Investment Guarantee Agency (MIGA)
http://www.miga.org/

National Liberation Movements
http://www.neravt.com/left/third.htm

Office for Outer Space Affairs (OOSA)
http://www.oosa.unvienna.org/

Office for the Coordination of Humanitarian Affairs (OCHA)
http://www.reliefweb.int/ocha_ol/index.html

Office of the United Nations High Commissioner for Human Rights (OHCHR)
http://www.unhchr.ch

Office of the United Nations High Commissioner for Refugees (OHCR)
http://www.unhcr.ch

Organization of American States
http://www.oas.org

Organization for the Prohibition of Chemical Weapons (OPCW)
http://www.opcw.org

Panel of External Auditors of the United Nations, the Specialized Agencies and the International Atomic Energy Agency
http://www.unsystem.org/auditors/external.htm

Permanent Court of Arbitration
http://pca-cpa.org

Report of the Panel on United Nations Peace Operations
http://www.un.org/peace/reports/peace_operations/

Rio Declaration
http://www.un.org/documents/ga/confl51/aconfl5126-lannexl.htm

Second Committee of the 56th General Assembly
http://www.un.org/ga/56/second

Senior Management Group
http://www.un.org/News/ossg/sg/pages/seniorstaff.html

Sixth Committee of the 56th General Assembly
http://www.un.org/law/cod/sixth/56/sixth55.htm

Statistical Yearbook
http://esa.un.org/unsd/pubs

Terrorism Website
http://www.un.org/terrorism

Third Committee of the 56th General Assembly
http://www.un.org/ga/56/third/

UN Framework Convention on Climate Change (UNFCCC)
http://www.unfccc.de/

UN General Assembly Resolutions
http://www.un.org/documents/ga/res/

UN Security Council Resolutions
http://www.un.org/documents/sc/res/

United Nations Advance mission in Cambodia
http://www.un.org/Depts/dpko/dpko/co_mission/unamic.htm

United Nations Angola Verification Mission (UNAVEM)
http://www.un.org/Depts/dpko/dpko/co_mission/unavem_p.htm

United Nations Assistance Mission in Sierra Leone (UNAMSIL)
http://www.un.org/Depts/dpko/unamsil/body_unamsil.htm

United Nations Board of Auditors
http://www.unsystem.org/auditors/

United Nations Capital Development Fund (UNCDF)
http://www.undp.org/uncdf

United Nations Centre for Human Settlements (Habitat) (UNCHS)
http://www.unchs.org/

United Nations Children's Fund (UNICEF)
http://www.unicef.org

United Nations Civilian Police Mission in Haiti
http://www.un.org/Depts/dpko/dpko/co_mission/miponuh.htm

United Nations Commission on International Trade Law (UNCITRAL)
http://www.uncitral.org

United Nations Common Supplier Database (UNCSD)
http://www.uncsd.org/

United Nations Compensation Commission (UNCC)
http://www.uncc.ch

United Nations Conference on Trade and Development (UNCTAD)
http://www.unctad.org/

United Nations Development Fund for Women (UNIFEM)
http://www.unifem.undp.org

United Nations Development Programme
http://www.undp.org/

United Nations Disarmament Commission (UNDC)
http://www.un.org/Depts/dda/UNDC/UNDC.htm

United Nations Disarmament Treaties
http://domino.un.org/TreatyStaus.nsf

United Nations Educational, Scientific and Cultural Organization (UNESCO)
http://www.unesco.org/

United Nations Environment Programme (UNEP)
http://www.unep.org/

United Nations Force in Cyprus (UNFICYP)
http://www.un.org/Depts/DPKO/Missions/unficyp/body_unficyp.htm

United Nations High Commissioner for Refugees (UNHCR)
http://www.unhcr.ch

United Nations Home Page
http://www.un.org/

United Nations India-Pakistan Observation Mission (UNIPOM)
http://www.un.org/Depts/dpko/dpko/co_mission/unipom.htm

United Nations Industrial Development Organization (UNIDO)
http://www.unido.org/

United Nations Institute for Disarmament Research (UNIDIR)
http://www.unog.ch/unidir

United Nations Institute for Training and Research (UNITAR)
http://www.unitar.org

United Nations Interim Administration Mission for Kosovo (UNMIK)
http://www.un.org/peace/kosovo/

United Nations Interim Force in Lebanon (UNIFIL)
http://www.un.org/Depts/DPKO/Missions/unifil

United Nations International Drug Control Programme (UNDCP)
http://www.undcp.org

United Nations International Research and Training Institute for the Advancement of Women (INSTRAW)
http://www.un.org/instraw

United Nations International School (UNIS)
http://www.unis.org/

United Nations Interregional Crime and Justice Research Institute (UNICRI)
http://www.unicri.it/

United Nations Joint Staff Pension Fund (UNJSPF)
http://www.un.org/unjspf/

United Nations Member States Website
http://www.un.org/members/index.html

United Nations Military Observer Group in India and Pakistan (UNMOGIP)
http://www.un.org/Depts/DPKO/Missions/unmogip/body_unmogip.htm

United Nations Non-governmental Liaison Service (NGLS)
http://www.unsystem.org/ngls/

United Nations Observer Mission in Angola (MONUA)
http://www.un.org/Depts/DPKO/Missions/Monua/monuabl.htm

United Nations Observer Mission in Sierra Leone (UNOMSIL)
http://www.un.org/Depts/DPKO/Missions/unomsil.htm

United Nations Office at Geneva (UNOG)
http://www.unog.ch

United Nations Office at Nairobi (UNON)
http://www.unon.org/

United Nations Office at Vienna (UNOV)
http://www.unvienna.org/

United Nations Office of Project Services (UNOPS)
http://www.unops.org

United Nations Operation in Mozambique (ONUMOZ)
http://www.un.org/Depts/DPKO/Missions/onumoz

United Nations Operation in Somalia (UNOSOM)
http://www.unsomalia.org

United Nations Population Fund (UNFPA)
http://www.unfpa.org/

United Nations Postal Administration (UNPA)
http://www.unpa.unvienna.org/

United Nations Preventive Deployment Force in the Former Yugoslav Republic of Macedonia (UNPREDEP)
http://www.un.org/Depts/DPKO/Missions/unpred

United Nations Relief and Works Agency for Palestine Refugees in the Near East (UNRWA)
http://www.unrwa.org

United Nations Research Institute for Social Development (UNRISD)
http://www.unrisd.org/

United Nations Secretariat of the Convention to Combat Desertification (CCD)
http://www.unccd.int/main.php

United Nations Staff College
http://www.itcilo.it/UNSCP/

United Nations System
http://www.unsystem.org

United Nations Transitional Administration in East Timor (UNTAET)
http://www.un.org/peace/etimor/etimor.htm

United Nations Transitional Authority in Cambodia
http://www.un.org/Depts/dpko/dpko/co_mission/untac.htm

United Nations Treaty Collection
http://untreaty.un.org/

United Nations Truce Supervision Organization (UNTSO)
http://www.un.org/Depts/DPKO/Missions/untso

United Nations University (UNU)
http://www.unu.edu

United Nations Volunteers
http://www.unv.org

Universal Postal Union (UPU)
http://www.upu.int/

Vienna Convention for the Protection of the Ozone Layer
http://www.unep.org/ozone/vienna

Women Watch
http://www.un.org/womenwatch/

World Bank Group
http://www.worldbank.org/

World Food Programme (WFP)
http://www.wfp.org

World Health Organization (WHO)
http://www.who.int/

World Intellectual Property Organization (WIPO)
http://www.wipo.int/

World Meteorological Organization (WMO)
http://www.wmo.ch/

World Tourism Organization (WTO/OMT)
http://www.world-tourism.org

World Trade Organization (WTO)
http://www.wto.org

SELECTED BIBLIOGRAPHY

AFRICA

Adelman, Howard, and Astri Suhrke, eds. *The Rwandan Crisis from Uganda to Zaire*. New Brunswick, N.J.: Transaction Publishers, 1999.

Berman, Eric G, and Katie E. Sams. *Peacekeeping in Africa: Capabilities and Culpabilities*. New York: United Nations Institute for Disarmament Research/Institute for Security Studies, 2000.

Ciment, James. *Angola and Mozambique: Postcolonial Wars in Southern Africa*. New York: Facts On File, 1997.

Cliffe, Lionel. *The Transition to Independence in Namibia*. Boulder, Colo.: Lynne Rienner, 1994.

Deng, Francis M., and Larry Minear. *The Challenges of Famine Relief*. Washington, D.C.: Brookings Institution 1992.

Donnelly, Jack. *Human Rights and International Relations*. Boulder, Colo.: Westview Press, 1993.

Dutt, Sagarika. *Africa at the Millennium: An Agenda for Mature Development*. New York: Palgrave, 2000.

Ezenwe, Uka. *ECOWAS and the Economic Integration of West Africa*. New York: St. Martin's, 1983.

Hodges, Tony. *African Issues: Angola from Afro-Stalinism to Petro-Diamond Capitalism*. Bloomington: Indiana University Press, 2001.

Kaela, Laurent. *The Question of Namibia*. New York: St. Martin's, 1996.

Nyangoni, Wellington. *Africa in the United Nations System*. London: Associated University Presses, 1975.

Senghor, Jeggan Colley. *ECOWAS: Perspectives on Treaty Revision and Reform*. Dakar: United Nations African Institute for Economic Development and Planning, 1999.

Shaw, Timothy M., and Julius Emeka Okolo. *The Political Economy of Foreign Policy in ECOWAS*. New York: St. Martin's, 1994.

Smilie, Ian, Lansana Gberie, and Ralph Hazleton. *The Heart of the Matter: Sierra Leone, Diamonds & Human Security*. Ottawa, Canada: Partnership Africa, January 2000.

United Nations. *Report of the Independent Inquiry into the Actions of the United Nations during the 1994 Genocide in Rwanda*. New York: United Nations, 1999.

———. *The United Nations and Rwanda 1993–1996*. Blue Books Series. Vol. 10. New York: United Nations, 1996.

United Nations Children's Fund. *Africa's Children, Africa's Future: Implementing the World Summit Declaration*. New York: UNICEF, 1990.

CHARTER OF THE UNITED NATIONS

Barros, James, ed. *The United Nations; Past, Present, and Future*. New York: The Free Press, 1972.

Cortright, David. *The Sanctions Decade: Assessing UN Strategies in the 1990s*. Boulder, Colo.: Lynne Rienner Publishers, 2000.

Freudenschuss, Helmut. "Article 39 of the UN Charter Revisited." *Austrian Journal of Public and International Law*, no. 46 (1993).

Goodrich, Leland, Edvard Hambro, and Anne Patricia Simons. *Charter of the United Nations*. New York: Columbia University Press, 1969.

Hilderbrand. Robert C. *Dumbarton Oaks: The Origins of the United Nations and the Search for Postwar Security*. Chapel Hill: University of North Carolina Press, 1990.

Krasno, Jean E. *The Founding of the United Nations. International Cooperation as an Evolutionary Process*. New Haven, Conn.: Academic Council on the United Nations System, 2001.

Lepgold, Joseph, and Thomas G. Weiss, eds. *Collective Conflict Management and Changing World Politics*. Albany: State University of New York Press, 1998.

Nicholas, H. G. *The United Nations as a Political Institution.* 5th ed. Oxford: Oxford University Press, 1975.

Russell, Ruth B. *A History of the United Nations Charter: The Role of the United States, 1940–1945.* Washington, D.C.: Brookings Institution, 1958.

Sarooshi, Danesh. *The United Nations and the Development of Collective Security: The Delegation by the UN Security Council of Its Chapter VII Powers.* Oxford: Clarendon, 2000.

Simma, Bruno, ed. *The Charter of the United Nations: A Commentary.* New York: Oxford University Press, 1994.

U.S. Department of State. *Postwar Foreign Policy Preparation, 1939–1945,* Department of State Publication 3580. Washington, D.C.: U.S. Government Printing Office, 1949.

Weiss, Thomas G, David P. Forsyth, and Roger A. Coate. *The United Nations and Changing World Politics.* Boulder, Colo.: Westview Press, 2000.

DECOLONIZATION, NATIONAL LIBERATION, AND THE DEVELOPING COUNTRIES

Mortimore, Robert. *The Third World Coalition in International Politics.* Boulder, Colo.: Westview Press, 1984.

Singh, Lalita Prasad. *India and Afro-Asian Independence: Liberation Diplomacy in the United Nations.* New Delhi: National Book Organization, 1993.

Urquhart, Brian. *Decolonization and World Peace.* Austin: University of Texas Press, 1989.

DEVELOPMENT

Bergesen, Helge Ole, Georg Parmann, and Oystein B. Thommessen. *Yearbook of International Cooperation on Environment and Development, 1999/2000.* London: Earthscan Publications Ltd., 1999.

Hoy, Paula. *Players and Issues in International Aid.* Bloomfield, Conn.: Kumarian Press, 1998.

Pinto, Anibal. "Raul Prebisch 1901–1986." *CEPAL Review,* no. 29 (August 1986): 9–11.

Rehnstrom, Joel. *Development Cooperation in Practice: The United Nations Volunteers in Nepal.* New York: United Nations University Press, 2000.

United Nations Conference on Trade and Development. *The Least Developed Countries Report.* New York and Geneva: United Nations, issued annually.

United Nations Conference on Trade and Development, Geneva. *The History of UNCTAD: 1964–1984.* New York: United Nations, 1985.

United Nations Development Programme. *Donor Organizations and Participatory Development.* New York: United Nations Development Programme, 1995.

Upton, Barbara. *The Multilateral Development Banks. Improving U.S. Leadership.* Washington, D.C.: Center for Strategic and International Studies, 2000.

Weiss, Thomas. *Multilateral Development Diplomacy in UNCTAD: The Lessons of Group Negotiations 1964–84.* London: Macmillan, 1986.

DIPLOMACY

Chronology, Bibliography and Index for the Group of 77 and the Non-aligned Movement. New York: Oceana, 1993.

Clement, Lee, ed. *Andrew Young at the United Nations.* Salisbury, Md.: Documentary, 1978.

Erisman, H. Michael. *Cuba's Foreign Relations in a Post-Soviet World.* Gainesville: University of Florida Press, 2000.

Hart, Michael. *Fifty Years of Canadian Statecraft: Canada at the GATT 1947–1997.* Ottawa: Centre for Trade Policy and Law, 1998.

Jackson, Richard L. *The Non-aligned, the UN, and the Superpowers.* New York: Praeger, 1983.

Kochler, Hans, ed. *The Principles of Non-Alignment.* London: Third World Center, 1982.

Mazuzan, George. *Warren R. Austin at the UN, 1946–1953.* Kent, Ohio: Kent State University Press, 1977.

Protocol and Liaison Service. *Permanent Missions to the United Nations.* New York: United Nations, 2000.

Sadri, Houman A. *Revolutionary States, Leaders, and Foreign Relations: A Comparative Study of China, Cuba, and Iran.* Westport, Conn.: Praeger Publishers, 1977.

Sauvant, Karl P. *The Group of 77: Evolution, Structure, Organization.* New York: Oceana, 1981.

Sauvant, Karl P., and Joachim Miller, eds. *The Third World without Superpowers: The Collected Documents of the Group of 77, 2nd Series.* New York: Oceana Publications, 1891–1995.

Schechter, Michael G. *United Nations–sponsored World Conference. Focus on Impact and Follow-up.* Tokyo: United Nations University Press, 2001.

United Nations Department of Public Information. *Un Briefing Papers: The World Conferences, Developing Priorities for the 21st Century.* New York: United Nations Department of Public Information, 1997.

Weiss, Thomas, and Leon Gordenker, eds. *NGOs, the UN, and Global Governance.* Boulder, Colo.: Lynne Rienner, 1996.

Willetts, Peter, ed. *The Conscience of the World: The Influence of Non-governmental Organizations in the UN System.* Washington, D.C.: Brookings Institution, 1996.

Williams, Marc. *Third World Cooperation: The Group of 77 in UNCTAD.* New York: St. Martin's, 1991.

DISARMAMENT

Bader, William. *The United States and the Spread of Nuclear Weapons.* New York: Pegasus, 1968.

Bechhoefer, Bernard. *Postwar Negotiations for Arms Control.* Washington, D.C.: Brookings Institution, 1961.

Beker, Avi. *Disarmament without Order*. Westport, Conn.: Greenwood, 1985.

Berman, Eric. *Managing Arms in Peace Processes: Mozambique*. New York: United Nations Institute for Disarmament Research, 1996.

Cameron, Maxwell A, Robert J. Lawson, and Brian W. Tomlin. *To Walk without Fear: The Global Movement to Ban Landmines*. Toronto: Oxford University Press, 1998.

Carle, Christophe, and Patricia Lewis. "Arms Control and Disarmament Mechanisms," *First Conference of the PfP Consortium of Defence Academies and Security Study Institutes*. Kongresshaus Zurich, Switzerland, October 18–21, 1998.

Cirincione, Joseph, ed. *Repairing the Regime: Preventing the Spread of Weapons of Mass Destruction*. New York: Routledge, 2000.

Clarfield, Gerard H., and William M. Wiecek. *Nuclear America*. New York: Harper and Row, 1984.

Clark, William, Jr., and Ryukichi Imai, eds. *Next Steps in Arms Control and Non-Proliferation: Report of the U.S.–Japan Study Group on Arms Control and Non-Proliferation after the Cold War*. Washington, D.C.: Carnegie Endowment for International Peace, 1997.

Compilation of All Texts of Principles, Guidelines or Recommendations on Subject Items Adopted Unanimously by the Disarmament Commission. New York: United Nations, 1999.

Compilation of Basic Documents of the Conference on Disarmament Relating to the Question of Transparency in Armaments. Geneva: United Nations, 1998.

Cordon, Pierce. "The Future of the Conference on Disarmament and Multilateral Arms Control." Center for Nonproliferation Studies; China-US Conference on Arms Control, Disarmament, and Nonproliferation, September 24–25, 1998.

Garcia Robles, Alfonso. *El Tratado de Tlatleloco*. Mexico City: El Collegio de Mexico, 1967.

Herken, Gregg. *The Winning Weapon: The Atomic Bomb in the Cold War, 1945–1950*. New York: Vintage Books, 1980.

Holloway, David. *The Soviet Union and the Arms Race*. New Haven, Conn.: Yale University Press, 1984.

Independent Commission on Disarmament and Security Issues. *Common Security: A Blueprint for Survival [Palme Report]*. New York: Simon and Schuster, 1982.

Johnson, Rebecca. "CD Writes Off 1999 with Hopes for 2000." *Disarmament Diplomacy*, no. 39.

Labrie, Roger P., ed. *SALT Handbook: Key Documents and Issues, 1972–1979*. Washington, D.C.: U.S. Arms Control and Disarmament Agency, 1979.

Larsen, Jeffrey A., and Gregory J. Rattray, eds. *Arms Control: Toward the 21st Century*. Boulder, Colo.: Lynne Rienner, 1996.

Larson, Thomas. *Disarmament and Soviet Policy, 1964–1968*. Englewood Cliffs, N.J.: Prentice Hall, 1969.

Rauf, Tariq, Mary Beth Nikitin, and Jenni Rissanen. *Inventory of International Nonproliferation Organizations and Regimes, 2000 Edition*. Monterey, Calif.: Program for Nonproliferation Studies, Monterey Institute of International Studies, 1993.

Rostow, Walt W. *Open Skies*. Austin: University of Texas Press, 1982.

Schmalberger, Thomas. In *Pursuit of a Nuclear Test Ban Treaty: A Guide to the Debate in the Conference on Disarmament*. New York: United Nations, 1991.

Sethi, Manpreet. "Conference on Disarmament: Groping Its Way Around." *Strategic Analysis* 23, no. 8 (November 1999).

Short, N. "The Role of NGOs in the Ottawa Process to Ban Landmines." *International Negotiation* 4, no. 3 (1999): 481–500.

Sigal, Leon V. *Disarming Strangers. Nuclear Diplomacy with North Korea*. Princeton, N.J.: Princeton University Press, 1997.

Stokke, Olav Schram, and Davor Vidas, eds. *Governing the Antarctic: The Effectiveness and Legitimacy of the Antarctic Treaty System*. New York: Cambridge University Press, 1996.

Sundararaman, S. "The Landmines Question: An Overview of the Ottawa Process." *Strategic Analysis* 22, no. 1 (April 1998): 17–33.

Thakur, R., and W. Maley. "The Ottawa Convention on Landmines: A Landmark Humanitarian Treaty in Arms Control?" *Global Governance: A Review of Multilateralism and International Organizations* 5, no. 3 (July–September 1999) 273–302.

Tucker, Jonathan B., ed. *The Chemical Weapons Convention: Implementation Challenges and Solutions*. Monterey, Calif.: Monterey Institute of International Studies' Center for Nonproliferation Studies, 2001.

United Nations Department of Public Information. *The United Nations and Disarmament, 1945–1965*. New York: United Nations Department of Public Information, 1967.

———. *The United Nations and Nuclear Non-Proliferation*. Vol. 3 of the United Nations Bluebook Series. New York: United Nations Department of Public Information, 1995.

———. *Verification and the United Nations: The Role of the Organization in Multilateral Arms Limitation and Disarmament Agreements*. New York: United Nations Department of Public Information, 1991.

United Nations Institute for Disarmament Research. "Electronic Conference on the Future of the Conference on Disarmament and Its Agenda." January 13–27, 1998.

United States Arms Control and Disarmament Agency. *Disarmament Document Series*. Washington, D.C.: U.S. Arms Control and Disarmament Agency.

Vines, A., and H. Thompson. "Beyond the Landmine Ban: Eradicating a Lethal Legacy." *Conflict Studies* 316 (March 1999): 1–37.

York, Herbert F. *The CTBT and Beyond*. New York: United Nations, 1994.

DIVISIONS AND AGENCIES OF THE UNITED NATIONS

Aggarwal-Khan, Sheila. *Promoting Coherence: Towards an Effective Global Environmental Facility.* Amsterdam: Netherlands Committee for IUCN, 1997.

Dijkzeul, Dennis. *Reforming for Results in the UN System. A Study of UNOPS.* New York: St. Martin's, 2000.

Global Environment Facility. *Introduction to the GEF.* Washington, D.C.: The Global Environmental Facility, 2000.

Lubin, Carol Riegelman, and Anne Winslow. *Social Justice for Women: The International Labor Organization and Women.* Durham, N.C.: Duke University Press, 1990.

New Zealand Ministry of Foreign Affairs. *United Nations Handbook.* Wellington, N.Z.: Ministry of Foreign Affairs and Trade, published annually.

Shaw, D. John, and Sir Hans W. Singer. "A Note on Some UN Achievements with Special Reference to the World Food Programme." *The United Nations at Work.* Edited by Martin Ira Glassner. Westport, Conn.: Praeger Publishers, 1998.

Sjeoberg, Helen. *From Idea to Reality: The Creation of the Global Environment Facility.* Washington, D.C.: The Global Environment Facility, 1994.

United Nations. *Analytical Guide to the Work of the International Law Commission, 1949–1997.* New York: United Nations, 1998.

United Nations. *The High Commissioner for Human Rights: An Introduction: Making Human Rights a Reality.* New York: United Nations, 1996.

United Nations. *The Work of the International Law Commission.* 5th ed. New York: United Nations, 1996.

United Nations Educational, Scientific and Cultural Organization and Human Rights: Standard-Setting Instruments, Major Meetings, Publications. Paris: United Nations Educational, Scientific and Cultural Organization, 1996.

Whitman, Jim, ed. *Peacekeeping and the UN Agencies.* London: Frank Cass, 1999.

ENVIRONMENT

Baker, Randall. *Research and Training for Desertification Control: The United Nations Effort.* Nairobi, Kenya: United Nations Environment Programme, 1985.

Biswas, Margaret R., and Asit K. Biswas. *Desertification: Associated Case Studies Prepared for the United Nations Conference on Desertification.* New York: Pergammon Press, 1980.

Caldwell, Lynton Keith. *International Environmental Policy, Emergence and Dimensions.* Durham, N.C.: Duke University Policy Studies, 1984.

Campiglio, Luigi, Laura Pineschi, Domenico Siniscalco, and Tullio Treves. *The Environment After Rio.* London: Graham and Trotman, 1994.

Chasek, Pamela S. *The Global Environment in the Twenty-first Century: Prospects for International Cooperation.* New York: United Nations University Press, 2000.

Elliott, Lorraine. *The Global Politics of the Environment.* New York: New York University Press, 1998.

Fletcher, Susan R. *Congressional Research Service Report for Congress. 98–2: Global Climate Change Treaty: The Kyoto Protocol.* Washington, D.C.: The National Council for Science and the Environment, 2000.

Grubb, Michael, Matthias Koch, Koy Thomson, Abby Manson, and Francis Sullivan. *The 'Earth Summit' Agreements: A Guide and Assessment.* London: Earthscan Publications, 1993.

Halpern, Shanna. *The United Nations Conference on Environment and Development: Process and Documentation.* Providence, R.I.: The Academic Council on the United Nations System, 1993.

Hurrell, Andrew, and Benedict Kingsbury, eds. *The International Politics of the Environment. Actors, Interests, and Institutions.* Oxford: Clarendon Press, 1992.

Imber, Mark F. *Environment, Security and UN Reform.* New York: St. Martin's, 1994.

Jones, Laura, ed. *Global Warming: The Science and the Politics.* Vancouver, B.C.: Fraser Institute, 1997.

Medina, Sarah. *Global Biodiversity.* Nairobi, Kenya: UNEP, 1993.

Minguet, Monique. *Desertification: Natural Background and Human Mismanagement.* Spring Study Edition. New York: Springer-Verlag, 1994.

Mintzer, Irving M., and J. Amber Leonard. *Negotiating Climate Change: The Inside Story of the Rio Convention.* New York: Cambridge University Press, 1994.

Mouat, David A., and Charles F. Hutchinson, eds. *Desertification in Developing Counties: International Symposium and Workshop on Desertification in Developing Countries.* The Hague: Kluwer Academic Publishers, 1996.

Paterson, Matthew. "Interpreting Trends in Global Environmental Governance." *International Affairs* 75 (October 1999): 793–802.

Sands, Philippe, ed. *Greening International Law.* New York: The New Press, 1994.

Scherl, Lea M. *Relationships and Partnerships among Governments, NGOs, CBOs and Indigenous Groups in the Context of the Convention to Combat Desertification and Drought.* Nairobi, Kenya: Environment Liaison Centre International, 1996.

Tessitore, John, and Susan Woolfson. *A Global Agenda. Issues Before the 54th General Assembly of the United Nations.* New York: Rowman and Littlefield, 1999.

United Nations. *Report of the United Nations Conference on Environment and Development.* Vol. III, A/CONF.151/26, August 12, 1992.

Victor, David G. *The Collapse of the Kyoto Protocol and the Struggle to Slow Global Warming.* Princeton, N.J.: Princeton University Press, 2001.

Victor, David G., Kal Raustiala, and Eugene B. Skolnikoff. *The Implementation and Effectiveness of International Environmental Commitments: Theory and Practice.* Cambridge, Mass.: MIT Press, 1998.

Vig, Norman J., and Regina S. Axelrod, eds. *The Global Environment: Institutions, Laws, and Policy.* Washington, D.C.: CQ Press, 1999.

Weiss, Edith Brown. *In Fairness to Future Generations: International Law, Common Patrimony and Intergenerational Equity.* New York: Transaction Publishers and United Nations University, 1989.

Werksman, Jacob. *Greening International Institutions.* London: Earthscan Publications, 1996.

World Commission on Environment and Development. *Our Common Future.* New York: Oxford University Press, 1987.

Young, Oran B. *International Governance. Protecting the Environment in a Stateless Society.* Ithaca, N.Y.: Cornell University Press, 1994.

GENERAL ASSEMBLY

Luján Flores, Maria del. "The Role of Law in the U.N. Decision-Making Process of the Sixth Committee of the General Assembly." *New York University Journal of International Law and Politics* 27, no. 3 (Spring 1995): 611–18.

Marin-Bosch, Miguel. "How Nations Vote in the General Assembly of the United Nations." *International Organization* 41, no. 4 (1987): 195–204.

Peterson, M.J. *The General Assembly in World Politics.* Boston: Allen and Unwin, 1986.

Puchala, Donald, ed. *Issues Before the General Assembly of the United Nations.* New York: United Nations Association of the United States of America, published annually.

Tessitore, John, and Susan Woolfson. *A Global Agenda. Issues before the General Assembly of the United Nations.* New York: Rowman and Littlefield, published annually.

United Nations. *International Instruments of the United Nations: A Compilation of Agreements, Charters, Conventions, Declarations, Principles, Proclamations, Protocols, Treaties, Adopted by the General Assembly of the United Nations, 1945–1995.* New York: United Nations, 1997.

GENERAL WORKS ON THE UNITED NATIONS AND ITS HISTORY

Abelson, Nathaniel. "Official Symbols of the United Nations." *Flag Bulletin.* 34, no. 4 (July–August 1995): 142–52.

Armstrong, James D. *From Versailles to Maastricht: International Organization in the Twentieth Century.* New York: St. Martin's, 1996.

Baehr, Peter R., and Leon Gordenker. *The United Nations in the 1990s.* 2d ed. New York: St. Martin's, 1994.

Bailey, Sydney D. *The United Nations: A Concise Political Guide.* 3d ed. Lanhan, Md.: Barnes and Noble, 1995.

Bennett, A. LeRoy. *International Organizations. Principles and Issues.* 4th ed. Englewood Cliffs, N.J.: Prentice Hall, 1988.

Bennett, Edward M. *Franklin D. Roosevelt and the Search for Victory: American-Soviet Relations, 1939–1945.* Wilmington, Del.: Scholarly Resources, 1990.

Bertrand, Maurice. *The United Nations: Past, Present and Future.* The Hague: Martinus Nijhoff Publishers, 1997.

Buhite, Russell D. *Decisions at Yalta: An Appraisal of Summit Diplomacy.* Wilmington, Del.: Scholarly Resources, 1986.

Claude, Inis. *Swords into Plowshares: The Problems and Progress of International Organization.* 4th ed. New York: Random House, 1971.

Conforti, Benedetto. *The Law and Practice of the United Nations.* Boston: Kluwer Law International, 2000.

De Henseler, Max. *The United Nations Emblem and Flag.* Addis Ababa: Mimeo, 1972.

Divine. Robert. *Second Chance: The Triumph of Internationalism in America during World War II.* New York: Atheneum, 1967.

Eagleton, Clyde, ed. *Annual Review of United Nations Affairs Series, 1949 to the Present.* Dobbs Ferry, N.Y.: Oceana, annually.

Eco'Diagnostic, Geneva. *International Geneva Yearbook.* Geneva: United Nations, published annually.

English, John. *The Life of Lester Pearson: Shadow of Heaven (1897–1948) and Worldly Years (1949–1972).* Toronto: Lester and Orphen Dennys and A.A. Knopf, 1989–1992.

Eubank, Keith. *Summit at Teheran.* New York: Morrow, 1985.

Gardner, Lloyd C. *Architects of Illusion.* Chicago: Quadrangle, 1970.

Gellman, Irwin F. *Secret Affairs: Franklin Roosevelt, Cordell Hull, and Sumner Welles.* Baltimore: Johns Hopkins University Press, 1995.

Gilbert, Martin, and Winston S. Churchill. *Road to Victory. 1944–1945.* Vol. 7. New York: Houghton Mifflin, 1986.

Haas, Ernst B. *Why We Still Need the United Nations: The Collective Management of International Conflict, 1945–1984.* Berkeley: University of California Press, 1986.

Hilderbrand, Robert C. *Dumbarton Oaks: The Origins of the United Nations and the Search for Postwar Security.* Chapel Hill: University of North Carolina Press, 1990.

Jonah, James O.C. "Differing State Perspectives on the United Nations in the Post–Cold War World." *Academic Council on the United Nations System, Reports and Papers,* nos. 4, 9, 1993.

Kimball, Warren. *The Juggler.* Princeton, N.J.: Princeton University Press, 1991.

Krasno, J. "A Step along an Evolutionary Path: The Founding of the United Nations." *Global Dialogue* 12, no. 2. (Spring 2000): 9–18.

Luard, Evan. *A History of the United Nations* Vol. 1, *The Years of Western Domination, 1945–1955.* New York: St. Martin's, 1982.

Macalister-Smith, Peter. "The United Nations Emblem and Flag." *Nordic Journal of International Law* 55, no. 35 (1986): 262–65.

Matsuura, Kumiko, Joachim W. Muller, Karl P. Sauvant, eds. *Chronology and Fact Book of the United Nations, 1941–1991.* Dobbs Ferry, N.Y.: Oceana, 1992.

May, Ernest R., and Angeliki E. Laiou, eds. *The Dumbarton Oaks Conversations and the United Nations, 1944–1994.* Cambridge, Mass.: Harvard University Press, 1998.

Meisler, Stanley. *United Nations: The First Fifty Years.* New York: Atlantic Monthly Press, 1995.

Mingst, Karen, and Margaret Karns. *The United Nations in the Post–Cold War Era, Dilemmas in World Politics.* Boulder, Colo.: Westview Press, 2000.

Muldoon, James P., JoAnn Fagot Aviel, Richard Reitano, and Earl Sullivan. *Multilateral Diplomacy and the United Nations Today.* Boulder, Colo.: Westview Press, 1999.

Plano, Jack C., and Robert E. Riggs. *Forging World Order. The Politics of International Organization.* New York: Macmillan, 1967.

Pratt, Julius W. *Cordell Hull, 1933–1944.* New York: Cooper Square Publishers, 1964.

Riggs, Robert E., and Jack C. Plano. *The United Nations.* Belmont, Calif.: Wadsworth, 1994.

———. *The United Nations. International Organization and World Politics.* Pacific Grove, Calif.: Brooks/Cole Publishing Company, 1988.

Rivlin, Benjamin, ed. *Ralph Bunche: The Man and His Times.* New York: Holmes and Meier, 1990.

Roberts, Adam, and Benedict Kingsbury, eds. *United Nations, Divided World: The UN's Roles in International Relations.* 2d ed. New York: Oxford University Press, 2000.

Ryan, Stephen. *The United Nations and International Politics.* New York: St. Martin's, 2000.

Schild, Georg. *Bretton Woods and Dumbarton Oaks: American Economic and Political Postwar Planning in the Summer of 1944.* New York: St. Martin's, 1995.

United Nations Department of Public Information. *Basic Facts about the United Nations.* New York: United Nations Department of Public Information, 1998.

———. *Everyone's United Nations; A Handbook on the Work of the United Nations.* New York: United Nations Department of Public Information, published periodically.

———. *Yearbook of the United Nations.* New York: United Nations Department of Public Information, 1945–1996.

———. *Yearbook of the United Nations. Special Edition, UN Fiftieth Anniversary, 1945–1995.* The Hague: Martinus Nijhoff Publishers, 1995.

Urquhart, Brian. *Ralph Bunche: An American Odyssey.* New York: W.W. Norton, 1998.

Ziring, Lawrence, Robert Riggs, and Jack Plano. *The United Nations: International Organization and World Politics.* Fort Worth, Tex.: Harcourt College Publishers, 2000.

GREAT POWERS IN THE UNITED NATIONS

Allison, Graham T. *The Essence of Decision: Explaining the Cuban Missile Crisis.* New York: Addison, Wesley, Longman, 1999.

Baker, James A. *The Politics of Diplomacy: Revolution, War and Peace, 1989–1992.* New York: Putnam, 1995.

Bemis, Samuel Flagg, ed. *American Secretaries of State and Their Policies.* New York: A.A. Knopf, 1958.

Bennis, Phyllis. *Calling the Shots: How Washington Dominates Today's UN.* New York: Olive Branch, 1996.

Campbell, Thomas M. *Masquerade Peace: America's UN Policy, 1944–1945.* Tallahassee: Florida State University Press, 1974.

Cohen, Warren I. *America's Response to China.* New York: Columbia University Press, 2000.

Divine, Robert A. *Second Chance: The Triumph of Internationalism in America during World War II.* New York: Atheneum, 1967.

Drummond, Donald F. "Cordell Hull." In *An Uncertain Tradition: American Secretaries of State in the Twentieth Century.* Edited by Norman A. Graebner. New York: McGraw Hill, 1961.

Dulles, Foster Rhea. *America's Rise to World Power, 1898–1954.* New York: Harper and Row, 1963.

Economy, Elizabeth, and Michel Oksenberg, eds. *China Joins the World: Progress and Prospects.* New York: Council on Foreign Relations Press, 1999.

Fairbank, John King, and Merle Goldman. *China: A New History.* Cambridge: Belknap Press, 1998.

Feis, Herbert. *Churchill. Roosevelt. Stalin; The War They Waged and the Peace They Sought.* Princeton, N.J.: Princeton University Press, 1957.

Finger, Seymour Maxwell. *Your Man at the UN.* New York: New York University Press, 1980.

Gaddis, Richard. *We Now Know, Rethinking Cold War History.* Oxford: Clarendon Press, 1998.

Garthoff, Raymond L. *Reflections on the Cuban Missile Crisis.* Washington, D.C.: Brookings Institution, 1990.

Gati, Toby Trister, ed. *The U.S. the UN, and the Management of Global Change.* New York: New York University Press, 1983.

Gregg, Robert W. *About Face? The United States and the United Nations.* Boulder, Colo.: Lynne Rienner, 1993.

Gross, Franz B. *The United States and the United Nations.* Norman: University of Oklahoma Press, 1964.

Harbert, Joseph R., and Seymour Maxwell Finger, eds. *U.S. Policy in International Institutions.* Boulder, Colo.: Westview, 1978.

Hoopes, Townsend, and Douglas Brinkley. *FDR and the Creation of the U.N.* New Haven, Conn.: Yale University Press, 1997.

Jensen, Erik, and Thomas Fisher, eds. *The United Kingdom, the United Nations.* London: Macmillan, 1990.

Johnson, Walter. "Edward R. Stettinius, Jr." In *An Uncertain Tradition: American Secretaries of State in the Twentieth Century.* Edited by Norman A. Graebner. New York: McGraw-Hill, 1961.

Karns, Margaret P., and Karen A. Mingst, eds. *The United States and Multilateral Institutions: Patterns of Changing Instrumentality and Influence.* Boston: Unwin Hyman, 1990.

Kay, David A., ed. *The Changing United Nations: Options for the United States.* New York: Praeger, 1977.

Kennedy, Robert F. *Thirteen Days: A Memoir of the Cuban Missile Crisis.* New York: W.W. Norton, 1999.

MacKinnon, Michael G. *The Evolution of U.S. Peacekeeping Policy under Clinton. A Fairweather Friend?* London: Frank Cass, 2000.

May, Ernest R., and Philip D. Zelikow, eds. *The Kennedy Tapes: Inside the White House during the Cuban Missile Crisis.* Cambridge, Mass.: Harvard University Press, 1998.

Moore, John Allphin, Jr., and Jerry Pubantz. *To Create a New World? American Presidents and the United Nations.* New York: Peter Lang Publishing, 1999.

Nathan, James A., ed. *The Cuban Missile Crisis Revisited.* New York: St. Martin's, 1993.

Ostrower, Gary B. *The United Nations and the United States.* New York: Twayne, 1998.

Pruden, Caroline. *Conditional Partners: Eisenhower, the United Nations, and the Search for a Permanent Peace.* Baton Rouge: Louisiana State University Press, 1998.

Public Papers of the Presidents of the United States. Washington, D.C.: U.S. Government Printing Office, published annually.

Sherwood, Robert. *Roosevelt and Hopkins: An Intimate Portrait.* New York: Harper, 1948.

Stoessinger, John G. *The United Nations and the Superpowers: China, Russia, and America.* 4th ed. New York: Random House, 1977.

United States Administration, Presidential Decision Directive. *Policy on Reforming Multilateral Peace Operations,* May 1994.

HUMAN RIGHTS

Alston, Philip, ed. *The United Nations and Human Rights: A Critical Appraisal.* Oxford: Oxford University Press, 1992.

Bayefsky, Anne F., ed. *The UN Human Rights Treaty System in the 21st Century.* The Hague: Kluwer Law International, 2000.

Burgers, Herman, and Hans Danelius. *United Nations Convention against Torture: A Handbook on the Convention against Torture and Other Cruel, Inhuman, or Degrading Treatment or Punishment.* The Hague: Kluwer Academic Publishers, 1988.

Dias, Clarence J. "The United Nations World Conference on Human Rights: Evaluation, Monitoring, and Review."

United Nations-Sponsored World Conferences: Focus on Impact and Follow-up. Edited by Michael G. Schechter. Tokyo: United Nations University, 2001.

Donnelly, Jack. *International Human Rights.* Boulder, Colo.: Westview Press, 1998.

Forsythe, David P. *Human Rights in International Relations.* New York: Cambridge University Press, 2000.

Gle-Ahanhanzo. *Report by the Special Rapporteur on Contemporary Forms of Racial Discrimination, Xenophobia and Related Intolerance.* UN Document CN.4/1997/71, January 16, 1997.

Glendon, Mary Ann. *A World Made New. Eleanor Roosevelt and the Universal Declaration of Human Rights.* New York: Random House, 2001.

Gourevitch, Philip. *We Wish to Inform You That Tomorrow We Will Be Killed with Our Families: Stories from Rwanda.* New York: St. Martin's, 1999.

Korey, William. *NGOs and the Universal Declaration of Human Rights, "A Curious Grapevine."* New York: St. Martin's, 1998.

Kuper, Leo. *Genocide: Its Political Use in the Twentieth Century.* Harmondsworth, U.K.: Penguin Books, 1981.

Langley, Winston E. *Encyclopedia of Human Rights Issues since 1945.* Westport, Conn.: Greenwood Press, 1999.

Lawson, Edward H. *Encyclopedia of Human Rights.* London: Taylor and Francis, 1991.

Malik, Habib C. *The Challenge of Human Rights: Charles Malik and the Universal Declaration.* Oxford: Center for Lebanese Studies, 2000.

Minow, Martha. *Between Vengeance and Forgiveness: Facing History after Genocide and Mass Violence.* Boston: Beacon Press, 1998.

Morsink, Johannes. *The Universal Declaration of Human Rights: Origins, Drafting and Intent.* Philadelphia: University of Pennsylvania Press, 1999.

Office of the High Commissioner for Human Rights. *Basic Human Rights Instruments.* Geneva: United Nations, 1998.

Osiel, Mark. *Mass Atrocity, Collective Memory, and the Law.* New Brunswick, N.J.: Transaction Publishers, 1997.

Paust, Jordan J. et al., eds. *International Criminal Law: Cases and Materials.* Durham, N.C.: Carolina Academic Press, 1996.

Power, Samantha, and Graham Allison, eds. *Realizing Human Rights: Movement from Inspiration to Impact.* New York: St. Martin's, 2000.

Stultz, Newell. "Evolution of the United Nations Anti-Apartheid Regime." *Human Rights Quarterly,* no. 13 (1991): 1–23.

Symonides, Janusz. *The Struggle against Discrimination: A Collection of International Instruments Adopted by the United Nations System.* Paris: United Nations Educational, Scientific and Cultural Organization, 1996.

United Nations. *Report of the World Conference on Human Rights. [Vienna, 14–25 June 1993].* New York: United Nations, 1993.

———. *The United Nations and Human Rights: 1945–1995.* New York: United Nations, 1995.

———. *Human Rights: A Compilation of International Instruments.* 2 vols. New York; Geneva: United Nations, 1994–1997.

———. *Human Rights: International Instruments: Chart of Ratifications as of 31 December 1997.* New York; Geneva: United Nations, 1998.

———. *Human Rights and Elections: A Handbook on the Legal, Technical and Human Rights Aspects of Elections.* New York; Geneva: United Nations, 1994.

———. *Manual on Human Rights Reporting under Six Major International Human Rights Instruments.* Geneva: United Nations, 1997.

United Nations Centre for Human Rights, and United Nations Institute for Training and Research. *Manual on Human Rights Reporting under Six Major International Human Rights Instruments.* New York: United Nations, 1991.

United Nations Development Programme. *Integrating Human Rights with Sustainable Human Development: A UNDP Policy Document.* New York: United Nations Development Programme, 1998.

INTERNATIONAL LAW

Ackerman, John E., and Eugene O'Sullivan. *Practice and Procedure of the International Criminal Tribunal for the Former Yugoslavia.* Boston: Kluwer Law International, 2000.

Anaya, S. James. *Indigenous Peoples in International Law.* New York: Oxford University Press, 2000.

Beck, Robert J. et al., eds. *International Rules: Approaches from International Law and International Relations.* New York: Oxford University Press, 1996.

Beigbeder, Yves, and Theo Von Boven. *Judging War Criminals: The Politics of International Justice.* New York: St. Martin's, 1999.

Bowett, D. W. et al. *The International Court of Justice: Process, Practice and Procedure.* London: British Institute of International and Comparative Law, 1997.

Brown, E. D. *The International Law of the Sea.* 2 vols. Aldershot, U.K.: Dartmouth, 1994.

Byers, Michael, ed. *The Role of Law in International Politics.* New York: Oxford University Press, 2001.

Castellino, Joshua. *International Law and Self-Determination.* Boston: Kluwer Law International, 2000.

Damrosch, Lori Fisler, Gennady M. Danilenko, and Rein Müllerson, eds. *Beyond Confrontation: International Law for the Post–Cold War Era.* Boulder, Colo.: Westview Press, 1995.

Degenhardt, Henry W. *Maritime Affairs—A World Handbook: A Reference Guide to Maritime Organizations, Conventions, and Disputes and to the International Politics of the Sea.* Harlow, U.K.: Longman, 1985.

"Developments in the Law—International Criminal Law." *Harvard Law Review* 114, no. 7 (May 2001): 1943–2073.

Elias, T.O. *New Horizons in International Law.* 2d rev. ed. Dordrecht, Netherlands: Nijhoff, 1992.

Frye, Alton, *Toward an International Criminal Court?: A Council Policy Initiative.* New York: Council on Foreign Relations, 2000.

Glassner, Martin Ira. *Neptune's Domain: A Political Geography of the Sea.* Boston: Unwin Hyman, 1990.

Hannikainen, Lauri. *Peremptory Norms (Jus Cogens) in International Law: Historical Development, Criteria, Present Status.* Helsinki: Finnish Lawyers' Publishing Company, 1988.

Henkin, Louis, ed. *Right v. Might: International Law and the Use of Force.* New York: Council on Foreign Relations, 1991.

International Court of Justice. *Yearbook, 1947– .* The Hague: International Court of Justice, published annually.

———. *Bibliography of the International Court of Justice.* The Hague: International Court of Justice, annual.

———. *The International Court of Justice.* 4th ed. The Hague: International Court of Justice, 1996.

Joyner, Christopher C. "Recommended Measures under the Antarctic Treaty: Hardening Compliance with Soft International Law." *Michigan Journal of International Law* 19 (1998): 401.

Lee, Roy S., ed. *The International Criminal Court: The Making of the Rome Statute Issues, Negotiations, Results.* The Hague: Kluwer Law International, 1999.

Miles, Edward L. *Global Ocean Politics: The Decision Process at the Third United Nations Conference on the Law of the Sea, 1973–1982.* The Hague: Martinus Nijhoff Publishers, 1998.

Morton, Jeffrey S. *The International Law Commission of the United Nations.* Columbia: University of South Carolina Press, 2000.

Nyiri, Nicolas. *The United Nations' Search for a Definition of Aggression.* New York: Peter Lang, 1989.

Oxman, Bernard H. "Complementary Agreements and Compulsory Jurisdiction." *American Journal of International Law* 95, no. 2 (April 2001): 277–312.

Rosenne, Shabtai. *The Law and Practice of the International Court, 1920–1996.* Boston: Martinus Nijhoff Publisher, 1997.

———. *The World Court: What It Is and How It Works.* 5th rev. ed. Boston: Martinus Nijhoff Publisher, 1995.

Sewall, Sarah B., and Carl Kaysen, eds. *The United States and the International Criminal Court: National Security and International Law.* Lanham, Md: Rowman and Littlefield, 2000.

Shaw, Malcolm N. *International Law.* 3d ed. Cambridge: Cambridge University Press, 1994.

Simma, Bruno. "The Antarctic Treaty as a Treaty Creating an Objective Regime." *Cornell International Law Journal* XIX (1985–86): 189–209.

United Nations. *Summaries of Judgments, Advisory Opinions and Orders of the International Court of Justice, 1948–1991.* New York: United Nations, 1992.

————. *Summaries of Judgments, Advisory Opinions and Orders of the International Court of Justice, 1992–1996.* New York: United Nations, 1998.

————. *Cumulative Index of the United Nations Juridical Yearbook.* Pt. I: 1962–1979; Pt. II: 1980–1986; Pt. III (selected legal opinions of the Secretariat of the United Nations): 1962–1986, 1990. New York: United Nations, 1998.

MIDDLE EAST

Andersen, Roy R., Robert F. Seibert, and Jon G. Wagner. *Politics and Change in the Middle East: Sources of Conflict and Accommodation.* 6th ed. Upper Saddle River, N.J.: Prentice Hall, 2001.

Bailey, Sydney D. *Four Arab-Israeli Wars and the Peace Process.* London: Macmillan, 1990.

Bentsur, Eytan. *Making Peace. A First-Hand Account of the Arab-Israeli Peace Process.* Westport, Conn.: Praeger Publishers, 2001.

Bickerton, Ian, and Carla Klausner. *A Concise History of the Arab-Israeli Conflict.* 2d ed. Englewood Cliffs, N.J.: Prentice Hall, 1995.

Butler, Richard. *Iraq. Weapons of Mass Destruction, and the Growing Crisis of Global Security.* New York: Public Affairs, 2000.

Christopher, Warren, et al. *American Hostages in Iran: The Conduct of a Crisis.* New Haven, Conn.: Yale University Press, 1985.

Conlon, Paul. *United Nations Sanctions Management: A Case Study of the Iraq Sanctions Committee. 1990–1994.* Ardsley, N.Y.: Transnational Publishers, 2000.

Dayan, Moshe. *Breakthrough: A Personal Account of the Egypt-Israel Peace Negotiations.* New York: Knopf, 1981.

Herzog, Chaim. *The Arab-Israeli Wars.* New York: Random House, 1982.

Lall, Arthur. *The UN and the Middle East Crisis, 1967.* New York: Columbia University Press, 1968.

Laqueur, Walter, and Barry Rubin. *The Israel-Arab Reader: A Documentary History of the Middle East Conflict.* New York: Penguin Books, 2000.

Pearson, Graham S. *The UNSCOM Saga: Chemical and Biological Weapons Non-proliferation.* Basingstoke, England: Macmillan, 2000.

Ritter, Scott. *Endgame: Solving the Iraq Problem—Once and for All.* New York: Simon and Schuster, 1999.

Said, Edward. *The Politics of Dispossession: The Struggle for Palestinian Self-Determination, 1969–1994.* New York: Vintage Books, 1995.

Shlaim, Avi. *The Iron Wall. Israel and the Arab World.* New York: W.W. Norton, 2001.

Simons, Geoff. *The United Nations: A Chronology of Conflict.* New York: St. Martin's, 1994.

Smith, Jean Edward. *George Bush's War.* New York: Holt, 1992.

NON-GOVERNMENTAL ORGANIZATIONS

Fisher, Julie. *Nongovernments. NGOs and the Political Development of the Third World.* Bloomfield, Conn.: Kumarian Press, 1997.

Foster, John W., and Anita Anand. *Whose World Is It Anyway? Civil Society, the United Nations and the Multilateral Future.* Bloomfield, Conn.: Kumarian Press, 1996.

Fox, Jonathan A., and L. David Brown, eds. *The Struggle for Accountability: The World Bank, NGOs, and Grassroots Movements.* Cambridge, Mass.: MIT Press, 1998.

Uvin, Peter, and Thomas G. Weiss. "The United Nations and NGOs: Global Civil Society and Institutional Change." In *The United Nations at Work.* Edited by Martin Ira Glassner. Westport, Conn.: Praeger Publishers, 1998.

Weiss, Thomas G., and Leon Gordenker, eds. *NGOs, the UN and Global Governance.* Boulder, Colo.: Lynne Rienner, 1996.

Welch, Claude E., Jr. *NGOs and Human Rights: Promise and Performance.* Philadelphia: University of Pennsylvania Press, 2001.

Willetts, Peter, ed. *"Conscience of the World": The Influence of Non-governmental Organizations in the UN System.* Washington, D.C.: Brookings Institution, 1996.

World Conference on Human Rights. *World Conference on Human Rights, Vienna, June 1993: The Contributions of NGOs: Reports and Documents.* Vienna: Manzsche Verlags und Universitätsbuchhandlung, 1994.

Young, Zoe. "NGOs and the Global Environmental Facility: Friendly Foes?" *Environmental Politics,* no. 8 (Spring 1999): 243–67.

PACIFIC SETTLEMENT

Lepgold, Joseph, and Thomas G. Weiss, eds. *Collective Conflict Management and Changing World Politics.* Albany: State University of New York Press, 1998.

Ratner, Steven R. "Image and Reality in the UN's Peaceful Settlement of Disputes." *European Journal of International Law* 6, no. 3 (1995): 426.

PARTICIPANTS' WORKS

Acheson, Dean. *Present at the Creation: My Years at the State Department.* New York: Norton, 1969.

Annan, Kofi. *Renewing the United Nations: A Programme for Reform.* UN Document A/51/950, July 16, 1997.

———. *Waging Peace, 1956–1961.* New York: Doubleday, 1965.

———. *We the Peoples: The Role of the United Nations in the 21st Century.* New York: United Nations Department of Public Information, 2000.

Baruch, Bernard M. *Baruch.* Vol. II, *The Public Years.* New York: Holt, Rinehart and Winston, 1960.

Boutros-Ghali, Boutros. *An Agenda for Peace.* New York: United Nations, 1992.

———. *An Agenda for Democratization.* New York: United Nations, 1996.

———. *An Agenda for Development.* New York: United Nations, 1995.

———. "Empowering the United Nations." *Foreign Affairs.* (winter 1992/93): 89–102.

———. "Global Leadership after the Cold War." *Foreign Affairs* (March–April 1996): 86–98.

———. *Unvanquished: A U.S.-U.N. Saga.* New York: Random House, 1999.

Boutros-Ghali, Boutros, and Nelson Mandela. *The United Nations and Apartheid.* New York: Department of Public Information, 1996.

Campbell, Thomas M., and George C. Herring, eds. *The Diaries of Edward R. Stettinius, Jr., 1943–1946.* New York: New Viewpoints, 1975.

Cassin, René. *La Pensée et l'Action.* Boulogne sur Seine, France: F. Lalou, 1972.

Eisenhower, Dwight D. *Mandate for Change, 1953–1956.* Garden City, N.Y.: Doubleday, 1963.

Hammarskjöld, Dag. *Markings.* Translated by Leif Sjöberg and W. H. Audon, with a forward by W. H. Audon. New York: Knopf, 1964.

Hampson, Fen Osler, and Maureen Appel Molot, eds. *Big Enough to Be Heard: Canada among Nations.* Ottawa: Carleton University Press, 1996.

Higgins, Rosalyn. *United Nations Peacekeeping, 1946–1967: Documents and Commentary.* 4 Vols. London; New York: Oxford University Press, 1969–1981.

Hiss, Alger. *Recollections of a Life.* New York: Seaver Books, 1988.

Holbrooke, Richard. *To End a War.* New York: Random House, 1998.

Hull, Cordell. *The Memoirs of Cordell Hull.* 2 Vols. New York: Macmillan, 1948.

Humphrey, John P. *Human Rights and the United Nations: A Great Adventure.* Dobbs Ferry, N.Y.: Transnational Publishing, 1984.

Kirkpatrick, Jeane J. *The Reagan Phenomenon—And Other Speeches on Foreign Policy.* Washington, D.C.: American Enterprise Institute, 1983.

Lie, Trygve. *In the Cause of Peace.* New York: Macmillan, 1954.

Moynihan, Daniel Patrick. *A Dangerous Place.* Boston: Little, Brown, 1978.

Pearson, Lester B. *Mike: The Memoirs of the Right Honourable Lester B. Pearson.* 3 Vols. New American Library of Canada, 1972

Pérez de Cuéllar, Javier. *Anarchy or Order: Annual Reports 1982–1991.* New York: United Nations, 1991.

———. *Pilgrimage for Peace: A Secretary-General's Memoir.* New York: St. Martin's, 1997.

Prebisch, Raul. "A Critique of Peripheral Capitalism." *CEPAL Review,* no. 1 (1976): 9–76.

———. "Five Stages in My Thinking on Development." In *Pioneers in Development.* Edited by Gerald M. Meier and Dudley Seers. New York: Oxford University Press, 1984.

———. "Notes on Trade from the Standpoint of the Periphery." *CEPAL Review,* no. 28 (April 1985): 203–214.

Romulo, Carlos, and Beth Day Romulo. *Forty Years: A Third World Soldier at the UN.* New York: Greenwood Press, 1986.

Roosevelt, Eleanor. *On My Own.* New York: Harper, 1958.

———. *This I Remember.* New York: Harper, 1949.

Stettinius, Edward R. Jr. *Roosevelt and the Russians; The Yalta Conference.* Edited by Walter Johnson. Westport, Conn.: Greenwood Press, 1970.

Thant, U. *Portfolio for Peace: Excerpts from the Writings and Speeches of U Thant, 1961–1968.* 2d ed. New York: United Nations, 1970.

———. *Toward World Peace: Addresses and Public Statements, 1957–1963.* New York: Thomas Yoseloff, 1964.

———. *View from the UN.* Garden City, N.Y.: Doubleday, 1978.

Tolba, Mostafa K., and Iwona Rummel-Bulska. *Global Environmental Diplomacy. Negotiating Environmental Agreements for the World, 1973–1992.* Cambridge, Mass.: MIT Press, 1998.

Truman, Harry S. *Memoirs.* Vol. 1, *Year of Decision.* Garden City, N.Y.: Doubleday, 1955.

Urquhart, Brian. *A Life in Peace and War.* New York: Harper and Row, 1987.

———. *Ralph Bunche: An American Life.* New York: Norton, 1993.

Urquhart, Brian, and Erskine Childers. *A World in Need of Leadership: Tomorrow's United Nations—A Fresh Appraisal.* Uppsala, Sweden: Dag Hammarskjöld Foundation, 1996.

Vance, Cyrus. *Hard Choices: Critical Years in America's Foreign Policy.* New York: Simon and Schuster, 1983.

Waldheim, Kurt. *Building the Future Order.* New York: The Free Press, 1980.

———. *In the Eye of the Storm: A Memoir.* Bethesda, Md.: Adler and Adler, 1986.

———. *The Challenge of Peace.* London: Weidenfeld and Nicolson, 1980.

PEACE AND WAR

Bailey, Stephen D. *The Korean Armistice.* New York: St. Martin's, 1992.

Berger, Carl. *The Korea Knot.* Philadelphia: University of Pennsylvania Press, 1964.

Bloomfield, Lincoln P. *The UN and Vietnam.* New York: Carnegie Endowment for International Peace, 1968.

Conlon, Paul. *United Nations Sanction Management: A Case Study of the Iraq Sanctions Committee, 1990–1994.* Ardsley, N.Y.: Transnational Publishers, 2000.

Foot, Rosemary. *The Wrong War: American Policy and the Dimensions of the Korean Conflict, 1950–1953.* Ithaca, N.Y.: Cornell University Press, 1985.

Haas, Michael E. *In The Devil's Shadow: UN Special Operations during the Korean War.* Annapolis, Md.: Naval Institute Press, 2000.

Hiro, Dilip. *Desert Shield to Desert Storm: The Second Gulf War.* London: Paladin, 1992.

Kaufman, Burton. *The Korean War: Challenges in Crisis, Credibility and Command.* New York: McGraw-Hill, 1997.

Maley, William. "The UN and Afghanistan: 'Doing Its Best' or 'Failure of a Mission'?" In *Fundamentalism Reborn: Afghanistan and the Taliban.* Edited by William Maley. New York: New York University Press, 1998.

Paige, Glenn D. *The Korean Decision.* New York: The Free Press, 1968.

Pak, Ch'i-yong. *Korea and the United Nations.* Cambridge: Kluwer Law International, 2000.

Khan, Riaz M. *Untying the Afghan Knot: Negotiating Soviet Withdrawal.* Durham, N.C.: Duke University Press, 1991.

Rubin, Barnett R. "Afghanistan under the Taliban." *Current History.* 98, no. 625 (February 1999): 79–91.

———. *The Search for Peace in Afghanistan: From Buffer State to Failed State.* New Haven, Conn.: Yale University Press, 1995.

Sifry, Micah L., and Christopher Cerf. *The Gulf War Reader: History, Documents, Opinions.* New York: Times Books, 1991.

Stueck, William. *The Korean War: An International History.* Princeton, N.J.: Princeton University Press, 1995.

Sutterlin, James S. *The United Nations and the Maintenance of International Security: A Challenge to Be Met.* Westport, Conn.: Praeger Publishers, 1995.

United Nations Educational, Scientific and Cultural Organization. *World Directory of Peace Research and Training Institutions,* 9th ed. Paris: United Nations Educational, Scientific and Cultural Organization, 2000.

PEACEKEEPING AND HUMANITARIAN INTERVENTION

Allsebrook, Mary. *Prototypes of Peacemaking: The First Forty Years of the United Nations.* Harlow, U.K.: Longman, 1986.

Benton, Barbara, ed. *Soldiers for Peace: Fifty Years of United Nations Peacekeeping.* New York: Facts On File, 1996.

Bertram, Eva. "Reinventing Governments: The Promise and Perils of United Nations Peacebuilding." *Journal of Conflict Resolution* 39, no. 3 (1995), 387–418.

Boulden, Jane. *The United Nations Experience in Congo, Somalia, and Bosnia.* Westport, Conn.: Praeger Publishers, 2001.

Chopra, Jarat. "United Nations Peace-Maintenance." In *The United Nations at Work.* Edited by Martin Ira Glassner. Westport, Conn.: Praeger Publishers, 1998.

Cliffe, Lionel. *The Transition to Independence in Namibia.* Boulder, Colo.: Lynne Rienner, 1994.

Dayal, R. *Mission for Hammarskjold: The Congo Crisis.* London: Oxford University Press, 1976.

Doyle, Michael W. *Peacekeeping in Cambodia: UNTAC's Civil Mandate.* Boulder, Colo.: Lynne Rienner, 1995.

Durch, William J., ed. *The Evolution of UN Peacekeeping: Case Studies and Comparative Analysis.* New York: St. Martin's, 1993.

Ginifer, Jeremy. *Beyond the Emergency: Development within UN Peace Missions.* London: Frank Cass, 1997.

Gordon, D. S., and F. H. Toase. *Aspects of Peacekeeping.* London: Frank Cass, 2001.

Hainsworth, Paul, and Stephen McCloske. *The East Timor Question: The Struggle for Independence from Indonesia.* London: I.B. Tauris, 2000.

Hare, Paul J. *Angola's Last Best Chance of Peace: An Insider's Account of the Peace Process.* Washington, D.C.: United States Institute of Peace Press, 1998.

Hill, Stephen M., and Shanin Malik. *Peacekeeping and the United Nations.* Aldershot, U.K.: Dartmouth, 1996.

Hirsch, John L., and Robert B. Oakley. *Somalia and Operation Restore Hope.* Washington, D.C.: United States Institute of Peace Press, 1995.

Holm, Tor Tanke, and Espen Barth Eide. *Peacebuilding and Police Reform.* London: Frank Cass, 2000.

Inter-Agency Standing Committee. *Humanitarian Action in the 21st Century.* New York: United Nations, 2000.

Jett, Dennis C. *Why Peacekeeping Fails.* New York: St Martin's, 2000.

Johnston, Ian. *Rights and Reconciliation: UN Strategies in El Salvador.* Boulder, Colo.: Lynn Rienner, 1995.

Krieger, Heike. *East Timor and the International Community: Basic Documents.* Cambridge: Research Centre for International Law, Cambridge University Press, 1997.

Lefever, Ernest. *Crisis in the Congo.* Washington, D.C.: Brookings Institution, 1965.

McWhinney, Edward. *The United Nations and the New World Order for a New Millennium: Self-Determination, State Succession, and Humanitarian Intervention.* Boston: Kluwer Law International, 2000.

Murphy, Sean D. *Humanitarian Intervention. The United Nations in an Evolving World Order.* Philadelphia: University of Pennsylvania Press, 1996.

Nicholson, Frances, and Patrick Twomey, eds. *Refugee Rights and Realities: Evolving International Concepts and Regimes.* Cambridge: Cambridge University Press, 1999.

Ontunnu, Olara A., and Michael W. Doyle, eds. *Peacemaking and Peacekeeping for the New Century,* Lanham, Md.: Rowman and Littlefield, 1996.

Perusse, Roland I. *Haitian Democracy Restored, 1991–1995.* Lanham, Md.: University Press of America, 1995.

Pugh, Michael. *The UN, Peace and Force.* London: Frank Cass, 1997.

Ratner, Steven R. *The New UN Peacekeeping: Building Peace in Land of Conflict after the Cold War.* New York: St. Martin's, 1995.

Richmond, Oliver P. *Mediating in Cyprus. The Cypriot Communities and the United Nations.* London: Frank Cass, 1998.

Rikhye, Indar Jit. *The Politics and Practice of United Nations Peacekeeping: Past, Present and Future.* Cornwallis Park, Nova Scotia: Canadian Peacekeeping Press, 2000.

Rikhye, Indar Jit, and Kjell Skjelsbaek, eds. *The United Nations and Peacekeeping: Results, Limitations and Prospects: The Lessons of 40 Years of Experience.* Basingbroke, England: Macmillan/International Peace Academy, 1990.

Rikhye, Indar Jit. *United Nations Peacekeeping and the Congo Crisis.* London: C. Hurst, 1990.

Schnabel, Albrecht, and Ramesh Thakur, eds. *Kosovo and the Challenge of Humanitarian Intervention.* New York: United Nations University, 2000.

Seikmann, Robert D. R. *Basic Documents on United Nations and Related Peace-Keeping Forces.* Dordrecht: Martinus Nijhoff, 1989.

Sharp, Walter Gary Sr. *Jus Paciarii: Emergent Legal Paradigms for U.N. Peace Operations in the 21st Century.* Stafford, Va.: Paciarii International, 1999.

Synge, Richard. *Mozambique. UN Peacekeeping in Action, 1992–94.* Herndon, Va.: United States Institute of Peace Press, 1997.

Thakur, Ramesh, and Albrecht Schnabel, eds. *United Nations Peacekeeping Operations: Ad Hoc Missions, Permanent Engagement.* Washington, D.C.: United Nations University Press, 2001.

Thayer, Carlyle A. "The UN Transitional Authority in Cambodia." In *A Crisis of Expectations: UN Peacekeeping in the 1990s.* Edited by Ramesh Thakur and Carlyle A. Thayer. Boulder, Colo.: Westview Press, 1995.

United Nations Department of Public Information. *The Blue Helmets: A Review of United Nations Peace-Keeping.* 3d ed. New York: United Nations Department of Public Information, 1996.

———. "The UN and Somalia, 1992–96." *The UN Blue Books Series.* Vol. 3. New York: United Nations Department of Public Information, 1996.

———. *UN Peacekeeping: 50 Years, 1948–1998.* New York: United Nations Publications, 1998.

———. *Agreements on a Comprehensive Political Settlement of the Cambodia Conflict, Paris, 23 October 1991.* New York: United Nations Department of Public Information, 1992.

———. Report of the Secretary-General. *Improving the Capacity of the United Nations for Peacekeeping.* A/48/403, S/26450, March 1994.

U.S. Senate. *Reform of United Nations Peacekeeping Operations: A Mandate for Change.* Staff Report, Committee on Foreign Relations, United States Senate. Washington, D.C.: U.S. Government Printing Office, 1993.

Weiss, Thomas G., and Cindy Collins. *Humanitarian Challenges and Intervention: World Politics and the Dilemmas of Help.* Boulder, Colo.: Westview Press, 1996.

White, N.D. *Keeping the Peace: The United Nations and the Maintenance of International Peace and Security.* Manchester, England: Manchester University Press, 1993.

Williams, Abiodun. *Preventing War: The United Nations and Macedonia.* Lanham, Md.: Rowman and Littlefield, 2000.

REFORM AND FINANCING

Beigbeder, Yves. *The Internal Management of United Nations Organizations.* New York: St. Martin's, 1997.

Bourantonis, Demitris, and Jarrod Weiner. *The United Nations and the New World Order.* New York: St. Martin's, 1995.

Drifte, Reinhard. *Japan's Quest for a Permanent Security Council Seat: A Matter of Pride or Justice?* New York: St. Martin's, 2000.

Fassbender, Bodo. *UN Security Council Reform and the Right of Veto.* The Hague: Kluwer Law International, 1998.

Franck, Thomas. *Nation against Nation: What Happened to the U.N. Dream and What the U.S. Can Do about It.* New York: Oxford University Press, 1985.

Gordon, Wendell. *The United Nations at the Crossroads of Reform.* Armonk, N.Y.: M.E. Sharpe, 1994.

Helms, Jesse. "Saving the U.N.: A Challenge to the Next Secretary-General." *Foreign Affairs* (September–October 1996): 2–7.

Knight, W. Andy. *A Changing United Nations: Multilateral Evolution and the Quest for Global Governance.* Houndsmill, U.K.: Macmillan Press, 2000.

Laurenti, Jeffrey. *Financing the United Nations.* New Haven, Conn.: Academic Council on the United Nations System, 2001.

Lichenstein, Charles M. *The United Nations: Its Problems and What to Do about Them.* Washington, D.C.: Heritage Foundation, 1986.

McDermott, Anthony. *The New Politics of Financing The UN.* Basingstoke, England: Macmillan, 2000.

Muller, Joachim. *The Reform of the United Nations.* 2 vols. New York: Oceana, 1992.

Peou, Sorpong. "The Subsidiarity Model of Global Governance in the UN-ASEAN Context." In *Global Governance: A Review of Multilateralism and International Organizations* 4, no. 4 (October–December 1998): 439–60.

Pines, Burton Yale, ed. *A World without a U.N.: What Would Happen If the U.N. Shut Down?* Washington, D.C.: Heritage Foundation, 1984.

South Centre. *For a Strong and Democratic United Nations: A South Perspective on UN Reform.* London: Zed Books, 1995.

Taylor, Paul, Sam Daws, and Ute Adamczick-Gerteis, eds. *Documents on Reform of the United Nations.* Brookfield, Vt.: Dartmouth, 1997.

Volker, Paul, and Shituro Ogata et al. *Financing an Effective United Nations.* New York: Ford Foundation, 1993.

REGIONALISM AND REGIONAL ORGANIZATIONS

Andemicael, Berhanykun, ed. *Regionalism and the United Nations.* Dobbs Ferry, N.Y.: Oceana Publications, 1979.

Cayuela, Jose. *ECLAC 40 Years (1948–1988).* Santiago, Chile: Economic Commission for Latin America and the Caribbean, 1988.

Cox, Robert. "Multilateralism and World Order." *Review of International Studies* 18, no. 2 (April 1992): 161–80.

El-Ayouty, Yassin, ed. *The Organization of African Unity after Thirty Years.* New York: Praeger, 1994.

Falk, Richard K., and Saul H. Mendlovitz, eds. *Regional Politics and World Order.* San Francisco: Freeman, 1973.

Houston, John A. *Latin America in the United Nations.* New York: Carnegie Endowment for International Peace, 1956.

Knight, W. Andy. *Adapting the United Nations to a Post Modern Era: Lessons Learned.* Houndmills, England: Macmillan Press, 2000.

Levin, Aida L. "The Organization of the American States and the United Nations." In *Regionalism and the United Nations.* Edited by Berhanykun Andemicael. Dobbs Ferry, N.Y.: Oceana Publications, 1979.

McCoubrey, Hilaire, and Justin Morris. *Regional Peacekeeping in the Post–Cold War Era.* Boston: Kluwer Law International, 2000.

Rosenthal, Gert. "The United Nations and ECLAC at the Half-Century Mark." *CEPAL Review,* no. 57 (December 1995): 7–15.

Ruggie, John. *Multilateralism Matters: The Theory and Praxis of an Institutional Form.* New York: Columbia University Press, 1993.

Santa Cruz, Hernan. "The Creation of the United Nations and ECLAC." *CEPAL Review,* no. 57 (December 1995): 17–33.

Solis, Leopoldo. *Raúl Prebisch at ECLA: Years of Creative Intellectual Effort.* San Francisco: International Center for Economic Growth, 1988.

United Nations. *Cooperation between the United Nations and the Organization of African Unity, Annual Report by the General Assembly.* New York: United Nations, 1998.

Wilson, Larman C., and David W. Dent. *Historical Dictionary of Inter-American Organizations.* Lanham, Md.: Scarecrow Press, 1998.

SECRETARIES-GENERAL

Barnes, James. *Trygve Lie and the Cold War: The UN Secretary-General Pursues Peace.* DeKalb: Northern Illinois University Press, 1989.

Boudreau, Thomas E. *Sheathing the Sword.* New York: Greenwood Press, 1991.

Finger, Seymour Maxwell, and Arnold A. Saltzman. *Bending with the Winds: Kurt Waldheim and the United Nations.* New York: Praeger, 1990.

Foote, Wilder, ed. *Servant of Peace; A Selection of the Speeches and Statements of Dag Hammarskjöld, Secretary-General of the United Nations, 1953–1961.* New York: Harper and Row, 1962.

Hazzard, Shirley. *Countenance of Truth: The United Nations and the Waldheim Case.* New York: Viking, 1990.

Herzstein, Robert Edwin. *Waldheim: The Missing Years.* New York: Paragon House, 1989.

Miller, Richard. *Dag Hammarskjold and Crisis Diplomacy.* New York: Oceana Publications, 1961.

Nassif, Ramses. *U Thant in New York, 1961–1971: A Portrait of the Third Secretary-General.* London: Hurst, 1988.

Newman, Edward. *The UN Secretary-General from the Cold War to the New Era: A Global Peace and Security Mandate?* New York: St. Martin's, 1998.

Public Papers of the Secretaries-General of the United Nations. 8 vols. New York: Columbia University Press.

Rivlin, Benjamin, and Leon Gordenker. *The Challenging Role of the UN Secretary-General.* Westport, Conn.: Praeger, 1993.

Tessitore, John. *Kofi Annan: The Peacekeeper.* New York: Franklin Watts, 2000.

United Nations. *Report of the Secretary-General on the Work of the Organization.* General Assembly. New York: United Nations, published annually.

Urquhart, Brian. *Hammarskjöld.* New York: Knopf, 1972.

Zacher, Mark W. *Dag Hammarskjöld's United Nations.* New York: Columbia University Press, 1970.

SECURITY COUNCIL

Bailey, Sydney D., and Sam Daws. *The Procedure of the UN Security Council.* 3d ed. New York: Oxford University Press, 1998.

Bedjaoui, Mohammed. *The New World Order and the Security Council: Testing the Legality of Its Acts.* Boston: M. Nijhoff Publishers, 1994.

Freudenschuss, Helmut. "Between Unilateralism and Collective Security: Authorizations of the Use of Force by the UN Security Council." *European Journal of International Law* 5, no. 4 (1994): 492–531.

Hoffmann, Walter. *United Nations Security Council Reform and Restructuring.* Livingston, N.J.: Center for U. N. Reform Education, 1994.

Köchler, Hans. *The Voting Procedure in the United Nations Security Council: Examining a Normative Contradiction in the UN Charter and Its Consequences on International Relations.* Vienna: International Progress Organization, 1991.

Patil, Anjali V. *The UN Veto in World Affairs 1946–1990: A Complete Record and Case Histories of the Security Council's Veto.* Sarasota, Fla.: Unifo, 1992.

Wellens, Karel C., ed. *Resolutions and Statements of the United Nations Security Council (1946–1992): A Thematic Guide.* 2d ed. Boston: Martinus Nijhoff Publishers, 1993.

SOCIAL ISSUES

Bastos, Cristiana. *Global Responses to AIDS: Science in Emergency.* Bloomington: Indiana University Press, 1999.

Castillo, Carlos. *The Children Here: Current Trends in the Decentralization of National Programmes of Action.* Florence, Italy: UNICEF International Child Development Centre, 1995.

Dutt, Mallika, ed. *From Vienna to Beijing: The Cairo Hearing on Reproductive Health and Human Rights.* New Brunswick, N.J.: Center for Women's Global Leadership, 1995.

Feldman, Douglas, and Julia Wang Miller. *The AIDS Crisis: A Documentary History.* Westport, Conn.: Greenwood Press, 1998.

Johnson, Stanley. *The Politics of Population: The International Conference on Population and Development, Cairo 1994.* London: Earthscan, 1995.

Leckie, Scott. *Towards an International Convention on Housing Rights: Options at Habitat II.* Washington, D.C.: American Society of International Law, 1994.

Mann, Jonathan, and Daniel Tarantola, eds. *AIDS in the World II.* New York: Oxford University Press, 1996.

McGovern, George. *The Third Freedom, Ending Hunger in Our Time.* New York: Simon and Schuster, 2001.

Paul, James. *Incorporating Human Rights into the Work of the World Summit for Social Development.* Washington, D.C.: American Society of International Law, 1995.

Smith, Raymond. *Encyclopedia of AIDS: A Social, Political, Cultural, and Scientific Record of the HIV Epidemic.* Chicago: Fitzroy Dearborn Publishers, 2000.

Stine, Gerald. *AIDS Update 2000.* Upper Saddle River, N.J.: Prentice Hall, 1999.

Taub, Nadine. *International Conference on Population and Development.* Washington, D.C.: American Society of International Law, 1994.

United Nations Children's Fund. *State of the World's Children.* New York: Oxford University Press, annually.

United Nations Conference on Human Settlements. *The City Summit: Habitat II, United Nations Conference on Human Settlements, Istanbul, Turkey, 3–14 June 1996.* New York: DPI, 1995.

United Nations Development Programme. *Poverty Eradication: A Policy Framework for Country Strategies.* New York: United Nations Development Programme, 1995.

———. *Progress against Poverty: A Report on Activities since Copenhagen.* New York: United Nations Development Programme, 1996.

United Nations High Commissioner for Refugees. *State of the World's Refugees.* New York: United Nations, issued every two years.

———. *Collection of International Instruments and Other Legal Texts concerning Refugees and Displaced Persons.* Geneva: United Nations High Commissioner for Refugees, 1995.

United Nations Office for Drug Control and Crime Prevention. *Global Report on Crime and Justice* New York: Oxford University Press, 1999.

———. *World Drug Report 2000.* New York: Oxford University Press, 2001.

SPECIALIZED AGENCIES

Beigbeder, Yves. *New Challenges for UNICEF: Children, Women, and Human Rights.* New York: Palgrave, 2001.

Black, Maggie. *Children First: The Story of UNICEF, Past and Present.* New York: Oxford University Press, 1996.

Convention on the IMO, IMO 013E, London: IMO Publishing Service, 1984.

Eco'Diagnostic, Geneva. *International Geneva Yearbook, 2000–2001.* Vol. 14. Geneva: United Nations, 2000.

Imber, Mark. *The USA, ILO, UNESCO, and IAEA: Politicization and Withdrawal in the Specialized Agencies.* London: Macmillan, 1989.

International Maritime Organization. *IMO: The First 50 Years.* London: International Maritime Organization, 1999.

Simmonds, K. R. *The International Maritime Organization.* London: Simmonds and Hill Publishers, 1994.

Wells, Clare. *The UN, UNESCO and the Politics of Knowledge.* London: Macmillan, 1987.

Williams, D. *The Specialized Agencies and the United Nations: The System in Crisis.* New York: St. Martin's, 1987.

World Health Organization. *Handbook of Resolutions and Decisions of the World Health Assembly and the Executive Board.* Geneva: World Health Organization, published annually.

TERRORISM

Combs, Cindy C., and Martin Slann. *Encyclopedia of Terrorism.* New York: Facts On File, 2001.

Elagab, Omer Y. *International Law Documents Relating to Terrorism.* London: Cavendish Publishers, 1995.

Gilbert, Geoff. "The 'Law' and 'Transnational Terrorism.'" *Netherlands Yearbook of International Law* 26 (1995): 3–32.

Higgins, Rosalyn, and Maurice Flory. *Terrorism and International Law.* New York: Routledge, 1997.

Kolosov, Yuri M., and Geoffrey M. Levitt. "International Cooperation against Terrorism." In *Beyond Confrontation: International Law for the Post–Cold War Era.* Edited by Lori Fisler Damrosch, Gennady M. Danilenko, and Rein Müllerson. Boulder, Colo.: Westview Press, 1995.

Kushner, Harvey W., ed. *The Future of Terrorism: Violence in the New Millennium.* Thousand Oaks, Calif.: Sage Publications, 1998.

Lopez, George A. "Terrorism and World Order." *Annual Editions: Violence and Terrorism.* Guilford, Conn.: Dushkin Publishers, 1993.

Nash, Jay Robert. *Terrorism in the 20th Century: A Narrative Encyclopedia from the Anarchists, through the Weathermen, to the Unabomber.* New York: M. Evans and Co., 1998.

Romanov, Valentin Aleksandrovich. "The United Nations and the Problem of Combatting International Terrorism." *Terrorism and Violence* 2, no. 3 (Autumn 1990): 289–304.

Taylor, Max, and John Horgan. *The Future of Terrorism.* London: Frank Cass, 2000.

Tucker, David. "Responding to Terrorism." *21 Debated Issues in World Politics.* Upper Saddle River, N.J.: Prentice Hall, 2000.

Tucker, Jonathan B., ed. *Toxic Terror: Assessing Terrorist Use of Chemical and Biological Weapons.* Cambridge: MIT Press, 2000.

TRADE AND INTERNATIONAL ECONOMICS

Culpepper, Roy. *Titans or Behemoths? The Multilateral Development Banks.* Ottawa: North South Institute, 1997.

Einhorn, Jessica. "The World Bank's Mission Creep." *Foreign Affairs* (September–October 2001): 22–35.

Grady, Patrick, and Kathleen Macmillan. *Seattle and Beyond: The WTO Millennium Round.* Ottawa: Global Economics Ltd., 1999.

Matejka, Harriet, and Mihály Sima. *Aspects of Transition.* Helsinki: United Nations University, 1999.

Micklethwait, John, and Adrian Wooldridge. *Future Perfect: The Challenge and Hidden Promise of Globalization.* New York: Crown Publishers, 2000.

Murphy, Craig. *The Emergence of the NIEO Ideology.* Boulder, Colo.: Westview Press, 1984.

O'Brien, Robert et al. *Contesting Global Governance: Multilateral Institutions and Global Movements.* New York: Cambridge University Press, 2000.

Sauvant, Karl P., and Hajo Hasenpflug. *The New International Economic Order: Confrontation or Cooperation between North and South.* Boulder, Colo.: Westview Press, 1977.

Schott, Jeffrey J., ed. *The WTO after Seattle.* Washington, D.C.: Institute for International Economics, 2000.

Schwartz, Herman M. *States versus Markets. History, Geography, and the Development of the International Political Economy.* New York: St. Martin's, 1994.

Upton, Barbara. *The Multilateral Development Banks. Improving U.S. Leadership.* Washington, D.C.: Center for Strategic and International Studies, 2000.

WAR CRIMES AND WAR CRIMES TRIBUNALS

Askin, Kelly D. *War Crimes Against Women: Prosecution in International War Crimes Tribunals.* The Hague: Martinus Nijhoff Publishers, 1997.

Ball, Howard. *Prosecuting War Crimes and Genocide: The Twentieth Century Experience.* Lawrence: University of Kansas Press, 1999.

Bass, Gary Jonathan. *Stay the Hand of Vengeance: The Politics of War Crimes Tribunals.* Princeton, N.J.: Princeton University Press, 2000.

Cooper, Belinda, ed. *War Crimes: The Legacy of Nuremberg.* New York: TV Books, 1999.

Jones, John R. W. D. *The Practice of the International Criminal Tribunals for the Former Yugoslavia and Rwanda.* Irvington, N.Y.: Transnational Publishers, 1999.

Magnarella, Paul J. *Justice in Africa: Rwanda's Genocide, Its Courts, and the UN Criminal Tribunal.* Aldershot, U.K.: Ashgate, 2000.

Morris, Virginia, and Michael P. Scharf. *International Criminal Tribunal for Rwanda.* Vols. 1 and 2. Irvington, N.Y.: Transnational Publishers, 1998.

Neier, Aryeh. *War Crimes: Brutality, Genocide, Terror, and the Struggle for Justice.* New York: Times Books, 1998.

WOMEN

Anand, Anita, with Gouri Salvi. *Beijing! UN Fourth World Conference on Women.* New Delhi: Women's Feature Service, 1998.

Askin, Kelly D., and Doreann M. Koenig, eds. *Women and International Human Rights Law,* Vol. 3, *Toward Empowerment.* Ardsley, N.Y.: Transnational Publishers, 2001.

Bunch, Charlotte, and Niamh Reilly. *Demanding Accountability: The Global Campaign and Vienna Tribunal for Women's Human Rights.* New Brunswick, N.J.: Center for Women's Global Leadership, 1994.

Byrnes, Andrew. "The Other Human Rights Body: The Work of the Committee on the Elimination of Discrimination against Women." *Yale Journal of International Law,* no. 14. (Winter 1989): 1–67.

Cook, Rebecca J. *The Elimination of Sexual Apartheid: Prospects for the Fourth World Conference on Women.*

Washington, D.C.: American Society of International Law, 1995.

Cooper, Mary H., "Women and Human Rights." *Congressional Quarterly* 9, no. 16 (April 30, 1999): 353.

Donnelly, Jack. "Human Rights at the United Nations, 1955–1988: The Question of Bias." *International Studies Quarterly,* no. 32 (1988): 275–303.

Fraser, Arvonne. *The UN Decade for Women.* Boulder, Colo.: Westview Press, 1987.

Meyer, Mary K., and Elisabeth Prügl. *Gender Politics in Global Governance.* Lanham, Md.: Rowman and Littlefield, 1999.

NGO Forum on Women. *Look at the World through Women's Eyes: Plenary Speeches from the NGO Forum on Women, Beijing '95.* New York: NGO Forum on Women, Beijing '95, Inc., 1996.

Pietilla, Hilkka, and Jeanne Vickers. *Making Women Matter: The Role of the United Nations.* London: Zed Books Ltd., 1996.

Reilly, Niamh, ed. *Testimonies of the Global Tribunal on Violations of Women's Human Rights at the United Nations World Conference on Human Rights, Vienna, June 1993.* New Brunswick, N.J.: Center for Women's Global Leadership, 1994.

Snyder, Margaret. *Women, Poverty and Politics: A UN Fund for Women.* London: Zed Books, 1995.

United Nations Department of Public Information. *The United Nations and the Advancement of Women, 1945–1996.* New York: United Nations Department of Public Information, 1996.

"United Nations Decade for Women 1976–1985: Really Only a Beginning. Mexico to Copenhagen, to Nairobi: An Irresistable Momentum…" *UN Chronicle* XXII, no. 7 (July–August 1985): ii–xxiv.

United Nations Educational, Scientific and Cultural Organization. *Droits des Femmes: Recueil de Textes Normatifs Internationaux* Women's law: A collection of international normative texts). Paris: United Nations Educational, Scientific and Cultural Organization, 1999.

Winslow, Anne, ed. *Women, Politics, and the United Nations.* Westport, Conn.: Greenwood Press, 1995.

"Women's Conference Adopts 'Beijing Declaration and Platform for Action,'" *UN Chronicle* XXXII, no. 4 (December 1995): 25–31.

Women's Environment and Development Organization. *Beyond Promises: Governments in Motion One Year after the Beijing Women's Conference.* New York: Women's Environment and Development Organization, 1996.

———. *Mapping Progress.* New York: Women's Environment and Development Organization, 1998.

Zoelle, Diana. *Globalizing Concern for Women's Human Rights.* New York: St. Martin's, 2000.

YUGOSLAVIA

Daalder, Ivo H. *Getting to Dayton: The Making of America's Bosnia Policy.* Washington, D.C.: Brookings Institution, 1999.

Meier, Viktor. *Yugoslavia: A History of Its Demise.* London: Routledge Books, 1999.

Rieff, David. *Slaughterhouse: Bosnia and the Failure of the West.* New York: Simon and Schuster, 1996.

Rogel, Carole. *The Breakup of Yugoslavia and the War in Bosnia.* Westport, Conn.: Greenwood Press, 1998.

Rohde, David. *Endgame: The Betrayal and Fall of Srebenica, Europe's Worst Massacre since World War II.* Boulder, Colo.: Westview Press, 2000.

Silber, Laura, and Allan Little. *Yugoslavia: Death of a Nation.* New York: Penguin Books, 1995.

Udovicki, Jasminka, and James Ridgeway, eds. *Burn This House: The Making and Unmaking of Yugoslavia.* Revised and expanded. Durham, N.C.: Duke University Press, 2000.

Williams, Abiodun. *Preventing War: The United Nations and Macedonia.* Lanham, Md.: Rowman and Littlefield, 2000.

INDEX

Italic page numbers indicate illustrations. **Boldface** page numbers indicate main headings.